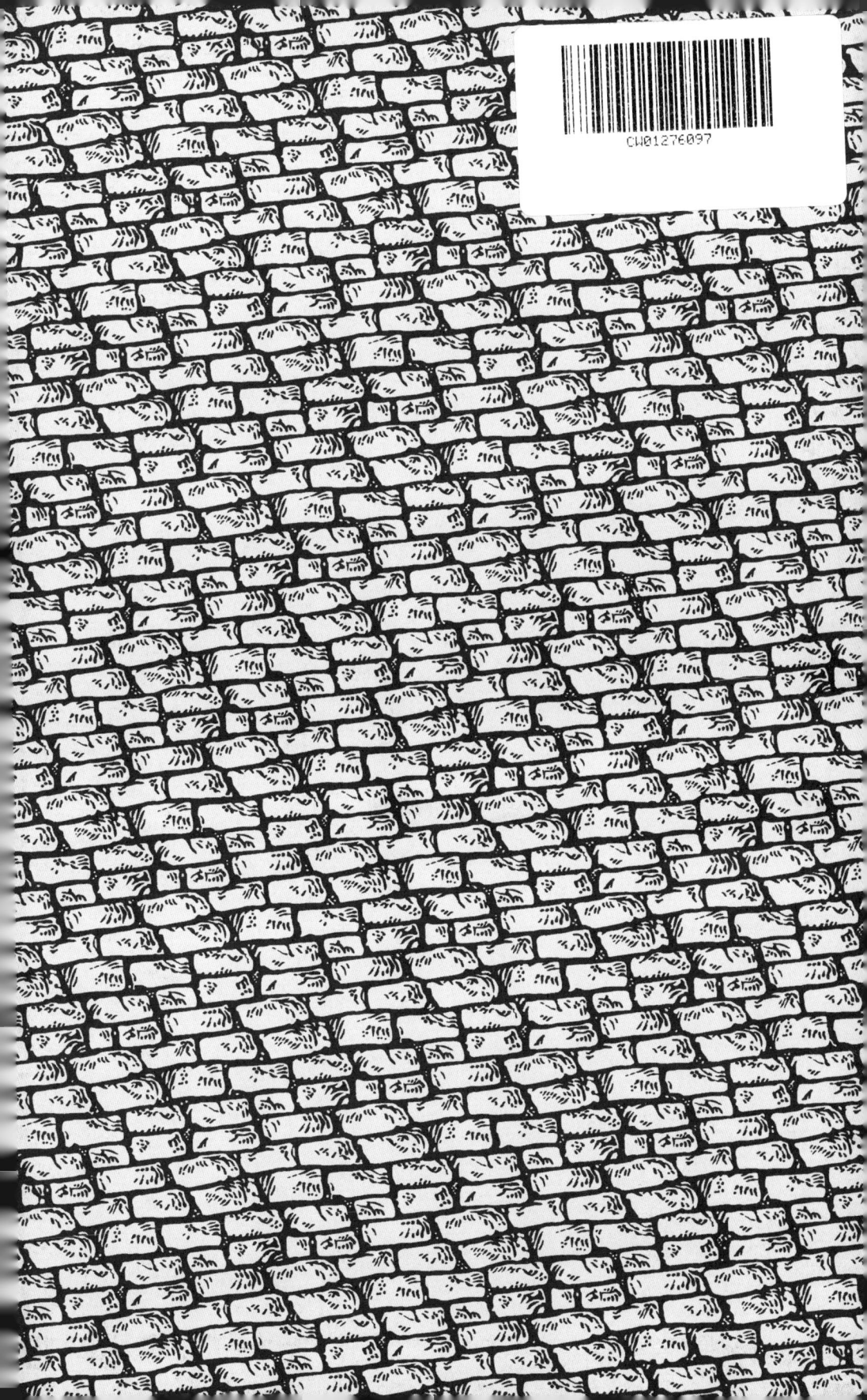

# THE ROAD BOOK
## 2021

A YEAR APART

# THE ROAD BOOK 2021

CYCLING ALMANACK

EDITED BY
NED BOULTING

First print run of the 2021 edition

First published in 2020 by The Road Book Ltd, 71 Gloucester Place, London W1U 8JW

www.theroadbook.co.uk

Copyright © The Road Book Ltd 2021

The Road Book Cycling Almanack is a registered trademark of The Road Book Limited

The moral right of The Road Book Ltd to be identified as the author of this work has been asserted in accordance with the Copyright, Designs and Patents Act 1988.

All rights reserved. No part of this publication may be reproduced or transmitted in any form or by any means, electronic or mechanical including photocopying, recording or any information storage or retrieval system, without prior permission in writing from the publishers.

No responsibility for loss caused to any individual or organisation acting on or refraining from action as a result of the material in this publication can be accepted by The Road Book Ltd.

ISBN 978-1-9164849-6-2

Design by conductorstudio.com
Typeset by seagulls.net
Printed and bound in the UK

# CONTENTS

**RIDER OF THE YEAR AWARDS** ix

**IN THE WINNERS' WORDS** xi

**EDITOR'S INTRODUCTION** by Ned Boulting 1

**JANUARY** 19

GP Cycliste la Marseillaise 20

**FEBRUARY** 21

Etoile de Bessèges 22
Tour de la Provence 25
Clásica de Almería 27
Tour des Alpes-Maritimes et du Var 28
UAE Tour 30

Omloop Het Nieuwsblad 37
Faun–Ardèche Classic 38
La Drôme Classic 39
Kuurne–Bruxelles–Kuurne 40

The End is Where We Start From by Kit Nicholson 41

**MARCH** 49

Le Samyn 50
Trofeo Laigueglia 51
Strade Bianche 52
Strade Bianche 53
GP Industria & Artigianato 54
GP Jean-Pierre Monseré 55
Paris–Nice 56
Tirreno–Adriatico 64
Danilith Nokere Koerse 71
Bredene Koksijde Classic 72
Milan–Sanremo 74

Trofeo Alfredo Binda 76
Per Sempre Alfredo 77
Volta Ciclista a Catalunya 78
Settimana Internazionale Coppi e Bartali 85
Brugge–De Panne 88
Brugge–De Panne 89
E3 Classic 90
Gent–Wevelgem 91
Gent–Wevelgem 92
Cholet – Pays de la Loire 93
Dwars door Vlaanderen 94

The Racemaker by Tomas Van Den Spiegel 95

## APRIL 99

GP Miguel Indurain  100
Tour of Flanders  102
Tour of Flanders  104
Trophée Harmonie Mutuelle  105
Itzulia Basque Country  106
Scheldeprijs  112
Presidential Tour of Turkey  113
De Brabantse Pijl  117
Volta a la Comunitat Valenciana  118
Amstel Gold Race  121

Amstel Gold Race  122
Tour of the Alps  123
La Flèche Wallonne  126
La Flèche Wallonne  127
Belgrade Banjaluka  128
Liège–Bastogne–Liège  130
Liège–Bastogne–Liège  132
Tour de Romandie  133
Vuelta Asturia  139

**Continental Drift – Africa's Greatest Race by Peter Kamasa**  141

## MAY 147

Tour du Rwanda  148
Volta ao Algarve  152
Giro d'Italia  156
Tour de Hongrie  200
Circuit de Wallonie  203
Trofeo Calvià  204
Trofeo Serra de Tramuntana  205
Trofeo Andratx  206
Tro-Bro Léon  207
Trofeo Alcudia  208

Vuelta a Andalucia  209
Vuelta a Burgos  212
Tour du Finistère  216
Vuelta a Murcia  217
Mercan'Tour Classic Alpes-Maritimes  218
Ronde van Limburg  219
Boucles de la Mayenne  220
Tour of Estonia  222
Critérium du Dauphiné  223

**Completing the Set by Dan Martin**  231

## JUNE 237

GP des Kantons Aargau  238
Dwars door het Hageland  239
Elfstedenronde  240
Tour de Suisse  241
Mont Ventoux Dénivelé Challenge  249
Tour of Slovenia  250
Baloise Belgium Tour  253

La Route d'Occitanie  256
Paris–Camembert  258
Adriatica Ionica Race  259
Giro dell'Appennino  261
La Course  262
Tour de France  264
GP Città di Lugan  308

**A Standing Start by Kathryn Bertine**  309

## JULY 315

Giro d'Italia Donne  316
Sibiu Cycling Tour  326
Settimana Ciclista Italiana  328
Tour de Wallonie  331
Olympic Games  334
Prueba Villafranca de Ordizia  339

Vuelta a Castilla y Leon  340
Tour de l'Ain  341
Donostia San Sebastián Klasikoa  343
Donostia San Sebastián Klasikoa  344
Heylen Vastgoed Heistse Pijl  345

## AUGUST 347

Circuito de Getxo  348
Vuelta a Burgos  349
Volta a Portugal  352
Arctic Race of Norway  358
Sazka Tour  360
Tour de Pologne  362
Tour of Denmark  369
Ladies Tour of Norway  372
Vuelta a España  376
GP Jef Scherens  420
La Polynormande  421
Egmont Cycling Race  422
Tour du Limousin  423

Tour of Norway  425
GP Marcel Kint  427
Tour Poitou–Charentes en Nouvelle Aquitaine  428
Simac Ladies Tour  431
Druivenkoers–Overijse  437
Deutschland Tour  438
Brussels Cycling Classic  440
Bretagne Classic – Ouest-France  441
GP de Plouay  442
Benelux Tour  443
Paralympic Games  450
Turul Romaniei  455

**A Pilgrim's Progress by Daniel Friebe**  458

## SEPTEMBER 463

Ceratizit Challenge  464
Classic Grand Besançon Doubs  468
Tour du Jura  469
Tour du Doubs  470
Tour of Britain  471
European Championships  475
GP de Fourmies  479
Antwerp Port Epic  480
Tour de Luxembourg  481
GP de Wallonie  484
Giro della Toscana  485
Tour de Slovaquie  486
Coppa Sabatini  489
Kampioenschap van Vlaanderen  490

Primus Classic  491
Memorial Marco Pantani  492
Eschborn–Frankfurt  493
Trofeo Matteotti  494
Gooikse Pijl  495
GP d'Isbergues  496
World Championships  497
GP de Denain  504
Omloop van het Houtland Middelkerke-Lichtervelde  505
Paris–Chauny  506
Giro di Sicilia  507
Cro Race  509
80° Eurométropole Tour  512

## OCTOBER 513

Route Adélie de Vitré 514
Paris–Roubaix 515
Giro dell'Emilia 516
Classic Loire Atlantique 517
Paris–Roubaix 518
Münsterland Giro 520
Coppa Bernocchi 521
Women's Tour 522
Tre Valli Varesine 528
Binche–Chimay–Binche 529
Milano–Torino 530
Gran Piemonte 531

Paris–Bourges 532
Il Lombardia 534
Tour de Vendée 536
Paris–Tours 537
Coppa Agostini 538
Giro del Veneto 539
GP de Plumelec-Morbihan 542
Boucles de l'Aulne 543
Chrono des Nations 544
Veneto Classic 545
Ronde van Drenthe 546
Ronde van Drenthe 547

## NATIONAL CHAMPIONS 549

Shaking My Confidence by Cecilie Uttrup Ludwig 555

## TEAMS 561

Men's WorldTour Teams 562
Women's WorldTour Teams 600
Men's Pro Continental Teams 630

Men's WorldTour End-of-season Rankings 650
Women's WorldTour End-of-season Rankings 652

## HISTORICAL RESULTS 655

Men's Historical WorldTour Results 656
Women's Historical WorldTour Results 702

## BRITISH DOMESTIC RACING 725

## CYCLOCROSS 741

In the Cross Fire by Tom Pidcock 749

## OBITUARIES 753

## CONTRIBUTORS 791

## ACKNOWLEDGEMENTS 793

# RIDERS OF THE YEAR 2021

Female Rider of the Year

LIZZIE DEIGNAN

Male Rider of the Year

JULIAN ALAPHILIPPE

Young Female Rider of the Year

ELISA BALSAMO

Young Male Rider of the Year

JONAS VINGEGAARD

Combative Female Rider of the Year

ELISA LONGO BORGHINI

Combative Male Rider of the Year

JULIAN ALAPHILIPPE

Road Book Society Readers' Award

MARK CAVENDISH

# IN THE WINNERS' WORDS
## JASPER STUYVEN

*Trek-Segafredo's Jasper Stuyven was born and bred in Leuven, in the heart of the Flemish Brabant. Throughout his career, he was tipped to win one of the cobbled Monuments, and often he had come close. At the start of 2020, he won Omloop Het Nieuwsblad, his biggest one-day race win to date. But nothing prepared him for the moment when, a year later, he sprang a surprise attack on the outskirts of Sanremo to fend off the chasing pack of favourites and ride out a maiden Monument victory.*

---

It was one of those nights at the hotel in Milan. We had a good dinner, talking with the guys. Everyone only spoke about the big three names. It was the same in our team. We had the meeting and we were all realistic: there were three guys who were doing really impressive stuff: Wout van Aert, Mathieu van der Poel and Julian Alaphilippe. But we had a goal, a plan. And we tried to do it as well as we possibly could.

I was confident. For a few days, I had been feeling really good. I spoke to Ryan Mullen for a long time. Ryan's on the Classics team with me, and we have a good relationship. I told him that I wanted to avoid every little bit of wind that I possibly could with him in front of me, that it might make a difference. I was counting on Ryan quite specifically to go to the next level to protect me. It might just give me a chance of winning the race. I truly believed it was possible. I came to the race with a little bit of a different mindset from in previous years, and I really had my views on how to race it.

You need to be wide awake at the start. In every team meeting they always mention the tram tracks in Milan. Every time I have raced Milan–Sanremo there have always been some crashes there. This year I didn't hear or see any, but there are always guys who don't make it to the official start because of a crash in the neutral roll-out. It has its charm.

Normally they stop the race at the official start, but this year they didn't. I'd been talking to Oliver Naesen and he stopped for a pee because he was expecting them to stop at the end of the neutral. But we went immediately. I didn't see him again until 20 minutes later, after he'd already had to chase back through the cars.

You don't want to start the race too relaxed. You don't want to end up riding in the wind, thinking, 'It's OK because we still have six hours to go.' You don't want to lose concentration, hit a bump and lose your handlebars. It's the same with eating and drinking. You can almost forget that you have to do it. All those small things make a big difference.

In Milan–Sanremo everyone feels this kind of laziness for the first six hours. And the first time you really have to push, you think, 'Woah, what's going on here?' The mental game is so important – not losing focus. You know it's normal that the body is a little bit lazy. You know it's normal that the body has to wake up. There's almost no other races where that is the case.

The first 80km were really fast, which was good. But then I had a little bit of mental crisis and was suffering a bit with how slowly the time was passing, from 80 to about 150km. But I talked to a lot of the guys: Oliver Naesen, Ryan Mullen, Yves Lampaert and Wout van Aert. It was important not just to be there looking around in silence. Some guys had been at Tirreno–Adriatico and so we talked about that. I spoke to Michael Gogl about how well he'd done at Strade Bianche, and with Yves we spoke about Paris–Nice, as well as about our girlfriends, who are very good friends with one another. And we talked about a TV show that was popular on Belgian television. There's always lots to talk about, not just cycling, and it's more than simply, 'Hello, how are you? What's your next race?'

The Turchino pass is a little bit harder than the route the race took this year. The valley road is less of a gradient, and I had the feeling that the peloton was a little bit less stressed. But the descent was quite technical and it stretched out the bunch.

All race I was stopping every 10km to have a pee. I don't know what was going on with me that day, but I stopped 13 times in total and it was driving Ryan crazy. We'd come back from a pee break, and five minutes later I'd tell him I needed to stop again. He thought I was kidding, until I told him that I really had to go again! Our sports director Kim Andersen said on the radio, after he'd seen me stop for the tenth or the eleventh time, 'Hey, Jasper! You're going to fly up the climb! You're so light after all those pee stops.'

Then, from the moment we hit the Capi climbs, the stress started. There were some tougher moments, but nothing that made me think, 'OK, this is *really* crazy.' The guys did a really good job in front, which meant I was able to conserve energy there. From the first of the Capi it really starts, and then the run-in to the Cipressa is quite impressive to be inside.

We lost each other a bit heading towards the Cipressa, and there it got a bit more dodgy. I had to take a few more risks than I would normally have done to be in the right position at the bottom of the climb. But it's a fight where everyone is trying to do the same thing, bumping shoulders. No one wants to be the first one to brake. I found a good gap right before the turn onto the Cipressa, so I hit the climb in maybe fifth or sixth. That was perfect.

Heading onto the Poggio I got a little bit boxed in. I was surprised by the way Ineos took control. Then I spotted Jasper de Buyst moving up on the right with Caleb Ewan. I've known Jasper for a long time, and we used to race on the same team. I know that's he's really good at being where he needs to be. So I jumped onto Caleb's wheel and that way I turned onto the Poggio in a really good position.

On the climb, Ewan stayed right behind the Ineos guys. I was a little bit further back, maybe five or six spots. I was happy where I was. Over the top there were about eight of us, and another four who chased on. I was quite surprised that it was such a big group as we hit the downhill. No one expected that, I don't think.

From the top of the climb, I knew that I was going to attack. Where I would attack would all depend on the moment that everyone would slow down and start looking. But I didn't know when that moment was going to come. I just wanted to try and stay open to taking the opportunity whenever it was there.

To be honest, I have a feeling we didn't go full speed downhill. There was a bit of hesitating. But what makes that descent so special is that you come over the top *à bloc* but then the downhill is so technical that, even though your body's on the limit physically, you still need to have the mental focus. And when your heart's beating at 190bpm, it's hard to keep it all under control. Pidcock went to the front and it went a little faster, and Schachmann opened up a little gap. But even then, I didn't feel I needed to start taking risks to stay up towards the front. Alaphilippe was the first one to try, and Pidcock immediately reacted and closed the door.

After that, I took my chance. My attack was really, really all-in.

For the first 30 seconds I felt amazing. I took the speed from the downhill, in the big gear, super fast. But then after 30 seconds the lactate reached my legs and I started fighting with myself to push. I had to tell myself, 'You need to go through this pain! This is all to win a Monument! This is your chance. You can't give it away now.'

I didn't look back until the moment that Søren Kragh Andersen caught up with me. I also felt it in my legs, so I knew that the way he'd closed the gap would have cost him a lot of energy. What I didn't know was how much room we had if he'd decided not to pull. Then I started to look around a lot to know where everyone was. With 1km to go, there is a kind of chicane. That was when I allowed myself just a moment to relieve a little of the pressure in my legs, take a deep breath and then go for the last 700 metres even with him on my wheel. So I did and that was what enabled me to jump on his wheel when he went to the other side of the road and attacked, though there are no TV pictures of that moment.

I knew I had to dig really deep to stay on his wheel. It was really painful. But I knew that if I could stay seated on his wheel, and if he just rode tempo, then I might be able to recover enough to take him on in the sprint. I knew how close the bunch was but I told myself, 'Don't get stressed. Because if you go too early then they'll roll you over on the line.' So I took a big gamble, but also I felt so in control of the situation. I wouldn't like to call it the 'killer instinct' because it's not as if I win a race every week, but I felt like I was doing the right thing. I took the right decision. It's what happens when you are on a good day. I am convinced that you see things more clearly when you are on a good day.

It's a beautiful finish line. It was so nice to throw my arms in the air. I only did it when I was sure that my front wheel was going to pass the line first. At that moment I felt alone in the world. You can see in the photos that I am not yet really going crazy, because at that point I was not really aware of what had just happened – that I'd just made the biggest achievement of my career. It was only in the following days that it became clear.

After the podium, everyone from the team was waiting for me at the parking lot. And then everyone just went home. They dropped me off in Monaco, where I live. My girlfriend was waiting there for me, and I handed over the flowers from the podium. Then we just cooked a normal dinner of pulled pork with some grilled potatoes and carrots, but I wasn't super hungry. We opened a bottle of champagne, which we enjoyed, and then we talked a lot about the day and how it went. She told me how she'd experienced the day. I got to spend that evening with the person I love and that makes it even more valuable – that we could enjoy it, just the two of us.

It was really strange actually: I still didn't realise what I'd just achieved. Even without winning Milan–Sanremo, I am proud of what I've achieved. I've always been up there, and I've had some nice victories and so many races where I was close, that I almost won. A rider should always appreciate those results, but in cycling it is about winning. But winning Sanremo was another level. It was not the Monument that was first on my list – I always thought more about Roubaix or Flanders – but that doesn't make it any less beautiful.

# IN THE WINNERS' WORDS
## DAME SARAH STOREY

*Dame Sarah Storey made history at the Tokyo Paralympic Games by winning a 17th Paralympic gold medal – more than any other athlete from Great Britain. Her debut at the Games dates back to 1992 when, aged 14, she picked up her first two gold medals as a swimmer. By 2008, she had switched to cycling and began to dominate across multiple disciplines. Her victory in the C4-5 road race in appalling weather conditions on Mount Fuji was one of her hardest fought. If she is still racing in Paris 2024, she will be 46 years old.*

---

It felt like I was going to do a job. There wasn't an expectation of any razzmatazz. I knew that the Games were going to be held in a very challenging environment for the Japanese hosts, so I knew we were going to have to be resourceful. There wasn't going to be any kind of party at the end. I went very prepared to be living in lockdown, which is what it was. I knew I was going to be travelling home by myself. It felt like I was going somewhere to do something and then come home: do your job; come home; control the controllable. For me it was very, very simple: just focus on what you do on two wheels.

There were so many things we had to do just in order to get on the plane. That was the first success. There was so much we had to do just to prove we should be there.

The hardest point of my preparation was not having any kind of data point that I knew I could rely on. The three-week training camp was the only thing that was at all similar to previous years. The longest race I'd done was only 70km. I'd had no proper road races for the two years or more since I'd come back to racing after having my second child. I'd had none of that sense of normality since the pandemic had struck so soon after he was born.

If it was all going to work, each of my races in Tokyo had to be treated with equal importance. They were such prolific performances. I was 4.3 seconds quicker than I'd ever been over the individual pursuit on the track. Then the time trial was the more controllable of the two on the road, and it was also the one that I had raced the most. And I had an absolute dream TT: the handling, the cornering, the speed. It was just the perfect time trial.

Once I'd got through the first of the stepping stones successfully, I had a lot of confidence going into the road race. But I was aware of the possibility of a mishap, especially with the weather forecast. I had to make sure that I was paying attention to every detail that was necessary.

I'd prepared everything that I needed the night before. I'd taken my own little rice cooker with me and made my own porridge in my room. It was all part of staying isolated, staying the right side of the playbook and making sure that I wasn't going to test positive for Covid.

I ate my porridge and then left in the car. On the side of Mount Fuji where we were the weather actually wasn't too bad. But we went through the tunnel and out the other side and it was like emerging into a different country! The rain lasted all through the day. The forecast was bad, but it got worse than that. It was a bit like approaching a race in the UK in the knowledge that we were definitely going to get very wet. There were suddenly no discussions about ice jackets for the heat any more. In fact, I could have done with a cup of tea! It was *awful*. I was so cold.

I was forced to go on the front and was the only person chasing the breakaway. It actually wasn't a problem riding on the front because it was the only way I could stay warm. It was 17 degrees and I was prepared for 35. So that was the surreal part – adjusting back to a normal UK temperature, having been so prepared to manage the heat.

The group was already down to six riders after the first lap anyway, and Kerstin Brachtendorf just kept attacking. She'd got a silver medal at the World Championships and was very keen to see a similar style of race. She's not as confident as me on the descents and corners, so she wanted to be up the road. It was always me who had to make sure she didn't go too far, and the one time I thought that someone else should chase, she got away. So I realised, 'Ah, OK. That didn't work. I am literally on my own here. Nobody's going to help close the gap to Kerstin.'

I was aware that my legs weren't feeling great because of the cold. I didn't feel as zippy up the climb as I had expected, which is normally my strength. So I had to think hard about which part of the race to use to shut her down, and I chose the technical bit because I was aware that I was the more confident and had the better skills. There's a picture of me with my eyes shut. I took a corner fast – at around 60kmph – but the rain was just coming straight into my face, so I thought, 'OK, just shut your eyes!'

Nobody else wanted to go around that corner so quickly in the rain. I didn't touch my brakes. I was rock solid, my weight distribution was just right. I didn't have a single 'sketchy' moment, to the extent that I started to question whether I was actually going fast enough. I had so many endorphins from just zooming around the circuit. It was brilliant!

Going into the bell lap, we were all together again. Then we got away – me and the other GB rider, Crystal Lane-Wright. She just wanted to make sure that we wouldn't be caught again, so I was on the front on the climb, keeping the pace high enough to hold them off but not so high that she would get dropped. She was saying, 'You've got to get me to that silver medal.'

None of it had gone according to how I had planned it. I had expected to attack on the climb and go solo. But that's what you have to do: work out a way to win the race with what you're given.

It was only with about 200 metres to go that I finally realised it was mine. Ever since, I've been thinking about the number of different ways I have had to use to win a bike race. There's never been two races that have been the same. All three of my Paralympic road titles have been very different strategies.

If I am absolutely honest, it's still taking me time to work it all out. Normally when you finish a race you feel as if your legs have worked the way you wanted them to. I'd never been in a championship race before when my legs have not done what I asked them to do: a combination of the lack of road racing preparation and maybe the cold, too. So slowly it's been sinking in that perhaps my brain was the winning factor. Though I was physically in great shape, I had to use my brain even more than normal. The tactics were not straightforward.

I feel huge pride. To be the greatest Paralympian in the UK – and still to be competing – that brings a huge smile to my face. I think of all the people I've worked with, trained with and raced against. The win in Tokyo has given me the opportunity to celebrate that while still racing. It's an insanely good feeling. I feel that as I've got older I've allowed myself to acknowledge and celebrate it more. Being a parent, and all the other things in my life, have given me a good balance and helped provide a clarity of thought, allowing me to make good decisions.

The future? Paris. I said even before Tokyo that, regardless of results, I couldn't imagine stopping in an empty stadium and with no crowd. You need to be prepared to win in an empty room, but I didn't anticipate that moment after the victory, which was empty as well. I hadn't imagined what that would feel like.

The chapter couldn't be closed – not on anything. There are so many reasons to keep going. And fewer reasons to stop.

# IN THE WINNERS' WORDS
## LIZZIE DEIGNAN

*The first-ever edition of the women's Paris–Roubaix had been anticipated with growing excitement by the cycling public, who were aware they would be witnessing a historic event. What comes as something of a surprise is that the emphatic winner of the race, Lizzie Deignan, was equally aware of the wider context of her achievement as she crossed the line and raised one bloodied hand skywards in a timeless victory salute.*

---

I started cycling when I was 15, and I didn't grow up in a cycling family. I grew up watching the London marathon and that kind of thing. That was the sort of sporting event we would watch. But when I moved to Belgium and tried to become a professional on the road, that's when I became aware of the iconic races. Obviously Flanders is huge, but the special thing about Roubaix was that we didn't have a women's one. So I was always available to watch it! I wasn't racing and always had a day off, so that meant it was a day on the sofa watching the race. It's one of those races that you watch from start to finish – and there's not that many that you do. You might watch a Tour de France stage and have a power nap in the middle. But, in Roubaix, you don't.

I think it's just a culmination of everything that a cyclist needs: they need to be skilful, they need to be strong, they need to have mental toughness and tactical awareness. That's why I love it: because it's more than just being the strongest bike rider. There are winners who puncture or crash, but you need it to go *more right* for you than anyone else, I suppose. It's just never over until it's over.

I was delighted and surprised when ASO announced in 2020 that they were going to hold a women's Paris–Roubaix. The news arrived in the middle of a pandemic. It was a huge motivator because we just didn't know what was going to happen: how the pandemic might affect women's cycling, and whether all the progress that had been made would be damaged by the financial insecurity of sponsors.

I had such an anti-climactic feeling after the Olympic Games because I'd put myself in the best possible physical shape and yet I couldn't control the race. And I knew going into the World Championships that actually my focus and my objective was Paris–Roubaix. In Trek-Segafredo, I knew we had a chance to win it, and I didn't know how strong a GB Team would be at the Worlds. They really surprised me and rode phenomenally but, in terms of being able to dictate the way a race can go, I didn't want to leave myself feeling like I had done after the Olympics again.

When I got to Roubaix our DS, Ina Teutenberg, told me I wasn't going to be a leader, and I had to accept that. Ellen van Dijk had just won the world time trial championship, and Elisa Longo

Borghini had been on such exceptional form. It was an ongoing conversation. We went to Roubaix on the Wednesday to do some recons, and it was quite clear from the language and the focus around the team that we were going to be riding for Ellen. So it didn't come as a surprise in the team meeting two days later to find out that I wasn't the leader.

We'd done a recon in the spring and I had been pleasantly surprised. I'd imagined the worst possible cobbles – and they are pretty ruthless – but I think having the specialist equipment just makes a massive difference. It's a huge advantage. I mean, you can't deny it: the technology has moved on from those iconic images of Roubaix that we all remember. It is different now. But it was still definitely different to anything we had ever done before, and I had some anxiety before the race – not knowing what we were getting into, I suppose.

In the team meeting, we were told to be 'OK with chaos'. That was what Ina said: 'You have to be OK in the chaos.' I think as a rider I'm pretty good in chaotic situations. I'm pretty level-headed. That probably helped in the race.

On the morning of the race, I felt excited. Genuine excitement. The weather forecast presented me with an opportunity. It's not something that I actually wanted – because obviously it leads to a more dangerous race, and no one wants that – but I wasn't scared by the possibility of rain. In the first 30km you could really feel the pressure. We were riding like we were setting up a bunch sprint. It was seriously hectic. You could feel the nervous energy in the peloton and some people don't cope well with that, obviously.

Our roles in the race were clearly defined. Our leaders were Elisa and Ellen. Audrey Cordon-Ragot and I were the last helpers. But there was a moment with about 5km to go until the first cobbled sector, when I turned to Audrey and said, 'Do I go back for them?' Elisa and Ellen just couldn't work their way through the bunch and were towards the back. It was all over the place, crashes were happening even on the tarmac. They were struggling to hold a position. Audrey made the perfect call and said that I should stay at the front. There was no good in us all being at the back. I at least needed to be an insurance tactic.

There was a moment when it all bottle-necked into the cobbles. I saw a gap opening up on the left-hand side and I did a full-on sprint and went into the sector in first place. I carried such a momentum that I created a gap. Lauretta Hanson was on my wheel and she made another really good call to just let me go.

At that point I know there were people looking at each other in the peloton and saying, 'She's crazy.' And of course, it was crazy. But I knew that, as long as I was off the front, I was buying Ellen and Elisa time to reorganise themselves in the peloton and then come across to me. On the radio Ina said, 'OK, Lizzie, you've got a gap. Just ride at 75 per cent. Get organised behind, girls.' But the gap kept just stretching out because the cobbles were so wet and slippery. Once the gap had gone out to a minute and a half, that's when Ina came on the radio and said, 'Lizzie, you've got to start riding at 100 per cent.' And that's what I did. I think I still had about 50km to go. I still felt like I was just the insurance policy because behind we still had Ellen, Audrey and Elisa. That was the idea, the whole time, until… I don't know. There were probably about 20km to go when Ina started saying to me, 'Lizzie, you've got this.' I thought I was hearing the radio wrong. I mean, what was she talking about?!

I was aware the whole time that I was one wrong move away from it all being over. But… I don't know. You have these days as a rider when you're just *on it*. I just felt in control, even when I was slipping. I didn't panic at any point. I also knew that I was going over these points as a solo rider and I could only imagine what was going on behind. I was definitely glad to be alone.

Then I got the information that Marianne Vos was coming across. When you hear that she is trying to ride you down, you feel as if you're being hunted. Elisa tried to stay on her wheel but couldn't. I didn't know that Ellen had crashed. So I knew at that point that I had to safely get over the cobbles with enough of a gap. I knew that she'd take time on me over the cobbles because she had fresh legs and she's technically such a very good rider. But, as long as I still had a minute, then I was confident. She took a big chunk of time out of me during her initial attack, but then I just held her. I felt incredibly proud to be standing on the podium next to her. We have a huge amount of respect for each other. Her palmarès is beyond anything I could dream of, but I've given her some good battles in my time.

I only felt I was going to win the race when I entered the velodrome. Watching the men's race the following day, I just thought, 'Thank god I was on my own!' To have to judge a sprint on the track when you've just had that many cobbles rattling your bones for that long! You're no longer able to make good decisions.

I never wear gloves to race. Not even in winter. I like to be able to feel the handlebars in my hands. I was the same on the track. I hadn't worn them on recon and I hadn't got blisters, so I didn't want to change. But obviously I paid for that decision. In the race I didn't feel my hands at all. The photos of the blood on my handlebar tape have gone everywhere and I suppose it makes the story even better.

I genuinely felt like the moment was bigger than me. I really felt like I was part of history. I said afterwards that I had felt the power of generations of women. I had Ina Teutenberg in the car behind me. She was a huge champion to me when I was growing up, watching her then racing alongside her. She won hundreds of races. Just to know that someone like her – who would absolutely have adored to race that race but never got the opportunity – was in our car made me so grateful even to be there. I am proud of the women before me who have raced just on passion. That race is all about passion.

As for the Roubaix showers, well, I have non-cycling friends who wonder what on earth that's all about! They can't believe there's a picture of me in the showers being auctioned for charity. But it *is* an iconic image – you're washing off the mud of the battle.

# IN THE WINNERS' WORDS
## TADEJ POGAČAR

*Tadej Pogačar has had quite the year. In July he won his second consecutive Tour de France, and in September he announced his engagement to his girlfriend, Urška Žigart. Either side of the big one, he picked up two of cycling's Monuments. Nothing seems to faze the 22-year-old phenomenon, who grew into something of a 'patron' during the three weeks of the Tour. Over 21 stages, there was just one brief moment when he was put under pressure. But other than that, it was perfection.*

---

I was quite relaxed coming into the Tour. I knew I had prepared well and have a good group of people around me and we all work really hard for each other. My target was to win the race again. I think that was a fair target after winning last year, though I knew it would be hard to achieve.

Before the Tour I was in Slovenia, where I had the time trial and road race National Championship, so it was a nice reason to go home and see the family. But also to put the final touches to my Tour prep. I love racing in Slovenia and representing the national team when I get the opportunity. It's really important for me and something I'm really proud of.

Allan Peiper has had a few health issues lately and so has been at fewer races than usual. He and I have a very good relationship. He was my *directeur sportif* at my first race for the team back in 2019 and also when I won the Tour last year. He has a lot of experience and his attention to detail and planning is something that really makes a big difference. He is a really good guy who I admire a lot.

The first few days at this year's Tour were really intense with all the crashes. We had our fair share of bad luck, with all of us touching the ground at some point, Hirschi and McNulty coming worst off in the crashes. We all look to beat our rivals but I can say that no rider wants to see other guys crash or hurt themselves. So when I heard Primož had crashed I was disappointed for him. At the end of the day, it's just sport and we all have families and loved ones who are more important.

I was delighted to win the time trial. I knew I had gone fast but there were a lot of specialists there so I didn't know exactly how I had done. When I found out I had won, it was a great feeling after such an intense first week. I also managed to take the white jersey that day, which was really nice as it's still an important one to wear and I have good memories in white jerseys.

We had spent a lot of time doing the recon of the stages in the Alps and knew what to expect pretty well. On the day we did the recon to Tignes the road was covered in snow and we had to walk across it in our cleats, carrying our bikes, to see the last part of the climb. The *directeur sportif* had to do a detour of over two hours to get around and collect us at the other side. On the actual day of the stage the weather was wet and cold, which was good for me as I know that it can suit me well.

On stage 11, on Ventoux, I went really deep. I couldn't follow Vingegaard so I let his wheel go. I knew we weren't so far from the top so it was a matter of getting into a good rhythm and limiting my losses. Then, when I saw Urán and Carapaz coming across, I knew we would have a good chance of catching Vingegaard on the descent because it was still far from the finish. We hit over 100kmph on that descent; it was one of the fastest speeds I've ever done on a bike.

The final time trial was a different sensation. In 2020 it was a feeling of shock and excitement because of the circumstances on the last time trial. But in 2021 I had a pretty healthy gap coming into the time trial, so it was a little bit more calm but also hugely emotional. Both feelings were great and I feel lucky to have had both experiences.

My girlfriend is a huge support for me also and she is usually the first person I call after the race. This year I also had my parents following a lot of the race in a campervan with my little sister, and my other two siblings also joined them for a few days. Obviously with the race bubble, I wasn't able to see much of them but once or twice I was able to go over and say hello from afar. It was nice having them there and it gives you an extra boost.

Standing on the podium in Paris is really beautiful. Speeches are not my strongest point. I always think that, no matter how much you prepare it, you always forget to thank somebody, but I did my best to speak from the heart.

One word is probably not enough to describe how I feel about my Tour victory, but it was really perfect.

# EDITOR'S INTRODUCTION

BY NED BOULTING

*Per Aspera (Through hardship)*

2021 wasn't really supposed to be like this. Even though those who had studied the consequences and effects of pandemics warned repeatedly and severally that we would be living with the aftershocks of Covid-19 for years to come, the unsilenceable optimist within us all refused to embrace the reality of their prognosis. The trauma of 2020 could not possibly be repeated – or so we believed. We were partially, but not completely, right.

The first inkling that the cycling calendar might once again be prised asunder came before the turning of the year. In fact, just as we at The Road Book were putting the finishing touches to the 2020 edition, in the naive expectation that its diminished size and fractured nature would be a unique volume, the organisation of the Tour Down Under fired off the first warning pistol into the ever-darkening November air. Australia's season-opening stage race would not take place in 2021. The cancellations, it seemed, had begun again.

The Tour de San Juan followed not long after, then the Tour Colombia. The two important early-season stage races, which had attracted such strong startlists in recent years and had offered wintry populations of the northern hemisphere a glimpse of the baking heat of Argentina and the sultry tropical warmth of Colombia, were simply erased from the calendar. Then, in order to get ahead of the third-wave curves of mounting Covid infection sweeping through much of the world, relatively minor races were suddenly being cancelled or at least postponed across Europe: in Belgium, the Netherlands, France, Italy and Spain. Paris–Camembert and the Tour de Normandie – both celebrated keystones of the French cycling year – were either struck off or delayed. In Germany, the 59th Eschborn–Frankfurt would not take place until September. The traditional Challenge Mallorca series of one-day races was shunted from its usual berth at the end of January to a rather hopeful-seeming new place in the calendar in May, as were the Volta ao Algarve and the Vuelta a Andalucia, with the Volta a la Comunitat Valenciana moving to mid-April. More emphatically still, Malaysia's Tour de Langkawi – Asia's most prestigious stage race – was dropped completely for the first time since its inaugural edition in 1996. The signs were not good.

And yet, there the wobbling edifice of another rapidly collapsing racing calendar seemed to steady itself. The worrying string of deferrals and cancellations stopped unfurling, and gradually a strong outline of the familiar race pattern started to emerge, set against a backdrop of patchy vaccination programmes being rolled out with staggering speed in certain territories and painful sluggishness in others. Not uncontroversially, the entire UAE Team Emirates squad, including their 2020 Tour de France champion Tadej Pogačar, were among some of the first people in the world to be vaccinated against Covid-19, receiving doses of the Chinese-developed Sinopharm vaccine at a training camp in Abu Dhabi in early January.

Regardless of when or where they might resume racing, teams prepared themselves for action, ready to perform as and when required. But the winter of 2020–21 had shaken the dice. There had been some big-name riders on the move in the men's peloton. In the women's equivalent, meanwhile, there had been just one that really mattered. Annemiek van Vleuten – entering her 14th year as a pro, at the age of 38 – had switched to ride for Movistar in an eye-catching move designed to deliver the Spanish team the kind of regular and repeated successes that had eluded them for the first three years of their existence. The European champion's new team – akin to the Mitchelton-Scott team she had left – would organise joint training camps for both the men's and the women's teams. Once again, therefore, Van Vleuten would benefit from the work she could do alongside both her male and female colleagues before her season got underway at the end of February in Omloop Het Nieuwsblad, a race she won in 2020 as she embarked on a five-race winning streak. Victory in that race was denied her in 2021, however, as both Van Vleuten and Lizzie Deignan made an uncharacteristic mistake in their positioning that saw them out the back and effectively out of the race when it split in the wind. That opened the way for Anna van der Breggen to pick up where she had left off in 2020: by winning.

Women's racing evolved fast in 2021. A minimum salary of €20,000 was applied throughout the WorldTour squads, though BikeExchange and Trek-Segafredo unilaterally raised their minimum to match that of their male riders, effectively doubling their female riders' pay. Trek-Segafredo also decided to match the prize money their riders could earn, where races had both male and female versions and a disparity existed. And Abi Van Twisk's case broke new ground when Trek-Segafredo honoured her salary throughout her pregnancy – something that Uno-X have also safeguarded for Elinor Barker, who is also pregnant and will ride for them in 2022. Each one of these steps moves the women's peloton towards a more enlightened and just future and, though they may be small gestures, they will make a huge difference in the lives of the individual athletes concerned.

The men's Omloop Het Nieuwsblad finished with a 45-rider bunch sprint, the biggest group to come to the line for years. Davide Ballerini confirmed his promise of 2020 by taking the victory, with young British rider Jake Stewart picking up a surprise second place. A few weeks later, Stewart would become embroiled in controversy when he was forced into the barriers by Nacer Bouhanni in the final of Cholet - Pays de la Loire. Stewart publicly took the French sprinter to task, and Bouhanni was fined and disqualified for the illegal and dangerous manoeuvre. Sometime later, Bouhanni revealed he had been on the receiving end of appalling racial abuse online. The cycling world was forced to take stock once more of its continuing problem with racism.

In the ranks of the men's WorldTour, one name in particular was generating more column inches than any other: Chris Froome. His move to Israel Start-Up Nation seemed, on the face of it, like a gamble. Nothing about his 2020 form had suggested the seven-time Grand Tour winner was even close to getting back to his best – or even close enough to be competitive. Yet Froome continued to talk up his chances and remained positive as the season got underway and for the first time in a decade he was not a Sky/Ineos rider.

As Froome continued his physical battle, another Grand Tour champion, Jumbo-Visma's Tom Dumoulin, pressed pause on his career, citing mental fatigue as his reasoning for stepping away from the sport. Whether he would ever be seen racing again remained uncertain. Aside from those two headliners, a number of significant others had been adjusting to a new environment, leaving TV commentators to grapple not only with new sponsors and new kits but also with familiar riders turning out in the colours of very unfamiliar teams: Greg Van Avermaet – into his fifth year as reigning Olympic champion, after the Tokyo Games were postponed in 2020 – had switched to AG2R Citroën, taking with him Oliver Naesen and Michael Schär. Roman Bardet had left that team, bound for DSM, while their star rider Marc Hirschi joined UAE Team Emirates in somewhat acrimonious and somewhat mysterious circumstances.

Team Ineos added yet more top-class firepower to their assault on the Grand Tours by signing Adam Yates and re-signing Richie Porte while also acquiring Dani Martínez and young British all-round talent Tom Pidcock. Thus, for the first time, the cycling world could anticipate the prospect of the Yates twins riding on opposing teams.

In the often turbulent world of sprinters' contracts, the only major change was Jasper Philipsen leaving the ranks of UAE Team Emirates for Mathieu van der Poel's Alpecin-Fenix, almost guaranteeing him a starting place at the Tour de France. The only other rumoured move never materialised: Wout van Aert was briefly thought to be leaving Jumbo-Visma, only to announce that he had signed a new long-term contract with the Dutch team. And it was Wout van Aert's rivalry with Mathieu van der Poel that would hold the cycling world enthralled through the misery of another Covid winter, even before the road calendar got underway. Along with the young pretender Tom Pidcock, a whole new audience found itself watching cyclocross for the first time. A venerable, distant, ancient and eccentric cousin of road racing, cyclocross has always been passionately advocated by those who understand its muddy peculiarities. Yet, to the outsider, its closed circuits have remained something of an eccentric mystery.

For the first time in our four-year history of The Road Book, we include a section on the World Cup cyclocross series and the UCI cyclocross World Championships, held this year behind closed doors – and partly through the North Sea. The remarkable sight of Wout van Aert chasing Mathieu van der Poel through the waves lapping the beach at Ostend was one of the most striking sights of the year and made a compelling case for the sub-set of cycling to be included in The Road Book, despite the lack of a visible road in the sand. The current generation of superstars in cyclocross are also such a dominant feature of the road racing scene that to omit their duelling in the mud and sand of the cross season would seem incomplete. To guide us through the hidden wonders of this arcane variant of the sport, we are delighted to include a thoughtful and funny piece of writing by Tom Pidcock. His tale of cruelly designed courses, appalling suffering and great victories brings the sport to life from the unique perspective of a young man in the thick of the action. For, in his words, 'Cross makes you fast. Strong and fast.' And just those attributes – as stripped-down and simple as they might sound – are the hallmark of the Van der Poel/Van Aert/Pidcock generation who are busily transforming the possible on the road.

There was one name missing from the roll call of exuberant young talent when racing finally got underway in the men's peloton: Remco Evenepoel. It is worth reminding ourselves of his achievements in 2020. He entered four stage races. He won every single one of them: San Juan, Algarve, Burgos and Poland. Along the way he took five stages, two of which were individual time trials. In Burgos, at the Picon Blanco, he'd proved beyond doubt that he was physiologically suited to long climbs when he won the stage ahead of specialist world-class climbers such as George Bennett, Mikel Landa and Esteban Chaves. And in Poland he'd humbled the GC opposition in the shape of Jakob Fuglsang and Simon Yates. But his broken pelvis at the August edition of Il Lombardia had denied him entry to his first Grand Tour and, as 2021 got going, his rehabilitation took a step back. Evenepoel had to scratch his early-season objectives, step off the bike and then slowly build again towards the Giro. By mid-April he was still yet to race, although this did not stop him putting his signature to a new five-year contract with Deceuninck-QuickStep.

With no racing in Mallorca, the cycling world had to wait until the end of January before the season stuttered into life, and then races started to come thick and fast. It felt like a throwback to a bygone age as, in the absence of the cancelled Saudi Tour and the southern hemisphere races, it was the traditional French races that became the focus of our attention. The GP Cycliste la Marseillaise, the Etoile de Bessèges and the Tour des Alpes-Maritimes et du Var served up a very early-season opportunity for new names to emerge, as was the case when AG2R Citroën's Aurélien Paret-Peintre finished with a rush to the line to thwart his compatriots Thomas Boudat and Bryan Coquard in Marseille. His name was virtually unknown before 2021, but not any longer. Established riders like Tim Wellens (who always seems to come out of the blocks flying) and Gianluca Brambilla chalked up GC wins, before the lure of a stuffed startlist drew the gaze towards the UAE, where Covid had first begun to wreak its own miserable havoc with the racing calendar a year previously.

The UAE Tour opened with a spectacular day's racing in strong crosswinds, the long straight roads of the desert perfectly aligned for the race to blow apart, which it did. From a reduced group of 20 riders, Mathieu van der Poel won the sprint ahead of 23-year-old David Dekker, who was making a hugely impressive WorldTour debut for Jumbo-Visma. But that was it for Van der Poel's race. A positive Covid result among the staff of his team forced the overnight withdrawal of Alpecin-Fenix and handed Dekker a surprise leader's jersey. The son of former Rabobank stalwart Erik Dekker was one of a clutch of more or less unheralded names who made their mark in the UAE Tour, including Swiss time triallist Stefan Bissegger and Jonas Vingegaard (who took the stage to Jebel Jais). These two riders would go on to serial successes throughout the year. Tadej Pogačar picked up his first GC win of 2021 in a race that – unlike in 2020 – ran its full distance.

Strade Bianche was returned to its natural spot in the early spring. The women's race set the tone for battles to come, with the powerful SD Worx team attacking in sequence. Former world road race champion Chantal van den Broek-Blaak emerged into the empty piazza in the heart of Siena in first place – a victory to sit alongside her notable Classics triumphs over half a decade. In the men's race, 2019 winner Julian Alaphilippe was left for dead by Mathieu van der Poel's almighty acceleration on the deserted Via Santa Caterina, and that was that.

While the women would have to wait a fortnight to race again, the men's peloton split into its traditional halves: one heading for Tirreno–Adriatico and the other to Paris–Nice. These two venerable stage races often vie for attention; the French race can be brutally hard and normally features strong winds on the march south from Paris, while its Italian cousin is a rather more elegant affair. Yet, up until the final stage of Paris–Nice in 2021, when Primož Roglič crashed on a descent and lost the race to 2020's victor Max Schachmann, it had been a fairly tepid affair.

Schachmann appeared at something of a loss to know how to celebrate the victory that had come at the expense of the previously invulnerable Slovenian. The early stages had been devoid of wind but enlivened by a brief attack by 11 Belgian riders (ten from West Flanders plus Philippe Gilbert) from different teams, orchestrated by Oliver Naesen. It was a moment of pure racing delight, both awe-inspiring and hilarious. But it only lasted for a few kilometres.

The stage race in Italy, however, was pure spectacle. Boasting arguably its best-ever startlist, its marvels ranged from the attacking spirit of world champion Alaphilippe, to Wout van Aert and Mathieu van der Poel knocking lumps out of one another, and Tadej Pogačar picking up where he'd left off in the UAE Tour. Van Aert's contribution to the race was perhaps the most notable: which other rider in the world would have been capable of taking the first stage in a bunch sprint and then the final time trial? It was a result that left him in second place on GC at a race that is invariably won by Grand Tour contenders. His extraordinary range continued to confound the conventions of modern racing.

Milan–Sanremo was broadcast in its entirety for the first time in its long history, to compensate for the request for the general public to stay away from the race and reduce the risk of spreading Covid. As is always the case, it wasn't until the Poggio that attempts were made to ride clear and win the race. A big group made it over the top together, from which Trek-Segafredo's Jasper Stuyven attacked as they came off the descent and into Sanremo. Somehow, the Belgian held on to take the first Monument of his career in dramatic fashion, as he recalls on the pages of this edition of The Road Book in his 'In The Winners' Words'.

After that came Belgium. The traditional shift from the Ligurian coast and the azure waters of the Mediterranean to the privations of Flanders, scarcely out of winter, marks a key moment in the developing narrative of any season, and this year the cobbled Classics heralded the resumption of the continuing rivalry between Van Aert and Van der Poel. But, by the time the Flanders Classics ended with the Brabanste Pijl, the duo had only managed one solitary victory between them (Wout van Aert took Gent–Wevelgem).

It is true that they both came extremely close to winning on numerous other occasions, but at the Tour of Flanders there was a sense that perhaps they were beatable after all. Kasper Asgreen of Deceuninck-QuickStep – the young man with the rock-solid position on a bike and curiously lugubrious air of someone who enjoys inflicting pain on others – sprang the biggest surprise of them all. He managed to do to Van der Poel what Van Aert had failed to do in 2020: namely, outsprint him. It was a stunningly self-confident end to the race. Asgreen's assuredness that he could match Van der Poel in a sprint flew in the face of conventional wisdom and, when it happened, silenced the millions watching at home who had been urging him to attack from distance.

It was the second year that the Tour of Flanders had been raced over bergs and cobbles devoid of its usual accompanying roadside whiff of chip fat and beer. For weeks, the messaging from the race organisation had been focused on stressing the need for spectators to stay at home and watch it on TV. For the man at the top of the Flanders Classics group that organises the Belgian spring Classics, Tomas Van Den Speigel, this was a period of great challenges. Writing exclusively for The Road Book, he offers an insight into the politics and challenges of staging the race in the middle of a pandemic, what the race means to *Flandriens*, and how it might develop in the future.

As the cobbled Classics made way for the Ardennes campaign, so a different assortment of riders came to the fore. First and foremost among them was the Slovenian phenomenon Tadej Pogačar. Already with two GC wins at WorldTour level to his name in 2021 (UAE and Tirreno–Adriatico), he unfussily won the first Monument of his absurdly accelerated career by taking Liège–Bastogne–Liège from under the nose of Flèche Wallonne winner Julian Alaphilippe and a high-class group of favourites. And he wasn't done yet (although his next Classics win would have to wait until October).

In the women's peloton, the victories continued to be shared among the star names. En route to Belgium, Elisa Longo Borghini – once again enjoying high visibility in the *tricolore* of the Italian national champion's jersey – had taken the Trofeo Alfredo Binda eight years after her first victory at the prestigious one-day race. Her 2013 win had announced her on the world stage at the age of 21; this repeat victory in 2021 was suggestive of more to come from the Italian.

But the continuing battle between the almighty SD Worx (Anna van der Breggen, Chantal van den Broek-Blaak, Demi Vollering et al) and their principal rivals (most notably Movistar, BikeExchange and Trek-Segafredo) would characterise the early clashes in the Women's WorldTour, as the peloton tried to figure out a solution to the dominance of the Dutch team. It seemed at first that their repeated numerical supremacy in the final selections in successive races was unanswerable, though as the season wore on, the results would be more evenly shared around the peloton. From inside the races, the irrepressible voice of Cecilie Uttrup Ludwig finds its distinctive expression (profanities and all) on these pages. The Danish rider – one of those select few challenging for major honours throughout the campaign – brings to life the drama, thrills, routine disappointments, occasional highs and frequent absurdities of a racing season like no other. She is searingly honest about the self-doubt that plagued her Classics campaign, but 2021 brought her a moment of pure vindication in Spain.

Across the world, Covid was beginning to spread again, as the Delta variant leapt from India to the UK and then was exported across the Channel. In France various local and regional authorities announced ever-tighter restrictions of public gatherings and freedom of movement, none of which augured particularly well for the prospects of Paris–Roubaix being raced in its rightful place in the calendar. Indeed, it wasn't long before it was postponed until October, which was the source of both regret and wild anticipation. Would there be rain at last on the cobbles? It seemed more likely somehow, yet the cycling world would have to wait a further six months to find out.

New UCI rules had been published in February concerning certain aspects of road racing, though they were not destined for enforcement until 1 April, allowing time for riders to become accustomed to not using the 'super-tuck' descending position popularised, though not invented, by Chris Froome in 2016. Gone too would be the habit of riders resting their forearms on their handlebars and crossing their hands in front. Both of these bike positions were deemed dangerous in race situations and, perhaps more significantly, were considered to be setting a bad example to impressionable young or amateur riders who might be persuaded to copy the pros after seeing their 'promotion' on the TV. There is scant evidence to suggest that what is seen on television actually translates into behaviour on the road, but this was the UCI taking a position of social responsibility. The new rules were generally met with a lot of harrumphing in both the women's and the men's pelotons, but by the summer everyone had got used to the changes.

Incidents of riders infringing these rules were few and far between. Richard Carapaz became the first rider to fall foul of the change to the 'super-tuck' regulations and was disqualified from

Liège–Bastogne–Liège, but it would be a further five months before anyone else suffered a similar fate. Yet the tinkering with the rules didn't stop there. In an effort to mitigate the often unhealthy optics of a peloton that liberally scatters plastic and wrappers across hundreds of kilometres of countryside as riders discard the contents of musettes and their back pockets, a new rule was introduced that expressly forbade any clothing from being thrown to the side of the road (an occasional but wasteful occurrence). Furthermore, picking up on Team Sky's 2018 campaign to 'Pass On Plastic', the practice of lobbing empty bidons at supporters by the side of the road was also banned. The most high-profile rider to be disqualified for rolling a water bottle to the side of the road was AG2R Citroën's Michael Schär. Off the back with a mechanical, and already effectively out of contention with 110km remaining, the Swiss spotted a clutch of teenagers reaching out their hands to ask for the bottle he had just emptied. Instinctively he obliged, before realising he was being followed at close quarters by a camera bike that had caught the whole transgression on film. Not long afterwards he was ordered to retire. For a day or two public opinion raged about the rights and wrongs (mostly the wrongs) of the ruling, before everyone forgot about it and got on with their lives.

Then, during the Giro d'Italia, another incident occurred that, in an indirect way, came about as a result of the new regulations. Deceuninck-QuickStep's Pieter Serry, having just lost contact with the GC group deep into a climb, was almost run over by a BikeExchange team vehicle that had driven up alongside the race director's car at the back of the bunch. Not concentrating on what was ahead of them on the road, all the occupants of both vehicles were seemingly focused on handing over a rain jacket that one of the Australian team's riders had given the race directors for safe keeping. They were in the process of returning it to its rightful owner when Serry, having suddenly decelerated, was struck from behind by the team car and could easily have fallen under its wheels. Instead, and very fortunately, the Belgian sprung to his feet, uninjured, and remonstrated with the driver, Gene Bates. The *directeur sportif* was thrown off the race, and his passenger Matt White was fined by the UCI. It could have been a whole lot worse.

The Giro was a race where rain jackets were in constant circulation. Despite a sunny start in Turin, which saw the mighty Filippo Ganna repeat his feat of 2020 and take the first *maglia rosa* in a time trial, the weather soon closed in. It stayed predominantly chilly and wet for the time of year all the way round a route that mostly shied away from southern Italy (the southernmost point being Foggia, in the very north of Puglia). Days without rain were few and far between, and in particular the stages to Sestola, Monte Zoncolan and Passo Giau were plagued by horrendous conditions. On the Giau stage, which should have featured three snowy ascents of over 2,000 metres, the race was shortened to omit the Pordoi and the Fedaia, and there was extremely limited TV coverage as neither the helicopters nor the accompanying signal-relay fixed-wing aircraft could get airborne. This was a shame, as it was on stage 16 that a hugely impressive Egan Bernal effectively ended any prospect of his race lead being usurped. It was the day he won the Giro d'Italia and set his sights on the Vuelta and a bid to take all three titles before his 25th birthday.

The race was full of bright detail, nevertheless. It was a somewhat chastening return to racing for Remco Evenepoel, who went into the race as one of the favourites despite having only just returned from serious injury and having never before raced a Grand Tour. His challenge came to a shuddering halt when he failed to find an answer to the pressure he was put under on the frightening downhill gravel sectors of a dramatic stage into Montalcino. Then there was Damiano Caruso's exceptional second place overall, Tim Merlier's emergence as a world-class sprinter, Leonardo Fortunato taking a first-ever Grand Tour stage win for Ivan Basso and Alberto

Contador's Eolo-Kometa team (prompting Contador to post a wildly excessive, tearful celebration on social media from in front of his TV in Spain), and a notable victory for Dan Martin. In claiming the stage to Sega di Ala, the Irishman completed the set of stage wins at all three Grand Tours, with a ride of astounding control and tactical mastery. He would later announce his retirement at the end of the season, ending a 14-year career that had yielded many noteworthy achievements, including two Monuments. Perhaps the stage victory in Italy clarified his thinking but, before making up his mind to quit, Dan agreed to write for The Road Book a first-person account of his Giro. The result is a candid, amusing and honest diary that brings to life the banal and epic experience of enduring a Grand Tour, triumphs, defeats and all. And it starts in the most unexpected way.

Even before the Giro had begun, there was a week of racing on the very fringe of Europe that was to have far-reaching consequences for how the entirety of the 2021 road race season would be remembered. The chain of events set in motion by the result of stage 2 of the Presidential Tour of Turkey would be as dramatic as they were unexpected. A 144km race around the still wintry-looking Anatolian city of Konya ended in a bunch sprint. It was won by Mark Cavendish ahead of Jasper Philipsen and his old rival and teammate André Greipel. That was Cavendish's first victory for three years, two months and four days – surely an unprecedentedly long drought for a top-class sprinter. The Tour of Turkey is the type of race that Cavendish used to deride as a 'shit, small race' – the very kind of event in which Greipel used to pick up the serial victories that didn't interest Cavendish when he and the German were both HTC Columbia teammates a decade previously. But in the context of 2021, and Cavendish's continuing belief that he could still return to winning ways, this victory was of great significance. It came only six months after he had tearfully suggested, in a televised interview at the end of the delayed 2020 Gent–Wevelgem, that he was very close to quitting the sport for good. By the end of the Tour of Turkey, Cavendish had picked up four stages. He was back.

In the meantime, March and April had yielded almost nothing but Dutch dominance in the women's WorldTour. With the notable exception of Grace Brown's impressive win at the catchily titled Oxyclean Classic Brugge–De Panne, the entire Classics campaign was dictated by riders whose surnames began with a 'V'. Between Marianne Vos, Annemiek van Vleuten, Anna van der Breggen and Demi Vollering, they had it sewn up. Vos proved at Gent–Wevelgem and at the Amstel Gold Race that, if a group comes to the line, her sprint remains her greatest weapon. Van Vleuten continued to rampage through the biggest races, though she had to do so without the support of the strongest team. Often, as was the case with her solo win at the Tour of Flanders, she would rely on one decisive acceleration to create a gap and leave her isolated rivals looking round at one another in a disorganised chase group. Van der Breggen captured a staggering seventh win at the Flèche Wallonne, making a convincing case that, when she retires at the end of the year, perhaps the race should be gently removed from the programme as there will surely never be another rider who has mastered the Mur de Huy like she has time and time again. And Vollering was busily making strides in 2021 that now firmly put her in the same bracket as her illustrious compatriots at the very top of their game. There was a certain equity in the way the four Dutch riders shared the spoils, but at times it must have felt like a closed shop.

Van der Breggen then took her form to the only WorldTour race in May, the Vuelta a Burgos, which she duly won. After that, with the cancellation of the horribly named Ride London Classique (why the feminine form?) and the Itzulia in Spain, the peloton would have to wait until La Course at the end of June to resume hostilities. This was to be the last edition of the much-maligned but often very engaging one-day race that had been shunted from pillar to post throughout its troubled eight-year existence. Even in 2021, it was moved from the opening Sunday of the Tour de France to an early-morning slot on the Saturday, on the pretext of not interfering with local elections being held in Brittany. (Quite why the men's race would not create difficulties, while the women's would, remained obscure.) It was won by Demi Vollering on the same uphill finish that Alaphilippe would dominate later on in the day. The Dutch rider will forever be remembered as the final winner of La Course; from 2022, it will be replaced by the Tour de France Femmes, an eight-day stage race to be held in the immediate aftermath of the men's race. The return to the calendar of an event that had seemingly disappeared for ever in 2009 was in part due to the lobbying efforts of a few committed individuals who applied pressure on ASO, the organisation behind the Tour de France. Those struggles are documented on these pages in the words of Kathryn Bertine, an ex-pro who actually lined up at the start of the first-ever La Course on the Champs-Élysées. In her recollections for the 2021 Road Book, she highlights the strains and stresses of her activism, the toll it took on her, and what the return of a women's Tour means for the sport.

Before the men's race got underway, there were the traditional warm-up races to complete. The Critérium du Dauphiné was won by Richie Porte. The Tasmanian looked to be on the same sparkling form that had characterised his third place at the 2020 Tour de France and led to his rejoining Ineos. The same could not be said, however, for his former teammate. Chris Froome – fresh from finishing the Tour de Romandie in 96th place – managed no better than 39th on any of the stages at the Dauphiné and was clearly so far off the pace that even he, with his relentless optimism, stopped talking about the possibility of competing for victory at the Tour de France. At times, as he was invariably one of the first riders to be dropped on the climbs, it was painful to watch.

If Froome was labouring, Alexey Lutsenko was flying. His victory on the race's individual time trial came so out of the blue that the TV director nearly missed it entirely. But it gave the Kazakh a temporary race lead, and made us all wonder whether he could race GC in the years to come, if not at Grand Tours then certainly in week-long stage races. His stage victory was a rare win for Astana in what amounted to a pretty miserable 2021 that saw turmoil behind the scenes and made little impact on the road. A few days before the Tour the team principal, Alexander Vinokourov, was ousted from his role, only to be reinstated later in the year as new owners fought over the future direction of a team short on success.

The Tour de Suisse was another GC success for Ineos Grenadiers, who must have believed their Tour preparations were pitch perfect a few weeks out from the grand départ. Richard Carapaz won the overall by 17 seconds to Rigoberto Urán. The Colombian surprised a few by riding to victory in the second ITT, which featured a long climb and a descent. He got the better of two Swiss time trial specialists in the Stefans Küng and Bissegger on home roads and in a race built in the image of Fabian Cancellara, boasting two time trials among its eight stages. Julian Alaphilippe was one of a few riders to race the time trial on a normal road bike, and still managed to come second, before promptly leaving the race to attend the birth of his and his partner Marion Rousse's son, Nino.

Finishing the Tour de Suisse in an unremarkable 41st place overall was the 2017 Giro d'Italia winner Tom Dumoulin. It was a welcome and heartening return to the peloton for the Dutchman after his five months of unpaid absence from the sport, at the start of which many observers questioned whether we'd seen the last of him on the road. Back in April, television viewers had been offered a brief glimpse of Dumoulin wearing a face mask and a black leather jacket, standing on the pavement near the Cauberg as the Amstel Gold Race passed by. There was a widespread sense of relief that Dumoulin's time away from the sport had not spelled the end. In the context of mental health, this was potentially a moment of great significance in a sport that is often rightly accused of ignoring the issue of its athletes' wellbeing.

In the immediate lead-up to the Tour de France teams announcing their line-ups, one name hogged the headlines like no other. Was there any possibility that Mark Cavendish might yet make it to the Tour? Much would depend on the fitness of Sam Bennett, Deceuninck-QuickStep's Irish sprinting star who had dominated the race in 2020 and had ended Peter Sagan's long stranglehold over the green jersey competition. Bennett had been scheduled to start the Baloise Belgium Tour at the beginning of June but had banged his knee against his handlebars in training – an injury that first appeared to be slight but then sidelined him from the week-long preparation race. That opened the door for Cavendish, who took a helicopter on the morning of the race in order to make the startline. He had to wait until the final stage, but on 13 June, in the Limburg city of Beringen, he won his fifth race of 2021, beating an indisputably world-class field that included Tim Merlier, fresh from his success at the Giro. If there wasn't a clamour for Cavendish's inclusion at the Tour before this result, there most assuredly was now. Collateral damage was being done to the relationship between Deceuninck-QuickStep's outspoken and autocratic boss Patrick Lefevere and Sam Bennett. With the Belgian now openly questioning Bennett's attitude and fitness, the momentum for selection appeared to be tilting the way of Cavendish, who was holding himself in readiness and keeping his counsel. On 21 June, eight days on from that victory in Beringen, it was announced that the Manxman would be returning to the race that had defined his career hitherto. After a two-year absence, Mark Cavendish was back at the Tour de France.

The fallout from Lefevere's public feuding with Bennett would endure until the end of the season, though Bennett would stoically resist the temptation to speak his mind in the press. When it became known that the Irishman would be returning to Bora-Hansgrohe in 2022, Lefevere likened his move to that of 'women who return home after domestic abuse'. Later in the season when Lefevere got wind of Bennett's intention to ride the European Championship road race for Ireland – his first race since early May – he publicly vowed to ensure that the team would punitively select Bennett for every available race between then and the end of the season. It was a sad and distasteful end to what had in 2020 been an excellent collaboration. If that year's successes are to be Sam Bennett's career apotheosis, then to have them remembered with such acrimony as was now being heaped upon him by Lefevere's continual public taunting is an unworthy conclusion indeed.

Lefevere's public contributions over the course of 2021 – and in previous years – had begun to attract more and more criticism. Often outspoken and occasionally irascible, his use of social media and his willingness to fire off in any number of directions at different targets seemed finally to have run its course when he gave an interview in which he dismissed the possibility of running a women's team, claiming that he was 'not a charity' and that he had neither the 'experience, time, money or desire' to invest in the sport. This would prompt an elegant response from Lizzie Deignan among others, who simply stated that she was 'pleased he has no interest in women's cycling because we have no interest in him either.' It was a classy riposte.

While the top women riders in the world, having briefly appeared in Brittany at La Course, now either headed for Italy to prepare for the Giro Rosa or simply vanished off the racing scene to ready themselves for the Olympics (as was the case for 2020 Giro Donne winner Annemiek van Vleuten), the Tour de France finally got underway. And for the three weeks of its duration, it pretty much obliterated all other racing headlines.

The opening weekend was both breathtaking and savage, with wins for Julian Alaphilippe and then Mathieu van der Poel constituting just about the most dramatic first two days of racing that anyone could recall. Van der Poel's victory in particular – with his impossible-seeming double attack of the Mur de Bretagne, which landed him in the first *maillot jaune* of his career – was perhaps the greatest memory of the 2021 Tour de France. His skyward gesture as he recalled his beloved grandfather Raymond Poulidor, having just taken the lead of the Tour on his debut at the race (a feat that had eluded 'Pou-Pou' throughout his career), was spine-tingling. The violence of his attacks was matched only by the violence of the series of crashes, most notably on stages 1 and 3, which broke bones and hopes and ultimately shaped the race. Co-favourite alongside Tadej Pogačar, Primož Roglič – who had skipped all the traditional warm-up races for the Tour in order to train at the team's base in Tignes – came down heavily on stage 1. He was one of a huge number of riders who hit the ground after Tony Martin was taken down by a supporter at the side of the road. The woman in question, whose identity remained a mystery for a few chaotic days, had been looking the wrong way as the peloton approached, holding a sign into the road that read 'Allez Opi-Omi', a message to her grandparents that she hoped might be seen on TV. The aftermath became a rather ugly trial by social media and a police enquiry before she eventually handed herself in.

Yet it was another more innocuous-seeming crash on his own on stage 3 that spelled the end of Roglič's hopes of victory. Though nothing was broken, he was clearly not the same rider thereafter, and lost time on multiple occasions. The same was true for Geraint Thomas who caused a crash all of his own (bringing down Tony Martin at the same time). He dislocated his shoulder, had it popped back in by the Tour doctors as he sat on the tarmac, and then resumed a Tour de France that was already over for him in terms of the GC. Two of Pogačar's biggest rivals were sunk before the battle had even begun.

What followed was effectively a procession to Paris for Pogačar, whose dominance was only questioned once – and even then only fleetingly. That was when Jumbo-Visma's Jonas Vingegaard, finding himself leading their team after Roglič abandoned, attacked the yellow jersey on Mont Ventoux and briefly put Pogačar on the back foot. But that was it – the only weak moment in three weeks that saw Pogačar increasingly assume the role of *patron* in the peloton, as befits a rider who has won more than Eddy Merckx at the same age and whose Tour de France record reads: raced two, won two.

At the same as the young Slovenian was turning the screw on the peloton of the Tour de France, the flagship women's stage race got underway in Piedmont, in Northern Italy. Though Trek-Segafredo took the opening team time trial of the Giro Rosa from Fassano to Cuneo, the rest of the race was a display of complete domination by a trio of riders from the all-conquering SD Worx team. When the race came to an end at Cormons, close to the border with Slovenia, the top three riders on the podium were all on the same team. Demi Vollering and Ashleigh Moolman-Pasio were third and second respectively. But the world champion Anna van der Breggen repeated her success of 2020 and rode to victory in the ten-day stage race for the fourth and final time in her career, picking up the first mountain stage to Prato Nevoso and, two days later, the only ITT of the race. After four stages, she'd established her winning margin. Despite her successes throughout the year, there appeared to be no reneging on Van der Breggen's avowed intention to call time on her racing career at the end of 2021. Indeed, when her autobiography, simply entitled *Anna*, was published later in the year, it seemed there could be no turning back. There was no Annemiek van Vleuten to challenge her, but some big-name riders picked up stages along the way – most notably

Emma Norsgaard and Lorena Wiebes, as well as two stages for Marianne Vos, who continued to produce a constant trickle of victories throughout her 16th year as a pro on the road.

Meanwhile, back in France, a rider who turned professional in 2005 – a year before Vos even – was setting about making history. Stage 4 of the Tour de France finished in the town of Fougères, which, like three other 2021 stage finishes (Châteauroux, Nîmes and Paris), had already witnessed victories by Mark Cavendish. And he duly did it again, crossing the line ahead of Nacer Bouhanni and Jasper Philipsen. His last wins at the Tour had come in 2016, when he had drawn to within touching distance of Eddy Merckx's record of 34 career stage wins in the Grande Boucle. But since then, Cavendish had been stuck on 30. In 2017 he'd crashed out in a collision with Peter Sagan. A year later, he'd been eliminated in the mountains. And in 2019 and 2020, he'd not made the team. Now, here he was again, picking up as if the intervening five years hadn't happened.

What followed was simply compelling. The victories piled up. He won again in Châteauroux, after which he implored the press not to invoke the name of Merckx: 'Don't say the name!' By win number three in Valence, he was within a single victory of drawing level with the Cannibal. And by Carcassonne, he had done it. What happened after that was almost agonising to watch. Shepherded through the Pyrenees by his lead-out man Michael Mørkøv and by Tim Declercq, Cavendish made it through the mountains. There were two more chances remaining on the race for him to take the decisive victory: a 200km flat stage through Les Landes to Libourne, and then Paris. But it wasn't to be. The bunch allowed the break to stay away on stage 19 despite (or perhaps because of) the presence of Merckx himself on the start line. And on the Champs-Élysées, Cavendish was outsprinted by Wout van Aert, who completed a remarkable trio of wins in a mountain stage, a time trial and a bunch sprint.

Cavendish had done the seemingly impossible. He'd taken four stages and the green jersey, exactly a decade on from his only other success in the points competition. Immediately thoughts turned to the future for the 36-year-old. Stuck on 34 wins, but without a contract for 2022, the negotiations began, with Patrick Lefevere routinely briefing the Belgian press about Cavendish's demands. They were, however, seemingly concluded by September: the Manxman appeared to be on the brink of signing again to ride in QuickStep blue the following year, albeit with no guarantee he'd be selected for the Tour. At the time of going to press, his future is still a little uncertain.

Kit Nicholson, who has contributed to every edition of The Road Book to date, has taken time to consider the comeback in all its forms, from Cavendish to Froome, Van Vleuten to Jakobsen and beyond. With a great deal of care, she observes the subtle difference in all the narratives, the challenge and rewards of picking oneself up and starting again, and why it is that a comeback resonates with the public like no other story does. We decided to include this essay and its themes back in the dark winter months and long before the season started to take shape, little knowing how relevant it might become.

Another feature of the 2021 Tour de France was the number of stages won by a solo rider's attack from a large and powerful breakaway. Whether it was Dylan Teuns, Bauke Mollema, Patrick Konrad, Sepp Kuss, Ben O'Connor, Wout van Aert, or the irrepressible Matej Mohorič, the pattern seemed to follow the same design. Mohorič's second win, in particular, was noteworthy for its unanswerable strength and for the message delivered at the line. The Slovenian, like all his Bahrain Victorious teammates, had been kept awake late into the night a few days previously after a police raid on their hotel rooms. At the time of writing, nothing has emerged to suggest that anything suspicious was unearthed. Mohorič made his feelings clear after his victory: he defended the principle of police checks and agreed that it was important for the authorities to act where the evidence demanded it, but was unhappy with what he considered to be invasive and heavy-handed police interventions. Perhaps Bahrain Victorious were victims of their own success because they were having an extremely good year, whether through Teuns, Sonny Colbrelli and Mohorič at the Tour and beyond, or Gino Mäder, Mark Padun, Mikel Landa and Phil Bauhaus in other races.

And so to Tokyo – reluctantly for some, with great anticipation for others. Whether or not the Games should have been cancelled given the well-documented public opposition to them among the Japanese population, will forever remain buried under the sheer weight of the reporting that accompanied the Olympics. Finally, after all the hand-wringing, the sport took centre stage and road racing was, as it almost always is, one of the first sports to start handing out medals. Richard Carapaz proved that he is a most unusual rider in the modern era: a Grand Tour champion with the heart of a one-day racer. His ascendant form from the final week of the Tour was confirmed by a devastating solo win in the men's road race as the Ecuadorian became only his country's second gold medallist at the Games (after Jefferson Pérez's gold in the 20km walk at Atlanta in 1996). The women's road race was exceptional – or exceptionally odd, depending on your take. The almost entirely unheralded Anna Kiesenhofer, a theoretical mathematician of great capacity, thwarted the entire chase, which was mismanaged spectacularly by the all-powerful Dutch team, who would go on to fail at the Worlds a little later. Annemiek van Vleuten's celebration for second place (she thought she'd won) was embarrassing to watch. On balance, the race was chaotic and made a questionable impression on the watching public.

The men's time trial was won by Primož Roglič, which was a little unexpected given the severity of the injuries that had only a few short weeks earlier spelled a premature end to his latest attempt to win the Tour de France. For the Slovenian, it augured well for the upcoming defence of his Vuelta title. Behind Roglič, the battle for silver and bronze was thrilling. Rohan Dennis and the returning Tom Dumoulin were involved in the tightest of tussles. The women's time trial went to Van Vleuten, who now finally had her hands on the longed-for gold medal.

A couple of weeks later, the Paralympics began. One athlete in particular proved yet again why she can legitimately claim to be one of the greatest Paralympians of all time. Dame Sarah Storey ticked off her three objectives by winning the individual pursuit on the track and both the time trial and road race on the road. The last of these was her 17th Paralympic gold medal. Now at 43 years of age, Storey has no intention of stopping and is eyeing her ninth Games, in Paris in 2024.

Two decades younger than Storey, Remco Evenepoel returned to racing in Belgium just before the Olympics and picked up where he had left off in 2020: by winning with audacious ease. The longer that 2021 went on, the more we began to understand his unique talent, which is never more apparent than when he is attacking from distance and growing an unassailable lead. The slight question marks about his descending skills that had accompanied his return to racing after injury at the 2020 Lombardia felt like nitpicking in the face of such devastating form. In June he'd won the Belgium Tour for the second edition in a row (2020's race having been cancelled). Then, after a fairly fruitless round trip to Tokyo, he returned to Europe and took the Tour of Denmark with a trademark display of strength. By the time the World Championships were to come around, the clamour surrounding him had once again reached fever pitch, especially when his fellow Brussels idol Eddy Merckx made somewhat dismissive comments about the young pretender that seemed designed to divide the Belgian sporting public into one or other faction: Van Aert or Remco. Every other country in the world would have longed for such a schism. Would they be able to work together in a team with a single goal? If this was a fraught point of discussion within the host nation for the Worlds, it was the stuff of dreams for everyone looking on from the outside.

However, before all that, there was the small matter of the Vuelta. Though Evenepoel did not go to Spain, his teammate Fabio Jakobsen did, buoyed by a brace of race wins in the Tour de Wallonie. The very fact that he was competing again, given the massive crash he had suffered at the Tour of Poland in 2020, was a testament to both the treatment the Dutchman had received and his own profound resilience. Jakobsen not only completed the race but came away from Spain with three stage wins and the green jersey. His accelerated return to winning ways, having very nearly lost his life in Katowice in early August the previous year, kickstarted an early jostling for primacy among Deceuninck-QuickStep's roster of sprinters for 2022. Both Cavendish (in all likelihood) and Jakobsen would be determinedly eyeing a berth in the Tour de France team. Team boss Patrick Lefevere would have another nuanced decision to make.

The final Grand Tour of the year was won by Primož Roglič for the third consecutive year. He took the leader's jersey with a display of dominance in the opening time trial in Burgos, before handing over temporary custodianship of the red jersey to Rein Taaramaë, Kenny Elissonde and, after regaining it briefly in the second week of racing, Odd Christian Eiking. (The Norwegian from close to the Arctic Circle spoke amusingly about almost melting in sweltering late-summer heat during a year of racing that traversed a continent once again setting record temperatures – further evidence of the gathering climate emergency that could have implications for the cycling calendar in years to come. This was a new and pressing worry whose potential to disrupt was something the sport was only just beginning to come to terms with.) In truth, Roglič's third Vuelta was never in any particular doubt, as a succession of his rivals fell short of putting him under sufficient pressure to reveal any weaknesses. From time to time over a typically mountainous race, riders such as Enric Mas (whose consistency earned him a valiant second place) and the GC challenge of Ineos (spearheaded by Adam Yates, who finished more strongly than a tiring Egan Bernal) would suggest they believed the fight was not over. In reality, it was never really close: the winning margin for Roglič of 4 minutes 42 seconds was the biggest since Alex Zülle's 5 minutes 7 seconds in 1997.

Miguel Ángel López, whose challenge spectacularly imploded on the penultimate day, provided some late drama. Finding himself the wrong side of a split in the peloton after some 50km of racing on stage 20, having had started the day in third, López simply quit the race within sight of the finish line after seemingly objecting to team orders 'not to chase'. By 1 October his contract had been terminated, ending an unhappy ten months with Movistar for the Colombian brought in to replace Nairo Quintana. Jack Haig took the final spot on the podium.

Podcaster and author Daniel Friebe was on the race and has written a beautiful account of the youngest, most ragged and unusual of the three Grand Tours. In his account of the Vuelta for The Road Book a fuller picture of an increasingly relaxed Primož Roglič emerges, as the road to Santiago de Compostela unwinds through a country of breathtaking beauty, occasional social unease and distinctive, lyrical character.

The European Championships were held in Trento, in the foothills of the Dolomites in northern Italy. Notable victories went to Ellen van Dijk and to Sonny Colbrelli, neither of whom were quite done yet with their campaigns for 2021. And then, a week later, the much-anticipated World

Championships were held in Flanders. It was, amazingly, the first time Belgium had hosted the competition since Mario Cippolini's victory in Zolder in 2002, almost a decade ago.

The time trials were run off to the north of Flanders, with a finish line in Bruges. The men's race produced the expected outcome, as victory went to Filippo Ganna once again, ahead of a ridiculously high-powered podium that held Wout van Aert and Remco Evenepoel. In the women's road race Ellen van Dijk – having fully recovered from Covid, which had badly affected her Classics campaign – rode to victory ahead of the newly crowned European ITT champion, Marlen Reusser of Switzerland, and Olympic gold medallist Annemiek van Vleuten.

The championships then switched their attention to the university town of Leuven in Brabant for the road races. In benign weather conditions, on the last few warm and sunny days of a European 'Indian summer', massive crowds lined the succession of cobbled climbs that characterise these very Flandrian races. There were notable performances in the development ranks, where Zoe Bäckstedt – younger daughter of Magnus – took the junior women's road race, having also finished second in the time trial. And in the men's Under-23 road race, Eritrean sprinter Biniam Ghirmay became the first-ever black African medallist at the World Championships when he came second. The whole issue of black African cycling has been explored for The Road Book by Kingali-based sportswriter Peter Kamasa. Seeing the continent through the filter of his home Tour du Rwanda, Kamasa assesses the historical and cultural significance of the race, set in the context of a varied and patchy relationship with the sport across a range of countries. The genocide is never far from the surface of the story, and Kamasa – whose family fled the country and who lost many relatives – deals with Rwanda's love for cycling with great sensitivity. For all the goodwill, it seems the development of black cyclists from Africa is still tortuous and full of hardships and obstacles. In 2021, for example, Qhubeka NextHash had just one black rider (Nic Dlamini) in their roster of 27. Would Ghirmay's achievements in Flanders fire the starting pistol for further successes, especially with the announcement that Rwanda would become the first African nation to host the World Championships in 2025 (a decision, incidentally, that was highly controversial, given the human rights record of the current government under the presidency of Paul Kagame)?

The women's road race in Flanders produced a thrilling finale in which Marianne Vos was thwarted in her attempt to claim a fourth rainbow jersey by a fearsome sprint from Elisa Balsamo, led out brilliantly by Elisa Longo Borghini. Vos – first a world champion in 2006 – was uncharacteristically distraught as she crossed the line, but she soon regained her composure and was seen behind the podium adjusting Balsamo's socks so that the Italian would present herself smartly for the world's photographers. Balsamo, at just 23, was a surprise winner perhaps, although her win was thoroughly merited and earned her a transfer to Trek-Segafredo for 2022. It didn't take long, however, before the inquiry started within the Dutch team as to how they could have squandered the title with such resources at their disposal.

The men's race was widely considered to be a vintage edition. As the groups were whittled down, it was the French who took up the responsibility to attack. To be more specific, Julian Alaphilippe, having dropped back to consult his DS, Thomas Voeckler, started to launch off the front in repeated forays. Later it would emerge that the tactic had been a kind of bluff: the constant attacks had been designed to look like the desperate moves of a rider not confident of his form, whereas in fact the defending world champion was in perfect condition. Having ridden a reasonably restrained Tour of Britain in preparation – unlike his big rival and clear race favourite Wout van Aert, who had dug extremely deep in order to win the week-long trip from Penzance to Aberdeen – the Frenchman was peaking exactly when he needed to. The decisive push came when his teammate Valentin Madouas set him up for the final attack, after which he was never seen again. Though the gap closed to around 8 seconds at one point, it then ballooned out as the chase quartet lost hope. And in front of massive, sometimes hostile crowds in Leuven, Alaphilippe produced a masterful display for the second successive year. He is a truly magical rider indeed.

A week later saw the much-delayed and longed-for return of Paris–Roubaix, raced for the first time by the men since Easter 2019 and, for the women, since the beginning of time. Not only that, but misery fetishists and fans of muddy melodrama were rubbing their hands together in delight at a weather forecast that promised – and delivered – strong winds and steady rain, especially for the men's race. Lizzie Deignan produced a ride of spontaneous brilliance in finishing alone to make history. Her immense solo ride, to which there was no answer, was perhaps her finest moment on a bike. And the outpouring of admiration and congratulations that overwhelmed her as she became the first woman to raise a cobble above her head in triumph is a testament to the esteem in which she is held, to the scope of her career and to the truly historic nature of her achievement.

With the huge success of this race, watched by record numbers of TV viewers across the world, 2021 felt in many ways like a significant stepping stone for women's racing. Anecdotally, since these things are often shrouded in secrecy, the salaries of the bigger-name riders took a leap across the peloton. More collaborations between men's and women's teams were announced and, as we look to 2022, the women's calendar appears busier than ever: the Tour de Romandie will be added, as will the Tour de France Femmes, and the Giro Rosa will return to WorldTour status. This welter of new commitments will start to pose questions as to whether the women's peloton has the depth, quality and number of riders to sustain such growth. Yet this is a good problem to have – and far better than 2020's spectacle of watching star riders in search of racing opportunities. Moreover, to add to the intrigue, another three high-profile women will become sports directors in 2022: Anna van der Breggen, Chantal van den Broek-Blaak and Jolien d'Hoore.

With Deignan's victory for Trek-Segafredo, 2021 increasingly felt like a season that had begun with domination by the SD Worx team had ended with the honours being more equitably shared than might first have seemed possible. So-called smaller teams enjoyed their moments, too. None of Cecilie Uttrup Ludwig, Marta Bastianelli, Mavi Garcia or Elisa Balsamo ride for the biggest outfits, yet all have enjoyed significant victories along the way.

Next it was the turn of the men. Paris–Roubaix did its best to provide the usual mind-blowing attrition. In the end, a group of three riders – all debutants – emerged blinking mud from their eyes and coated in wet Flandrian earth: one of Sonny Colbrelli, Florian Vermeersch and Mathieu van der Poel was going to win the cobbled Monument at the first time of asking. In the velodrome, Colbrelli outsprinted them all. Within seconds of winning the race he had collapsed on the ground, rolling from side to side, tearfully screaming in delight to the greyed-out heavens. Not far from him, Van der Poel, beaten into third place, lay face down in the turf, motionless. A soigneur gently placed a gilet across the Dutchman's broad shoulders. Not often had the famous race produced such a polarity of delight and despair. Never before had it been raced in October.

The final week of racing in the men's peloton saw the action switch to Italy, where its succession of one-day races culminated in the spectacle of Il Lombardia. A scorching solo attack from

Tadej Pogačar proved to be the race-winning move despite a challenge by Fausto Masnada, and the young Slovenian ended the year having picked up a Grand Tour and two Monuments. The Merckx-like accumulation of his success – at an age that even puts the great Belgian in the shade – continued unabated throughout 2021.

With that, our jury retired to vote on the fourth annual Road Book Riders of the Year awards. Christian Prudhomme, Giorgia Bronzini, David Millar, Sean Kelly, Orla Chennaoui, Rolf Sørensen, Ryder Hesjedal, Phil Liggett and Daniel Mangeas all deliberated and reached conclusions that were, in five of the six categories, on a knife edge; the Young Male Rider award was an absolute dead-heat and so, as editor, I had the casting vote.

The Road Book Society readership meanwhile decided by an overwhelming margin that their Rider of the Year was Mark Cavendish. The reasons given were principally based on the emotion associated with his four Tour de France stage wins, and are best summed up by Road Book reader Callum Devereux, who wrote that 'sport carries us, in various contortions, through life's ups and downs, though rarely reflecting our realities. But the Manx Missile's rearmament offers multi-generational motivation we didn't know we needed.'

The Female Rider of the Year was Lizzie Deignan. There was something about her victory in the velodrome of Roubaix that stood out above and beyond every other race win in 2021. It was a year in which there wasn't a dominant individual, and so Deignan's victory sat comfortably alongside all the other achievements of her peers and rivals throughout the calendar but had that extra quality of mystique about it that accompanies truly historic moments.

The Female Combative Rider of the Year, according to our jury, was Elisa Longo Borghini. Throughout the year, her consistency and her willingness to work for others – often to spectacular effect – did not escape the attention of the jurors. She took a couple of major one-day race wins, and doubled up in the Italian National Championships, winning both the road race and the time trial titles for the third and fifth times respectively.

Another Elisa won the Young Female Rider of the Year award. Elisa Balsamo had been led out by her Italian teammate Longo Borghini to take the World Championship ahead of Marianne Vos in Flanders. The 23-year-old Balsamo then won the final stage of the Women's Tour into Felixstowe – her first win in the rainbow jersey.

The Young Male Rider of the Year was Jonas Vingegaard. His wins throughout the year, starting with the ascent of Jebel Jais in the UAE, were confirmation of the promise he'd shown in support of Primož Roglič in the late 2020 Vuelta. But it was his emergence at the Tour de France as a genuine future contender that surprised pretty much everyone. His has been a rapid ascent through the ranks.

Julian Alaphilippe repeated his double of 2019 in taking home both the Male Combative Rider of the Year award and the Male Rider of the Year prize. All his remarkable qualities were on display in winning a second successive world title in Leuven – his waspish aggression and his astonishing, old-school racing style. Both that performance and his targeted brilliance of stage 1 of the Tour de France caught the eyes of the jury. The fact that he was chosen ahead of the likes of Cavendish, Pogačar, Van den Poel and Van Aert merely confirms the quality of the 2021 season. Many congratulations to Julian, Jonas, both Elisas, Lizzie and to Mark.

2021 was not perfect but it was pretty close at times. The road back to normality was longer, harder and more full of unexpected obstacles than we might have imagined, and the sense lingers that 2022 might yet be a fragile enterprise (the Tour Down Under has already been cancelled again). Along the way, the greatest names have lit up our shared experience of another year in which we sometimes can only sit back in admiration and respect: Van der Breggen, Vos, Alaphilippe, Cavendish, Van Aert, Van der Poel, Evenepoel, Colbrelli, Deignan… I could go on. We have come through hardship to reach this point in time, all of us. But over the course of 2021, the doubt that had dogged all our lives was being cast aside – sometimes cautiously, sometimes in the blink of an eye.

# JANUARY

January was underscored by absence and anxiety in 2021. No Tour Down Under nor Cadel Evans Great Ocean Road Race for the WorldTour; those races had been cancelled a long time in advance. Instead, a series of makeshift domestic competitions took their place, organised to satisfy the need to race for Australian riders who had 'wintered' down under and were about to depart for their European bases. As if it were needed, the Australian Open tennis tournament testified to the difficulties of organising safe international travel in a pandemic, with players forcibly quarantined in hotel rooms. Towards the end of the month, however, the racing began in Spain and in France.

| DATE | RACE TITLE | LOCATION | UCI CODE | PAGE |
|---|---|---|---|---|
| 31 January | GP Cycliste la Marseillaise | France | 1.1 | 20 |

JANUARY  .1 MEN'S RACE

# GP CYCLISTE LA MARSEILLAISE
31 January 2021
Marseille–Marseille
171.6km

## WEATHER

TEMPERATURE  WIND
12°C  W 11km/h

## RESULTS

| POS | NAME | TEAM | TIME |
|---|---|---|---|
| 1. | A. Paret-Peintre | ACT | 4:24:29 |
| 2. | T. Boudat | ARK | s.t. |
| 3. | B. Coquard | BBK | s.t. |
| 4. | F. Galván | EKP | s.t. |
| 5. | A. Livyns | WVA | s.t. |
| 6. | T. Wellens | LTS | s.t. |
| 7. | M. Trentin | UAD | s.t. |
| 8. | L. Calmejane | ACT | s.t. |
| 9. | J. El Fares | EFN | s.t. |
| 10. | O. C. Eiking | IWG | s.t. |
| 11. | M. Bouet | ARK | s.t. |
| 12. | A. Turgis | TDE | s.t. |
| 13. | T. Gallopin | ACT | s.t. |
| 14. | B. Thomas | GFC | s.t. |
| 15. | J. Bellicaud | IWG | s.t. |
| 16. | Je. Herrada | COF | s.t. |
| 17. | R. Gibbons | UAD | s.t. |
| 18. | A. Perez | COF | s.t. |
| 19. | E. Boasson Hagen | TDE | s.t. |
| 20. | A. Vuillermoz | TDE | s.t. |

# FEBRUARY

A single day of racing for the women's peloton, and not even at WorldTour level, was the meagre fare offered up in February – a month that saw a welter of races announcing their postponement until later in the year. The men, as ever, were better served. With no South American racing on offer, the UAE Tour represented the first chance for the WorldTour riders to develop their tan lines. Meanwhile, neighbouring European countries were adopting very different courses: most of Spain's regional stage races were postponed, much to the benefit of the early-season minor French stage races, which boasted stellar startlists and enjoyed considerable attention.

| DATE | RACE TITLE | LOCATION | UCI CODE | PAGE |
|---|---|---|---|---|
| 3–7 February | Etoile de Bessèges | France | 2.1 | 22 |
| 11–14 February | Tour de la Provence | France | 2.Pro | 25 |
| 14 February | Clásica de Almería | Spain | 1.Pro | 27 |
| 19–21 February | Tour des Alpes-Maritimes et du Var | France | 2.1 | 28 |
| 21–27 February | UAE Tour | UAE | 2.UWT | 30 |
| 27 February | Omloop Het Nieuwsblad | Belgium | 1.UWT | 37 |
| 27 February | Faun–Ardèche Classic | France | 1.Pro | 38 |
| 28 February | La Drôme Classic | France | 1.Pro | 39 |
| 28 February | Kuurne–Bruxelles–Kuurne | Belgium | 1.Pro | 40 |

FEBRUARY  .1 MEN'S RACE

## ETOILE DE BESSÈGES
Stage 1
3 February 2021
Bellegarde–Bellegarde
143.6km

## WEATHER

TEMPERATURE  WIND
14°C  SE 15km/h

### STAGE RESULTS

| POS | NAME | TEAM | TIME |
|---|---|---|---|
| 1. | C. Laporte | COF | 3:14:32 |
| 2. | N. Bouhanni | ARK | s.t. |
| 3. | M. Pedersen | TFS | 0:02 |
| 4. | G. Nizzolo | TQA | s.t. |
| 5. | M. Kwiatkowski | IGD | s.t. |
| 6. | J. Meeus | BOH | s.t. |
| 7. | B. Coquard | BBK | s.t. |
| 8. | J. Degenkolb | LTS | s.t. |
| 9. | J. Stewart | GFC | s.t. |
| 10. | D. van Poppel | IWG | s.t. |
| 11. | T. Merlier | AFC | s.t. |
| 12. | B. Vallée | WVA | s.t. |
| 13. | V. Nibali | TFS | s.t. |
| 14. | M. Würst Schmidt | ISN | s.t. |
| 15. | G. Van Avermaet | ACT | s.t. |
| 16. | C. Barthe | BBK | s.t. |
| 17. | M. Menten | WVA | s.t. |
| 18. | F. Galván | EKP | s.t. |
| 19. | A. Turgis | TDE | s.t. |
| 20. | A. Jensen | DKO | s.t. |

### GENERAL CLASSIFICATION

| POS | NAME | TEAM | TIME |
|---|---|---|---|
| 1. | C. Laporte | COF | 3:14:22 |
| 2. | N. Bouhanni | ARK | 0:04 |
| 3. | M. Pedersen | TFS | 0:08 |

### KING OF THE MOUNTAINS

| POS | NAME | TEAM | PTS |
|---|---|---|---|
| 1. | A. Delettre | DKO | 6 |
| 2. | T. Paquot | WVA | 4 |
| 3. | L. Louvet | AUB | 2 |

### POINTS

| POS | NAME | TEAM | PTS |
|---|---|---|---|
| 1. | C. Laporte | COF | 25 |
| 2. | N. Bouhanni | ARK | 20 |
| 3. | M. Pedersen | TFS | 16 |

### YOUNG RIDER

| POS | NAME | TEAM | TIME |
|---|---|---|---|
| 1. | J. Meeus | BOH | 3:14:34 |
| 2. | J. Stewart | GFC | s.t. |
| 3. | R. Adrià | EKP | s.t. |

## ETOILE DE BESSÈGES
Stage 2
4 February 2021
St Geniès–La Calmette
153.8km

## WEATHER

TEMPERATURE  WIND
11°C  SE 7km/h

### STAGE RESULTS

| POS | NAME | TEAM | TIME |
|---|---|---|---|
| 1. | T. Dupont | WVA | 3:35:15 |
| 2. | P. Barbier | DKO | s.t. |
| 3. | G. Nizzolo | TQA | s.t. |
| 4. | R. Barbier | ISN | s.t. |
| 5. | C. Laporte | COF | s.t. |
| 6. | N. Bouhanni | ARK | s.t. |
| 7. | M. Sarreau | ACT | s.t. |
| 8. | G. Thijssen | LTS | s.t. |
| 9. | S. Dillier | AFC | s.t. |
| 10. | E. Theuns | TFS | s.t. |
| 11. | B. Coquard | BBK | s.t. |
| 12. | E. Vermeulen | XRL | s.t. |
| 13. | T. Merlier | AFC | s.t. |
| 14. | M. Pelucchi | TQA | s.t. |
| 15. | J. Koch | IWG | s.t. |
| 16. | M. Menten | WVA | s.t. |
| 17. | Se. Bennett | TQA | s.t. |
| 18. | E. M. Grosu | DKO | s.t. |
| 19. | J. van den Berg | EFN | s.t. |
| 20. | J. Tesson | AUB | s.t. |

### GENERAL CLASSIFICATION

| POS | NAME | TEAM | TIME |
|---|---|---|---|
| 1. — | C. Laporte | COF | 6:49:37 |
| 2. ↑119 | T. Dupont | WVA | 0:02 |
| 3. ↓1 | N. Bouhanni | ARK | 0:04 |

### KING OF THE MOUNTAINS

| POS | NAME | TEAM | PTS |
|---|---|---|---|
| 1. — | A. Delettre | DKO | 28 |
| 2. — | L. Robeet | WVA | 12 |
| 3. — | V. Řepa | EKP | 8 |

### POINTS

| POS | NAME | TEAM | PTS |
|---|---|---|---|
| 1. — | C. Laporte | COF | 37 |
| 2. — | N. Bouhanni | ARK | 30 |
| 3. ↑1 | G. Nizzolo | TQA | 30 |

### YOUNG RIDER

| POS | NAME | TEAM | TIME |
|---|---|---|---|
| 1. ↑1 | J. Stewart | GFC | 6:49:49 |
| 2. ↑1 | R. Adrià | EKP | s.t. |
| 3. ↑2 | J. Rutsch | EFN | s.t. |

FEBRUARY  .1 MEN'S RACE

# ETOILE DE BESSÈGES
Stage 3
5 February 2021
Bessèges–Bessèges
156.9km

## WEATHER

| TEMPERATURE | WIND |
|---|---|
| 14°C | E 7km/h |

## STAGE RESULTS

| POS | NAME | TEAM | TIME |
|---|---|---|---|
| 1. | T. Wellens | LTS | 3:28:02 |
| 2. | E. Theuns | TFS | 0:37 |
| 3. | M. Würst Schmidt | ISN | s.t. |
| 4. | G. Van Avermaet | ACT | s.t. |
| 5. | P. Gilbert | LTS | s.t. |
| 6. | C. Barthe | BBK | s.t. |
| 7. | J. Stewart | GFC | s.t. |
| 8. | N. Politt | BOH | s.t. |
| 9. | M. Gogl | TQA | s.t. |
| 10. | M. Kwiatkowski | IGD | s.t. |
| 11. | O. C. Eiking | IWG | s.t. |
| 12. | M. Marquez | EKP | s.t. |
| 13. | C. Carisey | DKO | s.t. |
| 14. | S. Oldani | LTS | s.t. |
| 15. | E. Bernal | IGD | 1:02 |
| 16. | R. Cardis | AUB | 3:13 |
| 17. | I. Centrone | XRL | s.t. |
| 18. | Se. Bennett | TQA | s.t. |
| 19. | A. Jensen | DKO | s.t. |
| 20. | J. Le Bon | CCA | s.t. |

## GENERAL CLASSIFICATION

| POS | NAME | TEAM | TIME |
|---|---|---|---|
| 1. ↑67 | T. Wellens | LTS | 10:17:38 |
| 2. ↑31 | E. Theuns | TFS | 0:44 |
| 3. ↑34 | M. Würst Schmidt | ISN | 0:46 |

## KING OF THE MOUNTAINS

| POS | NAME | TEAM | PTS |
|---|---|---|---|
| 1. — | A. Delettre | DKO | 28 |
| 2. — | T. Wellens | LTS | 12 |
| 3. ↓1 | L. Robeet | WVA | 12 |

## POINTS

| POS | NAME | TEAM | PTS |
|---|---|---|---|
| 1. — | C. Laporte | COF | 37 |
| 2. — | T. Wellens | LTS | 31 |
| 3. ↓1 | N. Bouhanni | ARK | 30 |

## YOUNG RIDER

| POS | NAME | TEAM | TIME |
|---|---|---|---|
| 1. — | J. Stewart | GFC | 10:18:28 |
| 2. ↑4 | S. Oldani | LTS | s.t. |
| 3. ↓1 | R. Adrià | EKP | 2:36 |

# ETOILE DE BESSÈGES
Stage 4
6 February 2021
Rousson–St Siffret
152km

## WEATHER

| TEMPERATURE | WIND |
|---|---|
| 15°C | SE 22km/h |

## STAGE RESULTS

| POS | NAME | TEAM | TIME |
|---|---|---|---|
| 1. | F. Ganna | IGD | 3:22:59 |
| 2. | C. Laporte | COF | 0:17 |
| 3. | P. Ackermann | BOH | s.t. |
| 4. | G. Van Avermaet | ACT | s.t. |
| 5. | M. Menten | WVA | s.t. |
| 6. | B. Coquard | BBK | s.t. |
| 7. | C. Barthe | BBK | s.t. |
| 8. | N. Politt | BOH | s.t. |
| 9. | A. Jensen | DKO | s.t. |
| 10. | M. Würst Schmidt | ISN | s.t. |
| 11. | E. Theuns | TFS | s.t. |
| 12. | T. Wellens | LTS | s.t. |
| 13. | P. Gilbert | LTS | s.t. |
| 14. | R. Adrià | EKP | s.t. |
| 15. | G. Nizzolo | TQA | s.t. |
| 16. | D. Kowalski | XRL | s.t. |
| 17. | O. C. Eiking | IWG | s.t. |
| 18. | A. Livyns | WVA | s.t. |
| 19. | M. Kwiatkowski | IGD | s.t. |
| 20. | J. Stewart | GFC | s.t. |

## GENERAL CLASSIFICATION

| POS | NAME | TEAM | TIME |
|---|---|---|---|
| 1. — | T. Wellens | LTS | 13:40:54 |
| 2. — | E. Theuns | TFS | 0:44 |
| 3. — | M. Würst Schmidt | ISN | 0:46 |

## KING OF THE MOUNTAINS

| POS | NAME | TEAM | PTS |
|---|---|---|---|
| 1. — | A. Delettre | DKO | 28 |
| 2. ↑1 | L. Robeet | WVA | 18 |
| 3. ↓1 | T. Wellens | LTS | 12 |

## POINTS

| POS | NAME | TEAM | PTS |
|---|---|---|---|
| 1. — | C. Laporte | COF | 57 |
| 2. — | T. Wellens | LTS | 35 |
| 3. — | F. Ganna | IGD | 31 |

## YOUNG RIDER

| POS | NAME | TEAM | TIME |
|---|---|---|---|
| 1. — | J. Stewart | GFC | 13:41:44 |
| 2. — | S. Oldani | LTS | 0:39 |
| 3. — | R. Adrià | EKP | 2:36 |

FEBRUARY .1 MEN'S RACE

# ETOILE DE BESSÈGES
Stage 5 (ITT)
7 February 2021
Alès–Alès
10.74km

## WEATHER

TEMPERATURE  WIND
9°C          NW 15km/h

## STAGE RESULTS

| POS | NAME | TEAM | TIME |
|---|---|---|---|
| 1. | F. Ganna | IGD | 15:00 |
| 2. | B. Thomas | GFC | 0:10 |
| 3. | E. Hayter | IGD | 0:21 |
| 4. | T. Wellens | LTS | 0:29 |
| 5. | C. Laporte | COF | 0:31 |
| 6. | M. Kwiatkowski | IGD | 0:34 |
| 7. | A. Bettiol | EFN | 0:35 |
| 8. | O. Doull | IGD | 0:38 |
| 9. | N. Politt | BOH | s.t. |
| 10. | J. Stewart | GFC | 0:41 |
| 11. | R. Urán | EFN | 0:44 |
| 12. | P. Latour | TDE | s.t. |
| 13. | C. Swift | ARK | 0:47 |
| 14. | L. Pöstlberger | BOH | 0:49 |
| 15. | F. Großschartner | BOH | s.t. |
| 16. | B. Mollema | TFS | 0:51 |
| 17. | R. Adrià | EKP | s.t. |
| 18. | V. Nibali | TFS | 0:53 |
| 19. | M. Gogl | TQA | 0:55 |
| 20. | A. Brunel | GFC | s.t. |

## GENERAL CLASSIFICATION

| POS | | NAME | TEAM | TIME |
|---|---|---|---|---|
| 1. | — | T. Wellens | LTS | 13:56:23 |
| 2. | ↑2 | M. Kwiatkowski | IGD | 0:53 |
| 3. | ↑5 | N. Politt | BOH | 0:59 |

## KING OF THE MOUNTAINS

| POS | | NAME | TEAM | PTS |
|---|---|---|---|---|
| 1. | — | A. Delettre | DKO | 28 |
| 2. | — | L. Robeet | WVA | 18 |
| 3. | — | T. Wellens | LTS | 14 |

## POINTS

| POS | | NAME | TEAM | PTS |
|---|---|---|---|---|
| 1. | — | C. Laporte | COF | 69 |
| 2. | ↑1 | F. Ganna | IGD | 56 |
| 3. | ↓1 | T. Wellens | LTS | 49 |

## YOUNG RIDER

| POS | | NAME | TEAM | TIME |
|---|---|---|---|---|
| 1. | — | J. Stewart | GFC | 13:57:25 |
| 2. | — | S. Oldani | LTS | 1:26 |
| 3. | — | R. Adrià | EKP | 2:46 |

FEBRUARY .PRO MEN'S RACE

## TOUR DE LA PROVENCE
Stage 1
11 February 2021
Aubagne–Six-Fours-les-Plages
182.3km

### WEATHER

TEMPERATURE | WIND
11°C | NW 31km/h

### STAGE RESULTS

| POS | NAME | TEAM | TIME |
|---|---|---|---|
| 1. | D. Ballerini | DQT | 4:43:23 |
| 2. | A. Démare | GFC | s.t. |
| 3. | N. Bouhanni | ARK | s.t. |
| 4. | C. Venturini | ACT | s.t. |
| 5. | M. Walls | BOH | s.t. |
| 6. | I. Schelling | BOH | s.t. |
| 7. | B. Coquard | BBK | s.t. |
| 8. | P. Bauhaus | TBV | s.t. |
| 9. | M. Moschetti | TFS | s.t. |
| 10. | A. Kristoff | UAD | s.t. |
| 11. | P. Allegaert | COF | s.t. |
| 12. | B. Swift | IGD | s.t. |
| 13. | J. Haig | TBV | s.t. |
| 14. | N. Bonifazio | TDE | s.t. |
| 15. | A. Aranburu | APT | s.t. |
| 16. | J. Degenkolb | LTS | s.t. |
| 17. | Z. Štybar | DQT | s.t. |
| 18. | P. Konrad | BOH | s.t. |
| 19. | K. Asgreen | DQT | s.t. |
| 20. | F. Großschartner | BOH | s.t. |

### GENERAL CLASSIFICATION

| POS | NAME | TEAM | TIME |
|---|---|---|---|
| 1. | D. Ballerini | DQT | 4:43:13 |
| 2. | A. Démare | GFC | 0:04 |
| 3. | N. Bouhanni | ARK | 0:06 |

### KING OF THE MOUNTAINS

| POS | NAME | TEAM | PTS |
|---|---|---|---|
| 1. | L. Calmejane | ACT | 15 |
| 2. | D. Fernández | DKO | 9 |
| 3. | J. Alaphilippe | DQT | 5 |

### POINTS

| POS | NAME | TEAM | PTS |
|---|---|---|---|
| 1. | D. Ballerini | DQT | 15 |
| 2. | A. Démare | GFC | 12 |
| 3. | D. Fernández | DKO | 10 |

### YOUNG RIDER

| POS | NAME | TEAM | TIME |
|---|---|---|---|
| 1. | M. Walls | BOH | 4:43:23 |
| 2. | I. Schelling | BOH | s.t. |
| 3. | M. Moschetti | TFS | s.t. |

## TOUR DE LA PROVENCE
Stage 2
12 February 2021
Cassis–Manosque
174.7km

### WEATHER

TEMPERATURE | WIND
11°C | NE 9km/h

### STAGE RESULTS

| POS | NAME | TEAM | TIME |
|---|---|---|---|
| 1. | D. Ballerini | DQT | 4:21:49 |
| 2. | G. Ciccone | TFS | s.t. |
| 3. | A. Aranburu | APT | s.t. |
| 4. | D. Teuns | TBV | s.t. |
| 5. | P. Konrad | BOH | s.t. |
| 6. | A. Lutsenko | APT | s.t. |
| 7. | G. Moscon | IGD | s.t. |
| 8. | S. Oldani | LTS | s.t. |
| 9. | S. E. Bystrøm | UAD | s.t. |
| 10. | B. Mollema | TFS | s.t. |
| 11. | E. Bernal | IGD | s.t. |
| 12. | I. R. Sosa | IGD | s.t. |
| 13. | M. Scotson | GFC | s.t. |
| 14. | A. Paret-Peintre | ACT | s.t. |
| 15. | W. Barguil | ARK | s.t. |
| 16. | M. Vansevenant | DQT | s.t. |
| 17. | W. Poels | TBV | s.t. |
| 18. | B. O'Connor | ACT | s.t. |
| 19. | J. Haig | TBV | s.t. |
| 20. | P. Gilbert | LTS | s.t. |

### GENERAL CLASSIFICATION

| POS | NAME | TEAM | TIME |
|---|---|---|---|
| 1. — | D. Ballerini | DQT | 9:04:52 |
| 2. ↑17 | A. Aranburu | APT | 0:16 |
| 3. ↑2 | J. Alaphilippe | DQT | 0:17 |

### KING OF THE MOUNTAINS

| POS | NAME | TEAM | PTS |
|---|---|---|---|
| 1. — | L. Calmejane | ACT | 15 |
| 2. — | F. Conca | LTS | 15 |
| 3. ↓1 | D. Fernández | DKO | 9 |

### POINTS

| POS | NAME | TEAM | PTS |
|---|---|---|---|
| 1. — | D. Ballerini | DQT | 30 |
| 2. ↑12 | G. Ciccone | TFS | 15 |
| 3. ↓1 | A. Démare | GFC | 12 |

### YOUNG RIDER

| POS | NAME | TEAM | TIME |
|---|---|---|---|
| 1. ↑1 | I. Schelling | BOH | 9:05:12 |
| 2. ↑2 | A. Paret-Peintre | ACT | s.t. |
| 3. ↓2 | M. Walls | BOH | s.t. |

FEBRUARY .PRO MEN'S RACE

## TOUR DE LA PROVENCE
Stage 3
13 February 2021
Istres–Mont Ventoux/Chalet Reynard
153.9km

### WEATHER

TEMPERATURE: 6°C
WIND: NE 9km/h

### STAGE RESULTS

| POS | NAME | TEAM | TIME |
|---|---|---|---|
| 1. | I. R. Sosa | IGD | 4:08:14 |
| 2. | E. Bernal | IGD | 0:15 |
| 3. | J. Alaphilippe | DQT | 0:18 |
| 4. | W. Poels | TBV | 0:29 |
| 5. | Je. Herrada | COF | 0:48 |
| 6. | G. Ciccone | TFS | s.t. |
| 7. | B. Mollema | TFS | s.t. |
| 8. | M. Vansevenant | DQT | s.t. |
| 9. | J. Haig | TBV | s.t. |
| 10. | P. Konrad | BOH | s.t. |
| 11. | A. Vlasov | APT | s.t. |
| 12. | M. Jorgenson | MOV | 1:18 |
| 13. | W. Barguil | ARK | s.t. |
| 14. | A. Paret-Peintre | ACT | s.t. |
| 15. | M. Fabbro | BOH | 1:24 |
| 16. | D. Teuns | TBV | 1:50 |
| 17. | S. Rossetto | AUB | 2:08 |
| 18. | C. Rodriguez | IGD | s.t. |
| 19. | J. M. Díaz | DKO | s.t. |
| 20. | A. González | MOV | s.t. |

### GENERAL CLASSIFICATION

| POS | | NAME | TEAM | TIME |
|---|---|---|---|---|
| 1. | ↑15 | I. R. Sosa | IGD | 13:13:16 |
| 2. | ↑12 | E. Bernal | IGD | 0:19 |
| 3. | – | J. Alaphilippe | DQT | 0:21 |

### KING OF THE MOUNTAINS

| POS | | NAME | TEAM | PTS |
|---|---|---|---|---|
| 1. | ↑1 | F. Conca | LTS | 15 |
| 2. | ↑14 | J. Cousin | TDE | 9 |
| 3. | – | D. Fernández | DKO | 9 |

### POINTS

| POS | | NAME | TEAM | PTS |
|---|---|---|---|---|
| 1. | – | D. Ballerini | DQT | 30 |
| 2. | – | G. Ciccone | TFS | 18 |
| 3. | – | A. Démare | GFC | 12 |

### YOUNG RIDER

| POS | | NAME | TEAM | TIME |
|---|---|---|---|---|
| 1. | ↑4 | I. R. Sosa | IGD | 13:13:16 |
| 2. | ↑2 | E. Bernal | IGD | 0:19 |
| 3. | ↑4 | M. Vansevenant | DQT | 0:58 |

## TOUR DE LA PROVENCE
Stage 4
14 February 2021
Avignon–Salon-de-Provence
163.2km

### WEATHER

TEMPERATURE: 3°C
WIND: NE 9km/h

### STAGE RESULTS

| POS | NAME | TEAM | TIME |
|---|---|---|---|
| 1. | P. Bauhaus | TBV | 3:47:01 |
| 2. | D. Ballerini | DQT | s.t. |
| 3. | N. Bouhanni | ARK | s.t. |
| 4. | M. Moschetti | TFS | s.t. |
| 5. | J. Degenkolb | LTS | s.t. |
| 6. | B. Coquard | BBK | s.t. |
| 7. | M. Walls | BOH | s.t. |
| 8. | N. Bonifazio | TDE | s.t. |
| 9. | E. M. Grosu | DKO | s.t. |
| 10. | A. Kristoff | UAD | s.t. |
| 11. | Z. Štybar | DQT | s.t. |
| 12. | E. Vermeulen | XRL | s.t. |
| 13. | P. Allegaert | COF | s.t. |
| 14. | R. Cardis | AUB | s.t. |
| 15. | P. Konrad | BOH | s.t. |
| 16. | M. Jorgenson | MOV | s.t. |
| 17. | J. Alaphilippe | DQT | s.t. |
| 18. | C. Venturini | ACT | s.t. |
| 19. | E. Liepiņš | TFS | s.t. |
| 20. | W. Poels | TBV | s.t. |

### GENERAL CLASSIFICATION

| POS | | NAME | TEAM | TIME |
|---|---|---|---|---|
| 1. | – | I. R. Sosa | IGD | 17:00:17 |
| 2. | ↑1 | J. Alaphilippe | DQT | 0:18 |
| 3. | ↓1 | E. Bernal | IGD | 0:19 |

### KING OF THE MOUNTAINS

| POS | | NAME | TEAM | PTS |
|---|---|---|---|---|
| 1. | – | F. Conca | LTS | 15 |
| 2. | – | A. Leknessund | DSM | 15 |
| 3. | ↓1 | J. Cousin | TDE | 9 |

### POINTS

| POS | | NAME | TEAM | PTS |
|---|---|---|---|---|
| 1. | – | D. Ballerini | DQT | 42 |
| 2. | ↑22 | P. Bauhaus | TBV | 20 |
| 3. | ↑6 | N. Bouhanni | ARK | 20 |

### YOUNG RIDER

| POS | | NAME | TEAM | TIME |
|---|---|---|---|---|
| 1. | – | I. R. Sosa | IGD | 17:00:17 |
| 2. | – | E. Bernal | IGD | 0:19 |
| 3. | – | M. Vansevenant | DQT | 0:58 |

FEBRUARY .PRO MEN'S RACE

# CLÁSICA DE ALMERÍA
14 February 2021
Pueblo de Vicar–Roquetas de Mar
183.3km

## WEATHER

TEMPERATURE | WIND
19°C | E 24km/h

## RESULTS

| POS | NAME | TEAM | TIME |
|---|---|---|---|
| 1. | G. Nizzolo | TQA | 4:18:44 |
| 2. | F. Sénéchal | DQT | s.t. |
| 3. | M. Laas | BOH | s.t. |
| 4. | J. Aberasturi | CJR | s.t. |
| 5. | T. Dupont | WVA | s.t. |
| 6. | D. van Poppel | IWG | s.t. |
| 7. | G. Cullaigh | MOV | s.t. |
| 8. | E. Theuns | TFS | s.t. |
| 9. | M. Sarreau | ACT | s.t. |
| 10. | D. Cima | GAZ | s.t. |
| 11. | M. Canola | GAZ | s.t. |
| 12. | A. G. Jansen | BEX | s.t. |
| 13. | L. Manzin | TDE | s.t. |
| 14. | J. Warlop | SVB | s.t. |
| 15. | B. Van Lerberghe | DQT | s.t. |
| 16. | D. Touzé | ACT | s.t. |
| 17. | F. Gaviria | UAD | s.t. |
| 18. | F. Fiorelli | BCF | s.t. |
| 19. | J. Ezquerra | BBH | s.t. |
| 20. | C. Joyce | RLY | s.t. |

FEBRUARY .1 MEN'S RACE

## TOUR DES ALPES-MARITIMES ET DU VAR
Stage 1
19 February 2021
Biot–Gourdon
186.8km

### WEATHER

TEMPERATURE | WIND
15°C | SE 7km/h

### STAGE RESULTS

| POS | NAME | TEAM | TIME |
|---|---|---|---|
| 1. | B. Mollema | TFS | 4:50:20 |
| 2. | G. Van Avermaet | ACT | 0:01 |
| 3. | V. Madouas | GFC | s.t. |
| 4. | M. Woods | ISN | s.t. |
| 5. | G. Ciccone | TFS | s.t. |
| 6. | D. Godon | ACT | s.t. |
| 7. | R. Molard | GFC | s.t. |
| 8. | Je. Herrada | COF | s.t. |
| 9. | T. Pinot | GFC | s.t. |
| 10. | D. Gaudu | GFC | s.t. |
| 11. | A. Livyns | WVA | s.t. |
| 12. | J. Fuglsang | APT | s.t. |
| 13. | P. Vakoč | AFC | s.t. |
| 14. | M. Cort | EFN | s.t. |
| 15. | N. Quintana | ARK | s.t. |
| 16. | D. Martin | ISN | s.t. |
| 17. | R. Adrià | EKP | s.t. |
| 18. | J. Hivert | BBK | s.t. |
| 19. | G. Izaguirre | APT | s.t. |
| 20. | B. O'Connor | ACT | s.t. |

### GENERAL CLASSIFICATION

| POS | NAME | TEAM | TIME |
|---|---|---|---|
| 1. | B. Mollema | TFS | 4:50:20 |
| 2. | G. Van Avermaet | ACT | 0:01 |
| 3. | V. Madouas | GFC | s.t. |

### KING OF THE MOUNTAINS

| POS | NAME | TEAM | PTS |
|---|---|---|---|
| 1. | K. Neilands | ISN | 10 |
| 2. | O. Vergaerde | AFC | 10 |
| 3. | T. Pidcock | IGD | 8 |

### POINTS

| POS | NAME | TEAM | PTS |
|---|---|---|---|
| 1. | B. Mollema | TFS | 25 |
| 2. | G. Van Avermaet | ACT | 20 |
| 3. | V. Madouas | GFC | 16 |

### YOUNG RIDER

| POS | NAME | TEAM | TIME |
|---|---|---|---|
| 1. | V. Madouas | GFC | 4:50:21 |
| 2. | D. Godon | ACT | s.t. |
| 3. | D. Gaudu | GFC | s.t. |

## TOUR DES ALPES-MARITIMES ET DU VAR
Stage 2
20 February 2021
Fayence–Fayence
168.9km

### WEATHER

TEMPERATURE | WIND
16°C | SE 9km/h

### STAGE RESULTS

| POS | NAME | TEAM | TIME |
|---|---|---|---|
| 1. | M. Woods | ISN | 4:16:54 |
| 2. | B. Mollema | TFS | 0:02 |
| 3. | J. Narváez | IGD | 0:04 |
| 4. | D. Gaudu | GFC | 0:07 |
| 5. | A. Vuillermoz | TDE | 0:10 |
| 6. | R. Molard | GFC | s.t. |
| 7. | B. O'Connor | ACT | 0:11 |
| 8. | Je. Herrada | COF | 0:13 |
| 9. | A. Livyns | WVA | s.t. |
| 10. | P. Sivakov | IGD | s.t. |
| 11. | C. Laporte | COF | s.t. |
| 12. | N. Quintana | ARK | s.t. |
| 13. | G. Ciccone | TFS | s.t. |
| 14. | D. Martin | ISN | s.t. |
| 15. | J. Fuglsang | APT | s.t. |
| 16. | V. Madouas | GFC | s.t. |
| 17. | J. Hivert | BBK | s.t. |
| 18. | C. Champoussin | ACT | s.t. |
| 19. | G. Brambilla | TFS | s.t. |
| 20. | T. Pinot | GFC | s.t. |

### GENERAL CLASSIFICATION

| POS | NAME | TEAM | TIME |
|---|---|---|---|
| 1. ↑3 | M. Woods | ISN | 9:07:15 |
| 2. ↓1 | B. Mollema | TFS | 0:01 |
| 3. ↑7 | D. Gaudu | GFC | 0:07 |

### KING OF THE MOUNTAINS

| POS | NAME | TEAM | PTS |
|---|---|---|---|
| 1. — | B. Ghirmay | DKO | 16 |
| 2. ↑8 | A. Mifsud | SRA | 14 |
| 3. ↓2 | K. Neilands | ISN | 10 |

### POINTS

| POS | NAME | TEAM | PTS |
|---|---|---|---|
| 1. — | B. Mollema | TFS | 45 |
| 2. ↑2 | M. Woods | ISN | 39 |
| 3. ↑9 | D. Gaudu | GFC | 20 |

### YOUNG RIDER

| POS | NAME | TEAM | TIME |
|---|---|---|---|
| 1. ↑2 | D. Gaudu | GFC | 9:07:22 |
| 2. ↓1 | V. Madouas | GFC | 0:06 |
| 3. ↑4 | P. Sivakov | IGD | s.t. |

FEBRUARY  .1 MEN'S RACE

## TOUR DES ALPES-MARITIMES ET DU VAR
Stage 3
21 February 2021
Blausasc–Blausasc
136km

### WEATHER

TEMPERATURE  WIND
16°C  E 44km/h

### STAGE RESULTS

| POS | NAME | TEAM | TIME |
|---|---|---|---|
| 1. | G. Brambilla | TFS | 3:43:32 |
| 2. | T. Geoghegan Hart | IGD | 0:13 |
| 3. | B. O'Connor | ACT | s.t. |
| 4. | R. Molard | GFC | s.t. |
| 5. | V. Madouas | GFC | s.t. |
| 6. | J. Fuglsang | APT | 0:18 |
| 7. | D. Gaudu | GFC | s.t. |
| 8. | B. Mollema | TFS | s.t. |
| 9. | N. Quintana | ARK | s.t. |
| 10. | M. Woods | ISN | s.t. |
| 11. | G. Izaguirre | APT | 0:39 |
| 12. | C. Champoussin | ACT | 1:19 |
| 13. | M. Storer | DSM | 3:06 |
| 14. | A. Livyns | WVA | 3:53 |
| 15. | B. Tulett | AFC | s.t. |
| 16. | S. Armée | TQA | s.t. |
| 17. | A. Vuillermoz | TDE | s.t. |
| 18. | J. M. Díaz | DKO | s.t. |
| 19. | H. Houle | APT | s.t. |
| 20. | D. Martin | ISN | s.t. |

### GENERAL CLASSIFICATION

| POS | NAME | TEAM | TIME |
|---|---|---|---|
| 1. ↑16 | G. Brambilla | TFS | 12:51:00 |
| 2. ↓1 | M. Woods | ISN | 0:05 |
| 3. ↓1 | B. Mollema | TFS | 0:06 |

### KING OF THE MOUNTAINS

| POS | NAME | TEAM | PTS |
|---|---|---|---|
| 1. — | M. Tusveld | DSM | 25 |
| 2. — | V. Madouas | GFC | 22 |
| 3. — | R. Molard | GFC | 20 |

### POINTS

| POS | NAME | TEAM | PTS |
|---|---|---|---|
| 1. — | B. Mollema | TFS | 53 |
| 2. — | M. Woods | ISN | 45 |
| 3. ↑2 | R. Molard | GFC | 33 |

### YOUNG RIDER

| POS | NAME | TEAM | TIME |
|---|---|---|---|
| 1. — | D. Gaudu | GFC | 12:51:12 |
| 2. — | V. Madouas | GFC | 0:01 |
| 3. ↑5 | C. Champoussin | ACT | 1:26 |

FEBRUARY

FEBRUARY    WORLDTOUR MEN'S RACE

# UAE TOUR
Stage 1
21 February 2021
Al Dhafra Castle–Al Mirfa
176km

## WEATHER

| TEMPERATURE | WIND |
|---|---|
| 27°C | N 17km/h |

## PROFILE

Cycling fans had been forced to wait a little longer for WorldTour action than usual, after the Australian openers were cancelled due to the ongoing coronavirus pandemic, and the UAE Tour decided it would make up for lost time, crosswinds tearing the peloton apart from the off in the Middle East. The race then came back together but only for a moment, before Deceuninck-QuickStep put the hammer down, splitting the race for good this time. Tadej Pogačar and Adam Yates were the main GC beneficiaries, finding themselves at the right end of the split while others were caught behind. Around 25 riders were left to contest a reduced bunch sprint, and Mathieu van der Poel – fresh from defending his cyclocross rainbow jersey – wasted little time in transferring his winning ways to the road. The Dutchman outsprinted David Dekker, son of Erik, to take the first stage and race lead.

## STAGE RESULTS

| POS | NAME | TEAM | TIME |
|---|---|---|---|
| 1. | M. van der Poel | AFC | 3:45:47 |
| 2. | D. Dekker | TJV | s.t. |
| 3. | M. Mørkøv | DQT | s.t. |
| 4. | E. Liepiņš | TFS | s.t. |
| 5. | E. Viviani | COF | s.t. |
| 6. | T. Pogačar | UAD | s.t. |
| 7. | A. Roux | GFC | s.t. |
| 8. | C. Harper | TJV | 0:03 |
| 9. | J. Almeida | DQT | s.t. |
| 10. | F. Masnada | DQT | s.t. |
| 11. | S. Archbold | DQT | s.t. |
| 12. | A. Yates | IGD | s.t. |
| 13. | F. Gaviria | UAD | s.t. |
| 14. | M. Skjelmose Jensen | TFS | 0:06 |
| 15. | A. M. Richeze | UAD | s.t. |
| 16. | N. Powless | EFN | s.t. |
| 17. | G. Vermeersch | AFC | s.t. |
| 18. | M. Cattaneo | DQT | 0:03 |
| 19. | K. Reijnen | TFS | s.t. |
| 20. | R. Fernández | COF | s.t. |

## GENERAL CLASSIFICATION

| POS | NAME | TEAM | TIME |
|---|---|---|---|
| 1. | M. van der Poel | AFC | 3:45:37 |
| 2. | D. Dekker | TJV | 0:04 |
| 3. | M. Mørkøv | DQT | 0:06 |

## POINTS

| POS | NAME | TEAM | PTS |
|---|---|---|---|
| 1. | M. van der Poel | AFC | 20 |
| 2. | J. Almeida | DQT | 18 |
| 3. | D. Dekker | TJV | 16 |

## YOUNG RIDER

| POS | NAME | TEAM | TIME |
|---|---|---|---|
| 1. | D. Dekker | TJV | 3:45:41 |
| 2. | J. Almeida | DQT | 0:03 |
| 3. | T. Pogačar | UAD | 0:04 |

## BONUSES

| TYPE | NAME | | TEAM |
|---|---|---|---|
| Sprint 1 | J. Almeida | | DQT |
| Sprint 2 | J. Almeida | | DQT |

## TRIVIA

» Mathieu van der Poel also won his first road race of the year in 2019. In 2018, he finished second on his season opener, waiting until the next day to bag a first victory.

FEBRUARY    WORLDTOUR MEN'S RACE

# UAE TOUR
Stage 2 (ITT)
22 February 2021
Al Hudayriat Island–Al Hudayriat Island
13km

The big news at the start of the day was the withdrawal of Mathieu van der Poel's entire Alpecin-Fenix squad after a Covid-19 positive within the team camp. For the rest, a time trial would provide the first GC shake-up, and also a first opportunity to see the rainbow bands of world time trial champion Filippo Ganna at WorldTour level this season. The Ineos Grenadiers rider had already taken a first TT win of the year at Etoile de Bessèges and continued his dominance in the desert, putting 14 seconds into the next fastest man, Stefan Bissegger. Pogačar was strong enough for a fourth-placed finish, only 24 seconds slower than Ganna and enough to see him take the race lead, Deceuninck-QuickStep's João Almeida hot on his heels 5 seconds behind. Adam Yates shipped nearly 40 seconds to his Slovenian rival in a blow to his hopes for the overall.

## WEATHER

**TEMPERATURE**
29°C

**WIND**
NE 11km/h

## PROFILE

HUDAYRIAT ISLAND — HUDAYRIAT ISLAND

## STAGE RESULTS

| POS | NAME | TEAM | TIME |
|---|---|---|---|
| 1. | F. Ganna | IGD | 0:13:56 |
| 2. | S. Bissegger | EFN | 0:14 |
| 3. | M. Bjerg | UAD | 0:21 |
| 4. | T. Pogačar | UAD | 0:24 |
| 5. | L. L. Sanchez | APT | 0:30 |
| 6. | J. Almeida | DQT | s.t. |
| 7. | M. Walscheid | TQA | 0:32 |
| 8. | S. de Bod | APT | 0:33 |
| 9. | D. F. Martinez | IGD | 0:36 |
| 10. | M. Brändle | ISN | 0:38 |
| 11. | M. Cattaneo | DQT | 0:39 |
| 12. | L. Craddock | EFN | s.t. |
| 13. | J. Vingegaard | TJV | 0:43 |
| 14. | M. Sobrero | APT | 0:44 |
| 15. | J. van Emden | TJV | 0:46 |
| 16. | N. Arndt | DSM | 0:47 |
| 17. | A. Brunel | GFC | 0:48 |
| 18. | S. Higuita | EFN | s.t. |
| 19. | A. Tiberi | TFS | 0:49 |
| 20. | F. Wright | TBV | s.t. |

## GENERAL CLASSIFICATION

| POS | NAME | TEAM | TIME |
|---|---|---|---|
| 1. ↑4 | T. Pogačar | UAD | 4:00:05 |
| 2. ↑2 | J. Almeida | DQT | 0:05 |
| 3. ↑6 | M. Cattaneo | DQT | 0:18 |

## POINTS

| POS | NAME | TEAM | PTS |
|---|---|---|---|
| 1. ↑1 | J. Almeida | DQT | 23 |
| 2. — | F. Ganna | IGD | 20 |
| 3. ↑2 | T. Pogačar | UAD | 19 |

## YOUNG RIDER

| POS | NAME | TEAM | TIME |
|---|---|---|---|
| 1. ↑2 | T. Pogačar | UAD | 4:00:05 |
| 2. — | J. Almeida | DQT | 0:05 |
| 3. ↑2 | N. Powless | EFN | 0:41 |

## TRIVIA

» Filippo Ganna has won all five time trials he's competed in since taking the rainbow bands.

FEBRUARY    WORLDTOUR MEN'S RACE

# UAE TOUR
Stage 3
23 February 2021
Strata Manufactoring–Jebel Hafeet
166km

While the coronavirus pandemic still lingered over not just cycling but the whole world, stage 3 of the 2021 race took us back in time. Stage 5 was the last of the curtailed 2020 edition, Pogačar besting Adam Yates up the Jebel Hafeet climb, and 2021 saw history repeat itself. Yates gave it every bit of welly he could muster up the final 10km incline to the summit finish after an opening flat 155km, putting in dig after dig to try and dislodge the UAE Team Emirates rider. Pogačar hung on, though, waiting until the road dipped down in the final 400 metres, powering around Yates on a swooping bend and opening a gap that the Brit's weaker sprint couldn't hope to close in the final twisting corners. Pogačar had consolidated his race lead, Yates now the next best-placed rider on GC, 43 seconds in arrears.

## WEATHER

TEMPERATURE    WIND
30°C    NW 26km/h

## PROFILE

## BREAKAWAY
T. De Gendt (LTS), T. Gallopin (ACT)

## STAGE RESULTS

| POS | NAME | TEAM | TIME |
|---|---|---|---|
| 1. | T. Pogačar | UAD | 3:58:35 |
| 2. | A. Yates | IGD | s.t. |
| 3. | S. Higuita | EFN | 0:48 |
| 4. | E. Buchmann | BOH | s.t. |
| 5. | H. Vanhoucke | LTS | s.t. |
| 6. | J. Almeida | DQT | s.t. |
| 7. | F. Stork | DSM | 0:54 |
| 8. | N. Powless | EFN | s.t. |
| 9. | C. Harper | TJV | 1:00 |
| 10. | G. Bouchard | ACT | 1:09 |
| 11. | S. Kuss | TJV | s.t. |
| 12. | B. Hermans | ISN | 1:26 |
| 13. | V. Nibali | TFS | s.t. |
| 14. | N. Schultz | BEX | s.t. |
| 15. | D. Formolo | UAD | s.t. |
| 16. | L. Meintjes | IWG | s.t. |
| 17. | M. Skjelmose Jensen | TFS | 1:38 |
| 18. | D. Caruso | TBV | s.t. |
| 19. | W. Poels | TBV | 2:11 |
| 20. | R. Fernández | COF | s.t. |

## GENERAL CLASSIFICATION

| POS | NAME | TEAM | TIME |
|---|---|---|---|
| 1. — | T. Pogačar | UAD | 7:58:30 |
| 2. ↑3 | A. Yates | IGD | 0:43 |
| 3. ↓1 | J. Almeida | DQT | 1:03 |

## POINTS

| POS | NAME | TEAM | PTS |
|---|---|---|---|
| 1. ↑2 | T. Pogačar | UAD | 39 |
| 2. ↓1 | J. Almeida | DQT | 28 |
| 3. ↓1 | F. Ganna | IGD | 21 |

## YOUNG RIDER

| POS | NAME | TEAM | TIME |
|---|---|---|---|
| 1. — | T. Pogačar | UAD | 7:58:30 |
| 2. — | J. Almeida | DQT | 1:03 |
| 3. — | N. Powless | EFN | 1:45 |

## BONUSES

| TYPE | NAME | TEAM |
|---|---|---|
| Sprint 1 | T. Gallopin | ACT |
| Sprint 2 | T. Gallopin | ACT |

## TRIVIA

» This was Pogačar's first victory since winning the 2020 Tour de France.

FEBRUARY   WORLDTOUR MEN'S RACE

## UAE TOUR
Stage 4
24 February 2021
Al Marjan Island–Al Marjan Island
204km

The sprinters' reward for hauling themselves up Jebel Hafeet was an opportunity for stage victory the next day and, with the absence of both crosswinds and Mathieu van der Poel, they would get their chance for a bunch gallop to the line. They would have to earn it, though, on a hefty 204km coastal route. Two Frenchman – François Bidard and Olivier Le Gac – offered themselves up as the sacrificial lambs, flogging themselves off the front for the majority of the day. The sprint trains fanned across the yawning highways inside the final 10km. Bora-Hansgrohe tried to set it up for Pascal Ackermann, but Caleb Ewan and Elia Viviani flew around the right-hand side. It was Sam Bennett, however, who snuck up the inside, taking the quicker route to the line and subsequently his first victory of the year. Jumbo-Visma's David Dekker came in second once again.

### WEATHER

TEMPERATURE   WIND
27°C          NW 19km/h

### PROFILE

AL MARJAN ISLAND — UMM-AL-QUWAIN — RAS AL KHAIMAH — AL MARJAN ISLAND

### BREAKAWAY
F. Bidard (ACT), O. Le Gac (GFC)

### STAGE RESULTS

| POS | NAME | TEAM | TIME |
|---|---|---|---|
| 1. | S. Bennett | DQT | 4:51:51 |
| 2. | D. Dekker | TJV | s.t. |
| 3. | C. Ewan | LTS | s.t. |
| 4. | E. Viviani | COF | s.t. |
| 5. | M. Moschetti | TFS | s.t. |
| 6. | P. Ackermann | BOH | s.t. |
| 7. | P. Bauhaus | TBV | s.t. |
| 8. | G. Nizzolo | TQA | s.t. |
| 9. | F. Gaviria | UAD | s.t. |
| 10. | K. Groves | BEX | s.t. |
| 11. | A. Vendrame | ACT | s.t. |
| 12. | A. Greipel | ISN | s.t. |
| 13. | R. Minali | IWG | s.t. |
| 14. | C. Harper | TJV | s.t. |
| 15. | C. Bol | DSM | s.t. |
| 16. | J. Bauer | BEX | s.t. |
| 17. | M. Mørkøv | DQT | s.t. |
| 18. | Y. Gidich | APT | s.t. |
| 19. | M. Bjerg | UAD | s.t. |
| 20. | T. Pogačar | UAD | s.t. |

### GENERAL CLASSIFICATION

| POS | | NAME | TEAM | TIME |
|---|---|---|---|---|
| 1. | — | T. Pogačar | UAD | 12:50:21 |
| 2. | — | A. Yates | IGD | 0:43 |
| 3. | — | J. Almeida | DQT | 1:03 |

### POINTS

| POS | | NAME | TEAM | PTS |
|---|---|---|---|---|
| 1. | ↑6 | D. Dekker | TJV | 43 |
| 2. | ↓1 | T. Pogačar | UAD | 39 |
| 3. | ↓1 | J. Almeida | DQT | 28 |

### YOUNG RIDER

| POS | | NAME | TEAM | TIME |
|---|---|---|---|---|
| 1. | — | T. Pogačar | UAD | 12:50:21 |
| 2. | — | J. Almeida | DQT | 1:03 |
| 3. | — | N. Powless | EFN | 1:45 |

### BONUSES

| TYPE | NAME | TEAM |
|---|---|---|
| Sprint 1 | D. Dekker | TJV |
| Sprint 2 | O. Le Gac | GFC |

### TRIVIA
» This was Sam Bennett's 50th career win.

FEBRUARY   WORLDTOUR MEN'S RACE

# UAE TOUR
Stage 5
25 February 2021
Fujairah Marine Club–Jebel Jais
170km

Mathias Frank set off alone up the road at the start of stage 5 but was soon rescued by the likes of breakaway heavyweights Thomas De Gendt and Alexey Lutsenko as the day's escape formed. Ineos set the pace on the front, shadowed by UAE Team Emirates, and the race finally started to unfurl inside the last 5km up the 21km winding Jebel Jais, Chris Froome dropping. Jonas Vingegaard decided to take his chance with 1km to go, jumping free of the few riders remaining in the GC group. The young Dane caught up to Lutsenko's wheel, sharing a lighthearted word as he sat there looking fresh, the Kazakh's legs beginning to turn to lead. Vingegaard easily prised himself away to cross the line first while Pogačar and Yates sprinted for the next two podium spots, the Slovenian adding to his lead by taking a couple more bonification seconds than the Brit.

## WEATHER

TEMPERATURE  WIND
28°C         NE 15km/h

## PROFILE

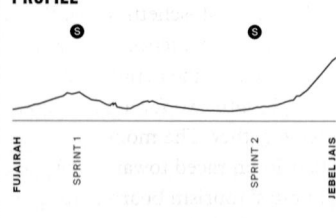

## BREAKAWAY

R. Kluge (LTS), L. Warbasse (ACT), O. Goldstein (ISN), T. De Gendt (LTS), K. Colleoni (BEX), L. N. Hansen (TQA), A. Lutsenko (APT), A. Dowsett (ISN)

## STAGE RESULTS

| POS | NAME | TEAM | TIME |
|---|---|---|---|
| 1. | J. Vingegaard | TJV | 4:19:08 |
| 2. | T. Pogačar | UAD | 0:03 |
| 3. | A. Yates | IGD | s.t. |
| 4. | S. Higuita | EFN | 0:05 |
| 5. | J. Almeida | DQT | 0:06 |
| 6. | N. Schultz | BEX | s.t. |
| 7. | S. Kuss | TJV | 0:08 |
| 8. | W. Poels | TBV | s.t. |
| 9. | B. Hermans | ISN | s.t. |
| 10. | G. Bouchard | ACT | s.t. |
| 11. | A. Lutsenko | APT | s.t. |
| 12. | M. Skjelmose Jensen | TFS | s.t. |
| 13. | L. Meintjes | IWG | s.t. |
| 14. | F. Stork | DSM | s.t. |
| 15. | C. Harper | TJV | s.t. |
| 16. | N. Powless | EFN | s.t. |
| 17. | D. Caruso | TBV | s.t. |
| 18. | G. Mäder | TBV | 0:15 |
| 19. | S. de Bod | APT | 0:22 |
| 20. | A. Valter | GFC | 0:26 |

## GENERAL CLASSIFICATION

| POS | | NAME | TEAM | TIME |
|---|---|---|---|---|
| 1. | — | T. Pogačar | UAD | 17:09:26 |
| 2. | — | A. Yates | IGD | 0:45 |
| 3. | — | J. Almeida | DQT | 1:12 |

## POINTS

| POS | | NAME | TEAM | PTS |
|---|---|---|---|---|
| 1. | ↑1 | T. Pogačar | UAD | 55 |
| 2. | ↓1 | D. Dekker | TJV | 48 |
| 3. | — | J. Almeida | DQT | 35 |

## YOUNG RIDER

| POS | | NAME | TEAM | TIME |
|---|---|---|---|---|
| 1. | — | T. Pogačar | UAD | 17:09:26 |
| 2. | — | J. Almeida | DQT | 1:12 |
| 3. | — | N. Powless | EFN | 1:56 |

## BONUSES

| TYPE | NAME | TEAM |
|---|---|---|
| Sprint 1 | M. Frank | ACT |
| Sprint 2 | T. De Gendt | LTS |

## TRIVIA

» Vingegaard ensures Jumbo-Visma's run of at least one stage win in the UAE continues, after Roglič took the spoils en route to the overall in 2019, and Dylan Groenewegen claimed a bunch sprint in 2020.

FEBRUARY    WORLDTOUR MEN'S RACE

# UAE TOUR
Stage 6
26 February 2021
Deira Island–Palm Jumeirah
165km

After a nasty-looking crash dumped Florian Stork and Matteo Moschetti out of the race early on, it took the re-emergence of crosswinds to animate the second half of the penultimate stage. The peloton was split into two for around 20km before coming back together. The monorail passed overhead as the peloton raced towards Palm Jumeirah, the Emirates' tourism board getting their money's worth as the helicopter showed picturesque shots of all the riches that oil money can amass. This time around Deceuninck-QuickStep led from the front heading to the finish line, David Dekker coming around early and making his bid for glory but tiring, as Sam Bennett persisted, winning his second sprint of the race ahead of Elia Viviani and Pascal Ackermann.

## WEATHER

TEMPERATURE    WIND
24°C           NW 20km/h

## PROFILE

DUBAI · SPRINGS VILLAGE · AL QUADRA CYCLE TRACK · PALM JUMEIRAH

## BREAKAWAY

T. Gallopin (ACT), A. Lutsenko (APT), L. L. Sanchez (APT), M. Ladagnous (GFC), A. Valter (GFC), I. Elosegui (MOV)

## STAGE RESULTS

| POS | NAME | TEAM | TIME |
|---|---|---|---|
| 1. | S. Bennett | DQT | 3:32:23 |
| 2. | E. Viviani | COF | s.t. |
| 3. | P. Ackermann | BOH | s.t. |
| 4. | D. Dekker | TJV | s.t. |
| 5. | F. Gaviria | UAD | s.t. |
| 6. | G. Nizzolo | TQA | s.t. |
| 7. | K. Groves | BEX | s.t. |
| 8. | A. Greipel | ISN | s.t. |
| 9. | C. Bol | DSM | s.t. |
| 10. | M. Mørkøv | DQT | s.t. |
| 11. | R. Minali | IWG | s.t. |
| 12. | C. Ewan | LTS | s.t. |
| 13. | E. Liepiņš | TFS | s.t. |
| 14. | Y. Gidich | APT | s.t. |
| 15. | A. Vendrame | ACT | s.t. |
| 16. | P. Bauhaus | TBV | s.t. |
| 17. | S. Bissegger | EFN | s.t. |
| 18. | J. Almeida | DQT | s.t. |
| 19. | N. Schultz | BEX | s.t. |
| 20. | R. Zabel | ISN | s.t. |

## GENERAL CLASSIFICATION

| POS | | NAME | TEAM | TIME |
|---|---|---|---|---|
| 1. | — | T. Pogačar | UAD | 20:41:59 |
| 2. | — | A. Yates | IGD | 0:35 |
| 3. | — | J. Almeida | DQT | 1:02 |

## POINTS

| POS | | NAME | TEAM | PTS |
|---|---|---|---|---|
| 1. | ↑1 | D. Dekker | TJV | 57 |
| 2. | ↓1 | T. Pogačar | UAD | 51 |
| 3. | ↑5 | S. Bennett | DQT | 40 |

## YOUNG RIDER

| POS | | NAME | TEAM | TIME |
|---|---|---|---|---|
| 1. | — | T. Pogačar | UAD | 20:41:59 |
| 2. | — | J. Almeida | DQT | 1:02 |
| 3. | — | N. Powless | EFN | 1:46 |

## BONUSES

| TYPE | NAME | TEAM |
|---|---|---|
| Sprint 1 | T. Gallopin | ACT |
| Sprint 2 | T. Gallopin | ACT |

## TRIVIA

» Elia Viviani has finished in the top five of a stage at the UAE Tour six times yet only won once.

FEBRUARY   WORLDTOUR MEN'S RACE

# UAE TOUR
Stage 7
27 February 2021
Yas Mall–Abu Dhabi Breakwater
147km

The third bout of crosswinds provided final-day excitement for viewers while the peloton was surely saying 'enough already'. With the finish giving a final chance for the sprinters, and many of the fast men's teams missing the front split, the race did come back together after momentarily parting. Pogačar was all but assured of the overall victory as second-place Adam Yates took an unpleasant tumble, his face colliding with the tarmac. Left bloodied, he told the TV camera he was all right before politely asking it to jog on and leave him alone. David Dekker confirmed his green jersey at the intermediate sprint, but once again couldn't quite manage the stage victory. Lotto Soudal's diminutive Caleb Ewan snuck out of the slipstream of his friend and neighbour Sam Bennett at the last to pip him on the line, ecstatic to not be leaving the UAE empty-handed.

## WEATHER

TEMPERATURE   WIND
23°C          NW 22km/h

## PROFILE

YAS MARINA / GOLF GARDENS / LOUVRE ABU DHABI / ABU DHABI BREAKWATER

## BREAKAWAY
S. Battistella (APT), M. Sobrero (APT), A. Brunel (GFC)

## STAGE RESULTS

| POS | NAME | TEAM | TIME |
|---|---|---|---|
| 1. | C. Ewan | LTS | 3:18:29 |
| 2. | S. Bennett | DQT | s.t. |
| 3. | P. Bauhaus | TBV | s.t. |
| 4. | M. Mørkøv | DQT | s.t. |
| 5. | C. Bol | DSM | s.t. |
| 6. | A. Greipel | ISN | s.t. |
| 7. | A. Vendrame | ACT | s.t. |
| 8. | L. Mezgec | BEX | s.t. |
| 9. | R. Minali | IWG | s.t. |
| 10. | Y. Gidich | APT | s.t. |
| 11. | P. Ackermann | BOH | s.t. |
| 12. | F. Gaviria | UAD | s.t. |
| 13. | E. Liepiņš | TFS | s.t. |
| 14. | D. Dekker | TJV | s.t. |
| 15. | E. Viviani | COF | s.t. |
| 16. | G. Nizzolo | TQA | s.t. |
| 17. | M. Laas | BOH | s.t. |
| 18. | M. Walscheid | TQA | s.t. |
| 19. | J. Bauer | BEX | s.t. |
| 20. | B. J. Lindeman | TQA | s.t. |

## GENERAL CLASSIFICATION

| POS | NAME | TEAM | TIME |
|---|---|---|---|
| 1. — | T. Pogačar | UAD | 24:00:28 |
| 2. — | A. Yates | IGD | 0:35 |
| 3. — | J. Almeida | DQT | 1:02 |

## POINTS

| POS | NAME | TEAM | PTS |
|---|---|---|---|
| 1. — | D. Dekker | TJV | 66 |
| 2. ↑1 | S. Bennett | DQT | 56 |
| 3. ↓1 | T. Pogačar | UAD | 51 |

## YOUNG RIDER

| POS | NAME | TEAM | TIME |
|---|---|---|---|
| 1. — | T. Pogačar | UAD | 24:00:28 |
| 2. — | J. Almeida | DQT | 1:02 |
| 3. — | N. Powless | EFN | 1:45 |

## BONUSES

| TYPE | NAME | TEAM |
|---|---|---|
| Sprint 1 | M. Sobrero | APT |
| Sprint 2 | D. Dekker | TJV |

## TRIVIA

» This was the second year in a row Caleb Ewan opened his account at the UAE Tour after not winning in Australia in January (the 2021 races being cancelled due to Covid). In 2020 he took his first win of the season on exactly the same day.

FEBRUARY    WORLDTOUR MEN'S RACE

## OMLOOP HET NIEUWSBLAD
27 February 2021
Ghent–Ninove
200.5km

It was a still, crisp, sunny edition of the race that is so often characterised by grey and wet Belgian weather of the most lugubrious sort. Perhaps the benign conditions were in keeping with the general fragile optimism with which the cycling world approached the opening of the Classics campaign. Would Paris–Roubaix possibly happen? Could Flanders yet be raced in its time-honoured berth? What would happen with the enduring rivalry between Mathieu van der Poel and Wout van Aert? Omloop het Nieuwsblad would answer none of those questions, however; Van Aert was heading to Strade Bianche, and Van der Poel pulled out of the race a few days beforehand, suffering from a high temperature (his team having been sent home from the UAE Tour following a positive Covid test among the staff). That left the door ajar for Deceuninck-QuickStep to dictate the terms all day on the bergs and cobbles of the venerable race. World champion Julian Alaphilippe had a characteristically combative race, but in the end a group of 45 riders came to the finish line together – the largest group in 12 years. It was Alaphilippe's versatile Italian teammate Davide Ballerini who won the sprint, confirming the promise he started to show post-lockdown in 2020. Immediately he catapulted his name up the order to become one of the favourites for still bigger prizes to come.

## WEATHER

TEMPERATURE    WIND
4°C            E 7km/h

## PROFILE

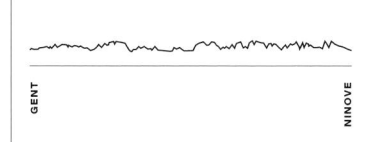

GENT                              NINOVE

## BREAKAWAY
Y. Federov (APT), R. Gibbons (UAD), K. De Ketele (SVB), B. De Backer (BBK), M. Louvel (ARK)

## RESULTS

| POS | NAME | TEAM | TIME |
|---|---|---|---|
| 1. | D. Ballerini | DQT | 4:43:03 |
| 2. | J. Stewart | GFC | s.t. |
| 3. | S. Vanmarcke | ISN | s.t. |
| 4. | H. Haussler | TBV | s.t. |
| 5. | P. Gilbert | LTS | s.t. |
| 6. | A. Aranburu | APT | s.t. |
| 7. | F. Sénéchal | DQT | s.t. |
| 8. | M. Trentin | UAD | s.t. |
| 9. | K. Geniets | GFC | s.t. |
| 10. | N. Politt | BOH | s.t. |
| 11. | I. García Cortina | MOV | s.t. |
| 12. | A. Capiot | ARK | s.t. |
| 13. | C. Laporte | COF | s.t. |
| 14. | S. Dillier | AFC | s.t. |
| 15. | A. Turgis | TDE | s.t. |
| 16. | B. Coquard | BBK | s.t. |
| 17. | C. Beullens | SVB | s.t. |
| 18. | T. Van Asbroeck | ISN | s.t. |
| 19. | O. Naesen | ACT | s.t. |
| 20. | D. De Bondt | AFC | s.t. |

## TRIVIA
» Davide Ballerini is only the fifth Italian to win this race – and the first since 1995.

FEBRUARY   .PRO MEN'S RACE

# FAUN-ARDÈCHE CLASSIC
27 February 2021
Guilherand-Granges–Guilherand-Granges
171.3km

## WEATHER

TEMPERATURE
6°C

WIND
NW 20km/h

## RESULTS

| POS | NAME | TEAM | TIME |
|---|---|---|---|
| 1. | D. Gaudu | GFC | 4:32:37 |
| 2. | C. Champoussin | ACT | s.t. |
| 3. | H. Carthy | EFN | 0:11 |
| 4. | M. F. Honoré | DQT | 0:28 |
| 5. | D. Godon | ACT | 0:40 |
| 6. | A. Vlasov | APT | s.t. |
| 7. | A. Paret-Peintre | ACT | 0:42 |
| 8. | T. Pinot | GFC | s.t. |
| 9. | J. Hivert | BBK | 0:46 |
| 10. | Q. Simmons | TFS | s.t. |
| 11. | W. Barguil | ARK | s.t. |
| 12. | R. Costa | UAD | s.t. |
| 13. | L. Huys | WVA | s.t. |
| 14. | B. Tulett | AFC | s.t. |
| 15. | S. Carr | EFN | s.t. |
| 16. | G. Martin | COF | s.t. |
| 17. | I. Izaguirre | APT | s.t. |
| 18. | J. Fuglsang | APT | s.t. |
| 19. | Je. Herrada | COF | 1:16 |
| 20. | L. Rota | IWG | s.t. |

FEBRUARY .PRO MEN'S RACE

# LA DRÔME CLASSIC

28 February 2021
Eurre–Eurre
179.2km

## WEATHER

TEMPERATURE | WIND
10°C | E 6km/h

## RESULTS

| POS | NAME | TEAM | TIME |
|---|---|---|---|
| 1. | A. Bagioli | DQT | 4:23:18 |
| 2. | D. Impey | ISN | 0:11 |
| 3. | M. F. Honoré | DQT | s.t. |
| 4. | J. Simon | TDE | s.t. |
| 5. | S. Clarke | TQA | s.t. |
| 6. | D. Godon | ACT | s.t. |
| 7. | B. Ghirmay | DKO | s.t. |
| 8. | C. Gautier | BBK | s.t. |
| 9. | W. Barguil | ARK | s.t. |
| 10. | P. Vakoč | AFC | s.t. |
| 11. | C. Venturini | ACT | s.t. |
| 12. | L. Rota | IWG | s.t. |
| 13. | A. Paret-Peintre | ACT | s.t. |
| 14. | S. Geschke | COF | s.t. |
| 15. | J. Bakelants | IWG | s.t. |
| 16. | Q. Simmons | TFS | s.t. |
| 17. | P. Serry | DQT | s.t. |
| 18. | G. Martin | COF | s.t. |
| 19. | A. Vlasov | APT | s.t. |
| 20. | D. Gaudu | GFC | s.t. |

FEBRUARY

FEBRUARY  .PRO MEN'S RACE

# KUURNE-BRUXELLES-KUURNE
28 February 2021
Kuurne–Kuurne
197km

## WEATHER

TEMPERATURE
8°C

WIND
NE 22km/h

## RESULTS

| POS | NAME | TEAM | TIME |
| --- | --- | --- | --- |
| 1. | M. Pedersen | TFS | 4:37:04 |
| 2. | A. Turgis | TDE | s.t. |
| 3. | T. Pidcock | IGD | s.t. |
| 4. | M. Trentin | UAD | s.t. |
| 5. | J. Biermans | ISN | s.t. |
| 6. | S. Colbrelli | TBV | s.t. |
| 7. | N. Politt | BOH | s.t. |
| 8. | G. Van Avermaet | ACT | s.t. |
| 9. | B. Van Lerberghe | DQT | s.t. |
| 10. | E. N. Resell | UXT | s.t. |
| 11. | I. Schelling | BOH | s.t. |
| 12. | M. van der Poel | AFC | s.t. |
| 13. | D. Claeys | TQA | s.t. |
| 14. | M. Hoelgaard | UXT | s.t. |
| 15. | A. G. Jansen | BEX | s.t. |
| 16. | O. Naesen | ACT | s.t. |
| 17. | J. Degenkolb | LTS | s.t. |
| 18. | J. I. Hvideberg | UXT | s.t. |
| 19. | A. Livyns | WVA | s.t. |
| 20. | S. Küng | GFC | s.t. |

# THE END IS WHERE WE START FROM

BY KIT NICHOLSON

It started at the end. It always does: Annemiek van Vleuten's 2016 Olympic dream ending on the side of the road, Greg LeMond's chest full of buckshot, Froome's Dauphiné recon crash, Marianne Vos's hiatus forced by overtraining. It looked very much like it was all over.

In the case of Mark Cavendish, the whole world had given up on him, confident that he was done, that he couldn't match the new generation of sprinters, that the best he could hope for was to share his wealth of experience with his successors and bow out with dignity.

'That's perhaps the last race of my career' were the words he uttered through tears after Gent–Wevelgem in October 2020. He'd endured three seasons riddled with injury, illness and clinical depression, instability in team set-ups and a global pandemic. He'd got into the breakaway of the Belgian Classic – a rare occurrence for the sprinter – but with no contract for the coming season, his future seemed very much in doubt. Then about two months later, his old team Deceuninck-QuickStep signed him up, offering the Manxman dignity and an opportunity to close the circle.

Cycling is a sport that asks a lot from its participants. Injuries and time away from the peloton are to be expected, and if you dig deep enough, there's a comeback story inside every jersey. Like underdog tales, the cult of the comeback is everywhere in sport, giving fans parables to live by. And after the 18 months Planet Earth has been through – bushfires, a pandemic and devastating floods – culture, sport and stories of renaissance, recovery and resurgence have become more important and more empowering than they've been in a long time.

2021 saw a number of unlikely as well as expected returns to form, and a few that were unfulfilled, but in a sport in which injury and time out of competition are inevitable, what really constitutes a comeback? By my reckoning, it starts with doubt (for example: will they ever walk again, never mind win races?). Then the individual has to return to the headlines, which might happen by winning or just by turning up, depending on the rider's circumstances, age, nature of their injury, length of their lay-off, etc. Every comeback is different.

At the start of 2021, Mark Cavendish barely featured in any predictions for the season, but what we've seen from the Manx Missile is the definitive comeback: a successful athlete on their way out and then written off altogether, before a resurgent performance when it seemed impossible. Any return to form seemed so unlikely that his re-signing with the 'winningest' team in the sport raised a fair few eyebrows. Surely Cavendish wouldn't get the chances he might once have expected, not with Sam Bennett on the same team? But that was perhaps the first glimmer of potential: no one expected anything of him any more, so it didn't matter. The pressure was off.

And then he started winning.

It wasn't immediate, but with a spring programme of smaller races, he was afforded the opportunity to be a bike racer in its purest form, with less support, bad weather and away from the prying eyes of the TV cameras. And in time that flourished into what the world – and Cav himself – thought might never happen again.

His first win – stage 2 at the Tour of Turkey – was a box ticked, a vindication, a finger wagged at the doubters. The three-year drought was over, but it still wasn't the Mark Cavendish of old, or rather the race wasn't. While that stage win – and then stages 3, and 4, and then 8 – at the Tour of Turkey saw him exit the purgatory he'd found himself in, there was a sense that he'd have to beat one of the world's top sprinters to 'complete the comeback'.

Hindsight is a wonderful thing. If winning breeds winning – which it certainly seems to do, especially at Deceuninck-QuickStep – then we should have known it was only a matter of time before Cavendish would cash in those Turkish victories for a much bigger one.

This is where luck comes in. Luck that brought with it the element of surprise. Sam Bennett's knee injury left an opening in the Baloise Belgium Tour line-up, a race that would be attended by a handful of the sprinters headed for the Tour de France. Cavendish was drafted in, carrying a little more expectation after the Tour of Turkey but still feeling light on pressure.

He'd conducted himself brilliantly as a teammate to race leader Remco Evenepoel until stage 5, which ended with a drag strip sprint on a wide road into Beringen. Caleb Ewan's Lotto Soudal team and Cavendish's Deceuninck-QuickStep led the race into the final kilometre of the local lap, the Manxman glued to the wheel of Michael Mørkøv. The wide and flat run-in invited the bunch to spread across the road, and as the sprint teams amassed on the front of the race, the Dane guided his sprinter through the mêlée. Tim Merlier (Alpecin-Fenix) started his sprint on the right side of the road as Cavendish was launched on the other and a good old-fashioned drag race ensued.

The foreshortening of the finishing straight and the impossibility of the result have rendered my memory of the sprint in slow motion. It's followed up with the image of Cavendish folding into teammate Remco Evenepoel's arms, looking as delighted as I was surprised to see him beat some of the world's best.

Yet the best was still to come. The Tour de France was due to start less than two weeks after his stage victory in Belgium, and initially there was no chance Cavendish would be on the start line of the Grand Tour. His contract was a limiting factor, and besides there was Sam Bennett: if the Irishman was fit, Cavendish would surely not make the trip to Brittany.

The news broke just days before the grand départ: Sam Bennett would be unable to defend his green jersey at the Tour de France and Mark Cavendish would go in his place. It was a big win in itself: a return to the race where he'd had so much success over the past decade, racking up 30 stage victories across eight appearances, the last of them in 2016. Anything more would be a bonus.

As if they'd known what was coming, the Tour de France organisers had put together a route that was something of a lap of honour for the Manx Missile. Stage 4 finished in Fougères, the site of Cavendish's stage 7 victory in 2015, a year after crashing out during the grand départ on home soil. Stage 6 finished in Châteauroux, home of his very first Tour de France victory 13 years ago.

The fairy tale began on stage 4. The lone Brent van Moer (Lotto Soudal) was caught deep inside the last kilometre, confirming a sprint that looked in doubt until 250 metres to go. As the gallop began, Cavendish had to edge round Van Moer on his way to the line in what now looks like a beautifully controlled and confident sprint that ended, inevitably, in victory.

Shock. Awe. Emotion. The stars had aligned and Cavendish – the man who had thought retirement was his only option just months earlier and who wasn't meant to be at the Tour – had achieved what so many had ruled out. And still, it was just the beginning.

Over a decade of experience came to the fore on stage 6 as Cavendish jumped from Mørkøv's wheel to Jasper Philipsen's, seeing the Alpecin-Fenix train take the winning line. With a second victory in three days – this time in the green jersey – the Cavendish who celebrated beyond the line seemed younger, more fired up, like the man of years past who would wag the proverbial finger at others, seeming almost to speak before thought had a chance to catch up.

He kept rolling back time as the race carried on, defying the weather and the terrain to beat the time cut on the first mountain stages, setting up himself and his (formerly Bennett's) perfectly configured sprint train in advance of the Tour's second week. A masterful sprint on stage 10 chalked up win number 33, stirring talk of the Merckx record into a frenzy, but Cavendish remained evasive. He was happy just to be back winning.

It seemed there was nothing he couldn't do now. There was a week and a half left of the Tour, and at least two chances to add to his list of wins. The fairy-tale ending only had to be enacted in reality.

Mark Cavendish inked his name alongside Eddy Merckx in Carcassonne on stage 13. At the end of an exhausting 219.9km, it looked like his biggest rival might be Michael Mørkøv, who kept sprinting after launching his teammate. But Cav stayed in front and the emotions that overcame him after the finish were an echo of ten days earlier and that first stage win. Shock and relief writ large.

That he was unable to break the record on stage 21 is a shame for the story, let alone his own perhaps concealed goals, but he'd already far exceeded the dreams of that rider at the end of Gent–Wevelgem. What's more, Cavendish knew after stage 13 that what he'd achieved would not only light up cycling, but it would transcend the sport: 'Don't let anybody say you can't do something.'

―

All comebacks are acts of defiance, but Annemiek van Vleuten's takes it a little further. She has been working away at hers for five years, with a few micro comebacks along the way.

Van Vleuten's crash when she was leading the Rio Olympic road race was the kind that almost overrides the result. The way she flew off her bike and crumpled into the kerb, where she stayed contorted and motionless, is a significantly more memorable scene than Anna van der Breggen's victory 10km later. It was a horrifying sight and one that would stay with her for years to come, in that it would be near-impossible to separate anything Van Vleuten might achieve from what we'd witnessed on that fast descent outside Rio de Janeiro.

In fact, her comeback was swift. She overcame severe concussion and three fractures in her spine to win her very first race back – the prologue of the Lotto Belgium Tour. Stage 3 victory into Geraardsbergen awarded Van Vleuten the overall title a few days later.

Van Vleuten has been one of the most prolific winners of the past decade, but she's no stranger to injury either – she came second in the 2020 World Championships road race a week after fracturing her wrist on stage 7 of the Giro Rosa (which she was leading at the time). But there was something else on her mind.

When Van Vleuten woke up in the Rio hospital, her first thought was of the gold medal that had been snatched from her on a corner she couldn't remember. Family, friends and fans were just happy she was alive and conscious, but all she felt was bitter disappointment. Ever since then, there was always something missing, even as she kept adding silverware to her trophy cabinet. Her Olympic dream has been something of a B story, and one that found its ending in 2021. Granted, it was maybe not the perfect final act she dreamed of nor planned for – and perhaps she'll be motivated to try again at Paris 2024 – but this time misfortune did not reach down and rob her of the chance.

There were plenty of factors that might have got in between Van Vleuten and the gold medal, not least the power struggle with her own teammates from the Netherlands. In the weeks before the Olympics, with her racing programme trimmed down to a minimum, she was pictured turbo training in a sauna to simulate the hot and humid conditions expected in Tokyo. And when it came to the race itself, Van Vleuten brushed herself off from an earlier crash before doing what she so often does and taking things into her own hands by attacking, not once but twice. First, into the gap between the disorganised peloton and the three-rider breakaway, chasing solo for 25km before being reeled back in by the peloton for some much-needed recovery. Her next attack came on the Fuji International Speedway, some of the weary early escapers dropping through the peloton after being caught.

Her intent was fierce, her position determined and when she crossed the line, her arms thrown wide, the joy was palpable. She apparently had no idea that Austria's Anna Kiesenhofer had already claimed the gold medal.

A thousand-yard stare. A minute before, Van Vleuten had been celebrating victory, redemption, a comeback years in the making. Would silver suffice? As it happened, she only had to endure a few days of disappointment before the time trial, where she was on another level entirely. She was 6 seconds up at the first time check, 28 at 15km and by the end of the 22.1km ITT, over a minute stood between Van Vleuten and the next fastest rider (yet to finish).

She would be Olympic champion, and she'd have known it was coming. With a handful of riders to follow her own ride, Van Vleuten watched them roll in, the last of them her teammate Anna van der Breggen. Even as the last riders' times ticked over into the red, Van Vleuten held the moment of elation at bay until she was absolutely sure. It wasn't until Van der Breggen crossed the line 1 minute 2 seconds down that the moment engulfed her. Van Vleuten finally had the gold medal.

The wait between her finish and knowing she was Olympic champion lasted about eight minutes but it must have felt like years. Then a short while later, the gold medal was hung around her neck, five years in the making. It's an extraordinarily determined comeback that, while less obvious than some, is perhaps even more romantic.

---

Crashes like Van Vleuten's descending disaster or Froome's high-speed collision with a wall strike fear throughout the peloton and all who revolve around it, from team staff to the farthest-flung fans. The incident on stage 1 of the 2020 Tour of Poland in which Dylan Groenewegen's sprint deviation sent Fabio Jakobsen plunging through the barriers is perhaps one of the worst crash scenes in recent memory. The fact that it occurred in the final moments of a sprint, filmed from all angles and replayed over and over again, etched it into the collective conscious.

Groenewegen was injured himself, riders and barriers everywhere, but what had happened to Jakobsen – mercifully hidden on the other side of the finish arch – was far worse. Florian Sénéchal quickly went to his friend's aid, apparently kneeling on the ground and cradling the young Dutchman's head as his injuries were attended to. Over the next couple of days the cycling world waited anxiously for news. It was all cautiously positive. The list of injuries was shocking, but at the same time it seemed a miracle he hadn't come off worse: brain contusion, fractured skull, broken nose, severe damage to upper and lower jaws, loss of ten teeth, cuts to his face and ear, heavily bruised buttock, shoulder contusion, broken thumb, lung contusion, vocal cord damage.

After being placed in an induced coma in the hospital in Poland, he soon returned home to begin his lengthy recovery and to undergo the first of many surgeries to his face. The fact that the only damage south of his shoulder was to his thumb meant that assumptions he might make a complete recovery and a return to racing were more than justified. He apparently doesn't remember the crash or the aftermath, but would the trauma of his injuries affect his sprint?

Jakobsen's was one of the most hotly anticipated comebacks of the 2021 season, and it began at the Tour of Turkey alongside his new teammate Mark Cavendish. His best stage finish was 39th, but he wasn't there to sprint, he was there to get his 'sea legs' back. He steadily and quietly worked away, turning up again and again, riding in the peloton once more, back where he belonged.

Then in July he headed to the Tour de Wallonie, a home race for his Deceuninck-QuickStep team, ready to get involved in the bunch gallop once more, and it all came together. It was two weeks before 5 August, the one-year anniversary of his crash. He won two stages in Belgium, but still – like Cavendish before him – there was a sense he had more to do.

The stage was set in Spain and only the second Grand Tour of Jakobsen's career, but one where he'd found success before. His biggest rival would be Jasper Philipsen of Alpecin-Fenix – and indeed, the young Belgian robbed Jakobsen of a fairy tale on stage 2. But just two days later,

Deceuninck-QuickStep perfectly navigated the frantic finale in Molina de Aragón and Jakobsen surged to a landmark victory, taking over the green jersey with it. One of the first to celebrate with him beyond the finish line was Florian Sénéchal, his teammate who had been with him from his very lowest point in Poland, right through his recovery and back to the very top.

By the end of the Vuelta a España, Jakobsen had won two more stages and the green jersey, with his team alongside him the whole way. One of the most memorable images of the whole race came at the end of stage 20 when all eight Deceuninck-QuickStep riders crossed the line shoulder to shoulder, bringing up the rear of the peloton after guiding their leader through 202.2km of turbulent Galician terrain. Twenty-four hours later, the Dutchman stood atop the podium before the Catedral de Santiago de Compostela, resplendent in green.

Jakobsen had been touted before his crash as one of the next great sprinters to make history in cycling. Now he wears his phenomenal comeback in the scars on his face, but he is back on track.

―――

One thing all comebacks – at least the ones we hear about – have in common is winning. The rider in question will either have been winning before or have won after, or both. The likes of Mark Cavendish, Annemiek van Vleuten and Chris Froome were at the top before their absence or incident, which makes their return to form a particularly steep climb. Not only that, but they're under the microscope the whole way. For proven winners, it's not enough just to return to competition; they have to return to the absolute top. Anything short of that and their very presence in the peloton is questioned.

Froome has seemed a shadow of his former self since 2019, still navigating the long road back from his devastating high-speed crash. Along with his new team, Israel Start-Up Nation, he had high hopes for some of the biggest races of the season – the major goal being the Tour de France. The litmus test would be the Critérium du Dauphiné, the same race at which his career so nearly came to an abrupt end two years earlier. But the writing was on the wall from the very start: every time the pace went up at the front, Froome dropped out of the back.

On the face of it, his performance was a sorry sight but, when we consider where he's come from, and the image of him laid out in intensive care, his return to racing is both hopeful and inspiring. Here's a man who just loves to race his bike, and he's seemed more relaxed and forthcoming in recent months as if to make that clear, never mind his poor results.

The talk of attempting a fifth Tour de France victory has not yet gone away, despite his advancing years and diminished form. But even if he never wins again – which looks more and more likely for the 36-year-old – his comeback is already sealed. There's a slender difference between 'he makes his racing comeback' and 'what a comeback!' In this instance, the results shouldn't matter.

Tom Dumoulin's return to the pro ranks was perhaps yet more surprising, even though a crash didn't play a significant role. Just 24 hours after he was listed as one of Team Jumbo-Visma's co-leaders for the 2021 Tour de France, Dumoulin announced that he would be taking a break from cycling. It was clear from his statement, recorded in a video from the team hotel, that it was something he'd been dwelling on for months: 'I have been doubting for quite some time – months, maybe even a year – how I should find my way as Tom Dumoulin the cyclist. The pressure, the expectations from different parties, I just want to do well for the team, for the sponsors, for my wife, for my family. I want to do well for everybody, but over the course of doing that I kind of forgot myself.'

He left the team training camp on 23 January to look after 'Tom Dumoulin the human'. His team had no indication of when he might return, and many suspected that we'd seen the last of Tom Dumoulin the cyclist.

The rangy time trial specialist has a healthy palmarès that peaked in 2017. With five Grand Tour stage wins under his belt, in both time trials and mountain stages, Dumoulin entered that season as a serious General Classification contender, despite having never won a race overall. He led the 2017 Giro d'Italia for nine days before relinquishing the pink jersey in the Dolomites. But still, he had the time trial on his side, and up against race leader Nairo Quintana, it seemed all he had to do was stay upright and in control to take back the lead. He raced the 29.3km like the Grand Tour leader he had become, pacing it not for the stage win but for the pink jersey.

As he was tossed in the air by his Sunweb teammates in front of the iconic backdrop of the Duomo di Milano, it looked like the beginning of something – someone to take on the dominant force of Team Sky, perhaps. But the 2017 Giro's stage 14 on 20 May was his last road stage win to date, and the BinckBank Tour later that year was his second and last overall victory. It seems that GC riders often have less to show for their efforts, and fewer trophies in the cabinet, so it's easy to forget that 2018 was perhaps even more consistent than the previous year. He finished a remarkable second overall at both the Giro and the Tour, but the ITT wins he took at each of those races were his only victories of 2018 and the last until 2021.

Stage 4 of the 2019 Giro d'Italia was the beginning of the end of Dumoulin's relationship with Team Sunweb, injury ruling him out of contention and then the race altogether. A few months later, he'd start the Critérium du Dauphiné only to withdraw before stage 7. He'd never race in Team Sunweb colours again.

It was 420 days before he'd race next. Surgery to remove a shard of gravel from his knee, a tricky contract negotiation that saw him transfer two years early, and then intestinal parasites and a global pandemic delayed his first appearance for Jumbo-Visma, which finally came about at the Tour de l'Ain. He had a solid season in 2020 – albeit on shaky ground thanks to the pandemic – that included seventh at the Dauphiné and Tour, but he later withdrew from the Vuelta citing fatigue. We now know that he was already having doubts by that point, and the announcement of his break came just three months later: 'The questions kept lingering all those months: if I want to continue as a pro cyclist, how am I going to continue? Do I want to win the Tour, and how? That's a question that has been bubbling up inside of me for several months really deep. I don't get to answer that question because life as a professional cyclist goes on. You're on an express train to the next training camp, to the next race, and the next goals… I am getting off this train now. I don't know if I will catch the next one or not.'

Fortunately, Dumoulin had the support he needed and was able to do what was best for him – 'It is really as if a backpack of 100kg has slipped off my shoulders' – and it was not the end. Time away from competition and the spotlight gave him the space to rediscover the joy of cycling. He made a VIP appearance at Amstel Gold Race near his home in the Netherlands, and a month later his return to the pro peloton was announced: he'd ride the Tour de Suisse to get some racing in the legs before taking on the National Championships with his eye on the Olympic Games. It wasn't a decision about his future just yet; that would come after Tokyo.

This storyline had a happy ending. Dumoulin won his fourth national time trial title in mid-June and a second Olympic silver medal at the end of July, beaten only by his teammate Primož Roglič. More importantly, he was visibly in a good place. He looked younger somehow, happy and brighter in himself – the cyclist *and* the human. And with his comeback begins a new chapter: he will continue cycling; he's back on the express train.

Froome and Dumoulin have a lot in common, and not just the 2019 Dauphiné's influence on their careers. They're both from the same era, they're out of the same mould, and they've both shown dignity in adversity. Regardless of results, both have exemplified a spiritual comeback, which is, to me, the most meaningful of the lot. The weight has fallen from their shoulders, lifted from their brows. They're doing what they have loved since they were small boys, having rediscovered their purpose after being forced to face the alternative: a life without.

———

2020 was a tough year for cycling, and on a greater scale there was an end to what we called 'normal', something that will likely take us years to come back from. But stories like these remind us of what's possible.

We like stories to have a clean beginning and end: what a beautiful mic-drop moment it would have been if Mark Cavendish had won that last stage on the Champs-Élysées, broken Merckx's record, unquestionably completed his comeback, and then retired on the spot.

The headlines were all about a 'fairy tale unfulfilled', but at the same time another rider's extraordinary story was unfolding, himself all too familiar with horrific injuries and laborious comebacks. That Cavendish was beaten by Wout van Aert at a race they both hold so dear – and so painful – was a fairy tale in itself. And knowing Cav as we do, the boy racer was never going to retire so soon. Maybe it was for our own sakes that we hoped he might; to rule out seeing another painful decline, a spiralling into illness and depression. But Cavendish had more to do and say, he had unfinished business in his career, just as life is itself unfinished business: it's always the beginning of something.

# MARCH

Finally, some normality. Races that the previous year had found themselves shunted into the late summer enjoyed their rightful places once more. Italy hosted its spring triumvirate of Classics and stage races. France saw Paris–Nice through to its planned conclusion, and then, as is traditional, the cycling world turned its attention to Belgium. The cobbled Classics got underway in benign weather conditions, restored to their normal berths in the calendar. But, with Covid cases starting to rise across mainland Europe, Italy and France went into various forms of lockdown, and Paris–Roubaix was postponed until October.

| DATE | RACE TITLE | LOCATION | UCI CODE | PAGE |
| --- | --- | --- | --- | --- |
| 2 March | Le Samyn | Belgium | 1.1 | 50 |
| 3 March | Trofeo Laigueglia | Italy | 1.Pro | 51 |
| 6 March | Strade Bianche | Italy | 1.UWT | 52 |
| 6 March | Strade Bianche | Italy | 1.WWT | 53 |
| 7 March | GP Industria & Artigianato | Italy | 1.Pro | 54 |
| 7 March | GP Jean-Pierre Monseré | Belgium | 1.1 | 55 |
| 7–14 March | Paris–Nice | France | 2.UWT | 56 |
| 10–16 March | Tirreno–Adriatico | Italy | 2.UWT | 64 |
| 17 March | Danilith Nokere Koerse | Belgium | 1.Pro | 71 |
| 19 March | Bredene Koksijde Classic | Belgium | 1.Pro | 72 |
| 20 March | Milan–Sanremo | Italy | 1.UWT | 74 |
| 21 March | Trofeo Alfredo Binda | Italy | 1.WWT | 76 |
| 21 March | Per Sempre Alfredo | Italy | 1.1 | 77 |
| 22–28 March | Volta Ciclista a Catalunya | Spain | 2.UWT | 78 |
| 23–27 March | Settimana Internazionale Coppi e Bartali | Italy | 2.1 | 85 |
| 24 March | Brugge–De Panne | Belgium | 1.UWT | 88 |
| 25 March | Brugge–De Panne | Belgium | 1.WWT | 89 |
| 26 March | E3 Classic | Belgium | 1.UWT | 90 |
| 28 March | Gent–Wevelgem | Belgium | 1.UWT | 91 |
| 28 March | Gent–Wevelgem | Belgium | 1.WWT | 92 |
| 28 March | Cholet – Pays de la Loire | France | 1.1 | 93 |
| 31 March | Dwars door Vlaanderen | Belgium | 1.UWT | 94 |

MARCH .1 MEN'S RACE

# LE SAMYN

2 March 2021
Quaregnon–Dour
205.4km

## WEATHER

TEMPERATURE
14°C

WIND
SE 11km/h

## RESULTS

| POS | NAME | TEAM | TIME |
|---|---|---|---|
| 1. | T. Merlier | AFC | 4:34:29 |
| 2. | R. Tiller | UXT | s.t. |
| 3. | A. Pasqualon | IWG | s.t. |
| 4. | S. Vanmarcke | ISN | s.t. |
| 5. | H. Hofstetter | ISN | s.t. |
| 6. | A. Capiot | ARK | s.t. |
| 7. | J. Degenkolb | LTS | s.t. |
| 8. | D. Claeys | TQA | s.t. |
| 9. | T. Dupont | WVA | s.t. |
| 10. | M. Menten | WVA | s.t. |
| 11. | J. Warlop | SVB | s.t. |
| 12. | D. Touzé | ACT | s.t. |
| 13. | L. Wiśniowski | TQA | s.t. |
| 14. | J. Drucker | COF | s.t. |
| 15. | F. Van den Bossche | SVB | s.t. |
| 16. | V. Campenaerts | TQA | s.t. |
| 17. | O. Kooij | TJV | s.t. |
| 18. | D. Hoole | SEG | s.t. |
| 19. | P. Allegaert | COF | s.t. |
| 20. | T. Willems | SVB | s.t. |

MARCH .PRO MEN'S RACE

# TROFEO LAIGUEGLIA

3 March 2021
Laigueglia–Laigueglia
202km

## WEATHER

TEMPERATURE | WIND
14°C | S 6km/h

## RESULTS

| POS | NAME | TEAM | TIME |
|---|---|---|---|
| 1. | B. Mollema | TFS | 4:57:05 |
| 2. | E. Bernal | IGD | 0:39 |
| 3. | M. Vansevenant | DQT | s.t. |
| 4. | C. Champoussin | ACT | s.t. |
| 5. | G. Ciccone | TFS | s.t. |
| 6. | M. Landa | TBV | s.t. |
| 7. | J. Knox | DQT | 0:57 |
| 8. | A. Vendrame | ACT | 1:01 |
| 9. | B. Ghirmay | DKO | s.t. |
| 10. | L. Rota | IWG | s.t. |
| 11. | Je. Herrada | COF | s.t. |
| 12. | V. Madouas | GFC | s.t. |
| 13. | G. Brambilla | TFS | s.t. |
| 14. | P. Bilbao | TBV | 1:03 |
| 15. | D. Devenyns | DQT | 1:28 |
| 16. | M. Mohorič | TBV | 1:32 |
| 17. | G. Martín | EUS | s.t. |
| 18. | C. Venturini | ACT | s.t. |
| 19. | N. Quintana | ARK | s.t. |
| 20. | M. Finetto | DKO | s.t. |

MARCH — WORLDTOUR MEN'S RACE

## STRADE BIANCHE
6 March 2021
Siena–Siena
184km

### WEATHER

TEMPERATURE: 12°C
WIND: NE 14km/h

### PROFILE

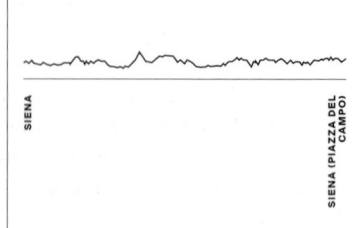

SIENA — SIENA (PIAZZA DEL CAMPO)

### BREAKAWAY

P. Walsleben (AFC), K. Ledanois (ARK), S. Bevilacqua (THR), S. Petilli (IWG), S. Zoccarato (BCF), T. Van der Sande (LTS), S. Rivi (EOK), F. Tagliani (ANS)

Cosmologists speculate what happens near the surface of a black hole. They should watch Mathieu van der Poel's astonishing acceleration on the Via Santa Caterina. With hindsight, the surprising thing is that there was ever any doubt over the final outcome. With 50km to go, a remarkable group emerged: reigning Strade Bianche champion Wout van Aert; his great rival – crowned cyclocross world champion for the fourth time on 30 January – Mathieu van der Poel; road world champion Julian Alaphilippe; the last two Tour de France champions Tadej Pogačar and Egan Bernal; 21-year-old Tom Pidcock, 19-year-old Quinn Simmons, and a glorious interloper in Qhubeka Assos's Austrian Michael Gogl. A puncture for Simmons took him out of the group, and a later crash with Gianni Vermeersch nearly took him out of the race. He finished 57th, but his ride proved his brilliance. An unexplained issue for Van Aert and Pidcock on the Colle Pinzuto left them trailing, after which the leaders made the chase back as hard as possible. On the 18 per cent gradients of Le Tolfe, Van der Poel darted away. Alaphilippe quickly made it onto his wheel, Bernal took a little longer, while Pogačar was the first to drop back. Van Aert, Pogačar, Pidcock and Gogl held them at 15 seconds but never closed. On the Via Santa Caterina, the Flying Dutchman went into warp drive to win Dante's race (*The Divine Comedy* mentions villages, battlefields and rivers on the stage route) on Michelangelo's birthday. How appropriate. (MR)

### RESULTS

| POS | NAME | TEAM | TIME |
|---|---|---|---|
| 1. | M. van der Poel | AFC | 4:40:29 |
| 2. | J. Alaphilippe | DQT | 0:05 |
| 3. | E. Bernal | IGD | 0:20 |
| 4. | W. van Aert | TJV | 0:51 |
| 5. | T. Pidcock | IGD | 0:54 |
| 6. | M. Gogl | TQA | s.t. |
| 7. | T. Pogačar | UAD | s.t. |
| 8. | S. Clarke | TQA | 2:25 |
| 9. | J. Fuglsang | APT | s.t. |
| 10. | P. Bilbao | TBV | 2:39 |
| 11. | S. Carr | EFN | 3:36 |
| 12. | R. Power | TQA | 3:45 |
| 13. | T. Wellens | LTS | 4:19 |
| 14. | G. Vermeersch | AFC | 4:21 |
| 15. | P. Vakoč | AFC | 4:26 |
| 16. | K. Geniets | GFC | 4:30 |
| 17. | C. Venturini | ACT | 6:26 |
| 18. | B. Mollema | TFS | s.t. |
| 19. | G. Van Avermaet | ACT | s.t. |
| 20. | R. Bardet | DSM | s.t. |

### TRIVIA

» This was only Van der Poel's second victory in Italy (after taking a stage at Tirreno–Adriatico last year).

MARCH   WORLDTOUR WOMEN'S RACE

# STRADE BIANCHE
6 March 2021
Siena–Siena
136km

The first Women's WorldTour race of the 2021 season took the peloton to Tuscany, where 31.6km of gravel roads on eight sectors provided the challenge in the 136km race. Chantal van den Broek-Blaak (Team SD Worx) and Elisa Longo Borghini (Trek-Segafredo) got away with a late attack, and Van den Broek-Blaak dropped the Italian champion on the final climb up the Via Santa Caterina to win. After several attacks and regroupings, a group of 15 riders reached the penultimate gravel sector together. Apart from Van den Broek-Blaak, Team SD Worx also had Anna van der Breggen, Demi Vollering and Ashleigh Moolman-Pasio in this group, and the team's strength in numbers would turn out to be decisive. Van den Broek-Blaak and Longo Borghini made a first move 15km from the finish but were quickly reeled in again. On the final gravel sector, Le Tolfe, Annemiek van Vleuten (Movistar Team) did a seated acceleration, and only Marianne Vos (Jumbo-Visma) was able to stay on her wheel. But with a determined chase group behind, this duo was caught inside the final 10km, starting a new flurry of attacks. Eventually, Van den Broek-Blaak broke free 6km from the line, and Longo Borghini bridged to her. As Van den Broek-Blaak had several teammates in the group behind, she forced Longo Borghini into doing the work, saving energy herself and then using the steep final kilometre to place her race-winning attack.

## WEATHER

**TEMPERATURE**
12°C

**WIND**
NE 14km/h

## PROFILE

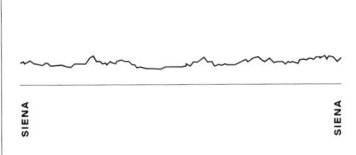

SIENA — SIENA

## BREAKAWAY
E. Pirrone (VAL)

## RESULTS

| POS | NAME | TEAM | TIME |
|---|---|---|---|
| 1. | C. van den Broek-Blaak | SDW | 3:54:40 |
| 2. | E. Longo Borghini | TFS | 0:07 |
| 3. | A. van der Breggen | SDW | 0:09 |
| 4. | A. van Vleuten | MOV | 0:11 |
| 5. | C. U. Ludwig | FDJ | s.t. |
| 6. | D. Vollering | SDW | s.t. |
| 7. | M. Vos | JVW | 0:23 |
| 8. | M. Cavalli | FDJ | 0:27 |
| 9. | K. Niewiadoma | CSR | 0:30 |
| 10. | E. van Dijk | TFS | 0:32 |
| 11. | A. Moolman | SDW | s.t. |
| 12. | A. Spratt | BEX | 0:46 |
| 13. | M. García | ALE | 1:52 |
| 14. | S. Paladin | LIV | 2:38 |
| 15. | S. Bertizzolo | LIV | s.t. |
| 16. | K. Faulkner | TIB | s.t. |
| 17. | L. Kopecky | LIV | 2:42 |
| 18. | L. Brennauer | WNT | 2:44 |
| 19. | E. Chabbey | CSR | s.t. |
| 20. | É. Muzic | FDJ | 2:47 |

## TRIVIA

» Chantal van den Broek-Blaak has now won a race every year since 2014, and since 2015 she's been at Boels Dolmans/SDWorx.

MARCH .PRO MEN'S RACE

## GP INDUSTRIA & ARTIGIANATO
7 March 2021
Larciano–Larciano
193.4km

## WEATHER

TEMPERATURE
13°C

WIND
SE 20km/h

## RESULTS

| POS | NAME | TEAM | TIME |
|---|---|---|---|
| 1. | M. Vansevenant | DQT | 4:26:26 |
| 2. | B. Mollema | TFS | s.t. |
| 3. | M. Landa | TBV | s.t. |
| 4. | N. Quintana | ARK | s.t. |
| 5. | I. Schelling | BOH | 0:03 |
| 6. | G. Brambilla | TFS | 0:04 |
| 7. | C. Rodriguez | IGD | 0:11 |
| 8. | A. Valverde | MOV | 0:16 |
| 9. | E. Dunbar | IGD | s.t. |
| 10. | V. Nibali | TFS | s.t. |
| 11. | M. Fabbro | BOH | s.t. |
| 12. | N. Tesfatsion | ANS | s.t. |
| 13. | S. Buitrago | TBV | s.t. |
| 14. | G. Aleotti | BOH | 1:08 |
| 15. | M. Finetto | DKO | s.t. |
| 16. | B. Ghirmay | DKO | s.t. |
| 17. | N. Schultz | BEX | s.t. |
| 18. | J. Romo | APT | s.t. |
| 19. | D. Savini | BCF | s.t. |
| 20. | J. Knox | DQT | s.t. |

MARCH .1 MEN'S RACE

# GP JEAN-PIERRE MONSERÉ

7 March 2021
Hooglede–Roeselare
202.1km

## WEATHER

| TEMPERATURE | WIND |
|---|---|
| 4°C | NE 14km/h |

## RESULTS

| POS | NAME | TEAM | TIME |
|---|---|---|---|
| 1. | T. Merlier | AFC | 4:34:44 |
| 2. | M. Cavendish | DQT | s.t. |
| 3. | T. Dupont | WVA | s.t. |
| 4. | P. Barbier | DKO | s.t. |
| 5. | R. Minali | IWG | s.t. |
| 6. | T. Boudat | ARK | s.t. |
| 7. | J. Warlop | SVB | s.t. |
| 8. | E. Vermeulen | XRL | s.t. |
| 9. | A. Marit | SVB | s.t. |
| 10. | R. Ärm | CGF | s.t. |
| 11. | J. W. van Schip | BCY | s.t. |
| 12. | J. Rasch | SEG | s.t. |
| 13. | T. Willems | SVB | s.t. |
| 14. | L. Mozzato | BBK | s.t. |
| 15. | S. Sajnok | COF | s.t. |
| 16. | T. Bayer | AFC | s.t. |
| 17. | O. Robinson | LCT | s.t. |
| 18. | W. Krul | SEG | s.t. |
| 19. | M. Van Staeyen | EVO | s.t. |
| 20. | A. Stockman | SVL | s.t. |

MARCH    WORLDTOUR MEN'S RACE

# PARIS-NICE
Stage 1
7 March 2021
St Cyr-L'École–St Cyr-L'École
165.8km

## WEATHER

TEMPERATURE: 7°C
WIND: NE 19km/h

## PROFILE

'The Race to the Sun' got under way on a very bright and fresh day in grand surroundings in front of the French army's former officer training school, with the magnificent palace of Versailles passed on the run-in to the finish. A sprint was always likely, which explained the general reluctance to accompany Total Direct Énergie's Fabien Doubey in the break. Even when Doubey was joined by Philippe Gilbert and Stefano Oldani, Anthony Perez and Chris Lawless late on, the peloton was chasing their heels. The sprinters' teams reeled them in on a high-speed and nervy approach to the finish, during which Richie Porte hit the deck and abandoned on his debut outing for Ineos Grenadiers. Groupama-FDJ set up Arnaud Démare for the uphill sprint to the line, but the Frenchman opened up too early and was unable to respond when Deceuninck-QuickStep's Sam Bennett breezed past him to win.

## BREAKAWAY

F. Doubey (TDE)

## STAGE RESULTS

| POS | NAME | TEAM | TIME |
|---|---|---|---|
| 1. | S. Bennett | DQT | 3:51:38 |
| 2. | A. Démare | GFC | s.t. |
| 3. | M. Pedersen | TFS | s.t. |
| 4. | J. Philipsen | AFC | s.t. |
| 5. | B. Coquard | BBK | s.t. |
| 6. | P. Ackermann | BOH | s.t. |
| 7. | P. Bauhaus | TBV | s.t. |
| 8. | C. Laporte | COF | s.t. |
| 9. | A. Greipel | ISN | s.t. |
| 10. | R. Barbier | ISN | s.t. |
| 11. | A. Turgis | TDE | s.t. |
| 12. | J. Degenkolb | LTS | s.t. |
| 13. | D. Touzé | ACT | s.t. |
| 14. | J. Meeus | BOH | s.t. |
| 15. | M. Trentin | UAD | s.t. |
| 16. | M. Jorgenson | MOV | s.t. |
| 17. | M. Matthews | BEX | s.t. |
| 18. | J. Jacobs | MOV | s.t. |
| 19. | B. McNulty | UAD | s.t. |
| 20. | G. Nizzolo | TQA | s.t. |

## GENERAL CLASSIFICATION

| POS | NAME | TEAM | TIME |
|---|---|---|---|
| 1. | S. Bennett | DQT | 3:51:28 |
| 2. | A. Démare | GFC | 0:04 |
| 3. | M. Matthews | BEX | 0:05 |

## KING OF THE MOUNTAINS

| POS | NAME | TEAM | PTS |
|---|---|---|---|
| 1. | F. Doubey | TDE | 9 |
| 2. | N. Politt | BOH | 3 |
| 3. | J. Bernard | TFS | 3 |

## POINTS

| POS | NAME | TEAM | PTS |
|---|---|---|---|
| 1. | S. Bennett | DQT | 15 |
| 2. | A. Démare | GFC | 12 |
| 3. | M. Pedersen | TFS | 9 |

## YOUNG RIDER

| POS | NAME | TEAM | TIME |
|---|---|---|---|
| 1. | J. Philipsen | AFC | 3:51:38 |
| 2. | D. Touzé | ACT | s.t. |
| 3. | J. Meeus | BOH | s.t. |

## TRIVIA

» Bennett is the first Irishman since Stephen Roche in 1990 to wear the overall leader's jersey at Paris-Nice.

## BONUSES

| TYPE | NAME | TEAM |
|---|---|---|
| KOM 1 | F. Doubey | TDE |
| KOM 2 | F. Doubey | TDE |
| KOM 3 | F. Doubey | TDE |
| KOM 4 | N. Politt | BOH |
| Sprint 1 | F. Doubey | TDE |
| Sprint 2 | M. Matthews | BEX |

MARCH  WORLDTOUR MEN'S RACE

# PARIS–NICE
Stage 2
8 March 2021
Oinville-sur-Montcient–Amilly
188km

In recent years, this stage across the flatlands to the south of Paris has witnessed carnage in the crosswinds. However, the sunny and benign conditions continued and made for rather more lacklustre fare. Sander Armée (Qhubeka Assos) and Dries De Bondt (Alpecin-Fenix) formed the break but were caught just beyond the halfway point as Trek-Segafredo tried to take advantage of what breeze there was to split the race. There were further brief flurries, which made the peloton very nervy, especially on smaller roads approaching the finish. The tension heightened on the twisting run through Amilly to the finishing straight, a crash 1km out stranding some sprinters. Set up perfectly by his teammates, Mads Pedersen was the first to launch his sprint but hit the slight headwind too soon, and Cees Bol powered by for the biggest win of his career, while bonus seconds put Michael Matthews in the yellow jersey.

## WEATHER

TEMPERATURE  WIND
6°C  NE 19km/h

## PROFILE

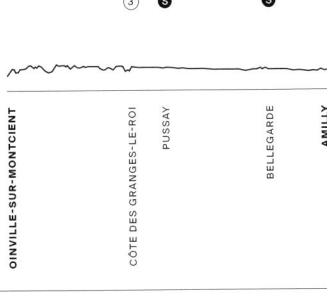

## BREAKAWAY
S. Armée (TQA), D. De Bondt (AFC)

## STAGE RESULTS

| POS | NAME | TEAM | TIME |
|---|---|---|---|
| 1. | C. Bol | DSM | 4:27:59 |
| 2. | M. Pedersen | TFS | s.t. |
| 3. | M. Matthews | BEX | s.t. |
| 4. | B. Coquard | BBK | s.t. |
| 5. | S. Bennett | DQT | s.t. |
| 6. | J. Degenkolb | LTS | s.t. |
| 7. | P. Ackermann | BOH | s.t. |
| 8. | P. Bauhaus | TBV | s.t. |
| 9. | J. Philipsen | AFC | s.t. |
| 10. | R. Barbier | ISN | s.t. |
| 11. | C. Laporte | COF | s.t. |
| 12. | S. Kragh Andersen | DSM | s.t. |
| 13. | S. Bissegger | EFN | s.t. |
| 14. | J. Stuyven | TFS | s.t. |
| 15. | M. Mørkøv | DQT | s.t. |
| 16. | N. Eekhoff | DSM | s.t. |
| 17. | A. Kristoff | UAD | s.t. |
| 18. | D. Touzé | ACT | s.t. |
| 19. | M. Jorgenson | MOV | s.t. |
| 20. | A. Turgis | TDE | s.t. |

## GENERAL CLASSIFICATION

| POS | NAME | TEAM | TIME |
|---|---|---|---|
| 1. ↑2 | M. Matthews | BEX | 8:19:23 |
| 2. ↑2 | M. Pedersen | TFS | 0:04 |
| 3. ↓2 | S. Bennett | DQT | s.t. |

## KING OF THE MOUNTAINS

| POS | NAME | TEAM | PTS |
|---|---|---|---|
| 1. — | F. Doubey | TDE | 10 |
| 2. — | N. Politt | BOH | 3 |
| 3. — | S. Armée | TQA | 3 |

## POINTS

| POS | NAME | TEAM | PTS |
|---|---|---|---|
| 1. — | S. Bennett | DQT | 21 |
| 2. ↑1 | M. Pedersen | TFS | 21 |
| 3. ↑3 | M. Matthews | BEX | 19 |

## YOUNG RIDER

| POS | NAME | TEAM | TIME |
|---|---|---|---|
| 1. ↑13 | F. Vermeersch | LTS | 8:19:35 |
| 2. ↓1 | J. Philipsen | AFC | 0:02 |
| 3. ↓1 | D. Touzé | ACT | s.t. |

## TRIVIA
» This was Team DSM's first win of the season.

## BONUSES

| TYPE | NAME | TEAM |
|---|---|---|
| KOM 1 | S. Armée | TQA |
| Sprint 1 | M. Matthews | BEX |
| Sprint 2 | A. Greipel | ISN |

MARCH  WORLDTOUR MEN'S RACE

# PARIS–NICE
Stage 3 (ITT)
9 March 2021
Gien–Gien
14.4km

## WEATHER

TEMPERATURE: 8°C
WIND: N 11km/h

## PROFILE

GIEN — GIEN

In the flat terrain of French climber Pierre Rolland's home town, the organisers did well to find two short but testing ramps to add some spice, the second rising up to the line alongside the Church of Joan of Arc overlooking the neat little town. Ineos Grenadiers' Rohan Dennis set the best mark early on, his time eventually bettered by teammate Dylan van Baarle, who was himself soon ousted by Søren Kragh Andersen. The Dane's short spell in the lead was quickly ended by Primož Roglič. Yet the Slovenian barely had time to park himself in the hot seat when Rémi Cavagna, who announced himself at the finish with a great roar of effort, improved Roglič's time by 6 seconds. As the Frenchman slumped on the barriers to recover, Swiss neo pro Stefan Bissegger chipped almost a second off Cavagna's time to scoop the stage and the yellow jersey. Ⓟ

## STAGE RESULTS

| POS | NAME | TEAM | TIME |
|---|---|---|---|
| 1. | S. Bissegger | EFN | 0:17:34 |
| 2. | R. Cavagna | DQT | s.t. |
| 3. | P. Roglič | TJV | 0:06 |
| 4. | B. McNulty | UAD | 0:09 |
| 5. | S. Kragh Andersen | DSM | 0:10 |
| 6. | R. Dennis | IGD | 0:13 |
| 7. | C. Laporte | COF | s.t. |
| 8. | D. van Baarle | IGD | 0:14 |
| 9. | Y. Lampaert | DQT | 0:16 |
| 10. | P. Bevin | ISN | s.t. |
| 11. | S. Kruijswijk | TJV | 0:20 |
| 12. | I. Izaguirre | APT | 0:21 |
| 13. | M. Schachmann | BOH | 0:22 |
| 14. | M. Pedersen | TFS | s.t. |
| 15. | M. Cattaneo | DQT | s.t. |
| 16. | A. Vlasov | APT | s.t. |
| 17. | M. Matthews | BEX | 0:23 |
| 18. | D. Teuns | TBV | 0:24 |
| 19. | M. Cort | EFN | 0:25 |
| 20. | J. van Emden | TJV | s.t. |

## GENERAL CLASSIFICATION

| POS | NAME | TEAM | TIME |
|---|---|---|---|
| 1. ↑27 | S. Bissegger | EFN | 8:37:11 |
| 2. ↑30 | R. Cavagna | DQT | s.t. |
| 3. ↑34 | P. Roglič | TJV | 0:06 |

## KING OF THE MOUNTAINS

| POS | NAME | TEAM | PTS |
|---|---|---|---|
| 1. — | F. Doubey | TDE | 10 |
| 2. — | N. Politt | BOH | 3 |
| 3. — | S. Armée | TQA | 3 |

## POINTS

| POS | NAME | TEAM | PTS |
|---|---|---|---|
| 1. — | S. Bennett | DQT | 21 |
| 2. — | M. Pedersen | TFS | 21 |
| 3. — | M. Matthews | BEX | 19 |

## YOUNG RIDER

| POS | NAME | TEAM | TIME |
|---|---|---|---|
| 1. ↑6 | S. Bissegger | EFN | 8:37:11 |
| 2. ↑4 | B. McNulty | UAD | 0:09 |
| 3. ↑6 | A. Vlasov | APT | 0:22 |

## TRIVIA

» This was Stefan Bissegger's first professional time trial victory.

MARCH  WORLDTOUR MEN'S RACE

# PARIS–NICE
Stage 4
10 March 2021
Chalon-sur-Saône–Chiroubles
187.6km

The first serious climbing test of the week brought seven climbs on the short but often steep hills of the Beaujolais wine country, the final one at Chiroubles the toughest of the lot. Julien Bernard proved the most durable of the day's six escapees, leading the race past his father Jean-François, who was spectating on the final hill, and staying clear until just 5km from home. Luis León Sánchez ended the Frenchman's hopes of victory as he bridged up and dropped him. Not far behind, the GC favourites were closing in too. Pierre Latour was the first to try his luck, but he was rapidly overhauled by Roglič in full flow through the vineyards. The Jumbo leader soon shot past Sánchez as well to claim maximum bonus seconds at the intermediate sprint, and then finished 12 seconds up on his rivals to take the overall lead. Ⓟ

## WEATHER

TEMPERATURE  WIND
9°C  SW 7km/h

## PROFILE

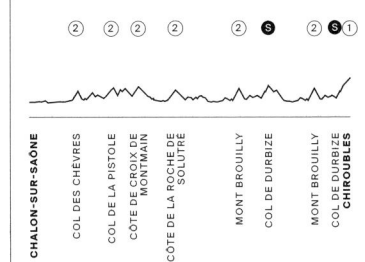

## BREAKAWAY
J. Bernard (TFS), A. Perez (COF), F. Doubey (TDE), J. J. Rojas (MOV), O. Naesen (ACT), O Riesebeek (AFC)

## STAGE RESULTS

| POS | NAME | TEAM | TIME |
|---|---|---|---|
| 1. | P. Roglič | TJV | 4:49:36 |
| 2. | M. Schachmann | BOH | 0:12 |
| 3. | G. Martin | COF | s.t. |
| 4. | T. Benoot | DSM | s.t. |
| 5. | A. Vlasov | APT | s.t. |
| 6. | L. Hamilton | BEX | s.t. |
| 7. | D. Gaudu | GFC | 0:16 |
| 8. | Q. Pacher | BBK | s.t. |
| 9. | P. Latour | TDE | s.t. |
| 10. | I. Izaguirre | APT | s.t. |
| 11. | A. Paret-Peintre | ACT | s.t. |
| 12. | J. Haig | TBV | s.t. |
| 13. | W. Barguil | ARK | s.t. |
| 14. | B. McNulty | UAD | 0:21 |
| 15. | S. Henao | TQA | s.t. |
| 16. | M. Jorgenson | MOV | 0:24 |
| 17. | H. Vanhoucke | LTS | s.t. |
| 18. | G. Mäder | TBV | s.t. |
| 19. | L. Meintjes | IWG | 0:26 |
| 20. | B. O'Connor | ACT | 0:28 |

## GENERAL CLASSIFICATION

| POS | NAME | TEAM | TIME |
|---|---|---|---|
| 1. ↑2 | P. Roglič | TJV | 13:26:40 |
| 2. ↑11 | M. Schachmann | BOH | 0:35 |
| 3. ↑1 | B. McNulty | UAD | 0:37 |

## KING OF THE MOUNTAINS

| POS | NAME | TEAM | PTS |
|---|---|---|---|
| 1. ↑5 | A. Perez | COF | 29 |
| 2. ↑2 | J. Bernard | TFS | 23 |
| 3. ↓2 | F. Doubey | TDE | 20 |

## POINTS

| POS | NAME | TEAM | PTS |
|---|---|---|---|
| 1. ↑8 | P. Roglič | TJV | 27 |
| 2. ↓1 | S. Bennett | DQT | 21 |
| 3. ↓1 | M. Pedersen | TFS | 21 |

## YOUNG RIDER

| POS | NAME | TEAM | TIME |
|---|---|---|---|
| 1. ↑1 | B. McNulty | UAD | 13:27:17 |
| 2. ↑1 | A. Vlasov | APT | 0:04 |
| 3. ↑1 | M. Jorgenson | MOV | 0:21 |

## BONUSES

| TYPE | NAME | TEAM |
|---|---|---|
| KOM 1 | A. Perez | COF |
| KOM 2 | A. Perez | COF |
| KOM 3 | A. Perez | COF |
| KOM 4 | A. Perez | COF |
| KOM 5 | A. Perez | COF |
| KOM 6 | J. Bernard | TFS |
| KOM 7 | P. Roglič | TJV |
| Sprint 1 | J. Bernard | TFS |
| Sprint 2 | P. Roglič | TJV |

## TRIVIA
» The last time Peter Sagan finished second on a stage of Paris–Nice it was also to a Spaniard: Xavier Tondo on stage 6 in 2010.

MARCH    WORLDTOUR MEN'S RACE

# PARIS–NICE
Stage 5
11 March 2021
Vienne–Bollène
200.2km

## WEATHER

TEMPERATURE: 15°C
WIND: S 7km/h

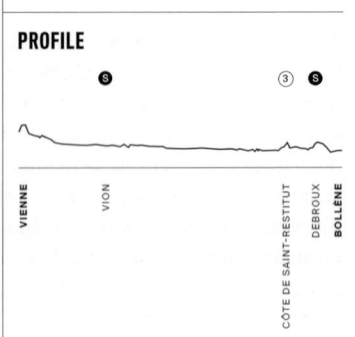

## PROFILE

VIENNE — VION — CÔTE DE SAINT-RESTITUT — DEBROUX — BOLLÈNE

A block headwind persuaded every rider to remain in the relative sanctuary of the peloton as the race moved southwards down the Rhône valley, the breeze so strong that there were whitecaps on the usually languid river. The riders barely covered 100km in the first three hours, and there was no action of note until 11 riders tried to force a split with 70km left. Riding into the teeth of the wind, they failed. Race leader Roglič had a scare, crashing after teammate Tony Martin went down in front of him. While Roglič escaped unscathed, Martin had to quit with a broken elbow. In the inevitable bunch sprint, Deceuninck-QuickStep guided Sam Bennett perfectly into the final kilometre, where the Irishman launched his sprint from lead-out man Michael Mørkøv's wheel and never looked likely to be caught, Nacer Bouhanni finishing a couple of bike lengths back in second. ℗

## STAGE RESULTS

| POS | NAME | TEAM | TIME |
|---|---|---|---|
| 1. | S. Bennett | DQT | 5:16:01 |
| 2. | N. Bouhanni | ARK | s.t. |
| 3. | P. Ackermann | BOH | s.t. |
| 4. | P. Bauhaus | TBV | s.t. |
| 5. | G. Nizzolo | TQA | s.t. |
| 6. | A. Kristoff | UAD | s.t. |
| 7. | B. Coquard | BBK | s.t. |
| 8. | C. Laporte | COF | s.t. |
| 9. | R. Barbier | ISN | s.t. |
| 10. | D. van Poppel | IWG | s.t. |
| 11. | J. Philipsen | AFC | s.t. |
| 12. | M. Pedersen | TFS | s.t. |
| 13. | M. Cort | EFN | s.t. |
| 14. | R. Oliveira | UAD | s.t. |
| 15. | D. Touzé | ACT | s.t. |
| 16. | M. Mørkøv | DQT | s.t. |
| 17. | J. Degenkolb | LTS | s.t. |
| 18. | K. Neilands | ISN | s.t. |
| 19. | M. Jorgenson | MOV | s.t. |
| 20. | R. Zabel | ISN | s.t. |

## TRIVIA

» This was Nacer Bouhanni's highest finish in a WorldTour race since his Vuelta stage win in 2018.

## GENERAL CLASSIFICATION

| POS | NAME | TEAM | TIME |
|---|---|---|---|
| 1. — | P. Roglič | TJV | 18:42:41 |
| 2. — | M. Schachmann | BOH | 0:31 |
| 3. — | B. McNulty | UAD | 0:37 |

## KING OF THE MOUNTAINS

| POS | NAME | TEAM | PTS |
|---|---|---|---|
| 1. — | A. Perez | COF | 29 |
| 2. — | J. Bernard | TFS | 23 |
| 3. — | F. Doubey | TDE | 20 |

## POINTS

| POS | NAME | TEAM | PTS |
|---|---|---|---|
| 1. ↑1 | S. Bennett | DQT | 36 |
| 2. ↓1 | P. Roglič | TJV | 27 |
| 3. — | M. Pedersen | TFS | 21 |

## YOUNG RIDER

| POS | NAME | TEAM | TIME |
|---|---|---|---|
| 1. — | B. McNulty | UAD | 18:43:18 |
| 2. — | A. Vlasov | APT | 0:04 |
| 3. — | M. Jorgenson | MOV | 0:21 |

## BONUSES

| TYPE | NAME | TEAM |
|---|---|---|
| KOM 1 | M. Schachmann | BOH |
| Sprint 1 | J. Sütterlin | DSM |
| Sprint 2 | I. Izaguirre | APT |

MARCH   WORLDTOUR MEN'S RACE

# PARIS–NICE
Stage 6
12 March 2021
Brignoles–Biot
202.4km

At the start, news began to filter through that Covid would result in significant changes to the race's final two stages. Thankfully, rather than leading to Paris–Nice ending prematurely (as in 2020), the organisers confirmed that the two final stages would be rerouted. On a stage that bumped all the way to Biot, close to Antibes, the riders raced as if this stage were the last. The pace was frenetic from the off, 50km passing before the break formed. It contained Kenny Elissonde, who became leader on the road and, ultimately alone, fended off the peloton until a dozen kilometres from home. Jonas Rutsch then made a brave solo bid, but the race came back together in the final kilometre. On the rise to the line, Guillaume Martin tried his luck from 400 metres out, only to see the imperious Roglič stomp past him for his second win. Ⓟ

## WEATHER

TEMPERATURE    WIND
16°C           W 26km/h

## PROFILE

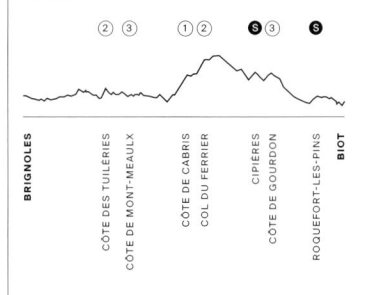

BRIGNOLES / CÔTE DES TUILERIES / CÔTE DE MONT-MEAULX / CÔTE DE CABRIS / COL DU FERRIER / CIPIÈRES / CÔTE DE GOURDON / ROQUEFORT-LES-PINS / BIOT

## BREAKAWAY

A. Perez (COF), K Elissonde (TFS), J. El Fares (EFN), A. Lutsenko (APT), J. Hivert (BBK), V. Campenaerts (TQA)

## STAGE RESULTS

| POS | NAME | TEAM | TIME |
|---|---|---|---|
| 1. | P. Roglič | TJV | 4:40:22 |
| 2. | C. Laporte | COF | s.t. |
| 3. | M. Matthews | BEX | s.t. |
| 4. | D. Teuns | TBV | s.t. |
| 5. | A. Paret-Peintre | ACT | s.t. |
| 6. | L. Hamilton | BEX | s.t. |
| 7. | B. Coquard | BBK | s.t. |
| 8. | Q. Pacher | BBK | s.t. |
| 9. | S. Henao | TQA | s.t. |
| 10. | K. Neilands | ISN | s.t. |
| 11. | I. Izagiurre | APT | s.t. |
| 12. | D. Godon | ACT | s.t. |
| 13. | P. Latour | TDE | s.t. |
| 14. | S. Geschke | COF | s.t. |
| 15. | D. van Baarle | IGD | s.t. |
| 16. | B. O'Connor | ACT | s.t. |
| 17. | G. Martin | COF | s.t. |
| 18. | T. Benoot | DSM | s.t. |
| 19. | M. Schachmann | BOH | s.t. |
| 20. | J. Philipsen | AFC | s.t. |

## GENERAL CLASSIFICATION

| POS | | NAME | TEAM | TIME |
|---|---|---|---|---|
| 1. | – | P. Roglič | TJV | 23:22:53 |
| 2. | – | M. Schachmann | BOH | 0:41 |
| 3. | ↑1 | I. Izaguirre | APT | 0:50 |

## KING OF THE MOUNTAINS

| POS | | NAME | TEAM | PTS |
|---|---|---|---|---|
| 1. | – | A. Perez | COF | 52 |
| 2. | – | J. Bernard | TFS | 23 |
| 3. | – | F. Doubey | TDE | 20 |

## POINTS

| POS | | NAME | TEAM | PTS |
|---|---|---|---|---|
| 1. | ↑1 | P. Roglič | TJV | 42 |
| 2. | ↓1 | S. Bennett | DQT | 36 |
| 3. | ↑1 | M. Matthews | BEX | 28 |

## YOUNG RIDER

| POS | | NAME | TEAM | TIME |
|---|---|---|---|---|
| 1. | ↑1 | A. Vlasov | APT | 23:23:44 |
| 2. | ↑1 | M. Jorgenson | MOV | 0:17 |
| 3. | ↑1 | L. Hamilton | BEX | 0:25 |

## TRIVIA

» Since his two stage victories in the 2016 edition, Michael Matthews has made the top ten in Paris–Nice stages 14 times without winning another stage.

## BONUSES

| TYPE | NAME | TEAM |
|---|---|---|
| KOM 1 | A. Perez | COF |
| KOM 2 | A. Perez | COF |
| KOM 3 | A. Perez | COF |
| KOM 4 | A. Perez | COF |
| KOM 5 | K. Elissonde | TFS |
| Sprint 1 | A. Lutsenko | APT |
| Sprint 2 | K. Elissonde | TFS |

MARCH    WORLDTOUR MEN'S RACE

# PARIS–NICE
Stage 7
13 March 2021
Le Broc–Valdeblore La Colmiane
119.2km

Although shortened by almost 50km due to the red 'no entry' Covid-19 zone imposed on the Nice area, stage 7 retained its summit finish on the race's highest climb, La Colmiane. The dash towards it was frantic, 13 riders joining the break; the peloton was never much more than a couple of minutes behind. The front 13 began to split on the final ascent, where Gino Mäder emerged as the strongest. The yellow group behind closed in on him in surges, an attack by one rider triggering the rest to up their pace, the catch producing a short lull before the next effort. This enabled young Mäder to get within range of the biggest win of his career. Yet two final surges by Roglič in the final 1.5km carried the race leader clear of his rivals and, with little more than 50 metres remaining, past the despairing Mäder as well. Ⓟ

## WEATHER

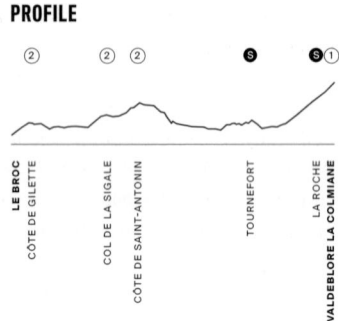

TEMPERATURE 14°C    WIND SW 11km/h

## PROFILE

## BREAKAWAY
S. Bennett (DQT), N. Powless (EFN), A. Amador (IGD), L. De Plus (IGD), A. Lutsenko (APT), A. Perez (COF), J. Bernard (TFS), K. Elissonde (TFS), T. De Gendt (LTS), D. De la Cruz (UAD), M. Cattaneo (DQT), D. Teuns (TBV), G. Mader (TBV)

## STAGE RESULTS

| POS | NAME | TEAM | TIME |
|---|---|---|---|
| 1. | P. Roglič | TJV | 3:09:18 |
| 2. | G. Mäder | TBV | 0:02 |
| 3. | M. Schachmann | BOH | 0:05 |
| 4. | L. Hamilton | BEX | 0:08 |
| 5. | A. Vlasov | APT | 0:10 |
| 6. | T. Benoot | DSM | s.t. |
| 7. | G. Martin | COF | 0:15 |
| 8. | I. Izaguirre | APT | s.t. |
| 9. | H. Vanhoucke | LTS | 0:22 |
| 10. | J. Hindley | DSM | 0:27 |
| 11. | S. Kruijswijk | TJV | s.t. |
| 12. | J. Haig | TBV | 0:35 |
| 13. | D. van Baarle | IGD | 0:38 |
| 14. | B. O'Connor | ACT | 0:40 |
| 15. | W. Barguil | ARK | 0:53 |
| 16. | A. Paret-Peintre | ACT | s.t. |
| 17. | L. Meintjes | IWG | 0:59 |
| 18. | M. Jorgenson | MOV | 1:03 |
| 19. | S. Henao | TQA | 1:14 |
| 20. | N. Powless | EFN | 1:27 |

## GENERAL CLASSIFICATION

| POS | NAME | TEAM | TIME |
|---|---|---|---|
| 1. — | P. Roglič | TJV | 26:32:01 |
| 2. — | M. Schachmann | BOH | 0:52 |
| 3. ↑1 | A. Vlasov | APT | 1:11 |

## KING OF THE MOUNTAINS

| POS | NAME | TEAM | PTS |
|---|---|---|---|
| 1. — | A. Perez | COF | 67 |
| 2. — | J. Bernard | TFS | 26 |
| 3. ↑2 | P. Roglič | TJV | 20 |

## POINTS

| POS | NAME | TEAM | PTS |
|---|---|---|---|
| 1. — | P. Roglič | TJV | 57 |
| 2. — | S. Bennett | DQT | 39 |
| 3. — | M. Matthews | BEX | 28 |

## YOUNG RIDER

| POS | NAME | TEAM | TIME |
|---|---|---|---|
| 1. — | A. Vlasov | APT | 26:33:12 |
| 2. ↑1 | L. Hamilton | BEX | 0:23 |
| 3. ↓1 | M. Jorgenson | MOV | 1:10 |

## TRIVIA
» This was Roglič's 50th career victory.

## BONUSES

| TYPE | NAME | TEAM |
|---|---|---|
| KOM 1 | A. Perez | COF |
| KOM 2 | A. Perez | COF |
| KOM 3 | A. Perez | COF |
| KOM 4 | P. Roglič | TJV |
| Sprint 1 | S. Bennett | DQT |
| Sprint 2 | G. Mader | TBV |

MARCH    WORLDTOUR MEN'S RACE

# PARIS–NICE
Stage 8
14 March 2021
Le Plan-du-Var–Levens
92.7km

Roglič's bid to claim a first Paris–Nice title was thwarted at the very last. His problems began when he crashed early on in this revamped final stage, his fall leaving him with a good deal of road rash. Approaching the final ascent of the Côte de Duranus, Roglič hit the deck again. As he tried to chase back up to the rear of the peloton, Bora and Astana pushed the pace up at the front. Although Roglič's teammates dropped back to assist him, their resources were quickly spent and he found himself in a pursuit up the twisting gorge to Levens that he was always going to lose. At the finish, Magnus Cort gave EF-Nippo their second stage win, with Bora's defending Paris–Nice champion Max Schachmann finishing just a few places behind the Dane. When Roglič rolled in more than 2 minutes down, the title was Schachmann's again. ⓅⒸ

## WEATHER

TEMPERATURE  WIND
18°C          NW 35km/h

## PROFILE

## BREAKAWAY
J. Rutsch (EFN), T. Declerq (DQT), S. E. Bystrøm (UAD), E. Theuns (TFS), W. Barguil (ARK), L. De Plus (IGD)

## STAGE RESULTS

| POS | NAME | TEAM | TIME |
|---|---|---|---|
| 1. | M. Cort | EFN | 2:16:58 |
| 2. | C. Laporte | COF | s.t. |
| 3. | P. Latour | TDE | s.t. |
| 4. | D. Teuns | TBV | s.t. |
| 5. | W. Barguil | ARK | s.t. |
| 6. | D. van Baarle | IGD | s.t. |
| 7. | I. Izaguirre | APT | s.t. |
| 8. | M. Jorgenson | MOV | s.t. |
| 9. | Y. Lampaert | DQT | s.t. |
| 10. | M. Schachmann | BOH | s.t. |
| 11. | T. Benoot | DSM | s.t. |
| 12. | A. Vlasov | APT | s.t. |
| 13. | A. Paret-Peintre | ACT | s.t. |
| 14. | L. Hamilton | BEX | s.t. |
| 15. | J. Haig | TBV | s.t. |
| 16. | Q. Pacher | BBK | s.t. |
| 17. | H. Vanhoucke | LTS | s.t. |
| 18. | G. Mäder | TBV | s.t. |
| 19. | G. Martin | COF | s.t. |
| 20. | L. L. Sanchez | APT | s.t. |

## GENERAL CLASSIFICATION

| POS | NAME | TEAM | TIME |
|---|---|---|---|
| 1. ↑1 | M. Schachmann | BOH | 28:49:51 |
| 2. ↑1 | A. Vlasov | APT | 0:19 |
| 3. ↑1 | I. Izaguirre | APT | 0:23 |

## KING OF THE MOUNTAINS

| POS | NAME | TEAM | PTS |
|---|---|---|---|
| 1. — | A. Perez | COF | 67 |
| 2. — | J. Bernard | TFS | 26 |
| 3. — | P. Roglič | TJV | 20 |

## POINTS

| POS | NAME | TEAM | PTS |
|---|---|---|---|
| 1. — | P. Roglič | TJV | 57 |
| 2. — | S. Bennett | DQT | 39 |
| 3. ↑2 | C. Laporte | COF | 34 |

## YOUNG RIDER

| POS | NAME | TEAM | TIME |
|---|---|---|---|
| 1. — | A. Vlasov | APT | 28:50:10 |
| 2. — | L. Hamilton | BEX | 0:22 |
| 3. — | M. Jorgenson | MOV | 1:10 |

## TRIVIA
» This was Schachmann's first win since taking the overall at Paris–Nice in 2020, exactly a year ago to the day.

## BONUSES

| TYPE | NAME | TEAM |
|---|---|---|
| KOM 1 | D. Van Baarle | IGD |
| KOM 2 | W. Barguil | ARK |
| KOM 3 | S. Geschke | COF |
| Sprint 1 | A. Paret-Peintre | ACT |
| Sprint 2 | W. Barguil | ARK |

MARCH  WORLDTOUR MEN'S RACE

# TIRRENO–ADRIATICO
Stage 1
10 March 2021
Lido di Camaiore–Lido di Camaiore
156km

## WEATHER

TEMPERATURE  WIND
14°C  W 6km/h

## PROFILE

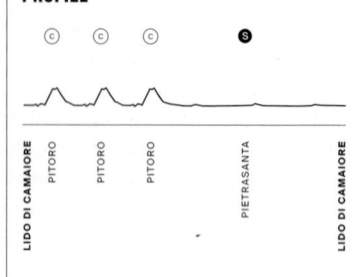

LIDO DI CAMAIORE — PITORO — PITORO — PITORO — PIETRASANTA — LIDO DI CAMAIORE

Mathieu van der Poel's aura was augmented by his Strade Bianche win. Meanwhile, on the sporza.be website, pre-stage, Merijn Zeeman, sports director of Jumbo-Visma, divulged his arch-rival Wout Van Aert's plan to ride this Tirreno–Adriatico for the overall win. To do so, he would have to outride Alaphilippe, Almeida, Bernal, Fuglsang, Nibali, Pogačar, Quintana, Geraint Thomas and Van der Poel. With the full Kluge–Van der Sande–De Buyst sprint train supporting Caleb Ewan, the wily Max Richeze working for Fernando Gaviria, and the Deceuninck-QuickStep wolf pack led today by Álvaro Hodeg, this presumably meant he would leave the bunch sprints to the specialists and worry about the three uphill finishes. Nothing could be further from the truth. Richeze gave Gaviria the perfect lead-out, but by the time Gaviria jumped, Van Aert had come off his wheel and won, with Ewan on his wheel but unable to come past. (MR)

## BREAKAWAY

G. Niv (ISN), M. Bais (ANS), V. Albanese (EOK), S. Rivi (EOK), S. Velasco (GAZ), J. Bakelants (IWG)

## STAGE RESULTS

| POS | NAME | TEAM | TIME |
|---|---|---|---|
| 1. | W. van Aert | TJV | 3:36:17 |
| 2. | C. Ewan | LTS | s.t. |
| 3. | F. Gaviria | UAD | s.t. |
| 4. | A. Vendrame | ACT | s.t. |
| 5. | L. Mezgec | BEX | s.t. |
| 6. | T. Merlier | AFC | s.t. |
| 7. | A. J. Hodeg | DQT | s.t. |
| 8. | D. Ballerini | DQT | s.t. |
| 9. | I. García Cortina | MOV | s.t. |
| 10. | H. Hofstetter | ISN | s.t. |
| 11. | P. Sagan | BOH | s.t. |
| 12. | M. Kanter | DSM | s.t. |
| 13. | L. Wiśniowski | TQA | s.t. |
| 14. | M. Malucelli | ANS | s.t. |
| 15. | F. Wright | TBV | s.t. |
| 16. | T. Boudat | ARK | s.t. |
| 17. | A. Petit | TDE | s.t. |
| 18. | N. Bonifazio | TDE | s.t. |
| 19. | M. Belletti | EOK | s.t. |
| 20. | E. Viviani | COF | s.t. |

## GENERAL CLASSIFICATION

| POS | NAME | TEAM | TIME |
|---|---|---|---|
| 1. | W. van Aert | TJV | 3:36:07 |
| 2. | C. Ewan | LTS | 0:04 |
| 3. | F. Gaviria | UAD | 0:06 |

## KING OF THE MOUNTAINS

| POS | NAME | TEAM | PTS |
|---|---|---|---|
| 1. | V. Albanese | EOK | 13 |
| 2. | J. Bakelants | IWG | 11 |
| 3. | S. Velasco | GAZ | 6 |

## POINTS

| POS | NAME | TEAM | PTS |
|---|---|---|---|
| 1. | W. van Aert | TJV | 12 |
| 2. | C. Ewan | LTS | 10 |
| 3. | F. Gaviria | UAD | 8 |

## YOUNG RIDER

| POS | NAME | TEAM | TIME |
|---|---|---|---|
| 1. | M. Bais | ANS | 3:36:15 |
| 2. | A. J. Hodeg | DQT | 0:02 |
| 3. | M. Kanter | DSM | s.t. |

## TRIVIA

» Since his stage win in 2017, Fernando Gaviria has finished in the top five at Tirreno–Adriatico six times without yet managing another win at the race.

## BONUSES

| TYPE | NAME | TEAM |
|---|---|---|
| KOM 1 | J. Bakelants | IWG |
| KOM 2 | V. Albanese | EOK |
| KOM 3 | V. Albanese | EOK |
| Sprint 1 | S. Velasco | GAZ |

MARCH  WORLDTOUR MEN'S RACE

# TIRRENO–ADRIATICO
Stage 2
11 March 2021
Camaiore–Chiusdino
202km

The early breakaway – including Velasco, fourth overall, just 7 seconds behind Van Aert – led by 5 minutes 46 but were caught on the Poggio alla Croce with 35km to go. Moments later, Bernal took off, joined by Asgreen and De Buyst. Scenting an opportunity, Almeida, Bilbao, Higuita, Konrad, Simmons, Sivakov, Soler, Vermeersch, Wellens and Simon Yates followed. Pogačar's teammate Jan Polanc closed the gap with 31.2km remaining, then Sivakov attacked again, followed by Almeida, Landa and Yates. With 2km left and the peloton almost on them, Yates dropped off the leaders, then the chasing group. Sivakov then Almeida attacked 300 metres later. With 1.1km left, Almeida went again. Behind him Geraint Thomas misread the signs and accelerated with 550 metres to go. Alaphilippe came off his wheel in the final 150 metres and opened several bike lengths as he passed his teammate Almeida. (MR)

## WEATHER

TEMPERATURE  13°C
WIND  SW 20km/h

## PROFILE

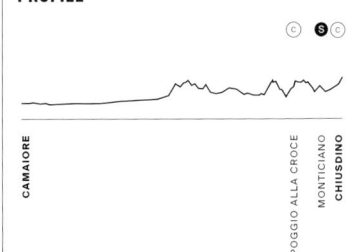

## BREAKAWAY
S. Pellaud (ANS), M. Burghard (BOH), V. Albanese (EOK), J. Archibald (EOK), S. Velasco (GAZ), P. Vanspeybroeck (IWG)

## STAGE RESULTS

| POS | NAME | TEAM | TIME |
|---|---|---|---|
| 1. | J. Alaphilippe | DQT | 5:01:32 |
| 2. | M. van der Poel | AFC | s.t. |
| 3. | W. van Aert | TJV | s.t. |
| 4. | T. Pogačar | UAD | s.t. |
| 5. | A. Aranburu | APT | s.t. |
| 6. | R. Stannard | BEX | s.t. |
| 7. | J. Almeida | DQT | s.t. |
| 8. | G. Van Avermaet | ACT | s.t. |
| 9. | T. Wellens | LTS | s.t. |
| 10. | G. Ciccone | TFS | s.t. |
| 11. | A. Vendrame | ACT | s.t. |
| 12. | E. Bernal | IGD | s.t. |
| 13. | G. Thomas | IGD | s.t. |
| 14. | S. Higuita | EFN | s.t. |
| 15. | G. Aleotti | BOH | s.t. |
| 16. | S. Clarke | TQA | s.t. |
| 17. | V. Nibali | TFS | s.t. |
| 18. | L. Vliegen | IWG | s.t. |
| 19. | M. Landa | TBV | s.t. |
| 20. | J. Fuglsang | APT | s.t. |

## GENERAL CLASSIFICATION

| POS | | NAME | TEAM | TIME |
|---|---|---|---|---|
| 1. | — | W. van Aert | TJV | 8:37:35 |
| 2. | ↑135 | J. Alaphilippe | DQT | 0:04 |
| 3. | ↑75 | M. van der Poel | AFC | 0:08 |

## KING OF THE MOUNTAINS

| POS | | NAME | TEAM | PTS |
|---|---|---|---|---|
| 1. | — | V. Albanese | EOK | 13 |
| 2. | — | J. Bakelants | IWG | 11 |
| 3. | — | S. Velasco | GAZ | 6 |

## POINTS

| POS | | NAME | TEAM | PTS |
|---|---|---|---|---|
| 1. | — | W. van Aert | TJV | 20 |
| 2. | — | J. Alaphilippe | DQT | 12 |
| 3. | — | M. van der Poel | AFC | 10 |

## YOUNG RIDER

| POS | | NAME | TEAM | TIME |
|---|---|---|---|---|
| 1. | ↑7 | P. Sivakov | IGD | 8:37:46 |
| 2. | ↑3 | R. Stannard | BEX | 0:03 |
| 3. | ↑3 | J. Almeida | DQT | s.t. |

## BONUSES

| TYPE | NAME | TEAM |
|---|---|---|
| KOM 1 | S. Yates | BEX |
| KOM 2 | J. Alaphilippe | DQT |
| Sprint 1 | P. Sivakov | IGD |

MARCH  WORLDTOUR MEN'S RACE

# TIRRENO–ADRIATICO
Stage 3
12 March 2021
Monticiano–Gualdo Tadino
219km

Davide Bais (the brother of Mattia, who was in the stage 1 breakaway) joined Boivin, Ludvigsson, Padun and Terpstra in the early attack, although the peloton was more concerned with the riders ahead than with the stragglers. With 114km still to ride, a kilometre before a 90-degree right-hander where there might just have been a breath of wind, Caleb Ewan was among the team cars. Pichon and Owsian, leading Quintana, increased the pace. As the domestiques began to reposition their leaders, Ewan's predicament came into focus and Van der Poel and Alaphilippe started pulling. Barely ten minutes after the first acceleration, Ewan climbed into his team car and started planning another way of preparing for Milan–Sanremo. With 2.2km to go, Alaphilippe was in second place on Štybar's wheel. He let a gap open 1km later and Štybar attacked. Van Aert reacted immediately, while a canny Van der Poel came off his wheel to win. ⓂⓇ

## WEATHER

TEMPERATURE  WIND
14°C  SE 7km/h

## PROFILE

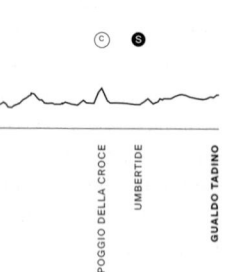

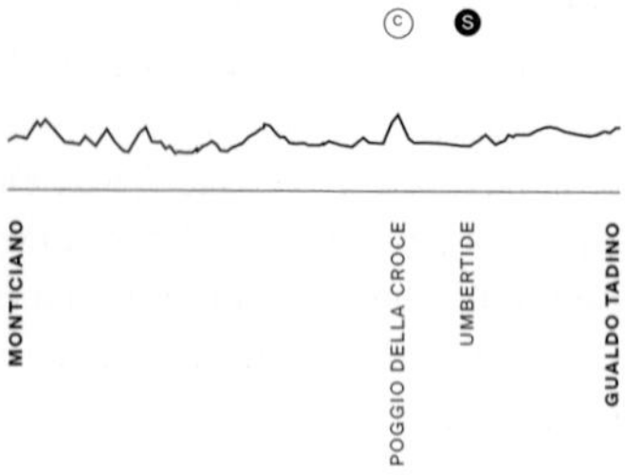

MONTICIANO — POGGIO DELLA CROCE — UMBERTIDE — GUALDO TADINO

## BREAKAWAY
M. Padun (TBV), D. Bais (EOK), T. Ludvigsson (GFC), G. Boivin (ISN), N. Terpstra (TDE)

## STAGE RESULTS

| POS | NAME | TEAM | TIME |
|---|---|---|---|
| 1. | M. van der Poel | AFC | 5:24:18 |
| 2. | W. van Aert | TJV | s.t. |
| 3. | D. Ballerini | DQT | s.t. |
| 4. | S. Higuita | EFN | s.t. |
| 5. | G. Van Avermaet | ACT | s.t. |
| 6. | J. de Buyst | LTS | s.t. |
| 7. | I. García Cortina | MOV | s.t. |
| 8. | T. Pogačar | UAD | s.t. |
| 9. | G. Serrano | MOV | s.t. |
| 10. | H. Hofstetter | ISN | s.t. |
| 11. | F. Felline | APT | s.t. |
| 12. | N. Bonifazio | TDE | s.t. |
| 13. | R. Stannard | BEX | s.t. |
| 14. | K. Geniets | GFC | s.t. |
| 15. | Z. Štybar | DQT | s.t. |
| 16. | A. Pasqualon | IWG | s.t. |
| 17. | N. Quintana | ARK | s.t. |
| 18. | J. Almeida | DQT | s.t. |
| 19. | P. Konrad | BOH | s.t. |
| 20. | M. Canola | GAZ | s.t. |

## GENERAL CLASSIFICATION

| POS | NAME | TEAM | TIME |
|---|---|---|---|
| 1. — | W. van Aert | TJV | 14:01:47 |
| 2. ↑1 | M. van der Poel | AFC | 0:04 |
| 3. ↓1 | J. Alaphilippe | DQT | 0:10 |

## KING OF THE MOUNTAINS

| POS | NAME | TEAM | PTS |
|---|---|---|---|
| 1. — | V. Albanese | EOK | 13 |
| 2. — | J. Bakelants | IWG | 11 |
| 3. — | S. Velasco | GAZ | 6 |

## POINTS

| POS | NAME | TEAM | PTS |
|---|---|---|---|
| 1. — | W. van Aert | TJV | 30 |
| 2. ↑1 | M. van der Poel | AFC | 22 |
| 3. ↓1 | J. Alaphilippe | DQT | 12 |

## YOUNG RIDER

| POS | NAME | TEAM | TIME |
|---|---|---|---|
| 1. ↑3 | T. Pogačar | UAD | 14:02:07 |
| 2. — | R. Stannard | BEX | s.t. |
| 3. — | J. Almeida | DQT | s.t. |

## BONUSES

| TYPE | NAME | TEAM |
|---|---|---|
| KOM 1 | D. Bais | EOK |
| Sprint 1 | D. Bais | EOK |

MARCH   WORLDTOUR MEN'S RACE

# TIRRENO–ADRIATICO
Stage 4
13 March 2021
Terni–Prati di Tivo
148km

The big mountain stage was a Pogačar masterclass in managing a small gap. With 7.5km left, Bernal attacked. Pogačar, pushing a much bigger gear, bridged across in an instant. The move brought back Mattia Bais, who had been in the breakaway, although it was Geraint Thomas who actually rode past him. Canola and Vinjebo had already been dropped, and Benjamin Thomas would be next, leaving only Würtz Schmidt out front. Pogačar rode everyone up to Thomas, who tried again. This time, a gap opened. Van Aert, asking and receiving no help, pulled the chasing group for the entire climb. With 5.6km remaining, Pogačar sped away, caught Thomas, led him past Würtz Schmidt and dropped him. Although the Slovenian's lead never exceeded 12 seconds, Bernal tried but failed to cross with 4.2km to go, then Yates did the same with 3.1km left. Pogačar led Yates by 6 seconds at the *flamme rouge* and at the finish line.

## WEATHER

**TEMPERATURE**  15°C
**WIND**  S 7km/h

## PROFILE

TERNI — PASSO CAPANNELLE — PIETRACAMELA — **PRATI DI TIVO**

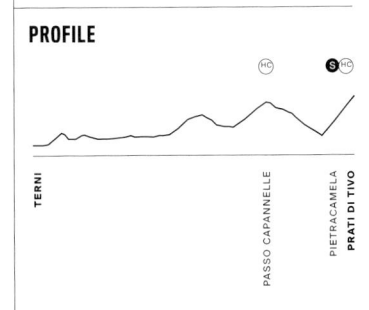

## BREAKAWAY
M. Bais (ANS), M. Würtz Schmidt (ISN), B. Thomas (GFC)

## STAGE RESULTS

| POS | NAME | TEAM | TIME |
|---|---|---|---|
| 1. | T. Pogačar | UAD | 3:51:24 |
| 2. | S. Yates | BEX | 0:06 |
| 3. | S. Higuita | EFN | 0:29 |
| 4. | M. Landa | TBV | s.t. |
| 5. | N. Quintana | ARK | 0:31 |
| 6. | J. Almeida | DQT | 0:35 |
| 7. | M. Fabbro | BOH | 0:42 |
| 8. | S. Carr | EFN | s.t. |
| 9. | W. van Aert | TJV | 0:45 |
| 10. | J. Fuglsang | APT | s.t. |
| 11. | E. Bernal | IGD | 0:58 |
| 12. | G. Thomas | IGD | s.t. |
| 13. | R. Bardet | DSM | 1:17 |
| 14. | G. Bouchard | ACT | 1:27 |
| 15. | D. Caruso | TBV | s.t. |
| 16. | V. Nibali | TFS | s.t. |
| 17. | J. Alaphilippe | DQT | 1:44 |
| 18. | T. Wellens | LTS | 2:05 |
| 19. | V. de la Parte | TDE | 2:06 |
| 20. | R. Molard | GFC | 3:03 |

## GENERAL CLASSIFICATION

| POS | NAME | TEAM | TIME |
|---|---|---|---|
| 1. ↑4 | T. Pogačar | UAD | 17:53:21 |
| 2. ↓1 | W. van Aert | TJV | 0:35 |
| 3. ↑5 | S. Higuita | EFN | s.t. |

## KING OF THE MOUNTAINS

| POS | NAME | TEAM | PTS |
|---|---|---|---|
| 1. ↑14 | T. Pogačar | UAD | 16 |
| 2. — | M. Würst Schmidt | ISN | 15 |
| 3. ↑2 | S. Yates | BEX | 15 |

## POINTS

| POS | NAME | TEAM | PTS |
|---|---|---|---|
| 1. — | W. van Aert | TJV | 32 |
| 2. ↑3 | T. Pogačar | UAD | 23 |
| 3. ↓1 | M. van der Poel | AFC | 22 |

## YOUNG RIDER

| POS | NAME | TEAM | TIME |
|---|---|---|---|
| 1. — | T. Pogačar | UAD | 17:53:21 |
| 2. ↑2 | S. Higuita | EFN | 0:35 |
| 3. — | J. Almeida | DQT | 0:45 |

## TRIVIA
» In the two stage races he's competed in so far this season, Pogačar has twice been on the top step of the podium with Yates second and Sergio Higuita third. Today it was Simon in second, while at the UAE Tour it was his twin, Adam.

## BONUSES

| TYPE | NAME | TEAM |
|---|---|---|
| KOM 1 | M. Würtz Schmidt | ISN |
| KOM 2 | T. Pogačar | UAD |
| Sprint 1 | M. Würtz Schmidt | ISN |

MARCH  WORLDTOUR MEN'S RACE

# TIRRENO–ADRIATICO
Stage 5
14 March 2021
Castellalto–Castelfidardo
205km

Continuous attacking pushed the average speed up to 57.4kmph for the first 30 minutes and 55kmph for the first hour. After 45km Ganna, Ballerini, Bilbao, Stannard and Rickaert stole away. The catch came with 56.5km left. Bernal darted away 400 metres later, joined by Higuita, Pogačar, Van Aert and Van der Poel. Van der Poel rode away alone 5km later and, with a 3 minutes 20 advantage 18km from the finish, victory seemed assured. Then Pogačar accelerated. For 3km, the gap remained unchanged. For the next 12.5km, Pogačar gained 11.5 seconds per kilometre. That left 48 seconds with 2.5km to go. He gained 20 seconds over the next 500 metres, and 12 seconds over the next kilometre, which left 16 seconds with 1km to go. With 500 metres remaining, the gap was still 13 seconds. Running on vapour, Van der Poel had been holding something back. It was enough to win the stage by 10 seconds.

## WEATHER

TEMPERATURE: 18°C
WIND: SW 22km/h

## PROFILE

## BREAKAWAY
F. Ganna (IGD), R. Stannard (BEX), J. Rickaert (AFC), P. Bilbao (TBV), D. Ballerini (DQT)

## STAGE RESULTS

| POS | NAME | TEAM | TIME |
|---|---|---|---|
| 1. | M. van der Poel | AFC | 4:48:17 |
| 2. | T. Pogačar | UAD | 0:10 |
| 3. | W. van Aert | TJV | 0:49 |
| 4. | F. Felline | APT | 1:26 |
| 5. | E. Bernal | IGD | 2:07 |
| 6. | D. Formolo | UAD | s.t. |
| 7. | T. Wellens | LTS | 2:18 |
| 8. | A. De Marchi | ISN | s.t. |
| 9. | M. Landa | TBV | 2:25 |
| 10. | M. Fabbro | BOH | 2:45 |
| 11. | M. Soler | MOV | 3:31 |
| 12. | P. Sivakov | IGD | 3:37 |
| 13. | R. Bardet | DSM | 3:39 |
| 14. | G. Van Avermaet | ACT | s.t. |
| 15. | S. Clarke | TQA | s.t. |
| 16. | H. Houle | APT | 3:51 |
| 17. | J. Almeida | DQT | 4:00 |
| 18. | G. Serrano | MOV | 4:17 |
| 19. | A. Aranburu | APT | s.t. |
| 20. | V. Nibali | TFS | 4:20 |

## GENERAL CLASSIFICATION

| POS | NAME | TEAM | TIME |
|---|---|---|---|
| 1. — | T. Pogačar | UAD | 22:41:41 |
| 2. — | W. van Aert | TJV | 1:15 |
| 3. ↑1 | M. Landa | TBV | 3:00 |

## KING OF THE MOUNTAINS

| POS | NAME | TEAM | PTS |
|---|---|---|---|
| 1. — | T. Pogačar | UAD | 24 |
| 2. ↑16 | M. van der Poel | AFC | 18 |
| 3. ↓1 | M. Würst Schmidt | ISN | 15 |

## POINTS

| POS | NAME | TEAM | PTS |
|---|---|---|---|
| 1. — | W. van Aert | TJV | 43 |
| 2. ↑1 | M. van der Poel | AFC | 39 |
| 3. ↓1 | T. Pogačar | UAD | 35 |

## YOUNG RIDER

| POS | NAME | TEAM | TIME |
|---|---|---|---|
| 1. — | T. Pogačar | UAD | 22:41:41 |
| 2. ↑3 | E. Bernal | IGD | 3:30 |
| 3. — | J. Almeida | DQT | 4:42 |

## BONUSES

| TYPE | NAME | TEAM |
|---|---|---|
| KOM 1 | P. Bilbao | TBV |
| KOM 2 | F. Ganna | IGD |
| KOM 3 | M. van der Poel | AFC |
| KOM 4 | M. van der Poel | AFC |
| KOM 5 | M. van der Poel | AFC |
| Sprint 1 | M. van der Poel | AFC |

MARCH    WORLDTOUR MEN'S RACE

# TIRRENO-ADRIATICO
Stage 6
15 March 2021
Castelraimondo–Lido di Fermo
169km

Mads Würtz Schmidt joined a doomed effort with Van Hooydonck and Mullen after 2km, before they got away after 23km. After 29km the gap was 4 minutes 7 seconds. With 20km to go and the gap still at 2 minutes 45, it was clear the winner would come from the breakaway. Oliveira (fourth, fifth, seventh and eighth in the world time trial championships), Würtz Schmidt (junior and under-23 world time trial champion in 2011 and 2015, respectively) and Van Moer (second in the 2018 under-23 world time trial championships) seemed to cancel each other out. On the little climb up to San Marco delle Paludi, Oliveira accelerated to 530 watts, distancing Liepiņš. Bakelants led them under the *flamme rouge*. Van Moer tore out of Würtz Schmidt's slipstream and came alongside, but weakened, leaving Würtz Schmidt to claim his first in-line stage as a pro, his first WorldTour win, and the fourth-fastest Tirreno–Adriatico road stage.

## WEATHER

**TEMPERATURE**  11°C
**WIND**  S 9km/h

## PROFILE

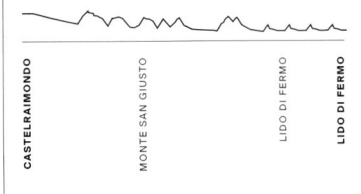

CASTELRAIMONDO — MONTE SAN GIUSTO — LIDO DI FERMO — LIDO DI FERMO

## BREAKAWAY

J. Bakelants (IWG), S. Velasco (GAZ), M. Würtz Schmidt (ISN), B. Van Moer (LTS), N. Oliveira (MOV), E. Liepiņš (TFS)

## STAGE RESULTS

| POS | NAME | TEAM | TIME |
|---|---|---|---|
| 1. | M. Würst Schmidt | ISN | 3:42:09 |
| 2. | B. Van Moer | LTS | s.t. |
| 3. | S. Velasco | GAZ | s.t. |
| 4. | J. Bakelants | IWG | s.t. |
| 5. | N. Oliveira | MOV | s.t. |
| 6. | E. Liepiņš | TFS | 0:25 |
| 7. | T. Merlier | AFC | 1:09 |
| 8. | D. Ballerini | DQT | s.t. |
| 9. | E. Viviani | COF | s.t. |
| 10. | M. Kanter | DSM | s.t. |
| 11. | H. Hofstetter | ISN | s.t. |
| 12. | A. Vendrame | ACT | s.t. |
| 13. | W. van Aert | TJV | s.t. |
| 14. | P. Sagan | BOH | s.t. |
| 15. | Q. Simmons | TFS | s.t. |
| 16. | I. Oliveira | UAD | s.t. |
| 17. | A. Pasqualon | IWG | s.t. |
| 18. | V. Albanese | EOK | s.t. |
| 19. | F. Wright | TBV | s.t. |
| 20. | L. Manzin | TDE | s.t. |

## GENERAL CLASSIFICATION

| POS | NAME | TEAM | TIME |
|---|---|---|---|
| 1. — | T. Pogačar | UAD | 26:24:59 |
| 2. — | W. van Aert | TJV | 1:15 |
| 3. — | M. Landa | TBV | 3:00 |

## KING OF THE MOUNTAINS

| POS | NAME | TEAM | PTS |
|---|---|---|---|
| 1. — | T. Pogačar | UAD | 24 |
| 2. ↑1 | M. Würst Schmidt | ISN | 20 |
| 3. ↓1 | M. van der Poel | AFC | 18 |

## POINTS

| POS | NAME | TEAM | PTS |
|---|---|---|---|
| 1. — | W. van Aert | TJV | 43 |
| 2. — | M. van der Poel | AFC | 39 |
| 3. — | T. Pogačar | UAD | 35 |

## YOUNG RIDER

| POS | NAME | TEAM | TIME |
|---|---|---|---|
| 1. — | T. Pogačar | UAD | 26:24:59 |
| 2. — | E. Bernal | IGD | 3:30 |
| 3. — | J. Almeida | DQT | 4:42 |

## TRIVIA

» Mads Würtz Schmidt is the only stage winner at this year's race to have never won a Monument.

## BONUSES

| TYPE | NAME | TEAM |
|---|---|---|
| KOM 1 | M. Würtz Schmidt | ISN |
| Sprint 1 | E. Liepiņš | TFS |

MARCH   WORLDTOUR MEN'S RACE

# TIRRENO–ADRIATICO
Stage 7 (ITT)
16 March 2021
San Benedetto del Tronto–San Benedetto del Tronto
10.1km

## WEATHER

TEMPERATURE
14°C

WIND
N 19km/h

European time trial champion Stefan Küng set the early best time of 11 minutes 12.45 seconds. Moments after he had finished, Filippo Ganna – the reigning time trial and the individual pursuit world champion, the last winner of the San Benedetto del Tronto time trial, and the course record holder – passed the intermediate timing point 4.67 seconds slower than Küng. He finished 4.99 seconds slower: it was the first off day Ganna had had in a time trial since San Juan 2020. Van Aert then powered through the intermediate timing point in 4 minutes 37.94, a second faster than even Küng. Van Aert eventually finished 6 seconds faster than Küng, 11 faster than Ganna, and 12 faster than Pogačar. The extraordinary Belgian had beaten Ewan in a bunch sprint and Ganna in a flat time trial, but he was no match for Pogačar, who took his second stage-race win of 2021.

## PROFILE

SAN BENEDETTO DEL TRONTO — SAN BENEDETTO DEL TRONTO

## STAGE RESULTS

| POS | NAME | TEAM | TIME |
|---|---|---|---|
| 1. | W. van Aert | TJV | 11:06 |
| 2. | S. Küng | GFC | 0:06 |
| 3. | F. Ganna | IGD | 0:11 |
| 4. | T. Pogačar | UAD | 0:12 |
| 5. | B. Thomas | GFC | 0:16 |
| 6. | A. Bettiol | EFN | 0:18 |
| 7. | J. Almeida | DQT | 0:24 |
| 8. | K. Asgreen | DQT | 0:26 |
| 9. | M. Hepburn | BEX | 0:27 |
| 10. | T. Ludvigsson | GFC | 0:28 |
| 11. | G. Thomas | IGD | s.t. |
| 12. | S. Langeveld | EFN | 0:30 |
| 13. | E. Affini | TJV | 0:32 |
| 14. | J. Tratnik | TBV | 0:33 |
| 15. | T. Pinot | GFC | 0:35 |
| 16. | D. Pozzovivo | TQA | 0:36 |
| 17. | N. Oliveira | MOV | s.t. |
| 18. | T. Foss | TJV | s.t. |
| 19. | M. Bodnar | BOH | 0:37 |
| 20. | I. Oliveira | UAD | s.t. |

## GENERAL CLASSIFICATION

| POS | NAME | TEAM | TIME |
|---|---|---|---|
| 1. — | T. Pogačar | UAD | 26:36:17 |
| 2. — | W. van Aert | TJV | 1:03 |
| 3. — | M. Landa | TBV | 3:57 |

## KING OF THE MOUNTAINS

| POS | NAME | TEAM | PTS |
|---|---|---|---|
| 1. — | T. Pogačar | UAD | 24 |
| 2. — | M. Würst Schmidt | ISN | 20 |
| 3. — | M. van der Poel | AFC | 18 |

## POINTS

| POS | NAME | TEAM | PTS |
|---|---|---|---|
| 1. — | W. van Aert | TJV | 55 |
| 2. ↑1 | T. Pogačar | UAD | 42 |
| 3. ↓1 | M. van der Poel | AFC | 39 |

## YOUNG RIDER

| POS | NAME | TEAM | TIME |
|---|---|---|---|
| 1. — | T. Pogačar | UAD | 26:36:17 |
| 2. — | E. Bernal | IGD | 4:13 |
| 3. — | J. Almeida | DQT | 4:54 |

## TRIVIA

» This is the first time trial Filippo Ganna has competed in without winning since the Vuelta a San Juan in January 2020.

MARCH .PRO MEN'S RACE

# DANILITH NOKERE KOERSE
17 March 2021
Deinze–Nokere
195km

## WEATHER

TEMPERATURE
7°C

WIND
N 25km/h

## RESULTS

| POS | NAME | TEAM | TIME |
|---|---|---|---|
| 1. | L. Robeet | WVA | 4:33:37 |
| 2. | D. Gaudin | TDE | 0:03 |
| 3. | L. Mozzato | BBK | 0:05 |
| 4. | J. Meeus | BOH | s.t. |
| 5. | T. Van Asbroeck | ISN | s.t. |
| 6. | J. Stewart | GFC | s.t. |
| 7. | M. Walscheid | TQA | s.t. |
| 8. | K. Halvorsen | UXT | s.t. |
| 9. | J. Narváez | IGD | s.t. |
| 10. | R. Barbier | ISN | s.t. |
| 11. | M. Bjerg | UAD | s.t. |
| 12. | P. Allegaert | COF | s.t. |
| 13. | E. Theuns | TFS | s.t. |
| 14. | P. Barbier | DKO | s.t. |
| 15. | W. Kreder | IWG | s.t. |
| 16. | E. M. Grosu | DKO | s.t. |
| 17. | O. Le Gac | GFC | s.t. |
| 18. | R. Oliveira | UAD | s.t. |
| 19. | M. Sarreau | ACT | s.t. |
| 20. | S. Vanmarcke | ISN | s.t. |

MARCH .PRO MEN'S RACE

# BREDENE KOKSIJDE CLASSIC
19 March 2021
Bredene–Koksijde
199.9km

## WEATHER

TEMPERATURE
6°C

WIND
NE 28km/h

## RESULTS

| POS | NAME | TEAM | TIME |
|---|---|---|---|
| 1. | T. Merlier | AFC | 4:13:43 |
| 2. | M. Pedersen | TFS | s.t. |
| 3. | F. Sénéchal | DQT | s.t. |
| 4. | T. Van Asbroeck | ISN | s.t. |
| 5. | E. M. Grosu | DKO | s.t. |
| 6. | S. Aniołkowski | WVA | s.t. |
| 7. | M. Walscheid | TQA | s.t. |
| 8. | B. Welten | ARK | s.t. |
| 9. | N. Politt | BOH | s.t. |
| 10. | C. Lemoine | BBK | s.t. |
| 11. | K. Halvorsen | UXT | s.t. |
| 12. | J. Stewart | GFC | s.t. |
| 13. | R. Oliveira | UAD | 0:02 |
| 14. | B. Declercq | ARK | s.t. |
| 15. | M. Bjerg | UAD | s.t. |
| 16. | H. Sweeny | LTS | s.t. |
| 17. | M. Gołaś | IGD | s.t. |
| 18. | J. Černý | DQT | 0:06 |
| 19. | A. Leknessund | DSM | s.t. |
| 20. | J. Rickaert | AFC | 0:10 |

# DOMINANT KIT COLOURS

Fashion trends will always come and go, and that's no different for the look of the professional peloton: one year everyone's wearing red, then blue, then black… the kaleidoscope continues to turn. Is it a case of a surplus of one colour at the imaginary factory where all the WorldTour jerseys are made? A secret cabal joining together to cut costs? Or do all of the teams turn up on start lines in the early spring and realise several other outfits have also had the same aesthetic inspiration for the new season?

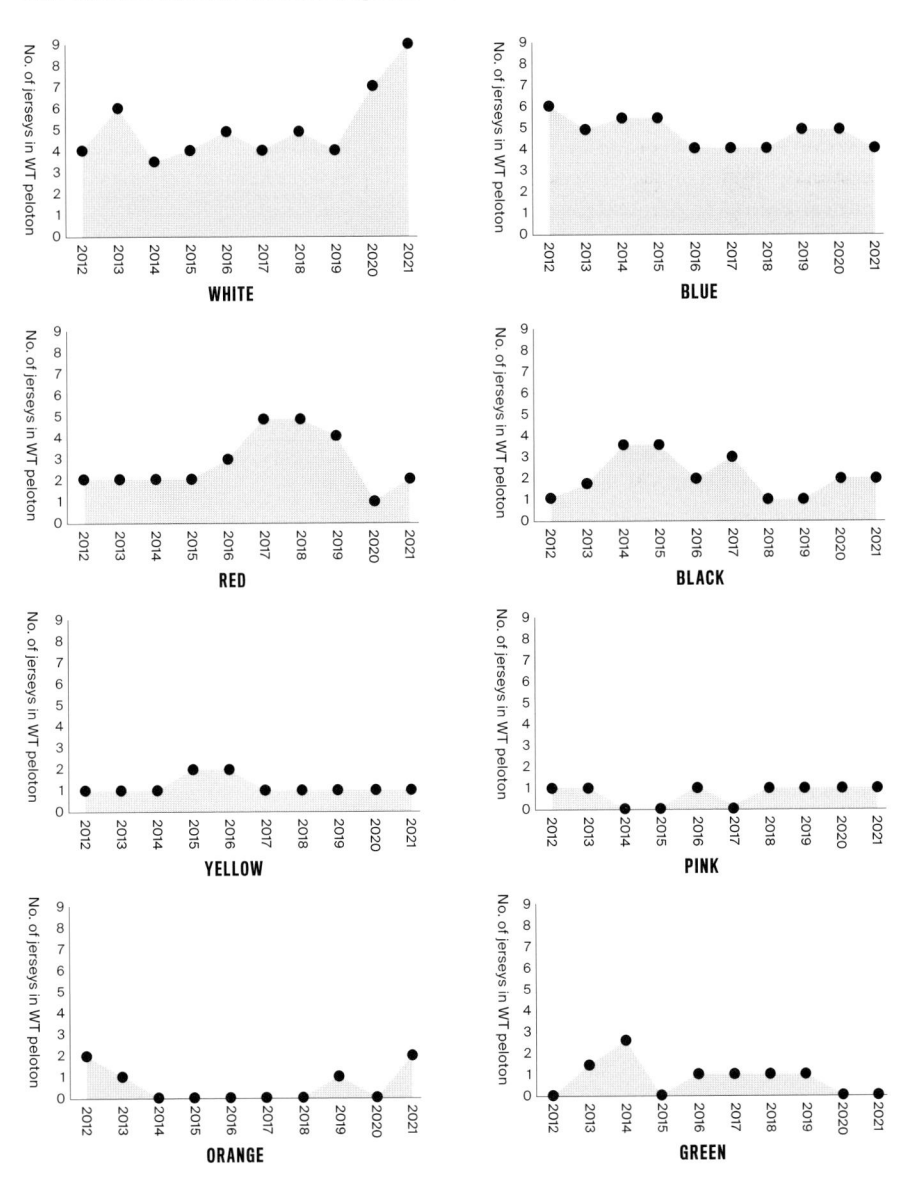

**WHITE**

**BLUE**

**RED**

**BLACK**

**YELLOW**

**PINK**

**ORANGE**

**GREEN**

MARCH   WORLDTOUR MEN'S RACE

# MILAN–SANREMO
20 March 2021
Milan–Sanremo
299km

## WEATHER

**TEMPERATURE**
10°C

**WIND**
SE 7km/h

## PROFILE

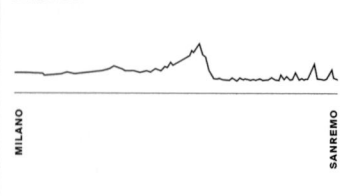

MILANO — SANREMO

## BREAKAWAY

N. Conci (TFS), A. Peron (TNN), C. Planet (TNN), M. Viel (ANS), A. Tonelli (BCF), T. Van der Hoorn (IWG), M. Norsgaard (MOV), F. Tagliani (BCF)

Three of the eight in the early breakaway were in last year's breakaway: Alessandro Tonelli, Charles Planet (his third in six Sanremos), and Filippo Tagliani, who chased and chased and finally made the group. The gap to them and their companions – Mattia Viel, Taco van der Hoorn, Mathias Norsgaard, Andrea Peron and Nicola Conci – stabilised at around 6 minutes 20, as Tim Declercq, Senne Leysen and Paul Martens led the peloton. Sam Oomen piloted Wout van Aert and the peloton past Van der Hoorn on the Cipressa, and the endgame began. Van Aert was glued to Alaphilippe's wheel on the Poggio. Ewan was so strong, he looked ready to attack on the climb. Pidcock led on the descent until, while he and the other leaders – Alaphilippe, Van Aert, Van der Poel, Schachmann, Kragh Andersen, Matthews, Aranburu, Colbrelli, Trentin, etc – paused to contemplate the Ewan conundrum, Jasper Stuyven attacked with 3.4km left. Pidcock gave chase with Turgis on his wheel, then desisted. Schachmann set off with Matthews on his wheel, then sat up. Van Avermaet followed, with Van Aert just behind, but no one would come through and commit. When Kragh Andersen darted away with 1.5km to go, Pidcock chased but, with Van Aert in his slipstream, he relented. Kragh Andersen reached Stuyven under the *flamme rouge* and they extended their lead on the final left–right chicane as the chasers dithered. Van der Poel unleashed his sprint with 250 metres remaining, but too late: with 100 metres left, Stuyven darted past Kragh Andersen, who had nothing left. (MR)

## TRIVIA

» This was Ewan's second runner-up placing at Milan–Sanremo, having finished behind Vincenzo Nibali in 2018.

# RESULTS

| POS | NAME | TEAM | TIME |
|---|---|---|---|
| 1. | J. Stuyven | TFS | 6:38:06 |
| 2. | C. Ewan | LTS | s.t. |
| 3. | W. van Aert | TJV | s.t. |
| 4. | P. Sagan | BOH | s.t. |
| 5. | M. van der Poel | AFC | s.t. |
| 6. | M. Matthews | BEX | s.t. |
| 7. | A. Aranburu | APT | s.t. |
| 8. | S. Colbrelli | TBV | s.t. |
| 9. | S. Kragh Andersen | DSM | s.t. |
| 10. | A. Turgis | TDE | s.t. |
| 11. | M. Mohorič | TBV | s.t. |
| 12. | M. Trentin | UAD | s.t. |
| 13. | G. Van Avermaet | ACT | s.t. |
| 14. | M. Schachmann | BOH | s.t. |
| 15. | T. Pidcock | IGD | s.t. |
| 16. | J. Alaphilippe | DQT | s.t. |
| 17. | M. Kwiatkowski | IGD | s.t. |
| 18. | G. Nizzolo | TQA | 0:06 |
| 19. | N. Bouhanni | ARK | s.t. |
| 20. | P. Ackermann | BOH | s.t. |
| 21. | O. Naesen | ACT | s.t. |
| 22. | C. Laporte | COF | s.t. |
| 23. | A. Vendrame | ACT | s.t. |
| 24. | G. Vermeersch | AFC | s.t. |
| 25. | G. Serrano | MOV | s.t. |
| 26. | A. Démare | GFC | s.t. |
| 27. | R. Bardet | DSM | s.t. |
| 28. | R. Stannard | BEX | s.t. |
| 29. | J. Simon | TDE | s.t. |
| 30. | I. García Cortina | MOV | s.t. |
| 31. | D. van Baarle | IGD | s.t. |
| 32. | J. Degenkolb | LTS | s.t. |
| 33. | D. Oss | BOH | s.t. |
| 34. | D. Formolo | UAD | 0:10 |
| 35. | V. Nibali | TFS | s.t. |
| 36. | S. Higuita | EFN | s.t. |
| 37. | Z. Štybar | DQT | 0:12 |
| 38. | S. Clarke | TQA | 0:18 |
| 39. | A. Covi | UAD | 0:21 |
| 40. | L. Rota | IWG | 0:29 |
| 41. | D. Ballerini | DQT | s.t. |
| 42. | S. Bennett | DQT | s.t. |
| 43. | D. Cimolai | ISN | s.t. |
| 44. | W. Barguil | ARK | s.t. |
| 45. | G. Izagirre | APT | s.t. |
| 46. | F. Felline | APT | s.t. |
| 47. | A. De Gendt | IWG | s.t. |
| 48. | F. Fiorelli | BCF | s.t. |
| 49. | L. Mezgec | BEX | s.t. |
| 50. | K. Geniets | GFC | s.t. |
| 51. | U. Marengo | BCF | s.t. |
| 52. | M. Valgren | EFN | s.t. |
| 53. | G. Martin | COF | s.t. |
| 54. | Y. Lampaert | DQT | s.t. |
| 55. | D. Caruso | TBV | s.t. |
| 56. | J. Mosca | TFS | 1:21 |
| 57. | L. Vliegen | IWG | 1:28 |
| 58. | L. Wiśniowski | TQA | s.t. |
| 59. | C. Russo | ARK | 1:38 |
| 60. | J. Rumac | ANS | s.t. |
| 61. | K. Sbaragli | AFC | s.t. |
| 62. | M. Cort | EFN | s.t. |
| 63. | N. Bonifazio | TDE | s.t. |
| 64. | F. Ganna | IGD | s.t. |
| 65. | M. Sobrero | APT | s.t. |
| 66. | I. Konovalovas | GFC | s.t. |
| 67. | H. Hofstetter | ISN | s.t. |
| 68. | E. Battaglin | BCF | s.t. |
| 69. | E. Viviani | COF | 1:45 |
| 70. | S. Oomen | TJV | s.t. |
| 71. | M. Burghardt | BOH | s.t. |
| 72. | P. Gilbert | LTS | s.t. |
| 73. | F. Zana | BCF | s.t. |
| 74. | Q. Simmons | TFS | s.t. |
| 75. | T. Skujiņš | TFS | s.t. |
| 76. | M. Gogl | TQA | s.t. |
| 77. | B. Swift | IGD | s.t. |
| 78. | T. Wellens | LTS | 2:39 |
| 79. | M. Tusveld | DSM | s.t. |
| 80. | T. Roosen | TJV | s.t. |
| 81. | V. Campenaerts | TQA | s.t. |
| 82. | A. De Marchi | ISN | 2:51 |
| 83. | A. Ponomar | ANS | 3:00 |
| 84. | L. Durbridge | BEX | 3:12 |
| 85. | N. Oliveira | MOV | 3:13 |
| 86. | D. Villella | MOV | s.t. |
| 87. | A. Pasqualon | IWG | s.t. |
| 88. | D. McLay | ARK | s.t. |
| 89. | A. Kristoff | UAD | s.t. |
| 90. | S. Dewulf | ACT | s.t. |
| 91. | L. G. Mas | MOV | s.t. |
| 92. | J. Koch | IWG | s.t. |
| 93. | C. Benedetti | BOH | s.t. |
| 94. | S. Puccio | IGD | s.t. |
| 95. | J. van Emden | TJV | s.t. |
| 96. | J. Guarnieri | GFC | s.t. |
| 97. | P. L. Périchon | COF | 4:30 |
| 98. | D. De Bondt | AFC | 5:02 |
| 99. | K. Asgreen | DQT | s.t. |
| 100. | M. Schär | ACT | s.t. |
| 101. | R. Kluge | LTS | 5:15 |
| 102. | J. de Buyst | LTS | s.t. |
| 103. | S. Bissegger | EFN | 6:25 |
| 104. | D. Martinelli | APT | 7:14 |
| 105. | N. Conci | TFS | s.t. |
| 106. | A. Tonelli | BCF | s.t. |
| 107. | M. Brändle | ISN | s.t. |
| 108. | S. E. Bystrøm | UAD | s.t. |
| 109. | A. Bettiol | EFN | s.t. |
| 110. | M. Scotson | GFC | s.t. |
| 111. | L. Chirico | ANS | s.t. |
| 112. | T. van der Hoorn | IWG | s.t. |
| 113. | F. Gaviria | UAD | s.t. |
| 114. | J. Sütterlin | DSM | s.t. |
| 115. | N. Roche | DSM | s.t. |
| 116. | D. Gruzdev | APT | s.t. |
| 117. | Y. Arashiro | TBV | s.t. |
| 118. | L. Rowe | IGD | s.t. |
| 119. | O. Vergaerde | AFC | 7:56 |
| 120. | C. Pedersen | DSM | s.t. |
| 121. | E. Vinjebo | TQA | s.t. |
| 122. | N. Venchiarutti | ANS | s.t. |
| 123. | R. Combaud | DSM | s.t. |
| 124. | M. Boaro | APT | s.t. |
| 125. | M. Norsgaard | MOV | s.t. |
| 126. | F. Sabatini | COF | s.t. |
| 127. | F. Frison | LTS | s.t. |
| 128. | J. Piccoli | ISN | s.t. |
| 129. | R. Mullen | TFS | s.t. |
| 130. | C. Juul-Jensen | BEX | 7:59 |
| 131. | S. Langeveld | EFN | s.t. |
| 132. | P. Vakoč | AFC | s.t. |
| 133. | M. Hepburn | BEX | 10:30 |
| 134. | A. Konychev | BEX | s.t. |
| 135. | J. Tratnik | TBV | s.t. |
| 136. | A. Gougeard | ACT | s.t. |
| 137. | E. Boasson Hagen | TDE | s.t. |
| 138. | A. Capiot | ARK | s.t. |
| 139. | N. Terpstra | TDE | s.t. |
| 140. | G. Van Hoecke | ACT | s.t. |
| 141. | M. Bodnar | BOH | s.t. |
| 142. | B. J. Lindeman | TQA | s.t. |
| 143. | P. Kusztor | TNN | s.t. |
| 144. | A. Torres | MOV | s.t. |
| 145. | G. Sagiv | ISN | s.t. |
| 146. | T. Scully | EFN | s.t. |
| 147. | A. M. Richeze | UAD | s.t. |
| 148. | F. Wright | TBV | s.t. |
| 149. | A. Petit | TDE | 10:58 |
| 150. | G. Visconti | BCF | s.t. |
| 151. | T. Declercq | DQT | s.t. |
| 152. | K. Vanbilsen | COF | s.t. |
| 153. | A. Viviani | COF | s.t. |
| 154. | P. Vanspeybrouck | IWG | s.t. |
| 155. | R. Sinkeldam | GFC | s.t. |
| 156. | L. Manzin | TDE | s.t. |
| 157. | H. Haussler | TBV | s.t. |
| 158. | E. Affini | TJV | 13:17 |
| 159. | C. Pfingsten | TJV | 14:55 |
| 160. | T. Guernalec | ARK | s.t. |
| 161. | S. Leysen | AFC | s.t. |
| 162. | C. Davy | GFC | 16:33 |
| 163. | P. Martens | TJV | s.t. |
| 164. | D. Lozano | TNN | 18:06 |
| 165. | U. Poli | TNN | 19:37 |
| 166. | F. Tagliani | ANS | s.t. |
| 167. | S. Brand | TNN | s.t. |
| 168. | A. Peron | TNN | s.t. |
| 169. | C. Planet | TNN | s.t. |

MARCH

MARCH  WORLDTOUR WOMEN'S RACE

## TROFEO ALFREDO BINDA
21 March 2021
Cocquio Trevisago–Cittiglio
141.8km

In the second Italian spring Classic, Elisa Longo Borghini (Trek-Segafredo) rode to a spectacular solo victory. The Italian champion attacked from the peloton with 25km to go, never to be seen again. The race around Cittiglio finished with four laps of a 17.5km circuit that included two climbs: the short, steep ascent to Casalzuigno and the longer, more gradual climb to Orino. Pauliena Rooijakkers (Liv Racing) and Tatiana Guderzo (Alé BTC Ljubljana) had attacked on the first of the finishing laps, holding a gap of just under 30 seconds. Marta Cavalli (FDJ Nouvelle-Aquitaine Futuroscope) and Audrey Cordon-Ragot (Trek-Segafredo) bridged the gap on the third-to-last lap, but the four riders were caught soon afterwards. Anouska Koster (Jumbo-Visma) was the next to initiate a move, but she never had a big advantage and was reeled in 29km from the finish. Longo Borghini's teammates Tayler Wiles and Ruth Winder strung out the peloton on the Orino climb, and after an attack by Katarzyna Niewiadoma (Canyon-SRAM), Longo Borghini countered and got away over the top of the climb and into the descent. Longo Borghini entered the final lap with an advantage of only 16 seconds on a five-woman chase group, but due to a lack of cooperation behind, she could celebrate a secure solo victory. One minute 42 seconds behind, Marianne Vos (Jumbo-Visma) beat Cecilie Uttrup Ludwig (FDJ Nouvelle-Aquitaine Futuroscope) in the sprint for second place.

## WEATHER

TEMPERATURE
7°C

WIND
SW 13km/h

## PROFILE

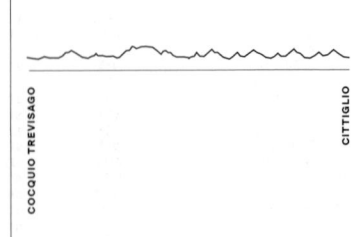

COCQUIO TREVISAGO — CITTIGLIO

## BREAKAWAY

T. Guderzo (ALE), M. Cavalli (FDJ), A. Cordon-Ragot (TFS), P. Rooijakkers (LIV)

## RESULTS

| POS | NAME | TEAM | TIME |
|---|---|---|---|
| 1. | E. Longo Borghini | TFS | 3:43:29 |
| 2. | M. Vos | JVW | 1:42 |
| 3. | C. U. Ludwig | FDJ | s.t. |
| 4. | K. Niewiadoma | CSR | s.t. |
| 5. | S. Paladin | LIV | s.t. |
| 6. | M. García | ALE | s.t. |
| 7. | E. Balsamo | VAL | 2:46 |
| 8. | S. Bertizzolo | LIV | s.t. |
| 9. | E. Fahlin | FDJ | s.t. |
| 10. | F. Mackaij | DSM | s.t. |
| 11. | J. Erić | MOV | s.t. |
| 12. | E. Deignan | TFS | s.t. |
| 13. | K. Ragusa | MNX | s.t. |
| 14. | A. Moolman | SDW | s.t. |
| 15. | H. Barnes | CSR | s.t. |
| 16. | L. Stephens | TIB | s.t. |
| 17. | D. Silvestri | TOP | s.t. |
| 18. | L. Thomas | MOV | s.t. |
| 19. | E. Magnaldi | WNT | s.t. |
| 20. | E. Cecchini | SDW | s.t. |

MARCH    .1 MEN'S RACE

# PER SEMPRE ALFREDO
21 March 2021
Firenze–Sesto Fiorentino
162km

## WEATHER

TEMPERATURE          WIND
9°C                  NE 22km/h

## RESULTS

| POS | NAME | TEAM | TIME |
|---|---|---|---|
| 1. | M. Moschetti | TFS | 3:48:10 |
| 2. | M. Aristi | EUS | s.t. |
| 3. | S. Zambelli | NAT | s.t. |
| 4. | J. Aberasturi | CJR | s.t. |
| 5. | L. Colnaghi | NAT | s.t. |
| 6. | G. Lonardi | BCF | s.t. |
| 7. | S. Gandin | ZEF | s.t. |
| 8. | T. Nencini | NAT | s.t. |
| 9. | N. Tesfatsion | ANS | s.t. |
| 10. | M. Mayrhofer | DSM | s.t. |
| 11. | D. Cima | GAZ | s.t. |
| 12. | E. Zambanini | ZEF | s.t. |
| 13. | K. Gradek | THR | s.t. |
| 14. | E. Onesti | GTS | s.t. |
| 15. | O. Aular | CJR | s.t. |
| 16. | K. Bonaldo | T4Q | s.t. |
| 17. | H. Mulubrhan | T4Q | s.t. |
| 18. | F. Gall | DSM | s.t. |
| 19. | M. Paluta | GLC | s.t. |
| 20. | D. González | CJR | s.t. |

MARCH  WORLDTOUR MEN'S RACE

## VOLTA CICLISTA A CATALUNYA
Stage 1
22 March 2021
Calella–Calella
178.4km

A casualty of the Covid-related racing shutdown in the spring of 2020, the Volta's 100th edition was initially dominated by a four-man break. The quartet's last member, Sylvain Moniquet, was reeled in on the descent of the category-1 Port de Santa Fe del Montseny, where Movistar's pace-making shed most of the sprinters. Several attempts were made to break clear in the final 30km and eventually one of them stuck. Luis León Sánchez initiated the move and was joined by Lennard Kämna, Rémy Rochas and Andreas Kron. As the chase failed to get properly organised, this foursome stayed clear. Kämna – a great climber but not so gifted in a sprint – tried his luck from 2km out but was quickly caught. At the line, the veteran Sánchez appeared the favourite, but he was outwitted and outpaced by 22-year-old Kron riding his first WorldTour stage race. (PC)

### WEATHER

TEMPERATURE: 16°C
WIND: NE 6km/h

### PROFILE

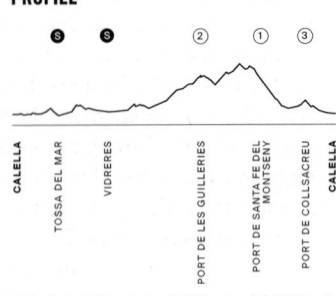

### BREAKAWAY
G. Martin (EUS), R. Taaramae (IWG), N. Berhane (COF), S. Moniquet (LTS)

### STAGE RESULTS

| POS | NAME | TEAM | TIME |
|---|---|---|---|
| 1. | A. Kron | LTS | 4:20:15 |
| 2. | L. L. Sanchez | APT | s.t. |
| 3. | R. Rochas | COF | s.t. |
| 4. | L. Kämna | BOH | s.t. |
| 5. | D. Smith | BEX | 0:16 |
| 6. | M. Mohorič | TBV | s.t. |
| 7. | I. Schelling | BOH | s.t. |
| 8. | A. Valverde | MOV | s.t. |
| 9. | A. Kamp | TFS | s.t. |
| 10. | M. Valgren | EFN | s.t. |
| 11. | M. Van Gils | LTS | s.t. |
| 12. | D. Impey | ISN | s.t. |
| 13. | R. Guerreiro | EFN | s.t. |
| 14. | F. Galván | EKP | s.t. |
| 15. | N. Quintana | ARK | s.t. |
| 16. | N. Roche | DSM | s.t. |
| 17. | É. Gesbert | ARK | s.t. |
| 18. | E. Mas | MOV | s.t. |
| 19. | H. Tejada | APT | s.t. |
| 20. | A. Delaplace | ARK | s.t. |

### GENERAL CLASSIFICATION

| POS | NAME | TEAM | TIME |
|---|---|---|---|
| 1. | A. Kron | LTS | 4:20:05 |
| 2. | L. L. Sanchez | APT | 0:04 |
| 3. | R. Rochas | COF | 0:06 |

### KING OF THE MOUNTAINS

| POS | NAME | TEAM | PTS |
|---|---|---|---|
| 1. | S. Moniquet | LTS | 11 |
| 2. | C. Verona | MOV | 8 |
| 3. | A. Pedrero | MOV | 6 |

### POINTS

| POS | NAME | TEAM | PTS |
|---|---|---|---|
| 1. | A. Kron | LTS | 10 |
| 2. | N. Berhane | COF | 6 |
| 3. | L. L. Sanchez | APT | 6 |

### YOUNG RIDER

| POS | NAME | TEAM | TIME |
|---|---|---|---|
| 1. | A. Kron | LTS | 4:20:05 |
| 2. | R. Rochas | COF | 0:06 |
| 3. | L. Kämna | BOH | 0:10 |

### TRIVIA
» This was Andreas Kron's first WorldTour victory.

### BONUSES

| TYPE | NAME | TEAM |
|---|---|---|
| KOM 1 | R. Taaramae | IWG |
| KOM 2 | S. Moniquet | LTS |
| KOM 3 | L. L. Sanchez | APT |
| Sprint 1 | N. Berhane | COF |
| Sprint 2 | N. Berhane | COF |

MARCH    WORLDTOUR MEN'S RACE

# VOLTA CICLISTA A CATALUNYA
Stage 2 (ITT)
23 March 2021
Banyoles–Banyoles
18.5km

Chris Boardman was the victor of the Volta's last mid-length time trial, way back in 1998, four years on from his success in the inaugural World Time Trial Championship. So it was fitting that victory in Banyoles went to another rider who has claimed that crown: 2019 champion Rohan Dennis, who hadn't won a time trial since that success in Yorkshire. Rémi Cavagna set the best time among the earlier starters, but Dennis soon improved on the Frenchman's mark, coming through the line 5 seconds quicker. No one got near challenging either rider's time; Cavagna's teammate João Almeida came the closest, 28 seconds down on Dennis. Brandon McNulty was just 1/100th of a second slower than the Portuguese, which proved the difference between them at the top of the General Classification.

## WEATHER

TEMPERATURE    WIND
15°C           S 15km/h

## PROFILE

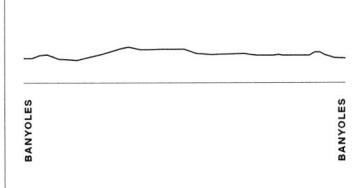

BANYOLES                              BANYOLES

## STAGE RESULTS

| POS | NAME | TEAM | TIME |
|---|---|---|---|
| 1. | R. Dennis | IGD | 0:22:27 |
| 2. | R. Cavagna | DQT | 0:05 |
| 3. | J. Almeida | DQT | 0:28 |
| 4. | B. McNulty | UAD | s.t. |
| 5. | S. Kruijswijk | TJV | 0:33 |
| 6. | R. Porte | IGD | 0:34 |
| 7. | A. Yates | IGD | 0:35 |
| 8. | J. Černý | DQT | 0:38 |
| 9. | S. de Bod | APT | s.t. |
| 10. | G. Thomas | IGD | 0:47 |
| 11. | F. Masnada | DQT | 0:48 |
| 12. | W. Kelderman | BOH | 0:52 |
| 13. | L. L. Sanchez | APT | 0:53 |
| 14. | T. van Garderen | EFN | 0:54 |
| 15. | J. Castroviejo | IGD | 0:55 |
| 16. | T. Arensman | DSM | 0:58 |
| 17. | K. Bouwman | TJV | 0:59 |
| 18. | T. De Gendt | LTS | 1:01 |
| 19. | D. Devenyns | DQT | 1:02 |
| 20. | R. Gesink | TJV | 1:05 |

## GENERAL CLASSIFICATION

| POS | | NAME | TEAM | TIME |
|---|---|---|---|---|
| 1. | ↑26 | J. Almeida | DQT | 4:43:26 |
| 2. | ↑44 | B. McNulty | UAD | s.t. |
| 3. | ↓1 | L. L. Sanchez | APT | 0:03 |

## KING OF THE MOUNTAINS

| POS | | NAME | TEAM | PTS |
|---|---|---|---|---|
| 1. | — | S. Moniquet | LTS | 11 |
| 2. | — | C. Verona | MOV | 8 |
| 3. | — | A. Pedrero | MOV | 6 |

## POINTS

| POS | | NAME | TEAM | PTS |
|---|---|---|---|---|
| 1. | — | A. Kron | LTS | 10 |
| 2. | — | R. Dennis | IGD | 10 |
| 3. | ↓1 | N. Berhane | COF | 6 |

## YOUNG RIDER

| POS | | NAME | TEAM | TIME |
|---|---|---|---|---|
| 1. | ↑11 | J. Almeida | DQT | 4:43:26 |
| 2. | ↑13 | B. McNulty | UAD | s.t. |
| 3. | ↑13 | S. de Bod | APT | 0:10 |

## TRIVIA

» Rohan Dennis's last victory was his world time trial title win in 2019.

MARCH — WORLDTOUR MEN'S RACE

# VOLTA CICLISTA A CATALUNYA
Stage 3
24 March 2021
Canal Olimpic de Catalunya–Vallter 2000
203.1km

Adam Yates repeated his 2019 success at Vallter 2000, taking his first victory in Ineos Grenadiers colours. For a long while, it appeared the breakaway might go the distance, as nine riders built up a lead of more than 12 minutes. Yet, at the foot of the final ascent, the favourites were already reeling the escapees in. Alejandro Valverde was the first of the big names to move. Chased down once, the Spanish veteran went again with 8km remaining. Yates waited until the steepest ramps arrived with 5km to go before making his move, Sepp Kuss tracking him. The pair soon breezed up to Valverde, this trio overhauling final escapee Thymen Arensman with 3.5km left. After Kuss made a vain attempt to go clear inside the final 2km, Yates made an acceleration of his own that proved the winning move and put him in the lead at João Almeida's expense. Ⓟ

## WEATHER

TEMPERATURE: 15°C
WIND: SW 13km/h

## PROFILE

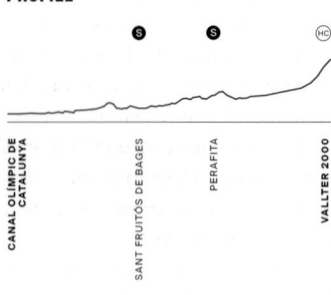

Canal Olímpic de Catalunya — Sant Fruitós de Bages — Perafita — Vallter 2000 (HC)

## BREAKAWAY

F. Galvan (EKP), A. Kamp (TFS), S. Bennett (TQA), C. Venturini (ACT), T. Champion (COF), R. Janse van Rensburg (TQA), C. Joyce (RLY), T. Arensman (DSM), A. Evans (IWG)

## STAGE RESULTS

| POS | NAME | TEAM | TIME |
|---|---|---|---|
| 1. | A. Yates | IGD | 5:00:58 |
| 2. | E. Chaves | BEX | 0:13 |
| 3. | A. Valverde | MOV | 0:19 |
| 4. | G. Thomas | IGD | 0:31 |
| 5. | H. Vanhoucke | LTS | s.t. |
| 6. | S. Kuss | TJV | s.t. |
| 7. | H. Carthy | EFN | s.t. |
| 8. | M. Woods | ISN | 0:36 |
| 9. | R. Porte | IGD | s.t. |
| 10. | G. Ciccone | TFS | s.t. |
| 11. | N. Quintana | ARK | s.t. |
| 12. | S. Yates | BEX | s.t. |
| 13. | L. Hamilton | BEX | s.t. |
| 14. | W. Kelderman | BOH | s.t. |
| 15. | E. Mas | MOV | 0:46 |
| 16. | J. Almeida | DQT | s.t. |
| 17. | M. Badilatti | GFC | 1:03 |
| 18. | M. Bizkarra | EUS | 1:09 |
| 19. | L. Kämna | BOH | s.t. |
| 20. | B. McNulty | UAD | 1:21 |

## GENERAL CLASSIFICATION

| POS | NAME | TEAM | TIME |
|---|---|---|---|
| 1. ↑5 | A. Yates | IGD | 9:44:21 |
| 2. ↑3 | R. Porte | IGD | 0:45 |
| 3. ↓2 | J. Almeida | DQT | 0:49 |

## KING OF THE MOUNTAINS

| POS | NAME | TEAM | PTS |
|---|---|---|---|
| 1. — | A. Yates | IGD | 26 |
| 2. ↑3 | E. Chaves | BEX | 24 |
| 3. ↑5 | A. Valverde | MOV | 18 |

## POINTS

| POS | NAME | TEAM | PTS |
|---|---|---|---|
| 1. — | A. Yates | IGD | 10 |
| 2. — | R. Dennis | IGD | 10 |
| 3. ↓2 | A. Kron | LTS | 10 |

## YOUNG RIDER

| POS | NAME | TEAM | TIME |
|---|---|---|---|
| 1. — | J. Almeida | DQT | 9:45:10 |
| 2. — | B. McNulty | UAD | 0:35 |
| 3. ↑5 | H. Vanhoucke | LTS | 0:41 |

## TRIVIA

» Yates had previously taken one stage win at this race: 2019's stage 3, which also finished at Vallter 2000.

## BONUSES

| TYPE | NAME | TEAM |
|---|---|---|
| KOM 1 | A. Yates | IGD |
| Sprint 1 | F. Galvan | EKP |
| Sprint 2 | A. Kamp | TFS |

MARCH   WORLDTOUR MEN'S RACE

# VOLTA CICLISTA A CATALUNYA
Stage 4
25 March 2021
Ripoll–Port Ainé
166.5km

There was a flurry of activity right from the off, as a dozen riders went clear on the Port de Toses, Lennard Kämna the best placed of them, barely 2 minutes down on race leader Adam Yates. On the Port del Cantó ascent, Kämna jumped clear on his own and reached the foot of the final climb with a lead of close to 2 minutes. Yates's teammates quickly set about trimming that deficit, Rohan Dennis and Richard Carapaz reeling the German back in. After Steven Kruijswijk tried and failed to go clear, Esteban Chaves managed to escape Ineos's stranglehold. Although the Colombian's advantage was never more than 30 seconds, he held on for his first win in two years. Michael Woods led in the chasing pack, 7 seconds behind Chaves, with Yates also close at hand, whose teammates Richie Porte and Geraint Thomas now filled the two other podium spots. ⓟ

## WEATHER

TEMPERATURE  WIND
18°C  S 24km/h

## PROFILE

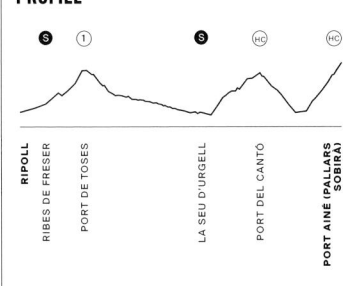

RIPOLL / RIBES DE FRESER / PORT DE TOSES / LA SEU D'URGELL / PORT DEL CANTÓ / PORT AINÉ (PALLARS SOBIRÀ)

## BREAKAWAY
T. De Gendt (LTS), L. Kamna (BOH), R. Urán (EFN), C. Champoussin (ACT), A. Tolhoek (TJV), K. Bouwman (TJV), S. Samitier (MOV), A. Pedrero (MOV), J. P. Lopez (TFS), A. Valter (GFC), J. Dombrowski (UAD), L. Meintjes (IWG)

## STAGE RESULTS

| POS | NAME | TEAM | TIME |
|---|---|---|---|
| 1. | E. Chaves | BEX | 4:29:47 |
| 2. | M. Woods | ISN | 0:07 |
| 3. | G. Thomas | IGD | s.t. |
| 4. | A. Yates | IGD | s.t. |
| 5. | S. Kuss | TJV | s.t. |
| 6. | A. Valverde | MOV | s.t. |
| 7. | R. Porte | IGD | s.t. |
| 8. | W. Kelderman | BOH | s.t. |
| 9. | N. Quintana | ARK | s.t. |
| 10. | L. Hamilton | BEX | s.t. |
| 11. | H. Carthy | EFN | 0:13 |
| 12. | S. Yates | BEX | 0:18 |
| 13. | J. Almeida | DQT | 0:25 |
| 14. | G. Ciccone | TFS | 0:31 |
| 15. | H. Vanhoucke | LTS | s.t. |
| 16. | M. Bizkarra | EUS | 0:51 |
| 17. | F. Masnada | DQT | 0:54 |
| 18. | B. McNulty | UAD | 1:02 |
| 19. | E. Mas | MOV | 1:34 |
| 20. | S. Buitrago | TBV | 2:03 |

## GENERAL CLASSIFICATION

| POS | NAME | TEAM | TIME |
|---|---|---|---|
| 1. — | A. Yates | IGD | 14:14:15 |
| 2. — | R. Porte | IGD | 0:45 |
| 3. ↑1 | G. Thomas | IGD | 0:49 |

## KING OF THE MOUNTAINS

| POS | NAME | TEAM | PTS |
|---|---|---|---|
| 1. ↑1 | E. Chaves | BEX | 50 |
| 2. ↓1 | A. Yates | IGD | 40 |
| 3. — | K. Bouwman | TJV | 30 |

## POINTS

| POS | NAME | TEAM | PTS |
|---|---|---|---|
| 1. ↑4 | E. Chaves | BEX | 16 |
| 2. ↓1 | A. Yates | IGD | 10 |
| 3. ↓1 | R. Dennis | IGD | 10 |

## YOUNG RIDER

| POS | NAME | TEAM | TIME |
|---|---|---|---|
| 1. — | J. Almeida | DQT | 14:15:22 |
| 2. ↑3 | L. Hamilton | BEX | 0:28 |
| 3. — | H. Vanhoucke | LTS | 0:47 |

## TRIVIA
» This was Esteban Chaves's first victory since stage 19 of the 2019 Giro d'Italia.

## BONUSES

| TYPE | NAME | TEAM |
|---|---|---|
| KOM 1 | K. Bouwman | TJV |
| KOM 2 | L. Kamna | BOH |
| KOM 3 | E. Chaves | BEX |
| Sprint 1 | A. Kron | LTS |
| Sprint 2 | J. P. Lopez | TFS |

MARCH   WORLDTOUR MEN'S RACE

# VOLTA CICLISTA A CATALUNYA
Stage 5
26 March 2021
La Pobla de Segur–Manresa
201.1km

This medium-mountain stage has a tendency to produce surprises in the GC battle, which perhaps explains why Ineos were keen to keep the peloton together early on. Yet, as the race descended the first pass, the Coll de Comiols, Rémi Cavagna and Matej Mohorič broke away off the front and no fewer than 39 riders managed to bridge up to them in the valley beyond, with Ineos not represented. The British team were aware, though, that none of their direct GC rivals had infiltrated the move and were happy to give the break some room. The in-form Cavagna went clear approaching the Port de Montserrat, but its category-1 slopes proved too much for the Frenchman. Several riders joined him, triggering a wave of attacks. With 12km left, Lennard Kämna tried his luck and, after being close twice already in this race, the German stayed away to claim the win. ⓟⓒ

## WEATHER

TEMPERATURE   WIND
17°C          SE 11km/h

## PROFILE

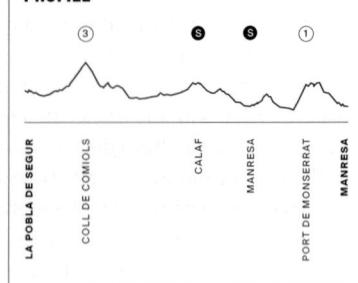

LA POBLA DE SEGUR · COLL DE COMIOLS · CALAF · MANRESA · PORT DE MONSERRAT · MANRESA

## BREAKAWAY

R. Cavagna (DQT), M. Mohorič (TBV), T. Arensman (DSM), I. Schelling (BOH)

## STAGE RESULTS

| POS | NAME | TEAM | TIME |
|---|---|---|---|
| 1. | L. Kämna | BOH | 4:29:13 |
| 2. | R. Guerreiro | EFN | 0:39 |
| 3. | M. Bizkarra | EUS | 0:42 |
| 4. | D. Smith | BEX | 0:44 |
| 5. | D. Martin | ISN | s.t. |
| 6. | M. Mohorič | TBV | s.t. |
| 7. | J. Knox | DQT | s.t. |
| 8. | A. Valter | GFC | s.t. |
| 9. | R. Urán | EFN | s.t. |
| 10. | S. Kruijswijk | TJV | s.t. |
| 11. | É. Gesbert | ARK | s.t. |
| 12. | N. Edet | COF | s.t. |
| 13. | M. Storer | DSM | s.t. |
| 14. | C. Verona | MOV | s.t. |
| 15. | S. Reichenbach | GFC | s.t. |
| 16. | D. Devenyns | DQT | s.t. |
| 17. | T. Kangert | BEX | 0:48 |
| 18. | G. Brambilla | TFS | 0:51 |
| 19. | B. Zwiehoff | BOH | 0:53 |
| 20. | H. Tejada | APT | s.t. |

## GENERAL CLASSIFICATION

| POS | NAME | TEAM | TIME |
|---|---|---|---|
| 1. — | A. Yates | IGD | 18:45:27 |
| 2. — | R. Porte | IGD | 0:45 |
| 3. — | G. Thomas | IGD | 0:49 |

## KING OF THE MOUNTAINS

| POS | NAME | TEAM | PTS |
|---|---|---|---|
| 1. — | E. Chaves | BEX | 50 |
| 2. — | A. Yates | IGD | 40 |
| 3. — | K. Bouwman | TJV | 33 |

## POINTS

| POS | NAME | TEAM | PTS |
|---|---|---|---|
| 1. — | E. Chaves | BEX | 16 |
| 2. — | A. Yates | IGD | 10 |
| 3. — | L. Kämna | BOH | 10 |

## YOUNG RIDER

| POS | NAME | TEAM | TIME |
|---|---|---|---|
| 1. — | J. Almeida | DQT | 18:46:34 |
| 2. — | L. Hamilton | BEX | 0:28 |
| 3. — | H. Vanhoucke | LTS | 0:47 |

## TRIVIA

» This was only Kämna's third career victory, although all three have been at WorldTour races (he won a stage of the Dauphiné and Tour de France in 2020).

## BONUSES

| TYPE | NAME | TEAM |
|---|---|---|
| KOM 1 | K. Bouwman | TJV |
| KOM 2 | R. Cavagna | DQT |
| Sprint 1 | R. Cavagna | DQT |
| Sprint 2 | B. Jungels | ACT |

MARCH  WORLDTOUR MEN'S RACE

# VOLTA CICLISTA A CATALUNYA
Stage 6
27 March 2021
Tarragona–Mataró
193.8km

Having struggled to get over the after-effects of the Covid-19 virus, which led to his decision to opt for Catalunya instead of following his traditional path through the northern Classics, Peter Sagan was rewarded with his first victory of the season. After his team had brought the race back together in the closing kilometres, the three-time world champion outstripped Daryl Impey and Juan Sebastián Molano in the bunch sprint. Five riders coalesced in the day's break, Dmitry Strakhov the last to yield 18km from home. On the descent from the final climb, Rémi Cavagna drew on his daring and power to forge a gap. Sensing the threat the Frenchman presented, Bora and UAE were quick to close him down, and to do the same when Cavagna's Deceuninck teammate Josef Černý attempted to counter. Bora's reward was a second consecutive stage victory, an important one for their team leader. ⓟⓒ

## WEATHER

TEMPERATURE  WIND
17°C  SW 17km/h

## PROFILE

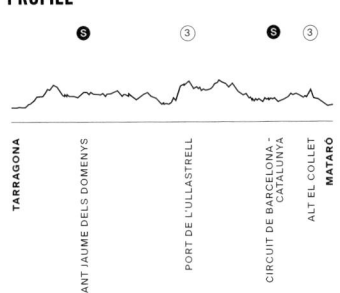

TARRAGONA — SANT JAUME DELS DOMENYS — PORT DE L'ULLASTRELL — CIRCUIT DE BARCELONA - CATALUNYA — ALT EL COLLET — MATARÓ

## BREAKAWAY
H. Tejada (APT), D. Strakhov (GAZ), M. Mohorič (TBV), M. Skjelmose Jensen (TFS), A. Duchesne (GFC)

## STAGE RESULTS

| POS | NAME | TEAM | TIME |
|---|---|---|---|
| 1. | P. Sagan | BOH | 4:23:18 |
| 2. | D. Impey | ISN | s.t. |
| 3. | J. S. Molano | UAD | s.t. |
| 4. | R. Janse Van Rensburg | TQA | s.t. |
| 5. | A. Kamp | TFS | s.t. |
| 6. | C. Venturini | ACT | s.t. |
| 7. | M. Kanter | DSM | s.t. |
| 8. | J. Almeida | DQT | s.t. |
| 9. | M. Valgren | EFN | s.t. |
| 10. | M. Van Gils | LTS | s.t. |
| 11. | A. Soto | EUS | s.t. |
| 12. | B. McNulty | UAD | s.t. |
| 13. | D. Smith | BEX | s.t. |
| 14. | S. Guglielmi | GFC | s.t. |
| 15. | A. Valverde | MOV | s.t. |
| 16. | W. Poels | TBV | s.t. |
| 17. | R. Cavagna | DQT | s.t. |
| 18. | H. Vanhoucke | LTS | s.t. |
| 19. | M. Louvel | ARK | s.t. |
| 20. | A. Yates | IGD | s.t. |

## GENERAL CLASSIFICATION

| POS | | NAME | TEAM | TIME |
|---|---|---|---|---|
| 1. | — | A. Yates | IGD | 23:08:45 |
| 2. | — | R. Porte | IGD | 0:45 |
| 3. | — | G. Thomas | IGD | 0:49 |

## KING OF THE MOUNTAINS

| POS | | NAME | TEAM | PTS |
|---|---|---|---|---|
| 1. | — | E. Chaves | BEX | 50 |
| 2. | — | A. Yates | IGD | 40 |
| 3. | — | K. Bouwman | TJV | 33 |

## POINTS

| POS | | NAME | TEAM | PTS |
|---|---|---|---|---|
| 1. | — | E. Chaves | BEX | 16 |
| 2. | — | A. Yates | IGD | 10 |
| 3. | — | L. Kämna | BOH | 10 |

## YOUNG RIDER

| POS | | NAME | TEAM | TIME |
|---|---|---|---|---|
| 1. | — | J. Almeida | DQT | 23:09:52 |
| 2. | — | L. Hamilton | BEX | 0:28 |
| 3. | — | H. Vanhoucke | LTS | 0:47 |

## TRIVIA
» Of Peter Sagan's 115 career wins, only five have been in Spain.

## BONUSES

| TYPE | NAME | TEAM |
|---|---|---|
| KOM 1 | M. Mohorič | TBV |
| KOM 2 | E. Gesbert | ARK |
| Sprint 1 | D. Strakhov | GAZ |
| Sprint 2 | A. Duchesne | GFC |

MARCH — WORLDTOUR MEN'S RACE

# VOLTA CICLISTA A CATALUNYA
Stage 7
28 March 2021
Barcelona–Barcelona
133km

The Volta's traditional finale, based on the Montjuich hill where many of the events took place during the 1992 Olympics, is always spectacular. On this occasion, however, the winning break went clear before the six laps of its 8km finishing circuit. There were 32 riders in it, none a threat to race leader Adam Yates. Cresting the Montjuich castle climb on the first lap, Thomas De Gendt and Matej Mohorič broke clear and set about establishing a stage-winning gap. Concerned that Mohorič might be too quick for him on the final drop off Montjuich, De Gendt attacked hard on the steepest section leading up to it and soloed away to his fifth stage win in what's one of his favourite races. Movistar tried all they could to make life difficult for Adam Yates, but the Ineos rider was relatively untroubled as he confirmed the biggest stage-race win of his career.

## WEATHER
TEMPERATURE: 17°C
WIND: E 15km/h

## PROFILE

## BREAKAWAY
H. Vanhoucke (LTS), M. Bizkarra (EUS), N. Edet (COF), S. Reichenbach (GFC), L. L. Sanchez (APT), D. De La Cruz (UAD), L. Kamna (BOH), M. Badilatti (GFC), E. Gesbert (ARK), J. Knox (DQT), C. Scotson (BEX), A. Valter (GFC), H. Pernsteiner (TBV), C. Champoussin (ACT), S. De Bod (APT), D. Smith (BEX), M. Mohorič (TBV), D. Devenyns (DQT), J. P. Lopez (TFS), M. Soler (MOV), K. Bouwman (TJV), J. Hanninen (ACT), L. Pichon (ARK), S. Samitier (MOV), D. Cataldo (MOV), I. Schelling (BOH), S. Bennett (TQA), L. Meintjes (IWG), F. Barcelo (COF), J. Černý (DQT)

## GENERAL CLASSIFICATION
| POS | | NAME | TEAM | TIME |
|---|---|---|---|---|
| 1. | – | A. Yates | IGD | 26:16:41 |
| 2. | – | R. Porte | IGD | 0:45 |
| 3. | – | G. Thomas | IGD | 0:49 |

## STAGE RESULTS
| POS | NAME | TEAM | TIME |
|---|---|---|---|
| 1. | T. De Gendt | LTS | 3:06:10 |
| 2. | M. Mohorič | TBV | 0:22 |
| 3. | A. Valter | GFC | 1:42 |
| 4. | S. Reichenbach | GFC | 1:46 |
| 5. | A. Valverde | MOV | s.t. |
| 6. | M. Woods | ISN | s.t. |
| 7. | M. Hirschi | UAD | s.t. |
| 8. | J. Almeida | DQT | s.t. |
| 9. | A. Yates | IGD | s.t. |
| 10. | C. Champoussin | ACT | s.t. |
| 11. | R. Porte | IGD | s.t. |
| 12. | N. Edet | COF | s.t. |
| 13. | B. McNulty | UAD | s.t. |
| 14. | L. L. Sanchez | APT | s.t. |
| 15. | E. Chaves | BEX | s.t. |
| 16. | H. Carthy | EFN | s.t. |
| 17. | E. Gesbert | ARK | s.t. |
| 18. | L. Hamilton | BEX | s.t. |
| 19. | W. Kelderman | BOH | s.t. |
| 20. | G. Thomas | IGD | s.t. |

## KING OF THE MOUNTAINS
| POS | | NAME | TEAM | PTS |
|---|---|---|---|---|
| 1. | – | E. Chaves | BEX | 50 |
| 2. | – | A. Yates | IGD | 40 |
| 3. | ↑19 | T. De Gendt | LTS | 38 |

## POINTS
| POS | | NAME | TEAM | PTS |
|---|---|---|---|---|
| 1. | – | E. Chaves | BEX | 16 |
| 2. | ↑20 | T. De Gendt | LTS | 13 |
| 3. | ↑2 | P. Sagan | BOH | 13 |

## YOUNG RIDER
| POS | | NAME | TEAM | TIME |
|---|---|---|---|---|
| 1. | – | J. Almeida | DQT | 26:17:46 |
| 2. | – | L. Hamilton | BEX | 0:30 |
| 3. | ↑1 | B. McNulty | UAD | 1:14 |

## BONUSES
| TYPE | NAME | TEAM |
|---|---|---|
| KOM 1 | A. Valter | GFC |
| KOM 2 | T. De Gendt | LTS |
| KOM 3 | T. De Gendt | LTS |
| KOM 4 | T. De Gendt | LTS |
| KOM 5 | T. De Gendt | LTS |
| KOM 6 | T. De Gendt | LTS |
| KOM 7 | T. De Gendt | LTS |
| Sprint 1 | P. Sagan | BOH |
| Sprint 2 | D. Smith | BEX |

## TRIVIA
» Thomas De Gendt has now won an equal number of races in France and Spain (six apiece).

MARCH  .1 MEN'S RACE

## SETTIMANA INTERNAZIONALE COPPI E BARTALI

Stage 1a
23 March 2021
Gatteo–Gatteo
97.8km

### WEATHER

TEMPERATURE | WIND
10°C | NE 22km/h

### STAGE RESULTS

| POS | NAME | TEAM | TIME |
|---|---|---|---|
| 1. | J. Mareczko | THR | 2:19:05 |
| 2. | M. Cavendish | DQT | s.t. |
| 3. | M. Mayrhofer | DSM | s.t. |
| 4. | L. Coati | T4Q | s.t. |
| 5. | E. Hayter | IGD | s.t. |
| 6. | M. Zecchin | IWM | s.t. |
| 7. | C. Rocchetta | GEF | s.t. |
| 8. | V. Albanese | EOK | s.t. |
| 9. | D. Cima | GAZ | s.t. |
| 10. | M. van Dijke | TJV | s.t. |
| 11. | T. Nencini | NAT | s.t. |
| 12. | J. Mosca | TFS | s.t. |
| 13. | D. Gabburo | BCF | s.t. |
| 14. | M. Baseggio | GEF | s.t. |
| 15. | E. A. Rubio | MOV | s.t. |
| 16. | A. González | MOV | s.t. |
| 17. | I. Van Wilder | DSM | s.t. |
| 18. | B. Swift | IGD | s.t. |
| 19. | M. Hessmann | TJV | s.t. |
| 20. | G. Brussenskiy | APT | s.t. |

### GENERAL CLASSIFICATION

| POS | NAME | TEAM | TIME |
|---|---|---|---|
| 1. | J. Mareczko | THR | 2:18:59 |
| 2. | M. Cavendish | DQT | 0:02 |
| 3. | M. Mayrhofer | DSM | 0:04 |

### KING OF THE MOUNTAINS

| POS | NAME | TEAM | PTS |
|---|---|---|---|
| 1. | R. Radice | MGK | 11 |
| 2. | F. Zandri | IWM | 10 |
| 3. | I. Garrison | DQT | 3 |

### POINTS

| POS | NAME | TEAM | PTS |
|---|---|---|---|
| 1. | J. Mareczko | THR | 10 |
| 2. | M. Cavendish | DQT | 8 |
| 3. | M. Mayrhofer | DSM | 6 |

### YOUNG RIDER

| POS | NAME | TEAM | TIME |
|---|---|---|---|
| 1. | M. Mayrhofer | DSM | 2:19:03 |
| 2. | L. Coati | T4Q | 0:02 |
| 3. | E. Hayter | IGD | s.t. |

## SETTIMANA INTERNAZIONALE COPPI E BARTALI

Stage 1b (TTT)
23 March 2021
Gatteo–Gatteo
10.8km

### WEATHER

TEMPERATURE | WIND
11°C | NE 17km/h

### STAGE RESULTS

| POS | NAME | TEAM | TIME |
|---|---|---|---|
| 1. | Israel Start-Up Nation | ISN | 11:36 |
| 2. | Astana Premier Tech | APT | 0:01 |
| 3. | Deceuninck-QuickStep | DQT | 0:02 |
| 4. | Team BikeExchange | BEX | 0:06 |
| 5. | Ineos Grenadiers | IGD | 0:08 |
| 6. | Jumbo-Visma | TJV | 0:11 |
| 7. | Italy | NAT | 0:14 |
| 8. | Movistar Team | MOV | 0:21 |
| 9. | Team Qhubeka Assos | T4Q | 0:22 |
| 10. | Trek-Segafredo | TFS | 0:23 |
| 11. | Vini Zabù | THR | 0:24 |
| 12. | Gazprom-RusVelo | GAZ | 0:30 |
| 13. | Caja Rural-Seguros RGA | CJR | s.t. |
| 14. | Team DSM | DSM | 0:32 |
| 15. | Eolo-Kometa Cycling Team | EOK | s.t. |
| 16. | Team Colpack Ballan | CPK | 0:35 |
| 17. | Russia | NAT | 0:38 |
| 18. | General Store-F.lli Curia-Essegibi | GEF | 0:42 |
| 19. | Euskaltel-Euskadi | EUS | s.t. |
| 20. | Beltrami TSA-Tre Colli | BTC | 0:43 |

### GENERAL CLASSIFICATION

| POS | NAME | TEAM | TIME |
|---|---|---|---|
| 1. ↑1 | M. Cavendish | DQT | 2:30:39 |
| 2. ↑24 | A. Dowsett | ISN | 0:02 |
| 3. ↑60 | B. Hermans | ISN | s.t. |

### KING OF THE MOUNTAINS

| POS | NAME | TEAM | PTS |
|---|---|---|---|
| 1. — | R. Radice | MGK | 11 |
| 2. — | F. Zandri | IWM | 10 |
| 3. — | I. Garrison | DQT | 3 |

### POINTS

| POS | NAME | TEAM | PTS |
|---|---|---|---|
| 1. — | J. Mareczko | THR | 10 |
| 2. — | M. Cavendish | DQT | 8 |
| 3. — | M. Mayrhofer | DSM | 6 |

### YOUNG RIDER

| POS | NAME | TEAM | TIME |
|---|---|---|---|
| 1. ↑61 | S. Berwick | ISN | 2:30:41 |
| 2. ↑11 | G. Brussenskiy | APT | 0:01 |
| 3. ↑11 | J. Romo | APT | s.t. |

MARCH .1 MEN'S RACE

## SETTIMANA INTERNAZIONALE COPPI E BARTALI
Stage 2
24 March 2021
Riccione–Sogliano al Rubicone
163.5km

### WEATHER

TEMPERATURE: 13°C  
WIND: E 19km/h

### STAGE RESULTS

| POS | NAME | TEAM | TIME |
|---|---|---|---|
| 1. | J. Vingegaard | TJV | 4:17:43 |
| 2. | I. R. Sosa | IGD | s.t. |
| 3. | N. Schultz | BEX | 0:04 |
| 4. | B. Hermans | ISN | s.t. |
| 5. | E. Hayter | IGD | s.t. |
| 6. | M. Vansevenant | DQT | 0:10 |
| 7. | I. Van Wilder | DSM | s.t. |
| 8. | M. Brenner | DSM | s.t. |
| 9. | S. Henao | T4Q | s.t. |
| 10. | J. Romo | APT | s.t. |
| 11. | N. Tesfatsion | ANS | 0:13 |
| 12. | J. Lastra | CJR | s.t. |
| 13. | M. F. Honoré | DQT | s.t. |
| 14. | E. Ravasi | EOK | s.t. |
| 15. | A. Fancellu | EOK | 0:15 |
| 16. | A. Ghebreigzabhier | TFS | s.t. |
| 17. | K. Colleoni | BEX | s.t. |
| 18. | J. Cepeda Ortiz | ANS | 0:18 |
| 19. | C. Rodriguez | IGD | 0:28 |
| 20. | M. Jorgenson | MOV | 0:31 |

### GENERAL CLASSIFICATION

| POS | NAME | TEAM | TIME |
|---|---|---|---|
| 1. ↑26 | J. Vingegaard | TJV | 6:48:25 |
| 2. ↑21 | I. R. Sosa | IGD | 0:01 |
| 3. – | B. Hermans | ISN | 0:03 |

### KING OF THE MOUNTAINS

| POS | NAME | TEAM | PTS |
|---|---|---|---|
| 1. – | M. Dina | EOK | 16 |
| 2. – | M. Petrucci | CPK | 11 |
| 3. ↓2 | R. Radice | MGK | 11 |

### POINTS

| POS | NAME | TEAM | PTS |
|---|---|---|---|
| 1. – | J. Vingegaard | TJV | 10 |
| 2. ↓1 | J. Mareczko | THR | 10 |
| 3. – | I. R. Sosa | IGD | 8 |

### YOUNG RIDER

| POS | NAME | TEAM | TIME |
|---|---|---|---|
| 1. ↑2 | J. Romo | APT | 6:48:35 |
| 2. ↑5 | E. Hayter | IGD | 0:01 |
| 3. ↑1 | M. Vansevenant | DQT | s.t. |

## SETTIMANA INTERNAZIONALE COPPI E BARTALI
Stage 3
25 March 2021
Riccione–Riccione
139km

### WEATHER

TEMPERATURE: 13°C  
WIND: E 17km/h

### STAGE RESULTS

| POS | NAME | TEAM | TIME |
|---|---|---|---|
| 1. | E. Hayter | IGD | 3:49:21 |
| 2. | S. Archbold | DQT | s.t. |
| 3. | N. Schultz | BEX | s.t. |
| 4. | J. Mosca | TFS | s.t. |
| 5. | N. Tesfatsion | ANS | s.t. |
| 6. | O. Aular | CJR | s.t. |
| 7. | V. Albanese | EOK | s.t. |
| 8. | D. Gabburo | BCF | s.t. |
| 9. | C. Scaroni | GAZ | s.t. |
| 10. | S. Velasco | GAZ | s.t. |
| 11. | J. Ayuso | CPK | s.t. |
| 12. | B. Swift | IGD | s.t. |
| 13. | M. Mayrhofer | DSM | s.t. |
| 14. | S. Ravanelli | ANS | s.t. |
| 15. | G. Brussenskiy | APT | s.t. |
| 16. | J. Romo | APT | s.t. |
| 17. | M. Jorgenson | MOV | s.t. |
| 18. | H. Mulubrhan | T4Q | s.t. |
| 19. | A. Puppio | T4Q | s.t. |
| 20. | A. Angulo | EUS | s.t. |

### GENERAL CLASSIFICATION

| POS | NAME | TEAM | TIME |
|---|---|---|---|
| 1. – | J. Vingegaard | TJV | 10:37:46 |
| 2. ↑4 | E. Hayter | IGD | 0:01 |
| 3. ↑1 | N. Schultz | BEX | s.t. |

### KING OF THE MOUNTAINS

| POS | NAME | TEAM | PTS |
|---|---|---|---|
| 1. – | M. Dina | EOK | 16 |
| 2. – | M. Petrucci | CPK | 11 |
| 3. – | R. Radice | MGK | 11 |

### POINTS

| POS | NAME | TEAM | PTS |
|---|---|---|---|
| 1. ↑3 | E. Hayter | IGD | 18 |
| 2. ↑4 | N. Schultz | BEX | 12 |
| 3. ↓2 | J. Vingegaard | TJV | 10 |

### YOUNG RIDER

| POS | NAME | TEAM | TIME |
|---|---|---|---|
| 1. ↑1 | E. Hayter | IGD | 10:37:47 |
| 2. ↓1 | J. Romo | APT | 0:09 |
| 3. – | M. Vansevenant | DQT | 0:10 |

MARCH .1 MEN'S RACE

## SETTIMANA INTERNAZIONALE COPPI E BARTALI

Stage 4
26 March 2021
San Marino–San Marino
154.8km

### WEATHER

TEMPERATURE: 13°C
WIND: NE 11km/h

### STAGE RESULTS

| POS | NAME | TEAM | TIME |
|---|---|---|---|
| 1. | J. Vingegaard | TJV | 4:26:37 |
| 2. | J. Romo | APT | s.t. |
| 3. | N. Schultz | BEX | s.t. |
| 4. | E. Hayter | IGD | s.t. |
| 5. | M. Vansevenant | DQT | s.t. |
| 6. | J. Ayuso | CPK | s.t. |
| 7. | B. Hermans | ISN | 0:02 |
| 8. | N. Tesfatsion | ANS | s.t. |
| 9. | S. Henao | T4Q | s.t. |
| 10. | A. Tiberi | TFS | s.t. |
| 11. | A. Cuadros Morata | CJR | s.t. |
| 12. | M. F. Honoré | DQT | s.t. |
| 13. | I. Van Wilder | DSM | s.t. |
| 14. | A. Ghebreigzabhier | TFS | s.t. |
| 15. | M. Jorgenson | MOV | s.t. |
| 16. | I. R. Sosa | IGD | 0:05 |
| 17. | J. Lastra | CJR | 0:07 |
| 18. | K. Colleoni | BEX | 0:09 |
| 19. | E. Ravasi | EOK | 0:13 |
| 20. | R. Contreras | APT | 0:14 |

### GENERAL CLASSIFICATION

| POS | NAME | TEAM | TIME |
|---|---|---|---|
| 1. — | J. Vingegaard | TJV | 15:04:13 |
| 2. ↑1 | N. Schultz | BEX | 0:07 |
| 3. ↓1 | E. Hayter | IGD | 0:11 |

### KING OF THE MOUNTAINS

| POS | NAME | TEAM | PTS |
|---|---|---|---|
| 1. — | M. Dina | EOK | 28 |
| 2. ↑4 | A. Osorio | CJR | 27 |
| 3. ↑2 | A. Nibali | TFS | 18 |

### POINTS

| POS | NAME | TEAM | PTS |
|---|---|---|---|
| 1. — | E. Hayter | IGD | 23 |
| 2. ↑1 | J. Vingegaard | TJV | 20 |
| 3. ↓1 | N. Schultz | BEX | 18 |

### YOUNG RIDER

| POS | NAME | TEAM | TIME |
|---|---|---|---|
| 1. — | E. Hayter | IGD | 15:04:24 |
| 2. — | J. Romo | APT | 0:03 |
| 3. — | M. Vansevenant | DQT | 0:10 |

## SETTIMANA INTERNAZIONALE COPPI E BARTALI

Stage 5
27 March 2021
Forlì–Forlì
166.2km

### WEATHER

TEMPERATURE: 18°C
WIND: S 11km/h

### STAGE RESULTS

| POS | NAME | TEAM | TIME |
|---|---|---|---|
| 1. | M. F. Honoré | DQT | 3:59:40 |
| 2. | J. Vingegaard | TJV | s.t. |
| 3. | S. Archbold | DQT | 0:19 |
| 4. | E. Hayter | IGD | s.t. |
| 5. | J. Ayuso | CPK | s.t. |
| 6. | J. Lastra | CJR | s.t. |
| 7. | I. Van Wilder | DSM | s.t. |
| 8. | J. Romo | APT | s.t. |
| 9. | P. Double | MGK | s.t. |
| 10. | B. Hermans | ISN | s.t. |
| 11. | A. Tiberi | TFS | s.t. |
| 12. | S. Henao | T4Q | s.t. |
| 13. | N. Schultz | BEX | s.t. |
| 14. | M. Vansevenant | DQT | s.t. |
| 15. | A. Ghebreigzabhier | TFS | s.t. |
| 16. | J. Cepeda Ortiz | ANS | s.t. |
| 17. | S. Velasco | GAZ | 0:36 |
| 18. | J. Mosca | TFS | s.t. |
| 19. | D. Gabburo | BCF | s.t. |
| 20. | H. Vandenabeele | DSM | s.t. |

### GENERAL CLASSIFICATION

| POS | NAME | TEAM | TIME |
|---|---|---|---|
| 1. — | J. Vingegaard | TJV | 19:03:47 |
| 2. ↑6 | M. F. Honoré | DQT | 0:22 |
| 3. ↓1 | N. Schultz | BEX | 0:32 |

### KING OF THE MOUNTAINS

| POS | NAME | TEAM | PTS |
|---|---|---|---|
| 1. ↑1 | A. Osorio | CJR | 32 |
| 2. ↓1 | M. Dina | EOK | 28 |
| 3. — | A. Nibali | TFS | 18 |

### POINTS

| POS | NAME | TEAM | PTS |
|---|---|---|---|
| 1. ↑1 | J. Vingegaard | TJV | 28 |
| 2. ↓1 | E. Hayter | IGD | 28 |
| 3. — | N. Schultz | BEX | 18 |

### YOUNG RIDER

| POS | NAME | TEAM | TIME |
|---|---|---|---|
| 1. — | E. Hayter | IGD | 19:04:23 |
| 2. — | J. Romo | APT | 0:03 |
| 3. — | M. Vansevenant | DQT | 0:10 |

MARCH  WORLDTOUR MEN'S RACE

# BRUGGE–DE PANNE
24 March 2021
Brugge–De Panne
203.9km

## WEATHER

**TEMPERATURE**
13°C

**WIND**
SW 17km/h

## PROFILE

BRUGGE — DE PANNE

## BREAKAWAY

W. Van Elzakker (THR), R. Apers (SVB), G. Thijssen (LTS), E. Nordsaeter Resell (UXT), B. Peak (BEX), A. Gougeard (ACT)

An early breakaway of six riders was brought back with more than 76km to go, and there was a brief lull for a few kilometres until Sebastián Mora attacked alone. The Spaniard would have preferred some company as he led the race onto the local laps, but it was the perfect outcome for the favourites. Mora managed a 25-second gap before the peloton started eating into his advantage, more as a consequence of their fight for position than any concerted chase. The leader was brought back with just under 50km remaining and the peloton kept the pace high as they entered the polder land (fields reclaimed from the sea through construction of dikes) of De Moeren for the last time. Lotto Soudal put the hammer down but they visibly wilted with the realisation the wind simply wasn't strong enough. Qhubeka Assos took over then but succeeded only in using up their resources for the now inevitable sprint. There were a few attacks inside the last 30km – first from Lluís Mas and Davide Martinelli, and then Brent Van Moer – but it was all together by 10km to go and the last passage of the dunes of Hoge Blekker. On the run-in, Tosh Van der Sande accelerated off the front and it was up to Deceuninck-QuickStep to chase him down, giving them the advantage under the *flamme rouge*. It went perfectly for Sam Bennett, who surged off Michael Mørkøv's wheel to take his first-ever WorldTour one-day victory.

## RESULTS

| POS | NAME | TEAM | TIME |
|---|---|---|---|
| 1. | S. Bennett | DQT | 4:27:40 |
| 2. | J. Philipsen | AFC | s.t. |
| 3. | P. Ackermann | BOH | s.t. |
| 4. | G. Nizzolo | TQA | s.t. |
| 5. | T. Dupont | WVA | s.t. |
| 6. | H. Hofstetter | ISN | s.t. |
| 7. | C. Bol | DSM | s.t. |
| 8. | M. Mørkøv | DQT | s.t. |
| 9. | E. Viviani | COF | s.t. |
| 10. | S. Aniołkowski | WVA | s.t. |
| 11. | C. Russo | ARK | s.t. |
| 12. | L. Manzin | TDE | s.t. |
| 13. | J. Lecroq | BBK | s.t. |
| 14. | F. Gaviria | UAD | s.t. |
| 15. | F. Vermeersch | LTS | s.t. |
| 16. | S. Colbrelli | TBV | s.t. |
| 17. | D. McLay | ARK | s.t. |
| 18. | K. Halvorsen | UXT | s.t. |
| 19. | M. Moschetti | TFS | s.t. |
| 20. | G. Van Hoecke | ACT | s.t. |

## TRIVIA

» Sam Bennett has never previously in his career won five races before the end of March.

WORLDTOUR WOMEN'S RACE

# BRUGGE–DE PANNE
25 March 2021
Brugge–De Panne
158.8km

Held in pancake-flat West Flanders, Brugge–De Panne was shaped by crosswinds in the exposed area of De Moeren, tearing the peloton apart and leaving just 12 riders fighting for victory. Grace Brown (Team BikeExchange) attacked in the final and held off the chasers to take her first Women's WorldTour victory. Racing into a headwind on the first stretch from Brugge to De Panne meant that no escapees ever got far, and the peloton entered the two laps of a 45km circuit around De Panne together. The first time through De Moeren with 80km to go, the peloton broke apart into two groups, but things came back together. On the final lap, a crash on a narrow road held up many riders and split the race, with strong crosswinds wreaking even more havoc. By 32km from the finish, only 13 riders remained in the first group, though Lisa Brennauer (Ceratizit-WNT) crashed out of contention around the 20km mark. Despite this, the front group kept a gap of 30 seconds on the next group, where several sprinters' teams were chasing hard. Brown then took the rest of the group by surprise with an attack when 10km remained, quickly building a sizable gap as the chase did not get organised for a while. In the end, Brown crossed the line 7 seconds ahead of Emma Norsgaard (Movistar) who won the sprint for second place against Jolien D'hoore (Team SD Worx).

## WEATHER

TEMPERATURE: 11°C
WIND: W 19km/h

## PROFILE

BRUGGE — DE PANNE

## BREAKAWAY

J. D'hoore (SDW), A. Pieters (SDW), L. Hanson (TFS), C. Hosking (TFS), E. Norsgaard (MOV), A. Biannic (MOV), G. Brown (BEX), A. Barnes (CSR), K. Wild (WNT), J. Leth (WNT), L. Brennauer (WNT), E. Balsamo (VAL), L. Kopecky (LIV)

## RESULTS

| POS | NAME | TEAM | TIME |
|---|---|---|---|
| 1. | G. Brown | BEX | 4:03:17 |
| 2. | E. Norsgaard | MOV | 0:07 |
| 3. | J. D'hoore | SDW | s.t. |
| 4. | L. Kopecky | LIV | s.t. |
| 5. | E. Balsamo | VAL | s.t. |
| 6. | K. Wild | WNT | s.t. |
| 7. | C. Hosking | TFS | s.t. |
| 8. | A. Barnes | CSR | s.t. |
| 9. | A. Pieters | SDW | s.t. |
| 10. | J. Leth | WNT | s.t. |
| 11. | A. Biannic | MOV | s.t. |
| 12. | L. Hanson | TFS | 0:25 |
| 13. | L. Wiebes | DSM | 0:40 |
| 14. | E. Moberg | DRP | s.t. |
| 15. | C. Majerus | SDW | s.t. |
| 16. | S. Borgli | FDJ | s.t. |
| 17. | A. Sierra | MNX | s.t. |
| 18. | K. Ragusa | MNX | s.t. |
| 19. | M. de Zoete | NXG | s.t. |
| 20. | F. Markus | PHV | s.t. |

## TRIVIA

» This was Grace Brown's first WorldTour win.

MARCH  WORLDTOUR MEN'S RACE

# E3 CLASSIC
26 March 2021
Harelbeke–Harelbeke
203.9km

Considered the dress rehearsal for the Tour of Flanders, the E3 Saxo Bank Classic always delivers non-stop action in one of cycling's most beloved heartlands. The peloton took on the first of 17 *hellingen* together before a 12-strong breakaway formed, including André Greipel and former winner Niki Terpstra, but their advantage was short-lived. Deceuninck-QuickStep performed a team time trial-esque effort onto the Taaienberg, setting up attacks and ultimately bringing back the breakaway. The combined strengths of Deceuninck and the stiff wind forced splits in the race, culminating in an attack by Kasper Asgreen with 66km to go. As the Dane enjoyed his breathing space out front, the small group of favourites fought each other behind while defending champion Zdenek Štybar and Florian Sénéchal policed things. Then, with little over 25km remaining, Yves Lampaert made it across to the chasers with Dylan van Baarle, handing Deceuninck four cards to play – at least until Lampaert punctured. What's more, the only work they were required to do was mark their rivals, giving Mathieu van der Poel and Wout van Aert the lion's share of the work. The latter rode himself out of contention by the time Asgreen was caught with 12km left, the Dane tucking himself onto last wheel. After 7km of well-earned recovery, Asgreen accelerated hard from the back. With two teammates in the group, there wasn't anyone with the resources to follow and the Danish national champion soloed to a famous victory, rewarding a phenomenal team effort.

## TRIVIA

» Kasper Asgreen is the first rider to be presented his medal by a podium robot, as the UCI looked to enforce their ban on hugs.

## WEATHER

**TEMPERATURE**  12°C
**WIND**  SW 29km/h

## PROFILE

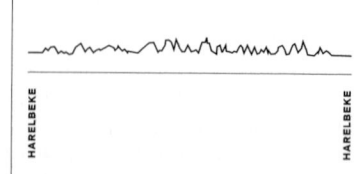

HARELBEKE — HARELBEKE

## BREAKAWAY

N. Terpstra (TDE), A. Greipel (ISN), T. Van der Hoorn (IWG), M. Haller (TBV), J. Milan (TBV), J. Wallays (COF), J. Van den Berg (EFN), A. Brunel (GFC), J. Jacobs (MOV), L. Mas (MOV), L. De Vylder (SVB), R. Tiller (UXT)

## RESULTS

| POS | NAME | TEAM | TIME |
|---|---|---|---|
| 1. | K. Asgreen | DQT | 4:42:56 |
| 2. | F. Sénéchal | DQT | 0:32 |
| 3. | M. van der Poel | AFC | s.t. |
| 4. | O. Naesen | ACT | s.t. |
| 5. | Z. Štybar | DQT | s.t. |
| 6. | G. Van Avermaet | ACT | s.t. |
| 7. | D. van Baarle | IGD | s.t. |
| 8. | M. Hoelgaard | UXT | 1:28 |
| 9. | G. Vermeersch | AFC | 1:30 |
| 10. | M. Haller | TBV | s.t. |
| 11. | W. van Aert | TJV | s.t. |
| 12. | A. Turgis | TDE | 1:34 |
| 13. | Y. Lampaert | DQT | 2:12 |
| 14. | J. Stuyven | TFS | s.t. |
| 15. | T. Benoot | DSM | s.t. |
| 16. | F. Vermeersch | LTS | 2:47 |
| 17. | J. de Buyst | LTS | s.t. |
| 18. | M. Trentin | UAD | s.t. |
| 19. | D. Claeys | TQA | s.t. |
| 20. | S. Küng | GFC | s.t. |

MARCH    WORLDTOUR MEN'S RACE

## GENT–WEVELGEM
28 March 2021
Ypres–Wevelgem
250km

Wind played a key role in the race through Flanders Fields, cutting echelons across the road and allowing a very strong group of 25 to go clear of the peloton with 173km still to race, joining the early breakaway after about 20km. Nearly all the favourites were there, with the notable exception of 2020 winner Mads Pedersen and Milan–Sanremo champion Jasper Stuyven, whose team joined Bora-Hansgrohe on the sidelines after a positive Covid-19 test. It was Wout van Aert who made the decisive move on the second ascent of the Kemmelberg, jettisoning the passengers in the lead group, which had 54km left to race. His teammate Nathan Van Hooydonck made the selection, along with Stefan Küng, Michael Matthews, Giacomo Nizzolo, Danny van Poppel, Matteo Trentin, Sam Bennett and Sonny Colbrelli. They took almost a minute's advantage onto the fast open road back to Wevelgem with 33km remaining, but Bennett looked to be in some discomfort off the back and he threw up before clawing his way back into the group. He lasted another 15km before dropping out of contention along with Van Poppel, as Anthony Turgis accelerated out of the fracturing chase group, but he had his work cut out. In the closing kilometres, Van Aert benefited from teammate Van Hooydonck's ability to both drive the pace and wear down his rivals with testing attacks. The Jumbo-Visma leader carried his freshness into the finishing straight, sprinting right down the middle and leaving Nizzolo and Trentin to find second and third in his slipstream. ⓚⓃ

### TRIVIA
» This was Wout van Aert's 20th career victory – and his eighth in his native Belgium.

### WEATHER

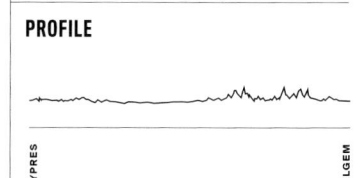

TEMPERATURE    WIND
12°C           SW 32km/h

### PROFILE
YPRES — WEVELGEM

### BREAKAWAY
S. Bissegger (EFN), J. Rutsch (EFN), Y. Federov (APT), L. Rex (BWB), S. Bennett (DQT), J. De Buyst (LTS), D. Van Poppel (IWG), W. van Aert (TJV), N. Van Hooydonck (TJV), S. Colbrelli (TBV), J. Bauer (BEX), L. Mezgec (BEX), M. Matthews (BEX), R. Stannard (BEX), I. Erviti (MOV), L. Mas (MOV), J. Sütterlin (MOV), G. Nizzolo (TQA), S. E. Bystrøm (UAD), M. Trentin (UAD), S. Küng (GFC), M. Golas (IGD), T. Dupont (BWB), J. Lecroq (BBK), C. Lemoine (BBK)

### RESULTS
| POS | NAME | TEAM | TIME |
|---|---|---|---|
| 1. | W. van Aert | TJV | 5:45:11 |
| 2. | G. Nizzolo | TQA | s.t. |
| 3. | M. Trentin | UAD | s.t. |
| 4. | S. Colbrelli | TBV | s.t. |
| 5. | M. Matthews | BEX | s.t. |
| 6. | S. Küng | GFC | s.t. |
| 7. | N. Van Hooydonck | TJV | 0:03 |
| 8. | D. van Baarle | IGD | 0:52 |
| 9. | A. Turgis | TDE | 0:54 |
| 10. | G. Vermeersch | AFC | 1:25 |
| 11. | J. Lecroq | BBK | s.t. |
| 12. | G. Van Avermaet | ACT | s.t. |
| 13. | S. E. Bystrøm | UAD | s.t. |
| 14. | Y. Lampaert | DQT | s.t. |
| 15. | J. Bauer | BEX | s.t. |
| 16. | O. Naesen | ACT | 1:27 |
| 17. | O. Doull | IGD | 1:52 |
| 18. | I. García Cortina | MOV | 1:56 |
| 19. | D. Van Gestel | TDE | 1:57 |
| 20. | B. Van Lerberghe | DQT | s.t. |

MARCH  WORLDTOUR WOMEN'S RACE

# GENT–WEVELGEM
28 March 2021
Ypres–Wevelgem
141.7km

## WEATHER

TEMPERATURE  WIND
12°C  SW 32km/h

## PROFILE

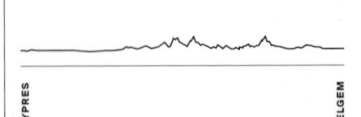

YPRES  WEVELGEM

Despite echelons and attacks, the race came down to a sprint where Jumbo-Visma's Marianne Vos followed up on Wout van Aert's victory in the men's race to make it two from two for the Dutch team. The first passage of the steep and cobbled Kemmelberg led to a front group of 17 riders, but the race quickly came back together as there was still a long way to go. The Plugstreet gravel sections did not change the race as nobody wanted to push the pace. The second time up the Kemmelberg, Elisa Longo Borghini (Trek-Segafredo) strung out the peloton, and in the kilometres after the climb, several groups united to form one peloton of 20 riders. Anna Henderson (Jumbo-Visma) attacked from this group, gaining an advantage of 20 seconds into Ypres where the route turned east towards Wevelgem, giving a cross-tailwind. Trek-Segafredo put the race in the gutter, quickly catching Henderson and putting three riders into the first echelon of eight. Longo Borghini got away 20km from the finish as her teammates left a gap behind her, and only Soraya Paladin (Liv Racing) was able to bridge. The two Italians cooperated well until Paladin was too exhausted to contribute much to the work, and they were caught on the final kilometre. Vos then started her sprint early with 300 metres to go, holding off Lotte Kopecky and Lisa Brennauer for the win.

## RESULTS

| POS | NAME | TEAM | TIME |
|---|---|---|---|
| 1. | M. Vos | JVW | 3:45:08 |
| 2. | L. Kopecky | LIV | s.t. |
| 3. | L. Brennauer | WNT | s.t. |
| 4. | E. Balsamo | VAL | s.t. |
| 5. | M. Bastianelli | ALE | s.t. |
| 6. | E. Fahlin | FDJ | s.t. |
| 7. | K. Faulkner | TIB | s.t. |
| 8. | S. Roy | BEX | s.t. |
| 9. | E. Norsgaard | MOV | s.t. |
| 10. | L. Stephens | TIB | s.t. |
| 11. | A. Pieters | SDW | s.t. |
| 12. | L. Lippert | DSM | s.t. |
| 13. | M. Reusser | ALE | s.t. |
| 14. | K. Ragusa | MNX | s.t. |
| 15. | A. Sierra | MNX | s.t. |
| 16. | M. Novolodskaia | MNX | s.t. |
| 17. | E. Deignan | TFS | s.t. |
| 18. | H. Barnes | CSR | s.t. |
| 19. | F. Mackaij | DSM | s.t. |
| 20. | E. van Dijk | TFS | s.t. |

## TRIVIA

» This was Marianne Vos's 232nd career victory – and Jumbo-Visma women's first.

MARCH  .1 MEN'S RACE

## CHOLET – PAYS DE LA LOIRE
28 March 2021
Cholet–Cholet
201.8km

## WEATHER

TEMPERATURE  WIND
15°C  SW 19km/h

## RESULTS

| POS | NAME | TEAM | TIME |
|---|---|---|---|
| 1. | E. Viviani | COF | 4:43:35 |
| 2. | J. Aberasturi | CJR | s.t. |
| 3. | P. Barbier | DKO | s.t. |
| 4. | D. Godon | ACT | s.t. |
| 5. | M. Sarreau | ACT | s.t. |
| 6. | A. Vogel | SRA | s.t. |
| 7. | M. Bostock | DHB | s.t. |
| 8. | T. Boudat | ARK | s.t. |
| 9. | R. Cardis | AUB | s.t. |
| 10. | M. Malucelli | ANS | s.t. |
| 11. | M. Lammertink | IWG | s.t. |
| 12. | P. A. Coté | RLY | s.t. |
| 13. | N. Bonifazio | TDE | s.t. |
| 14. | S. Aniołkowski | BWB | s.t. |
| 15. | J. Tesson | AUB | s.t. |
| 16. | J. Ezquerra | BBH | s.t. |
| 17. | D. Kowalski | XRL | s.t. |
| 18. | T. Kongstad | RIW | s.t. |
| 19. | J. Hansen | RIW | s.t. |
| 20. | J. Leveau | XRL | s.t. |

MARCH    WORLDTOUR MEN'S RACE

# DWARS DOOR VLAANDEREN
31 March 2021
Roeselare–Waregem
184.1km

## WEATHER

TEMPERATURE  WIND
10°C         SE 11km/h

## PROFILE

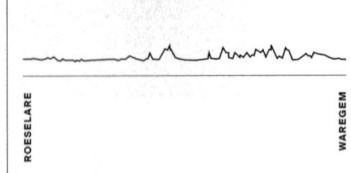

ROESELARE — WAREGEM

The final build-up before the Tour of Flanders saw the likes of Mathieu van der Poel, Julian Alaphilippe and Greg Van Avermaet in attendance. Elia Viviani and Davide Ballerini were two of the fast men caught out early on in a crash off to the side of a cobbled sector, and they may have stood a chance at taking the victory had it not been for a certain Ineos Grenadier. No, not Tom Pidcock, who was shot out the back just as his teammate Dylan van Baarle was going off the front with around 50km to the line. The likes of Van Avermaet began to tussle to get back on terms with 30km remaining, yet this main group of contenders were more concerned with those around them than the Dutchman off the front, given that he was less than a minute out of their reach. Even Mathieu van der Poel's white shorts couldn't stem his fatigue as Van Baarle tirelessly pushed on, defending his advantage until the finish line. It was a deserved win for the man so often employed in service of others' victories. Christophe Laporte and Tim Merlier led the charge behind, crossing the line 26 seconds later.

## BREAKAWAY

E. Hayter (IGD), J. Wallays (COF), F. Vermeersch (LTS)

## RESULTS

| POS | NAME | TEAM | TIME |
|---|---|---|---|
| 1. | D. van Baarle | IGD | 3:58:59 |
| 2. | C. Laporte | COF | 0:26 |
| 3. | T. Merlier | AFC | s.t. |
| 4. | Y. Lampaert | DQT | s.t. |
| 5. | T. Van der Sande | LTS | s.t. |
| 6. | A. Kristoff | UAD | s.t. |
| 7. | G. Van Avermaet | ACT | s.t. |
| 8. | A. Turgis | TDE | s.t. |
| 9. | F. Sénéchal | DQT | s.t. |
| 10. | J. Stuyven | TFS | s.t. |
| 11. | E. Hayter | IGD | s.t. |
| 12. | B. van Poppel | IWG | s.t. |
| 13. | L. Durbridge | BEX | s.t. |
| 14. | B. Coquard | BBK | s.t. |
| 15. | G. Nizzolo | TQA | s.t. |
| 16. | J. Warlop | SVB | s.t. |
| 17. | A. Livyns | BWB | s.t. |
| 18. | H. Haussler | TBV | s.t. |
| 19. | O. Naesen | ACT | s.t. |
| 20. | M. Trentin | UAD | s.t. |

## TRIVIA

» This was Dylan van Baarle's fifth victory of his 11-year career so far, and only his second at WorldTour level.

# THE RACEMAKER

BY TOMAS VAN DEN SPIEGEL

If you're born in Flanders, there's a bigger chance than anywhere else in the world that you will become a cycling fan. That's exactly what happened to me.

My earliest cycling memory dates back to the sacred year of 1986. My uncle took me to go and see the Under-23 Tour of Flanders. It was a hectic day in which we did the traditional thing of trying to watch the riders come past as many times as possible, before getting to the finish in time to see Edwig Van Hooydonck take the win. Van Hooydonck would go on to become a local hero by repeating his feat in the professional race in 1989 and 1991.

My education as a cycling fan was further defined, at least in my eyes, by the dominance of the Panasonic team of Peter Post, Eric Vanderaerden, Eddy Planckaert and all the others. Their kit was beautiful and their Mercedes cars set them apart from the rest. And, of course, I clearly remember the great LeMond–Fignon duel at the 1989 Tour de France.

I would have loved to become a cyclist. They're the real heroes in Flanders. But my talent lay elsewhere, namely on a basketball court. That led to a professional career that lasted 18 years, during which I experienced cycling passively. I was a passionate fan of the sport, and would never miss a big race, especially not the *Ronde van Vlaanderen*, or Tour of Flanders.

There was not a single bit of me that imagined that the course my life had taken would one day intersect with the cycling world in the way it has done. But after several twists and turns, I find myself enormously grateful to be in a position where I can help to build cycling. It is something so close to our hearts, something that we in Flanders consider to be a part of who we are. It's often said that cycling in Flanders is a religion, and that's not far from the truth. Not a day goes by without cycling featuring prominently in the newspapers. And for most of us the names Koppenberg, Oude Kwaremont and Muur van Geraardsbergen mean so much more than just a series of cobbled climbs to be visited and ticked off a bucket list.

At Flanders Classics we are involved in about 70 to 80 events a year that revolve around cycling. We're not the biggest professional cycling organiser in the world – we don't have a Tour de France or a Giro d'Italia, for example – but we do aim to be the most inspiring and innovative for all fans, regardless of their age, race or gender. Sport in general has become part of the entertainment industry in recent years and the battle for fans' attention is very fierce. That's a boat that cycling in general simply cannot afford to miss, and we at Flanders Classics in particular owe it to ourselves to challenge one another to innovate, rejuvenate and become more and more inclusive.

The Ronde is by far our biggest event (with the exception of the Road World Championships 2021, but we don't organise them every year!). We have seen the Ronde grow year by year on all fronts. Every spring around a million people gather by the side of the road to try and catch a glimpse of their heroes.

In 2011 to we took the bold decision to make Oudenaarde the centre of the experience for 2012, with three climbs of the Oude Kwaremont and two of the Paterberg, which meant that the Muur van Geraardsbergen was no longer the final obstacle. It was met with a lot of misunderstanding at the time, but it has since proved to be entirely the right decision. The thing is that when you touch the race, you are actually touching the identity of the Flemish people. But such emotions should never stand in the way of progress and the sport's best interests. Over the last ten years there has been a steady rise in the crowd sizes, with more for them all to experience, and every year the race has provided an opportunity for the best riders to race it in their own way.

I made my debut at the Ronde – sadly not as a rider but as an organiser – in 2019. The men's edition was won by Alberto Bettiol, with Marta Bastianelli taking the women's race. It was, for Bettiol, a first-ever professional win. But even though he had been riding well all spring, including finishing fourth in Harelbeke a week earlier, his victory was not enjoyed as much by the fans as if, say, Greg Van Avermaet or a rider from a Belgian team had won. But, as an organiser, you try to look at things in a more rational way. In the context of hosting an international race, having two Italian winners could hardly be a bad thing. And in the meantime, Alberto has of course gone on to become an absolutely top-class rider, as well as being a fantastic ambassador for the Ronde.

Now we are almost three years and two editions of the race further on: two editions that will be recorded in the annals of history as having been raced without a crowd. But two editions that also signalled the definitive breakthrough of a clutch of superstars of today's global cycling: Wout van Aert, Mathieu van der Poel, Julian Alaphilippe and Kasper Asgreen. Two editions that have also put us on the map, that have shown us to be a strong organisation. Not even a global pandemic, with its first and second waves, could stop us – not even when others, like Paris–Roubaix, were repeatedly halted.

But this year's edition was even more challenging than the previous year. We had managed, in October 2020, to get cycling fans to stay at home. We had done it once. But how do you do that twice? The discipline shown by the fans last year in not coming to the race and only following it on television showed just how important we Flemish think the Ronde is. Of course, none of this would have been possible without the support of the authorities, the media and the virologists, who were all too aware that the Ronde – even without fans by the side of the road – would be a welcome diversion after months of lockdown. We consistently referred to those races of October 2020 (we also organised the Gent–Wevelgem, the Brabantse Pijl and the Scheldeprijs during that period) as our test events for 2021. People got tired of hearing me recite over and over again in newspapers or on the television: 'Stay home, stay home and stay home!' We knew that if we could all pull together to do this, then there would be no hesitation from the government's side in allowing us to organise the entire Flemish spring of 2021. And that's exactly what happened.

But in 2021 – even more so than in 2020, when I had been proud and happy just to have been able to organise the race – I couldn't help thinking one thing: if only these stars of cycling could tackle the Oude Kwaremont flanked by two walls of people shouting their encouragement and with the smell of chips and beer. We got nothing of the sort. It was surreal. A deafening silence, broken only by the sound of the riders' breathing and their gearsets working.

The best photographers from across the world were producing beautiful imagery and, on television, the race was still going strong. In fact, it had never been watched more on TV. Personally, I had never followed more of the race with my own eyes than I did in this edition, not even when I had been a fan. The climbs of the Flemish Ardennes were so empty that I could pass easily from one spot to the next, and watch from a number of different places. I saw the riders at the start, in Sint-Niklaas, on the Paddestraat, three times up the Oude Kwaremont, twice on the Hotond, on the Steenbeekdries and then at the finish. But this wasn't what we wanted. We wanted the public, the emotion. We hoped we'd never repeat our little trick again. Every day I cross my fingers that it'll never happen like that again.

And yet, there were a number of reasons to be very proud of the 2021 edition of the Ronde. It wasn't just the men's race (and what a bear Kasper Asgreen is – Wout, your turn will come!), but also the women's race, won by Annemiek van Vleuten. Annemiek and I share the same very ambitious but also rational view of the development and huge potential of women's cycling. It starts with respectful organisation: what you provide for the men, you should also provide for the women. But it's also about the constant search for better and longer broadcasts and more optimal TV slots, generating extra attention and attracting additional resources to the sport in every possible way. I couldn't have wished for a better winner than Annemiek, who did it again ten years after her first victory at the Ronde.

The 2021 Tour of Flanders will also be remembered as the edition where, after lengthy negotiations, we were able to announce that we would be reinstating a traditional piece of the Ronde's past. From 2022 onwards, the start of the race will alternate between Antwerp and Bruges, its former start city. There's no doubt about what this will mean to people from Bruges and its surrounds, because the loss of the annual start to *Vlaanderens Mooiste* (Flanders' Most Beautiful) in 2017 is still a sensitive issue there. This new formula will allow us to be creative with the route and make even more Flemings periodically happy with a passage of the race through their neighbourhood. It's a win–win–win.

2021 is also the year in which we (and others, by the way, not just us) really took important steps in the field of security, not just at the Ronde but at other races too. We rethought all our processes and implemented them successfully. Because, if there is one thing that had kept me awake at night all year, it was the thought that something might happen to the riders in one of our races, or even to the public, and that we hadn't done everything in our power to prevent it. For the time being, racing still takes place on public roads and these are becoming less and less suitable for professional cycling. Because of the increasing traffic volume and the corresponding structural interventions designed for general traffic safety, the roads are increasingly unsafe for the peloton. This is an issue that requires more than ad hoc thinking. It needs the stakeholders from the cycling world, together with government, to anticipate problems and give them due consideration. And that would be good for my sleeping pattern!

The Ronde is the Ronde. It belongs to everyone, and everyone is proud to be a small cog in this great machine. Thousands of people work on it every year. When I had a beer on the Sunday night after the race, I enjoyed a feeling of satisfaction and passion that I don't think I could have matched in any other job. Ever since I stopped playing basketball I have said that the trap most professional athletes fall into is trying to replicate the feeling of victory in their later lives. That first blissful minute after an important win is so unmatchable for the rest of their lives that retired sportspeople often mount a comeback, successfully or not. You have to be able to let go of that feeling in order to be successful in your second career. It's a feeling that will probably never return, so don't go looking for it again. That said, I found a feeling that finished a pretty close second. In fact, it was only just beaten on the line.

# APRIL

New UCI regulations came into force at the beginning of April, to almost universal ridicule from the teams and the fans of the sport. Gone was the 'super tuck' descending position, and gone too was the tradition of riders throwing bottles for fans by the side of the road to collect. It didn't take long for riders to fall foul of both regulations. If the rule changes made the racing experience altered, the race programme was much more familiar, as the cobbled Classics gave way to the Ardennes race programme for both the women and the men. In Spain, the Volta al País Vasco provided the star attraction for stage racers.

| DATE | RACE TITLE | LOCATION | UCI CODE | PAGE |
|---|---|---|---|---|
| 3 April | GP Miguel Indurain | Spain | 1.Pro | 100 |
| 4 April | Tour of Flanders | Belgium | 1.UWT | 102 |
| 4 April | Tour of Flanders | Belgium | 1.WWT | 104 |
| 4 April | Trophée Harmonie Mutuelle | France | 1.1 | 105 |
| 5–10 April | Itzulia Basque Country | Spain | 2.UWT | 106 |
| 7 April | Scheldeprijs | Netherlands/Belgium | 1.Pro | 112 |
| 11–18 April | Presidential Tour of Turkey | Turkey | 2.Pro | 113 |
| 14 April | De Brabantse Pijl | Belgium | 1.Pro | 117 |
| 14–18 April | Volta a la Comunitat Valenciana | Spain | 2.Pro | 118 |
| 18 April | Amstel Gold Race | Netherlands | 1.UWT | 121 |
| 18 April | Amstel Gold Race | Netherlands | 1.WWT | 122 |
| 19–23 April | Tour of the Alps | Austria/Italy | 2.Pro | 123 |
| 21 April | La Flèche Wallonne | Belgium | 1.UWT | 126 |
| 21 April | La Flèche Wallonne | Belgium | 1.WWT | 127 |
| 22–25 April | Belgrade Banjaluka | Serbia/Bosnia & Herzegovina | 2.1 | 128 |
| 25 April | Liège–Bastogne–Liège | Belgium | 1.UWT | 130 |
| 25 April | Liège–Bastogne–Liège | Belgium | 1.WWT | 132 |
| 27 April–2 May | Tour de Romandie | Switzerland | 2.UWT | 133 |
| 30 April–2 May | Vuelta Asturias | Spain | 2.1 | 139 |

APRIL — PRO MEN'S RACE

# GP MIGUEL INDURAIN

3 April 2021
Estella–Estella
203.2km

## WEATHER

TEMPERATURE: 15°C
WIND: NW 33km/h

## RESULTS

| POS | NAME | TEAM | TIME |
|---|---|---|---|
| 1. | A. Valverde | MOV | 5:10:47 |
| 2. | A. Lutsenko | APT | 0:06 |
| 3. | L. L. Sanchez | APT | 0:15 |
| 4. | P. Bilbao | TBV | 0:17 |
| 5. | É. Gesbert | ARK | 0:18 |
| 6. | K. Neilands | ISN | 0:21 |
| 7. | B. Mollema | TFS | s.t. |
| 8. | Je. Herrada | COF | s.t. |
| 9. | O. Fraile | APT | s.t. |
| 10. | L. De Plus | IGD | 0:30 |
| 11. | B. Hermans | ISN | s.t. |
| 12. | G. Mäder | TBV | 0:31 |
| 13. | P. Latour | TDE | 0:49 |
| 14. | G. Martin | COF | 0:53 |
| 15. | A. Delaplace | ARK | 0:54 |
| 16. | R. Adrià | EKP | 0:59 |
| 17. | T. Skujiņš | TFS | 1:03 |
| 18. | J. Ezquerra | BBH | 1:04 |
| 19. | M. Burgaudeau | TDE | s.t. |
| 20. | S. Henao | IGD | s.t. |

## CALENDAR MONTH WINNERS

There are many accolades a rider can win during their career, from Grand Tour stage wins and Monument victories to the *ruban jaune* and *lanterne rouge*. But what about the achievement of winning a road race in every calendar month? With the calendar becoming more international, and races in far-flung locations defying the bitterness of the European winter, some active riders have come very close to completing the set. The coronavirus pandemic pushing the end of the 2020 Vuelta a España also leaves stage winner in that race Tim Wellens with just one month missing.

| | JAN | FEB | MAR | APR | MAY | JUN | JUL | AUG | SEP | OCT | NOV | DEC |
|---|---|---|---|---|---|---|---|---|---|---|---|---|
| **WELLENS** | ✓ | ✓ | ✓ | ✓ | ✓ | ✓ | ✓ | ✓ | ✓ | ✓ | | ✓ |
| **ACKERMANN** | | ✓ | ✓ | ✓ | ✓ | ✓ | ✓ | ✓ | ✓ | ✓ | ✓ | |
| **ALAPHILIPPE** | ✓ | ✓ | ✓ | ✓ | ✓ | ✓ | ✓ | ✓ | ✓ | ✓ | | |
| **CAVENDISH** | ✓ | ✓ | ✓ | ✓ | ✓ | ✓ | ✓ | ✓ | ✓ | | | |
| **EWAN** | ✓ | ✓ | ✓ | ✓ | ✓ | ✓ | ✓ | ✓ | ✓ | ✓ | | |
| **GILBERT** | ✓ | ✓ | ✓ | ✓ | ✓ | ✓ | ✓ | ✓ | ✓ | ✓ | | |
| **GREIPEL** | ✓ | ✓ | ✓ | ✓ | ✓ | ✓ | ✓ | ✓ | ✓ | ✓ | | |
| **NIBALI** | ✓ | ✓ | ✓ | ✓ | ✓ | ✓ | ✓ | ✓ | ✓ | ✓ | | |
| **ROGLIČ** | | ✓ | ✓ | ✓ | ✓ | ✓ | ✓ | ✓ | ✓ | ✓ | ✓ | |
| **SAGAN** | ✓ | ✓ | ✓ | ✓ | ✓ | ✓ | ✓ | ✓ | ✓ | ✓ | | |
| **VIVIANI** | ✓ | ✓ | ✓ | ✓ | ✓ | ✓ | ✓ | ✓ | ✓ | ✓ | | |
| **VAN VLEUTEN** | ✓ | ✓ | ✓ | ✓ | ✓ | ✓ | ✓ | ✓ | ✓ | | | |
| **BRAND** | | ✓ | ✓ | ✓ | ✓ | ✓ | ✓ | ✓ | ✓ | | | |
| **VOS** | | | | ✓ | ✓ | ✓ | ✓ | ✓ | ✓ | ✓ | | |

APRIL　　WORLDTOUR MEN'S RACE

# TOUR OF FLANDERS
4 April 2021
Antwerp–Oudenaarde
254.3km

Proving once again that success in the GP E3 is a good indicator of form for the Tour of Flanders, Kasper Asgreen (Elegant-QuickStep) emulated the likes of Tom Boonen, Fabian Cancellara and Niki Terpstra by the adding the Ronde title to the E3 crown he'd taken a week earlier, outsprinting defending champion Mathieu van der Poel (Alpecin-Fenix) in a two-up sprint. This pair initially showed that they were the strongest when they dropped their rivals the second time over the Oude Kwaremont and the Paterberg, Wout van Aert (Jumbo-Visma) leading the chase back up to them on both occasions. This trio went clear topping the Kruisberg, with 27km remaining. When Van der Poel accelerated once more on the final ascent of the Oude Kwaremont, Van Aert was unable to follow the pace. But Asgreen managed to stay with the Dutchman, the pair then riding side by side up the Paterberg and cooperating all the way to the end. Coming into the finish, the Dane manoeuvred his rival to the front. When Asgreen launched his sprint from Van der Poel's rear wheel, the Dutch rider responded quickly, drawing alongside him, only to find he'd expended his last joules of energy in the process. As Van der Poel slumped in his saddle, Asgreen powered on to clinch his first Monument.

## WEATHER

TEMPERATURE
7°C

WIND
N 6km/h

## PROFILE

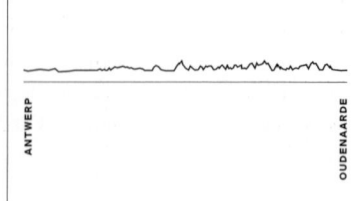

ANTWERP — OUDENAARDE

## BREAKAWAY
S. Bissegger (EFN), M. Norsgaard (MOV), J. Wallays (COF), F. Van Den Bossche (SVB), M. Paasschens (BWB), H. Houle (APT), N. Denz (DSM)

## TRIVIA
» Asgreen is only the second Dane to win the Tour of Flanders (after Rolf Sørensen in 1997).

# RESULTS

| POS | NAME | TEAM | TIME |
|---|---|---|---|
| 1. | K. Asgreen | DQT | 6:02:12 |
| 2. | M. van der Poel | AFC | s.t. |
| 3. | G. Van Avermaet | ACT | 0:32 |
| 4. | J. Stuyven | TFS | 0:33 |
| 5. | S. Vanmarcke | ISN | 0:47 |
| 6. | W. van Aert | TJV | s.t. |
| 7. | G. Vermeersch | AFC | s.t. |
| 8. | A. Turgis | TDE | s.t. |
| 9. | F. Sénéchal | DQT | s.t. |
| 10. | D. van Baarle | IGD | s.t. |
| 11. | C. Laporte | COF | s.t. |
| 12. | T. Benoot | DSM | 0:49 |
| 13. | D. Claeys | TQA | 2:15 |
| 14. | M. Burghardt | BOH | s.t. |
| 15. | P. Sagan | BOH | s.t. |
| 16. | D. van Poppel | IWG | s.t. |
| 17. | Y. Lampaert | DQT | s.t. |
| 18. | A. Kristoff | UAD | s.t. |
| 19. | T. Van Asbroeck | ISN | s.t. |
| 20. | H. Haussler | TBV | s.t. |
| 21. | M. Matthews | BEX | s.t. |
| 22. | N. Politt | BOH | s.t. |
| 23. | I. García Cortina | MOV | s.t. |
| 24. | H. Hofstetter | ISN | s.t. |
| 25. | T. Wellens | LTS | s.t. |
| 26. | J. Biermans | ISN | s.t. |
| 27. | M. Walscheid | TQA | s.t. |
| 28. | A. Bettiol | EFN | s.t. |
| 29. | C. Russo | ARK | s.t. |
| 30. | J. Degenkolb | LTS | s.t. |
| 31. | A. Livyns | BWB | s.t. |
| 32. | D. Van Gestel | TDE | s.t. |
| 33. | O. Naesen | ACT | s.t. |
| 34. | A. De Gendt | IWG | s.t. |
| 35. | D. Teuns | TBV | s.t. |
| 36. | W. Barguil | ARK | 2:20 |
| 37. | S. E. Byström | UAD | s.t. |
| 38. | V. Campenaerts | TQA | s.t. |
| 39. | V. Madouas | GFC | s.t. |
| 40. | M. Haller | TBV | 2:24 |
| 41. | T. Pidcock | IGD | 2:35 |
| 42. | J. Alaphilippe | DQT | s.t. |
| 43. | M. Gogl | TQA | 2:52 |
| 44. | S. Küng | GFC | 3:19 |
| 45. | M. Norsgaard | MOV | s.t. |
| 46. | C. Lemoine | BBK | s.t. |
| 47. | C. Beullens | SVB | 4:00 |
| 48. | C. Barthe | BBK | s.t. |
| 49. | D. De Bondt | AFC | s.t. |
| 50. | S. Dewulf | ACT | s.t. |
| 51. | R. Stannard | BEX | s.t. |
| 52. | K. Geniets | GFC | s.t. |
| 53. | D. Touzé | ACT | s.t. |
| 54. | E. Hayter | IGD | s.t. |
| 55. | S. Colbrelli | TBV | s.t. |
| 56. | R. Oliveira | UAD | s.t. |
| 57. | M. Trentin | UAD | 9:00 |
| 58. | S. Kragh Andersen | DSM | s.t. |
| 59. | E. Theuns | TFS | s.t. |
| 60. | T. Willems | SVB | s.t. |
| 61. | P. Allegaert | COF | s.t. |
| 62. | N. Van Hooydonck | TJV | s.t. |
| 63. | N. Denz | DSM | s.t. |
| 64. | R. Gibbons | UAD | s.t. |
| 65. | O. Le Gac | GFC | s.t. |
| 66. | J. Hollmann | MOV | s.t. |
| 67. | G. Serrano | MOV | s.t. |
| 68. | J. Wallays | COF | s.t. |
| 69. | L. Wirtgen | BWB | s.t. |
| 70. | B. Perry | APT | s.t. |
| 71. | M. Paasschens | BWB | s.t. |
| 72. | M. Gołaś | IGD | s.t. |
| 73. | C. Swift | ARK | s.t. |
| 74. | B. van Poppel | IWG | s.t. |
| 75. | B. Van Lerberghe | DQT | s.t. |
| 76. | L. Wiśniowski | TQA | s.t. |
| 77. | M. Louvel | ARK | s.t. |
| 78. | J. Jacobs | MOV | s.t. |
| 79. | H. Houle | APT | s.t. |
| 80. | J. Vanendert | BWB | s.t. |
| 81. | D. Gruzdev | APT | s.t. |
| 82. | J. Bauer | BEX | s.t. |
| 83. | L. G. Mas | MOV | s.t. |
| 84. | E. Boasson Hagen | TDE | s.t. |
| 85. | L. Vliegen | IWG | s.t. |
| 86. | N. Terpstra | TDE | s.t. |
| 87. | L. Durbridge | BEX | s.t. |
| 88. | D. Oss | BOH | s.t. |
| 89. | S. Bissegger | EFN | s.t. |
| 90. | J. Rickaert | AFC | s.t. |
| 91. | A. Zakharov | APT | 13:00 |
| 92. | M. Wynants | TJV | s.t. |
| 93. | D. Dekker | TJV | s.t. |
| 94. | P. Eenkhoorn | TJV | s.t. |
| 95. | B. De Backer | BBK | s.t. |
| 96. | K. de Kort | TFS | s.t. |
| 97. | T. Roosen | TJV | s.t. |
| 98. | G. Boivin | ISN | s.t. |
| 99. | M. Sieberg | TBV | s.t. |
| 100. | T. Ludvigsson | GFC | s.t. |
| 101. | T. van der Hoorn | IWG | s.t. |
| 102. | F. Backaert | BBK | s.t. |
| 103. | C. Noppe | ARK | s.t. |
| 104. | M. Bodnar | BOH | s.t. |
| 105. | V. S. Laengen | UAD | s.t. |
| 106. | W. Kreder | IWG | s.t. |
| 107. | D. McLay | ARK | s.t. |
| 108. | P. Vanspeybrouck | IWG | s.t. |
| 109. | S. Langeveld | EFN | s.t. |
| 110. | F. Van den Bossche | SVB | s.t. |
| 111. | A. Carvalho | COF | s.t. |
| 112. | F. Wright | TBV | s.t. |
| 113. | D. Gaudin | TDE | s.t. |

APRIL    WORLDTOUR WOMEN'S RACE

# TOUR OF FLANDERS
4 April 2021
Oudenaarde–Oudenaarde
152km

## WEATHER

TEMPERATURE
7°C

WIND
N 7km/h

Ten years after her first victory, Annemiek van Vleuten won her second Tour of Flanders, attacking from a small group of favourites on the Paterberg and soloing to the finish. Van Vleuten's first attack came on the Kanarieberg, an asphalted climb 44km from the finish, but a headwind made her stop right away. The next move came from Audrey Cordon-Ragot, who held a 30-second advantage on a peloton of 40 riders for a long time. Soraya Paladin went on a solo chase, but both were eventually reeled in just before the Oude Kwaremont. Anna van der Breggen led the race up the long, cobbled climb, with only seven riders able to hold her wheel. Grace Brown made a move on the way to the Paterberg, and Van Vleuten bridged to her. However, the rest of the group came up to them just before the final climb. Van Vleuten launched her attack, dropping everyone and cresting the top with an 8-second lead. Pushing hard all the way to the finish and with little cooperation in the group behind, she won 26 seconds ahead of Lisa Brennauer and Brown.

## PROFILE

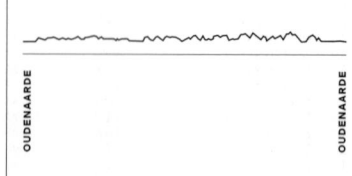

OUDENAARDE — OUDENAARDE

## BREAKAWAY
A. Cordon-Ragot (TFS), S. Paladin (LIV)

## RESULTS

| POS | NAME | TEAM | TIME |
|---|---|---|---|
| 1. | A. van Vleuten | MOV | 4:01:11 |
| 2. | L. Brennauer | WNT | 0:26 |
| 3. | G. Brown | BEX | s.t. |
| 4. | E. Longo Borghini | TFS | s.t. |
| 5. | D. Vollering | SDW | s.t. |
| 6. | M. Cavalli | FDJ | s.t. |
| 7. | C. U. Ludwig | FDJ | 0:28 |
| 8. | A. van der Breggen | SDW | 0:35 |
| 9. | M. Reusser | ALE | 0:51 |
| 10. | K. Faulkner | TIB | 0:55 |
| 11. | L. Thomas | MOV | 0:57 |
| 12. | M. Vos | JVW | 1:00 |
| 13. | L. Kopecky | LIV | s.t. |
| 14. | A. Pieters | SDW | s.t. |
| 15. | E. Balsamo | VAL | s.t. |
| 16. | M. G. Confalonieri | WNT | s.t. |
| 17. | F. Mackaij | DSM | s.t. |
| 18. | E. Deignan | TFS | s.t. |
| 19. | C. van den Broek-Blaak | SDW | s.t. |
| 20. | K. Niewiadoma | CSR | 1:03 |

## TRIVIA
» Annemiek van Vleuten has now won the Tour of Flanders twice. The first time was ten years ago, in 2011.

APRIL  .1 MEN'S RACE

# TROPHÉE HARMONIE MUTUELLE
4 April 2021
Ste-Maure-de-Touraine–Tours
204km

## WEATHER

TEMPERATURE
12°C

WIND
NE 15km/h

## RESULTS

| POS | NAME | TEAM | TIME |
|---|---|---|---|
| 1. | A. Démare | GFC | 4:52:59 |
| 2. | N. Bouhanni | ARK | s.t. |
| 3. | M. Sarreau | ACT | s.t. |
| 4. | B. Welten | ARK | s.t. |
| 5. | S. Consonni | COF | s.t. |
| 6. | B. Ghirmay | DKO | s.t. |
| 7. | A. Pasqualon | IWG | s.t. |
| 8. | L. Mozzato | BBK | s.t. |
| 9. | M. Menten | BWB | s.t. |
| 10. | L. Manzin | TDE | s.t. |
| 11. | P. A. Coté | RLY | s.t. |
| 12. | S. Wærenskjold | UXT | s.t. |
| 13. | O. Aular | CJR | s.t. |
| 14. | R. Cardis | AUB | s.t. |
| 15. | J. J. Lobato | EUS | s.t. |
| 16. | E. Vermeulen | XRL | s.t. |
| 17. | T. Ferasse | BBK | s.t. |
| 18. | J. Leveau | XRL | s.t. |
| 19. | T. Boudat | ARK | s.t. |
| 20. | A. Jullien | ACT | s.t. |

APRIL  WORLDTOUR MEN'S RACE

# ITZULIA BASQUE COUNTRY
Stage 1 (ITT)
5 April 2021
Bilbao–Bilbao
13.89km

## WEATHER

| TEMPERATURE | WIND |
|---|---|
| 15°C | NW 11km/h |

## PROFILE

Making his first appearance since his final day setback at Paris–Nice, when a crash not only cost him overall victory but left him with a dislocated shoulder, Primož Roglič was quickly back in winning form in the race-opening time trial in Bilbao. The Jumbo-Visma leader finished 2 seconds clear of Brandon McNulty (UAE Team Emirates), with Roglič's young teammate Jonas Vingegaard 18 seconds back in third place. The Slovenian went off early, his speed on the final sharp ramp up to the finish critical to him setting a new best mark. Ultimately, McNulty was the only rider who went close to challenging Roglič, although the American's teammate Tadej Pogačar had been expected to. The 2020 Tour de France champion went off fast, setting the quickest time at the intermediate check but steadily lost time from that point. He finished 28 seconds down on Roglič and fifth on the day. ⓟ

## STAGE RESULTS

| POS | NAME | TEAM | TIME |
|---|---|---|---|
| 1. | P. Roglič | TJV | 17:17 |
| 2. | B. McNulty | UAD | 0:02 |
| 3. | J. Vingegaard | TJV | 0:18 |
| 4. | T. Foss | TJV | 0:24 |
| 5. | T. Pogačar | UAD | 0:28 |
| 6. | A. Yates | IGD | s.t. |
| 7. | P. Bevin | ISN | s.t. |
| 8. | I. Schelling | BOH | 0:29 |
| 9. | A. Aranburu | APT | 0:30 |
| 10. | M. Schachmann | BOH | 0:31 |
| 11. | W. Kelderman | BOH | 0:36 |
| 12. | M. Hirschi | UAD | 0:37 |
| 13. | P. Bilbao | TBV | 0:38 |
| 14. | J. Fuglsang | APT | 0:39 |
| 15. | M. Cattaneo | DQT | 0:40 |
| 16. | O. Fraile | APT | s.t. |
| 17. | P. Latour | TDE | 0:43 |
| 18. | M. Vansevenant | DQT | s.t. |
| 19. | A. Valverde | MOV | s.t. |
| 20. | P. Konrad | BOH | s.t. |

## GENERAL CLASSIFICATION

| POS | NAME | TEAM | TIME |
|---|---|---|---|
| 1. | P. Roglič | TJV | 17:17 |
| 2. | B. McNulty | UAD | 0:02 |
| 3. | J. Vingegaard | TJV | 0:18 |

## KING OF THE MOUNTAINS

| POS | NAME | TEAM | PTS |
|---|---|---|---|
| 1. | T. Pogačar | UAD | 3 |
| 2. | A. Yates | IGD | 2 |
| 3. | B. McNulty | UAD | 1 |

## POINTS

| POS | NAME | TEAM | PTS |
|---|---|---|---|
| 1. | P. Roglič | TJV | 25 |
| 2. | B. McNulty | UAD | 20 |
| 3. | J. Vingegaard | TJV | 16 |

## YOUNG RIDER

| POS | NAME | TEAM | TIME |
|---|---|---|---|
| 1. | B. McNulty | UAD | 17:19 |
| 2. | J. Vingegaard | TJV | 0:16 |
| 3. | T. Foss | TJV | 0:22 |

## TRIVIA

» This was Roglič's 12th professional time trial win.

## BONUSES

| TYPE | NAME | TEAM |
|---|---|---|
| KOM 1 | T. Pogačar | UAD |

APRIL  WORLDTOUR MEN'S RACE

# ITZULIA BASQUE COUNTRY
Stage 2
6 April 2021
Zalla–Sestao
154.8km

Wet weather added significantly to the difficulty of a tricky course. The pivotal point proved to be the final climb, La Asturiana. Tadej Pogačar and David Gaudu provided the trigger, attacking on the lower slopes. The lead group stretched, then came back together, but with fewer members in it. Max Schachmann was the next to move, joined by Primož Roglič, Brandon McNulty and Sergio Higuita. Several riders bridged up to them on the short plateau beyond the crest of the climb, Astana-Premier Tech's turquoise jerseys very apparent close to the front. Omar Fraile was the first from the Kazakh team to try to go clear. When he was brought to heel, Alex Aranburu punched clear. Drawing on knowledge of his home roads, Aranburu flew into Sestao, his lead big enough to ensure him an emotional stage win but not quite sufficient to displace Roglič from the overall lead.

## WEATHER

TEMPERATURE: 11°C
WIND: W 7km/h

## PROFILE

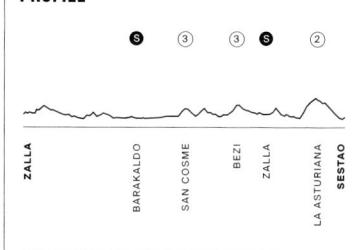

ZALLA – BARAKALDO – SAN COSME – BEZI – ZALLA – LA ASTURIANA – SESTAO

## BREAKAWAY

Q. Hermans (IWG), M. Tusveld (DSM), B. Gastauer (ACT), J. Irisarri (CJR), O. Cabedo (BBH), M. Iturria (EUS), K. Vermaerke (DSM)

## STAGE RESULTS

| POS | NAME | TEAM | TIME |
|---|---|---|---|
| 1. | A. Aranburu | APT | 3:45:32 |
| 2. | O. Fraile | APT | 0:15 |
| 3. | T. Pogačar | UAD | s.t. |
| 4. | D. Gaudu | GFC | s.t. |
| 5. | M. Woods | ISN | s.t. |
| 6. | P. Roglič | TJV | s.t. |
| 7. | M. Schachmann | BOH | s.t. |
| 8. | M. Landa | TBV | s.t. |
| 9. | S. Higuita | EFN | s.t. |
| 10. | A. Valverde | MOV | s.t. |
| 11. | I. Izaguirre | APT | s.t. |
| 12. | P. Latour | TDE | s.t. |
| 13. | A. Yates | IGD | s.t. |
| 14. | A. Paret-Peintre | ACT | s.t. |
| 15. | I. Van Wilder | DSM | 0:19 |
| 16. | J. Knox | DQT | s.t. |
| 17. | P. Bilbao | TBV | s.t. |
| 18. | E. Chaves | BEX | s.t. |
| 19. | B. McNulty | UAD | s.t. |
| 20. | J. Fuglsang | APT | s.t. |

## GENERAL CLASSIFICATION

| POS | NAME | TEAM | TIME |
|---|---|---|---|
| 1. – | P. Roglič | TJV | 4:03:04 |
| 2. ↑7 | A. Aranburu | APT | 0:05 |
| 3. ↓1 | B. McNulty | UAD | 0:06 |

## KING OF THE MOUNTAINS

| POS | NAME | TEAM | PTS |
|---|---|---|---|
| 1. – | M. Schachmann | BOH | 6 |
| 2. – | Q. Hermans | IWG | 6 |
| 3. – | P. Roglič | TJV | 4 |

## POINTS

| POS | NAME | TEAM | PTS |
|---|---|---|---|
| 1. – | P. Roglič | TJV | 35 |
| 2. ↑7 | A. Aranburu | APT | 32 |
| 3. ↑2 | T. Pogačar | UAD | 28 |

## YOUNG RIDER

| POS | NAME | TEAM | TIME |
|---|---|---|---|
| 1. – | B. McNulty | UAD | 4:03:10 |
| 2. ↑2 | T. Pogačar | UAD | 0:18 |
| 3. ↓1 | J. Vingegaard | TJV | 0:26 |

## TRIVIA

» This was Alex Aranburu's first WorldTour victory.

## BONUSES

| TYPE | NAME | TEAM |
|---|---|---|
| KOM 1 | Q. Hermans | IWG |
| KOM 2 | Q. Hermans | IWG |
| KOM 3 | M. Schachmann | BOH |
| Sprint 1 | B. Gastauer | ACT |
| Sprint 2 | M. Iturria | EUS |

APRIL WORLDTOUR MEN'S RACE

# ITZULIA BASQUE COUNTRY
Stage 3
7 April 2021
Amurrio–Ermualde (Laudio)
167.7km

The steep ramps of the Ermualde looked likely to deliver the first big contest between the GC favourites, but that didn't stop seven hopefuls getting into the break with the aim of thwarting the favourites: Mikkel Honoré, Théo Delacroix, Larry Warbasse, Oier Lazkano, Daniel Navarro, Gotzon Martín and Felix Gall. Their lead reached 6 minutes, but all were brought back into line by the penultimate climb of the Malkuartu. Approaching the final ascent, Magnus Cort, Sergio Higuita, Aurélien Paret-Peintre and Richard Carapaz broke clear. As Primož Roglič and Tadej Pogačar closed in, Carapaz pressed on alone, but the Ecuadorean couldn't hold off the double-headed Slovenian express, and the two favourites swept past. When rival riders closed in, Pogačar and Roglič went again, then a third time, Roglič in the vanguard until Pogačar edged by to claim a thrilling victory. ⓟⓒ

## WEATHER

TEMPERATURE 11°C
WIND E 22km/h

## PROFILE

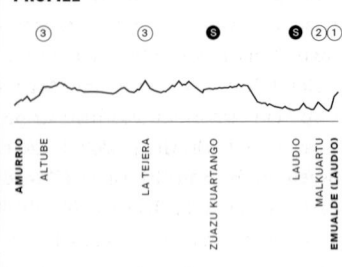

## BREAKAWAY
M. Honoré (DQT), T. Delacroix (IWG), L. Warbasse (ACT), O. Lazkano (CJR), D. Navarro (BBH), G. Martin (EUS), F. Gall (DSM)

## STAGE RESULTS

| POS | NAME | TEAM | TIME |
|---|---|---|---|
| 1. | T. Pogačar | UAD | 4:04:50 |
| 2. | P. Roglič | TJV | s.t. |
| 3. | A. Valverde | MOV | 0:05 |
| 4. | A. Yates | IGD | s.t. |
| 5. | M. Landa | TBV | s.t. |
| 6. | D. Gaudu | GFC | 0:08 |
| 7. | J. Knox | DQT | 0:16 |
| 8. | J. Vingegaard | TJV | s.t. |
| 9. | M. Vansevenant | DQT | s.t. |
| 10. | B. McNulty | UAD | 0:18 |
| 11. | S. Higuita | EFN | 0:20 |
| 12. | P. Bilbao | TBV | s.t. |
| 13. | E. Chaves | BEX | s.t. |
| 14. | M. Schachmann | BOH | 0:32 |
| 15. | J. Fuglsang | APT | s.t. |
| 16. | H. Carthy | EFN | s.t. |
| 17. | I. Van Wilder | DSM | 0:34 |
| 18. | E. Buchmann | BOH | 0:36 |
| 19. | I. Izaguirre | APT | s.t. |
| 20. | G. Mäder | TBV | 0:50 |

## GENERAL CLASSIFICATION

| POS | NAME | TEAM | TIME |
|---|---|---|---|
| 1. — | P. Roglič | TJV | 8:07:48 |
| 2. ↑2 | T. Pogačar | UAD | 0:20 |
| 3. — | B. McNulty | UAD | 0:30 |

## KING OF THE MOUNTAINS

| POS | NAME | TEAM | PTS |
|---|---|---|---|
| 1. ↑4 | T. Pogačar | UAD | 13 |
| 2. — | Q. Hermans | IWG | 12 |
| 3. — | P. Roglič | TJV | 12 |

## POINTS

| POS | NAME | TEAM | PTS |
|---|---|---|---|
| 1. — | P. Roglič | TJV | 55 |
| 2. ↑1 | T. Pogačar | UAD | 53 |
| 3. ↓1 | A. Aranburu | APT | 32 |

## YOUNG RIDER

| POS | NAME | TEAM | TIME |
|---|---|---|---|
| 1. ↑1 | T. Pogačar | UAD | 8:08:08 |
| 2. ↓1 | B. McNulty | UAD | 0:10 |
| 3. — | J. Vingegaard | TJV | 0:34 |

## TRIVIA
» Since he turned professional in 2019, 15 of Pogačar's 22 career wins have been at WorldTour level.

## BONUSES

| TYPE | NAME | TEAM |
|---|---|---|
| KOM 1 | O. Lazkano | CJR |
| KOM 2 | O. Lazkano | CJR |
| KOM 3 | Q. Hermans | IWG |
| KOM 4 | T. Pogačar | UAD |
| Sprint 1 | D. Navarro | BBH |
| Sprint 2 | O. Lazkano | CJR |

APRIL    WORLDTOUR MEN'S RACE

# ITZULIA BASQUE COUNTRY
Stage 4
8 April 2021
Vitoria-Gasteiz–Hondarribia
189.2km

Racing into the very north-east corner of the Basque region, this was another frantic stage. More than 100km passed before the break went clear – Ben O'Connor, Guillaume Martin, Jefferson Cepeda Hernández and Juan López Pérez the quartet in it. On the Jaizkibel, the emblematic ascent of the San Sebastián Classic, O'Connor and López pushed on. Topping it, their lead was just 40 seconds. Soon after they reached the next climb, the Erlaitz, the bunch was on them. As the race rolled back towards the coast and Hondarribia, Pello Bilbao, Esteban Chaves, Brandon McNulty, Ion Izaguirre and Emanuel Buchmann slipped clear, marked by Jumbo's Jonas Vingegaard. This looked a strange move on the Dutch team's part, with race leader Roglič isolated in the group behind, and it cost them. The sextet were never caught, Izaguirre pipping fellow Basque Bilbao for the stage win as McNulty nudged Roglič out of the leader's jersey.

## WEATHER

TEMPERATURE: 13°C
WIND: SW 15km/h

## PROFILE

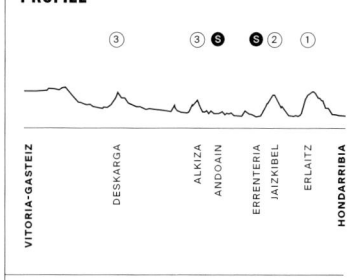

## BREAKAWAY
B. O'Connor (ACT), G. Martin (COF), J. Cepeda (CJR), J. P. Lopez (TFS)

## GENERAL CLASSIFICATION

| POS | NAME | TEAM | TIME |
|---|---|---|---|
| 1. ↑2 | B. McNulty | UAD | 12:25:21 |
| 2. ↓1 | P. Roglič | TJV | 0:23 |
| 3. ↑3 | J. Vingegaard | TJV | 0:28 |

## STAGE RESULTS

| POS | NAME | TEAM | TIME |
|---|---|---|---|
| 1. | I. Izaguirre | APT | 4:17:07 |
| 2. | P. Bilbao | TBV | s.t. |
| 3. | B. McNulty | UAD | s.t. |
| 4. | J. Vingegaard | TJV | s.t. |
| 5. | E. Buchmann | BOH | s.t. |
| 6. | E. Chaves | BEX | 0:02 |
| 7. | P. Bevin | ISN | 0:49 |
| 8. | J. Knox | DQT | s.t. |
| 9. | Q. Hermans | IWG | s.t. |
| 10. | A. Valverde | MOV | s.t. |
| 11. | A. Aranburu | APT | s.t. |
| 12. | T. Pogačar | UAD | s.t. |
| 13. | S. Geschke | COF | s.t. |
| 14. | P. Roglič | TJV | s.t. |
| 15. | I. Van Wilder | DSM | s.t. |
| 16. | S. Higuita | EFN | s.t. |
| 17. | A. Osorio | CJR | s.t. |
| 18. | P. Latour | TDE | s.t. |
| 19. | J. Lastra | CJR | s.t. |
| 20. | M. Schachmann | BOH | s.t. |

## KING OF THE MOUNTAINS

| POS | NAME | TEAM | PTS |
|---|---|---|---|
| 1. — | T. Pogačar | UAD | 17 |
| 2. — | Q. Hermans | IWG | 14 |
| 3. — | P. Roglič | TJV | 14 |

## POINTS

| POS | NAME | TEAM | PTS |
|---|---|---|---|
| 1. — | P. Roglič | TJV | 57 |
| 2. — | T. Pogačar | UAD | 57 |
| 3. ↑2 | B. McNulty | UAD | 42 |

## YOUNG RIDER

| POS | NAME | TEAM | TIME |
|---|---|---|---|
| 1. ↑1 | B. McNulty | UAD | 12:25:21 |
| 2. ↑1 | J. Vingegaard | TJV | 0:28 |
| 3. ↓2 | T. Pogačar | UAD | 0:43 |

## TRIVIA
» Having not won so far all season, Astana turned things around by taking two stages at this race.

## BONUSES

| TYPE | NAME | TEAM |
|---|---|---|
| KOM 1 | J. P. Lopez | TFS |
| KOM 2 | G. Martin | COF |
| KOM 3 | B. O'Connor | ACT |
| KOM 4 | B. McNulty | UAD |
| Sprint 1 | B. O'Connor | ACT |
| Sprint 2 | G. Martin | COF |

APRIL   WORLDTOUR MEN'S RACE

# ITZULIA BASQUE COUNTRY
Stage 5
9 April 2021
Hondarribia–Ondarroa
160.2km

The most straightforward stage of the race presented the best chance of a breakaway group going the distance, with the favourites focused primarily on the critical final day to come. Six riders made the cut: Deceuninck-QuickStep's Mikkel Honoré and Josef Černý, Julien Bernard (Trek-Segafredo), Andrey Amador (Ineos Grenadiers), Andreas Leknessund (Team DSM) and Ide Schelling (Bora-Hansgrohe). The peloton kept their advantage to less than 3 minutes. Sensing they had to move before the peloton closed in, the Deceuninck duo accelerated on the final category-3 climb, Bernard the only one capable of following them. With 10km left, Bernard's collaboration stopped, prompting an attack from Honoré. As the Frenchman began to wilt, Černý jumped away from him too and bridged up to his Danish teammate. There was no final sprint, the pair celebrating well before they reached the line, Honoré rolling across it first.

## WEATHER

TEMPERATURE | WIND
18°C | SE 15km/h

## PROFILE

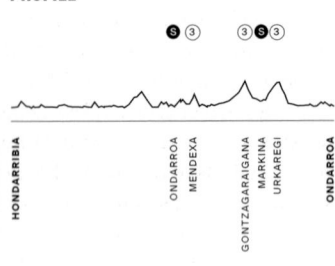

HONDARRIBIA — ONDARROA / MENDEXA — GONTZAGARAIGANA — MARKINA / URKAREGI — ONDARROA

## BREAKAWAY
J. Bernard (TFS), I. Schelling (BOH), M. Honoré (DQT), J. Černý (DQT), A. Amador (IGD), A. Leknessund (DSM)

## STAGE RESULTS

| POS | NAME | TEAM | TIME |
|---|---|---|---|
| 1. | M. F. Honoré | DQT | 3:39:54 |
| 2. | J. Černý | DQT | s.t. |
| 3. | J. Bernard | TFS | 0:17 |
| 4. | D. Impey | ISN | 0:28 |
| 5. | S. Clarke | TQA | s.t. |
| 6. | S. Oldani | LTS | s.t. |
| 7. | P. Roglič | TJV | s.t. |
| 8. | J. Simon | TDE | s.t. |
| 9. | M. Cort | EFN | s.t. |
| 10. | T. Pogačar | UAD | s.t. |
| 11. | J. Ezquerra | BBH | s.t. |
| 12. | L. Rota | IWG | s.t. |
| 13. | M. Tusveld | DSM | s.t. |
| 14. | A. Lutsenko | APT | s.t. |
| 15. | P. Konrad | BOH | s.t. |
| 16. | I. Van Wilder | DSM | s.t. |
| 17. | Q. Hermans | IWG | s.t. |
| 18. | G. Martin | COF | s.t. |
| 19. | M. Scotson | GFC | s.t. |
| 20. | R. Combaud | DSM | s.t. |

## GENERAL CLASSIFICATION

| | | | | |
|---|---|---|---|---|
| 1. | — | B. McNulty | UAD | 16:05:43 |
| 2. | — | P. Roglič | TJV | 0:23 |
| 3. | — | J. Vingegaard | TJV | 0:28 |

## KING OF THE MOUNTAINS

| POS | | NAME | TEAM | PTS |
|---|---|---|---|---|
| 1. | — | T. Pogačar | UAD | 17 |
| 2. | — | Q. Hermans | IWG | 14 |
| 3. | — | P. Roglič | TJV | 14 |

## POINTS

| POS | | NAME | TEAM | PTS |
|---|---|---|---|---|
| 1. | — | P. Roglič | TJV | 66 |
| 2. | — | T. Pogačar | UAD | 63 |
| 3. | — | B. McNulty | UAD | 42 |

## YOUNG RIDER

| POS | | NAME | TEAM | TIME |
|---|---|---|---|---|
| 1. | — | B. McNulty | UAD | 16:05:43 |
| 2. | — | J. Vingegaard | TJV | 0:28 |
| 3. | — | T. Pogačar | UAD | 0:43 |

## TRIVIA
» This was Deceuninck-QuickStep's second win this season with a 1-2 on the podium.

## BONUSES

| TYPE | NAME | TEAM |
|---|---|---|
| KOM 1 | J. Černý | DQT |
| KOM 2 | J. Bernard | TFS |
| KOM 3 | J. Černý | DQT |
| Sprint 1 | I. Schelling | BOH |
| Sprint 2 | J. Bernard | TFS |

APRIL   WORLDTOUR MEN'S RACE

# ITZULIA BASQUE COUNTRY
Stage 6
10 April 2021
Ondarroa–Arrate (Eibar)
111.9km

UAE Team Emirates played their hand as poorly as Jumbo-Visma had two days earlier. The attacks began almost from the off, and the turning point came on the descent of the Elosua-Gorla. Astana were chasing a small breakaway group when the 30-strong peloton split, Primož Roglič in the front part, UAE's Brandon McNulty and Tadej Pogačar stranded in the second. UAE called Marc Hirschi back from the break, put Pogačar on the front to chase, but Roglič remained out of reach. On the brutally steep Krabelin, Roglič was left with just David Gaudu and Hugh Carthy for company. Behind, McNulty cracked, leaving Pogačar to try to close down Roglič's advantage – in vain. When the front trio reached the climb, Gaudu jumped away and Roglič scampered after him, the pair sharing the work to the summit. Gaudu won the stage; just behind him, Roglič celebrated his second Itzulia Basque Country title. ⓡⓒ

## WEATHER

TEMPERATURE | WIND
17°C | S 11km/h

## PROFILE

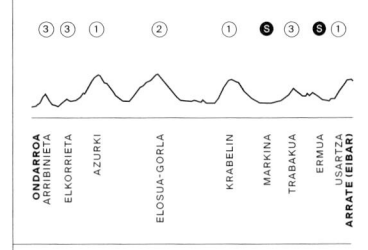

ONDARROA ARRIBINIETA · ELKORRIETA · AZURKI · ELOSUA-GORLA · KRABELIN · MARKINA · TRABAKUA · ERMUA · USARTZA ARRATE (EIBAR)

## BREAKAWAY

E. Mas (MOV), R. Carapaz (IGD), P. Bevin (ISN), H. Carthy (EFN), B. O'Connor (ACT), O. Fraile (APT), A. Tolhoek (TJV), M. Padun (TBV), C. Verona (MOV), G. Martin (COF), S. Oomen (TJV), M. Hirschi (UAD)

## GENERAL CLASSIFICATION

| POS | NAME | TEAM | TIME |
|---|---|---|---|
| 1. ↑1 | P. Roglič | TJV | 19:11:36 |
| 2. ↑1 | J. Vingegaard | TJV | 0:52 |
| 3. ↑2 | T. Pogačar | UAD | 1:07 |

## STAGE RESULTS

| POS | NAME | TEAM | TIME |
|---|---|---|---|
| 1. | D. Gaudu | GFC | 3:05:42 |
| 2. | P. Roglič | TJV | s.t. |
| 3. | A. Valverde | MOV | 0:35 |
| 4. | A. Yates | IGD | s.t. |
| 5. | T. Pogačar | UAD | s.t. |
| 6. | J. Vingegaard | TJV | s.t. |
| 7. | P. Bilbao | TBV | 1:03 |
| 8. | E. Chaves | BEX | 1:05 |
| 9. | M. Landa | TBV | s.t. |
| 10. | M. Vansevenant | DQT | 1:55 |
| 11. | I. Izaguirre | APT | s.t. |
| 12. | B. O'Connor | ACT | 1:57 |
| 13. | H. Carthy | EFN | 1:59 |
| 14. | R. Fernández | COF | 2:47 |
| 15. | J. Knox | DQT | 3:42 |
| 16. | E. Buchmann | BOH | 4:05 |
| 17. | J. Fuglsang | APT | 4:21 |
| 18. | R. Carapaz | IGD | 4:40 |
| 19. | E. Mas | MOV | s.t. |
| 20. | P. Bevin | ISN | 5:21 |

## KING OF THE MOUNTAINS

| POS | NAME | TEAM | PTS |
|---|---|---|---|
| 1. ↑2 | P. Roglič | TJV | 34 |
| 2. ↓1 | T. Pogačar | UAD | 27 |
| 3. ↑22 | D. Gaudu | GFC | 20 |

## POINTS

| POS | NAME | TEAM | PTS |
|---|---|---|---|
| 1. — | P. Roglič | TJV | 106 |
| 2. — | T. Pogačar | UAD | 75 |
| 3. ↑9 | D. Gaudu | GFC | 61 |

## YOUNG RIDER

| POS | NAME | TEAM | TIME |
|---|---|---|---|
| 1. ↑1 | J. Vingegaard | TJV | 19:12:28 |
| 2. ↑1 | T. Pogačar | UAD | 0:15 |
| 3. ↑3 | D. Gaudu | GFC | 0:35 |

## BONUSES

| TYPE | NAME | TEAM |
|---|---|---|
| KOM 1 | C. Verona | MOV |
| KOM 2 | A. Tolhoek | TJV |
| KOM 3 | A. Tolhoek | TJV |
| KOM 4 | P. Bevin | ISN |
| KOM 5 | P. Roglič | TJV |
| KOM 6 | H. Carthy | EFN |
| KOM 7 | D. Gaudu | GFC |
| Sprint 1 | P. Roglič | TJV |
| Sprint 2 | P. Roglič | TJV |

## TRIVIA

» This was the first time in 2021 that Groupama-FDJ claimed victory outside France.

APRIL .PRO MEN'S RACE

# SCHELDEPRIJS
7 April 2021
Terneuzen–Schoten
193.8km

## WEATHER

TEMPERATURE | WIND
5°C | W 28km/h

## RESULTS

| POS | NAME | TEAM | TIME |
|---|---|---|---|
| 1. | J. Philipsen | AFC | 4:03:30 |
| 2. | S. Bennett | DQT | s.t. |
| 3. | M. Cavendish | DQT | s.t. |
| 4. | D. van Poppel | IWG | s.t. |
| 5. | C. Russo | ARK | s.t. |
| 6. | P. Ackermann | BOH | s.t. |
| 7. | L. Mozzato | BBK | s.t. |
| 8. | G. Nizzolo | TQA | s.t. |
| 9. | M. Sarreau | ACT | s.t. |
| 10. | D. Van Gestel | TDE | s.t. |
| 11. | E. Šiškevičius | DKO | s.t. |
| 12. | M. Walscheid | TQA | s.t. |
| 13. | J. Rickaert | AFC | s.t. |
| 14. | N. Politt | BOH | s.t. |
| 15. | J. W. van Schip | BCY | s.t. |
| 16. | N. Vahtra | ISN | s.t. |
| 17. | L. Bugter | BCY | s.t. |
| 18. | P. Havik | BCY | s.t. |
| 19. | B. Van Moer | LTS | s.t. |
| 20. | C. Bol | DSM | s.t. |

APRIL  .PRO MEN'S RACE

# PRESIDENTIAL TOUR OF TURKEY
Stage 1
11 April 2021
Konya–Konya
72.4km

## WEATHER

TEMPERATURE | WIND
3°C | NW 22km/h

## STAGE RESULTS

| POS | NAME | TEAM | TIME |
|---|---|---|---|
| 1. | A. de Kleijn | RLY | 1:35:38 |
| 2. | K. Halvorsen | UXT | s.t. |
| 3. | P. Barbier | DKO | s.t. |
| 4. | M. Cavendish | DQT | s.t. |
| 5. | J. Philipsen | AFC | s.t. |
| 6. | A. Greipel | ISN | s.t. |
| 7. | G. Lonardi | BCF | s.t. |
| 8. | M. Belletti | EOK | s.t. |
| 9. | M. Peñalver | BBH | s.t. |
| 10. | E. M. Grosu | DKO | s.t. |
| 11. | J. J. Lobato | EUS | s.t. |
| 12. | M. Pluto | ABC | s.t. |
| 13. | L. Kulbe | SVL | s.t. |
| 14. | A. Peron | TNN | s.t. |
| 15. | S. Wærenskjold | UXT | s.t. |
| 16. | S. Aniołkowski | BWB | s.t. |
| 17. | G. Brussenskiy | APT | s.t. |
| 18. | A. J. Hodeg | DQT | s.t. |
| 19. | M. Frapporti | EOK | s.t. |
| 20. | M. Stash | STC | s.t. |

## GENERAL CLASSIFICATION

| POS | NAME | TEAM | TIME |
|---|---|---|---|
| 1. | A. de Kleijn | RLY | 1:35:28 |
| 2. | K. Halvorsen | UXT | 0:04 |
| 3. | P. Barbier | DKO | 0:06 |

## KING OF THE MOUNTAINS

| POS | NAME | TEAM | PTS |
|---|---|---|---|
| 1. | I. Slik | ABC | 3 |
| 2. | S. De Bie | BWB | 2 |
| 3. | V. Buts | SBB | 1 |

## POINTS

| POS | NAME | TEAM | PTS |
|---|---|---|---|
| 1. | A. de Kleijn | RLY | 15 |
| 2. | K. Halvorsen | UXT | 14 |
| 3. | P. Barbier | DKO | 13 |

# PRESIDENTIAL TOUR OF TURKEY
Stage 2
12 April 2021
Konya–Konya
144.9km

## WEATHER

TEMPERATURE | WIND
5°C | N 15km/h

## STAGE RESULTS

| POS | NAME | TEAM | TIME |
|---|---|---|---|
| 1. | M. Cavendish | DQT | 3:17:26 |
| 2. | J. Philipsen | AFC | s.t. |
| 3. | A. Greipel | ISN | s.t. |
| 4. | A. de Kleijn | RLY | s.t. |
| 5. | S. Aniołkowski | BWB | s.t. |
| 6. | M. Peñalver | BBH | s.t. |
| 7. | G. Lonardi | BCF | s.t. |
| 8. | L. Mozzato | BBK | s.t. |
| 9. | R. Zabel | ISN | s.t. |
| 10. | S. Wærenskjold | UXT | s.t. |
| 11. | P. Barbier | DKO | s.t. |
| 12. | L. Taminiaux | AFC | s.t. |
| 13. | M. Pluto | ABC | s.t. |
| 14. | B. Del Grosso | ABC | s.t. |
| 15. | E. M. Grosu | DKO | s.t. |
| 16. | J. J. Lobato | EUS | s.t. |
| 17. | D. Cima | GAZ | s.t. |
| 18. | U. Marengo | BCF | s.t. |
| 19. | A. Peron | TNN | s.t. |
| 20. | J. Vine | AFC | s.t. |

## GENERAL CLASSIFICATION

| POS | NAME | TEAM | TIME |
|---|---|---|---|
| 1. ↑6 | M. Cavendish | DQT | 4:52:54 |
| 2. ↓1 | A. de Kleijn | RLY | s.t. |
| 3. ↑5 | J. Philipsen | AFC | 0:04 |

## KING OF THE MOUNTAINS

| POS | NAME | TEAM | PTS |
|---|---|---|---|
| 1. ↑2 | V. Buts | SBB | 9 |
| 2. — | S. Zoccarato | BCF | 4 |
| 3. ↓2 | I. Slik | ABC | 3 |

## POINTS

| POS | NAME | TEAM | PTS |
|---|---|---|---|
| 1. ↑3 | M. Cavendish | DQT | 27 |
| 2. ↓1 | A. de Kleijn | RLY | 27 |
| 3. ↑2 | J. Philipsen | AFC | 25 |

APRIL .PRO MEN'S RACE

# PRESIDENTIAL TOUR OF TURKEY
Stage 3
13 April 2021
Beysehir–Alanya
212.6km

## WEATHER

TEMPERATURE: 10°C
WIND: NE 7km/h

## STAGE RESULTS

| POS | NAME | TEAM | TIME |
|---|---|---|---|
| 1. | M. Cavendish | DQT | 5:10:30 |
| 2. | J. Philipsen | AFC | s.t. |
| 3. | S. Aniołkowski | BWB | s.t. |
| 4. | K. Halvorsen | UXT | s.t. |
| 5. | A. Greipel | ISN | s.t. |
| 6. | M. Belletti | EOK | s.t. |
| 7. | A. de Kleijn | RLY | s.t. |
| 8. | L. Taminiaux | AFC | s.t. |
| 9. | E. M. Grosu | DKO | s.t. |
| 10. | G. Lonardi | BCF | s.t. |
| 11. | M. Peñalver | BBH | s.t. |
| 12. | D. González | CJR | s.t. |
| 13. | L. Kulbe | SVL | s.t. |
| 14. | W. Vercamst | BWB | s.t. |
| 15. | N. Granigan | WGC | s.t. |
| 16. | M. Stash | STC | s.t. |
| 17. | P. Barbier | DKO | s.t. |
| 18. | S. Shauchenka | MCC | s.t. |
| 19. | S. Wærenskjold | UXT | s.t. |
| 20. | D. Cima | GAZ | s.t. |

## GENERAL CLASSIFICATION

| POS | NAME | TEAM | TIME |
|---|---|---|---|
| 1. — | M. Cavendish | DQT | 10:03:14 |
| 2. ↑1 | J. Philipsen | AFC | 0:08 |
| 3. ↓1 | A. de Kleijn | RLY | 0:10 |

## KING OF THE MOUNTAINS

| POS | NAME | TEAM | PTS |
|---|---|---|---|
| 1. — | V. Buts | SBB | 9 |
| 2. — | N. Venchiarutti | ANS | 8 |
| 3. ↑2 | U. A. Castillo | WGC | 7 |

## POINTS

| POS | NAME | TEAM | PTS |
|---|---|---|---|
| 1. — | M. Cavendish | DQT | 42 |
| 2. ↑1 | J. Philipsen | AFC | 39 |
| 3. ↓1 | A. de Kleijn | RLY | 36 |

# PRESIDENTIAL TOUR OF TURKEY
Stage 4
14 April 2021
Alanya–Kemer
184.4km

## WEATHER

TEMPERATURE: 18°C
WIND: SW 13km/h

## STAGE RESULTS

| POS | NAME | TEAM | TIME |
|---|---|---|---|
| 1. | M. Cavendish | DQT | 4:09:38 |
| 2. | J. Philipsen | AFC | s.t. |
| 3. | S. Aniołkowski | BWB | s.t. |
| 4. | A. de Kleijn | RLY | s.t. |
| 5. | P. Barbier | DKO | s.t. |
| 6. | D. González | CJR | s.t. |
| 7. | L. Kulbe | SVL | s.t. |
| 8. | L. Mozzato | BBK | s.t. |
| 9. | M. Pluto | ABC | s.t. |
| 10. | D. Cima | GAZ | s.t. |
| 11. | M. Peñalver | BBH | s.t. |
| 12. | K. Halvorsen | UXT | s.t. |
| 13. | Y. Gidich | APT | s.t. |
| 14. | W. Vercamst | BWB | s.t. |
| 15. | L. Taminiaux | AFC | s.t. |
| 16. | M. Malucelli | ANS | s.t. |
| 17. | P. Münstermann | SVL | s.t. |
| 18. | B. Del Grosso | ABC | s.t. |
| 19. | G. Bouglas | SBB | s.t. |
| 20. | W. Smit | BBH | s.t. |

## GENERAL CLASSIFICATION

| POS | NAME | TEAM | TIME |
|---|---|---|---|
| 1. — | M. Cavendish | DQT | 14:12:42 |
| 2. — | J. Philipsen | AFC | 0:12 |
| 3. — | A. de Kleijn | RLY | 0:20 |

## KING OF THE MOUNTAINS

| POS | NAME | TEAM | PTS |
|---|---|---|---|
| 1. — | V. Buts | SBB | 9 |
| 2. — | N. Venchiarutti | ANS | 8 |
| 3. — | U. A. Castillo | WGC | 7 |

## POINTS

| POS | NAME | TEAM | PTS |
|---|---|---|---|
| 1. — | M. Cavendish | DQT | 57 |
| 2. — | J. Philipsen | AFC | 53 |
| 3. — | A. de Kleijn | RLY | 48 |

APRIL .PRO MEN'S RACE

## PRESIDENTIAL TOUR OF TURKEY
Stage 5
15 April 2021
Kemer–Elmalı (Göğübeli)
160.3km

### WEATHER

| TEMPERATURE | WIND |
|---|---|
| 19°C | S 15km/h |

### STAGE RESULTS

| POS | NAME | TEAM | TIME |
|---|---|---|---|
| 1. | J. M. Díaz | DKO | 4:25:25 |
| 2. | J. Vine | AFC | s.t. |
| 3. | E. Sepúlveda | ANS | s.t. |
| 4. | A. H. Johannessen | UXT | 0:15 |
| 5. | J. García | CJR | s.t. |
| 6. | M. Kudus | APT | 0:18 |
| 7. | A. Charmig | UXT | 0:20 |
| 8. | D. Fernández | DKO | 0:23 |
| 9. | Q. Pacher | BBK | 0:38 |
| 10. | A. Nych | GAZ | 0:42 |
| 11. | G. Mannion | RLY | 0:45 |
| 12. | G. Bravo | EUS | 0:54 |
| 13. | J. Romo | APT | 1:11 |
| 14. | A. Hoehn | WGC | 1:19 |
| 15. | R. Contreras | APT | s.t. |
| 16. | M. Finetto | DKO | 1:21 |
| 17. | J. Bol | BBH | 1:23 |
| 18. | P. Rolland | BBK | 1:31 |
| 19. | S. Berwick | ISN | 1:40 |
| 20. | N. Cherkasov | GAZ | 1:59 |

### GENERAL CLASSIFICATION

| POS | | NAME | TEAM | TIME |
|---|---|---|---|---|
| 1. | ↑48 | J. M. Díaz | DKO | 18:38:27 |
| 2. | ↑89 | J. Vine | AFC | 0:04 |
| 3. | ↑44 | E. Sepúlveda | ANS | 0:06 |

### KING OF THE MOUNTAINS

| POS | | NAME | TEAM | PTS |
|---|---|---|---|---|
| 1. | — | V. Buts | SBB | 19 |
| 2. | — | J. M. Díaz | DKO | 10 |
| 3. | — | M. Maestri | BCF | 10 |

### POINTS

| POS | | NAME | TEAM | PTS |
|---|---|---|---|---|
| 1. | — | M. Cavendish | DQT | 57 |
| 2. | — | J. Philipsen | AFC | 53 |
| 3. | — | A. de Kleijn | RLY | 45 |

## PRESIDENTIAL TOUR OF TURKEY
Stage 6
16 April 2021
Fethiye–Marmaris
129.1km

### WEATHER

| TEMPERATURE | WIND |
|---|---|
| 19°C | SW 19km/h |

### STAGE RESULTS

| POS | NAME | TEAM | TIME |
|---|---|---|---|
| 1. | J. Philipsen | AFC | 2:55:50 |
| 2. | A. Greipel | ISN | s.t. |
| 3. | K. Halvorsen | UXT | s.t. |
| 4. | M. Cavendish | DQT | s.t. |
| 5. | S. Aniołkowski | BWB | s.t. |
| 6. | L. Mozzato | BBK | s.t. |
| 7. | G. Lonardi | BCF | s.t. |
| 8. | V. Albanese | EOK | s.t. |
| 9. | I. Boev | GAZ | s.t. |
| 10. | M. Pluto | ABC | s.t. |
| 11. | E. M. Grosu | DKO | s.t. |
| 12. | N. Venchiarutti | ANS | s.t. |
| 13. | K. Reza | BBK | s.t. |
| 14. | D. González | CJR | s.t. |
| 15. | J. Rumac | ANS | s.t. |
| 16. | Y. Gidich | APT | s.t. |
| 17. | S. Shauchenka | MCC | s.t. |
| 18. | D. Cimolai | ISN | s.t. |
| 19. | A. Örken | TSC | s.t. |
| 20. | J. J. Lobato | EUS | s.t. |

### GENERAL CLASSIFICATION

| POS | | NAME | TEAM | TIME |
|---|---|---|---|---|
| 1. | — | J. M. Díaz | DKO | 21:34:17 |
| 2. | — | J. Vine | AFC | 0:04 |
| 3. | — | E. Sepúlveda | ANS | 0:06 |

### KING OF THE MOUNTAINS

| POS | | NAME | TEAM | PTS |
|---|---|---|---|---|
| 1. | — | V. Buts | SBB | 22 |
| 2. | ↑3 | J. Vine | AFC | 11 |
| 3. | ↓1 | J. M. Díaz | DKO | 10 |

### POINTS

| POS | | NAME | TEAM | PTS |
|---|---|---|---|---|
| 1. | — | M. Cavendish | DQT | 69 |
| 2. | — | J. Philipsen | AFC | 68 |
| 3. | ↑2 | A. Greipel | ISN | 48 |

APRIL .PRO MEN'S RACE

# PRESIDENTIAL TOUR OF TURKEY
Stage 7
17 April 2021
Marmaris–Turgutreis
180km

## WEATHER

TEMPERATURE | WIND
24°C | SW 17km/h

## STAGE RESULTS

| POS | NAME | TEAM | TIME |
|---|---|---|---|
| 1. | J. Philipsen | AFC | 4:20:45 |
| 2. | A. Greipel | ISN | s.t. |
| 3. | M. Cavendish | DQT | s.t. |
| 4. | S. Aniołkowski | BWB | s.t. |
| 5. | V. Albanese | EOK | s.t. |
| 6. | R. Zabel | ISN | s.t. |
| 7. | L. Wackermann | EOK | s.t. |
| 8. | G. Brussenskiy | APT | s.t. |
| 9. | G. Lonardi | BCF | s.t. |
| 10. | A. Örken | TSC | s.t. |
| 11. | D. González | CJR | s.t. |
| 12. | J. Vine | AFC | s.t. |
| 13. | K. Halvorsen | UXT | s.t. |
| 14. | I. Azurmendi | EUS | s.t. |
| 15. | J. Bol | BBH | s.t. |
| 16. | L. Taminiaux | AFC | s.t. |
| 17. | S. Bazhkou | MCC | s.t. |
| 18. | N. Venchiarutti | ANS | s.t. |
| 19. | S. Steels | DQT | s.t. |
| 20. | A. H. Johannessen | UXT | s.t. |

## GENERAL CLASSIFICATION

| POS | | NAME | TEAM | TIME |
|---|---|---|---|---|
| 1. | – | J. M. Díaz | DKO | 25:55:02 |
| 2. | – | J. Vine | AFC | 0:01 |
| 3. | – | E. Sepúlveda | ANS | 0:06 |

## KING OF THE MOUNTAINS

| POS | | NAME | TEAM | PTS |
|---|---|---|---|---|
| 1. | – | V. Buts | SBB | 22 |
| 2. | – | D. Celano | TSC | 15 |
| 3. | ↓1 | J. Vine | AFC | 11 |

## POINTS

| POS | | NAME | TEAM | PTS |
|---|---|---|---|---|
| 1. | ↑1 | J. Philipsen | AFC | 86 |
| 2. | ↓1 | M. Cavendish | DQT | 82 |
| 3. | – | A. Greipel | ISN | 62 |

# PRESIDENTIAL TOUR OF TURKEY
Stage 8
18 April 2021
Bodrum–Kusadasi
160.3km

## WEATHER

TEMPERATURE | WIND
27°C | SE 22km/h

## STAGE RESULTS

| POS | NAME | TEAM | TIME |
|---|---|---|---|
| 1. | M. Cavendish | DQT | 3:24:38 |
| 2. | J. Philipsen | AFC | s.t. |
| 3. | K. Halvorsen | UXT | s.t. |
| 4. | A. Greipel | ISN | s.t. |
| 5. | G. Lonardi | BCF | s.t. |
| 6. | V. Albanese | EOK | s.t. |
| 7. | S. Aniołkowski | BWB | s.t. |
| 8. | D. Cima | GAZ | s.t. |
| 9. | J. Aranburu | EUS | s.t. |
| 10. | A. Örken | TSC | s.t. |
| 11. | A. Peron | TNN | s.t. |
| 12. | D. González | CJR | s.t. |
| 13. | D. Cimolai | ISN | s.t. |
| 14. | J. García | CJR | s.t. |
| 15. | S. Wærenskjold | UXT | s.t. |
| 16. | M. Kudus | APT | s.t. |
| 17. | C. Raileanu | TSC | s.t. |
| 18. | A. Hoehn | WGC | s.t. |
| 19. | S. Zoccarato | BCF | s.t. |
| 20. | J. Bol | BBH | s.t. |

## GENERAL CLASSIFICATION

| POS | | NAME | TEAM | TIME |
|---|---|---|---|---|
| 1. | – | J. M. Díaz | DKO | 29:19:40 |
| 2. | – | J. Vine | AFC | 0:01 |
| 3. | – | E. Sepúlveda | ANS | 0:06 |

## KING OF THE MOUNTAINS

| POS | | NAME | TEAM | PTS |
|---|---|---|---|---|
| 1. | – | V. Buts | SBB | 25 |
| 2. | – | D. Celano | TSC | 22 |
| 3. | ↑2 | M. Maestri | BCF | 11 |

## POINTS

| POS | | NAME | TEAM | PTS |
|---|---|---|---|---|
| 1. | – | J. Philipsen | AFC | 101 |
| 2. | – | M. Cavendish | DQT | 97 |
| 3. | – | A. Greipel | ISN | 74 |

APRIL  .PRO MEN'S RACE

# DE BRABANTSE PIJL
14 April 2021
Leuven–Overijse
201.7km

## WEATHER

TEMPERATURE  
8°C

WIND  
S 4km/h

## RESULTS

| POS | NAME | TEAM | TIME |
|---|---|---|---|
| 1. | T. Pidcock | IGD | 4:36:27 |
| 2. | W. van Aert | TJV | s.t. |
| 3. | M. Trentin | UAD | 0:02 |
| 4. | I. Schelling | BOH | 0:07 |
| 5. | T. Skujiņš | TFS | s.t. |
| 6. | R. Stannard | BEX | s.t. |
| 7. | D. Teuns | TBV | s.t. |
| 8. | B. Cosnefroy | ACT | s.t. |
| 9. | O. Riesebeek | AFC | s.t. |
| 10. | A. Leknessund | DSM | 0:12 |
| 11. | R. Cavagna | DQT | 0:25 |
| 12. | G. Van Avermaet | ACT | 0:48 |
| 13. | D. De Bondt | AFC | s.t. |
| 14. | V. Madouas | GFC | s.t. |
| 15. | M. Menten | BWB | s.t. |
| 16. | S. Moniquet | LTS | s.t. |
| 17. | V. Campenaerts | TQA | 0:51 |
| 18. | C. Laporte | COF | 0:53 |
| 19. | M. Burghardt | BOH | s.t. |
| 20. | R. Molard | GFC | s.t. |

APRIL .PRO MEN'S RACE

## VOLTA A LA COMUNITAT VALENCIANA
Stage 1
14 April 2021
Elche–Ondara
168.9km

### WEATHER

TEMPERATURE  WIND
16°C  NE 19km/h

### STAGE RESULTS

| POS | NAME | TEAM | TIME |
|---|---|---|---|
| 1. | M. Scotson | GFC | 4:14:57 |
| 2. | J. Degenkolb | LTS | 0:28 |
| 3. | A. Riou | ARK | s.t. |
| 4. | C. Joyce | RLY | s.t. |
| 5. | S. Consonni | COF | s.t. |
| 6. | T. Ferasse | BBK | s.t. |
| 7. | S. Küng | GFC | s.t. |
| 8. | F. Bonnamour | BBK | s.t. |
| 9. | J. Lastra | CJR | s.t. |
| 10. | R. Mertz | BWB | s.t. |
| 11. | P. Wright | MGK | s.t. |
| 12. | M. Louvel | ARK | s.t. |
| 13. | A. Raugel | GFC | s.t. |
| 14. | J. López | EKP | s.t. |
| 15. | A. Molenaar | BBH | s.t. |
| 16. | J. Hivert | BBK | s.t. |
| 17. | S. Novikov | EKP | s.t. |
| 18. | É. Gesbert | ARK | s.t. |
| 19. | J. Ezquerra | BBH | s.t. |
| 20. | V. Lafay | COF | s.t. |

### GENERAL CLASSIFICATION

| POS | NAME | TEAM | TIME |
|---|---|---|---|
| 1. | M. Scotson | GFC | 4:14:47 |
| 2. | J. Degenkolb | LTS | 0:32 |
| 3. | A. Riou | ARK | 0:34 |

### KING OF THE MOUNTAINS

| POS | NAME | TEAM | PTS |
|---|---|---|---|
| 1. | I. Ruiz | EKP | 21 |
| 2. | L. Teugels | TIS | 8 |
| 3. | S. Bassett | RLY | 6 |

### POINTS

| POS | NAME | TEAM | PTS |
|---|---|---|---|
| 1. | M. Scotson | GFC | 25 |
| 2. | J. Degenkolb | LTS | 20 |
| 3. | A. Riou | ARK | 16 |

### YOUNG RIDER

| POS | NAME | TEAM | TIME |
|---|---|---|---|
| 1. | A. Riou | ARK | 4:15:21 |
| 2. | V. Lafay | COF | 0:03 |
| 3. | P. Wright | MGK | 0:04 |

## VOLTA A LA COMUNITAT VALENCIANA
Stage 2
15 April 2021
Alicante–Alicante
179km

### WEATHER

TEMPERATURE  WIND
32°C  NW 17km/h

### STAGE RESULTS

| POS | NAME | TEAM | TIME |
|---|---|---|---|
| 1. | A. Démare | GFC | 4:09:23 |
| 2. | T. Dupont | BWB | s.t. |
| 3. | C. Ewan | LTS | s.t. |
| 4. | S. Consonni | COF | s.t. |
| 5. | S. Mora | MOV | s.t. |
| 6. | J. Guarnieri | GFC | s.t. |
| 7. | E. Ávila | BBH | s.t. |
| 8. | C. Joyce | RLY | s.t. |
| 9. | F. Orts | BBH | s.t. |
| 10. | G. D'heygere | TIS | s.t. |
| 11. | J. J. Rojas | MOV | s.t. |
| 12. | M. Louvel | ARK | s.t. |
| 13. | Á. Fuentes | BBH | s.t. |
| 14. | M. Aristi | EUS | s.t. |
| 15. | Á. Jaime | EKP | s.t. |
| 16. | A. De Decker | TIS | s.t. |
| 17. | O. Nisu | EVO | s.t. |
| 18. | A. Riou | ARK | s.t. |
| 19. | A. Molenaar | BBH | s.t. |
| 20. | F. Bonnamour | BBK | s.t. |

### GENERAL CLASSIFICATION

| POS | | NAME | TEAM | TIME |
|---|---|---|---|---|
| 1. | — | M. Scotson | GFC | 8:24:10 |
| 2. | — | J. Degenkolb | LTS | 0:32 |
| 3. | — | A. Riou | ARK | 0:34 |

### KING OF THE MOUNTAINS

| POS | | NAME | TEAM | PTS |
|---|---|---|---|---|
| 1. | — | I. Ruiz | EKP | 27 |
| 2. | — | L. Teugels | TIS | 8 |
| 3. | — | S. Bassett | RLY | 6 |

### POINTS

| POS | | NAME | TEAM | PTS |
|---|---|---|---|---|
| 1. | ↑4 | S. Consonni | COF | 26 |
| 2. | ↓1 | M. Scotson | GFC | 25 |
| 3. | — | A. Démare | GFC | 25 |

### YOUNG RIDER

| POS | | NAME | TEAM | TIME |
|---|---|---|---|---|
| 1. | — | A. Riou | ARK | 8:24:44 |
| 2. | — | V. Lafay | COF | 0:03 |
| 3. | ↑1 | M. Louvel | ARK | 0:04 |

APRIL   .PRO MEN'S RACE

## VOLTA A LA COMUNITAT VALENCIANA
Stage 3
16 April 2021
Torrent–Alto de la Reina
165km

### WEATHER

TEMPERATURE | WIND
15°C | E 11km/h

### STAGE RESULTS

| POS | NAME | TEAM | TIME |
|---|---|---|---|
| 1. | E. Mas | MOV | 4:11:47 |
| 2. | V. Lafay | COF | 0:02 |
| 3. | É. Gesbert | ARK | 0:08 |
| 4. | L. A. Maté | EUS | 0:29 |
| 5. | G. Martín | EUS | 0:31 |
| 6. | R. Mertz | BWB | s.t. |
| 7. | N. Oliveira | MOV | 0:35 |
| 8. | R. Rochas | COF | 0:38 |
| 9. | S. Küng | GFC | s.t. |
| 10. | M. Iturria | EUS | 1:33 |
| 11. | J. Lastra | CJR | 1:35 |
| 12. | A. González | MOV | 2:05 |
| 13. | J. Vanendert | BWB | s.t. |
| 14. | D. Navarro | BBH | s.t. |
| 15. | J. Cepeda Hernández | CJR | 2:09 |
| 16. | J. D. Alba | MOV | s.t. |
| 17. | L. Huys | BWB | 2:11 |
| 18. | D. Lopez | EKP | s.t. |
| 19. | M. Louvel | ARK | 2:14 |
| 20. | E. Lietaer | BBK | s.t. |

### GENERAL CLASSIFICATION

| POS | | NAME | TEAM | TIME |
|---|---|---|---|---|
| 1. | ↑3 | E. Mas | MOV | 12:36:22 |
| 2. | ↑4 | V. Lafay | COF | 0:08 |
| 3. | ↑13 | É. Gesbert | ARK | 0:17 |

### KING OF THE MOUNTAINS

| POS | | NAME | TEAM | PTS |
|---|---|---|---|---|
| 1. | – | I. Ruiz | EKP | 30 |
| 2. | – | E. Mas | MOV | 12 |
| 3. | – | V. Lafay | COF | 8 |

### POINTS

| POS | | NAME | TEAM | PTS |
|---|---|---|---|---|
| 1. | ↑21 | E. Mas | MOV | 29 |
| 2. | ↓1 | S. Consonni | COF | 26 |
| 3. | ↓1 | M. Scotson | GFC | 25 |

### YOUNG RIDER

| POS | | NAME | TEAM | TIME |
|---|---|---|---|---|
| 1. | ↑1 | V. Lafay | COF | 12:36:30 |
| 2. | ↑3 | R. Rochas | COF | 0:43 |
| 3. | ↑13 | G. Martín | EUS | 1:47 |

## VOLTA A LA COMUNITAT VALENCIANA
Stage 4 (ITT)
17 April 2021
Xilxes–Playa Almenara
14.3km

### WEATHER

TEMPERATURE | WIND
14°C | SW 13km/h

### STAGE RESULTS

| POS | NAME | TEAM | TIME |
|---|---|---|---|
| 1. | S. Küng | GFC | 16:12 |
| 2. | N. Oliveira | MOV | 0:11 |
| 3. | T. Guernalec | ARK | 0:40 |
| 4. | M. Scotson | GFC | 0:41 |
| 5. | A. Démare | GFC | 1:03 |
| 6. | M. Louvel | ARK | 1:08 |
| 7. | S. Mora | MOV | 1:09 |
| 8. | A. Riou | ARK | 1:12 |
| 9. | X. M. Azparren | EUS | 1:13 |
| 10. | D. Lopez | EKP | 1:14 |
| 11. | S. Sajnok | COF | 1:17 |
| 12. | S. Novikov | EKP | 1:18 |
| 13. | J. Degenkolb | LTS | 1:21 |
| 14. | M. Sheffield | RLY | 1:26 |
| 15. | E. Mas | MOV | 1:27 |
| 16. | V. Lafay | COF | 1:28 |
| 17. | C. García | EKP | 1:34 |
| 18. | É. Gesbert | ARK | 1:35 |
| 19. | Jo. Herrada | COF | 1:36 |
| 20. | I. Erviti | MOV | 1:38 |

### GENERAL CLASSIFICATION

| POS | | NAME | TEAM | TIME |
|---|---|---|---|---|
| 1. | ↑6 | S. Küng | GFC | 12:53:25 |
| 2. | ↑4 | N. Oliveira | MOV | 0:06 |
| 3. | ↓2 | E. Mas | MOV | 0:36 |

### KING OF THE MOUNTAINS

| POS | | NAME | TEAM | PTS |
|---|---|---|---|---|
| 1. | – | I. Ruiz | EKP | 30 |
| 2. | – | E. Mas | MOV | 12 |
| 3. | – | V. Lafay | COF | 8 |

### POINTS

| POS | | NAME | TEAM | PTS |
|---|---|---|---|---|
| 1. | ↑10 | S. Küng | GFC | 41 |
| 2. | ↑1 | M. Scotson | GFC | 39 |
| 3. | ↑1 | A. Démare | GFC | 37 |

### YOUNG RIDER

| POS | | NAME | TEAM | TIME |
|---|---|---|---|---|
| 1. | – | V. Lafay | COF | 12:54:10 |
| 2. | – | R. Rochas | COF | 1:18 |
| 3. | ↑5 | M. Louvel | ARK | 1:58 |

APRIL

APRIL · PRO MEN'S RACE

# VOLTA A LA COMUNITAT VALENCIANA
Stage 5
18 April 2021
Paterna–Valencia
91.2km

## WEATHER

TEMPERATURE: 16°C
WIND: SE 6km/h

## STAGE RESULTS

| POS | NAME | TEAM | TIME |
|---|---|---|---|
| 1. | A. Démare | GFC | 1:56:25 |
| 2. | J. Aberasturi | CJR | s.t. |
| 3. | T. Dupont | BWB | s.t. |
| 4. | S. Consonni | COF | s.t. |
| 5. | C. Joyce | RLY | s.t. |
| 6. | C. Ewan | LTS | s.t. |
| 7. | A. Molenaar | BBH | s.t. |
| 8. | B. Welten | ARK | s.t. |
| 9. | G. Thijssen | LTS | s.t. |
| 10. | F. Di Felice | MGK | s.t. |
| 11. | A. Angulo | EUS | s.t. |
| 12. | X. M. Azparren | EUS | s.t. |
| 13. | A. Viviani | COF | s.t. |
| 14. | A. De Decker | TIS | s.t. |
| 15. | J. J. Rojas | MOV | s.t. |
| 16. | O. Nisu | EVO | s.t. |
| 17. | F. Carollo | MGK | s.t. |
| 18. | J. Guarnieri | GFC | s.t. |
| 19. | M. Louvel | ARK | s.t. |
| 20. | M. Aristi | EUS | s.t. |

## GENERAL CLASSIFICATION

| POS | | NAME | TEAM | TIME |
|---|---|---|---|---|
| 1. | – | S. Küng | GFC | 14:49:50 |
| 2. | – | N. Oliveira | MOV | 0:06 |
| 3. | – | E. Mas | MOV | 0:36 |

## KING OF THE MOUNTAINS

| POS | | NAME | TEAM | PTS |
|---|---|---|---|---|
| 1. | – | I. Ruiz | EKP | 30 |
| 2. | – | E. Mas | MOV | 12 |
| 3. | – | V. Lafay | COF | 8 |

## POINTS

| POS | | NAME | TEAM | PTS |
|---|---|---|---|---|
| 1. | ↑2 | A. Démare | GFC | 62 |
| 2. | ↓1 | S. Küng | GFC | 41 |
| 3. | ↑3 | S. Consonni | COF | 40 |

## YOUNG RIDER

| POS | | NAME | TEAM | TIME |
|---|---|---|---|---|
| 1. | – | V. Lafay | COF | 14:50:35 |
| 2. | – | R. Rochas | COF | 1:18 |
| 3. | – | M. Louvel | ARK | 1:58 |

APRIL WORLDTOUR MEN'S RACE

# AMSTEL GOLD RACE
18 April 2021
Valkenburg–Berg en Terblijt
218.6km

## WEATHER

TEMPERATURE  WIND
11°C         W 13km/h

The 55th edition broke from tradition by replacing the usual course with 12 laps of a circuit that included the Geulhemmerberg, Bemelerberg and iconic Cauberg. A 13th shorter loop would bring an end to the race, missing out the Cauberg in favour of Matthieu van der Poel Allee, its namesake not in attendance. The peloton was happy to hold the breakaway at about 4 minutes until the ninth ascent of the Bemelerberg, where Power (Qhubeka) accelerated off the front, marking the start of a flurry of attacks and the steady crumbling of the breakaway's lead. A small number of attackers bridged to the leaders inside the last 40km, but the group began to disintegrate almost immediately. The on-form Schelling (Bora) sounded the death knell for the last fragments of the breakaway, enjoying the pointy end of affairs until he was caught on the last time up the Cauberg. As Roglič fell victim to a mechanical, his co-leader Van Aert rode away with a small group of favourites, including three Ineos riders who began a series of determined accelerations. When Pidcock attacked, only Schachmann (Bora) and Van Aert could follow, and the trio went all the way to the finish. With Schachmann third wheel and fading, Van Aert opened his sprint from the front and Pidcock came up alongside with a ferocious turn of pace. A controversial photo finish showed that the race was just 2mm too short for the Brit, who had to settle for second.

## PROFILE

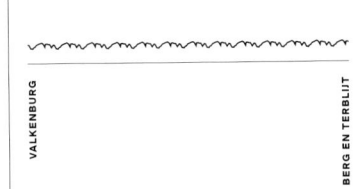

VALKENBURG — BERG EN TERBLIJT

## BREAKAWAY

E. Theuns (TFS), J. Bernard (TFS), S. Dewulf (ACT), S. Grignard (LTS), M. Lammertink (IWG), L. Vliegen (IWG), C. Haga (DSM), R. Gibbons (UAD), K. Molly (BWB), A. Skaarseth (UXT)

## RESULTS

| POS | NAME | TEAM | TIME |
|---|---|---|---|
| 1. | W. van Aert | TJV | 5:03:29 |
| 2. | T. Pidcock | IGD | s.t. |
| 3. | M. Schachmann | BOH | s.t. |
| 4. | M. Matthews | BEX | 0:03 |
| 5. | A. Valverde | MOV | s.t. |
| 6. | J. Alaphilippe | DQT | s.t. |
| 7. | K. Sbaragli | AFC | s.t. |
| 8. | M. Kwiatkowski | IGD | s.t. |
| 9. | M. Mohorič | TBV | s.t. |
| 10. | T. Van der Sande | LTS | s.t. |
| 11. | A. Aranburu | APT | s.t. |
| 12. | M. Trentin | UAD | s.t. |
| 13. | M. Valgren | EFN | s.t. |
| 14. | P. Konrad | BOH | s.t. |
| 15. | T. Benoot | DSM | s.t. |
| 16. | G. Martin | COF | s.t. |
| 17. | B. Tulett | AFC | s.t. |
| 18. | A. Paret-Peintre | ACT | s.t. |
| 19. | M. Hoelgaard | UXT | s.t. |
| 20. | Q. Hermans | IWG | s.t. |

## TRIVIA

» This was Tom Pidcock's fourth top-five finish in his debut season as a pro.

APRIL  WORLDTOUR WOMEN'S RACE

# AMSTEL GOLD RACE
18 April 2021
Valkenburg–Berg en Terblijt
116.3km

## WEATHER

TEMPERATURE
7°C

WIND
W 6km/h

## PROFILE

VALKENBURG

BERG EN TERBLIJT

## BREAKAWAY

L. Kennedy (BEX), E. Chabbey (CSR), M. Bastianelli (ALE), T. Wiles (TFS)

With the absence of Amstel Gold Race in 2020 due to the Covid-19 pandemic, the riders lined up for a traditional spring edition with gratitude, excitement and uncertainty due to a modified course. The 116.3km event was moved to a circuit for 2021, untraditionally starting in Valkenburg with an opening 14.9km lap followed by six laps of 16.9km featuring three main climbs: the Geulhemmerberg, Bemelerberg and Cauberg. A large breakaway of 19 riders animated the early proceedings, but the move was eventually shut down when world champion Anna van der Breggen bridged across, taking Team BikeExchange's Grace Brown with her on the Cauberg. A flurry of moves then followed, with Trek-Segafredo using their numbers to attack one after the other before Brown launched her own strong and dangerous counter-attack while Pauliena Rooijakkers followed. The duo quickly opened up a gap with the peloton in a panic behind. Brown soon dropped Rooijakkers and went for it solo, only to be caught with less than 3km to go when Annemiek van Vleuten launched a fierce attack the final time up the Cauberg. Katarzyna Niewiadoma followed the European champion before flying straight past her with Elisa Longo Borghini tight on the wheel as, behind, Van Vleuten began to fade. It looked like the race-winning move had established; however, the duo began to stall on the finishing straight and their chances were quickly over once Marianne Vos charged past to take the race victory in her home country.

## RESULTS

| POS | NAME | TEAM | TIME |
|---|---|---|---|
| 1. | M. Vos | JVW | 3:00:20 |
| 2. | D. Vollering | SDW | s.t. |
| 3. | A. van Vleuten | MOV | s.t. |
| 4. | A. Spratt | BEX | s.t. |
| 5. | S. Paladin | LIV | s.t. |
| 6. | M. García | ALE | s.t. |
| 7. | C. U. Ludwig | FDJ | 0:01 |
| 8. | E. Longo Borghini | TFS | s.t. |
| 9. | A. Moolman | SDW | s.t. |
| 10. | K. Niewiadoma | CSR | 0:02 |
| 11. | K. Aalerud | MOV | 0:09 |
| 12. | N. Fisher-Black | SDW | s.t. |
| 13. | M. Novolodskaia | MNX | 0:10 |
| 14. | E. Magnaldi | WNT | s.t. |
| 15. | K. Faulkner | TIB | 0:16 |
| 16. | J. Labous | DSM | 0:18 |
| 17. | A. Shackley | SDW | 0:19 |
| 18. | L. Kennedy | BEX | 0:26 |
| 19. | G. Brown | BEX | 0:55 |
| 20. | R. Winder | TFS | 1:00 |

## TRIVIA

» Riders from the Netherlands have now won five of the seven editions of AGR (with riders from Poland and the UK grabbing the other two).

APRIL .PRO MEN'S RACE

## TOUR OF THE ALPS
Stage 1
19 April 2021
Brixen–Innsbruck
140.6km

### WEATHER

TEMPERATURE | WIND
15°C | NW 9km/h

### STAGE RESULTS

| POS | NAME | TEAM | TIME |
|---|---|---|---|
| 1. | G. Moscon | IGD | 3:29:24 |
| 2. | I. Andersen | UXT | s.t. |
| 3. | A. Riabushenko | UAD | s.t. |
| 4. | F. Felline | APT | s.t. |
| 5. | N. Schultz | BEX | s.t. |
| 6. | E. Battaglin | BCF | s.t. |
| 7. | G. Brambilla | TFS | s.t. |
| 8. | R. Guerreiro | EFN | s.t. |
| 9. | N. Tesfatsion | ANS | s.t. |
| 10. | R. Janse Van Rensburg | TQA | s.t. |
| 11. | L. L. Sanchez | APT | s.t. |
| 12. | N. Quintana | ARK | s.t. |
| 13. | P. Bilbao | TBV | s.t. |
| 14. | D. Savini | BCF | s.t. |
| 15. | O. Goldstein | ISN | s.t. |
| 16. | L. Chirico | ANS | s.t. |
| 17. | D. Bais | EOK | s.t. |
| 18. | F. Großschartner | BOH | s.t. |
| 19. | L. Warbasse | ACT | s.t. |
| 20. | L. van den Berg | GFC | s.t. |

### GENERAL CLASSIFICATION

| POS | NAME | TEAM | TIME |
|---|---|---|---|
| 1. | G. Moscon | IGD | 3:29:14 |
| 2. | I. Andersen | UXT | 0:04 |
| 3. | A. Riabushenko | UAD | 0:06 |

### KING OF THE MOUNTAINS

| POS | NAME | TEAM | PTS |
|---|---|---|---|
| 1. | A. De Marchi | ISN | 9 |
| 2. | M. Dina | EOK | 6 |
| 3. | F. Engelhardt | TIR | 3 |

### YOUNG RIDER

| POS | NAME | TEAM | TIME |
|---|---|---|---|
| 1. | I. Andersen | UXT | 3:29:18 |
| 2. | N. Tesfatsion | ANS | 0:06 |
| 3. | D. Bais | EOK | s.t. |

## TOUR OF THE ALPS
Stage 2
20 April 2021
Innsbruck–Feichten im Kaunertal
121.5km

### WEATHER

TEMPERATURE | WIND
11°C | NE 17km/h

### STAGE RESULTS

| POS | NAME | TEAM | TIME |
|---|---|---|---|
| 1. | S. Yates | BEX | 3:17:42 |
| 2. | P. Sivakov | IGD | 0:41 |
| 3. | D. Martin | ISN | 0:58 |
| 4. | A. Vlasov | APT | s.t. |
| 5. | J. Cepeda Ortiz | ANS | s.t. |
| 6. | J. Hindley | DSM | 1:17 |
| 7. | H. Carthy | EFN | s.t. |
| 8. | N. Schultz | BEX | 1:42 |
| 9. | R. Bardet | DSM | s.t. |
| 10. | R. Guerreiro | EFN | s.t. |
| 11. | P. Bilbao | TBV | s.t. |
| 12. | I. R. Sosa | IGD | s.t. |
| 13. | N. Quintana | ARK | s.t. |
| 14. | G. Bouchard | ACT | 1:59 |
| 15. | D. F. Martínez | IGD | 2:08 |
| 16. | T. H. Johannessen | UXT | s.t. |
| 17. | G. Brambilla | TFS | 2:49 |
| 18. | A. Osorio | CJR | s.t. |
| 19. | A. Ghebreigzabhier | TFS | s.t. |
| 20. | M. Nieve | BEX | s.t. |

### GENERAL CLASSIFICATION

| POS | NAME | TEAM | TIME |
|---|---|---|---|
| 1. ↑60 | S. Yates | BEX | 6:46:56 |
| 2. ↑28 | P. Sivakov | IGD | 0:45 |
| 3. ↑46 | D. Martin | ISN | 1:04 |

### KING OF THE MOUNTAINS

| POS | NAME | TEAM | PTS |
|---|---|---|---|
| 1. — | S. Yates | BEX | 10 |
| 2. ↓1 | A. De Marchi | ISN | 9 |
| 3. — | P. Sivakov | IGD | 8 |

### YOUNG RIDER

| POS | NAME | TEAM | TIME |
|---|---|---|---|
| 1. ↑15 | J. Cepeda Ortiz | ANS | 6:48:04 |
| 2. ↑4 | T. H. Johannessen | UXT | 1:10 |
| 3. ↑9 | A. Osorio | CJR | 1:51 |

APRIL    .PRO MEN'S RACE

# TOUR OF THE ALPS
Stage 3
21 April 2021
Imst–Naturns
162km

## WEATHER

TEMPERATURE: 17°C    WIND: W 4km/h

## STAGE RESULTS

| POS | NAME | TEAM | TIME |
|---|---|---|---|
| 1. | G. Moscon | IGD | 4:04:25 |
| 2. | F. Großschartner | BOH | s.t. |
| 3. | M. Storer | DSM | 0:01 |
| 4. | M. Fabbro | BOH | s.t. |
| 5. | A. De Marchi | ISN | s.t. |
| 6. | A. Nibali | TFS | s.t. |
| 7. | F. Bidard | ACT | s.t. |
| 8. | P. Bilbao | TBV | s.t. |
| 9. | L. L. Sanchez | APT | s.t. |
| 10. | H. Pernsteiner | TBV | 0:13 |
| 11. | N. Roche | DSM | 0:49 |
| 12. | M. Padun | TBV | s.t. |
| 13. | R. Guerreiro | EFN | s.t. |
| 14. | G. Brambilla | TFS | s.t. |
| 15. | C. Scaroni | GAZ | s.t. |
| 16. | L. Warbasse | ACT | s.t. |
| 17. | A. Tiberi | TFS | s.t. |
| 18. | E. Battaglin | BCF | s.t. |
| 19. | R. Bardet | DSM | s.t. |
| 20. | H. Vandenabeele | DSM | s.t. |

## GENERAL CLASSIFICATION

| POS | NAME | TEAM | TIME |
|---|---|---|---|
| 1. — | S. Yates | BEX | 10:52:10 |
| 2. — | P. Sivakov | IGD | 0:45 |
| 3. ↑7 | P. Bilbao | TBV | 1:04 |

## KING OF THE MOUNTAINS

| POS | NAME | TEAM | PTS |
|---|---|---|---|
| 1. ↑1 | A. De Marchi | ISN | 15 |
| 2. ↓1 | S. Yates | BEX | 10 |
| 3. ↑1 | R. Thompson | GFC | 10 |

## YOUNG RIDER

| POS | NAME | TEAM | TIME |
|---|---|---|---|
| 1. — | J. Cepeda Ortiz | ANS | 10:53:18 |
| 2. ↑1 | A. Osorio | CJR | 1:51 |
| 3. ↑1 | M. Ries | TFS | 2:13 |

# TOUR OF THE ALPS
Stage 4
22 April 2021
Naturns–Pieve di Bono
168.6km

## WEATHER

TEMPERATURE: 19°C    WIND: S 6km/h

## STAGE RESULTS

| POS | NAME | TEAM | TIME |
|---|---|---|---|
| 1. | P. Bilbao | TBV | 4:39:42 |
| 2. | A. Vlasov | APT | s.t. |
| 3. | S. Yates | BEX | s.t. |
| 4. | N. Quintana | ARK | 0:58 |
| 5. | J. Cepeda Ortiz | ANS | 1:06 |
| 6. | H. Carthy | EFN | s.t. |
| 7. | R. Guerreiro | EFN | 1:16 |
| 8. | R. Bardet | DSM | s.t. |
| 9. | G. Brambilla | TFS | s.t. |
| 10. | M. Fabbro | BOH | 1:22 |
| 11. | A. Osorio | CJR | s.t. |
| 12. | D. Pozzovivo | TQA | 1:36 |
| 13. | N. Schultz | BEX | 1:40 |
| 14. | G. Bouchard | ACT | s.t. |
| 15. | P. Sivakov | IGD | 1:48 |
| 16. | D. F. Martínez | IGD | 1:52 |
| 17. | F. Lipowitz | TIR | 2:06 |
| 18. | J. Hindley | DSM | 2:19 |
| 19. | E. Ravasi | EOK | 2:35 |
| 20. | A. C. Ardila | UAD | 2:48 |

## GENERAL CLASSIFICATION

| POS | NAME | TEAM | TIME |
|---|---|---|---|
| 1. — | S. Yates | BEX | 15:31:48 |
| 2. ↑1 | P. Bilbao | TBV | 0:58 |
| 3. ↑2 | A. Vlasov | APT | 1:06 |

## KING OF THE MOUNTAINS

| POS | NAME | TEAM | PTS |
|---|---|---|---|
| 1. ↑5 | M. Dina | EOK | 16 |
| 2. ↓1 | A. De Marchi | ISN | 15 |
| 3. ↓1 | S. Yates | BEX | 14 |

## YOUNG RIDER

| POS | NAME | TEAM | TIME |
|---|---|---|---|
| 1. — | J. Cepeda Ortiz | ANS | 15:34:06 |
| 2. — | A. Osorio | CJR | 2:07 |
| 3. ↑3 | F. Lipowitz | TIR | 3:38 |

APRIL .PRO MEN'S RACE

# TOUR OF THE ALPS

Stage 5
23 April 2021
Valle del Chiese/Idroland–Riva del Garda
120.9km

## WEATHER

TEMPERATURE  WIND
19°C  SE 11km/h

## STAGE RESULTS

| POS | NAME | TEAM | TIME |
|---|---|---|---|
| 1. | F. Großschartner | BOH | 3:03:38 |
| 2. | N. Roche | DSM | 0:34 |
| 3. | A. De Marchi | ISN | s.t. |
| 4. | G. Moscon | IGD | 0:40 |
| 5. | A. Osorio | CJR | s.t. |
| 6. | R. Bardet | DSM | s.t. |
| 7. | L. L. Sanchez | APT | s.t. |
| 8. | R. Guerreiro | EFN | s.t. |
| 9. | M. Padun | TBV | s.t. |
| 10. | M. Fabbro | BOH | s.t. |
| 11. | H. Vandenabeele | DSM | s.t. |
| 12. | S. Yates | BEX | s.t. |
| 13. | N. Schultz | BEX | s.t. |
| 14. | P. Bilbao | TBV | s.t. |
| 15. | A. Vlasov | APT | s.t. |
| 16. | D. Pozzovivo | TQA | s.t. |
| 17. | G. Bouchard | ACT | s.t. |
| 18. | N. Quintana | ARK | s.t. |
| 19. | A. Valter | GFC | s.t. |
| 20. | H. Carthy | EFN | s.t. |

## GENERAL CLASSIFICATION

| POS | NAME | TEAM | TIME |
|---|---|---|---|
| 1. — | S. Yates | BEX | 18:36:06 |
| 2. — | P. Bilbao | TBV | 0:58 |
| 3. — | A. Vlasov | APT | 1:06 |

## KING OF THE MOUNTAINS

| POS | NAME | TEAM | PTS |
|---|---|---|---|
| 1. ↑1 | A. De Marchi | ISN | 25 |
| 2. ↓1 | M. Dina | EOK | 16 |
| 3. — | S. Yates | BEX | 14 |

## YOUNG RIDER

| POS | NAME | TEAM | TIME |
|---|---|---|---|
| 1. — | J. Cepeda Ortiz | ANS | 18:38:31 |
| 2. — | A. Osorio | CJR | 2:00 |
| 3. — | F. Lipowitz | TIR | 4:03 |

APRIL   WORLDTOUR MEN'S RACE

# LA FLÈCHE WALLONNE
21 April 2021
Charleroi–Mur de Huy
193.6km

## WEATHER

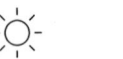

**TEMPERATURE** 14°C   **WIND** N 11km/h

## PROFILE

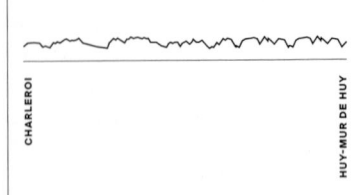

CHARLEROI — HUY-MUR DE HUY

The race got underway without defending champion Hirschi due to a positive Covid-19 test in the UAE Team Emirates camp. Once the eight-man breakaway was established, positioning before the climbs was the priority in the peloton. The leaders carried 3 minutes onto the first of three ascents of the Mur de Huy, Louis Vervaeke looking like the strongest among them. As the breakaway crossed the finish line for the penultimate time, Simon Geschke accelerated out of the peloton, marked by Tao Geoghegan Hart with Krists Neilands, Jan Tratnik and Mauri Vansevenant close behind. It was all together again by 30km to go, but their efforts effectively carried the race into the third act. While Tom Pidcock chased back after a crash, the gap to the breakaway fell under a minute with Jumbo-Visma driving the peloton. Tim Wellens jumped away on the Côte d'Ereffe, drawing out Omar Fraile and Ilan Van Wilder. Richard Carapaz launched next, and it fell to James Knox to patiently haul in the attackers inside the last 10km. The surviving breakaway rider, Maurits Lammertink, was caught just before the bottom of the Mur de Huy, the peloton led by Tratnik and Mikkel Honoré. First-timer Primož Roglič chose to tail two-time winner Julian Alaphilippe up the climb but made the mistake of accelerating first. The world champion knew exactly what he was doing, climbing up to Roglič with Alejandro Valverde on his wheel, before opening his sprint at the 50-metre mark to take a definitive victory. (KN)

## BREAKAWAY

A. Howes (EFN), S. Moniquet (LTS), S. Armée (TQA), M. Lammertink (IWG), J. Mertens (SVB), D. Rosa (ARK), L. Vervaeke (AFC), S. Velasco (GAZ)

## TRIVIA

» Alaphilippe is now equal on three wins at Flèche Wallonne alongside Eddy Merckx, Marcel Kint, Moreno Argentin and Davide Rebellin. Only Alejandro Valverde has more, with five.

## RESULTS

| POS | NAME | TEAM | TIME |
|---|---|---|---|
| 1. | J. Alaphilippe | DQT | 4:36:25 |
| 2. | P. Roglič | TJV | s.t. |
| 3. | A. Valverde | MOV | 0:06 |
| 4. | M. Woods | ISN | 0:08 |
| 5. | W. Barguil | ARK | 0:11 |
| 6. | T. Pidcock | IGD | s.t. |
| 7. | D. Gaudu | GFC | s.t. |
| 8. | E. Chaves | BEX | s.t. |
| 9. | R. Carapaz | IGD | s.t. |
| 10. | M. Schachmann | BOH | 0:16 |
| 11. | B. Mollema | TFS | s.t. |
| 12. | B. Tulett | AFC | s.t. |
| 13. | A. Aranburu | APT | s.t. |
| 14. | Q. Hermans | IWG | s.t. |
| 15. | P. Konrad | BOH | s.t. |
| 16. | G. Martin | COF | s.t. |
| 17. | J. Fuglsang | APT | 0:19 |
| 18. | B. Cosnefroy | ACT | 0:21 |
| 19. | J. Haig | TBV | s.t. |
| 20. | A. Yates | IGD | 0:27 |

APRIL  WORLDTOUR WOMEN'S RACE

# LA FLÈCHE WALLONNE
21 April 2021
Huy–Mur de Huy
130.2km

It wasn't until the final 50km of racing, ahead of the first ascent of the brutal Mur de Huy, when the first real dangerous move established. Three riders, Elise Chabbey of (Canyon-SRAM), Lucinda Brand (Trek-Segafredo) and Anna Henderson (Jumbo-Visma) attacked away from the bunch and opened up a gap of 40 seconds. The trio remained ahead for the next 30km but, after a hard chase from SD Worx, the group was reeled back in by the reduced peloton with 20km remaining. Immediately as the catch was made, Trek-Segafredo made their move sending American champion Ruth Winder up the road. Winder dangled ahead as the peloton approached the final 10km, and on the Côte du Chemin des Gueuses European champion Annemiek van Vleuten was the next rider to attack, with only eight race favourites able to follow her acceleration. There, the race-winning move was born. Despite the fast pace as more attacks came and went, Winder remained ahead as she entered the base of the Mur de Huy, but with a slim 15-second lead after a hard chase by Demi Vollering (SD Worx). As soon as the road headed north, Winder was caught and gaps began to open up in the group with every pedal stroke. Katarzyna Niewiadoma and Anna van der Breggen proved to be the strongest, distancing the others into the final 400 metres before Van der Breggen accelerated again, crossing the line to claim a phenomenal seventh consecutive win at La Flèche Wallonne Feminine.

## WEATHER

TEMPERATURE  WIND
11°C  N 7km/h

## PROFILE

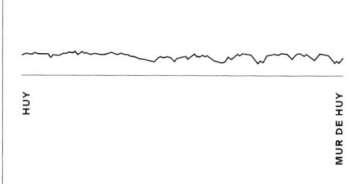

HUY — MUR DE HUY

## BREAKAWAY
M. Lach (WNT), F. Gerritse (PHV)

## TRIVIA
» Anna van der Breggen has now won every edition of La Flèche Wallonne since 2015.

## RESULTS

| POS | NAME | TEAM | TIME |
|---|---|---|---|
| 1. | A. van der Breggen | SDW | 3:28:27 |
| 2. | K. Niewiadoma | CSR | 0:02 |
| 3. | E. Longo Borghini | TFS | 0:06 |
| 4. | A. van Vleuten | MOV | s.t. |
| 5. | M. García | ALE | 0:22 |
| 6. | J. Labous | DSM | 0:28 |
| 7. | R. Winder | TFS | 0:31 |
| 8. | C. U. Ludwig | FDJ | 0:32 |
| 9. | A. Spratt | BEX | 0:35 |
| 10. | D. Vollering | SDW | 0:42 |
| 11. | M. Vos | JVW | 1:32 |
| 12. | A. Moolman | SDW | 1:36 |
| 13. | E. Magnaldi | WNT | 1:38 |
| 14. | K. Doebel-Hickok | RLW | 1:39 |
| 15. | K. Aalerud | MOV | 1:42 |
| 16. | L. Thomas | MOV | s.t. |
| 17. | K. Faulkner | TIB | 1:43 |
| 18. | S. Stultiens | LIV | 1:45 |
| 19. | L. Kennedy | BEX | 1:48 |
| 20. | É. Muzic | FDJ | 1:50 |

APRIL  .1 MEN'S RACE

## BELGRADE BANJALUKA
Stage 1
22 April 2021
Belgrade–Sabac
96km

### WEATHER

TEMPERATURE | WIND
19°C | SW 6km/h

### STAGE RESULTS

| POS | NAME | TEAM | TIME |
| --- | --- | --- | --- |
| 1. | J. Wolf | BAI | 1:52:44 |
| 2. | P. Stosz | VOS | 0:10 |
| 3. | F. Fiorelli | BCF | s.t. |
| 4. | A. Guardini | GTS | s.t. |
| 5. | M. Van Staeyen | EVO | s.t. |
| 6. | D. Rajović | NAT | s.t. |
| 7. | D. Per | ADR | s.t. |
| 8. | S. Daniels | XSU | s.t. |
| 9. | L. Marchiori | ANS | s.t. |
| 10. | M. Heming | PBS | s.t. |
| 11. | A. Banaszek | MSP | s.t. |
| 12. | M. Nikitin | VAM | s.t. |
| 13. | C. Planet | TNN | s.t. |
| 14. | F. Tagliani | ANS | s.t. |
| 15. | T. Vančo | DKB | s.t. |
| 16. | Ž. Jerman | ANS | s.t. |
| 17. | A. Foltan | DKB | s.t. |
| 18. | T. Loderer | HAC | s.t. |
| 19. | Ž. Horvat | ADR | s.t. |
| 20. | R. Jenko | NAT | s.t. |

### GENERAL CLASSIFICATION

| POS | NAME | TEAM | TIME |
| --- | --- | --- | --- |
| 1. | J. Wolf | BAI | 1:52:34 |
| 2. | P. Stosz | VOS | 0:14 |
| 3. | F. Fiorelli | BCF | 0:16 |

### KING OF THE MOUNTAINS

| POS | NAME | TEAM | PTS |
| --- | --- | --- | --- |
| 1. | L. Pajek | HAC | 5 |
| 2. | M. Schmidbauer | WSA | 3 |
| 3. | T. Wollenberg | PBS | 1 |

### YOUNG RIDER

| POS | NAME | TEAM | TIME |
| --- | --- | --- | --- |
| 1. | M. Heming | PBS | 1:52:54 |
| 2. | T. Vančo | DKB | s.t. |
| 3. | A. Foltan | DKB | s.t. |

## BELGRADE BANJALUKA
Stage 2
23 April 2021
Obrenovac–Bijeljina
122km

### WEATHER

TEMPERATURE | WIND
15°C | NW 30km/h

### STAGE RESULTS

| POS | NAME | TEAM | TIME |
| --- | --- | --- | --- |
| 1. | P. Stosz | VOS | 2:37:39 |
| 2. | M. Räim | MSP | s.t. |
| 3. | A. Guardini | GTS | s.t. |
| 4. | F. Fiorelli | BCF | s.t. |
| 5. | P. Simion | GTS | s.t. |
| 6. | M. Van Staeyen | EVO | s.t. |
| 7. | L. Marchiori | ANS | s.t. |
| 8. | Ž. Jerman | ANS | s.t. |
| 9. | F. Tagliani | ANS | s.t. |
| 10. | L. Kubiš | DKB | s.t. |
| 11. | R. Jenko | NAT | s.t. |
| 12. | D. Per | ADR | s.t. |
| 13. | P. Taebling | PBS | s.t. |
| 14. | V. Götzinger | WSA | s.t. |
| 15. | T. Wollenberg | PBS | s.t. |
| 16. | T. Loderer | HAC | s.t. |
| 17. | E. Burtnik | XSU | s.t. |
| 18. | S. Kolb | HAC | s.t. |
| 19. | M. Heming | PBS | s.t. |
| 20. | O. Nisu | EVO | s.t. |

### GENERAL CLASSIFICATION

| POS | NAME | TEAM | TIME |
| --- | --- | --- | --- |
| 1. — | J. Wolf | BAI | 4:30:13 |
| 2. — | P. Stosz | VOS | 0:04 |
| 3. ↑37 | M. Räim | MSP | 0:14 |

### KING OF THE MOUNTAINS

| POS | NAME | TEAM | PTS |
| --- | --- | --- | --- |
| 1. — | L. Pajek | HAC | 6 |
| 2. — | J. Primožič | NAT | 5 |
| 3. — | T. Wollenberg | PBS | 4 |

### YOUNG RIDER

| POS | NAME | TEAM | TIME |
| --- | --- | --- | --- |
| 1. — | M. Heming | PBS | 4:30:33 |
| 2. ↑3 | V. Götzinger | WSA | s.t. |
| 3. ↓1 | T. Vančo | DKB | s.t. |

APRIL .1 MEN'S RACE

## BELGRADE BANJALUKA
Stage 3
24 April 2021
Bijeljina–Vlasenica
124.1km

### WEATHER

TEMPERATURE | WIND
17°C | E 15km/h

### STAGE RESULTS

| POS | NAME | TEAM | TIME |
|---|---|---|---|
| 1. | D. Auer | WSA | 2:37:31 |
| 2. | C. Monk | EVO | s.t. |
| 3. | M. Räim | MSP | s.t. |
| 4. | P. Franczak | VOS | s.t. |
| 5. | N. Venchiarutti | ANS | s.t. |
| 6. | F. Tagliani | ANS | s.t. |
| 7. | L. Kubiš | DKB | s.t. |
| 8. | J. Rapp | HAC | s.t. |
| 9. | J. Primožič | NAT | s.t. |
| 10. | K. J. Yustre | GTS | s.t. |
| 11. | M. Čanecký | DKB | s.t. |
| 12. | F. Fiorelli | BCF | s.t. |
| 13. | P. Stosz | VOS | s.t. |
| 14. | J. Eyskens | EVO | s.t. |
| 15. | D. Per | ADR | s.t. |
| 16. | U. Marengo | BCF | s.t. |
| 17. | P. Tybor | DKB | s.t. |
| 18. | M. Lavrič | NAT | s.t. |
| 19. | Ž. Jerman | ANS | s.t. |
| 20. | J. Wolf | BAI | s.t. |

### GENERAL CLASSIFICATION

| POS | NAME | TEAM | TIME |
|---|---|---|---|
| 1. — | J. Wolf | BAI | 7:07:44 |
| 2. — | P. Stosz | VOS | 0:04 |
| 3. — | M. Räim | MSP | 0:10 |

### KING OF THE MOUNTAINS

| POS | NAME | TEAM | PTS |
|---|---|---|---|
| 1. — | L. Pajek | HAC | 6 |
| 2. — | J. Primožič | NAT | 5 |
| 3. — | A. Tonelli | BCF | 5 |

### YOUNG RIDER

| POS | NAME | TEAM | TIME |
|---|---|---|---|
| 1. ↑8 | L. Kubiš | DKB | 7:08:04 |
| 2. ↑9 | A. Ponomar | ANS | s.t. |
| 3. ↑10 | W. Mol | XSU | s.t. |

## BELGRADE BANJALUKA
Stage 4
25 April 2021
Prijedor–Banjaluka
163.5km

### WEATHER

TEMPERATURE | WIND
19°C | NE 9km/h

### STAGE RESULTS

| POS | NAME | TEAM | TIME |
|---|---|---|---|
| 1. | M. Räim | MSP | 3:32:43 |
| 2. | A. Guardini | GTS | s.t. |
| 3. | L. Marchiori | ANS | s.t. |
| 4. | M. Van Staeyen | EVO | s.t. |
| 5. | S. Daniels | XSU | s.t. |
| 6. | Ž. Jerman | ANS | s.t. |
| 7. | F. Fiorelli | BCF | s.t. |
| 8. | M. Benhamouda | TNN | s.t. |
| 9. | F. Tagliani | ANS | s.t. |
| 10. | B. Rhim | EVO | s.t. |
| 11. | M. Heming | PBS | s.t. |
| 12. | M. Lavrič | NAT | s.t. |
| 13. | M. Debesay | BAI | s.t. |
| 14. | O. Nisu | EVO | s.t. |
| 15. | K. J. Yustre | GTS | s.t. |
| 16. | T. Vančo | DKB | s.t. |
| 17. | R. Jenko | NAT | s.t. |
| 18. | J. Rapp | HAC | s.t. |
| 19. | A. Piasetski | MCC | s.t. |
| 20. | A. Gratzer | WSA | s.t. |

### GENERAL CLASSIFICATION

| POS | NAME | TEAM | TIME |
|---|---|---|---|
| 1. ↑2 | M. Räim | MSP | 10:40:27 |
| 2. ↓1 | J. Wolf | BAI | s.t. |
| 3. ↓1 | P. Stosz | VOS | 0:04 |

### KING OF THE MOUNTAINS

| POS | NAME | TEAM | PTS |
|---|---|---|---|
| 1. ↑3 | D. Auer | WSA | 10 |
| 2. ↓1 | L. Pajek | HAC | 9 |
| 3. ↓1 | J. Primožič | NAT | 6 |

### YOUNG RIDER

| POS | NAME | TEAM | TIME |
|---|---|---|---|
| 1. ↑1 | A. Ponomar | ANS | 10:40:47 |
| 2. ↓1 | L. Kubiš | DKB | s.t. |
| 3. ↑2 | R. A. Sinza | GTS | 0:47 |

APRIL

APRIL  WORLDTOUR MEN'S RACE

# LIÈGE-BASTOGNE-LIÈGE
25 April 2021
Liège–Liège
259.1km

Harm Vanhoucke and Marks Donovan and Padun got things going inside the final 60km, peeling off the front to chase down a breakaway formed mostly of Belgian riders whose jerseys advertised cement, sealants and mayonnaise – important not to get that trio confused. Tao Geoghegan Hart then decided to stretch his legs as Ineos Grenadiers kicked off their plan of attack, Jonas Vingegaard following as Loïc Vliegen's legs finally gave up, having spent each of the three Ardennes Classics in the day's break. Adam Yates then ratcheted things up before Richard Carapaz took a flyer with 20km to go, managing to eke out an advantage of half a minute at one stage. After James Knox had done the first bit of work to bring the Ecuadorian back, Davide Formolo finished the job, both working for their respective team leaders. Things were now finely poised for fireworks on the Côte de la Roche-aux-Faucons, Michael Woods launching his move near the top to take the decisive group clear, defending champion Primož Roglič unable to follow. Accompanying the Canadian to contest the victory were world champion Julian Alaphilippe, Tour champion Tadej Pogačar, four-time Liège victor Alejandro Valverde and upcoming Frenchman David Gaudu. Woods and Gaudu blinked first, Valverde left on the front to open up the sprint, but his legs weren't up to the task on his 41st birthday. Alaphilippe picked his moment well, but had Pogačar glued to his wheel, the Slovenian nicking it on the line, his hands on his head in disbelief as he took his first Monument victory.

## WEATHER

TEMPERATURE  WIND
8°C  NE 22km/h

## PROFILE

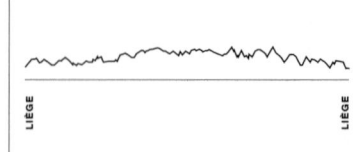

LIÈGE  LIÈGE

## BREAKAWAY

L. Huys (BWB), M. Paasschens (BWB), L. Vliegen (IWG), L. Rota (IWG), S. Chernetski (GAZ), T. Marczynski (LTS), A. Van Poucke (SVB)

## TRIVIA

» In only his fourth appearance at a Monument, Pogačar claimed his first victory.

## RESULTS

| POS | NAME | TEAM | TIME |
|---|---|---|---|
| 1. | T. Pogačar | UAD | 6:39:26 |
| 2. | J. Alaphilippe | DQT | s.t. |
| 3. | D. Gaudu | GFC | s.t. |
| 4. | A. Valverde | MOV | s.t. |
| 5. | M. Woods | ISN | s.t. |
| 6. | M. Hirschi | UAD | 0:07 |
| 7. | T. Benoot | DSM | s.t. |
| 8. | B. Mollema | TFS | s.t. |
| 9. | M. Schachmann | BOH | 0:09 |
| 10. | M. Mohorič | TBV | s.t. |
| 11. | M. Kwiatkowski | IGD | s.t. |
| 12. | J. Fuglsang | APT | s.t. |
| 13. | P. Roglič | TJV | s.t. |
| 14. | E. Chaves | BEX | s.t. |
| 15. | G. Martin | COF | s.t. |
| 16. | D. Formolo | UAD | s.t. |
| 17. | J. Haig | TBV | 0:12 |
| 18. | A. Yates | IGD | 0:37 |
| 19. | M. Matthews | BEX | 1:21 |
| 20. | P. Konrad | BOH | s.t. |
| 21. | A. Aranburu | APT | s.t. |
| 22. | T. Skujiņš | TFS | s.t. |
| 23. | A. Paret-Peintre | ACT | s.t. |
| 24. | T. Wellens | LTS | s.t. |
| 25. | K. Neilands | ISN | s.t. |
| 26. | W. Barguil | ARK | s.t. |
| 27. | W. Kelderman | BOH | s.t. |
| 28. | J. Vingegaard | TJV | s.t. |
| 29. | O. Fraile | APT | s.t. |
| 30. | S. Higuita | EFN | s.t. |
| 31. | S. Clarke | TQA | 1:44 |
| 32. | J. Knox | DQT | s.t. |
| 33. | D. Teuns | TBV | 1:45 |
| 34. | T. Geoghegan Hart | IGD | 1:47 |
| 35. | Q. Hermans | IWG | 2:42 |
| 36. | Je. Herrada | COF | s.t. |
| 37. | M. Donovan | DSM | 2:43 |
| 38. | A. Kamp | TFS | 3:06 |
| 39. | G. Van Avermaet | ACT | s.t. |
| 40. | J. Simon | TDE | s.t. |
| 41. | L. Rota | IWG | s.t. |
| 42. | L. Pichon | ARK | s.t. |
| 43. | F. Barceló | COF | s.t. |
| 44. | N. Conci | TFS | s.t. |
| 45. | L. Wirtgen | BWB | s.t. |
| 46. | R. Gesink | TJV | s.t. |
| 47. | B. Cosnefroy | ACT | s.t. |
| 48. | M. Tusveld | DSM | s.t. |
| 49. | M. F. Honoré | DQT | s.t. |
| 50. | K. Sbaragli | AFC | s.t. |
| 51. | D. Rosa | ARK | s.t. |
| 52. | I. Zakarin | GAZ | s.t. |
| 53. | B. Tulett | AFC | s.t. |
| 54. | I. Schelling | BOH | s.t. |
| 55. | M. Jorgenson | MOV | s.t. |
| 56. | R. Power | TQA | s.t. |
| 57. | M. Valgren | EFN | s.t. |
| 58. | S. Geschke | COF | s.t. |
| 59. | D. Pozzovivo | TQA | s.t. |
| 60. | F. Aru | TQA | s.t. |
| 61. | R. Molard | GFC | s.t. |
| 62. | R. Costa | UAD | s.t. |
| 63. | V. Ferron | TDE | s.t. |
| 64. | J. Almeida | DQT | s.t. |
| 65. | R. Seigle | GFC | s.t. |
| 66. | L. L. Sanchez | APT | s.t. |
| 67. | H. Vanhoucke | LTS | s.t. |
| 68. | C. Hamilton | DSM | s.t. |
| 69. | D. Impey | ISN | s.t. |
| 70. | C. Verona | MOV | s.t. |
| 71. | J. Vanendert | BWB | s.t. |
| 72. | C. Juul-Jensen | BEX | s.t. |
| 73. | L. Hamilton | BEX | s.t. |
| 74. | M. Nieve | BEX | s.t. |
| 75. | R. Fernández | COF | s.t. |
| 76. | S. Henao | TQA | s.t. |
| 77. | P. Latour | TDE | s.t. |
| 78. | M. Padun | TBV | s.t. |
| 79. | M. Vansevenant | DQT | 3:45 |
| 80. | J. Bakelants | IWG | 4:15 |
| 81. | Ł. Owsian | ARK | s.t. |
| 82. | V. Madouas | GFC | s.t. |
| 83. | R. Mertz | BWB | s.t. |
| 84. | S. Moniquet | LTS | s.t. |
| 85. | D. Godon | ACT | 5:02 |
| 86. | J. Bernard | TFS | s.t. |
| 87. | J. Janssens | AFC | s.t. |
| 88. | A. Lutsenko | APT | s.t. |
| 89. | S. Chernetski | GAZ | s.t. |
| 90. | T. Marczyński | LTS | s.t. |
| 91. | L. Vliegen | IWG | 6:17 |
| 92. | A. Van Poucke | SVB | 6:58 |
| 93. | S. Oomen | TJV | s.t. |
| 94. | M. Burgaudeau | TDE | 7:56 |
| 95. | A. Perez | COF | s.t. |
| 96. | S. Velasco | GAZ | 7:59 |
| 97. | N. Arndt | DSM | s.t. |
| 98. | A. Howes | EFN | s.t. |
| 99. | S. de Bod | APT | s.t. |
| 100. | O. Goldstein | ISN | s.t. |
| 101. | P. Gilbert | LTS | s.t. |
| 102. | T. Sprengers | SVB | s.t. |
| 103. | B. Bookwalter | BEX | s.t. |
| 104. | M. Ladagnous | GFC | s.t. |
| 105. | M. Lammertink | IWG | s.t. |
| 106. | J. K. Caicedo | EFN | s.t. |
| 107. | B. O'Connor | ACT | s.t. |
| 108. | W. Poels | TBV | s.t. |
| 109. | S. Armée | TQA | s.t. |
| 110. | F. Doubey | TDE | s.t. |
| 111. | T. Kangert | BEX | s.t. |
| 112. | N. Eg | TFS | s.t. |
| 113. | K. Ledanois | ARK | s.t. |
| 114. | C. Benedetti | BOH | s.t. |
| 115. | E. Mas | MOV | s.t. |
| 116. | X. Meurisse | AFC | 9:32 |
| 117. | G. Serrano | MOV | s.t. |
| 118. | M. Schär | ACT | s.t. |
| 119. | R. Hollenstein | ISN | s.t. |
| 120. | F. Grellier | TDE | s.t. |
| 121. | K. Molly | BWB | 10:28 |
| 122. | M. Paasschens | BWB | s.t. |
| 123. | E. Dunbar | IGD | s.t. |
| 124. | L. Huys | BWB | s.t. |
| 125. | R. Herregodts | SVB | 12:13 |
| 126. | M. Fabbro | BOH | s.t. |
| 127. | J. Mertens | SVB | s.t. |
| 128. | J. Arcas | MOV | s.t. |
| 129. | M. Ries | TFS | s.t. |
| 130. | S. Carr | EFN | s.t. |
| 131. | V. S. Laengen | UAD | s.t. |
| 132. | A. Riou | ARK | s.t. |
| 133. | L. Rowe | IGD | s.t. |
| 134. | M. Gołaś | IGD | s.t. |
| 135. | R. Apers | SVB | s.t. |
| 136. | T. Guernalec | ARK | s.t. |
| 137. | P. Serry | DQT | s.t. |
| 138. | L. Craddock | EFN | s.t. |
| 139. | K. Vermaerke | DSM | s.t. |
| 140. | S. Grignard | LTS | s.t. |
| 141. | L. Hofstede | TJV | s.t. |
| 142. | R. Rochas | COF | s.t. |
| 143. | D. Strakhov | GAZ | s.t. |
| 144. | Se. Bennett | TQA | s.t. |
| 145. | T. Van der Sande | LTS | s.t. |
| 146. | A. Colman | SVB | 12:37 |

APRIL

APRIL  WORLDTOUR WOMEN'S RACE

# LIÈGE–BASTOGNE–LIÈGE
25 April 2021
Bastogne–Liège
140.9km

One of the most iconic races of the UCI WorldTour calendar began with two riders – Claire Faber and Silvia Zanardi – opening up a lead of 3 minutes before being reeled back in ahead of the first climb of the day. The next move was a strong acceleration by Niamh Fisher-Black, taking with her six riders; however, their efforts failed and the catch was made with 50km to go on the Côte de Desnié. As predicted, on the iconic Côte de La Redoute the peloton significantly reduced after multiple attacks, and by the time the race entered the final 15km, on the Côte de la Roche-aux-Faucons, only 30 riders remained together. Over the top of the climb five riders led the race when La Flèche Wallonne winner Anna van der Breggen set a strong tempo. Ashleigh Moolman-Pasio and Cecilie Uttrup Ludwig tried to get back on terms with the leaders but were unable to do so and it was left to Demi Vollering, Elisa Longo Borghini, Katarzyna Niewiadoma and Annemiek van Vleuten and Van der Breggen to challenge for the victory. The race came down to a sprint with 24-year-old Vollering coming out on top for the victory, the biggest Classic of her career. After consistence throughout the Ardennes Classics, Longo Borghini concluded the week as the UCI Women's WorldTour leader, with Maria Novolodskaya leading the Under-23 category.

## WEATHER

TEMPERATURE  WIND
8°C  NE 19km/h

## PROFILE

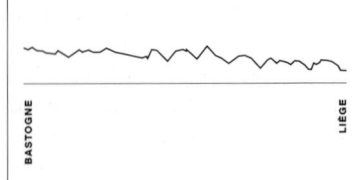

BASTOGNE – LIÈGE

## BREAKAWAY

C. Faber (ASC), S. Zanardi (BPK)

## RESULTS

| POS | NAME | TEAM | TIME |
|---|---|---|---|
| 1. | D. Vollering | SDW | 3:54:31 |
| 2. | A. van Vleuten | MOV | s.t. |
| 3. | E. Longo Borghini | TFS | s.t. |
| 4. | K. Niewiadoma | CSR | s.t. |
| 5. | A. van der Breggen | SDW | 0:02 |
| 6. | M. Vos | JVW | 1:27 |
| 7. | A. Moolman | SDW | s.t. |
| 8. | C. U. Ludwig | FDJ | s.t. |
| 9. | L. Brand | TFS | 1:59 |
| 10. | A. Spratt | BEX | s.t. |
| 11. | S. Paladin | LIV | s.t. |
| 12. | R. Markus | JVW | s.t. |
| 13. | E. Chabbey | CSR | s.t. |
| 14. | M. Cavalli | FDJ | s.t. |
| 15. | M. Novolodskaia | MNX | s.t. |
| 16. | E. Magnaldi | WNT | s.t. |
| 17. | N. Fisher-Black | SDW | s.t. |
| 18. | A. Santesteban | BEX | s.t. |
| 19. | M. García | ALE | s.t. |
| 20. | L. Thomas | MOV | s.t. |

## TRIVIA

» Demi Vollering is the seventh different SDWorx rider to win this season so far.

APRIL  WORLDTOUR MEN'S RACE

# TOUR DE ROMANDIE
Prologue
27 April 2021
Oron–Oron
4.05km

Stefan Bissegger (EF-Nippo) spent almost an hour in the hot seat before Rohan Dennis put in a massive ride to chop a whopping 10 seconds off the Swiss neo pro's benchmark. It was a good day for Ineos Grenadiers, whose reported investment in their time trial wheels was certainly paying off. Richie Porte clocked the second-best time until being nudged into third by Geraint Thomas, who went a fraction of a second faster. World champion Filippo Ganna was the only Grenadier to come away disappointed, finishing 15 seconds down in ninth. The only man who looked likely to threaten the throne was Rémi Cavagna. The French ITT champion was fastest through the intermediate time check, but he faded in the second half of the course and came home fourth, the best of the rest after the Ineos trio. ⓚⓝ

## WEATHER

TEMPERATURE  WIND
16°C  E 9km/h

## PROFILE

## STAGE RESULTS

| POS | NAME | TEAM | TIME |
|---|---|---|---|
| 1. | R. Dennis | IGD | 5:26 |
| 2. | G. Thomas | IGD | 0:09 |
| 3. | R. Porte | IGD | s.t. |
| 4. | R. Cavagna | DQT | 0:11 |
| 5. | S. Bissegger | EFN | s.t. |
| 6. | J. Tratnik | TBV | 0:13 |
| 7. | Je. Herrada | COF | 0:14 |
| 8. | M. Hirschi | UAD | 0:15 |
| 9. | M. Cattaneo | DQT | s.t. |
| 10. | F. Ganna | IGD | s.t. |
| 11. | W. Kelderman | BOH | 0:16 |
| 12. | I. Van Wilder | DSM | s.t. |
| 13. | S. Kuss | TJV | s.t. |
| 14. | S. Küng | GFC | 0:17 |
| 15. | M. Cort | EFN | s.t. |
| 16. | P. Bevin | ISN | 0:18 |
| 17. | J. Černý | DQT | s.t. |
| 18. | R. Costa | UAD | 0:19 |
| 19. | A. Lutsenko | APT | s.t. |
| 20. | M. A. López | MOV | s.t. |

## GENERAL CLASSIFICATION

| POS | NAME | TEAM | TIME |
|---|---|---|---|
| 1. | R. Dennis | IGD | 5:26 |
| 2. | G. Thomas | IGD | 0:09 |
| 3. | R. Porte | IGD | s.t. |

## POINTS

| POS | NAME | TEAM | PTS |
|---|---|---|---|
| 1. | R. Dennis | IGD | 30 |
| 2. | G. Thomas | IGD | 25 |
| 3. | R. Porte | IGD | 22 |

## YOUNG RIDER

| POS | NAME | TEAM | TIME |
|---|---|---|---|
| 1. | S. Bissegger | EFN | 5:37 |
| 2. | M. Hirschi | UAD | 0:04 |
| 3. | I. Van Wilder | DSM | 0:05 |

## TRIVIA

» This was Rohan Dennis's 30th career win – 20 of which have been time trial victories.

APRIL  WORLDTOUR MEN'S RACE

# TOUR DE ROMANDIE
Stage 1
28 April 2021
Aigle–Martigny
168.1km

The first road stage took place in the backyard of the UCI headquarters, heading south from Aigle and onto four laps punctuated by two category-3 climbs in the valley north-east of Martigny. A breakaway of Thymen Arensmen, Manuele Boaro, Filippo Conca, Alexis Gougeard, Robert Power and Joel Suter got away quickly, the latter on a mission for KOM points. The stage passed fairly uneventfully – the promised rain even held off for most of the day – and a bunch finish began to look ever more likely. Arensmen was the last man standing after climbing away from his breakaway companions on the steep penultimate climb, caught by a peloton determined to keep the dropped sprinters from regaining contact. There were several probing attacks on the run-in, but Bora-Hansgrohe and Bahrain-Victorious were too strong. In the bunch sprint, Peter Sagan was perfectly placed to jump off Sonny Colbrelli's wheel to take the victory.

## STAGE RESULTS

| POS | NAME | TEAM | TIME |
|---|---|---|---|
| 1. | P. Sagan | BOH | 4:12:40 |
| 2. | S. Colbrelli | TBV | s.t. |
| 3. | P. Bevin | ISN | s.t. |
| 4. | A. Pasqualon | IWG | s.t. |
| 5. | A. Covi | UAD | s.t. |
| 6. | M. Cort | EFN | s.t. |
| 7. | D. Smith | BEX | s.t. |
| 8. | C. Venturini | ACT | s.t. |
| 9. | M. Cattaneo | DQT | s.t. |
| 10. | J. Mosca | TFS | s.t. |
| 11. | R. Costa | UAD | s.t. |
| 12. | M. Hirschi | UAD | s.t. |
| 13. | J. Bakelants | IWG | s.t. |
| 14. | C. Barbero | TQA | s.t. |
| 15. | D. Villella | MOV | s.t. |
| 16. | S. Kuss | TJV | s.t. |
| 17. | W. Kelderman | BOH | s.t. |
| 18. | J. Haig | TBV | s.t. |
| 19. | D. Devenyns | DQT | s.t. |
| 20. | F. Masnada | DQT | s.t. |

## TRIVIA
» Sagan has taken 19 wins in Switzerland: 17 at the Tour de Suisse, bookended by victories at the Tour de Romandie.

## WEATHER

TEMPERATURE: 13°C
WIND: SW 13km/h

## PROFILE

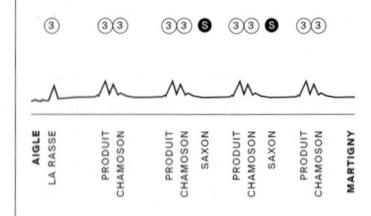

AIGLE – LA RASSE – PRODUIT CHAMOSON – PRODUIT CHAMOSON SAXON – PRODUIT CHAMOSON – PRODUIT CHAMOSON SAXON – PRODUIT CHAMOSON – MARTIGNY

## BREAKAWAY
F. Conca (LTS), J. Suter (NAT), M. Boaro (APT), A. Gougeard (ACT), T. Arensman (DSM), R. Power (TQA)

## GENERAL CLASSIFICATION

| POS | | NAME | TEAM | TIME |
|---|---|---|---|---|
| 1. | – | R. Dennis | IGD | 4:18:06 |
| 2. | – | G. Thomas | IGD | 0:09 |
| 3. | – | R. Porte | IGD | s.t. |

## KING OF THE MOUNTAINS

| POS | NAME | TEAM | PTS |
|---|---|---|---|
| 1. | J. Suter | NAT | 38 |
| 2. | M. Boaro | APT | 19 |
| 3. | R. Power | TQA | 12 |

## POINTS

| POS | | NAME | TEAM | PTS |
|---|---|---|---|---|
| 1. | – | P. Sagan | BOH | 50 |
| 2. | ↓1 | R. Dennis | IGD | 30 |
| 3. | – | M. Boaro | APT | 30 |

## YOUNG RIDER

| POS | | NAME | TEAM | TIME |
|---|---|---|---|---|
| 1. | ↑1 | M. Hirschi | UAD | 4:18:21 |
| 2. | ↑1 | I. Van Wilder | DSM | 0:01 |
| 3. | ↑1 | T. Arensman | DSM | 0:06 |

## BONUSES

| TYPE | NAME | TEAM |
|---|---|---|
| KOM 1 | J. Suter | NAT |
| KOM 2 | J. Suter | NAT |
| KOM 3 | J. Suter | NAT |
| KOM 4 | J. Suter | NAT |
| KOM 5 | J. Suter | NAT |
| KOM 6 | J. Suter | NAT |
| KOM 7 | J. Suter | NAT |
| KOM 8 | T. Arensman | DSM |
| KOM 9 | T. Arensman | DSM |
| Sprint 1 | M. Boaro | APT |
| Sprint 2 | M. Boaro | APT |

APRIL  WORLDTOUR MEN'S RACE

# TOUR DE ROMANDIE
Stage 2
29 April 2021
La Neuveville–Saint-Imier
165.7km

This was a curious day of racing, playing out in many ways like a dry run for the coming days, at least on the inclines. There were six classified climbs on the menu, the longest and last of them, La Vue-des-Alpes, weighing in at 7.8km with an average of 6.7 per cent and topping out 17km from the finish. But it was on the second passage of the flat finish just inside the last 50km that Rein Taaramäe left the rest of the breakaway behind, staying away for almost 30km before letting the peloton catch him on the final climb. A flurry of attacks followed from some of the GC favourites but, with race leader Dennis working for his teammates, no one was allowed much breathing room and a reduced bunch sprint beckoned. This time Colbrelli had enough to take the win ahead of Patrick Bevin and Marc Hirschi. (KN)

## WEATHER

TEMPERATURE: 14°C
WIND: E 6km/h

## PROFILE

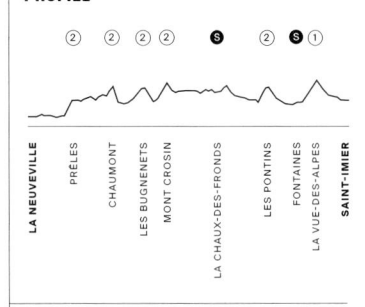

LA NEUVEVILLE · PRÊLES · CHAUMONT · LES BUGNENETS · MONT CROSIN · LA CHAUX-DES-FONDS · LES PONTINS · FONTAINES · LA VUE-DES-ALPES · SAINT-IMIER

## BREAKAWAY

H. Pernsteiner (TBV), C. Hamilton (BEX), A. Tolhoek (TJV), D. Villella (MOV), J. Caicedo (EFN), R. Taarame (IWG)

## STAGE RESULTS

| POS | NAME | TEAM | TIME |
|---|---|---|---|
| 1. | S. Colbrelli | TBV | 4:21:42 |
| 2. | P. Bevin | ISN | s.t. |
| 3. | M. Hirschi | UAD | s.t. |
| 4. | C. Champoussin | ACT | s.t. |
| 5. | D. Ulissi | UAD | s.t. |
| 6. | W. Kelderman | BOH | s.t. |
| 7. | I. Van Wilder | DSM | s.t. |
| 8. | F. Masnada | DQT | s.t. |
| 9. | R. Costa | UAD | s.t. |
| 10. | M. Soler | MOV | s.t. |
| 11. | D. Cataldo | MOV | s.t. |
| 12. | M. Cattaneo | DQT | s.t. |
| 13. | M. Skjelmose Jensen | TFS | s.t. |
| 14. | S. Kuss | TJV | s.t. |
| 15. | S. Petilli | IWG | s.t. |
| 16. | I. Izaguirre | APT | s.t. |
| 17. | D. Howson | BEX | s.t. |
| 18. | Je. Herrada | COF | s.t. |
| 19. | G. Thomas | IGD | s.t. |
| 20. | K. Elissonde | TFS | s.t. |

## GENERAL CLASSIFICATION

| POS | | NAME | TEAM | TIME |
|---|---|---|---|---|
| 1. | — | R. Dennis | IGD | 8:39:48 |
| 2. | ↑5 | P. Bevin | ISN | 0:08 |
| 3. | ↓1 | G. Thomas | IGD | 0:09 |

## KING OF THE MOUNTAINS

| POS | | NAME | TEAM | PTS |
|---|---|---|---|---|
| 1. | — | J. Suter | NAT | 38 |
| 2. | — | D. Villella | MOV | 34 |
| 3. | — | R. Taaramäe | IWG | 26 |

## POINTS

| POS | | NAME | TEAM | PTS |
|---|---|---|---|---|
| 1. | ↑3 | S. Colbrelli | TBV | 80 |
| 2. | ↓1 | P. Sagan | BOH | 50 |
| 3. | ↑4 | P. Bevin | ISN | 50 |

## YOUNG RIDER

| POS | | NAME | TEAM | TIME |
|---|---|---|---|---|
| 1. | — | M. Hirschi | UAD | 8:39:59 |
| 2. | — | I. Van Wilder | DSM | 0:05 |
| 3. | — | T. Arensman | DSM | 0:10 |

## BONUSES

| TYPE | NAME | TEAM |
|---|---|---|
| KOM 1 | A. Tolhoek | TJV |
| KOM 2 | D. Villella | MOV |
| KOM 3 | D. Villella | MOV |
| KOM 4 | D. Villella | MOV |
| KOM 5 | R. Taaramae | IWG |
| KOM 6 | R. Dennis | IGD |
| Sprint 1 | A. Tolhoek | TJV |
| Sprint 2 | R. Taaramae | IWG |

## TRIVIA

» This is Marc Hirschi's first podium since arriving at UAE Team Emirates.

APRIL  WORLDTOUR MEN'S RACE

# TOUR DE ROMANDIE
Stage 3
30 April 2021
Estavayer–Estavayer
168.7km

## WEATHER

| TEMPERATURE | WIND |
|---|---|
| 10°C | NW 20km/h |

The Tour de Romandie finally settled into normal service on stage 3 with torrential rain and Stefan Küng winning a place in the breakaway, the first of many battles in a race of attrition. The lead group started to disintegrate with 50km to go, and by the penultimate climb only Küng, Kobe Goossens and Johan Jacobs were left. With just a 25-second advantage over the peloton, the Swiss national champion pushed on and only Goossens could follow. But then disaster struck on the descent, a wet white line sending Küng sliding into the verge at a stomach-churning speed. With Goossens caught, the strung-out favourites group tested each other on the last climb until Marc Soler surprised them all with a particularly hard acceleration off the front with 10km to go. Every second counted for the Spaniard, who took both the stage win and the yellow jersey.

## PROFILE

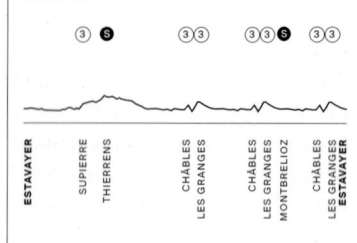

## BREAKAWAY
S. Küng (GFC), S. Bissegger (EFN), K. Goossens (LTS), S. Armée (TQA), M. Reutimann (NAT), C. Quarterman (TFS), J. Jacobs (MOV)

## STAGE RESULTS

| POS | NAME | TEAM | TIME |
|---|---|---|---|
| 1. | M. Soler | MOV | 3:58:35 |
| 2. | M. Cort | EFN | 0:22 |
| 3. | P. Sagan | BOH | s.t. |
| 4. | S. Colbrelli | TBV | s.t. |
| 5. | G. Izaguirre | APT | s.t. |
| 6. | D. Ulissi | UAD | s.t. |
| 7. | I. Van Wilder | DSM | s.t. |
| 8. | S. Kuss | TJV | s.t. |
| 9. | I. Izaguirre | APT | s.t. |
| 10. | R. Costa | UAD | s.t. |
| 11. | M. Skjelmose Jensen | TFS | s.t. |
| 12. | C. Champoussin | ACT | s.t. |
| 13. | W. Kelderman | BOH | s.t. |
| 14. | M. Cattaneo | DQT | s.t. |
| 15. | M. Woods | ISN | s.t. |
| 16. | F. Masnada | DQT | s.t. |
| 17. | M. Hirschi | UAD | s.t. |
| 18. | G. Thomas | IGD | s.t. |
| 19. | K. Goossens | LTS | s.t. |
| 20. | L. Hamilton | BEX | s.t. |

## GENERAL CLASSIFICATION

| POS | NAME | TEAM | TIME |
|---|---|---|---|
| 1. ↑22 | M. Soler | MOV | 12:38:40 |
| 2. ↑1 | G. Thomas | IGD | 0:14 |
| 3. ↑1 | R. Porte | IGD | s.t. |

## KING OF THE MOUNTAINS

| POS | NAME | TEAM | PTS |
|---|---|---|---|
| 1. — | J. Suter | NAT | 38 |
| 2. — | D. Villella | MOV | 34 |
| 3. — | R. Taaramäe | IWG | 26 |

## POINTS

| POS | NAME | TEAM | PTS |
|---|---|---|---|
| 1. — | S. Colbrelli | TBV | 98 |
| 2. — | P. Sagan | BOH | 70 |
| 3. ↑30 | M. Soler | MOV | 57 |

## YOUNG RIDER

| POS | NAME | TEAM | TIME |
|---|---|---|---|
| 1. — | M. Hirschi | UAD | 12:38:56 |
| 2. — | I. Van Wilder | DSM | 0:05 |
| 3. — | T. Arensman | DSM | 0:10 |

## BONUSES

| TYPE | NAME | TEAM |
|---|---|---|
| KOM 1 | Reutimann | NAT |
| KOM 2 | K. Goossens | LTS |
| KOM 3 | K. Goossens | LTS |
| KOM 4 | K. Goossens | LTS |
| KOM 5 | K. Goossens | LTS |
| KOM 6 | K. Goossens | LTS |
| Sprint 1 | C. Quarterman | TFS |
| Sprint 2 | J. Jacobs | NAT |

## TRIVIA
» Marc Soler bagged Movistar's third win of the year here, surpassing their total of two for the whole of 2020 (both of which were thanks to him).

APRIL — WORLDTOUR MEN'S RACE

# TOUR DE ROMANDIE
Stage 4
1 May 2021
Sion–Thyon 2000
161.3km

Snow forecast at the finish persuaded the organisers to bring the start forward, but the weather still played a defining role. With six of the seven original escapees holding less than 4 minutes on the foggy penultimate climb, the news broke that part of the descent would be neutralised. By the time they were let off the leash, their lead had grown by well over a minute, and by the foot of the final 20km climb they had 5 minutes 40. Magnus Cort and Simone Petilli lasted longest, but the breakaway's role was all but over as the GC race began in earnest. Thomas proved one of the strongest of the favourites, leading Michael Woods under the *flamme rouge* with Ben O'Connor chasing, the race lead up for grabs. Then within reach of the summit, the Welshman lost his grip and hit the sodden tarmac, leaving Woods to take victory. (KN)

## WEATHER

TEMPERATURE: 9°C
WIND: NE 9km/h

## PROFILE

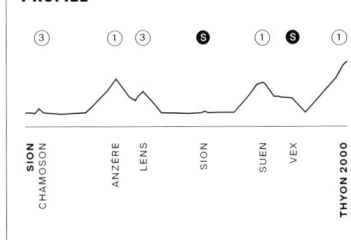

SION CHAMOSON — ANZÈRE — LENS — SION — SUEN — VEX — THYON 2000

## BREAKAWAY

K. Goossens (LTS), S. Pellaud (NAT), M. Holmes (LTS), M. Cort (EFN), J. Černý (DQT), S. Petilli (IWG), M. Würtz Schmidt (ISN)

## STAGE RESULTS

| POS | NAME | TEAM | TIME |
|---|---|---|---|
| 1. | M. Woods | ISN | 4:58:35 |
| 2. | B. O'Connor | ACT | 0:17 |
| 3. | G. Thomas | IGD | 0:21 |
| 4. | L. Hamilton | BEX | 0:34 |
| 5. | F. Masnada | DQT | 0:37 |
| 6. | R. Porte | IGD | 0:42 |
| 7. | I. Izaguirre | APT | s.t. |
| 8. | D. Caruso | TBV | 0:52 |
| 9. | M. Soler | MOV | 0:53 |
| 10. | T. Arensman | DSM | 1:57 |
| 11. | W. Kelderman | BOH | s.t. |
| 12. | S. Petilli | IWG | 2:20 |
| 13. | S. Kuss | TJV | 2:45 |
| 14. | R. Costa | UAD | 3:00 |
| 15. | M. Skjelmose Jensen | TFS | 3:25 |
| 16. | M. Cattaneo | DQT | 3:28 |
| 17. | S. Reichenbach | GFC | 4:17 |
| 18. | L. Meintjes | IWG | 4:40 |
| 19. | M. Badilatti | GFC | 5:00 |
| 20. | S. Pellaud | NAT | 5:34 |

## GENERAL CLASSIFICATION

| POS | NAME | TEAM | TIME |
|---|---|---|---|
| 1. ↑15 | M. Woods | ISN | 17:37:35 |
| 2. — | G. Thomas | IGD | 0:11 |
| 3. ↑14 | B. O'Connor | ACT | 0:21 |

## KING OF THE MOUNTAINS

| POS | NAME | TEAM | PTS |
|---|---|---|---|
| 1. ↑3 | K. Goossens | LTS | 48 |
| 2. ↓1 | J. Suter | NAT | 43 |
| 3. ↑9 | G. Thomas | IGD | 34 |

## POINTS

| POS | NAME | TEAM | PTS |
|---|---|---|---|
| 1. — | S. Colbrelli | TBV | 98 |
| 2. ↑2 | M. Cort | EFN | 76 |
| 3. ↓1 | P. Sagan | BOH | 70 |

## YOUNG RIDER

| POS | NAME | TEAM | TIME |
|---|---|---|---|
| 1. ↑2 | T. Arensman | DSM | 17:39:38 |
| 2. ↑2 | M. Skjelmose Jensen | TFS | 1:34 |
| 3. ↓1 | I. Van Wilder | DSM | 4:16 |

## BONUSES

| TYPE | NAME | TEAM |
|---|---|---|
| KOM 1 | J. Suter | NAT |
| KOM 2 | S. Pellaud | NAT |
| KOM 3 | S. Pellaud | NAT |
| KOM 4 | K. Goossens | LTS |
| KOM 5 | G. Thomas | IGD |
| Sprint 1 | M. Cort | EFN |
| Sprint 2 | M. Cort | EFN |

## TRIVIA

» This was Michael Woods' second win of the year, already equalling his total number of victories in each of the past two seasons.

APRIL  WORLDTOUR MEN'S RACE

# TOUR DE ROMANDIE
Stage 5 (ITT)
2 May 2021
Fribourg–Fribourg
16.19km

## WEATHER

| TEMPERATURE | WIND |
| --- | --- |
| 9°C | S 17km/h |

Both the early leader Bissegger and ultimately unbeatable Cavagna enjoyed dry conditions, separated by just 6 seconds at the finish, and as rain began to fall at the halfway point, attention turned to the fight for yellow. 'Recovery' was the big question of the day and with the top eight all within a minute, it was all to play for. The way Thomas's ride played out was reminiscent of the last ITT of the 2018 Tour de France. Just like that day, he came through the intermediate time check fastest but then opted for caution, all thoughts trained on overall victory, which would be his first since the Tour. Woods had a comparably disastrous ITT, going almost a minute slower than the Welshman and tumbling to fifth overall. Thomas was the only consistent figure on the overall podium, joined by teammate Porte and Fausto Masnada, who both posted blistering times.

## PROFILE

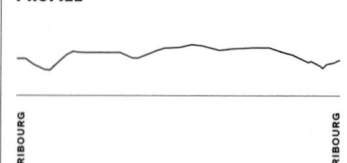

FRIBOURG — FRIBOURG

## STAGE RESULTS

| POS | NAME | TEAM | TIME |
| --- | --- | --- | --- |
| 1. | R. Cavagna | DQT | 21:54 |
| 2. | S. Bissegger | EFN | 0:06 |
| 3. | G. Thomas | IGD | 0:17 |
| 4. | I. Van Wilder | DSM | 0:18 |
| 5. | R. Porte | IGD | 0:20 |
| 6. | F. Masnada | DQT | 0:21 |
| 7. | M. Cattaneo | DQT | 0:29 |
| 8. | M. Soler | MOV | 0:34 |
| 9. | R. Dennis | IGD | 0:35 |
| 10. | F. Ganna | IGD | 0:37 |
| 11. | I. Izaguirre | APT | 0:48 |
| 12. | A. Tiberi | TFS | 0:49 |
| 13. | W. Kelderman | BOH | 0:50 |
| 14. | A. Amador | IGD | 0:51 |
| 15. | S. Küng | GFC | s.t. |
| 16. | B. O'Connor | ACT | 0:52 |
| 17. | D. Caruso | TBV | 0:54 |
| 18. | R. Contreras | APT | 0:55 |
| 19. | J. Tratnik | TBV | s.t. |
| 20. | M. Cort | EFN | 0:57 |

## GENERAL CLASSIFICATION

| POS | NAME | TEAM | TIME |
| --- | --- | --- | --- |
| 1. ↑1 | G. Thomas | IGD | 17:59:57 |
| 2. ↑3 | R. Porte | IGD | 0:28 |
| 3. ↑3 | F. Masnada | DQT | 0:38 |

## KING OF THE MOUNTAINS

| POS | NAME | TEAM | PTS |
| --- | --- | --- | --- |
| 1. – | K. Goossens | LTS | 48 |
| 2. – | J. Suter | NAT | 43 |
| 3. – | G. Thomas | IGD | 34 |

## POINTS

| POS | NAME | TEAM | PTS |
| --- | --- | --- | --- |
| 1. – | S. Colbrelli | TBV | 98 |
| 2. ↑2 | M. Soler | MOV | 77 |
| 3. ↓1 | M. Cort | EFN | 76 |

## YOUNG RIDER

| POS | NAME | TEAM | TIME |
| --- | --- | --- | --- |
| 1. – | T. Arensman | DSM | 18:02:45 |
| 2. – | M. Skjelmose Jensen | TFS | 1:37 |
| 3. – | I. Van Wilder | DSM | 3:21 |

## TRIVIA

» This was Geraint Thomas's first win since his 2018 Tour de France victory.

APRIL .1 MEN'S RACE

## VUELTA ASTURIAS
Stage 1
30 April 2021
Oviedo–Pola de Lena
184.5km

### STAGE RESULTS

| POS | NAME | TEAM | TIME |
|---|---|---|---|
| 1. | N. Quintana | ARK | 5:03:45 |
| 2. | A. Pedrero | MOV | 0:26 |
| 3. | P. Latour | TDE | 0:27 |
| 4. | G. Martín | EUS | 0:49 |
| 5. | A. Osorio | CJR | s.t. |
| 6. | C. Scaroni | GAZ | s.t. |
| 7. | R. Adrià | EKP | s.t. |
| 8. | N. Oliveira | MOV | s.t. |
| 9. | E. A. Rubio | MOV | s.t. |
| 10. | J. Amezqueta | CJR | s.t. |
| 11. | I. Zakarin | GAZ | s.t. |
| 12. | J. T. Hernandez | MED | s.t. |
| 13. | V. de la Parte | TDE | s.t. |
| 14. | J. García | CJR | s.t. |
| 15. | L. A. Maté | EUS | 1:32 |
| 16. | L. Fortunato | EOK | s.t. |
| 17. | F. Gavazzi | EOK | s.t. |
| 18. | D. Rosa | ARK | s.t. |
| 19. | Ó. Cabedo | BBH | s.t. |
| 20. | T. Juaristi | EUS | s.t. |

### WEATHER

TEMPERATURE   WIND
12°C          NW 11km/h

### GENERAL CLASSIFICATION

| POS | NAME | TEAM | TIME |
|---|---|---|---|
| 1. | N. Quintana | ARK | 5:03:35 |
| 2. | A. Pedrero | MOV | 0:30 |
| 3. | P. Latour | TDE | 0:33 |

### KING OF THE MOUNTAINS

| POS | NAME | TEAM | PTS |
|---|---|---|---|
| 1. | J. M. Gutierrez | GIS | 19 |
| 2. | D. Viegas | EOK | 13 |
| 3. | L. A. Maté | EUS | 7 |

### POINTS

| POS | NAME | TEAM | PTS |
|---|---|---|---|
| 1. | N. Quintana | ARK | 25 |
| 2. | A. Pedrero | MOV | 20 |
| 3. | P. Latour | TDE | 16 |

## VUELTA ASTURIAS
Stage 2
1 May 2021
Candás–Cangas del Narcea
200.5km

### STAGE RESULTS

| POS | NAME | TEAM | TIME |
|---|---|---|---|
| 1. | H. Carretero | MOV | 5:30:57 |
| 2. | N. Quintana | ARK | s.t. |
| 3. | E. A. Rubio | MOV | s.t. |
| 4. | R. Adrià | EKP | s.t. |
| 5. | J. M. Díaz | DKO | s.t. |
| 6. | A. Pedrero | MOV | s.t. |
| 7. | V. de la Parte | TDE | s.t. |
| 8. | I. Zakarin | GAZ | 0:03 |
| 9. | P. Latour | TDE | 0:37 |
| 10. | G. Martín | EUS | s.t. |
| 11. | N. Oliveira | MOV | s.t. |
| 12. | A. Osorio | CJR | s.t. |
| 13. | J. Amezqueta | CJR | s.t. |
| 14. | M. Iturria | EUS | s.t. |
| 15. | D. Rosa | ARK | s.t. |
| 16. | L. Fortunato | EOK | s.t. |
| 17. | D. Navarro | BBH | s.t. |
| 18. | A. Nych | GAZ | 1:09 |
| 19. | J. T. Hernandez | MED | s.t. |
| 20. | M. Finetto | DKO | 1:38 |

### WEATHER

TEMPERATURE   WIND
11°C          W 11km/h

### GENERAL CLASSIFICATION

| POS | | NAME | TEAM | TIME |
|---|---|---|---|---|
| 1. | — | N. Quintana | ARK | 10:34:26 |
| 2. | — | A. Pedrero | MOV | 0:36 |
| 3. | ↑6 | E. A. Rubio | MOV | 1:01 |

### KING OF THE MOUNTAINS

| POS | | NAME | TEAM | PTS |
|---|---|---|---|---|
| 1. | — | J. M. Gutierrez | GIS | 19 |
| 2. | — | D. Viegas | EOK | 13 |
| 3. | — | V. de la Parte | TDE | 10 |

### POINTS

| POS | | NAME | TEAM | PTS |
|---|---|---|---|---|
| 1. | — | N. Quintana | ARK | 45 |
| 2. | — | A. Pedrero | MOV | 30 |
| 3. | — | H. Carretero | MOV | 25 |

APRIL  .1 MEN'S RACE

# VUELTA ASTURIAS
Stage 3
2 May 2021
Cangas del Narcea–Alto del Naranco
125.3km

## WEATHER

TEMPERATURE | WIND
13°C | NE 7km/h

## STAGE RESULTS

| POS | NAME | TEAM | TIME |
|---|---|---|---|
| 1. | P. Latour | TDE | 2:59:49 |
| 2. | A. Osorio | CJR | 0:02 |
| 3. | V. de la Parte | TDE | 0:12 |
| 4. | A. Pedrero | MOV | s.t. |
| 5. | N. Quintana | ARK | s.t. |
| 6. | E. A. Rubio | MOV | 0:19 |
| 7. | L. Fortunato | EOK | 0:59 |
| 8. | J. García | CJR | s.t. |
| 9. | R. Adrià | EKP | s.t. |
| 10. | D. Navarro | BBH | s.t. |
| 11. | I. Zakarin | GAZ | 1:04 |
| 12. | J. T. Hernandez | MED | s.t. |
| 13. | T. Juaristi | EUS | 1:14 |
| 14. | N. Oliveira | MOV | 1:19 |
| 15. | J. M. Díaz | DKO | 1:30 |
| 16. | M. Iturria | EUS | 1:33 |
| 17. | J. Amezqueta | CJR | s.t. |
| 18. | L. A. Maté | EUS | 1:54 |
| 19. | A. Fedeli | DKO | 2:13 |
| 20. | A. Nych | GAZ | 2:29 |

## GENERAL CLASSIFICATION

| POS | NAME | TEAM | TIME |
|---|---|---|---|
| 1. — | N. Quintana | ARK | 13:34:27 |
| 2. — | A. Pedrero | MOV | 0:36 |
| 3. ↑4 | P. Latour | TDE | 0:54 |

## KING OF THE MOUNTAINS

| POS | NAME | TEAM | PTS |
|---|---|---|---|
| 1. — | J. M. Gutierrez | GIS | 19 |
| 2. ↑1 | V. de la Parte | TDE | 16 |
| 3. ↑7 | P. Latour | TDE | 15 |

## POINTS

| POS | NAME | TEAM | PTS |
|---|---|---|---|
| 1. — | N. Quintana | ARK | 57 |
| 2. ↑4 | P. Latour | TDE | 48 |
| 3. ↓1 | A. Pedrero | MOV | 44 |

# CONTINENTAL DRIFT – AFRICA'S GREATEST RACE

BY PETER KAMASA

*Peter Kamasa was born and raised in exile, in Tanzania. His parents, both Tutsis, had fled Rwanda before the genocide. Of the family who remained, more than 20 close relatives were murdered in April 1994. On the family's return to Rwanda, Kamasa studied International Relations Science at Kigali Independent University. A qualified and extremely successful volleyball coach, Kamasa has now been working for over a decade as a sport journalist, latterly with the New Times of Rwanda. He has covered nine editions of the Tour du Rwanda as well as numerous other cycling events in Africa.*

———

With or without coronavirus, the 13th edition of the Tour du Rwanda lived up to its billing.

The race was initially due to be held in February but it was postponed till early May following a spike in new Covid-19 cases. Widely considered to be the biggest UCI 2.1 cycling race in Africa, this year's edition attracted 75 riders competing in 15 teams from across the world. Known for creating massive hype and support from cycling fans at the side of the road, the Tour du Rwanda is showing signs of soon overtaking all other sports in terms of bringing joy and happiness and simply a smile to Rwandans' faces. While football arguably remains the global community's favourite sport, cycling is increasingly challenging that top spot and attracts the attention of people of all ages ahead of all other events on Rwandan soil.

The Tour du Rwanda is also the biggest cycling showpiece on the African continent. It continues to attract internationally renowned cycling clubs including teams that are used to big cycling events on the international calendar. The likes of Israel Start-Up Nation, where Chris Froome had just signed, as well as Total Direct Énergie and B&B Hotels – all teams that take part in the Tour de France – were committed to participating in the 2021 Tour du Rwanda.

This year's eight-stage route took the race to all corners of the country, including four stages dedicated to climbers, two for sprinters, one for puncheurs, and a time trial, for a total of 913km with almost 16,400 metres of climbing. The passages of the famous Mount Kigali would once again make the Tour du Rwanda one of the most testing races of the early 2021 season.

---

A victory for a Rwandan rider is a victory for all Rwandans. Cycling has played a big part in bringing hope back to genocide survivors who lost loved ones, through a memorial bike race paying tribute to the victims slain. The story of the 1994 genocide deeply touches all domestic riders who participate in the Tour du Rwanda. But at the same time, visiting riders from overseas are profoundly impressed by the way in which the country is building a united and reconciled society.

'When you consider the atrocities that this country and its people experienced almost 30 years ago, it is incredible,' Pierre Rolland, the star climber of B&B Hotels, observed before the race got underway.

The race began in 1988 with just three participating teams. But Rwanda was then torn apart by genocide in 1994, with up to a million people being murdered in the central African country within 100 days. In this 27th anniversary year, the peloton continues to play its part in helping the country move on from such a sad and difficult past.

It has clearly not been easy. There have been many problems a normal bike team wouldn't have encountered. Many of the local riders have experienced trauma, having been young children during the genocide. Former national cycling team captain, Adrien Niyonshuti is a central figure in Rwandan cycling. The four-time national champion and former Dimension Data rider won the 2008 Tour du Rwanda – the final edition of the race before it became a UCI event. He also become the first and only Rwandan cyclist to represent his country at the Olympic Games more than once. Though Niyonshuti's status in the sport is unrivalled within Rwanda, his story is tragically typical. He finds it hard to explain and can never resolve the issues fully. As a result of what happened to his family in April 1994, he suffers from profound depression. Cycling, he says, has played a significant role in helping him deal with the wounds of the genocide.

Niyonshuti, a Tutsi, fled the Hutu killers who came to his village, but six of his brothers were murdered and up to 60 of his wider family perished. He miraculously escaped with his mother and father, living off scraps in the countryside, almost starving to death before aid came in the form of the rebel Tutsi army from neighbouring Uganda.

'It was hard for me to remember how we lived in the bush. We hid in the countryside after they came to destroy us and loot our home. After a few days, we took to the road to seek refuge in the city. I was seven years old. I remember having to hide all the food until we came to Rwamagana where we were able to find another place to hide. The memory of the genocide is a really hard time for me and for a lot of people in Rwanda. Cycling gave me the opportunity to keep my past at a distance and really focus on what I wanted to do.'

Racing became a special calling after the loss of his family and siblings, and he recalls wanting to make his family proud to set a foot in their shoes. 'It was difficult,' he says, 'a difficult history. God has helped us for years in peace.'

Not only did Niyonshuti survive one of the worst atrocities in modern history, but he went on to become a national sporting hero, overcoming all the odds and eventually carrying his country's flag at London 2012 Olympic Games.

---

The national Team Rwanda is making a huge difference to the lives of young Rwandan riders. They've been able to buy houses with their race winnings; they can support their families. And it's not just the cyclists – the team is helping train mechanics and coaches, trying to create something sustainable for the future. Yet progress being made by African riders is slow – and almost appears to be stalling or going backwards. There is a total of just nine Africans (four of whom are white South Africans) in the WorldTour.

Much of the reason for this is practicalities. According to Niyonshuti, one of the main obstacles remains documentation to travel to the cycling heartlands of Europe: 'If you are a South African you can get a visa quickly to represent your country in the USA and UK. But if you come from Rwanda the same application for a visa can take so long that you will fail to get to the race.'

Racism in competitive cycling is nothing new but the emergence of more high-level black riders has unmasked some particularly ugly racism that the sport has yet to tackle full-on. In 2015, the MTN-Qhubeka Tour of Austria team complained of racism after members of the team were racially abused. In what was described as a 'heat of the battle' exchange, an MTN-Qhubeka rider was issued with an apology but the offending cyclist, Belarusian Branislau Samoilau, was not expelled from the race. There have been claims of institutional racism within the sport. Those barriers to wider participation from black, Asian and minority ethnic groups sadly continue to exist – for amateur cyclists as well as professional competitors.

Then there is the culture of cycling. It is a predominantly a white European sport, and it is hard for black Rwandans to gain an understanding of what is meant by a cycling life. In Morocco, and in the ex-French colonies of North Africa, this culture is better understood than in Rwanda. Morocco has been a cycling nation for a long time, having hosted at least 43 editions of its flagship Tour du Maroc race since 1937. The race was reserved for amateurs between 1957 and 1993 but has since been integrated as a 2.2 event into the UCI Africa Tour.

But it is Eritreans who have found themselves in a league of their own in recent years. The country has established itself as the cycling giant of Africa, excelling in all the continent's main cycling events – including the Tour du Rwanda, which was won by Eritreans (Merhawi Kudus in 2019, and the 2020 champion Natnael Tesfatsion) since being upgraded to a 2.1 UCI race. Those two Eritrean victories ended a five-year domination of the event by Rwandans.

It is no surprise that Eritrea has been touted by many as the 'Cycling Heaven' or the 'Bicycle Horn of Africa', given that Eritreans have for years welcomed cycling as part of their culture. When you visit Asmara, you are struck by the presence of bikes on the capital city's roads. Asmara only has about 500,000 inhabitants. Combined with low salaries, high import taxes and fuel shortages, this means the city has few vehicles and some roads are relatively empty of cars. Eritreans – young and old, women and men – all seem to embrace the cycling culture they have inherited from their Italy colonizers, and cycling is now a part of Eritrean identity.

On the other side of the continent, Sierra Leone has similar potential to become a flagship for Western African cycling. Much of its population relies on the bicycle for essential transport: riding to work, to school or to the next town. A bicycle is easier to own than a car and remains the common means of transport for the majority of Sierra Leone citizens in either urban or rural areas. With no competitive cyclists yet, Sierra Leone is nonetheless home to a handful of cycling clubs in Freetown – the most prominent of which, Lunsar, organises a non-UCI stage race.

In South Africa, cycling means business. Here, rich clubs invest millions of dollars in attracting the best riders. Former Tour du Rwanda participants – including winners Merhawi Kudus and Natnael Tesfatsion, as well as Daniel Teklehaimanot, who also rode the Tour de France – all made their path to the top level through South African teams.

The national stage race of Rwanda has also historically been the launch pad for local riders to impress. The likes of Joseph Areruya (formerly of Dimension Data and Delko Marseilles Provence), Samuel Mugisha (La Roche-sur-Yon Vendée Cyclisme), Valens Ndayisenga (a former Dimension Data for Qhubeka rider) and Adrien Niyonshuti still thank the Tour du Rwanda for playing a key part in securing professional contracts from foreign teams. It has been an irreplaceable showcase. However, talent exposure is still limited. Some riders, despite their talent and hard work, lack a strategic scouting system in which they can flourish and raise the country's flag high. Opportunities are limited, yet young riders' hunger to become great cyclists continues to grow. If the doors remain closed for opportunities, the passion for cycling could vanish.

Another persistent issue is the lack of funding. The majority of cycling teams continue to struggle for financial partnerships from businesses and sponsors, meaning talent development in the sport remains a big challenge that will persist for many more years to come should no funds be invested in this area, with only a handful of youngsters given a platform to shine. There seems to be gold in Rwandan cycling, but the strategies to exploit it are still substandard, and a large number of young riders see their talent go to waste as clubs cannot afford to set up a development model that can reach all parts of the country.

―――

Covid-19 may have been a huge blow to the 2021 Tour du Rwanda. The principal sponsor, SKOL Brewery Ltd, withdrew from their title sponsorship at the last minute. But, in tough times, the race organisation responded well and held a successful event, despite missing the atmosphere from fans on the streets. It was characterised by unending competition, fighting spirit and ferocious sprints. Breton puncheur rider Alan Boileau claimed three stages – the first three professional wins for the 21-year-old from B&B Hotels. His experienced team leader, Pierre Rolland, picked up stage 6, and Jhonatan Restrepo was one of two Colombian stage winners.

At the start of the last day, more than five riders were still in contention for the podium and the yellow jersey remained up for grabs. In the end, Total Énergie's Cristián Rodríguez won the 75km eighth and final stage to become the first Spanish and European rider to win the Tour du Rwanda. For the 26-year-old climber, newly signed from Caja Rural, it was a landmark achievement and his biggest victory to date. He took it by a slender 17 seconds over Canadian James Piccoli from Israel Start-Up Nation.

But no African riders won any stages. It seems that, as the importance and stature of the race has grown, the harder it is for local Rwandan riders to make an impact. Yet its purpose is still unique.

Nowadays, Adrien Niyonshuti is the *directeur sportif* of a development team of young Rwandan riders that bears his name. He remembers how, at the age of 16, his uncle lent him an old steel bike. Niyonshuti was elated but did not yet know that this combination of small metallic cylinders would change his life and destiny, or that he would use cycling as an escape from the realities of his past.

'At the end of the genocide, my uncle used to tell me "since you are my sister's child, I will try to help you." I was young, the bicycle was some form of game for me. Never did I think it would be a career that would take me places.'

The Tour du Rwanda goes to those places that other races cannot reach.

# WORLDTOUR AVERAGE AGES

All professional teams are a mixture of youth and experience, but which teams are closer to the crib and which are closer to the retirement home? Interestingly, there are similarities across the men's and women's peloton. DSM are the youngest in both, while BikeExchange would be the oldest in both if it weren't for Israel Start-Up Nation. Meanwhile, Trek-Segafredo have the third-youngest men's squad but the second-oldest women's team. The difference in age between the oldest on average in the men's peloton is more than four years, while in the women's it's more than five.

| Men | Average Age | Women | Average Age |
| --- | --- | --- | --- |
| TEAM DSM | 24.5 | TEAM DSM | 23.1 |
| LOTTO SOUDAL | 26 | FDJ NOUVELLE-AQUITAINE | 24.8 |
| TREK-SEGAFREDO | 26.3 | FUTUROSCOPE | |
| ASTANA-PREMIER TECH | 26.6 | CANYON-SRAM RACING | 25 |
| UAE TEAM EMIRATES | 26.8 | LIV RACING | 25.6 |
| AG2R CITROËN TEAM | 26.9 | MOVISTAR TEAM | 26.6 |
| INTERMARCHÉ-WANTY-GOBERT MATÉRIAUX | 26.9 | TEAM SD WORX | 26.8 |
| | | ALÉ BTC LJUBLJANA | 27.9 |
| MOVISTAR TEAM | 27.2 | TREK-SEGAFREDO | 27.9 |
| INEOS GRENADIERS | 27.3 | TEAM BIKEEXCHANGE | 28.5 |
| COFIDIS | 27.4 | | |
| DECEUNINCK-QUICKSTEP | 27.5 | | |
| BORA-HANSGROHE | 27.6 | | |
| EF EDUCATION-NIPPO | 27.6 | | |
| JUMBO-VISMA | 27.7 | | |
| GROUPAMA-FDJ | 27.8 | | |
| BAHRAIN VICTORIOUS | 28.1 | | |
| TEAM QHUBEKA ASSOS | 28.1 | | |
| TEAM BIKEEXCHANGE | 28.3 | | |
| ISRAEL START-UP NATION | 28.9 | | |

Average age 27.2 years

Average age 26.2 years

# MAY

Restored to its rightful place in the calendar, the Giro d'Italia dominated the month, generating headlines that eclipsed almost everything else. A route that largely ignored the south of the peninsula offered up its usual late-spring mixture of sunshine and sleet, with extreme weather conditions in the Dolomites. The first stage race of the women's calendar was the Vuelta a Burgos, after the cancellation of the Itzulia Basque Country Women. With Covid-19 vaccination programmes gathering pace across Europe, hopes were growing that the remainder of the racing programme could survive intact.

| DATE | RACE TITLE | LOCATION | UCI CODE | PAGE |
|---|---|---|---|---|
| 2–9 May | Tour du Rwanda | Rwanda | 2.1 | 148 |
| 5–9 May | Volta ao Algarve | Portugal | 2.Pro | 152 |
| 8–30 May | Giro d'Italia | Italy | 2.UWT | 156 |
| 12–16 May | Tour de Hongrie | Hungary | 2.1 | 200 |
| 13 May | Circuit de Wallonie | Belgium | 1.1 | 203 |
| 13 May | Trofeo Calvià | Spain | 1.1 | 204 |
| 14 May | Trofeo Serra de Tramuntana | Spain | 1.1 | 205 |
| 15 May | Trofeo Andratx | Spain | 1.1 | 206 |
| 16 May | Tro-Bro Léon | France | 1.Pro | 207 |
| 16 May | Trofeo Alcudia | Spain | 1.1 | 208 |
| 18–22 May | Vuelta a Andalucia | Spain | 2.Pro | 209 |
| 20–23 May | Vuelta a Burgos | Spain | 2.WWT | 212 |
| 22 May | Tour du Finistère | France | 1.1 | 216 |
| 23 May | Vuelta a Murcia | Spain | 1.1 | 217 |
| 24 May | Mercan'Tour Classic Alpes-Maritimes | France | 1.1 | 218 |
| 24 May | Ronde van Limburg | Belgium | 1.1 | 219 |
| 27–30 May | Boucles de la Mayenne | France | 2.Pro | 220 |
| 28–29 May | Tour of Estonia | Estonia | 2.1 | 222 |
| 30 May–6 June | Critérium du Dauphiné | France | 2.UWT | 223 |

MAY  .1 MEN'S RACE

## TOUR DU RWANDA
Stage 1
2 May 2021
Kigali–Rwamagana
115.6km

### WEATHER

TEMPERATURE  WIND
27°C  S 13km/h

### STAGE RESULTS

| POS | NAME | TEAM | TIME |
|---|---|---|---|
| 1. | B. Sánchez | MED | 2:33:43 |
| 2. | A. Hoehn | WGC | s.t. |
| 3. | W. A. Roldán | MED | s.t. |
| 4. | Q. Pacher | BBK | s.t. |
| 5. | J. Restrepo | ANS | s.t. |
| 6. | D. Muñoz | ANS | s.t. |
| 7. | G. Basson | PRO | s.t. |
| 8. | S. Umba | ANS | s.t. |
| 9. | A. De Decker | TIS | s.t. |
| 10. | A. Vuillermoz | TDE | s.t. |
| 11. | N. Holler | BAI | s.t. |
| 12. | J. Hivert | BBK | s.t. |
| 13. | S. Kipkemboi | BAI | s.t. |
| 14. | S. Hakizimana | SAC | s.t. |
| 15. | R. Byiza Uhiriwe | NAT | s.t. |
| 16. | C. Gautier | BBK | s.t. |
| 17. | J. Piccoli | ISN | s.t. |
| 18. | N. Saidi | NAT | s.t. |
| 19. | P. Rolland | BBK | s.t. |
| 20. | Ó. Sevilla | MED | s.t. |

### GENERAL CLASSIFICATION

| POS | NAME | TEAM | TIME |
|---|---|---|---|
| 1. | B. Sánchez | MED | 2:33:43 |
| 2. | A. Hoehn | WGC | s.t. |
| 3. | W. A. Roldán | MED | s.t. |

### KING OF THE MOUNTAINS

| POS | NAME | TEAM | PTS |
|---|---|---|---|
| 1. | M. N. A. Mohd Zariff | TSG | 3 |
| 2. | B. Suaza | MED | 1 |

### YOUNG RIDER

| POS | NAME | TEAM | TIME |
|---|---|---|---|
| 1. | S. Umba | ANS | 2:33:43 |
| 2. | S. Kipkemboi | BAI | s.t. |
| 3. | R. Byiza Uhiriwe | NAT | s.t. |

## TOUR DU RWANDA
Stage 2
3 May 2021
Kigali–Huye
120.5km

### WEATHER

TEMPERATURE  WIND
27°C  S 11km/h

### STAGE RESULTS

| POS | NAME | TEAM | TIME |
|---|---|---|---|
| 1. | A. Boileau | BBK | 3:07:14 |
| 2. | S. Umba | ANS | 0:06 |
| 3. | B. Sánchez | MED | 0:08 |
| 4. | N. Vahtra | ISN | s.t. |
| 5. | G. Marchand | TIS | s.t. |
| 6. | A. Hoehn | WGC | s.t. |
| 7. | J. Restrepo | ANS | s.t. |
| 8. | S. Kipkemboi | BAI | s.t. |
| 9. | Q. Pacher | BBK | s.t. |
| 10. | V. Ferron | TDE | s.t. |
| 11. | L. Teugels | TIS | s.t. |
| 12. | N. Zerai | NAT | s.t. |
| 13. | J. Piccoli | ISN | s.t. |
| 14. | A. Lagab | NAT | s.t. |
| 15. | A. Van Engelen | BAI | s.t. |
| 16. | Ó. Sevilla | MED | s.t. |
| 17. | A. Bisolti | ANS | s.t. |
| 18. | K. Main | PRO | s.t. |
| 19. | C. Quintero | TSG | s.t. |
| 20. | R. Byiza Uhiriwe | NAT | s.t. |

### GENERAL CLASSIFICATION

| POS | NAME | TEAM | TIME |
|---|---|---|---|
| 1. ↑7 | S. Umba | ANS | 5:41:03 |
| 2. ↓1 | B. Sánchez | MED | 0:02 |
| 3. ↓2 | A. Hoehn | WGC | s.t. |

### KING OF THE MOUNTAINS

| POS | NAME | TEAM | PTS |
|---|---|---|---|
| 1. — | E. Manizabayo | BIG | 11 |
| 2. — | J. B. Nsengimana | NAT | 9 |
| 3. — | C. Quintero | TSG | 3 |

### YOUNG RIDER

| POS | NAME | TEAM | TIME |
|---|---|---|---|
| 1. — | S. Umba | ANS | 5:41:03 |
| 2. — | S. Kipkemboi | BAI | 0:02 |
| 3. ↑1 | V. Ferron | TDE | s.t. |

MAY  .1 MEN'S RACE

# TOUR DU RWANDA
Stage 3
4 May 2021
Nyanza–Gicumbi
171.6km

## WEATHER

TEMPERATURE | WIND
26°C | SW 11km/h

## STAGE RESULTS

| POS | NAME | TEAM | TIME |
|---|---|---|---|
| 1. | A. Boileau | BBK | 4:23:57 |
| 2. | C. Quintero | TSG | s.t. |
| 3. | J. Piccoli | ISN | s.t. |
| 4. | B. Sánchez | MED | s.t. |
| 5. | M. Eyob | TSG | s.t. |
| 6. | A. Hoehn | WGC | s.t. |
| 7. | A. Vuillermoz | TDE | s.t. |
| 8. | Ó. Sevilla | MED | s.t. |
| 9. | C. Rodríguez | TDE | s.t. |
| 10. | Q. Pacher | BBK | s.t. |
| 11. | J. Restrepo | ANS | s.t. |
| 12. | N. Zerai | NAT | 0:06 |
| 13. | S. Weldemicael | NAT | 0:09 |
| 14. | G. Marchand | TIS | s.t. |
| 15. | A. Ovechkin | TSG | 0:20 |
| 16. | J. Hivert | BBK | 0:24 |
| 17. | B. Suaza | MED | 0:29 |
| 18. | C. Ormiston | PRO | 0:37 |
| 19. | E. Bergstrom Frisk | BAI | 0:55 |
| 20. | K. Main | PRO | 0:58 |

## GENERAL CLASSIFICATION

| POS | NAME | TEAM | TIME |
|---|---|---|---|
| 1. ↑1 | B. Sánchez | MED | 10:05:02 |
| 2. ↑1 | A. Hoehn | WGC | s.t. |
| 3. ↑2 | Q. Pacher | BBK | s.t. |

## KING OF THE MOUNTAINS

| POS | NAME | TEAM | PTS |
|---|---|---|---|
| 1. — | L. Teugels | TIS | 21 |
| 2. ↑1 | C. Quintero | TSG | 19 |
| 3. — | P. Byukusenge | BIG | 15 |

## YOUNG RIDER

| POS | NAME | TEAM | TIME |
|---|---|---|---|
| 1. ↑5 | N. Zerai | NAT | 10:05:08 |
| 2. ↑7 | A. Boileau | BBK | 0:27 |
| 3. ↑2 | E. Bergstrom Frisk | BAI | 0:49 |

# TOUR DU RWANDA
Stage 4
5 May 2021
Kigali–Musanze
123.9km

## WEATHER

TEMPERATURE | WIND
25°C | S 11km/h

## STAGE RESULTS

| POS | NAME | TEAM | TIME |
|---|---|---|---|
| 1. | V. Ferron | TDE | 3:13:47 |
| 2. | P. Rolland | BBK | s.t. |
| 3. | E. Manizabayo | BIG | 0:04 |
| 4. | T. Goytom | NAT | 0:18 |
| 5. | A. Lagab | NAT | 0:22 |
| 6. | L. Teugels | TIS | 0:27 |
| 7. | J. B. Nsengimana | NAT | 0:46 |
| 8. | B. Sánchez | MED | 1:29 |
| 9. | A. Boileau | BBK | s.t. |
| 10. | J. Restrepo | ANS | s.t. |
| 11. | Q. Pacher | BBK | s.t. |
| 12. | J. Piccoli | ISN | s.t. |
| 13. | C. Quintero | TSG | s.t. |
| 14. | A. Hoehn | WGC | s.t. |
| 15. | Ó. Sevilla | MED | s.t. |
| 16. | C. Rodríguez | TDE | s.t. |
| 17. | A. Vuillermoz | TDE | s.t. |
| 18. | K. Main | PRO | s.t. |
| 19. | S. Umba | ANS | s.t. |
| 20. | N. Zerai | NAT | s.t. |

## GENERAL CLASSIFICATION

| POS | NAME | TEAM | TIME |
|---|---|---|---|
| 1. — | B. Sánchez | MED | 13:20:18 |
| 2. — | A. Hoehn | WGC | s.t. |
| 3. ↑1 | J. Restrepo | ANS | s.t. |

## KING OF THE MOUNTAINS

| POS | NAME | TEAM | PTS |
|---|---|---|---|
| 1. — | L. Teugels | TIS | 35 |
| 2. ↑2 | E. Manizabayo | BIG | 26 |
| 3. ↓1 | C. Quintero | TSG | 20 |

## YOUNG RIDER

| POS | NAME | TEAM | TIME |
|---|---|---|---|
| 1. — | N. Zerai | NAT | 13:20:24 |
| 2. — | A. Boileau | BBK | 0:27 |
| 3. — | E. Bergstrom Frisk | BAI | 1:04 |

MAY   .1 MEN'S RACE

## TOUR DU RWANDA
Stage 5
6 May 2021
Nyagatare–Kigali (Kimironko)
149.3km

### WEATHER

TEMPERATURE 24°C   WIND NE 15km/h

### STAGE RESULTS

| POS | NAME | TEAM | TIME |
|---|---|---|---|
| 1. | A. Boileau | BBK | 3:28:45 |
| 2. | A. Vuillermoz | TDE | s.t. |
| 3. | M. Eyob | TSG | 0:02 |
| 4. | C. Rodríguez | TDE | 0:04 |
| 5. | K. Main | PRO | 0:06 |
| 6. | A. Hoehn | WGC | s.t. |
| 7. | J. Piccoli | ISN | s.t. |
| 8. | J. Restrepo | ANS | s.t. |
| 9. | Q. Pacher | BBK | s.t. |
| 10. | S. Weldemicael | NAT | 0:11 |
| 11. | Ó. Sevilla | MED | s.t. |
| 12. | N. Zerai | NAT | 0:14 |
| 13. | C. Quintero | TSG | 0:22 |
| 14. | C. Kagimu | BAI | s.t. |
| 15. | A. Bisolti | ANS | s.t. |
| 16. | B. Sánchez | MED | s.t. |
| 17. | G. Marchand | TIS | s.t. |
| 18. | A. Van Engelen | BAI | s.t. |
| 19. | C. Ormiston | PRO | s.t. |
| 20. | P. Byukusenge | BIG | 0:28 |

### GENERAL CLASSIFICATION

| POS | | NAME | TEAM | TIME |
|---|---|---|---|---|
| 1. | ↑8 | M. Eyob | TSG | 16:49:05 |
| 2. | ↑6 | C. Rodríguez | TDE | 0:02 |
| 3. | ↓1 | A. Hoehn | WGC | 0:04 |

### KING OF THE MOUNTAINS

| POS | | NAME | TEAM | PTS |
|---|---|---|---|---|
| 1. | — | L. Teugels | TIS | 35 |
| 2. | — | E. Manizabayo | BIG | 26 |
| 3. | — | C. Quintero | TSG | 20 |

### YOUNG RIDER

| POS | | NAME | TEAM | TIME |
|---|---|---|---|---|
| 1. | — | N. Zerai | NAT | 16:49:23 |
| 2. | — | A. Boileau | BBK | 0:13 |
| 3. | ↑1 | C. Ormiston | PRO | 1:17 |

## TOUR DU RWANDA
Stage 6
7 May 2021
Kigali–Mont Kigali
152.6km

### WEATHER

TEMPERATURE 21°C   WIND NW 11km/h

### STAGE RESULTS

| POS | NAME | TEAM | TIME |
|---|---|---|---|
| 1. | P. Rolland | BBK | 3:46:03 |
| 2. | A. Vuillermoz | TDE | 0:50 |
| 3. | A. Van Engelen | BAI | 2:36 |
| 4. | L. Teugels | TIS | 2:45 |
| 5. | C. Rodríguez | TDE | 3:00 |
| 6. | J. Piccoli | ISN | 3:05 |
| 7. | A. Boileau | BBK | 3:07 |
| 8. | J. Restrepo | ANS | 3:11 |
| 9. | Q. Pacher | BBK | 3:31 |
| 10. | N. Zerai | NAT | s.t. |
| 11. | S. Umba | ANS | 3:35 |
| 12. | K. Main | PRO | 3:38 |
| 13. | C. Quintero | TSG | s.t. |
| 14. | A. Hoehn | WGC | 3:41 |
| 15. | Ó. Sevilla | MED | 3:44 |
| 16. | A. Bisolti | ANS | 4:09 |
| 17. | S. Mugisha | NAT | 4:17 |
| 18. | M. Gaillard | TDE | 4:18 |
| 19. | B. Sánchez | MED | 4:26 |
| 20. | E. Bergstrom Frisk | BAI | s.t. |

### GENERAL CLASSIFICATION

| POS | | NAME | TEAM | TIME |
|---|---|---|---|---|
| 1. | ↑1 | C. Rodríguez | TDE | 20:38:10 |
| 2. | ↑4 | J. Piccoli | ISN | 0:07 |
| 3. | ↑1 | J. Restrepo | ANS | 0:13 |

### KING OF THE MOUNTAINS

| POS | | NAME | TEAM | PTS |
|---|---|---|---|---|
| 1. | — | L. Teugels | TIS | 54 |
| 2. | ↑9 | P. Rolland | BBK | 32 |
| 3. | ↓1 | E. Manizabayo | BIG | 26 |

### YOUNG RIDER

| POS | | NAME | TEAM | TIME |
|---|---|---|---|---|
| 1. | ↑1 | A. Boileau | BBK | 20:38:46 |
| 2. | ↓1 | N. Zerai | NAT | 0:11 |
| 3. | — | C. Ormiston | PRO | 2:25 |

MAY  .1 MEN'S RACE

## TOUR DU RWANDA
Stage 7 (ITT)
8 May 2021
Kigali–Kwa Mutwe
4.5km

### STAGE RESULTS

| POS | NAME | TEAM | TIME |
|---|---|---|---|
| 1. | J. Restrepo | ANS | 6:27 |
| 2. | A. Hoehn | WGC | 0:01 |
| 3. | A. Boileau | BBK | 0:02 |
| 4. | A. Geniez | TDE | 0:05 |
| 5. | J. Piccoli | ISN | 0:06 |
| 6. | C. Rodríguez | TDE | 0:08 |
| 7. | A. Vuillermoz | TDE | 0:10 |
| 8. | Q. Pacher | BBK | 0:11 |
| 9. | C. Quintero | TSG | 0:12 |
| 10. | J. Hivert | BBK | s.t. |
| 11. | Ó. Sevilla | MED | 0:13 |
| 12. | V. Ferron | TDE | 0:16 |
| 13. | K. Main | PRO | 0:17 |
| 14. | C. McGeough | WGC | s.t. |
| 15. | B. Sánchez | MED | 0:19 |
| 16. | E. Bergstrom Frisk | BAI | s.t. |
| 17. | G. Marchand | TIS | 0:20 |
| 18. | S. Tvetcov | WGC | 0:22 |
| 19. | A. Goeman | TIS | s.t. |
| 20. | E. Van Breussegem | TIS | 0:23 |

### WEATHER

TEMPERATURE: 24°C
WIND: NE 11km/h

### GENERAL CLASSIFICATION

| POS | NAME | TEAM | TIME |
|---|---|---|---|
| 1. — | C. Rodríguez | TDE | 20:44:45 |
| 2. ↑1 | J. Restrepo | ANS | 0:05 |
| 3. ↓1 | J. Piccoli | ISN | s.t. |

### KING OF THE MOUNTAINS

| POS | NAME | TEAM | PTS |
|---|---|---|---|
| 1. — | L. Teugels | TIS | 54 |
| 2. — | P. Rolland | BBK | 32 |
| 3. — | E. Manizabayo | BIG | 26 |

### YOUNG RIDER

| POS | NAME | TEAM | TIME |
|---|---|---|---|
| 1. — | A. Boileau | BBK | 20:45:15 |
| 2. — | N. Zerai | NAT | 0:53 |
| 3. — | C. Ormiston | PRO | 2:49 |

## TOUR DU RWANDA
Stage 8
9 May 2021
Kigali–Kigali
75.3km

### STAGE RESULTS

| POS | NAME | TEAM | TIME |
|---|---|---|---|
| 1. | C. Rodríguez | TDE | 2:05:06 |
| 2. | J. Piccoli | ISN | 0:12 |
| 3. | N. Zerai | NAT | 0:14 |
| 4. | A. Hoehn | WGC | s.t. |
| 5. | A. Vuillermoz | TDE | 0:21 |
| 6. | A. Boileau | BBK | s.t. |
| 7. | Ó. Sevilla | MED | 0:29 |
| 8. | Q. Pacher | BBK | s.t. |
| 9. | C. Kagimu | BAI | 0:44 |
| 10. | J. Restrepo | ANS | 0:46 |
| 11. | K. Main | PRO | 0:57 |
| 12. | G. Marchand | TIS | 1:05 |
| 13. | E. Bergstrom Frisk | BAI | s.t. |
| 14. | S. Umba | ANS | 1:17 |
| 15. | A. Van Engelen | BAI | s.t. |
| 16. | W. Vargas | MED | s.t. |
| 17. | P. Rolland | BBK | s.t. |
| 18. | A. Goeman | TIS | 1:51 |
| 19. | M. Tewelde | NAT | 1:54 |
| 20. | A. Geniez | TDE | 1:56 |

### WEATHER

TEMPERATURE: 20°C
WIND: N 15km/h

### GENERAL CLASSIFICATION

| POS | NAME | TEAM | TIME |
|---|---|---|---|
| 1. — | C. Rodríguez | TDE | 22:49:51 |
| 2. ↑1 | J. Piccoli | ISN | 0:17 |
| 3. ↑2 | A. Hoehn | WGC | 0:50 |

### KING OF THE MOUNTAINS

| POS | NAME | TEAM | PTS |
|---|---|---|---|
| 1. — | L. Teugels | TIS | 68 |
| 2. ↑1 | E. Manizabayo | BIG | 36 |
| 3. ↓1 | P. Rolland | BBK | 35 |

### YOUNG RIDER

| POS | NAME | TEAM | TIME |
|---|---|---|---|
| 1. — | A. Boileau | BBK | 22:50:42 |
| 2. — | N. Zerai | NAT | 0:46 |
| 3. ↑1 | E. Bergstrom Frisk | BAI | 3:41 |

MAY .PRO MEN'S RACE

## VOLTA AO ALGARVE
Stage 1
5 May 2021
Lagos–Portimão
189.5km

### WEATHER

TEMPERATURE: 22°C
WIND: SW 17km/h

### STAGE RESULTS

| POS | NAME | TEAM | TIME |
|---|---|---|---|
| 1. | S. Bennett | DQT | 4:37:41 |
| 2. | D. van Poppel | IWG | s.t. |
| 3. | J. Aberasturi | CJR | s.t. |
| 4. | S. Aniołkowski | BWB | s.t. |
| 5. | L. Leitão | TAV | s.t. |
| 6. | M. Mørkøv | DQT | s.t. |
| 7. | J. Drizners | HBA | s.t. |
| 8. | R. Oliveira | UAD | s.t. |
| 9. | E. Hayter | IGD | s.t. |
| 10. | M. Aristi | EUS | s.t. |
| 11. | M. Schwarzmann | BOH | s.t. |
| 12. | M. Menten | BWB | s.t. |
| 13. | T. Boudat | ARK | s.t. |
| 14. | I. Oliveira | UAD | s.t. |
| 15. | J. Ezquerra | BBH | s.t. |
| 16. | M. Sarreau | ACT | s.t. |
| 17. | D. Freitas | RPB | s.t. |
| 18. | E. Sanz | EKP | s.t. |
| 19. | É. Gesbert | ARK | s.t. |
| 20. | S. J. Caldeira | W52 | s.t. |

### GENERAL CLASSIFICATION

| POS | NAME | TEAM | TIME |
|---|---|---|---|
| 1. | S. Bennett | DQT | 4:37:41 |
| 2. | D. van Poppel | IWG | s.t. |
| 3. | J. Aberasturi | CJR | s.t. |

### KING OF THE MOUNTAINS

| POS | NAME | TEAM | PTS |
|---|---|---|---|
| 1. | J. Irisarri | CJR | 4 |
| 2. | C. Canal | BBH | 3 |
| 3. | H. Nunes | RPB | 2 |

### POINTS

| POS | NAME | TEAM | PTS |
|---|---|---|---|
| 1. | S. Bennett | DQT | 25 |
| 2. | D. van Poppel | IWG | 20 |
| 3. | J. Aberasturi | CJR | 16 |

### YOUNG RIDER

| POS | NAME | TEAM | TIME |
|---|---|---|---|
| 1. | J. Drizners | HBA | 4:37:41 |
| 2. | S. Quinn | HBA | s.t. |
| 3. | C. Rodriguez | IGD | s.t. |

## VOLTA AO ALGARVE
Stage 2
6 May 2021
Sagres–Fóia
182.8km

### WEATHER

TEMPERATURE: 24°C
WIND: SW 15km/h

### STAGE RESULTS

| POS | NAME | TEAM | TIME |
|---|---|---|---|
| 1. | E. Hayter | IGD | 4:48:43 |
| 2. | J. Rodrigues | W52 | s.t. |
| 3. | J. Lastra | CJR | s.t. |
| 4. | É. Gesbert | ARK | 0:04 |
| 5. | I. R. Sosa | IGD | 0:09 |
| 6. | S. Henao | IGD | 0:20 |
| 7. | A. Antunes | W52 | 0:30 |
| 8. | O. C. Eiking | IWG | 0:34 |
| 9. | L. Fernandes | RPB | 0:35 |
| 10. | N. Prodhomme | ACT | s.t. |
| 11. | J. M. Díaz | DKO | 0:37 |
| 12. | F. Figueiredo | EFP | s.t. |
| 13. | M. Bouet | ARK | s.t. |
| 14. | D. Fernández | DKO | s.t. |
| 15. | J. Brandão | W52 | 0:40 |
| 16. | D. Navarro | BBH | s.t. |
| 17. | I. Moreno | EKP | 0:42 |
| 18. | K. Asgreen | DQT | 0:44 |
| 19. | S. Quinn | HBA | 0:48 |
| 20. | G. Zimmermann | IWG | 1:02 |

### GENERAL CLASSIFICATION

| POS | NAME | TEAM | TIME |
|---|---|---|---|
| 1. ↑8 | E. Hayter | IGD | 9:26:24 |
| 2. ↑19 | J. Rodrigues | W52 | s.t. |
| 3. ↑20 | J. Lastra | CJR | s.t |

### KING OF THE MOUNTAINS

| POS | NAME | TEAM | PTS |
|---|---|---|---|
| 1. — | J. Rodrigues | W52 | 11 |
| 2. — | E. Hayter | IGD | 10 |
| 3. — | K. Molly | BWB | 8 |

### POINTS

| POS | NAME | TEAM | PTS |
|---|---|---|---|
| 1. — | S. Bennett | DQT | 25 |
| 2. — | D. van Poppel | IWG | 20 |
| 3. ↑8 | E. Hayter | IGD | 17 |

### YOUNG RIDER

| POS | NAME | TEAM | TIME |
|---|---|---|---|
| 1. ↑1 | S. Quinn | HBA | 9:27:12 |
| 2. ↑10 | M. Riccitello | HBA | 0:56 |
| 3. ↑11 | P. Andrade | HBA | s.t. |

MAY .PRO MEN'S RACE

# VOLTA AO ALGARVE
Stage 3
7 May 2021
Faro–Tavira
203.1km

## WEATHER

TEMPERATURE | WIND
21°C | SW 15km/h

## STAGE RESULTS

| POS | NAME | TEAM | TIME |
|---|---|---|---|
| 1. | S. Bennett | DQT | 5:02:14 |
| 2. | D. van Poppel | IWG | s.t. |
| 3. | M. Mørkøv | DQT | s.t. |
| 4. | J. Aberasturi | CJR | s.t. |
| 5. | P. Ackermann | BOH | s.t. |
| 6. | E. M. Grosu | DKO | s.t. |
| 7. | T. Boudat | ARK | s.t. |
| 8. | R. Oliveira | UAD | s.t. |
| 9. | L. Leitão | TAV | 0:02 |
| 10. | R. Gibbons | UAD | s.t. |
| 11. | M. Sarreau | ACT | s.t. |
| 12. | D. Touzé | ACT | s.t. |
| 13. | C. Martingil | ATM | s.t. |
| 14. | D. González | CJR | s.t. |
| 15. | M. van den Berg | GFC | s.t. |
| 16. | M. Alonso | EUS | s.t. |
| 17. | J. Drizners | HBA | s.t. |
| 18. | V. García de Mateos | CDF | s.t. |
| 19. | E. Sanz | EKP | s.t. |
| 20. | C. Joyce | RLY | s.t. |

## GENERAL CLASSIFICATION

| POS | | NAME | TEAM | TIME |
|---|---|---|---|---|
| 1. | – | E. Hayter | IGD | 14:28:40 |
| 2. | – | J. Rodrigues | W52 | s.t. |
| 3. | – | J. Lastra | CJR | s.t. |

## KING OF THE MOUNTAINS

| POS | | NAME | TEAM | PTS |
|---|---|---|---|---|
| 1. | – | J. Rodrigues | W52 | 11 |
| 2. | – | E. Hayter | IGD | 10 |
| 3. | – | K. Molly | BWB | 8 |

## POINTS

| POS | | NAME | TEAM | PTS |
|---|---|---|---|---|
| 1. | – | S. Bennett | DQT | 50 |
| 2. | – | D. van Poppel | IWG | 40 |
| 3. | ↑1 | J. Aberasturi | CJR | 29 |

## YOUNG RIDER

| POS | | NAME | TEAM | TIME |
|---|---|---|---|---|
| 1. | – | S. Quinn | HBA | 14:29:28 |
| 2. | – | M. Riccitello | HBA | 0:56 |
| 3. | – | P. Andrade | HBA | s.t. |

# VOLTA AO ALGARVE
Stage 4 (ITT)
8 May 2021
Lagoa–Lagoa
20.3km

## WEATHER

TEMPERATURE | WIND
20°C | SW 13km/h

## STAGE RESULTS

| POS | NAME | TEAM | TIME |
|---|---|---|---|
| 1. | K. Asgreen | DQT | 23:52 |
| 2. | R. Reis | EFP | 0:03 |
| 3. | B. Thomas | GFC | 0:09 |
| 4. | T. Guernalec | ARK | 0:19 |
| 5. | N. Politt | BOH | 0:28 |
| 6. | I. Oliveira | UAD | 0:37 |
| 7. | R. Gibbons | UAD | 0:52 |
| 8. | D. Lopez | EKP | 0:53 |
| 9. | E. Hayter | IGD | 1:02 |
| 10. | C. Rodriguez | IGD | 1:13 |
| 11. | J. Rodrigues | W52 | 1:14 |
| 12. | C. Davy | GFC | 1:16 |
| 13. | A. Brunel | GFC | s.t. |
| 14. | M. Bouet | ARK | 1:18 |
| 15. | X. M. Azparren | EUS | 1:23 |
| 16. | D. Mestre | W52 | s.t. |
| 17. | M. Louvel | ARK | 1:24 |
| 18. | J. Rosskopf | RLY | 1:27 |
| 19. | L. Kämna | BOH | 1:28 |
| 20. | P. Ackermann | BOH | 1:30 |

## GENERAL CLASSIFICATION

| POS | | NAME | TEAM | TIME |
|---|---|---|---|---|
| 1. | – | E. Hayter | IGD | 14:53:34 |
| 2. | – | J. Rodrigues | W52 | 0:12 |
| 3. | ↑22 | K. Asgreen | DQT | 0:21 |

## KING OF THE MOUNTAINS

| POS | | NAME | TEAM | PTS |
|---|---|---|---|---|
| 1. | – | J. Rodrigues | W52 | 11 |
| 2. | – | E. Hayter | IGD | 10 |
| 3. | – | K. Molly | BWB | 8 |

## POINTS

| POS | | NAME | TEAM | PTS |
|---|---|---|---|---|
| 1. | – | S. Bennett | DQT | 50 |
| 2. | ↑1 | J. Aberasturi | CJR | 29 |
| 3. | ↑1 | M. Mørkøv | DQT | 24 |

## YOUNG RIDER

| POS | | NAME | TEAM | TIME |
|---|---|---|---|---|
| 1. | – | S. Quinn | HBA | 14:55:11 |
| 2. | – | M. Riccitello | HBA | 1:16 |
| 3. | – | P. Andrade | HBA | 2:26 |

MAY .PRO MEN'S RACE

## VOLTA AO ALGARVE
Stage 5
9 May 2021
Albufeira–Malhão
170.1km

## WEATHER

TEMPERATURE  WIND
20°C  W 33km/h

## STAGE RESULTS

| POS | NAME | TEAM | TIME |
|---|---|---|---|
| 1. | É. Gesbert | ARK | 4:10:10 |
| 2. | J. Rodrigues | W52 | s.t. |
| 3. | J. Brandão | W52 | 0:09 |
| 4. | J. Lastra | CJR | 0:11 |
| 5. | A. Antunes | W52 | 0:15 |
| 6. | J. Silva | TAV | 0:17 |
| 7. | N. Prodhomme | ACT | s.t. |
| 8. | K. Asgreen | DQT | 0:19 |
| 9. | S. Henao | IGD | 0:21 |
| 10. | E. Hayter | IGD | s.t. |
| 11. | D. Fernández | DKO | s.t. |
| 12. | J. Neves Fernandes | W52 | 0:23 |
| 13. | D. Navarro | BBH | s.t. |
| 14. | M. Lammertink | IWG | 0:27 |
| 15. | M. Bouet | ARK | 0:32 |
| 16. | R. Mertz | BWB | 0:38 |
| 17. | T. Guernalec | ARK | s.t. |
| 18. | G. Zimmermann | IWG | s.t. |
| 19. | E. Duarte | ATM | s.t. |
| 20. | G. Mannion | RLY | s.t. |

## GENERAL CLASSIFICATION

| POS | | NAME | TEAM | TIME |
|---|---|---|---|---|
| 1. | ↑1 | J. Rodrigues | W52 | 19:03:56 |
| 2. | ↓1 | E. Hayter | IGD | 0:09 |
| 3. | — | K. Asgreen | DQT | 0:28 |

## KING OF THE MOUNTAINS

| POS | | NAME | TEAM | PTS |
|---|---|---|---|---|
| 1. | ↑5 | L. Fernandes | RPB | 16 |
| 2. | ↓1 | J. Rodrigues | W52 | 15 |
| 3. | — | M. Schwarzmann | BOH | 13 |

## POINTS

| POS | | NAME | TEAM | PTS |
|---|---|---|---|---|
| 1. | — | S. Bennett | DQT | 50 |
| 2. | — | J. Aberasturi | CJR | 29 |
| 3. | ↑2 | J. Rodrigues | W52 | 25 |

## YOUNG RIDER

| POS | | NAME | TEAM | TIME |
|---|---|---|---|---|
| 1. | — | S. Quinn | HBA | 19:06:26 |
| 2. | ↑2 | C. Rodriguez | IGD | 3:05 |
| 3. | — | P. Andrade | HBA | 5:12 |

# WORLDTOUR POINTS COMPETITION

Amassing the most green-jersey points from all the WorldTour stage races over the season doesn't garner a specific prize, but what it does seem to show is who was the most competitive, getting in the mix to try and win bike races. Of course, the weighting is massively in favour of succeeding at the Tour de France, but the difficulty of the task at hand should always be compensated generously. The strength of Sonny Colbrelli beats out the resurgent Mark Cavendish, while Michael Matthews' consistency without that final edge sees him towards the top but just missing out on first position. And Michael Mørkøv deserves a special mention, having managed to make the top 15 despite almost exclusively riding in support of others.

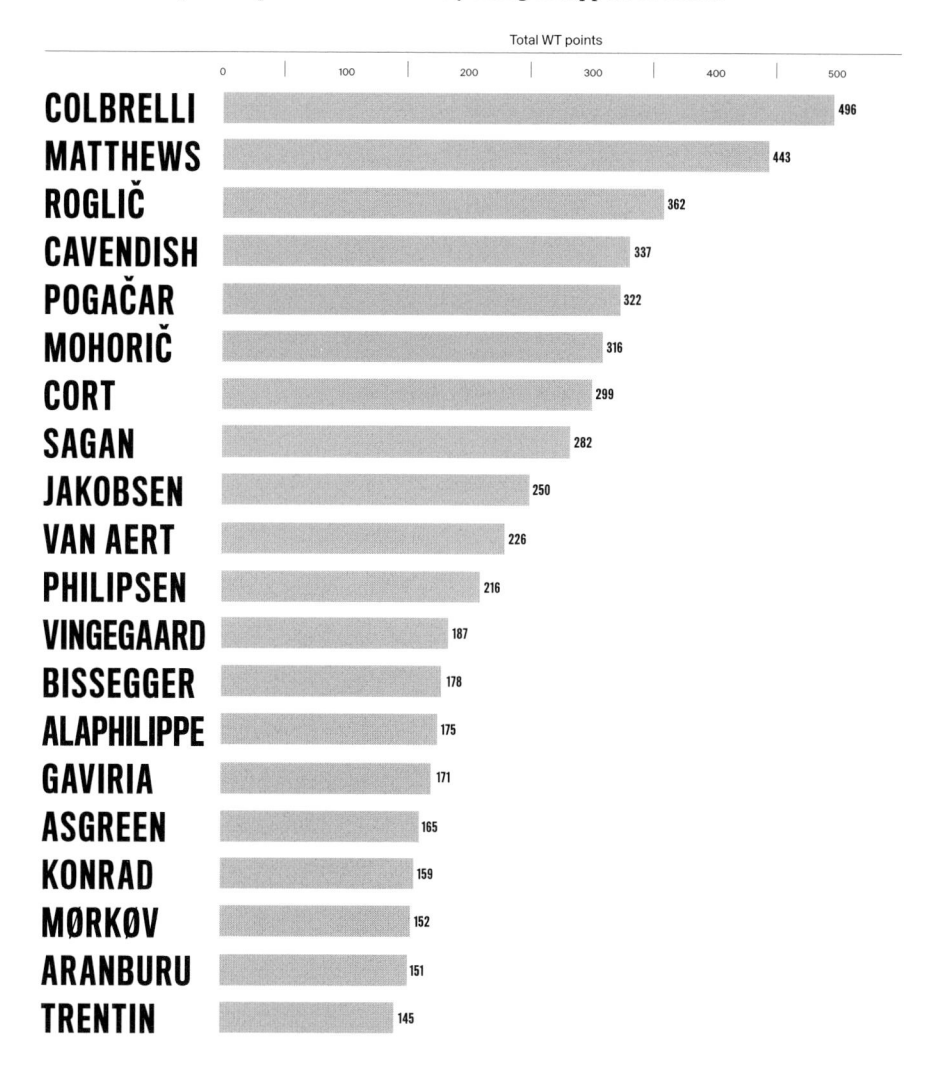

Total WT points

| Rider | Points |
|---|---|
| COLBRELLI | 496 |
| MATTHEWS | 443 |
| ROGLIČ | 362 |
| CAVENDISH | 337 |
| POGAČAR | 322 |
| MOHORIČ | 316 |
| CORT | 299 |
| SAGAN | 282 |
| JAKOBSEN | 250 |
| VAN AERT | 226 |
| PHILIPSEN | 216 |
| VINGEGAARD | 187 |
| BISSEGGER | 178 |
| ALAPHILIPPE | 175 |
| GAVIRIA | 171 |
| ASGREEN | 165 |
| KONRAD | 159 |
| MØRKØV | 152 |
| ARANBURU | 151 |
| TRENTIN | 145 |

MAY  WORLDTOUR MEN'S RACE

# GIRO D'ITALIA
Stage 1 (ITT)
8 May 2021
Turin–Turin
8.6km

**WEATHER**

TEMPERATURE
17°C

WIND
NE 13km/h

**PROFILE**

TORINO — TORINO

Beneath the smothering helmet, the time trial is an orgy of violence turned inwards. Even those whose physique is robust enough to take it are faced with aligning the lived experience of time with the mechanical means that measure it. In the words of Edoardo Affini, who replaced his teammate Tobias Foss's best time and kept it for 3 minutes short of an hour, 'You have to destroy yourself. You have to push yourself over the limit. It's really intense, and it's really hard for the body to take it.' If the violence is inward, its cleansing power is numinous, and Filippo Ganna's achievement almost spiritual. The pressure, the knowledge that his every move was being scrutinised, the presence of his rival Remco Evenepoel (his vanquisher in the time trial at San Juan in January 2020) just a minute ahead of him – none of this distorted his perception or dented his mental discipline. Yet his win was a triumph of improvisation and the inner child. 'We started with one little radio, but it didn't work at all. So I said, "Listen, Filippo, go full gas, and listen to the people at the roadside. If they shout your name loudly, you are going fast enough." It worked.' It made him the first to win four consecutive time trials at the Giro since Francesco Moser. And not even Eddy Merckx won four time trials at the Giro before his 25th birthday. Aleksandr Vlasov emerged an even more credible contender, with the best time trial in his career to date: 11th in the stage, he conceded 7 seconds to João Almeida and 5 to Evenepoel. Pozzovivo, Formolo and Sivakov all finished within 19 seconds of Almeida, with Martínez, Carthy, Yates, Bernal, Nibali, Bennett and Mollema separated by no more than 5 seconds, although Emanuel Buchmann and Dan Martin lost rather more. In short, an impressive start by Deceuninck-QuickStep's pair. Ineos took the win and put six riders – including Sivakov, Martínez and Bernal – within 22 seconds of Almeida. The Giro started well for both teams. (MR)

**GENERAL CLASSIFICATION**

| POS | NAME | TEAM | TIME |
|---|---|---|---|
| 1. | F. Ganna | IGD | 8:47 |
| 2. | E. Affini | TJV | 0:10 |
| 3. | T. Foss | TJV | 0:13 |
| 4. | J. Almeida | DQT | 0:17 |
| 5. | R. Cavagna | DQT | 0:18 |
| 6. | J. van Emden | TJV | s.t. |
| 7. | R. Evenepoel | DQT | 0:19 |
| 8. | M. Walscheid | TQA | s.t. |
| 9. | M. Brändle | ISN | 0:22 |
| 10. | G. Moscon | IGD | 0:23 |

**POINTS**

| POS | NAME | TEAM | PTS |
|---|---|---|---|
| 1. | F. Ganna | IGD | 15 |
| 2. | E. Affini | TJV | 12 |
| 3. | T. Foss | TJV | 9 |

**YOUNG RIDER**

| POS | NAME | TEAM | TIME |
|---|---|---|---|
| 1. | F. Ganna | IGD | 8:47 |
| 2. | E. Affini | TJV | 0:10 |
| 3. | T. Foss | TJV | 0:13 |

# TRIVIA
» Filippo Ganna's win was the third-fastest ITT performance in the history of the Giro.

## STAGE RESULTS

| POS | NAME | TEAM | TIME |
|---|---|---|---|
| 1. | F. Ganna | IGD | 8:47 |
| 2. | E. Affini | TJV | 0:10 |
| 3. | T. Foss | TJV | 0:13 |
| 4. | J. Almeida | DQT | 0:17 |
| 5. | R. Cavagna | DQT | 0:18 |
| 6. | J. van Emden | TJV | s.t. |
| 7. | R. Evenepoel | DQT | 0:19 |
| 8. | M. Walscheid | TQA | s.t. |
| 9. | M. Brändle | ISN | 0:22 |
| 10. | G. Moscon | IGD | 0:23 |
| 11. | A. Vlasov | APT | 0:24 |
| 12. | A. Bettiol | EFN | 0:26 |
| 13. | J. Castroviejo | IGD | 0:27 |
| 14. | A. Dowsett | ISN | s.t. |
| 15. | M. Bodnar | BOH | 0:28 |
| 16. | N. Oliveira | MOV | 0:29 |
| 17. | D. Ulissi | UAD | s.t. |
| 18. | R. Kluge | LTS | 0:30 |
| 19. | A. De Marchi | ISN | s.t. |
| 20. | F. Felline | APT | 0:31 |
| 21. | D. Pozzovivo | TQA | s.t. |
| 22. | V. Conti | UAD | s.t. |
| 23. | J. Tratnik | TBV | 0:32 |
| 24. | V. Campenaerts | TQA | s.t. |
| 25. | D. Caruso | TBV | s.t. |
| 26. | D. Dekker | TJV | s.t. |
| 27. | M. F. Honoré | DQT | 0:33 |
| 28. | S. Battistella | APT | s.t. |
| 29. | D. Formolo | UAD | s.t. |
| 30. | M. Sobrero | APT | s.t. |
| 31. | M. Hepburn | BEX | 0:34 |
| 32. | P. Sivakov | IGD | s.t. |
| 33. | D. F. Martínez | IGD | 0:36 |
| 34. | M. Jorgenson | MOV | s.t. |
| 35. | H. Carthy | EFN | 0:38 |
| 36. | P. Bilbao | TBV | s.t. |
| 37. | S. Yates | BEX | s.t. |
| 38. | M. Mohorič | TBV | s.t. |
| 39. | F. Masnada | DQT | s.t. |
| 40. | E. Bernal | IGD | 0:39 |
| 41. | R. Seigle | GFC | s.t. |
| 42. | T. van Garderen | EFN | s.t. |
| 43. | J. van den Berg | EFN | s.t. |
| 44. | F. Großschartner | BOH | s.t. |
| 45. | G. Izagirre | APT | 0:40 |
| 46. | N. Roche | DSM | s.t. |
| 47. | S. Carr | EFN | s.t. |
| 48. | R. Molard | GFC | s.t. |
| 49. | F. Gaviria | UAD | 0:41 |
| 50. | V. Nibali | TFS | s.t. |
| 51. | P. Sagan | BOH | s.t. |
| 52. | G. Bennett | TJV | s.t. |
| 53. | H. Tejada | APT | s.t. |
| 54. | B. Mollema | TFS | s.t. |
| 55. | G. Mäder | TBV | s.t. |
| 56. | M. Soler | MOV | 0:42 |
| 57. | N. Arndt | DSM | s.t. |
| 58. | O. Riesebeek | AFC | s.t. |
| 59. | C. Meyer | BEX | s.t. |
| 60. | T. Kangert | BEX | 0:43 |
| 61. | M. Schmid | TQA | s.t. |
| 62. | T. Gallopin | ACT | s.t. |
| 63. | S. Leysen | AFC | s.t. |
| 64. | A. M. Richeze | UAD | 0:44 |
| 65. | P. Bevin | ISN | s.t. |
| 66. | J. S. Molano | UAD | s.t. |
| 67. | S. Reichenbach | GFC | 0:45 |
| 68. | H. Vanhoucke | LTS | s.t. |
| 69. | C. Juul-Jensen | BEX | s.t. |
| 70. | N. Denz | DSM | s.t. |
| 71. | J. Keukeleire | EFN | s.t. |
| 72. | C. Champoussin | ACT | 0:46 |
| 73. | J. Hindley | DSM | s.t. |
| 74. | R. Guerreiro | EFN | 0:47 |
| 75. | K. Bouwman | TJV | s.t. |
| 76. | G. Nizzolo | TQA | 0:48 |
| 77. | M. Landa | TBV | 0:49 |
| 78. | L. van den Berg | GFC | s.t. |
| 79. | K. Frankiny | TQA | s.t. |
| 80. | J. Narváez | IGD | 0:50 |
| 81. | K. Goossens | LTS | s.t. |
| 82. | L. Wiśniowski | TQA | s.t. |
| 83. | Q. Hermans | IWG | s.t. |
| 84. | S. Puccio | IGD | s.t. |
| 85. | A. Covi | UAD | s.t. |
| 86. | P. Martens | TJV | s.t. |
| 87. | L. Warbasse | ACT | s.t. |
| 88. | L. Vervaeke | AFC | s.t. |
| 89. | E. Viviani | COF | 0:51 |
| 90. | G. Aleotti | BOH | s.t. |
| 91. | R. Bardet | DSM | 0:52 |
| 92. | P. Serry | DQT | s.t. |
| 93. | M. Fabbro | BOH | s.t. |
| 94. | T. De Gendt | LTS | s.t. |
| 95. | A. Valter | GFC | 0:53 |
| 96. | A. Vendrame | ACT | s.t. |
| 97. | Y. Arashiro | TBV | s.t. |
| 98. | J. K. Caicedo | EFN | s.t. |
| 99. | C. Scotson | BEX | s.t. |
| 100. | A. Torres | MOV | s.t. |
| 101. | R. Taaramäe | IWG | 0:54 |
| 102. | V. Albanese | EOK | s.t. |
| 103. | C. Hamilton | DSM | 0:55 |
| 104. | E. Buchmann | BOH | s.t. |
| 105. | K. Neilands | ISN | s.t. |
| 106. | D. Oss | BOH | 0:56 |
| 107. | G. Ciccone | TFS | s.t. |
| 108. | D. Martin | ISN | 0:57 |
| 109. | C. Benedetti | BOH | s.t. |
| 110. | A. Duchesne | GFC | s.t. |
| 111. | I. Keisse | DQT | s.t. |
| 112. | T. Merlier | AFC | 0:58 |
| 113. | M. Storer | DSM | s.t. |
| 114. | J. Janssens | AFC | s.t. |
| 115. | S. Consonni | COF | s.t. |
| 116. | G. Bouchard | ACT | 0:59 |
| 117. | V. Pronskiy | APT | s.t. |
| 118. | M. Moschetti | TFS | s.t. |
| 119. | N. Schultz | BEX | s.t. |
| 120. | G. Vermeersch | AFC | 1:01 |
| 121. | S. Ravanelli | ANS | s.t. |
| 122. | M. Christian | EOK | s.t. |
| 123. | R. Rochas | COF | s.t. |
| 124. | A. Ponomar | ANS | 1:02 |
| 125. | A. Gougeard | ACT | s.t. |
| 126. | J. Knox | DQT | s.t. |
| 127. | T. Marczyński | LTS | s.t. |
| 128. | N. Edet | COF | 1:03 |
| 129. | J. de Buyst | LTS | s.t. |
| 130. | F. Sabatini | COF | 1:04 |
| 131. | A. Pasqualon | IWG | s.t. |
| 132. | V. Lafay | COF | s.t. |
| 133. | K. de Kort | TFS | 1:05 |
| 134. | M. Kanter | DSM | 1:06 |
| 135. | J. Hirt | IWG | s.t. |
| 136. | A. Ghebreigzabhier | TFS | s.t. |
| 137. | G. Carboni | BCF | s.t. |
| 138. | D. Villella | MOV | 1:08 |
| 139. | J. Dombrowski | UAD | 1:09 |
| 140. | D. De Bondt | AFC | s.t. |
| 141. | F. Bidard | ACT | s.t. |
| 142. | F. Zana | BCF | 1:10 |
| 143. | D. Cimolai | ISN | s.t. |
| 144. | S. Petilli | IWG | s.t. |
| 145. | M. Badilatti | GFC | s.t. |
| 146. | D. Cataldo | MOV | s.t. |
| 147. | C. Ewan | LTS | 1:11 |
| 148. | S. Oldani | LTS | s.t. |
| 149. | J. Mosca | TFS | 1:12 |
| 150. | A. Krieger | AFC | s.t. |
| 151. | M. Dina | EOK | 1:13 |
| 152. | D. Groenewegen | TJV | s.t. |
| 153. | R. Valls | TBV | s.t. |
| 154. | L. Naesen | ACT | 1:14 |
| 155. | S. Guglielmi | GFC | s.t. |
| 156. | A. Pedrero | MOV | 1:15 |
| 157. | F. Gavazzi | EOK | s.t. |
| 158. | E. Sepúlveda | ANS | s.t. |
| 159. | R. Minali | IWG | 1:16 |
| 160. | B. J. Lindeman | TQA | s.t. |
| 161. | S. Rivi | EOK | 1:17 |
| 162. | G. Brambilla | TFS | 1:18 |
| 163. | N. Tesfatsion | ANS | 1:19 |
| 164. | T. van der Hoorn | IWG | 1:21 |
| 165. | S. Pellaud | ANS | s.t. |
| 166. | W. Kreder | IWG | 1:22 |
| 167. | N. Berhane | COF | 1:23 |
| 168. | U. Marengo | BCF | s.t. |
| 169. | E. Ravasi | EOK | 1:24 |
| 170. | M. Nieve | BEX | s.t. |
| 171. | F. Fiorelli | BCF | 1:25 |
| 172. | S. Zoccarato | BCF | 1:26 |
| 173. | E. A. Rubio | MOV | s.t. |
| 174. | G. Visconti | BCF | 1:27 |
| 175. | J. Cepeda Ortiz | ANS | 1:28 |
| 176. | D. Gabburo | BCF | 1:30 |
| 177. | E. Battaglin | BCF | s.t. |
| 178. | N. Venchiarutti | ANS | 1:31 |
| 179. | M. Belletti | EOK | 1:32 |
| 180. | L. Fortunato | EOK | s.t. |
| 181. | A. Viviani | COF | 1:33 |
| 182. | F. Tagliani | ANS | 1:34 |
| 183. | G. Niv | ISN | s.t. |
| 184. | L. L. Sanchez | APT | 1:37 |

MAY   WORLDTOUR MEN'S RACE

# GIRO D'ITALIA
Stage 2
9 May 2021
Stupinigi–Novara
179km

As Tim Merlier crossed the line to win the first sprint finish in the first Grand Tour of his career, he made the 'W' sign and pointed to the sky. 9 May will always be remembered as the day Wouter Weylandt died after crashing on the Passo del Bocco in 2011. His race number, 108, was removed from the startlist (hence Tejay van Garderen wearing 109 this year). Behind Merlier, Giacomo Nizzolo broke many unwanted records: the tenth second place of his Giro career – he already had five thirds – without ever taking a stage win. It took him ahead of Pietro Rimoldi, with four second places and nine thirds between 1936 and 1940. Then again, every bike race is a multiverse; its many parallel realities sometimes touch but often live entirely independent lives. Take the second intermediate sprint at Vercelli today. Filippo Ganna was quick to see Deceuninck riders moving to the front: he darted through to deny Remco Evenepoel the 3 bonus seconds, accidentally extending his lead overall from 10 to 13 seconds. The first intermediate sprint might itself have taken place in a parallel universe. Gaviria, Viviani, Sagan and Pasqualon swaggered towards the '40km to go' banner, where Viviani thought he had won the sprint, at which point Gaviria noticed that the intermediate sprint line was actually 400 yards away and so darted ahead to take 6 *maglia ciclamino* points, 3 points towards the *traguardo volanti* (hotspot sprint) competition and 3 towards the *premio della combattività* (combativity prize) in the wake of the breakaway riders Filippo Tagliani and Umberto Marengo. After their cock-up, the four lined up so that their smiles of embarrassment could be caught by the race photographers. It was not the last red face in a sprint. As Sebastián Molano shed speed after his lead-out in the final kilometre, he drifted towards the barrier and blocked his teammate Gaviria. Finishing the way Nizzolo did today, and suffering what Gaviria had to, are very different ways of losing a race. (MR)

## TRIVIA
» Tim Merlier is the first Belgian to win a stage of the Giro d'Italia since 2018.

## WEATHER

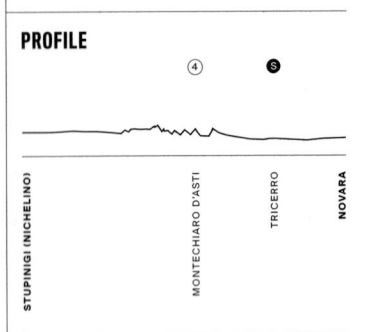

TEMPERATURE   WIND
19°C          SE 6km/h

## PROFILE

## BREAKAWAY
F. Tagliani (ANS), U. Marengo (BCF), V. Albanese (EOK)

## GENERAL CLASSIFICATION

| POS | | NAME | TEAM | TIME |
|---|---|---|---|---|
| 1. | — | F. Ganna | IGD | 4:29:53 |
| 2. | — | E. Affini | TJV | 0:13 |
| 3. | — | T. Foss | TJV | 0:16 |
| 4. | ↑3 | R. Evenepoel | DQT | 0:20 |
| 5. | ↓1 | J. Almeida | DQT | s.t. |
| 6. | ↓1 | R. Cavagna | DQT | 0:21 |
| 7. | ↓1 | J. van Emden | TJV | s.t. |
| 8. | — | M. Walscheid | TQA | 0:22 |
| 9. | — | M. Brändle | ISN | 0:25 |
| 10. | — | G. Moscon | IGD | 0:26 |

## KING OF THE MOUNTAINS

| POS | NAME | TEAM | PTS |
|---|---|---|---|
| 1. | V. Albanese | EOK | 3 |
| 2. | F. Tagliani | ANS | 2 |
| 3. | U. Marengo | BCF | 1 |

## POINTS

| POS | | NAME | TEAM | PTS |
|---|---|---|---|---|
| 1. | — | T. Merlier | AFC | 50 |
| 2. | — | G. Nizzolo | TQA | 35 |
| 3. | — | E. Viviani | COF | 30 |

## YOUNG RIDER

| POS | | NAME | TEAM | TIME |
|---|---|---|---|---|
| 1. | — | F. Ganna | IGD | 4:29:53 |
| 2. | — | E. Affini | TJV | 0:13 |
| 3. | — | T. Foss | TJV | 0:16 |

## BONUSES

| TYPE | NAME | TEAM |
|---|---|---|
| KOM 1 | V. Albanese | EOK |
| Sprint 1 | F. Tagliani | ANS |

# STAGE RESULTS

| POS | NAME | TEAM | TIME |
|---|---|---|---|
| 1. | T. Merlier | AFC | 4:21:09 |
| 2. | G. Nizzolo | TQA | s.t. |
| 3. | E. Viviani | COF | s.t. |
| 4. | D. Groenewegen | TJV | s.t. |
| 5. | P. Sagan | BOH | s.t. |
| 6. | M. Moschetti | TFS | s.t. |
| 7. | F. Fiorelli | BCF | s.t. |
| 8. | L. Naesen | ACT | s.t. |
| 9. | D. Cimolai | ISN | s.t. |
| 10. | C. Ewan | LTS | s.t. |
| 11. | J. S. Molano | UAD | s.t. |
| 12. | M. Kanter | DSM | s.t. |
| 13. | M. Belletti | EOK | s.t. |
| 14. | J. de Buyst | LTS | s.t. |
| 15. | R. Minali | IWG | s.t. |
| 16. | E. Bernal | IGD | s.t. |
| 17. | Q. Hermans | IWG | s.t. |
| 18. | D. Dekker | TJV | s.t. |
| 19. | M. Soler | MOV | s.t. |
| 20. | F. Ganna | IGD | s.t. |
| 21. | S. Consonni | COF | s.t. |
| 22. | A. Pasqualon | IWG | s.t. |
| 23. | A. M. Richeze | UAD | s.t. |
| 24. | F. Gaviria | UAD | s.t. |
| 25. | N. Denz | DSM | s.t. |
| 26. | D. Gabburo | BCF | s.t. |
| 27. | G. Ciccone | TFS | s.t. |
| 28. | G. Vermeersch | AFC | s.t. |
| 29. | L. Warbasse | ACT | s.t. |
| 30. | A. Covi | UAD | s.t. |
| 31. | A. Krieger | AFC | s.t. |
| 32. | D. Ulissi | UAD | s.t. |
| 33. | F. Sabatini | COF | s.t. |
| 34. | V. Nibali | TFS | s.t. |
| 35. | R. Bardet | DSM | s.t. |
| 36. | J. Mosca | TFS | s.t. |
| 37. | J. Hindley | DSM | s.t. |
| 38. | A. Ghebreigzabhier | TFS | s.t. |
| 39. | P. Bevin | ISN | s.t. |
| 40. | E. Battaglin | BCF | s.t. |
| 41. | L. Wiśniowski | TQA | s.t. |
| 42. | F. Großschartner | BOH | s.t. |
| 43. | N. Arndt | DSM | s.t. |
| 44. | D. De Bondt | AFC | s.t. |
| 45. | P. Sivakov | IGD | s.t. |
| 46. | V. Campenaerts | TQA | s.t. |
| 47. | A. Vlasov | APT | s.t. |
| 48. | D. Formolo | UAD | s.t. |
| 49. | M. F. Honoré | DQT | s.t. |
| 50. | J. Almeida | DQT | s.t. |
| 51. | M. Bodnar | BOH | s.t. |
| 52. | N. Berhane | COF | s.t. |
| 53. | F. Felline | APT | s.t. |
| 54. | J. Keukeleire | EFN | s.t. |
| 55. | G. Moscon | IGD | s.t. |
| 56. | G. Mäder | TBV | s.t. |
| 57. | D. F. Martínez | IGD | s.t. |
| 58. | E. Ravasi | EOK | s.t. |
| 59. | R. Guerreiro | EFN | s.t. |
| 60. | J. van Emden | TJV | s.t. |
| 61. | S. Oldani | LTS | s.t. |
| 62. | N. Oliveira | MOV | s.t. |
| 63. | H. Carthy | EFN | s.t. |
| 64. | D. Martin | ISN | s.t. |
| 65. | N. Venchiarutti | ANS | s.t. |
| 66. | A. Dowsett | ISN | s.t. |
| 67. | D. Villella | MOV | s.t. |
| 68. | A. Bettiol | EFN | s.t. |
| 69. | J. Dombrowski | UAD | s.t. |
| 70. | M. Sobrero | APT | s.t. |
| 71. | F. Gavazzi | EOK | s.t. |
| 72. | M. Landa | TBV | s.t. |
| 73. | M. Fabbro | BOH | s.t. |
| 74. | R. Kluge | LTS | s.t. |
| 75. | R. Molard | GFC | s.t. |
| 76. | E. Buchmann | BOH | s.t. |
| 77. | M. Hepburn | BEX | s.t. |
| 78. | P. Bilbao | TBV | s.t. |
| 79. | R. Cavagna | DQT | s.t. |
| 80. | R. Seigle | GFC | s.t. |
| 81. | K. Goossens | LTS | s.t. |
| 82. | M. Walscheid | TQA | s.t. |
| 83. | L. L. Sanchez | APT | s.t. |
| 84. | S. Yates | BEX | s.t. |
| 85. | W. Kreder | IWG | s.t. |
| 86. | C. Meyer | BEX | s.t. |
| 87. | N. Schultz | BEX | s.t. |
| 88. | M. Schmid | TQA | s.t. |
| 89. | K. Bouwman | TJV | s.t. |
| 90. | G. Izagirre | APT | s.t. |
| 91. | A. Viviani | COF | s.t. |
| 92. | D. Cataldo | MOV | s.t. |
| 93. | H. Vanhoucke | LTS | s.t. |
| 94. | J. K. Caicedo | EFN | s.t. |
| 95. | N. Roche | DSM | s.t. |
| 96. | T. van Garderen | EFN | s.t. |
| 97. | J. van den Berg | EFN | s.t. |
| 98. | I. Keisse | DQT | s.t. |
| 99. | J. Cepeda Ortiz | ANS | s.t. |
| 100. | T. Foss | TJV | s.t. |
| 101. | E. Affini | TJV | s.t. |
| 102. | F. Masnada | DQT | s.t. |
| 103. | G. Bennett | TJV | s.t. |
| 104. | R. Evenepoel | DQT | s.t. |
| 105. | E. A. Rubio | MOV | s.t. |
| 106. | G. Niv | ISN | s.t. |
| 107. | A. Duchesne | GFC | s.t. |
| 108. | J. Tratnik | TBV | s.t. |
| 109. | A. De Marchi | ISN | s.t. |
| 110. | G. Brambilla | TFS | s.t. |
| 111. | D. Caruso | TBV | s.t. |
| 112. | V. Pronskiy | APT | s.t. |
| 113. | M. Brändle | ISN | s.t. |
| 114. | A. Pedrero | MOV | s.t. |
| 115. | G. Aleotti | BOH | s.t. |
| 116. | S. Pellaud | ANS | s.t. |
| 117. | L. Vervaeke | AFC | s.t. |
| 118. | T. van der Hoorn | IWG | s.t. |
| 119. | G. Bouchard | ACT | s.t. |
| 120. | T. Kangert | BEX | s.t. |
| 121. | R. Rochas | COF | s.t. |
| 122. | S. Guglielmi | GFC | s.t. |
| 123. | D. Oss | BOH | s.t. |
| 124. | G. Carboni | BCF | s.t. |
| 125. | Y. Arashiro | TBV | s.t. |
| 126. | F. Bidard | ACT | s.t. |
| 127. | M. Mohorič | TBV | s.t. |
| 128. | S. Ravanelli | ANS | s.t. |
| 129. | J. Hirt | IWG | s.t. |
| 130. | K. Frankiny | TQA | s.t. |
| 131. | A. Ponomar | ANS | s.t. |
| 132. | C. Champoussin | ACT | s.t. |
| 133. | D. Pozzovivo | TQA | s.t. |
| 134. | F. Zana | BCF | s.t. |
| 135. | A. Valter | GFC | s.t. |
| 136. | R. Taaramäe | IWG | s.t. |
| 137. | L. van den Berg | GFC | s.t. |
| 138. | S. Petilli | IWG | s.t. |
| 139. | U. Marengo | BCF | s.t. |
| 140. | V. Conti | UAD | s.t. |
| 141. | N. Tesfatsion | ANS | s.t. |
| 142. | T. Gallopin | ACT | s.t. |
| 143. | E. Sepúlveda | ANS | s.t. |
| 144. | T. Marczyński | LTS | s.t. |
| 145. | F. Tagliani | ANS | s.t. |
| 146. | C. Juul-Jensen | BEX | s.t. |
| 147. | J. Knox | DQT | s.t. |
| 148. | S. Battistella | APT | s.t. |
| 149. | H. Tejada | APT | s.t. |
| 150. | M. Nieve | BEX | s.t. |
| 151. | A. Gougeard | ACT | s.t. |
| 152. | S. Carr | EFN | s.t. |
| 153. | L. Fortunato | EOK | s.t. |
| 154. | B. Mollema | TFS | s.t. |
| 155. | S. Rivi | EOK | s.t. |
| 156. | N. Edet | COF | s.t. |
| 157. | V. Lafay | COF | s.t. |
| 158. | J. Narváez | IGD | s.t. |
| 159. | G. Visconti | BCF | s.t. |
| 160. | C. Scotson | BEX | s.t. |
| 161. | M. Jorgenson | MOV | s.t. |
| 162. | A. Vendrame | ACT | s.t. |
| 163. | S. Puccio | IGD | s.t. |
| 164. | C. Hamilton | DSM | s.t. |
| 165. | M. Storer | DSM | s.t. |
| 166. | S. Leysen | AFC | s.t. |
| 167. | M. Dina | EOK | s.t. |
| 168. | O. Riesebeek | AFC | s.t. |
| 169. | J. Castroviejo | IGD | s.t. |
| 170. | S. Zoccarato | BCF | s.t. |
| 171. | P. Martens | TJV | s.t. |
| 172. | J. Janssens | AFC | s.t. |
| 173. | M. Christian | EOK | s.t. |
| 174. | T. De Gendt | LTS | s.t. |
| 175. | V. Albanese | EOK | s.t. |
| 176. | B. J. Lindeman | TQA | s.t. |
| 177. | K. de Kort | TFS | s.t. |
| 178. | R. Valls | TBV | 0:35 |
| 179. | C. Benedetti | BOH | s.t. |
| 180. | S. Reichenbach | GFC | s.t. |
| 181. | M. Badilatti | GFC | s.t. |
| 182. | A. Torres | MOV | 0:45 |
| 183. | P. Serry | DQT | 2:33 |

MAY — WORLDTOUR MEN'S RACE

# GIRO D'ITALIA
Stage 3
10 May 2021
Biella–Canale
190km

Taco van der Hoorn spent two years at Jumbo-Visma as a domestique for Wout van Aert, before Intermarché-Wanty-Gobert Matériaux promised him more freedom. Freedom? Did no one tell him they can monitor core temperature and blood sugar in real time and correlate them to power output? Or that comparative work rates prove the futility of breaking away when, in the belly of the peloton, a few tens of watts are enough to match the speed of the straining fugitives? Or that swarms of all-seeing, geostationary satellites are relaying the position of every rider to computers that calculate convergence rates? In short, that there is no freedom? There is enormous pressure in the peloton to surrender to nomolatry (or code fetishism), the belief – in life as in sport – that a single code can tell us how to act in every situation. In this version of cycling and modernity, attacking is for the small teams who scrap for airtime early in the stage and probably won't make the highlights package. So, with 50km to go, Bora-Hansgrohe moved to the front of the peloton *en bloc*, setting a pace so high that the sprinters could not follow. Sagan eventually finished second in the sprint behind Davide Cimolai. But the sprint was for second place; ahead of it, Van der Hoorn had attacked the eight-man breakaway. After abstaining from the battle for points along the way, he set off after the irrepressible Swiss-Colombian Simon Pellaud on the climb up to the final intermediate sprint at Guarene, worked with him until there were 7km remaining, then darted away. With 1km left, an advantage of 14 seconds, and the peloton on his wheel, he discovered a source of strength unavailable to riders who had spent all day riding tactically and saving their legs as the code dictates – a righteous, sweary self-assurance: 'With 1km to go, I was looking behind and I was thinking, "Oh f★★★! I'm going to make it, what the f★★★!"'

## TRIVIA
» This was Intermarché-Wanty-Gobert Matériaux's first-ever Grand Tour stage victory.

## WEATHER
TEMPERATURE: 13°C
WIND: N 6km/h

## PROFILE

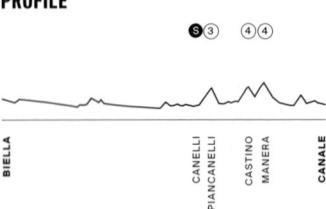

## BREAKAWAY
V. Albanese (EOK), S. Rivi (EOK), T. van der Hoorn (IWG), L. van den Berg (GFC), S. Zoccarato (BCF), A. Gougeard (ACT), S. Pellaud (ANS), A. Ponomar (ANS)

## GENERAL CLASSIFICATION

| POS | | NAME | TEAM | TIME |
|---|---|---|---|---|
| 1. | — | F. Ganna | IGD | 8:51:26 |
| 2. | ↑1 | T. Foss | TJV | 0:16 |
| 3. | ↑1 | R. Evenepoel | DQT | 0:20 |
| 4. | ↑1 | J. Almeida | DQT | s.t. |
| 5. | ↑1 | R. Cavagna | DQT | 0:21 |
| 6. | ↑4 | G. Moscon | IGD | 0:26 |
| 7. | ↑4 | A. Vlasov | APT | 0:27 |
| 8. | ↑4 | A. Bettiol | EFN | 0:29 |
| 9. | ↑4 | J. Castroviejo | IGD | 0:30 |
| 10. | ↑6 | D. Ulissi | UAD | 0:32 |

## KING OF THE MOUNTAINS

| POS | | NAME | TEAM | PTS |
|---|---|---|---|---|
| 1. | — | V. Albanese | EOK | 16 |
| 2. | — | S. Pellaud | ANS | 6 |
| 3. | — | L. van den Berg | GFC | 6 |

## POINTS

| POS | | NAME | TEAM | PTS |
|---|---|---|---|---|
| 1. | — | T. Merlier | AFC | 50 |
| 2. | ↑1 | E. Viviani | COF | 38 |
| 3. | ↓1 | G. Nizzolo | TQA | 35 |

## YOUNG RIDER

| POS | | NAME | TEAM | TIME |
|---|---|---|---|---|
| 1. | — | F. Ganna | IGD | 8:51:26 |
| 2. | ↑1 | T. Foss | TJV | 0:16 |
| 3. | ↑1 | R. Evenepoel | DQT | 0:20 |

## BONUSES

| TYPE | NAME | TEAM |
|---|---|---|
| KOM 1 | V. Albanese | EOK |
| KOM 2 | V. Albanese | EOK |
| KOM 3 | S. Pellaud | ANS |
| Sprint 1 | S. Pellaud | ANS |

## STAGE RESULTS

| POS | NAME | TEAM | TIME |
|---|---|---|---|
| 1. | T. van der Hoorn | IWG | 4:21:29 |
| 2. | D. Cimolai | ISN | 0:04 |
| 3. | P. Sagan | BOH | s.t. |
| 4. | E. Viviani | COF | s.t. |
| 5. | P. Bevin | ISN | s.t. |
| 6. | G. Vermeersch | AFC | s.t. |
| 7. | F. Gaviria | UAD | s.t. |
| 8. | A. Bettiol | EFN | s.t. |
| 9. | S. Oldani | LTS | s.t. |
| 10. | J. Mosca | TFS | s.t. |
| 11. | A. Vendrame | ACT | s.t. |
| 12. | Q. Hermans | IWG | s.t. |
| 13. | A. Pasqualon | IWG | s.t. |
| 14. | G. Moscon | IGD | s.t. |
| 15. | K. Bouwman | TJV | s.t. |
| 16. | E. Battaglin | BCF | s.t. |
| 17. | F. Felline | APT | s.t. |
| 18. | N. Tesfatsion | ANS | s.t. |
| 19. | M. Soler | MOV | s.t. |
| 20. | F. Gavazzi | EOK | s.t. |
| 21. | N. Arndt | DSM | s.t. |
| 22. | L. Vervaeke | AFC | s.t. |
| 23. | G. Brambilla | TFS | s.t. |
| 24. | M. Sobrero | APT | s.t. |
| 25. | L. Warbasse | ACT | s.t. |
| 26. | M. F. Honoré | DQT | s.t. |
| 27. | E. Bernal | IGD | s.t. |
| 28. | S. Zoccarato | BCF | s.t. |
| 29. | M. Mohorič | TBV | s.t. |
| 30. | G. Ciccone | TFS | s.t. |
| 31. | G. Izaguirre | APT | s.t. |
| 32. | V. Campenaerts | TQA | s.t. |
| 33. | F. Masnada | DQT | s.t. |
| 34. | J. Almeida | DQT | s.t. |
| 35. | D. Formolo | UAD | s.t. |
| 36. | S. Consonni | COF | s.t. |
| 37. | D. Martin | ISN | s.t. |
| 38. | D. Ulissi | UAD | s.t. |
| 39. | P. Sivakov | IGD | s.t. |
| 40. | J. Dombrowski | UAD | s.t. |
| 41. | A. Vlasov | APT | s.t. |
| 42. | L. L. Sanchez | APT | s.t. |
| 43. | G. Carboni | BCF | s.t. |
| 44. | E. Ravasi | EOK | s.t. |
| 45. | L. Fortunato | EOK | s.t. |
| 46. | V. Nibali | TFS | s.t. |
| 47. | R. Bardet | DSM | s.t. |
| 48. | H. Vanhoucke | LTS | s.t. |
| 49. | D. Caruso | TBV | s.t. |
| 50. | T. Foss | TJV | s.t. |
| 51. | F. Ganna | IGD | s.t. |
| 52. | A. Valter | GFC | s.t. |
| 53. | N. Oliveira | MOV | s.t. |
| 54. | G. Bennett | TJV | s.t. |
| 55. | J. Hindley | DSM | s.t. |
| 56. | M. Landa | TBV | s.t. |
| 57. | P. Bilbao | TBV | s.t. |
| 58. | D. Villella | MOV | s.t. |
| 59. | R. Molard | GFC | s.t. |
| 60. | A. Covi | UAD | s.t. |
| 61. | Y. Arashiro | TBV | s.t. |
| 62. | R. Cavagna | DQT | s.t. |
| 63. | N. Roche | DSM | s.t. |
| 64. | R. Taaramäe | IWG | s.t. |
| 65. | H. Carthy | EFN | s.t. |
| 66. | E. Buchmann | BOH | s.t. |
| 67. | A. Pedrero | MOV | s.t. |
| 68. | J. Knox | DQT | s.t. |
| 69. | E. A. Rubio | MOV | s.t. |
| 70. | R. Guerreiro | EFN | s.t. |
| 71. | G. Mäder | TBV | s.t. |
| 72. | T. Kangert | BEX | s.t. |
| 73. | M. Christian | EOK | s.t. |
| 74. | D. Cataldo | MOV | s.t. |
| 75. | D. Pozzovivo | TQA | s.t. |
| 76. | J. K. Caicedo | EFN | s.t. |
| 77. | S. Yates | BEX | s.t. |
| 78. | N. Schultz | BEX | s.t. |
| 79. | R. Evenepoel | DQT | s.t. |
| 80. | D. F. Martínez | IGD | s.t. |
| 81. | S. Puccio | IGD | s.t. |
| 82. | M. Nieve | BEX | s.t. |
| 83. | J. Cepeda Ortiz | ANS | s.t. |
| 84. | S. Reichenbach | GFC | s.t. |
| 85. | C. Champoussin | ACT | s.t. |
| 86. | H. Tejada | APT | s.t. |
| 87. | G. Bouchard | ACT | s.t. |
| 88. | E. Sepúlveda | ANS | s.t. |
| 89. | T. Gallopin | ACT | s.t. |
| 90. | J. Hirt | IWG | s.t. |
| 91. | A. De Marchi | ISN | s.t. |
| 92. | T. van Garderen | EFN | s.t. |
| 93. | G. Niv | ISN | s.t. |
| 94. | M. Fabbro | BOH | s.t. |
| 95. | M. Jorgenson | MOV | s.t. |
| 96. | M. Badilatti | GFC | s.t. |
| 97. | L. van den Berg | GFC | s.t. |
| 98. | C. Hamilton | DSM | s.t. |
| 99. | S. Ravanelli | ANS | s.t. |
| 100. | B. Mollema | TFS | s.t. |
| 101. | S. Pellaud | ANS | s.t. |
| 102. | N. Edet | COF | s.t. |
| 103. | V. Conti | UAD | s.t. |
| 104. | J. Castroviejo | IGD | s.t. |
| 105. | J. Narváez | IGD | s.t. |
| 106. | K. Frankiny | TQA | s.t. |
| 107. | C. Scotson | BEX | s.t. |
| 108. | V. Lafay | COF | s.t. |
| 109. | C. Meyer | BEX | s.t. |
| 110. | M. Storer | DSM | s.t. |
| 111. | V. Albanese | EOK | 0:46 |
| 112. | P. Serry | DQT | 0:59 |
| 113. | N. Berhane | COF | 1:36 |
| 114. | R. Rochas | COF | s.t. |
| 115. | D. Oss | BOH | 1:56 |
| 116. | R. Valls | TBV | 8:49 |
| 117. | A. Gougeard | ACT | s.t. |
| 118. | G. Nizzolo | TQA | 9:36 |
| 119. | M. Moschetti | TFS | s.t. |
| 120. | V. Pronskiy | APT | s.t. |
| 121. | A. Krieger | AFC | s.t. |
| 122. | J. Tratnik | TBV | s.t. |
| 123. | G. Aleotti | BOH | s.t. |
| 124. | F. Zana | BCF | s.t. |
| 125. | F. Bidard | ACT | s.t. |
| 126. | F. Großschartner | BOH | s.t. |
| 127. | A. Ponomar | ANS | s.t. |
| 128. | D. De Bondt | AFC | s.t. |
| 129. | L. Naesen | ACT | s.t. |
| 130. | C. Benedetti | BOH | s.t. |
| 131. | E. Affini | TJV | s.t. |
| 132. | A. Ghebreigzabhier | TFS | s.t. |
| 133. | J. S. Molano | UAD | s.t. |
| 134. | S. Petilli | IWG | s.t. |
| 135. | M. Kanter | DSM | s.t. |
| 136. | J. van Emden | TJV | s.t. |
| 137. | P. Martens | TJV | s.t. |
| 138. | S. Carr | EFN | s.t. |
| 139. | S. Guglielmi | GFC | s.t. |
| 140. | M. Schmid | TQA | s.t. |
| 141. | B. J. Lindeman | TQA | s.t. |
| 142. | J. de Buyst | LTS | s.t. |
| 143. | C. Juul-Jensen | BEX | s.t. |
| 144. | S. Rivi | EOK | s.t. |
| 145. | T. De Gendt | LTS | 10:34 |
| 146. | F. Sabatini | COF | s.t. |
| 147. | J. Keukeleire | EFN | s.t. |
| 148. | N. Venchiarutti | ANS | s.t. |
| 149. | I. Keisse | DQT | s.t. |
| 150. | A. M. Richeze | UAD | s.t. |
| 151. | M. Walscheid | TQA | s.t. |
| 152. | D. Gabburo | BCF | s.t. |
| 153. | F. Fiorelli | BCF | 13:05 |
| 154. | F. Tagliani | ANS | s.t. |
| 155. | K. de Kort | TFS | s.t. |
| 156. | G. Visconti | BCF | s.t. |
| 157. | A. Duchesne | GFC | s.t. |
| 158. | A. Dowsett | ISN | s.t. |
| 159. | M. Brändle | ISN | s.t. |
| 160. | L. Wiśniowski | TQA | s.t. |
| 161. | O. Riesebeek | AFC | s.t. |
| 162. | S. Battistella | APT | s.t. |
| 163. | R. Seigle | GFC | s.t. |
| 164. | K. Goossens | LTS | s.t. |
| 165. | T. Merlier | AFC | 14:06 |
| 166. | U. Marengo | BCF | s.t. |
| 167. | T. Marczyński | LTS | s.t. |
| 168. | M. Hepburn | BEX | s.t. |
| 169. | A. Viviani | COF | s.t. |
| 170. | N. Denz | DSM | s.t. |
| 171. | J. van den Berg | EFN | s.t. |
| 172. | D. Dekker | TJV | s.t. |
| 173. | S. Leysen | AFC | s.t. |
| 174. | W. Kreder | IWG | s.t. |
| 175. | M. Bodnar | BOH | s.t. |
| 176. | R. Minali | IWG | s.t. |
| 177. | C. Ewan | LTS | s.t. |
| 178. | D. Groenewegen | TJV | s.t. |
| 179. | M. Belletti | EOK | s.t. |
| 180. | M. Dina | EOK | s.t. |
| 181. | A. Torres | MOV | s.t. |
| 182. | R. Kluge | LTS | s.t. |
| 183. | J. Janssens | AFC | s.t. |

MAY  WORLDTOUR MEN'S RACE

## GIRO D'ITALIA
Stage 4
11 May 2021
Piacenza–Sestola
187km

### WEATHER

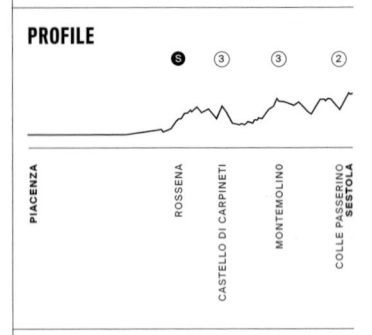

| TEMPERATURE | WIND |
|---|---|
| 16°C | E 9km/h |

### PROFILE

PIACENZA — ROSSENA — CASTELLO DI CARPINETI — MONTEMOLINO — COLLE PASSERINO — SESTOLA

Before the stage, asked just how strong he felt after impressing Filippo Ganna yesterday by climbing on the big ring, Remco Evenepoel played it down: 'I don't know. Maybe I just forgot to shift gear.' Hours later, with 20km to go, the camera peered through the rain into Remco's face. He was wearing no dark glasses, and black stress lines under his eyes were plainly visible. It became clear what we were looking at: an excruciating, old-fashioned ordeal. It was only after many decades of cycling history – some say in the 1920s with the Pelissier brothers, and men like Ottavio Bottecchia – that speed became the principle feature of professional cycling. Until then, it had more in common with shuffling to the South Pole. Rarely does the Tour de France, which bagged the July calendar slot early in the game, revert to its gruelling origins. But the Italian Apennines can be cruel in May. Remember last year's carnage in the Cesenatico stage? With 5km remaining, João Almeida – so impressive in 2020 – began to lose ground. He would finish 49th, 4 minutes 21 behind Egan Bernal, one of the most resistant to the conditions today. With 5.5km to go, Ciccone attacked. A kilometre later, Landa set off after him. With 3km left, Vlasov darted out of the group, Caruso on his wheel. Then, like a bird of prey, Bernal flashed away from the nest formed by his teammates. He flew by the Russian and his shadow, and, in a matter of seconds, joined Landa and Ciccone. Presently, Carthy followed, with Vlasov on his wheel. Bernal jumped again but ran out of gradient. It was the first time we have seen his dazzling acceleration since the 2019 Tour de France. It gained him only 11 seconds on Remco today, but his resilience augured well. One minute 37 seconds before Bernal finished, Joe Dombrowski won his first professional race outside the USA, after joining the right, 25-man breakaway. Behind him, his fellow escapee Alessandro De Marchi took the *maglia rosa*. (MR)

### BREAKAWAY

R. Taaramaë (IWG), C. Juul-Jensen (BEX), A. De Marchi (ISN), P. Serry (DQT), J. Dombrowski (UAD), N. Oliveira (MOV), A. Vendrame (ACT), L. Vervaeke (AFC), N. Edet (COF), J. Tratnik (TBV), F. Zana (BCF), F. Fiorelli (BCF), A. Ghebreigzabhier (TFS), J. Mosca (TFS), F. Gavazzi (EOK), M. Dina (EOK), A. Valter (GFC), N. Denz (DSM), Q. Hermans (IWG), K. de Kort (TFS), V. Conti (UAD), V. Campenaerts (TQA), N. Venchiarutti (ANS)

### GENERAL CLASSIFICATION

| POS | NAME | TEAM | TIME |
|---|---|---|---|
| 1. ↑11 | A. De Marchi | ISN | 13:50:44 |
| 2. ↑88 | J. Dombrowski | UAD | 0:22 |
| 3. ↑58 | L. Vervaeke | AFC | 0:42 |
| 4. ↑7 | N. Oliveira | MOV | 0:48 |
| 5. ↑59 | A. Valter | GFC | 1:00 |
| 6. ↑76 | N. Edet | COF | 1:15 |
| 7. – | A. Vlasov | APT | 1:24 |
| 8. ↓5 | R. Evenepoel | DQT | 1:28 |
| 9. ↓1 | A. Bettiol | EFN | 1:37 |
| 10.↑15 | H. Carthy | EFN | 1:38 |

### KING OF THE MOUNTAINS

| POS | NAME | TEAM | PTS |
|---|---|---|---|
| 1. – | J. Dombrowski | UAD | 18 |
| 2. ↓1 | V. Albanese | EOK | 16 |
| 3. – | R. Taaramäe | IWG | 13 |

### POINTS

| POS | NAME | TEAM | PTS |
|---|---|---|---|
| 1. – | T. Merlier | AFC | 50 |
| 2. – | E. Viviani | COF | 38 |
| 3. – | G. Nizzolo | TQA | 35 |

### YOUNG RIDER

| POS | NAME | TEAM | TIME |
|---|---|---|---|
| 1. ↑19 | A. Valter | GFC | 13:51:44 |
| 2. ↑3 | A. Vlasov | APT | 0:24 |
| 3. – | R. Evenepoel | DQT | 0:28 |

### BONUSES

| TYPE | NAME | TEAM |
|---|---|---|
| KOM 1 | F. Gavazzi | EOK |
| KOM 2 | R. Taaramäe | IWG |
| KOM 3 | J. Dombrowski | UAD |
| Sprint 1 | F. Tagliani | ANS |

### TRIVIA

» In his ninth Grand Tour – after 728 hours of racing – Joe Dombrowski finally claimed a stage win. That's enough time to watch US sitcom *Friends* 8.22 times over.

# STAGE RESULTS

| POS | NAME | TEAM | TIME |
|---|---|---|---|
| 1. | J. Dombrowski | UAD | 4:58:38 |
| 2. | A. De Marchi | ISN | 0:13 |
| 3. | F. Fiorelli | BCF | 0:27 |
| 4. | L. Vervaeke | AFC | 0:29 |
| 5. | J. Tratnik | TBV | s.t. |
| 6. | A. Valter | GFC | 0:44 |
| 7. | N. Edet | COF | 0:49 |
| 8. | N. Oliveira | MOV | 0:57 |
| 9. | R. Taaramäe | IWG | 1:33 |
| 10. | C. Juul-Jensen | BEX | 1:36 |
| 11. | E. Bernal | IGD | 1:37 |
| 12. | G. Ciccone | TFS | s.t. |
| 13. | A. Vlasov | APT | s.t. |
| 14. | M. Landa | TBV | s.t. |
| 15. | H. Carthy | EFN | s.t. |
| 16. | R. Evenepoel | DQT | 1:48 |
| 17. | R. Bardet | DSM | s.t. |
| 18. | S. Yates | BEX | s.t. |
| 19. | D. Martin | ISN | s.t. |
| 20. | D. Formolo | UAD | s.t. |
| 21. | A. Bettiol | EFN | s.t. |
| 22. | D. Caruso | TBV | s.t. |
| 23. | G. Moscon | IGD | 2:05 |
| 24. | A. Vendrame | ACT | s.t. |
| 25. | D. Pozzovivo | TQA | 2:11 |
| 26. | E. Buchmann | BOH | s.t. |
| 27. | V. Nibali | TFS | s.t. |
| 28. | P. Sivakov | IGD | s.t. |
| 29. | J. Hindley | DSM | s.t. |
| 30. | D. F. Martínez | IGD | s.t. |
| 31. | M. Soler | MOV | s.t. |
| 32. | N. Schultz | BEX | s.t. |
| 33. | P. Bilbao | TBV | s.t. |
| 34. | F. Masnada | DQT | 2:51 |
| 35. | G. Mäder | TBV | s.t. |
| 36. | J. Mosca | TFS | s.t. |
| 37. | T. Foss | TJV | 3:06 |
| 38. | G. Bennett | TJV | s.t. |
| 39. | R. Guerreiro | EFN | s.t. |
| 40. | D. Ulissi | UAD | 3:31 |
| 41. | H. Tejada | APT | 3:52 |
| 42. | T. Kangert | BEX | s.t. |
| 43. | F. Großschartner | BOH | 4:07 |
| 44. | M. Dina | EOK | s.t. |
| 45. | K. Bouwman | TJV | 5:02 |
| 46. | J. Narváez | IGD | s.t. |
| 47. | J. Hirt | IWG | 5:20 |
| 48. | J. Knox | DQT | 5:58 |
| 49. | J. Almeida | DQT | s.t. |
| 50. | L. L. Sanchez | APT | s.t. |
| 51. | R. Molard | GFC | s.t. |
| 52. | M. Nieve | BEX | s.t. |
| 53. | P. Serry | DQT | s.t. |
| 54. | M. Storer | DSM | s.t. |
| 55. | F. Gavazzi | EOK | s.t. |
| 56. | L. Fortunato | EOK | 6:12 |
| 57. | P. Bevin | ISN | 6:59 |
| 58. | M. Mohorič | TBV | 7:56 |
| 59. | V. Lafay | COF | 8:24 |
| 60. | M. F. Honoré | DQT | 8:52 |
| 61. | C. Scotson | BEX | s.t. |
| 62. | G. Brambilla | TFS | s.t. |
| 63. | G. Izagirre | APT | s.t. |
| 64. | M. Sobrero | APT | s.t. |
| 65. | J. Castroviejo | IGD | s.t. |
| 66. | J. K. Caicedo | EFN | s.t. |
| 67. | F. Bidard | ACT | 9:16 |
| 68. | G. Bouchard | ACT | s.t. |
| 69. | D. Villella | MOV | 12:22 |
| 70. | E. A. Rubio | MOV | s.t. |
| 71. | N. Venchiarutti | ANS | s.t. |
| 72. | F. Zana | BCF | s.t. |
| 73. | G. Aleotti | BOH | 12:36 |
| 74. | M. Fabbro | BOH | s.t. |
| 75. | N. Roche | DSM | s.t. |
| 76. | J. Keukeleire | EFN | 13:55 |
| 77. | G. Vermeersch | AFC | s.t. |
| 78. | M. Schmid | TQA | s.t. |
| 79. | K. Frankiny | TQA | s.t. |
| 80. | C. Hamilton | DSM | s.t. |
| 81. | T. Gallopin | ACT | s.t. |
| 82. | A. Covi | UAD | s.t. |
| 83. | L. Warbasse | ACT | s.t. |
| 84. | V. Pronskiy | APT | s.t. |
| 85. | A. Pasqualon | IWG | s.t. |
| 86. | S. Reichenbach | GFC | s.t. |
| 87. | S. Petilli | IWG | s.t. |
| 88. | S. Ravanelli | ANS | s.t. |
| 89. | R. Cavagna | DQT | s.t. |
| 90. | N. Denz | DSM | s.t. |
| 91. | G. Niv | ISN | s.t. |
| 92. | B. Mollema | TFS | s.t. |
| 93. | S. Guglielmi | GFC | s.t. |
| 94. | R. Seigle | GFC | s.t. |
| 95. | E. Ravasi | EOK | s.t. |

| POS | NAME | TEAM | TIME |
|---|---|---|---|
| 96. | A. Ghebreigzabhier | TFS | s.t. |
| 97. | V. Campenaerts | TQA | s.t. |
| 98. | J. Cepeda Ortiz | ANS | s.t. |
| 99. | A. Pedrero | MOV | s.t. |
| 100. | R. Valls | TBV | 15:08 |
| 101. | Q. Hermans | IWG | 18:07 |
| 102. | M. Badilatti | GFC | 18:29 |
| 103. | D. Oss | BOH | 20:36 |
| 104. | K. de Kort | TFS | s.t. |
| 105. | M. Hepburn | BEX | s.t. |
| 106. | R. Rochas | COF | s.t. |
| 107. | S. Puccio | IGD | s.t. |
| 108. | L. van den Berg | GFC | s.t. |
| 109. | N. Tesfatsion | ANS | s.t. |
| 110. | E. Affini | TJV | s.t. |
| 111. | D. Cataldo | MOV | s.t. |
| 112. | G. Carboni | BCF | s.t. |
| 113. | T. van Garderen | EFN | s.t. |
| 114. | H. Vanhoucke | LTS | s.t. |
| 115. | F. Ganna | IGD | 21:08 |
| 116. | V. Conti | UAD | 21:25 |
| 117. | P. Sagan | BOH | 23:06 |
| 118. | L. Wiśniowski | TQA | s.t. |
| 119. | L. Naesen | ACT | s.t. |
| 120. | S. Oldani | LTS | s.t. |
| 121. | D. Gabburo | BCF | s.t. |
| 122. | A. Ponomar | ANS | s.t. |
| 123. | G. Visconti | BCF | s.t. |
| 124. | F. Tagliani | ANS | s.t. |
| 125. | N. Berhane | COF | s.t. |
| 126. | A. Duchesne | GFC | s.t. |
| 127. | U. Marengo | BCF | s.t. |
| 128. | S. Pellaud | ANS | s.t. |
| 129. | N. Arndt | DSM | s.t. |
| 130. | C. Benedetti | BOH | s.t. |
| 131. | M. Walscheid | TQA | s.t. |
| 132. | G. Nizzolo | TQA | s.t. |
| 133. | B. J. Lindeman | TQA | s.t. |
| 134. | S. Leysen | AFC | s.t. |
| 135. | E. Sepúlveda | ANS | s.t. |
| 136. | E. Battaglin | BCF | s.t. |
| 137. | F. Gaviria | UAD | s.t. |
| 138. | M. Jorgenson | MOV | s.t. |
| 139. | M. Christian | EOK | s.t. |
| 140. | J. van Emden | TJV | s.t. |
| 141. | A. Dowsett | ISN | s.t. |
| 142. | P. Martens | TJV | s.t. |
| 143. | M. Brändle | ISN | s.t. |
| 144. | S. Battistella | APT | s.t. |
| 145. | D. Groenewegen | TJV | s.t. |
| 146. | A. Gougeard | ACT | s.t. |
| 147. | C. Champoussin | ACT | s.t. |
| 148. | M. Kanter | DSM | s.t. |
| 149. | D. Dekker | TJV | s.t. |
| 150. | D. Cimolai | ISN | s.t. |
| 151. | K. Goossens | LTS | s.t. |
| 152. | J. van den Berg | EFN | s.t. |
| 153. | S. Carr | EFN | s.t. |
| 154. | V. Albanese | EOK | s.t. |
| 155. | T. Marczyński | LTS | s.t. |
| 156. | I. Keisse | DQT | s.t. |
| 157. | F. Felline | APT | s.t. |
| 158. | Y. Arashiro | TBV | s.t. |
| 159. | W. Kreder | IWG | s.t. |
| 160. | T. van der Hoorn | IWG | s.t. |
| 161. | O. Riesebeek | AFC | s.t. |
| 162. | T. Merlier | AFC | s.t. |
| 163. | J. S. Molano | UAD | s.t. |
| 164. | M. Bodnar | BOH | s.t. |
| 165. | J. de Buyst | LTS | s.t. |
| 166. | J. Janssens | AFC | s.t. |
| 167. | C. Meyer | BEX | s.t. |
| 168. | A. Krieger | AFC | 24:35 |
| 169. | A. Torres | MOV | 24:48 |
| 170. | F. Sabatini | COF | 25:42 |
| 171. | S. Zoccarato | BCF | s.t. |
| 172. | S. Rivi | EOK | 26:53 |
| 173. | M. Belletti | EOK | s.t. |
| 174. | M. Minali | IWG | s.t. |
| 175. | A. M. Richeze | UAD | 27:53 |
| 176. | D. De Bondt | AFC | 28:10 |
| 177. | T. De Gendt | LTS | 29:00 |
| 178. | M. Moschetti | TFS | s.t. |
| 179. | R. Kluge | LTS | 30:48 |
| 180. | C. Ewan | LTS | s.t. |
| 181. | S. Consonni | COF | 30:56 |
| 182. | E. Viviani | COF | s.t. |
| 183. | A. Viviani | COF | s.t. |

MAY  WORLDTOUR MEN'S RACE

## GIRO D'ITALIA
Stage 5
12 May 2021
Modena–Cattolica
177km

### WEATHER

TEMPERATURE | WIND
19°C | NW 11km/h

### PROFILE

MODENA — IMOLA — CATTOLICA

Three moments. First, Bologna, kilometre 35: Lorenzo Fortunato, born in the city on 5 September 1996, talks to the *maglia rosa* Alessandro De Marchi, and is granted permission to enter his hometown ahead of the peloton. Second, Savignano sul Rubicone, kilometre 136: if he wins the second intermediate sprint, Simon Pellaud will replace his teammate Tagliani at the head of the *traguardi volanti* and the *premio della combattività* standings. He is poised on the wheel of his breakaway companion Davide Gabburo and, just before the sprint line, he turns to the camera, smiles… and does not sprint. He has already visited the podium and so decides to let a teammate do the same. Third, Rimini, kilometre 153: the *maglia rosa* is moving to the front of the peloton to begin working for his sprinter, Davide Cimolai, who finished second in stage 3. The Spanish national champion Luis León Sánchez looks over, sees the jersey, reaches out an arm and helps him through with a smile. It is impossible to watch these minor episodes, of virtually no sporting significance, without feeling slightly uplifted. Three more moments. First, just inside 16km to go, the motorbike regulator warns of a hazard. The pace slackens, the peloton bunches and veers left, and Pavel Sivakov performs a somersault, landing on his back. It recalls his crash on stage 1 of his debut Tour. Second, just inside 5km, the marshal on a traffic island waves an orange pennant. A rider hits him full on, then careers across the road. François Bidard, *maglia azzurra* Joe Dombrowski, and Mikel Landa end up on the ground. Landa's Giro is over. Third, with 200 metres left, Giacomo Nizzolo flies past Elia Viviani and the other sprinters. The voracious Caleb Ewan somehow finds the strength and speed to draw level and ease past, winning by half a bike length. A sporting moment at last, yet it is hard not to feel more for Giacomo – second yet again – than for Caleb, yet again first. This is the paradox that today's stage revealed so starkly: so much of what sport is about is not about sport. (MR)

### BREAKAWAY
F. Tagliani (ANS), U. Marengo (BCF)

### GENERAL CLASSIFICATION

| POS | | NAME | TEAM | TIME |
|---|---|---|---|---|
| 1. | – | A. De Marchi | ISN | 17:57:45 |
| 2. | ↑1 | L. Vervaeke | AFC | 0:42 |
| 3. | ↑1 | N. Oliveira | MOV | 0:48 |
| 4. | ↑1 | A. Valter | GFC | 1:00 |
| 5. | ↑1 | N. Edet | COF | 1:15 |
| 6. | ↑1 | A. Vlasov | APT | 1:24 |
| 7. | ↑1 | R. Evenepoel | DQT | 1:28 |
| 8. | ↑1 | A. Bettiol | EFN | 1:37 |
| 9. | ↑1 | H. Carthy | EFN | 1:38 |
| 10. | ↑1 | E. Bernal | IGD | 1:39 |

### KING OF THE MOUNTAINS

| POS | | NAME | TEAM | PTS |
|---|---|---|---|---|
| 1. | – | J. Dombrowski | UAD | 18 |
| 2. | – | V. Albanese | EOK | 16 |
| 3. | – | R. Taaramäe | IWG | 13 |

### POINTS

| POS | | NAME | TEAM | PTS |
|---|---|---|---|---|
| 1. | ↑2 | G. Nizzolo | TQA | 72 |
| 2. | – | E. Viviani | COF | 68 |
| 3. | ↓2 | T. Merlier | AFC | 58 |

### YOUNG RIDER

| POS | | NAME | TEAM | TIME |
|---|---|---|---|---|
| 1. | – | A. Valter | GFC | 17:58:45 |
| 2. | – | A. Vlasov | APT | 0:24 |
| 3. | – | R. Evenepoel | DQT | 0:28 |

### TRIVIA
» Caleb Ewan has now won a stage at each of the seven Grand Tours he's lined up at, except for the 2016 Giro d'Italia.

### BONUSES

| TYPE | NAME | TEAM |
|---|---|---|
| Sprint 1 | F. Tagliani | ANS |

## STAGE RESULTS

| POS | NAME | TEAM | TIME |
|---|---|---|---|
| 1. | C. Ewan | LTS | 4:07:01 |
| 2. | G. Nizzolo | TQA | s.t. |
| 3. | E. Viviani | COF | s.t. |
| 4. | P. Sagan | BOH | s.t. |
| 5. | F. Gaviria | UAD | s.t. |
| 6. | M. Moschetti | TFS | s.t. |
| 7. | A. Pasqualon | IWG | s.t. |
| 8. | D. Groenewegen | TJV | s.t. |
| 9. | M. Belletti | EOK | s.t. |
| 10. | D. Cimolai | ISN | s.t. |
| 11. | S. Consonni | COF | s.t. |
| 12. | T. Merlier | AFC | s.t. |
| 13. | F. Tagliani | ANS | s.t. |
| 14. | M. Kanter | DSM | s.t. |
| 15. | L. Naesen | ACT | s.t. |
| 16. | G. Moscon | IGD | s.t. |
| 17. | E. Bernal | IGD | s.t. |
| 18. | P. Bevin | ISN | s.t. |
| 19. | N. Oliveira | MOV | s.t. |
| 20. | A. M. Richeze | UAD | s.t. |
| 21. | A. Vlasov | APT | s.t. |
| 22. | R. Bardet | DSM | s.t. |
| 23. | A. Krieger | AFC | s.t. |
| 24. | N. Arndt | DSM | s.t. |
| 25. | R. Minali | IWG | s.t. |
| 26. | D. Dekker | TJV | s.t. |
| 27. | M. Soler | MOV | s.t. |
| 28. | J. S. Molano | UAD | s.t. |
| 29. | J. van Emden | TJV | s.t. |
| 30. | L. L. Sanchez | APT | s.t. |
| 31. | A. Vendrame | ACT | s.t. |
| 32. | F. Felline | APT | s.t. |
| 33. | D. Martin | ISN | s.t. |
| 34. | G. Izagirre | APT | s.t. |
| 35. | R. Cavagna | DQT | s.t. |
| 36. | V. Nibali | TFS | s.t. |
| 37. | L. Vervaeke | AFC | s.t. |
| 38. | G. Bennett | TJV | s.t. |
| 39. | H. Tejada | APT | s.t. |
| 40. | J. Almeida | DQT | s.t. |
| 41. | M. Sobrero | APT | s.t. |
| 42. | A. De Marchi | ISN | s.t. |
| 43. | T. Foss | TJV | s.t. |
| 44. | J. Mosca | TFS | s.t. |
| 45. | J. Hindley | DSM | s.t. |
| 46. | E. Buchmann | BOH | s.t. |
| 47. | A. Bettiol | EFN | s.t. |
| 48. | L. Warbasse | ACT | s.t. |
| 49. | A. Covi | UAD | s.t. |
| 50. | D. Ulissi | UAD | s.t. |
| 51. | H. Carthy | EFN | s.t. |
| 52. | P. Bilbao | TBV | s.t. |
| 53. | D. Formolo | UAD | s.t. |
| 54. | J. K. Caicedo | EFN | s.t. |
| 55. | D. Caruso | TBV | s.t. |
| 56. | S. Yates | BEX | s.t. |
| 57. | M. Hepburn | BEX | s.t. |
| 58. | M. Fabbro | BOH | s.t. |
| 59. | S. Battistella | APT | s.t. |
| 60. | R. Evenepoel | DQT | s.t. |
| 61. | D. F. Martínez | IGD | s.t. |
| 62. | D. Pozzovivo | TQA | s.t. |
| 63. | G. Ciccone | TFS | s.t. |
| 64. | D. Villella | MOV | s.t. |
| 65. | D. Cataldo | MOV | s.t. |
| 66. | R. Taaramäe | IWG | s.t. |
| 67. | F. Masnada | DQT | s.t. |
| 68. | R. Molard | GFC | s.t. |
| 69. | N. Roche | DSM | s.t. |
| 70. | C. Benedetti | BOH | s.t. |
| 71. | F. Gavazzi | EOK | s.t. |
| 72. | D. Oss | BOH | s.t. |
| 73. | I. Keisse | DQT | s.t. |
| 74. | G. Vermeersch | AFC | s.t. |
| 75. | M. F. Honoré | DQT | s.t. |
| 76. | N. Schultz | BEX | s.t. |
| 77. | E. Battaglin | BCF | s.t. |
| 78. | A. Valter | GFC | s.t. |
| 79. | U. Marengo | BCF | s.t. |
| 80. | E. Sepúlveda | ANS | s.t. |
| 81. | A. Ponomar | ANS | s.t. |
| 82. | E. A. Rubio | MOV | s.t. |
| 83. | N. Edet | COF | s.t. |
| 84. | F. Großschartner | BOH | s.t. |
| 85. | Q. Hermans | IWG | s.t. |
| 86. | V. Albanese | EOK | s.t. |
| 87. | K. Frankiny | TQA | s.t. |
| 88. | N. Berhane | COF | s.t. |
| 89. | G. Aleotti | BOH | s.t. |
| 90. | S. Guglielmi | GFC | s.t. |
| 91. | G. Bouchard | ACT | s.t. |
| 92. | V. Lafay | COF | s.t. |
| 93. | J. Keukeleire | EFN | s.t. |
| 94. | R. Seigle | GFC | s.t. |
| 95. | R. Guerreiro | EFN | s.t. |

| POS | NAME | TEAM | TIME |
|---|---|---|---|
| 96. | A. Viviani | COF | s.t. |
| 97. | N. Denz | DSM | s.t. |
| 98. | S. Petilli | IWG | s.t. |
| 99. | D. De Bondt | AFC | s.t. |
| 100. | V. Campenaerts | TQA | s.t. |
| 101. | W. Kreder | IWG | s.t. |
| 102. | B. Mollema | TFS | s.t. |
| 103. | M. Brändle | ISN | s.t. |
| 104. | A. Dowsett | ISN | s.t. |
| 105. | M. Walscheid | TQA | s.t. |
| 106. | E. Ravasi | EOK | s.t. |
| 107. | N. Venchiarutti | ANS | s.t. |
| 108. | V. Conti | UAD | s.t. |
| 109. | A. Duchesne | GFC | s.t. |
| 110. | G. Carboni | BCF | s.t. |
| 111. | S. Ravanelli | ANS | s.t. |
| 112. | L. van den Berg | GFC | s.t. |
| 113. | S. Oldani | LTS | s.t. |
| 114. | T. Gallopin | ACT | s.t. |
| 115. | R. Rochas | COF | s.t. |
| 116. | L. Fortunato | EOK | s.t. |
| 117. | F. Sabatini | COF | s.t. |
| 118. | F. Zana | BCF | s.t. |
| 119. | T. Kangert | BEX | s.t. |
| 120. | K. Bouwman | TJV | s.t. |
| 121. | T. van der Hoorn | IWG | s.t. |
| 122. | A. Torres | MOV | s.t. |
| 123. | S. Leysen | AFC | s.t. |
| 124. | J. Hirt | IWG | s.t. |
| 125. | M. Jorgenson | MOV | s.t. |
| 126. | P. Martens | TJV | s.t. |
| 127. | A. Pedrero | MOV | s.t. |
| 128. | K. de Kort | TFS | s.t. |
| 129. | V. Pronskiy | APT | s.t. |
| 130. | L. Wiśniowski | TQA | s.t. |
| 131. | M. Bodnar | BOH | s.t. |
| 132. | J. Knox | DQT | s.t. |
| 133. | M. Christian | EOK | s.t. |
| 134. | N. Tesfatsion | ANS | s.t. |
| 135. | S. Reichenbach | GFC | s.t. |
| 136. | M. Dina | EOK | s.t. |
| 137. | M. Badilatti | GFC | s.t. |
| 138. | M. Schmid | TQA | s.t. |
| 139. | G. Brambilla | TFS | 0:43 |
| 140. | G. Visconti | BCF | s.t. |
| 141. | G. Mäder | TBV | 1:03 |
| 142. | S. Carr | EFN | s.t. |
| 143. | M. Nieve | BEX | s.t. |
| 144. | C. Champoussin | ACT | s.t. |
| 145. | J. de Buyst | LTS | s.t. |
| 146. | A. Ghebreigzabhier | TFS | s.t. |
| 147. | D. Gabburo | BCF | s.t. |
| 148. | J. Janssens | AFC | s.t. |
| 149. | M. van den Berg | EFN | 1:17 |
| 150. | A. Gougeard | ACT | 1:29 |
| 151. | E. Affini | TJV | s.t. |
| 152. | S. Puccio | IGD | s.t. |
| 153. | T. Marczyński | LTS | 1:37 |
| 154. | O. Riesebeek | AFC | s.t. |
| 155. | J. Cepeda Ortiz | ANS | 1:44 |
| 156. | T. De Gendt | LTS | 1:51 |
| 157. | C. Hamilton | DSM | 2:04 |
| 158. | M. Storer | DSM | s.t. |
| 159. | G. Niv | ISN | s.t. |
| 160. | S. Rivi | EOK | s.t. |
| 161. | B. J. Lindeman | TQA | s.t. |
| 162. | S. Pellaud | ANS | s.t. |
| 163. | C. Scotson | BEX | 2:22 |
| 164. | C. Meyer | BEX | s.t. |
| 165. | C. Juul-Jensen | BEX | 2:34 |
| 166. | R. Kluge | LTS | 2:49 |
| 167. | F. Ganna | IGD | 3:03 |
| 168. | P. Serry | DQT | 3:35 |
| 169. | J. Castroviejo | IGD | s.t. |
| 170. | T. van Garderen | EFN | 4:00 |
| 171. | S. Zoccarato | BCF | 4:51 |
| 172. | K. Goossens | LTS | 4:56 |
| 173. | H. Vanhoucke | LTS | s.t. |
| 174. | J. Tratnik | TBV | 5:05 |
| 175. | M. Mohorič | TBV | s.t. |
| 176. | R. Valls | TBV | s.t. |
| 177. | Y. Arashiro | TBV | s.t. |
| 178. | F. Fiorelli | BCF | 7:31 |
| 179. | F. Bidard | ACT | 8:00 |
| 180. | J. Dombrowski | UAD | 8:15 |
| 181. | J. Narváez | IGD | 13:08 |
| 182. | P. Sivakov | IGD | s.t. |

MAY  WORLDTOUR MEN'S RACE

## GIRO D'ITALIA
Stage 6
13 May 2021
Grotte di Frasassi–Ascoli Piceno (San Giacomo)
160km

We are caught in cross-pressures by the old and the new, which tear the world apart the way the astonishing Filippo Ganna tore the peloton apart for 50km today, dispossessing poor Alessandro De Marchi of his treasured *maglia rosa*. Our supply lines to the past allow us to define our identities; without them, we are lost. Today the peloton took the ancient Via Salaria, built by the Italic people of the Sabines before the foundation of Rome, to a finish line in San Giacomo on the border between the Italian regions of Abruzzo and Le Marche. A milestone laid in 1847 shows the position of the ancient boundary defined by Roger II, 'King of Sicily and Africa', some time between 1140 and 1143 to put an end to disputes between Rome and Naples. Today it was all change in the Giro. Gino Mäder became only the second Gino have won a Giro stage. No Attilas had ridden the Giro before this year, let alone donned any of its jerseys, until stage 4, when Attila Valter took the *maglia bianca*. Today – by finishing with Carthy, Vlasov and Yates, 17 seconds behind Bernal, Dan Martin and Evenepoel – he swapped it for a pink one and made Hungary the ninth nation in the past decade to take its first *maglia rosa*, after Belarus (2011), Canada (2012), Lithuania (2012), Colombia (2014), Costa Rica (2016), Austria (2017), Ecuador (2019) and Slovenia (2019). No Remcos or Egans have ever ridden the Giro before (and only one Hugh, the same one). After today's wet stage, Attila, Remco, Egan and Hugh now lay first, second, third and sixth, with Aleksandr Vlasov and Louis Vervaeke in fourth and fifth. There were 45 *maglia azzurra* points available. After stage 16, which would offer 170 of them, today's first mountain finish would seem a distant memory. But we should cherish memory. The Giro – the bicycle, that elementary piece of industrial heritage, now designed by F1 engineers and built by robots – helps us balance the cross-pressures. (MR)

### TRIVIA
» Attila Valter is the first-ever Hungarian to wear a Grand Tour leader's jersey.

### WEATHER

TEMPERATURE 21°C
WIND SW 19km/h

### PROFILE

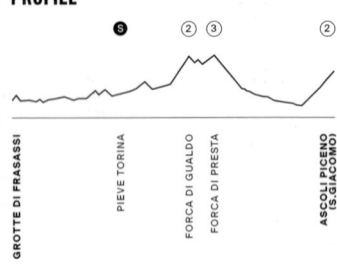

### BREAKAWAY
M. Mohorič (TBV), G. Mäder (TBV), D. Cataldo (MOV), S. Guglielmi (GFC), J. Janssens (AFC), S. Ravanelli (ANS), B. Mollema (TFS), G. Bouchard (ACT)

### GENERAL CLASSIFICATION
| POS | NAME | TEAM | TIME |
|---|---|---|---|
| 1. ↑3 | A. Valter | GFC | 22:17:06 |
| 2. ↑5 | R. Evenepoel | DQT | 0:11 |
| 3. ↑7 | E. Bernal | IGD | 0:16 |
| 4. ↑2 | A. Vlasov | APT | 0:24 |
| 5. ↓3 | L. Vervaeke | AFC | 0:25 |
| 6. ↑3 | H. Carthy | EFN | 0:38 |
| 7. ↑4 | D. Caruso | TBV | 0:39 |
| 8. ↑8 | G. Ciccone | TFS | 0:41 |
| 9. ↑10 | D. Martin | ISN | 0:47 |
| 10.↑4 | S. Yates | BEX | 0:49 |

### KING OF THE MOUNTAINS
| POS | NAME | TEAM | PTS |
|---|---|---|---|
| 1. — | G. Mäder | TBV | 26 |
| 2. — | G. Bouchard | ACT | 18 |
| 3. ↓1 | V. Albanese | EOK | 16 |

### POINTS
| POS | NAME | TEAM | PTS |
|---|---|---|---|
| 1. — | G. Nizzolo | TQA | 72 |
| 2. — | E. Viviani | COF | 68 |
| 3. — | T. Merlier | AFC | 58 |

### YOUNG RIDER
| POS | NAME | TEAM | TIME |
|---|---|---|---|
| 1. — | A. Valter | GFC | 22:17:06 |
| 2. ↑1 | R. Evenepoel | DQT | 0:11 |
| 3. ↑1 | E. Bernal | IGD | 0:16 |

### BONUSES
| TYPE | NAME | TEAM |
|---|---|---|
| KOM 1 | G. Bouchard | GFC |
| KOM 2 | M. Mohorič | TBV |
| KOM 3 | G. Mäder | TBV |
| Sprint 1 | S. Ravanelli | ANS |

## STAGE RESULTS

| POS | NAME | TEAM | TIME |
|---|---|---|---|
| 1. | G. Mäder | TBV | 4:17:52 |
| 2. | E. Bernal | IGD | 0:12 |
| 3. | D. Martin | ISN | s.t. |
| 4. | R. Evenepoel | DQT | s.t. |
| 5. | G. Ciccone | TFS | 0:14 |
| 6. | D. Caruso | TBV | 0:25 |
| 7. | D. F. Martínez | IGD | s.t. |
| 8. | M. Soler | MOV | 0:27 |
| 9. | H. Carthy | EFN | 0:29 |
| 10. | A. Vlasov | APT | s.t. |
| 11. | S. Yates | BEX | s.t. |
| 12. | A. Valter | GFC | s.t. |
| 13. | E. Buchmann | BOH | 0:40 |
| 14. | R. Bardet | DSM | s.t. |
| 15. | T. Foss | TJV | s.t. |
| 16. | J. Almeida | DQT | s.t. |
| 17. | D. Formolo | UAD | s.t. |
| 18. | V. Nibali | TFS | 0:57 |
| 19. | N. Schultz | BEX | s.t. |
| 20. | E. A. Rubio | MOV | 1:10 |
| 21. | L. Fortunato | EOK | 1:12 |
| 22. | L. Vervaeke | AFC | s.t. |
| 23. | R. Taaramäe | IWG | 1:14 |
| 24. | P. Bilbao | TBV | 1:18 |
| 25. | R. Guerreiro | EFN | 1:19 |
| 26. | A. Pedrero | MOV | 1:26 |
| 27. | G. Moscon | IGD | 1:41 |
| 28. | F. Masnada | DQT | 1:46 |
| 29. | M. Fabbro | BOH | s.t. |
| 30. | H. Tejada | APT | s.t. |
| 31. | B. Mollema | TFS | 2:02 |
| 32. | D. Cataldo | MOV | 2:07 |
| 33. | T. Kangert | BEX | 2:15 |
| 34. | J. Hindley | DSM | 2:38 |
| 35. | K. Goossens | LTS | s.t. |
| 36. | J. K. Caicedo | EFN | s.t. |
| 37. | D. Villella | MOV | 4:21 |
| 38. | D. Ulissi | UAD | 5:12 |
| 39. | M. Storer | DSM | 5:55 |
| 40. | J. Castroviejo | IGD | 6:30 |
| 41. | K. Bouwman | TJV | 7:12 |
| 42. | G. Bennett | TJV | 7:14 |
| 43. | M. Mohorič | TBV | 8:45 |
| 44. | P. Bevin | ISN | 10:27 |
| 45. | V. Lafay | COF | s.t. |
| 46. | S. Guglielmi | GFC | 12:57 |
| 47. | T. Gallopin | ACT | 14:37 |
| 48. | G. Bouchard | ACT | s.t. |
| 49. | N. Roche | DSM | s.t. |
| 50. | M. F. Honoré | DQT | s.t. |
| 51. | K. Frankiny | TQA | s.t. |
| 52. | G. Brambilla | TFS | s.t. |
| 53. | F. Gavazzi | EOK | s.t. |
| 54. | F. Großschartner | BOH | s.t. |
| 55. | L. Warbasse | ACT | s.t. |
| 56. | N. Oliveira | MOV | s.t. |
| 57. | Q. Hermans | IWG | s.t. |
| 58. | E. Ravasi | EOK | s.t. |
| 59. | J. Knox | DQT | s.t. |
| 60. | J. Janssens | AFC | s.t. |
| 61. | P. Serry | DQT | s.t. |
| 62. | G. Izaguirre | APT | s.t. |
| 63. | M. Nieve | BEX | s.t. |
| 64. | J. Mosca | TFS | s.t. |
| 65. | F. Felline | APT | s.t. |
| 66. | S. Petilli | IWG | s.t. |
| 67. | J. Hirt | IWG | s.t. |
| 68. | G. Carboni | BCF | 16:29 |
| 69. | J. Keukeleire | EFN | 18:42 |
| 70. | C. Juul-Jensen | BEX | s.t. |
| 71. | S. Puccio | IGD | 18:52 |
| 72. | A. Bettiol | EFN | s.t. |
| 73. | J. Narváez | IGD | s.t. |
| 74. | S. Ravanelli | ANS | s.t. |
| 75. | F. Fiorelli | BCF | 19:18 |
| 76. | A. Covi | UAD | s.t. |
| 77. | J. van Emden | TJV | s.t. |
| 78. | A. Pasqualon | IWG | s.t. |
| 79. | F. Ganna | IGD | 19:36 |
| 80. | M. Sobrero | APT | s.t. |
| 81. | S. Reichenbach | GFC | 20:20 |
| 82. | N. Edet | COF | s.t. |
| 83. | R. Seigle | GFC | s.t. |
| 84. | R. Molard | GFC | s.t. |
| 85. | C. Hamilton | DSM | s.t. |
| 86. | D. Pozzovivo | TQA | s.t. |
| 87. | T. De Gendt | LTS | s.t. |
| 88. | T. van Garderen | EFN | s.t. |
| 89. | L. van den Berg | GFC | 21:08 |
| 90. | F. Zana | BCF | 21:47 |
| 91. | E. Affini | TJV | s.t. |
| 92. | E. Sepúlveda | ANS | s.t. |
| 93. | N. Arndt | DSM | s.t. |
| 94. | J. Cepeda Ortiz | ANS | s.t. |
| 95. | O. Riesebeek | AFC | 22:06 |

| POS | NAME | TEAM | TIME |
|---|---|---|---|
| 96. | S. Battistella | APT | s.t. |
| 97. | A. Vendrame | ACT | s.t. |
| 98. | M. Dina | EOK | s.t. |
| 99. | P. Sagan | BOH | 24:49 |
| 100. | F. Sabatini | COF | s.t. |
| 101. | A. Duchesne | GFC | s.t. |
| 102. | C. Benedetti | BOH | s.t. |
| 103. | G. Visconti | BCF | s.t. |
| 104. | G. Aleotti | BOH | s.t. |
| 105. | V. Conti | UAD | s.t. |
| 106. | M. Hepburn | BEX | s.t. |
| 107. | S. Pellaud | ANS | s.t. |
| 108. | R. Valls | TBV | s.t. |
| 109. | S. Oldani | LTS | s.t. |
| 110. | D. Oss | BOH | s.t. |
| 111. | V. Pronskiy | APT | s.t. |
| 112. | B. J. Lindeman | TQA | s.t. |
| 113. | C. Champoussin | ACT | s.t. |
| 114. | Y. Arashiro | TBV | s.t. |
| 115. | P. Martens | TJV | s.t. |
| 116. | T. van der Hoorn | IWG | s.t. |
| 117. | A. Ponomar | ANS | s.t. |
| 118. | E. Battaglin | BCF | s.t. |
| 119. | M. Jorgenson | MOV | s.t. |
| 120. | D. Gabburo | BCF | s.t. |
| 121. | S. Leysen | AFC | s.t. |
| 122. | G. Vermeersch | AFC | s.t. |
| 123. | W. Kreder | IWG | s.t. |
| 124. | M. Badilatti | GFC | s.t. |
| 125. | M. Christian | EOK | s.t. |
| 126. | L. L. Sanchez | APT | s.t. |
| 127. | I. Koisse | DQT | s.t. |
| 128. | C. Scotson | BEX | s.t. |
| 129. | A. Ghebreigzabhier | TFS | s.t. |
| 130. | V. Campenaerts | TQA | s.t. |
| 131. | R. Cavagna | DQT | s.t. |
| 132. | V. Albanese | EOK | s.t. |
| 133. | S. Carr | EFN | s.t. |
| 134. | M. Kanter | DSM | s.t. |
| 135. | J. van den Berg | EFN | s.t. |
| 136. | A. De Marchi | ISN | s.t. |
| 137. | N. Denz | DSM | 26:04 |
| 138. | N. Berhane | COF | s.t. |
| 139. | M. Brändle | ISN | 27:32 |
| 140. | R. Minali | IWG | s.t. |
| 141. | A. Gougeard | ACT | s.t. |
| 142. | R. Rochas | COF | s.t. |
| 143. | A. Dowsett | ISN | s.t. |
| 144. | K. de Kort | TFS | s.t. |
| 145. | N. Tesfatsion | ANS | s.t. |
| 146. | L. Naesen | ACT | s.t. |
| 147. | C. Ewan | LTS | s.t. |
| 148. | T. Marczyński | LTS | s.t. |
| 149. | D. Groenewegen | TJV | s.t. |
| 150. | N. Venchiarutti | ANS | s.t. |
| 151. | J. de Buyst | LTS | s.t. |
| 152. | S. Zoccarato | BCF | s.t. |
| 153. | M. Moschetti | TFS | s.t. |
| 154. | F. Tagliani | ANS | s.t. |
| 155. | U. Marengo | BCF | s.t. |
| 156. | L. Wiśniowski | TQA | s.t. |
| 157. | E. Viviani | COF | s.t. |
| 158. | G. Niv | ISN | s.t. |
| 159. | H. Vanhoucke | LTS | s.t. |
| 160. | M. Schmid | TQA | s.t. |
| 161. | M. Walscheid | TQA | s.t. |
| 162. | J. Tratnik | TBV | s.t. |
| 163. | S. Rivi | EOK | s.t. |
| 164. | G. Nizzolo | TQA | s.t. |
| 165. | T. Merlier | AFC | s.t. |
| 166. | D. Cimolai | ISN | s.t. |
| 167. | D. De Bondt | AFC | s.t. |
| 168. | A. Viviani | COF | s.t. |
| 169. | A. Torres | MOV | s.t. |
| 170. | M. Bodnar | BOH | s.t. |
| 171. | A. Krieger | AFC | s.t. |
| 172. | D. Dekker | TJV | s.t. |
| 173. | S. Consonni | COF | 27:45 |
| 174. | R. Kluge | LTS | s.t. |
| 175. | F. Gaviria | UAD | 27:48 |
| 176. | J. S. Molano | UAD | s.t. |
| 177. | A. M. Richeze | UAD | s.t. |
| 178. | C. Meyer | BEX | s.t. |

MAY    WORLDTOUR MEN'S RACE

# GIRO D'ITALIA
Stage 7
14 May 2021
Notaresco–Termoli
181km

In 1862, Torino – 128.6km into today's stage on the Adriatic coast – added the local river to its name and became Torino di Sangro, to avoid confusion with the newly adopted capital of the newborn nation state, Italy. Before the first intermediate sprint, Peter Sagan and Daniel Oss made a mischievous attack to pick up the 5 *maglia ciclamino* points awarded for fourth place, behind the three leaders, who had no interest at all in the *maglia ciclamino* but wanted the *traguardi volanti* and *combattività* points. As it happened, Simon Pellaud – who had moved ahead of Vincenzo Albanese at the top of the *fuga bianchi* breakaway competition after 25km of the stage – picked up enough of each to take the lead in both competitions, despite losing the sprint to the Umberto Marengo. If he could have left the *maglia ciclamino* points for Sagan, he probably would have but – unlike Torino in Piedmont and Torino in Abruzzo – the categories are melded together. The three breakaway riders (the trio completed by the Manxman Mark Christian) sped along the recently rebranded 'Costa dei Trabocchi', spreading the good news of its tourist potential. The *trabocco* is a wooden platform jutting out into the sea from which two long, catapult-like arms manipulate a huge, narrow-mesh fishing net. Modernity can never wait to humiliate such traditional technologies with its hi-tech alternatives but, like the modern racing bicycle, the underlying design concept still catches our imagination. Caleb Ewan's winning sprint – despite Fernando Gaviria's attempt to foil it with an early attack – was the perfectly realised embodiment of an underlying plan: 'I had all my guys there from a long way out, because there was a few points in the last 10km when we really needed to be at the front, so we didn't have to brake or anything. The most important point for me, I told them, was the start of the climb because, if I got a free run there, then I'd save a lot of energy.' (MR)

## TRIVIA
» Caleb Ewan now has five stage wins at both the Giro d'Italia and Tour de France, but only one at the Vuelta a España.

## WEATHER

| TEMPERATURE | WIND |
|---|---|
| 22°C | E 22km/h |

## PROFILE

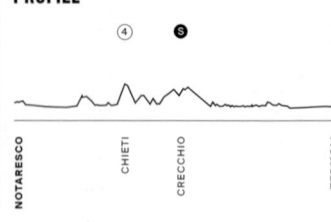

NOTARESCO — CHIETI — CRECCHIO — TERMOLI

## BREAKAWAY
U. Marengo (BCF), S. Pellaud (ANS), M. Christian (EOK)

## GENERAL CLASSIFICATION

| POS | NAME | TEAM | TIME |
|---|---|---|---|
| 1. — | A. Valter | GFC | 26:59:18 |
| 2. — | R. Evenepoel | DQT | 0:11 |
| 3. — | E. Bernal | IGD | 0:16 |
| 4. — | A. Vlasov | APT | 0:24 |
| 5. — | L. Vervaeke | AFC | 0:25 |
| 6. — | H. Carthy | EFN | 0:38 |
| 7. — | D. Caruso | TBV | 0:39 |
| 8. — | G. Ciccone | TFS | 0:41 |
| 9. — | D. Martin | ISN | 0:47 |
| 10.— | S. Yates | BEX | 0:49 |

## KING OF THE MOUNTAINS

| POS | NAME | TEAM | PTS |
|---|---|---|---|
| 1. — | G. Mäder | TBV | 26 |
| 2. — | G. Bouchard | ACT | 18 |
| 3. — | V. Albanese | EOK | 16 |

## POINTS

| POS | NAME | TEAM | PTS |
|---|---|---|---|
| 1. ↑3 | C. Ewan | LTS | 106 |
| 2. ↑1 | T. Merlier | AFC | 83 |
| 3. ↓2 | G. Nizzolo | TQA | 76 |

## YOUNG RIDER

| POS | NAME | TEAM | TIME |
|---|---|---|---|
| 1. — | A. Valter | GFC | 26:59:18 |
| 2. — | R. Evenepoel | DQT | 0:11 |
| 3. — | E. Bernal | IGD | 0:16 |

## BONUSES

| TYPE | NAME | TEAM |
|---|---|---|
| KOM 1 | S. Pellaud | ANS |
| Sprint 1 | U. Marengo | BCF |

# STAGE RESULTS

| POS | NAME | TEAM | TIME |
|---|---|---|---|
| 1. | C. Ewan | LTS | 4:42:12 |
| 2. | D. Cimolai | ISN | s.t. |
| 3. | T. Merlier | AFC | s.t. |
| 4. | M. Moschetti | TFS | s.t. |
| 5. | A. Pasqualon | IWG | s.t. |
| 6. | F. Gaviria | UAD | s.t. |
| 7. | D. Groenewegen | TJV | s.t. |
| 8. | M. Kanter | DSM | s.t. |
| 9. | F. Fiorelli | BCF | s.t. |
| 10. | J. S. Molano | UAD | s.t. |
| 11. | F. Felline | APT | s.t. |
| 12. | G. Nizzolo | TQA | s.t. |
| 13. | G. Moscon | IGD | s.t. |
| 14. | P. Sagan | BOH | s.t. |
| 15. | E. Viviani | COF | s.t. |
| 16. | M. Mohorič | TBV | s.t. |
| 17. | A. Vendrame | ACT | s.t. |
| 18. | E. Bernal | IGD | s.t. |
| 19. | J. Mosca | TFS | s.t. |
| 20. | L. Naesen | ACT | s.t. |
| 21. | R. Cavagna | DQT | s.t. |
| 22. | T. Foss | TJV | s.t. |
| 23. | D. Gabburo | BCF | s.t. |
| 24. | R. Seigle | GFC | s.t. |
| 25. | R. Bardet | DSM | s.t. |
| 26. | D. Ulissi | UAD | s.t. |
| 27. | J. Hindley | DSM | s.t. |
| 28. | D. Caruso | TBV | s.t. |
| 29. | D. Formolo | UAD | s.t. |
| 30. | M. Soler | MOV | s.t. |
| 31. | V. Nibali | TFS | s.t. |
| 32. | J. Almeida | DQT | s.t. |
| 33. | D. F. Martínez | IGD | s.t. |
| 34. | D. Martin | ISN | s.t. |
| 35. | F. Tagliani | ANS | s.t. |
| 36. | A. Valter | GFC | s.t. |
| 37. | L. L. Sanchez | APT | s.t. |
| 38. | L. van den Berg | GFC | s.t. |
| 39. | S. Yates | BEX | s.t. |
| 40. | G. Izagirre | APT | s.t. |
| 41. | G. Ciccone | TFS | s.t. |
| 42. | A. Vlasov | APT | s.t. |
| 43. | N. Schultz | BEX | s.t. |
| 44. | E. Buchmann | BOH | s.t. |
| 45. | I. Keisse | DQT | s.t. |
| 46. | M. Hepburn | BEX | s.t. |
| 47. | V. Pronskiy | APT | s.t. |
| 48. | P. Bilbao | TBV | s.t. |
| 49. | L. Vervaeke | AFC | s.t. |
| 50. | R. Evenepoel | DQT | s.t. |
| 51. | M. F. Honoré | DQT | s.t. |
| 52. | M. Fabbro | BOH | s.t. |
| 53. | F. Masnada | DQT | s.t. |
| 54. | G. Vermeersch | AFC | s.t. |
| 55. | R. Taaramäe | IWG | s.t. |
| 56. | A. M. Richeze | UAD | s.t. |
| 57. | K. Bouwman | TJV | s.t. |
| 58. | H. Tejada | APT | s.t. |
| 59. | G. Bennett | TJV | s.t. |
| 60. | V. Albanese | EOK | s.t. |
| 61. | N. Venchiarutti | ANS | s.t. |
| 62. | Y. Arashiro | TBV | s.t. |
| 63. | L. Warbasse | ACT | 0:23 |
| 64. | A. Ghebreigzabhier | TFS | s.t. |
| 65. | F. Großschartner | BOH | s.t. |
| 66. | J. Narváez | IGD | s.t. |
| 67. | J. de Buyst | LTS | s.t. |
| 68. | D. Oss | BOH | s.t. |
| 69. | T. Kangert | BEX | 0:35 |
| 70. | V. Campenaerts | TQA | s.t. |
| 71. | G. Brambilla | TFS | 0:39 |
| 72. | G. Aleotti | BOH | s.t. |
| 73. | A. Ponomar | ANS | s.t. |
| 74. | G. Carboni | BCF | s.t. |
| 75. | J. Keukeleire | EFN | s.t. |
| 76. | E. Battaglin | BCF | s.t. |
| 77. | M. Walscheid | TQA | 0:54 |
| 78. | N. Arndt | DSM | s.t. |
| 79. | W. Kreder | IWG | s.t. |
| 80. | A. Krieger | AFC | s.t. |
| 81. | F. Ganna | IGD | s.t. |
| 82. | V. Lafay | COF | s.t. |
| 83. | A. Viviani | COF | s.t. |
| 84. | R. Molard | GFC | s.t. |
| 85. | B. Mollema | TFS | s.t. |
| 86. | M. Nieve | BEX | s.t. |
| 87. | F. Gavazzi | EOK | s.t. |
| 88. | M. Bodnar | BOH | s.t. |
| 89. | N. Tesfatsion | ANS | s.t. |
| 90. | L. Fortunato | EOK | s.t. |
| 91. | D. Cataldo | MOV | s.t. |
| 92. | T. Gallopin | ACT | s.t. |
| 93. | G. Bouchard | ACT | s.t. |
| 94. | F. Sabatini | COF | s.t. |
| 95. | K. Frankiny | TQA | s.t. |
| 96. | S. Reichenbach | GFC | s.t. |
| 97. | E. Sepúlveda | ANS | s.t. |
| 98. | Q. Hermans | IWG | s.t. |
| 99. | M. Dina | EOK | s.t. |
| 100. | A. Covi | UAD | s.t. |
| 101. | J. van Emden | TJV | s.t. |
| 102. | G. Niv | ISN | s.t. |
| 103. | P. Bevin | ISN | s.t. |
| 104. | S. Leysen | AFC | s.t. |
| 105. | S. Petilli | IWG | s.t. |
| 106. | A. Pedrero | MOV | s.t. |
| 107. | F. Zana | BCF | 1:13 |
| 108. | M. Jorgenson | MOV | s.t. |
| 109. | S. Guglielmi | GFC | s.t. |
| 110. | N. Berhane | COF | s.t. |
| 111. | A. Duchesne | GFC | s.t. |
| 112. | J. Knox | DQT | s.t. |
| 113. | M. Sobrero | APT | s.t. |
| 114. | A. Gougeard | ACT | s.t. |
| 115. | J. Hirt | IWG | s.t. |
| 116. | D. Villella | MOV | s.t. |
| 117. | N. Denz | DSM | s.t. |
| 118. | E. A. Rubio | MOV | s.t. |
| 119. | J. K. Caicedo | EFN | s.t. |
| 120. | N. Edet | COF | s.t. |
| 121. | S. Ravanelli | ANS | s.t. |
| 122. | J. Janssens | AFC | s.t. |
| 123. | O. Riesebeek | AFC | s.t. |
| 124. | S. Zoccarato | BCF | s.t. |
| 125. | C. Benedetti | BOH | s.t. |
| 126. | J. Cepeda Ortiz | ANS | s.t. |
| 127. | G. Mäder | TBV | s.t. |
| 128. | M. Brändle | ISN | s.t. |
| 129. | A. Dowsett | ISN | s.t. |
| 130. | N. Oliveira | MOV | s.t. |
| 131. | U. Marengo | BCF | 1:42 |
| 132. | G. Visconti | BCF | s.t. |
| 133. | T. van der Hoorn | IWG | s.t. |
| 134. | R. Minali | IWG | s.t. |
| 135. | B. J. Lindeman | TQA | 1:48 |
| 136. | T. De Gendt | LTS | s.t. |
| 137. | R. Valls | TBV | s.t. |
| 138. | C. Champoussin | ACT | s.t. |
| 139. | R. Rochas | COF | s.t. |
| 140. | K. de Kort | TFS | s.t. |
| 141. | M. Badilatti | GFC | s.t. |
| 142. | S. Battistella | APT | s.t. |
| 143. | M. Schmid | TQA | s.t. |
| 144. | S. Rivi | EOK | s.t. |
| 145. | A. De Marchi | ISN | s.t. |
| 146. | P. Martens | TJV | s.t. |
| 147. | S. Consonni | COF | s.t. |
| 148. | L. Wiśniowski | TQA | s.t. |
| 149. | J. Tratnik | TBV | s.t. |
| 150. | S. Pellaud | ANS | s.t. |
| 151. | M. Christian | EOK | s.t. |
| 152. | M. Storer | DSM | 2:05 |
| 153. | K. Goossens | LTS | 2:09 |
| 154. | S. Oldani | LTS | s.t. |
| 155. | T. Marczyński | LTS | s.t. |
| 156. | H. Vanhoucke | LTS | s.t. |
| 157. | R. Kluge | LTS | s.t. |
| 158. | V. Conti | UAD | 2:14 |
| 159. | D. Dekker | TJV | s.t. |
| 160. | J. van den Berg | EFN | 2:21 |
| 161. | A. Bettiol | EFN | s.t. |
| 162. | H. Carthy | EFN | 0:00 |
| 163. | T. van Garderen | EFN | 2:21 |
| 164. | E. Ravasi | EOK | 2:37 |
| 165. | S. Carr | EFN | s.t. |
| 166. | R. Guerreiro | EFN | 2:43 |
| 167. | C. Scotson | BEX | s.t. |
| 168. | D. De Bondt | AFC | 2:53 |
| 169. | S. Juul-Jensen | BEX | 2:56 |
| 170. | S. Puccio | IGD | s.t. |
| 171. | J. Castroviejo | IGD | s.t. |
| 172. | P. Serry | DQT | 3:12 |
| 173. | A. Torres | MOV | s.t. |
| 174. | C. Hamilton | DSM | s.t. |
| 175. | N. Roche | DSM | s.t. |
| 176. | C. Meyer | BEX | 3:27 |
| 177. | E. Affini | TJV | 3:35 |

MAY    WORLDTOUR MEN'S RACE

# GIRO D'ITALIA
Stage 8
15 May 2021
Foggia–Guardia Sanframondi
170km

In 1806 Napoleon's brother Joseph Bonaparte, King of Naples, abolished feudalism. Until then, towns, villages and inhabitants had been passed between feudal overlords like chattels. The peloton's own dynasties behave the same way. The 22-year-old *maglia rosa*, Attila Valter, said after the stage, 'I could never get used to this feeling. I mean, at the start of the Giro I wondered what it must feel like to be Filippo Ganna in Italy. Now I have some idea!' In his own version of events, 'We let the perfect breakaway go – nine riders with a large gap in the GC – and then we controlled the whole day.' Ganna might dispute that. With Egan Bernal on his wheel, the gladiatorial Ganna covered 44.5km in the first hour – most of it uphill – controlling the race almost singlehandedly until a breakaway he deemed acceptable was allowed to go. By the time it did, Caleb Ewan had abandoned. Meanwhile, world hour record-holder Victor Campenaerts – already the author of a heroic two-man attack with Quinten Hermans on stage 4, around which the successful breakaway eventually formed – chased the eight-man group for about 10km before finally making it across and joining Victor Lafay, whose Cofidis had not won a Giro stage since 2010. Knowing his forte was the intense 10-minute effort, Lafay attacked with 3km to go, rode past Giovanni Carboni and sped away to make his first pro win a stage in a Grand Tour – like Van Den Hoorn four days ago. Behind them, the feudal dynasties eyed each other suspiciously, Martínez escorting Bernal up most of the final climb, Almeida doing the same for Evenepoel.

## WEATHER

TEMPERATURE    WIND
18°C           NW 26km/h

## PROFILE

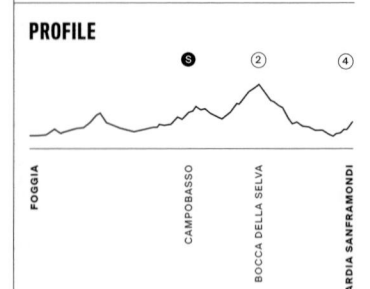

FOGGIA – CAMPOBASSO – BOCCA DELLA SELVA – GUARDIA SANFRAMONDI

## BREAKAWAY

N. Oliveira (MOV), K. Goossens (LTS), A. Gougeard (ACT), N. Arndt (DSM), V. Lafay (COF), G. Carboni (BCF), F. Gavazzi (EOK), F. Gaviria (UAD)

## GENERAL CLASSIFICATION

| POS | | NAME | TEAM | TIME |
|---|---|---|---|---|
| 1. | – | A. Valter | GFC | 31:10:53 |
| 2. | – | R. Evenepoel | DQT | 0:11 |
| 3. | – | E. Bernal | IGD | 0:16 |
| 4. | – | A. Vlasov | APT | 0:24 |
| 5. | ↑1 | H. Carthy | EFN | 0:38 |
| 6. | ↑1 | D. Caruso | TBV | 0:39 |
| 7. | ↑1 | G. Ciccone | TFS | 0:41 |
| 8. | ↑1 | D. Martin | ISN | 0:47 |
| 9. | ↑1 | S. Yates | BEX | 0:49 |
| 10. | ↓5 | L. Vervaeke | AFC | 0:50 |

## KING OF THE MOUNTAINS

| POS | | NAME | TEAM | PTS |
|---|---|---|---|---|
| 1. | – | G. Mäder | TBV | 26 |
| 2. | – | G. Bouchard | ACT | 18 |
| 3. | – | K. Goossens | LTS | 18 |

## POINTS

| POS | | NAME | TEAM | PTS |
|---|---|---|---|---|
| 1. | ↑1 | T. Merlier | AFC | 83 |
| 2. | ↑1 | G. Nizzolo | TQA | 76 |
| 3. | ↑1 | E. Viviani | COF | 69 |

## YOUNG RIDER

| POS | | NAME | TEAM | TIME |
|---|---|---|---|---|
| 1. | – | A. Valter | GFC | 31:10:53 |
| 2. | – | R. Evenepoel | DQT | 0:11 |
| 3. | – | E. Bernal | IGD | 0:16 |

## TRIVIA

» Nominative determinism struck twice today, with Victor Lafay taking the Giro stage win and Winner Anacona triumphant at Trofeo Andratx.

## BONUSES

| TYPE | NAME | TEAM |
|---|---|---|
| KOM 1 | K. Goossens | LTS |
| KOM 2 | V. Lafay | COF |
| Sprint 1 | F. Gaviria | UAD |

## STAGE RESULTS

| POS | NAME | TEAM | TIME |
|---|---|---|---|
| 1. | V. Lafay | COF | 4:06:47 |
| 2. | F. Gavazzi | EOK | 0:36 |
| 3. | N. Arndt | DSM | 0:37 |
| 4. | N. Oliveira | MOV | 0:41 |
| 5. | G. Carboni | BCF | 0:44 |
| 6. | K. Goossens | LTS | 0:58 |
| 7. | V. Campenaerts | TQA | 1:00 |
| 8. | A. Gougeard | ACT | 1:54 |
| 9. | F. Gaviria | UAD | 3:04 |
| 10. | J. Almeida | DQT | 4:48 |
| 11. | A. Vlasov | APT | s.t. |
| 12. | D. Ulissi | UAD | s.t. |
| 13. | R. Evenepoel | DQT | s.t. |
| 14. | G. Moscon | IGD | s.t. |
| 15. | D. Caruso | TBV | s.t. |
| 16. | M. Soler | MOV | s.t. |
| 17. | E. Bernal | IGD | s.t. |
| 18. | S. Yates | BEX | s.t. |
| 19. | N. Schultz | BEX | s.t. |
| 20. | R. Bardet | DSM | s.t. |
| 21. | G. Ciccone | TFS | s.t. |
| 22. | E. Buchmann | BOH | s.t. |
| 23. | H. Carthy | EFN | s.t. |
| 24. | L. Fortunato | EOK | s.t. |
| 25. | T. Foss | TJV | s.t. |
| 26. | D. Martin | ISN | s.t. |
| 27. | D. Formolo | UAD | s.t. |
| 28. | G. Bennett | TJV | s.t. |
| 29. | A. Valter | GFC | s.t. |
| 30. | V. Nibali | TFS | s.t. |
| 31. | D. F. Martínez | IGD | s.t. |
| 32. | S. Reichenbach | GFC | s.t. |
| 33. | K. Bouwman | TJV | s.t. |
| 34. | L. L. Sanchez | APT | s.t. |
| 35. | F. Masnada | DQT | s.t. |
| 36. | M. Nieve | BEX | 4:54 |
| 37. | M. Storer | DSM | 4:59 |
| 38. | J. Hindley | DSM | s.t. |
| 39. | Q. Hermans | IWG | 5:06 |
| 40. | R. Taaramäe | IWG | s.t. |
| 41. | T. Kangert | BEX | s.t. |
| 42. | R. Guerreiro | EFN | 5:10 |
| 43. | L. Vervaeke | AFC | 5:13 |
| 44. | C. Champoussin | ACT | 5:16 |
| 45. | P. Bilbao | TBV | 5:18 |
| 46. | G. Niv | ISN | s.t. |
| 47. | M. Badilatti | GFC | s.t. |
| 48. | J. Hirt | IWG | s.t. |
| 49. | N. Edet | COF | 5:27 |
| 50. | G. Brambilla | TFS | 5:38 |
| 51. | G. Izaguirre | APT | s.t. |
| 52. | L. van den Berg | GFC | 5:40 |
| 53. | V. Pronskiy | APT | 5:43 |
| 54. | A. Ghebreigzabhier | TFS | 5:48 |
| 55. | H. Tejada | APT | s.t. |
| 56. | A. Pedrero | MOV | s.t. |
| 57. | C. Hamilton | DSM | 5:58 |
| 58. | G. Mäder | TBV | 6:02 |
| 59. | C. Scotson | BEX | 6:05 |
| 60. | A. Ponomar | ANS | 6:18 |
| 61. | G. Bouchard | ACT | s.t. |
| 62. | B. Mollema | TFS | s.t. |
| 63. | L. Warbasse | ACT | 6:35 |
| 64. | H. Vanhoucke | LTS | 6:45 |
| 65. | R. Molard | GFC | 6:53 |
| 66. | F. Fiorelli | BCF | s.t. |
| 67. | E. Battaglin | BCF | s.t. |
| 68. | M. Mohorič | TBV | 7:26 |
| 69. | P. Bevin | ISN | s.t. |
| 70. | R. Rochas | COF | s.t. |
| 71. | V. Albanese | EOK | 8:08 |
| 72. | J. Mosca | TFS | 8:27 |
| 73. | A. Bettiol | EFN | s.t. |
| 74. | T. van Garderen | EFN | s.t. |
| 75. | E. Sepúlveda | ANS | s.t. |
| 76. | S. Carr | EFN | s.t. |
| 77. | J. K. Caicedo | EFN | s.t. |
| 78. | J. Cepeda Ortiz | ANS | s.t. |
| 79. | J. Narváez | IGD | s.t. |
| 80. | J. Janssens | AFC | s.t. |
| 81. | M. Fabbro | BOH | s.t. |
| 82. | G. Aleotti | BOH | s.t. |
| 83. | A. Dowsett | ISN | 8:44 |
| 84. | M. Brändle | ISN | s.t. |
| 85. | Y. Arashiro | TBV | s.t. |
| 86. | A. Vendrame | ACT | s.t. |
| 87. | J. van Emden | TJV | s.t. |
| 88. | F. Großschartner | BOH | s.t. |
| 89. | K. Frankiny | TQA | s.t. |
| 90. | E. A. Rubio | MOV | s.t. |
| 91. | T. Gallopin | ACT | s.t. |
| 92. | D. Gabburo | BCF | 8:50 |
| 93. | R. Cavagna | DQT | 8:55 |
| 94. | J. Keukeleire | EFN | 9:32 |
| 95. | N. Roche | DSM | 9:40 |
| 96. | P. Martens | TJV | s.t. |
| 97. | F. Zana | BCF | s.t. |
| 98. | E. Affini | TJV | s.t. |
| 99. | D. Cataldo | MOV | s.t. |
| 100. | M. Jorgenson | MOV | s.t. |
| 101. | D. Villella | MOV | s.t. |
| 102. | F. Felline | APT | s.t. |
| 103. | M. Sobrero | APT | s.t. |
| 104. | A. De Marchi | ISN | 9:43 |
| 105. | J. Castroviejo | IGD | s.t. |
| 106. | P. Serry | DQT | 10:14 |
| 107. | D. De Bondt | AFC | 10:16 |
| 108. | T. De Gendt | LTS | s.t. |
| 109. | R. Valls | TBV | 10:28 |
| 110. | M. F. Honoré | DQT | s.t. |
| 111. | G. Vermeersch | AFC | s.t. |
| 112. | A. Pasqualon | IWG | s.t. |
| 113. | C. Benedetti | BOH | s.t. |
| 114. | J. Knox | DQT | s.t. |
| 115. | R. Seigle | GFC | 10:40 |
| 116. | S. Puccio | IGD | 10:46 |
| 117. | N. Denz | DSM | 11:14 |
| 118. | M. Dina | EOK | s.t. |
| 119. | A. Covi | UAD | 11:29 |
| 120. | J. van den Berg | EFN | 11:36 |
| 121. | M. Hepburn | BEX | 12:12 |
| 122. | V. Conti | UAD | 13:00 |
| 123. | S. Leysen | AFC | s.t. |
| 124. | F. Sabatini | COF | 13:49 |
| 125. | B. J. Lindeman | TQA | s.t. |
| 126. | A. Duchesne | GFC | s.t. |
| 127. | G. Visconti | BCF | s.t. |
| 128. | N. Berhane | COF | s.t. |
| 129. | U. Marengo | BCF | s.t. |
| 130. | I. Keisse | DQT | s.t. |
| 131. | L. Naesen | ACT | s.t. |
| 132. | N. Tesfatsion | ANS | s.t. |
| 133. | D. Cimolai | ISN | s.t. |
| 134. | S. Battistella | APT | s.t. |
| 135. | F. Tagliani | ANS | s.t. |
| 136. | K. de Kort | TFS | s.t. |
| 137. | S. Pellaud | ANS | s.t. |
| 138. | W. Kreder | IWG | s.t. |
| 139. | O. Riesebeek | AFC | s.t. |
| 140. | R. Minali | IWG | s.t. |
| 141. | M. Kanter | DSM | s.t. |
| 142. | S. Zoccarato | BCF | s.t. |
| 143. | E. Ravasi | EOK | s.t. |
| 144. | J. Tratnik | TBV | s.t. |
| 145. | L. Wiśniowski | TQA | s.t. |
| 146. | D. Oss | BOH | s.t. |
| 147. | N. Venchiarutti | ANS | s.t. |
| 148. | M. Walscheid | TQA | s.t. |
| 149. | M. Christian | EOK | s.t. |
| 150. | C. Juul-Jensen | BEX | s.t. |
| 151. | A. M. Richeze | UAD | s.t. |
| 152. | M. Moschetti | TFS | s.t. |
| 153. | S. Ravanelli | ANS | s.t. |
| 154. | T. Marczyński | LTS | s.t. |
| 155. | J. de Buyst | LTS | s.t. |
| 156. | G. Nizzolo | TQA | 14:11 |
| 157. | P. Sagan | BOH | s.t. |
| 158. | E. Viviani | COF | s.t. |
| 159. | S. Oldani | LTS | s.t. |
| 160. | S. Consonni | COF | s.t. |
| 161. | M. Bodnar | BOH | s.t. |
| 162. | S. Rivi | EOK | s.t. |
| 163. | M. Schmid | TQA | s.t. |
| 164. | J. S. Molano | UAD | s.t. |
| 165. | T. van der Hoorn | IWG | s.t. |
| 166. | S. Guglielmi | GFC | s.t. |
| 167. | F. Ganna | IGD | s.t. |
| 168. | A. Krieger | AFC | s.t. |
| 169. | S. Petilli | IWG | s.t. |
| 170. | C. Meyer | BEX | s.t. |
| 171. | A. Torres | MOV | s.t. |
| 172. | D. Dekker | TJV | 17:19 |
| 173. | D. Groenewegen | TJV | s.t. |
| 174. | A. Viviani | COF | s.t. |
| 175. | T. Merlier | AFC | s.t. |
| 176. | R. Kluge | LTS | 18:00 |

MAY    WORLDTOUR MEN'S RACE

# GIRO D'ITALIA
Stage 9
16 May 2021
Castel di Sangro–Campo Felice (Rocca di Cambio)
158km

Stage 9 wove through the ancient settlements of the upper Sangro river, inhabited since the upper Palaeolithic period, from 36,000 to 10,000 years ago. The start town, Castel di Sangro, was founded in the seventh century BC, Alfedena (km 4.5) dates back to the sixth century BC. At Cocullo (km 69.9), in a ritual that has been included in UNESCO's list of intangible human heritage, a statue of St Dominic is covered in live snakes and paraded through its streets. The original snake rite goes back thousands of years. At Castel di Ieri (km 89.4) – 'yesterday's castle' – the Italic people built a temple in the eighth century BC. After back pain destroyed his Tour de France and put his future in doubt, Egan Bernal returned to his castle of yesterday with a stunning acceleration that won him his first Grand Tour stage, and the *maglia rosa*. Ritual life in those ancient societies was often defined by numinous violence: against rival clans and invaders, but also in purifying sacrifices. Two or three thousand years later, in the modern ritual that is professional cycling, the riders turn the violence on themselves. They take huge risks – indeed, an acrobatic crash ended Matej Mohorič's Giro d'Italia on the descent from the Passo Godi. Elsewhere, it took close to 90km of constant attacking and reacting over three big climbs for the breakaway to form today, and there were still three big climbs to come. Keon Bouwman, the best of the breakaway riders, was caught at the last gasp and ended the stage just 31 seconds from victory. But the day belonged to Egan, whose tears during his post-stage interview told a story: 'A lot has happened to get me here, and my teammates had more confidence in me today than I did. This victory is more for them than for me. There is a long way to go in the Giro, but this win, and this *maglia rosa*, makes it all worth it.'

## TRIVIA
» Egan Bernal's 18th pro win was his first Grand Tour stage victory.

## WEATHER

TEMPERATURE
19°C

WIND
NE 13km/h

## PROFILE

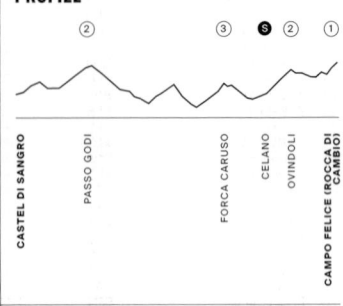

## BREAKAWAY
R. Guerreiro (EFN), D. Ulissi (UAD), G. Bennett (TJV), K. Bouwman (TJV), M. Storer (DSM), M. Fabbro (BOH), B. Mollema (TFS), N. Edet (COF), G. Bouchard (GFC), L. L. Sánchez (APT), T. Gallopin (ACT), F. Zana (BCF), S. Carr (EFN), T. Kangert (BEX), G. Visconti (BCF)

## GENERAL CLASSIFICATION

| POS | NAME | TEAM | TIME |
|---|---|---|---|
| 1. ↑2 | E. Bernal | IGD | 35:19:22 |
| 2. — | R. Evenepoel | DQT | 0:15 |
| 3. ↑1 | A. Vlasov | APT | 0:21 |
| 4. ↑3 | G. Ciccone | TFS | 0:36 |
| 5. ↓4 | A. Valter | GFC | 0:43 |
| 6. ↓1 | H. Carthy | EFN | 0:44 |
| 7. ↓1 | D. Caruso | TBV | 0:45 |
| 8. — | D. Martin | ISN | 0:51 |
| 9. — | S. Yates | BEX | 0:55 |
| 10. ↑1 | D. Formolo | UAD | 1:01 |

## KING OF THE MOUNTAINS

| POS | NAME | TEAM | PTS |
|---|---|---|---|
| 1. ↑1 | G. Bouchard | ACT | 51 |
| 2. ↑9 | E. Bernal | IGD | 48 |
| 3. ↓2 | G. Mäder | TBV | 44 |

## POINTS

| POS | NAME | TEAM | PTS |
|---|---|---|---|
| 1. — | T. Merlier | AFC | 83 |
| 2. — | G. Nizzolo | TQA | 76 |
| 3. — | E. Viviani | COF | 69 |

## YOUNG RIDER

| POS | NAME | TEAM | TIME |
|---|---|---|---|
| 1. ↑2 | E. Bernal | IGD | 35:19:22 |
| 2. — | R. Evenepoel | DQT | 0:15 |
| 3. ↑1 | A. Vlasov | APT | 0:21 |

## BONUSES

| TYPE | NAME | TEAM |
|---|---|---|
| KOM 1 | G. Mäder | TBV |
| KOM 2 | G. Bouchard | GFC |
| KOM 3 | G. Bouchard | GFC |
| KOM 4 | E. Bernal | IGD |
| Sprint 1 | T. Gallopin | ACT |

# STAGE RESULTS

| POS | NAME | TEAM | TIME |
|---|---|---|---|
| 1. | E. Bernal | IGD | 4:08:23 |
| 2. | G. Ciccone | TFS | 0:07 |
| 3. | A. Vlasov | APT | s.t. |
| 4. | R. Evenepoel | DQT | 0:10 |
| 5. | D. Martin | ISN | s.t. |
| 6. | D. Caruso | TBV | 0:12 |
| 7. | R. Bardet | DSM | s.t. |
| 8. | M. Soler | MOV | s.t. |
| 9. | D. F. Martínez | IGD | s.t. |
| 10. | J. Almeida | DQT | s.t. |
| 11. | D. Formolo | UAD | s.t. |
| 12. | H. Carthy | EFN | s.t. |
| 13. | E. Buchmann | BOH | s.t. |
| 14. | S. Yates | BEX | s.t. |
| 15. | K. Bouwman | TJV | 0:31 |
| 16. | G. Moscon | IGD | s.t. |
| 17. | R. Taaramäe | IWG | s.t. |
| 18. | T. Foss | TJV | 0:35 |
| 19. | N. Schultz | BEX | s.t. |
| 20. | A. Bettiol | EFN | s.t. |
| 21. | V. Nibali | TFS | s.t. |
| 22. | G. Bouchard | ACT | 0:38 |
| 23. | L. Fortunato | EOK | 0:49 |
| 24. | L. Vervaeke | AFC | s.t. |
| 25. | A. Valter | GFC | s.t. |
| 26. | S. Reichenbach | GFC | s.t. |
| 27. | J. Hindley | DSM | 0:53 |
| 28. | E. Ravasi | EOK | 1:00 |
| 29. | P. Bilbao | TBV | 1:01 |
| 30. | M. Badilatti | GFC | s.t. |
| 31. | M. Nieve | BEX | 1:07 |
| 32. | R. Guerreiro | EFN | 1:13 |
| 33. | F. Großschartner | BOH | 1:16 |
| 34. | J. Hirt | IWG | 1:18 |
| 35. | N. Edet | COF | 1:34 |
| 36. | G. Bennett | TJV | 1:44 |
| 37. | A. Pedrero | MOV | 1:47 |
| 38. | B. Mollema | TFS | 1:49 |
| 39. | T. Kangert | BEX | 1:50 |
| 40. | T. Gallopin | ACT | s.t. |
| 41. | M. Fabbro | BOH | 2:13 |
| 42. | L. Warbasse | ACT | 2:21 |
| 43. | Q. Hermans | IWG | 2:25 |
| 44. | M. Storer | DSM | 2:27 |
| 45. | H. Tejada | APT | s.t. |
| 46. | A. Ghebreigzabhier | TFS | 2:34 |
| 47. | R. Rochas | COF | 2:45 |
| 48. | J. Castroviejo | IGD | 2:51 |
| 49. | E. A. Rubio | MOV | s.t. |
| 50. | S. Carr | EFN | 2:57 |
| 51. | F. Masnada | DQT | s.t. |
| 52. | V. Pronskiy | APT | 3:13 |
| 53. | J. Janssens | AFC | 3:14 |
| 54. | C. Hamilton | DSM | 3:21 |
| 55. | K. Frankiny | TQA | 4:02 |
| 56. | S. Petilli | IWG | 4:08 |
| 57. | L. van den Berg | GFC | 4:28 |
| 58. | G. Brambilla | TFS | 5:14 |
| 59. | J. Mosca | TFS | s.t. |
| 60. | Y. Arashiro | TBV | s.t. |
| 61. | J. Narváez | IGD | 5:25 |
| 62. | G. Carboni | BCF | 5:28 |
| 63. | G. Izagirre | APT | 6:42 |
| 64. | L. L. Sanchez | APT | s.t. |
| 65. | D. Villella | MOV | 6:49 |
| 66. | J. Keukeleire | EFN | 7:09 |
| 67. | G. Niv | ISN | 7:24 |
| 68. | H. Vanhoucke | LTS | 7:31 |
| 69. | N. Roche | DSM | s.t. |
| 70. | D. Ulissi | UAD | 7:44 |
| 71. | D. Cataldo | MOV | s.t. |
| 72. | J. K. Caicedo | EFN | s.t. |
| 73. | P. Serry | DQT | 7:46 |
| 74. | F. Zana | BCF | 7:56 |
| 75. | G. Aleotti | BOH | 7:58 |
| 76. | A. De Marchi | ISN | s.t. |
| 77. | N. Oliveira | MOV | 8:42 |
| 78. | S. Pellaud | ANS | s.t. |
| 79. | O. Riesebeek | AFC | 8:44 |
| 80. | J. van Emden | TJV | 8:45 |
| 81. | G. Visconti | BCF | s.t. |
| 82. | R. Molard | GFC | s.t. |
| 83. | A. Covi | UAD | 8:49 |
| 84. | T. van Garderen | EFN | s.t. |
| 85. | A. Vendrame | ACT | 8:55 |
| 86. | S. Guglielmi | GFC | 9:02 |
| 87. | R. Valls | TBV | 9:08 |
| 88. | C. Scotson | BEX | s.t. |
| 89. | J. Tratnik | TBV | 9:16 |
| 90. | E. Sepúlveda | ANS | 9:33 |
| 91. | F. Felline | APT | 10:44 |
| 92. | S. Puccio | IGD | 14:54 |
| 93. | G. Mäder | TBV | s.t. |
| 94. | M. Sobrero | APT | s.t. |
| 95. | R. Cavagna | DQT | 14:56 |
| 96. | C. Juul-Jensen | BEX | 15:11 |
| 97. | T. De Gendt | LTS | 16:44 |
| 98. | F. Gavazzi | EOK | 16:54 |
| 99. | P. Bevin | ISN | s.t. |
| 100. | N. Berhane | COF | s.t. |
| 101. | M. Jorgenson | MOV | 17:01 |
| 102. | V. Conti | UAD | s.t. |
| 103. | I. Keisse | DQT | 17:42 |
| 104. | A. Pasqualon | IWG | s.t. |
| 105. | D. De Bondt | AFC | s.t. |
| 106. | M. Schmid | TQA | s.t. |
| 107. | N. Denz | DSM | 17:46 |
| 108. | S. Leysen | AFC | 17:52 |
| 109. | R. Seigle | GFC | 18:17 |
| 110. | P. Martens | TJV | 18:23 |
| 111. | J. Knox | DQT | s.t. |
| 112. | S. Battistella | APT | s.t. |
| 113. | S. Zoccarato | BCF | s.t. |
| 114. | E. Battaglin | BCF | s.t. |
| 115. | F. Fiorelli | BCF | s.t. |
| 116. | C. Benedetti | BOH | 18:28 |
| 117. | E. Affini | TJV | 18:59 |
| 118. | V. Lafay | COF | 22:22 |
| 119. | M. Dina | EOK | s.t. |
| 120. | A. Duchesne | GFC | s.t. |
| 121. | K. Goossens | LTS | s.t. |
| 122. | J. van den Berg | EFN | 22:24 |
| 123. | M. Hepburn | BEX | s.t. |
| 124. | M. Kanter | DSM | s.t. |
| 125. | M. Christian | EOK | s.t. |
| 126. | N. Tesfatsion | ANS | s.t. |
| 127. | S. Ravanelli | ANS | 22:30 |
| 128. | S. Oldani | LTS | s.t. |
| 129. | G. Vermeersch | AFC | s.t. |
| 130. | D. Oss | BOH | s.t. |
| 131. | A. Gougeard | ACT | s.t. |
| 132. | D. Cimolai | ISN | s.t. |
| 133. | V. Albanese | EOK | s.t. |
| 134. | A. Torres | MOV | s.t. |
| 135. | T. van der Hoorn | IWG | 22:34 |
| 136. | C. Meyer | BEX | s.t. |
| 137. | P. Sagan | BOH | 22:52 |
| 138. | M. Bodnar | BOH | s.t. |
| 139. | N. Arndt | DSM | 24:51 |
| 140. | R. Kluge | LTS | s.t. |
| 141. | K. de Kort | TFS | 25:10 |
| 142. | M. F. Honoré | DQT | 25:12 |
| 143. | D. Gabburo | BCF | s.t. |
| 144. | A. Dowsett | ISN | 25:14 |
| 145. | U. Marengo | BCF | s.t. |
| 146. | M. Brändle | ISN | s.t. |
| 147. | A. Ponomar | ANS | s.t. |
| 148. | L. Naesen | ACT | s.t. |
| 149. | F. Sabatini | COF | s.t. |
| 150. | N. Venchiarutti | ANS | 25:23 |
| 151. | B. J. Lindeman | TQA | s.t. |
| 152. | L. Wiśniowski | TQA | s.t. |
| 153. | W. Kreder | IWG | s.t. |
| 154. | D. Dekker | TJV | 25:26 |
| 155. | A. Viviani | COF | 25:37 |
| 156. | F. Ganna | IGD | 25:53 |
| 157. | M. Walscheid | TQA | 25:55 |
| 158. | J. Cepeda Ortiz | ANS | 25:57 |
| 159. | F. Tagliani | ANS | s.t. |
| 160. | J. S. Molano | UAD | s.t. |
| 161. | R. Minali | IWG | s.t. |
| 162. | T. Merlier | AFC | s.t. |
| 163. | A. Krieger | AFC | s.t. |
| 164. | M. Moschetti | TFS | 26:02 |
| 165. | E. Viviani | COF | 26:03 |
| 166. | S. Consonni | COF | s.t. |
| 167. | F. Gaviria | UAD | s.t. |
| 168. | V. Campenaerts | TQA | s.t. |
| 169. | S. Rivi | EOK | s.t. |
| 170. | A. M. Richeze | UAD | 26:08 |
| 171. | D. Groenewegen | TJV | 26:11 |
| 172. | G. Nizzolo | TQA | 26:30 |

MAY    WORLDTOUR MEN'S RACE

# GIRO D'ITALIA

Stage 10
17 May 2021
L'Aquila–Foligno
139km

## WEATHER

**TEMPERATURE**  **WIND**
24°C            NE 17km/h

## PROFILE

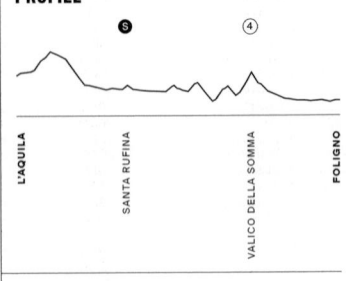

L'AQUILA — SANTA RUFINA — VALICO DELLA SOMMA — FOLIGNO

Before the stage, Elia Viviani said: 'There is a climb with 40km to go, where a guy like Sagan can set a nice pace.' Knowing what is coming is one thing; doing anything about it is an entirely different matter. Simon Pellaud tasted the truth of this earlier in the stage. Before the first intermediate sprint at Santa Rufina, he was up against two better sprinters in Samuele Rivi and Umberto Marengo. His only recourse was to attack early, but they caught him, regrouped, and then the whole ordeal started all over again, leaving Pellaud with empty legs and trailing in third place. The breakaway was swept up when Sagan's Bora-Hansgrohe team raised the pace, dropping Groenewegen, Merlier, Dekker and Nizzolo on the Valico della Somma. Israel sent Brändle, then Dowsett and De Marchi, to contribute to the speed. At the sprint for the finish line, Molano went early, leaving his teammate Gaviria on Sagan's wheel, but there was no stopping the Slovakian. Gaviria was second, Cimolai third. The intermediate sprint at Campello sul Clitunno 17.8km earlier was, if anything, even more compelling: as Iljo Keisse led out Evenepoel, Ganna burst past with Bernal on his wheel and opened a gap. Evenepoel himself sprinted after them then darted past, with Egan trailing, before Egan's teammate Jhonatan Narváez took the situation in hand and seized the 3 seconds himself. Evenepoel came through for 2 seconds and Bernal took 1. Bernal's post-race summary was a classic example of the unreliable narrator: 'I was just following Pippo. I saw the opportunity to take a second for minimum effort, so why not? We are here to enjoy the race and that's what we are doing.' No mention of Evenepoel or the dropped second. (MR)

## BREAKAWAY

U. Marengo (BCF), S. Pellaud (ANS), T. van der Hoorn (IWG), S. Rivi (EOK), K. Goossens (LTS)

## GENERAL CLASSIFICATION

| POS | NAME | TEAM | TIME |
|---|---|---|---|
| 1. — | E. Bernal | IGD | 38:30:17 |
| 2. — | R. Evenepoel | DQT | 0:14 |
| 3. — | A. Vlasov | APT | 0:22 |
| 4. — | G. Ciccone | TFS | 0:37 |
| 5. — | A. Valter | GFC | 0:44 |
| 6. — | H. Carthy | EFN | 0:45 |
| 7. — | D. Caruso | TBV | 0:46 |
| 8. — | D. Martin | ISN | 0:52 |
| 9. — | S. Yates | BEX | 0:56 |
| 10.— | D. Formolo | UAD | 1:02 |

## KING OF THE MOUNTAINS

| POS | NAME | TEAM | PTS |
|---|---|---|---|
| 1. — | G. Bouchard | ACT | 51 |
| 2. — | E. Bernal | IGD | 48 |
| 3. — | G. Mäder | TBV | 44 |

## POINTS

| POS | NAME | TEAM | PTS |
|---|---|---|---|
| 1. ↑4 | P. Sagan | BOH | 108 |
| 2. ↑4 | F. Gaviria | UAD | 91 |
| 3. ↑1 | D. Cimolai | ISN | 91 |

## YOUNG RIDER

| POS | NAME | TEAM | TIME |
|---|---|---|---|
| 1. — | E. Bernal | IGD | 38:30:17 |
| 2. — | R. Evenepoel | DQT | 0:14 |
| 3. — | A. Vlasov | APT | 0:22 |

## TRIVIA

» This was Peter Sagan's 18th Grand Tour stage victory, but only his first bunch sprint win at the Giro d'Italia.

## BONUSES

| TYPE | NAME | TEAM |
|---|---|---|
| KOM 1 | G. Aleotti | BOH |
| Sprint 1 | S. Rivi | EOK |

## STAGE RESULTS

| POS | NAME | TEAM | TIME |
|---|---|---|---|
| 1. | P. Sagan | BOH | 3:10:56 |
| 2. | F. Gaviria | UAD | s.t. |
| 3. | D. Cimolai | ISN | s.t. |
| 4. | S. Oldani | LTS | s.t. |
| 5. | G. Vermeersch | AFC | s.t. |
| 6. | D. De Bondt | AFC | s.t. |
| 7. | A. Vendrame | ACT | s.t. |
| 8. | V. Albanese | EOK | s.t. |
| 9. | E. Viviani | COF | s.t. |
| 10. | J. S. Molano | UAD | s.t. |
| 11. | N. Arndt | DSM | s.t. |
| 12. | Q. Hermans | IWG | s.t. |
| 13. | A. Vlasov | APT | s.t. |
| 14. | G. Moscon | IGD | s.t. |
| 15. | M. Brändle | ISN | s.t. |
| 16. | M. Soler | MOV | s.t. |
| 17. | N. Tesfatsion | ANS | s.t. |
| 18. | A. Covi | UAD | s.t. |
| 19. | L. L. Sanchez | APT | s.t. |
| 20. | R. Bardet | DSM | s.t. |
| 21. | D. Oss | BOH | s.t. |
| 22. | M. Bodnar | BOH | s.t. |
| 23. | S. Consonni | COF | s.t. |
| 24. | D. Ulissi | UAD | s.t. |
| 25. | V. Nibali | TFS | s.t. |
| 26. | E. Buchmann | BOH | s.t. |
| 27. | A. Valter | GFC | s.t. |
| 28. | R. Molard | GFC | s.t. |
| 29. | N. Oliveira | MOV | s.t. |
| 30. | G. Ciccone | TFS | s.t. |
| 31. | M. Jorgenson | MOV | s.t. |
| 32. | L. Fortunato | EOK | s.t. |
| 33. | J. Mosca | TFS | s.t. |
| 34. | P. Bevin | ISN | s.t. |
| 35. | L. Vervaeke | AFC | s.t. |
| 36. | D. Formolo | UAD | s.t. |
| 37. | T. Foss | TJV | s.t. |
| 38. | E. Bernal | IGD | s.t. |
| 39. | L. van den Berg | GFC | s.t. |
| 40. | T. Gallopin | ACT | s.t. |
| 41. | F. Gavazzi | EOK | s.t. |
| 42. | A. Bettiol | EFN | s.t. |
| 43. | N. Schultz | BEX | s.t. |
| 44. | J. Hindley | DSM | s.t. |
| 45. | S. Reichenbach | GFC | s.t. |
| 46. | G. Bennett | TJV | s.t. |
| 47. | F. Masnada | DQT | s.t. |
| 48. | R. Rochas | COF | s.t. |
| 49. | F. Felline | APT | s.t. |
| 50. | E. Sepúlveda | ANS | s.t. |
| 51. | J. Almeida | DQT | s.t. |
| 52. | G. Izagirre | APT | s.t. |
| 53. | G. Brambilla | TFS | s.t. |
| 54. | L. Warbasse | ACT | s.t. |
| 55. | S. Yates | BEX | s.t. |
| 56. | D. Villella | MOV | s.t. |
| 57. | R. Taaramäe | IWG | s.t. |
| 58. | D. Martin | ISN | s.t. |
| 59. | R. Guerreiro | EFN | s.t. |
| 60. | H. Carthy | EFN | s.t. |
| 61. | Y. Arashiro | TBV | s.t. |
| 62. | S. Puccio | IGD | s.t. |
| 63. | R. Evenepoel | DQT | s.t. |
| 64. | D. Caruso | TBV | s.t. |
| 65. | T. Kangert | BEX | s.t. |
| 66. | P. Bilbao | TBV | s.t. |
| 67. | M. Badilatti | GFC | s.t. |
| 68. | D. F. Martínez | IGD | s.t. |
| 69. | M. Nieve | BEX | s.t. |
| 70. | N. Roche | DSM | s.t. |
| 71. | H. Tejada | APT | s.t. |
| 72. | M. Christian | EOK | s.t. |
| 73. | C. Scotson | BEX | s.t. |
| 74. | B. Mollema | TFS | s.t. |
| 75. | K. Bouwman | TJV | s.t. |
| 76. | A. Pedrero | MOV | s.t. |
| 77. | A. Ghebreigzabhier | TFS | s.t. |
| 78. | G. Mäder | TBV | s.t. |
| 79. | J. Hirt | IWG | s.t. |
| 80. | J. van Emden | TJV | s.t. |
| 81. | F. Fiorelli | BCF | s.t. |
| 82. | G. Visconti | BCF | s.t. |
| 83. | T. De Gendt | LTS | s.t. |
| 84. | D. Cataldo | MOV | s.t. |
| 85. | F. Zana | BCF | s.t. |
| 86. | H. Vanhoucke | LTS | s.t. |
| 87. | M. Fabbro | BOH | s.t. |
| 88. | V. Conti | UAD | s.t. |
| 89. | M. Storer | DSM | s.t. |
| 90. | C. Meyer | BEX | s.t. |
| 91. | R. Cavagna | DQT | s.t. |
| 92. | M. F. Honoré | DQT | s.t. |
| 93. | M. Sobrero | APT | s.t. |
| 94. | S. Battistella | APT | s.t. |
| 95. | E. Ravasi | EOK | s.t. |

| POS | NAME | TEAM | TIME |
|---|---|---|---|
| 96. | J. K. Caicedo | EFN | s.t. |
| 97. | E. A. Rubio | MOV | s.t. |
| 98. | J. Narváez | IGD | s.t. |
| 99. | J. Castroviejo | IGD | s.t. |
| 100. | R. Valls | TBV | s.t. |
| 101. | E. Battaglin | BCF | s.t. |
| 102. | G. Carboni | BCF | s.t. |
| 103. | M. Kanter | DSM | s.t. |
| 104. | A. De Marchi | ISN | 2:01 |
| 105. | G. Aleotti | BOH | s.t. |
| 106. | P. Serry | DQT | s.t. |
| 107. | J. Knox | DQT | s.t. |
| 108. | C. Hamilton | DSM | 3:00 |
| 109. | F. Großschartner | BOH | s.t. |
| 110. | F. Ganna | IGD | 3:08 |
| 111. | S. Pellaud | ANS | 5:36 |
| 112. | R. Seigle | GFC | s.t. |
| 113. | K. Frankiny | TQA | s.t. |
| 114. | L. Wiśniowski | TQA | s.t. |
| 115. | S. Carr | EFN | s.t. |
| 116. | J. Keukeleire | EFN | s.t. |
| 117. | A. Gougeard | ACT | s.t. |
| 118. | L. Naesen | ACT | s.t. |
| 119. | M. Walscheid | TQA | s.t. |
| 120. | V. Pronskiy | APT | s.t. |
| 121. | C. Benedetti | BOH | s.t. |
| 122. | G. Niv | ISN | s.t. |
| 123. | O. Riesebeek | AFC | s.t. |
| 124. | S. Petilli | IWG | s.t. |
| 125. | N. Edet | COF | s.t. |
| 126. | J. Tratnik | TBV | s.t. |
| 127. | A. Pasqualon | IWG | s.t. |
| 128. | I. Keisse | DQT | s.t. |
| 129. | G. Nizzolo | TQA | s.t. |
| 130. | B. J. Lindeman | TQA | s.t. |
| 131. | T. Merlier | AFC | s.t. |
| 132. | S. Leysen | AFC | s.t. |
| 133. | D. Dekker | TJV | s.t. |
| 134. | A. M. Richeze | UAD | s.t. |
| 135. | F. Sabatini | COF | s.t. |
| 136. | M. Moschetti | TFS | s.t. |
| 137. | T. van Garderen | EFN | s.t. |
| 138. | T. van der Hoorn | IWG | s.t. |
| 139. | J. Cepeda Ortiz | ANS | s.t. |
| 140. | S. Ravanelli | ANS | s.t. |
| 141. | M. Schmid | TQA | s.t. |
| 142. | K. Goossens | LTS | s.t. |
| 143. | V. Campenaerts | TQA | s.t. |
| 144. | A. Krieger | AFC | s.t. |
| 145. | J. Janssens | AFC | s.t. |
| 146. | S. Rivi | EOK | s.t. |
| 147. | C. Juul-Jensen | BEX | s.t. |
| 148. | J. van den Berg | EFN | s.t. |
| 149. | R. Kluge | LTS | 8:01 |
| 150. | E. Affini | TJV | s.t. |
| 151. | G. Bouchard | ACT | 10:11 |
| 152. | N. Denz | DSM | s.t. |
| 153. | N. Berhane | COF | s.t. |
| 154. | U. Marengo | BCF | s.t. |
| 155. | K. de Kort | TFS | s.t. |
| 156. | F. Tagliani | ANS | s.t. |
| 157. | S. Zoccarato | BCF | s.t. |
| 158. | A. Dowsett | ISN | s.t. |
| 159. | A. Ponomar | ANS | s.t. |
| 160. | M. Dina | EOK | s.t. |
| 161. | P. Martens | TJV | s.t. |
| 162. | N. Venchiarutti | ANS | s.t. |
| 163. | V. Lafay | COF | s.t. |
| 164. | A. Viviani | COF | s.t. |
| 165. | D. Gabburo | BCF | s.t. |
| 166. | A. Duchesne | GFC | s.t. |
| 167. | S. Guglielmi | GFC | s.t. |
| 168. | D. Groenewegen | TJV | s.t. |
| 169. | A. Torres | MOV | s.t. |
| 170. | R. Minali | IWG | 12:30 |
| 171. | W. Kreder | IWG | s.t. |
| 172. | M. Hepburn | BEX | s.t. |

MAY

MAY WORLDTOUR MEN'S RACE

# GIRO D'ITALIA
Stage 11
19 May 2021
Perugia–Montalcino
162km

On the approach to the first sector of white road, Remco seemed to be sitting too far back in the peloton, eating a lot more dust there than second wheel like Bernal. You wondered if it was a tactic: keep the team together, let Ganna tear his own formation apart, then counter-attack as a group. When it all came together and Ganna dropped off, you wondered if it had worked… except that Deceuninck too had been if not decimated then quartered, as in hung and drawn. Something in the team was not working, and there were still 50 of the hardest kilometres of the Giro to come. Just before the '25km to go' banner, through the clouds of dust, Remco dropped back to last place in the *maglia rosa* group with Dani Martínez keeping a wary eye. A gap opened. Bernal moved to the front of the group and raised the pace. At that moment, Remco lost contact and the Giro. When Vlasov attacked with 4.5km remaining, Bernal followed then exploded past. In a flash, he was with Buchmann, who had attacked beforehand, and they rode off to a 20-second lead over the other GC contenders and an advantage of 2 minutes 8 seconds over Remco. The stage had been won minutes before by 21-year-old Mauro Schmid, who took his first professional win. There are now so many champions barely in their twenties – and cyclocross champions who borrow a road bike and tear the peloton to shreds, track riders who win mountain stages, not to mention all those young Colombians – that it has come to seem the norm. We forget that, until stage 15 of last year's Tour de France, Bernal had been very much a contender: he'd gone into stage 15 third overall (with three other Colombians from fourth to sixth in GC) behind the two Slovenians, only to fall out of contention with unbearable back pain. Suddenly, we were swamped with Slovenian success, and Bernal's record-breaking Tour win in 2019 began to sound like ancient history. But in 2021 Bernal was proving to be very much the man of the moment.

## WEATHER

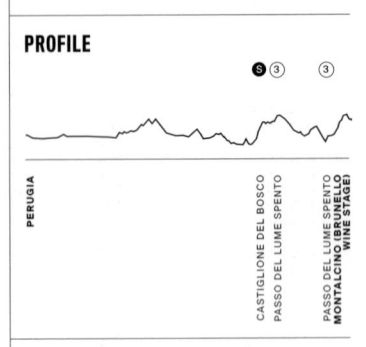

TEMPERATURE
19°C

WIND
N 26km/h

## PROFILE

## BREAKAWAY
D. De Bondt (AFC), A. Covi (UAD), S. Guglielmi (GFC),
L. Naesen (ACT), H. Vanhoucke (LTS), R. Kluge (LTS),
T. van der Hoorn (IWG), B. J. Lindeman (TQA),
M. Schmid (TQA), E. Battaglin (BCF), F. Gavazzi (EOK)

## GENERAL CLASSIFICATION

| POS | | NAME | TEAM | TIME |
|---|---|---|---|---|
| 1. | — | E. Bernal | IGD | 42:35:21 |
| 2. | ↑1 | A. Vlasov | APT | 0:45 |
| 3. | ↑4 | D. Caruso | TBV | 1:12 |
| 4. | ↑2 | H. Carthy | EFN | 1:17 |
| 5. | ↑4 | S. Yates | BEX | 1:22 |
| 6. | ↑9 | E. Buchmann | BOH | 1:50 |
| 7. | ↓5 | R. Evenepoel | DQT | 2:22 |
| 8. | ↓4 | G. Ciccone | TFS | 2:24 |
| 9. | ↑9 | T. Foss | TJV | 2:49 |
| 10. | ↑1 | D. F. Martínez | IGD | 3:15 |

## KING OF THE MOUNTAINS

| POS | | NAME | TEAM | PTS |
|---|---|---|---|---|
| 1. | — | G. Bouchard | ACT | 51 |
| 2. | — | E. Bernal | IGD | 48 |
| 3. | — | G. Mäder | TBV | 44 |

## POINTS

| POS | | NAME | TEAM | PTS |
|---|---|---|---|---|
| 1. | — | P. Sagan | BOH | 108 |
| 2. | — | F. Gaviria | UAD | 91 |
| 3. | — | D. Cimolai | ISN | 91 |

## YOUNG RIDER

| POS | | NAME | TEAM | TIME |
|---|---|---|---|---|
| 1. | — | E. Bernal | IGD | 42:35:21 |
| 2. | ↑1 | A. Vlasov | APT | 0:45 |
| 3. | ↓1 | R. Evenepoel | DQT | 2:22 |

## BONUSES

| TYPE | NAME | TEAM |
|---|---|---|
| KOM 1 | H. Vanhoucke | LTS |
| KOM 2 | M. Schmid | TQA |
| Sprint 1 | F. Gavazzi | EOK |

## STAGE RESULTS

| POS | NAME | TEAM | TIME |
|---|---|---|---|
| 1. | M. Schmid | TQA | 4:01:55 |
| 2. | A. Covi | UAD | 0:01 |
| 3. | H. Vanhoucke | LTS | 0:26 |
| 4. | D. De Bondt | AFC | 0:41 |
| 5. | S. Guglielmi | GFC | s.t. |
| 6. | E. Battaglin | BCF | 0:44 |
| 7. | R. Kluge | LTS | 1:23 |
| 8. | F. Gavazzi | EOK | 1:37 |
| 9. | T. van der Hoorn | IWG | 1:43 |
| 10. | L. Naesen | ACT | 1:59 |
| 11. | E. Bernal | IGD | 3:09 |
| 12. | E. Buchmann | BOH | 3:12 |
| 13. | A. Vlasov | APT | 3:32 |
| 14. | D. Caruso | TBV | 3:35 |
| 15. | S. Yates | BEX | s.t. |
| 16. | T. Foss | TJV | s.t. |
| 17. | R. Guerreiro | EFN | 3:39 |
| 18. | H. Carthy | EFN | 3:41 |
| 19. | G. Ciccone | TFS | 4:56 |
| 20. | A. Bettiol | EFN | s.t. |
| 21. | G. Moscon | IGD | 5:05 |
| 22. | M. Soler | MOV | 5:07 |
| 23. | K. Bouwman | TJV | s.t. |
| 24. | V. Nibali | TFS | s.t. |
| 25. | D. F. Martínez | IGD | 5:11 |
| 26. | R. Evenepoel | DQT | 5:17 |
| 27. | R. Bardet | DSM | s.t. |
| 28. | J. Almeida | DQT | s.t. |
| 29. | R. Molard | GFC | 6:16 |
| 30. | A. Valter | GFC | s.t. |
| 31. | L. L. Sanchez | APT | 6:27 |
| 32. | G. Izaguirre | APT | s.t. |
| 33. | N. Oliveira | MOV | 6:33 |
| 34. | R. Taaramäe | IWG | 6:36 |
| 35. | J. Hindley | DSM | s.t. |
| 36. | T. Kangert | BEX | s.t. |
| 37. | G. Carboni | BCF | 7:00 |
| 38. | P. Bilbao | TBV | 7:05 |
| 39. | D. Formolo | UAD | 9:23 |
| 40. | D. Martin | ISN | s.t. |
| 41. | N. Schultz | BEX | s.t. |
| 42. | A. Ghebreigzabhier | TFS | 9:32 |
| 43. | M. Nieve | BEX | 9:37 |
| 44. | C. Hamilton | DSM | 9:39 |
| 45. | S. Reichenbach | GFC | 9:40 |
| 46. | S. Battistella | APT | 11:59 |
| 47. | M. Sobrero | APT | s.t. |
| 48. | Q. Hermans | IWG | 13:59 |
| 49. | G. Bennett | TJV | s.t. |
| 50. | D. Ulissi | UAD | 15:20 |
| 51. | J. Mosca | TFS | s.t. |
| 52. | A. Pasqualon | IWG | s.t. |
| 53. | S. Zoccarato | BCF | s.t. |
| 54. | R. Seigle | GFC | s.t. |
| 55. | D. Cataldo | MOV | 17:33 |
| 56. | M. Jorgenson | MOV | s.t. |
| 57. | G. Brambilla | TFS | s.t. |
| 58. | D. Villella | MOV | s.t. |
| 59. | B. J. Lindeman | TQA | 17:35 |
| 60. | A. Pedrero | MOV | s.t. |
| 61. | L. van den Berg | GFC | 18:59 |
| 62. | M. F. Honoré | DQT | s.t. |
| 63. | R. Cavagna | DQT | s.t. |
| 64. | B. Mollema | TFS | s.t. |
| 65. | Y. Arashiro | TBV | s.t. |
| 66. | F. Zana | BCF | s.t. |
| 67. | P. Martens | TJV | s.t. |
| 68. | A. De Marchi | ISN | s.t. |
| 69. | L. Vervaeke | AFC | s.t. |
| 70. | J. Knox | DQT | s.t. |
| 71. | O. Riesebeek | AFC | s.t. |
| 72. | F. Felline | APT | s.t. |
| 73. | J. van Emden | TJV | s.t. |
| 74. | E. A. Rubio | MOV | s.t. |
| 75. | M. Dina | EOK | s.t. |
| 76. | N. Roche | DSM | s.t. |
| 77. | J. Cepeda Ortiz | ANS | s.t. |
| 78. | V. Albanese | EOK | s.t. |
| 79. | J. Narváez | IGD | 19:12 |
| 80. | G. Vermeersch | AFC | 21:24 |
| 81. | J. Keukeleire | EFN | 22:35 |
| 82. | M. Brändle | ISN | s.t. |
| 83. | M. Fabbro | BOH | s.t. |
| 84. | G. Aleotti | BOH | s.t. |
| 85. | P. Sagan | BOH | s.t. |
| 86. | T. De Gendt | LTS | s.t. |
| 87. | P. Bevin | ISN | s.t. |
| 88. | S. Pellaud | ANS | s.t. |
| 89. | R. Valls | TBV | s.t. |
| 90. | G. Bouchard | ACT | s.t. |
| 91. | M. Hepburn | BEX | s.t. |
| 92. | N. Arndt | DSM | s.t. |
| 93. | D. Dekker | TJV | s.t. |
| 94. | M. Walscheid | TQA | s.t. |
| 95. | K. Frankiny | TQA | s.t. |
| 96. | T. Gallopin | ACT | s.t. |
| 97. | L. Warbasse | ACT | s.t. |
| 98. | S. Leysen | AFC | s.t. |
| 99. | A. Duchesne | GFC | s.t. |
| 100. | L. Fortunato | EOK | s.t. |
| 101. | L. Wiśniowski | TQA | s.t. |
| 102. | C. Benedetti | BOH | s.t. |
| 103. | J. Castroviejo | IGD | s.t. |
| 104. | A. Torres | MOV | s.t. |
| 105. | D. Gabburo | BCF | s.t. |
| 106. | F. Gaviria | UAD | s.t. |
| 107. | A. Viviani | COF | s.t. |
| 108. | I. Keisse | DQT | s.t. |
| 109. | A. Vendrame | ACT | s.t. |
| 110. | S. Ravanelli | ANS | s.t. |
| 111. | C. Juul-Jensen | BEX | s.t. |
| 112. | V. Campenaerts | TQA | s.t. |
| 113. | P. Serry | DQT | s.t. |
| 114. | J. Tratnik | TBV | s.t. |
| 115. | V. Pronskiy | APT | s.t. |
| 116. | A. Gougeard | ACT | s.t. |
| 117. | A. Ponomar | ANS | s.t. |
| 118. | J. van den Berg | EFN | s.t. |
| 119. | F. Großschartner | BOH | s.t. |
| 120. | S. Carr | EFN | s.t. |
| 121. | K. Goossens | LTS | s.t. |
| 122. | T. van Garderen | EFN | s.t. |
| 123. | C. Scotson | BEX | s.t. |
| 124. | W. Kreder | IWG | s.t. |
| 125. | F. Masnada | DQT | 22:52 |
| 126. | S. Oldani | LTS | 23:16 |
| 127. | H. Tejada | APT | 23:25 |
| 128. | M. Bodnar | BOH | s.t. |
| 129. | F. Ganna | IGD | s.t. |
| 130. | D. Oss | BOH | s.t. |
| 131. | F. Sabatini | COF | 26:00 |
| 132. | V. Lafay | COF | s.t. |
| 133. | N. Denz | DSM | s.t. |
| 134. | R. Rochas | COF | s.t. |
| 135. | U. Marengo | BCF | s.t. |
| 136. | F. Fiorelli | BCF | s.t. |
| 137. | G. Visconti | BCF | s.t. |
| 138. | N. Venchiarutti | ANS | s.t. |
| 139. | F. Tagliani | ANS | s.t. |
| 140. | M. Kanter | DSM | s.t. |
| 141. | K. de Kort | TFS | s.t. |
| 142. | S. Puccio | IGD | s.t. |
| 143. | M. Christian | EOK | s.t. |
| 144. | R. Minali | IWG | s.t. |
| 145. | N. Tesfatsion | ANS | s.t. |
| 146. | N. Berhane | COF | s.t. |
| 147. | A. Dowsett | ISN | s.t. |
| 148. | N. Edet | COF | s.t. |
| 149. | M. Moschetti | TFS | s.t. |
| 150. | M. Storer | DSM | s.t. |
| 151. | E. Sepúlveda | ANS | 26:09 |
| 152. | G. Nizzolo | TQA | 26:15 |
| 153. | E. Ravasi | EOK | s.t. |
| 154. | E. Viviani | COF | s.t. |
| 155. | G. Niv | ISN | s.t. |
| 156. | D. Cimolai | ISN | s.t. |
| 157. | E. Affini | TJV | s.t. |
| 158. | S. Petilli | IWG | s.t. |
| 159. | M. Badilatti | GFC | s.t. |
| 160. | V. Conti | UAD | s.t. |
| 161. | A. M. Richeze | UAD | s.t. |
| 162. | J. S. Molano | UAD | s.t. |
| 163. | J. Janssens | AFC | s.t. |
| 164. | S. Rivi | EOK | s.t. |
| 165. | J. Hirt | IWG | s.t. |
| 166. | C. Meyer | BEX | s.t. |
| 167. | A. Krieger | AFC | s.t. |
| 168. | D. Groenewegen | TJV | s.t. |
| 169. | S. Consonni | COF | 26:20 |
| 170. | G. Mäder | TBV | 26:27 |

## TRIVIA

» This was Switzerland's second Giro stage win of this edition. Before this year, their last was on stage 6 in 2017 courtesy of Silvan Dillier.

MAY — WORLDTOUR MEN'S RACE

## GIRO D'ITALIA
Stage 12
20 May 2021
Siena–Bagno di Romagna
212km

The profile looked hilly, with no climbs over 1,295 metres. Yet Nico Roche said before the start, 'With 4,000-plus metres of climbing, if you don't call it a mountain stage, then we don't have a mountain stage.' The breakaway did not form for 60km. When it did, AG2R roommates Andrea Vendrame and Geoffrey Bouchard were in it. In the spring of 2019, Vendrame seemed ready for a breakthrough. In the final week of the Giro, he was the fastest finisher in a three-man breakaway with Esteban Chaves and Amaro Antunes but shipped his chain and came away second. He started the 2021 Giro wearing number 17, unlucky since the Battle of the Teutoburg Forest in 9 AD, when the German tribes ambushed Legion XVII of the Roman army and completely annihilated it. The Roman army did not use the number again. Number 17 had not won a Giro stage since 1987, when Marco Vitali outfoxed two breakaway companions at Rive del Garda. Until today. Vendrame led out Bouchard for the mountains points, helping him equal Raphaël Géminiani – twice King of the Mountains at the Giro d'Italia in the 1950s – on seven GPM wins. Then it was down to Vendrame. On the final climb, a four-man group of Vendrame, Hamilton, Brambilla and Bennett formed. On the run-in to the finish, as Brambilla and Bennett bickered, Vendrame and Hamilton stole away. Even working at the front himself, Vendrame had enough left to win the sprint. The GC contenders declared a truce until the final climb, where Nibali and Ciccone attacked in tandem. Team Ineos closed them down, before Nibali went again on the descent. It was, if nothing else, a show of defiance – towards Bernal, his rivals, and the passing years. Meanwhile, Vendrame would be able to pass through his birthplace of Conegliano on stage 14 with some satisfaction.
In Roman times, to ward off bad luck, stonemasons often changed the number XVII to 'VIXI', meaning 'I have lived'. After today's win, Andrea Vendrame can certainly say the same.

**WEATHER**

TEMPERATURE: 21°C
WIND: NW 7km/h

**PROFILE**

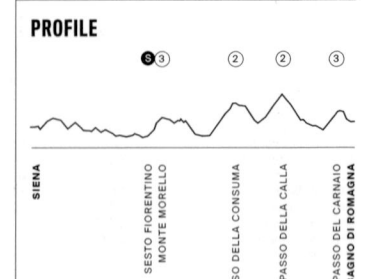

SIENA — SESTO FIORENTINO / MONTE MORELLO — PASSO DELLA CONSUMA — PASSO DELLA CALLA — PASSO DEL CARNAIO — BAGNO DI ROMAGNA

**BREAKAWAY**

G. Bennett (TJV), G. Brambilla (TFS), D. Ulissi (UAD), C. Hamilton (DSM), G. Bouchard (ACT), A. Vendrame (ACT), M. Honoré (DQT), S. Petilli (IWG), G. Niv (ISN), V. Campenaerts (TQA), D. De Bondt (AFC), V. Albanese (EOK), S. Ravanelli (ANS), N. Tesfatsion (ANS), G. Visconti (BCF), N. Edet (COF)

**GENERAL CLASSIFICATION**

| POS | NAME | TEAM | TIME |
|---|---|---|---|
| 1. — | E. Bernal | IGD | 48:29:23 |
| 2. — | A. Vlasov | APT | 0:45 |
| 3. — | D. Caruso | TBV | 1:12 |
| 4. — | H. Carthy | EFN | 1:17 |
| 5. — | S. Yates | BEX | 1:22 |
| 6. — | E. Buchmann | BOH | 1:50 |
| 7. — | R. Evenepoel | DQT | 2:22 |
| 8. — | G. Ciccone | TFS | 2:24 |
| 9. — | T. Foss | TJV | 2:49 |
| 10.— | D. F. Martínez | IGD | 3:15 |

**KING OF THE MOUNTAINS**

| POS | NAME | TEAM | PTS |
|---|---|---|---|
| 1. — | G. Bouchard | ACT | 96 |
| 2. — | E. Bernal | IGD | 48 |
| 3. ↑28 | D. De Bondt | AFC | 24 |

**POINTS**

| POS | NAME | TEAM | PTS |
|---|---|---|---|
| 1. — | P. Sagan | BOH | 108 |
| 2. — | F. Gaviria | UAD | 91 |
| 3. — | D. Cimolai | ISN | 91 |

**YOUNG RIDER**

| POS | NAME | TEAM | TIME |
|---|---|---|---|
| 1. — | E. Bernal | IGD | 48:29:23 |
| 2. — | A. Vlasov | APT | 0:45 |
| 3. — | R. Evenepoel | DQT | 2:22 |

**BONUSES**

| TYPE | NAME | TEAM |
|---|---|---|
| KOM 1 | G. Bouchard | GFC |
| KOM 2 | G. Bouchard | GFC |
| KOM 3 | G. Bouchard | GFC |
| KOM 4 | G. Brambilla | TFS |
| Sprint 1 | D. De Bondt | AFC |

## STAGE RESULTS

| POS | NAME | TEAM | TIME |
|---|---|---|---|
| 1. | A. Vendrame | ACT | 5:43:48 |
| 2. | C. Hamilton | DSM | s.t. |
| 3. | G. Bennett | TJV | 0:15 |
| 4. | G. Brambilla | TFS | s.t. |
| 5. | G. Visconti | BCF | 1:12 |
| 6. | G. Bouchard | ACT | 1:25 |
| 7. | N. Edet | COF | 1:47 |
| 8. | S. Petilli | IWG | s.t. |
| 9. | M. F. Honoré | DQT | 3:00 |
| 10. | S. Ravanelli | ANS | 4:19 |
| 11. | D. De Bondt | AFC | 7:07 |
| 12. | G. Niv | ISN | s.t. |
| 13. | N. Tesfatsion | ANS | 7:13 |
| 14. | V. Albanese | EOK | s.t. |
| 15. | V. Nibali | TFS | 10:07 |
| 16. | J. Narváez | IGD | 10:14 |
| 17. | E. Bernal | IGD | s.t. |
| 18. | L. L. Sanchez | APT | s.t. |
| 19. | M. Storer | DSM | s.t. |
| 20. | K. Bouwman | TJV | s.t. |
| 21. | F. Großschartner | BOH | s.t. |
| 22. | G. Izagirre | APT | s.t. |
| 23. | A. Valter | GFC | s.t. |
| 24. | A. Covi | UAD | s.t. |
| 25. | E. Buchmann | BOH | s.t. |
| 26. | N. Schultz | BEX | s.t. |
| 27. | D. Caruso | TBV | s.t. |
| 28. | A. Vlasov | APT | s.t. |
| 29. | M. Fabbro | BOH | s.t. |
| 30. | D. F. Martínez | IGD | s.t. |
| 31. | V. Pronskiy | APT | s.t. |
| 32. | R. Bardet | DSM | s.t. |
| 33. | J. Almeida | DQT | s.t. |
| 34. | G. Ciccone | TFS | s.t. |
| 35. | M. Badilatti | GFC | s.t. |
| 36. | S. Yates | BEX | s.t. |
| 37. | T. Foss | TJV | s.t. |
| 38. | D. Formolo | UAD | s.t. |
| 39. | R. Guerreiro | EFN | s.t. |
| 40. | R. Evenepoel | DQT | s.t. |
| 41. | M. Nieve | BEX | s.t. |
| 42. | T. Kangert | BEX | s.t. |
| 43. | R. Taaramäe | IWG | s.t. |
| 44. | H. Carthy | EFN | s.t. |
| 45. | D. Martin | ISN | s.t. |
| 46. | A. Pedrero | MOV | s.t. |
| 47. | G. Moscon | IGD | s.t. |
| 48. | J. Hirt | IWG | s.t. |
| 49. | J. Castroviejo | IGD | s.t. |
| 50. | S. Pellaud | ANS | 11:45 |
| 51. | S. Reichenbach | GFC | 11:47 |
| 52. | L. Fortunato | EOK | 11:55 |
| 53. | L. Warbasse | ACT | s.t. |
| 54. | K. Frankiny | TQA | s.t. |
| 55. | L. Vervaeke | AFC | s.t. |
| 56. | D. Villella | MOV | s.t. |
| 57. | G. Carboni | BCF | 11:58 |
| 58. | P. Bilbao | TBV | 12:23 |
| 59. | S. Carr | EFN | 13:38 |
| 60. | F. Gavazzi | EOK | 15:28 |
| 61. | E. Ravasi | EOK | s.t. |
| 62. | P. Bevin | ISN | s.t. |
| 63. | T. van Garderen | EFN | s.t. |
| 64. | J. Mosca | TFS | s.t. |
| 65. | F. Felline | APT | s.t. |
| 66. | P. Serry | DQT | s.t. |
| 67. | R. Molard | GFC | s.t. |
| 68. | G. Aleotti | BOH | s.t. |
| 69. | N. Roche | DSM | s.t. |
| 70. | A. Ponomar | ANS | s.t. |
| 71. | L. van den Berg | GFC | s.t. |
| 72. | N. Oliveira | MOV | s.t. |
| 73. | T. Gallopin | ACT | s.t. |
| 74. | E. A. Rubio | MOV | s.t. |
| 75. | E. Sepúlveda | ANS | s.t. |
| 76. | J. Cepeda Ortiz | ANS | s.t. |
| 77. | M. Sobrero | APT | s.t. |
| 78. | B. Mollema | TFS | 16:33 |
| 79. | J. Janssens | AFC | s.t. |
| 80. | T. De Gendt | LTS | 17:46 |
| 81. | C. Benedetti | BOH | s.t. |
| 82. | J. Hindley | DSM | s.t. |
| 83. | J. Knox | DQT | s.t. |
| 84. | Y. Arashiro | TBV | s.t. |
| 85. | D. Ulissi | UAD | s.t. |
| 86. | A. Bettiol | EFN | 19:59 |
| 87. | P. Martens | TJV | 20:47 |
| 88. | S. Puccio | IGD | s.t. |
| 89. | H. Tejada | APT | s.t. |
| 90. | R. Cavagna | DQT | s.t. |
| 91. | C. Meyer | BEX | s.t. |
| 92. | J. Keukeleire | EFN | 21:24 |
| 93. | R. Rochas | COF | s.t. |
| 94. | N. Denz | DSM | 22:57 |
| 95. | N. Arndt | DSM | s.t. |
| 96. | A. Pasqualon | IWG | s.t. |
| 97. | W. Kreder | IWG | s.t. |
| 98. | E. Battaglin | BCF | 25:21 |
| 99. | E. Viviani | COF | 26:05 |
| 100. | E. Affini | TJV | s.t. |
| 101. | B. J. Lindeman | TQA | s.t. |
| 102. | F. Zana | BCF | s.t. |
| 103. | F. Fiorelli | BCF | s.t. |
| 104. | U. Marengo | BCF | s.t. |
| 105. | F. Tagliani | ANS | s.t. |
| 106. | F. Sabatini | COF | s.t. |
| 107. | V. Lafay | COF | s.t. |
| 108. | N. Venchiarutti | ANS | s.t. |
| 109. | M. Walscheid | TQA | s.t. |
| 110. | G. Nizzolo | TQA | s.t. |
| 111. | M. Kanter | DSM | s.t. |
| 112. | M. Christian | EOK | s.t. |
| 113. | R. Valls | TBV | s.t. |
| 114. | J. Tratnik | TBV | s.t. |
| 115. | S. Zoccarato | BCF | s.t. |
| 116. | V. Campenaerts | TQA | s.t. |
| 117. | S. Leysen | AFC | s.t. |
| 118. | D. Cataldo | MOV | s.t. |
| 119. | D. Gabburo | BCF | s.t. |
| 120. | A. Viviani | COF | s.t. |
| 121. | A. Duchesne | GFC | s.t. |
| 122. | D. Cimolai | ISN | s.t. |
| 123. | S. Battistella | APT | s.t. |
| 124. | Q. Hermans | IWG | s.t. |
| 125. | G. Vermeersch | AFC | s.t. |
| 126. | K. de Kort | TFS | s.t. |
| 127. | O. Riesebeek | AFC | s.t. |
| 128. | M. Hepburn | BEX | s.t. |
| 129. | N. Berhane | COF | s.t. |
| 130. | A. Ghebreigzabhier | TFS | s.t. |
| 131. | C. Scotson | BEX | s.t. |
| 132. | M. Brändle | ISN | s.t. |
| 133. | A. Krieger | AFC | s.t. |
| 134. | A. M. Richeze | UAD | s.t. |
| 135. | F. Gaviria | UAD | s.t. |
| 136. | S. Oldani | LTS | s.t. |
| 137. | J. S. Molano | UAD | s.t. |
| 138. | M. Moschetti | TFS | s.t. |
| 139. | D. Oss | BOH | s.t. |
| 140. | M. Dina | EOK | s.t. |
| 141. | S. Rivi | EOK | s.t. |
| 142. | I. Keisse | DQT | s.t. |
| 143. | L. Naesen | ACT | s.t. |
| 144. | A. Gougeard | ACT | s.t. |
| 145. | M. Bodnar | BOH | s.t. |
| 146. | J. van Emden | TJV | s.t. |
| 147. | D. Groenewegen | TJV | s.t. |
| 148. | T. van der Hoorn | IWG | s.t. |
| 149. | C. Juul-Jensen | BEX | s.t. |
| 150. | D. Dekker | TJV | s.t. |
| 151. | J. van den Berg | EFN | s.t. |
| 152. | H. Vanhoucke | LTS | s.t. |
| 153. | R. Kluge | LTS | s.t. |
| 154. | S. Guglielmi | GFC | s.t. |
| 155. | R. Seigle | GFC | s.t. |
| 156. | S. Consonni | COF | 26:13 |
| 157. | F. Ganna | IGD | s.t. |
| 158. | A. Torres | MOV | s.t. |
| 159. | P. Sagan | BOH | s.t. |
| 160. | R. Minali | IWG | 27:08 |
| 161. | V. Conti | UAD | s.t. |
| 162. | M. Schmid | TQA | 27:10 |
| 163. | M. Jorgenson | MOV | s.t. |
| 164. | L. Wiśniowski | TQA | s.t. |

## TRIVIA

» Before Andrea Vendrame won stage 12 there was a danger the 2021 Giro would see the joint-lowest number of Italian stage winners since the turn of the millennium. 2017 saw only Vincenzo Nibali take a stage, while every other edition since 2000 has had at least five Italian stage winners.

MAY  WORLDTOUR MEN'S RACE

# GIRO D'ITALIA
Stage 13
21 May 2021
Ravenna–Verona
198km

Since the Second World War, only 12 riders have won their first Giro stage older than Giacomo Nizzolo. Although 32 years and 111 days is no age at all, to quote a line of verse known to 99.9 per cent of Italians, it can certainly be called *Nel mezzo del camin di nostra vita* – midway along the path through life. That feels appropriate on the stage dedicated to Dante Alighieri, whose *Divine Comedy* is sometimes considered a commentary on the male midlife crisis. Not that there is ever only one path, as proved by the soigneur who was waiting for Nizzolo on the finish line. Five seasons a WorldTour rider, all of them as Nizzolo's teammate at Trek-Segafredo, Eugenio Alafaci retrained as a sports masseur but remains Giacomo's faithful *gregario*. The breakaway riders were fully aware of the different paths that lay ahead of them today. Defeated in the first intermediate sprint by Umberto Marengo, and displaced from the top of the hotspot sprint standings, Simon Pellaud took another tack by setting a punitive solo ride that gained him 17 *fuga bianchi* kilometres, at least guaranteeing him leadership in that competition for another day. Behind them, Fernando Gaviria regained three *maglia ciclamino* points on Peter Sagan. When Dries De Bondt drifted ahead of the bunch to pick up some combativity points at the second intermediate sprint, Thomas De Gendt accelerated, trying to form a counter-attack. The peloton would not let them go and spent the rest of the stage trying *not* to catch Pellaud, Marengo and their breakaway companion Samuele Rivi (from Trento but half-Tyrolese). On the day the Italian national anthem was played before the roll-out to celebrate Elia Viviani's appointment as the Italian flagbearer at the Tokyo Olympics, it was good to be reminded of Italy's many identities. Rather than Dante's singular path through life, the Giro follows the philosophy of the Portuguese poet Fernando Pessoa, who wrote, 'Countless lives inhabit us.' (MR)

## WEATHER

TEMPERATURE  WIND
24°C  W 22km/h

## PROFILE

RAVENNA  FERRARA  VERONA

## BREAKAWAY

S. Rivi (EOK), U. Marengo (BCF), S. Pellaud (ANS)

## GENERAL CLASSIFICATION

| POS | NAME | TEAM | TIME |
|---|---|---|---|
| 1. — | E. Bernal | IGD | 53:11:42 |
| 2. — | A. Vlasov | APT | 0:45 |
| 3. — | D. Caruso | TBV | 1:12 |
| 4. — | H. Carthy | EFN | 1:17 |
| 5. — | S. Yates | BEX | 1:22 |
| 6. — | E. Buchmann | BOH | 1:50 |
| 7. — | R. Evenepoel | DQT | 2:22 |
| 8. — | G. Ciccone | TFS | 2:24 |
| 9. — | T. Foss | TJV | 2:49 |
| 10.— | D. F. Martinez | IGD | 3:15 |

## KING OF THE MOUNTAINS

| POS | NAME | TEAM | PTS |
|---|---|---|---|
| 1. — | G. Bouchard | ACT | 96 |
| 2. — | E. Bernal | IGD | 48 |
| 3. — | D. De Bondt | AFC | 24 |

## POINTS

| POS | NAME | TEAM | PTS |
|---|---|---|---|
| 1. — | P. Sagan | BOH | 135 |
| 2. ↑3 | G. Nizzolo | TQA | 126 |
| 3. — | D. Cimolai | ISN | 113 |

## YOUNG RIDER

| POS | NAME | TEAM | TIME |
|---|---|---|---|
| 1. — | E. Bernal | IGD | 53:11:42 |
| 2. — | A. Vlasov | APT | 0:45 |
| 3. — | R. Evenepoel | DQT | 2:22 |

## TRIVIA

» Giacomo Nizzolo no longer holds the record for the most top-three stage finishes without ever winning (16). Now it belongs to Pietro Rimoldi (with 14), who was a pro between 1932 and 1942.

## BONUSES

| TYPE | NAME | TEAM |
|---|---|---|
| Sprint 1 | U. Marengo | BCF |

## STAGE RESULTS

| POS | NAME | TEAM | TIME |
|---|---|---|---|
| 1. | G. Nizzolo | TQA | 4:42:19 |
| 2. | E. Affini | TJV | s.t. |
| 3. | P. Sagan | BOH | s.t. |
| 4. | D. Cimolai | ISN | s.t. |
| 5. | F. Gaviria | UAD | s.t. |
| 6. | S. Oldani | LTS | s.t. |
| 7. | A. Pasqualon | IWG | s.t. |
| 8. | M. Kanter | DSM | s.t. |
| 9. | E. Viviani | COF | s.t. |
| 10. | D. Groenewegen | TJV | s.t. |
| 11. | A. Krieger | AFC | s.t. |
| 12. | L. Naesen | ACT | s.t. |
| 13. | V. Albanese | EOK | s.t. |
| 14. | M. Moschetti | TFS | s.t. |
| 15. | F. Fiorelli | BCF | s.t. |
| 16. | F. Tagliani | ANS | s.t. |
| 17. | M. Walscheid | TQA | s.t. |
| 18. | R. Kluge | LTS | s.t. |
| 19. | N. Denz | DSM | s.t. |
| 20. | V. Campenaerts | TQA | s.t. |
| 21. | J. Tratnik | TBV | s.t. |
| 22. | F. Felline | APT | s.t. |
| 23. | J. S. Molano | UAD | s.t. |
| 24. | A. M. Richeze | UAD | s.t. |
| 25. | S. Consonni | COF | s.t. |
| 26. | R. Minali | IWG | s.t. |
| 27. | L. L. Sanchez | APT | s.t. |
| 28. | A. Vlasov | APT | s.t. |
| 29. | D. Formolo | UAD | s.t. |
| 30. | G. Ciccone | TFS | s.t. |
| 31. | L. Warbasse | ACT | s.t. |
| 32. | D. Caruso | TBV | s.t. |
| 33. | D. Gabburo | BCF | s.t. |
| 34. | E. Bernal | IGD | s.t. |
| 35. | T. van der Hoorn | IWG | s.t. |
| 36. | N. Arndt | DSM | s.t. |
| 37. | I. Keisse | DQT | s.t. |
| 38. | F. Ganna | IGD | s.t. |
| 39. | M. Hepburn | BEX | s.t. |
| 40. | V. Nibali | TFS | s.t. |
| 41. | R. Evenepoel | DQT | s.t. |
| 42. | C. Meyer | BEX | s.t. |
| 43. | D. Dekker | TJV | s.t. |
| 44. | R. Bardet | DSM | s.t. |
| 45. | P. Bevin | ISN | s.t. |
| 46. | G. Moscon | IGD | s.t. |
| 47. | J. Almeida | DQT | s.t. |
| 48. | G. Izaguirre | APT | s.t. |
| 49. | Y. Arashiro | TBV | s.t. |
| 50. | J. van Emden | TJV | s.t. |
| 51. | D. F. Martínez | IGD | s.t. |
| 52. | T. Foss | TJV | s.t. |
| 53. | D. Oss | BOH | s.t. |
| 54. | S. Yates | BEX | s.t. |
| 55. | N. Schultz | BEX | s.t. |
| 56. | R. Taaramäe | IWG | s.t. |
| 57. | A. Valter | GFC | s.t. |
| 58. | K. Bouwman | TJV | s.t. |
| 59. | J. Keukeleire | EFN | s.t. |
| 60. | R. Seigle | GFC | s.t. |
| 61. | M. Fabbro | BOH | s.t. |
| 62. | E. Buchmann | BOH | s.t. |
| 63. | A. Viviani | COF | s.t. |
| 64. | M. Brändle | ISN | s.t. |
| 65. | D. Martin | ISN | s.t. |
| 66. | G. Aleotti | BOH | s.t. |
| 67. | G. Bennett | TJV | s.t. |
| 68. | R. Cavagna | DQT | s.t. |
| 69. | A. Bettiol | EFN | s.t. |
| 70. | T. Kangert | BEX | s.t. |
| 71. | H. Carthy | EFN | s.t. |
| 72. | E. Battaglin | BCF | s.t. |
| 73. | J. van den Berg | EFN | s.t. |
| 74. | J. Mosca | TFS | s.t. |
| 75. | B. J. Lindeman | TQA | s.t. |
| 76. | L. Vervaeke | AFC | s.t. |
| 77. | N. Venchiarutti | ANS | s.t. |
| 78. | D. Ulissi | UAD | s.t. |
| 79. | N. Oliveira | MOV | s.t. |
| 80. | A. Covi | UAD | s.t. |
| 81. | F. Gavazzi | EOK | s.t. |
| 82. | E. Sepúlveda | ANS | s.t. |
| 83. | S. Puccio | IGD | s.t. |
| 84. | M. Schmid | TQA | s.t. |
| 85. | G. Vermeersch | AFC | s.t. |
| 86. | R. Guerreiro | EFN | s.t. |
| 87. | A. Vendrame | ACT | s.t. |
| 88. | S. Zoccarato | BCF | s.t. |
| 89. | U. Marengo | BCF | s.t. |
| 90. | T. De Gendt | LTS | s.t. |
| 91. | G. Niv | ISN | s.t. |
| 92. | S. Pellaud | ANS | s.t. |
| 93. | A. Ponomar | ANS | s.t. |
| 94. | S. Leysen | AFC | s.t. |
| 95. | M. F. Honoré | DQT | s.t. |
| 96. | R. Molard | GFC | s.t. |
| 97. | A. Duchesne | GFC | s.t. |
| 98. | N. Edet | COF | s.t. |
| 99. | F. Großschartner | BOH | s.t. |
| 100. | M. Sobrero | APT | s.t. |
| 101. | M. Bodnar | BOH | s.t. |
| 102. | F. Zana | BCF | s.t. |
| 103. | Q. Hermans | IWG | s.t. |
| 104. | W. Kreder | IWG | s.t. |
| 105. | F. Sabatini | COF | s.t. |
| 106. | E. Ravasi | EOK | 0:32 |
| 107. | D. Villella | MOV | 0:37 |
| 108. | S. Battistella | APT | s.t. |
| 109. | V. Pronskiy | APT | s.t. |
| 110. | D. De Bondt | AFC | 0:43 |
| 111. | G. Bouchard | ACT | 0:51 |
| 112. | L. Fortunato | EOK | s.t. |
| 113. | A. Gougeard | ACT | s.t. |
| 114. | T. Gallopin | ACT | s.t. |
| 115. | G. Carboni | BCF | s.t. |
| 116. | K. de Kort | TFS | s.t. |
| 117. | B. Mollema | TFS | s.t. |
| 118. | K. Frankiny | TQA | s.t. |
| 119. | M. Storer | DSM | s.t. |
| 120. | S. Ravanelli | ANS | s.t. |
| 121. | N. Tesfatsion | ANS | s.t. |
| 122. | N. Roche | DSM | s.t. |
| 123. | C. Scotson | BEX | s.t. |
| 124. | J. Narváez | IGD | s.t. |
| 125. | J. Janssens | AFC | s.t. |
| 126. | L. Wiśniowski | TQA | 1:07 |
| 127. | C. Benedetti | BOH | s.t. |
| 128. | D. Cataldo | MOV | s.t. |
| 129. | G. Visconti | BCF | s.t. |
| 130. | V. Conti | UAD | s.t. |
| 131. | R. Rochas | COF | s.t. |
| 132. | P. Bilbao | TBV | s.t. |
| 133. | N. Berhane | COF | s.t. |
| 134. | E. A. Rubio | MOV | s.t. |
| 135. | L. van den Berg | GFC | s.t. |
| 136. | S. Reichenbach | GFC | s.t. |
| 137. | P. Martens | TJV | s.t. |
| 138. | M. Badilatti | GFC | s.t. |
| 139. | A. Ghebreigzabhier | TFS | s.t. |
| 140. | A. Pedrero | MOV | s.t. |
| 141. | J. Cepeda Ortiz | ANS | s.t. |
| 142. | G. Brambilla | TFS | s.t. |
| 143. | M. Nieve | BEX | s.t. |
| 144. | M. Dina | EOK | s.t. |
| 145. | S. Petilli | IWG | s.t. |
| 146. | S. Carr | EFN | s.t. |
| 147. | M. Jorgenson | MOV | s.t. |
| 148. | J. Knox | DQT | s.t. |
| 149. | M. Christian | EOK | s.t. |
| 150. | T. van Garderen | EFN | s.t. |
| 151. | H. Vanhoucke | LTS | s.t. |
| 152. | J. Hirt | IWG | s.t. |
| 153. | O. Riesebeek | AFC | s.t. |
| 154. | H. Tejada | APT | s.t. |
| 155. | J. Castroviejo | IGD | s.t. |
| 156. | R. Valls | TBV | 1:37 |
| 157. | S. Guglielmi | GFC | 1:45 |
| 158. | P. Serry | DQT | 1:50 |
| 159. | C. Juul-Jensen | BEX | s.t. |
| 160. | V. Lafay | COF | 2:15 |
| 161. | C. Hamilton | DSM | s.t. |
| 162. | J. Hindley | DSM | s.t. |
| 163. | A. Torres | MOV | s.t. |
| 164. | S. Rivi | EOK | 2:58 |

MAY  WORLDTOUR MEN'S RACE

# GIRO D'ITALIA
Stage 14
22 May 2021
Cittadella–Monte Zoncolan
205km

## WEATHER

TEMPERATURE  WIND
19°C  SW 7km/h

## PROFILE

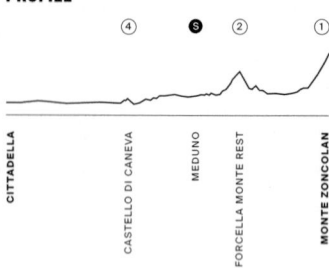

CITTADELLA — CASTELLO DI CANEVA — MEDUNO — FORCELLA MONTE REST — MONTE ZONCOLAN

Today brought Lorenzo Fortunato – last seen saluting Bologna on stage 5 – his first professional race win. Bernal gained 11 seconds on Yates, 39 seconds on Caruso and Ciccone, and 44 on Dan Martin. Yet the mere facts of the matter were an insignificant distraction today. A stage like this is better covered by crackling radio or comic book than high definition. Or seen in a daydream – or a nightmare, for Zoncolan is a name for a monster not a sports facility. At least there was the mist, which removed the events of the day from the cold, analytic light of plain view and into the realm of the imagination. That said, Jan Tratnik has something of the bogeyman about him. He attacked with a sort of naive, bumbling menace, yet rode away from affirmed climbers like Mollema and Bennett. When Fortunato finally decided not to wait for the more accomplished chasers (that is, all of them, given that the last race he won was the Trofeo Guido Dorigo in 2013, just over eight years ago), he set off after him and, 2.5km later, caught him. With 2.4km to go, on the steepest section of the climb, it was the Italian's turn to ride away. Behind, Astana had been threatening to tear things apart for 50km. Descending from the Forcella Monte Rest, they split the peloton: four of their riders, plus Bernal, Castroviejo and Pello Bilbao, formed a leading group. Tellingly, Remco Evenepoel was not in the next group but in the group after that. But the attack had nowhere to go and, despite leading up the final climb, Moscon, Narváez, Castroviejo and Martínez took control. With 1,500 metres remaining, Simon Yates attacked. Martínez moved aside, allowing the *maglia rosa* to follow. Buchmann, next in line, allowed a gap to open. Inside the final 300 metres, Bernal darted past the Englishman and away. (MR)

## BREAKAWAY

A. Ponomar (ANS), J. Tratnik (TBV), R. Rochas (COF), V. Albanese (EOK), L. Fortunato (EOK), G. Bennett (TJV), E. Affini (TJV), N. Oliveira (MOV), B. Mollema (TFS), J. Mosca (TFS), A. Covi (UAD)

## GENERAL CLASSIFICATION

| POS | NAME | TEAM | TIME |
|---|---|---|---|
| 1. — | E. Bernal | IGD | 58:30:47 |
| 2. ↑3 | S. Yates | BEX | 1:33 |
| 3. — | D. Caruso | TBV | 1:51 |
| 4. ↓2 | A. Vlasov | APT | 1:57 |
| 5. ↓1 | H. Carthy | EFN | 2:11 |
| 6. — | E. Buchmann | BOH | 2:36 |
| 7. ↑1 | G. Ciccone | TFS | 3:03 |
| 8. ↓1 | R. Evenepoel | DQT | 3:52 |
| 9. ↑1 | D. F. Martínez | IGD | 3:54 |
| 10. ↑1 | R. Bardet | DSM | 4:31 |

## KING OF THE MOUNTAINS

| POS | NAME | TEAM | PTS |
|---|---|---|---|
| 1. — | G. Bouchard | ACT | 96 |
| 2. — | E. Bernal | IGD | 57 |
| 3. ↑1 | B. Mollema | TFS | 50 |

## POINTS

| POS | NAME | TEAM | PTS |
|---|---|---|---|
| 1. — | P. Sagan | BOH | 135 |
| 2. — | G. Nizzolo | TQA | 126 |
| 3. — | D. Cimolai | ISN | 113 |

## YOUNG RIDER

| POS | NAME | TEAM | TIME |
|---|---|---|---|
| 1. — | E. Bernal | IGD | 58:30:47 |
| 2. — | A. Vlasov | APT | 1:57 |
| 3. — | R. Evenepoel | DQT | 3:52 |

## TRIVIA

» Lorenzo Fortunato is the second-youngest of the nine winners atop Monte Zoncolan. The youngest was also the first-ever winner, Fabiana Luperini at the 1997 Giro.

## BONUSES

| TYPE | NAME | TEAM |
|---|---|---|
| KOM 1 | B. Mollema | TFS |
| KOM 2 | B. Mollema | TFS |
| KOM 3 | L. Fortunato | EOK |
| Sprint 1 | J. Tratnik | TBV |

## STAGE RESULTS

| POS | NAME | TEAM | TIME |
|---|---|---|---|
| 1. | L. Fortunato | EOK | 5:17:22 |
| 2. | J. Tratnik | TBV | 0:26 |
| 3. | A. Covi | UAD | 0:59 |
| 4. | E. Bernal | IGD | 1:43 |
| 5. | B. Mollema | TFS | 1:47 |
| 6. | S. Yates | BEX | 1:54 |
| 7. | G. Bennett | TJV | 2:10 |
| 8. | N. Oliveira | MOV | 2:18 |
| 9. | D. F. Martínez | IGD | 2:22 |
| 10. | D. Caruso | TBV | s.t. |
| 11. | G. Ciccone | TFS | s.t. |
| 12. | D. Martin | ISN | 2:27 |
| 13. | E. Buchmann | BOH | 2:29 |
| 14. | H. Carthy | EFN | 2:37 |
| 15. | R. Bardet | DSM | 2:45 |
| 16. | A. Vlasov | APT | 2:55 |
| 17. | A. Pedrero | MOV | 3:07 |
| 18. | J. Almeida | DQT | 3:11 |
| 19. | R. Evenepoel | DQT | 3:13 |
| 20. | N. Schultz | BEX | s.t. |
| 21. | R. Guerreiro | EFN | s.t. |
| 22. | J. Hirt | IWG | 3:32 |
| 23. | V. Lafay | COF | 4:04 |
| 24. | D. Formolo | UAD | 4:19 |
| 25. | M. Nieve | BEX | 4:26 |
| 26. | K. Bouwman | TJV | 4:31 |
| 27. | T. Foss | TJV | s.t. |
| 28. | A. Ponomar | ANS | 4:52 |
| 29. | E. A. Rubio | MOV | 5:37 |
| 30. | M. Badilatti | GFC | 5:39 |
| 31. | S. Reichenbach | GFC | 5:41 |
| 32. | A. Valter | GFC | s.t. |
| 33. | M. Christian | EOK | 5:53 |
| 34. | F. Großschartner | BOH | 6:59 |
| 35. | J. Castroviejo | IGD | s.t. |
| 36. | L. Vervaeke | AFC | 7:27 |
| 37. | P. Bilbao | TBV | 7:47 |
| 38. | G. Izagirre | APT | 8:41 |
| 39. | E. Sepúlveda | ANS | 9:05 |
| 40. | S. Carr | EFN | 9:45 |
| 41. | T. Kangert | BEX | 9:47 |
| 42. | E. Ravasi | EOK | 10:25 |
| 43. | C. Hamilton | DSM | 10:46 |
| 44. | M. Fabbro | BOH | 12:04 |
| 45. | V. Nibali | TFS | s.t. |
| 46. | R. Taaramäe | IWG | s.t. |
| 47. | L. Warbasse | ACT | 12:54 |
| 48. | L. L. Sanchez | APT | 13:29 |
| 49. | J. Narváez | IGD | 13:52 |
| 50. | J. Cepeda Ortiz | ANS | s.t. |
| 51. | G. Brambilla | TFS | 14:07 |
| 52. | P. Serry | DQT | 14:58 |
| 53. | R. Molard | GFC | 15:04 |
| 54. | N. Roche | DSM | 15:10 |
| 55. | T. Gallopin | ACT | 15:43 |
| 56. | P. Bevin | ISN | s.t. |
| 57. | D. Ulissi | UAD | 15:58 |
| 58. | F. Gavazzi | EOK | 16:19 |
| 59. | S. Petilli | IWG | s.t. |
| 60. | G. Moscon | IGD | 17:03 |
| 61. | G. Niv | ISN | 19:18 |
| 62. | J. Mosca | TFS | 20:57 |
| 63. | A. Ghebreigzabhier | TFS | s.t. |
| 64. | N. Arndt | DSM | s.t. |
| 65. | D. Villella | MOV | s.t. |
| 66. | A. Bettiol | EFN | s.t. |
| 67. | V. Pronskiy | APT | s.t. |
| 68. | R. Rochas | COF | s.t. |
| 69. | T. van Garderen | EFN | s.t. |
| 70. | Q. Hermans | IWG | s.t. |
| 71. | J. Knox | DQT | s.t. |
| 72. | R. Cavagna | DQT | s.t. |
| 73. | V. Albanese | EOK | 21:03 |
| 74. | M. F. Honoré | DQT | 22:27 |
| 75. | E. Affini | TJV | 24:33 |
| 76. | J. Keukeleire | EFN | 24:55 |
| 77. | S. Puccio | IGD | s.t. |
| 78. | H. Tejada | APT | 25:32 |
| 79. | S. Battistella | APT | 25:48 |
| 80. | L. van den Berg | GFC | 31:11 |
| 81. | F. Felline | APT | 31:20 |
| 82. | T. De Gendt | LTS | 31:31 |
| 83. | J. Janssens | AFC | 31:34 |
| 84. | S. Pellaud | ANS | 31:37 |
| 85. | R. Seigle | GFC | s.t. |
| 86. | Y. Arashiro | TBV | 31:45 |
| 87. | A. Vendrame | ACT | 32:10 |
| 88. | R. Valls | TBV | 32:12 |
| 89. | G. Aleotti | BOH | 32:23 |
| 90. | M. Dina | EOK | 32:48 |
| 91. | N. Venchiarutti | ANS | 34:24 |
| 92. | G. Bouchard | ACT | s.t. |
| 93. | I. Keisse | DQT | s.t. |
| 94. | J. van Emden | TJV | s.t. |
| 95. | M. Hepburn | BEX | s.t. |
| 96. | C. Benedetti | BOH | s.t. |
| 97. | C. Juul-Jensen | BEX | s.t. |
| 98. | N. Tesfatsion | ANS | s.t. |
| 99. | M. Sobrero | APT | 34:30 |
| 100. | F. Zana | BCF | s.t. |
| 101. | E. Battaglin | BCF | s.t. |
| 102. | K. de Kort | TFS | 34:43 |
| 103. | P. Martens | TJV | 34:52 |
| 104. | G. Vermeersch | AFC | 34:55 |
| 105. | G. Carboni | BCF | 35:05 |
| 106. | N. Denz | DSM | 35:19 |
| 107. | M. Storer | DSM | s.t. |
| 108. | J. van den Berg | EFN | 35:25 |
| 109. | S. Guglielmi | GFC | 35:28 |
| 110. | F. Sabatini | COF | 35:35 |
| 111. | A. Duchesne | GFC | s.t. |
| 112. | N. Berhane | COF | s.t. |
| 113. | K. Frankiny | TQA | s.t. |
| 114. | M. Schmid | TQA | s.t. |
| 115. | D. Gabburo | BCF | s.t. |
| 116. | S. Ravanelli | ANS | s.t. |
| 117. | F. Tagliani | ANS | s.t. |
| 118. | D. Cataldo | MOV | s.t. |
| 119. | S. Leysen | AFC | s.t. |
| 120. | S. Zoccarato | BCF | s.t. |
| 121. | A. Pasqualon | IWG | 35:51 |
| 122. | A. Viviani | COF | s.t. |
| 123. | A. Gougeard | ACT | 35:57 |
| 124. | U. Marengo | BCF | 36:10 |
| 125. | G. Visconti | BCF | 36:11 |
| 126. | B. J. Lindeman | TQA | 36:21 |
| 127. | F. Fiorelli | BCF | 36:30 |
| 128. | M. Jorgenson | MOV | 36:32 |
| 129. | M. Kanter | DSM | 36:38 |
| 130. | W. Kreder | IWG | 36:50 |
| 131. | R. Minali | IWG | s.t. |
| 132. | D. Oss | BOH | 36:57 |
| 133. | D. De Bondt | AFC | s.t. |
| 134. | M. Brändle | ISN | 37:16 |
| 135. | D. Cimolai | ISN | 37:17 |
| 136. | E. Viviani | COF | 37:38 |
| 137. | F. Gaviria | UAD | s.t. |
| 138. | L. Naesen | ACT | s.t. |
| 139. | S. Rivi | EOK | s.t. |
| 140. | M. Moschetti | TFS | s.t. |
| 141. | O. Riesebeek | AFC | s.t. |
| 142. | V. Campenaerts | TQA | 37:41 |
| 143. | M. Walscheid | TQA | 37:44 |
| 144. | G. Nizzolo | TQA | s.t. |
| 145. | A. Krieger | AFC | 37:46 |
| 146. | T. van der Hoorn | IWG | s.t. |
| 147. | V. Conti | UAD | 37:48 |
| 148. | P. Sagan | BOH | 38:33 |
| 149. | L. Wiśniowski | TQA | 38:35 |
| 150. | S. Consonni | COF | s.t. |
| 151. | F. Ganna | IGD | s.t. |
| 152. | J. S. Molano | UAD | s.t. |
| 153. | A. M. Richeze | UAD | s.t. |
| 154. | H. Vanhoucke | LTS | s.t. |
| 155. | S. Oldani | LTS | s.t. |
| 156. | M. Bodnar | BOH | 38:40 |
| 157. | C. Meyer | BEX | s.t. |
| 158. | C. Scotson | BEX | s.t. |
| 159. | A. Torres | MOV | 38:43 |

MAY — WORLDTOUR MEN'S RACE

## GIRO D'ITALIA
Stage 15
23 May 2021
Grado–Gorizia
147km

For a day, the Giro d'Italia was a tour of a border region, where every hamlet has five names or more. Gornje Cerovo – the category-4 climb of the day, repeated three times – was once called Cerovo Gorenje but is Cerò di Sopra in Italian (although formerly Cerou di Sopra or Cerou Superiore); in German it is, or was, Ober Cerou, and in Friulan it is Cerò di Sore. It has been part of the Holy Roman Empire, the Ostrogoth Kingdom, the Byzantine Empire, the Kingdom of the Lombards, the Duchy of Friuli, the *Roegnum Italiae*, the Austro-Italian Marches, the Kingdom of Italy, *Italica*, the Republic of Venice, the Habsburg Empire, the Napoleonic Kingdom of Italy, the Operational Zone of the Adriatic Littoral (a Nazi German district on the northern Adriatic coast created during the Second World War in 1943, formed out of territories that were previously under Fascist Italian control until its takeover by Germany), Zone A of Venezia Giulia under the British-American control of the Allied Military Government, then Yugoslavia, and now Slovenia. History runs deep in these parts, and people have learned to adapt to a changing world. With three riders in the 15-man breakaway, Team Qhubeka Assos faced one of the hardest tactical conundrums in cycling: how to make a numerical advantage count. When Campenaerts attacked before a right-hand bend with 22.5km to go, only Albert Torres, the track specialist, and Oscar Riesebeek, the 28-year-old with no wins on the road, went with him. Dries De Bondt – who had been burning energy at the intermediate sprints and climbs, picking up points in the *combattività* standings, which he was once again leading – held up the chasers in the bend, allowing the three to get away. In teeming rain, Campenaerts seemed to squander his energy with ineffectual attacks. With 300 metres left, Riesebeek sprinted past. But it was too early, and his rival had time to come back at him and take his first Giro stage win, after four second places and a third. With three stage wins so far, his team too has learned to adapt.

## WEATHER

TEMPERATURE: 21°C
WIND: SW 28km/h

## PROFILE

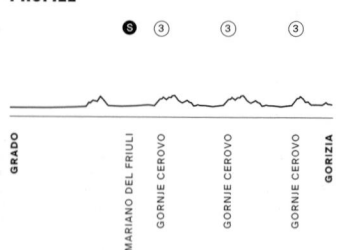

GRADO — MARIANO DEL FRIULI — GORNJE CEROVO — GORNJE CEROVO — GORNJE CEROVO — GORIZIA

## BREAKAWAY

D. De Bondt (AFC), O. Riesebeek (AFC), S. Consonni (COF), L. van den Berg (GFC), Q. Hermans (IWG), S. Oldani (LTS), H. Vanhoucke (LTS), D. Cataldo (MOV), A. Torres (MOV), N. Arndt (DSM), V. Campenaerts (TQA), M. Walscheid (TQA), Ł. Wiśniowski (TQA), B. Mollema (TFS), J. S. Molano (UAD)

## GENERAL CLASSIFICATION

| POS | NAME | TEAM | TIME |
|---|---|---|---|
| 1. — | E. Bernal | IGD | 62:13:33 |
| 2. — | S. Yates | BEX | 1:33 |
| 3. — | D. Caruso | TBV | 1:51 |
| 4. — | A. Vlasov | APT | 1:57 |
| 5. — | H. Carthy | EFN | 2:11 |
| 6. ↑1 | G. Ciccone | TFS | 3:03 |
| 7. ↑1 | R. Evenepoel | DQT | 3:52 |
| 8. ↑1 | D. F. Martínez | IGD | 3:54 |
| 9. ↑1 | R. Bardet | DSM | 4:31 |
| 10.↑1 | T. Foss | TJV | 5:37 |

## KING OF THE MOUNTAINS

| POS | NAME | TEAM | PTS |
|---|---|---|---|
| 1. — | G. Bouchard | ACT | 96 |
| 2. — | E. Bernal | IGD | 57 |
| 3. — | B. Mollema | TFS | 53 |

## POINTS

| POS | NAME | TEAM | PTS |
|---|---|---|---|
| 1. — | P. Sagan | BOH | 135 |
| 2. ↑1 | D. Cimolai | ISN | 113 |
| 3. ↑1 | F. Gaviria | UAD | 110 |

## YOUNG RIDER

| POS | NAME | TEAM | TIME |
|---|---|---|---|
| 1. — | E. Bernal | IGD | 62:13:33 |
| 2. — | A. Vlasov | APT | 1:57 |
| 3. — | R. Evenepoel | DQT | 3:52 |

## BONUSES

| TYPE | NAME | TEAM |
|---|---|---|
| KOM 1 | D. De Bondt | AFC |
| KOM 2 | D. De Bondt | AFC |
| KOM 3 | V. Campenaerts | TQA |
| Sprint 1 | D. De Bondt | AFC |

## STAGE RESULTS

| POS | NAME | TEAM | TIME |
|---|---|---|---|
| 1. | V. Campenaerts | TQA | 3:25:25 |
| 2. | O. Riesebeek | AFC | s.t. |
| 3. | N. Arndt | DSM | 0:07 |
| 4. | S. Consonni | COF | s.t. |
| 5. | Q. Hermans | IWG | s.t. |
| 6. | D. Cataldo | MOV | s.t. |
| 7. | B. Mollema | TFS | 0:09 |
| 8. | A. Torres | MOV | 0:44 |
| 9. | J. S. Molano | UAD | 1:02 |
| 10. | M. Walscheid | TQA | s.t. |
| 11. | D. De Bondt | AFC | s.t. |
| 12. | L. Wiśniowski | TQA | s.t. |
| 13. | S. Oldani | LTS | s.t. |
| 14. | L. van den Berg | GFC | s.t. |
| 15. | H. Vanhoucke | LTS | 1:09 |
| 16. | S. Puccio | IGD | 17:21 |
| 17. | F. Ganna | IGD | s.t. |
| 18. | J. Castroviejo | IGD | s.t. |
| 19. | J. Narváez | IGD | s.t. |
| 20. | C. Juul-Jensen | BEX | s.t. |
| 21. | E. Bernal | IGD | s.t. |
| 22. | G. Moscon | IGD | s.t. |
| 23. | D. F. Martínez | IGD | s.t. |
| 24. | M. Hepburn | BEX | s.t. |
| 25. | S. Yates | BEX | s.t. |
| 26. | N. Schultz | BEX | s.t. |
| 27. | A. Vlasov | APT | s.t. |
| 28. | T. Kangert | BEX | s.t. |
| 29. | M. Nieve | BEX | s.t. |
| 30. | F. Felline | APT | s.t. |
| 31. | J. Tratnik | TBV | s.t. |
| 32. | D. Caruso | TBV | s.t. |
| 33. | J. Mosca | TFS | s.t. |
| 34. | G. Ciccone | TFS | s.t. |
| 35. | L. L. Sanchez | APT | s.t. |
| 36. | N. Denz | DSM | s.t. |
| 37. | Y. Arashiro | TBV | s.t. |
| 38. | G. Izaguirre | APT | s.t. |
| 39. | K. de Kort | TFS | s.t. |
| 40. | P. Serry | DQT | s.t. |
| 41. | V. Pronskiy | APT | s.t. |
| 42. | J. Keukeleire | EFN | s.t. |
| 43. | R. Rochas | COF | s.t. |
| 44. | S. Zoccarato | BCF | s.t. |
| 45. | R. Molard | GFC | s.t. |
| 46. | H. Carthy | EFN | s.t. |
| 47. | A. Bettiol | EFN | s.t. |
| 48. | A. Valter | GFC | s.t. |
| 49. | P. Bevin | ISN | s.t. |
| 50. | J. van den Berg | EFN | s.t. |
| 51. | R. Seigle | GFC | s.t. |
| 52. | T. Foss | TJV | s.t. |
| 53. | G. Carboni | BCF | s.t. |
| 54. | D. Formolo | UAD | s.t. |
| 55. | R. Taaramäe | IWG | s.t. |
| 56. | F. Sabatini | COF | s.t. |
| 57. | R. Bardet | DSM | s.t. |
| 58. | S. Leysen | AFC | s.t. |
| 59. | P. Martens | TJV | s.t. |
| 60. | R. Evenepoel | DQT | s.t. |
| 61. | M. Sobrero | APT | s.t. |
| 62. | V. Nibali | TFS | s.t. |
| 63. | D. Ulissi | UAD | s.t. |
| 64. | D. Martin | ISN | s.t. |
| 65. | E. Sepúlveda | ANS | s.t. |
| 66. | L. Fortunato | EOK | s.t. |
| 67. | S. Guglielmi | GFC | s.t. |
| 68. | N. Oliveira | MOV | s.t. |
| 69. | E. Viviani | COF | s.t. |
| 70. | J. Almeida | DQT | s.t. |
| 71. | A. Ponomar | ANS | s.t. |
| 72. | E. Affini | TJV | s.t. |
| 73. | F. Zana | BCF | s.t. |
| 74. | L. Warbasse | ACT | s.t. |
| 75. | M. Fabbro | BOH | s.t. |
| 76. | A. Covi | UAD | s.t. |
| 77. | F. Gavazzi | EOK | s.t. |
| 78. | S. Pellaud | ANS | s.t. |
| 79. | N. Venchiarutti | ANS | s.t. |
| 80. | F. Großschartner | BOH | s.t. |
| 81. | F. Tagliani | ANS | s.t. |
| 82. | E. A. Rubio | MOV | s.t. |
| 83. | C. Benedetti | BOH | s.t. |
| 84. | K. Bouwman | TJV | s.t. |
| 85. | A. Krieger | AFC | s.t. |
| 86. | P. Bilbao | TBV | s.t. |
| 87. | A. Vendrame | ACT | s.t. |
| 88. | J. Knox | DQT | s.t. |
| 89. | L. Vervaeke | AFC | s.t. |
| 90. | D. Villella | MOV | s.t. |
| 91. | M. Jorgenson | MOV | s.t. |
| 92. | G. Bennett | TJV | s.t. |
| 93. | A. Pasqualon | IWG | s.t. |
| 94. | G. Bouchard | ACT | s.t. |
| 95. | M. Kanter | DSM | s.t. |
| 96. | C. Hamilton | DSM | 17:39 |
| 97. | K. Frankiny | TQA | s.t. |
| 98. | R. Valls | TBV | s.t. |
| 99. | U. Marengo | BCF | s.t. |
| 100. | S. Ravanelli | ANS | s.t. |
| 101. | S. Battistella | APT | s.t. |
| 102. | G. Aleotti | BOH | s.t. |
| 103. | E. Battaglin | BCF | s.t. |
| 104. | A. Duchesne | GFC | s.t. |
| 105. | S. Petilli | IWG | s.t. |
| 106. | S. Carr | EFN | s.t. |
| 107. | M. Badilatti | GFC | s.t. |
| 108. | T. van Garderen | EFN | s.t. |
| 109. | R. Cavagna | DQT | s.t. |
| 110. | M. Christian | EOK | s.t. |
| 111. | A. Viviani | COF | s.t. |
| 112. | B. J. Lindeman | TQA | s.t. |
| 113. | E. Ravasi | EOK | s.t. |
| 114. | M. Storer | DSM | s.t. |
| 115. | D. Gabburo | BCF | s.t. |
| 116. | M. Dina | EOK | s.t. |
| 117. | J. Cepeda Ortiz | ANS | s.t. |
| 118. | A. Gougeard | ACT | s.t. |
| 119. | F. Gaviria | UAD | s.t. |
| 120. | R. Minali | IWG | s.t. |
| 121. | D. Oss | BOH | s.t. |
| 122. | A. Pedrero | MOV | s.t. |
| 123. | J. Janssens | AFC | s.t. |
| 124. | G. Vermeersch | AFC | s.t. |
| 125. | S. Rivi | EOK | s.t. |
| 126. | W. Kreder | IWG | s.t. |
| 127. | N. Roche | DSM | s.t. |
| 128. | T. De Gendt | LTS | s.t. |
| 129. | V. Lafay | COF | s.t. |
| 130. | A. Ghebreigzabhier | TFS | s.t. |
| 131. | J. Hirt | IWG | s.t. |
| 132. | S. Reichenbach | GFC | s.t. |
| 133. | N. Tesfatsion | ANS | s.t. |
| 134. | H. Tejada | APT | s.t. |
| 135. | L. Naesen | ACT | s.t. |
| 136. | V. Albanese | EOK | s.t. |
| 137. | C. Scotson | BEX | 17:52 |
| 138. | G. Visconti | BCF | s.t. |
| 139. | F. Fiorelli | BCF | s.t. |
| 140. | I. Keisse | DQT | s.t. |
| 141. | T. van der Hoorn | IWG | s.t. |
| 142. | V. Conti | UAD | s.t. |
| 143. | P. Sagan | BOH | s.t. |
| 144. | D. Cimolai | ISN | s.t. |
| 145. | T. Gallopin | ACT | 18:50 |
| 146. | C. Meyer | BEX | 19:13 |
| 147. | A. M. Richeze | UAD | 20:04 |
| 148. | G. Brambilla | TFS | s.t. |
| 149. | M. Brändle | ISN | s.t. |
| 150. | G. Niv | ISN | s.t. |
| 151. | M. Bodnar | BOH | s.t. |
| 152. | M. Moschetti | TFS | 23:13 |
| 153. | M. F. Honoré | DQT | s.t. |
| 154. | M. Schmid | TQA | 23:16 |

## TRIVIA

» Hour record-holder Victor Campenaerts is known more as a time trial specialist, and this victory was only his second non-TT victory out of eight total career wins.

MAY — WORLDTOUR MEN'S RACE

# GIRO D'ITALIA
Stage 16
24 May 2021
Sacile–Cortina d'Ampezzo
153km

Every day in the Giro, Egan Bernal seems to have different adversaries. At Montalcino it was Buchmann, at Campo Felice it was Vlasov, on the Zoncolan it was Yates, today it was Caruso and Bardet. Every time, the answer is the same. 'I wanted to show I'm still in the game,' he said after the stage. On the day that Egan decided to do something special – 'It's not every day you win a stage in the Giro wearing the *maglia rosa*' – rain, snow and freezing temperatures forced changes on the race organisers. A 59km loop containing the Passo Fedaia and the Passo Pordoi was cut from the route. That removed this year's Pantani Climb and *Cima Coppi*. By way of compensation, 800 extra metres were added in the first 8km, allowing the stage to roll through Colle Umberto, the birthplace of Ottavio Bottecchia, the first Italian to win the Tour de France. That was not all that was cut. On a day when the helicopters that relay the television signal could not fly, we were deprived of what we most cherish: the evidence put before our own eyes. We forget how easily they can be deceived, especially when camera lenses are involved. TV cameras flatten gradients, lower speeds, reduce distance, fatten bodies, frame out the damp, the cold and the stress. Any impression their images may give of real presence is a false one. When they fail, instead of wringing our hands in frustration, we should raise our palms in thanks and revert to our imagination for normal service. With 60km remaining, the advantage of the six front riders reached 5 minutes 53. It took 10km to reduce it to 4 minutes 20, then 10km more to cut it to 4 minutes 3 seconds, and 10km more to bring it down to 1 minute 38. By then, the *maglia rosa* group was in tatters: Vlasov had gone, Yates was losing time, but Martínez was still there as the surprising Simon Carr drove the pace for Carthy. When he pulled aside, so too did Martínez, and Egan Bernal pounced.

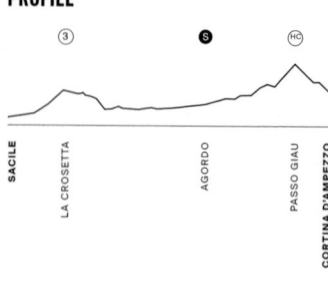

## TRIVIA
» Egan Bernal has now won three times in four countries: Romania, USA, Switzerland and Italy. His most successful country is France, where he has bagged four wins.

## WEATHER
TEMPERATURE: 14°C
WIND: NE 13km/h

## PROFILE
SACILE — LA CROSETTA — AGORDO — PASSO GIAU — CORTINA D'AMPEZZO

## BREAKAWAY
G. Bouchard (ACT), L. Vervaeke (AFC), N. Tesfatsion (ANS), G. Izaguirre (APT), J. Tratnik (TBV), M. Fabbro (BOH), F. Großschartner (BOH), J. Almeida (DQT), L. Fortunato (EOK), J. Hirt (IWG), K. Bouwman (TJV), H. Vanhoucke (LTS), A. Pedrero (MOV), E. Rubio (MOV), D. Villella (MOV), T. Kangert (BEX), N. Roche (DSM), V. Nibali (TFS), G. Brambilla (TFS), A. Ghebreigzabhier (TFS), D. Formolo (UAD), D. Martin (ISN), G. Visconti (BCF), S. Zoccarato (BCF)

## GENERAL CLASSIFICATION
| POS | NAME | TEAM | TIME |
|---|---|---|---|
| 1. – | E. Bernal | IGD | 66:36:04 |
| 2. ↑1 | D. Caruso | TBV | 2:24 |
| 3. ↑2 | H. Carthy | EFN | 3:40 |
| 4. – | A. Vlasov | APT | 4:18 |
| 5. ↓3 | S. Yates | BEX | 4:20 |
| 6. – | G. Ciccone | TFS | 4:31 |
| 7. ↑2 | R. Bardet | DSM | 5:02 |
| 8. – | D. F. Martínez | IGD | 7:17 |
| 9. ↑1 | T. Foss | TJV | 8:20 |
| 10.↑3 | J. Almeida | DQT | 10:01 |

## KING OF THE MOUNTAINS
| POS | NAME | TEAM | PTS |
|---|---|---|---|
| 1. – | G. Bouchard | ACT | 136 |
| 2. – | E. Bernal | IGD | 107 |
| 3. – | B. Mollema | TFS | 53 |

## POINTS
| POS | NAME | TEAM | PTS |
|---|---|---|---|
| 1. – | P. Sagan | BOH | 135 |
| 2. – | D. Cimolai | ISN | 113 |
| 3. – | F. Gaviria | UAD | 110 |

## YOUNG RIDER
| POS | NAME | TEAM | TIME |
|---|---|---|---|
| 1. – | E. Bernal | IGD | 66:36:04 |
| 2. – | A. Vlasov | APT | 4:18 |
| 3. ↑1 | D. F. Martínez | IGD | 7:17 |

## BONUSES
| TYPE | NAME | TEAM |
|---|---|---|
| KOM 1 | G. Bouchard | GFC |
| KOM 2 | E. Bernal | IGD |
| Sprint 1 | G. Izaguirre | APT |

## STAGE RESULTS

| POS | NAME | TEAM | TIME |
|---|---|---|---|
| 1. | E. Bernal | IGD | 4:22:41 |
| 2. | R. Bardet | DSM | 0:27 |
| 3. | D. Caruso | TBV | s.t. |
| 4. | G. Ciccone | TFS | 1:18 |
| 5. | H. Carthy | EFN | 1:19 |
| 6. | J. Almeida | DQT | 1:21 |
| 7. | A. Vlasov | APT | 2:11 |
| 8. | G. Izaguirre | APT | 2:31 |
| 9. | D. Formolo | UAD | 2:33 |
| 10. | T. Foss | TJV | s.t. |
| 11. | S. Yates | BEX | 2:37 |
| 12. | A. Pedrero | MOV | 2:51 |
| 13. | D. F. Martínez | IGD | 3:13 |
| 14. | G. Bennett | TJV | 6:12 |
| 15. | M. Nieve | BEX | s.t. |
| 16. | D. Martin | ISN | 7:10 |
| 17. | V. Nibali | TFS | 7:16 |
| 18. | E. Sepúlveda | ANS | 7:25 |
| 19. | K. Bouwman | TJV | 7:33 |
| 20. | G. Brambilla | TFS | 8:22 |
| 21. | A. Valter | GFC | 8:24 |
| 22. | L. Fortunato | EOK | s.t. |
| 23. | J. Castroviejo | IGD | 10:17 |
| 24. | P. Bilbao | TBV | s.t. |
| 25. | S. Carr | EFN | 10:32 |
| 26. | M. Sobrero | APT | 11:40 |
| 27. | V. Pronskiy | APT | s.t. |
| 28. | G. Carboni | BCF | 11:48 |
| 29. | K. Frankiny | TQA | s.t. |
| 30. | L. Vervaeke | AFC | s.t. |
| 31. | S. Petilli | IWG | 12:11 |
| 32. | C. Scotson | BEX | 16:03 |
| 33. | H. Tejada | APT | s.t. |
| 34. | N. Schultz | BEX | 16:47 |
| 35. | F. Gavazzi | EOK | s.t. |
| 36. | J. Narváez | IGD | s.t. |
| 37. | A. Pasqualon | IWG | 17:44 |
| 38. | N. Oliveira | MOV | 17:55 |
| 39. | F. Felline | APT | 18:32 |
| 40. | L. Warbasse | ACT | s.t. |
| 41. | D. Ulissi | UAD | 18:49 |
| 42. | A. Ghebreigzabhier | TFS | 18:54 |
| 43. | M. Storer | DSM | s.t. |
| 44. | J. Janssens | AFC | 19:19 |
| 45. | S. Leysen | AFC | 19:49 |
| 46. | T. Kangert | BEX | s.t. |
| 47. | M. Badilatti | GFC | 19:57 |
| 48. | J. Cepeda Ortiz | ANS | 20:16 |
| 49. | A. Vendrame | ACT | 21:06 |
| 50. | S. Pellaud | ANS | s.t. |
| 51. | S. Ravanelli | ANS | s.t. |
| 52. | T. Gallopin | ACT | s.t. |
| 53. | A. Ponomar | ANS | s.t. |
| 54. | C. Juul-Jensen | BEX | 23:19 |
| 55. | M. Hepburn | BEX | s.t. |
| 56. | P. Bevin | ISN | s.t. |
| 57. | A. Bettiol | EFN | 23:45 |
| 58. | R. Evenepoel | DQT | 24:05 |
| 59. | J. Knox | DQT | s.t. |
| 60. | Q. Hermans | IWG | s.t. |
| 61. | R. Seigle | GFC | s.t. |
| 62. | P. Serry | DQT | s.t. |
| 63. | R. Cavagna | DQT | s.t. |
| 64. | L. L. Sanchez | APT | s.t. |
| 65. | G. Moscon | IGD | s.t. |
| 66. | M. Jorgenson | MOV | s.t. |
| 67. | C. Meyer | BEX | 26:42 |
| 68. | R. Valls | TBV | 27:29 |
| 69. | E. Battaglin | BCF | 27:41 |
| 70. | S. Zoccarato | BCF | s.t. |
| 71. | S. Oldani | LTS | s.t. |
| 72. | A. Covi | UAD | s.t. |
| 73. | V. Albanese | EOK | 27:50 |
| 74. | M. Dina | EOK | s.t. |
| 75. | J. Hirt | IWG | s.t. |
| 76. | F. Zana | BCF | 28:17 |
| 77. | J. Mosca | TFS | s.t. |
| 78. | G. Visconti | BCF | s.t. |
| 79. | R. Molard | GFC | s.t. |
| 80. | S. Battistella | APT | 28:49 |
| 81. | F. Großschartner | BOH | 29:29 |
| 82. | D. Villella | MOV | s.t. |
| 83. | E. A. Rubio | MOV | s.t. |
| 84. | G. Vermeersch | AFC | 29:53 |
| 85. | N. Denz | DSM | 30:10 |
| 86. | D. Gabburo | BCF | 30:19 |
| 87. | A. Duchesne | GFC | 31:42 |
| 88. | Y. Arashiro | TBV | 32:26 |
| 89. | N. Arndt | DSM | s.t. |
| 90. | C. Hamilton | DSM | 32:36 |
| 91. | G. Aleotti | BOH | 32:42 |
| 92. | M. Fabbro | BOH | s.t. |
| 93. | P. Sagan | BOH | s.t. |
| 94. | D. Oss | BOH | s.t. |
| 95. | J. Tratnik | TBV | s.t. |
| 96. | H. Vanhoucke | LTS | 33:03 |
| 97. | J. van den Berg | EFN | 33:45 |
| 98. | T. van Garderen | EFN | s.t. |
| 99. | J. Keukeleire | EFN | s.t. |
| 100. | M. Christian | EOK | s.t. |
| 101. | S. Rivi | EOK | s.t. |
| 102. | E. Ravasi | EOK | s.t. |
| 103. | M. Kanter | DSM | 34:15 |
| 104. | B. Mollema | TFS | 34:30 |
| 105. | N. Roche | DSM | 35:25 |
| 106. | P. Martens | TJV | 36:16 |
| 107. | E. Affini | TJV | s.t. |
| 108. | D. Cataldo | MOV | s.t. |
| 109. | F. Ganna | IGD | 40:17 |
| 110. | S. Puccio | IGD | s.t. |
| 111. | M. F. Honoré | DQT | 41:28 |
| 112. | G. Bouchard | ACT | s.t. |
| 113. | I. Keisse | DQT | s.t. |
| 114. | C. Benedetti | BOH | s.t. |
| 115. | R. Taaramäe | IWG | s.t. |
| 116. | V. Conti | UAD | s.t. |
| 117. | N. Tesfatsion | ANS | 41:32 |
| 118. | U. Marengo | BCF | 41:43 |
| 119. | T. van der Hoorn | IWG | 41:45 |
| 120. | R. Rochas | COF | 41:57 |
| 121. | M. Brändle | ISN | s.t. |
| 122. | E. Viviani | COF | 42:06 |
| 123. | F. Sabatini | COF | s.t. |
| 124. | A. Viviani | COF | s.t. |
| 125. | M. Moschetti | TFS | s.t. |
| 126. | N. Venchiarutti | ANS | s.t. |
| 127. | K. de Kort | TFS | s.t. |
| 128. | F. Tagliani | ANS | s.t. |
| 129. | M. Walscheid | TQA | s.t. |
| 130. | D. Cimolai | ISN | s.t. |
| 131. | B. J. Lindeman | TQA | 42:13 |
| 132. | M. Bodnar | BOH | 42:15 |
| 133. | W. Kreder | IWG | s.t. |
| 134. | L. Naesen | ACT | 43:07 |
| 135. | A. Gougeard | ACT | s.t. |
| 136. | R. Minali | IWG | s.t. |
| 137. | G. Niv | ISN | s.t. |
| 138. | F. Fiorelli | BCF | 44:07 |
| 139. | M. Schmid | TQA | 44:33 |
| 140. | S. Consonni | COF | 44:37 |
| 141. | V. Lafay | COF | 44:50 |
| 142. | A. Krieger | AFC | s.t. |
| 143. | O. Riesebeek | AFC | 45:05 |
| 144. | J. S. Molano | UAD | 45:17 |
| 145. | A. M. Richeze | UAD | s.t. |
| 146. | F. Gaviria | UAD | s.t. |
| 147. | A. Torres | MOV | 45:19 |
| 148. | D. De Bondt | AFC | 47:40 |
| 149. | L. Wiśniowski | TQA | 48:17 |
| 150. | V. Campenaerts | TQA | s.t. |
| 151. | S. Guglielmi | GFC | 49:00 |
| 152. | L. van den Berg | GFC | s.t. |

MAY • WORLDTOUR MEN'S RACE

# GIRO D'ITALIA
Stage 17
26 May 2021
Canazei–Sega di Ala
193km

## WEATHER

**TEMPERATURE**
22°C

**WIND**
SE 9km/h

Gianni Moscon celebrated riding on home roads by joining the breakaway. With 5km left on the final climb, he slotted onto the front of the group alongside Egan Bernal, who, in Castroviejo and Martínez, already had two helpers with him. In Brentonico, the cheese-rolling town, Remco Evenepoel had somersaulted over the barrier. After Montalcino, Almeida had preferred not to say what he thought about having to wait for Remco. Now, with his co-leader out of the equation, he darted away, stirring Simon Yates to respond with 4km to go. The *maglia rosa* and his helper Dani Martínez were quickly on his wheel. Each time Yates led them up to Almeida, the Portuguese rider launched a Henry Rono-style acceleration, eventually stealing off to take second place in the stage. His jolting attacks prised Yates free of Bernal, who was suddenly unable to follow. The only question left seemed to be whether Dan Martin – still a minute or more ahead of Yates – would stay away to take his first Giro d'Italia stage win. Martin had promised his wife before the Montalcino stage that he would not risk his neck. His GC hopes went up in a cloud of dust that day, although, when Alex Dowsett was asked the following morning how disappointed the team was, he said, 'Not as much as you'd think.' Today, Martin provided the explanation: 'This is what I came here for, to try and win a stage. Everybody worked for it. I had information from [DS] Nicki [Sørensen] the whole climb, and I knew from my recon to go full gas with 2.5km to go.' After losing Krists Neilands on the first day, taking the *maglia rosa* with Alessandro De Marchi, then losing him to a horrific crash and Dowsett to illness, Dan Martin had given Israel Start-Up Nation something special to celebrate. After today's stage, Egan played down what had happened: 'Yates was impressive, the stage was perfect for him. I had a bad day but I didn't lose much time.' Ⓜ

## PROFILE

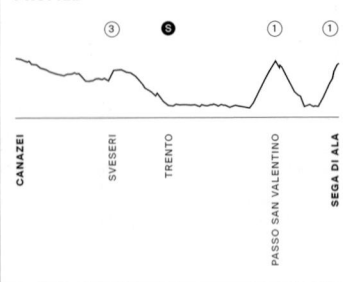

CANAZEI – SVESERI – TRENTO – PASSO SAN VALENTINO – SEGA DI ALA

## BREAKAWAY

G. Moscon (IGD), G. Bouchard (ACT), D. De Bondt (AFC), S. Ravanelli (ANS), L. L. Sánchez (APT), G. Carboni (BCF), F. Großschartner (BOH), J. Knox (DQT), P. Serry (DQT), M. Badilatti (GFC), J. Hirt (IWG), A. Pasqualon (IWG), Q. Hermans (IWG), M. Jorgenson (MOV), A. P. López (MOV), J. Mosca (TFS), V. Conti (UAD), A. Covi (UAD), D. Martin (ISN)

## GENERAL CLASSIFICATION

| POS | NAME | TEAM | TIME |
|---|---|---|---|
| 1. – | E. Bernal | IGD | 71:32:05 |
| 2. – | D. Caruso | TBV | 2:21 |
| 3. ↑2 | S. Yates | BEX | 3:23 |
| 4. – | A. Vlasov | APT | 6:03 |
| 5. ↓2 | H. Carthy | EFN | 6:09 |
| 6. ↑1 | R. Bardet | DSM | 6:31 |
| 7. ↑1 | D. F. Martínez | IGD | 7:17 |
| 8. ↑2 | J. Almeida | DQT | 8:45 |
| 9. – | T. Foss | TJV | 9:18 |
| 10. ↓4 | G. Ciccone | TFS | 11:26 |

## KING OF THE MOUNTAINS

| POS | NAME | TEAM | PTS |
|---|---|---|---|
| 1. – | G. Bouchard | ACT | 180 |
| 2. – | E. Bernal | IGD | 109 |
| 3. ↑7 | D. Martin | ISN | 79 |

## POINTS

| POS | NAME | TEAM | PTS |
|---|---|---|---|
| 1. – | P. Sagan | BOH | 135 |
| 2. – | D. Cimolai | ISN | 113 |
| 3. – | F. Gaviria | UAD | 110 |

## YOUNG RIDER

| POS | NAME | TEAM | TIME |
|---|---|---|---|
| 1. – | E. Bernal | IGD | 71:32:05 |
| 2. – | A. Vlasov | APT | 6:03 |
| 3. – | D. F. Martínez | IGD | 7:17 |

## BONUSES

| TYPE | NAME | TEAM |
|---|---|---|
| KOM 1 | D. De Bondt | AFC |
| KOM 2 | G. Bouchard | GFC |
| KOM 3 | D. Martin | ISN |
| Sprint 1 | D. De Bondt | AFC |

## TRIVIA
» Dan Martin is the 102nd rider in history to win a stage at all three Grand Tours.

## STAGE RESULTS

| POS | NAME | TEAM | TIME |
|---|---|---|---|
| 1. | D. Martin | ISN | 4:54:38 |
| 2. | J. Almeida | DQT | 0:13 |
| 3. | S. Yates | BEX | 0:30 |
| 4. | D. Ulissi | UAD | 1:20 |
| 5. | D. Caruso | TBV | s.t. |
| 6. | D. F. Martinez | IGD | 1:23 |
| 7. | E. Bernal | IGD | s.t. |
| 8. | A. Pedrero | MOV | 1:38 |
| 9. | P. Bilbao | TBV | 1:43 |
| 10. | G. Bennett | TJV | 2:21 |
| 11. | T. Foss | TJV | s.t. |
| 12. | L. Fortunato | EOK | 2:47 |
| 13. | G. Bouchard | ACT | 2:49 |
| 14. | R. Bardet | DSM | 2:52 |
| 15. | G. Moscon | IGD | s.t. |
| 16. | M. Storer | DSM | 3:05 |
| 17. | A. Vlasov | APT | 3:08 |
| 18. | J. Castroviejo | IGD | 3:10 |
| 19. | E. Ravasi | EOK | 3:18 |
| 20. | A. Bettiol | EFN | 3:52 |
| 21. | H. Carthy | EFN | s.t. |
| 22. | K. Bouwman | TJV | 5:16 |
| 23. | G. Carboni | BCF | 5:53 |
| 24. | V. Pronskiy | APT | 6:17 |
| 25. | M. Badilatti | GFC | s.t. |
| 26. | L. Vervaeke | AFC | s.t. |
| 27. | M. Fabbro | BOH | 7:58 |
| 28. | G. Ciccone | TFS | s.t. |
| 29. | T. Kangert | BEX | 9:16 |
| 30. | S. Ravanelli | ANS | 10:44 |
| 31. | J. Hirt | IWG | 11:18 |
| 32. | F. Felline | APT | 12:58 |
| 33. | R. Molard | GFC | 15:24 |
| 34. | P. Serry | DQT | s.t. |
| 35. | V. Conti | UAD | s.t. |
| 36. | J. Knox | DQT | 15:37 |
| 37. | N. Oliveira | MOV | 16:30 |
| 38. | G. Izagirre | APT | s.t. |
| 39. | T. Gallopin | ACT | s.t. |
| 40. | L. L. Sanchez | APT | s.t. |
| 41. | N. Roche | DSM | s.t. |
| 42. | Q. Hermans | IWG | 16:51 |
| 43. | P. Bevin | ISN | 17:04 |
| 44. | B. Mollema | TFS | s.t. |
| 45. | M. Christian | EOK | s.t. |
| 46. | K. Frankiny | TQA | 17:21 |
| 47. | F. Tagliani | ANS | s.t. |
| 48. | A. Ghebreigzabhier | TFS | 17:51 |
| 49. | D. Formolo | UAD | 17:55 |
| 50. | S. Petilli | IWG | 18:49 |
| 51. | C. Hamilton | DSM | 19:09 |
| 52. | F. Gavazzi | EOK | 19:24 |
| 53. | C. Benedetti | BOH | s.t. |
| 54. | L. Warbasse | ACT | s.t. |
| 55. | A. Ponomar | ANS | s.t. |
| 56. | D. Gabburo | BCF | s.t. |
| 57. | S. Zoccarato | BCF | 19:54 |
| 58. | L. van den Berg | GFC | 20:12 |
| 59. | A. Valter | GFC | s.t. |
| 60. | D. Cataldo | MOV | 20:52 |
| 61. | M. Nieve | BEX | s.t. |
| 62. | R. Valls | TBV | 22:29 |
| 63. | Y. Arashiro | TBV | s.t. |
| 64. | P. Martens | TJV | s.t. |
| 65. | A. Duchesne | GFC | 23:06 |
| 66. | M. Dina | EOK | 24:01 |
| 67. | N. Arndt | DSM | 24:38 |
| 68. | J. Mosca | TFS | 24:45 |
| 69. | G. Brambilla | TFS | s.t. |
| 70. | V. Nibali | TFS | s.t. |
| 71. | J. Narváez | IGD | s.t. |
| 72. | J. Cepeda Ortiz | ANS | s.t. |
| 73. | R. Taaramäe | IWG | s.t. |
| 74. | N. Schultz | BEX | s.t. |
| 75. | G. Aleotti | BOH | 27:16 |
| 76. | A. Vendrame | ACT | s.t. |
| 77. | M. Schmid | TQA | s.t. |
| 78. | H. Tejada | APT | 28:29 |
| 79. | E. A. Rubio | MOV | s.t. |
| 80. | S. Battistella | APT | s.t. |
| 81. | M. Sobrero | APT | s.t. |
| 82. | E. Battaglin | BCF | s.t. |
| 83. | A. Pasqualon | IWG | s.t. |
| 84. | G. Niv | ISN | s.t. |
| 85. | D. Villella | MOV | s.t. |
| 86. | E. Sepúlveda | ANS | s.t. |
| 87. | G. Visconti | BCF | 29:59 |
| 88. | U. Marengo | BCF | s.t. |
| 89. | H. Vanhoucke | LTS | 30:39 |
| 90. | F. Zana | BCF | 30:45 |
| 91. | S. Pellaud | ANS | 31:25 |
| 92. | D. De Bondt | AFC | s.t. |
| 93. | A. Gougeard | ACT | 31:27 |
| 94. | L. Naesen | ACT | s.t. |
| 95. | K. de Kort | TFS | 31:30 |

| POS | NAME | TEAM | TIME |
|---|---|---|---|
| 96. | F. Sabatini | COF | s.t. |
| 97. | N. Tesfatsion | ANS | s.t. |
| 98. | S. Leysen | AFC | s.t. |
| 99. | J. Keukeleire | EFN | s.t. |
| 100. | T. van Garderen | EFN | s.t. |
| 101. | N. Venchiarutti | ANS | s.t. |
| 102. | S. Puccio | IGD | s.t. |
| 103. | M. Brändle | ISN | s.t. |
| 104. | J. Janssens | AFC | s.t. |
| 105. | G. Vermeersch | AFC | s.t. |
| 106. | R. Seigle | GFC | 32:11 |
| 107. | S. Carr | EFN | 32:41 |
| 108. | V. Lafay | COF | s.t. |
| 109. | A. Viviani | COF | s.t. |
| 110. | S. Guglielmi | GFC | s.t. |
| 111. | B. J. Lindeman | TQA | 33:32 |
| 112. | N. Denz | DSM | 34:01 |
| 113. | W. Kreder | IWG | s.t. |
| 114. | F. Großschartner | BOH | 35:34 |
| 115. | M. Kanter | DSM | s.t. |
| 116. | O. Riesebeek | AFC | s.t. |
| 117. | A. Covi | UAD | 35:51 |
| 118. | A. Krieger | AFC | 35:59 |
| 119. | D. Oss | BOH | 36:28 |
| 120. | E. Viviani | COF | s.t. |
| 121. | F. Fiorelli | BCF | s.t. |
| 122. | D. Cimolai | ISN | s.t. |
| 123. | S. Oldani | LTS | s.t. |
| 124. | E. Affini | TJV | s.t. |
| 125. | J. Tratnik | TBV | s.t. |
| 126. | L. Wiśniowski | TQA | s.t. |
| 127. | M. Bodnar | BOH | s.t. |
| 128. | P. Sagan | BOH | s.t. |
| 129. | F. Ganna | IGD | s.t. |
| 130. | S. Consonni | COF | s.t. |
| 131. | R. Minali | IWG | s.t. |
| 132. | R. Evenepoel | DQT | s.t. |
| 133. | I. Keisse | DQT | s.t. |
| 134. | M. F. Honoré | DQT | s.t. |
| 135. | F. Gaviria | UAD | s.t. |
| 136. | A. M. Richeze | UAD | s.t. |
| 137. | J. S. Molano | UAD | s.t. |
| 138. | J. van den Berg | EFN | s.t. |
| 139. | T. van der Hoorn | IWG | s.t. |
| 140. | R. Cavagna | DQT | s.t. |
| 141. | V. Albanese | EOK | s.t. |
| 142. | S. Rivi | EOK | s.t. |
| 143. | C. Meyer | BEX | s.t. |
| 144. | C. Scotson | BEX | s.t. |
| 145. | M. Jorgenson | MOV | s.t. |
| 146. | C. Juul-Jensen | BEX | s.t. |
| 147. | A. Torres | MOV | s.t. |
| 148. | M. Hepburn | BEX | 37:14 |
| 149. | M. Walscheid | TQA | 37:43 |
| 150. | M. Moschetti | TFS | 38:10 |

MAY  WORLDTOUR MEN'S RACE

## GIRO D'ITALIA
Stage 18
27 May 2021
Rovereto–Stradella
231km

The fastest stage of the Giro, and the longest, and a stage for wine, poetry, music and lingerie lovers, passing Ala (where Mozart stayed), Castel Goffredo (Virgil's birthplace and Italy's lingerie capital), and Cremona (where Stradivarius and Guarneri built their violins). Between the towns and vineyards, the peloton strode single file like a fairy-tale millipede a quarter of a mile long, led by the smiling face of Filippo Ganna. It took 29km for 23 riders to win the lottery prize of a place in the breakaway. Peter Sagan was not one of them: 'It's no sense for me because if I go to break away, also Gaviria and Cimolai go with me, you know? It's better to… well, it always depends on the goal that you have, and now I have this *ciclamino* jersey as a goal, and it was like it was.' With 26km to go, the various groups came together and Cavagna darted away, opening a lead of about half a minute. With 14km left, Alberto Bettiol – the Ronde winner, who has been one of 'Huge' Hugh Carthy's best mountain helpers this Giro – set off after him. With 6.9km remaining, Bettiol caught him. Then, 300 metres later, Cavagna blew. Bettiol darted past, followed by Nico Roche, who never quite caught the Tuscan and conceded second place in the final 100 metres to Simone Consonni. Ganna led the *maglia rosa* group home 23 minutes 30 seconds after possibly the most popular win of the race: the boyish, charming Tuscan, Alberto Bettiol, dressed in a jersey that looked like a thrown-together patchwork of flags. After the stage, as Bettiol embraced third-placed Nico Roche (who he described in his macaronic English as 'a friend of mine, but in the final didn't really help me, it's OK, like, but I dropped him on the last climb'), Colombian fans on social media noted the position of their flag on the EF Education-Nippo jersey and joked that to them belonged the armpit of victory. (MR)

### TRIVIA
» Six Italians finished in the top ten today, the joint-most this Giro with stages 5 and 13.

### WEATHER

TEMPERATURE
22°C

WIND
SW 9km/h

### PROFILE

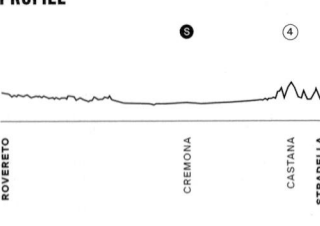

### BREAKAWAY
A. Vendrame (ACT), G. Vermeersch (AFC), S. Pellaud (ANS), A. Ponomar (ANS), N. Tesfatsion (ANS), S. Battistella (APT), G. Izagirre (APT), F. Zana (BCF), S. Consonni (COF), R. Cavagna (DDQT), A. Bettiol (EFN), F. Gavazzi (EOK), S. Rivi (EOK), W. Kreder (IWG), P. Bevin (ISN), S. Oldani (LTS), D. Cataldo (MOV), N. Arndt (DSM), N. Denz (DSM), N. Roche (DSM), J. Mosca (TFS), A. Covi (UAD), D. Ulissi (UAD)

### GENERAL CLASSIFICATION

| POS | NAME | TEAM | TIME |
|---|---|---|---|
| 1. — | E. Bernal | IGD | 77:10:18 |
| 2. — | D. Caruso | TBV | 2:21 |
| 3. — | S. Yates | BEX | 3:23 |
| 4. — | A. Vlasov | APT | 6:03 |
| 5. — | H. Carthy | EFN | 6:09 |
| 6. — | R. Bardet | DSM | 6:31 |
| 7. — | D. F. Martínez | IGD | 7:17 |
| 8. — | J. Almeida | DQT | 8:45 |
| 9. — | T. Foss | TJV | 9:18 |
| 10.↑1 | D. Martin | ISN | 13:37 |

### KING OF THE MOUNTAINS

| POS | NAME | TEAM | PTS |
|---|---|---|---|
| 1. — | G. Bouchard | ACT | 180 |
| 2. — | E. Bernal | IGD | 109 |
| 3. — | D. Martin | ISN | 79 |

### POINTS

| POS | NAME | TEAM | PTS |
|---|---|---|---|
| 1. — | P. Sagan | BOH | 135 |
| 2. — | D. Cimolai | ISN | 113 |
| 3. — | F. Gaviria | UAD | 110 |

### YOUNG RIDER

| POS | NAME | TEAM | TIME |
|---|---|---|---|
| 1. — | E. Bernal | IGD | 77:10:18 |
| 2. — | A. Vlasov | APT | 6:03 |
| 3. — | D. F. Martínez | IGD | 7:17 |

### BONUSES

| TYPE | NAME | TEAM |
|---|---|---|
| KOM 1 | R. Cavagna | DQT |
| Sprint 1 | G. Vermeersch | AFC |

# STAGE RESULTS

| POS | NAME | TEAM | TIME |
|---|---|---|---|
| 1. | A. Bettiol | EFN | 5:14:43 |
| 2. | S. Consonni | COF | 0:17 |
| 3. | N. Roche | DSM | 0:18 |
| 4. | N. Arndt | DSM | s.t. |
| 5. | D. Ulissi | UAD | s.t. |
| 6. | S. Battistella | APT | s.t. |
| 7. | F. Zana | BCF | s.t. |
| 8. | N. Tesfatsion | ANS | s.t. |
| 9. | R. Cavagna | DQT | 0:24 |
| 10. | J. Mosca | TFS | 1:12 |
| 11. | S. Oldani | LTS | 1:34 |
| 12. | D. Cataldo | MOV | s.t. |
| 13. | S. Pellaud | ANS | s.t. |
| 14. | A. Vendrame | ACT | 2:11 |
| 15. | N. Denz | DSM | 2:36 |
| 16. | S. Rivi | EOK | 2:58 |
| 17. | P. Bevin | ISN | 3:16 |
| 18. | A. Ponomar | ANS | 3:50 |
| 19. | G. Vermeersch | AFC | s.t. |
| 20. | F. Gavazzi | EOK | 7:09 |
| 21. | G. Izaguirre | APT | s.t. |
| 22. | A. M. Richeze | UAD | 8:37 |
| 23. | W. Kreder | IWG | 10:29 |
| 24. | F. Ganna | IGD | 23:30 |
| 25. | S. Puccio | IGD | s.t. |
| 26. | G. Moscon | IGD | s.t. |
| 27. | J. Narváez | IGD | s.t. |
| 28. | J. Castroviejo | IGD | s.t. |
| 29. | E. Bernal | IGD | s.t. |
| 30. | D. F. Martínez | IGD | s.t. |
| 31. | R. Valls | TBV | s.t. |
| 32. | J. Tratnik | TBV | s.t. |
| 33. | D. Caruso | TBV | s.t. |
| 34. | G. Visconti | BCF | s.t. |
| 35. | Y. Arashiro | TBV | s.t. |
| 36. | P. Bilbao | TBV | s.t. |
| 37. | M. Hepburn | BEX | s.t. |
| 38. | S. Yates | BEX | s.t. |
| 39. | C. Meyer | BEX | s.t. |
| 40. | M. F. Honoré | DQT | s.t. |
| 41. | J. Almeida | DQT | s.t. |
| 42. | C. Juul-Jensen | BEX | s.t. |
| 43. | J. Keukeleire | EFN | s.t. |
| 44. | M. Nieve | BEX | s.t. |
| 45. | A. Vlasov | APT | s.t. |
| 46. | L. L. Sanchez | APT | s.t. |
| 47. | C. Hamilton | DSM | s.t. |
| 48. | M. Sobrero | APT | s.t. |
| 49. | T. Kangert | BEX | s.t. |
| 50. | V. Pronskiy | APT | s.t. |
| 51. | F. Tagliani | ANS | s.t. |
| 52. | H. Carthy | EFN | s.t. |
| 53. | F. Sabatini | COF | s.t. |
| 54. | T. van Garderen | EFN | s.t. |
| 55. | G. Brambilla | TFS | s.t. |
| 56. | A. Valter | GFC | s.t. |
| 57. | S. Carr | EFN | s.t. |
| 58. | B. J. Lindeman | TQA | s.t. |
| 59. | R. Bardet | DSM | s.t. |
| 60. | G. Carboni | BCF | s.t. |
| 61. | P. Martens | TJV | s.t. |
| 62. | G. Aleotti | BOH | s.t. |
| 63. | M. Storer | DSM | s.t. |
| 64. | C. Benedetti | BOH | s.t. |
| 65. | E. Ravasi | EOK | s.t. |
| 66. | R. Molard | GFC | s.t. |
| 67. | T. Foss | TJV | s.t. |
| 68. | E. Sepúlveda | ANS | s.t. |
| 69. | A. Krieger | AFC | s.t. |
| 70. | L. Fortunato | EOK | s.t. |
| 71. | D. Formolo | UAD | s.t. |
| 72. | F. Felline | APT | s.t. |
| 73. | J. Knox | DQT | s.t. |
| 74. | G. Bennett | TJV | s.t. |
| 75. | G. Niv | ISN | s.t. |
| 76. | L. van den Berg | GFC | s.t. |
| 77. | L. Warbasse | ACT | s.t. |
| 78. | D. Martin | ISN | s.t. |
| 79. | A. Duchesne | GFC | s.t. |
| 80. | K. de Kort | TFS | s.t. |
| 81. | L. Wiśniowski | TQA | s.t. |
| 82. | B. Mollema | TFS | s.t. |
| 83. | M. Fabbro | BOH | s.t. |
| 84. | H. Tejada | APT | s.t. |
| 85. | N. Oliveira | MOV | s.t. |
| 86. | M. Kanter | DSM | s.t. |
| 87. | M. Dina | EOK | s.t. |
| 88. | R. Taaramäe | IWG | s.t. |
| 89. | D. Oss | BOH | s.t. |
| 90. | E. A. Rubio | MOV | s.t. |
| 91. | L. Naesen | ACT | s.t. |
| 92. | T. Gallopin | ACT | s.t. |
| 93. | M. Badilatti | GFC | s.t. |
| 94. | Q. Hermans | IWG | s.t. |
| 95. | A. Gougeard | ACT | s.t. |
| 96. | U. Marengo | BCF | s.t. |
| 97. | V. Nibali | TFS | s.t. |
| 98. | F. Großschartner | BOH | s.t. |
| 99. | A. Viviani | COF | s.t. |
| 100. | L. Vervaeke | AFC | s.t. |
| 101. | A. Covi | UAD | s.t. |
| 102. | S. Leysen | AFC | s.t. |
| 103. | F. Gaviria | UAD | s.t. |
| 104. | M. Moschetti | TFS | s.t. |
| 105. | D. Gabburo | BCF | s.t. |
| 106. | E. Viviani | COF | s.t. |
| 107. | A. Pasqualon | IWG | s.t. |
| 108. | R. Seigle | GFC | s.t. |
| 109. | D. Villella | MOV | s.t. |
| 110. | J. S. Molano | UAD | s.t. |
| 111. | M. Walscheid | TQA | s.t. |
| 112. | M. Bodnar | BOH | s.t. |
| 113. | P. Sagan | BOH | s.t. |
| 114. | F. Fiorelli | BCF | s.t. |
| 115. | K. Frankiny | TQA | s.t. |
| 116. | E. Battaglin | BCF | s.t. |
| 117. | S. Petilli | IWG | s.t. |
| 118. | S. Ravanelli | ANS | s.t. |
| 119. | N. Venchiarutti | ANS | s.t. |
| 120. | J. Cepeda Ortiz | ANS | s.t. |
| 121. | M. Christian | EOK | s.t. |
| 122. | E. Affini | TJV | s.t. |
| 123. | K. Bouwman | TJV | s.t. |
| 124. | R. Minali | IWG | s.t. |
| 125. | M. Jorgenson | MOV | s.t. |
| 126. | A. Ghebreigzabhier | TFS | s.t. |
| 127. | D. Cimolai | ISN | s.t. |
| 128. | A. Torres | MOV | s.t. |
| 129. | A. Pedrero | MOV | s.t. |
| 130. | H. Vanhoucke | LTS | s.t. |
| 131. | J. Janssens | AFC | s.t. |
| 132. | S. Zoccarato | BCF | s.t. |
| 133. | V. Conti | UAD | s.t. |
| 134. | G. Bouchard | ACT | s.t. |
| 135. | V. Lafay | COF | s.t. |
| 136. | J. Hirt | IWG | s.t. |
| 137. | I. Keisse | DQT | s.t. |
| 138. | S. Guglielmi | GFC | s.t. |
| 139. | V. Albanese | EOK | s.t. |
| 140. | M. Brändle | ISN | s.t. |
| 141. | T. van der Hoorn | IWG | s.t. |
| 142. | O. Riesebeek | AFC | s.t. |
| 143. | D. De Bondt | AFC | s.t. |
| 144. | P. Serry | DQT | 24:18 |
| 145. | J. van den Berg | EFN | s.t. |
| 146. | C. Scotson | BEX | s.t. |
| 147. | M. Schmid | TQA | s.t. |

MAY     WORLDTOUR MEN'S RACE

# GIRO D'ITALIA
Stage 19
28 May 2021
Abbiategrasso–Alpe di Mera (Valsesia)
166km

In 2019 Egan Bernal won a high-altitude Tour de France that visited the Tourmalet (2115m), the Vars (2109m), the Izoard (2360m), the Galibier (2642m), the Iseran (2770m), Tignes (2113m) and Val Thorens (2365m). Even before the cancellation of the Fedaia and the Pordoi in stage 16, there were few sections above 2,000 metres in this year's Giro: about 500 metres of uphill on the Passo Fedaia, 3.1km uphill on the Passo Pordoi, 2.7km uphill on the Passo Giau – a total of 6.3km going uphill, with probably about the same descending – then, on stage 20, about 2.6km of uphill on the Passo San Bernardino and maybe 1.2km on the Passo Spluga, a total of 3.8km uphill, and, again, perhaps about the same descending. That made a total of 20km out of a total of 3,470km. If he could hold on to win this low-lying Giro, Bernal would prove he doesn't need long sections over 2,000 metres to beat sea-level natives. The Mottarone cable-car tragedy meant the stage was rerouted through Gignese (km 85.3 / 80.7km to go), where a small section of descending, unknown to all but the locals, suddenly appeared on the race route. Deceuninck sent riders to the front and took the descent at high speed, splitting the peloton. The main rider distanced was Egan Bernal's teammate Dani Martínez. Filippo Ganna was sent back for him and, after a struggle, the gap was closed. Egan's core mountain management team of Castroviejo and Martínez was reunited, and their plan survived. The script from Sega di Ala was good for another day. Almeida attacked early – with 7km to go this time – and Simon Yates attacked 500 metres higher up. This time, Egan stayed with his management team, allowed the Englishman a 30-second advantage, and held him there for the rest of the climb.

## TRIVIA
» Simon Yates hasn't won a bike race outside of Italy since 2019, taking five victories in the last two seasons.

## WEATHER

**TEMPERATURE**
23°C

**WIND**
NE 7km/h

## PROFILE

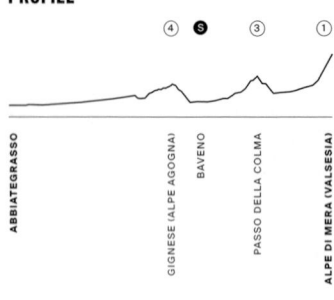

## BREAKAWAY
L. Warbasse (ACT), M. Christian (EOK), G. Aleotti (BOH), A. Pasqualon (IWG), N. Venchiarutti (ANS), Q. Hermans (AFC).

## GENERAL CLASSIFICATION
| POS | NAME | TEAM | TIME |
|---|---|---|---|
| 1. | E. Bernal | IGD | 81:13:37 |
| 2. | D. Caruso | TBV | 2:29 |
| 3. | S. Yates | BEX | 2:49 |
| 4. | A. Vlasov | APT | 6:11 |
| 5. | H. Carthy | EFN | 7:10 |
| 6. | R. Bardet | DSM | 7:32 |
| 7. | D. F. Martínez | IGD | 7:42 |
| 8. | J. Almeida | DQT | 8:26 |
| 9. | T. Foss | TJV | 10:19 |
| 10.– | D. Martin | ISN | 13:55 |

## KING OF THE MOUNTAINS
| POS | NAME | TEAM | PTS |
|---|---|---|---|
| 1. – | G. Bouchard | ACT | 180 |
| 2. – | E. Bernal | IGD | 121 |
| 3. – | D. Martin | ISN | 83 |

## POINTS
| POS | NAME | TEAM | PTS |
|---|---|---|---|
| 1. – | P. Sagan | BOH | 135 |
| 2. – | D. Cimolai | ISN | 113 |
| 3. – | F. Gaviria | UAD | 110 |

## YOUNG RIDER
| POS | NAME | TEAM | TIME |
|---|---|---|---|
| 1. – | E. Bernal | IGD | 81:13:37 |
| 2. – | A. Vlasov | APT | 6:11 |
| 3. – | D. F. Martínez | IGD | 7:42 |

## BONUSES
| TYPE | NAME | TEAM |
|---|---|---|
| KOM 1 | M. Christian | EOK |
| KOM 2 | L. Warbasse | ACT |
| KOM 3 | S. Yates | BEX |
| Sprint 1 | A. Pasqualon | IWG |

# STAGE RESULTS

| POS | NAME | TEAM | TIME |
|---|---|---|---|
| 1. | S. Yates | BEX | 4:02:55 |
| 2. | J. Almeida | DQT | 0:11 |
| 3. | E. Bernal | IGD | 0:28 |
| 4. | D. Caruso | TBV | 0:32 |
| 5. | A. Vlasov | APT | s.t. |
| 6. | D. Martin | ISN | 0:42 |
| 7. | D. F. Martínez | IGD | 0:49 |
| 8. | K. Bouwman | TJV | 1:25 |
| 9. | T. Foss | TJV | s.t. |
| 10. | R. Bardet | DSM | s.t. |
| 11. | H. Carthy | EFN | s.t. |
| 12. | G. Bennett | TJV | 2:46 |
| 13. | A. Covi | UAD | 3:20 |
| 14. | J. Hirt | IWG | 3:23 |
| 15. | E. Sepúlveda | ANS | s.t. |
| 16. | A. Valter | GFC | 3:30 |
| 17. | M. Badilatti | GFC | 3:34 |
| 18. | F. Großschartner | BOH | 4:01 |
| 19. | L. Fortunato | EOK | 4:12 |
| 20. | J. Castroviejo | IGD | 4:37 |
| 21. | S. Oldani | LTS | 4:48 |
| 22. | M. Storer | DSM | 4:56 |
| 23. | V. Nibali | TFS | 5:14 |
| 24. | D. Ulissi | UAD | s.t. |
| 25. | L. L. Sanchez | APT | s.t. |
| 26. | J. Janssens | AFC | s.t. |
| 27. | P. Bilbao | TBV | s.t. |
| 28. | R. Molard | GFC | 6:03 |
| 29. | T. Kangert | BEX | 6:11 |
| 30. | B. Mollema | TFS | 6:58 |
| 31. | C. Hamilton | DSM | 7:00 |
| 32. | M. Christian | EOK | 7:21 |
| 33. | V. Pronskiy | APT | s.t. |
| 34. | K. Frankiny | TQA | 8:11 |
| 35. | S. Petilli | IWG | s.t. |
| 36. | J. Narváez | IGD | 8:19 |
| 37. | G. Izaguirre | APT | 9:40 |
| 38. | H. Tejada | APT | s.t. |
| 39. | A. Pasqualon | IWG | 11:16 |
| 40. | Q. Hermans | IWG | s.t. |
| 41. | L. Warbasse | ACT | s.t. |
| 42. | J. Tratnik | TBV | 11:44 |
| 43. | J. Knox | DQT | s.t. |
| 44. | D. Formolo | UAD | 12:23 |
| 45. | V. Conti | UAD | s.t. |
| 46. | N. Oliveira | MOV | s.t. |
| 47. | D. Villella | MOV | s.t. |
| 48. | E. A. Rubio | MOV | s.t. |
| 49. | G. Carboni | BCF | 12:30 |
| 50. | L. van den Berg | GFC | s.t. |
| 51. | M. Nieve | BEX | 13:53 |
| 52. | M. Sobrero | APT | 13:54 |
| 53. | J. Keukeleire | EFN | s.t. |
| 54. | F. Felline | APT | s.t. |
| 55. | E. Ravasi | EOK | s.t. |
| 56. | L. Vervaeke | AFC | s.t. |
| 57. | P. Serry | DQT | s.t. |
| 58. | A. Ghebreigzabhier | TFS | s.t. |
| 59. | M. Fabbro | BOH | s.t. |
| 60. | F. Gaviria | UAD | s.t. |
| 61. | A. Vendrame | ACT | s.t. |
| 62. | N. Arndt | DSM | s.t. |
| 63. | P. Martens | TJV | 14:22 |
| 64. | G. Aleotti | BOH | 14:24 |
| 65. | F. Gavazzi | EOK | 14:35 |
| 66. | V. Albanese | EOK | 14:36 |
| 67. | Y. Arashiro | TBV | 15:48 |
| 68. | J. Mosca | TFS | 16:37 |
| 69. | G. Moscon | IGD | s.t. |
| 70. | C. Scotson | BEX | 17:14 |
| 71. | T. van Garderen | EFN | 17:32 |
| 72. | C. Meyer | BEX | 17:42 |
| 73. | F. Tagliani | ANS | 21:22 |
| 74. | M. Kanter | DSM | 21:57 |
| 75. | D. De Bondt | AFC | 22:29 |
| 76. | F. Ganna | IGD | 22:39 |
| 77. | A. Bettiol | EFN | s.t. |
| 78. | M. F. Honoré | DQT | s.t. |
| 79. | N. Roche | DSM | s.t. |
| 80. | F. Zana | BCF | 23:54 |
| 81. | G. Visconti | BCF | s.t. |
| 82. | B. J. Lindeman | TQA | 25:06 |
| 83. | F. Sabatini | COF | s.t. |
| 84. | P. Bevin | ISN | s.t. |
| 85. | A. Duchesne | GFC | s.t. |
| 86. | K. de Kort | TFS | s.t. |
| 87. | M. Jorgenson | MOV | s.t. |
| 88. | S. Leysen | AFC | s.t. |
| 89. | N. Tesfatsion | ANS | s.t. |
| 90. | A. Gougeard | ACT | s.t. |
| 91. | G. Vermeersch | AFC | s.t. |
| 92. | R. Valls | TBV | s.t. |
| 93. | S. Pellaud | ANS | s.t. |
| 94. | L. Naesen | ACT | s.t. |
| 95. | E. Battaglin | BCF | s.t. |
| 96. | M. Moschetti | TFS | s.t. |
| 97. | S. Puccio | IGD | s.t. |
| 98. | S. Ravanelli | ANS | s.t. |
| 99. | A. Ponomar | ANS | s.t. |
| 100. | G. Bouchard | ACT | s.t. |
| 101. | R. Taaramäe | IWG | s.t. |
| 102. | R. Seigle | GFC | s.t. |
| 103. | D. Gabburo | BCF | s.t. |
| 104. | C. Benedetti | BOH | s.t. |
| 105. | L. Wiśniowski | TQA | s.t. |
| 106. | N. Denz | DSM | s.t. |
| 107. | M. Schmid | TQA | s.t. |
| 108. | U. Marengo | BCF | s.t. |
| 109. | M. Dina | EOK | s.t. |
| 110. | G. Niv | ISN | s.t. |
| 111. | A. Viviani | COF | s.t. |
| 112. | T. Gallopin | ACT | s.t. |
| 113. | W. Kreder | IWG | s.t. |
| 114. | A. Pedrero | MOV | s.t. |
| 115. | D. Cataldo | MOV | s.t. |
| 116. | R. Cavagna | DQT | s.t. |
| 117. | T. van der Hoorn | IWG | 26:11 |
| 118. | I. Keisse | DQT | 26:14 |
| 119. | C. Juul-Jensen | BEX | 26:23 |
| 120. | S. Battistella | APT | 26:34 |
| 121. | R. Minali | IWG | s.t. |
| 122. | M. Hepburn | BEX | 26:57 |
| 123. | H. Vanhoucke | LTS | 27:22 |
| 124. | S. Carr | EFN | 27:26 |
| 125. | S. Guglielmi | GFC | s.t. |
| 126. | J. van den Berg | EFN | 28:11 |
| 127. | E. Affini | TJV | 28:26 |
| 128. | D. Oss | BOH | 28:33 |
| 129. | P. Sagan | BOH | s.t. |
| 130. | E. Viviani | COF | 28:38 |
| 131. | A. M. Richeze | UAD | s.t. |
| 132. | J. S. Molano | UAD | s.t. |
| 133. | F. Fiorelli | BCF | s.t. |
| 134. | M. Bodnar | BOH | s.t. |
| 135. | M. Brändle | ISN | 28:40 |
| 136. | O. Riesebeek | AFC | 28:47 |
| 137. | A. Krieger | AFC | s.t. |
| 138. | S. Consonni | COF | 29:16 |
| 139. | D. Cimolai | ISN | s.t. |
| 140. | M. Walscheid | TQA | s.t. |
| 141. | A. Torres | MOV | s.t. |
| 142. | N. Venchiarutti | ANS | s.t. |
| 143. | S. Zoccarato | BCF | s.t. |
| 144. | S. Rivi | EOK | s.t. |

MAY  WORLDTOUR MEN'S RACE

# GIRO D'ITALIA
Stage 20
29 May 2021
Verbania–Valle Spluga-Alpe Motta
164km

The intermediate sprints were two of the most enjoyable moments of the stage. When Dries De Bondt followed Umberto Marengo across the first of them at Cannobio, he secured the *traguardi volanti* title. Peter Sagan had no need to monitor the sprint but did so anyway, perhaps as a nod to his agent, Giovanni Lombardi, who won a stage out of Cannobio in 2003. It allowed him finally to celebrate winning the *maglia ciclamino*. When last year's *traguardi volanti* winner, Simon Pellaud, made it into the leading group, he ensured he would win the *fuga bianchi* breakaway competition. Meanwhile, Geoffrey Bouchard crossed the Passo San Bernardino sixth, taking 4 points. This left Bernal needing to win both final climbs to deprive the Frenchman of the jersey. On the descent, Team DSM's Chris Hamilton, Michael Storer and Romain Bardet attacked with over 57km to go, and Damiano Caruso's instinct was to follow. Bilbao set the pace on the descent from the Splügenpass, then Caruso dropped Bardet just before the second intermediate sprint, in Madesimo, 2.5km from the finish. He took maximum bonus seconds there, then pressed on towards a well-deserved victory. Behind him, Egan Bernal's final domestique, Dani Martínez, pulled aside to let his leader take the final bonus second then resumed his position at the front. It showed the clarity of thought he retained, despite riding at a pace that, moments later, Simon Yates and João Almeida would find themselves unable to follow. Martínez led the *maglia rosa* past Bardet under the *flamme rouge*, then Bernal darted away to limit his losses to his closest rival. To Caruso he conceded 24 seconds plus 4 bonus seconds. On his most feared rival, Simon Yates, he gained 51 seconds plus 6 bonus seconds. When Caruso won the stage, Dries De Bondt secured victory in the *combattività* competition. Egan Bernal would go into tomorrow's 30.3km time trial with a 1 minute 59 advantage over Caruso, who gained 6.46 seconds on him in the first time trial, or 0.722 seconds per kilometre. At the same rate, Bernal could expect to lose 21.9 seconds tomorrow. (MR)

## WEATHER

TEMPERATURE: 24°C
WIND: SW 15km/h

## PROFILE

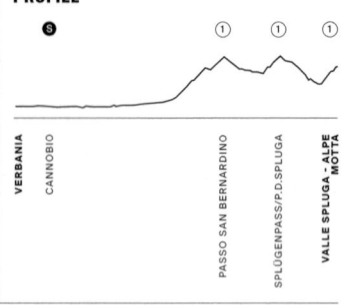

## BREAKAWAY
L. Vervaeke (AFC), F. Großschartner (BOH), S. Pellaud (ANS), V. Albanese (EOK), D. De Bondt (AFC), G. Visconti (BCF), M. Jorgenson (MOV), N. Denz (DSM), T. van der Hoorn (IWG)

## GENERAL CLASSIFICATION

| POS | NAME | TEAM | TIME |
|---|---|---|---|
| 1. — | E. Bernal | IGD | 85:41:47 |
| 2. — | D. Caruso | TBV | 1:59 |
| 3. — | S. Yates | BEX | 3:23 |
| 4. — | A. Vlasov | APT | 7:07 |
| 5. ↑1 | R. Bardet | DSM | 7:48 |
| 6. ↑1 | D. F. Martínez | IGD | 7:56 |
| 7. ↓2 | H. Carthy | EFN | 8:22 |
| 8. — | J. Almeida | DQT | 8:50 |
| 9. — | T. Foss | TJV | 12:39 |
| 10.— | D. Martin | ISN | 16:48 |

## KING OF THE MOUNTAINS

| POS | NAME | TEAM | PTS |
|---|---|---|---|
| 1. — | G. Bouchard | ACT | 184 |
| 2. — | E. Bernal | IGD | 140 |
| 3. ↑4 | D. Caruso | TBV | 99 |

## POINTS

| POS | NAME | TEAM | PTS |
|---|---|---|---|
| 1. — | P. Sagan | BOH | 136 |
| 2. — | D. Cimolai | ISN | 118 |
| 3. — | F. Gaviria | UAD | 116 |

## YOUNG RIDER

| POS | NAME | TEAM | TIME |
|---|---|---|---|
| 1. — | E. Bernal | IGD | 85:41:47 |
| 2. — | A. Vlasov | APT | 7:07 |
| 3. — | D. F. Martínez | IGD | 7:56 |

## BONUSES

| TYPE | NAME | TEAM |
|---|---|---|
| KOM 1 | G. Visconti | BCF |
| KOM 2 | M Storer | DSM |
| KOM 3 | D. Caruso | TBV |
| Sprint 1 | U. Marengo | EOK |

## STAGE RESULTS

| POS | NAME | TEAM | TIME |
|---|---|---|---|
| 1. | D. Caruso | TBV | 4:27:53 |
| 2. | E. Bernal | IGD | 0:24 |
| 3. | D. F. Martínez | IGD | 0:35 |
| 4. | R. Bardet | DSM | s.t. |
| 5. | J. Almeida | DQT | 0:41 |
| 6. | S. Yates | BEX | 0:51 |
| 7. | A. Vlasov | APT | 1:13 |
| 8. | H. Carthy | EFN | 1:29 |
| 9. | L. Fortunato | EOK | 2:07 |
| 10. | A. Pedrero | MOV | 2:23 |
| 11. | J. Hirt | IWG | s.t. |
| 12. | T. Foss | TJV | 2:37 |
| 13. | K. Bouwman | TJV | s.t. |
| 14. | D. Martin | ISN | 3:10 |
| 15. | G. Bennett | TJV | 3:42 |
| 16. | V. Pronskiy | APT | s.t. |
| 17. | P. Bilbao | TBV | 4:08 |
| 18. | E. A. Rubio | MOV | 4:10 |
| 19. | H. Tejada | APT | 4:44 |
| 20. | F. Großschartner | BOH | 5:29 |
| 21. | M. Nieve | BEX | 6:01 |
| 22. | D. Formolo | UAD | 6:25 |
| 23. | D. Cataldo | MOV | 6:41 |
| 24. | M. Storer | DSM | 6:46 |
| 25. | A. Valter | GFC | 6:50 |
| 26. | M. Fabbro | BOH | s.t. |
| 27. | S. Petilli | IWG | 6:55 |
| 28. | G. Bouchard | ACT | 6:56 |
| 29. | M. Badilatti | GFC | 7:00 |
| 30. | E. Sepúlveda | ANS | 7:33 |
| 31. | D. Ulissi | UAD | 8:02 |
| 32. | M. Schmid | TQA | s.t. |
| 33. | J. Knox | DQT | s.t. |
| 34. | L. Vervaeke | AFC | 8:15 |
| 35. | J. Castroviejo | IGD | 8:18 |
| 36. | E. Ravasi | EOK | 9:05 |
| 37. | G. Carboni | BCF | 12:28 |
| 38. | V. Nibali | TFS | 13:42 |
| 39. | B. Mollema | TFS | s.t. |
| 40. | A. Covi | UAD | s.t. |
| 41. | R. Molard | GFC | s.t. |
| 42. | P. Serry | DQT | s.t. |
| 43. | L. L. Sanchez | APT | s.t. |
| 44. | G. Izaguirre | APT | s.t. |
| 45. | T. Kangert | BEX | s.t. |
| 46. | L. Warbasse | ACT | 14:00 |
| 47. | F. Gavazzi | EOK | 14:18 |
| 48. | J. Janssens | AFC | 14:30 |
| 49. | S. Guglielmi | GFC | 14:53 |
| 50. | D. Villella | MOV | 14:55 |
| 51. | Q. Hermans | IWG | 17:58 |
| 52. | S. Leysen | AFC | s.t. |
| 53. | G. Niv | ISN | s.t. |
| 54. | J. Narváez | IGD | s.t. |
| 55. | S. Pellaud | ANS | s.t. |
| 56. | G. Moscon | IGD | 18:01 |
| 57. | K. Frankiny | TQA | 18:47 |
| 58. | V. Conti | UAD | 20:13 |
| 59. | N. Oliveira | MOV | 22:06 |
| 60. | M. Sobrero | APT | s.t. |
| 61. | P. Bevin | ISN | 22:10 |
| 62. | R. Seigle | GFC | 22:18 |
| 63. | A. Bettiol | EFN | 24:06 |
| 64. | J. Tratnik | TBV | s.t. |
| 65. | P. Martens | TJV | 24:25 |
| 66. | J. Keukeleire | EFN | 24:59 |
| 67. | S. Carr | EFN | s.t. |
| 68. | M. Jorgenson | MOV | s.t. |
| 69. | C. Hamilton | DSM | 25:38 |
| 70. | A. Pasqualon | IWG | 26:43 |
| 71. | S. Ravanelli | ANS | s.t. |
| 72. | C. Juul-Jensen | BEX | 27:09 |
| 73. | S. Puccio | IGD | 27:55 |
| 74. | F. Zana | BCF | 28:25 |
| 75. | A. Gougeard | ACT | s.t. |
| 76. | T. Gallopin | ACT | s.t. |
| 77. | A. Vendrame | ACT | s.t. |
| 78. | M. Dina | EOK | 29:50 |
| 79. | V. Albanese | EOK | s.t. |
| 80. | G. Aleotti | BOH | 31:17 |
| 81. | S. Battistella | APT | s.t. |
| 82. | Y. Arashiro | TBV | s.t. |
| 83. | R. Valls | TBV | s.t. |
| 84. | F. Fiorelli | BCF | s.t. |
| 85. | E. Battaglin | BCF | s.t. |
| 86. | G. Visconti | BCF | s.t. |
| 87. | B. J. Lindeman | TQA | s.t. |
| 88. | G. Vermeersch | AFC | s.t. |
| 89. | I. Keisse | DQT | 31:37 |
| 90. | A. Duchesne | GFC | s.t. |
| 91. | L. van den Berg | GFC | s.t. |
| 92. | M. Christian | EOK | s.t. |
| 93. | C. Benedetti | BOH | 31:39 |
| 94. | A. Ponomar | ANS | s.t. |
| 95. | D. Gabburo | BCF | s.t. |
| 96. | O. Riesebeek | AFC | s.t. |
| 97. | N. Denz | DSM | 32:05 |
| 98. | N. Arndt | DSM | s.t. |
| 99. | K. de Kort | TFS | 32:48 |
| 100. | T. van der Hoorn | IWG | s.t. |
| 101. | N. Roche | DSM | 32:58 |
| 102. | A. Ghebreigzabhier | TFS | 33:29 |
| 103. | N. Tesfatsion | ANS | s.t. |
| 104. | T. van Garderen | EFN | 33:45 |
| 105. | S. Oldani | LTS | 34:07 |
| 106. | M. Hepburn | BEX | 34:17 |
| 107. | C. Scotson | BEX | s.t. |
| 108. | M. Kanter | DSM | 34:18 |
| 109. | M. F. Honoré | DQT | 34:47 |
| 110. | J. van den Berg | EFN | 35:18 |
| 111. | D. Oss | BOH | 35:38 |
| 112. | F. Sabatini | COF | 37:36 |
| 113. | R. Minali | IWG | s.t. |
| 114. | L. Naesen | ACT | s.t. |
| 115. | N. Venchiarutti | ANS | s.t. |
| 116. | D. De Bondt | AFC | s.t. |
| 117. | U. Marengo | BCF | s.t. |
| 118. | J. Mosca | TFS | s.t. |
| 119. | M. Moschetti | TFS | s.t. |
| 120. | A. Viviani | COF | s.t. |
| 121. | F. Tagliani | ANS | s.t. |
| 122. | S. Zoccarato | BCF | s.t. |
| 123. | R. Taaramäe | IWG | 37:42 |
| 124. | E. Viviani | COF | 37:47 |
| 125. | F. Gaviria | UAD | s.t. |
| 126. | L. Wiśniowski | TQA | s.t. |
| 127. | W. Kreder | IWG | s.t. |
| 128. | E. Affini | TJV | s.t. |
| 129. | R. Cavagna | DQT | 37:53 |
| 130. | S. Consonni | COF | 38:05 |
| 131. | F. Ganna | IGD | s.t. |
| 132. | A. M. Richeze | UAD | s.t. |
| 133. | J. S. Molano | UAD | s.t. |
| 134. | M. Walscheid | TQA | s.t. |
| 135. | A. Krieger | AFC | s.t. |
| 136. | H. Vanhoucke | LTS | s.t. |
| 137. | M. Brändle | ISN | s.t. |
| 138. | C. Meyer | BEX | s.t. |
| 139. | S. Rivi | EOK | s.t. |
| 140. | A. Torres | MOV | 38:09 |
| 141. | M. Bodnar | BOH | 38:21 |
| 142. | P. Sagan | BOH | s.t. |
| 143. | D. Cimolai | ISN | s.t. |

## TRIVIA

» This was only Damiano Caruso's third professional win, and his first Grand Tour stage victory.

MAY  WORLDTOUR MEN'S RACE

# GIRO D'ITALIA
Stage 21 (ITT)
30 May 2021
Senago–Milan
30.3km

## WEATHER

TEMPERATURE  WIND
23°C  SE 7km/h

## PROFILE

SENAGO — MILANO

A puncture punctuated Filippo Ganna's performance, giving Rémi Cavagna the rare opportunity of a time trial win against the great Italian. But the Frenchman rode too hard, forgot the left-hand bend 500 metres from the finish, and rode straight into the barrier. After the stage, Ganna – now the only rider in history to have won five consecutive Giro time trials – observed, 'We played with the same hand, and the result is the same as if I hadn't punctured and he hadn't crashed.' If a half-hour time trial can be shaped by such drama, how much can go wrong in 86 hours, 17 minutes and 28 seconds? As someone said on social media, if the story of 2020 was Bernal's back, the story so far of 2021 is 'Bernal's back!' The Colombian conceded 30 seconds to Damiano Caruso, but gained 52 seconds on Simon Yates, who said sportingly, 'I came up against two guys who were much better than me, and this was the best I could do, so I'm happy.' Elsewhere in the top ten, Almeida jumped two places and Bardet dropped two. Yesterday's super-domestique, Dani Martínez, conceded 54 seconds to Almeida, exactly his GC advantage before the stage. The Colombian took fifth place overall by 0.053 seconds. Egan – who became the first rider to win the Giro wearing dossard 1 since Miguel Induráin in 1992 – joined Bartali, Gimondi and Merckx as the only riders in history to win the Giro and the Tour before their 25th birthdays. 'It is my first Giro, and it was very special because of the way we rode and the way I returned to being a contender after nearly two years,' he said. Peter Sagan said his *maglia ciclamino* win was 'Amazing for me. It was missing in my collection,' while *maglia azzurra* Geoffrey Bouchard whispered, 'It's wonderful to live moments like this. I've dreamed about this since I was a child.' (MR)

## GENERAL CLASSIFICATION

| POS | | NAME | TEAM | TIME |
|---|---|---|---|---|
| 1. | — | E. Bernal | IGD | 86:17:28 |
| 2. | — | D. Caruso | TBV | 1:29 |
| 3. | — | S. Yates | BEX | 4:15 |
| 4. | — | A. Vlasov | APT | 6:40 |
| 5. | ↑1 | D. F. Martínez | IGD | 7:24 |
| 6. | ↑2 | J. Almeida | DQT | s.t. |
| 7. | ↓2 | R. Bardet | DSM | 8:05 |
| 8. | ↓1 | H. Carthy | EFN | 8:56 |
| 9. | — | T. Foss | TJV | 11:44 |
| 10. | — | D. Martin | ISN | 18:35 |

## KING OF THE MOUNTAINS

| POS | | NAME | TEAM | PTS |
|---|---|---|---|---|
| 1. | — | G. Bouchard | ACT | 184 |
| 2. | — | E. Bernal | IGD | 140 |
| 3. | — | D. Caruso | TBV | 99 |

## POINTS

| POS | | NAME | TEAM | PTS |
|---|---|---|---|---|
| 1. | — | P. Sagan | BOH | 136 |
| 2. | — | D. Cimolai | ISN | 118 |
| 3. | — | F. Gaviria | UAD | 116 |

## TRIVIA

» The last time a Giro d'Italia time trial wasn't won by Filippo Ganna (stage 21, 2019) Remco Evenepoel hadn't won a professional bike race, Wout van Aert hadn't won a WorldTour race and Tadej Pogačar hadn't even raced a Grand Tour.

## YOUNG RIDER

| POS | | NAME | TEAM | TIME |
|---|---|---|---|---|
| 1. | — | E. Bernal | IGD | 86:17:28 |
| 2. | — | A. Vlasov | APT | 6:40 |
| 3. | — | D. F. Martínez | IGD | 7:24 |

## STAGE RESULTS

| POS | NAME | TEAM | TIME |
|---|---|---|---|
| 1. | F. Ganna | IGD | 33:48 |
| 2. | R. Cavagna | DQT | 0:12 |
| 3. | E. Affini | TJV | 0:13 |
| 4. | M. Sobrero | APT | 0:14 |
| 5. | J. Almeida | DQT | 0:27 |
| 6. | M. Walscheid | TQA | 0:33 |
| 7. | A. Bettiol | EFN | 0:34 |
| 8. | J. Tratnik | TBV | 0:42 |
| 9. | G. Moscon | IGD | 0:44 |
| 10. | I. Keisse | DQT | 0:47 |
| 11. | M. Bodnar | BOH | 0:54 |
| 12. | T. Foss | TJV | 0:58 |
| 13. | N. Arndt | DSM | 1:02 |
| 14. | D. F. Martínez | IGD | 1:21 |
| 15. | D. Ulissi | UAD | 1:23 |
| 16. | M. Brändle | ISN | s.t. |
| 17. | D. Caruso | TBV | s.t. |
| 18. | F. Großschartner | BOH | s.t. |
| 19. | A. Vlasov | APT | 1:26 |
| 20. | J. van den Berg | EFN | 1:38 |
| 21. | K. Bouwman | TJV | 1:45 |
| 22. | D. Formolo | UAD | 1:50 |
| 23. | M. Hepburn | BEX | 1:52 |
| 24. | E. Bernal | IGD | 1:53 |
| 25. | J. Castroviejo | IGD | 1:57 |
| 26. | N. Denz | DSM | 2:00 |
| 27. | P. Serry | DQT | 2:04 |
| 28. | R. Seigle | GFC | 2:05 |
| 29. | O. Riesebeek | AFC | 2:07 |
| 30. | L. L. Sanchez | APT | 2:09 |
| 31. | R. Bardet | DSM | 2:10 |
| 32. | G. Izagirre | APT | 2:11 |
| 33. | L. Wisniowski | TQA | 2:12 |
| 34. | M. F. Honoré | DQT | 2:13 |
| 35. | S. Battistella | APT | 2:19 |
| 36. | M. Jorgenson | MOV | 2:22 |
| 37. | H. Tejada | APT | 2:25 |
| 38. | V. Nibali | TFS | s.t. |
| 39. | H. Carthy | EFN | 2:27 |
| 40. | N. Oliveira | MOV | 2:28 |
| 41. | A. Covi | UAD | 2:29 |
| 42. | A. Valter | GFC | 2:32 |
| 43. | G. Bennett | TJV | 2:33 |
| 44. | S. Leysen | AFC | 2:34 |
| 45. | J. S. Molano | UAD | s.t. |
| 46. | L. Warbasse | ACT | 2:35 |
| 47. | S. Carr | EFN | 2:36 |
| 48. | J. Janssens | AFC | 2:38 |
| 49. | V. Pronskiy | APT | 2:41 |
| 50. | M. Kanter | DSM | 2:43 |
| 51. | S. Yates | BEX | 2:45 |
| 52. | P. Bevin | ISN | 2:46 |
| 53. | C. Juul-Jensen | BEX | 2:47 |
| 54. | A. Gougeard | ACT | 2:52 |
| 55. | A. Torres | MOV | 2:53 |
| 56. | A. Vendrame | ACT | 2:54 |
| 57. | P. Sagan | BOH | 2:59 |
| 58. | D. Cataldo | MOV | 3:01 |
| 59. | F. Gaviria | UAD | 3:02 |
| 60. | M. Fabbro | BOH | 3:04 |
| 61. | A. Ponomar | ANS | s.t. |
| 62. | G. Aleotti | BOH | 3:06 |
| 63. | M. Storer | DSM | 3:10 |
| 64. | J. Knox | DQT | s.t. |
| 65. | F. Zana | BCF | 3:14 |
| 66. | L. van den Berg | GFC | 3:15 |
| 67. | V. Conti | UAD | 3:20 |
| 68. | T. Kangert | BEX | 3:21 |
| 69. | S. Puccio | IGD | 3:22 |
| 70. | J. Hirt | IWG | s.t. |
| 71. | P. Martens | TJV | 3:23 |
| 72. | S. Consonni | COF | 3:26 |
| 73. | J. Keukeleire | EFN | s.t. |
| 74. | A. Pasqualon | IWG | 3:27 |
| 75. | R. Taaramäe | IWG | 3:28 |
| 76. | D. De Bondt | AFC | 3:30 |
| 77. | E. Sepúlveda | ANS | s.t. |
| 78. | F. Sabatini | COF | 3:32 |
| 79. | C. Scotson | BEX | 3:33 |
| 80. | A. M. Richeze | UAD | s.t. |
| 81. | A. Krieger | AFC | 3:38 |
| 82. | R. Minali | IWG | 3:39 |
| 83. | V. Albanese | EOK | 3:40 |
| 84. | D. Oss | BOH | s.t. |
| 85. | P. Bilbao | TBV | s.t. |
| 86. | D. Martin | ISN | s.t. |
| 87. | A. Ghebreigzabhier | TFS | 3:41 |
| 88. | S. Rivi | EOK | 3:42 |
| 89. | F. Tagliani | ANS | s.t. |
| 90. | J. Narváez | IGD | 3:43 |
| 91. | L. Vervaeke | AFC | s.t. |
| 92. | E. Viviani | COF | 3:45 |
| 93. | C. Hamilton | DSM | 3:47 |
| 94. | N. Roche | DSM | 3:48 |
| 95. | B. Mollema | TFS | 3:50 |

| POS | NAME | TEAM | TIME |
|---|---|---|---|
| 96. | J. Mosca | TFS | 3:51 |
| 97. | D. Villella | MOV | 3:52 |
| 98. | W. Kreder | IWG | s.t. |
| 99. | C. Meyer | BEX | 3:53 |
| 100. | Y. Arashiro | TBV | 3:55 |
| 101. | Q. Hermans | IWG | s.t. |
| 102. | D. Cimolai | ISN | 3:58 |
| 103. | F. Gavazzi | EOK | 3:59 |
| 104. | T. Gallopin | ACT | 4:01 |
| 105. | G. Bouchard | ACT | 4:03 |
| 106. | G. Carboni | BCF | 4:04 |
| 107. | M. Badilatti | GFC | 4:08 |
| 108. | S. Petilli | IWG | 4:09 |
| 109. | R. Molard | GFC | s.t. |
| 110. | M. Moschetti | TFS | 4:10 |
| 111. | E. Ravasi | EOK | s.t. |
| 112. | S. Ravanelli | ANS | 4:11 |
| 113. | A. Pedrero | MOV | 4:18 |
| 114. | A. Duchesne | GFC | s.t. |
| 115. | L. Naesen | ACT | 4:21 |
| 116. | S. Oldani | LTS | 4:22 |
| 117. | C. Benedetti | BOH | 4:23 |
| 118. | T. van Garderen | EFN | s.t. |
| 119. | M. Schmid | TQA | 4:25 |
| 120. | G. Visconti | BCF | 4:27 |
| 121. | K. Frankiny | TQA | 4:30 |
| 122. | B. J. Lindeman | TQA | 4:31 |
| 123. | M. Nieve | BEX | s.t. |
| 124. | K. de Kort | TFS | 4:36 |
| 125. | R. Valls | TBV | 4:37 |
| 126. | U. Marengo | BCF | 4:47 |
| 127. | A. Viviani | COF | 4:50 |
| 128. | E. Battaglin | BCF | 5:01 |
| 129. | G. Niv | ISN | 5:04 |
| 130. | D. Gabburo | BCF | 5:07 |
| 131. | S. Zoccarato | BCF | 5:08 |
| 132. | G. Vermeersch | AFC | 5:13 |
| 133. | L. Fortunato | EOK | 5:15 |
| 134. | S. Pellaud | ANS | 5:19 |
| 135. | T. van der Hoorn | IWG | 5:21 |
| 136. | S. Guglielmi | GFC | 5:24 |
| 137. | F. Fiorelli | BCF | 5:28 |
| 138. | M. Christian | EOK | 5:33 |
| 139. | M. Dina | EOK | 5:34 |
| 140. | N. Tesfatsion | ANS | s.t. |
| 141. | H. Vanhoucke | LTS | 5:40 |
| 142. | N. Venchiarutti | ANS | 5:50 |
| 143. | E. A. Rubio | MOV | 6:20 |

MAY

MAY  WORLDTOUR MEN'S RACE

# GIRO D'ITALIA
Final Classifications

## GENERAL CLASSIFICATION

| POS | NAME | TEAM | TIME |
|---|---|---|---|
| 1. | E. Bernal | IGD | 86:17:28 |
| 2. | D. Caruso | TBV | 1:29 |
| 3. | S. Yates | BEX | 4:15 |
| 4. | A. Vlasov | APT | 6:40 |
| 5. | D. F. Martínez | IGD | 7:24 |
| 6. | J. Almeida | DQT | s.t. |
| 7. | R. Bardet | DSM | 8:05 |
| 8. | H. Carthy | EFN | 8:56 |
| 9. | T. Foss | TJV | 11:44 |
| 10. | D. Martin | ISN | 18:35 |
| 11. | G. Bennett | TJV | 25:35 |
| 12. | K. Bouwman | TJV | 30:56 |
| 13. | P. Bilbao | TBV | 37:58 |
| 14. | A. Valter | GFC | 45:30 |
| 15. | D. Formolo | UAD | 47:21 |
| 16. | L. Fortunato | EOK | 47:31 |
| 17. | D. Ulissi | UAD | 56:32 |
| 18. | V. Nibali | TFS | 1:03:59 |
| 19. | G. Izagirre | APT | 1:04:12 |
| 20. | L. Vervaeke | AFC | 1:05:19 |
| 21. | T. Kangert | BEX | 1:07:25 |
| 22. | A. Pedrero | MOV | 1:07:50 |
| 23. | J. Castroviejo | IGD | 1:18:16 |
| 24. | G. Moscon | IGD | 1:18:17 |
| 25. | M. Nieve | BEX | 1:20:58 |
| 26. | J. Hirt | IWG | 1:32:42 |
| 27. | N. Oliveira | MOV | 1:36:27 |
| 28. | B. Mollema | TFS | 1:36:47 |
| 29. | F. Gavazzi | EOK | 1:40:19 |
| 30. | A. Bettiol | EFN | 1:43:43 |
| 31. | M. Storer | DSM | 1:49:05 |
| 32. | M. Fabbro | BOH | 1:49:23 |
| 33. | L. L. Sanchez | APT | 1:49:52 |
| 34. | M. Badilatti | GFC | 1:51:47 |
| 35. | G. Carboni | BCF | 2:00:45 |
| 36. | H. Tejada | APT | 2:01:12 |
| 37. | R. Molard | GFC | 2:02:01 |
| 38. | A. Covi | UAD | 2:03:30 |
| 39. | E. A. Rubio | MOV | 2:03:56 |
| 40. | V. Pronskiy | APT | 2:03:59 |
| 41. | L. Warbasse | ACT | 2:05:59 |
| 42. | L. Großschartner | BOH | 2:12:10 |
| 43. | Q. Hermans | IWG | 2:13:57 |
| 44. | S. Petilli | IWG | 2:14:12 |
| 45. | C. Hamilton | DSM | 2:17:55 |
| 46. | E. Ravasi | EOK | 2:18:40 |
| 47. | E. Sepúlveda | ANS | 2:20:12 |
| 48. | P. Bevin | ISN | 2:21:29 |
| 49. | J. Narváez | IGD | 2:21:53 |
| 50. | A. Vendrame | ACT | 2:23:42 |
| 51. | J. Taaramäe | IWG | 2:24:46 |
| 52. | J. Mosca | TFS | 2:27:00 |
| 53. | J. Knox | DQT | 2:29:17 |
| 54. | D. Cataldo | MOV | 2:29:24 |
| 55. | D. Villella | MOV | 2:29:51 |
| 56. | P. Serry | DQT | 2:30:40 |
| 57. | K. Frankiny | TQA | 2:34:36 |
| 58. | G. Bouchard | ACT | 2:36:35 |
| 59. | N. Roche | DSM | 2:41:13 |
| 60. | T. Gallopin | ACT | 2:46:05 |
| 61. | M. Sobrero | APT | 2:47:16 |
| 62. | N. Arndt | DSM | 2:56:04 |
| 63. | A. Ghebreigzabhier | TFS | 2:59:03 |
| 64. | L. van den Berg | GFC | 3:13:49 |
| 65. | J. Janssens | AFC | 3:15:06 |
| 66. | S. Carr | EFN | 3:18:32 |
| 67. | A. Ponomar | ANS | 3:18:33 |
| 68. | R. Cavagna | DQT | 3:19:43 |
| 69. | S. Pellaud | ANS | 3:20:10 |
| 70. | J. Tratnik | TBV | 3:22:28 |
| 71. | S. Ravanelli | ANS | 3:22:30 |
| 72. | A. Pasqualon | IWG | 3:23:57 |
| 73. | F. Zana | BCF | 3:28:45 |
| 74. | G. Niv | ISN | 3:33:32 |
| 75. | V. Albanese | EOK | 3:34:13 |
| 76. | M. Christian | EOK | 3:35:44 |
| 77. | Y. Arashiro | TBV | 3:36:24 |
| 78. | J. Keukeleire | EFN | 3:37:24 |
| 79. | S. Oldani | LTS | 3:39:11 |
| 80. | G. Aleotti | BOH | 3:40:28 |
| 81. | M. F. Honoré | DQT | 3:41:43 |
| 82. | S. Battistella | APT | 3:45:57 |
| 83. | C. Scotson | BEX | 3:46:05 |
| 84. | T. van Garderen | EFN | 3:46:16 |
| 85. | E. Battaglin | BCF | 3:47:55 |
| 86. | H. Vanhoucke | LTS | 3:49:07 |
| 87. | G. Vermeersch | AFC | 3:52:52 |
| 88. | R. Seigle | GFC | 3:55:23 |
| 89. | V. Conti | UAD | 3:58:45 |
| 90. | S. Guglielmi | GFC | 3:59:46 |
| 91. | D. De Bondt | AFC | 4:03:03 |
| 92. | N. Tesfatsion | ANS | 4:03:27 |
| 93. | M. Schmid | TQA | 4:03:47 |
| 94. | S. Puccio | IGD | 4:04:23 |
| 95. | G. Visconti | BCF | 4:04:45 |
| 96. | R. Valls | TBV | 4:04:52 |
| 97. | C. Juul-Jensen | BEX | 4:05:47 |
| 98. | M. Jorgenson | MOV | 4:05:48 |
| 99. | P. Martens | TJV | 4:09:07 |
| 100. | M. Dina | EOK | 4:11:55 |
| 101. | S. Leysen | AFC | 4:15:22 |
| 102. | N. Denz | DSM | 4:16:02 |
| 103. | C. Benedetti | BOH | 4:26:44 |
| 104. | O. Riesebeek | AFC | 4:33:33 |
| 105. | S. Zoccarato | BCF | 4:33:49 |
| 106. | D. Gabburo | BCF | 4:35:44 |
| 107. | T. van der Hoorn | IWG | 4:35:49 |
| 108. | F. Fiorelli | BCF | 4:36:05 |
| 109. | F. Gaviria | UAD | 4:37:48 |
| 110. | S. Consonni | COF | 4:38:16 |
| 111. | C. Meyer | BEX | 4:38:42 |
| 112. | D. Oss | BOH | 4:42:49 |
| 113. | E. Affini | TJV | 4:43:51 |
| 114. | A. Gougeard | ACT | 4:43:57 |
| 115. | A. Duchesne | GFC | 4:43:58 |
| 116. | M. Kanter | DSM | 4:46:24 |
| 117. | P. Sagan | BOH | s.t. |
| 118. | F. Ganna | IGD | 4:47:40 |
| 119. | L. Naesen | ACT | 4:47:48 |
| 120. | M. Hepburn | BEX | 4:47:58 |
| 121. | I. Keisse | DQT | 4:50:45 |
| 122. | B. J. Lindeman | TQA | 4:58:29 |
| 123. | F. Tagliani | ANS | 4:59:05 |
| 124. | M. Walscheid | TQA | 4:59:37 |
| 125. | J. van den Berg | EFN | 5:00:11 |
| 126. | J. S. Molano | UAD | 5:01:04 |
| 127. | D. Cimolai | ISN | 5:02:16 |
| 128. | W. Kreder | IWG | 5:02:43 |
| 129. | S. Rivi | EOK | 5:02:59 |
| 130. | M. Brändle | ISN | 5:03:34 |
| 131. | L. Wiśniowski | TQA | 5:08:11 |
| 132. | N. Venchiarutti | ANS | 5:08:13 |
| 133. | F. Sabatini | COF | 5:09:16 |
| 134. | K. de Kort | TFS | 5:11:05 |
| 135. | E. Viviani | COF | 5:12:15 |
| 136. | M. Bodnar | BOH | 5:14:42 |
| 137. | A. M. Richeze | UAD | 5:17:22 |
| 138. | A. Torres | MOV | 5:17:26 |
| 139. | U. Marengo | BCF | 5:19:06 |
| 140. | A. Krieger | AFC | 5:25:02 |
| 141. | M. Moschetti | TFS | 5:29:21 |
| 142. | A. Viviani | COF | 5:29:40 |
| 143. | R. Minali | IWG | 5:35:49 |

## KING OF THE MOUNTAINS

| POS | NAME | TEAM | PTS |
|---|---|---|---|
| 1. | G. Bouchard | ACT | 184 |
| 2. | E. Bernal | IGD | 140 |
| 3. | D. Caruso | TBV | 99 |
| 4. | D. Martin | ISN | 83 |
| 5. | S. Yates | BEX | 61 |
| 6. | J. Almeida | DQT | 54 |
| 7. | B. Mollema | TFS | 53 |
| 8. | L. Fortunato | EOK | 52 |
| 9. | R. Bardet | DSM | 49 |
| 10. | M. Storer | DSM | 46 |

## POINTS

| POS | NAME | TEAM | PTS |
|---|---|---|---|
| 1. | P. Sagan | BOH | 136 |
| 2. | D. Cimolai | ISN | 118 |
| 3. | F. Gaviria | UAD | 116 |
| 4. | E. Viviani | COF | 86 |
| 5. | E. Bernal | IGD | 80 |
| 6. | D. De Bondt | AFC | 71 |
| 7. | A. Pasqualon | IWG | 61 |
| 8. | S. Consonni | COF | 60 |
| 9. | E. Affini | TJV | 59 |
| 10. | A. Bettiol | EFN | 57 |

## YOUNG RIDER

| POS | NAME | TEAM | TIME |
|---|---|---|---|
| 1. | E. Bernal | IGD | 86:17:28 |
| 2. | A. Vlasov | APT | 6:40 |
| 3. | D. F. Martínez | IGD | 7:24 |
| 4. | J. Almeida | DQT | s.t. |
| 5. | T. Foss | TJV | 11:44 |
| 6. | A. Valter | GFC | 45:30 |
| 7. | L. Fortunato | EOK | 47:31 |
| 8. | M. Storer | DSM | 1:49:05 |
| 9. | H. Tejada | APT | 2:01:12 |
| 10. | A. Covi | UAD | 2:03:30 |

## TEAMS

| POS | NAME | TEAM | TIME |
|---|---|---|---|
| 1. | Ineos Grenadiers | IGD | 259:30:31 |
| 2. | Jumbo-Visma | TJV | 26:52 |
| 3. | Team DSM | DSM | 29:09 |
| 4. | Astana Premier Tech | APT | 33:05 |
| 5. | Team BikeExchange | BEX | 1:15:12 |
| 6. | Trek-Segafredo | TFS | 1:27:09 |
| 7. | Movistar Team | MOV | 1:28:18 |
| 8. | Deceuninck-QuickStep | DQT | 1:37:51 |
| 9. | Bahrain Victorious | TBV | 1:51:05 |
| 10. | UAE Team Emirates | UAD | 1:54:04 |
| 11. | EF Education-Nippo | EFN | 2:00:35 |
| 12. | Groupama-FDJ | GFC | 2:27:17 |
| 13. | Eolo-Kometa Cycling Team | EOK | 2:41:05 |
| 14. | Intermarché-Wanty-Gobert Matériaux | IWG | 2:46:29 |
| 15. | AG2R Citroën Team | ACT | 4:37:06 |
| 16. | Bora-Hansgrohe | BOH | 4:38:43 |
| 17. | Israel Start-Up Nation | ISN | 4:45:33 |
| 18. | Alpecin-Fenix | AFC | 5:12:49 |
| 19. | Androni Giocattoli-Sidermec | ANS | 5:19:23 |
| 20. | Bardiani CSF Faizane | BCF | 6:55:15 |
| 21. | Team Qhubeka Assos | TQA | 8:44:05 |
| 22. | Cofidis | COF | 9:37:59 |

## ABANDONS

| | |
|---|---|
| Stage 2 | K. Neilands (ISN) |
| Stage 5 | M. Landa (TBV) |
| Stage 6 | M. Belletti (EOK), F. Bidard (ACT), P. Sivakov (IGD), J. Dombrowski (UAD) |
| Stage 7 | D. Pozzovivo (TQA) |
| Stage 8 | C. Ewan (LTS) |
| Stage 9 | C. Champoussin (ACT), M. Mohorič (TBV), J. de Buyst (LTS), T. Marczyński (LTS) |
| Stage 11 | J. K. Caicedo (EFN), T. Merlier (AFC) |
| Stage 12 | G. Mäder (TBV), F. Masnada (DQT), A. De Marchi (ISN), A. Dowsett (ISN), K. Goossens (LTS), M. Soler (MOV) |
| Stage 14 | N. Edet (COF), R. Kluge (LTS), D. Dekker (TJV), D. Groenewegen (TJV), J. Hindley (DSM) |
| Stage 15 | E. Buchmann (BOH), N. Berhane (COF), R. Guerreiro (EFN), J. van Emden (TJV), G. Nizzolo (TQA) |
| Stage 16 | S. Reichenbach (GFC), T. De Gendt (LTS) |
| Stage 17 | R. Rochas (COF), V. Campenaerts (TQA) |
| Stage 18 | R. Evenepoel (DQT), N. Schultz (BEX), G. Ciccone (TFS) |
| Stage 19 | G. Brambilla (TFS), V. Lafay (COF), J. Cepeda Ortiz (ANS) |
| Stage 20 | F. Felline (APT) |

MAY  .1 MEN'S RACE

# TOUR DE HONGRIE
Stage 1
12 May 2021
Siófok–Kaposvár
173km

## WEATHER

TEMPERATURE: 17°C
WIND: S 11km/h

## STAGE RESULTS

| POS | NAME | TEAM | TIME |
|---|---|---|---|
| 1. | P. Bauhaus | TBV | 3:54:22 |
| 2. | J. Mareczko | THR | s.t. |
| 3. | J. Meeus | BOH | s.t. |
| 4. | R. Barbier | ISN | s.t. |
| 5. | T. Dupont | BWB | s.t. |
| 6. | K. Groves | BEX | s.t. |
| 7. | O. Kooij | TJV | s.t. |
| 8. | N. Larsen | UXT | s.t. |
| 9. | E. Blikra | UXT | s.t. |
| 10. | A. Dainese | DSM | s.t. |
| 11. | M. Malucelli | ANS | s.t. |
| 12. | S. Weemaes | SVB | s.t. |
| 13. | A. Banaszek | MSP | s.t. |
| 14. | E. Theuns | TFS | s.t. |
| 15. | D. González | CJR | s.t. |
| 16. | D. Cima | GAZ | s.t. |
| 17. | A. K. Karl | NAT | s.t. |
| 18. | A. Marit | SVB | s.t. |
| 19. | P. Simion | GTS | s.t. |
| 20. | L. Pacioni | EOK | s.t. |

## GENERAL CLASSIFICATION

| POS | NAME | TEAM | TIME |
|---|---|---|---|
| 1. | P. Bauhaus | TBV | 3:54:12 |
| 2. | J. Mareczko | THR | 0:04 |
| 3. | P. Stosz | VOS | s.t. |

## KING OF THE MOUNTAINS

| POS | NAME | TEAM | PTS |
|---|---|---|---|
| 1. | P. Stosz | VOS | 5 |
| 2. | D. P. Sevilla | EOK | 3 |
| 3. | F. Van den Bossche | SVB | 1 |

## POINTS

| POS | NAME | TEAM | PTS |
|---|---|---|---|
| 1. | P. Bauhaus | TBV | 15 |
| 2. | J. Mareczko | THR | 12 |
| 3. | P. Stosz | VOS | 10 |

# TOUR DE HONGRIE
Stage 2
13 May 2021
Balatonfüred–Nagykanizsa
182.6km

## WEATHER

TEMPERATURE: 17°C
WIND: N 7km/h

## STAGE RESULTS

| POS | NAME | TEAM | TIME |
|---|---|---|---|
| 1. | J. Meeus | BOH | 4:03:55 |
| 2. | A. Dainese | DSM | s.t. |
| 3. | P. Bauhaus | TBV | s.t. |
| 4. | O. Kooij | TJV | s.t. |
| 5. | K. Groves | BEX | s.t. |
| 6. | R. Barbier | ISN | s.t. |
| 7. | E. Theuns | TFS | s.t. |
| 8. | T. Dupont | BWB | s.t. |
| 9. | D. González | CJR | s.t. |
| 10. | J. Warlop | SVB | s.t. |
| 11. | O. Aular | CJR | s.t. |
| 12. | D. Martinelli | APT | s.t. |
| 13. | P. Stosz | VOS | s.t. |
| 14. | A. Banaszek | MSP | s.t. |
| 15. | F. Wright | TBV | s.t. |
| 16. | A. Marit | SVB | s.t. |
| 17. | C. Quarterman | TFS | s.t. |
| 18. | Y. Fedorov | APT | s.t. |
| 19. | E. Liepiņš | TFS | s.t. |
| 20. | P. Simion | GTS | s.t. |

## GENERAL CLASSIFICATION

| POS | NAME | TEAM | TIME |
|---|---|---|---|
| 1. ↑3 | J. Meeus | BOH | 7:58:03 |
| 2. ↓1 | P. Bauhaus | TBV | s.t. |
| 3. ↑30 | M. Paterski | VOS | 0:06 |

## KING OF THE MOUNTAINS

| POS | NAME | TEAM | PTS |
|---|---|---|---|
| 1. – | M. Paterski | VOS | 10 |
| 2. – | S. R. Martín | CJR | 6 |
| 3. ↓2 | P. Stosz | VOS | 5 |

## POINTS

| POS | NAME | TEAM | PTS |
|---|---|---|---|
| 1. ↑3 | J. Meeus | BOH | 25 |
| 2. ↓1 | P. Bauhaus | TBV | 25 |
| 3. – | M. Paterski | VOS | 13 |

MAY  .1 MEN'S RACE

## TOUR DE HONGRIE
Stage 3
14 May 2021
Veszprém–Tata
141.9km

## WEATHER

| TEMPERATURE | WIND |
|---|---|
| 9°C | NW 24km/h |

### STAGE RESULTS

| POS | NAME | TEAM | TIME |
|---|---|---|---|
| 1. | P. Bauhaus | TBV | 3:17:30 |
| 2. | M. Teunissen | TJV | s.t. |
| 3. | F. Wright | TBV | s.t. |
| 4. | D. Martinelli | APT | s.t. |
| 5. | M. Räim | MSP | s.t. |
| 6. | J. Warlop | SVB | s.t. |
| 7. | T. Dupont | BWB | s.t. |
| 8. | K. Halvorsen | UXT | s.t. |
| 9. | L. Pacioni | EOK | s.t. |
| 10. | T. Jones | ISN | s.t. |
| 11. | M. van Dijke | TJV | s.t. |
| 12. | H. Haussler | TBV | s.t. |
| 13. | E. Theuns | TFS | s.t. |
| 14. | E. Onesti | GTS | s.t. |
| 15. | S. Weemaes | SVB | s.t. |
| 16. | A. K. Karl | NAT | s.t. |
| 17. | P. Rikunov | GAZ | s.t. |
| 18. | K. Gradek | THR | s.t. |
| 19. | G. Katrašnik | ADR | s.t. |
| 20. | I. Boev | GAZ | s.t. |

### GENERAL CLASSIFICATION

| POS | NAME | TEAM | TIME |
|---|---|---|---|
| 1. ↑1 | P. Bauhaus | TBV | 11:15:23 |
| 2. ↓1 | J. Meeus | BOH | 0:10 |
| 3. ↑3 | P. Stosz | VOS | 0:15 |

### KING OF THE MOUNTAINS

| POS | NAME | TEAM | PTS |
|---|---|---|---|
| 1. — | M. Paterski | VOS | 15 |
| 2. ↑1 | P. Stosz | VOS | 13 |
| 3. ↓1 | S. R. Martín | CJR | 7 |

### POINTS

| POS | NAME | TEAM | PTS |
|---|---|---|---|
| 1. ↑1 | P. Bauhaus | TBV | 40 |
| 2. ↓1 | J. Meeus | BOH | 25 |
| 3. ↑6 | P. Stosz | VOS | 15 |

## TOUR DE HONGRIE
Stage 4
15 May 2021
Balassagyarmat–Gyöngyös-Kékestető
202.2km

## WEATHER

| TEMPERATURE | WIND |
|---|---|
| 15°C | S 11km/h |

### STAGE RESULTS

| POS | NAME | TEAM | TIME |
|---|---|---|---|
| 1. | D. Howson | BEX | 4:55:50 |
| 2. | B. Hermans | ISN | 0:09 |
| 3. | A. Tiberi | TFS | 0:15 |
| 4. | J. García | CJR | 0:19 |
| 5. | S. de Bod | APT | 0:32 |
| 6. | L. Huys | BWB | 0:38 |
| 7. | P. Cieślik | VOS | 0:41 |
| 8. | J. Romo | APT | s.t. |
| 9. | K. Colleoni | BEX | 0:44 |
| 10. | S. Buitrago | TBV | 0:46 |
| 11. | E. Fetter | EOK | 0:54 |
| 12. | K. Vermaerke | DSM | 0:56 |
| 13. | F. Van den Bossche | SVB | 1:00 |
| 14. | L. Wirtgen | BWB | 1:06 |
| 15. | G. Leemreize | TJV | 1:08 |
| 16. | O. Aular | CJR | 1:10 |
| 17. | K. Gradek | THR | s.t. |
| 18. | A. Ropero | EOK | s.t. |
| 19. | S. Rekita | VOS | 1:13 |
| 20. | P. Brożyna | MSP | 1:14 |

### GENERAL CLASSIFICATION

| POS | NAME | TEAM | TIME |
|---|---|---|---|
| 1. ↑33 | D. Howson | BEX | 16:11:24 |
| 2. ↑61 | B. Hermans | ISN | 0:16 |
| 3. ↑29 | A. Tiberi | TFS | 0:24 |

### KING OF THE MOUNTAINS

| POS | NAME | TEAM | PTS |
|---|---|---|---|
| 1. — | M. Paterski | VOS | 21 |
| 2. — | P. Stosz | VOS | 13 |
| 3. — | D. Howson | BEX | 10 |

### POINTS

| POS | NAME | TEAM | PTS |
|---|---|---|---|
| 1. — | P. Bauhaus | TBV | 45 |
| 2. — | J. Meeus | BOH | 25 |
| 3. — | D. Howson | BEX | 20 |

# TOUR DE HONGRIE

Stage 5
16 May 2021
Budapest–Budapest
92.4km

## WEATHER

| TEMPERATURE | WIND |
|---|---|
| 16°C | NW 18km/h |

## STAGE RESULTS

| POS | NAME | TEAM | TIME |
|---|---|---|---|
| 1. | E. Theuns | TFS | 1:55:46 |
| 2. | O. Kooij | TJV | s.t. |
| 3. | T. Dupont | BWB | s.t. |
| 4. | P. Bauhaus | TBV | s.t. |
| 5. | M. Malucelli | ANS | s.t. |
| 6. | J. Meeus | BOH | s.t. |
| 7. | S. Weemaes | SVB | s.t. |
| 8. | R. Barbier | ISN | s.t. |
| 9. | M. Teunissen | TJV | s.t. |
| 10. | O. Aular | CJR | s.t. |
| 11. | K. Groves | BEX | s.t. |
| 12. | D. González | CJR | s.t. |
| 13. | D. Martinelli | APT | s.t. |
| 14. | A. Tiberi | TFS | s.t. |
| 15. | P. Stosz | VOS | s.t. |
| 16. | D. Cima | GAZ | s.t. |
| 17. | J. Warlop | SVB | s.t. |
| 18. | A. Banaszek | MSP | s.t. |
| 19. | J. Mareczko | THR | s.t. |
| 20. | A. K. Karl | NAT | s.t. |

## GENERAL CLASSIFICATION

| POS | | NAME | TEAM | TIME |
|---|---|---|---|---|
| 1. | — | D. Howson | BEX | 18:07:10 |
| 2. | — | B. Hermans | ISN | 0:16 |
| 3. | — | A. Tiberi | TFS | 0:24 |

## KING OF THE MOUNTAINS

| POS | | NAME | TEAM | PTS |
|---|---|---|---|---|
| 1. | — | M. Paterski | VOS | 21 |
| 2. | — | P. Stosz | VOS | 13 |
| 3. | — | D. Howson | BEX | 10 |

## POINTS

| POS | | NAME | TEAM | PTS |
|---|---|---|---|---|
| 1. | — | P. Bauhaus | TBV | 53 |
| 2. | — | J. Meeus | BOH | 30 |
| 3. | ↑13 | E. Theuns | TFS | 24 |

## CIRCUIT DE WALLONIE

13 May 2021
Charleroi–Charleroi
194.2km

## WEATHER

TEMPERATURE
10°C

WIND
SW 24km/h

## RESULTS

| POS | NAME | TEAM | TIME |
|---|---|---|---|
| 1. | C. Laporte | COF | 4:18:42 |
| 2. | M. Sarreau | ACT | s.t. |
| 3. | L. Pithie | CGF | s.t. |
| 4. | S. Aniołkowski | BWB | s.t. |
| 5. | S. Wærenskjold | UXT | s.t. |
| 6. | M. Budding | BCY | s.t. |
| 7. | S. Van Tricht | SEG | s.t. |
| 8. | F. Vermeersch | LTS | s.t. |
| 9. | D. McLay | ARK | s.t. |
| 10. | M. Bostock | DHB | s.t. |
| 11. | L. Kubiš | DKB | s.t. |
| 12. | B. Planckaert | IWG | s.t. |
| 13. | M. Meisen | AFC | s.t. |
| 14. | B. Turner | TRI | s.t. |
| 15. | T. Roosen | JVD | s.t. |
| 16. | P. Penhoët | CGF | s.t. |
| 17. | J. Fouché | BSC | s.t. |
| 18. | I. Andersen | UXT | s.t. |
| 19. | C. Russo | ARK | s.t. |
| 20. | R. Townsend | DHB | s.t. |

MAY  .1 MEN'S RACE

## TROFEO CALVIÀ
13 May 2021
Peguera–Palmanova
168.7km

## WEATHER

**TEMPERATURE**
21°C

**WIND**
SW 24km/h

## RESULTS

| POS | NAME | TEAM | TIME |
|---|---|---|---|
| 1. | R. Gibbons | UAD | 4:21:04 |
| 2. | A. Delaplace | ARK | s.t. |
| 3. | R. Herregodts | SVB | 0:41 |
| 4. | E. Lietaer | BBK | 0:44 |
| 5. | J. López | EKP | s.t. |
| 6. | S. E. Byström | UAD | s.t. |
| 7. | J. J. Lobato | EUS | s.t. |
| 8. | K. Ledanois | ARK | s.t. |
| 9. | M. Lammertink | IWG | s.t. |
| 10. | W. Smit | BBH | s.t. |
| 11. | D. Claeys | TQA | s.t. |
| 12. | T. Sprengers | SVB | s.t. |
| 13. | S. Velasco | GAZ | s.t. |
| 14. | R. Hardy | ARK | s.t. |
| 15. | J. Bouček | ISN | s.t. |
| 16. | S. Chernetski | GAZ | s.t. |
| 17. | M. Chevalier | BBK | s.t. |
| 18. | D. Savini | BCF | s.t. |
| 19. | F. Bonnamour | BBK | s.t. |
| 20. | J. Maas | LPC | s.t. |

MAY　　　.1 MEN'S RACE

# TROFEO SERRA DE TRAMUNTANA
14 May 2021
Lloseta–Deià
158.6km

## WEATHER

TEMPERATURE
20°C

WIND
NW 24km/h

## RESULTS

| POS | NAME | TEAM | TIME |
|---|---|---|---|
| 1. | Je. Herrada | COF | 3:52:21 |
| 2. | J. Lastra | CJR | s.t. |
| 3. | H. Carretero | MOV | 0:11 |
| 4. | M. Würst Schmidt | ISN | 0:20 |
| 5. | A. Kristoff | UAD | s.t. |
| 6. | R. Hardy | ARK | s.t. |
| 7. | G. Zimmermann | IWG | s.t. |
| 8. | G. Serrano | MOV | s.t. |
| 9. | C. Scaroni | GAZ | s.t. |
| 10. | F. Bonnamour | BBK | s.t. |
| 11. | R. Gibbons | UAD | s.t. |
| 12. | R. Thalmann | NAT | s.t. |
| 13. | D. Savini | BCF | s.t. |
| 14. | A. Garosio | BCF | s.t. |
| 15. | F. Barceló | COF | s.t. |
| 16. | M. Chevalier | BBK | s.t. |
| 17. | J. López | EKP | s.t. |
| 18. | D. Strakhov | GAZ | s.t. |
| 19. | S. Kipkemboi | BAI | s.t. |
| 20. | S. Chernetski | GAZ | s.t. |

MAY  .1 MEN'S RACE

# TROFEO ANDRATX
15 May 2021
Andratx–Mirador d'Es Colomer (Pollença)
161.3km

## WEATHER

TEMPERATURE  WIND
21°C         SW 26km/h

## RESULTS

| POS | NAME | TEAM | TIME |
| --- | --- | --- | --- |
| 1. | W. Anacona | ARK | 4:04:30 |
| 2. | V. S. Laengen | UAD | 0:10 |
| 3. | M. Iturria | EUS | 0:13 |
| 4. | Je. Herrada | COF | 1:34 |
| 5. | R. Herregodts | SVB | 1:39 |
| 6. | G. Mannion | RLY | s.t. |
| 7. | M. Chevalier | BBK | s.t. |
| 8. | G. Zimmermann | IWG | s.t. |
| 9. | J. Bellicaud | IWG | s.t. |
| 10. | Se. Bennett | TQA | 1:44 |
| 11. | J. Maas | LPC | 1:46 |
| 12. | A. Delaplace | ARK | s.t. |
| 13. | R. Gibbons | UAD | s.t. |
| 14. | J. López | EKP | 1:49 |
| 15. | S. Velasco | GAZ | 1:51 |
| 16. | F. Bonnamour | BBK | 1:54 |
| 17. | J. F. Parra | EKP | 1:55 |
| 18. | M. Bizkarra | EUS | 1:57 |
| 19. | A. González | MOV | 2:00 |
| 20. | A. Garosio | BCF | 2:03 |

MAY  .PRO MEN'S RACE

# TRO-BRO LÉON

16 May 2021
Lannilis–Lannilis
207km

## WEATHER

TEMPERATURE | WIND
12°C | W 39km/h

## RESULTS

| POS | NAME | TEAM | TIME |
|---|---|---|---|
| 1. | C. Swift | ARK | 5:18:38 |
| 2. | P. Allegaert | COF | s.t. |
| 3. | B. Planckaert | IWG | s.t. |
| 4. | O. Le Gac | GFC | s.t. |
| 5. | R. Tiller | UXT | s.t. |
| 6. | J. Degenkolb | LTS | 0:26 |
| 7. | O. Naesen | ACT | s.t. |
| 8. | B. Welten | ARK | s.t. |
| 9. | C. Laporte | COF | s.t. |
| 10. | K. Geniets | GFC | s.t. |
| 11. | P. Gilbert | LTS | s.t. |
| 12. | J. Leveau | XRL | s.t. |
| 13. | B. Thomas | GFC | s.t. |
| 14. | C. Russo | ARK | s.t. |
| 15. | R. Cardis | AUB | s.t. |
| 16. | V. Ferron | TDE | s.t. |
| 17. | E. Planckaert | AFC | s.t. |
| 18. | L. Eriksson | RIW | s.t. |
| 19. | J. El Fares | EFN | s.t. |
| 20. | J. Bouts | BCY | s.t. |

MAY   .1 MEN'S RACE

## TROFEO ALCUDIA
16 May 2021
Alcudia–Alcudia
169.8km

## WEATHER

TEMPERATURE
25°C

WIND
SW 22km/h

## RESULTS

| POS | NAME | TEAM | TIME |
|---|---|---|---|
| 1. | A. Greipel | ISN | 3:50:24 |
| 2. | A. Kristoff | UAD | s.t. |
| 3. | C. Noppe | ARK | s.t. |
| 4. | R. Janse Van Rensburg | TQA | s.t. |
| 5. | G. Cullaigh | MOV | s.t. |
| 6. | H. Hofstetter | ISN | s.t. |
| 7. | G. Lonardi | BCF | s.t. |
| 8. | T. Devriendt | IWG | s.t. |
| 9. | X. Cañellas | GIS | s.t. |
| 10. | E. Vernon | NAT | s.t. |
| 11. | E. Zanoncello | BCF | s.t. |
| 12. | S. Thurau | TDA | s.t. |
| 13. | Ó. Pelegrí | EHE | s.t. |
| 14. | L. De Vylder | SVB | s.t. |
| 15. | A. Van Poucke | SVB | s.t. |
| 16. | S. De Pestel | SVB | s.t. |
| 17. | S. Sajnok | COF | s.t. |
| 18. | M. Canola | GAZ | s.t. |
| 19. | D. Grondin | ARK | s.t. |
| 20. | J. J. Lobato | EUS | s.t. |

MAY    .PRO MEN'S RACE

## VUELTA A ANDALUCIA
Stage 1
18 May 2021
Mijas–Zahara de la Sierra
152.1km

### STAGE RESULTS

| POS | NAME | TEAM | TIME |
|---|---|---|---|
| 1. | G. Serrano | MOV | 3:54:25 |
| 2. | O. Aular | CJR | s.t. |
| 3. | D. Impey | ISN | s.t. |
| 4. | E. Hayter | IGD | s.t. |
| 5. | R. Stannard | BEX | 0:03 |
| 6. | M. Canola | GAZ | s.t. |
| 7. | J. Cepeda Hernández | CJR | s.t. |
| 8. | T. Skujiņš | TFS | s.t. |
| 9. | M. A. López | MOV | s.t. |
| 10. | A. Tolhoek | TJV | s.t. |
| 11. | S. E. Bystrøm | UAD | s.t. |
| 12. | J. Lastra | CJR | s.t. |
| 13. | J. F. Parra | EKP | s.t. |
| 14. | L. A. Maté | EUS | s.t. |
| 15. | R. Gibbons | UAD | 0:07 |
| 16. | R. Herregodts | SVB | s.t. |
| 17. | C. Rodriguez | IGD | s.t. |
| 18. | G. Martín | EUS | s.t. |
| 19. | R. Adrià | EKP | s.t. |
| 20. | H. Carretero | MOV | 0:12 |

### WEATHER

TEMPERATURE  WIND
22°C         SE 19km/h

### GENERAL CLASSIFICATION

| POS | NAME | TEAM | TIME |
|---|---|---|---|
| 1. | G. Serrano | MOV | 3:54:25 |
| 2. | O. Aular | CJR | s.t. |
| 3. | D. Impey | ISN | s.t. |

### KING OF THE MOUNTAINS

| POS | NAME | TEAM | PTS |
|---|---|---|---|
| 1. | R. Oliveira | UAD | 12 |
| 2. | A. Soto | EUS | 8 |
| 3. | T. Sprengers | SVB | 4 |

### POINTS

| POS | NAME | TEAM | PTS |
|---|---|---|---|
| 1. | G. Serrano | MOV | 25 |
| 2. | O. Aular | CJR | 20 |
| 3. | D. Impey | ISN | 16 |

## VUELTA A ANDALUCIA
Stage 2
19 May 2021
Iznájar–Alcalá la Real
184.8km

### STAGE RESULTS

| POS | NAME | TEAM | TIME |
|---|---|---|---|
| 1. | E. Hayter | IGD | 5:04:30 |
| 2. | M. A. López | MOV | 0:07 |
| 3. | S. E. Bystrøm | UAD | 0:10 |
| 4. | C. Rodriguez | IGD | 0:14 |
| 5. | J. Amezqueta | CJR | s.t. |
| 6. | J. Lastra | CJR | 0:17 |
| 7. | R. Stannard | BEX | 0:18 |
| 8. | O. Rodríguez | APT | 0:23 |
| 9. | T. Skujiņš | TFS | 0:25 |
| 10. | R. Adrià | EKP | s.t. |
| 11. | G. Serrano | MOV | s.t. |
| 12. | A. Tolhoek | TJV | s.t. |
| 13. | D. Impey | ISN | 0:31 |
| 14. | F. Fisher-Black | TJV | 0:33 |
| 15. | J. Gregaard | APT | 0:35 |
| 16. | Á. Madrazo | BBH | 0:37 |
| 17. | A. Nibali | TFS | 0:43 |
| 18. | R. Gibbons | UAD | s.t. |
| 19. | R. Herregodts | SVB | s.t. |
| 20. | J. Cepeda Hernández | CJR | 0:51 |

### WEATHER

TEMPERATURE  WIND
28°C         N 6km/h

### GENERAL CLASSIFICATION

| POS | NAME | TEAM | TIME |
|---|---|---|---|
| 1. ↑3 | E. Hayter | IGD | 8:58:55 |
| 2. ↑7 | M. A. López | MOV | 0:10 |
| 3. ↑8 | S. E. Bystrøm | UAD | 0:13 |

### KING OF THE MOUNTAINS

| POS | NAME | TEAM | PTS |
|---|---|---|---|
| 1. — | R. Oliveira | UAD | 26 |
| 2. — | A. Cuadros Morata | CJR | 11 |
| 3. ↓1 | A. Soto | EUS | 8 |

### POINTS

| POS | NAME | TEAM | PTS |
|---|---|---|---|
| 1. ↑3 | E. Hayter | IGD | 39 |
| 2. ↓1 | G. Serrano | MOV | 30 |
| 3. ↑6 | M. A. López | MOV | 27 |

MAY .PRO MEN'S RACE

## VUELTA A ANDALUCIA
Stage 3
20 May 2021
Beas de Segura–Villarrodrigo (Puerto de Onsares)
176.9km

### WEATHER

TEMPERATURE | WIND
27°C | E 4km/h

### STAGE RESULTS

| POS | NAME | TEAM | TIME |
|---|---|---|---|
| 1. | M. A. López | MOV | 5:03:26 |
| 2. | A. Tolhoek | TJV | 0:02 |
| 3. | J. Piccoli | ISN | 0:06 |
| 4. | J. Amezqueta | CJR | 0:17 |
| 5. | M. Bizkarra | EUS | 0:28 |
| 6. | H. Carretero | MOV | 1:25 |
| 7. | C. Rodríguez | IGD | 1:29 |
| 8. | T. Skujiņš | TFS | s.t. |
| 9. | J. Lastra | CJR | 1:41 |
| 10. | O. Rodríguez | APT | 2:07 |
| 11. | R. Herregodts | SVB | 2:23 |
| 12. | E. Hayter | IGD | s.t. |
| 13. | R. Adrià | EKP | s.t. |
| 14. | R. Gibbons | UAD | s.t. |
| 15. | J. Cepeda Hernández | CJR | 2:25 |
| 16. | J. Gregaard | APT | 2:28 |
| 17. | U. Cuadrado | EUS | s.t. |
| 18. | F. De Tier | AFC | s.t. |
| 19. | T. Grmay | BEX | 2:33 |
| 20. | D. Nekrasov | GAZ | 2:34 |

### GENERAL CLASSIFICATION

| POS | | NAME | TEAM | TIME |
|---|---|---|---|---|
| 1. | ↑1 | M. A. López | MOV | 14:02:31 |
| 2. | ↑7 | A. Tolhoek | TJV | 0:20 |
| 3. | ↑10 | J. Amezqueta | CJR | 0:55 |

### KING OF THE MOUNTAINS

| POS | | NAME | TEAM | PTS |
|---|---|---|---|---|
| 1. | ↑16 | L. A. Maté | EUS | 27 |
| 2. | ↓1 | R. Oliveira | UAD | 27 |
| 3. | ↑4 | T. Sprengers | SVB | 15 |

### POINTS

| POS | | NAME | TEAM | PTS |
|---|---|---|---|---|
| 1. | ↑2 | M. A. López | MOV | 52 |
| 2. | ↓1 | E. Hayter | IGD | 43 |
| 3. | ↓1 | G. Serrano | MOV | 30 |

## VUELTA A ANDALUCIA
Stage 4
21 May 2021
Baza–Cúllar Vega
182.9km

### WEATHER

TEMPERATURE | WIND
28°C | W 7km/h

### STAGE RESULTS

| POS | NAME | TEAM | TIME |
|---|---|---|---|
| 1. | A. Greipel | ISN | 4:37:12 |
| 2. | A. J. Hodeg | DQT | s.t. |
| 3. | M. Pedersen | TFS | s.t. |
| 4. | A. Kristoff | UAD | s.t. |
| 5. | A. Kirsch | TFS | s.t. |
| 6. | R. Zabel | ISN | s.t. |
| 7. | E. Sanz | EKP | s.t. |
| 8. | E. Hayter | IGD | s.t. |
| 9. | A. Konychev | BEX | s.t. |
| 10. | T. Bayer | AFC | s.t. |
| 11. | B. Van Lerberghe | DQT | s.t. |
| 12. | R. Gibbons | UAD | s.t. |
| 13. | J. J. Lobato | EUS | s.t. |
| 14. | P. Eenkhoorn | TJV | s.t. |
| 15. | M. Canola | GAZ | s.t. |
| 16. | G. Serrano | MOV | s.t. |
| 17. | R. Stannard | BEX | s.t. |
| 18. | G. Brussenskiy | APT | s.t. |
| 19. | M. A. López | MOV | s.t. |
| 20. | C. Canal | BBH | s.t. |

### GENERAL CLASSIFICATION

| POS | | NAME | TEAM | TIME |
|---|---|---|---|---|
| 1. | — | M. A. López | MOV | 18:39:43 |
| 2. | — | A. Tolhoek | TJV | 0:20 |
| 3. | — | J. Amezqueta | CJR | 0:55 |

### KING OF THE MOUNTAINS

| POS | | NAME | TEAM | PTS |
|---|---|---|---|---|
| 1. | — | L. A. Maté | EUS | 33 |
| 2. | — | R. Oliveira | UAD | 27 |
| 3. | — | T. Sprengers | SVB | 15 |

### POINTS

| POS | | NAME | TEAM | PTS |
|---|---|---|---|---|
| 1. | — | M. A. López | MOV | 52 |
| 2. | — | E. Hayter | IGD | 51 |
| 3. | — | G. Serrano | MOV | 30 |

## VUELTA A ANDALUCIA

Stage 5
22 May 2021
Vera–Pulpí
107km

### WEATHER

TEMPERATURE | WIND
22°C | S 9km/h

### STAGE RESULTS

| POS | NAME | TEAM | TIME |
|---|---|---|---|
| 1. | E. Hayter | IGD | 2:27:12 |
| 2. | P. Walsleben | AFC | s.t. |
| 3. | T. Skujiņš | TFS | s.t. |
| 4. | M. A. López | MOV | s.t. |
| 5. | S. E. Bystrøm | UAD | s.t. |
| 6. | G. Serrano | MOV | s.t. |
| 7. | O. Rodríguez | APT | s.t. |
| 8. | A. Tolhoek | TJV | s.t. |
| 9. | T. Grmay | BEX | s.t. |
| 10. | C. Rodriguez | IGD | 0:03 |
| 11. | P. Eenkhoorn | TJV | 0:10 |
| 12. | S. Archbold | DQT | s.t. |
| 13. | R. Gibbons | UAD | s.t. |
| 14. | N. Van Hooydonck | TJV | s.t. |
| 15. | H. Carretero | MOV | 0:15 |
| 16. | J. Gregaard | APT | s.t. |
| 17. | J. Lastra | CJR | s.t. |
| 18. | J. J. Rojas | MOV | s.t. |
| 19. | J. Amezqueta | CJR | s.t. |
| 20. | M. Bizkarra | EUS | 0:24 |

### GENERAL CLASSIFICATION

| POS | | NAME | TEAM | TIME |
|---|---|---|---|---|
| 1. | — | M. A. López | MOV | 21:06:55 |
| 2. | — | A. Tolhoek | TJV | 0:20 |
| 3. | — | J. Amezqueta | CJR | 1:10 |

### KING OF THE MOUNTAINS

| POS | | NAME | TEAM | PTS |
|---|---|---|---|---|
| 1. | — | L. A. Maté | EUS | 33 |
| 2. | — | R. Oliveira | UAD | 27 |
| 3. | — | T. Sprengers | SVB | 15 |

### POINTS

| POS | | NAME | TEAM | PTS |
|---|---|---|---|---|
| 1. | ↑1 | E. Hayter | IGD | 76 |
| 2. | ↓1 | M. A. López | MOV | 66 |
| 3. | — | G. Serrano | MOV | 40 |

MAY  WORLDTOUR WOMEN'S RACE

# VUELTA A BURGOS
Stage 1
20 May 2021
Villadiego–Sargentes de la Lora
100km

Stage 1 covered 100 rolling kilometres and finished at the Geoparque Las Loras after the Alto de la Lora climb, followed by another 6km of gentle but steady climbing. After an early breakaway of three riders had been reeled in with 45km to go, Amalie Dideriksen went on a short-lived solo. This was followed by an attack by her Trek-Segafredo teammate Shirin van Anrooij, who built a gap of over a minute but was caught just before the start of the Alto de La Lora climb. There were no moves until Grace Brown (Team BikeExchange) and Elise Chabbey (Canyon-SRAM) attacked just before the top. They were joined by Niamh Fisher-Black (Team SD Worx) on a short downhill. The front trio never was more than 20 seconds ahead but held off the chasing peloton to the finish, where Brown won the stage.

## WEATHER

TEMPERATURE: 19°C
WIND: SW 11km/h

## PROFILE

VILLADIEGO — ALTO DE COCULINA (3) — ALTO DE LA LORA (3) / SARGENTES DE LA LORA

## BREAKAWAY
M. Benito (MAT), H. Franz (RLW), V. Looser (ILP)

## STAGE RESULTS

| POS | NAME | TEAM | TIME |
|---|---|---|---|
| 1. | G. Brown | BEX | 2:28:28 |
| 2. | E. Chabbey | CSR | s.t. |
| 3. | N. Fisher-Black | SDW | s.t. |
| 4. | A. Sierra | MNX | 0:05 |
| 5. | S. Paladin | LIV | s.t. |
| 6. | S. Bertizzolo | LIV | s.t. |
| 7. | E. Longo Borghini | TFS | s.t. |
| 8. | D. Vollering | SDW | s.t. |
| 9. | T. Neumanova | WCS | s.t. |
| 10. | A. van Vleuten | MOV | s.t. |
| 11. | T. Dronova-Balabolina | CGS | s.t. |
| 12. | K. Niewiadoma | CSR | s.t. |
| 13. | A. Spratt | BEX | s.t. |
| 14. | É. Muzic | FDJ | s.t. |
| 15. | K. Doebel-Hickok | RLW | s.t. |
| 16. | M. García | ALE | s.t. |
| 17. | A. Santesteban | BEX | s.t. |
| 18. | A. Moolman | SDW | s.t. |
| 19. | M. Harvey | CSR | s.t. |
| 20. | Š. Kern | MAT | s.t. |

## GENERAL CLASSIFICATION

| POS | NAME | TEAM | TIME |
|---|---|---|---|
| 1. | G. Brown | BEX | 2:28:28 |
| 2. | E. Chabbey | CSR | s.t. |
| 3. | N. Fisher-Black | SDW | s.t. |

## QUEEN OF THE MOUNTAINS

| POS | NAME | TEAM | PTS |
|---|---|---|---|
| 1. | G. Brown | BEX | 6 |
| 2. | H. Franz | RLW | 6 |
| 3. | E. Chabbey | CSR | 4 |

## POINTS

| POS | NAME | TEAM | PTS |
|---|---|---|---|
| 1. | G. Brown | BEX | 25 |
| 2. | E. Chabbey | CSR | 20 |
| 3. | N. Fisher-Black | SDW | 16 |

## YOUNG RIDER

| POS | NAME | TEAM | TIME |
|---|---|---|---|
| 1. | N. Fisher-Black | SDW | 2:28:28 |
| 2. | T. Neumanova | WCS | 0:05 |
| 3. | É. Muzic | FDJ | s.t. |

## TRIVIA
» This was Grace Brown's second WorldTour win this season – and the first two of her career.

## BONUSES

| TYPE | NAME | TEAM |
|---|---|---|
| QOM 1 | H. Franz | RLW |
| QOM 2 | G. Brown | BEX |

MAY — WORLDTOUR WOMEN'S RACE

# VUELTA A BURGOS
Stage 2
21 May 2021
Pedrosa de Valdeporres–Villarcayo
97km

On a stage with a flat finish, one rider from the break of the day went all the way to the finish while her two companions were caught by the chasing peloton. Anastasia Chursina (Alé BTC Ljubljana), Heidi Franz (Rally Cycling), and Antri Christoforou (Women Cycling Sport) had attacked just after the day's first classified climb and increased their advantage to 4 minutes 10 seconds, putting Chursina into the virtual overall lead. On the final climb, the Alto Retuerta, Chursina dropped Franz and Christoforou, and when Franz came back on the descent, the Russian attacked again and soloed to the finish to win the stage 1 minute 11 seconds ahead of the peloton that had reeled in the other two escapees in the final. As there were no time bonifications in the race, Elise Chabbey took over the GC leader's jersey due to a better stage placing than Brown. ⓘⓚ

## WEATHER

TEMPERATURE: 20°C
WIND: SW 26km/h

## PROFILE

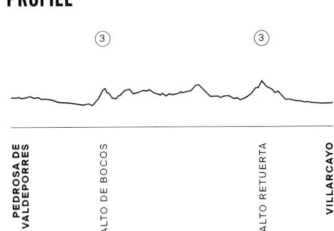

PEDROSA DE VALDEPORRES — ALTO DE BOCOS (3) — ALTO RETUERTA (3) — VILLARCAYO

## STAGE RESULTS

| POS | NAME | TEAM | TIME |
|---|---|---|---|
| 1. | A. Chursina | ALE | 2:29:28 |
| 2. | A. Barnes | CSR | 1:11 |
| 3. | A. Diderikson | TFS | s.t. |
| 4. | A. Sierra | MNX | s.t. |
| 5. | S. Alonso | BDU | s.t. |
| 6. | L. Tomasi | ALE | s.t. |
| 7. | E. Duval | FDJ | s.t. |
| 8. | J. Erić | MOV | s.t. |
| 9. | D. Vollering | SDW | s.t. |
| 10. | M. Le Net | FDJ | s.t. |
| 11. | S. Persico | VAL | s.t. |
| 12. | M. Lach | WNT | s.t. |
| 13. | A. Fidanza | BEX | s.t. |
| 14. | E. Chabbey | CSR | s.t. |
| 15. | K. Niewiadoma | CSR | s.t. |
| 16. | T. Neumanova | WCS | s.t. |
| 17. | T. Dronova-Balabolina | CGS | s.t. |
| 18. | K. Ragusa | MNX | s.t. |
| 19. | A. Moolman | SDW | s.t. |
| 20. | N. Fisher-Black | SDW | s.t. |

## GENERAL CLASSIFICATION

| POS | NAME | TEAM | TIME |
|---|---|---|---|
| 1. ↑1 | E. Chabbey | CSR | 4:59:07 |
| 2. ↑1 | N. Fisher-Black | SDW | s.t. |
| 3. ↓2 | G. Brown | BEX | s.t. |

## QUEEN OF THE MOUNTAINS

| POS | NAME | TEAM | PTS |
|---|---|---|---|
| 1. ↑1 | H. Franz | RLW | 10 |
| 2. ↑3 | N. Fisher-Black | SDW | 9 |
| 3. ↓2 | G. Brown | BEX | 6 |

## POINTS

| POS | NAME | TEAM | PTS |
|---|---|---|---|
| 1. ↑3 | A. Sierra | MNX | 28 |
| 2. ↓1 | G. Brown | BEX | 25 |
| 3. — | A. Chursina | ALE | 25 |

## YOUNG RIDER

| POS | NAME | TEAM | TIME |
|---|---|---|---|
| 1. — | N. Fisher-Black | SDW | 4:59:07 |
| 2. — | T. Neumanova | WCS | 0:05 |
| 3. ↑1 | M. Harvey | CSR | s.t. |

## TRIVIA
» This was Chursina's first victory outside her native Russia.

## BONUSES

| TYPE | NAME | TEAM |
|---|---|---|
| QOM 1 | N. Fisher-Black | SDW |
| QOM 2 | A. Chursina | ALE |

MAY · WORLDTOUR WOMEN'S RACE

# VUELTA A BURGOS
Stage 3
22 May 2021
Medina de Pomar–Ojo Guareña
115.4km

No breakaway was let go on the first 90km before an aggressive finale on the last 27km. After a first attack by Mavi García, Niamh Fisher-Black led Cecilie Uttrup Ludwig and Pauliena Rooijakkers (Liv Racing) over the Alto de las Hoyas, but they were caught again on the descent. The next move by Evita Muzic (FDJ Nouvelle-Aquitaine Futuroscope) and Sabrina Stultiens (Liv Racing) was followed by attacks from Erica Magnaldi (Ceratizit-WNT), Tayler Wiles (Trek-Segafredo) and Karol-Ann Canuel (Team SD Worx). Canuel went on another move with GC leader Elise Chabbey, but they were caught on the finishing climb. Grace Brown led the peloton into the uphill sprint, and Fisher-Black was the first to open up. She was quickly passed by Katarzyna Niewiadoma but the Pole was then overtaken by Uttrup Ludwig, who took her first Women's WorldTour victory. Fisher-Black took the overall lead ahead of the final stage.

## WEATHER

TEMPERATURE: 24°C
WIND: NE 7km/h

## PROFILE

## STAGE RESULTS

| POS | NAME | TEAM | TIME |
|---|---|---|---|
| 1. | C. U. Ludwig | FDJ | 3:00:28 |
| 2. | K. Niewiadoma | CSR | s.t. |
| 3. | A. van der Breggen | SDW | s.t. |
| 4. | E. Longo Borghini | TFS | s.t. |
| 5. | N. Fisher-Black | SDW | 0:03 |
| 6. | M. García | ALE | s.t. |
| 7. | D. Vollering | SDW | s.t. |
| 8. | A. van Vleuten | MOV | s.t. |
| 9. | A. Moolman | SDW | s.t. |
| 10. | S. Paladin | LIV | s.t. |
| 11. | G. Brown | BEX | s.t. |
| 12. | A. Santesteban | BEX | s.t. |
| 13. | K. Doebel-Hickok | RLW | s.t. |
| 14. | A. Sierra | MNX | 0:11 |
| 15. | E. Magnaldi | WNT | s.t. |
| 16. | K. Aalerud | MOV | s.t. |
| 17. | É. Muzic | FDJ | s.t. |
| 18. | S. Persico | VAL | s.t. |
| 19. | S. Stultiens | LIV | s.t. |
| 20. | T. Dronova-Balabolina | CGS | 0:14 |

## GENERAL CLASSIFICATION

| POS | NAME | TEAM | TIME |
|---|---|---|---|
| 1. ↑1 | N. Fisher-Black | SDW | 7:59:38 |
| 2. ↑1 | G. Brown | BEX | s.t. |
| 3. ↑4 | K. Niewiadoma | CSR | 0:02 |

## QUEEN OF THE MOUNTAINS

| POS | NAME | TEAM | PTS |
|---|---|---|---|
| 1. ↑1 | N. Fisher-Black | SDW | 15 |
| 2. — | C. U. Ludwig | FDJ | 10 |
| 3. ↓2 | H. Franz | RLW | 10 |

## POINTS

| POS | NAME | TEAM | PTS |
|---|---|---|---|
| 1. ↑1 | G. Brown | BEX | 30 |
| 2. ↓1 | A. Sierra | MNX | 30 |
| 3. ↑3 | N. Fisher-Black | SDW | 28 |

## YOUNG RIDER

| POS | NAME | TEAM | TIME |
|---|---|---|---|
| 1. — | N. Fisher-Black | SDW | 7:59:38 |
| 2. ↑2 | É. Muzic | FDJ | 0:13 |
| 3. ↓1 | T. Neumanova | WCS | 0:16 |

## TRIVIA

» This was Cecilie Uttrup Ludwig's tenth career win, and her only one at WorldTour level.

## BONUSES

| TYPE | NAME | TEAM |
|---|---|---|
| QOM 1 | N. Fisher-Black | SDW |
| QOM 2 | C. U. Ludwig | FDJ |

MAY     WORLDTOUR WOMEN'S RACE

# VUELTA A BURGOS
Stage 4
23 May 2021
Quintanar de la Sierra–Lagunas de Neila
121.6km

The Vuelta a Burgos ended with a mountain-top finish at the Lagunas de Neila atop a 12.5km climb. A group of 30 riders had gone away 50km from the finish, and 14 of them were still 45 seconds ahead when the climb started. Halfway up, only Amanda Spratt (Team BikeExchange), Katrine Aalerud (Movistar Team), Anna Shackley (Team SD Worx) and Clara Koppenburg (Rally Cycling) remained. They attacked each other on the climb several times but always came back together. In what remained of the peloton, Karol-Ann Canuel worked hard to reduce the gap, and Demi Vollering's work caught the last escapees on the final kilometre. Anna van der Breggen held off Annemiek van Vleuten on the last metres of the climb to win the stage and the GC plus the points and mountain jerseys. Niamh Fisher-Black was the best Under-23 rider.

## WEATHER

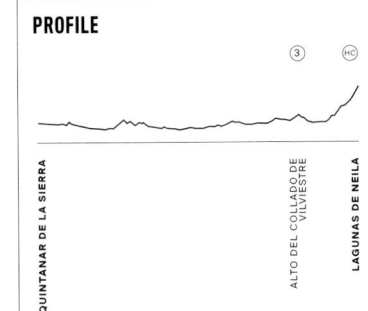

TEMPERATURE     WIND
14°C            N 9km/h

## PROFILE

## BREAKAWAY
A. Spratt (BEX), K. Aalerud (MOV), A. Shackley (SDW), C. Koppenburg (RLW)

## STAGE RESULTS

| POS | NAME | TEAM | TIME |
|---|---|---|---|
| 1. | A. van der Breggen | SDW | 3:24:15 |
| 2. | A. van Vleuten | MOV | s.t. |
| 3. | D. Vollering | SDW | 0:20 |
| 4. | P. Rooijakkers | LIV | 0:35 |
| 5. | C. Koppenburg | RLW | 0:37 |
| 6. | K. Aalerud | MOV | 0:51 |
| 7. | C. U. Ludwig | FDJ | 1:04 |
| 8. | A. Moolman | SDW | 1:06 |
| 9. | G. Brown | BEX | 1:09 |
| 10. | A. Spratt | BEX | 1:17 |
| 11. | K. Niewiadoma | CSR | 1:25 |
| 12. | E. Longo Borghini | TFS | 1:27 |
| 13. | O. Zabelinskaya | CGS | s.t. |
| 14. | É. Muzic | FDJ | 1:34 |
| 15. | N. Fisher-Black | SDW | 1:43 |
| 16. | S. Stultiens | LIV | 1:42 |
| 17. | E. Chabbey | CSR | 1:46 |
| 18. | M. Harvey | CSR | s.t. |
| 19. | K. Doebel-Hickok | RLW | 1:51 |
| 20. | M. Reusser | ALE | 1:54 |

## GENERAL CLASSIFICATION

| POS | NAME | TEAM | TIME |
|---|---|---|---|
| 1. ↑5 | A. van der Breggen | SDW | 11:23:55 |
| 2. ↑10 | A. van Vleuten | MOV | 0:03 |
| 3. ↑4 | D. Vollering | SDW | 0:23 |

## QUEEN OF THE MOUNTAINS

| POS | NAME | TEAM | PTS |
|---|---|---|---|
| 1. ↑9 | A. van der Breggen | SDW | 32 |
| 2. — | A. van Vleuten | MOV | 25 |
| 3. — | D. Vollering | SDW | 20 |

## POINTS

| POS | NAME | TEAM | PTS |
|---|---|---|---|
| 1. ↑11 | A. van der Breggen | SDW | 41 |
| 2. ↑5 | D. Vollering | SDW | 40 |
| 3. ↓2 | G. Brown | BEX | 37 |

## YOUNG RIDER

| POS | NAME | TEAM | TIME |
|---|---|---|---|
| 1. — | N. Fisher-Black | SDW | 11:25:36 |
| 2. — | É. Muzic | FDJ | 0:04 |
| 3. ↑1 | M. Harvey | CSR | 0:27 |

## TRIVIA
» This was Anna van der Breggen's 12th GC victory of her career.

## BONUSES

| TYPE | NAME | TEAM |
|---|---|---|
| QOM 1 | A. Spratt | BEX |
| QOM 2 | A. van der Breggen | SDW |

MAY  .1 MEN'S RACE

## TOUR DU FINISTÈRE
22 May 2021
Saint-Evarzec–Quimper
196.3km

## WEATHER

TEMPERATURE
12°C

WIND
W 24km/h

## RESULTS

| POS | NAME | TEAM | TIME |
|---|---|---|---|
| 1. | B. Cosnefroy | ACT | 4:58:43 |
| 2. | S. De Bie | BWB | s.t. |
| 3. | R. Tiller | UXT | s.t. |
| 4. | A. Vuillermoz | TDE | s.t. |
| 5. | B. Planckaert | IWG | s.t. |
| 6. | J. Simon | TDE | s.t. |
| 7. | R. Hardy | ARK | s.t. |
| 8. | J. Hivert | BBK | s.t. |
| 9. | C. Barthe | BBK | s.t. |
| 10. | D. Touzé | ACT | s.t. |
| 11. | R. Cardis | AUB | 0:03 |
| 12. | F. Lienhard | GFC | s.t. |
| 13. | B. Coquard | BBK | s.t. |
| 14. | V. Ferron | TDE | s.t. |
| 15. | L. Rota | IWG | s.t. |
| 16. | A. Jensen | DKO | s.t. |
| 17. | E. Morin | COF | s.t. |
| 18. | M. Burgaudeau | TDE | s.t. |
| 19. | D. Godon | ACT | s.t. |
| 20. | A. Goeman | TIS | 0:14 |

## VUELTA A MURCIA

23 May 2021
Los Alcázares–Alcantarilla
192.4km

## WEATHER

TEMPERATURE
18°C

WIND
NE 30km/h

### RESULTS

| POS | NAME | TEAM | TIME |
|---|---|---|---|
| 1. | A. Soto | EUS | 4:42:19 |
| 2. | Á. Madrazo | BBH | 0:31 |
| 3. | G. Serrano | MOV | s.t. |
| 4. | J. J. Rojas | MOV | s.t. |
| 5. | R. Gibbons | UAD | s.t. |
| 6. | J. Ezquerra | BBH | s.t. |
| 7. | C. Canal | BBH | s.t. |
| 8. | G. Martín | EUS | s.t. |
| 9. | J. Gregaard | APT | s.t. |
| 10. | U. Cuadrado | EUS | s.t. |
| 11. | J. Amezqueta | CJR | s.t. |
| 12. | J. Lastra | CJR | s.t. |
| 13. | A. Berlin | GLC | s.t. |
| 14. | A. Cuadros Morata | CJR | s.t. |
| 15. | K. Swirbul | RLY | s.t. |
| 16. | U. Berrade | EKP | 0:41 |
| 17. | M. A. Ballesteros | EHE | 1:51 |
| 18. | A. Kristoff | UAD | 2:02 |
| 19. | M. Vacek | GAZ | s.t. |
| 20. | A. Okamika | BBH | s.t. |

MAY    .1 MEN'S RACE

## MERCAN'TOUR CLASSIC ALPES-MARITIMES
24 May 2021
Saint-Sauveur-sur-Tinée–Col de Valberg
149.9km

## WEATHER

TEMPERATURE
15°C

WIND
SW 6km/h

## RESULTS

| POS | NAME | TEAM | TIME |
|---|---|---|---|
| 1. | G. Martin | COF | 4:23:56 |
| 2. | A. Paret-Peintre | ACT | 1:42 |
| 3. | B. Armirail | GFC | s.t. |
| 4. | A. Perez | COF | 2:40 |
| 5. | M. Frank | ACT | 2:43 |
| 6. | A. Moreno | VBG | 2:53 |
| 7. | J. Cabot | TDE | 2:56 |
| 8. | R. Thalmann | VBG | 3:05 |
| 9. | I. Andersen | UXT | 3:20 |
| 10. | J. Hänninen | ACT | 3:36 |
| 11. | J. M. Díaz | DKO | 4:14 |
| 12. | L. Morton | EFN | s.t. |
| 13. | D. Rosa | ARK | 4:52 |
| 14. | A. Guerin | VBG | 4:54 |
| 15. | S. Rossetto | AUB | 5:26 |
| 16. | E. Lietaer | BBK | 5:43 |
| 17. | V. Langellotti | BBH | 6:00 |
| 18. | R. Fernández | COF | 6:59 |
| 19. | N. Prodhomme | ACT | 7:57 |
| 20. | C. Berthet | DKO | 8:38 |

MAY  .1 MEN'S RACE

# RONDE VAN LIMBURG
24 May 2021
Hasselt–Tongeren
199.8km

## WEATHER

TEMPERATURE  WIND
12°C  S 28km/h

## RESULTS

| POS | NAME | TEAM | TIME |
|---|---|---|---|
| 1. | T. Merlier | AFC | 4:41:35 |
| 2. | D. McLay | ARK | s.t. |
| 3. | J. Degenkolb | LTS | s.t. |
| 4. | R. Janse Van Rensburg | TQA | s.t. |
| 5. | B. Welten | ARK | s.t. |
| 6. | M. Menten | BWB | s.t. |
| 7. | S. Van Tricht | SEG | s.t. |
| 8. | B. van Poppel | IWG | s.t. |
| 9. | J. Lecroq | BBK | s.t. |
| 10. | R. Townsend | DHB | s.t. |
| 11. | C. van Uden | DDS | s.t. |
| 12. | A. Marit | SVB | s.t. |
| 13. | W. Vanhoof | SVB | s.t. |
| 14. | T. Paquot | BWB | s.t. |
| 15. | R. Apers | SVB | s.t. |
| 16. | A. Stokbro | TQA | s.t. |
| 17. | F. Van den Bossche | SVB | s.t. |
| 18. | J. Fouché | BSC | s.t. |
| 19. | J. Drizners | HBA | s.t. |
| 20. | T. Aerts | TBL | s.t. |

MAY .PRO MEN'S RACE

## BOUCLES DE LA MAYENNE
Stage 1
27 May 2021
Le Genest-Saint-Isle–Ambrières-les-Vallées
175km

### WEATHER

TEMPERATURE | WIND
16°C | E 4km/h

### STAGE RESULTS

| POS | NAME | TEAM | TIME |
|---|---|---|---|
| 1. | P. Walsleben | AFC | 3:59:48 |
| 2. | D. Rubio | BBH | 0:07 |
| 3. | A. Démare | GFC | 0:11 |
| 4. | K. Halvorsen | UXT | s.t. |
| 5. | B. Coquard | BBK | s.t. |
| 6. | P. Allegaert | COF | s.t. |
| 7. | M. Sarreau | ACT | s.t. |
| 8. | N. Eekhoff | DSM | s.t. |
| 9. | B. Welten | ARK | 0:15 |
| 10. | J. Aberasturi | CJR | 0:17 |
| 11. | C. Barthe | BBK | s.t. |
| 12. | E. Vermeulen | XRL | s.t. |
| 13. | B. Cosnefroy | ACT | s.t. |
| 14. | F. Maurelet | AUB | s.t. |
| 15. | J. Trarieux | DKO | s.t. |
| 16. | D. McLay | ARK | s.t. |
| 17. | K. Reza | BBK | s.t. |
| 18. | R. Tiller | UXT | s.t. |
| 19. | D. Kowalski | XRL | s.t. |
| 20. | K. Van Rooy | SVB | s.t. |

### GENERAL CLASSIFICATION

| POS | NAME | TEAM | TIME |
|---|---|---|---|
| 1. | P. Walsleben | AFC | 3:59:33 |
| 2. | D. Rubio | BBH | 0:16 |
| 3. | A. Démare | GFC | 0:22 |

### KING OF THE MOUNTAINS

| POS | NAME | TEAM | PTS |
|---|---|---|---|
| 1. | M. Urruty | XRL | 30 |
| 2. | R. Adrià | EKP | 10 |
| 3. | D. Rubio | BBH | 9 |

### POINTS

| POS | NAME | TEAM | PTS |
|---|---|---|---|
| 1. | P. Walsleben | AFC | 35 |
| 2. | D. Rubio | BBH | 20 |
| 3. | A. Démare | GFC | 16 |

### YOUNG RIDER

| POS | NAME | TEAM | TIME |
|---|---|---|---|
| 1. | N. Eekhoff | DSM | 3:59:59 |
| 2. | B. Welten | ARK | 0:04 |
| 3. | M. Peñalver | BBH | 0:06 |

## BOUCLES DE LA MAYENNE
Stage 2
28 May 2021
Vaiges–Évron
173km

### WEATHER

TEMPERATURE | WIND
21°C | E 17km/h

### STAGE RESULTS

| POS | NAME | TEAM | TIME |
|---|---|---|---|
| 1. | A. Démare | GFC | 4:11:32 |
| 2. | N. Bonifazio | TDE | s.t. |
| 3. | K. Halvorsen | UXT | s.t. |
| 4. | J. Koch | IWG | s.t. |
| 5. | S. Aniołkowski | BWB | s.t. |
| 6. | P. Allegaert | COF | s.t. |
| 7. | M. Malucelli | ANS | s.t. |
| 8. | E. Vermeulen | XRL | s.t. |
| 9. | J. Aberasturi | CJR | s.t. |
| 10. | N. Eekhoff | DSM | s.t. |
| 11. | B. Welten | ARK | s.t. |
| 12. | J. Guarnieri | GFC | s.t. |
| 13. | A. de Kleijn | RLY | s.t. |
| 14. | K. Van Rooy | SVB | s.t. |
| 15. | C. Barthe | BBK | s.t. |
| 16. | J. Drucker | COF | s.t. |
| 17. | J. Leveau | XRL | s.t. |
| 18. | A. Delettre | DKO | s.t. |
| 19. | T. Willems | SVB | s.t. |
| 20. | S. Velasco | GAZ | s.t. |

### GENERAL CLASSIFICATION

| POS | NAME | TEAM | TIME |
|---|---|---|---|
| 1. — | P. Walsleben | AFC | 8:11:05 |
| 2. ↑1 | A. Démare | GFC | 0:12 |
| 3. ↓1 | D. Rubio | BBH | 0:16 |

### KING OF THE MOUNTAINS

| POS | NAME | TEAM | PTS |
|---|---|---|---|
| 1. — | M. Urruty | XRL | 30 |
| 2. — | S. Dewulf | ACT | 29 |
| 3. — | M. van Niekerk | AUB | 22 |

### POINTS

| POS | NAME | TEAM | PTS |
|---|---|---|---|
| 1. ↑2 | A. Démare | GFC | 41 |
| 2. ↓1 | P. Walsleben | AFC | 35 |
| 3. ↑1 | K. Halvorsen | UXT | 30 |

### YOUNG RIDER

| POS | NAME | TEAM | TIME |
|---|---|---|---|
| 1. — | N. Eekhoff | DSM | 8:11:31 |
| 2. — | B. Welten | ARK | 0:04 |
| 3. ↑2 | S. Aniołkowski | BWB | 0:06 |

MAY .PRO MEN'S RACE

# BOUCLES DE LA MAYENNE
Stage 3
29 May 2021
Saint-Berthevin–Craon
182km

## WEATHER

TEMPERATURE | WIND
22°C | E 11km/h

## STAGE RESULTS

| POS | NAME | TEAM | TIME |
|---|---|---|---|
| 1. | A. Démare | GFC | 4:18:48 |
| 2. | K. Halvorsen | UXT | s.t. |
| 3. | N. Eekhoff | DSM | s.t. |
| 4. | A. de Kleijn | RLY | s.t. |
| 5. | S. Aniołkowski | BWB | s.t. |
| 6. | P. Allegaert | COF | s.t. |
| 7. | D. McLay | ARK | s.t. |
| 8. | E. Vermeulen | XRL | s.t. |
| 9. | S. Weemaes | SVB | s.t. |
| 10. | J. Aberasturi | CJR | s.t. |
| 11. | B. Coquard | BBK | s.t. |
| 12. | T. Bayer | AFC | s.t. |
| 13. | P. Barbier | DKO | s.t. |
| 14. | C. Barthe | BBK | s.t. |
| 15. | D. Kowalski | XRL | s.t. |
| 16. | M. Malucelli | ANS | s.t. |
| 17. | F. Maurelet | AUB | s.t. |
| 18. | N. Bonifazio | TDE | s.t. |
| 19. | L. De Vylder | SVB | s.t. |
| 20. | J. Trarieux | DKO | s.t. |

## GENERAL CLASSIFICATION

| POS | NAME | TEAM | TIME |
|---|---|---|---|
| 1. ↑1 | A. Démare | GFC | 12:29:55 |
| 2. ↓1 | P. Walsleben | AFC | 0:02 |
| 3. ↑1 | K. Halvorsen | UXT | 0:14 |

## KING OF THE MOUNTAINS

| POS | NAME | TEAM | PTS |
|---|---|---|---|
| 1. — | M. Urruty | XRL | 30 |
| 2. — | S. Dewulf | ACT | 29 |
| 3. — | J. Restrepo | ANS | 28 |

## POINTS

| POS | NAME | TEAM | PTS |
|---|---|---|---|
| 1. — | A. Démare | GFC | 66 |
| 2. ↑1 | K. Halvorsen | UXT | 50 |
| 3. ↓1 | P. Walsleben | AFC | 35 |

## YOUNG RIDER

| POS | NAME | TEAM | TIME |
|---|---|---|---|
| 1. — | N. Eekhoff | DSM | 12:30:15 |
| 2. ↑3 | T. Bayer | AFC | 0:06 |
| 3. — | S. Aniołkowski | BWB | 0:10 |

# BOUCLES DE LA MAYENNE
Stage 4
30 May 2021
Méral–Laval
181km

## WEATHER

TEMPERATURE | WIND
22°C | E 15km/h

## STAGE RESULTS

| POS | NAME | TEAM | TIME |
|---|---|---|---|
| 1. | A. Démare | GFC | 4:14:55 |
| 2. | D. McLay | ARK | s.t. |
| 3. | B. Coquard | BBK | s.t. |
| 4. | N. Eekhoff | DSM | s.t. |
| 5. | S. Aniołkowski | BWB | s.t. |
| 6. | N. Bonifazio | TDE | s.t. |
| 7. | K. Halvorsen | UXT | s.t. |
| 8. | J. Aberasturi | CJR | s.t. |
| 9. | M. Sarreau | ACT | s.t. |
| 10. | J. Warlop | SVB | s.t. |
| 11. | S. Weemaes | SVB | s.t. |
| 12. | E. Vermeulen | XRL | s.t. |
| 13. | M. Malucelli | ANS | s.t. |
| 14. | J. Koch | IWG | s.t. |
| 15. | S. Velasco | GAZ | s.t. |
| 16. | J. Trarieux | DKO | s.t. |
| 17. | T. Bayer | AFC | s.t. |
| 18. | A. Delettre | DKO | s.t. |
| 19. | C. Barthe | BBK | s.t. |
| 20. | T. Willems | SVB | s.t. |

## GENERAL CLASSIFICATION

| POS | NAME | TEAM | TIME |
|---|---|---|---|
| 1. — | A. Démare | GFC | 16:44:40 |
| 2. — | P. Walsleben | AFC | 0:17 |
| 3. — | K. Halvorsen | UXT | 0:24 |

## KING OF THE MOUNTAINS

| POS | NAME | TEAM | PTS |
|---|---|---|---|
| 1. ↑2 | J. Restrepo | ANS | 36 |
| 2. ↑6 | R. Adrià | EKP | 34 |
| 3. ↓1 | S. Dewulf | ACT | 31 |

## POINTS

| POS | NAME | TEAM | PTS |
|---|---|---|---|
| 1. — | A. Démare | GFC | 92 |
| 2. — | K. Halvorsen | UXT | 59 |
| 3. ↑3 | B. Coquard | BBK | 45 |

## YOUNG RIDER

| POS | NAME | TEAM | TIME |
|---|---|---|---|
| 1. — | N. Eekhoff | DSM | 16:45:10 |
| 2. — | T. Bayer | AFC | 0:06 |
| 3. ↑2 | A. Delettre | DKO | 0:08 |

MAY  .1 MEN'S RACE

# TOUR OF ESTONIA
Stage 1
28 May 2021
Tallinn–Tartu
193.3km

## WEATHER

TEMPERATURE | WIND
11°C | NW 19km/h

## STAGE RESULTS

| POS | NAME | TEAM | TIME |
|---|---|---|---|
| 1. | K. P. Lauk | NAT | 4:07:36 |
| 2. | M. Boguslawski | MSP | 0:07 |
| 3. | P. Tzortzakis | KPT | 0:08 |
| 4. | J. Murias | VOS | 0:12 |
| 5. | O. Nisu | NAT | 0:15 |
| 6. | N. Vahtra | NAT | 0:16 |
| 7. | M. Laas | NAT | 0:20 |
| 8. | E. Liepiņš | NAT | 0:24 |
| 9. | A. J. Juntunen | ADT | 0:26 |
| 10. | M. Gibson | RWC | 0:27 |
| 11. | M. Räim | MSP | s.t. |
| 12. | M. Paterski | VOS | 0:28 |
| 13. | E. Šiškevičius | NAT | 0:29 |
| 14. | D. Babor | SKC | 0:32 |
| 15. | M. Pluto | NAT | 0:33 |
| 16. | K. Ansons | ADT | 0:34 |
| 17. | A. Peron | TNN | s.t. |
| 18. | C. Page | RWC | 0:35 |
| 19. | A. Banaszek | MSP | s.t. |
| 20. | P. Rubenis | ADT | s.t. |

## GENERAL CLASSIFICATION

| POS | NAME | TEAM | TIME |
|---|---|---|---|
| 1. | K. P. Lauk | NAT | 4:07:26 |
| 2. | M. Boguslawski | MSP | 0:11 |
| 3. | P. Tzortzakis | KPT | 0:12 |

## KING OF THE MOUNTAINS

| POS | NAME | TEAM | PTS |
|---|---|---|---|
| 1. | M. Boguslawski | MSP | 6 |
| 2. | J. Beniušis | NAT | 3 |
| 3. | J. Murias | VOS | 2 |

## POINTS

| POS | NAME | TEAM | PTS |
|---|---|---|---|
| 1. | K. P. Lauk | NAT | 10 |
| 2. | P. Tzortzakis | KPT | 10 |
| 3. | M. Boguslawski | MSP | 9 |

## YOUNG RIDER

| POS | NAME | TEAM | TIME |
|---|---|---|---|
| 1. | A. J. Juntunen | ADT | 4:08:02 |
| 2. | D. Babor | SKC | 0:06 |
| 3. | K. Ansons | ADT | 0:08 |

# TOUR OF ESTONIA
Stage 2
29 May 2021
Tartu–Tartu
163km

## WEATHER

TEMPERATURE | WIND
7°C | N 11km/h

## STAGE RESULTS

| POS | NAME | TEAM | TIME |
|---|---|---|---|
| 1. | M. Laas | NAT | 3:55:23 |
| 2. | A. Banaszek | MSP | 0:03 |
| 3. | M. Paterski | VOS | s.t. |
| 4. | M. Pluto | NAT | s.t. |
| 5. | A. J. Juntunen | ADT | 0:05 |
| 6. | P. Tzortzakis | KPT | s.t. |
| 7. | K. P. Lauk | NAT | 0:10 |
| 8. | M. Podlaski | NAT | 0:11 |
| 9. | A. Flaksis | NAT | s.t. |
| 10. | K. Ansons | ADT | s.t. |
| 11. | E. Šiškevičius | NAT | s.t. |
| 12. | M. Boguslawski | MSP | s.t. |
| 13. | H. Forssell | NAT | 0:14 |
| 14. | N. Vahtra | NAT | 0:16 |
| 15. | P. Gruber | SKC | 0:20 |
| 16. | M. Gibson | RWC | 0:23 |
| 17. | T. Pawlak | MSP | 0:25 |
| 18. | M. Räim | MSP | 0:33 |
| 19. | P. Pruus | NAT | 0:38 |
| 20. | D. Bigham | RWC | 0:56 |

## GENERAL CLASSIFICATION

| POS | NAME | TEAM | TIME |
|---|---|---|---|
| 1. | K. P. Lauk | NAT | 8:02:59 |
| 2. | M. Laas | NAT | 0:07 |
| 3. | P. Tzortzakis | KPT | s.t. |

## KING OF THE MOUNTAINS

| POS |  | NAME | TEAM | PTS |
|---|---|---|---|---|
| 1. | — | M. Boguslawski | MSP | 6 |
| 2. | — | M. Räim | MSP | 3 |
| 3. | — | D. Babor | SKC | 3 |

## POINTS

| POS |  | NAME | TEAM | PTS |
|---|---|---|---|---|
| 1. | ↑3 | M. Laas | NAT | 17 |
| 2. | — | P. Tzortzakis | KPT | 15 |
| 3. | ↓2 | K. P. Lauk | NAT | 14 |

## YOUNG RIDER

| POS |  | NAME | TEAM | TIME |
|---|---|---|---|---|
| 1. | — | A. J. Juntunen | ADT | 8:03:30 |
| 2. | ↑1 | K. Ansons | ADT | 0:14 |
| 3. | ↑6 | H. Forssell | NAT | 0:40 |

MAY — WORLDTOUR MEN'S RACE

# CRITÉRIUM DU DAUPHINÉ
Stage 1
30 May 2021
Issoire–Issoire
181.8km

This was the day that young Lotto Soudal rouleur Brent Van Moer properly introduced himself to the WorldTour peloton. The Belgian had just been in the headlines when sent off course by a marshal as he closed on victory at the Ronde van Limburg. Here, he went clear with Ian Garrison (Deceuninck-QuickStep), Cyril Gautier (B&B Hotels) and Patrick Gamper (Bora-Hansgrohe). Garrison dropped away before they reached the final circuit, covered three times. As the bunch closed in, Van Moer punched clear, ostensibly looking for mountains points. Although his advantage was chopped to a minute with a dozen kilometres left, he refused to yield, producing the kind of performance that's long been the hallmark of his hugely experienced teammate Thomas De Gendt. Making the most of the narrow lanes and tight turns, Van Moer hung on, collecting the full set of jerseys to go with his stage win. ⓟⓒ

## WEATHER

TEMPERATURE  
22°C

WIND  
NE 11km/h

## PROFILE

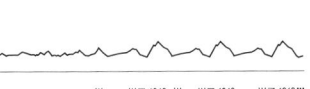

## BREAKAWAY
B. Van Moer (LTS), I. Garrison (DQT), P. Gamper (BOH), C. Gautier (BBK)

## GENERAL CLASSIFICATION

| POS | NAME | TEAM | TIME |
|---|---|---|---|
| 1. | B. Van Moer | LTS | 4:12:49 |
| 2. | S. Colbrelli | TBV | 0:30 |
| 3. | C. Venturini | ACT | 0:32 |

## STAGE RESULTS

| POS | NAME | TEAM | TIME |
|---|---|---|---|
| 1. | B. Van Moer | LTS | 4:13:00 |
| 2. | S. Colbrelli | TBV | 0:25 |
| 3. | C. Venturini | ACT | s.t. |
| 4. | J. Stuyven | TFS | s.t. |
| 5. | K. Groves | BEX | s.t. |
| 6. | N. Politt | BOH | s.t. |
| 7. | M. Kwiatkowski | IGD | s.t. |
| 8. | K. Asgreen | DQT | s.t. |
| 9. | A. Aranburu | APT | s.t. |
| 10. | A. Valverde | MOV | s.t. |
| 11. | C. Barbero | TQA | s.t. |
| 12. | E. Lietaer | BBK | s.t. |
| 13. | W. Barguil | ARK | s.t. |
| 14. | G. Martin | COF | s.t. |
| 15. | M. Gogl | TQA | s.t. |
| 16. | M. Valgren | EFN | s.t. |
| 17. | K. Vermaerke | DSM | s.t. |
| 18. | P. Konrad | BOH | s.t. |
| 19. | L. Hofstede | TJV | s.t. |
| 20. | O. Goldstein | ISN | s.t. |

## KING OF THE MOUNTAINS

| POS | NAME | TEAM | PTS |
|---|---|---|---|
| 1. | B. Van Moer | LTS | 10 |
| 2. | C. Gautier | BBK | 2 |
| 3. | P. Gamper | BOH | 1 |

## POINTS

| POS | NAME | TEAM | PTS |
|---|---|---|---|
| 1. | B. Van Moer | LTS | 29 |
| 2. | S. Colbrelli | TBV | 22 |
| 3. | C. Venturini | ACT | 20 |

## YOUNG RIDER

| POS | NAME | TEAM | TIME |
|---|---|---|---|
| 1. | B. Van Moer | LTS | 4:12:49 |
| 2. | P. Gamper | BOH | 0:33 |
| 3. | K. Groves | BEX | 0:36 |

## TRIVIA
» This was Brent Van Moer's first professional victory.

## BONUSES

| TYPE | NAME | TEAM |
|---|---|---|
| KOM 1 | B. Van Moer | LTS |
| KOM 2 | B. Van Moer | LTS |
| KOM 3 | B. Van Moer | LTS |
| KOM 4 | B. Van Moer | LTS |
| KOM 5 | B. Van Moer | LTS |
| KOM 6 | B. Van Moer | LTS |
| KOM 7 | B. Van Moer | LTS |
| Sprint 1 | P. Gamper | BOH |

MAY  WORLDTOUR MEN'S RACE

# CRITÉRIUM DU DAUPHINÉ
Stage 2
31 May 2021
Brioude–Sauges
172.8km

The break once again got the better of the peloton, Bora-Hansgrohe's Lukas Pöstlberger emulating Van Moer as a solo winner and, in the process, removing the leader's yellow-and-blue jersey from the Belgian's shoulders. Racing through the steep dips and gorges of the beautiful Allier region, the Austrian went clear with Anthony Delaplace (Arkéa-Samsic), Matt Holmes (Lotto Soudal), Shane Archbold (Deceuninck-QuickStep) and Robert Power (Qhubeka Assos). As the bunch began to close, Pöstlberger adopted the Van Moer tactic, dropping his companions in turn, Archbold the last to cede on the penultimate ascent. He crested the final climb, 4km from home, with a narrow lead but it was sufficient for him to hold on the fast drop into Sauges, claiming his first WorldTour victory since the opening stage of the 2017 Giro d'Italia, with Bahrain Victorious sprinter Sonny Colbrelli best of the rest as he had been in Issoire. ⓟⓒ

## WEATHER

TEMPERATURE   WIND
21°C          NE 11km/h

## PROFILE

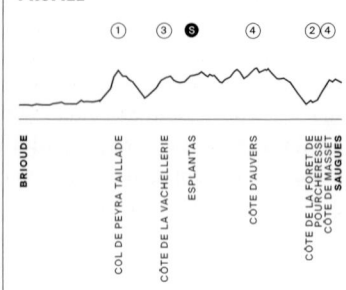

## BREAKAWAY
L. Pöstlberger (BOH), A. Delaplace (ARK), M. Holmes (LTS), S. Archbold (DQT), R. Power (TQA)

## GENERAL CLASSIFICATION

| POS | NAME | TEAM | TIME |
|---|---|---|---|
| 1. ↑33 | L. Pöstlberger | BOH | 8:38:32 |
| 2. — | S. Colbrelli | TBV | 0:12 |
| 3. ↑8 | A. Valverde | MOV | 0:20 |

## STAGE RESULTS

| POS | NAME | TEAM | TIME |
|---|---|---|---|
| 1. | L. Pöstlberger | BOH | 4:25:20 |
| 2. | S. Colbrelli | TBV | 0:11 |
| 3. | A. Valverde | MOV | s.t. |
| 4. | K. Asgreen | DQT | s.t. |
| 5. | S. E. Byström | UAD | s.t. |
| 6. | P. Konrad | BOH | s.t. |
| 7. | I. Van Wilder | DSM | s.t. |
| 8. | G. Van Avermaet | ACT | s.t. |
| 9. | A. Aranburu | APT | s.t. |
| 10. | D. Gaudu | GFC | s.t. |
| 11. | S. Kruijswijk | TJV | s.t. |
| 12. | B. McNulty | UAD | s.t. |
| 13. | A. Lutsenko | APT | s.t. |
| 14. | M. Valgren | EFN | s.t. |
| 15. | F. Gall | DSM | s.t. |
| 16. | N. Quintana | ARK | s.t. |
| 17. | G. Thomas | IGD | s.t. |
| 18. | Q. Pacher | BBK | s.t. |
| 19. | G. Martin | COF | s.t. |
| 20. | S. Kuss | TJV | s.t. |

## KING OF THE MOUNTAINS

| POS | NAME | TEAM | PTS |
|---|---|---|---|
| 1. — | M. Holmes | LTS | 13 |
| 2. — | L. Pöstlberger | BOH | 12 |
| 3. ↓2 | B. Van Moer | LTS | 10 |

## POINTS

| POS | NAME | TEAM | PTS |
|---|---|---|---|
| 1. ↑1 | S. Colbrelli | TBV | 44 |
| 2. — | L. Pöstlberger | BOH | 35 |
| 3. ↓2 | B. Van Moer | LTS | 29 |

## YOUNG RIDER

| POS | NAME | TEAM | TIME |
|---|---|---|---|
| 1. ↑6 | I. Van Wilder | DSM | 8:38:56 |
| 2. ↑6 | A. Paret-Peintre | ACT | s.t. |
| 3. ↑6 | M. Skjelmose Jensen | TFS | s.t. |

## TRIVIA
» Bora-Hansgrohe have now won a stage of the Dauphiné every year since 2018.

## BONUSES

| TYPE | NAME | TEAM |
|---|---|---|
| KOM 1 | M. Holmes | LTS |
| KOM 2 | M. Holmes | LTS |
| KOM 3 | M. Holmes | LTS |
| KOM 4 | L. Pöstlberger | BOH |
| KOM 5 | L. Pöstlberger | BOH |
| Sprint 1 | L. Pöstlberger | BOH |

MAY | WORLDTOUR MEN'S RACE

## CRITÉRIUM DU DAUPHINÉ
Stage 3
1 June 2021
Langeac–Saint-Haon-Le-Vieux
172.2km

One fellow pro described Sonny Colbrelli as looking 'as strong as a cow' coming into the Dauphiné, although the Italian looked every inch a thoroughbred as he steamed up the short but sharp hill into St-Haon-le-Vieux, leaving Brandon McNulty (UAE Team Emirates) and Alex Aranburu (Astana Premier Tech) well beaten in his wake. Though Colbrelli took the victory garlands, the finale was notable too for the presence of Dutch sprinter Fabio Jakobsen. Almost a year on from his horrific crash at the Tour of Poland, the Deceuninck rider felt he had the stamina, speed and nerve to get involved in a bunch finale once again. In the end, that steep final ramp proved too much for Jakobsen, but he looked just as delighted as stage winner Colbrelli at the finish, having been at the business end of a bunch sprint for the first time this season. ⓟ

### WEATHER

TEMPERATURE: 19°C
WIND: SE 24km/h

### PROFILE

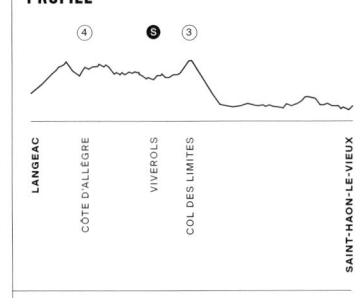

LANGEAC — CÔTE D'ALLÈGRE — VIVEROLS — COL DES LIMITES — SAINT-HAON-LE-VIEUX

### BREAKAWAY
O. Goldstein (ISN), L. Vliegen (IWG)

### STAGE RESULTS

| POS | NAME | TEAM | TIME |
|---|---|---|---|
| 1. | S. Colbrelli | TBV | 3:56:36 |
| 2. | A. Aranburu | APT | s.t. |
| 3. | B. McNulty | UAD | s.t. |
| 4. | J. Stuyven | TFS | s.t. |
| 5. | W. Kelderman | BOH | s.t. |
| 6. | C. Venturini | ACT | s.t. |
| 7. | C. Barbero | TQA | s.t. |
| 8. | C. Russo | ARK | s.t. |
| 9. | T. Wellens | LTS | s.t. |
| 10. | K. Asgreen | DQT | s.t. |
| 11. | A. Valverde | MOV | s.t. |
| 12. | Q. Pacher | BBK | s.t. |
| 13. | I. Izagirre | APT | s.t. |
| 14. | F. Bonnamour | BBK | s.t. |
| 15. | M. Schwarzmann | BOH | s.t. |
| 16. | S. Kruijswijk | TJV | s.t. |
| 17. | D. Gaudu | GFC | s.t. |
| 18. | G. Van Avermaet | ACT | s.t. |
| 19. | G. Thomas | IGD | s.t. |
| 20. | I. Van Wilder | DSM | s.t. |

### GENERAL CLASSIFICATION

| POS | | NAME | TEAM | TIME |
|---|---|---|---|---|
| 1. | — | L. Pöstlberger | BOH | 12:35:08 |
| 2. | — | S. Colbrelli | TBV | 0:02 |
| 3. | ↑2 | A. Aranburu | APT | 0:18 |

### KING OF THE MOUNTAINS

| POS | | NAME | TEAM | PTS |
|---|---|---|---|---|
| 1. | — | M. Holmes | LTS | 13 |
| 2. | — | L. Pöstlberger | BOH | 12 |
| 3. | — | B. Van Moer | LTS | 10 |

### POINTS

| POS | | NAME | TEAM | PTS |
|---|---|---|---|---|
| 1. | — | S. Colbrelli | TBV | 69 |
| 2. | ↑6 | A. Aranburu | APT | 38 |
| 3. | ↑1 | K. Asgreen | DQT | 38 |

### YOUNG RIDER

| POS | | NAME | TEAM | TIME |
|---|---|---|---|---|
| 1. | — | I. Van Wilder | DSM | 12:35:32 |
| 2. | ↑3 | D. Gaudu | GFC | s.t. |
| 3. | ↓1 | A. Paret-Peintre | ACT | s.t. |

### BONUSES

| TYPE | NAME | TEAM |
|---|---|---|
| KOM 1 | O. Goldstein | ISN |
| KOM 2 | O. Goldstein | ISN |
| Sprint 1 | O. Goldstein | ISN |

MAY  WORLDTOUR MEN'S RACE

## CRITÉRIUM DU DAUPHINÉ
Stage 4 (ITT)
2 June 2021
Firminy–Roche-La-Molière
16.4km

### WEATHER

TEMPERATURE  WIND
21°C  S 20km/h

### PROFILE

FIRMINY — ROCHE-LA-MOLIÈRE

Held in the steep-sided and wooded valleys just to the west of St-Étienne, this was a most unusual time trial, full of twists, dips and steep climbs, making it almost impossible to find and maintain a rhythm. In short, it was a test that suited no one in particular, and was an enthralling watch as a result of that. Pacing was crucial. Geraint Thomas was among the many who misjudged it. Quickest at the intermediate checkpoint, the Ineos Grenadier laboured up the final climb. Surprisingly, two Astana riders emerged as the pick of the day's racers. Ion Izaguirre first nudged Kasper Asgreen out of first place, then Alexey Lutsenko revealed that he'd judged his effort perfectly by going 8 seconds quicker than his teammate. Last off, Pöstlberger got the pacing right too, retaining the lead by just a second from the Kazakh. (PC)

### STAGE RESULTS

| POS | NAME | TEAM | TIME |
|---|---|---|---|
| 1. | A. Lutsenko | APT | 21:36 |
| 2. | I. Izaguirre | APT | 0:08 |
| 3. | K. Asgreen | DQT | 0:09 |
| 4. | W. Kelderman | BOH | 0:12 |
| 5. | I. Van Wilder | DSM | 0:13 |
| 6. | R. Porte | IGD | 0:15 |
| 7. | J. Vingegaard | TJV | 0:17 |
| 8. | B. McNulty | UAD | 0:21 |
| 9. | L. Pöstlberger | BOH | 0:23 |
| 10. | G. Thomas | IGD | s.t. |
| 11. | M. Kwiatkowski | IGD | 0:28 |
| 12. | P. Konrad | BOH | 0:31 |
| 13. | B. O'Connor | ACT | 0:33 |
| 14. | J. Haig | TBV | 0:34 |
| 15. | M. Bjerg | UAD | 0:35 |
| 16. | A. Paret-Peintre | ACT | 0:37 |
| 17. | T. Wellens | LTS | 0:38 |
| 18. | L. Craddock | EFN | 0:39 |
| 19. | S. Kruijswijk | TJV | s.t. |
| 20. | M. A. López | MOV | 0:42 |

### GENERAL CLASSIFICATION

| POS | NAME | TEAM | TIME |
|---|---|---|---|
| 1. — | L. Pöstlberger | BOH | 12:57:07 |
| 2. ↑10 | A. Lutsenko | APT | 0:01 |
| 3. ↑2 | K. Asgreen | DQT | 0:09 |

### KING OF THE MOUNTAINS

| POS | NAME | TEAM | PTS |
|---|---|---|---|
| 1. — | M. Holmes | LTS | 13 |
| 2. — | L. Pöstlberger | BOH | 12 |
| 3. — | B. Van Moer | LTS | 10 |

### POINTS

| POS | NAME | TEAM | PTS |
|---|---|---|---|
| 1. — | S. Colbrelli | TBV | 69 |
| 2. ↑1 | K. Asgreen | DQT | 48 |
| 3. ↓1 | A. Aranburu | APT | 38 |

### YOUNG RIDER

| POS | NAME | TEAM | TIME |
|---|---|---|---|
| 1. — | I. Van Wilder | DSM | 12:57:21 |
| 2. ↑1 | A. Paret-Peintre | ACT | 0:24 |
| 3. ↑1 | M. Skjelmose Jensen | TFS | 0:35 |

MAY  WORLDTOUR MEN'S RACE

# CRITÉRIUM DU DAUPHINÉ
Stage 5
3 June 2021
Saint-Chamond–Saint-Vallier
175.4km

Geraint Thomas bounced straight back from his TT disappointment with a cunningly constructed and well-finished stage victory in the Rhône valley. After lone breakaway Lawson Craddock (EF Education-Nippo) had been reeled back in 2km from home, Ineos riders gathered on the front of the lined-out bunch. With 1km to go, the route turned a 270-degree corner. Thomas was right at the front, with teammate Michal Kwiatkowski on his wheel. As the Welshman accelerated, the Pole eased off, enabling Thomas to increase his advantage. The principal fall guy was Sonny Colbrelli, who quickly realised he'd been ambushed and, with no teammates in support, was left with no option but to chase Thomas. The Italian would have overhauled the Ineos leader if he had another five metres of road, but Thomas held on for his first win since Alpe d'Huez in the 2018 Tour de France.

## WEATHER

TEMPERATURE  WIND
25°C  SE 7km/h

## PROFILE

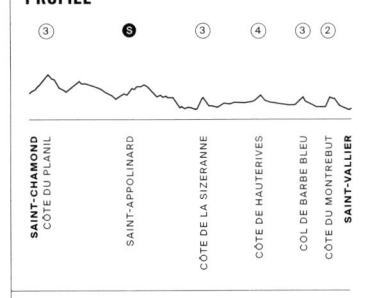

SAINT-CHAMOND / CÔTE DU PLANIL
SAINT-APPOLINARD
CÔTE DE LA SIZERANNE
CÔTE DE HAUTERIVES
COL DE BARBE BLEU
CÔTE DU MONTREBUT
SAINT-VALLIER

## BREAKAWAY
K. Asgreen (DQT), T. Wellens (LTS), T. Grmay (BEX), J. Bernard (TFS), C. Gautier (BBK), R. Mullen (TFS), J. Stuyven (TFS), J. Černý (DQT)

## STAGE RESULTS

| POS | NAME | TEAM | TIME |
|---|---|---|---|
| 1. | G. Thomas | IGD | 4:02:15 |
| 2. | S. Colbrelli | TBV | s.t. |
| 3. | A. Aranburu | APT | s.t. |
| 4. | C. Barbero | TQA | s.t. |
| 5. | M. Würst Schmidt | ISN | s.t. |
| 6. | M. Valgren | EFN | s.t. |
| 7. | P. Konrad | BOH | s.t. |
| 8. | A. Valverde | MOV | s.t. |
| 9. | H. Sweeny | LTS | s.t. |
| 10. | F. Bonnamour | BBK | s.t. |
| 11. | Se. Bennett | TQA | s.t. |
| 12. | S. Kuss | TJV | s.t. |
| 13. | Q. Pacher | BBK | s.t. |
| 14. | B. McNulty | UAD | s.t. |
| 15. | K. Vermaerke | DSM | s.t. |
| 16. | K. Asgreen | DQT | s.t. |
| 17. | L. Pöstlberger | BOH | s.t. |
| 18. | A. Lutsenko | APT | s.t. |
| 19. | B. Van Moer | LTS | s.t. |
| 20. | G. Martin | COF | s.t. |

## GENERAL CLASSIFICATION

| POS | NAME | TEAM | TIME |
|---|---|---|---|
| 1. — | L. Pöstlberger | BOH | 16:59:22 |
| 2. — | A. Lutsenko | APT | 0:01 |
| 3. — | K. Asgreen | DQT | 0:06 |

## KING OF THE MOUNTAINS

| POS | NAME | TEAM | PTS |
|---|---|---|---|
| 1. — | M. Holmes | LTS | 13 |
| 2. — | L. Pöstlberger | BOH | 12 |
| 3. — | B. Van Moer | LTS | 10 |

## POINTS

| POS | NAME | TEAM | PTS |
|---|---|---|---|
| 1. — | S. Colbrelli | TBV | 91 |
| 2. — | K. Asgreen | DQT | 58 |
| 3. — | A. Aranburu | APT | 58 |

## YOUNG RIDER

| POS | NAME | TEAM | TIME |
|---|---|---|---|
| 1. — | I. Van Wilder | DSM | 16:59:36 |
| 2. — | A. Paret-Peintre | ACT | 0:24 |
| 3. — | M. Skjelmose Jensen | TFS | 0:35 |

## TRIVIA
» Although Geraint Thomas has won the Critérium du Dauphiné before, this is his first stage victory at the French race.

## BONUSES

| TYPE | NAME | TEAM |
|---|---|---|
| KOM 1 | T. Wellens | LTS |
| KOM 2 | J. Bernard | TFS |
| KOM 3 | J. Černý | DQT |
| KOM 4 | S. E. Bystrøm | UAD |
| KOM 5 | L. Craddock | EFN |
| Sprint 1 | K. Asgreen | DQT |

MAY    WORLDTOUR MEN'S RACE

# CRITÉRIUM DU DAUPHINÉ
Stage 6
4 June 2021
Loriol-sur-Drome–Le Sappey-en-Chartreuse
167.2km

Often ridiculed for their lack of tactical coherence, Movistar got their strategy exactly right on a stage that featured four categorised climbs in its last quarter through the rugged Chartreuse massif. Aiming to set up Alejandro Valverde for the uphill finish, they began by first whittling down the size of the peloton. On the final two climbs, they pushed the pace even higher, thanks to Carlos Verona and, particularly, Miguel Ángel López. Coming into the finish, it meant there were just two dozen riders left in the front group. Tao Geoghegan Hart was the first to attack but he never looked likely to hold off Valverde once the 41-year-old Spaniard countered. Valverde breezed by the Ineos rider to claim his first WorldTour win for almost two seasons. By finishing in the pack behind him, Lutsenko took the overall lead from Pöstlberger. PC

## WEATHER

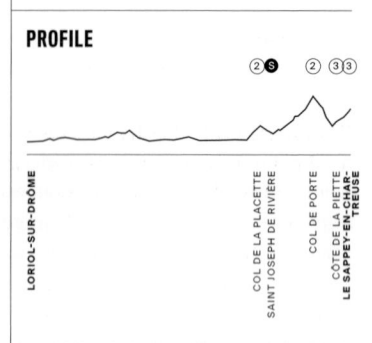

TEMPERATURE   WIND
25°C          SW 11km/h

## PROFILE

## BREAKAWAY
G. Van Avermaet (ACT), M. Holmes (LTS), L. Craddock (EFN), O. Le Gac (GFC), A. Perez (COF), O. Goldstein (ISN), L. Pichon (ARK), S. E. Byström (UAD), J. Černý (DQT), J. Bernard (TFS), B. Peak (BEX), M. Salmon (DSM), F. Bonnamour (BBK), J. Bakelants (IWG)

## STAGE RESULTS

| POS | NAME | TEAM | TIME |
|---|---|---|---|
| 1. | A. Valverde | MOV | 3:52:53 |
| 2. | T. Geoghegan Hart | IGD | s.t. |
| 3. | P. Konrad | BOH | s.t. |
| 4. | W. Kelderman | BOH | s.t. |
| 5. | E. Mas | MOV | s.t. |
| 6. | S. Kuss | TJV | s.t. |
| 7. | A. Lutsenko | APT | s.t. |
| 8. | J. Haig | TBV | s.t. |
| 9. | B. Hermans | ISN | s.t. |
| 10. | S. Kruijswijk | TJV | s.t. |
| 11. | G. Thomas | IGD | s.t. |
| 12. | N. Quintana | ARK | s.t. |
| 13. | R. Porte | IGD | s.t. |
| 14. | D. Gaudu | GFC | s.t. |
| 15. | I. Izaguirre | APT | s.t. |
| 16. | I. Van Wilder | DSM | s.t. |
| 17. | D. Howson | BEX | s.t. |
| 18. | L. Meintjes | IWG | s.t. |
| 19. | G. Martin | COF | s.t. |
| 20. | M. A. López | MOV | s.t. |

## GENERAL CLASSIFICATION

| POS | NAME | TEAM | TIME |
|---|---|---|---|
| 1. ↑1 | A. Lutsenko | APT | 20:52:16 |
| 2. ↑2 | I. Izaguirre | APT | 0:08 |
| 3. ↑2 | W. Kelderman | BOH | 0:12 |

## KING OF THE MOUNTAINS

| POS | NAME | TEAM | PTS |
|---|---|---|---|
| 1. — | M. Holmes | LTS | 21 |
| 2. ↑3 | L. Craddock | EFN | 13 |
| 3. ↓1 | L. Pöstlberger | BOH | 12 |

## POINTS

| POS | NAME | TEAM | PTS |
|---|---|---|---|
| 1. — | S. Colbrelli | TBV | 91 |
| 2. — | K. Asgreen | DQT | 58 |
| 3. — | A. Aranburu | APT | 58 |

## YOUNG RIDER

| POS | NAME | TEAM | TIME |
|---|---|---|---|
| 1. — | I. Van Wilder | DSM | 20:52:29 |
| 2. — | A. Paret-Peintre | ACT | 0:37 |
| 3. ↑1 | D. Gaudu | GFC | 0:46 |

## TRIVIA
» This was Alejandro Valverde's third Dauphiné stage win of his career. The other two were in 2008.

## BONUSES

| TYPE | NAME | TEAM |
|---|---|---|
| KOM 1 | M. Holmes | LTS |
| KOM 2 | L. Craddock | EFN |
| KOM 3 | L. Craddock | EFN |
| KOM 4 | A. Valverde | MOV |
| Sprint 1 | G. Van Avermaet | ACT |

MAY  WORLDTOUR MEN'S RACE

# CRITÉRIUM DU DAUPHINÉ
Stage 7
5 June 2021
Saint-Martin-le-Vinoux–La Plagne
171.1km

Richie Porte rejoined Ineos in order to support the team's leaders in the Grand Tours. But the veteran Australian was also eyeing victory in the Dauphiné, a title that had always proved elusive to him. On this, the toughest mountain stage, he instigated the stage-winning move with 8km remaining. He was joined by Sepp Kuss, Enric Mas and the unfamiliar figure of Ukraine's Mark Padun. Although Kuss and Padun soon went clear, neither was a GC threat, and Porte didn't need to react when Padun dropped the American and powered away to a surprising victory. Porte was focused on distancing race leader Lutsenko and the other overall favourites, principally Miguel Ángel López. In the final kilometre through what may be the ugliest ski station in the French Alps, Porte accelerated away from the little Colombian to take the race lead. ⓟ

## WEATHER

TEMPERATURE: 20°C
WIND: NW 19km/h

## PROFILE

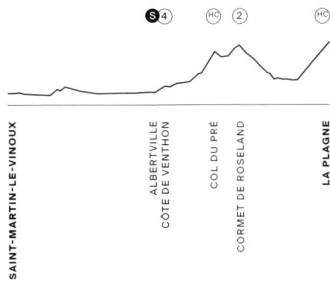

SAINT-MARTIN-LE-VINOUX — ALBERTVILLE CÔTE DE VENTHON — COL DU PRÉ — CORMET DE ROSELAND — LA PLAGNE

## BREAKAWAY
M. Haller (TBV), A. Renard (ISN), M. Salmon (DSM), P. Rolland (BBK), F. Bonnamour (BBK)

## STAGE RESULTS

| POS | NAME | TEAM | TIME |
|---|---|---|---|
| 1. | M. Padun | TBV | 4:35:07 |
| 2. | R. Porte | IGD | 0:34 |
| 3. | M. A. López | MOV | 0:43 |
| 4. | J. Haig | TBV | s.t. |
| 5. | B. O'Connor | ACT | 0:47 |
| 6. | S. Kuss | TJV | 0:52 |
| 7. | D. Gaudu | GFC | 0:56 |
| 8. | E. Mas | MOV | s.t. |
| 9. | G. Thomas | IGD | 0:59 |
| 10. | A. Lutsenko | APT | 1:00 |
| 11. | A. Valverde | MOV | 1:04 |
| 12. | W. Kelderman | BOH | s.t. |
| 13. | A. Paret-Peintre | ACT | 1:10 |
| 14. | T. Geoghegan Hart | IGD | s.t. |
| 15. | N. Quintana | ARK | 1:13 |
| 16. | I. Izagirre | APT | s.t. |
| 17. | D. Howson | BEX | 1:39 |
| 18. | S. Kruijswijk | TJV | s.t. |
| 19. | L. Meintjes | IWG | s.t. |
| 20. | F. Gall | DSM | 2:08 |

## GENERAL CLASSIFICATION

| POS | | NAME | TEAM | TIME |
|---|---|---|---|---|
| 1. | ↑5 | R. Porte | IGD | 25:28:06 |
| 2. | ↓1 | A. Lutsenko | APT | 0:17 |
| 3. | ↑1 | G. Thomas | IGD | 0:29 |

## KING OF THE MOUNTAINS

| POS | | NAME | TEAM | PTS |
|---|---|---|---|---|
| 1. | ↑1 | L. Craddock | EFN | 33 |
| 2. | ↓1 | M. Holmes | LTS | 21 |
| 3. | — | M. Padun | TBV | 15 |

## POINTS

| POS | | NAME | TEAM | PTS |
|---|---|---|---|---|
| 1. | — | S. Colbrelli | TBV | 91 |
| 2. | — | K. Asgreen | DQT | 58 |
| 3. | — | A. Aranburu | APT | 58 |

## YOUNG RIDER

| POS | | NAME | TEAM | TIME |
|---|---|---|---|---|
| 1. | ↑2 | D. Gaudu | GFC | 25:29:18 |
| 2. | — | A. Paret-Peintre | ACT | 0:05 |
| 3. | ↑1 | M. Skjelmose Jensen | TFS | 1:42 |

## TRIVIA
» This was Mark Padun's first WorldTour win.

## BONUSES

| TYPE | NAME | TEAM |
|---|---|---|
| KOM 1 | F. Bonnamour | BBK |
| KOM 2 | L. Craddock | EFN |
| KOM 3 | L. Craddock | EFN |
| KOM 4 | M. Padun | TBV |
| Sprint 1 | M. Haller | TBV |

MAY     WORLDTOUR MEN'S RACE

# CRITÉRIUM DU DAUPHINÉ
Stage 8
6 June 2021
La Léchère-Les-Bains–Les Gets
147km

The Dauphiné's final stage confirmed what the previous one had suggested: that Padun was in untouchable form in the high mountains and Porte was the pick of the GC favourites. The Ukrainian made his move from the break, surging clear on the early slopes of the race's final climb, the fearsome Col de Joux Plane. His style isn't pretty – akin to someone on a butcher's bike rather than a state-of-the-art machine – but it proved hugely effective. In the GC group, Porte, who famously saw victory in the 2017 Dauphiné slip from his grasp on the final day, fended off his rivals' attacks quite comfortably, assisted by Thomas and Geoghegan Hart. There was brief concern when Thomas slid off on the descent into the finish, leaving the Australian isolated, but the Welshman quickly regained contact and shepherded the GC group home, helping to secure Porte's overall victory.

## WEATHER

TEMPERATURE: 20°C
WIND: N 11km/h

## PROFILE

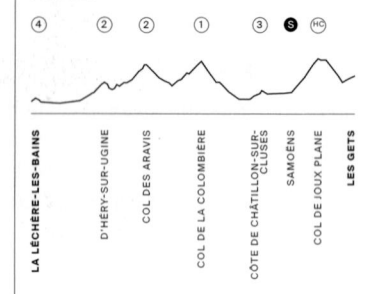

(4) (2) (2) (1) (3) S HC

LA LÉCHÈRE-LES-BAINS
D'HÉRY-SUR-UGINE
COL DES ARAVIS
COL DE LA COLOMBIÈRE
CÔTE DE CHÂTILLON-SUR-CLUSES
SAMOËNS
COL DE JOUX PLANE
LES GETS

## BREAKAWAY

J. Bernard (TFS), F. Bonnamour (BBK), V. Madouas (GFC), G. Martin (COF), J. Vingegaard (TJV), J. Arcas (MOV), I. Erviti (MOV), P. Konrad (BOH), N. Politt (BOH), D. Godon (ACT), W. Barguil (ARK), H. Sweeny (LTS), M. Padun (TBV), K. Elissonde (TFS), P. Rolland (BBK), S. Armée (TQA), M. Valgren (EFN), M. Tusveld (DSM), J. Bakelants (IWG)

## STAGE RESULTS

| POS | NAME | TEAM | TIME |
|---|---|---|---|
| 1. | M. Padun | TBV | 4:06:49 |
| 2. | J. Vingegaard | TJV | 1:36 |
| 3. | P. Konrad | BOH | s.t. |
| 4. | B. O'Connor | ACT | 1:57 |
| 5. | D. Gaudu | GFC | 2:10 |
| 6. | G. Thomas | IGD | s.t. |
| 7. | A. Lutsenko | APT | s.t. |
| 8. | R. Porte | IGD | s.t. |
| 9. | J. Haig | TBV | s.t. |
| 10. | G. Martin | COF | s.t. |
| 11. | M. A. López | MOV | s.t. |
| 12. | W. Kelderman | BOH | s.t. |
| 13. | I. Izaguirre | APT | s.t. |
| 14. | T. Geoghegan Hart | IGD | 2:43 |
| 15. | E. Mas | MOV | 2:50 |
| 16. | K. Elissonde | TFS | 3:04 |
| 17. | L. Meintjes | IWG | 4:04 |
| 18. | A. Paret-Peintre | ACT | s.t. |
| 19. | D. Howson | BEX | s.t. |
| 20. | A. Valverde | MOV | s.t. |

## GENERAL CLASSIFICATION

| POS | | NAME | TEAM | TIME |
|---|---|---|---|---|
| 1. | — | R. Porte | IGD | 29:37:05 |
| 2. | — | A. Lutsenko | APT | 0:17 |
| 3. | — | G. Thomas | IGD | 0:29 |

## KING OF THE MOUNTAINS

| POS | | NAME | TEAM | PTS |
|---|---|---|---|---|
| 1. | ↑2 | M. Padun | TBV | 50 |
| 2. | ↓1 | L. Craddock | EFN | 33 |
| 3. | ↑1 | M. Valgren | EFN | 26 |

## POINTS

| POS | | NAME | TEAM | PTS |
|---|---|---|---|---|
| 1. | — | S. Colbrelli | TBV | 91 |
| 2. | — | K. Asgreen | DQT | 58 |
| 3. | — | A. Aranburu | APT | 58 |

## YOUNG RIDER

| POS | | NAME | TEAM | TIME |
|---|---|---|---|---|
| 1. | — | D. Gaudu | GFC | 29:38:17 |
| 2. | — | A. Paret-Peintre | ACT | 1:59 |
| 3. | — | M. Skjelmose Jensen | TFS | 5:44 |

## TRIVIA

» Richie Porte adds the Dauphiné to his burgeoning list of major stage-race victories: Paris-Nice, Volta a Catalunya, Tour de Romandie and the Tour de Suisse.

## BONUSES

| TYPE | NAME | TEAM |
|---|---|---|
| KOM 1 | M. Schwarzmann | BOH |
| KOM 2 | M. Padun | TBV |
| KOM 3 | M. Padun | TBV |
| KOM 4 | M. Padun | TBV |
| KOM 5 | N. Politt | BOH |
| KOM 6 | M. Padun | TBV |
| SPRINT1 | P. Konrad | BOH |

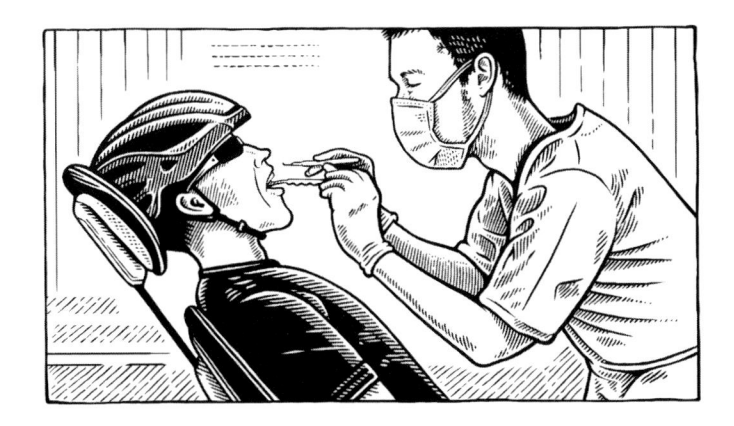

# COMPLETING THE SET

BY DAN MARTIN

The pink jersey. *La maglia rosa.* This icon of cycling makes frequent appearances in my earliest childhood cycling memories, generally appearing through the mist on top of some impossibly steep mountain pass. I remember Mario Cipollini, Marco Pantani, Miguel Induráin, Evgeni Berzin, Gilberto Simoni; I grew up watching the Giro, not necessarily dreaming of being there one day. I'm not sure what I was thinking.

Fast-forward to 2010 and an impromptu appearance at the Giro d'Italia, sprung on me just ten days before with little time to prepare. I set off on the expedition across one of the most beautiful countries in the world and got my arse kicked, splattered all over Italy. I returned from that race, after days of horrendous weather and epic mountain stages, with my tail between my legs and a firm determination to not return.

I'm not sure why I took such a dislike to the race but it persisted. The race started in Ireland in 2014 and I was persuaded to make an appearance that quite possibly ranks as one of the shortest Grand Tour appearances in history, making it just 15km into the race before I crashed and took down most of my team in the opening team time trial, breaking my collarbone in the process. Normally, when I watch a race from the comfort of my sofa – except for perhaps the northern Classics or Strade Bianche – the competitor in me wants to be there, and questions if I would have won if I was present. Not at the Giro.

I loved spending my May training hard at home, my afternoons relaxing, content to enjoy the suffering of others. But alas, 2021 arrived and it hit me that I was in the twilight of my career and that I needed to return to at least attempt to complete my hattrick: my collection of Grand Tour stage victories, having already succeeded – twice, in fact – in the Tour and the Vuelta. Buoyed by a successful campaign at the 2020 Vuelta, I even dared to wonder if grabbing that pink jersey was at all a possibility.

9:05am Saturday 8 May. Hours before I'm due to roll down the start ramp of the prologue, I find myself in a dentist's chair, surrounded by unilingual (only Italian, of course) dental nurses, attempting to glue back in its rightful place a molar crown that had somehow come unstuck in an unusually sticky piece of 85 per cent dark chocolate the previous night. It was a quick procedure and within the hour I was back at the hotel, but it was one of the more bizarre starts to a Grand Tour that I have experienced. I can happily report that the tooth stayed intact for the remainder of the race. Still unsure as to whether he had cleaned it thoroughly, though.

To the race. Beginning with a prologue has always seemed quite romantic, although an increasingly rare occurrence these last years. Starting a Grand Tour should be an occasion and allowing each of the participants their moment in the spotlight as they roll down the start ramp increases the sensation of this being a big deal. Butterflies flutter as you question what lies ahead, anxious to not make a fool of yourself or make any silly mistakes. It's a pure test of power but also skill in judging pace and the level of risk to take in the corners. In the grand scheme of things, the prologue rarely counts for much more than a morale boost, but there is always so much scrutiny over the results that the pressure is high; nobody wants to begin the three weeks on a bad note.

Unfortunately for us, the race started worse than for just about any other team. I have always been against riding back to the hotel during a race. So many things can go wrong, especially when riding through a busy city. Even when the hotel is a matter of a few kilometres from the finish, I prefer the safety and comfort of the team bus. Krists Neilands decided to ride the 15km back to our team hotel as he was the first rider to finish. He made it perfectly safely 14.9km before a freak crash meant he tumbled to the floor within view of the hotel, snapping his collarbone in the process. He is an incredibly talented rider and we missed him throughout the race. Small things like this can damage morale but we had a strong group and, although we were down a rider before the race had really started, we hit the reset button and it gelled us together as a team.

My experience in the French and Spanish Grand Tours is well documented. I had forgotten how different the Giro is in character. The first glaring difference is that the Italians design stages to be a sprint. No hidden surprises. Big wide flat roads with zero hope of the breakaway actually making it to the finish line. The speed always picks up in the last 20km with the jostle for position and the inevitable handful of corners in the very last kilometres, but generally speaking, days like these don't exist in the Tour and Vuelta. They are almost a day off with low power and heartrate numbers (I'm talking less than 100bpm average). The fatigue comes from the concentration and fight for position towards the end so I wouldn't say they are easy, and it is on days like these that mistakes are often made, with silly little crashes taking out riders.

The finishes are always hotly contested with, it seemed this year, an abundance of road furniture catching out the likes of Mikel Landa and Pavel Sivakov. My team did a great job of navigating me through these hectic final stretches, but at times you do emerge from the bubble – a mix of extreme concentration, adrenaline and lactic acid, as you race through narrow streets at 65kmph, inches from traffic islands and other road furniture (more commonly known as 'form fuckers') – and realise what we are doing is actually insane. There are no practice laps for us. It's testament to the skill of the peloton that there are not more incidents. Every one of these finishes that you tick off without incident is a relief as a GC rider. It's not just about staying out of trouble; you are always in fear of missing a split and losing time because of poor positioning.

One thing that I remember vividly from 2010 is that it rained – a lot. Nearly every day, in fact. I heard stories of some Giros with no bad weather, and crossed every finger I had for this miracle to repeat itself. It didn't. In 2021 we had very few days without any precipitation. I don't mind the rain but my body just seems to function better when it's warm and sunny. Plus, let's face it, it is much more pleasant to ride under sunny skies than sodden grey darkness overhead. It became a common thread during this Giro, and actually a standing joke, that even with the most minimal possibility of rain in the forecast, it would rain. Stage 4 to Sestola was epic. Pouring rain all day, technical downhills. I was super focused all throughout the stage and never out of position. My teammate De Marchi, up ahead in the breakaway, was on his way to taking the pink jersey and finishing second on the stage. I was content to survive a small time loss as the rain and cold sucked the energy out of me after five long hours in the saddle. Fifteen minutes after the finish, the sun made an appearance.

On stage 6 our director proudly announced only a 10 per cent probability of light showers. Cue one of the most ferocious downpours I have ever raced through. It did, however, dry up again after about ten minutes of torrential rain, only for the storm to return with a vengeance just as we crested the highest climb of the day. Ineos attacked as the wind swept across the plateau and we were pelted with hailstones. A routine ride to the final climb became an epic battle. I was shivering uncontrollably on the fast wet descent. Ordinarily the 20km towards the bottom of the climb was simple but the false-flat descent on a big road in the rain, doing 70kmph with little effort and no team cars behind to get extra clothes due to splits, meant I was properly cold, concentrating hard not to shake too much.

In hindsight, the shot of adrenaline I got when Felix Großschartner decided to take a lie-down on a corner directly in front of me, knocking me off, probably rejuvenated me because when I hit the climb immediately afterwards I felt really good and began taking off all my extra clothing. The climb shouldn't have been decisive but the conditions made it that the race blew to pieces on the final steeper ramps. It caught me by surprise but I was happy to be right up there with Egan Bernal and grab third on the stage. I was just hanging on to his back wheel in the final kilometre as he rode into the headwind but I can always rustle up a sprint. Once again, minutes after we finished, the sky broke up and the sun appeared, at least making the extremely picturesque drive to the hotel more enjoyable.

Does gravel have a place in stage racing? When RCS announced the Giro route I was far from enamoured with stage 11 but was set on coping and surviving the stage. The fight to be in the front going into the first sector was incredibly intense and that's where me and my team made our big mistake. We underestimated the importance of sector 1. I entered near the front but crucially not at the front. The lack of visibility and faith in my colleagues meant I effectively shat myself. Going 60kmph on an unpredictable surface, and witnessing a number of guys crash around me, I began to envisage a mass pile-up whereby one rider would lose control and create a sequence of crashes causing other riders to hit the brakes and also lose control.

The sector was actually a descent on gravel, with tight corners and a surface that in places was reasonably good, almost as hard packed as tarmac, but these sections were interspersed by deep patches of gravel and sand, ruts where you effectively lost control of the bike momentarily. The race was in pieces after the first sector and from this point on I was in TT mode. I kept focus and just got to the finish as fast as possible, catching and passing groups of riders at a time. This persistence paid off in Milan. Without this dogged determination I would not have finished in the top ten on GC. It's a lesson to never give up. Experience has taught me not to be affected by time losses. In victory or defeat you need to refocus quickly and continue fighting. I was safe and still in the game.

There is bad weather and then there is unrideable weather. One of the stages I was most looking forward to in order to complete my Giro experience was stage 16, an epic jaunt through the Dolomites with more than 5700m of altitude gain over 212km. You don't get stages like this in any other race. Sadly, the weather forecast was horrific. Pouring rain and 10 degrees at the start altitude of 200m, it didn't take a genius to figure out what was going on up in the mountains. Murmurs began among the riders' WhatsApp group to decide an action plan as we faced up to three long descents above 2000m in freezing conditions and precipitation that would more than likely be snow at that altitude. Unfortunately, it seems the organisers and UCI are incapable of making a decision, so it fell to the riders to propose a shortening of the stage or we would not leave the team buses. Faced with this ultimatum, the proposal was accepted. I hope that organisers learn from how the stage panned out as it was actually an aggressive exciting stage, which was mostly missed by the television cameras due to the weather conditions. Shorter stages mean we can race harder. We still raced for five hours in the pouring rain over some brutal terrain and there was a worthy winner. The images of gaunt, weather-beaten, exhausted faces crossing the finish line were still beamed across the world. It would have otherwise been a painfully slow seven-hour procession with less attacking as by the end everybody would have been too shattered to attack.

After racing the Tour of the Alps in April, I saw on the map that we were really close to the finish of stage 17 to Alpe di Mera and suggested that, together with our somewhat eccentric Italian director, we take a drive up the final climb at least. My initial thoughts were 'wow, what a beautiful climb.' I got goosebumps when we approached the proposed finish line; I immediately called my wife and proclaimed that something special would happen there. I looked at the race situation on the rest day and made a plan for how to win the stage. This was my opportunity. Perhaps the last opportunity to take home a stage victory. I was far enough out of the GC picture to be allowed freedom, so I planned to use the most aerodynamic bike set-up possible in order to save energy on the first 100km of flat and downhill but also to make it easier to infiltrate the breakaway. The problem on a day like this is that the majority of the peloton has the same idea, so we raced at 70kmph on the slightly downhill valley roads.

It was pretty terrifying but I kept focused, followed multiple attacks until I made it into the right group. Part one of the mission complete. One thing I hadn't planned on was the strong headwind that would hit us in the valley, along with a determined chase by BikeExchange. I have a calculating brain, and after changing to my lightweight climbing set-up, and seeing the gap to the peloton begin to tumble, I set off on a mission to eke out more time. I calculated that I needed at least 3 minutes at the top of the penultimate climb to have a chance, but with the strong headwind I couldn't go alone. It was a delicate balancing act between pushing hard to take time but not so hard that I would drop the whole group. I needed help to maintain a big enough gap.

The final climb became a time trial and somehow I held on. I was getting constant updates on the radio both on the time gap and the road ahead, despite knowing the road. My experience as a GC rider also meant that I understood how the race would unfold behind, and that even when the attacks came – as long as they didn't catch me – the effort of making that strong acceleration would take it out of my pursuers. With the final 2km being an easier gradient, I planned to save as much energy on the steeper sections without getting caught and then reaccelerate on the flatter final part, hopefully breaking the morale of those behind.

It was a beautiful moment in my career. The attention you get when you cross the line first in a big race like the Giro is unreal, the happiness that it brings to the whole organisation and the back-room people who work so hard; that one moment of glory makes the weeks and months of toil disappear. As a GC rider there is never much time to enjoy the moment as you need to refocus for the next stage, but for me it was mission accomplished. I had achieved what I had ambitiously set out to at the start of the race in Turin, so anything more was a huge bonus.

Two big mountain stages to go. I had slipped into the top ten on GC so was determined to hold on to it now.

The main feature of the final two stages seemed to be teams attacking on tricky descents to split the peloton – Deceuninck-QuickStep on stage 19 and then Team DSM on stage 20 who were then accompanied by Damiano Caruso and Pello Bilbao of Bahrain. Descending is a part of the sport and we always push the limits but I'm not a big fan of tactics such as these. It all comes down to positioning, and the proximity of the TV motorbike also aids a descending attack. On stage 19 the peloton split but regrouped for a typical mountain-top finish battle between the best climbers.

Stage 20 threatened at one point to upend the whole race as Caruso crept closer to taking the pink jersey. Personally I had a good day on stage 19, although I definitely felt my exertions from my stage win. Stage 20 was brutal from the start with changeable weather conditions and drastic fluctuations in temperature, beginning in balmy sunshine before being hit by a freezing rain shower once we got up into the mountains, meaning tricky wet descents. After three weeks I was done. Nothing left. Grand Tour racing is as much about the mental battle as physical; the need to keep fighting to preserve your three weeks of work. I didn't have the legs to win the stage and I had an 8-minute buffer to 11th place on GC. The short final ascent was one of the more interesting climbs I've done, with a series of vicious switchbacks that resembled a multi-storey car park followed by a flat section before a final steep pitch packed with delirious fans screaming in our faces. No masks here. Crossing the line, I was satisfied. Just the TT to go now into the centre of Milan.

Unusually we even had a short 120km transfer from the finish to the final race hotel. We settled into our seats before being reminded one last time that this was indeed the Giro. The bus was parked at the bottom of the final climb but our driver informed us that the route to the hotel involved a somewhat challenging road. There was a series of tight hairpin bends between us and Milan – ordinarily not a problem… unless you are in a 13-metre team bus. Each of the 15–20 switchbacks involved every bus shimmying back and forth to make the turn – a fact made even more difficult by the constant stream of oncoming traffic that was becoming equally frustrated. It took us two hours to drive 18km. Any other day and the atmosphere would have been one of frustration, but at this point we were done so there was nothing left to do but sit back and enjoy the ride.

The Piazza del Duomo is a truly amazing place to finish a race and as I said about the prologue, a TT gives each and every rider their moment in the spotlight and makes each individual who has suffered all the way to the finish line feel special. Most riders would simply cruise around the flat city streets and enjoy the moment, with a select few racing for a result. I was able to enjoy myself, crossing the line with a mixture of relief and happiness. It had been a special three weeks with a great group of guys.

The Giro truly has a character that is missing from other races. It's all very… Italian.

# COMEBACKS

One defining theme of the 2021 season has been comebacks: from Mark Cavendish picking himself up from wintry tears in Belgium at the end of 2020 to winning again in Turkey and then returning to the top of the sport at the Tour de France, or Tom Dumoulin taking a national time trial title after several months away from the sport. Then there's Geraint Thomas and Rigoberto Urán – two riders you wouldn't necessarily expect to have been on such lengthy winless streaks. The likes of Dylan Groenewegen and Fabio Jakobsen have both returned to winning ways after last year's incident at the Tour of Poland, and Remco Evenepoel has wasted no time in riding to seemingly effortless victories in feats that are beyond the realms of what appears possible. The longest notable comeback of all, however, is that of Romain Bardet, winning his first race in 1,258 days at a new team and then going on to take a glorious stage victory at the Vuelta a España.

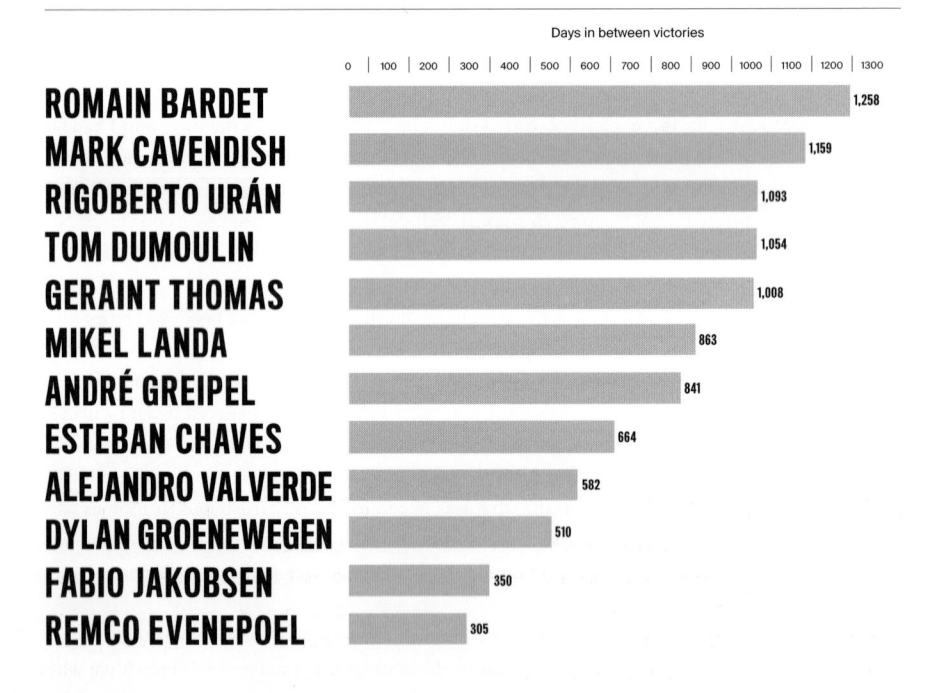

Days in between victories

|  |  |
|---|---|
| ROMAIN BARDET | 1,258 |
| MARK CAVENDISH | 1,159 |
| RIGOBERTO URÁN | 1,093 |
| TOM DUMOULIN | 1,054 |
| GERAINT THOMAS | 1,008 |
| MIKEL LANDA | 863 |
| ANDRÉ GREIPEL | 841 |
| ESTEBAN CHAVES | 664 |
| ALEJANDRO VALVERDE | 582 |
| DYLAN GROENEWEGEN | 510 |
| FABIO JAKOBSEN | 350 |
| REMCO EVENEPOEL | 305 |

# JUNE

For a second successive year, the Tour de France started in June, a week earlier than its longstanding and traditional berth over the opening weekend in July. This adjustment in the calendar was necessitated by the Tokyo Olympics, postponed by a year but scheduled to start a week after the Tour. In the Women's World Tour, there was just a single day's racing, as the final running of La Course was held early in the morning of stage 1 of the Tour. Before both of those races, though, there was (with a few exceptions, including Great Britain) an almost-complete programme of National Championships.

| DATE | RACE TITLE | LOCATION | UCI CODE | PAGE |
| --- | --- | --- | --- | --- |
| 4 June | GP des Kantons Aargau | Switzerland | 1.1 | 238 |
| 5 June | Dwars door het Hageland | Belgium | 1.Pro | 239 |
| 6 June | Elfstedenronde | Belgium | 1.1 | 240 |
| 6–13 June | Tour de Suisse | Switzerland | 2.UWT | 241 |
| 8 June | Mont Ventoux Dénivelé Challenge | France | 1.1 | 249 |
| 9–13 June | Tour of Slovenia | Slovenia | 2.Pro | 250 |
| 9–13 June | Baloise Belgium Tour | Belgium | 2.Pro | 253 |
| 10–13 June | La Route d'Occitanie | France | 2.1 | 256 |
| 15 June | Paris–Camembert | France | 1.1 | 258 |
| 15–17 June | Adriatica Ionica Race | Spain | 2.1 | 259 |
| 24 June | Giro dell'Appennino | Italy | 1.1 | 261 |
| 26 June | La Course | France | 1.WWT | 262 |
| 26 June–18 July | Tour de France | France | 2.UWT | 264 |
| 27 June | GP Città di Lugano | Switzerland | 1.1 | 308 |

JUNE    .1 MEN'S RACE

# GP DES KANTONS AARGAU
4 June 2021
Leuggern–Leuggern
172km

## WEATHER

TEMPERATURE
20°C

WIND
SW 7km/h

## RESULTS

| POS | NAME | TEAM | TIME |
|---|---|---|---|
| 1. | I. Schelling | BOH | 4:05:45 |
| 2. | R. Costa | UAD | s.t. |
| 3. | E. Chaves | BEX | s.t. |
| 4. | G. Nizzolo | TQA | 0:15 |
| 5. | P. Ackermann | BOH | s.t. |
| 6. | M. Matthews | BEX | s.t. |
| 7. | M. Tizza | AMO | s.t. |
| 8. | A. Pasqualon | IWG | s.t. |
| 9. | G. Van Hoecke | ACT | s.t. |
| 10. | J. Simon | TDE | s.t. |
| 11. | M. Canola | GAZ | s.t. |
| 12. | R. Hardy | ARK | s.t. |
| 13. | J. Maas | LPC | s.t. |
| 14. | L. Ruegg | SRA | s.t. |
| 15. | J. Suter | BWB | s.t. |
| 16. | T. Willems | SVB | s.t. |
| 17. | A. Vuillermoz | TDE | s.t. |
| 18. | R. Gibbons | UAD | s.t. |
| 19. | M. Lammertink | IWG | s.t. |
| 20. | M. Schär | ACT | s.t. |

JUNE .PRO MEN'S RACE

# DWARS DOOR HET HAGELAND
5 June 2021
Aarschot–Diest
177km

## WEATHER

TEMPERATURE  WIND
14°C  W 17km/h

## RESULTS

| POS | NAME | TEAM | TIME |
|---|---|---|---|
| 1. | R. Tiller | UXT | 3:58:27 |
| 2. | D. van Poppel | IWG | 0:01 |
| 3. | Y. Lampaert | DQT | 0:02 |
| 4. | J. Rickaert | AFC | s.t. |
| 5. | P. Allegaert | COF | s.t. |
| 6. | C. Swift | ARK | 0:05 |
| 7. | B. van Poppel | IWG | 0:16 |
| 8. | D. Van Gestel | TDE | 0:47 |
| 9. | T. Merlier | AFC | 0:51 |
| 10. | K. Halvorsen | UXT | s.t. |
| 11. | T. Aerts | TBL | s.t. |
| 12. | M. Menten | BWB | s.t. |
| 13. | T. Nys | TBL | 0:53 |
| 14. | A. Capiot | ARK | s.t. |
| 15. | C. van Kessel | IWG | s.t. |
| 16. | T. van der Hoorn | IWG | 0:56 |
| 17. | N. Eekhoff | DSM | s.t. |
| 18. | J. Koch | IWG | s.t. |
| 19. | N. Arndt | DSM | s.t. |
| 20. | L. Mozzato | BBK | s.t. |

JUNE  .1 MEN'S RACE

# ELFSTEDENRONDE
6 June 2021
Bruges–Bruges
193.1km

## WEATHER

TEMPERATURE  WIND
20°C  NE 15km/h

## RESULTS

| POS | NAME | TEAM | TIME |
|---|---|---|---|
| 1. | T. Merlier | AFC | 4:16:30 |
| 2. | M. Cavendish | DQT | s.t. |
| 3. | S. Weemaes | SVB | s.t. |
| 4. | P. Ackermann | BOH | s.t. |
| 5. | M. Mørkøv | DQT | s.t. |
| 6. | D. van Poppel | IWG | s.t. |
| 7. | D. McLay | ARK | s.t. |
| 8. | L. Mozzato | BBK | s.t. |
| 9. | J. Warlop | SVB | s.t. |
| 10. | D. Groenewegen | TJV | s.t. |
| 11. | J. de Buyst | LTS | s.t. |
| 12. | J. Hesters | BCY | s.t. |
| 13. | A. Dainese | DSM | s.t. |
| 14. | M. Van Staeyen | EVO | s.t. |
| 15. | S. Aniołkowski | BWB | s.t. |
| 16. | J. Philipsen | AFC | s.t. |
| 17. | O. Nisu | EVO | s.t. |
| 18. | M. Pluto | ABC | 0:03 |
| 19. | G. D'heygere | TIS | s.t. |
| 20. | P. Gilbert | LTS | s.t. |

JUNE    WORLDTOUR MEN'S RACE

# TOUR DE SUISSE
Stage 1 (ITT)
6 June 2021
Frauenfeld–Frauenfeld
10.9km

## WEATHER

TEMPERATURE: 16°C
WIND: N 9km/h

## PROFILE

FRAUENFELD — FRAUENFELD

The customary opening time trial in and around Frauenfeld gave the peloton a taste of the weather to come in the Tour de Suisse. Early starter Stefan Bissegger got some of the worst of the rain, but he still managed to set a benchmark that was unassailable by all but one. Now six months into his first full season as a pro, Bissegger spent over an hour warming the hot seat for compatriot Stefan Küng, who celebrated victory on home roads, also taking the race lead. Mattia Cattaneo continued his run of strong form with third, and a little further down the results sheet was Tom Dumoulin in 16th, marking a satisfying return to racing after his six-month hiatus from the sport. (KN)

## STAGE RESULTS

| POS | NAME | TEAM | TIME |
|---|---|---|---|
| 1. | S. Küng | GFC | 12:00 |
| 2. | S. Bissegger | EFN | 0:04 |
| 3. | M. Cattaneo | DQT | 0:12 |
| 4. | T. Scully | EFN | 0:15 |
| 5. | J. Alaphilippe | DQT | 0:19 |
| 6. | J. Rutsch | EFN | 0:22 |
| 7. | J. Steimle | DQT | s.t. |
| 8. | F. Vermeersch | LTS | s.t. |
| 9. | S. Kragh Andersen | DSM | s.t. |
| 10. | R. Dennis | IGD | 0:23 |
| 11. | N. Powless | EFN | 0:25 |
| 12. | M. Schachmann | BOH | 0:29 |
| 13. | D. Devenyns | DQT | 0:30 |
| 14. | I. García Cortina | MOV | s.t. |
| 15. | R. Carapaz | IGD | 0:31 |
| 16. | T. Dumoulin | TJV | 0:32 |
| 17. | M. Boaro | APT | 0:33 |
| 18. | B. Jungels | ACT | s.t. |
| 19. | G. Serrano | MOV | 0:34 |
| 20. | S. de Bod | APT | s.t. |

## GENERAL CLASSIFICATION

| POS | NAME | TEAM | TIME |
|---|---|---|---|
| 1. | S. Küng | GFC | 12:00 |
| 2. | S. Bissegger | EFN | 0:04 |
| 3. | M. Cattaneo | DQT | 0:12 |

## POINTS

| POS | NAME | TEAM | PTS |
|---|---|---|---|
| 1. | S. Küng | GFC | 12 |
| 2. | S. Bissegger | EFN | 8 |
| 3. | M. Cattaneo | DQT | 6 |

## YOUNG RIDER

| POS | NAME | TEAM | TIME |
|---|---|---|---|
| 1. | S. Bissegger | EFN | 12:04 |
| 2. | J. Rutsch | EFN | 0:18 |
| 3. | J. Steimle | DQT | s.t. |

## TRIVIA

» More than half of Stefan Küng's 20 career victories have been achieved in his homeland of Switzerland.

JUNE    WORLDTOUR MEN'S RACE

# TOUR DE SUISSE
Stage 2
7 June 2021
Neuhausen am Rheinfall–Lachen
178km

A four-man breakaway fought over the first mountains jersey of the race, before Deceuninck-QuickStep took over in the last 10km. Julian Alaphilippe's inevitable attack drew out a group of GC favourites and Classics specialists, which included Michael Woods, Max Schachmann, Richard Carapaz and the ever-threatening Mathieu van der Poel. The group seemed desperate to shake the Dutch national champion before the flat finish, but he was more than equal to the task, and accelerated away just outside 3km to go. Schachmann alone could bridge up to Van der Poel's wheel, but the German seemed unable to do much work. Those left behind looked worn out by their own attacks, not to mention the gunmetal rainfall. In the end, there was no stopping Van der Poel, who threw his arms wide as he took a convincing stage win, with Schachmann one second behind and Wout Poels third. (KN)

## WEATHER

TEMPERATURE  WIND
19°C          N 9km/h

## PROFILE

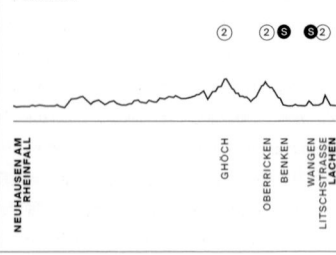

## BREAKAWAY
C. Imhof (NAT), T. Bohli (COF), N. Zukowsky (RLY), M Dal-Cin (RLY)

## STAGE RESULTS

| POS | NAME | TEAM | TIME |
|---|---|---|---|
| 1. | M. van der Poel | AFC | 4:12:30 |
| 2. | M. Schachmann | BOH | 0:01 |
| 3. | W. Poels | TBV | 0:04 |
| 4. | I. García Cortina | MOV | s.t. |
| 5. | M. Hirschi | UAD | s.t. |
| 6. | R. Carapaz | IGD | s.t. |
| 7. | M. Woods | ISN | s.t. |
| 8. | J. Alaphilippe | DQT | s.t. |
| 9. | J. Fuglsang | APT | s.t. |
| 10. | A. Kron | LTS | 0:09 |
| 11. | B. Cosnefroy | ACT | 0:11 |
| 12. | G. Mäder | TBV | s.t. |
| 13. | R. Urán | EFN | s.t. |
| 14. | M. Matthews | BEX | 0:22 |
| 15. | G. Serrano | MOV | s.t. |
| 16. | A. Vuillermoz | TDE | s.t. |
| 17. | E. Dunbar | IGD | s.t. |
| 18. | A. Kamp | TFS | s.t. |
| 19. | M. Cattaneo | DQT | s.t. |
| 20. | L. Rota | IWG | s.t. |

## GENERAL CLASSIFICATION

| POS | NAME | TEAM | TIME |
|---|---|---|---|
| 1. — | S. Küng | GFC | 4:24:52 |
| 2. ↑3 | J. Alaphilippe | DQT | 0:01 |
| 3. ↑9 | M. Schachmann | BOH | 0:02 |

## KING OF THE MOUNTAINS

| POS | NAME | TEAM | PTS |
|---|---|---|---|
| 1. | T. Bohli | COF | 10 |
| 2. | N. Zukowsky | RLY | 10 |
| 3. | M. Schachmann | BOH | 6 |

## POINTS

| POS | NAME | TEAM | PTS |
|---|---|---|---|
| 1. — | S. Küng | GFC | 12 |
| 2. — | M. van der Poel | AFC | 12 |
| 3. — | C. Imhof | NAT | 8 |

## YOUNG RIDER

| POS | NAME | TEAM | TIME |
|---|---|---|---|
| 1. ↑4 | N. Powless | EFN | 4:25:17 |
| 2. ↑5 | G. Mäder | TBV | 0:05 |
| 3. ↑10 | A. Kron | LTS | 0:08 |

## TRIVIA
» Mathieu van der Poel has now won a road race in nine different countries.

## BONUSES

| TYPE | NAME | TEAM |
|---|---|---|
| KOM 1 | N. Zukowsky | RLY |
| KOM 2 | T. Bohli | COF |
| KOM 3 | G. Mäder | TBV |
| Sprint 1 | C. Imhof | NAT |
| Sprint 2 | C. Imhof | NAT |

JUNE     WORLDTOUR MEN'S RACE

## TOUR DE SUISSE
Stage 3
8 June 2021
Lachen–Pfaffnau
182.1km

A four-man breakaway was let out early in the mercifully dry day, with the same teams represented as on the previous stage, only with the addition of Mathias Frank in his last stage race before retirement. A couple of unpleasant crashes upset the rhythm in the peloton before, with 25km to go, Mathieu van der Poel created more chaos when he accelerated, forcing all those who'd tried to shake him on stage 2 to follow. Julian Alaphilippe launched a furious attack just as they were about to be caught but, unfortunately for the world champion, the swollen chase had him pegged. Iván García made the most convincing escape inside the last 10km, but it was heartbreak for the Spaniard who was overcome by the bunch under the *flamme rouge*. A frantic sprint followed but Van der Poel was untouchable, his back-to-back stage wins giving him the race lead. (KN)

### WEATHER

TEMPERATURE: 21°C
WIND: NW 9km/h

### PROFILE

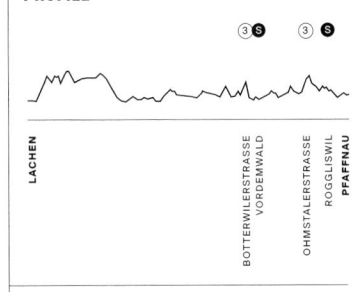

### BREAKAWAY
R. Rochas (COF), C. Imhof (NAT), B. King (RLY), M. Frank (ACT)

### STAGE RESULTS

| POS | NAME | TEAM | TIME |
|---|---|---|---|
| 1. | M. van der Poel | AFC | 4:24:26 |
| 2. | C. Laporte | COF | s.t. |
| 3. | J. Alaphilippe | DQT | s.t. |
| 4. | M. Matthews | BEX | s.t. |
| 5. | M. Schachmann | BOH | s.t. |
| 6. | A. Kamp | TFS | s.t. |
| 7. | T. Benoot | DSM | s.t. |
| 8. | O. Fraile | APT | s.t. |
| 9. | A. Turgis | TDE | s.t. |
| 10. | M. Woods | ISN | s.t. |
| 11. | L. Rota | IWG | s.t. |
| 12. | R. Carapaz | IGD | s.t. |
| 13. | E. Chaves | BEX | s.t. |
| 14. | W. Poels | TBV | s.t. |
| 15. | A. Kron | LTS | s.t. |
| 16. | B. Tulett | AFC | s.t. |
| 17. | R. Urán | EFN | s.t. |
| 18. | M. Hirschi | UAD | s.t. |
| 19. | E. Dunbar | IGD | s.t. |
| 20. | J. Fuglsang | APT | s.t. |

### GENERAL CLASSIFICATION

| POS | NAME | TEAM | TIME |
|---|---|---|---|
| 1. ↑3 | M. van der Poel | AFC | 8:49:14 |
| 2. — | J. Alaphilippe | DQT | 0:01 |
| 3. ↓2 | S. Küng | GFC | 0:04 |

### KING OF THE MOUNTAINS

| POS | NAME | TEAM | PTS |
|---|---|---|---|
| 1. ↑1 | N. Zukowsky | RLY | 10 |
| 2. ↓1 | T. Bohli | COF | 10 |
| 3. — | M. Schachmann | BOH | 6 |

### POINTS

| POS | NAME | TEAM | PTS |
|---|---|---|---|
| 1. ↑1 | M. van der Poel | AFC | 24 |
| 2. ↓1 | S. Küng | GFC | 12 |
| 3. — | C. Imhof | NAT | 12 |

### YOUNG RIDER

| POS | NAME | TEAM | TIME |
|---|---|---|---|
| 1. — | N. Powless | EFN | 8:49:43 |
| 2. ↑1 | A. Kron | LTS | 0:08 |
| 3. ↑1 | M. Hirschi | UAD | 0:23 |

### BONUSES

| TYPE | NAME | TEAM |
|---|---|---|
| KOM 1 | B. King | RLY |
| KOM 2 | R. Rochas | COF |
| Sprint 1 | C. Imhof | NAT |
| Sprint 2 | M. Cattaneo | DQT |

JUNE   WORLDTOUR MEN'S RACE

# TOUR DE SUISSE
Stage 4
9 June 2021
Sankt Urban–Gstaad
171km

## WEATHER

TEMPERATURE | WIND
15°C | NW 9km/h

## PROFILE

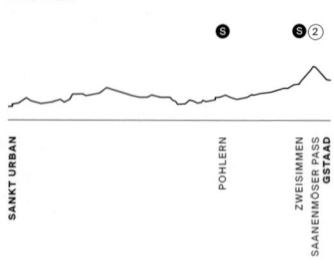

SANKT URBAN — POHLERN — ZWEISIMMEN — SAANENMOSER PASS — GSTAAD

The sun shone on the start line in Saint Urban, but heavy rain played a key role in the finale once again. Another four-man breakaway enjoyed a healthy advantage and – after a short-lived and somewhat half-hearted chase – the peloton let the breakaway have what fun they could. Joel Suter (of the Swiss national team) couldn't match the pace of his companions when they started testing each other inside the last 15km, and it fell to Stefan Bissegger, Benjamin Thomas and Joey Rosskopf to fight over the podium. Up against superior sprinters, Rosskopf tried his luck in the run-in, but his rivals were never far off his wheel and the American ended up leading them into the final straight. Thomas tried to react when Bissegger opened up his sprint, but he could not come round the young Swiss rider, who took his first road stage victory on the runway.

## BREAKAWAY
J. Suter (NAT), J. Rosskopf (RLY), B. Thomas (GFC), S. Bissegger (EFN)

## STAGE RESULTS

| POS | NAME | TEAM | TIME |
|---|---|---|---|
| 1. | S. Bissegger | EFN | 3:46:21 |
| 2. | B. Thomas | GFC | s.t. |
| 3. | J. Rosskopf | RLY | s.t. |
| 4. | J. Suter | NAT | 0:23 |
| 5. | E. Theuns | TFS | 5:16 |
| 6. | J. S. Molano | UAD | s.t. |
| 7. | O. Fraile | APT | s.t. |
| 8. | M. Teunissen | TJV | s.t. |
| 9. | F. Wright | TBV | s.t. |
| 10. | M. Matthews | BEX | s.t. |
| 11. | A. Stokbro | TQA | s.t. |
| 12. | G. Serrano | MOV | s.t. |
| 13. | A. Tiberi | TFS | s.t. |
| 14. | J. Stewart | GFC | s.t. |
| 15. | B. Tulett | AFC | s.t. |
| 16. | M. Van Gils | LTS | s.t. |
| 17. | E. Dunbar | IGD | s.t. |
| 18. | A. Kron | LTS | s.t. |
| 19. | L. Ruegg | NAT | s.t. |
| 20. | R. Thalmann | NAT | s.t. |

## GENERAL CLASSIFICATION

| POS | NAME | TEAM | TIME |
|---|---|---|---|
| 1. — | M. van der Poel | AFC | 12:40:51 |
| 2. — | J. Alaphilippe | DQT | 0:01 |
| 3. — | S. Küng | GFC | 0:04 |

## KING OF THE MOUNTAINS

| POS | NAME | TEAM | PTS |
|---|---|---|---|
| 1. — | N. Zukowsky | RLY | 10 |
| 2. — | T. Bohli | COF | 10 |
| 3. — | M. Schachmann | BOH | 6 |

## POINTS

| POS | NAME | TEAM | PTS |
|---|---|---|---|
| 1. — | M. van der Poel | AFC | 24 |
| 2. ↑6 | S. Bissegger | EFN | 21 |
| 3. ↓1 | S. Küng | GFC | 12 |

## YOUNG RIDER

| POS | NAME | TEAM | TIME |
|---|---|---|---|
| 1. — | N. Powless | EFN | 12:41:20 |
| 2. — | A. Kron | LTS | 0:08 |
| 3. ↑20 | S. Bissegger | EFN | 0:09 |

## BONUSES

| TYPE | NAME | TEAM |
|---|---|---|
| KOM 1 | J. Suter | NAT |
| Sprint 1 | J. Rosskopf | RLY |
| Sprint 2 | B. Thomas | GFC |

JUNE     WORLDTOUR MEN'S RACE

# TOUR DE SUISSE
Stage 5
10 June 2021
Gstaad–Leukerbad
175.2km

The first truly mountainous day staged an unlikely story starring Mathieu van der Poel, who got himself into the day's four-man breakaway knowing he was unlikely to hold on to the race lead. The stage otherwise unfolded as expected and the escape was caught by the penultimate climb, where Antwan Tolhoek's attack provided a springboard for Esteban Chaves. The Colombian led the race over the category-1 climb of Erschmatt but his margin was slim, and one ill-judged corner on the descent made it much easier for lone chaser Jakob Fuglsang to join and then drop him just outside 5km to go. Unfortunately for Fuglsang, the peloton was not far behind and Michael Woods' acceleration drew out Richard Carapaz. In the uphill sprint, Carapaz positioned himself on the Dane's wheel, ready to surge past him at the very last minute, taking the race lead with a smart stage victory.

## WEATHER

TEMPERATURE     WIND
24°C     NE 20km/h

## PROFILE

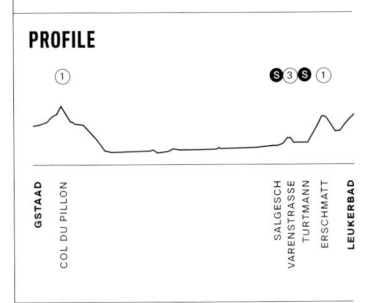

GSTAAD — COL DU PILLON — SALGESCH — VARENSTRASSE — TURTMANN — ERSCHMATT — LEUKERBAD

## BREAKAWAY

C. Imhof (NAT), S. Samitier (MOV), H. Pernsteiner (TBV), M. van der Poel (AFC)

## STAGE RESULTS

| POS | NAME | TEAM | TIME |
|---|---|---|---|
| 1. | R. Carapaz | IGD | 4:01:52 |
| 2. | J. Fuglsang | APT | s.t. |
| 3. | M. Woods | ISN | 0:39 |
| 4. | L. Hamilton | BEX | s.t. |
| 5. | R. Urán | EFN | s.t. |
| 6. | M. Schachmann | BOH | s.t. |
| 7. | J. Alaphilippe | DQT | s.t. |
| 8. | D. Pozzovivo | TQA | s.t. |
| 9. | E. Chaves | BEX | 0:49 |
| 10. | S. Oomen | TJV | 1:22 |
| 11. | A. Tolhoek | TJV | 2:17 |
| 12. | E. Dunbar | IGD | 3:39 |
| 13. | T. Benoot | DSM | s.t. |
| 14. | M. Badilatti | GFC | 4:04 |
| 15. | R. Costa | UAD | s.t. |
| 16. | N. Eg | TFS | 4:13 |
| 17. | A. Vuillermoz | TDE | 4:31 |
| 18. | G. Serrano | MOV | s.t. |
| 19. | J. Piccoli | ISN | s.t. |
| 20. | X. Meurisse | AFC | s.t. |

## GENERAL CLASSIFICATION

| POS | NAME | TEAM | TIME |
|---|---|---|---|
| 1. ↑6 | R. Carapaz | IGD | 16:42:50 |
| 2. ↑10 | J. Fuglsang | APT | 0:26 |
| 3. ↑1 | M. Schachmann | BOH | 0:38 |

## KING OF THE MOUNTAINS

| POS | NAME | TEAM | PTS |
|---|---|---|---|
| 1. — | E. Chaves | BEX | 12 |
| 2. — | G. Mannion | RLY | 12 |
| 3. ↓2 | N. Zukowsky | RLY | 10 |

## POINTS

| POS | NAME | TEAM | PTS |
|---|---|---|---|
| 1. — | M. van der Poel | AFC | 26 |
| 2. — | S. Bissegger | EFN | 21 |
| 3. ↑1 | C. Imhof | NAT | 16 |

## YOUNG RIDER

| POS | NAME | TEAM | TIME |
|---|---|---|---|
| 1. ↑5 | L. Hamilton | BEX | 16:44:21 |
| 2. ↑3 | E. Dunbar | IGD | 2:57 |
| 3. ↑5 | S. Williams | TBV | 4:26 |

## TRIVIA

» This was Richard Carapaz's first win of the season, and only the second since his Giro d'Italia victory in 2019.

## BONUSES

| TYPE | NAME | TEAM |
|---|---|---|
| KOM 1 | G. Mannion | RLY |
| KOM 2 | S. Samitier | MOV |
| KOM 3 | E. Chaves | BEX |
| Sprint 1 | C. Imhof | NAT |
| Sprint 2 | M. Cattaneo | DQT |

JUNE     WORLDTOUR MEN'S RACE

# TOUR DE SUISSE
Stage 6
11 June 2021
Fiesch–Disentis Sedrun
130.1km

The first of three rerouted stages following heavy snowfall in the high mountains, stage 6 took on the Gotthardpass straight out of the blocks and a very large group made short work of the escape. The peloton was happy to let the breakaway have the day to themselves, and the attacks began on the Lukmanierpass, the escapees trading blows and jettisoning passengers before the final ramp. The winning move came in the last 5km when three-time Tour de Suisse champion Rui Costa jumped away with Andreas Kron and Hermann Pernsteiner. Costa opened his sprint as he rounded the final bend 200m from the line, swinging into the path of Kron who had to ease off in a crucial moment. Even Costa's celebration was slightly flat and, sure enough, the win was awarded to the 23-year-old Dane.

## WEATHER

**TEMPERATURE** 14°C
**WIND** N 4km/h

## PROFILE

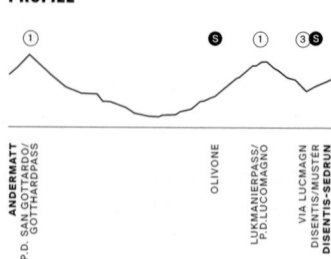

## BREAKAWAY
J. Alaphilippe (DQT), M. Cattaneo (DQT), M. Soler (MOV), A. Nibali (TFS)

## STAGE RESULTS

| POS | NAME | TEAM | TIME |
|---|---|---|---|
| 1. | A. Kron | LTS | 3:14:52 |
| 2. | R. Costa | UAD | s.t. |
| 3. | H. Pernsteiner | TBV | 0:01 |
| 4. | G. Serrano | MOV | 0:03 |
| 5. | P. Latour | TDE | s.t. |
| 6. | H. Houle | APT | s.t. |
| 7. | N. Powless | EFN | s.t. |
| 8. | A. Tolhoek | TJV | s.t. |
| 9. | M. Fabbro | BOH | 0:50 |
| 10. | A. Leknessund | DSM | 1:00 |
| 11. | F. Wright | TBV | 1:15 |
| 12. | M. Matthews | BEX | s.t. |
| 13. | M. Vansevenant | DQT | s.t. |
| 14. | S. Samitier | MOV | s.t. |
| 15. | M. Hirschi | UAD | s.t. |
| 16. | O. Fraile | APT | 1:19 |
| 17. | J. Piccoli | ISN | 1:37 |
| 18. | K. Murphy | RLY | 1:41 |
| 19. | M. Donovan | DSM | 2:16 |
| 20. | J. Simon | TDE | 2:49 |

## GENERAL CLASSIFICATION

| POS | NAME | TEAM | TIME |
|---|---|---|---|
| 1. – | R. Carapaz | IGD | 20:00:31 |
| 2. – | J. Fuglsang | APT | 0:26 |
| 3. – | M. Schachmann | BOH | 0:38 |

## KING OF THE MOUNTAINS

| POS | NAME | TEAM | PTS |
|---|---|---|---|
| 1. ↑7 | A. Nibali | TFS | 20 |
| 2. – | D. de la Cruz | UAD | 15 |
| 3. ↑2 | S. Samitier | MOV | 15 |

## POINTS

| POS | NAME | TEAM | PTS |
|---|---|---|---|
| 1. ↑1 | S. Bissegger | EFN | 21 |
| 2. ↑1 | C. Imhof | NAT | 16 |
| 3. – | A. Kron | LTS | 14 |

## YOUNG RIDER

| POS | NAME | TEAM | TIME |
|---|---|---|---|
| 1. ↑3 | A. Leknessund | DSM | 20:05:10 |
| 2. – | E. Dunbar | IGD | 0:09 |
| 3. ↑2 | N. Powless | EFN | 1:42 |

## BONUSES

| TYPE | NAME | TEAM |
|---|---|---|
| KOM 1 | D. de la Cruz | UAD |
| KOM 2 | A. Nibali | TFS |
| KOM 3 | D. de la Cruz | UAD |
| Sprint 1 | M. Matthews | BEX |
| Sprint 2 | D. de la Cruz | UAD |

JUNE  WORLDTOUR MEN'S RACE

# TOUR DE SUISSE
Stage 7 (ITT)
12 June 2021
Disentis Sedrun–Andermatt
23.2km

The impending Tour de France hovered in the periphery of stage 7, the 23.2km mountain test representing an important gauge of form two weeks from the grand départ. With the 9.5km Oberalppass (average 6.4 per cent) to contend with before a fast descent into Andermatt, equipment was a hot topic, the riders choosing from a pick-and-mix of time trial rigs, disc wheels and tri bar-equipped road bikes, aero and climbing helmets, and bike changes at the summit. Tom Dumoulin laid down a strong marker but was soon pipped by a flying Gino Mäder despite a nervy descent. Rigoberto Urán then obliterated the fastest intermediate time and flew his full TT set-up down the mountain to his first win in three years, jumping up to second overall and slashing the advantage Richard Carapaz had before the stage. Julian Alaphilippe wrestled his road bike to second place, 40 seconds down, and Gino Mäder took third.

## WEATHER

TEMPERATURE
28°C

WIND
S 9km/h

## PROFILE

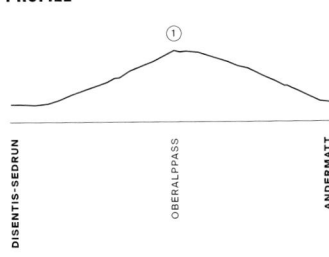

DISENTIS-SEDRUN — OBERALPPASS — ANDERMATT

## STAGE RESULTS

| POS | NAME | TEAM | TIME |
|---|---|---|---|
| 1. | R. Urán | EFN | 36:02 |
| 2. | J. Alaphilippe | DQT | 0:40 |
| 3. | G. Mäder | TBV | 0:54 |
| 4. | R. Carapaz | IGD | s.t. |
| 5. | T. Dumoulin | TJV | 0:56 |
| 6. | M. Cattaneo | DQT | 0:58 |
| 7. | D. Pozzovivo | TQA | 1:00 |
| 8. | R. Costa | UAD | s.t. |
| 9. | S. Kragh Andersen | DSM | 1:04 |
| 10. | S. Küng | GFC | 1:05 |
| 11. | W. Poels | TBV | 1:14 |
| 12. | V. de la Parte | TDE | 1:16 |
| 13. | M. Schachmann | BOH | 1:23 |
| 14. | P. Latour | TDE | 1:32 |
| 15. | J. Rutsch | EFN | 1:35 |
| 16. | J. Fuglsang | APT | 1:43 |
| 17. | H. Pernsteiner | TBV | 1:46 |
| 18. | N. Powless | EFN | 1:52 |
| 19. | A. Leknessund | DSM | s.t. |
| 20. | R. Dennis | IGD | 1:58 |

## GENERAL CLASSIFICATION

| POS | NAME | TEAM | TIME |
|---|---|---|---|
| 1. — | R. Carapaz | IGD | 20:37:27 |
| 2. ↑3 | R. Urán | EFN | 0:17 |
| 3. ↑1 | J. Alaphilippe | DQT | 0:39 |

## KING OF THE MOUNTAINS

| POS | NAME | TEAM | PTS |
|---|---|---|---|
| 1. — | A. Nibali | TFS | 20 |
| 2. ↑4 | J. Alaphilippe | DQT | 20 |
| 3. ↑17 | R. Urán | EFN | 16 |

## POINTS

| POS | NAME | TEAM | PTS |
|---|---|---|---|
| 1. — | S. Bissegger | EFN | 21 |
| 2. ↑3 | R. Carapaz | IGD | 16 |
| 3. ↓1 | C. Imhof | NAT | 16 |

## YOUNG RIDER

| POS | NAME | TEAM | TIME |
|---|---|---|---|
| 1. — | A. Leknessund | DSM | 20:43:04 |
| 2. — | E. Dunbar | IGD | 0:38 |
| 3. — | N. Powless | EFN | 1:42 |

## TRIVIA
» This was Rigoberto Urán's first win since the 2018 Tour of Slovenia.

## BONUSES

| TYPE | NAME | TEAM |
|---|---|---|
| KOM 1 | R. Urán | EFN |

JUNE — WORLDTOUR MEN'S RACE

# TOUR DE SUISSE
Stage 8
13 June 2021
Andermatt–Andermatt
159.5km

The final stage went back over familiar ground, taking the peloton over the past two stages tacked together. The GC race was much closer than it had been before the previous day's time trial, even without third-place Julian Alaphilippe, who was on his way home for the birth of his first child. With the early breakaway caught, Richard Carapaz was put under pressure by the likes of Rigoberto Urán on the Gotthardpass, but he was too strong to shake. Michael Woods then attacked near the top, drawing out Mattia Cattaneo and Gino Mäder, who caught up to the Canadian on the sweeping descent. With the GC group only seconds behind, Woods was forced to lead the pair into Andermatt, which allowed Mäder to time his sprint to perfection. Woods settled for second, also taking the final KOM jersey, and Cattaneo led the favourites home a slender 9 seconds later.

## WEATHER

TEMPERATURE: 19°C
WIND: N 12km/h

## PROFILE

ANDERMATT / OBERALPPASS — P.D. LUCOMAGNO/LUKMANIERPASS — GIORNICO — AMBRI (QUINTO) — GOTTHARDPASS/P.SAN GOTTARDO — ANDERMATT

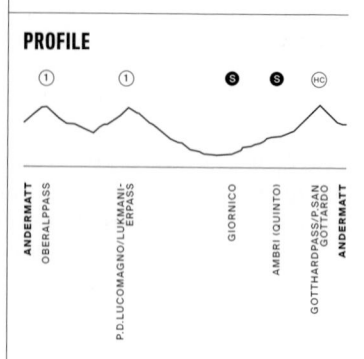

## BREAKAWAY

A. Leknessund (DSM), W. Poels (TBV), T. Benoot (DSM), H. Pernsteiner (TBV), O. Fraile (APT), N. Peters (ACT), S. Küng (GFC), D. Devenyns (DQT), M. Vansevenant (DQT), S. Samitier (MOV), D. de la Cruz (UAD), S. Kragh Andersen (DSM), F. Doubey (TDE), M. Soler (MOV), A. Nibali (TFS)

## STAGE RESULTS

| POS | NAME | TEAM | TIME |
|---|---|---|---|
| 1. | G. Mäder | TBV | 4:06:25 |
| 2. | M. Woods | ISN | s.t. |
| 3. | M. Cattaneo | DQT | 0:09 |
| 4. | E. Dunbar | IGD | s.t. |
| 5. | R. Carapaz | IGD | s.t. |
| 6. | R. Costa | UAD | s.t. |
| 7. | R. Urán | EFN | s.t. |
| 8. | D. Pozzovivo | TQA | s.t. |
| 9. | J. Fuglsang | APT | s.t. |
| 10. | M. Schachmann | BOH | 0:21 |
| 11. | N. Powless | EFN | 0:44 |
| 12. | S. Oomen | TJV | 0:46 |
| 13. | E. Chaves | BEX | 1:13 |
| 14. | G. Serrano | MOV | 1:36 |
| 15. | P. Latour | TDE | s.t. |
| 16. | M. Van Gils | LTS | s.t. |
| 17. | H. Carretero | MOV | s.t. |
| 18. | H. Pernsteiner | TBV | 1:38 |
| 19. | G. Mannion | RLY | s.t. |
| 20. | A. Kron | LTS | 3:20 |

## GENERAL CLASSIFICATION

| POS | | NAME | TEAM | TIME |
|---|---|---|---|---|
| 1. | – | R. Carapaz | IGD | 24:44:01 |
| 2. | – | R. Urán | EFN | 0:17 |
| 3. | ↑2 | J. Fuglsang | APT | 1:15 |

## KING OF THE MOUNTAINS

| POS | | NAME | TEAM | PTS |
|---|---|---|---|---|
| 1. | ↑10 | M. Woods | ISN | 29 |
| 2. | ↑2 | D. de la Cruz | UAD | 29 |
| 3. | ↑2 | S. Samitier | MOV | 29 |

## POINTS

| POS | | NAME | TEAM | PTS |
|---|---|---|---|---|
| 1. | – | S. Bissegger | EFN | 21 |
| 2. | ↑5 | M. Cattaneo | DQT | 20 |
| 3. | ↓1 | R. Carapaz | IGD | 18 |

## YOUNG RIDER

| POS | | NAME | TEAM | TIME |
|---|---|---|---|---|
| 1. | ↑1 | E. Dunbar | IGD | 24:50:16 |
| 2. | ↑1 | N. Powless | EFN | 1:39 |
| 3. | ↑1 | A. Kron | LTS | 7:26 |

## TRIVIA

» Ineos Grenadiers have now won four WorldTour stage races in a row (Tour de Romandie, Giro, Dauphiné and now Tour de Suisse), each with a different rider.

## BONUSES

| TYPE | NAME | TEAM |
|---|---|---|
| KOM 1 | W. Poels | TBV |
| KOM 2 | W. Poels | TBV |
| KOM 3 | M. Woods | ISN |
| Sprint 1 | G. Mäder | TBV |
| Sprint 2 | S. Küng | GFC |

JUNE  .1 MEN'S RACE

# MONT VENTOUX DÉNIVELÉ CHALLENGE

8 June 2021
Vaison-la-Romaine–Mont Ventoux
153km

## WEATHER

TEMPERATURE | WIND
28°C | SE 9km/h

## RESULTS

| POS | NAME | TEAM | TIME |
|---|---|---|---|
| 1. | M. A. López | MOV | 4:30:04 |
| 2. | O. Rodríguez | APT | 2:26 |
| 3. | E. Mas | MOV | 2:33 |
| 4. | B. O'Connor | ACT | 3:30 |
| 5. | C. Rodríguez | TDE | s.t. |
| 6. | K. Elissonde | TFS | 4:02 |
| 7. | M. Ries | TFS | 4:45 |
| 8. | S. Carr | EFN | 5:41 |
| 9. | C. Verona | MOV | 5:48 |
| 10. | G. Bouchard | ACT | 6:10 |
| 11. | M. Chevalier | BBK | 6:17 |
| 12. | J. Bernard | TFS | 6:32 |
| 13. | C. Berthet | DKO | 6:50 |
| 14. | M. Kudus | APT | 7:38 |
| 15. | M. Iturria | EUS | 7:53 |
| 16. | A. Okamika | BBH | 8:58 |
| 17. | M. A. Ballesteros | EHE | 9:04 |
| 18. | J. García | CJR | 9:11 |
| 19. | J. Cabot | TDE | 9:27 |
| 20. | Q. Pacher | BBK | 9:31 |

JUNE .PRO MEN'S RACE

## TOUR OF SLOVENIA
Stage 1
9 June 2021
Ptuj–Rogaška Slatina
151.5km

### WEATHER

TEMPERATURE: 27°C
WIND: NE 4km/h

### STAGE RESULTS

| POS | NAME | TEAM | TIME |
|---|---|---|---|
| 1. | P. Bauhaus | TBV | 3:33:45 |
| 2. | J. Aberasturi | CJR | s.t. |
| 3. | R. Oliveira | UAD | s.t. |
| 4. | S. Aniołkowski | BWB | s.t. |
| 5. | M. Malucelli | ANS | s.t. |
| 6. | A. Edmondson | BEX | s.t. |
| 7. | A. Banaszek | MSP | s.t. |
| 8. | R. Christensen | DHB | s.t. |
| 9. | M. Bostock | DHB | s.t. |
| 10. | M. Alonso | EUS | s.t. |
| 11. | H. Haussler | TBV | s.t. |
| 12. | R. Stannard | BEX | s.t. |
| 13. | J. Primožič | NAT | s.t. |
| 14. | M. Gibson | RWC | s.t. |
| 15. | O. W. Frederiksen | TCQ | s.t. |
| 16. | L. Kubiš | DKB | s.t. |
| 17. | S. Kolze Changizi | TCQ | s.t. |
| 18. | D. Ulissi | UAD | s.t. |
| 19. | T. Finkšt | LGS | s.t. |
| 20. | V. Kuznetsov | GAZ | s.t. |

### GENERAL CLASSIFICATION

| POS | NAME | TEAM | TIME |
|---|---|---|---|
| 1. | P. Bauhaus | TBV | 3:33:35 |
| 2. | J. Aberasturi | CJR | 0:04 |
| 3. | R. Oliveira | UAD | 0:06 |

### KING OF THE MOUNTAINS

| POS | NAME | TEAM | PTS |
|---|---|---|---|
| 1. | M. Paasschens | BWB | 3 |
| 2. | J. Scott | DHB | 2 |
| 3. | A. Bagües | CJR | 1 |

### POINTS

| POS | NAME | TEAM | PTS |
|---|---|---|---|
| 1. | P. Bauhaus | TBV | 25 |
| 2. | J. Aberasturi | CJR | 20 |
| 3. | R. Oliveira | UAD | 16 |

### YOUNG RIDER

| POS | NAME | TEAM | TIME |
|---|---|---|---|
| 1. | J. I. Hvideberg | UXT | 3:33:42 |
| 2. | O. W. Frederiksen | TCQ | 0:03 |
| 3. | L. Kubiš | DKB | s.t. |

## TOUR OF SLOVENIA
Stage 2
10 June 2021
Žalec–Celje (Celjski Grad)
147km

### WEATHER

TEMPERATURE: 25°C
WIND: N 6km/h

### STAGE RESULTS

| POS | NAME | TEAM | TIME |
|---|---|---|---|
| 1. | T. Pogačar | UAD | 3:32:03 |
| 2. | M. Mohorič | TBV | 1:22 |
| 3. | D. Ulissi | UAD | s.t. |
| 4. | M. Sobrero | APT | s.t. |
| 5. | T. Kangert | BEX | 1:25 |
| 6. | J. Shaw | RWC | s.t. |
| 7. | R. Majka | UAD | s.t. |
| 8. | G. Carboni | BCF | s.t. |
| 9. | J. Lastra | CJR | s.t. |
| 10. | J. Polanc | UAD | 1:30 |
| 11. | R. Stannard | BEX | 1:57 |
| 12. | J. Tratnik | TBV | 3:27 |
| 13. | L. Chirico | ANS | 3:30 |
| 14. | J. A. Pallesen | TCQ | 3:32 |
| 15. | K. Hočevar | ADR | s.t. |
| 16. | S. R. Martín | CJR | s.t. |
| 17. | D. Muñoz | ANS | 3:36 |
| 18. | A. Zeits | BEX | s.t. |
| 19. | A. Garosio | BCF | s.t. |
| 20. | D. Strakhov | GAZ | s.t. |

### GENERAL CLASSIFICATION

| POS | | NAME | TEAM | TIME |
|---|---|---|---|---|
| 1. | ↑45 | T. Pogačar | UAD | 7:05:37 |
| 2. | ↑29 | M. Mohorič | TBV | 1:24 |
| 3. | ↑4 | D. Ulissi | UAD | 1:28 |

### KING OF THE MOUNTAINS

| POS | | NAME | TEAM | PTS |
|---|---|---|---|---|
| 1. | – | T. Pogačar | UAD | 6 |
| 2. | – | K. Molly | BWB | 6 |
| 3. | – | M. Sobrero | APT | 4 |

### POINTS

| POS | | NAME | TEAM | PTS |
|---|---|---|---|---|
| 1. | – | P. Bauhaus | TBV | 28 |
| 2. | – | T. Pogačar | UAD | 26 |
| 3. | – | M. Mohorič | TBV | 25 |

### YOUNG RIDER

| POS | | NAME | TEAM | TIME |
|---|---|---|---|---|
| 1. | ↑9 | K. Hočevar | ADR | 7:09:20 |
| 2. | ↑7 | R. García Pierna | EKP | 0:09 |
| 3. | ↑8 | W. B. Levy | TCQ | 3:26 |

JUNE .PRO MEN'S RACE

## TOUR OF SLOVENIA
Stage 3
11 June 2021
Brežice–Krško
165.8km

### WEATHER

TEMPERATURE | WIND
26°C | W 6km/h

### STAGE RESULTS

| POS | NAME | TEAM | TIME |
| --- | --- | --- | --- |
| 1. | J. Aberasturi | CJR | 3:50:26 |
| 2. | M. Mohorič | TBV | s.t. |
| 3. | M. Trentin | UAD | s.t. |
| 4. | R. Mertz | BWB | s.t. |
| 5. | J. A. Pallesen | TCQ | s.t. |
| 6. | J. Shaw | RWC | s.t. |
| 7. | D. Muñoz | ANS | s.t. |
| 8. | G. Carboni | BCF | s.t. |
| 9. | D. Strakhov | GAZ | s.t. |
| 10. | J. Romo | APT | s.t. |
| 11. | M. Hoelgaard | UXT | s.t. |
| 12. | D. Peyskens | BWB | s.t. |
| 13. | M. Stedman | DHB | s.t. |
| 14. | L. Chirico | ANS | s.t. |
| 15. | M. Sobrero | APT | s.t. |
| 16. | P. Brożyna | MSP | s.t. |
| 17. | A. Zeits | BEX | s.t. |
| 18. | I. Moreno | EKP | s.t. |
| 19. | T. Pogačar | UAD | s.t. |
| 20. | S. R. Martín | CJR | s.t. |

### GENERAL CLASSIFICATION

| POS | NAME | TEAM | TIME |
| --- | --- | --- | --- |
| 1. — | T. Pogačar | UAD | 10:56:03 |
| 2. — | M. Mohorič | TBV | 1:15 |
| 3. — | D. Ulissi | UAD | 1:26 |

### KING OF THE MOUNTAINS

| POS | NAME | TEAM | PTS |
| --- | --- | --- | --- |
| 1. ↑1 | K. Molly | BWB | 9 |
| 2. ↓1 | T. Pogačar | UAD | 8 |
| 3. ↑3 | R. Majka | UAD | 5 |

### POINTS

| POS | NAME | TEAM | PTS |
| --- | --- | --- | --- |
| 1. ↑2 | M. Mohorič | TBV | 50 |
| 2. ↑2 | J. Aberasturi | CJR | 45 |
| 3. ↓2 | P. Bauhaus | TBV | 28 |

### YOUNG RIDER

| POS | NAME | TEAM | TIME |
| --- | --- | --- | --- |
| 1. — | K. Hočevar | ADR | 10:59:46 |
| 2. — | R. García Pierna | EKP | 2:09 |
| 3. ↑2 | J. Romo | APT | 4:22 |

## TOUR OF SLOVENIA
Stage 4
12 June 2021
Ajdovščina–Nova Gorica
164.1km

### WEATHER

TEMPERATURE | WIND
28°C | SW 13km/h

### STAGE RESULTS

| POS | NAME | TEAM | TIME |
| --- | --- | --- | --- |
| 1. | D. Ulissi | UAD | 4:15:28 |
| 2. | T. Pogačar | UAD | 0:01 |
| 3. | M. Sobrero | APT | s.t. |
| 4. | R. Majka | UAD | 0:27 |
| 5. | J. Shaw | RWC | 0:48 |
| 6. | T. Kangert | BEX | 0:53 |
| 7. | G. Carboni | BCF | 1:05 |
| 8. | M. Mohorič | TBV | 1:19 |
| 9. | J. Romo | APT | 1:28 |
| 10. | J. Polanc | UAD | 1:35 |
| 11. | I. Zakarin | GAZ | 1:47 |
| 12. | I. Moreno | EKP | 1:56 |
| 13. | A. Nych | GAZ | 2:09 |
| 14. | A. Zeits | BEX | 2:15 |
| 15. | A. Bisolti | ANS | 2:27 |
| 16. | M. Hoelgaard | UXT | 2:32 |
| 17. | S. R. Martín | CJR | 2:45 |
| 18. | J. Tratnik | TBV | 2:48 |
| 19. | T. Træen | UXT | 2:52 |
| 20. | L. Chirico | ANS | 3:04 |

### GENERAL CLASSIFICATION

| POS | NAME | TEAM | TIME |
| --- | --- | --- | --- |
| 1. — | T. Pogačar | UAD | 15:11:26 |
| 2. ↑1 | D. Ulissi | UAD | 1:21 |
| 3. ↑1 | M. Sobrero | APT | 1:35 |

### KING OF THE MOUNTAINS

| POS | NAME | TEAM | PTS |
| --- | --- | --- | --- |
| 1. ↑1 | T. Pogačar | UAD | 16 |
| 2. ↑1 | R. Majka | UAD | 13 |
| 3. — | D. Ulissi | UAD | 12 |

### POINTS

| POS | NAME | TEAM | PTS |
| --- | --- | --- | --- |
| 1. — | M. Mohorič | TBV | 58 |
| 2. ↑2 | T. Pogačar | UAD | 46 |
| 3. ↑2 | D. Ulissi | UAD | 45 |

### YOUNG RIDER

| POS | NAME | TEAM | TIME |
| --- | --- | --- | --- |
| 1. — | K. Hočevar | ADR | 15:18:30 |
| 2. ↑1 | J. Romo | APT | 2:34 |
| 3. ↓1 | R. García Pierna | EKP | 8:13 |

JUNE .PRO MEN'S RACE

# TOUR OF SLOVENIA
Stage 5
13 June 2021
Ljubljana–Novo Mesto
175.3km

## WEATHER

| TEMPERATURE | WIND |
|---|---|
| 22°C | SE 11km/h |

## STAGE RESULTS

| POS | NAME | TEAM | TIME |
|---|---|---|---|
| 1. | P. Bauhaus | TBV | 4:12:05 |
| 2. | A. Edmondson | BEX | s.t. |
| 3. | H. Haussler | TBV | s.t. |
| 4. | M. Trentin | UAD | s.t. |
| 5. | J. Aberasturi | CJR | s.t. |
| 6. | E. Sanz | EKP | s.t. |
| 7. | M. Gibson | RWC | s.t. |
| 8. | R. Oliveira | UAD | s.t. |
| 9. | A. Banaszek | MSP | s.t. |
| 10. | M. Sobrero | APT | s.t. |
| 11. | S. Aniołkowski | BWB | s.t. |
| 12. | M. Malucelli | ANS | s.t. |
| 13. | Ž. Jerman | ANS | s.t. |
| 14. | D. Martinelli | APT | s.t. |
| 15. | R. Mertz | BWB | s.t. |
| 16. | E. Zanoncello | BCF | s.t. |
| 17. | J. Shaw | RWC | s.t. |
| 18. | A. Soto | EUS | s.t. |
| 19. | S. Kolze Changizi | TCQ | s.t. |
| 20. | M. Bostock | DHB | s.t. |

## GENERAL CLASSIFICATION

| POS | NAME | TEAM | TIME |
|---|---|---|---|
| 1. — | T. Pogačar | UAD | 19:23:31 |
| 2. — | D. Ulissi | UAD | 1:21 |
| 3. — | M. Sobrero | APT | 1:35 |

## KING OF THE MOUNTAINS

| POS | NAME | TEAM | PTS |
|---|---|---|---|
| 1. — | T. Pogačar | UAD | 16 |
| 2. — | R. Majka | UAD | 13 |
| 3. — | D. Ulissi | UAD | 12 |

## POINTS

| POS | NAME | TEAM | PTS |
|---|---|---|---|
| 1. — | M. Mohorič | TBV | 58 |
| 2. ↑2 | J. Aberasturi | CJR | 57 |
| 3. ↑4 | P. Bauhaus | TBV | 53 |

## YOUNG RIDER

| POS | NAME | TEAM | TIME |
|---|---|---|---|
| 1. — | K. Hočevar | ADR | 19:30:35 |
| 2. — | J. Romo | APT | 2:34 |
| 3. — | R. García Pierna | EKP | 8:13 |

JUNE .PRO MEN'S RACE

## BALOISE BELGIUM TOUR
Stage 1
9 June 2021
Beveren–Maarkedal
175.3km

## WEATHER

TEMPERATURE | WIND
23°C | W 11km/h

### STAGE RESULTS

| POS | NAME | TEAM | TIME |
|---|---|---|---|
| 1. | R. Ghys | SVB | 4:05:15 |
| 2. | R. Evenepoel | DQT | s.t. |
| 3. | G. Marchand | TIS | s.t. |
| 4. | J. Philipsen | AFC | 0:28 |
| 5. | J. de Buyst | LTS | s.t. |
| 6. | T. Aerts | TBL | s.t. |
| 7. | I. Schelling | BOH | s.t. |
| 8. | B. van Poppel | IWG | s.t. |
| 9. | B. Coquard | BBK | s.t. |
| 10. | P. Eenkhoorn | TJV | s.t. |
| 11. | N. Bouhanni | ARK | s.t. |
| 12. | Y. Lampaert | DQT | s.t. |
| 13. | F. Van den Bossche | SVB | s.t. |
| 14. | E. Iserbyt | PSB | s.t. |
| 15. | D. Claeys | TQA | s.t. |
| 16. | D. Van Gestel | TDE | s.t. |
| 17. | L. Vliegen | IWG | s.t. |
| 18. | F. Fisher-Black | TJV | s.t. |
| 19. | F. Fiorelli | BCF | s.t. |
| 20. | C. Swift | ARK | s.t. |

### GENERAL CLASSIFICATION

| POS | NAME | TEAM | TIME |
|---|---|---|---|
| 1. | R. Evenepoel | DQT | 4:05:00 |
| 2. | R. Ghys | SVB | 0:05 |
| 3. | G. Marchand | TIS | 0:08 |

### POINTS

| POS | NAME | TEAM | PTS |
|---|---|---|---|
| 1. | R. Ghys | SVB | 30 |
| 2. | R. Evenepoel | DQT | 25 |
| 3. | G. Marchand | TIS | 22 |

## BALOISE BELGIUM TOUR
Stage 2 (ITT)
10 June 2021
Knokke-Heist–Knokke-Heist
11.2km

## WEATHER

TEMPERATURE | WIND
20°C | NW 13km/h

### STAGE RESULTS

| POS | NAME | TEAM | TIME |
|---|---|---|---|
| 1. | R. Evenepoel | DQT | 12:00 |
| 2. | Y. Lampaert | DQT | 0:02 |
| 3. | F. Fisher-Black | TJV | 0:18 |
| 4. | R. Herregodts | SVB | 0:19 |
| 5. | F. Frison | LTS | s.t. |
| 6. | T. Guernalec | ARK | 0:21 |
| 7. | L. N. Hansen | TQA | s.t. |
| 8. | K. Bouwman | TJV | 0:24 |
| 9. | D. Ballerini | DQT | 0:25 |
| 10. | C. Swift | ARK | 0:26 |
| 11. | R. Mullen | TFS | s.t. |
| 12. | I. Schelling | BOH | 0:27 |
| 13. | O. Riesebeek | AFC | s.t. |
| 14. | N. Eekhoff | DSM | s.t. |
| 15. | P. Eenkhoorn | TJV | s.t. |
| 16. | M. van Dijke | TJV | s.t. |
| 17. | C. Quarterman | TFS | 0:28 |
| 18. | T. Aerts | TBL | 0:32 |
| 19. | D. Dekker | TJV | s.t. |
| 20. | E. Vinjebo | TQA | s.t. |

### GENERAL CLASSIFICATION

| POS | NAME | TEAM | TIME |
|---|---|---|---|
| 1. — | R. Evenepoel | DQT | 4:17:00 |
| 2. ↑10 | Y. Lampaert | DQT | 0:45 |
| 3. — | G. Marchand | TIS | 0:53 |

### POINTS

| POS | NAME | TEAM | PTS |
|---|---|---|---|
| 1. ↑1 | R. Evenepoel | DQT | 45 |
| 2. ↓1 | R. Ghys | SVB | 30 |
| 3. — | G. Marchand | TIS | 22 |

JUNE .PRO MEN'S RACE

## BALOISE BELGIUM TOUR
Stage 3
11 June 2021
Gingelom–Scherpenheuvel-Zichem
174.4km

### WEATHER

TEMPERATURE | WIND
23°C | W 13km/h

### STAGE RESULTS

| POS | NAME | TEAM | TIME |
|---|---|---|---|
| 1. | C. Ewan | LTS | 3:56:43 |
| 2. | M. Mørkøv | DQT | s.t. |
| 3. | D. van Poppel | IWG | s.t. |
| 4. | M. Moschetti | TFS | s.t. |
| 5. | T. Dupont | BWB | s.t. |
| 6. | O. Kooij | TJV | s.t. |
| 7. | B. Coquard | BBK | s.t. |
| 8. | T. Nys | TBL | s.t. |
| 9. | N. Eekhoff | DSM | s.t. |
| 10. | N. Bonifazio | TDE | s.t. |
| 11. | L. Bugter | BCY | s.t. |
| 12. | E. Liepiņš | TFS | s.t. |
| 13. | F. Fiorelli | BCF | s.t. |
| 14. | Y. Havik | BCY | s.t. |
| 15. | R. Kamp | PSB | s.t. |
| 16. | M. Menten | BWB | s.t. |
| 17. | G. D'heygere | TIS | s.t. |
| 18. | D. Van Gestel | TDE | s.t. |
| 19. | D. Groenewegen | TJV | s.t. |
| 20. | J. Van den Brande | TIS | s.t. |

### GENERAL CLASSIFICATION

| POS | | NAME | TEAM | TIME |
|---|---|---|---|---|
| 1. | — | R. Evenepoel | DQT | 8:13:43 |
| 2. | — | Y. Lampaert | DQT | 0:45 |
| 3. | — | G. Marchand | TIS | 0:53 |

### POINTS

| POS | | NAME | TEAM | PTS |
|---|---|---|---|---|
| 1. | — | R. Evenepoel | DQT | 45 |
| 2. | — | R. Ghys | SVB | 30 |
| 3. | — | C. Ewan | LTS | 30 |

## BALOISE BELGIUM TOUR
Stage 4
12 June 2021
Hamoir–Hamoir
152.7km

### WEATHER

TEMPERATURE | WIND
17°C | W 17km/h

### STAGE RESULTS

| POS | NAME | TEAM | TIME |
|---|---|---|---|
| 1. | C. Ewan | LTS | 3:37:48 |
| 2. | B. Coquard | BBK | s.t. |
| 3. | D. Ballerini | DQT | s.t. |
| 4. | G. Nizzolo | TQA | s.t. |
| 5. | J. de Buyst | LTS | s.t. |
| 6. | I. Schelling | BOH | s.t. |
| 7. | L. Vliegen | IWG | s.t. |
| 8. | F. Fiorelli | BCF | s.t. |
| 9. | A. Livyns | BWB | s.t. |
| 10. | C. Barthe | BBK | s.t. |
| 11. | C. Pedersen | DSM | s.t. |
| 12. | D. De Bondt | AFC | s.t. |
| 13. | D. Van Gestel | TDE | s.t. |
| 14. | R. Evenepoel | DQT | s.t. |
| 15. | C. Swift | ARK | s.t. |
| 16. | T. Wirtgen | BWB | s.t. |
| 17. | K. Sbaragli | AFC | s.t. |
| 18. | J. Bouts | BCY | s.t. |
| 19. | E. Iserbyt | PSB | s.t. |
| 20. | F. Van den Bossche | SVB | s.t. |

### GENERAL CLASSIFICATION

| POS | | NAME | TEAM | TIME |
|---|---|---|---|---|
| 1. | — | R. Evenepoel | DQT | 11:51:31 |
| 2. | — | Y. Lampaert | DQT | 0:45 |
| 3. | — | G. Marchand | TIS | 0:53 |

### POINTS

| POS | | NAME | TEAM | PTS |
|---|---|---|---|---|
| 1. | ↑2 | C. Ewan | LTS | 60 |
| 2. | ↑3 | B. Coquard | BBK | 49 |
| 3. | ↓2 | R. Evenepoel | DQT | 45 |

## BALOISE BELGIUM TOUR
Stage 5
13 June 2021
Turnhout–Beringen
178.7km

## WEATHER

| TEMPERATURE | WIND |
|---|---|
| 21°C | NW 7km/h |

### STAGE RESULTS

| POS | NAME | TEAM | TIME |
|---|---|---|---|
| 1. | M. Cavendish | DQT | 3:50:31 |
| 2. | T. Merlier | AFC | s.t. |
| 3. | P. Ackermann | BOH | s.t. |
| 4. | D. Groenewegen | TJV | s.t. |
| 5. | N. Bouhanni | ARK | s.t. |
| 6. | B. Coquard | BBK | s.t. |
| 7. | S. Weemaes | SVB | s.t. |
| 8. | N. Bonifazio | TDE | s.t. |
| 9. | C. Ewan | LTS | s.t. |
| 10. | D. van Poppel | IWG | s.t. |
| 11. | J. Mareczko | THR | s.t. |
| 12. | O. Kooij | TJV | s.t. |
| 13. | J. Rickaert | AFC | s.t. |
| 14. | M. Mørkøv | DQT | s.t. |
| 15. | G. Nizzolo | TQA | s.t. |
| 16. | F. Fiorelli | BCF | s.t. |
| 17. | B. van Poppel | IWG | s.t. |
| 18. | D. McLay | ARK | s.t. |
| 19. | O. Riesebeek | AFC | s.t. |
| 20. | R. Evenepoel | DQT | s.t. |

### GENERAL CLASSIFICATION

| POS | NAME | TEAM | TIME |
|---|---|---|---|
| 1. — | R. Evenepoel | DQT | 15:41:59 |
| 2. — | Y. Lampaert | DQT | 0:46 |
| 3. — | G. Marchand | TIS | 0:56 |

### POINTS

| POS | NAME | TEAM | PTS |
|---|---|---|---|
| 1. — | C. Ewan | LTS | 71 |
| 2. — | B. Coquard | BBK | 64 |
| 3. — | R. Evenepoel | DQT | 45 |

JUNE  .1 MEN'S RACE

# LA ROUTE D'OCCITANIE
Stage 1
10 June 2021
Cazouls-Lès-Béziers–Lacaune Les Bains
156.5km

## WEATHER

TEMPERATURE | WIND
31°C | NW 19km/h

## STAGE RESULTS

| POS | NAME | TEAM | TIME |
|---|---|---|---|
| 1. | A. Vendrame | ACT | 3:59:41 |
| 2. | M. Cort | EFN | 0:04 |
| 3. | J. Mosca | TFS | s.t. |
| 4. | L. L. Sanchez | APT | s.t. |
| 5. | Je. Herrada | COF | s.t. |
| 6. | B. Swift | IGD | s.t. |
| 7. | T. Gallopin | ACT | s.t. |
| 8. | R. Hardy | ARK | s.t. |
| 9. | D. Lopez | EKP | s.t. |
| 10. | J. García | CJR | s.t. |
| 11. | R. Adrià | EKP | s.t. |
| 12. | C. Champoussin | ACT | s.t. |
| 13. | J. Cabot | TDE | s.t. |
| 14. | J. Bou | EUS | s.t. |
| 15. | O. Rodríguez | APT | s.t. |
| 16. | É. Gesbert | ARK | s.t. |
| 17. | J. Murguialday | CJR | s.t. |
| 18. | Y. Natarov | APT | s.t. |
| 19. | M. Debesay | BAI | s.t. |
| 20. | J. M. Díaz | DKO | s.t. |

## GENERAL CLASSIFICATION

| POS | NAME | TEAM | TIME |
|---|---|---|---|
| 1. | A. Vendrame | ACT | 3:59:31 |
| 2. | M. Cort | EFN | 0:08 |
| 3. | J. Mosca | TFS | 0:10 |

## KING OF THE MOUNTAINS

| POS | NAME | TEAM | PTS |
|---|---|---|---|
| 1. | A. Cuadros Morata | CJR | 10 |
| 2. | G. Bravo | EUS | 8 |
| 3. | C. García | EKP | 6 |

## POINTS

| POS | NAME | TEAM | PTS |
|---|---|---|---|
| 1. | A. Vendrame | ACT | 20 |
| 2. | M. Cort | EFN | 17 |
| 3. | J. Mosca | TFS | 15 |

## YOUNG RIDER

| POS | NAME | TEAM | TIME |
|---|---|---|---|
| 1. | J. Agirre | EKP | 3:59:43 |
| 2. | D. Lopez | EKP | 0:02 |
| 3. | J. García | CJR | s.t. |

# LA ROUTE D'OCCITANIE
Stage 2
11 June 2021
Villefranche-De-Rouergue–Auch
198.7km

## WEATHER

TEMPERATURE | WIND
26°C | NW 11km/h

## STAGE RESULTS

| POS | NAME | TEAM | TIME |
|---|---|---|---|
| 1. | A. Démare | GFC | 5:01:31 |
| 2. | O. Aular | CJR | s.t. |
| 3. | J. Mosca | TFS | s.t. |
| 4. | L. Manzin | TDE | s.t. |
| 5. | D. González | CJR | s.t. |
| 6. | R. Hardy | ARK | s.t. |
| 7. | T. Boudat | ARK | s.t. |
| 8. | A. Vendrame | ACT | s.t. |
| 9. | E. Vermeulen | XRL | s.t. |
| 10. | L. G. Mas | MOV | s.t. |
| 11. | G. Mühlberger | MOV | s.t. |
| 12. | F. Maurelet | AUB | s.t. |
| 13. | A. Boileau | BBK | s.t. |
| 14. | J. Trarieux | DKO | s.t. |
| 15. | B. Swift | IGD | s.t. |
| 16. | Je. Herrada | COF | s.t. |
| 17. | G. Ciccone | TFS | s.t. |
| 18. | M. Kudus | APT | s.t. |
| 19. | R. Adrià | EKP | s.t. |
| 20. | L. L. Sanchez | APT | s.t. |

## GENERAL CLASSIFICATION

| POS | | NAME | TEAM | TIME |
|---|---|---|---|---|
| 1. | — | A. Vendrame | ACT | 9:01:02 |
| 2. | ↑1 | J. Mosca | TFS | 0:06 |
| 3. | ↓1 | M. Cort | EFN | 0:08 |

## KING OF THE MOUNTAINS

| POS | | NAME | TEAM | PTS |
|---|---|---|---|---|
| 1. | — | A. Cuadros Morata | CJR | 13 |
| 2. | — | Á. Madrazo | BBH | 9 |
| 3. | ↓1 | G. Bravo | EUS | 8 |

## POINTS

| POS | | NAME | TEAM | PTS |
|---|---|---|---|---|
| 1. | ↑2 | J. Mosca | TFS | 30 |
| 2. | ↓1 | A. Vendrame | ACT | 28 |
| 3. | — | A. Démare | GFC | 20 |

## YOUNG RIDER

| POS | | NAME | TEAM | TIME |
|---|---|---|---|---|
| 1. | — | J. Agirre | EKP | 9:01:14 |
| 2. | ↑2 | R. Adrià | EKP | 0:02 |
| 3. | ↑5 | A. Boileau | BBK | s.t. |

JUNE    .1 MEN'S RACE

## LA ROUTE D'OCCITANIE
Stage 3
12 June 2021
Pierrefitte-Nestalas–Le Mourtis
191.8km

### WEATHER
TEMPERATURE  WIND
22°C  N 6km/h

### STAGE RESULTS

| POS | NAME | TEAM | TIME |
|---|---|---|---|
| 1. | A. Pedrero | MOV | 5:22:05 |
| 2. | Je. Herrada | COF | 0:40 |
| 3. | O. Rodríguez | APT | 0:43 |
| 4. | C. Rodríguez | TDE | 0:46 |
| 5. | S. Carr | EFN | s.t. |
| 6. | G. Ciccone | TFS | s.t. |
| 7. | M. Kudus | APT | 1:18 |
| 8. | É. Gesbert | ARK | 1:21 |
| 9. | M. Bizkarra | EUS | 1:23 |
| 10. | J. Amezqueta | CJR | 1:26 |
| 11. | C. Berthet | DKO | 1:32 |
| 12. | J. Bou | EUS | 1:54 |
| 13. | J. F. Parra | EKP | 2:06 |
| 14. | J. Agirre | EKP | 2:31 |
| 15. | G. Mühlberger | MOV | 2:50 |
| 16. | R. Adrià | EKP | s.t. |
| 17. | J. García | CJR | 2:52 |
| 18. | Y. Natarov | APT | 2:53 |
| 19. | H. Toumire | NAT | 2:55 |
| 20. | G. Brambilla | TFS | 3:03 |

### GENERAL CLASSIFICATION

| POS | NAME | TEAM | TIME |
|---|---|---|---|
| 1. ↑29 | A. Pedrero | MOV | 14:23:11 |
| 2. ↑6 | Je. Herrada | COF | 0:44 |
| 3. ↑20 | O. Rodríguez | APT | 0:49 |

### KING OF THE MOUNTAINS

| POS | NAME | TEAM | PTS |
|---|---|---|---|
| 1. — | A. Cuadros Morata | CJR | 40 |
| 2. — | D. Navarro | BBH | 16 |
| 3. — | M. Iturria | EUS | 14 |

### POINTS

| POS | NAME | TEAM | PTS |
|---|---|---|---|
| 1. — | J. Mosca | TFS | 30 |
| 2. — | A. Vendrame | ACT | 28 |
| 3. ↑7 | Je. Herrada | COF | 24 |

### YOUNG RIDER

| POS | NAME | TEAM | TIME |
|---|---|---|---|
| 1. ↑13 | S. Carr | EFN | 14:24:30 |
| 2. ↑6 | C. Berthet | DKO | 0:23 |
| 3. ↑1 | J. Bou | EUS | 0:45 |

## LA ROUTE D'OCCITANIE
Stage 4
13 June 2021
Lavelanet-Pays d'Olmes–Duilhac-Sous-Peyrepertuse
151.2km

### WEATHER
TEMPERATURE  WIND
32°C  W 19km/h

### STAGE RESULTS

| POS | NAME | TEAM | TIME |
|---|---|---|---|
| 1. | M. Cort | EFN | 3:42:54 |
| 2. | G. Brambilla | TFS | 0:18 |
| 3. | T. Gallopin | ACT | 0:34 |
| 4. | Je. Herrada | COF | 0:52 |
| 5. | O. Rodríguez | APT | 0:56 |
| 6. | C. Champoussin | ACT | 0:58 |
| 7. | C. Rodríguez | TDE | s.t. |
| 8. | J. Amezqueta | CJR | 1:04 |
| 9. | É. Gesbert | ARK | 1:08 |
| 10. | A. Pedrero | MOV | 1:11 |
| 11. | J. F. Parra | EKP | s.t. |
| 12. | M. Kudus | APT | 1:13 |
| 13. | G. Ciccone | TFS | s.t. |
| 14. | S. Carr | EFN | 1:23 |
| 15. | M. Bizkarra | EUS | s.t. |
| 16. | R. Adrià | EKP | 1:28 |
| 17. | J. Bou | EUS | 1:32 |
| 18. | A. Jousseaume | NAT | 1:41 |
| 19. | C. Berthet | DKO | 2:06 |
| 20. | H. Toumire | NAT | 2:10 |

### GENERAL CLASSIFICATION

| POS | NAME | TEAM | TIME |
|---|---|---|---|
| 1. — | A. Pedrero | MOV | 18:07:16 |
| 2. — | Je. Herrada | COF | 0:25 |
| 3. — | O. Rodríguez | APT | 0:34 |

### KING OF THE MOUNTAINS

| POS | NAME | TEAM | PTS |
|---|---|---|---|
| 1. — | A. Cuadros Morata | CJR | 40 |
| 2. — | T. Gallopin | ACT | 16 |
| 3. ↓1 | D. Navarro | BBH | 16 |

### POINTS

| POS | NAME | TEAM | PTS |
|---|---|---|---|
| 1. ↑1 | A. Vendrame | ACT | 34 |
| 2. ↑4 | M. Cort | EFN | 32 |
| 3. — | Je. Herrada | COF | 32 |

### YOUNG RIDER

| POS | NAME | TEAM | TIME |
|---|---|---|---|
| 1. — | S. Carr | EFN | 18:08:47 |
| 2. ↑2 | J. F. Parra | EKP | 0:45 |
| 3. — | J. Bou | EUS | 0:54 |

JUNE .1 MEN'S RACE

# PARIS–CAMEMBERT
15 June 2021
Pont-Audemer–Camembert
210km

## WEATHER

TEMPERATURE | WIND
21°C | W 13km/h

## RESULTS

| POS | NAME | TEAM | TIME |
|---|---|---|---|
| 1. | D. Godon | ACT | 5:19:08 |
| 2. | P. L. Périchon | COF | s.t. |
| 3. | G. Bouchard | ACT | 0:46 |
| 4. | L. van den Berg | GFC | s.t. |
| 5. | L. Manzin | TDE | 0:55 |
| 6. | G. Vermeersch | AFC | s.t. |
| 7. | A. Capiot | ARK | s.t. |
| 8. | G. Van Avermaet | ACT | s.t. |
| 9. | F. Bonnamour | BBK | s.t. |
| 10. | N. Haas | COF | s.t. |
| 11. | A. Delettre | DKO | s.t. |
| 12. | L. Rota | IWG | s.t. |
| 13. | R. Molard | GFC | s.t. |
| 14. | R. Seigle | GFC | s.t. |
| 15. | J. Leveau | XRL | s.t. |
| 16. | A. Delaplace | ARK | s.t. |
| 17. | M. Urruty | XRL | s.t. |
| 18. | O. Naesen | ACT | s.t. |
| 19. | V. Lafay | COF | 3:02 |
| 20. | M. Cam | BBK | s.t. |

JUNE   .1 MEN'S RACE

# ADRIATICA IONICA RACE

Stage 1
15 June 2021
Trieste–Sulle Rotte della Serenissima
178km

## WEATHER

TEMPERATURE | WIND
24°C | NW 9km/h

## STAGE RESULTS

| POS | NAME | TEAM | TIME |
|---|---|---|---|
| 1. | E. Viviani | NAT | 4:02:02 |
| 2. | D. Persico | CPK | s.t. |
| 3. | L. Pacioni | EOK | s.t. |
| 4. | J. Mareczko | THR | s.t. |
| 5. | E. Zanoncello | BCF | s.t. |
| 6. | A. D'Amato | IRC | s.t. |
| 7. | D. Boscaro | CPK | s.t. |
| 8. | N. Furlan | IRC | s.t. |
| 9. | D. Martinelli | APT | s.t. |
| 10. | S. Di Benedetto | IWM | s.t. |
| 11. | S. Zambelli | IRC | s.t. |
| 12. | R. Ceurens | TNN | s.t. |
| 13. | D. Cimolai | NAT | s.t. |
| 14. | M. Canola | GAZ | s.t. |
| 15. | F. Gamper | TIR | s.t. |
| 16. | L. Regalli | IRC | s.t. |
| 17. | F. Dignani | IWM | s.t. |
| 18. | S. Quaranta | CPK | s.t. |
| 19. | C. Rocchetta | GEF | s.t. |
| 20. | S. Velasco | GAZ | s.t. |

## GENERAL CLASSIFICATION

| POS | NAME | TEAM | TIME |
|---|---|---|---|
| 1. | E. Viviani | NAT | 4:01:52 |
| 2. | D. Persico | CPK | 0:04 |
| 3. | L. Pacioni | EOK | 0:06 |

## KING OF THE MOUNTAINS

| POS | NAME | TEAM | PTS |
|---|---|---|---|
| 1. | D. P. Sevilla | EOK | 5 |
| 2. | L. Rastelli | CPK | 4 |
| 3. | M. Donegà | CTF | 3 |

## POINTS

| POS | NAME | TEAM | PTS |
|---|---|---|---|
| 1. | E. Viviani | NAT | 25 |
| 2. | D. Persico | CPK | 18 |
| 3. | M. Donegà | CTF | 16 |

## YOUNG RIDER

| POS | NAME | TEAM | TIME |
|---|---|---|---|
| 1. | D. Persico | CPK | 4:01:56 |
| 2. | A. D'Amato | IRC | 0:06 |
| 3. | D. Boscaro | CPK | s.t. |

# ADRIATICA IONICA RACE

Stage 2
16 June 2021
Vittorio Veneto–Cima Grappa
144.2km

## WEATHER

TEMPERATURE | WIND
29°C | W 4km/h

## STAGE RESULTS

| POS | NAME | TEAM | TIME |
|---|---|---|---|
| 1. | L. Fortunato | EOK | 3:58:38 |
| 2. | M. Kudus | APT | 0:01 |
| 3. | V. Pronskiy | APT | 0:03 |
| 4. | G. Carboni | BCF | 0:07 |
| 5. | F. Zana | BCF | 0:35 |
| 6. | A. Monaco | BCF | 0:40 |
| 7. | L. Covili | BCF | 1:07 |
| 8. | E. Sepúlveda | ANS | 1:19 |
| 9. | A. Garosio | BCF | 1:27 |
| 10. | D. Rebellin | IWM | 1:32 |
| 11. | R. Lucca | GEF | 1:45 |
| 12. | L. Chirico | ANS | 2:01 |
| 13. | F. Lipowitz | TIR | 2:03 |
| 14. | S. Velasco | GAZ | 2:13 |
| 15. | D. Merchan | NAT | 2:43 |
| 16. | D. Orrico | THR | 3:09 |
| 17. | A. Ropero | EOK | 3:34 |
| 18. | N. Tesfatsion | ANS | 3:43 |
| 19. | D. Muñoz | ANS | 4:16 |
| 20. | F. Romano | NAT | 4:39 |

## GENERAL CLASSIFICATION

| POS | | NAME | TEAM | TIME |
|---|---|---|---|---|
| 1. | ↑78 | L. Fortunato | EOK | 8:00:30 |
| 2. | ↑25 | M. Kudus | APT | 0:05 |
| 3. | ↑29 | V. Pronskiy | APT | 0:09 |

## KING OF THE MOUNTAINS

| POS | | NAME | TEAM | PTS |
|---|---|---|---|---|
| 1. | — | L. Fortunato | EOK | 10 |
| 2. | — | M. Kudus | APT | 8 |
| 3. | ↓1 | L. Rastelli | CPK | 8 |

## POINTS

| POS | | NAME | TEAM | PTS |
|---|---|---|---|---|
| 1. | — | E. Viviani | NAT | 25 |
| 2. | — | D. Persico | CPK | 18 |
| 3. | — | M. Donegà | CTF | 16 |

## YOUNG RIDER

| POS | | NAME | TEAM | TIME |
|---|---|---|---|---|
| 1. | ↑19 | V. Pronskiy | APT | 8:00:39 |
| 2. | ↑17 | F. Zana | BCF | 0:36 |
| 3. | ↑29 | A. Monaco | BCF | 0:41 |

JUNE .1 MEN'S RACE

# ADRIATICA IONICA RACE
Stage 3
17 June 2021
Ferrara–Comacchio
149.5km

## WEATHER

TEMPERATURE: 30°C
WIND: N 7km/h

## STAGE RESULTS

| POS | NAME | TEAM | TIME |
|---|---|---|---|
| 1. | E. Viviani | NAT | 3:19:23 |
| 2. | J. Mareczko | THR | s.t. |
| 3. | D. Martinelli | APT | s.t. |
| 4. | E. Zanoncello | BCF | s.t. |
| 5. | M. Canola | GAZ | s.t. |
| 6. | G. Masotto | ZEF | s.t. |
| 7. | M. Govekar | TIR | s.t. |
| 8. | L. Pacioni | EOK | s.t. |
| 9. | V. Pronskiy | APT | s.t. |
| 10. | C. Rocchetta | GEF | s.t. |
| 11. | F. Burchio | IWM | s.t. |
| 12. | S. Zambelli | IRC | s.t. |
| 13. | M. Kudus | APT | s.t. |
| 14. | U. Poli | TNN | s.t. |
| 15. | D. Gabburo | BCF | s.t. |
| 16. | L. Chirico | ANS | s.t. |
| 17. | F. Zana | BCF | s.t. |
| 18. | J. D. Peña | NAT | s.t. |
| 19. | B. A. Rojas Vega | NAT | s.t. |
| 20. | N. Tesfatsion | ANS | s.t. |

## GENERAL CLASSIFICATION

| POS | | NAME | TEAM | TIME |
|---|---|---|---|---|
| 1. | — | L. Fortunato | EOK | 11:19:56 |
| 2. | — | M. Kudus | APT | 0:02 |
| 3. | — | V. Pronskiy | APT | 0:06 |

## KING OF THE MOUNTAINS

| POS | | NAME | TEAM | PTS |
|---|---|---|---|---|
| 1. | — | L. Fortunato | EOK | 10 |
| 2. | — | M. Kudus | APT | 8 |
| 3. | ↑1 | V. Pronskiy | APT | 6 |

## POINTS

| POS | | NAME | TEAM | PTS |
|---|---|---|---|---|
| 1. | — | E. Viviani | NAT | 56 |
| 2. | ↑9 | J. Mareczko | THR | 26 |
| 3. | — | R. Bobbo | IWM | 22 |

## YOUNG RIDER

| POS | | NAME | TEAM | TIME |
|---|---|---|---|---|
| 1. | — | V. Pronskiy | APT | 11:20:02 |
| 2. | — | F. Zana | BCF | 0:36 |
| 3. | — | A. Monaco | BCF | 0:44 |

JUNE .1 MEN'S RACE

# GIRO DELL'APPENNINO

24 June 2021
Pasturana–Genoa
192.1km

## WEATHER

TEMPERATURE | WIND
24°C | SE 19km/h

## RESULTS

| POS | NAME | TEAM | TIME |
|---|---|---|---|
| 1. | B. Hermans | ISN | 4:50:22 |
| 2. | V. Conti | UAD | 0:30 |
| 3. | E. Battaglin | BCF | s.t. |
| 4. | S. Velasco | GAZ | s.t. |
| 5. | J. Polanc | UAD | 0:31 |
| 6. | H. Mulubrhan | T4Q | s.t. |
| 7. | D. Ulissi | UAD | s.t. |
| 8. | L. Chirico | ANS | s.t. |
| 9. | A. Ropero | EOK | s.t. |
| 10. | E. Sepúlveda | ANS | s.t. |
| 11. | A. Fedeli | NAT | s.t. |
| 12. | D. Rebellin | IWM | s.t. |
| 13. | M. Tizza | AMO | s.t. |
| 14. | M. Trentin | UAD | 0:34 |
| 15. | A. Garosio | BCF | 0:42 |
| 16. | G. Carboni | BCF | 0:46 |
| 17. | J. Ayuso | UAD | 0:52 |
| 18. | N. Cherkasov | GAZ | s.t. |
| 19. | G. Moscon | IGD | 1:00 |
| 20. | M. Louvel | ARK | 3:37 |

JUNE  WORLDTOUR WOMEN'S RACE

## LA COURSE
26 June 2021
Brest–Landerneau
107.4km

Held in the morning ahead of the first stage of the men's Tour de France, the 2021 edition of La Course will probably be the last one, as the inaugural edition of the Tour de France Femmes is planned for 2022.

An attack by Lucinda Brand (Trek-Segafredo) on the first of four ascents of the Côte de la Fosse aux Loups led to a group of 11 that caught the early attackers and stayed ahead of the peloton until Anna van der Breggen closed the gap on the second ascent. Ruth Winder (Trek-Segafredo) then initiated a move of ten riders, with two more bridging later. After the third ascent of the Côte de la Fosse aux Loups, the group of 12 started the final lap with a 40-second advantage. Jumbo-Visma and Canyon-SRAM took up the chase and reduced this to 14 seconds with 5km to go, and another attack by Brand brought everything back together. Katarzyna Niewiadoma attacked on the climb and took Grace Brown, Cecilie Uttrup Ludwig, and Anna van der Breggen with her. Soraya Paladin, Marianne Vos, Demi Vollering and Liane Lippert came back as the climb flattened out, and after a couple of attacks were shut down, Van der Breggen started the sprint very early, forcing Vos to react and enabling Vollering to come around and win. Uttrup Ludwig also came past Vos in the final metres to take second place.

## WEATHER

TEMPERATURE  WIND
16°C  N 9km/h

## PROFILE

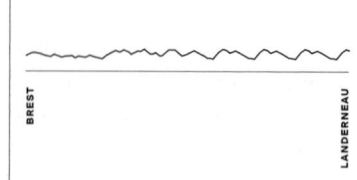

BREST — LANDERNEAU

## BREAKAWAY
C. Kerbaol (ARK), E. Pirrone (VAL)

## RESULTS

| POS | NAME | TEAM | TIME |
|---|---|---|---|
| 1. | D. Vollering | SDW | 2:50:29 |
| 2. | C. U. Ludwig | FDJ | s.t. |
| 3. | M. Vos | JVW | s.t. |
| 4. | A. van der Breggen | SDW | s.t. |
| 5. | G. Brown | BEX | s.t. |
| 6. | K. Niewiadoma | CSR | s.t. |
| 7. | S. Paladin | LIV | s.t. |
| 8. | L. Lippert | DSM | s.t. |
| 9. | E. Deignan | TFS | 0:04 |
| 10. | S. Bertizzolo | LIV | s.t. |
| 11. | L. Thomas | MOV | s.t. |
| 12. | C. Rivera | DSM | 0:08 |
| 13. | M. Cavalli | FDJ | s.t. |
| 14. | N. Fisher-Black | SDW | s.t. |
| 15. | M. Harvey | CSR | s.t. |
| 16. | T. Guderzo | ALE | s.t. |
| 17. | A. Henderson | JVW | s.t. |
| 18. | J. Labous | DSM | s.t. |
| 19. | P. Rooijakkers | LIV | s.t. |
| 20. | A. Spratt | BEX | s.t. |

## TRIVIA
» Demi Vollering's is likely to be the last La Course victory because a women's Tour de France stage race is scheduled to return next year. The Dutch have won six of the eight editions of the one-day offering.

# THE CLOSEST QUICKSTEP VICTORY TO A LIDL

Sponsors are the lifeblood of pro cycling, and few are as recognisable or relatable as the Lidl logo that Deceuninck-QuickStep sport on the shoulders of their jerseys. After all, how many people are really buying grouting materials every week? But the question that is, of course, constantly on everyone's lips is which of Deceuninck-QuickStep's many victories was the closest to a Lidl store in 2021? Irish sprinter Sam Bennett is responsible for both the furthest away and the closest, winning at the UAE Tour (where one would need to hot-foot it over to Cyprus to find a branch of the supermarket chain) and at the Volta ao Algarve (just 300 metres down the street from a branch).

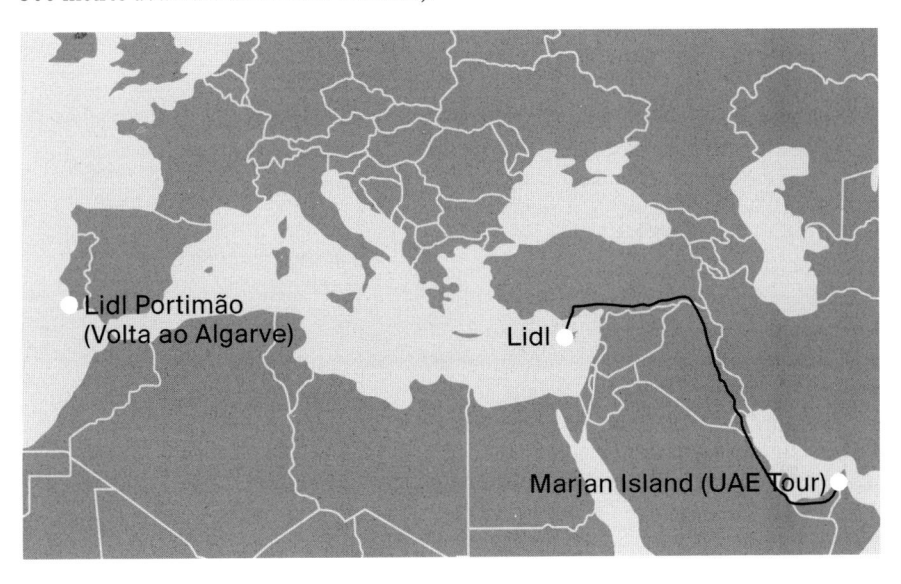

| Race | Rider | Distance to nearest Lidl |
|---|---|---|
| Volta ao Algarve stage 1 | Sam Bennett | 300m |
| GP Marcel Kint | Álvaro José Hodeg | 800m |
| Tour of Slovakia stage 1 | Álvaro José Hodeg | 950m |
| Tour of Flanders | Kasper Asgreen | 1km |
| Brugge–De Panne | Sam Bennett | 1km |
| Tour de Pologne stage 2 | João Almeida | 1km |
| Vuelta a España stage 13 | Fabio Jakobsen | 1.3km |
| Tour of Denmark stage 5 (ITT) | Remco Evenepoel | 1.5km |
| Tour of Britain stage 7 | Yves Lampaert | 1.9km |
| La Vuelta a España stage 8 | Fabio Jakobsen | 2km |
| Tour de Pologne stage 6 (ITT) | Rémi Cavagna | 2km |
| Tour of Denmark | Remco Evenepoel | 2km |
| Tour de l'Ain stage 1 | Álvaro José Hodeg | 2km |
| Tour de France stage 13 | Mark Cavendish | 2km |
| Tour de France stage 6 | Mark Cavendish | 2km |
| Tour de France stage 4 | Mark Cavendish | 2km |
| Volta ao Algarve stage 3 | Sam Bennett | 2km |
| Itzulia Basque Country stage 5 | Mikkel Frølich Honoré | 2km |
| Settimana Inter. Coppi e Bartali stage 5 | Mikkel Frølich Honoré | 2km |
| E3 Classic | Kasper Asgreen | 2km |
| Brussels Cycling Classic | Remco Evenepoel | 2.2km |
| Omloop Het Nieuwsblad | Davide Ballerini | 2.5km |
| Tour de Wallonie stage 5 | Fabio Jakobsen | 2.5km |
| Eurométropole Tour | Fabio Jakobsen | 2.5km |
| Coppa Bernocchi | Remco Evenepoel | 2.5km |
| Tour de France stage 10 | Mark Cavendish | 3km |
| Paris–Nice stage 1 | Sam Bennett | 3.5km |
| Gooikse Pijl | Fabio Jakobsen | 3.6km |
| Vuelta a España stage 16 | Fabio Jakobsen | 4km |
| Tour de France stage 1 | Julian Alaphilippe | 4km |
| Tour de la Provence stage 1 | Davide Ballerini | 4km |
| Tour of Luxembourg stage 1 | João Almeida | 5km |
| Tour de Wallonie stage 2 | Fabio Jakobsen | 5km |
| Baloise Belgium Tour stage 5 | Mark Cavendish | 5km |
| Tour of Slovakia stage 2 | Jannik Steilme | 5.1km |
| Primus Classic | Florian Sénéchal | 5.2km |
| Baloise Belgium Tour stage 2 (ITT) | Remco Evenepoel | 5.5km |
| Flèche Wallonne | Julian Alaphilippe | 6km |
| Tour de la Provence stage 2 | Davide Ballerini | 6.5km |
| Tour de Romandie stage 5 (ITT) | Rémi Cavagna | 7km |
| Volta ao Algarve stage 4 (ITT) | Kasper Asgreen | 7.5km |
| Tour of Luxembourg stage 4 (ITT) | Mattia Cattaneo | 8km |
| Sparkassen Münsterland Giro | Mark Cavendish | 8.2km |
| Druivenkoers–Overijse | Remco Evenepoel | 8.3km |
| Paris–Nice stage 5 | Sam Bennett | 9km |
| Tour de Pologne stage 4 | João Almeida | 15km |
| La Drôme Classic | Andrea Bagioli | 15km |
| GP Industria & Artigianato | Mari Vansevenant | 20km |
| Tirreno–Adriatico stage 2 | Julian Alaphilippe | 50km |
| La Vuelta a España stage 4 | Fabio Jakobsen | 100km |
| Pres. Cycling Tour of Turkey stage 3 | Mark Cavendish | 223km |
| Pres. Cycling Tour of Turkey stage 4 | Mark Cavendish | 404km |
| Pres. Cycling Tour of Turkey stage 2 | Mark Cavendish | 486km |
| Pres. Cycling Tour of Turkey stage 8 | Mark Cavendish | 501km |
| UAE Tour stage 6 | Sam Bennett | 3,485km |
| UAE Tour stage 4 | Sam Bennett | 3,553km |

JUNE　　WORLDTOUR MEN'S RACE

# TOUR DE FRANCE
Stage 1
26 June 2021
Brest–Landerneau
197.8km

The Tour began with a celebration of Breton cycling. The region hosted the first four stages, one in each of its four *départements*, each with a distinct set of characteristics and challenges. On day one in Finisterre, the principal difficulty for most in a nervy peloton was simply to get to the finish line unscathed. Few observers of the sport could recall such a violent opening day of racing. Twice the peloton crumpled in the middle, struck by savage and unavoidable crashes that resulted in broken bones, shattered hopes and, ultimately, a national manhunt involving the police. It was the first of the crashes, brought about by a spectator holding a sign into the road while looking away from the onrushing peloton, that will be remembered and replayed for many years. Jumbo-Visma's Tony Martin was the first to collide with her, followed by his team leader and pre-race favourite Primož Roglič. And on his wheel, half of the Tour de France. After the race was over, the hunt for the perpetrator began – a search that would end with her arrest in Landerneau some four days later. Despite another huge pile-up on the run-in to the finish line, the race eventually reached the final climb, the Côte de la Fosse aux Loups, which loosely translates as the Wolf-Pit Hill. How fitting, therefore, that world champion Julian Alaphilippe, riding for the self-styled 'Wolfpack', aka Deceuninck-QuickStep, delivered an unanswerably vicious attack and rode clear of a group of GC favourites, soloing to victory and taking another yellow jersey in the process. Most of the favourites finished in a group 8 seconds down, along with a disappointed Tour debutant Mathieu van der Poel. Richard Carapaz of Ineos Grenadiers lost a further 5 seconds. A total of 12 riders, including Chris Froome, were taken to hospital in Brest that evening for further examination.

---

### TRIVIA
» The last world champion to take yellow on the first day was Frenchman Bernard Hinault in the 1981 prologue in Nice.

## WEATHER

**TEMPERATURE**　16°C
**WIND**　N 9km/h

## PROFILE

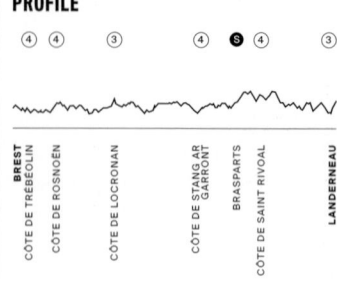

BREST · CÔTE DE TREBEOLIN · CÔTE DE ROSNOËN · CÔTE DE LOCRONAN · CÔTE DE STANG AR GARRONT · BRASPARTS · CÔTE DE SAINT RIVOAL · LANDERNEAU

## BREAKAWAY
F. Bonnamour (BBK), C. Rodríguez (TEN), D. van Poppel (IWG), A. Perez (COF), I. Schelling (BOH), C. Swift (ARK)

## GENERAL CLASSIFICATION

| POS | NAME | TEAM | TIME |
|---|---|---|---|
| 1. | J. Alaphilippe | DQT | 4:38:55 |
| 2. | M. Matthews | BEX | 0:12 |
| 3. | P. Roglič | TJV | 0:14 |
| 4. | J. Haig | TBV | 0:18 |
| 5. | W. Kelderman | BOH | s.t. |
| 6. | T. Pogačar | UAD | s.t. |
| 7. | D. Gaudu | GFC | s.t. |
| 8. | S. Higuita | EFN | s.t. |
| 9. | B. Mollema | TFS | s.t. |
| 10. | G. Thomas | IGD | s.t. |

## KING OF THE MOUNTAINS

| POS | NAME | TEAM | PTS |
|---|---|---|---|
| 1. | I. Schelling | BOH | 3 |
| 2. | J. Alaphilippe | DQT | 2 |
| 3. | A. Perez | COF | 2 |

## POINTS

| POS | NAME | TEAM | PTS |
|---|---|---|---|
| 1. | J. Alaphilippe | DQT | 50 |
| 2. | M. Matthews | BEX | 43 |
| 3. | I. Schelling | BOH | 20 |

## YOUNG RIDER

| POS | NAME | TEAM | TIME |
|---|---|---|---|
| 1. | T. Pogačar | UAD | 4:39:13 |
| 2. | D. Gaudu | GFC | s.t. |
| 3. | S. Higuita | EFN | s.t. |

## BONUSES

| TYPE | NAME | TEAM |
|---|---|---|
| KOM 1 | V. Campenaerts | TQA |
| KOM 2 | D. van Poppel | IWG |
| KOM 3 | A. Perez | COF |
| KOM 4 | I. Schelling | BOH |
| KOM 5 | I. Schelling | BOH |
| KOM 6 | J. Alaphilippe | DQT |
| Sprint 1 | I. Schelling | BOH |

## STAGE RESULTS

| POS | NAME | TEAM | TIME |
|---|---|---|---|
| 1. | J. Alaphilippe | DQT | 4:39:05 |
| 2. | M. Matthews | BEX | 0:08 |
| 3. | P. Roglič | TJV | s.t. |
| 4. | J. Haig | TBV | s.t. |
| 5. | W. Kelderman | BOH | s.t. |
| 6. | T. Pogačar | UAD | s.t. |
| 7. | D. Gaudu | GFC | s.t. |
| 8. | S. Higuita | EFN | s.t. |
| 9. | B. Mollema | TFS | s.t. |
| 10. | G. Thomas | IGD | s.t. |
| 11. | E. Chaves | BEX | s.t. |
| 12. | P. Bilbao | TBV | s.t. |
| 13. | J. Vingegaard | TJV | s.t. |
| 14. | A. Lutsenko | APT | s.t. |
| 15. | E. Mas | MOV | s.t. |
| 16. | R. Urán | EFN | s.t. |
| 17. | N. Quintana | ARK | s.t. |
| 18. | V. Nibali | TFS | s.t. |
| 19. | K. Asgreen | DQT | s.t. |
| 20. | M. van der Poel | AFC | s.t. |
| 21. | J. Fuglsang | APT | s.t. |
| 22. | R. Carapaz | IGD | 0:13 |
| 23. | A. Aranburu | APT | s.t. |
| 24. | W. van Aert | TJV | s.t. |
| 25. | P. Latour | TEN | s.t. |
| 26. | T. Benoot | DSM | 0:16 |
| 27. | A. Turgis | TEN | 0:28 |
| 28. | L. Hamilton | BEX | 0:38 |
| 29. | B. Van Moer | LTS | 0:46 |
| 30. | T. Skujiņš | TFS | 0:51 |
| 31. | G. Boivin | ISN | s.t. |
| 32. | J. Stuyven | TFS | 0:54 |
| 33. | S. Colbrelli | TBV | s.t. |
| 34. | B. van Poppel | IWG | 1:24 |
| 35. | S. Kragh Andersen | DSM | 1:49 |
| 36. | R. Gesink | TJV | s.t. |
| 37. | I. García Cortina | MOV | s.t. |
| 38. | M. Valgren | EFN | s.t. |
| 39. | M. Gogl | TQA | s.t. |
| 40. | B. O'Connor | ACT | s.t. |
| 41. | M. A. López | MOV | s.t. |
| 42. | E. Buchmann | BOH | s.t. |
| 43. | S. Henao | TQA | s.t. |
| 44. | S. Kruijswijk | TJV | s.t. |
| 45. | M. Mohorič | TBV | s.t. |
| 46. | G. Martin | COF | s.t. |
| 47. | P. Rolland | BBK | s.t. |
| 48. | M. Cattaneo | DQT | s.t. |
| 49. | S. Küng | GFC | s.t. |
| 50. | C. Laporte | COF | s.t. |
| 51. | M. Donovan | DSM | s.t. |
| 52. | J. Nieuwenhuis | DSM | s.t. |
| 53. | S. Bissegger | EFN | s.t. |
| 54. | N. Eekhoff | DSM | 1:57 |
| 55. | D. Devenyns | DQT | 2:03 |
| 56. | R. Guerreiro | EFN | 2:10 |
| 57. | N. Powless | EFN | s.t. |
| 58. | O. Naesen | ACT | 2:16 |
| 59. | G. Van Avermaet | ACT | s.t. |
| 60. | A. Paret-Peintre | ACT | s.t. |
| 61. | L. Meintjes | IWG | s.t. |
| 62. | C. Barthe | BBK | s.t. |
| 63. | Q. Pacher | BBK | s.t. |
| 64. | W. Poels | TBV | s.t. |
| 65. | R. Porte | IGD | s.t. |
| 66. | P. Gilbert | LTS | s.t. |
| 67. | S. de Bod | APT | s.t. |
| 68. | X. Meurisse | AFC | s.t. |
| 69. | D. Formolo | UAD | s.t. |
| 70. | H. Houle | APT | s.t. |
| 71. | J. Rickaert | AFC | s.t. |
| 72. | D. van Baarle | IGD | 3:02 |
| 73. | P. Sagan | BOH | 3:17 |
| 74. | L. Mezgec | BEX | s.t. |
| 75. | S. Yates | BEX | s.t. |
| 76. | S. Geschke | COF | s.t. |
| 77. | J. Bakelants | IWG | s.t. |
| 78. | A. Delaplace | ARK | s.t. |
| 79. | L. Rowe | IGD | 3:30 |
| 80. | M. Kwiatkowski | IGD | s.t. |
| 81. | C. Swift | ARK | 3:55 |
| 82. | J. Rutsch | EFN | s.t. |
| 83. | T. De Gendt | LTS | 4:10 |
| 84. | D. Teuns | TBV | s.t. |
| 85. | L. Pöstlberger | BOH | s.t. |
| 86. | Se. Bennett | TQA | s.t. |
| 87. | M. Cort | EFN | 4:24 |
| 88. | C. Juul-Jensen | BEX | s.t. |
| 89. | V. S. Laengen | UAD | 4:57 |
| 90. | B. Armirail | GFC | 5:00 |
| 91. | J. Wallays | COF | 5:21 |
| 92. | D. Ballerini | DQT | 5:26 |
| 93. | A. Valverde | MOV | 5:33 |
| 94. | C. Barbero | TQA | s.t. |
| 95. | I. Erviti | MOV | s.t. |

| POS | NAME | TEAM | TIME |
|---|---|---|---|
| 96. | R. Costa | UAD | s.t. |
| 97. | R. Majka | UAD | s.t. |
| 98. | N. Dlamini | TQA | s.t. |
| 99. | J. Bernard | TFS | s.t. |
| 100. | K. Elissonde | TFS | s.t. |
| 101. | A. Perez | COF | s.t. |
| 102. | N. Bouhanni | ARK | s.t. |
| 103. | J. Philipsen | AFC | s.t. |
| 104. | R. Fernández | COF | s.t. |
| 105. | F. Bonnamour | BBK | s.t. |
| 106. | C. Gautier | BBK | s.t. |
| 107. | F. Doubey | TEN | s.t. |
| 108. | É. Gesbert | ARK | s.t. |
| 109. | V. Madouas | GFC | s.t. |
| 110. | C. Rodríguez | TEN | s.t. |
| 111. | V. de la Parte | TEN | s.t. |
| 112. | A. Démare | GFC | s.t. |
| 113. | O. Fraile | APT | s.t. |
| 114. | E. Boasson Hagen | TEN | s.t. |
| 115. | T. Van der Sande | LTS | s.t. |
| 116. | M. Scotson | GFC | s.t. |
| 117. | C. Verona | MOV | s.t. |
| 118. | F. Wright | TBV | s.t. |
| 119. | J. Guarnieri | GFC | s.t. |
| 120. | P. Vakoč | AFC | s.t. |
| 121. | D. Martin | ISN | s.t. |
| 122. | J. Cabot | TEN | s.t. |
| 123. | T. Geoghegan Hart | IGD | s.t. |
| 124. | J. Castroviejo | IGD | s.t. |
| 125. | J. Koch | IWG | s.t. |
| 126. | M. Walscheid | TQA | 6:01 |
| 127. | D. Oss | BOH | 6:07 |
| 128. | R. Kluge | LTS | s.t. |
| 129. | C. Ewan | LTS | s.t. |
| 130. | W. Barguil | ARK | s.t. |
| 131. | T. Declercq | DQT | s.t. |
| 132. | M. Cavendish | DQT | s.t. |
| 133. | M. Mørkøv | DQT | s.t. |
| 134. | L. Durbridge | BEX | 6:31 |
| 135. | V. Campenaerts | TQA | 6:47 |
| 136. | J. de Buyst | LTS | 6:57 |
| 137. | S. Clarke | TQA | s.t. |
| 138. | B. McNulty | UAD | s.t. |
| 139. | J. Simon | TEN | s.t. |
| 140. | L. Vliegen | IWG | s.t. |
| 141. | D. van Poppel | IWG | s.t. |
| 142. | J. Arcas | MOV | s.t. |
| 143. | L. Rota | IWG | 7:00 |
| 144. | M. Schär | ACT | s.t. |
| 145. | N. Peters | ACT | 7:50 |
| 146. | D. Godon | ACT | s.t. |
| 147. | M. Chevalier | BBK | s.t. |
| 148. | S. Dillier | AFC | 8:10 |
| 149. | M. Bjerg | UAD | 8:49 |
| 150. | N. Politt | BOH | s.t. |
| 151. | P. Konrad | BOH | s.t. |
| 152. | T. Merlier | AFC | s.t. |
| 153. | H. Sweeny | LTS | s.t. |
| 154. | M. Woods | ISN | s.t. |
| 155. | C. Pedersen | DSM | 9:19 |
| 156. | K. Sbaragli | AFC | 9:32 |
| 157. | Je. Herrada | COF | s.t. |
| 158. | C. Bol | DSM | 9:47 |
| 159. | B. Cosnefroy | ACT | 9:52 |
| 160. | G. Zimmermann | IWG | 10:55 |
| 161. | D. Gruzdev | APT | 11:05 |
| 162. | I. Izagirre | APT | s.t. |
| 163. | A. Greipel | ISN | 11:16 |
| 164. | E. Theuns | TFS | s.t. |
| 165. | P. L. Périchon | COF | s.t. |
| 166. | M. Haller | TBV | 11:21 |
| 167. | I. Schelling | BOH | 11:52 |
| 168. | B. Coquard | BBK | 13:04 |
| 169. | C. Russo | ARK | 14:22 |
| 170. | D. McLay | ARK | s.t. |
| 171. | C. Froome | ISN | 14:37 |
| 172. | O. Goldstein | ISN | s.t. |
| 173. | M. Pedersen | TFS | s.t. |
| 174. | R. Hollenstein | ISN | s.t. |
| 175. | R. Zabel | ISN | 16:29 |
| 176. | T. Martin | TJV | s.t. |
| 177. | S. Kuss | TJV | s.t. |
| 178. | M. Teunissen | TJV | s.t. |
| 179. | A. G. Jansen | BEX | s.t. |
| 180. | M. Hirschi | UAD | 18:09 |
| 181. | M. Soler | MOV | 24:38 |

JUNE · WORLDTOUR MEN'S RACE

# TOUR DE FRANCE
Stage 2
27 June 2021
Perros-Guirec–Mûr-de-Bretagne Guerlédan
183.7km

A double ascent of the famous climb outside the village of Mûr de Bretagne sparked a somewhat pedantic debate as to what exactly the climb, dubbed the 'Alpe d'Huez of Brittany', was actually to be called. With the consensus settling on the Breton title *Menez Hiez*, attention then turned to the race itself and what might happen both the first time and the second time up its steep and steady 2km slopes. For the *maillot jaune*, Julian Alaphilippe, thoughts would have been returning to the same date in 2020, on which his beloved father Jo had died. For Mathieu van der Poel, the emotional pressure of trying to claim a yellow jersey in memory of his recently departed grandfather Raymond Poulidor (who famously never once led the race) was immense. But the climb, with its maximum 8 bonus seconds the first time up, offered an opportunity for the Dutchman to win the stage and possibly – just possibly – take the jersey from Alaphilippe. However, in order to make up the 18-second gap on GC, he would have to take all the bonus seconds available and win the stage with at least a second's gap to the race leader. Nothing else would do. As soon as they hit the climb for the first time, he attacked, picked up the bonus seconds and then slowed up to recover in the peloton for an even more powerful attack on the final ascent, some 13km later. He won the stage with a 6-second advantage over Tadej Pogačar in second place and, as he crossed the line, he pointed skywards in memory of Poulidor. It was a second day of scintillating racing and high emotion.

## WEATHER

TEMPERATURE: 17°C
WIND: NE 13km/h

## PROFILE

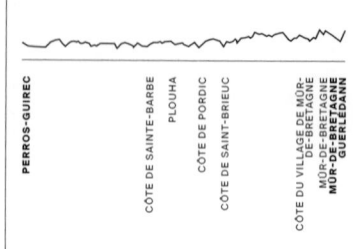

Perros-Guirec — Côte de Sainte-Barbe — Plouha — Côte de Pordic — Côte de Saint-Brieuc — Côte du village de Mûr-de-Bretagne — Mûr-de-Bretagne Guerlédann

## BREAKAWAY
A. Perez (COF), E. Theuns (TFS), S. Clarke (TQA), J. Koch (IWG), I. Schelling (BOH), J. Cabot (TEN)

## GENERAL CLASSIFICATION

| POS | NAME | TEAM | TIME |
|---|---|---|---|
| 1. ↑19 | M. van der Poel | AFC | 8:57:25 |
| 2. ↓1 | J. Alaphilippe | DQT | 0:08 |
| 3. ↑3 | T. Pogačar | UAD | 0:13 |
| 4. ↓1 | P. Roglič | TJV | 0:14 |
| 5. — | W. Kelderman | BOH | 0:24 |
| 6. ↓2 | J. Haig | TBV | 0:26 |
| 7. ↑2 | B. Mollema | TFS | s.t. |
| 8. — | S. Higuita | EFN | s.t. |
| 9. ↑4 | J. Vingegaard | TJV | s.t. |
| 10. ↓3 | D. Gaudu | GFC | s.t. |

## KING OF THE MOUNTAINS

| POS | NAME | TEAM | PTS |
|---|---|---|---|
| 1. — | M. van der Poel | AFC | 4 |
| 2. ↓1 | I. Schelling | BOH | 4 |
| 3. — | A. Perez | COF | 3 |

## POINTS

| POS | NAME | TEAM | PTS |
|---|---|---|---|
| 1. — | J. Alaphilippe | DQT | 66 |
| 2. — | M. van der Poel | AFC | 50 |
| 3. ↓1 | M. Matthews | BEX | 45 |

## YOUNG RIDER

| POS | NAME | TEAM | TIME |
|---|---|---|---|
| 1. — | T. Pogačar | UAD | 8:57:38 |
| 2. ↑1 | S. Higuita | EFN | 0:13 |
| 3. ↑1 | J. Vingegaard | TJV | s.t. |

## TRIVIA
» This was the fourth time the Tour de France has been up the Mûr-de-Bretagne in the race's history. A remarkable 15 riders of the current Tour peloton have raced up it on each of the previous three times – that's 8.3 per cent of the bunch.

## BONUSES

| TYPE | NAME | TEAM |
|---|---|---|
| KOM 1 | A. Perez | COF |
| KOM 2 | I. Schelling | BOH |
| KOM 3 | E. Theuns | TFS |
| KOM 4 | E. Theuns | TFS |
| KOM 5 | M. van der Poel | AFC |
| KOM 6 | M. van der Poel | AFC |
| Sprint 1 | E. Theuns | TFS |

# STAGE RESULTS

| POS | NAME | TEAM | TIME |
|---|---|---|---|
| 1. | M. van der Poel | AFC | 4:18:30 |
| 2. | T. Pogačar | UAD | 0:06 |
| 3. | P. Roglič | TJV | s.t. |
| 4. | W. Kelderman | BOH | s.t. |
| 5. | J. Alaphilippe | DQT | 0:08 |
| 6. | B. Mollema | TFS | s.t. |
| 7. | J. Vingegaard | TJV | s.t. |
| 8. | S. Higuita | EFN | s.t. |
| 9. | P. Latour | TEN | s.t. |
| 10. | J. Haig | TBV | s.t. |
| 11. | M. Woods | ISN | s.t. |
| 12. | R. Carapaz | IGD | s.t. |
| 13. | E. Mas | MOV | s.t. |
| 14. | D. Gaudu | GFC | s.t. |
| 15. | N. Quintana | ARK | s.t. |
| 16. | A. Lutsenko | APT | s.t. |
| 17. | A. Valverde | MOV | s.t. |
| 18. | P. Bilbao | TBV | s.t. |
| 19. | S. Kruijswijk | TJV | s.t. |
| 20. | D. Teuns | TBV | s.t. |
| 21. | E. Chaves | BEX | s.t. |
| 22. | E. Buchmann | BOH | s.t. |
| 23. | W. van Aert | TJV | s.t. |
| 24. | G. Martin | COF | s.t. |
| 25. | R. Urán | EFN | s.t. |
| 26. | S. Henao | TQA | s.t. |
| 27. | S. Colbrelli | TBV | s.t. |
| 28. | G. Thomas | IGD | 0:23 |
| 29. | I. Izaguirre | APT | s.t. |
| 30. | M. A. López | MOV | s.t. |
| 31. | J. Fuglsang | APT | s.t. |
| 32. | R. Guerreiro | EFN | s.t. |
| 33. | V. Nibali | TFS | s.t. |
| 34. | A. Paret-Peintre | ACT | s.t. |
| 35. | L. Meintjes | IWG | s.t. |
| 36. | A. Aranburu | APT | s.t. |
| 37. | W. Poels | TBV | s.t. |
| 38. | Q. Pacher | BBK | s.t. |
| 39. | L. Hamilton | BEX | 0:28 |
| 40. | D. Martin | ISN | 0:36 |
| 41. | É. Gesbert | ARK | 0:42 |
| 42. | R. Porte | IGD | s.t. |
| 43. | F. Bonnamour | BBK | 0:49 |
| 44. | S. Kragh Andersen | DSM | 0:51 |
| 45. | T. Benoot | DSM | s.t. |
| 46. | K. Asgreen | DQT | 0:59 |
| 47. | X. Meurisse | AFC | s.t. |
| 48. | K. Elissonde | TFS | s.t. |
| 49. | T. Skujiņš | TFS | s.t. |
| 50. | J. Bakelants | IWG | s.t. |
| 51. | G. Van Avermaet | ACT | s.t. |
| 52. | B. O'Connor | ACT | 1:06 |
| 53. | S. de Bod | APT | 1:11 |
| 54. | W. Barguil | ARK | 1:14 |
| 55. | M. Mohorič | TBV | 1:30 |
| 56. | D. Formolo | UAD | 1:35 |
| 57. | S. Yates | BEX | 1:44 |
| 58. | J. Simon | TEN | 1:45 |
| 59. | P. Rolland | BBK | s.t. |
| 60. | N. Powless | EFN | s.t. |
| 61. | V. Madouas | GFC | s.t. |
| 62. | J. Bernard | TFS | s.t. |
| 63. | R. Costa | UAD | 2:10 |
| 64. | S. Geschke | COF | 2:26 |
| 65. | R. Majka | UAD | s.t. |
| 66. | F. Doubey | TEN | s.t. |
| 67. | A. Turgis | TEN | s.t. |
| 68. | D. Devenyns | DQT | s.t. |
| 69. | V. de la Parte | TEN | s.t. |
| 70. | M. Gogl | TQA | s.t. |
| 71. | M. Valgren | EFN | s.t. |
| 72. | B. McNulty | UAD | s.t. |
| 73. | S. Küng | GFC | s.t. |
| 74. | R. Fernández | COF | 2:38 |
| 75. | P. Konrad | BOH | s.t. |
| 76. | M. Matthews | BEX | 2:40 |
| 77. | M. Kwiatkowski | IGD | 3:48 |
| 78. | C. Rodríguez | TEN | s.t. |
| 79. | I. García Cortina | MOV | s.t. |
| 80. | K. Sbaragli | AFC | s.t. |
| 81. | O. Fraile | APT | s.t. |
| 82. | T. Geoghegan Hart | IGD | s.t. |
| 83. | C. Verona | MOV | s.t. |
| 84. | J. Castroviejo | IGD | s.t. |
| 85. | M. Donovan | DSM | s.t. |
| 86. | S. Kuss | TJV | s.t. |
| 87. | M. Cattaneo | DQT | s.t. |
| 88. | L. Mezgec | BEX | s.t. |
| 89. | S. Dillier | AFC | 3:51 |
| 90. | D. van Baarle | IGD | 4:03 |
| 91. | R. Gesink | TJV | 4:49 |
| 92. | J. Nieuwenhuis | DSM | s.t. |
| 93. | C. Swift | ARK | s.t. |
| 94. | N. Peters | ACT | s.t. |
| 95. | P. Gilbert | LTS | s.t. |
| 96. | D. Godon | ACT | s.t. |
| 97. | G. Boivin | ISN | s.t. |
| 98. | A. Delaplace | ARK | s.t. |
| 99. | E. Boasson Hagen | TEN | s.t. |
| 100. | P. Sagan | BOH | s.t. |
| 101. | B. Armirail | GFC | 5:23 |
| 102. | B. Cosnefroy | ACT | s.t. |
| 103. | M. Cort | EFN | 5:58 |
| 104. | H. Houle | APT | s.t. |
| 105. | J. Rickaert | AFC | 6:18 |
| 106. | O. Naesen | ACT | s.t. |
| 107. | C. Barthe | BBK | s.t. |
| 108. | C. Gautier | BBK | s.t. |
| 109. | M. Chevalier | BBK | s.t. |
| 110. | L. Vliegen | IWG | 6:56 |
| 111. | B. Van Moer | LTS | s.t. |
| 112. | B. van Poppel | IWG | 7:03 |
| 113. | Je. Herrada | COF | 7:41 |
| 114. | O. Goldstein | ISN | s.t. |
| 115. | S. Clarke | TQA | s.t. |
| 116. | J. Rutsch | EFN | s.t. |
| 117. | M. Schär | ACT | s.t. |
| 118. | S. Bissegger | EFN | s.t. |
| 119. | P. L. Périchon | COF | s.t. |
| 120. | C. Laporte | COF | s.t. |
| 121. | D. Gruzdev | APT | s.t. |
| 122. | V. Campenaerts | TQA | s.t. |
| 123. | Se. Bennett | TQA | s.t. |
| 124. | N. Eekhoff | DSM | 9:06 |
| 125. | T. De Gendt | LTS | s.t. |
| 126. | I. Erviti | MOV | s.t. |
| 127. | J. Arcas | MOV | s.t. |
| 128. | F. Wright | TBV | s.t. |
| 129. | M. Teunissen | TJV | s.t. |
| 130. | D. Oss | BOH | s.t. |
| 131. | V. S. Laengen | UAD | s.t. |
| 132. | L. Rota | IWG | s.t. |
| 133. | B. Coquard | BBK | s.t. |
| 134. | M. Hirschi | UAD | s.t. |
| 135. | N. Politt | BOH | 11:21 |
| 136. | R. Zabel | ISN | s.t. |
| 137. | J. Wallays | COF | s.t. |
| 138. | C. Froome | ISN | s.t. |
| 139. | C. Barbero | TQA | s.t. |
| 140. | A. Perez | COF | s.t. |
| 141. | M. Haller | TBV | s.t. |
| 142. | P. Vakoč | AFC | 11:44 |
| 143. | J. Stuyven | TFS | 11:51 |
| 144. | L. Pöstlberger | BOH | 12:30 |
| 145. | I. Schelling | BOH | 12:55 |
| 146. | N. Dlamini | TQA | s.t. |
| 147. | T. Van der Sande | LTS | s.t. |
| 148. | D. van Poppel | IWG | s.t. |
| 149. | T. Declercq | DQT | s.t. |
| 150. | G. Zimmermann | IWG | s.t. |
| 151. | J. Philipsen | AFC | s.t. |
| 152. | A. Greipel | ISN | s.t. |
| 153. | C. Russo | ARK | s.t. |
| 154. | T. Merlier | AFC | s.t. |
| 155. | J. de Buyst | LTS | s.t. |
| 156. | L. Rowe | IGD | s.t. |
| 157. | M. Cavendish | DQT | s.t. |
| 158. | C. Ewan | LTS | 13:06 |
| 159. | M. Mørkøv | DQT | s.t. |
| 160. | M. Pedersen | TFS | s.t. |
| 161. | C. Juul-Jensen | BEX | s.t. |
| 162. | H. Sweeny | LTS | s.t. |
| 163. | R. Hollenstein | ISN | s.t. |
| 164. | N. Bouhanni | ARK | s.t. |
| 165. | T. Martin | TJV | s.t. |
| 166. | M. Bjerg | UAD | s.t. |
| 167. | C. Pedersen | DSM | s.t. |
| 168. | M. Walscheid | TQA | s.t. |
| 169. | J. Guarnieri | GFC | s.t. |
| 170. | D. Ballerini | DQT | s.t. |
| 171. | M. Scotson | GFC | s.t. |
| 172. | A. Démare | GFC | s.t. |
| 173. | J. Koch | IWG | s.t. |
| 174. | R. Kluge | LTS | s.t. |
| 175. | A. G. Jansen | BEX | s.t. |
| 176. | L. Durbridge | BEX | s.t. |
| 177. | D. McLay | ARK | s.t. |
| 178. | J. Cabot | TEN | s.t. |
| 179. | E. Theuns | TFS | s.t. |
| 180. | C. Bol | DSM | s.t. |

JUNE

JUNE — WORLDTOUR MEN'S RACE

## TOUR DE FRANCE
Stage 3
28 June 2021
Lorient–Pontivy
182.9km

A flatter day, as the race passed through Morbihan towards a final approach to the line in Pontivy, that would do still greater damage to the prospects of some significant names in the peloton and would result in a riders' protest the following day. But before any of that late drama, Geraint Thomas – one of at least two co-leaders of Ineos Grenadiers – contrived to crash at the most innocuous moment as a becalmed peloton was rolling through a Breton town. Thomas also brought down Tony Martin as well as Martin's Dutch teammate Robert Gesink, who was forced to abandon as a result. Thomas himself was seen seated on the ground, pointing at his right shoulder and seemingly suggesting to his teammate and compatriot Luke Rowe that he was about to abandon. However, the race doctors swiftly ascertained that, instead of having broken any bones, the Welshman had dislocated his left shoulder. And with that, they popped it back in. Before long, Rowe was piloting Thomas back towards the peloton. He somehow managed to finish the day in 48th place, in the same time as most of the GC favourites. Tim Merlier of Alpecin-Fenix, making his Tour de France debut, repeated his feat from the Giro d'Italia of winning a Grand Tour sprint at the first possible opportunity, ahead of a decimated group of sprinters in which Caleb Ewan crashed violently into Peter Sagan. Ewan was forced to abandon the following day. Before they even reached Pontivy Primož Roglič had crashed hard again, this time with even more serious consequences for his Tour. He finished the stage almost a minute down on Tadej Pogačar and the rest. Jack Haig of Bahrain Victorious was, along with Gesink, unable to complete the stage, having crashed shortly after Roglič. ⓝⓑ

### TRIVIA
» Tim Merlier has now won a stage at each of the two Grand Tours he's lined up for so far in his career.

### WEATHER

TEMPERATURE: 17°C
WIND: SW 11km/h

### PROFILE

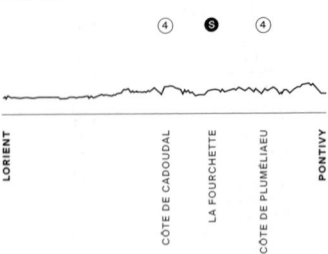

LORIENT – CÔTE DE CADOUDAL – LA FOURCHETTE – CÔTE DE PLUMÉLIAU – PONTIVY

### BREAKAWAY
I. Schelling (BOH), C. Barthe (BBK), M. Chevalier (BBK), J. Wallays (COF), M. Schär (ACT)

### GENERAL CLASSIFICATION

| POS | | NAME | TEAM | TIME |
|---|---|---|---|---|
| 1. | — | M. van der Poel | AFC | 12:58:53 |
| 2. | — | J. Alaphilippe | DQT | 0:08 |
| 3. | ↑15 | R. Carapaz | IGD | 0:31 |
| 4. | ↑15 | W. van Aert | TJV | s.t. |
| 5. | — | W. Kelderman | BOH | 0:38 |
| 6. | ↓3 | T. Pogačar | UAD | 0:39 |
| 7. | ↑4 | E. Mas | MOV | 0:40 |
| 8. | ↑6 | N. Quintana | ARK | s.t. |
| 9. | ↑8 | P. Latour | TEN | 0:45 |
| 10. | ↓2 | S. Higuita | EFN | 0:52 |

### KING OF THE MOUNTAINS

| POS | | NAME | TEAM | PTS |
|---|---|---|---|---|
| 1. | ↑1 | I. Schelling | BOH | 5 |
| 2. | ↓1 | M. van der Poel | AFC | 4 |
| 3. | — | A. Perez | COF | 3 |

### POINTS

| POS | | NAME | TEAM | PTS |
|---|---|---|---|---|
| 1. | — | J. Alaphilippe | DQT | 80 |
| 2. | — | M. van der Poel | AFC | 62 |
| 3. | — | T. Merlier | AFC | 50 |

### YOUNG RIDER

| POS | | NAME | TEAM | TIME |
|---|---|---|---|---|
| 1. | — | T. Pogačar | UAD | 12:59:32 |
| 2. | — | S. Higuita | EFN | 0:13 |
| 3. | ↑1 | D. Gaudu | GFC | s.t. |

### BONUSES

| TYPE | NAME | TEAM |
|---|---|---|
| KOM 1 | I. Schelling | BOH |
| KOM 2 | J. Wallays | COF |
| Sprint 1 | C. Barthe | BBK |

## STAGE RESULTS

| POS | NAME | TEAM | TIME |
|---|---|---|---|
| 1. | T. Merlier | AFC | 4:01:28 |
| 2. | J. Philipsen | AFC | s.t. |
| 3. | N. Bouhanni | ARK | s.t. |
| 4. | D. Ballerini | DQT | s.t. |
| 5. | S. Colbrelli | TBV | s.t. |
| 6. | J. Alaphilippe | DQT | s.t. |
| 7. | M. van der Poel | AFC | s.t. |
| 8. | C. Bol | DSM | s.t. |
| 9. | A. Turgis | TEN | s.t. |
| 10. | M. Walscheid | TQA | s.t. |
| 11. | M. Mohorič | TBV | s.t. |
| 12. | M. Scotson | GFC | s.t. |
| 13. | R. Carapaz | IGD | s.t. |
| 14. | S. Kragh Andersen | DSM | s.t. |
| 15. | W. van Aert | TJV | s.t. |
| 16. | J. Rickaert | AFC | s.t. |
| 17. | N. Eekhoff | DSM | s.t. |
| 18. | M. Matthews | BEX | 0:14 |
| 19. | E. Mas | MOV | s.t. |
| 20. | B. van Poppel | IWG | s.t. |
| 21. | V. Nibali | TFS | s.t. |
| 22. | J. Fuglsang | APT | s.t. |
| 23. | G. Boivin | ISN | s.t. |
| 24. | F. Doubey | TEN | s.t. |
| 25. | N. Quintana | ARK | s.t. |
| 26. | W. Kelderman | BOH | s.t. |
| 27. | P. Latour | TEN | s.t. |
| 28. | V. Campenaerts | TQA | s.t. |
| 29. | S. Henao | TQA | s.t. |
| 30. | L. Vliegen | IWG | s.t. |
| 31. | J. Bakelants | IWG | s.t. |
| 32. | J. Koch | IWG | s.t. |
| 33. | D. van Poppel | IWG | s.t. |
| 34. | C. Barbero | TQA | s.t. |
| 35. | T. Pogačar | UAD | 0:26 |
| 36. | M. Bjerg | UAD | s.t. |
| 37. | S. Higuita | EFN | s.t. |
| 38. | I. García Cortina | MOV | s.t. |
| 39. | M. Cort | EFN | s.t. |
| 40. | B. Mollema | TFS | s.t. |
| 41. | L. Mezgec | BEX | s.t. |
| 42. | D. Gaudu | GFC | s.t. |
| 43. | A. Lutsenko | APT | s.t. |
| 44. | R. Urán | EFN | s.t. |
| 45. | T. Skujiņš | TFS | s.t. |
| 46. | G. Van Avermaet | ACT | s.t. |
| 47. | J. Nieuwenhuis | DSM | s.t. |
| 48. | G. Thomas | IGD | s.t. |
| 49. | E. Chaves | BEX | s.t. |
| 50. | L. Meintjes | IWG | s.t. |
| 51. | J. Bernard | TFS | s.t. |
| 52. | E. Buchmann | BOH | s.t. |
| 53. | W. Poels | TBV | s.t. |
| 54. | C. Gautier | BBK | s.t. |
| 55. | F. Wright | TBV | s.t. |
| 56. | V. S. Laengen | UAD | s.t. |
| 57. | A. Paret-Peintre | ACT | s.t. |
| 58. | X. Meurisse | AFC | s.t. |
| 59. | O. Naesen | ACT | s.t. |
| 60. | D. Godon | ACT | s.t. |
| 61. | É. Gesbert | ARK | s.t. |
| 62. | K. Asgreen | DQT | s.t. |
| 63. | S. Küng | GFC | s.t. |
| 64. | E. Boasson Hagen | TEN | s.t. |
| 65. | J. Simon | TEN | s.t. |
| 66. | M. Donovan | DSM | s.t. |
| 67. | L. Hamilton | BEX | s.t. |
| 68. | D. Formolo | UAD | s.t. |
| 69. | R. Porte | IGD | s.t. |
| 70. | R. Guerreiro | EFN | s.t. |
| 71. | J. Guarnieri | GFC | s.t. |
| 72. | M. Cattaneo | DQT | s.t. |
| 73. | B. O'Connor | ACT | s.t. |
| 74. | Q. Pacher | BBK | s.t. |
| 75. | G. Martin | COF | s.t. |
| 76. | A. Delaplace | ARK | s.t. |
| 77. | M. Mørkov | DQT | 0:38 |
| 78. | C. Barthe | BBK | 0:44 |
| 79. | J. Stuyven | TFS | 0:53 |
| 80. | P. Sagan | BOH | 0:00 |
| 81. | F. Bonnamour | BBK | 1:06 |
| 82. | M. Kwiatkowski | IGD | 1:13 |
| 83. | R. Zabel | ISN | 1:15 |
| 84. | G. Zimmermann | IWG | s.t. |
| 85. | A. Greipel | ISN | s.t. |
| 86. | K. Elissonde | TFS | s.t. |
| 87. | M. Valgren | EFN | s.t. |
| 88. | S. Bissegger | EFN | s.t. |
| 89. | L. Rota | IWG | s.t. |
| 90. | A. Valverde | MOV | 1:21 |
| 91. | M. Teunissen | TJV | s.t. |
| 92. | P. Roglič | TJV | s.t. |
| 93. | M. A. López | MOV | s.t. |
| 94. | P. Bilbao | TBV | s.t. |
| 95. | D. Teuns | TBV | s.t. |

| POS | NAME | TEAM | TIME |
|---|---|---|---|
| 96. | J. Vingegaard | TJV | s.t. |
| 97. | S. Dillier | AFC | s.t. |
| 98. | S. Kruijswijk | TJV | s.t. |
| 99. | P. Rolland | BBK | s.t. |
| 100. | I. Erviti | MOV | s.t. |
| 101. | R. Costa | UAD | 1:27 |
| 102. | N. Dlamini | TQA | 1:35 |
| 103. | C. Swift | ARK | 1:45 |
| 104. | C. Verona | MOV | 1:56 |
| 105. | N. Powless | EFN | s.t. |
| 106. | S. de Bod | APT | s.t. |
| 107. | M. Pedersen | TFS | 1:59 |
| 108. | E. Theuns | TFS | s.t. |
| 109. | J. Castroviejo | IGD | 2:03 |
| 110. | O. Fraile | APT | s.t. |
| 111. | I. Izagirre | APT | s.t. |
| 112. | N. Peters | ACT | 2:06 |
| 113. | T. Benoot | DSM | s.t. |
| 114. | C. Rodríguez | TEN | 2:07 |
| 115. | V. de la Parte | TEN | s.t. |
| 116. | B. Cosnefroy | ACT | s.t. |
| 117. | P. Konrad | BOH | s.t. |
| 118. | J. Wallays | COF | s.t. |
| 119. | K. Sbaragli | AFC | s.t. |
| 120. | P. Vakoč | AFC | s.t. |
| 121. | D. Martin | ISN | 2:11 |
| 122. | L. Rowe | IGD | s.t. |
| 123. | C. Froome | ISN | s.t. |
| 124. | R. Hollenstein | ISN | s.t. |
| 125. | M. Woods | ISN | s.t. |
| 126. | M. Schär | ACT | s.t. |
| 127. | C. Laporte | COF | s.t. |
| 128. | S. Geschke | COF | s.t. |
| 129. | C. Pedersen | DSM | s.t. |
| 130. | S. Yates | BEX | s.t. |
| 131. | T. Martin | TJV | 2:15 |
| 132. | B. McNulty | UAD | s.t. |
| 133. | R. Majka | UAD | s.t. |
| 134. | M. Gogl | TQA | 2:22 |
| 135. | P. Gilbert | LTS | 2:32 |
| 136. | R. Fernández | COF | 2:37 |
| 137. | T. Van der Sande | LTS | s.t. |
| 138. | H. Houle | APT | 2:39 |
| 139. | L. Pöstlberger | BOH | 2:42 |
| 140. | T. Geoghegan Hart | IGD | 2:46 |
| 141. | L. Durbridge | BEX | 2:47 |
| 142. | D. van Baarle | IGD | s.t. |
| 143. | N. Politt | BOH | 2:56 |
| 144. | T. Declercq | DQT | s.t. |
| 145. | Je. Herrada | COF | 2:59 |
| 146. | A. Perez | COF | s.t. |
| 147. | D. Gruzdev | APT | 3:00 |
| 148. | M. Hirschi | UAD | s.t. |
| 149. | A. Aranburu | APT | s.t. |
| 150. | B. Van Moer | LTS | 3:51 |
| 151. | H. Sweeny | LTS | 3:52 |
| 152. | C. Juul-Jensen | BEX | s.t. |
| 153. | B. Armirail | GFC | 4:11 |
| 154. | A. Démare | GFC | s.t. |
| 155. | J. Arcas | MOV | 4:57 |
| 156. | D. Devenyns | DQT | s.t. |
| 157. | O. Goldstein | ISN | s.t. |
| 158. | J. Cabot | TEN | s.t. |
| 159. | V. Madouas | GFC | 5:01 |
| 160. | P. L. Périchon | COF | s.t. |
| 161. | S. Clarke | TQA | s.t. |
| 162. | Se. Bennett | TQA | s.t. |
| 163. | A. G. Jansen | BEX | s.t. |
| 164. | S. Kuss | TJV | s.t. |
| 165. | J. Rutsch | EFN | 5:03 |
| 166. | M. Chevalier | BBK | 5:20 |
| 167. | B. Coquard | BBK | 5:21 |
| 168. | M. Cavendish | DQT | 5:28 |
| 169. | T. De Gendt | LTS | 6:07 |
| 170. | R. Kluge | LTS | 6:08 |
| 171. | W. Barguil | ARK | 6:37 |
| 172. | D. McLay | ARK | 6:39 |
| 173. | C. Russo | ARK | 7:36 |
| 174. | J. de Buyst | LTS | s.t. |
| 175. | D. Oss | BOH | 7:39 |
| 176. | I. Schelling | BOH | 7:41 |
| 177. | M. Haller | TBV | 8:36 |
| 178. | C. Ewan | LTS | 0:00 |

JUNE

JUNE  WORLDTOUR MEN'S RACE

## TOUR DE FRANCE
Stage 4
29 June 2021
Redon–Fougères
150.4km

Thus began the Mark Cavendish Nostalgia Tour. Fougères, the final Breton stage finish in 2021, was one of four stage finishes on the race route where Cavendish had already won at the Tour (along with Chateauroux, Nîmes and Paris). The intervening six years since his last win in Fougères had been characterised by such a steep decline in his fortunes that he had been left on the brink of retirement from the sport – demoralised and very nearly without a place on a team for 2021, let alone the prospect of starting the Tour de France. And yet, here he was: the most prolific sprinter in the history of the sport, at the age of 36, supported by a phenomenally cohesive Deceuninck-QuickStep team and piloted to the line by the unique brilliance of Danish lead-out expert Michael Mørkøv. Much like in Cavendish's first-ever Tour victory, in 2008, a lone rider from the breakaway almost thwarted the sprint. Back then it was Nicolas Vogondy who had been caught 50 metres from the line. In 2021, it was 'the new Thomas De Gendt' (according to Thomas De Gendt), Lotto Soudal's Brent Van Moer who almost stayed away, as he had done so brilliantly just a few weeks earlier at the Dauphiné. But Cavendish was simply not to be denied. He outsprinted Nacer Bouhanni to the line, and afterwards was uncharacteristically almost unable to articulate the scale of his achievement. 'No words' were some of his first words. And with victory number 31, the talk of hunting down Eddy Merckx's all-time record of 34 stage wins at the Tour was instantly reactivated, even if it was rejected by the sprinter in question.

### TRIVIA
» This was the same Fougères finish line as in the 2015 Tour, where Mark Cavendish also won.

### WEATHER

| TEMPERATURE | WIND |
|---|---|
| 19°C | W 11km/h |

### PROFILE

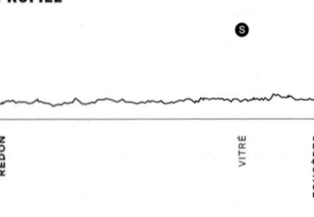

### BREAKAWAY
B. Van Moer (LTS), P. L. Périchon (COF)

### GENERAL CLASSIFICATION

| POS | | NAME | TEAM | TIME |
|---|---|---|---|---|
| 1. | — | M. van der Poel | AFC | 16:19:10 |
| 2. | — | J. Alaphilippe | DQT | 0:08 |
| 3. | — | R. Carapaz | IGD | 0:31 |
| 4. | — | W. van Aert | TJV | s.t. |
| 5. | — | W. Kelderman | BOH | 0:38 |
| 6. | — | T. Pogačar | UAD | 0:39 |
| 7. | — | E. Mas | MOV | 0:40 |
| 8. | — | N. Quintana | ARK | s.t. |
| 9. | — | P. Latour | TEN | 0:45 |
| 10. | ↑2 | D. Gaudu | GFC | 0:52 |

### KING OF THE MOUNTAINS

| POS | | NAME | TEAM | PTS |
|---|---|---|---|---|
| 1. | — | I. Schelling | BOH | 5 |
| 2. | — | M. van der Poel | AFC | 4 |
| 3. | — | A. Perez | COF | 3 |

### POINTS

| POS | | NAME | TEAM | PTS |
|---|---|---|---|---|
| 1. | ↑13 | M. Cavendish | DQT | 89 |
| 2. | ↓1 | J. Alaphilippe | DQT | 82 |
| 3. | ↑1 | M. Matthews | BEX | 78 |

### YOUNG RIDER

| POS | | NAME | TEAM | TIME |
|---|---|---|---|---|
| 1. | — | T. Pogačar | UAD | 16:19:49 |
| 2. | ↑1 | D. Gaudu | GFC | 0:13 |
| 3. | ↓1 | S. Higuita | EFN | s.t. |

### BONUSES

| TYPE | NAME | TEAM |
|---|---|---|
| Sprint 1 | B. Van Moer | LTS |

# STAGE RESULTS

| POS | NAME | TEAM | TIME |
|---|---|---|---|
| 1. | M. Cavendish | DQT | 3:20:17 |
| 2. | N. Bouhanni | ARK | s.t. |
| 3. | J. Philipsen | AFC | s.t. |
| 4. | M. Matthews | BEX | s.t. |
| 5. | P. Sagan | BOH | s.t. |
| 6. | C. Bol | DSM | s.t. |
| 7. | C. Laporte | COF | s.t. |
| 8. | M. Pedersen | TFS | s.t. |
| 9. | B. van Poppel | IWG | s.t. |
| 10. | A. Greipel | ISN | s.t. |
| 11. | S. Colbrelli | TBV | s.t. |
| 12. | M. van der Poel | AFC | s.t. |
| 13. | N. Eekhoff | DSM | s.t. |
| 14. | A. Lutsenko | APT | s.t. |
| 15. | R. Zabel | ISN | s.t. |
| 16. | M. Walscheid | TQA | s.t. |
| 17. | B. Coquard | BBK | s.t. |
| 18. | W. Poels | TBV | s.t. |
| 19. | C. Barthe | BBK | s.t. |
| 20. | I. García Cortina | MOV | s.t. |
| 21. | G. Boivin | ISN | s.t. |
| 22. | D. Gaudu | GFC | s.t. |
| 23. | A. Paret-Peintre | ACT | s.t. |
| 24. | E. Boasson Hagen | TEN | s.t. |
| 25. | W. van Aert | TJV | s.t. |
| 26. | C. Russo | ARK | s.t. |
| 27. | K. Asgreen | DQT | s.t. |
| 28. | T. Pogačar | UAD | s.t. |
| 29. | J. Simon | TEN | s.t. |
| 30. | E. Mas | MOV | s.t. |
| 31. | V. Nibali | TFS | s.t. |
| 32. | R. Carapaz | IGD | s.t. |
| 33. | C. Swift | ARK | s.t. |
| 34. | N. Quintana | ARK | s.t. |
| 35. | T. Merlier | AFC | s.t. |
| 36. | S. Dillier | AFC | s.t. |
| 37. | O. Naesen | ACT | s.t. |
| 38. | S. Kragh Andersen | DSM | s.t. |
| 39. | J. Alaphilippe | DQT | s.t. |
| 40. | D. Formolo | UAD | s.t. |
| 41. | J. Rickaert | AFC | s.t. |
| 42. | W. Kelderman | BOH | s.t. |
| 43. | M. Mohorič | TBV | s.t. |
| 44. | S. Higuita | EFN | s.t. |
| 45. | B. Mollema | TFS | s.t. |
| 46. | A. Démare | GFC | s.t. |
| 47. | L. Rowe | IGD | s.t. |
| 48. | V. Campenaerts | TQA | s.t. |
| 49. | B. Van Moer | LTS | s.t. |
| 50. | P. Latour | TEN | s.t. |
| 51. | L. Hamilton | BEX | s.t. |
| 52. | J. Koch | IWG | s.t. |
| 53. | L. Meintjes | IWG | s.t. |
| 54. | J. Vingegaard | TJV | s.t. |
| 55. | G. Thomas | IGD | s.t. |
| 56. | B. O'Connor | ACT | s.t. |
| 57. | G. Martin | COF | s.t. |
| 58. | S. Henao | TQA | s.t. |
| 59. | F. Bonnamour | BBK | s.t. |
| 60. | F. Doubey | TEN | s.t. |
| 61. | P. Roglič | TJV | s.t. |
| 62. | M. Teunissen | TJV | s.t. |
| 63. | V. S. Laengen | UAD | s.t. |
| 64. | J. Stuyven | TFS | s.t. |
| 65. | R. Urán | EFN | s.t. |
| 66. | L. Vliegen | IWG | s.t. |
| 67. | M. Cort | EFN | s.t. |
| 68. | E. Buchmann | BOH | s.t. |
| 69. | J. Arcas | MOV | s.t. |
| 70. | E. Chaves | BEX | s.t. |
| 71. | M. Valgren | EFN | s.t. |
| 72. | A. Turgis | TEN | s.t. |
| 73. | R. Guerreiro | EFN | s.t. |
| 74. | P. Bilbao | TBV | s.t. |
| 75. | I. Erviti | MOV | s.t. |
| 76. | L. Mezgec | BEX | s.t. |
| 77. | J. Bakelants | IWG | s.t. |
| 78. | M. Donovan | DSM | s.t. |
| 79. | S. Kruijswijk | TJV | s.t. |
| 80. | J. Fuglsang | APT | s.t. |
| 81. | R. Porte | IGD | s.t. |
| 82. | M. A. López | MOV | s.t. |
| 83. | P. Gilbert | LTS | s.t. |
| 84. | T. Skujiņš | TFS | s.t. |
| 85. | Q. Pacher | BBK | s.t. |
| 86. | R. Fernández | COF | s.t. |
| 87. | G. Van Avermaet | ACT | s.t. |
| 88. | T. Benoot | DSM | s.t. |
| 89. | D. Godon | ACT | s.t. |
| 90. | T. Martin | TJV | s.t. |
| 91. | M. Schär | ACT | s.t. |
| 92. | B. McNulty | UAD | s.t. |
| 93. | N. Politt | BOH | s.t. |
| 94. | S. de Bod | APT | s.t. |
| 95. | É. Gesbert | ARK | s.t. |
| 96. | A. Valverde | MOV | s.t. |
| 97. | S. Küng | GFC | s.t. |
| 98. | B. Cosnefroy | ACT | s.t. |
| 99. | N. Peters | ACT | s.t. |
| 100. | P. Konrad | BOH | s.t. |
| 101. | O. Goldstein | ISN | s.t. |
| 102. | N. Powless | EFN | s.t. |
| 103. | D. Teuns | TBV | s.t. |
| 104. | S. Geschke | COF | s.t. |
| 105. | D. Gruzdev | APT | s.t. |
| 106. | C. Gautier | BBK | s.t. |
| 107. | H. Sweeny | LTS | s.t. |
| 108. | M. Woods | ISN | s.t. |
| 109. | K. Elissonde | TFS | s.t. |
| 110. | M. Cattaneo | DQT | s.t. |
| 111. | H. Houle | APT | s.t. |
| 112. | P. Rolland | BBK | s.t. |
| 113. | W. Barguil | ARK | s.t. |
| 114. | J. Bernard | TFS | s.t. |
| 115. | M. Scotson | GFC | s.t. |
| 116. | M. Chevalier | BBK | s.t. |
| 117. | V. de la Parte | TEN | s.t. |
| 118. | J. Rutsch | EFN | s.t. |
| 119. | D. Martin | ISN | s.t. |
| 120. | M. Mørkøv | DQT | s.t. |
| 121. | K. Sbaragli | AFC | s.t. |
| 122. | A. Delaplace | ARK | s.t. |
| 123. | V. Madouas | GFC | s.t. |
| 124. | J. Guarnieri | GFC | 0:26 |
| 125. | C. Rodríguez | TEN | 0:41 |
| 126. | T. De Gendt | LTS | s.t. |
| 127. | C. Froome | ISN | s.t. |
| 128. | D. Devenyns | DQT | 0:43 |
| 129. | D. McLay | ARK | s.t. |
| 130. | J. Nieuwenhuis | DSM | s.t. |
| 131. | C. Barbero | TQA | s.t. |
| 132. | T. Van der Sande | LTS | 0:47 |
| 133. | J. de Buyst | LTS | s.t. |
| 134. | J. Wallays | COF | 0:50 |
| 135. | F. Wright | TBV | 1:04 |
| 136. | M. Haller | TBV | s.t. |
| 137. | D. van Baarle | IGD | 1:07 |
| 138. | D. Oss | BOH | s.t. |
| 139. | R. Majka | UAD | s.t. |
| 140. | L. Rota | IWG | s.t. |
| 141. | R. Costa | UAD | s.t. |
| 142. | N. Dlamini | TQA | s.t. |
| 143. | L. Durbridge | BEX | s.t. |
| 144. | S. Bissegger | EFN | s.t. |
| 145. | D. van Poppel | IWG | s.t. |
| 146. | Je. Herrada | COF | s.t. |
| 147. | I. Izaguirre | APT | s.t. |
| 148. | O. Fraile | APT | s.t. |
| 149. | A. Aranburu | APT | s.t. |
| 150. | A. G. Jansen | BEX | s.t. |
| 151. | C. Verona | MOV | s.t. |
| 152. | M. Hirschi | UAD | s.t. |
| 153. | A. Perez | COF | s.t. |
| 154. | G. Zimmermann | IWG | 1:23 |
| 155. | E. Theuns | TFS | s.t. |
| 156. | R. Hollenstein | ISN | 1:28 |
| 157. | L. Pöstlberger | BOH | s.t. |
| 158. | M. Kwiatkowski | IGD | s.t. |
| 159. | M. Gogl | TQA | s.t. |
| 160. | J. Castroviejo | IGD | s.t. |
| 161. | S. Kuss | TJV | s.t. |
| 162. | Se. Bennett | TQA | s.t. |
| 163. | B. Armirail | GFC | s.t. |
| 164. | T. Declercq | DQT | s.t. |
| 165. | I. Schelling | BOH | s.t. |
| 166. | T. Geoghegan Hart | IGD | 1:33 |
| 167. | C. Pedersen | DSM | s.t. |
| 168. | P. Vakoč | AFC | s.t. |
| 169. | S. Yates | BEX | s.t. |
| 170. | S. Clarke | TQA | s.t. |
| 171. | J. Cabot | TEN | s.t. |
| 172. | X. Meurisse | AFC | 1:38 |
| 173. | M. Bjerg | UAD | 1:47 |
| 174. | C. Juul-Jensen | BEX | s.t. |
| 175. | P. L. Périchon | COF | 1:57 |
| 176. | D. Ballerini | DQT | 0:00 |
| 177. | R. Kluge | LTS | 7:16 |

JUNE

271

JUNE  WORLDTOUR MEN'S RACE

# TOUR DE FRANCE
Stage 5 (ITT)
30 June 2021
Changé–Laval Espace Mayenne
27.2km

The first of two fairly long, mostly flat individual time trials would certainly provide the first major shake-up in the General Classification, with a host of pure climbers among the GC contingent susceptible to substantial time losses. Groupama-FDJ's Swiss time-trialling star Stefan Küng – the reigning European champion in the discipline – was one of the big favourites. With the notable absences of the Ineos duo of Rohan Dennis and the seemingly unbeatable Filippo Ganna on the startlist, this appeared to be a great opportunity for Küng finally to win a stage of the biggest race of them all. And for a long time, that seemed a distinct possibility. On the hot seat for a lengthy shift after posting the best time in an average speed of 50.5kmph, and having seen off the challenges of Kasper Asgreen, Wout van Aert and Mathieu van der Poel, Küng's hopes of victory were dashed by a dominant Tadej Pogačar, who picked up where he left off in the 2020 Tour de France, winning back-to-back time trials over very different parcours. The young Slovenian put a further 44 seconds into a battling Primož Roglič who, despite his injuries, finished ahead of almost all the other GC riders. Van der Poel's outstanding fifth place in a discipline he had rarely raced meant that, much to Pogačar's evident annoyance, the Dutchman defended his yellow jersey and would seemingly be taking it into the Alps. Finishing in a quietly brilliant third was Jonas Vingegaard, whose performance was indicative not just of what was still to come in this edition of the race, but also retrospectively analysed for what he might go on to achieve in a career that was just beginning to take off.

## WEATHER

TEMPERATURE  WIND
20°C  NW 9km/h

## PROFILE

CHANGÉ — LAVAL (ESPACE MAYENNE)

## GENERAL CLASSIFICATION

| POS | | NAME | TEAM | TIME |
|---|---|---|---|---|
| 1. | — | M. van der Poel | AFC | 16:51:41 |
| 2. | ↑4 | T. Pogačar | UAD | 0:08 |
| 3. | ↑1 | W. van Aert | TJV | 0:30 |
| 4. | ↓2 | J. Alaphilippe | DQT | 0:48 |
| 5. | ↑6 | A. Lutsenko | APT | 1:21 |
| 6. | ↑3 | P. Latour | TEN | 1:28 |
| 7. | ↑7 | R. Urán | EFN | 1:29 |
| 8. | ↑15 | J. Vingegaard | TJV | 1:43 |
| 9. | ↓6 | R. Carapaz | IGD | 1:44 |
| 10. | ↑10 | P. Roglič | TJV | 1:48 |

## KING OF THE MOUNTAINS

| POS | | NAME | TEAM | PTS |
|---|---|---|---|---|
| 1. | — | I. Schelling | BOH | 5 |
| 2. | — | M. van der Poel | AFC | 4 |
| 3. | — | A. Perez | COF | 3 |

## POINTS

| POS | | NAME | TEAM | PTS |
|---|---|---|---|---|
| 1. | — | M. Cavendish | DQT | 89 |
| 2. | — | J. Alaphilippe | DQT | 84 |
| 3. | ↑2 | M. van der Poel | AFC | 78 |

## TRIVIA

» Mark Cavendish finished ahead of both Tony Martin and Chris Froome in today's time trial. Only once before has this happened – the prologue of the 2010 Volta Ciclista a Catalunya.

## YOUNG RIDER

| POS | | NAME | TEAM | TIME |
|---|---|---|---|---|
| 1. | — | T. Pogačar | UAD | 16:51:49 |
| 2. | ↑3 | J. Vingegaard | TJV | 1:35 |
| 3. | ↓1 | D. Gaudu | GFC | 2:27 |

## STAGE RESULTS

| POS | NAME | TEAM | TIME |
|---|---|---|---|
| 1. | T. Pogačar | UAD | 32:00 |
| 2. | S. Küng | GFC | 0:19 |
| 3. | J. Vingegaard | TJV | 0:27 |
| 4. | W. van Aert | TJV | 0:30 |
| 5. | M. van der Poel | AFC | 0:31 |
| 6. | K. Asgreen | DQT | 0:37 |
| 7. | P. Roglič | TJV | 0:44 |
| 8. | M. Cattaneo | DQT | 0:55 |
| 9. | R. Porte | IGD | s.t. |
| 10. | A. Lutsenko | APT | 1:00 |
| 11. | M. Bjerg | UAD | 1:01 |
| 12. | M. Cort | EFN | 1:07 |
| 13. | R. Urán | EFN | 1:08 |
| 14. | J. Alaphilippe | DQT | 1:11 |
| 15. | P. Latour | TEN | 1:14 |
| 16. | G. Thomas | IGD | 1:18 |
| 17. | S. Kragh Andersen | DSM | 1:19 |
| 18. | S. Bissegger | EFN | 1:22 |
| 19. | N. Powless | EFN | 1:40 |
| 20. | L. Durbridge | BEX | 1:42 |
| 21. | S. Kruijswijk | TJV | s.t. |
| 22. | A. Perez | COF | s.t. |
| 23. | R. Carapaz | IGD | 1:44 |
| 24. | O. Fraile | APT | 1:46 |
| 25. | B. Mollema | TFS | 1:47 |
| 26. | E. Mas | MOV | 1:49 |
| 27. | W. Kelderman | BOH | s.t. |
| 28. | M. Walscheid | TQA | s.t. |
| 29. | J. Fuglsang | APT | 1:52 |
| 30. | H. Sweeny | LTS | 1:53 |
| 31. | B. O'Connor | ACT | 1:56 |
| 32. | T. De Gendt | LTS | 1:57 |
| 33. | S. Kuss | TJV | s.t. |
| 34. | H. Houle | APT | 1:58 |
| 35. | L. Pöstlberger | BOH | 2:00 |
| 36. | M. Mohorič | TBV | 2:01 |
| 37. | X. Meurisse | AFC | 2:04 |
| 38. | S. Henao | TQA | 2:05 |
| 39. | D. Teuns | TBV | 2:07 |
| 40. | M. A. López | MOV | 2:08 |
| 41. | P. Bilbao | TBV | s.t. |
| 42. | R. Guerreiro | EFN | 2:09 |
| 43. | J. Rutsch | EFN | 2:14 |
| 44. | D. Gaudu | GFC | s.t. |
| 45. | S. de Bod | APT | 2:19 |
| 46. | D. Ballerini | DQT | 2:24 |
| 47. | S. Yates | BEX | 2:25 |
| 48. | E. Buchmann | BOH | 2:29 |
| 49. | V. Nibali | TFS | 2:31 |
| 50. | T. Skujiņš | TFS | 2:34 |
| 51. | N. Quintana | ARK | 2:36 |
| 52. | A. Paret-Peintre | ACT | 2:38 |
| 53. | W. Poels | TBV | 2:41 |
| 54. | S. Higuita | EFN | 2:45 |
| 55. | A. Aranburu | APT | 2:47 |
| 56. | L. Hamilton | BEX | 2:48 |
| 57. | M. Valgren | EFN | s.t. |
| 58. | J. Cabot | TEN | 2:51 |
| 59. | A. Turgis | TEN | s.t. |
| 60. | L. Meintjes | IWG | 2:56 |
| 61. | D. Godon | ACT | 3:03 |
| 62. | E. Chaves | BEX | s.t. |
| 63. | P. L. Périchon | COF | 3:05 |
| 64. | M. Schär | ACT | 3:07 |
| 65. | I. Izaguirre | APT | s.t. |
| 66. | J. Bakelants | IWG | 3:08 |
| 67. | B. Cosnefroy | ACT | 3:11 |
| 68. | A. Delaplace | ARK | 3:13 |
| 69. | G. Van Avermaet | ACT | s.t. |
| 70. | G. Martin | COF | 3:15 |
| 71. | M. Donovan | DSM | 3:18 |
| 72. | J. Rickaert | AFC | 3:21 |
| 73. | C. Swift | ARK | 3:22 |
| 74. | N. Eekhoff | DSM | s.t. |
| 75. | M. Teunissen | TJV | s.t. |
| 76. | N. Politt | BOH | s.t. |
| 77. | M. Cavendish | DQT | 3:24 |
| 78. | S. Dillier | AFC | 3:25 |
| 79. | F. Bonnamour | BBK | 3:32 |
| 80. | A. Valverde | MOV | s.t. |
| 81. | T. Martin | TJV | 3:33 |
| 82. | O. Goldstein | ISN | 3:37 |
| 83. | T. Benoot | DSM | 3:41 |
| 84. | J. Nieuwenhuis | DSM | s.t. |
| 85. | N. Peters | ACT | 3:42 |
| 86. | V. de la Parte | TEN | s.t. |
| 87. | S. Colbrelli | TBV | s.t. |
| 88. | D. Oss | BOH | 3:43 |
| 89. | M. Haller | TBV | 3:44 |
| 90. | D. van Poppel | IWG | 3:47 |
| 91. | É. Gesbert | ARK | 3:48 |
| 92. | I. Erviti | MOV | s.t. |
| 93. | Je. Herrada | COF | 3:49 |
| 94. | Q. Pacher | BBK | 3:51 |
| 95. | V. Campenaerts | TQA | 3:52 |
| 96. | M. Mørkøv | DQT | s.t. |
| 97. | C. Pedersen | DSM | s.t. |
| 98. | M. Matthews | BEX | 3:53 |
| 99. | M. Chevalier | BBK | 3:54 |
| 100. | F. Doubey | TEN | 3:55 |
| 101. | D. van Baarle | IGD | s.t. |
| 102. | G. Boivin | ISN | 3:59 |
| 103. | W. Barguil | ARK | 4:00 |
| 104. | R. Fernández | COF | 4:01 |
| 105. | D. Martin | ISN | 4:02 |
| 106. | P. Sagan | BOH | 4:04 |
| 107. | L. Rota | IWG | 4:05 |
| 108. | V. Madouas | GFC | 4:06 |
| 109. | M. Woods | ISN | s.t. |
| 110. | S. Geschke | COF | 4:07 |
| 111. | P. Rolland | BBK | 4:08 |
| 112. | C. Russo | ARK | 4:10 |
| 113. | E. Boasson Hagen | TEN | 4:11 |
| 114. | D. Formolo | UAD | s.t. |
| 115. | D. Gruzdev | APT | s.t. |
| 116. | C. Juul-Jensen | BEX | 4:12 |
| 117. | S. Clarke | TQA | 4:13 |
| 118. | O. Naesen | ACT | 4:15 |
| 119. | Se. Bennett | TQA | 4:16 |
| 120. | F. Wright | TBV | s.t. |
| 121. | C. Froome | ISN | 4:20 |
| 122. | L. Vliegen | IWG | 4:21 |
| 123. | M. Scotson | GFC | 4:24 |
| 124. | D. Devenyns | DQT | 4:26 |
| 125. | T. Declercq | DQT | s.t. |
| 126. | P. Vakoč | AFC | s.t. |
| 127. | J. de Buyst | LTS | 4:27 |
| 128. | T. Van der Sande | LTS | s.t. |
| 129. | R. Majka | UAD | s.t. |
| 130. | M. Hirschi | UAD | 4:28 |
| 131. | J. Bernard | TFS | 4:29 |
| 132. | C. Barthe | BBK | 4:30 |
| 133. | N. Dlamini | TQA | 4:31 |
| 134. | J. Philipsen | AFC | 4:36 |
| 135. | L. Rowe | IGD | s.t. |
| 136. | I. García Cortina | MOV | 4:39 |
| 137. | B. Van Moer | LTS | 4:40 |
| 138. | B. van Poppel | IWG | s.t. |
| 139. | M. Gogl | TQA | 4:43 |
| 140. | V. S. Laengen | UAD | s.t. |
| 141. | R. Costa | UAD | 4:45 |
| 142. | J. Simon | TEN | 4:46 |
| 143. | B. Armirail | GFC | 4:48 |
| 144. | A. Greipel | ISN | 4:49 |
| 145. | A. Démare | GFC | 4:53 |
| 146. | C. Gautier | BBK | 4:54 |
| 147. | R. Zabel | ISN | s.t. |
| 148. | P. Gilbert | LTS | 4:55 |
| 149. | C. Rodríguez | TEN | 4:56 |
| 150. | J. Koch | IWG | 4:58 |
| 151. | J. Arcas | MOV | s.t. |
| 152. | G. Zimmermann | IWG | 5:01 |
| 153. | C. Bol | DSM | 5:03 |
| 154. | E. Theuns | TFS | s.t. |
| 155. | A. G. Jansen | BEX | 5:04 |
| 156. | J. Guarnieri | GFC | 5:05 |
| 157. | J. Stuyven | TFS | 5:07 |
| 158. | T. Geoghegan Hart | IGD | 5:10 |
| 159. | C. Barbero | TQA | 5:13 |
| 160. | C. Laporte | COF | 5:14 |
| 161. | J. Wallays | COF | 5:21 |
| 162. | P. Konrad | BOH | s.t. |
| 163. | L. Mezgec | BEX | 5:28 |
| 164. | D. McLay | ARK | 5:29 |
| 165. | J. Castroviejo | IGD | s.t. |
| 166. | I. Schelling | BOH | 5:31 |
| 167. | T. Merlier | AFC | 5:33 |
| 168. | K. Sbaragli | AFC | 5:38 |
| 169. | M. Kwiatkowski | IGD | 5:41 |
| 170. | R. Hollenstein | ISN | s.t. |
| 171. | K. Elissonde | TFS | 5:44 |
| 172. | N. Bouhanni | ARK | 5:51 |
| 173. | B. Coquard | BBK | 5:55 |
| 174. | M. Pedersen | TFS | 5:58 |
| 175. | R. Kluge | LTS | 6:13 |
| 176. | C. Verona | MOV | 6:23 |
| 177. | B. McNulty | UAD | 6:55 |

JUNE    WORLDTOUR MEN'S RACE

## TOUR DE FRANCE
Stage 6
1 July 2021
Tours–Châteauroux
160.4km

Mark Cavendish's third ever race into Chateauroux got underway in the kind of blazing sense of expectation rather than hope that used to characterise his years of serial successes in the colours of HTC Colombia, Sky and QuickStep. On both previous occasions he had contested a bunch sprint in Chateauroux, he won. In 2011 he won there during his final campaign with HTC, resulting in the green jersey. But in 2008 he had tasted victory at the Tour for the first time in his career. From that peloton, only five riders were still racing in 2021: Cavendish, Philippe Gilbert, Vincenzo Nibali, Alejandro Valverde and Chris Froome (who had made his debut at the race). While Froome's comeback race was turning into something of a humbling sufferfest, Cavendish's was just starting to ignite. Confused tactics by Alpecin-Fenix arguably contributed to the apparent ease with which Deceuninck-QuickStep once again delivered Cavendish to victory. The Dutch team, for whom the yellow jersey of Mathieu van der Poel had worked as an early lead-out man, seemed unsure which of their Belgian sprinters to back in the final. Instead of fully committing to either Jasper Philipsen or Tim Merlier, in the end both sprinted and both were beaten by Cavendish, though Philipsen, finishing in second, seemed at first to suggest that Cavendish had deviated from his line in the sprint. The victory stood, and Cavendish – already in green after winning stage 4 – consolidated his lead in the points competition and moved to within two of the Merckx record. 'Don't say his name!' he warned inquiring journalists. And with that, no one did for a further week at least.

### WEATHER

TEMPERATURE | WIND
23°C | W 6km/h

### PROFILE

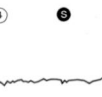

### BREAKAWAY
R. Kluge (LTS), G. Van Avermaet (ACT)

### GENERAL CLASSIFICATION

| POS | NAME | TEAM | TIME |
|---|---|---|---|
| 1. — | M. van der Poel | AFC | 20:09:17 |
| 2. — | T. Pogačar | UAD | 0:08 |
| 3. — | W. van Aert | TJV | 0:30 |
| 4. — | J. Alaphilippe | DQT | 0:48 |
| 5. — | A. Lutsenko | APT | 1:21 |
| 6. — | P. Latour | TEN | 1:28 |
| 7. — | R. Urán | EFN | 1:29 |
| 8. — | J. Vingegaard | TJV | 1:43 |
| 9. — | R. Carapaz | IGD | 1:44 |
| 10.— | P. Roglič | TJV | 1:48 |

### KING OF THE MOUNTAINS

| POS | NAME | TEAM | PTS |
|---|---|---|---|
| 1. — | I. Schelling | BOH | 5 |
| 2. — | M. van der Poel | AFC | 4 |
| 3. — | A. Perez | COF | 3 |

### POINTS

| POS | NAME | TEAM | PTS |
|---|---|---|---|
| 1. — | M. Cavendish | DQT | 148 |
| 2. ↑5 | J. Philipsen | AFC | 102 |
| 3. ↑2 | N. Bouhanni | ARK | 99 |

### YOUNG RIDER

| POS | NAME | TEAM | TIME |
|---|---|---|---|
| 1. — | T. Pogačar | UAD | 20:09:25 |
| 2. — | J. Vingegaard | TJV | 1:35 |
| 3. — | D. Gaudu | GFC | 2:27 |

### TRIVIA
» This was Cavendish's 50th Grand Tour stage victory.

### BONUSES

| TYPE | NAME | TEAM |
|---|---|---|
| KOM 1 | G. Van Avermaet | ACT |
| Sprint 1 | G. Van Avermaet | ACT |

## STAGE RESULTS

| POS | NAME | TEAM | TIME |
|---|---|---|---|
| 1. | M. Cavendish | DQT | 3:17:36 |
| 2. | J. Philipsen | AFC | s.t. |
| 3. | N. Bouhanni | ARK | s.t. |
| 4. | A. Démare | GFC | s.t. |
| 5. | P. Sagan | BOH | s.t. |
| 6. | C. Bol | DSM | s.t. |
| 7. | T. Merlier | AFC | s.t. |
| 8. | W. van Aert | TJV | s.t. |
| 9. | M. Matthews | BEX | s.t. |
| 10. | M. Pedersen | TFS | s.t. |
| 11. | S. Colbrelli | TBV | s.t. |
| 12. | J. de Buyst | LTS | s.t. |
| 13. | M. Walscheid | TQA | s.t. |
| 14. | R. Zabel | ISN | s.t. |
| 15. | M. Teunissen | TJV | s.t. |
| 16. | B. Coquard | BBK | s.t. |
| 17. | T. Van der Sande | LTS | s.t. |
| 18. | D. van Poppel | IWG | s.t. |
| 19. | A. Turgis | TEN | s.t. |
| 20. | I. García Cortina | MOV | s.t. |
| 21. | M. Mørkøv | DQT | s.t. |
| 22. | C. Laporte | COF | s.t. |
| 23. | A. Greipel | ISN | s.t. |
| 24. | M. Mohorič | TBV | s.t. |
| 25. | T. Pogačar | UAD | s.t. |
| 26. | L. Mezgec | BEX | s.t. |
| 27. | C. Barthe | BBK | s.t. |
| 28. | J. Rickaert | AFC | s.t. |
| 29. | N. Eekhoff | DSM | s.t. |
| 30. | B. Cosnefroy | ACT | s.t. |
| 31. | R. Carapaz | IGD | s.t. |
| 32. | E. Mas | MOV | s.t. |
| 33. | J. Nieuwenhuis | DSM | s.t. |
| 34. | M. van der Poel | AFC | s.t. |
| 35. | W. Kelderman | BOH | s.t. |
| 36. | V. Campenaerts | TQA | s.t. |
| 37. | S. Dillier | AFC | s.t. |
| 38. | J. Stuyven | TFS | s.t. |
| 39. | A. G. Jansen | BEX | s.t. |
| 40. | H. Sweeny | LTS | s.t. |
| 41. | N. Peters | ACT | s.t. |
| 42. | D. Ballerini | DQT | s.t. |
| 43. | E. Boasson Hagen | TEN | s.t. |
| 44. | S. Kragh Andersen | DSM | s.t. |
| 45. | D. McLay | ARK | s.t. |
| 46. | G. Thomas | IGD | s.t. |
| 47. | J. Simon | TEN | s.t. |
| 48. | D. Gaudu | GFC | s.t. |
| 49. | V. Nibali | TFS | s.t. |
| 50. | A. Lutsenko | APT | s.t. |
| 51. | G. Boivin | ISN | s.t. |
| 52. | I. Erviti | MOV | s.t. |
| 53. | A. Valverde | MOV | s.t. |
| 54. | D. Godon | ACT | s.t. |
| 55. | D. Formolo | UAD | s.t. |
| 56. | G. Van Avermaet | ACT | s.t. |
| 57. | P. Latour | TEN | s.t. |
| 58. | F. Doubey | TEN | s.t. |
| 59. | L. Hamilton | BEX | s.t. |
| 60. | B. O'Connor | ACT | s.t. |
| 61. | J. Fuglsang | APT | s.t. |
| 62. | N. Quintana | ARK | s.t. |
| 63. | V. S. Laengen | UAD | s.t. |
| 64. | C. Barbero | TQA | s.t. |
| 65. | S. Henao | TQA | s.t. |
| 66. | J. Alaphilippe | DQT | s.t. |
| 67. | G. Martin | COF | s.t. |
| 68. | L. Durbridge | BEX | s.t. |
| 69. | A. Paret-Peintre | ACT | s.t. |
| 70. | P. Gilbert | LTS | s.t. |
| 71. | F. Bonnamour | BBK | s.t. |
| 72. | E. Buchmann | BOH | s.t. |
| 73. | M. Scotson | GFC | s.t. |
| 74. | P. Roglič | TJV | s.t. |
| 75. | N. Politt | BOH | s.t. |
| 76. | K. Asgreen | DQT | s.t. |
| 77. | W. Barguil | ARK | s.t. |
| 78. | M. Valgren | EFN | s.t. |
| 79. | M. A. López | MOV | s.t. |
| 80. | J. Vingegaard | TJV | s.t. |
| 81. | C. Pedersen | DSM | s.t. |
| 82. | S. Bissegger | EFN | s.t. |
| 83. | R. Urán | EFN | s.t. |
| 84. | L. Meintjes | IWG | s.t. |
| 85. | P. Bilbao | TBV | s.t. |
| 86. | J. Rutsch | EFN | s.t. |
| 87. | M. Cort | EFN | s.t. |
| 88. | J. Bakelants | IWG | s.t. |
| 89. | S. Kruijswijk | TJV | s.t. |
| 90. | W. Poels | TBV | s.t. |
| 91. | E. Chaves | BEX | s.t. |
| 92. | T. Skujiņš | TFS | s.t. |
| 93. | T. Benoot | DSM | s.t. |
| 94. | H. Houle | APT | s.t. |
| 95. | M. Chevalier | BBK | s.t. |
| 96. | R. Porte | IGD | s.t. |
| 97. | B. Mollema | TFS | s.t. |
| 98. | P. Konrad | BOH | s.t. |
| 99. | B. Van Moer | LTS | s.t. |
| 100. | R. Guerreiro | EFN | s.t. |
| 101. | Q. Pacher | BBK | s.t. |
| 102. | D. Teuns | TBV | s.t. |
| 103. | V. Madouas | GFC | s.t. |
| 104. | M. Woods | ISN | s.t. |
| 105. | M. Schär | ACT | s.t. |
| 106. | B. van Poppel | IWG | s.t. |
| 107. | K. Elissonde | TFS | s.t. |
| 108. | O. Goldstein | ISN | s.t. |
| 109. | M. Cattaneo | DQT | s.t. |
| 110. | C. Rodríguez | TEN | s.t. |
| 111. | R. Fernández | COF | s.t. |
| 112. | J. Bernard | TFS | s.t. |
| 113. | S. Higuita | EFN | s.t. |
| 114. | N. Dlamini | TQA | s.t. |
| 115. | S. de Bod | APT | s.t. |
| 116. | C. Swift | ARK | s.t. |
| 117. | V. de la Parte | TEN | s.t. |
| 118. | P. Rolland | BBK | s.t. |
| 119. | D. Martin | ISN | s.t. |
| 120. | O. Naesen | ACT | s.t. |
| 121. | T. Martin | TJV | s.t. |
| 122. | S. Kuss | TJV | s.t. |
| 123. | A. Delaplace | ARK | s.t. |
| 124. | C. Gautier | BBK | 0:22 |
| 125. | C. Russo | ARK | 0:24 |
| 126. | É. Gesbert | ARK | s.t. |
| 127. | J. Koch | IWG | 0:40 |
| 128. | B. McNulty | UAD | 0:46 |
| 129. | E. Theuns | TFS | 0:52 |
| 130. | D. Gruzdev | APT | s.t. |
| 131. | C. Froome | ISN | s.t. |
| 132. | F. Wright | TBV | 1:03 |
| 133. | S. Geschke | COF | 1:06 |
| 134. | T. De Gendt | LTS | 1:07 |
| 135. | N. Powless | EFN | s.t. |
| 136. | K. Sbaragli | AFC | s.t. |
| 137. | L. Rowe | IGD | s.t. |
| 138. | R. Kluge | LTS | s.t. |
| 139. | D. van Baarle | IGD | s.t. |
| 140. | M. Donovan | DSM | s.t. |
| 141. | R. Hollenstein | ISN | s.t. |
| 142. | S. Küng | GFC | s.t. |
| 143. | J. Arcas | MOV | s.t. |
| 144. | L. Pöstlberger | BOH | 1:13 |
| 145. | M. Kwiatkowski | IGD | 1:51 |
| 146. | G. Zimmermann | IWG | s.t. |
| 147. | M. Gogl | TQA | s.t. |
| 148. | L. Rota | IWG | s.t. |
| 149. | L. Vliegen | IWG | s.t. |
| 150. | J. Wallays | COF | s.t. |
| 151. | J. Castroviejo | IGD | s.t. |
| 152. | Je. Herrada | COF | s.t. |
| 153. | T. Geoghegan Hart | IGD | s.t. |
| 154. | S. Yates | BEX | s.t. |
| 155. | R. Costa | UAD | s.t. |
| 156. | S. Clarke | TQA | s.t. |
| 157. | X. Meurisse | AFC | s.t. |
| 158. | R. Majka | UAD | s.t. |
| 159. | P. Vakoč | AFC | s.t. |
| 160. | A. Aranburu | APT | s.t. |
| 161. | C. Verona | MOV | s.t. |
| 162. | I. Izaguirre | APT | s.t. |
| 163. | P. L. Périchon | COF | s.t. |
| 164. | O. Fraile | APT | s.t. |
| 165. | B. Armirail | GFC | s.t. |
| 166. | M. Hirschi | UAD | s.t. |
| 167. | Se. Bennett | TQA | s.t. |
| 168. | T. Declercq | DQT | s.t. |
| 169. | D. Devenyns | DQT | s.t. |
| 170. | D. Oss | BOH | s.t. |
| 171. | I. Schelling | BOH | s.t. |
| 172. | J. Cabot | TEN | s.t. |
| 173. | C. Juul-Jensen | BEX | 1:56 |
| 174. | M. Bjerg | UAD | 2:13 |
| 175. | M. Haller | TBV | 2:30 |
| 176. | J. Guarnieri | GFC | 3:42 |
| 177. | A. Perez | COF | 4:24 |

JUNE   WORLDTOUR MEN'S RACE

# TOUR DE FRANCE
Stage 7
2 July 2021
Vierzon–Le Creusot
249.1km

## WEATHER

TEMPERATURE: 27°C
WIND: SW 7km/h

## PROFILE

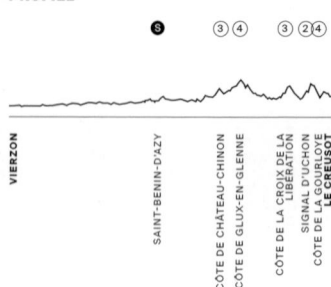

VIERZON · SAINT-BENIN-D'AZY · CÔTE DE CHÂTEAU-CHINON · CÔTE DE GLUX-EN-GLENNE · CÔTE DE LA CROIX DE LA LIBÉRATION · SIGNAL D'UCHON · CÔTE DE LA GOURLOYE · LE CREUSOT

At just under 250km, stage 7 to Le Creusot was the longest on the race for a staggering 21 years. And, as befitted a stage of such grandeur, a 29-man breakaway of ridiculous strength eventually stole away to make this a brutal day out for all concerned, as UAE Team Emirates had the whole team on the front in order to limit the GC gains being made by the riders on the attack. In the end, Kasper Asgreen of Deceuninck-QuickStep would finish the day second on GC with a decent lead over some of the climbers as the race headed for the Alps. Mark Cavendish managed to sneak into the move as well and was able to pick up the maximum 20 points at the day's intermediate sprint, extending his lead over all of his rivals. The day's racing was significant for the overall picture of the race in a few ways, not least UAE Team Emirates' assumption as the dominant of the peloton, working for the interests of the pre-eminent rider. It was a reversal from the pattern of 2020, which had seen Jumbo-Visma do just that. Instead, they were having to rethink their race entirely. Their bruised and battered team leader, Primož Roglič, was dropped on the penultimate climb, the Signal d'Uchon. This time, unlike on stage 4, no riders from his team dropped back to support him. His GC challenge was definitely over by the end of the day. At the front of the race, his compatriot, the Slovenian road race champion Matej Mohorič, took flight with 18km remaining and was never seen again. Once more, emotions overcame the winner when he was interviewed at the finish. Tears were becoming a theme of the race. This solo stage win was not the end of the story for Bahrain Victorious or Mohorič. ⓝⓑ

## GENERAL CLASSIFICATION

| POS | NAME | TEAM | TIME |
|---|---|---|---|
| 1. — | M. van der Poel | AFC | 25:39:17 |
| 2. ↑1 | W. van Aert | TJV | 0:30 |
| 3. ↑8 | K. Asgreen | DQT | 1:49 |
| 4. ↑29 | M. Mohorič | TBV | 3:01 |
| 5. ↓3 | T. Pogačar | UAD | 3:43 |
| 6. ↑13 | V. Nibali | TFS | 4:12 |
| 7. ↓3 | J. Alaphilippe | DQT | 4:23 |
| 8. ↓3 | A. Lutsenko | APT | 4:56 |
| 9. ↓3 | P. Latour | TEN | 5:03 |
| 10. ↓3 | R. Urán | EFN | 5:04 |

## KING OF THE MOUNTAINS

| POS | NAME | TEAM | PTS |
|---|---|---|---|
| 1. — | M. Mohorič | TBV | 11 |
| 2. ↓1 | I. Schelling | BOH | 5 |
| 3. ↓1 | M. van der Poel | AFC | 4 |

## POINTS

| POS | NAME | TEAM | PTS |
|---|---|---|---|
| 1. — | M. Cavendish | DQT | 168 |
| 2. ↑4 | M. van der Poel | AFC | 103 |
| 3. ↓1 | J. Philipsen | AFC | 102 |

## YOUNG RIDER

| POS | NAME | TEAM | TIME |
|---|---|---|---|
| 1. — | T. Pogačar | UAD | 25:43:00 |
| 2. — | J. Vingegaard | TJV | 1:35 |
| 3. — | D. Gaudu | GFC | 2:27 |

## BREAKAWAY

M. Cavendish (DQT), V. Nibali (TFS), P. Gilbert (LTS), S. Yates (BEX), M. Cort (EFN), W. van Aert (TJV), I. Erviti (MOV), M. Mohorič (TBV), S. Kragh Andersen (DSM), R. Guerreiro (EFN), V. Campenaerts (TQA), J. Bakelants (IWG), J. Stuyven (TFS), M. Teunissen (TJV), M. van der Poel (AFC), H. Houle (APT), I. García Cortina (MOV), T. Skujiņš (TFS), H. Sweeny (LTS), P. Konrad (BOH), B. Van Moer (LTS), D. Godon (ACT), C. Laporte (COF), B. van Poppel (IWG), K. Asgreen (DQT), M. Schär (ACT), F. Bonnamour (BBK), D. van Baarle (IGD), X. Meurisse (AFC)

## BONUSES

| TYPE | NAME | TEAM |
|---|---|---|
| KOM 1 | M. Mohorič | TBV |
| KOM 2 | M. Mohorič | TBV |
| KOM 3 | M. Mohorič | TBV |
| KOM 4 | M. Mohorič | TBV |
| KOM 5 | M. Mohorič | TBV |
| Sprint 1 | M. Cavendish | DQT |

## STAGE RESULTS

| POS | NAME | TEAM | TIME |
|---|---|---|---|
| 1. | M. Mohorič | TBV | 5:28:20 |
| 2. | J. Stuyven | TFS | 1:20 |
| 3. | M. Cort | EFN | 1:40 |
| 4. | M. van der Poel | AFC | s.t. |
| 5. | K. Asgreen | DQT | s.t. |
| 6. | F. Bonnamour | BBK | s.t. |
| 7. | P. Konrad | BOH | s.t. |
| 8. | W. van Aert | TJV | s.t. |
| 9. | B. Van Moer | LTS | 1:44 |
| 10. | D. Godon | ACT | 2:45 |
| 11. | T. Skujiņš | TFS | s.t. |
| 12. | H. Houle | APT | 2:57 |
| 13. | V. Nibali | TFS | s.t. |
| 14. | S. Yates | BEX | s.t. |
| 15. | X. Meurisse | AFC | 4:22 |
| 16. | P. Gilbert | LTS | s.t. |
| 17. | J. Bakelants | IWG | 4:25 |
| 18. | S. Kragh Andersen | DSM | 4:32 |
| 19. | J. Alaphilippe | DQT | 5:15 |
| 20. | E. Mas | MOV | s.t. |
| 21. | R. Carapaz | IGD | s.t. |
| 22. | P. Latour | TEN | s.t. |
| 23. | S. Higuita | EFN | s.t. |
| 24. | A. Lutsenko | APT | s.t. |
| 25. | J. Vingegaard | TJV | s.t. |
| 26. | T. Pogačar | UAD | s.t. |
| 27. | S. Henao | TQA | s.t. |
| 28. | B. Mollema | TFS | s.t. |
| 29. | P. Bilbao | TBV | s.t. |
| 30. | E. Chaves | BEX | s.t. |
| 31. | B. O'Connor | ACT | s.t. |
| 32. | K. Elissonde | TFS | s.t. |
| 33. | L. Meintjes | IWG | s.t. |
| 34. | R. Porte | IGD | s.t. |
| 35. | E. Buchmann | BOH | s.t. |
| 36. | A. Paret-Peintre | ACT | s.t. |
| 37. | R. Urán | FFN | s.t. |
| 38. | J. Fuglsang | APT | s.t. |
| 39. | D. Gaudu | GFC | s.t. |
| 40. | G. Martin | COF | s.t. |
| 41. | G. Thomas | IGD | s.t. |
| 42. | S. Kruijswijk | TJV | s.t. |
| 43. | J. Bernard | TFS | s.t. |
| 44. | P. Rolland | BBK | s.t. |
| 45. | R. Majka | UAD | s.t. |
| 46. | L. Hamilton | BEX | s.t. |
| 47. | C. Rodríguez | TEN | s.t. |
| 48. | W. Kelderman | BOH | s.t. |
| 49. | M. A. López | MOV | s.t. |
| 50. | A. Valverde | MOV | s.t. |
| 51. | M. Kwiatkowski | IGD | 5:26 |
| 52. | J. Castroviejo | IGD | 5:44 |
| 53. | I. Erviti | MOV | 6:22 |
| 54. | D. van Baarle | IGD | 7:00 |
| 55. | W. Poels | TBV | s.t. |
| 56. | I. García Cortina | MOV | 7:02 |
| 57. | V. Madouas | GFC | 7:31 |
| 58. | N. Powless | EFN | 7:57 |
| 59. | T. De Gendt | LTS | 8:02 |
| 60. | Q. Pacher | BBK | s.t. |
| 61. | M. Cattaneo | DQT | s.t. |
| 62. | M. Donovan | DSM | s.t. |
| 63. | S. Geschke | COF | 9:03 |
| 64. | W. Barguil | ARK | s.t. |
| 65. | P. Roglič | TJV | s.t. |
| 66. | D. Martin | ISN | 9:42 |
| 67. | M. Schär | ACT | 10:53 |
| 68. | V. Campenaerts | TQA | s.t. |
| 69. | É. Gesbert | ARK | s.t. |
| 70. | H. Sweeny | LTS | s.t. |
| 71. | D. Devenyns | DQT | 11:35 |
| 72. | D. Cosnefroy | ACT | s.t. |
| 73. | D. Teuns | TBV | s.t. |
| 74. | M. Teunissen | TJV | s.t. |
| 75. | L. Vliegen | IWG | 13:19 |
| 76. | L. Rota | IWG | s.t. |
| 77. | M. Valgren | EFN | s.t. |
| 78. | C. Barthe | BBK | s.t. |
| 79. | P. L. Périchon | COF | s.t. |
| 80. | R. Fernández | COF | s.t. |
| 81. | G. Van Avermaet | ACT | s.t. |
| 82. | Je. Herrada | COF | s.t. |
| 83. | B. Armirail | GFC | s.t. |
| 84. | S. Kuss | TJV | s.t. |
| 85. | S. Colbrelli | TBV | 15:32 |
| 86. | N. Politt | BOH | s.t. |
| 87. | S. Küng | GFC | s.t |
| 88. | I. Izaguirre | APT | s.t. |
| 89. | T. Declercq | DQT | s.t. |
| 90. | O. Fraile | APT | s.t. |
| 91. | A. Aranburu | APT | s.t. |
| 92. | D. Gruzdev | APT | s.t. |
| 93. | A. Delaplace | ARK | s.t. |
| 94. | M. Haller | TBV | s.t. |
| 95. | B. van Poppel | IWG | s.t. |
| 96. | V. de la Parte | TEN | s.t. |
| 97. | C. Verona | MOV | 16:43 |
| 98. | S. de Bod | APT | 17:34 |
| 99. | J. Arcas | MOV | s.t. |
| 100. | M. Woods | ISN | s.t. |
| 101. | J. Rickaert | AFC | s.t. |
| 102. | C. Laporte | COF | 18:05 |
| 103. | A. Perez | COF | s.t. |
| 104. | A. G. Jansen | BEX | 18:37 |
| 105. | E. Boasson Hagen | TEN | s.t. |
| 106. | N. Peters | ACT | s.t. |
| 107. | J. Wallays | COF | s.t. |
| 108. | S. Dillier | AFC | s.t. |
| 109. | K. Sbaragli | AFC | s.t. |
| 110. | C. Froome | ISN | s.t. |
| 111. | R. Zabel | ISN | s.t. |
| 112. | A. Greipel | ISN | s.t. |
| 113. | N. Eekhoff | DSM | s.t. |
| 114. | J. Philipsen | AFC | s.t. |
| 115. | D. van Poppel | IWG | s.t. |
| 116. | O. Goldstein | ISN | s.t. |
| 117. | M. Matthews | BEX | s.t. |
| 118. | L. Mezgec | BEX | s.t. |
| 119. | P. Sagan | BOH | s.t. |
| 120. | D. Oss | BOH | s.t. |
| 121. | R. Guerreiro | EFN | s.t. |
| 122. | A. Turgis | TEN | s.t. |
| 123. | C. Swift | ARK | s.t. |
| 124. | G. Boivin | ISN | s.t. |
| 125. | M. Scotson | GFC | s.t. |
| 126. | L. Durbridge | BEX | s.t. |
| 127. | M. Walscheid | TQA | s.t. |
| 128. | R. Hollenstein | ISN | s.t. |
| 129. | T. Martin | TJV | s.t. |
| 130. | S. Clarke | TQA | s.t. |
| 131. | T. Van der Sande | LTS | s.t. |
| 132. | C. Barbero | TQA | s.t. |
| 133. | T. Geoghegan Hart | IGD | s.t. |
| 134. | N. Dlamini | TQA | s.t. |
| 135. | N. Quintana | ARK | s.t. |
| 136. | T. Merlier | AFC | s.t. |
| 137. | O. Naesen | ACT | s.t. |
| 138. | C. Juul-Jensen | BEX | s.t. |
| 139. | E. Theuns | TFS | s.t. |
| 140. | G. Zimmermann | IWG | s.t. |
| 141. | J. de Buyst | LTS | s.t. |
| 142. | B. Coquard | BBK | s.t. |
| 143. | M. Chevalier | BBK | s.t. |
| 144. | C. Gautier | BBK | s.t. |
| 145. | M. Gogl | TQA | s.t. |
| 146. | L. Pöstlberger | BOH | s.t. |
| 147. | I. Schelling | BOH | s.t. |
| 148. | Se. Bennett | TQA | s.t. |
| 149. | J. Koch | IWG | s.t. |
| 150. | R. Costa | UAD | s.t. |
| 151. | P. Vakoč | AFC | s.t. |
| 152. | D. Ballerini | DQT | s.t. |
| 153. | M. Cavendish | DQT | 21:13 |
| 154. | D. McLay | ARK | 23:47 |
| 155. | J. Nieuwenhuis | DSM | s.t. |
| 156. | M. Bjerg | UAD | s.t. |
| 157. | M. Pedersen | TFS | s.t. |
| 158. | J. Rutsch | EFN | s.t. |
| 159. | B. McNulty | UAD | s.t. |
| 160. | J. Gaugnieri | GFC | s.t. |
| 161. | D. Formolo | UAD | s.t. |
| 162. | N. Bouhanni | ARK | s.t. |
| 163. | J. Simon | TEN | s.t. |
| 164. | C. Russo | ARK | s.t. |
| 165. | A. Démare | GFC | s.t. |
| 166. | T. Benoot | DSM | s.t. |
| 167. | C. Pedersen | DSM | s.t. |
| 168. | F. Doubey | TEN | s.t. |
| 169. | V. S. Laengen | UAD | 24:43 |
| 170. | L. Rowe | IGD | s.t. |
| 171. | F. Wright | TBV | s.t. |
| 172. | M. Mørkøv | DQT | s.t. |
| 173. | M. Hirschi | UAD | s.t. |
| 174. | S. Bissegger | EFN | s.t. |
| 175. | C. Bol | DSM | s.t. |
| 176. | J. Cabot | TEN | s.t. |
| 177. | R. Kluge | LTS | 25:03 |

## TRIVIA

» Today's stage was the longest for 21 years, at 249.1km. In 2000, the 254.5km stage 20 was won by Erik Zabel. Here, 21 years later, his son Rick was on the start line.

JUNE

JUNE    WORLDTOUR MEN'S RACE

## TOUR DE FRANCE
Stage 8
3 July 2021
Oyonnax–Le Grand-Bornand
150.8km

Into the Alps, skirting the Plateau des Glières in the Massif des Aravis, the race was heading over a total of five climbs, including three category-1s, towards a familiar finish in Le Grand Bornand, where Julian Alaphilippe had first ridden to victory at the Tour in 2018. It took a frantic 70km for the break to form; when it did eventually go, it contained the stage winner Dylan Teuns, in the dark red of Bahrain Victorious, buoyed by the success of their teammate Matej Mohorič from the previous day. Teuns' teammate Wout Poels was also in the breakaway, trying – and succeeding – to wrestle the King of the Mountains jersey from Mohorič. With racing this hard there would be casualties. Geraint Thomas found himself in the *gruppetto* early on, having been dropped along with the sprinters. Eventually Primož Roglič found himself in the same group of stragglers. This would be his last day at the Tour, before he departed the race and prepared for his assault on the Tokyo Olympics, where he would go on to claim the individual time trial. On the final climb of the day, the Col de la Colombière, Teuns attacked Michael Woods and went clear on the descent as he rode to victory. But it was on the previous climb that Tadej Pogačar made his single most decisive move of the entire Tour: he attacked on the Col de Romme and went clear. By the top of the Colombière he was within 15 seconds of Teuns and seemed intent on catching him, before sagely relenting on the descent, content with the huge gains he had made on GC. He took the yellow jersey, and now led the race by a staggering margin. Of the true GC riders, none were within 4 and a half minutes of the 22-year-old Slovenian.

## WEATHER

TEMPERATURE: 19°C
WIND: W 2km/h

## PROFILE

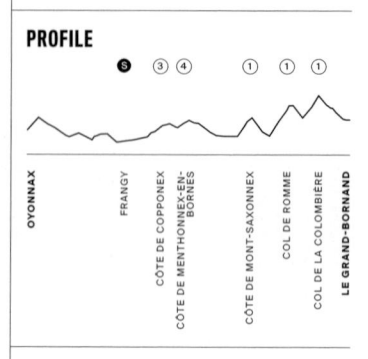

OYONNAX — FRANGY — CÔTE DE COPPONEX — CÔTE DE MENTHONNEX-EN-BORNES — CÔTE DE MONT-SAXONNEX — COL DE ROMME — COL DE LA COLOMBIÈRE — LE GRAND-BORNAND

## BREAKAWAY

S. Kragh Andersen (DSM), T. Benoot (DSM), M. Cattaneo (DQT), S. Yates (BEX), C. Juul-Jensen (BEX), J. Castroviejo (IGD), A. Valverde (MOV), N. Quintana (ARK), K. Elissonde (TFS), S. Henao (TQA), G. Martin (COF), A. Paret-Peintre (ACT), S. Kuss (TJV), B. Armirail (GFC), I. Izaguirre (APT), D. Teuns (TBV)

## GENERAL CLASSIFICATION

| POS | NAME | TEAM | TIME |
|---|---|---|---|
| 1. ↑4 | T. Pogačar | UAD | 29:38:25 |
| 2. — | W. van Aert | TJV | 1:48 |
| 3. ↑5 | A. Lutsenko | APT | 4:38 |
| 4. ↑6 | R. Urán | EFN | 4:46 |
| 5. ↑6 | J. Vingegaard | TJV | 5:00 |
| 6. ↑6 | R. Carapaz | IGD | 5:01 |
| 7. ↑7 | W. Kelderman | BOH | 5:13 |
| 8. ↑7 | E. Mas | MOV | 5:15 |
| 9. ↑10 | D. Gaudu | GFC | 5:52 |
| 10. ↑12 | P. Bilbao | TBV | 6:41 |

## KING OF THE MOUNTAINS

| POS | NAME | TEAM | PTS |
|---|---|---|---|
| 1. — | W. Poels | TBV | 23 |
| 2. — | M. Woods | ISN | 22 |
| 3. — | N. Quintana | ARK | 14 |

## POINTS

| POS | NAME | TEAM | PTS |
|---|---|---|---|
| 1. — | M. Cavendish | DQT | 168 |
| 2. ↑3 | M. Matthews | BEX | 113 |
| 3. ↓1 | M. van der Poel | AFC | 103 |

## YOUNG RIDER

| POS | NAME | TEAM | TIME |
|---|---|---|---|
| 1. — | T. Pogačar | UAD | 29:38:25 |
| 2. — | J. Vingegaard | TJV | 5:00 |
| 3. — | D. Gaudu | GFC | 5:52 |

## BONUSES

| TYPE | NAME | TEAM |
|---|---|---|
| KOM 1 | W. Poels | TBV |
| KOM 2 | W. Poels | TBV |
| KOM 3 | W. Poels | TBV |
| KOM 4 | M. Woods | ISN |
| KOM 5 | D. Teuns | TBV |
| Sprint 1 | S. Colbrelli | TBV |

## STAGE RESULTS

| POS | NAME | TEAM | TIME |
|---|---|---|---|
| 1. | D. Teuns | TBV | 3:54:41 |
| 2. | I. Izaguirre | APT | 0:44 |
| 3. | M. Woods | ISN | 0:47 |
| 4. | T. Pogačar | UAD | 0:49 |
| 5. | W. Poels | TBV | 2:33 |
| 6. | S. Yates | BEX | 2:43 |
| 7. | A. Paret-Peintre | ACT | 3:03 |
| 8. | G. Martin | COF | s.t. |
| 9. | M. Cattaneo | DQT | 4:07 |
| 10. | J. Vingegaard | TJV | 4:09 |
| 11. | A. Lutsenko | APT | s.t. |
| 12. | E. Mas | MOV | s.t. |
| 13. | R. Carapaz | IGD | s.t. |
| 14. | R. Urán | EFN | s.t. |
| 15. | D. Gaudu | GFC | s.t. |
| 16. | P. Bilbao | TBV | s.t. |
| 17. | W. Kelderman | BOH | s.t. |
| 18. | B. O'Connor | ACT | s.t. |
| 19. | S. Henao | TQA | 4:13 |
| 20. | D. Formolo | UAD | 4:18 |
| 21. | W. van Aert | TJV | 5:45 |
| 22. | N. Quintana | ARK | 8:34 |
| 23. | J. Castroviejo | IGD | s.t. |
| 24. | E. Chaves | BEX | 10:19 |
| 25. | B. Mollema | TFS | s.t. |
| 26. | L. Meintjes | IWG | 12:21 |
| 27. | B. Armirail | GFC | 12:23 |
| 28. | N. Peters | ACT | 14:14 |
| 29. | J. Fuglsang | APT | 15:50 |
| 30. | O. Fraile | APT | s.t. |
| 31. | K. Elissonde | TFS | 16:01 |
| 32. | S. Kragh Andersen | DSM | 17:00 |
| 33. | T. Benoot | DSM | s.t. |
| 34. | S. Kruijswijk | TJV | 18:22 |
| 35. | T. Geoghegan Hart | IGD | 18:55 |
| 36. | F. Bonnamour | BBK | s.t. |
| 37. | J. Alaphilippe | DQT | s.t. |
| 38. | R. Guerreiro | EFN | s.t. |
| 39. | R. Porte | IGD | s.t. |
| 40. | Q. Pacher | BBK | 21:15 |
| 41. | V. Nibali | TFS | 21:47 |
| 42. | M. A. López | MOV | s.t. |
| 43. | S. Kuss | TJV | s.t. |
| 44. | M. van der Poel | AFC | s.t. |
| 45. | I. Schelling | BOH | 22:19 |
| 46. | M. Donovan | DSM | 23:18 |
| 47. | V. de la Parte | TEN | s.t. |
| 48. | S. Geschke | COF | 25:30 |
| 49. | K. Asgreen | DQT | 27:56 |
| 50. | F. Doubey | TEN | s.t. |
| 51. | B. McNulty | UAD | 28:26 |
| 52. | T. De Gendt | LTS | 28:41 |
| 53. | D. Ballerini | DQT | s.t. |
| 54. | X. Meurisse | AFC | s.t. |
| 55. | N. Politt | BOH | s.t. |
| 56. | D. Martin | ISN | s.t. |
| 57. | E. Buchmann | BOH | s.t. |
| 58. | C. Rodríguez | TEN | s.t. |
| 59. | G. Zimmermann | IWG | s.t. |
| 60. | É. Gesbert | ARK | s.t. |
| 61. | C. Swift | ARK | s.t. |
| 62. | S. Küng | GFC | s.t. |
| 63. | H. Houle | APT | s.t. |
| 64. | M. Valgren | EFN | s.t. |
| 65. | F. Wright | TBV | s.t. |
| 66. | M. Chevalier | BBK | s.t. |
| 67. | S. Colbrelli | TBV | s.t. |
| 68. | L. Hamilton | BEX | s.t. |
| 69. | M. Mohorič | TBV | s.t. |
| 70. | C. Juul-Jensen | BEX | s.t. |
| 71. | A. Perez | COF | s.t. |
| 72. | P. Konrad | BOH | s.t. |
| 73. | P. L. Périchon | COF | s.t. |
| 74. | J. Bernard | TFS | s.t. |
| 75. | Je. Herrada | COF | s.t. |
| 76. | D. van Baarle | IGD | 29:52 |
| 77. | A. Turgis | TEN | 30:21 |
| 78. | P. Latour | TEN | s.t. |
| 79. | A. Aranburu | APT | s.t. |
| 80. | S. de Bod | APT | 31:25 |
| 81. | R. Fernández | COF | 32:41 |
| 82. | L. Durbridge | BEX | 34:04 |
| 83. | M. Matthews | BEX | 34:06 |
| 84. | D. Oss | BOH | s.t. |
| 85. | D. Devenyns | DQT | 34:34 |
| 86. | R. Costa | UAD | 34:46 |
| 87. | M. Kwiatkowski | IGD | 34:55 |
| 88. | S. Higuita | EFN | s.t. |
| 89. | G. Boivin | ISN | 35:01 |
| 90. | L. Rowe | IGD | s.t. |
| 91. | A. Valverde | MOV | s.t. |
| 92. | I. García Cortina | MOV | s.t. |
| 93. | J. Bakelants | IWG | s.t. |
| 94. | C. Barbero | TQA | s.t. |
| 95. | C. Barthe | BBK | s.t. |
| 96. | H. Sweeny | LTS | s.t. |
| 97. | I. Erviti | MOV | s.t. |
| 98. | W. Barguil | ARK | s.t. |
| 99. | P. Rolland | BBK | s.t. |
| 100. | K. Sbaragli | AFC | s.t. |
| 101. | C. Verona | MOV | s.t. |
| 102. | P. Gilbert | LTS | s.t. |
| 103. | O. Naesen | ACT | s.t. |
| 104. | M. Hirschi | UAD | s.t. |
| 105. | R. Zabel | ISN | s.t. |
| 106. | A. Greipel | ISN | s.t. |
| 107. | V. S. Laengen | UAD | s.t. |
| 108. | J. Nieuwenhuis | DSM | s.t. |
| 109. | J. Rutsch | EFN | s.t. |
| 110. | J. Philipsen | AFC | s.t. |
| 111. | P. Vakoč | AFC | s.t. |
| 112. | D. Godon | ACT | s.t. |
| 113. | C. Gautier | BBK | s.t. |
| 114. | C. Laporte | COF | s.t. |
| 115. | S. Dillier | AFC | s.t. |
| 116. | B. Cosnefroy | ACT | s.t. |
| 117. | M. Teunissen | TJV | s.t. |
| 118. | S. Bissegger | EFN | s.t. |
| 119. | N. Eekhoff | DSM | s.t. |
| 120. | M. Cort | EFN | s.t. |
| 121. | J. Rickaert | AFC | s.t. |
| 122. | B. Coquard | BBK | s.t. |
| 123. | V. Madouas | GFC | s.t. |
| 124. | P. Sagan | BOH | s.t. |
| 125. | T. Van der Sande | LTS | s.t. |
| 126. | B. Van Moer | LTS | s.t. |
| 127. | M. Scotson | GFC | s.t. |
| 128. | E. Theuns | TFS | s.t. |
| 129. | J. Stuyven | TFS | s.t. |
| 130. | J. de Buyst | LTS | s.t. |
| 131. | D. van Poppel | IWG | s.t. |
| 132. | J. Arcas | MOV | s.t. |
| 133. | R. Hollenstein | ISN | s.t. |
| 134. | J. Wallays | COF | s.t. |
| 135. | D. McLay | ARK | s.t. |
| 136. | D. Gruzdev | APT | s.t. |
| 137. | L. Mezgec | BEX | s.t. |
| 138. | M. Schär | ACT | s.t. |
| 139. | A. Delaplace | ARK | s.t. |
| 140. | C. Russo | ARK | s.t. |
| 141. | L. Rota | IWG | s.t. |
| 142. | J. Guarnieri | GFC | s.t. |
| 143. | G. van Avermaet | ACT | s.t. |
| 144. | L. Vliegen | IWG | s.t. |
| 145. | M. Haller | TBV | s.t. |
| 146. | T. Merlier | AFC | s.t. |
| 147. | J. Koch | IWG | s.t. |
| 148. | A. G. Jansen | BEX | s.t. |
| 149. | T. Martin | TJV | s.t. |
| 150. | M. Mørkøv | DQT | s.t. |
| 151. | M. Cavendish | DQT | s.t. |
| 152. | T. Declercq | DQT | s.t. |
| 153. | E. Boasson Hagen | TEN | s.t. |
| 154. | M. Walscheid | TQA | s.t. |
| 155. | B. van Poppel | IWG | s.t. |
| 156. | C. Froome | ISN | s.t. |
| 157. | O. Goldstein | ISN | s.t. |
| 158. | J. Simon | TEN | s.t. |
| 159. | N. Dlamini | TQA | s.t. |
| 160. | S. Clarke | TQA | s.t. |
| 161. | M. Bjerg | UAD | s.t. |
| 162. | C. Pedersen | DSM | s.t. |
| 163. | Se. Bennett | TQA | s.t. |
| 164. | L. Pöstlberger | BOH | s.t. |
| 165. | T. Skujiņš | TFS | s.t. |
| 166. | M. Pedersen | TFS | s.t. |
| 167. | R. Majka | UAD | s.t. |
| 168. | C. Bol | DSM | s.t. |
| 169. | R. Kluge | LTS | s.t. |
| 170. | M. Gogl | TQA | s.t. |
| 171. | N. Bouhanni | ARK | s.t. |
| 172. | V. Campenaerts | TQA | s.t. |
| 173. | J. Cabot | TEN | s.t. |
| 174. | G. Thomas | IGD | s.t. |
| 175. | P. Roglič | TJV | s.t. |
| 176. | N. Powless | EFN | s.t. |
| 177. | A. Démare | GFC | 35:34 |

JUNE   WORLDTOUR MEN'S RACE

# TOUR DE FRANCE
Stage 9
4 July 2021
Cluses–Tignes
144.9km

And so to Tignes, which had featured in 2019 on the day that Egan Bernal knew he had won the Tour de France. Tignes, which Jumbo-Visma use as their annual altitude training camp (though Primož Roglič would not start the stage, along with Mathieu van der Poel), was the first summit finish of the 2021 Tour, crowning a stage that already featured the ascent of the Col des Saisies, the Col du Pré and the Cormet de Roselend. The weather was appalling, with plummeting temperatures and heavy rain throughout. After the race many a seasoned campaigner would declare they had never been so cold in a race. On French television, the former *maillot jaune* Thomas Voeckler said that, in his long experience of the Tour, he had never known conditions like these. A huge breakaway established itself, including Wout Poels, Michael Woods and Nairo Quintana, who were engaged in an intriguing tussle for the polka-dot jersey. But the best-placed rider in the move was AG2R Citroën's young Australian signing, Ben O'Connor, at 8 minutes 13. He won the stage with a stunning solo ride on a climb eminently suited to his characteristics and, up until the final few kilometres, when the GC race behind suddenly exploded into life, he was in the virtual race lead. As it was, he still finished the day second overall, but now with a Tour de France stage win to add to his Giro victory from a breakaway the previous year. As O'Connor crossed the line, Richard Carapaz attacked the group of favourites 4km down the mountain. That provoked a response from Tadej Pogačar, who had hitherto seemed content to ride with a becalmed group of GC favourites. At the end of the day, he extended his lead over those in his group still further. With the considerable benefit of hindsight, it might well be argued that Pogačar had won the Tour before they had left the Alps.

## TRIVIA

» The past three editions of the Tour have seen the yellow jersey on the first rest day not wearing it on the podium in Paris. The previous six editions all saw the rider in the race lead resplendent in yellow on the Champs-Élysées.

## WEATHER

TEMPERATURE   WIND
18°C   SW 7km/h

## PROFILE

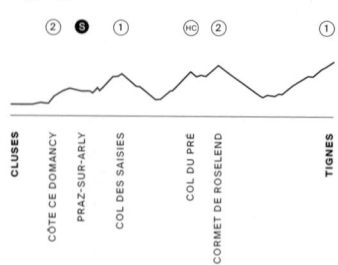

## BREAKAWAY

M. Woods (ISN), S. Higuita (EFN), N. Quintana (ARK), B. O'Connor (ACT)

## GENERAL CLASSIFICATION

| POS | NAME | TEAM | TIME |
|---|---|---|---|
| 1. – | T. Pogačar | UAD | 34:11:10 |
| 2. ↑12 | B. O'Connor | ACT | 2:01 |
| 3. ↑1 | R. Urán | EFN | 5:18 |
| 4. ↑1 | J. Vingegaard | TJV | 5:32 |
| 5. ↑1 | R. Carapaz | IGD | 5:33 |
| 6. ↑2 | E. Mas | MOV | 5:47 |
| 7. – | W. Kelderman | BOH | 5:58 |
| 8. ↓5 | A. Lutsenko | APT | 6:12 |
| 9. ↑3 | G. Martin | COF | 7:02 |
| 10. ↓1 | D. Gaudu | GFC | 7:22 |

## KING OF THE MOUNTAINS

| POS | NAME | TEAM | PTS |
|---|---|---|---|
| 1. ↑2 | N. Quintana | ARK | 50 |
| 2. – | M. Woods | ISN | 42 |
| 3. ↓2 | W. Poels | TBV | 39 |

## POINTS

| POS | NAME | TEAM | PTS |
|---|---|---|---|
| 1. – | M. Cavendish | DQT | 168 |
| 2. – | M. Matthews | BEX | 130 |
| 3. ↑3 | S. Colbrelli | TBV | 121 |

## YOUNG RIDER

| POS | NAME | TEAM | TIME |
|---|---|---|---|
| 1. – | T. Pogačar | UAD | 34:11:10 |
| 2. – | J. Vingegaard | TJV | 5:32 |
| 3. – | D. Gaudu | GFC | 7:22 |

## BONUSES

| TYPE | NAME | TEAM |
|---|---|---|
| KOM 1 | P. Latour | TEN |
| KOM 2 | W. Poels | TBV |
| KOM 3 | N. Quintana | ARK |
| KOM 4 | N. Quintana | ARK |
| KOM 5 | B. O'Connor | ACT |
| Sprint 1 | S. Colbrelli | TBV |

## STAGE RESULTS

| POS | NAME | TEAM | TIME |
|---|---|---|---|
| 1. | B. O'Connor | ACT | 4:26:43 |
| 2. | M. Cattaneo | DQT | 5:07 |
| 3. | S. Colbrelli | TBV | 5:34 |
| 4. | G. Martin | COF | 5:36 |
| 5. | F. Bonnamour | BBK | 6:02 |
| 6. | T. Pogačar | UAD | s.t. |
| 7. | R. Carapaz | IGD | 6:34 |
| 8. | J. Vingegaard | TJV | s.t. |
| 9. | E. Mas | MOV | s.t. |
| 10. | R. Urán | EFN | s.t. |
| 11. | N. Quintana | ARK | 6:38 |
| 12. | R. Guerreiro | EFN | 6:47 |
| 13. | W. Kelderman | BOH | s.t. |
| 14. | D. Gaudu | GFC | 7:32 |
| 15. | A. Lutsenko | APT | 7:36 |
| 16. | P. Konrad | BOH | s.t. |
| 17. | P. Bilbao | TBV | 7:59 |
| 18. | A. Valverde | MOV | s.t. |
| 19. | G. Thomas | IGD | 9:41 |
| 20. | B. Cosnefroy | ACT | 10:23 |
| 21. | A. Paret-Peintre | ACT | s.t. |
| 22. | P. Rolland | BBK | s.t. |
| 23. | V. Madouas | GFC | s.t. |
| 24. | J. Castroviejo | IGD | s.t. |
| 25. | J. Stuyven | TFS | 11:15 |
| 26. | J. Rutsch | EFN | 12:50 |
| 27. | I. Izaguirre | APT | s.t. |
| 28. | S. Higuita | EFN | 12:54 |
| 29. | W. Barguil | ARK | 13:17 |
| 30. | D. Teuns | TBV | 14:21 |
| 31. | N. Politt | BOH | 15:27 |
| 32. | L. Rota | IWG | 15:33 |
| 33. | L. Meintjes | IWG | s.t. |
| 34. | E. Chaves | BEX | s.t. |
| 35. | R. Majka | UAD | 17:12 |
| 36. | D. Formolo | UAD | 17:49 |
| 37. | R. Costa | UAD | s.t. |
| 38. | V. de la Parte | TEN | 21:14 |
| 39. | A. Perez | COF | s.t. |
| 40. | J. Arcas | MOV | 23:10 |
| 41. | W. Poels | TBV | s.t. |
| 42. | S. Küng | GFC | s.t. |
| 43. | M. Valgren | EFN | s.t. |
| 44. | D. Martin | ISN | 25:27 |
| 45. | M. Woods | ISN | s.t. |
| 46. | F. Doubey | TEN | 25:55 |
| 47. | S. Dillier | AFC | s.t. |
| 48. | J. Fuglsang | APT | s.t. |
| 49. | I. Erviti | MOV | s.t. |
| 50. | J. Bakelants | IWG | s.t. |
| 51. | V. Nibali | TFS | s.t. |
| 52. | H. Houle | APT | s.t. |
| 53. | K. Elissonde | TFS | 27:12 |
| 54. | M. Pedersen | TFS | s.t. |
| 55. | J. Bernard | TFS | s.t. |
| 56. | M. Bjerg | UAD | 28:09 |
| 57. | M. Cort | EFN | s.t. |
| 58. | D. van Baarle | IGD | 28:25 |
| 59. | T. De Gendt | LTS | 29:22 |
| 60. | S. Kuss | TJV | 30:27 |
| 61. | B. Mollema | TFS | s.t. |
| 62. | R. Zabel | ISN | 31:37 |
| 63. | C. Barthe | BBK | s.t. |
| 64. | C. Rodríguez | TEN | s.t. |
| 65. | P. Gilbert | LTS | s.t. |
| 66. | S. Kruijswijk | TJV | s.t. |
| 67. | J. Nieuwenhuis | DSM | s.t. |
| 68. | X. Meurisse | AFC | s.t. |
| 69. | Q. Pacher | BBK | s.t. |
| 70. | C. Barbero | TQA | s.t. |
| 71. | C. Verona | MOV | s.t. |
| 72. | G. Boivin | ISN | s.t. |
| 73. | M. Chevalier | BBK | s.t. |
| 74. | R. Fernández | COF | s.t. |
| 75. | C. Russo | ARK | s.t. |
| 76. | K. Sbaragli | AFC | s.t. |
| 77. | D. Godon | ACT | s.t. |
| 78. | M. Schär | ACT | s.t. |
| 79. | L. Rowe | IGD | s.t. |
| 80. | S. Clarke | TQA | s.t. |
| 81. | F. Wright | TBV | s.t. |
| 82. | M. Kwiatkowski | IGD | s.t. |
| 83. | C. Laporte | COF | s.t. |
| 84. | P. Latour | TEN | s.t. |
| 85. | O. Goldstein | ISN | s.t. |
| 86. | W. van Aert | TJV | s.t. |
| 87. | D. Ballerini | DQT | s.t. |
| 88. | S. Bissegger | EFN | s.t. |
| 89. | K. Asgreen | DQT | s.t. |
| 90. | J. Rickaert | AFC | s.t. |
| 91. | S. Henao | TQA | s.t. |
| 92. | M. Donovan | DSM | s.t. |
| 93. | H. Sweeny | LTS | s.t. |
| 94. | L. Hamilton | BEX | s.t. |
| 95. | D. van Poppel | IWG | s.t. |
| 96. | É. Gesbert | ARK | s.t. |
| 97. | E. Buchmann | BOH | s.t. |
| 98. | B. Van Moer | LTS | s.t. |
| 99. | E. Theuns | TFS | s.t. |
| 100. | C. Gautier | BBK | s.t. |
| 101. | M. Teunissen | TJV | s.t. |
| 102. | O. Naesen | ACT | s.t. |
| 103. | L. Pöstlberger | BOH | s.t. |
| 104. | L. Durbridge | BEX | s.t. |
| 105. | R. Porte | IGD | s.t. |
| 106. | B. Armirail | GFC | s.t. |
| 107. | P. Vakoč | AFC | s.t. |
| 108. | C. Swift | ARK | s.t. |
| 109. | L. Mezgec | BEX | s.t. |
| 110. | M. Mohorič | TBV | s.t. |
| 111. | P. Sagan | BOH | s.t. |
| 112. | T. Martin | TJV | s.t. |
| 113. | J. Philipsen | AFC | s.t. |
| 114. | M. Matthews | BEX | s.t. |
| 115. | S. Yates | BEX | s.t. |
| 116. | P. L. Périchon | COF | s.t. |
| 117. | M. Hirschi | UAD | s.t. |
| 118. | T. Geoghegan Hart | IGD | s.t. |
| 119. | N. Powless | EFN | s.t. |
| 120. | D. Oss | BOH | s.t. |
| 121. | C. Juul-Jensen | BEX | s.t. |
| 122. | D. Gruzdev | APT | s.t. |
| 123. | O. Fraile | APT | s.t. |
| 124. | I. García Cortina | MOV | s.t. |
| 125. | I. Schelling | BOH | s.t. |
| 126. | S. Geschke | COF | s.t. |
| 127. | J. Koch | IWG | s.t. |
| 128. | C. Froome | ISN | 32:21 |
| 129. | T. Benoot | DSM | s.t. |
| 130. | R. Hollenstein | ISN | s.t. |
| 131. | S. Kragh Andersen | DSM | s.t. |
| 132. | A. Turgis | TEN | s.t. |
| 133. | B. McNulty | UAD | s.t. |
| 134. | E. Boasson Hagen | TEN | s.t. |
| 135. | M. Walscheid | TQA | s.t. |
| 136. | Je. Herrada | COF | s.t. |
| 137. | Se. Bennett | TQA | s.t. |
| 138. | C. Bol | DSM | s.t. |
| 139. | A. Aranburu | APT | s.t. |
| 140. | T. Van der Sande | LTS | 33:06 |
| 141. | M. Haller | TBV | 33:21 |
| 142. | M. Gogl | TQA | s.t. |
| 143. | G. Zimmermann | IWG | 33:54 |
| 144. | D. McLay | ARK | 34:11 |
| 145. | V. S. Laengen | UAD | s.t. |
| 146. | J. Alaphilippe | DQT | 34:13 |
| 147. | M. Scotson | GFC | s.t. |
| 148. | C. Pedersen | DSM | s.t. |
| 149. | M. A. López | MOV | s.t. |
| 150. | N. Eekhoff | DSM | 34:39 |
| 151. | B. van Poppel | IWG | 35:03 |
| 152. | T. Skujiņš | TFS | s.t. |
| 153. | R. Kluge | LTS | 35:33 |
| 154. | N. Bouhanni | ARK | s.t. |
| 155. | J. Simon | TEN | s.t. |
| 156. | J. Cabot | TEN | 35:34 |
| 157. | D. Devenyns | DQT | 35:43 |
| 158. | T. Declercq | DQT | 35:49 |
| 159. | M. Mørkøv | DQT | s.t. |
| 160. | M. Cavendish | DQT | s.t. |
| 161. | A. Greipel | ISN | 36:28 |
| 162. | V. Campenaerts | TQA | 37:15 |
| 163. | J. Wallays | COF | s.t. |
| 164. | A. G. Jansen | BEX | s.t. |
| 165. | G. Van Avermaet | ACT | s.t. |

JUNE  WORLDTOUR MEN'S RACE

## TOUR DE FRANCE
Stage 10
6 July 2021
Albertville–Valence
190.7km

### WEATHER

TEMPERATURE: 21°C
WIND: SW 7km/h

### PROFILE

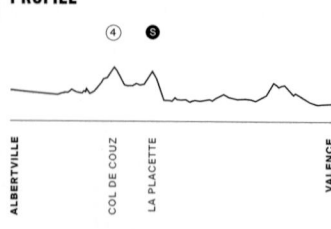

ALBERTVILLE — COL DE COUZ — LA PLACETTE — VALENCE

The wind routinely blows down along the Rhone valley, which, together with the Isère, must be crossed as the race travels from the Alps to the Pyrenees. The wind affected the race briefly in the final 30km, though without significance in the GC or among the stage favourites. Instead, it was a calmer stage, as is often the case after a rest day. Two riders snuck away and stayed off the front for most of the day: Tosh Van der Sande and Hugo Houle, who would be the last surviving rider of the pair. He was swept up on the top of an uncategorised climb with 40km to go, shortly after another crash had brought down Richie Porte and Geraint Thomas among others (though without any grave consequences on this occasion). Mark Cavendish was aware that the last time he had tried to contest a sprint into Valence, he'd been dropped in the wind and André Greipel had won (in 2015). Taking no such chances, Cavendish's Deceuninck-QuickStep team kept a very aggressive position at the front of the bunch as the race hurtled towards its conclusion. And Cavendish – led out once again to perfection by Michael Mørkøv – struck for the third time in 2021, taking his overall tally to 33 stage wins, one short of the Merckx record, with four stages still to come in which a bunch sprint could be expected. However, he was pushed hard to the line by Jasper Philipsen in third and, ominously, Wout van Aert who was now free to ride for himself.

### BREAKAWAY
T. Van der Sande (LTS), H. Houle (APT)

### GENERAL CLASSIFICATION

| POS | NAME | TEAM | TIME |
|---|---|---|---|
| 1. — | T. Pogačar | UAD | 38:25:17 |
| 2. — | B. O'Connor | ACT | 2:01 |
| 3. — | R. Urán | EFN | 5:18 |
| 4. — | J. Vingegaard | TJV | 5:32 |
| 5. — | R. Carapaz | IGD | 5:33 |
| 6. — | E. Mas | MOV | 5:47 |
| 7. — | W. Kelderman | BOH | 5:58 |
| 8. — | A. Lutsenko | APT | 6:12 |
| 9. — | G. Martin | COF | 7:02 |
| 10. — | D. Gaudu | GFC | 7:22 |

### KING OF THE MOUNTAINS

| POS | NAME | TEAM | PTS |
|---|---|---|---|
| 1. — | N. Quintana | ARK | 50 |
| 2. — | M. Woods | ISN | 42 |
| 3. — | W. Poels | TBV | 39 |

### POINTS

| POS | NAME | TEAM | PTS |
|---|---|---|---|
| 1. — | M. Cavendish | DQT | 218 |
| 2. — | M. Matthews | BEX | 159 |
| 3. — | S. Colbrelli | TBV | 136 |

### YOUNG RIDER

| POS | NAME | TEAM | TIME |
|---|---|---|---|
| 1. — | T. Pogačar | UAD | 38:25:17 |
| 2. — | J. Vingegaard | TJV | 5:32 |
| 3. — | D. Gaudu | GFC | 7:22 |

### TRIVIA
» Today saw Mark Cavendish move to within one win of equalling Eddy Merckx's all-time Tour stage-victory record.

### BONUSES

| TYPE | NAME | TEAM |
|---|---|---|
| KOM 1 | H. Houle | APT |
| Sprint 1 | T. Van der Sande | LTS |

## STAGE RESULTS

| POS | NAME | TEAM | TIME |
|---|---|---|---|
| 1. | M. Cavendish | DQT | 4:14:07 |
| 2. | W. van Aert | TJV | s.t. |
| 3. | J. Philipsen | AFC | s.t. |
| 4. | N. Bouhanni | ARK | s.t. |
| 5. | M. Matthews | BEX | s.t. |
| 6. | M. Mørkøv | DQT | s.t. |
| 7. | A. Greipel | ISN | s.t. |
| 8. | P. Sagan | BOH | s.t. |
| 9. | A. Turgis | TEN | s.t. |
| 10. | C. Bol | DSM | s.t. |
| 11. | B. van Poppel | IWG | s.t. |
| 12. | I. García Cortina | MOV | s.t. |
| 13. | E. Theuns | TFS | s.t. |
| 14. | C. Laporte | COF | s.t. |
| 15. | C. Barthe | BBK | s.t. |
| 16. | F. Bonnamour | BBK | s.t. |
| 17. | S. Colbrelli | TBV | s.t. |
| 18. | M. Walscheid | TQA | s.t. |
| 19. | C. Barbero | TQA | s.t. |
| 20. | W. Kelderman | BOH | s.t. |
| 21. | S. Bissegger | EFN | s.t. |
| 22. | B. Van Moer | LTS | s.t. |
| 23. | O. Naesen | ACT | s.t. |
| 24. | S. Küng | GFC | s.t. |
| 25. | T. Pogačar | UAD | s.t. |
| 26. | D. Gaudu | GFC | s.t. |
| 27. | R. Guerreiro | EFN | s.t. |
| 28. | S. Dillier | AFC | s.t. |
| 29. | J. Vingegaard | TJV | s.t. |
| 30. | G. Van Avermaet | ACT | s.t. |
| 31. | P. Gilbert | LTS | s.t. |
| 32. | M. Schär | ACT | s.t. |
| 33. | B. O'Connor | ACT | s.t. |
| 34. | A. Paret-Peintre | ACT | s.t. |
| 35. | K. Sbaragli | AFC | s.t. |
| 36. | H. Sweeny | LTS | s.t. |
| 37. | D. McLay | ARK | s.t. |
| 38. | V. S. Laengen | UAD | s.t. |
| 39. | A. Lutsenko | APT | s.t. |
| 40. | P. Latour | TEN | s.t. |
| 41. | D. Ballerini | DQT | s.t. |
| 42. | M. Valgren | EFN | s.t. |
| 43. | R. Carapaz | IGD | s.t. |
| 44. | J. Wallays | COF | s.t. |
| 45. | P. Bilbao | TBV | s.t. |
| 46. | E. Chaves | BEX | s.t. |
| 47. | G. Martin | COF | s.t. |
| 48. | R. Urán | EFN | s.t. |
| 49. | J. Rutsch | EFN | s.t. |
| 50. | M. Cort | EFN | s.t. |
| 51. | L. Meintjes | IWG | s.t. |
| 52. | S. Higuita | EFN | s.t. |
| 53. | J. Bakelants | IWG | s.t. |
| 54. | I. Erviti | MOV | s.t. |
| 55. | E. Mas | MOV | s.t. |
| 56. | S. Kruijswijk | TJV | s.t. |
| 57. | P. Konrad | BOH | s.t. |
| 58. | D. Formolo | UAD | s.t. |
| 59. | M. Teunissen | TJV | s.t. |
| 60. | W. Poels | TBV | s.t. |
| 61. | J. Rickaert | AFC | s.t. |
| 62. | M. Chevalier | BBK | s.t. |
| 63. | D. Godon | ACT | s.t. |
| 64. | M. Cattaneo | DQT | s.t. |
| 65. | D. Teuns | TBV | s.t. |
| 66. | P. L. Périchon | COF | s.t. |
| 67. | F. Doubey | TEN | s.t. |
| 68. | W. Barguil | ARK | s.t. |
| 69. | G. Boivin | ISN | s.t. |
| 70. | N. Politt | BOH | s.t. |
| 71. | N. Powless | EFN | s.t. |
| 72. | S. Henao | TQA | s.t. |
| 73. | X. Meurisse | AFC | s.t. |
| 74. | R. Hollenstein | ISN | s.t. |
| 75. | J. Stuyven | TFS | s.t. |
| 76. | R. Zabel | ISN | s.t. |
| 77. | C. Swift | ARK | s.t. |
| 78. | C. Russo | ARK | 0:29 |
| 79. | K. Asgreen | DQT | 0:32 |
| 80. | J. Nieuwenhuis | DSM | s.t. |
| 81. | M. Mohorič | TBV | s.t. |
| 82. | D. Oss | BOH | 0:47 |
| 83. | M. Kwiatkowski | IGD | s.t. |
| 84. | D. van Baarle | IGD | s.t. |
| 85. | L. Mezgec | BEX | s.t. |
| 86. | P. Vakoč | AFC | s.t. |
| 87. | F. Wright | TBV | s.t. |
| 88. | N. Quintana | ARK | s.t. |
| 89. | S. Clarke | TQA | s.t. |
| 90. | C. Pedersen | DSM | 1:06 |
| 91. | L. Durbridge | BEX | 1:20 |
| 92. | E. Boasson Hagen | TEN | s.t. |
| 93. | J. Arcas | MOV | 1:28 |
| 94. | I. Schelling | BOH | s.t. |
| 95. | J. Alaphilippe | DQT | 1:51 |
| 96. | M. Bjerg | UAD | 1:55 |
| 97. | D. Devenyns | DQT | 2:15 |
| 98. | M. A. López | MOV | 3:46 |
| 99. | C. Gautier | BBK | s.t. |
| 100. | Q. Pacher | BBK | s.t. |
| 101. | G. Zimmermann | IWG | s.t. |
| 102. | O. Goldstein | ISN | s.t. |
| 103. | T. Skujiņš | TFS | s.t. |
| 104. | T. Benoot | DSM | s.t. |
| 105. | B. Mollema | TFS | s.t. |
| 106. | N. Eekhoff | DSM | s.t. |
| 107. | M. Hirschi | UAD | s.t. |
| 108. | L. Rowe | IGD | s.t. |
| 109. | T. Declercq | DQT | s.t. |
| 110. | L. Pöstlberger | BOH | s.t. |
| 111. | M. Haller | TBV | s.t. |
| 112. | J. Castroviejo | IGD | s.t. |
| 113. | K. Elissonde | TFS | 4:38 |
| 114. | S. Geschke | COF | s.t. |
| 115. | T. Geoghegan Hart | IGD | s.t. |
| 116. | C. Rodríguez | TEN | s.t. |
| 117. | M. Scotson | GFC | s.t. |
| 118. | J. Bernard | TFS | s.t. |
| 119. | T. De Gendt | LTS | s.t. |
| 120. | A. Valverde | MOV | s.t. |
| 121. | A. Aranburu | APT | s.t. |
| 122. | R. Majka | UAD | s.t. |
| 123. | N. Houle | APT | s.t. |
| 124. | J. Fuglsang | APT | s.t. |
| 125. | Je. Herrada | COF | s.t. |
| 126. | R. Fernández | COF | s.t. |
| 127. | B. McNulty | UAD | s.t. |
| 128. | B. Armirail | GFC | s.t. |
| 129. | G. Thomas | IGD | s.t. |
| 130. | V. Nibali | TFS | s.t. |
| 131. | S. Kragh Andersen | DSM | s.t. |
| 132. | R. Porte | IGD | s.t. |
| 133. | C. Froome | ISN | s.t. |
| 134. | D. Martin | ISN | s.t. |
| 135. | É. Gesbert | ARK | s.t. |
| 136. | O. Fraile | APT | s.t. |
| 137. | I. Izaguirre | APT | s.t. |
| 138. | V. Madouas | GFC | s.t. |
| 139. | P. Rolland | BBK | s.t. |
| 140. | V. de la Parte | TEN | s.t. |
| 141. | B. Cosnefroy | ACT | s.t. |
| 142. | R. Costa | UAD | s.t. |
| 143. | E. Buchmann | BOH | s.t. |
| 144. | T. Martin | TJV | s.t. |
| 145. | S. Kuss | TJV | s.t. |
| 146. | M. Woods | ISN | s.t. |
| 147. | D. Gruzdev | APT | s.t. |
| 148. | M. Donovan | DSM | s.t. |
| 149. | J. Cabot | TEN | s.t. |
| 150. | M. Gogl | TQA | s.t. |
| 151. | L. Rota | IWG | s.t. |
| 152. | L. Hamilton | BEX | s.t. |
| 153. | S. Yates | BEX | s.t. |
| 154. | C. Juul-Jensen | BEX | s.t. |
| 155. | A. Perez | COF | s.t. |
| 156. | A. G. Jansen | BEX | s.t. |
| 157. | Se. Bennett | TQA | s.t. |
| 158. | R. Kluge | LTS | s.t. |
| 159. | C. Verona | MOV | s.t. |
| 160. | T. Van der Sande | LTS | 7:59 |
| 161. | M. Pedersen | TFS | s.t. |
| 162. | J. Simon | TEN | s.t. |
| 163. | V. Campenaerts | TQA | s.t. |
| 164. | D. van Poppel | IWG | s.t. |

JUNE — WORLDTOUR MEN'S RACE

## TOUR DE FRANCE
Stage 11
7 July 2021
Sorgues–Malaucène
198.9km

Ventoux twice. In a fascinating reworking of the classic Mont Ventoux stage, the race organisers had decided to take the riders to the renowned summit – with its red and white meteorological station, its rocky slopes and its wind – first from the eastern approach then from the conventional route to the south. That meant the climb from Sault, a 22km drag, would act as a sapping hors d'oeuvre to the famous route through Bedoin and on to the unrelenting passage across the forest before shooting the treeline at Chalet Reynard. But the race wouldn't finish at the top; instead a descent to Malaucène would provide the opportunity for an attack, or a chance for any riders who'd been dropped near the top to get back on. This it did, and in the most unexpected fashion. From the breakaway, a select group of riders were still in contention as the race hit the final climb, including the world champion Julian Alaphilippe. But it was Wout van Aert who attacked and was not seen again. Having contested, and very nearly won, a bunch sprint the previous day, Van Aert rode clear of an elite group of climbing talent on perhaps the single most fearsome and redoubtable climb in all of the Tour de France's long history. From the moment he crested the summit alone, his victory was a foregone conclusion. It was an astonishing ride from an astonishing rider. Not far behind him, the GC group started to do battle: Pogačar skirmished with Carapaz, only to find Jonas Vingegaard suddenly in a position to attack, which he duly did. Pale-faced and ghostly in his white jersey, the young Dane looked back in amazement to see that he had dropped Pogačar. And so he pressed on. Over the top of the climb, and onto the descent, the yellow jersey dropped back to join a small group of chasers who ultimately nullified Vingegaard's advantage on GC. But for the first time in the race, albeit only fleetingly, Pogačar had hinted at weakness. And Vingegaard had announced himself as a GC name to be taken extremely seriously.

## WEATHER

**TEMPERATURE**: 28°C
**WIND**: NE 9km/h

## PROFILE

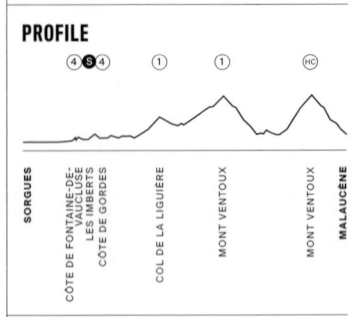

SORGUES — CÔTE DE FONTAINE-DE-VAUCLUSE — CÔTE DES IMBERTS — CÔTE DE GORDES — COL DE LA LIGUIÈRE — MONT VENTOUX — MONT VENTOUX — MALAUCÈNE

## BREAKAWAY

J. Alaphilippe (DQT), N. Quintana (ARK), D. Martin (ISN), J. Fuglsang (APT), A. Perez (COF), E. Gesbert (ARK), V. S. Laengen (UAD), J. Bernard (TFS), B. Mollema (TFS), N. Politt (BOH), X. Meurisse (AFC), K. Sbaragli (AFC), L. Durbridge (BEX), Q. Pacher (BBK), W. van Aert (TJV), K. Elissonde (TFS), P. L. Périchon (COF), B. Cosnegroy (ACT), G. Van Avermaet (ACT)

## GENERAL CLASSIFICATION

| POS | NAME | TEAM | TIME |
|---|---|---|---|
| 1. — | T. Pogačar | UAD | 43:44:38 |
| 2. ↑1 | R. Urán | EFN | 5:18 |
| 3. ↑1 | J. Vingegaard | TJV | 5:32 |
| 4. ↑1 | R. Carapaz | IGD | 5:33 |
| 5. ↓3 | B. O'Connor | ACT | 5:58 |
| 6. ↑1 | W. Kelderman | BOH | 6:16 |
| 7. ↑1 | A. Lutsenko | APT | 6:30 |
| 8. ↓2 | E. Mas | MOV | 7:11 |
| 9. — | G. Martin | COF | 9:29 |
| 10. ↑1 | P. Bilbao | TBV | 10:28 |

## KING OF THE MOUNTAINS

| POS | NAME | TEAM | PTS |
|---|---|---|---|
| 1. — | N. Quintana | ARK | 50 |
| 2. — | W. van Aert | TJV | 43 |
| 3. ↓1 | M. Woods | ISN | 42 |

## POINTS

| POS | NAME | TEAM | PTS |
|---|---|---|---|
| 1. — | M. Cavendish | DQT | 218 |
| 2. — | M. Matthews | BEX | 160 |
| 3. ↑1 | J. Philipsen | AFC | 142 |

## YOUNG RIDER

| POS | NAME | TEAM | TIME |
|---|---|---|---|
| 1. — | T. Pogačar | UAD | 43:44:38 |
| 2. — | J. Vingegaard | TJV | 5:32 |
| 3. ↑1 | A. Paret-Peintre | ACT | 24:44 |

## BONUSES

| TYPE | NAME | TEAM |
|---|---|---|
| KOM 1 | J. Alaphilippe | DQT |
| KOM 2 | J. Alaphilippe | DQT |
| KOM 3 | D. Martin | ISN |
| KOM 4 | J. Alaphilippe | DQT |
| KOM 5 | W. van Aert | TJV |
| Sprint 1 | J. Alaphilippe | DQT |

## STAGE RESULTS

| POS | NAME | TEAM | TIME |
|---|---|---|---|
| 1. | W. van Aert | TJV | 5:17:43 |
| 2. | K. Elissonde | TFS | 1:14 |
| 3. | B. Mollema | TFS | s.t. |
| 4. | T. Pogačar | UAD | 1:38 |
| 5. | R. Urán | EFN | s.t. |
| 6. | R. Carapaz | IGD | s.t. |
| 7. | J. Vingegaard | TJV | s.t. |
| 8. | A. Lutsenko | APT | 1:56 |
| 9. | W. Kelderman | BOH | s.t. |
| 10. | E. Mas | MOV | 3:02 |
| 11. | P. Bilbao | TBV | 3:28 |
| 12. | G. Martin | COF | 4:05 |
| 13. | X. Meurisse | AFC | 5:09 |
| 14. | E. Chaves | BEX | s.t. |
| 15. | B. O'Connor | ACT | 5:35 |
| 16. | M. Cattaneo | DQT | s.t. |
| 17. | A. Valverde | MOV | s.t. |
| 18. | R. Majka | UAD | 5:46 |
| 19. | L. Meintjes | IWG | 7:18 |
| 20. | M. Woods | ISN | 7:34 |
| 21. | S. Kruijswijk | TJV | 11:32 |
| 22. | M. Kwiatkowski | IGD | 12:18 |
| 23. | J. Alaphilippe | DQT | s.t. |
| 24. | S. Higuita | EFN | s.t. |
| 25. | R. Guerreiro | EFN | s.t. |
| 26. | R. Porte | IGD | s.t. |
| 27. | C. Rodríguez | TEN | 13:07 |
| 28. | O. Naesen | ACT | 14:28 |
| 29. | S. Kuss | TJV | s.t. |
| 30. | S. Dillier | AFC | s.t. |
| 31. | P. Rolland | BBK | s.t. |
| 32. | C. Gautier | BBK | s.t. |
| 33. | M. Donovan | DSM | s.t. |
| 34. | J. Rutsch | EFN | s.t. |
| 35. | A. Paret-Peintre | ACT | s.t. |
| 36. | M. A. López | MOV | s.t. |
| 37. | J. Fuglsang | APT | s.t. |
| 38. | P. Konrad | BOH | s.t. |
| 39. | W. Poels | TBV | s.t. |
| 40. | E. Buchmann | BOH | s.t. |
| 41. | J. Castroviejo | IGD | 14:46 |
| 42. | W. Barguil | ARK | 18:30 |
| 43. | A. Perez | COF | 19:40 |
| 44. | L. Durbridge | BEX | s.t. |
| 45. | S. Henao | TQA | 19:44 |
| 46. | J. Bernard | TFS | 19:59 |
| 47. | B. McNulty | UAD | 21:52 |
| 48. | Q. Pacher | BBK | 22:18 |
| 49. | Je. Herrada | COF | s.t. |
| 50. | S. Geschke | COF | s.t. |
| 51. | A. Turgis | TEN | 23:27 |
| 52. | N. Powless | EFN | 24:20 |
| 53. | H. Houle | APT | 24:38 |
| 54. | I. Izagirre | APT | s.t. |
| 55. | G. Zimmermann | IWG | s.t. |
| 56. | M. Valgren | EFN | s.t. |
| 57. | V. Nibali | TFS | s.t. |
| 58. | M. Teunissen | TJV | s.t. |
| 59. | D. Teuns | TBV | s.t. |
| 60. | M. Hirschi | UAD | s.t. |
| 61. | M. Cort | EFN | s.t. |
| 62. | M. Schär | ACT | s.t. |
| 63. | R. Costa | UAD | s.t. |
| 64. | D. Formolo | UAD | s.t. |
| 65. | T. Geoghegan Hart | IGD | s.t. |
| 66. | G. Van Avermaet | ACT | s.t. |
| 67. | K. Sbaragli | AFC | s.t. |
| 68. | C. Pedersen | DSM | s.t. |
| 69. | D. Martin | ISN | s.t. |
| 70. | N. Politt | BOH | s.t. |
| 71. | P. Vakoč | AFC | s.t. |
| 72. | V. Madouas | GFC | 25:07 |
| 73. | D. Gaudu | GFC | s.t. |
| 74. | V. S. Laengen | UAD | 26:00 |
| 75. | P. Latour | TEN | 26:16 |
| 76. | P. L. Périchon | COF | 26:58 |
| 77. | S. Küng | GFC | s.t. |
| 78. | M. Bjerg | UAD | s.t. |
| 79. | J. Rickaert | AFC | 27:08 |
| 80. | C. Barthe | BBK | s.t. |
| 81. | K. Asgreen | DQT | 28:15 |
| 82. | S. Yates | BEX | s.t. |
| 83. | R. Hollenstein | ISN | s.t. |
| 84. | A. Aranburu | APT | s.t. |
| 85. | V. de la Parte | TEN | s.t. |
| 86. | O. Fraile | APT | s.t. |
| 87. | D. van Baarle | IGD | s.t. |
| 88. | I. Erviti | MOV | s.t. |
| 89. | C. Verona | MOV | s.t. |
| 90. | É. Gesbert | ARK | s.t. |
| 91. | D. Gruzdev | APT | s.t. |
| 92. | L. Rota | IWG | s.t. |
| 93. | S. Bissegger | EFN | s.t. |
| 94. | B. Cosnefroy | ACT | s.t. |
| 95. | E. Boasson Hagen | TEN | 29:04 |
| 96. | M. Chevalier | BBK | 29:53 |
| 97. | L. Hamilton | BEX | 29:58 |
| 98. | H. Sweeny | LTS | 30:00 |
| 99. | J. Arcas | MOV | 30:48 |
| 100. | C. Froome | ISN | 31:09 |
| 101. | G. Boivin | ISN | s.t. |
| 102. | J. Stuyven | TFS | s.t. |
| 103. | E. Theuns | TFS | s.t. |
| 104. | M. Mohorič | TBV | s.t. |
| 105. | J. Wallays | COF | s.t. |
| 106. | R. Fernández | COF | s.t. |
| 107. | F. Doubey | TEN | 32:55 |
| 108. | J. Bakelants | IWG | 33:05 |
| 109. | L. Pöstlberger | BOH | 33:10 |
| 110. | M. Gogl | TQA | s.t. |
| 111. | S. Clarke | TQA | s.t. |
| 112. | B. Van Moer | LTS | s.t. |
| 113. | P. Gilbert | LTS | s.t. |
| 114. | B. Armirail | GFC | s.t. |
| 115. | N. Quintana | ARK | s.t. |
| 116. | D. Godon | ACT | 34:24 |
| 117. | C. Swift | ARK | 34:26 |
| 118. | C. Laporte | COF | 36:55 |
| 119. | T. De Gendt | LTS | 37:13 |
| 120. | R. Kluge | LTS | s.t. |
| 121. | S. Colbrelli | TBV | 37:26 |
| 122. | B. van Poppel | IWG | s.t. |
| 123. | R. Zabel | ISN | s.t. |
| 124. | D. van Poppel | IWG | s.t. |
| 125. | D. Oss | BOH | s.t. |
| 126. | J. Philipsen | AFC | s.t. |
| 127. | T. Skujiņš | TFS | s.t. |
| 128. | L. Mezgec | BEX | s.t. |
| 129. | A. G. Jansen | BEX | s.t. |
| 130. | I. Schelling | BOH | s.t. |
| 131. | A. Greipel | ISN | s.t. |
| 132. | M. Walscheid | TQA | s.t. |
| 133. | M. Matthews | BEX | s.t. |
| 134. | N. Eekhoff | DSM | s.t. |
| 135. | C. Juul-Jensen | BEX | s.t. |
| 136. | O. Goldstein | ISN | s.t. |
| 137. | F. Bonnamour | BBK | s.t. |
| 138. | G. Thomas | IGD | s.t. |
| 139. | C. Bol | DSM | s.t. |
| 140. | P. Sagan | BOH | s.t. |
| 141. | M. Haller | TBV | s.t. |
| 142. | F. Wright | TBV | s.t. |
| 143. | J. Simon | TEN | 39:13 |
| 144. | J. Nieuwenhuis | DSM | s.t. |
| 145. | Se. Bennett | TQA | 39:58 |
| 146. | D. Ballerini | DQT | 40:40 |
| 147. | M. Cavendish | DQT | s.t. |
| 148. | M. Mørkøv | DQT | s.t. |
| 149. | T. Declercq | DQT | s.t. |
| 150. | I. García Cortina | MOV | s.t. |
| 151. | D. Devenyns | DQT | s.t. |
| 152. | C. Barbero | TQA | s.t. |
| 153. | M. Pedersen | TFS | s.t. |
| 154. | J. Cabot | TEN | s.t. |
| 155. | N. Bouhanni | ARK | 43:25 |
| 156. | S. Kragh Andersen | DSM | 47:36 |

## TRIVIA

» Of the six previous times the Giant of Provence has featured in the race but not as a summit finish, only once did the yellow jersey at the end of the day held on to the race lead until the final stage (Louison Bobet in 1955).

JUNE   WORLDTOUR MEN'S RACE

# TOUR DE FRANCE
Stage 12
8 July 2021
Saint-Paul-Trois-Châteaux–Nîmes
159.4km

## WEATHER

**TEMPERATURE** 26°C   **WIND** NW 15km/h

## PROFILE

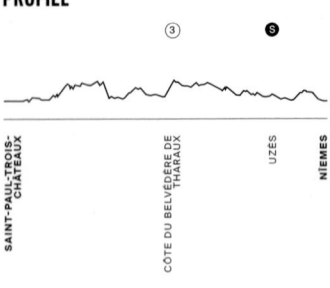

So strong was the wind on the morning of stage 10 that the race organisation delayed the start in anticipation of a freakishly fast average speed, hoping the race would still finish close to the allotted hour so important for global TV schedules. The hot wind's direction and strength were perfectly aligned, being both a crosswind and a tailwind for much of the day. In the end, and though it is hard to explain, the race was not ripped apart. The opening phase of racing was ridiculously fast, the wind meaning that riders were spinning out in their top gear and that consequently it was hard to make a breakaway stick and too easy for the bunch to come back. From time to time, Mark Cavendish seemed intent on creating havoc in the bunch by showing his green jersey towards the fore, hinting that he might make the move of the day. Yet it all calmed down once a 13-rider breakaway had gone clear. The gaps that had appeared in the peloton were quickly brought back, and in the end the race allowed the attackers to contest the stage. With no serious intent to do one another harm in the crosswinds, which seemed to allow for such tactics, the GC race was neutralised too and the bunch rolled in over a quarter of an hour down on the race winner. He was Nils Politt, the likeable German whose work at the Tour – and indeed throughout the year – is normally in the service of his leader, Peter Sagan. However, the three-time world champion, having looked off the pace (he had, after all, raced the Giro in May), stepped off with persistent knee pain. Up stepped Politt to fill the void. He attacked a three-man group, the strongest in the breakaway, and – after Mohorič, Teuns and O'Connor – became the fourth rider to pull off a long-range solo victory (his first at Grand Tour level).

## BREAKAWAY

A. Greipel (ISN), E. Theuns (TFS), S. Küng (GFC), S. Bissegger (EFN), C. Swift (ARK), B. Van Moer (LTS), L. Mezgec (BEX), S. Henao (TQA), E. Boasson Hagen (TEN), I. Erviti (MOV), H. Sweeny (LTS), N. Politt (BOH), J. Alaphilippe (DQT)

## GENERAL CLASSIFICATION

| POS | NAME | TEAM | TIME |
|---|---|---|---|
| 1. — | T. Pogačar | UAD | 47:22:43 |
| 2. — | R. Urán | EFN | 5:18 |
| 3. — | J. Vingegaard | TJV | 5:32 |
| 4. — | R. Carapaz | IGD | 5:33 |
| 5. — | B. O'Connor | ACT | 5:58 |
| 6. — | W. Kelderman | BOH | 6:16 |
| 7. — | A. Lutsenko | APT | 6:30 |
| 8. — | E. Mas | MOV | 7:11 |
| 9. — | G. Martin | COF | 9:29 |
| 10. — | P. Bilbao | TBV | 10:28 |

## KING OF THE MOUNTAINS

| POS | NAME | TEAM | PTS |
|---|---|---|---|
| 1. — | N. Quintana | ARK | 50 |
| 2. — | W. van Aert | TJV | 43 |
| 3. — | M. Woods | ISN | 42 |

## POINTS

| POS | NAME | TEAM | PTS |
|---|---|---|---|
| 1. — | M. Cavendish | DQT | 221 |
| 2. — | M. Matthews | BEX | 162 |
| 3. — | J. Philipsen | AFC | 142 |

## YOUNG RIDER

| POS | NAME | TEAM | TIME |
|---|---|---|---|
| 1. — | T. Pogačar | UAD | 47:22:43 |
| 2. — | J. Vingegaard | TJV | 5:32 |
| 3. — | A. Paret-Peintre | ACT | 24:44 |

## TRIVIA

» This was only Nils Politt's second win of his career, the other being in 2018 at the Deutschland Tour.

## BONUSES

| TYPE | NAME | TEAM |
|---|---|---|
| KOM 1 | N. Politt | BOH |
| Sprint 1 | N. Politt | BOH |

## STAGE RESULTS

| POS | NAME | TEAM | TIME |
|---|---|---|---|
| 1. | N. Politt | BOH | 3:22:12 |
| 2. | I. Erviti | MOV | 0:31 |
| 3. | H. Sweeny | LTS | s.t. |
| 4. | S. Küng | GFC | 1:58 |
| 5. | L. Mezgec | BEX | 2:06 |
| 6. | A. Greipel | ISN | s.t. |
| 7. | E. Theuns | TFS | s.t. |
| 8. | B. Van Moer | LTS | s.t. |
| 9. | J. Alaphilippe | DQT | s.t. |
| 10. | S. Henao | TQA | s.t. |
| 11. | C. Swift | ARK | s.t. |
| 12. | E. Boasson Hagen | TEN | 2:09 |
| 13. | S. Bissegger | EFN | 5:22 |
| 14. | M. Cavendish | DQT | 15:53 |
| 15. | M. Matthews | BEX | s.t. |
| 16. | J. Philipsen | AFC | s.t. |
| 17. | C. Barbero | TQA | s.t. |
| 18. | J. Rickaert | AFC | s.t. |
| 19. | C. Barthe | BBK | s.t. |
| 20. | D. Ballerini | DQT | s.t. |
| 21. | T. Pogačar | UAD | s.t. |
| 22. | T. Declercq | DQT | s.t. |
| 23. | M. Teunissen | TJV | s.t. |
| 24. | K. Asgreen | DQT | s.t. |
| 25. | J. Vingegaard | TJV | s.t. |
| 26. | A. Lutsenko | APT | s.t. |
| 27. | D. Oss | BOH | s.t. |
| 28. | M. Schär | ACT | s.t. |
| 29. | M. Cort | EFN | s.t. |
| 30. | W. Kelderman | BOH | s.t. |
| 31. | R. Carapaz | IGD | s.t. |
| 32. | A. Paret-Peintre | ACT | s.t. |
| 33. | S. Dillier | AFC | s.t. |
| 34. | D. Godon | ACT | s.t. |
| 35. | N. Eekhoff | DSM | s.t. |
| 36. | D. van Baarle | IGD | s.t. |
| 37. | M. Valgren | EFN | s.t. |
| 38. | K. Sbaragli | AFC | s.t. |
| 39. | E. Mas | MOV | s.t. |
| 40. | B. O'Connor | ACT | s.t. |
| 41. | R. Urán | EFN | s.t. |
| 42. | W. van Aert | TJV | s.t. |
| 43. | B. McNulty | UAD | s.t. |
| 44. | G. Martin | COF | s.t. |
| 45. | M. Mohorič | TBV | s.t. |
| 46. | C. Rodríguez | TEN | s.t. |
| 47. | R. Costa | UAD | s.t. |
| 48. | D. Gaudu | GFC | s.t. |
| 49. | E. Chaves | BEX | s.t. |
| 50. | J. Rutsch | EFN | s.t. |
| 51. | F. Bonnamour | BBK | s.t. |
| 52. | R. Guerreiro | EFN | s.t. |
| 53. | D. Formolo | UAD | s.t. |
| 54. | V. Madouas | GFC | s.t. |
| 55. | S. Colbrelli | TBV | s.t. |
| 56. | N. Bouhanni | ARK | s.t. |
| 57. | L. Durbridge | BEX | s.t. |
| 58. | P. Bilbao | TBV | s.t. |
| 59. | I. Izagirre | APT | s.t. |
| 60. | R. Fernández | COF | s.t. |
| 61. | M. Hirschi | UAD | s.t. |
| 62. | F. Wright | TBV | s.t. |
| 63. | T. Skujiņš | TFS | s.t. |
| 64. | V. de la Parte | TEN | s.t. |
| 65. | G. Van Avermaet | ACT | s.t. |
| 66. | O. Naesen | ACT | s.t. |
| 67. | J. Bakelants | IWG | s.t. |
| 68. | M. Chevalier | BBK | s.t. |
| 69. | P. Konrad | BOH | s.t. |
| 70. | J. Fuglsang | APT | s.t. |
| 71. | W. Poels | TBV | s.t. |
| 72. | W. Barguil | ARK | s.t. |
| 73. | S. Clarke | TQA | s.t. |
| 74. | R. Hollenstein | ISN | s.t. |
| 75. | N. Powless | EFN | s.t. |
| 76. | J. Wallays | COF | s.t. |
| 77. | D. van Poppel | IWG | s.t. |
| 78. | C. Pedersen | DSM | s.t. |
| 79. | S. Kragh Andersen | DSM | s.t. |
| 80. | M. Haller | TBV | s.t. |
| 81. | I. García Cortina | MOV | s.t. |
| 82. | J. Nieuwenhuis | DSM | s.t. |
| 83. | H. Houle | APT | s.t. |
| 84. | B. Mollema | TFS | s.t. |
| 85. | S. Higuita | EFN | s.t. |
| 86. | S. Kuss | TJV | s.t. |
| 87. | G. Zimmermann | IWG | s.t. |
| 88. | L. Meintjes | IWG | s.t. |
| 89. | C. Laporte | COF | s.t. |
| 90. | O. Goldstein | ISN | s.t. |
| 91. | B. van Poppel | IWG | s.t. |
| 92. | D. Teuns | TBV | s.t. |
| 93. | P. Gilbert | LTS | s.t. |
| 94. | L. Rota | IWG | s.t. |
| 95. | L. Pöstlberger | BOH | s.t. |
| 96. | V. Nibali | TFS | s.t. |
| 97. | S. Geschke | COF | s.t. |
| 98. | C. Froome | ISN | s.t. |
| 99. | M. Kwiatkowski | IGD | s.t. |
| 100. | M. Cattaneo | DQT | s.t. |
| 101. | R. Majka | UAD | s.t. |
| 102. | A. Valverde | MOV | s.t. |
| 103. | J. Castroviejo | IGD | s.t. |
| 104. | I. Schelling | BOH | s.t. |
| 105. | X. Meurisse | AFC | s.t. |
| 106. | G. Boivin | ISN | s.t. |
| 107. | P. Latour | TEN | s.t. |
| 108. | M. Donovan | DSM | s.t. |
| 109. | C. Bol | DSM | s.t. |
| 110. | M. Woods | ISN | s.t. |
| 111. | E. Buchmann | BOH | s.t. |
| 112. | T. De Gendt | LTS | s.t. |
| 113. | S. Kruijswijk | TJV | s.t. |
| 114. | F. Doubey | TEN | s.t. |
| 115. | Se. Bennett | TQA | s.t. |
| 116. | J. Bernard | TFS | s.t. |
| 117. | R. Zabel | ISN | s.t. |
| 118. | A. Turgis | TEN | s.t. |
| 119. | C. Gautier | BBK | s.t. |
| 120. | P. L. Périchon | COF | s.t. |
| 121. | Q. Pacher | BBK | s.t. |
| 122. | V. S. Laengen | UAD | s.t. |
| 123. | Je. Herrada | COF | s.t. |
| 124. | M. Mørkøv | DQT | s.t. |
| 125. | T. Geoghegan Hart | IGD | s.t. |
| 126. | D. Devenyns | DQT | s.t. |
| 127. | P. Vakoč | AFC | s.t. |
| 128. | J. Simon | TEN | s.t. |
| 129. | D. Gruzdev | APT | s.t. |
| 130. | D. Martin | ISN | s.t. |
| 131. | A. Perez | COF | s.t. |
| 132. | J. Cabot | TEN | s.t. |
| 133. | P. Rolland | BBK | s.t. |
| 134. | B. Armirail | GFC | s.t. |
| 135. | O. Fraile | APT | s.t. |
| 136. | R. Porte | IGD | s.t. |
| 137. | L. Hamilton | BEX | s.t. |
| 138. | B. Cosnefroy | ACT | s.t. |
| 139. | S. Yates | BEX | s.t. |
| 140. | K. Elissonde | TFS | s.t. |
| 141. | M. Bjerg | UAD | 16:26 |
| 142. | A. G. Jansen | BEX | s.t. |
| 143. | A. Aranburu | APT | s.t. |
| 144. | J. Arcas | MOV | s.t. |
| 145. | M. A. López | MOV | s.t. |
| 146. | C. Juul-Jensen | BEX | s.t. |
| 147. | J. Stuyven | TFS | s.t. |
| 148. | M. Pedersen | TFS | s.t. |
| 149. | G. Thomas | IGD | s.t. |
| 150. | M. Walscheid | TQA | s.t. |
| 151. | É. Gesbert | ARK | 17:19 |
| 152. | N. Quintana | ARK | s.t. |
| 153. | R. Kluge | LTS | 17:30 |
| 154. | M. Gogl | TQA | s.t. |
| 155. | C. Verona | MOV | s.t. |

JUNE   WORLDTOUR MEN'S RACE

## TOUR DE FRANCE
Stage 13
9 July 2021
Nîmes–Carcassonne
219.9km

Carcassonne was the finish line of stage 13, the heavily restored Cathar citadel. Normally, when the race is routed there, it drops down over the climbs of the Massif Central and a small group comes to the line. The winner often comes from a breakaway, given the city's location as something of a Pyrenean launch pad – the Carcassonne stage being the final calm before the GC storm of days to come. A three-rider breakaway was off the front after a 30km fight to get in the move, including the former Israeli national road race champion Omer Goldstein. He and the ever-willing Pierre Latour, who would get stronger and stronger in the Pyrenees, battled each other hard for the honour of being the last rider standing, after the pair had dropped the American debutant Sean Bennett. Both were caught with around 50km to go. Before the catch, a brief injection of pace from Philippe Gilbert woke the peloton from its soporific state and caused a number of riders to crash spectacularly on a section of road covered in loose gravel. Deceuninck-QuickStep's Tim Declercq came off worst of all and faced a long solo ride off the back. Meanwhile his teammates took control of the run-in to the sprint, though they were challenged for position by both Bahrain Victorious and DSM. It was a scrappy affair in the end, which briefly threatened to produce a surprise result when Cavendish's teammate Davide Ballerini sprinted for the win from a long way out. That forced Iván García Cortina to chase, which in turn dragged Michael Mørkøv and Cavendish back into the frame. Cavendish duly won, but only just. His lead-out man finished in second, with Jasper Philipsen once again coming agonisingly close. And with that, Cavendish had done the seemingly impossible and drawn level with Eddy Merckx's long-standing record of 34 stage victories at the Tour de France. It was an outlandish turn of events that would have seemed unimaginable before the race had got underway two weeks previously. (NB)

### WEATHER

TEMPERATURE  WIND
28°C         N 20km/h

### PROFILE

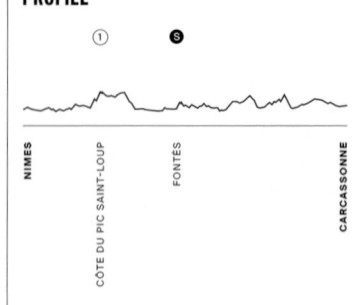

### BREAKAWAY
O. Goldstein (ISN), P. Latour (TEN), S. Bennett (TQA)

### GENERAL CLASSIFICATION

| POS | NAME | TEAM | TIME |
|---|---|---|---|
| 1. — | T. Pogačar | UAD | 52:27:12 |
| 2. — | R. Urán | EFN | 5:18 |
| 3. — | J. Vingegaard | TJV | 5:32 |
| 4. — | R. Carapaz | IGD | 5:33 |
| 5. — | B. O'Connor | ACT | 5:58 |
| 6. — | W. Kelderman | BOH | 6:16 |
| 7. — | A. Lutsenko | APT | 6:30 |
| 8. — | E. Mas | MOV | 7:11 |
| 9. — | G. Martin | COF | 9:29 |
| 10.— | P. Bilbao | TBV | 10:28 |

### KING OF THE MOUNTAINS

| POS | NAME | TEAM | PTS |
|---|---|---|---|
| 1. — | N. Quintana | ARK | 50 |
| 2. — | W. van Aert | TJV | 43 |
| 3. — | M. Woods | ISN | 42 |

### POINTS

| POS | NAME | TEAM | PTS |
|---|---|---|---|
| 1. — | M. Cavendish | DQT | 279 |
| 2. — | M. Matthews | BEX | 178 |
| 3. — | J. Philipsen | AFC | 171 |

### YOUNG RIDER

| POS | NAME | TEAM | TIME |
|---|---|---|---|
| 1. — | T. Pogačar | UAD | 52:27:12 |
| 2. — | J. Vingegaard | TJV | 5:32 |
| 3. — | A. Paret-Peintre | ACT | 24:44 |

### BONUSES

| TYPE | NAME | TEAM |
|---|---|---|
| KOM 1 | P. Latour | TEN |
| Sprint 1 | O. Goldstein | ISN |

## STAGE RESULTS

| POS | NAME | TEAM | TIME |
|---|---|---|---|
| 1. | M. Cavendish | DQT | 5:04:29 |
| 2. | M. Mørkøv | DQT | s.t. |
| 3. | J. Philipsen | AFC | s.t. |
| 4. | I. García Cortina | MOV | s.t. |
| 5. | D. van Poppel | IWG | s.t. |
| 6. | A. Aranburu | APT | s.t. |
| 7. | C. Laporte | COF | s.t. |
| 8. | A. Greipel | ISN | s.t. |
| 9. | M. Cort | EFN | s.t. |
| 10. | J. Stuyven | TFS | s.t. |
| 11. | N. Bouhanni | ARK | s.t. |
| 12. | M. Matthews | BEX | s.t. |
| 13. | C. Barthe | BBK | s.t. |
| 14. | M. Walscheid | TQA | s.t. |
| 15. | W. van Aert | TJV | s.t. |
| 16. | J. Rickaert | AFC | s.t. |
| 17. | P. Gilbert | LTS | s.t. |
| 18. | D. Ballerini | DQT | s.t. |
| 19. | C. Bol | DSM | s.t. |
| 20. | A. Turgis | TEN | s.t. |
| 21. | G. Van Avermaet | ACT | s.t. |
| 22. | R. Urán | EFN | s.t. |
| 23. | R. Guerreiro | EFN | s.t. |
| 24. | S. Colbrelli | TBV | s.t. |
| 25. | W. Kelderman | BOH | s.t. |
| 26. | T. Pogačar | UAD | s.t. |
| 27. | V. Madouas | GFC | s.t. |
| 28. | D. Oss | BOH | s.t. |
| 29. | E. Mas | MOV | s.t. |
| 30. | A. Paret-Peintre | ACT | s.t. |
| 31. | J. Vingegaard | TJV | s.t. |
| 32. | A. Lutsenko | APT | s.t. |
| 33. | R. Carapaz | IGD | s.t. |
| 34. | D. Gaudu | GFC | s.t. |
| 35. | N. Eekhoff | DSM | s.t. |
| 36. | B. O'Connor | ACT | s.t. |
| 37. | E. Theuns | TFS | s.t. |
| 38. | S. Dillier | AFC | s.t. |
| 39. | G. Martin | COF | s.t. |
| 40. | J. Rutsch | EFN | s.t. |
| 41. | G. Zimmermann | IWG | s.t. |
| 42. | F. Doubey | TEN | s.t. |
| 43. | S. Kruijswijk | TJV | s.t. |
| 44. | P. Bilbao | TBV | s.t. |
| 45. | L. Rota | IWG | s.t. |
| 46. | L. Meintjes | IWG | s.t. |
| 47. | E. Chaves | BEX | s.t. |
| 48. | I. Erviti | MOV | s.t. |
| 49. | A. Valverde | MOV | s.t. |
| 50. | M. Teunissen | TJV | s.t. |
| 51. | H. Sweeny | LTS | s.t. |
| 52. | M. Schär | ACT | s.t. |
| 53. | D. Teuns | TBV | s.t. |
| 54. | B. Mollema | TFS | s.t. |
| 55. | P. Konrad | BOH | s.t. |
| 56. | M. Cattaneo | DQT | s.t. |
| 57. | J. Simon | TEN | s.t. |
| 58. | C. Swift | ARK | 0:18 |
| 59. | G. Boivin | ISN | s.t. |
| 60. | S. Bissegger | EFN | s.t. |
| 61. | C. Gautier | BBK | s.t. |
| 62. | M. Mohorič | TBV | s.t. |
| 63. | R. Zabel | ISN | s.t. |
| 64. | J. Bakelants | IWG | s.t. |
| 65. | M. Chevalier | BBK | s.t. |
| 66. | K. Sbaragli | AFC | s.t. |
| 67. | X. Meurisse | AFC | s.t. |
| 68. | S. Henao | TQA | s.t. |
| 69. | O. Naesen | ACT | s.t. |
| 70. | M. A. López | MOV | s.t. |
| 71. | B. van Poppel | IWG | s.t. |
| 72. | L. Mezgec | BEX | s.t. |
| 73. | J. Wallays | COF | s.t. |
| 74. | É. Gesbert | ARK | s.t. |
| 75. | S. Higuita | EFN | s.t. |
| 76. | E. Boasson Hagen | TEN | 0:28 |
| 77. | K. Asgreen | DQT | 0:32 |
| 78. | B. McNulty | UAD | 0:35 |
| 79. | V. S. Laengen | UAD | 0:36 |
| 80. | L. Pöstlberger | BOH | 1:07 |
| 81. | B. Van Moer | LTS | 1:11 |
| 82. | F. Wright | TBV | 1:13 |
| 83. | M. Haller | TBV | s.t. |
| 84. | O. Fraile | APT | s.t. |
| 85. | N. Powless | EFN | 1:28 |
| 86. | M. Valgren | EFN | s.t. |
| 87. | P. L. Périchon | COF | s.t. |
| 88. | D. Formolo | UAD | 1:31 |
| 89. | V. Nibali | TFS | s.t. |
| 90. | T. Skujiņš | TFS | 1:32 |
| 91. | J. Arcas | MOV | 2:17 |
| 92. | J. Castroviejo | IGD | s.t. |
| 93. | F. Bonnamour | BBK | s.t. |
| 94. | M. Kwiatkowski | IGD | 2:23 |
| 95. | T. Geoghegan Hart | IGD | s.t. |
| 96. | D. Godon | ACT | s.t. |
| 97. | S. Kuss | TJV | s.t. |
| 98. | J. Fuglsang | APT | s.t. |
| 99. | R. Costa | UAD | s.t. |
| 100. | G. Thomas | IGD | s.t. |
| 101. | J. Cabot | TEN | s.t. |
| 102. | N. Politt | BOH | 4:03 |
| 103. | S. Geschke | COF | s.t. |
| 104. | M. Woods | ISN | s.t. |
| 105. | O. Goldstein | ISN | s.t. |
| 106. | N. Quintana | ARK | s.t. |
| 107. | C. Rodríguez | TEN | s.t. |
| 108. | R. Porte | IGD | s.t. |
| 109. | W. Poels | TBV | s.t. |
| 110. | J. Bernard | TFS | s.t. |
| 111. | M. Hirschi | UAD | s.t. |
| 112. | P. Rolland | BBK | s.t. |
| 113. | K. Elissonde | TFS | s.t. |
| 114. | M. Pedersen | TFS | s.t. |
| 115. | D. van Baarle | IGD | s.t. |
| 116. | S. Clarke | TQA | s.t. |
| 117. | W. Barguil | ARK | s.t. |
| 118. | C. Juul-Jensen | BEX | s.t. |
| 119. | Q. Pacher | BBK | 4:49 |
| 120. | E. Buchmann | BOH | s.t. |
| 121. | S. Küng | GFC | s.t. |
| 122. | Je. Herrada | COF | s.t. |
| 123. | M. Bjerg | UAD | s.t. |
| 124. | P. Latour | TEN | s.t. |
| 125. | R. Fernández | COF | s.t. |
| 126. | I. Izagirre | APT | s.t. |
| 127. | L. Durbridge | BEX | s.t. |
| 128. | I. Schelling | BOH | 4:53 |
| 129. | C. Pedersen | DSM | 5:17 |
| 130. | D. Devenyns | DQT | 5:25 |
| 131. | T. De Gendt | LTS | 6:15 |
| 132. | C. Froome | ISN | s.t. |
| 133. | M. Donovan | DSM | s.t. |
| 134. | R. Hollenstein | ISN | s.t. |
| 135. | H. Houle | APT | s.t. |
| 136. | P. Vakoč | AFC | s.t. |
| 137. | D. Martin | ISN | s.t. |
| 138. | A. G. Jansen | BEX | s.t. |
| 139. | Se. Bennett | TQA | s.t. |
| 140. | C. Barbero | TQA | s.t. |
| 141. | B. Cosnefroy | ACT | 6:19 |
| 142. | A. Perez | COF | s.t. |
| 143. | D. Gruzdev | APT | s.t. |
| 144. | V. de la Parte | TEN | s.t. |
| 145. | C. Verona | MOV | s.t. |
| 146. | R. Majka | UAD | 6:21 |
| 147. | B. Armirail | GFC | s.t. |
| 148. | J. Nieuwenhuis | DSM | 6:33 |
| 149. | J. Alaphilippe | DQT | s.t. |
| 150. | S. Kragh Andersen | DSM | 16:28 |
| 151. | T. Declercq | DQT | 21:38 |

## TRIVIA

» With today's win, Mark Cavendish equalled Eddy Merckx's Tour stage-victory record.

JUNE　　WORLDTOUR MEN'S RACE

## TOUR DE FRANCE
Stage 14
10 July 2021
Carcassonne–Quillan
183.7km

A medium mountain stage into the foothills of the Pyrenees took the Tour onto roads that are not often raced. Five categorised climbs on the profile, but none any harder than a category 2, meant there was little to gain or lose for the riders on GC, especially not in view of the four consecutive big mountain stages to come. So another day for a breakaway in a race that had already produced five victories from attackers. The continuing battle for the King of the Mountains jersey provided much of the interest for the bulk of the day's action, with Michael Woods and Wout Poels duelling over three consecutive climbs (the Canadian ending the day in the temporary lead of the classification). But it was Bauke Mollema who stole away over the top of the Col de Saint Louis, the stage's final climb, over the top of which he had only 17km to ride to a victory that closely resembled his only previous Tour win (into Le Puy-en-Velay in 2017). The Dutchman had been ever-present in breakaways for the best part of a week, and this was his just reward. The other winner of the day was Cofidis's Guillaume Martin. The French climber had started the day in ninth place at 9 minutes and 29 seconds. He got himself in the breakaway and held on to finish the stage in 11th place, propelling him up to second on GC, just over 4 minutes down on the race leader Tadej Pogačar. Asked about his elevated status after the race, Martin made it clear that he would need all the minutes he had gained on the stage in his attempt to hang on to a top-ten finish, something that had eluded him for the past two years.

### WEATHER

TEMPERATURE　　WIND
29°C　　NW 9km/h

### PROFILE

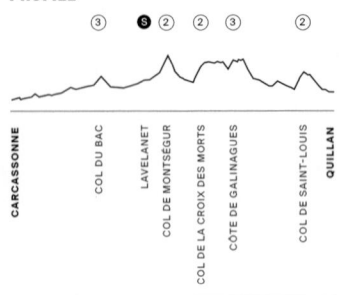

CARCASSONNE · COL DU BAC · LAVELANET · COL DE MONTSÉGUR · COL DE LA CROIX DES MORTS · CÔTE DE GALINAGUES · COL DE SAINT-LOUIS · QUILLAN

### BREAKAWAY

W. Poels (TBV), M. Cattaneo (DQT), M. Woods (EFN), E. Chaves (BEX), G. Martin (COF), S. Higuita (EFN), P. Konrad (BOH), O. Fraile (APT), L. Meintjes (IWG), B. Mollema (TFS), P. Rolland (BBK), Q. Pacher (BBK), E. Gesbert (ARK), V. Madouas (GFC)

### GENERAL CLASSIFICATION

| POS | NAME | TEAM | TIME |
|---|---|---|---|
| 1. — | T. Pogačar | UAD | 56:50:21 |
| 2. ↑7 | G. Martin | COF | 4:04 |
| 3. ↓1 | R. Urán | EFN | 5:18 |
| 4. ↓1 | J. Vingegaard | TJV | 5:32 |
| 5. ↓1 | R. Carapaz | IGD | 5:33 |
| 6. ↓1 | B. O'Connor | ACT | 5:58 |
| 7. ↓1 | W. Kelderman | BOH | 6:16 |
| 8. ↓1 | A. Lutsenko | APT | 6:30 |
| 9. ↓1 | E. Mas | MOV | 7:11 |
| 10. ↑1 | M. Cattaneo | DQT | 9:48 |

### KING OF THE MOUNTAINS

| POS | NAME | TEAM | PTS |
|---|---|---|---|
| 1. ↑2 | M. Woods | ISN | 54 |
| 2. ↓1 | N. Quintana | ARK | 50 |
| 3. ↑1 | W. Poels | TBV | 49 |

### POINTS

| POS | NAME | TEAM | PTS |
|---|---|---|---|
| 1. — | M. Cavendish | DQT | 279 |
| 2. — | M. Matthews | BEX | 187 |
| 3. — | J. Philipsen | AFC | 174 |

### YOUNG RIDER

| POS | NAME | TEAM | TIME |
|---|---|---|---|
| 1. — | T. Pogačar | UAD | 56:50:21 |
| 2. — | J. Vingegaard | TJV | 5:32 |
| 3. — | A. Paret-Peintre | ACT | 24:44 |

### TRIVIA

» If the podium were to remain the same until Paris, it would be the first time in 40 years that the countries of the top three have boasted populations under 20 million.

### BONUSES

| TYPE | NAME | TEAM |
|---|---|---|
| KOM 1 | K. Sbaragli | AFC |
| KOM 2 | W. Poels | TBV |
| KOM 3 | M. Woods | ISN |
| KOM 4 | W. Poels | TBV |
| KOM 5 | B. Mollema | TFS |
| Sprint 1 | J. Rickaert | AFC |

## STAGE RESULTS

| POS | NAME | TEAM | TIME |
|---|---|---|---|
| 1. | B. Mollema | TFS | 4:16:16 |
| 2. | P. Konrad | BOH | 1:04 |
| 3. | S. Higuita | EFN | s.t. |
| 4. | M. Cattaneo | DQT | 1:06 |
| 5. | M. Woods | ISN | 1:10 |
| 6. | O. Fraile | APT | 1:25 |
| 7. | É. Gesbert | ARK | s.t. |
| 8. | Q. Pacher | BBK | s.t. |
| 9. | L. Meintjes | IWG | 1:26 |
| 10. | E. Chaves | BEX | 1:28 |
| 11. | G. Martin | COF | s.t. |
| 12. | V. Madouas | GFC | 3:32 |
| 13. | W. Poels | TBV | s.t. |
| 14. | P. Rolland | BBK | 6:23 |
| 15. | B. McNulty | UAD | 6:53 |
| 16. | R. Costa | UAD | s.t. |
| 17. | R. Majka | UAD | s.t. |
| 18. | T. Pogačar | UAD | s.t. |
| 19. | D. van Baarle | IGD | s.t. |
| 20. | R. Carapaz | IGD | s.t. |
| 21. | R. Porte | IGD | s.t. |
| 22. | J. Castroviejo | IGD | s.t. |
| 23. | J. Stuyven | TFS | s.t. |
| 24. | K. Elissonde | TFS | s.t. |
| 25. | E. Mas | MOV | s.t. |
| 26. | R. Guerreiro | EFN | s.t. |
| 27. | A. Valverde | MOV | s.t. |
| 28. | E. Buchmann | BOH | s.t. |
| 29. | M. Donovan | DSM | s.t. |
| 30. | W. Kelderman | BOH | s.t. |
| 31. | R. Urán | EFN | s.t. |
| 32. | D. Teuns | TBV | s.t. |
| 33. | S. Kruijswijk | TJV | s.t. |
| 34. | J. Bakelants | IWG | s.t. |
| 35. | S. Kuss | TJV | s.t. |
| 36. | C. Gautier | BBK | s.t. |
| 37. | J. Vingegaard | TJV | s.t. |
| 38. | I. Izaguirre | APT | s.t. |
| 39. | L. Rota | IWG | s.t. |
| 40. | C. Rodriguez | TEN | s.t. |
| 41. | N. Powless | EFN | s.t. |
| 42. | A. Lutsenko | APT | s.t. |
| 43. | B. O'Connor | ACT | s.t. |
| 44. | D. Gaudu | GFC | s.t. |
| 45. | A. Paret-Peintre | ACT | s.t. |
| 46. | V. Nibali | TFS | s.t. |
| 47. | P. Bilbao | TBV | s.t. |
| 48. | M. Kwiatkowski | IGD | s.t. |
| 49. | S. Henao | TQA | s.t. |
| 50. | D. Formolo | UAD | s.t. |
| 51. | J. Bernard | TFS | 9:15 |
| 52. | M. Schär | ACT | 9:52 |
| 53. | T. Geoghegan Hart | IGD | s.t. |
| 54. | J. Arcas | MOV | s.t. |
| 55. | M. A. López | MOV | s.t. |
| 56. | H. Houle | APT | s.t. |
| 57. | D. Martin | ISN | s.t. |
| 58. | G. Zimmermann | IWG | s.t. |
| 59. | N. Politt | BOH | s.t. |
| 60. | C. Juul-Jensen | BEX | s.t. |
| 61. | J. Fuglsang | APT | 12:57 |
| 62. | K. Asgreen | DQT | 13:15 |
| 63. | Je. Herrada | COF | s.t. |
| 64. | M. Valgren | EFN | s.t. |
| 65. | N. Quintana | ARK | s.t. |
| 66. | R. Fernández | COF | s.t. |
| 67. | S. Colbrelli | TBV | s.t. |
| 68. | D. Gruzdev | APT | s.t. |
| 69. | C. Verona | MOV | s.t. |
| 70. | S. Küng | GFC | s.t. |
| 71. | J. Alaphilippe | DQT | s.t. |
| 72. | W. van Aert | TJV | s.t. |
| 73. | F. Bonnamour | BBK | s.t. |
| 74. | M. Hirschi | UAD | s.t. |
| 75. | S. Geschke | COF | s.t. |
| 76. | I. Schelling | BOH | s.t. |
| 77. | T. Skujiņš | TFS | s.t. |
| 78. | G. Thomas | IGD | s.t. |
| 79. | J. Rutsch | EFN | 16:47 |
| 80. | M. Cort | EFN | s.t. |
| 81. | M. Matthews | BEX | 17:04 |
| 82. | L. Mezgec | BEX | s.t. |
| 83. | L. Durbridge | BEX | s.t. |
| 84. | M. Bjerg | UAD | s.t. |
| 85. | T. De Gendt | LTS | 17:42 |
| 86. | K. Sbaragli | AFC | s.t. |
| 87. | A. Greipel | ISN | s.t. |
| 88. | M. Chevalier | BBK | s.t. |
| 89. | M. Teunissen | TJV | s.t. |
| 90. | R. Zabel | ISN | s.t. |
| 91. | S. Clarke | TQA | s.t. |
| 92. | D. Godon | ACT | s.t. |
| 93. | D. Oss | BOH | s.t. |
| 94. | C. Froome | ISN | s.t. |
| 95. | C. Laporte | COF | s.t. |

| POS | NAME | TEAM | TIME |
|---|---|---|---|
| 96. | S. Dillier | AFC | s.t. |
| 97. | O. Goldstein | ISN | s.t. |
| 98. | C. Swift | ARK | s.t. |
| 99. | C. Barthe | BBK | s.t. |
| 100. | J. Philipsen | AFC | s.t. |
| 101. | F. Wright | TBV | s.t. |
| 102. | X. Meurisse | AFC | s.t. |
| 103. | G. Van Avermaet | ACT | s.t. |
| 104. | L. Aranburu | APT | s.t. |
| 105. | P. Gilbert | LTS | s.t. |
| 106. | D. van Poppel | IWG | s.t. |
| 107. | P. L. Périchon | COF | s.t. |
| 108. | B. Van Moer | LTS | s.t. |
| 109. | P. Latour | TEN | s.t. |
| 110. | H. Sweeny | LTS | s.t. |
| 111. | M. Mohorič | TBV | s.t. |
| 112. | I. García Cortina | MOV | s.t. |
| 113. | F. Doubey | TEN | s.t. |
| 114. | L. Pöstlberger | BOH | s.t. |
| 115. | M. Haller | TBV | s.t. |
| 116. | J. Wallays | COF | s.t. |
| 117. | O. Naesen | ACT | s.t. |
| 118. | I. Erviti | MOV | s.t. |
| 119. | G. Boivin | ISN | s.t. |
| 120. | B. van Poppel | IWG | s.t. |
| 121. | V. S. Laengen | UAD | s.t. |
| 122. | P. Vakoč | AFC | s.t. |
| 123. | Se. Bennett | TQA | s.t. |
| 124. | B. Armirail | GFC | s.t. |
| 125. | B. Cosnefroy | ACT | s.t. |
| 126. | A. Perez | COF | s.t. |
| 127. | J. Cabot | TEN | s.t. |
| 128. | D. Ballerini | DQT | 25:34 |
| 129. | C. Pedersen | DSM | s.t. |
| 130. | N. Eekhoff | DSM | s.t. |
| 131. | R. Hollenstein | ISN | s.t. |
| 132. | E. Boasson Hagen | TEN | s.t. |
| 133. | M. Mørkøv | DQT | s.t. |
| 134. | A. Turgis | TEN | s.t. |
| 135. | D. Devenyns | DQT | s.t. |
| 136. | J. Simon | TEN | s.t. |
| 137. | T. Declercq | DQT | s.t. |
| 138. | E. Theuns | TFS | s.t. |
| 139. | M. Walscheid | TQA | s.t. |
| 140. | J. Nieuwenhuis | DSM | s.t. |
| 141. | V. de la Parte | TEN | s.t. |
| 142. | S. Bissegger | EFN | s.t. |
| 143. | C. Barbero | TQA | s.t. |
| 144. | M. Cavendish | DQT | s.t. |
| 145. | M. Pedersen | TFS | s.t. |
| 146. | J. Rickaert | AFC | s.t. |
| 147. | N. Bouhanni | ARK | 36:46 |
| 148. | A. G. Jansen | BEX | s.t. |
| 149. | C. Bol | DSM | s.t. |

JUNE    WORLDTOUR MEN'S RACE

# TOUR DE FRANCE
Stage 15
11 July 2021
Céret–Andorra la Vella
191.3km

## WEATHER

TEMPERATURE: 28°C
WIND: E 17km/h

## PROFILE

CÉRET · OLETTE · MONTÉE DE MONT-LOUIS · COL DE PUYMORENS · PORT D'ENVALIRA · COL DE BEIXALIS · ANDORRE-LA-VIEILLE

Into the Pyrenees proper for the first of four huge mountain stages. For around 80 riders in the peloton, the race was heading onto home roads, given that it finished in Andorra, the tax-efficient choice of domicile for the professional bike rider of the age. In particular, the final climb of the Col de Beixalis, with its rough road surface and tough gradients, would be the focus for virtually all the riders who found themselves in a 34-man group that prised itself clear of the peloton. Jumbo-Visma placed three of their remaining riders in the breakaway, with the sole exception of the isolated Jonas Vingegaard, who began the stage in fourth place on GC. It was Sepp Kuss, though, who produced the ride of the day. An attack over the final climb was all he needed to ride clear of the rest and solo to a win in the grey streets of Andorra La Vieille. It was a ride that saw him overcome more than 4,500 metres of altitude gain, including the Port d'Envalira – at 2,408 metres the Souvenir Henri Desgranges climb of this year's race (taken by Nairo Quintana, who was still hunting points in the King of the Mountains). For Kuss this was an unexpected chance to double his tally of Grand Tour stage wins, having previously won at the Vuelta on a summit finish. But for Jumbo-Visma, it was further reward for their imaginative rethinking of race tactics after their Tour had unravelled with the abandon of Primož Roglič. Back in the GC race, it was Richard Carapaz who tried but failed to break clear over the final climb. Then Vingegaard attempted once more to put Pogačar under pressure as he had on the slopes of Mont Ventoux – this time to no avail. The race leader had things firmly under control. The same could not be said for Guillaume Martin, who lost nearly 4 minutes and dropped from second to ninth on GC, which meant that everyone else shuffled up a place. At the end of the day, Jumbo-Visma had ridden to a stage win and a podium place on GC with Vingegaard.

## GENERAL CLASSIFICATION

| POS | NAME | TEAM | TIME |
|---|---|---|---|
| 1. — | T. Pogačar | UAD | 62:07:18 |
| 2. ↑1 | R. Urán | EFN | 5:18 |
| 3. ↑1 | J. Vingegaard | TJV | 5:32 |
| 4. ↑1 | R. Carapaz | IGD | 5:33 |
| 5. ↑1 | B. O'Connor | ACT | 5:58 |
| 6. ↑1 | W. Kelderman | BOH | 6:16 |
| 7. ↑1 | A. Lutsenko | APT | 7:01 |
| 8. ↑1 | E. Mas | MOV | 7:11 |
| 9. ↓7 | G. Martin | COF | 7:58 |
| 10.↑1 | P. Bilbao | TBV | 10:59 |

## KING OF THE MOUNTAINS

| POS | NAME | TEAM | PTS |
|---|---|---|---|
| 1. ↑2 | W. Poels | TBV | 74 |
| 2. ↓1 | M. Woods | ISN | 66 |
| 3. ↓1 | N. Quintana | ARK | 64 |

## POINTS

| POS | NAME | TEAM | PTS |
|---|---|---|---|
| 1. — | M. Cavendish | DQT | 279 |
| 2. — | M. Matthews | BEX | 207 |
| 3. — | J. Philipsen | AFC | 174 |

## YOUNG RIDER

| POS | NAME | TEAM | TIME |
|---|---|---|---|
| 1. — | T. Pogačar | UAD | 62:07:18 |
| 2. — | J. Vingegaard | TJV | 5:32 |
| 3. — | A. Paret-Peintre | ACT | 21:15 |

## BONUSES

| TYPE | NAME | TEAM |
|---|---|---|
| KOM 1 | W. Poels | TBV |
| KOM 2 | W. van Aert | TJV |
| KOM 3 | N. Quintana | ARK |
| KOM 4 | S. Kuss | TJV |
| Sprint 1 | M. Matthews | BEX |

## TRIVIA

» Sepp Kuss now only needs a Giro d'Italia stage win to complete his Grand Tour set.

## STAGE RESULTS

| POS | NAME | TEAM | TIME |
|---|---|---|---|
| 1. | S. Kuss | TJV | 5:12:06 |
| 2. | A. Valverde | MOV | 0:23 |
| 3. | W. Poels | TBV | 1:15 |
| 4. | I. Izagirre | APT | s.t. |
| 5. | R. Guerreiro | EFN | s.t. |
| 6. | N. Quintana | ARK | s.t. |
| 7. | D. Gaudu | GFC | s.t. |
| 8. | D. Martin | ISN | 1:22 |
| 9. | F. Bonnamour | BBK | s.t. |
| 10. | A. Paret-Peintre | ACT | s.t. |
| 11. | V. Nibali | TFS | s.t. |
| 12. | J. Alaphilippe | DQT | s.t. |
| 13. | N. Powless | EFN | 3:00 |
| 14. | M. Donovan | DSM | 3:02 |
| 15. | D. Teuns | TBV | 4:11 |
| 16. | K. Elissonde | TFS | s.t. |
| 17. | J. Bernard | TFS | s.t. |
| 18. | S. Henao | TQA | s.t. |
| 19. | W. van Aert | TJV | 4:51 |
| 20. | E. Mas | MOV | s.t. |
| 21. | J. Vingegaard | TJV | s.t. |
| 22. | T. Pogačar | UAD | s.t. |
| 23. | R. Carapaz | IGD | s.t. |
| 24. | R. Urán | EFN | s.t. |
| 25. | W. Kelderman | BOH | s.t. |
| 26. | B. O'Connor | ACT | s.t. |
| 27. | A. Lutsenko | APT | 5:22 |
| 28. | P. Bilbao | TBV | s.t. |
| 29. | M. Mohorič | TBV | 5:25 |
| 30. | M. Woods | ISN | 6:19 |
| 31. | L. Meintjes | IWG | 7:14 |
| 32. | E. Chaves | BEX | s.t. |
| 33. | G. Martin | COF | 8:45 |
| 34. | V. Madouas | GFC | s.t. |
| 35. | S. Kruijswijk | TJV | s.t. |
| 36. | J. Castroviejo | IGD | s.t. |
| 37. | M. Cattaneo | DQT | 9:48 |
| 38. | G. Thomas | IGD | s.t. |
| 39. | D. Ballerini | DQT | 13:13 |
| 40. | T. De Gendt | LTS | s.t. |
| 41. | S. Higuita | EFN | s.t. |
| 42. | E. Buchmann | BOH | 14:35 |
| 43. | M. Schär | ACT | s.t. |
| 44. | J. Stuyven | TFS | s.t. |
| 45. | P. Konrad | BOH | s.t. |
| 46. | P. Latour | TEN | s.t. |
| 47. | X. Meurisse | AFC | 15:57 |
| 48. | J. Bakelants | IWG | s.t. |
| 49. | C. Rodríguez | TEN | s.t. |
| 50. | D. van Baarle | IGD | s.t. |
| 51. | M. A. López | MOV | 17:04 |
| 52. | S. Geschke | COF | 18:06 |
| 53. | R. Fernández | COF | s.t. |
| 54. | M. Matthews | BEX | 19:17 |
| 55. | J. Fuglsang | APT | 20:06 |
| 56. | R. Porte | IGD | s.t. |
| 57. | Q. Pacher | BBK | s.t. |
| 58. | A. Aranburu | APT | s.t. |
| 59. | J. Rutsch | EFN | s.t. |
| 60. | R. Costa | UAD | s.t. |
| 61. | M. Cort | EFN | s.t. |
| 62. | B. Mollema | TFS | s.t. |
| 63. | T. Geoghegan Hart | IGD | s.t. |
| 64. | M. Teunissen | TJV | s.t. |
| 65. | Se. Bennett | TQA | s.t. |
| 66. | Je. Herrada | COF | s.t. |
| 67. | L. Pöstlberger | BOH | 22:50 |
| 68. | S. Dillier | AFC | 23:07 |
| 69. | S. Küng | GFC | s.t. |
| 70. | F. Wright | TBV | s.t. |
| 71. | C. Barthe | BBK | s.t. |
| 72. | C. Froome | ISN | s.t. |
| 73. | M. Haller | TBV | s.t. |
| 74. | J. Arcas | MOV | s.t. |
| 75. | L. Durbridge | BEX | s.t. |
| 76. | I. Erviti | MOV | s.t. |
| 77. | C. Juul-Jensen | BEX | s.t. |
| 78. | B. Van Moer | LTS | 23:45 |
| 79. | J. Philipsen | AFC | s.t. |
| 80. | H. Sweeny | LTS | s.t. |
| 81. | L. Rota | IWG | s.t. |
| 82. | D. Godon | ACT | s.t. |
| 83. | F. Doubey | TEN | s.t. |
| 84. | M. Valgren | EFN | s.t. |
| 85. | H. Houle | APT | s.t. |
| 86. | É. Gesbert | ARK | s.t. |
| 87. | K. Asgreen | DQT | s.t. |
| 88. | M. Kwiatkowski | IGD | s.t. |
| 89. | C. Barbero | TQA | s.t. |
| 90. | D. Formolo | UAD | s.t. |
| 91. | M. Hirschi | UAD | s.t. |
| 92. | P. L. Périchon | COF | s.t. |
| 93. | P. Rolland | BBK | s.t. |
| 94. | O. Goldstein | ISN | s.t. |
| 95. | R. Majka | UAD | s.t. |
| 96. | C. Verona | MOV | s.t. |
| 97. | B. McNulty | UAD | s.t. |
| 98. | J. Cabot | TEN | s.t. |
| 99. | O. Fraile | APT | s.t. |
| 100. | J. Rickaert | AFC | s.t. |
| 101. | I. García Cortina | MOV | 24:27 |
| 102. | G. Zimmermann | IWG | s.t. |
| 103. | O. Naesen | ACT | s.t. |
| 104. | C. Laporte | COF | 24:31 |
| 105. | D. Oss | BOH | s.t. |
| 106. | I. Schelling | BOH | s.t. |
| 107. | B. Armirail | GFC | s.t. |
| 108. | A. Turgis | TEN | 25:35 |
| 109. | N. Politt | BOH | s.t. |
| 110. | M. Chevalier | BBK | 25:55 |
| 111. | M. Bjerg | UAD | 26:01 |
| 112. | M. Pedersen | TFS | 26:27 |
| 113. | C. Pedersen | DSM | s.t. |
| 114. | T. Skujinš | TFS | s.t. |
| 115. | D. van Poppel | IWG | s.t. |
| 116. | C. Gautier | BBK | s.t. |
| 117. | C. Swift | ARK | s.t. |
| 118. | L. Mezgec | BEX | s.t. |
| 119. | S. Colbrelli | TBV | s.t. |
| 120. | A. Perez | COF | s.t. |
| 121. | D. Gruzdev | APT | 27:10 |
| 122. | G. Boivin | ISN | 28:19 |
| 123. | A. Greipel | ISN | 30:49 |
| 124. | S. Clarke | TQA | s.t. |
| 125. | R. Hollenstein | ISN | s.t. |
| 126. | R. Zabel | ISN | s.t. |
| 127. | J. Simon | TEN | s.t. |
| 128. | K. Sbaragli | AFC | s.t. |
| 129. | P. Gilbert | LTS | s.t. |
| 130. | B. van Poppel | IWG | s.t. |
| 131. | G. Van Avermaet | ACT | s.t. |
| 132. | E. Theuns | TFS | s.t. |
| 133. | V. de la Parte | TEN | s.t. |
| 134. | P. Vakoč | AFC | s.t. |
| 135. | J. Nieuwenhuis | DSM | 30:52 |
| 136. | N. Eekhoff | DSM | s.t. |
| 137. | C. Bol | DSM | s.t. |
| 138. | S. Bissegger | EFN | 31:37 |
| 139. | J. Wallays | COF | 33:20 |
| 140. | M. Walscheid | TQA | s.t. |
| 141. | V. S. Laengen | UAD | s.t. |
| 142. | A. G. Jansen | BEX | 34:48 |
| 143. | B. Cosnefroy | ACT | s.t. |
| 144. | M. Mørkøv | DQT | 34:57 |
| 145. | T. Declercq | DQT | s.t. |
| 146. | D. Devenyns | DQT | s.t. |
| 147. | M. Cavendish | DQT | s.t. |

## BREAKAWAY

S. Kruijswijk (TJV), S. Kuss (TJV), W. van Aert (TJV), J. Castroviejo (IGD), D. van Baarle (IGD), D. Martin (ISN), M. Woods (ISN), V. Nibali (TFS), J. Bernard (TFS), K. Elissonde (TFS), J. Alaphilippe (DQT), D. Ballerini (DQT), A. Valverde (MOV), L. Pöstlberger (BOH), D. Gaudu (GFC), B. Armirail (GFC), V. Madouas (GFC), R. Fernández (COF), A. Paret-Peintre (ACT), N. Quintana (ARK), R. Guerreiro (EFN), N. Powless (EFN), M. Donovan (DSM), T. De Gendt (LTS), M. Mohorič (TBV), W. Poels (TBV), D. Teuns (TBV), M. Matthews (BEX), I. Izagirre (APT), S. Henao (TQA), P. Latour (TEN), F. Bonnamour (BBK)

JUNE    WORLDTOUR MEN'S RACE

# TOUR DE FRANCE
Stage 16
13 July 2021
El Pas de la Casa–Saint-Gaudens
169km

After the second rest day, stage 16 was the last downhill finish in the Pyrenees before two monstrous summit finishes. It would perhaps prove to be the final opportunity for a breakaway to make it all the way to the line. On this occasion, the race was already more than 80km old before the definitive move of the day was formed after a dozen riders bridged across to a trio including Chris Juul-Jensen, Fabien Doubey and Jan Bakelants. In part, this was because of the battle between Michael Matthews and Sonny Colbrelli for green jersey points at the intermediate sprint halfway through the stage. It was a feature of the points competition throughout the campaign that Mark Cavendish would mostly rely on the large number of points at the finish lines, whereas his closest (but nonetheless distant) rivals were almost duty-bound to go hunting points on every stage, including the mountains. On the lower slopes of the Col de Portet d'Aspet, it was the Austrian champion Patrick Konrad from Bora-Hansgrohe who attacked and went clear. No one would see him again, despite the best efforts of David Gaudu, who was about to step up in the Pyrenees and provide confirmation of his growing pre-eminence in a team beginning to move on from the Thibaut Pinot years. Konrad was too strong for them all, though. His 35km solo ride was Bora-Hansgrohe's second win (after Nils Politt claimed stage 12), and the third consecutive day on which a solo attacker had stayed away. The GC riders finished in a group behind, fully 12 minutes after the race had been won.

## WEATHER

TEMPERATURE: 10°C
WIND: NW 6km/h

## PROFILE

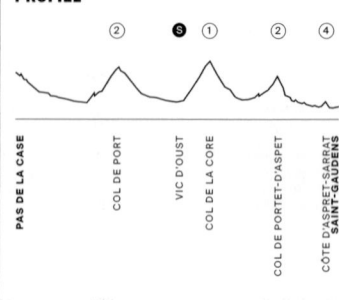

PAS DE LA CASE — COL DE PORT — VIC D'OUST — COL DE LA CORE — COL DE PORTET-D'ASPET — CÔTE D'ASPRET-SARRAT — SAINT-GAUDENS

## BREAKAWAY
P. Konrad (BOH), C. Juul-Jensen (BEX), F. Doubey (TEN), J. Bakelants (IWG)

## GENERAL CLASSIFICATION

| POS | NAME | TEAM | TIME |
|---|---|---|---|
| 1. — | T. Pogačar | UAD | 66:23:06 |
| 2. — | R. Urán | EFN | 5:18 |
| 3. — | J. Vingegaard | TJV | 5:32 |
| 4. — | R. Carapaz | IGD | 5:33 |
| 5. — | B. O'Connor | ACT | 5:58 |
| 6. — | W. Kelderman | BOH | 6:16 |
| 7. — | A. Lutsenko | APT | 7:01 |
| 8. — | E. Mas | MOV | 7:11 |
| 9. — | G. Martin | COF | 8:02 |
| 10.— | P. Bilbao | TBV | 10:59 |

## KING OF THE MOUNTAINS

| POS | NAME | TEAM | PTS |
|---|---|---|---|
| 1. — | W. Poels | TBV | 74 |
| 2. — | M. Woods | ISN | 66 |
| 3. — | N. Quintana | ARK | 64 |

## POINTS

| POS | NAME | TEAM | PTS |
|---|---|---|---|
| 1. — | M. Cavendish | DQT | 279 |
| 2. — | M. Matthews | BEX | 242 |
| 3. ↑1 | S. Colbrelli | TBV | 195 |

## YOUNG RIDER

| POS | NAME | TEAM | TIME |
|---|---|---|---|
| 1. — | T. Pogačar | UAD | 66:23:06 |
| 2. — | J. Vingegaard | TJV | 5:32 |
| 3. ↑1 | D. Gaudu | GFC | 14:13 |

## TRIVIA
» Since his last stage win (stage 16 in 2017), this was Michael Matthews' 16th top-ten finish without another victory at the Tour de France.

## BONUSES

| TYPE | NAME | TEAM |
|---|---|---|
| KOM 1 | M. Cattaneo | DQT |
| KOM 2 | P. Konrad | BOH |
| KOM 3 | P. Konrad | BOH |
| KOM 4 | P. Konrad | BOH |
| Sprint 1 | J. Bakelants | IWG |

## STAGE RESULTS

| POS | NAME | TEAM | TIME |
|---|---|---|---|
| 1. | P. Konrad | BOH | 4:01:59 |
| 2. | S. Colbrelli | TBV | 0:42 |
| 3. | M. Matthews | BEX | s.t. |
| 4. | P. L. Périchon | COF | s.t. |
| 5. | F. Bonnamour | BBK | s.t. |
| 6. | A. Aranburu | APT | s.t. |
| 7. | T. Skujiņš | TFS | 0:45 |
| 8. | J. Bakelants | IWG | s.t. |
| 9. | D. Gaudu | GFC | 0:47 |
| 10. | L. Rota | IWG | 1:03 |
| 11. | F. Doubey | TEN | 4:39 |
| 12. | F. Wright | TBV | 4:41 |
| 13. | R. Carapaz | IGD | 13:49 |
| 14. | T. Pogačar | UAD | s.t. |
| 15. | A. Lutsenko | APT | s.t. |
| 16. | J. Vingegaard | TJV | s.t. |
| 17. | R. Urán | EFN | s.t. |
| 18. | W. Kelderman | BOH | s.t. |
| 19. | B. O'Connor | ACT | s.t. |
| 20. | M. Cattaneo | DQT | s.t. |
| 21. | E. Mas | MOV | s.t. |
| 22. | P. Bilbao | TBV | s.t. |
| 23. | G. Martin | COF | 13:53 |
| 24. | D. Formolo | UAD | 14:12 |
| 25. | W. van Aert | TJV | 14:22 |
| 26. | D. Godon | ACT | 14:44 |
| 27. | M. Schär | ACT | s.t. |
| 28. | E. Theuns | TFS | s.t. |
| 29. | M. Cort | EFN | s.t. |
| 30. | D. Teuns | TBV | s.t. |
| 31. | L. Meintjes | IWG | s.t. |
| 32. | C. Barthe | BBK | s.t. |
| 33. | A. Paret-Peintre | ACT | s.t. |
| 34. | J. Bernard | TFS | s.t. |
| 35. | N. Powless | EFN | s.t. |
| 36. | Q. Pacher | BBK | s.t. |
| 37. | S. Dillier | AFC | s.t. |
| 38. | R. Guerreiro | EFN | s.t. |
| 39. | J. Rutsch | EFN | s.t. |
| 40. | M. Teunissen | TJV | s.t. |
| 41. | X. Meurisse | AFC | s.t. |
| 42. | B. Mollema | TFS | s.t. |
| 43. | E. Chaves | BEX | s.t. |
| 44. | S. Henao | TQA | s.t. |
| 45. | A. Valverde | MOV | s.t. |
| 46. | C. Barbero | TQA | s.t. |
| 47. | G. Van Avermaet | ACT | s.t. |
| 48. | K. Elissonde | TFS | s.t. |
| 49. | R. Fernández | COF | 14:57 |
| 50. | G. Zimmermann | IWG | s.t. |
| 51. | E. Buchmann | BOH | s.t. |
| 52. | J. Castroviejo | IGD | s.t. |
| 53. | M. A. López | MOV | s.t. |
| 54. | M. Hirschi | UAD | s.t. |
| 55. | M. Valgren | EFN | s.t. |
| 56. | T. Geoghegan Hart | IGD | 15:08 |
| 57. | S. Geschke | COF | s.t. |
| 58. | D. van Baarle | IGD | s.t. |
| 59. | O. Naesen | ACT | s.t. |
| 60. | H. Houle | APT | 15:14 |
| 61. | M. Mohorič | TBV | 15:17 |
| 62. | B. McNulty | UAD | 15:20 |
| 63. | N. Politt | BOH | s.t. |
| 64. | I. Izaguirre | APT | 15:24 |
| 65. | S. Kuss | TJV | 15:40 |
| 66. | A. Perez | COF | 16:31 |
| 67. | R. Majka | UAD | 16:33 |
| 68. | R. Costa | UAD | s.t. |
| 69. | T. De Gendt | LTS | 16:42 |
| 70. | J. Fuglsang | APT | s.t. |
| 71. | I. García Cortina | MOV | s.t. |
| 72. | R. Porte | IGD | s.t. |
| 73. | P. Gilbert | LTS | s.t. |
| 74. | D. Oss | BOH | s.t. |
| 75. | J. Simon | TEN | s.t. |
| 76. | O. Fraile | APT | s.t. |
| 77. | B. Van Moer | LTS | s.t. |
| 78. | J. Philipsen | AFC | s.t. |
| 79. | N. Quintana | ARK | s.t. |
| 80. | P. Vakoč | AFC | s.t. |
| 81. | K. Asgreen | DQT | s.t. |
| 82. | I. Erviti | MOV | s.t. |
| 83. | K. Sbaragli | AFC | s.t. |
| 84. | J. Arcas | MOV | s.t. |
| 85. | C. Rodríguez | TEN | s.t. |
| 86. | V. de la Parte | TEN | s.t. |
| 87. | J. Nieuwenhuis | DSM | s.t. |
| 88. | Je. Herrada | COF | s.t. |
| 89. | C. Verona | MOV | s.t. |
| 90. | B. Cosnefroy | ACT | s.t. |
| 91. | M. Chevalier | BBK | s.t. |
| 92. | S. Higuita | EFN | s.t. |
| 93. | P. Latour | TEN | s.t. |
| 94. | J. Rickaert | AFC | s.t. |
| 95. | V. Madouas | GFC | s.t. |
| 96. | L. Mezgec | BEX | s.t. |
| 97. | S. Bissegger | EFN | s.t. |
| 98. | W. Poels | TBV | s.t. |
| 99. | M. Haller | TBV | s.t. |
| 100. | M. Donovan | DSM | s.t. |
| 101. | G. Thomas | IGD | s.t. |
| 102. | D. Martin | ISN | s.t. |
| 103. | P. Rolland | BBK | s.t. |
| 104. | D. van Poppel | IWG | s.t. |
| 105. | S. Küng | GFC | s.t. |
| 106. | O. Goldstein | ISN | s.t. |
| 107. | C. Gautier | BBK | s.t. |
| 108. | É. Gesbert | ARK | s.t. |
| 109. | I. Schelling | BOH | 16:50 |
| 110. | M. Bjerg | UAD | 17:56 |
| 111. | H. Sweeny | LTS | s.t. |
| 112. | S. Kruijswijk | TJV | s.t. |
| 113. | L. Durbridge | BEX | s.t. |
| 114. | V. S. Laengen | UAD | s.t. |
| 115. | J. Alaphilippe | DQT | s.t. |
| 116. | J. Stuyven | TFS | s.t. |
| 117. | M. Pedersen | TFS | s.t. |
| 118. | M. Kwiatkowski | IGD | s.t. |
| 119. | C. Laporte | COF | s.t. |
| 120. | L. Pöstlberger | BOH | s.t. |
| 121. | C. Pedersen | DSM | s.t. |
| 122. | B. Armirail | GFC | s.t. |
| 123. | A. Turgis | TEN | s.t. |
| 124. | D. Gruzdev | APT | s.t. |
| 125. | J. Cabot | TEN | s.t. |
| 126. | C. Swift | ARK | s.t. |
| 127. | M. Woods | ISN | s.t. |
| 128. | C. Juul-Jensen | BEX | 18:02 |
| 129. | R. Hollenstein | ISN | 23:40 |
| 130. | G. Boivin | ISN | s.t. |
| 131. | C. Froome | ISN | s.t. |
| 132. | M. Walscheid | TQA | s.t. |
| 133. | A. Greipel | ISN | s.t. |
| 134. | R. Zabel | ISN | s.t. |
| 135. | M. Cavendish | DQT | s.t. |
| 136. | S. Clarke | TQA | s.t. |
| 137. | Se. Bennett | TQA | s.t. |
| 138. | D. Ballerini | DQT | s.t. |
| 139. | T. Declercq | DQT | s.t. |
| 140. | M. Mørkøv | DQT | s.t. |
| 141. | J. Wallays | COF | s.t. |
| 142. | B. van Poppel | IWG | s.t. |
| 143. | D. Devenyns | DQT | s.t. |
| 144. | C. Bol | DSM | s.t. |
| 145. | N. Eekhoff | DSM | s.t. |

JUNE    WORLDTOUR MEN'S RACE

## TOUR DE FRANCE
Stage 17
14 July 2021
Muret–Saint-Lary-Soulan (Col du Portet)
178.4km

On 32 previous occasions French riders had taken stage wins on Bastille Day, the last of which had been in 2017, when Warren Barguil rode to victory in the Alps. In that spirit, Pierre Rolland was the first rider to attack. However, he didn't make it into the definitive breakaway when at last it established itself. Six riders – including four Frenchmen: Dorian Godon, Anthony Perez, Anthony Turgis and Maxime Chevalier – went clear and built up a healthy lead. There was a skirmish once again for green jersey points in Luchon, and then a counter-attack shortly thereafter from Nairo Quintana and Wout Poels, joined by Élie Gesbert and Pierre Latour. That move was neutralised by UAE Team Emirates. When the race hit the huge final climb of the Col du Portet, it was only Perez out front on his own. The Cofidis rider acquitted himself well but was no match for a GC race that, for once, targeted the stage win. Close to the top of the climb a curious trio of the race's three strongest riders went clear as second-placed Rigoberto Urán fell away. Tadej Pogačar once again found Jonas Vingegaard was undroppable. But so too, as both Pogačar and Vingegaard now established, was Richard Carapaz. The Slovenian and the Dutchman briefly communicated to one another their frustration and suspicion that the Ineos rider might be bluffing. The Ecuadorian sat on the back of the trio, declined the invitation to share the work and then, on the entry to a short tunnel close to the finish line, attacked. It was a bold move but one that was shut down by Pogačar. The yellow jersey swept past Carapaz to take his second stage win of the Tour. Vingegaard countered to finish second and Richard Carapaz third. And that was the podium order at the end of the day.

### WEATHER

TEMPERATURE: 19°C
WIND: W 24km/h

### PROFILE

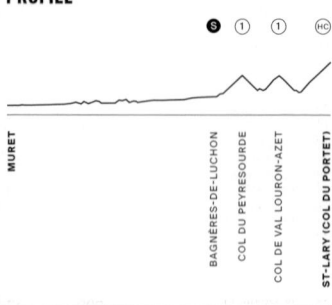

### BREAKAWAY
L. Pöstlberger (BOH), A. Perez (COF), D. van Poppel (IWG), D. Godon (ACT), A. Turgis (TEN), M. Chevalier (BBK)

### GENERAL CLASSIFICATION

| POS | | NAME | TEAM | TIME |
|---|---|---|---|---|
| 1. | — | T. Pogačar | UAD | 71:26:27 |
| 2. | ↑1 | J. Vingegaard | TJV | 5:39 |
| 3. | ↑1 | R. Carapaz | IGD | 5:43 |
| 4. | ↓2 | R. Urán | EFN | 7:17 |
| 5. | — | B. O'Connor | ACT | 7:34 |
| 6. | — | W. Kelderman | BOH | 8:06 |
| 7. | ↑1 | E. Mas | MOV | 9:48 |
| 8. | ↓1 | A. Lutsenko | APT | 10:04 |
| 9. | — | G. Martin | COF | 11:51 |
| 10. | — | P. Bilbao | TBV | 12:53 |

### KING OF THE MOUNTAINS

| POS | | NAME | TEAM | PTS |
|---|---|---|---|---|
| 1. | — | W. Poels | TBV | 78 |
| 2. | ↑5 | T. Pogačar | UAD | 67 |
| 3. | — | N. Quintana | ARK | 66 |

### POINTS

| POS | | NAME | TEAM | PTS |
|---|---|---|---|---|
| 1. | — | M. Cavendish | DQT | 287 |
| 2. | — | M. Matthews | BEX | 251 |
| 3. | — | S. Colbrelli | TBV | 201 |

### YOUNG RIDER

| POS | | NAME | TEAM | TIME |
|---|---|---|---|---|
| 1. | — | T. Pogačar | UAD | 71:26:27 |
| 2. | — | J. Vingegaard | TJV | 5:39 |
| 3. | — | D. Gaudu | GFC | 15:42 |

### TRIVIA
» This was Jonas Vingegaard's fifth top-ten finish in his debut Tour.

### BONUSES

| TYPE | NAME | TEAM |
|---|---|---|
| KOM 1 | A. Turgis | TEN |
| KOM 2 | A. Perez | COF |
| KOM 3 | T. Pogačar | UAD |
| Sprint 1 | D. van Poppel | IWG |

## STAGE RESULTS

| POS | NAME | TEAM | TIME |
|---|---|---|---|
| 1. | T. Pogačar | UAD | 5:03:31 |
| 2. | J. Vingegaard | TJV | 0:03 |
| 3. | R. Carapaz | IGD | 0:04 |
| 4. | D. Gaudu | GFC | 1:19 |
| 5. | B. O'Connor | ACT | 1:26 |
| 6. | W. Kelderman | BOH | 1:40 |
| 7. | P. Bilbao | TBV | 1:44 |
| 8. | S. Higuita | EFN | 1:49 |
| 9. | R. Urán | EFN | s.t. |
| 10. | D. Teuns | TBV | s.t. |
| 11. | E. Mas | MOV | 2:27 |
| 12. | A. Lutsenko | APT | 2:53 |
| 13. | G. Martin | COF | 3:39 |
| 14. | L. Meintjes | IWG | 3:41 |
| 15. | R. Guerreiro | EFN | 3:55 |
| 16. | E. Chaves | BEX | 4:46 |
| 17. | M. Cattaneo | DQT | s.t. |
| 18. | W. Poels | TBV | 5:26 |
| 19. | J. Castroviejo | IGD | 6:38 |
| 20. | B. Mollema | TFS | 7:27 |
| 21. | X. Meurisse | AFC | 7:35 |
| 22. | S. Kuss | TJV | 8:08 |
| 23. | Q. Pacher | BBK | 8:26 |
| 24. | A. Paret-Peintre | ACT | 9:28 |
| 25. | R. Majka | UAD | 9:33 |
| 26. | D. Godon | ACT | 11:47 |
| 27. | M. A. López | MOV | 11:50 |
| 28. | S. Henao | TQA | 12:14 |
| 29. | A. Valverde | MOV | s.t. |
| 30. | G. Thomas | IGD | 13:27 |
| 31. | E. Buchmann | BOH | s.t. |
| 32. | N. Quintana | ARK | 14:15 |
| 33. | R. Porte | IGD | 14:17 |
| 34. | M. Woods | ISN | 15:29 |
| 35. | A. Turgis | TEN | 15:37 |
| 36. | A. Perez | COF | 16:09 |
| 37. | V. de la Parte | TEN | 17:36 |
| 38. | P. Latour | TEN | s.t. |
| 39. | J. Alaphilippe | DQT | 18:56 |
| 40. | W. van Aert | TJV | s.t. |
| 41. | S. Geschke | COF | s.t. |
| 42. | D. van Baarle | IGD | s.t. |
| 43. | O. Fraile | APT | 19:28 |
| 44. | I. Izaguirre | APT | s.t. |
| 45. | J. Fuglsang | APT | 20:59 |
| 46. | F. Bonnamour | BBK | s.t. |
| 47. | B. Armirail | GFC | s.t. |
| 48. | T. Geoghegan Hart | IGD | 21:12 |
| 49. | M. Donovan | DSM | 21:55 |
| 50. | M. Mohorič | TBV | 21:58 |
| 51. | D. Formolo | UAD | 23:02 |
| 52. | S. Küng | GFC | 23:34 |
| 53. | T. De Gendt | LTS | s.t. |
| 54. | M. Schär | ACT | s.t. |
| 55. | M. Hirschi | UAD | 23:36 |
| 56. | G. Zimmermann | IWG | s.t. |
| 57. | D. Martin | ISN | 23:51 |
| 58. | B. McNulty | UAD | 24:31 |
| 59. | Je. Herrada | COF | 25:24 |
| 60. | C. Verona | MOV | s.t. |
| 61. | N. Politt | BOH | 25:36 |
| 62. | M. Chevalier | BBK | 26:13 |
| 63. | C. Rodriguez | TEN | 27:29 |
| 64. | R. Fernández | COF | 27:33 |
| 65. | M. Cort | EFN | 27:47 |
| 66. | S. Dillier | AFC | 28:06 |
| 67. | J. Rickaert | AFC | s.t. |
| 68. | J. Stuyven | TFS | 28:59 |
| 69. | T. Skujiņš | TFS | s.t. |
| 70. | K. Elissonde | TFS | s.t. |
| 71. | J. Arcas | MOV | s.t. |
| 72. | I. Erviti | MOV | s.t. |
| 73. | L. Rota | IWG | s.t. |
| 74. | G. Boivin | ISN | s.t. |
| 75. | M. Matthews | BEX | s.t. |
| 76. | J. Rutsch | EFN | s.t. |
| 77. | D. Oss | BOH | s.t. |
| 78. | K. Sbaragli | AFC | s.t. |
| 79. | C. Barthe | BBK | s.t. |
| 80. | H. Houle | APT | s.t. |
| 81. | M. Valgren | EFN | s.t. |
| 82. | V. Madouas | GFC | s.t. |
| 83. | C. Laporte | COF | s.t. |
| 84. | D. van Poppel | IWG | s.t. |
| 85. | É. Gesbert | ARK | s.t. |
| 86. | M. Teunissen | TJV | s.t. |
| 87. | J. Bakelants | IWG | s.t. |
| 88. | O. Naesen | ACT | s.t. |
| 89. | J. Nieuwenhuis | DSM | s.t. |
| 90. | P. Konrad | BOH | s.t. |
| 91. | O. Goldstein | ISN | s.t. |
| 92. | C. Gautier | BBK | s.t. |
| 93. | H. Sweeny | LTS | s.t. |
| 94. | J. Bernard | TFS | s.t. |
| 95. | F. Wright | TBV | s.t. |
| 96. | N. Powless | EFN | s.t. |
| 97. | K. Asgreen | DQT | s.t. |
| 98. | F. Doubey | TEN | s.t. |
| 99. | M. Bjerg | UAD | s.t. |
| 100. | P. Rolland | BBK | s.t. |
| 101. | L. Durbridge | BEX | s.t. |
| 102. | V. S. Laengen | UAD | s.t. |
| 103. | P. L. Périchon | COF | s.t. |
| 104. | L. Pöstlberger | BOH | s.t. |
| 105. | R. Costa | UAD | s.t. |
| 106. | J. Cabot | TEN | s.t. |
| 107. | J. Simon | TEN | s.t. |
| 108. | S. Colbrelli | TBV | 29:11 |
| 109. | I. Schelling | BOH | s.t. |
| 110. | A. Aranburu | APT | s.t. |
| 111. | B. Van Moer | LTS | 29:18 |
| 112. | C. Juul-Jensen | BEX | 29:28 |
| 113. | I. García Cortina | MOV | 30:03 |
| 114. | C. Pedersen | DSM | s.t. |
| 115. | J. Philipsen | AFC | 30:05 |
| 116. | P. Vakoč | AFC | s.t. |
| 117. | N. Eekhoff | DSM | 30:12 |
| 118. | Se. Bennett | TQA | 30:56 |
| 119. | M. Haller | TBV | 31:47 |
| 120. | P. Gilbert | LTS | s.t. |
| 121. | R. Zabel | ISN | s.t. |
| 122. | S. Bissegger | EFN | 32:22 |
| 123. | A. Greipel | ISN | s.t. |
| 124. | C. Barbero | TQA | s.t. |
| 125. | C. Swift | ARK | s.t. |
| 126. | M. Pedersen | TFS | s.t. |
| 127. | E. Theuns | TFS | s.t. |
| 128. | R. Hollenstein | ISN | s.t. |
| 129. | C. Froome | ISN | s.t. |
| 130. | D. Gruzdev | APT | s.t. |
| 131. | J. Wallays | COF | 33:44 |
| 132. | B. Cosnefroy | ACT | 33:52 |
| 133. | D. Devenyns | DQT | 34:10 |
| 134. | T. Declercq | DQT | s.t. |
| 135. | D. Ballerini | DQT | s.t. |
| 136. | M. Mørkøv | DQT | s.t. |
| 137. | G. Van Avermaet | ACT | s.t. |
| 138. | M. Kwiatkowski | IGD | s.t. |
| 139. | B. van Poppel | IWG | s.t. |
| 140. | M. Cavendish | DQT | s.t. |
| 141. | S. Clarke | TQA | s.t. |
| 142. | M. Walscheid | TQA | s.t. |
| 143. | L. Mezgec | BEX | s.t. |
| 144. | C. Bol | DSM | s.t. |

JUNE    WORLDTOUR MEN'S RACE

# TOUR DE FRANCE
Stage 18
15 July 2021
Pau–Luz Ardiden
129.7km

News broke in the morning that the Bahrain Victorious team hotel had been raided by police overnight. Acting on undisclosed evidence, they had searched the premises and examined personal belongings. The team's successes – not just at the Tour de France but across multiple races throughout the first half of 2021 – had generated considerable interest and, in the ever-wary circles of professional road racing, the odd raised eyebrow of suspicion. Many of the riders had not been left alone to get any sleep until the early hours of the morning. Fortunately perhaps for those sleep-deprived riders, this was the shortest of the mountain stages, at 129.7km. But the final 50km took the race over Tourmalet and straight onto the final climb of Luz Ardiden, both hors catégorie mountains. A succession of strong breakaways went clear on Tourmalet, every single one featuring an outstanding climber in the likes of Ruben Guerreiro and Julian Alaphilippe. In a defiant showing, Bahrain Victorious's Matej Mohorič was among their number, just as his teammate Wout Poels had been off the front earlier in the stage. But it was David Gaudu of Groupama-FDJ who took his chance best of all, having been paced across to the front of the race by his Breton teammate Valentin Madouas. Gaudu went clear over the top of Tourmalet and attacked the descent but, by the time he reached the final climb, his gap was negligible. The ensuing GC race saw Enric Mas attack with real intent for the first time in the race. But Pogačar rode him down and then attacked the rest, and for the second day in a row took a summit finish in the Pyrenees, with Vingegaard and Carapaz once again in second and third as the pecking order solidified. With all the climbing done, Pogačar had extended his lead on GC to a mighty 5 minutes 45 seconds with the final time trial still to come.

## TRIVIA
» Tadej Pogačar has now won three stages at each of the three Grand Tours he's competed in.

## WEATHER

TEMPERATURE  WIND
20°C  N 6km/h

## PROFILE

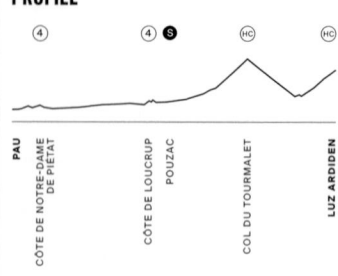

## BREAKAWAY
M. Mohorič (TBV), C. Juul-Jensen (BEX), S. Bennett (TQA), J. Alaphilippe (DQT), P. L. Périchon (COF)

## GENERAL CLASSIFICATION

| POS | | NAME | TEAM | TIME |
|---|---|---|---|---|
| 1. | — | T. Pogačar | UAD | 75:00:02 |
| 2. | — | J. Vingegaard | TJV | 5:45 |
| 3. | — | R. Carapaz | IGD | 5:51 |
| 4. | ↑1 | B. O'Connor | ACT | 8:18 |
| 5. | ↑1 | W. Kelderman | BOH | 8:50 |
| 6. | ↑1 | E. Mas | MOV | 10:11 |
| 7. | ↑1 | A. Lutsenko | APT | 11:22 |
| 8. | ↑1 | G. Martin | COF | 12:46 |
| 9. | ↑1 | P. Bilbao | TBV | 13:48 |
| 10. | ↓6 | R. Urán | EFN | 16:25 |

## KING OF THE MOUNTAINS

| POS | | NAME | TEAM | PTS |
|---|---|---|---|---|
| 1. | ↑1 | T. Pogačar | UAD | 107 |
| 2. | ↓1 | W. Poels | TBV | 88 |
| 3. | ↑3 | J. Vingegaard | TJV | 82 |

## POINTS

| POS | | NAME | TEAM | PTS |
|---|---|---|---|---|
| 1. | — | M. Cavendish | DQT | 298 |
| 2. | — | M. Matthews | BEX | 260 |
| 3. | — | S. Colbrelli | TBV | 208 |

## YOUNG RIDER

| POS | | NAME | TEAM | TIME |
|---|---|---|---|---|
| 1. | — | T. Pogačar | UAD | 75:00:02 |
| 2. | — | J. Vingegaard | TJV | 5:45 |
| 3. | — | D. Gaudu | GFC | 18:42 |

## BONUSES

| TYPE | NAME | TEAM |
|---|---|---|
| KOM 1 | C. Juul-Jensen | BEX |
| KOM 2 | J. Alaphilippe | DQT |
| KOM 3 | P. Latour | TEN |
| KOM 4 | T. Pogačar | UAD |
| Sprint 1 | J. Alaphilippe | DQT |

## STAGE RESULTS

| POS | NAME | TEAM | TIME |
|---|---|---|---|
| 1. | T. Pogačar | UAD | 3:33:45 |
| 2. | J. Vingegaard | TJV | 0:02 |
| 3. | R. Carapaz | IGD | s.t. |
| 4. | E. Mas | MOV | 0:13 |
| 5. | D. Martin | ISN | 0:24 |
| 6. | S. Kuss | TJV | 0:30 |
| 7. | S. Higuita | EFN | 0:33 |
| 8. | B. O'Connor | ACT | 0:34 |
| 9. | W. Kelderman | BOH | s.t. |
| 10. | A. Valverde | MOV | 0:40 |
| 11. | P. Bilbao | TBV | 0:45 |
| 12. | G. Martin | COF | s.t. |
| 13. | A. Lutsenko | APT | 1:08 |
| 14. | E. Buchmann | BOH | 1:15 |
| 15. | L. Meintjes | IWG | 1:43 |
| 16. | R. Majka | UAD | 1:46 |
| 17. | J. Castroviejo | IGD | 1:56 |
| 18. | W. Poels | TBV | 2:32 |
| 19. | D. Gaudu | GFC | 2:50 |
| 20. | X. Meurisse | AFC | 3:07 |
| 21. | E. Chaves | BEX | 3:15 |
| 22. | R. Guerreiro | EFN | s.t. |
| 23. | D. Teuns | TBV | s.t. |
| 24. | M. Cattaneo | DQT | 3:45 |
| 25. | F. Bonnamour | BBK | 3:57 |
| 26. | C. Rodríguez | TEN | s.t. |
| 27. | B. Mollema | TFS | 4:05 |
| 28. | M. Hirschi | UAD | s.t. |
| 29. | T. Geoghegan Hart | IGD | 4:34 |
| 30. | A. Paret-Peintre | ACT | 5:23 |
| 31. | N. Quintana | ARK | 5:57 |
| 32. | M. Schär | ACT | 6:18 |
| 33. | V. de la Parte | TEN | s.t. |
| 34. | P. Konrad | BOH | s.t. |
| 35. | M. Mohorič | TBV | 6:31 |
| 36. | W. van Aert | TJV | 6:37 |
| 37. | Q. Pacher | BBK | 7:15 |
| 38. | B. McNulty | UAD | 8:09 |
| 39. | S. Henao | TQA | s.t. |
| 40. | M. A. López | MOV | s.t. |
| 41. | M. Woods | ISN | 8:58 |
| 42. | M. Cort | EFN | s.t. |
| 43. | R. Urán | EFN | s.t. |
| 44. | N. Powless | EFN | s.t. |
| 45. | O. Naesen | ACT | s.t. |
| 46. | P. Latour | TEN | 10:27 |
| 47. | V. Madouas | GFC | 11:02 |
| 48. | I. Izagirre | APT | 12:05 |
| 49. | S. Dillier | AFC | 13:43 |
| 50. | S. Küng | GFC | s.t. |
| 51. | J. Arcas | MOV | s.t. |
| 52. | L. Rota | IWG | 14:05 |
| 53. | M. Chevalier | BBK | s.t. |
| 54. | O. Fraile | APT | 14:07 |
| 55. | H. Houle | APT | 14:15 |
| 56. | D. van Baarle | IGD | 14:47 |
| 57. | M. Kwiatkowski | IGD | s.t. |
| 58. | S. Geschke | COF | 16:12 |
| 59. | G. Thomas | IGD | 16:37 |
| 60. | Je. Herrada | COF | s.t. |
| 61. | C. Verona | MOV | s.t. |
| 62. | T. De Gendt | LTS | 17:05 |
| 63. | S. Colbrelli | TBV | 18:35 |
| 64. | M. Teunissen | TJV | s.t. |
| 65. | J. Bakelants | IWG | s.t. |
| 66. | J. Bernard | TFS | s.t. |
| 67. | R. Fernández | COF | s.t. |
| 68. | I. Erviti | MOV | s.t. |
| 69. | F. Doubey | TEN | s.t. |
| 70. | J. Stuyven | TFS | s.t. |
| 71. | J. Rutsch | EFN | s.t. |
| 72. | H. Sweeny | LTS | s.t. |
| 73. | J. Fuglsang | APT | s.t. |
| 74. | M. Valgren | EFN | s.t. |
| 75. | T. Skujiņš | TFS | s.t. |
| 76. | P. Rolland | BBK | s.t. |
| 77. | K. Elissonde | TFS | 19:54 |
| 78. | J. Alaphilippe | DQT | s.t. |
| 79. | D. Gruzdev | APT | 20:48 |
| 80. | I. Schelling | BOH | 21:08 |
| 81. | I. García Cortina | MOV | 23:13 |
| 82. | D. Oss | BOH | s.t. |
| 83. | G. Boivin | ISN | s.t. |
| 84. | C. Barthe | BBK | s.t. |
| 85. | S. Bissegger | EFN | s.t. |
| 86. | M. Haller | TBV | s.t. |
| 87. | D. Formolo | UAD | s.t. |
| 88. | K. Sbaragli | AFC | s.t. |
| 89. | D. Godon | ACT | s.t. |
| 90. | O. Goldstein | ISN | s.t. |
| 91. | C. Gautier | BBK | s.t. |
| 92. | J. Rickaert | AFC | s.t. |
| 93. | F. Wright | TBV | s.t. |
| 94. | C. Barbero | TQA | s.t. |
| 95. | É. Gesbert | ARK | s.t. |
| 96. | B. Van Moer | LTS | s.t. |
| 97. | J. Philipsen | AFC | s.t. |
| 98. | G. Zimmermann | IWG | s.t. |
| 99. | M. Donovan | DSM | s.t. |
| 100. | D. van Poppel | IWG | s.t. |
| 101. | R. Porte | IGD | s.t. |
| 102. | B. van Poppel | IWG | s.t. |
| 103. | J. Simon | TEN | s.t. |
| 104. | C. Swift | ARK | s.t. |
| 105. | L. Durbridge | BEX | s.t. |
| 106. | C. Juul-Jensen | BEX | s.t. |
| 107. | V. S. Laengen | UAD | s.t. |
| 108. | A. Aranburu | APT | s.t. |
| 109. | B. Armirail | GFC | s.t. |
| 110. | R. Costa | UAD | s.t. |
| 111. | J. Cabot | TEN | s.t. |
| 112. | A. Turgis | TEN | s.t. |
| 113. | C. Pedersen | DSM | s.t. |
| 114. | S. Clarke | TQA | s.t. |
| 115. | M. Bjerg | UAD | s.t. |
| 116. | P. Vakoč | AFC | s.t. |
| 117. | N. Politt | BOH | s.t. |
| 118. | C. Laporte | COF | 24:34 |
| 119. | M. Matthews | BEX | 24:49 |
| 120. | N. Eekhoff | DSM | 25:03 |
| 121. | G. Van Avermaet | ACT | s.t. |
| 122. | A. Perez | COF | 26:37 |
| 123. | K. Asgreen | DQT | 27:36 |
| 124. | J. Nieuwenhuis | DSM | s.t. |
| 125. | P. Gilbert | LTS | 27:57 |
| 126. | A. Greipel | ISN | s.t. |
| 127. | R. Zabel | ISN | s.t. |
| 128. | R. Hollenstein | ISN | s.t. |
| 129. | C. Froome | ISN | s.t. |
| 130. | B. Cosnefroy | ACT | s.t. |
| 131. | L. Mezgec | BEX | s.t. |
| 132. | P. L. Périchon | COF | s.t. |
| 133. | M. Pedersen | TFS | s.t. |
| 134. | E. Theuns | TFS | s.t. |
| 135. | M. Walscheid | TQA | s.t. |
| 136. | L. Pöstlberger | BOH | s.t. |
| 137. | J. Wallays | COF | s.t. |
| 138. | Se. Bennett | TQA | 28:10 |
| 139. | C. Bol | DSM | 29:35 |
| 140. | M. Mørkøv | DQT | 32:06 |
| 141. | T. Declercq | DQT | s.t. |
| 142. | D. Devenyns | DQT | s.t. |
| 143. | D. Ballerini | DQT | s.t. |
| 144. | M. Cavendish | DQT | s.t. |

JUNE  WORLDTOUR MEN'S RACE

## TOUR DE FRANCE
Stage 19
16 July 2021
Mourenx–Libourne
207km

Eddy Merckx was at the start line next to the eponymous Merckx velodrome in Mourenx, the site of one the Belgian's greatest solo victories in the 1969 Tour de France. It was a coincidence that the race was to start there, but that his pre-planned visit to the Tour would coincide with Mark Cavendish's penultimate opportunity to better the Merckx record was nothing short of extraordinary serendipity. The two men exchanged a hug for the cameras at the start line, during which Merckx was heard to tell Cavendish that he hoped he'd break the record that day. The course was certainly well designed for a bunch sprint: a long, straight, flat northbound slog through Les Landes. But, with such a depleted sprinters' field, it was not clear that Deceuninck-QuickStep could expect much, if any, support as they tried to control the race. After the intermediate sprint, the race really started and Cavendish's team looked content to let a big breakaway go. They placed Davide Ballerini in the move, and the Italian seemed to be working, which sent a signal to the rest of the peloton that Deceuninck-QuickStep were not interested in controlling the race. That led to a prolonged tug-of-war between a break of well over 20 mostly committed riders and a chase organised mostly by Israel Start-Up Nation and Ineos Grenadiers. It was a telling sight, watching former Tour de France winners Chris Froome and Geraint Thomas doing so much work in a doomed attempt to get a rider in the breakaway. Bahrain Victorious were also part of the unsuccessful chase, which was curious given that, in Matej Mohorič, they had a proven race winner up the road. And Mohorič used the rolling terrain on the road to Libourne to his advantage, pulling clear, and then holding on to his lead as the chase behind formed, re-formed and generally squabbled. Crossing the line to take his second victory at the race, the Slovenian made a gesture towards those who doubted the team's propriety, by 'zipping up' his mouth with a finger drawn from right to left. He went on very articulately to explain that, while he was fully behind the need for anti-doping vigilance, the attitude of the police who had raided his room had, he claimed, been heavy-handed.

## WEATHER

TEMPERATURE   WIND
23°C          N 9km/h

## PROFILE

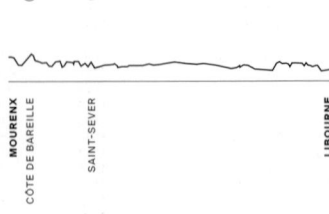

MOURENX · CÔTE DE BAREILLE · SAINT-SEVER · LIBOURNE

## BREAKAWAY

N. Politt (BOH), E. Theuns (TFS), M. Teunissen (TJV), J. Stuyven (TFS), D. Ballerini (DQT), C. Laporte (COF), S. Dillier (AFC), M. Valgren (EFN), E. Gesbert (ARK), C. Pedersen (DSM), B. Van Moer (LTS), O. Fraile (APT), I. Izaguirre (APT), D. Gruzdev (APT), M. Walscheid (TQA), A. Turgis (TEN), A. Valverde (MOV), J. Arcas (MOV), I. García Cortina (MOV), G. Van Avermaet (ACT)

## GENERAL CLASSIFICATION

| POS | NAME | TEAM | TIME |
|---|---|---|---|
| 1. — | T. Pogačar | UAD | 79:40:09 |
| 2. — | J. Vingegaard | TJV | 5:45 |
| 3. — | R. Carapaz | IGD | 5:51 |
| 4. — | B. O'Connor | ACT | 8:18 |
| 5. — | W. Kelderman | BOH | 8:50 |
| 6. — | E. Mas | MOV | 10:11 |
| 7. — | A. Lutsenko | APT | 11:22 |
| 8. — | G. Martin | COF | 12:46 |
| 9. — | P. Bilbao | TBV | 13:48 |
| 10.— | R. Urán | EFN | 16:25 |

## KING OF THE MOUNTAINS

| POS | NAME | TEAM | PTS |
|---|---|---|---|
| 1. — | T. Pogačar | UAD | 107 |
| 2. — | W. Poels | TBV | 88 |
| 3. — | J. Vingegaard | TJV | 82 |

## POINTS

| POS | NAME | TEAM | PTS |
|---|---|---|---|
| 1. — | M. Cavendish | DQT | 304 |
| 2. — | M. Matthews | BEX | 269 |
| 3. — | S. Colbrelli | TBV | 216 |

## YOUNG RIDER

| POS | NAME | TEAM | TIME |
|---|---|---|---|
| 1. — | T. Pogačar | UAD | 79:40:09 |
| 2. — | J. Vingegaard | TJV | 5:45 |
| 3. — | D. Gaudu | GFC | 18:42 |

## BONUSES

| TYPE | NAME | TEAM |
|---|---|---|
| KOM 1 | J. Rutsch | EFN |
| Sprint 1 | G. Zimmermann | IWG |

## STAGE RESULTS

| POS | NAME | TEAM | TIME |
|---|---|---|---|
| 1. | M. Mohorič | TBV | 4:19:17 |
| 2. | C. Laporte | COF | 0:58 |
| 3. | C. Pedersen | DSM | s.t. |
| 4. | M. Teunissen | TJV | 1:02 |
| 5. | N. Politt | BOH | 1:08 |
| 6. | E. Theuns | TFS | s.t. |
| 7. | M. Valgren | EFN | s.t. |
| 8. | G. Zimmermann | IWG | s.t. |
| 9. | A. Turgis | TEN | 1:10 |
| 10. | J. Stuyven | TFS | s.t. |
| 11. | J. Bernard | TFS | 2:37 |
| 12. | M. Walscheid | TQA | s.t. |
| 13. | D. Ballerini | DQT | s.t. |
| 14. | S. Dillier | AFC | s.t. |
| 15. | J. Rutsch | EFN | s.t. |
| 16. | É. Gesbert | ARK | s.t. |
| 17. | B. Van Moer | LTS | s.t. |
| 18. | I. Izagirre | APT | 2:43 |
| 19. | F. Bonnamour | BBK | 2:57 |
| 20. | S. Clarke | TQA | 10:05 |
| 21. | M. Hirschi | UAD | 20:50 |
| 22. | R. Costa | UAD | s.t. |
| 23. | R. Majka | UAD | s.t. |
| 24. | V. S. Laengen | UAD | s.t. |
| 25. | M. Bjerg | UAD | s.t. |
| 26. | T. Pogačar | UAD | s.t. |
| 27. | B. McNulty | UAD | s.t. |
| 28. | D. Formolo | UAD | s.t. |
| 29. | J. Arcas | MOV | s.t. |
| 30. | A. Valverde | MOV | s.t. |
| 31. | I. García Cortina | MOV | s.t. |
| 32. | L. Rota | IWG | s.t. |
| 33. | S. Colbrelli | TBV | s.t. |
| 34. | E. Mas | MOV | s.t. |
| 35. | F. Wright | TBV | s.t. |
| 36. | P. Bilbao | TBV | s.t. |
| 37. | I. Erviti | MOV | s.t. |
| 38. | D. Gruzdev | APT | s.t. |
| 39. | C. Verona | MOV | s.t. |
| 40. | M. Kwiatkowski | IGD | s.t. |
| 41. | J. Fuglsang | APT | s.t. |
| 42. | Q. Pacher | BBK | s.t. |
| 43. | W. van Aert | TJV | s.t. |
| 44. | M. Chevalier | BBK | s.t. |
| 45. | A. Lutsenko | APT | s.t. |
| 46. | J. Vingegaard | TJV | s.t. |
| 47. | S. Kuss | TJV | s.t. |
| 48. | H. Houle | APT | s.t. |
| 49. | P. Gilbert | LTS | s.t. |
| 50. | J. Castroviejo | IGD | s.t. |
| 51. | R. Carapaz | IGD | s.t. |
| 52. | G. Thomas | IGD | s.t. |
| 53. | A. Paret-Peintre | ACT | s.t. |
| 54. | T. De Gendt | LTS | s.t. |
| 55. | M. Schär | ACT | s.t. |
| 56. | D. van Baarle | IGD | s.t. |
| 57. | D. Gaudu | GFC | s.t. |
| 58. | D. Teuns | TBV | s.t. |
| 59. | B. Cosnefroy | ACT | s.t. |
| 60. | C. Rodríguez | TEN | s.t. |
| 61. | T. Geoghegan Hart | IGD | s.t. |
| 62. | B. O'Connor | ACT | s.t. |
| 63. | D. Godon | ACT | s.t. |
| 64. | V. Madouas | GFC | s.t. |
| 65. | C. Barthe | BBK | s.t. |
| 66. | N. Powless | EFN | s.t. |
| 67. | B. Armirail | GFC | s.t. |
| 68. | R. Zabel | ISN | s.t. |
| 69. | E. Buchmann | BOH | s.t. |
| 70. | G. Van Avermaet | ACT | s.t. |
| 71. | T. Declercq | DQT | s.t. |
| 72. | R. Hollenstein | ISN | s.t. |
| 73. | M. Haller | TBV | s.t. |
| 74. | K. Sbaragli | AFC | s.t. |
| 75. | J. Wallays | COF | s.t. |
| 76. | M. Cort | EFN | s.t. |
| 77. | J. Philipsen | AFC | s.t. |
| 78. | G. Martin | COF | s.t. |
| 79. | L. Meintjes | IWG | s.t. |
| 80. | H. Sweeny | LTS | s.t. |
| 81. | R. Porte | IGD | s.t. |
| 82. | D. Oss | BOH | s.t. |
| 83. | W. Kelderman | BOH | s.t. |
| 84. | J. Bakelants | IWG | s.t. |
| 85. | R. Guerreiro | EFN | s.t. |
| 86. | E. Chaves | BEX | s.t. |
| 87. | R. Fernández | COF | s.t. |
| 88. | P. Konrad | BOH | s.t. |
| 89. | S. Bissegger | EFN | s.t. |
| 90. | P. L. Périchon | COF | s.t. |
| 91. | C. Gautier | BBK | s.t. |
| 92. | W. Poels | TBV | s.t. |
| 93. | P. Rolland | BBK | s.t. |
| 94. | R. Urán | EFN | s.t. |
| 95. | J. Simon | TEN | s.t. |
| 96. | Je. Herrada | COF | s.t. |
| 97. | B. Mollema | TFS | s.t. |
| 98. | S. Geschke | COF | s.t. |
| 99. | O. Fraile | APT | s.t. |
| 100. | V. de la Parte | TEN | s.t. |
| 101. | P. Vakoč | AFC | s.t. |
| 102. | P. Latour | TEN | s.t. |
| 103. | F. Doubey | TEN | s.t. |
| 104. | J. Alaphilippe | DQT | s.t. |
| 105. | M. Cattaneo | DQT | s.t. |
| 106. | X. Meurisse | AFC | s.t. |
| 107. | O. Naesen | ACT | s.t. |
| 108. | M. Matthews | BEX | s.t. |
| 109. | D. Devenyns | DQT | s.t. |
| 110. | L. Mezgec | BEX | s.t. |
| 111. | M. Cavendish | DQT | s.t. |
| 112. | B. van Poppel | IWG | s.t. |
| 113. | D. van Poppel | IWG | s.t. |
| 114. | A. Aranburu | APT | s.t. |
| 115. | M. Mørkøv | DQT | s.t. |
| 116. | S. Küng | GFC | s.t. |
| 117. | C. Juul-Jensen | BEX | s.t. |
| 118. | A. Greipel | ISN | s.t. |
| 119. | O. Goldstein | ISN | s.t. |
| 120. | C. Bol | DSM | s.t. |
| 121. | T. Skujiņš | TFS | s.t. |
| 122. | M. Pedersen | TFS | s.t. |
| 123. | J. Nieuwenhuis | DSM | s.t. |
| 124. | C. Barbero | TQA | s.t. |
| 125. | N. Quintana | ARK | s.t. |
| 126. | S. Higuita | EFN | s.t. |
| 127. | C. Swift | ARK | s.t. |
| 128. | C. Froome | ISN | s.t. |
| 129. | G. Boivin | ISN | s.t. |
| 130. | L. Durbridge | BEX | s.t. |
| 131. | D. Martin | ISN | s.t. |
| 132. | M. Donovan | DSM | s.t. |
| 133. | Se. Bennett | TQA | s.t. |
| 134. | S. Henao | TQA | s.t. |
| 135. | N. Eekhoff | DSM | s.t. |
| 136. | A. Perez | COF | s.t. |
| 137. | K. Elissonde | TFS | s.t. |
| 138. | I. Schelling | BOH | s.t. |
| 139. | L. Pöstlberger | BOH | s.t. |
| 140. | J. Cabot | TEN | s.t. |
| 141. | J. Rickaert | AFC | s.t. |
| 142. | K. Asgreen | DQT | s.t. |

## TRIVIA

» All of the three Slovenian Tour de France stage winners (Mohorič, Roglič and Pogačar) have now won more than one stage each.

JUNE    WORLDTOUR MEN'S RACE

## TOUR DE FRANCE
Stage 20 (ITT)
17 July 2021
Libourne–Saint-Émilion
30.8km

### WEATHER

TEMPERATURE  WIND
26°C         N 9km/h

### PROFILE

LIBOURNE — SAINT-ÉMILION

For those with nothing much at stake in the GC, this was simply a beautiful ride through the vineyards of Pomerol and St Emilion. During a similarly long test to stage 5's ITT, there hung over the race a sense that there was not much that could move on GC; the gaps between the key riders seemed baked in – particularly the podium places. One cameo that caught the eye was the low-key battle fought by Guillaume Martin to hold off Pello Bilbao in ninth place, something the Frenchman achieved with 31 seconds in hand, allowing him to finish a hugely creditable eighth overall. In fact, nothing changed on GC. Pogačar – understandably not as fresh as he had been in the opening week – was unable to replicate his success from Laval. But that opened the door to the stage hunters, most notably Kasper Asgreen, who found himself in the hot seat for a prolonged stay. Stefan Küng appeared to be going faster than the Dane but then faded over the second half of the course. Jonas Vingegaard, setting off second from last, pulled off another attention-grabbing time trial that will have been noted by all his future Grand Tour rivals, Pogačar included. Vingegaard finished third once again, 25 seconds faster than Pogačar, but it was Wout van Aert who once more stole the day. The Belgian, who had undergone appendix surgery in May, appeared to be getting stronger the longer the race went on. He put 21 seconds into Asgreen's time to take the stage, adding it to his victory on the Mont Ventoux stage, and notching up a third win from Jumbo-Visma. But the time trial acted as long-known confirmation that in 2021 no one was in the same class as 22-year-old Tadej Pogačar, who had raced two Tours de France and won them both. And he'd done that earlier in his career than even the great Eddy Merckx. ⓝⓑ

### GENERAL CLASSIFICATION

| POS | NAME | TEAM | TIME |
|---|---|---|---|
| 1. — | T. Pogačar | UAD | 80:16:59 |
| 2. — | J. Vingegaard | TJV | 5:20 |
| 3. — | R. Carapaz | IGD | 7:03 |
| 4. — | B. O'Connor | ACT | 10:02 |
| 5. — | W. Kelderman | BOH | 10:13 |
| 6. — | E. Mas | MOV | 11:43 |
| 7. — | A. Lutsenko | APT | 12:23 |
| 8. — | G. Martin | COF | 15:33 |
| 9. — | P. Bilbao | TBV | 16:04 |
| 10.— | R. Urán | EFN | 18:34 |

### KING OF THE MOUNTAINS

| POS | NAME | TEAM | PTS |
|---|---|---|---|
| 1. — | T. Pogačar | UAD | 107 |
| 2. — | W. Poels | TBV | 88 |
| 3. — | J. Vingegaard | TJV | 82 |

### POINTS

| POS | NAME | TEAM | PTS |
|---|---|---|---|
| 1. — | M. Cavendish | DQT | 304 |
| 2. — | M. Matthews | BEX | 269 |
| 3. — | S. Colbrelli | TBV | 216 |

### TRIVIA

» Wout van Aert is the first Belgian in 36 years to win a Tour de France ITT stage since Eric Vanderaerden in 1985.

### YOUNG RIDER

| POS | NAME | TEAM | TIME |
|---|---|---|---|
| 1. — | T. Pogačar | UAD | 80:16:59 |
| 2. — | J. Vingegaard | TJV | 5:20 |
| 3. — | D. Gaudu | GFC | 21:21 |

## STAGE RESULTS

| POS | NAME | TEAM | TIME |
|---|---|---|---|
| 1. | W. van Aert | TJV | 35:53 |
| 2. | K. Asgreen | DQT | 0:21 |
| 3. | J. Vingegaard | TJV | 0:32 |
| 4. | S. Küng | GFC | 0:38 |
| 5. | S. Bissegger | EFN | 0:44 |
| 6. | M. Cattaneo | DQT | 0:49 |
| 7. | M. Bjerg | UAD | 0:52 |
| 8. | T. Pogačar | UAD | 0:57 |
| 9. | M. Cort | EFN | 1:00 |
| 10. | D. van Baarle | IGD | 1:21 |
| 11. | B. McNulty | UAD | 1:35 |
| 12. | B. Armirail | GFC | 1:46 |
| 13. | J. Castroviejo | IGD | 1:47 |
| 14. | O. Fraile | APT | s.t. |
| 15. | F. Wright | TBV | 1:56 |
| 16. | A. Lutsenko | APT | 1:58 |
| 17. | M. Walscheid | TQA | 2:01 |
| 18. | H. Sweeny | LTS | s.t. |
| 19. | J. Alaphilippe | DQT | 2:05 |
| 20. | A. Perez | COF | s.t. |
| 21. | L. Durbridge | BEX | s.t. |
| 22. | D. Devenyns | DQT | 2:06 |
| 23. | R. Carapaz | IGD | 2:09 |
| 24. | N. Powless | EFN | 2:16 |
| 25. | J. Rickaert | AFC | 2:19 |
| 26. | W. Kelderman | BOH | 2:20 |
| 27. | E. Mas | MOV | 2:29 |
| 28. | B. Mollema | TFS | 2:32 |
| 29. | H. Houle | APT | 2:33 |
| 30. | X. Meurisse | AFC | 2:40 |
| 31. | B. O'Connor | ACT | 2:41 |
| 32. | R. Guerreiro | EFN | s.t. |
| 33. | T. De Gendt | LTS | 2:42 |
| 34. | C. Swift | ARK | 2:43 |
| 35. | P. Latour | TEN | 2:45 |
| 36. | A. Paret-Peintre | ACT | s.t. |
| 37. | J. Stuyven | TFS | 2:47 |
| 38. | C. Laporte | COF | 3:04 |
| 39. | D. Teuns | TBV | s.t. |
| 40. | R. Urán | EFN | 3:06 |
| 41. | L. Meintjes | IWG | 3:11 |
| 42. | P. Bilbao | TBV | 3:13 |
| 43. | R. Porte | IGD | 3:15 |
| 44. | R. Costa | UAD | 3:19 |
| 45. | M. Valgren | EFN | 3:22 |
| 46. | S. Higuita | EFN | 3:23 |
| 47. | G. Thomas | IGD | 3:28 |
| 48. | J. Fuglsang | APT | 3:35 |
| 49. | D. Gaudu | GFC | 3:36 |
| 50. | P. L. Périchon | COF | 3:41 |
| 51. | M. Mørkøv | DQT | 3:42 |
| 52. | S. Kuss | TJV | 3:44 |
| 53. | G. Martin | COF | s.t. |
| 54. | N. Eekhoff | DSM | 3:47 |
| 55. | V. Madouas | GFC | 3:52 |
| 56. | V. S. Laengen | UAD | 3:54 |
| 57. | J. Rutsch | EFN | s.t. |
| 58. | B. Van Moer | LTS | 3:56 |
| 59. | D. Oss | BOH | 3:58 |
| 60. | R. Majka | UAD | 4:00 |
| 61. | D. Godon | ACT | s.t. |
| 62. | O. Goldstein | ISN | 4:01 |
| 63. | P. Gilbert | LTS | s.t. |
| 64. | M. Chevalier | BBK | 4:07 |
| 65. | C. Barthe | BBK | 4:11 |
| 66. | M. Cavendish | DQT | 4:12 |
| 67. | O. Naesen | ACT | 4:13 |
| 68. | J. Bakelants | IWG | 4:17 |
| 69. | I. Izaguirre | APT | 4:18 |
| 70. | J. Bernard | TFS | s.t. |
| 71. | L. Rota | IWG | 4:20 |
| 72. | N. Politt | BOH | 4:22 |
| 73. | A. Valverde | MOV | 4:23 |
| 74. | T. Geoghegan Hart | IGD | s.t. |
| 75. | M. Pedersen | TFS | 4:24 |
| 76. | M. Schär | ACT | 4:25 |
| 77. | C. Rodríguez | TEN | s.t. |
| 78. | M. Matthews | BEX | 4:26 |
| 79. | K. Elissonde | TFS | s.t. |
| 80. | Q. Pacher | BBK | s.t. |
| 81. | I. Erviti | MOV | 4:27 |
| 82. | T. Declercq | DQT | s.t. |
| 83. | B. van Poppel | IWG | 4:28 |
| 84. | D. van Poppel | IWG | s.t. |
| 85. | E. Buchmann | BOH | 4:30 |
| 86. | D. Ballerini | DQT | s.t. |
| 87. | J. Wallays | COF | s.t. |
| 88. | T. Skujiņš | TFS | s.t. |
| 89. | F. Doubey | TEN | 4:31 |
| 90. | R. Zabel | ISN | 4:32 |
| 91. | W. Poels | TBV | s.t. |
| 92. | D. Martin | ISN | 4:33 |
| 93. | I. García Cortina | MOV | 4:34 |
| 94. | D. Formolo | UAD | 4:38 |
| 95. | S. Clarke | TQA | 4:39 |
| 96. | M. Donovan | DSM | s.t. |
| 97. | J. Arcas | MOV | 4:40 |
| 98. | V. de la Parte | TEN | 4:43 |
| 99. | C. Juul-Jensen | BEX | 4:44 |
| 100. | L. Pöstlberger | BOH | 4:45 |
| 101. | M. Hirschi | UAD | s.t. |
| 102. | K. Sbaragli | AFC | 4:49 |
| 103. | A. Turgis | TEN | 4:50 |
| 104. | R. Hollenstein | ISN | 4:56 |
| 105. | Je. Herrada | COF | 4:58 |
| 106. | S. Colbrelli | TBV | 5:00 |
| 107. | E. Theuns | TFS | 5:04 |
| 108. | A. Aranburu | APT | 5:07 |
| 109. | J. Nieuwenhuis | DSM | s.t. |
| 110. | F. Bonnamour | BBK | 5:11 |
| 111. | C. Pedersen | DSM | s.t. |
| 112. | G. Van Avermaet | ACT | 5:12 |
| 113. | A. Greipel | ISN | 5:14 |
| 114. | C. Gautier | BBK | s.t. |
| 115. | P. Vakoč | AFC | 5:15 |
| 116. | M. Teunissen | TJV | 5:16 |
| 117. | G. Zimmermann | IWG | 5:17 |
| 118. | L. Mezgec | BEX | s.t. |
| 119. | C. Bol | DSM | 5:23 |
| 120. | J. Simon | TEN | s.t. |
| 121. | P. Konrad | BOH | 5:24 |
| 122. | D. Gruzdev | APT | 5:25 |
| 123. | C. Froome | ISN | 5:28 |
| 124. | G. Boivin | ISN | 5:32 |
| 125. | R. Fernández | COF | 5:33 |
| 126. | I. Schelling | BOH | 5:40 |
| 127. | S. Henao | TQA | 5:43 |
| 128. | N. Quintana | ARK | 5:44 |
| 129. | C. Barbero | TQA | 5:46 |
| 130. | M. Kwiatkowski | IGD | s.t. |
| 131. | J. Philipsen | AFC | 5:47 |
| 132. | J. Cabot | TEN | 5:50 |
| 133. | S. Geschke | COF | s.t. |
| 134. | M. Haller | TBV | 5:53 |
| 135. | P. Rolland | BBK | 5:54 |
| 136. | C. Verona | MOV | 5:56 |
| 137. | B. Cosnefroy | ACT | 5:57 |
| 138. | S. Dillier | AFC | 6:04 |
| 139. | Se. Bennett | TQA | 6:09 |
| 140. | M. Mohorič | TBV | 6:11 |
| 141. | É. Gesbert | ARK | 6:14 |
| 142. | E. Chaves | BEX | 6:38 |

JUNE  WORLDTOUR MEN'S RACE

## TOUR DE FRANCE
Stage 21
18 July 2021
Chatou–Paris Champs-Élysées
108.4km

It was an afternoon of immense pressure for Mark Cavendish, who had seen his chance of bettering the Merckx record slip through his fingers on stage 19. The Champs-Élysées stage, however, was not an opportunity to spurn. Four times in the past, Cavendish had ridden to victory on the renowned cobbles. But this time, the race organisation had moved the finish line further up the avenue, away from the Place de la Concorde. This slight adjustment would change everything about the sprint, doubling the distance from the final corner onto the finishing straight. Was that what unsettled the smooth workings of the Deceuninck-QuickStep lead-out? Or was it the work they'd already had to do to control a race that was so short of dominant sprinters' teams? Either way, Cavendish had been dislodged from his lead-out train before entering the tunnel under the Jardin des Tuileries for the final time. Though he regained his position, he lost Michael Mørkøv again as they hit the Place de la Concorde, opting instead to take the wheel of Wout van Aert. Cavendish later confessed that perhaps this had been a tactical error. But, more pertinently, he was up against a fearsome opponent in Van Aert. The Belgian – a decade younger than Cavendish – was that bit fresher, that much stronger, and held all the other sprinters at bay to take a famous win. In doing so, he emulated Bernard Hinault and Eddy Merckx, the only other riders in Tour history to have won a sprint, a mountain stage and a time trial all in the same race. Though Cavendish would have to wait another year to try and take the record outright, his green jersey and four stage wins were historic and rank among the greatest comebacks of all time. The man in yellow, though, Tadej Pogačar, had crushed the life out of the race and won more emphatically than anyone in a generation. The legacy he was building was happening at warp speed: twice inside a year he had won the Tour de France. (NB)

### TRIVIA
» The last rider to win a sprint, TT and mountain stage in the same Tour was Bernard Hinault in 1979. Eddy Merckx also did it in 1974.

### WEATHER
TEMPERATURE  WIND
27°C  NE 22km/h

### PROFILE

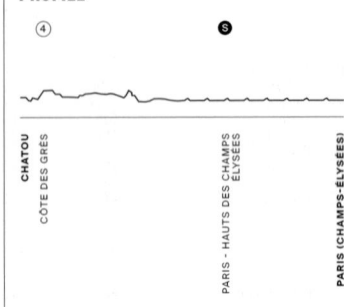

### BREAKAWAY
H. Sweeny (LTS), S. Bissegger (EFN), C. Pedersen (DSM), I. Schelling (BOH), M. Valgren (EFN), B. Van Moer (LTS), F. Bonnamour (BBK)

### GENERAL CLASSIFICATION
| POS | NAME | TEAM | TIME |
|---|---|---|---|
| 1. — | T. Pogačar | UAD | 82:56:36 |
| 2. — | J. Vingegaard | TJV | 5:20 |
| 3. — | R. Carapaz | IGD | 7:03 |
| 4. — | B. O'Connor | ACT | 10:02 |
| 5. — | W. Kelderman | BOH | 10:13 |
| 6. — | E. Mas | MOV | 11:43 |
| 7. — | A. Lutsenko | APT | 12:23 |
| 8. — | G. Martin | COF | 15:33 |
| 9. — | P. Bilbao | TBV | 16:04 |
| 10.— | R. Urán | EFN | 18:34 |

### KING OF THE MOUNTAINS
| POS | NAME | TEAM | PTS |
|---|---|---|---|
| 1. — | T. Pogačar | UAD | 107 |
| 2. — | W. Poels | TBV | 88 |
| 3. — | J. Vingegaard | TJV | 82 |

### POINTS
| POS | NAME | TEAM | PTS |
|---|---|---|---|
| 1. — | M. Cavendish | DQT | 337 |
| 2. — | M. Matthews | BEX | 291 |
| 3. — | S. Colbrelli | TBV | 227 |

### YOUNG RIDER
| POS | NAME | TEAM | TIME |
|---|---|---|---|
| 1. — | T. Pogačar | UAD | 82:56:36 |
| 2. — | J. Vingegaard | TJV | 5:20 |
| 3. — | D. Gaudu | GFC | 21:50 |

### BONUSES
| TYPE | NAME | TEAM |
|---|---|---|
| KOM 1 | M. Bjerg | UAD |
| Sprint 1 | S. Bissegger | EFN |

## STAGE RESULTS

| POS | NAME | TEAM | TIME |
|---|---|---|---|
| 1. | W. van Aert | TJV | 2:39:37 |
| 2. | J. Philipsen | AFC | s.t. |
| 3. | M. Cavendish | DQT | s.t. |
| 4. | L. Mezgec | BEX | s.t. |
| 5. | A. Greipel | ISN | s.t. |
| 6. | D. van Poppel | IWG | s.t. |
| 7. | M. Matthews | BEX | s.t. |
| 8. | A. Aranburu | APT | s.t. |
| 9. | C. Barthe | BBK | s.t. |
| 10. | M. Walscheid | TQA | s.t. |
| 11. | D. Oss | BOH | s.t. |
| 12. | I. García Cortina | MOV | s.t. |
| 13. | S. Colbrelli | TBV | s.t. |
| 14. | S. Dillier | AFC | s.t. |
| 15. | M. Cort | EFN | s.t. |
| 16. | L. Pöstlberger | BOH | s.t. |
| 17. | A. Perez | COF | s.t. |
| 18. | M. Pedersen | TFS | s.t. |
| 19. | C. Swift | ARK | s.t. |
| 20. | J. Arcas | MOV | s.t. |
| 21. | C. Bol | DSM | s.t. |
| 22. | M. Teunissen | TJV | s.t. |
| 23. | R. Zabel | ISN | s.t. |
| 24. | J. Simon | TEN | s.t. |
| 25. | N. Eekhoff | DSM | s.t. |
| 26. | É. Gesbert | ARK | s.t. |
| 27. | M. Schär | ACT | s.t. |
| 28. | K. Sbaragli | AFC | s.t. |
| 29. | G. Boivin | ISN | s.t. |
| 30. | D. Godon | ACT | s.t. |
| 31. | N. Politt | BOH | s.t. |
| 32. | B. O'Connor | ACT | s.t. |
| 33. | W. Kelderman | BOH | s.t. |
| 34. | D. van Baarle | IGD | s.t. |
| 35. | V. Madouas | GFC | s.t. |
| 36. | S. Kuss | TJV | s.t. |
| 37. | C. Laporte | COF | s.t. |
| 38. | M. Haller | TBV | s.t. |
| 39. | J. Stuyven | TFS | s.t. |
| 40. | J. Bakelants | IWG | s.t. |
| 41. | J. Rickaert | AFC | s.t. |
| 42. | M. Mørkøv | DQT | s.t. |
| 43. | F. Wright | TBV | s.t. |
| 44. | A. Lutsenko | APT | s.t. |
| 45. | J. Bernard | TFS | s.t. |
| 46. | S. Küng | GFC | s.t. |
| 47. | I. Erviti | MOV | s.t. |
| 48. | G. Martin | COF | s.t. |
| 49. | L. Meintjes | IWG | s.t. |
| 50. | G. Van Avermaet | ACT | s.t. |
| 51. | P. Gilbert | LTS | s.t. |
| 52. | A. Valverde | MOV | s.t. |
| 53. | B. van Poppel | IWG | s.t. |
| 54. | C. Rodríguez | TEN | s.t. |
| 55. | J. Wallays | COF | s.t. |
| 56. | E. Mas | MOV | s.t. |
| 57. | B. Armirail | GFC | s.t. |
| 58. | V. de la Parte | TEN | s.t. |
| 59. | T. Skujiņš | TFS | s.t. |
| 60. | M. Bjerg | UAD | s.t. |
| 61. | B. McNulty | UAD | s.t. |
| 62. | R. Guerreiro | EFN | s.t. |
| 63. | S. Bissegger | EFN | s.t. |
| 64. | J. Rutsch | EFN | s.t. |
| 65. | V. S. Laengen | UAD | s.t. |
| 66. | A. Paret-Peintre | ACT | s.t. |
| 67. | E. Chaves | BEX | s.t. |
| 68. | M. Hirschi | UAD | s.t. |
| 69. | D. Formolo | UAD | s.t. |
| 70. | R. Majka | UAD | s.t. |
| 71. | N. Quintana | ARK | s.t. |
| 72. | T. Pogačar | UAD | s.t. |
| 73. | R. Costa | UAD | s.t. |
| 74. | P. Latour | TEN | s.t. |
| 75. | P. Bilbao | TBV | s.t. |
| 76. | L. Rota | IWG | s.t. |
| 77. | R. Hollenstein | ISN | s.t. |
| 78. | J. Castroviejo | IGD | s.t. |
| 79. | D. Ballerini | DQT | s.t. |
| 80. | Se. Bennett | TQA | s.t. |
| 81. | N. Powless | EFN | s.t. |
| 82. | C. Gautier | BBK | s.t. |
| 83. | F. Bonnamour | BBK | s.t. |
| 84. | C. Barbero | TQA | s.t. |
| 85. | I. Izagirre | APT | s.t. |
| 86. | M. Chevalier | BBK | s.t. |
| 87. | X. Meurisse | AFC | s.t. |
| 88. | R. Carapaz | IGD | s.t. |
| 89. | O. Goldstein | ISN | s.t. |
| 90. | C. Froome | ISN | s.t. |
| 91. | D. Teuns | TBV | s.t. |
| 92. | R. Urán | EFN | s.t. |
| 93. | P. Konrad | BOH | s.t. |
| 94. | R. Fernández | COF | s.t. |
| 95. | D. Gruzdev | APT | s.t. |
| 96. | P. Rolland | BBK | s.t. |
| 97. | J. Vingegaard | TJV | s.t. |
| 98. | S. Henao | TQA | s.t. |
| 99. | O. Naesen | ACT | s.t. |
| 100. | D. Gaudu | GFC | 0:29 |
| 101. | T. Geoghegan Hart | IGD | 0:36 |
| 102. | J. Nieuwenhuis | DSM | 0:39 |
| 103. | L. Durbridge | BEX | s.t. |
| 104. | C. Pedersen | DSM | s.t. |
| 105. | B. Mollema | TFS | s.t. |
| 106. | K. Asgreen | DQT | s.t. |
| 107. | E. Theuns | TFS | 0:45 |
| 108. | W. Poels | TBV | 0:00 |
| 109. | T. De Gendt | LTS | 0:47 |
| 110. | Q. Pacher | BBK | s.t. |
| 111. | M. Mohorič | TBV | 0:59 |
| 112. | P. L. Périchon | COF | 1:05 |
| 113. | O. Fraile | APT | s.t. |
| 114. | R. Porte | IGD | 1:26 |
| 115. | G. Thomas | IGD | s.t. |
| 116. | M. Kwiatkowski | IGD | s.t. |
| 117. | E. Buchmann | BOH | s.t. |
| 118. | D. Martin | ISN | s.t. |
| 119. | Je. Herrada | COF | s.t. |
| 120. | S. Geschke | COF | s.t. |
| 121. | B. Cosnefroy | ACT | 1:30 |
| 122. | G. Zimmermann | IWG | s.t. |
| 123. | M. Cattaneo | DQT | s.t. |
| 124. | D. Devenyns | DQT | 1:56 |
| 125. | C. Juul-Jensen | BEX | 2:07 |
| 126. | F. Doubey | TEN | 2:11 |
| 127. | H. Sweeny | LTS | 2:27 |
| 128. | S. Clarke | TQA | s.t. |
| 129. | C. Verona | MOV | 2:31 |
| 130. | J. Cabot | TEN | 2:35 |
| 131. | B. Van Moer | LTS | 2:37 |
| 132. | M. Donovan | DSM | 2:48 |
| 133. | I. Schelling | BOH | 3:01 |
| 134. | P. Vakoč | AFC | 3:29 |
| 135. | J. Alaphilippe | DQT | s.t. |
| 136. | M. Valgren | EFN | 3:49 |
| 137. | S. Higuita | EFN | s.t. |
| 138. | T. Declercq | DQT | 4:24 |
| 139. | H. Houle | APT | s.t. |
| 140. | K. Elissonde | TFS | 5:58 |
| 141. | A. Turgis | TEN | 12:33 |

JUNE — WORLDTOUR MEN'S RACE

# TOUR DE FRANCE
Final Classifications

## GENERAL CLASSIFICATION

| POS | NAME | TEAM | TIME |
|---|---|---|---|
| 1. | T. Pogačar | UAD | 82:56:36 |
| 2. | J. Vingegaard | TJV | 5:20 |
| 3. | R. Carapaz | IGD | 7:03 |
| 4. | B. O'Connor | ACT | 10:02 |
| 5. | W. Kelderman | BOH | 10:13 |
| 6. | E. Mas | MOV | 11:43 |
| 7. | A. Lutsenko | APT | 12:23 |
| 8. | G. Martin | COF | 15:33 |
| 9. | P. Bilbao | TBV | 16:04 |
| 10. | R. Urán | EFN | 18:34 |
| 11. | D. Gaudu | GFC | 21:50 |
| 12. | M. Cattaneo | DQT | 24:58 |
| 13. | E. Chaves | BEX | 37:48 |
| 14. | L. Meintjes | IWG | 38:09 |
| 15. | A. Paret-Peintre | ACT | 39:09 |
| 16. | W. Poels | TBV | 50:35 |
| 17. | D. Teuns | TBV | 51:40 |
| 18. | R. Guerreiro | EFN | 54:10 |
| 19. | W. van Aert | TJV | 57:02 |
| 20. | B. Mollema | TFS | 1:02:18 |
| 21. | S. Henao | TQA | 1:03:12 |
| 22. | F. Bonnamour | BBK | 1:04:35 |
| 23. | J. Castroviejo | IGD | 1:06:20 |
| 24. | A. Valverde | MOV | 1:07:50 |
| 25. | S. Higuita | EFN | 1:09:16 |
| 26. | I. Izagirre | APT | 1:23:39 |
| 27. | P. Konrad | BOH | 1:27:06 |
| 28. | N. Quintana | ARK | 1:33:11 |
| 29. | X. Meurisse | AFC | 1:40:48 |
| 30. | J. Alaphilippe | DQT | 1:43:06 |
| 31. | M. Mohorič | TBV | 1:50:04 |
| 32. | S. Kuss | TJV | s.t. |
| 33. | E. Buchmann | BOH | 1:51:05 |
| 34. | R. Majka | UAD | 1:54:04 |
| 35. | Q. Pacher | BBK | 1:55:34 |
| 36. | K. Elissonde | TFS | 1:56:33 |
| 37. | J. Bernard | TFS | 2:03:32 |
| 38. | R. Porte | IGD | 2:06:39 |
| 39. | J. Stuyven | TFS | 2:07:39 |
| 40. | D. Martin | ISN | 2:09:35 |
| 41. | G. Thomas | IGD | 2:11:37 |
| 42. | V. Madouas | GFC | 2:11:39 |
| 43. | N. Powless | EFN | 2:13:33 |
| 44. | D. Formolo | UAD | 2:15:56 |
| 45. | M. Donovan | DSM | 2:17:40 |
| 46. | C. Rodríguez | TEN | 2:19:31 |
| 47. | P. Latour | TEN | 2:19:36 |
| 48. | J. Bakelants | IWG | 2:21:30 |
| 49. | S. Küng | GFC | 2:22:03 |
| 50. | N. Politt | BOH | 2:22:44 |
| 51. | P. Rolland | BBK | 2:23:11 |
| 52. | S. Colbrelli | TBV | 2:24:39 |
| 53. | M. Valgren | EFN | 2:26:16 |
| 54. | D. van Baarle | IGD | 2:27:07 |
| 55. | J. Rutsch | EFN | 2:29:33 |
| 56. | M. Cort | EFN | 2:30:23 |
| 57. | O. Fraile | APT | 2:31:14 |
| 58. | M. Schär | ACT | 2:35:18 |
| 59. | S. Dillier | AFC | 2:35:43 |
| 60. | T. Geoghegan Hart | IGD | 2:37:02 |
| 61. | É. Gesbert | ARK | 2:38:28 |
| 62. | S. Geschke | COF | 2:38:51 |
| 63. | L. Rota | IWG | 2:39:57 |
| 64. | K. Asgreen | DQT | 2:43:41 |
| 65. | B. Van Moer | LTS | 2:43:49 |
| 66. | H. Houle | APT | 2:44:39 |
| 67. | I. Erviti | MOV | 2:49:07 |
| 68. | M. Kwiatkowski | IGD | 2:49:22 |
| 69. | B. McNulty | UAD | 2:50:53 |
| 70. | O. Naesen | ACT | 2:52:25 |
| 71. | T. Skujiņš | TFS | 2:52:56 |
| 72. | V. de la Parte | TEN | 2:54:28 |
| 73. | A. Turgis | TEN | 2:55:51 |
| 74. | A. Aranburu | APT | 2:56:44 |
| 75. | D. Godon | ACT | 2:57:11 |
| 76. | M. Teunissen | TJV | 2:58:25 |
| 77. | R. Costa | UAD | 2:58:29 |
| 78. | F. Doubey | TEN | 3:02:45 |
| 79. | M. Matthews | BEX | 3:03:30 |
| 80. | G. Zimmermann | IWG | 3:05:48 |
| 81. | C. Gautier | BBK | 3:08:30 |
| 82. | T. De Gendt | LTS | 3:08:46 |
| 83. | B. Armirail | GFC | 3:09:58 |
| 84. | R. Fernández | COF | 3:10:43 |
| 85. | H. Sweeny | LTS | 3:10:52 |
| 86. | A. Perez | COF | 3:10:56 |
| 87. | Je. Herrada | COF | 3:11:15 |
| 88. | C. Barthe | BBK | 3:12:31 |
| 89. | C. Swift | ARK | 3:13:48 |
| 90. | J. Arcas | MOV | 3:14:41 |
| 91. | C. Laporte | COF | 3:15:03 |
| 92. | P. L. Périchon | COF | 3:16:27 |
| 93. | M. Chevalier | BBK | 3:16:54 |
| 94. | I. García Cortina | MOV | 3:21:25 |
| 95. | J. Rickaert | AFC | 3:22:36 |
| 96. | F. Wright | TBV | 3:24:19 |
| 97. | G. Van Avermaet | ACT | 3:24:29 |
| 98. | M. Hirschi | UAD | 3:24:38 |
| 99. | P. Gilbert | LTS | 3:27:22 |
| 100. | L. Durbridge | BEX | 3:28:05 |
| 101. | C. Verona | MOV | 3:28:40 |
| 102. | L. Mezgec | BEX | 3:30:17 |
| 103. | S. Bissegger | EFN | 3:31:35 |
| 104. | E. Theuns | TFS | 3:33:31 |
| 105. | G. Boivin | ISN | 3:33:42 |
| 106. | K. Sbaragli | AFC | 3:34:19 |
| 107. | B. Cosnefroy | ACT | 3:34:54 |
| 108. | D. Ballerini | DQT | 3:35:13 |
| 109. | J. Philipsen | AFC | 3:42:11 |
| 110. | M. Bjerg | UAD | 3:42:21 |
| 111. | C. Pedersen | DSM | 3:42:52 |
| 112. | V. S. Laengen | UAD | 3:43:33 |
| 113. | D. Gruzdev | APT | 3:44:49 |
| 114. | C. Juul-Jensen | BEX | 3:45:07 |
| 115. | D. Oss | BOH | 3:46:53 |
| 116. | L. Pöstlberger | BOH | 3:47:12 |
| 117. | B. van Poppel | IWG | 3:50:25 |
| 118. | P. Vakoč | AFC | 3:51:06 |
| 119. | I. Schelling | BOH | 3:51:16 |
| 120. | D. van Poppel | IWG | 3:52:53 |
| 121. | M. Walscheid | TQA | 3:53:05 |
| 122. | O. Goldstein | ISN | 3:55:26 |
| 123. | S. Clarke | TQA | 3:56:08 |
| 124. | C. Barbero | TQA | 4:00:20 |
| 125. | A. Greipel | ISN | 4:01:26 |
| 126. | N. Eekhoff | DSM | 4:02:44 |
| 127. | M. Haller | TBV | 4:03:01 |
| 128. | J. Nieuwenhuis | DSM | 4:03:22 |
| 129. | J. Simon | TEN | 4:05:49 |
| 130. | Se. Bennett | TQA | 4:07:42 |
| 131. | J. Wallays | COF | 4:09:46 |
| 132. | J. Cabot | TEN | 4:11:35 |
| 133. | C. Froome | ISN | 4:12:01 |
| 134. | R. Zabel | ISN | 4:13:07 |
| 135. | D. Devenyns | DQT | 4:20:49 |
| 136. | R. Hollenstein | ISN | 4:24:19 |
| 137. | M. Pedersen | TFS | 4:29:17 |
| 138. | M. Mørkøv | DQT | 4:32:45 |
| 139. | M. Cavendish | DQT | 4:34:14 |
| 140. | C. Bol | DSM | 4:36:39 |
| 141. | T. Declercq | DQT | 5:01:09 |

## KING OF THE MOUNTAINS

| POS | NAME | TEAM | PTS |
|---|---|---|---|
| 1. | T. Pogačar | UAD | 107 |
| 2. | W. Poels | TBV | 88 |
| 3. | J. Vingegaard | TJV | 82 |
| 4. | W. van Aert | TJV | 68 |
| 5. | N. Quintana | ARK | 66 |
| 6. | R. Carapaz | IGD | 56 |
| 7. | B. O'Connor | ACT | 44 |
| 8. | B. Mollema | TFS | 41 |
| 9. | D. Gaudu | GFC | 41 |
| 10. | A. Perez | COF | 37 |

## POINTS

| POS | NAME | TEAM | PTS |
|---|---|---|---|
| 1. | M. Cavendish | DQT | 337 |
| 2. | M. Matthews | BEX | 291 |
| 3. | S. Colbrelli | TBV | 227 |
| 4. | J. Philipsen | AFC | 216 |
| 5. | W. van Aert | TJV | 171 |
| 6. | M. Mohorič | TBV | 163 |
| 7. | J. Alaphilippe | DQT | 163 |
| 8. | T. Pogačar | UAD | 154 |
| 9. | M. Mørkøv | DQT | 124 |
| 10. | J. Vingegaard | TJV | 103 |

## YOUNG RIDER

| POS | NAME | TEAM | TIME |
|---|---|---|---|
| 1. | T. Pogačar | UAD | 82:56:36 |
| 2. | J. Vingegaard | TJV | 5:20 |
| 3. | D. Gaudu | GFC | 21:50 |
| 4. | A. Paret-Peintre | ACT | 39:09 |
| 5. | S. Higuita | EFN | 1:09:16 |
| 6. | V. Madouas | GFC | 2:11:39 |
| 7. | N. Powless | EFN | 2:13:33 |
| 8. | M. Donovan | DSM | 2:17:40 |
| 9. | J. Rutsch | EFN | 2:29:33 |
| 10. | B. Van Moer | LTS | 2:43:49 |

## TEAMS

| POS | NAME | TEAM | TIME |
|---|---|---|---|
| 1. | Bahrain Victorious | TBV | 249:16:47 |
| 2. | EF Education-Nippo | EFN | 19:12 |
| 3. | Jumbo-Visma | TJV | 1:11:35 |
| 4. | Ineos Grenadiers | IGD | 1:27:10 |
| 5. | AG2R Citroën Team | ACT | 1:31:54 |
| 6. | Bora-Hansgrohe | BOH | 1:36:44 |
| 7. | Trek-Segafredo | TFS | 1:47:04 |
| 8. | Astana Premier Tech | APT | 2:01:45 |
| 9. | Movistar Team | MOV | 2:04:28 |
| 10. | UAE Team Emirates | UAD | 2:38:08 |
| 11. | Deceuninck-QuickStep | DQT | 3:36:47 |
| 12. | B&B Hotels p/b KTM | BBK | 3:43:10 |
| 13. | Groupama-FDJ | GFC | 3:46:26 |
| 14. | Cofidis | COF | 3:50:22 |
| 15. | Intermarché-Wanty-Gobert Matériaux | IWG | 4:15:34 |
| 16. | Team BikeExchange | BEX | 4:31:31 |
| 17. | TotalEnergies | TEN | 5:02:02 |
| 18. | Team Arkéa-Samsic | ARK | 5:50:38 |
| 19. | Israel Start-Up Nation | ISN | 5:52:16 |
| 20. | Alpecin-Fenix | AFC | 6:07:29 |
| 21. | Team Qhubeka NextHash | TQA | 6:55:52 |
| 22. | Team DSM | DSM | 7:33:29 |
| 23. | Lotto Soudal | LTS | 7:45:44 |

## ABANDONS

| | |
|---|---|
| Stage 1 | I. Konovalovas (GFC), J. Sütterlin (DSM), C. Lemoine (BBK) |
| Stage 2 | M. Soler (MOV) |
| Stage 3 | J. Haig (TBV), R. Gesink (TJV) |
| Stage 4 | C. Ewan (LTS) |
| Stage 9 | B. Coquard (BBK), S. de Bod (APT), A. Démare (GFC), L. Vliegen (IWG), J. Guarnieri (GFC), A. Delaplace (ARK), N. Dlamini (TQA), N. Peters (ACT), T. Merlier (AFC), J. de Buyst (LTS), P. Roglič (TJV), M. van der Poel (AFC) |
| Stage 10 | J. Koch (IWG) |
| Stage 11 | M. Scotson (GFC), C. Russo (ARK), T. Van der Sande (LTS), T. Martin (TJV), D. McLay (ARK), T. Benoot (DSM), V. Campenaerts (TQA), L. Rowe (IGD) |
| Stage 12 | P. Sagan (BOH) |
| Stage 13 | L. Hamilton (BEX), R. Kluge (LTS), S. Yates (BEX), M. Gogl (TQA) |
| Stage 14 | W. Barguil (ARK), S. Kragh Andersen (DSM) |
| Stage 15 | N. Bouhanni (ARK), E. Boasson Hagen (TEN) |
| Stage 16 | A. G. Jansen (BEX), V. Nibali (TFS) |
| Stage 17 | S. Kruijswijk (TJV) |
| Stage 19 | M. A. López (MOV), M. Woods (ISN) |
| Stage 21 | J. Fuglsang (APT) |

JUNE .1 MEN'S RACE

# GP CITTÀ DI LUGANO
27 June 2021
Lugano–Lugano
179.2km

## WEATHER

TEMPERATURE  WIND
29°C  S 7km/h

## RESULTS

| POS | NAME | TEAM | TIME |
|---|---|---|---|
| 1. | G. Moscon | IGD | 4:53:00 |
| 2. | V. Conti | UAD | 0:20 |
| 3. | B. Hermans | ISN | s.t. |
| 4. | S. Pellaud | ANS | 0:32 |
| 5. | D. Ulissi | UAD | 0:56 |
| 6. | S. Velasco | GAZ | 0:57 |
| 7. | D. Smith | BEX | 1:27 |
| 8. | D. Orrico | THR | s.t. |
| 9. | M. Tizza | AMO | 1:28 |
| 10. | M. Wildauer | VBG | 1:33 |
| 11. | Ł. Owsian | ARK | 1:37 |
| 12. | D. P. Sevilla | EOK | s.t. |
| 13. | M. Canola | GAZ | s.t. |
| 14. | F. Aru | TQA | s.t. |
| 15. | R. Thalmann | VBG | s.t. |
| 16. | M. Bais | ANS | s.t. |
| 17. | O. El Gouzi | IRC | s.t. |
| 18. | A. Ropero | EOK | s.t. |
| 19. | A. Garosio | BCF | 2:25 |
| 20. | A. Zeits | BEX | 2:31 |

# A STANDING START

BY KATHRYN BERTINE

*Kathryn Bertine is a retired professional road racer based in Tucson, Arizona. She rode at the highest level from 2012 to 2017 on four UCI Women's WorldTour teams, including Wiggle-Honda in 2014. As a dual-citizen, she is a six-time national champion of St Kitts and Nevis. Bertine is also a driving force behind the push for equality in cycling and was heavily involved in the lobbying for change that brought about the creation of La Course by Tour de France. After eight years, 2021 saw the final edition of La Course, as it segues into the long-awaited 2022 Tour de France Femmes. But the pressures of her decade-long equality campaign were immense. The following excerpt is from her book* **STAND: A Memoir on Activism. A Manual for Progress.**

---

'The most pivotal day of my journey in activism went by way too fast, no matter how hard I try to slow the incalculable speed of memory. July 27, 2014. *Flashes of colour, noise and blurry people as crowds pressed against the cycling barriers lining the Champs-Élysées. Wind in my ears and the whir of gears as we encircled the Arc d'Triomphe. Pounding heart and burning lungs in sync with the peloton of women around me.* We were racing at the Tour de France. A race that once banned women. For the last five years, I'd taken up arms – alongside fellow athletes and supporters around the world – against the discriminatory regulations and the bureaucratic dinosaurs that barred us from the roadways of France while men competed in the most iconic cycling race in the world. Finally, on this momentous day, here we were. 125 female professional cyclists in the heart of Paris, racing down the cobblestones of the Champs-Élysées. I revelled in every moment of our prodigious, triumphant day. Inside, though, I was cracking.

A photographer snapped a picture of me on my bike that day – appearing invincible, victorious, joyful and as though I had my shit together as I rolled towards the start line of the inaugural La Course by Tour de France. *All smiles! All strength! All confidence!* All lies.

What cannot be seen in that photograph are the tears streaming down behind my glasses. Beneath my glove, the wedding ring I cannot bear to take off. The fractures and fissures deep within. My body, strong. My soul, lost. I am weak, empty, scared, scarred, scripted, rehearsed and acting triumphant, fulfilled, confident, collected. In the fleeting pause between each cobblestone, despair seeps through the cracks of stillness and movement. On the outside, I am a warrior for justice. Inside, stone-cold fucking broken. That day, the weight of worthlessness consumed me. Hiding it seemed better. So I wore the historic victory of our presence at the Tour de France like a mask over the private, ugly pain of advocacy.

When I sat down to write this story – about what we achieved for women's equality that day – I thought: *People don't want to read about worthlessness. The Brokenness. The Empties. Better to skip that stuff. Vulnerability isn't important.* Took me five years to find the courage to disagree.

To write about creating change takes data, and I had plenty of that. But to write about activism requires a mirror. And a steel gut. And a box of tissues. And a reckoning with Vulnerability. In 2019 I taped the photograph of myself, on the bike in Paris, above my computer. As I sat down to write, the woman in the photograph whispered from under her mask:

*You want to talk about what it takes to make change happen? You want to stop throwing away shitty first drafts? Fine. Then start writing about what really happens when we stand up and fight for what we believe. All of it. What happened in public. What happened in private. About your plan to walk in the woods and not come out. Write about what we need to talk about in our culture, our society, right now, today. That's how change happens. Facts, schmacts. That's not enough. Remember what Quixote said? "Facts get in the way of truth." You've got plenty of facts. Now bring in the truth. If you want to write anything worthwhile and meaningful about activism, then you're going to need to step onto that terrifyingly thin tightrope of vulnerability strung across the abyss of truth and authenticity. Ready?*

No.

*Ready?*

Nope.

*Ready?*

Ooof.

OK, Voice. Here we go…

We need to talk about what really happens when we stand up and fight for what we believe. We need to talk about the nasty underbelly of activism. And its beautiful, beautiful wings. We need to talk about the myth of strength, the truth of masks and the dark side of progress. We need to talk about being broken. Because the universal truth of adulthood is that we're all a little bit broken. We need to look closely at photographs and wonder about what isn't there, and shine a light into the cracks and caves of all the things we cannot see. We don't all need to be activists. But we do all need to talk about how to support those who are out there standing on the frontlines of Change.

We need to stop thinking that happy people don't carry the weight of despair. We need to check in on our strongest friends and ask how they're really doing. We need to tell those who have their Shit Together that it's OK to Come Undone. We need to talk about demons; ours and others. We need to talk about suicide. We need to ask *Why* and embrace *How*, so we can be the Who, What and Where if someone needs us. Even if they don't ask. We need to talk about the frailty of strength and the armour of vulnerability. No, I don't have those mixed up.

We need to talk about divorce. We need to talk about divorce. We need to talk about it twice because there are two. The one we go through in public, the one we go through in private. We need to talk about pain. And how to channel it. We need to talk about sensitivity. And how to unchain it. We need to talk about the wardrobe of Masks, and when to wear them. Or not. We need to talk about depression until we cry tears of laugher from the sweet release of authenticity when we say, out loud, how truly fucking bad it is. We need to laugh. Not just because it feels good, but because Humour is the golden chariot of activism and laughter is how we hail a cab through the ugly, gridlocked traffic on the road to Progress.

We need to talk about demons, again. Not just talk about them, but *to* them. We need to talk to our inner beasts until we can look them straight in the eyes, pet their scaly hides, throw a saddle across their razored spines, grab tight the reins, and ride those crazy ogres wherever we so choose. Because we can choose. We need to stop trying to slay our demons and start building stables. We need to talk about how Activism just might be the great big barn where beasts and demons grow into Change and Progress. We need to understand the reality and consequence of what happens when we stand, lead and fight. We need to talk about it all.

At least I do. How activism bore me, broke me, rebuilt me and became my cornerstone of Self. Stepping onto the tightrope of vulnerability, I wrote this book because standing up and speaking out matters. And also, this: I was lost for a long time and I needed to write myself home. To figure stuff out. To find peace and clarity. To lock eyes with authenticity. To snuggle with my demons. To confront truth. To help others plot their route into the wilds of activism. To maybe help us all rise. To finally answer the question… Yes, our struggles are worth the journey. At least I've got that much figured out.'

---

In 2009, I had dreams of becoming a professional cyclist and racing the Tour de France. Only to find out there was no Tour de France for women. (Not any more. There had been one in the 1980s.) I was 34 years old at the time, and also found out UCI had a ridiculous rule that no women's UCI team could average over the age of 28. OK, wait a minute. No Tour for women? Age medians for teams? No women's base salary wage? At races where women were 'allowed', the distances were half that of men's events? Prize money for professional women that was a mere fraction of the men's event? Oh boy. My journalism brain went haywire, asking *why, why, why?* When there were no plausible answers to be found, I switched into activism mode.

Little did I know that an email I sent ASO in 2009 asking to collaborate on reinstating women at the Tour de France (which went unanswered, of course) would be the first step in a decade-long journey of fighting for women's rights in sport. In 2012, I did receive that coveted professional road racing team contract, despite being deemed an ol' hag at the age of 37. In 2014, I stood on the start line of my dreams at La Course by Tour de France. A race my activism group, Le Tour

Entier – consisting of Marianne Vos, Emma Pooley, Chrissie Wellington and myself – created with ASO during 2013. This effort was very much a behind-the-scenes endeavour after a worldwide viral petition, calculated planning and countless draft manifestos, emails and secret meetings culminated in ASO finally engaging with our demands for a women's race. While ASO never credited us for doing the lion's share of the work, rendering us 'hidden figures', we often laughed about the fact that 100,000 people signed our petition and knew exactly what women were doing behind the scenes. La Course was a huge success but the activism wasn't done yet.

By 2015, the documentary film we made on women's pro cycling, *Half the Road: The passion, pitfalls and power of women's pro cycling*, was acquired and distributed worldwide. Visibility was happening and the world was responding. So were the UCI. The women's team age median was finally eliminated. In 2016, I had my best pro cycling season at the 'ancient' age of 40. Then suffered a near-life-ending brain injury in a crash at the Vuelta Mexico Feminil. That was one lucky break. Well, four: two bones in my skull, one collarbone, one in an arm. Quite a year. In 2017, I retired from pro cycling and founded Homestretch Foundation, which assists female pro cyclists who struggle with the gender pay gap… and behind the scenes, we lobbied UCI to change their archaic stance that women on WorldTour teams simply didn't need to be paid a liveable wage. In 2020, we won. In 2023, women will have a base salary equal to the Pro Continental men.

Perhaps the biggest victory, though, is what stemmed from the proof that La Course by Le Tour de France was indeed a marketable, sustainable and incredible race. After years of pressuring ASO to keep their failed promise to grow La Course into a multi-day race, finally in 2022 we will see an eight-day race for women at Tour de France Femmes, which will begin at the end of the men's Tour de France. Progress? Yes. Equality? Not quite. Eight days is not 21 days, like in the men's edition. There is still an antiquated idea at ASO that women simply can't do such a gruelling number of kilometres and days, despite the fact that women from 1984 to 1989 indeed conquered 21 days without issue. Till the women's race grows – or the men's race is shortened! – to equal days and distance, we'll keep the pressure on up to the point at which professional women are equally welcomed at the most prestigious stage race in the world. La Course by Le Tour de France opened that door.

Sounds victorious, doesn't it? On paper, La Course looks that way. We shook things up and made shit happen. We changed the system. Fixed some broken parts. Bent the will of authority. Those were great victories. But there were other broken parts. Namely, me. When I sent that email to ASO in 2009, I had no idea that lobbying for a better, fairer world for women would also change my own personal world. In the beginning, I thought the hardest part of this journey would be convincing traditionalist French businessmen to change their ways. Never did it occur to me how much change I would go through. Among the victories along the battlefield of international progress, there were personal, private setbacks I never anticipated. Divorce. Depression. Bullying. Worthlessness. Benched careers. Demons. Suicides. Therapy. Healing. Never in a million years did I think standing up for what we believe in would become a public journey laced with personal landmines.

In 2018, I sat down to write my entire journey of a decade in cycling and activism. No holds barred. The personal stuff, the public stuff and all the crazy, funny, sad, angry, happy stuff that happened behind the scenes. Turns out there was a lot of stuff. *STAND* was gonna be a long one! It was my fourth book, though, so I figured my literary agent would find a willing publishing house to buy the proposal. My three previous books had done well, so what could go wrong? What happened next dumbfounded me.

More than 20 rejections came in, all with the same response from corporate publishers: 'We don't believe a book about women who stand up and fight for change is marketable. It won't sell. No room on the shelf.' *What?! Is anyone paying attention to our social and political climate? Strong, feisty, outspoken women are everywhere.* My gut knew the publishers were wrong. Still, I was left with two possibilities: 1) Forget it. Don't write the book. 2) Write the book. Prove 'em wrong. Build your own damn shelf.

I went with option 2. Without a book advance, I wrote during my spare time around my other work schedules. *STAND* took three years to complete. Then another six months of hiring editors, a graphic designer, publicists and tech gurus to actually create the book. (Apparently elves don't sew them together. Bummer.) What we created as a team in that tangible, rectangular, paper brick of words was truly beautiful. And eerily reminiscent of the book's content itself: what happens when the Powers That Be decree you're not welcome as an equal? Band together with others and prove we are.

The truth is that we – the non-famous, non-wealthy, non-Olympians, non-InstaInfluencers – can truly create change and move the dial forward in this weird, crazy world. I did this, a little bit, in the cycling universe. Whether or not I'm personally remembered for bringing women back to the Tour de France doesn't matter much in the long run. What matters most is that I helped clear a path for the next generation of cyclists – and non-cyclists – to follow suit, and to stand for what they believe in. We're all capable of doing so. If I did, anyone can.

## CAVENDISH'S VANQUISHED 34

Mark Cavendish wrote his name into the history books once again with his return to the Tour de France, winning four stages and the green jersey to equal Eddy Merckx's record tally of stage victories. But who were the 34 vanquished riders he swatted into second place? The 20 pros hold 84 stage wins between them, proving their quality. André Greipel and Tyler Farrar were those who most often found themselves on the receiving end of a Cavendish sprint victory.

**4    ANDRÉ GREIPEL**
      **TYLER FARRAR**

**3    ALESSANDRO PETACCHI**
      **THOR HUSHOVD**

**2    EDVALD BOASSON HAGEN**
      **MARCEL KITTEL**
      **GERALD CIOLEK**
      **PETER SAGAN**

**1    PHILIPPE GILBERT**
      **MARK RENSHAW**
      **ÓSCAR FREIRE**
      **SÉBASTIAN CHAVANEL**
      **ROBBIE McEWEN**
      **JULIAN DEAN**
      **MATTHEW GOSS**
      **ALEXANDER KRISTOFF**
      **NACER BOUHANNI**
      **JASPER PHILIPSEN**
      **WOUT VAN AERT**
      **MICHAEL MØRKØV**

# JULY

The Olympics were the central focus of the women's peloton but, before the Games got underway, the women's Giro Rosa – denied WorldTour status in 2021 – was still the preeminent stage race on the calendar. In men's racing, the Tour de France came to an end in the middle of the month, having started in June. Scarcely a week later, a fair percentage of both pelotons had travelled to Japan to compete for gold medals on the slopes of Mount Fuji.

| DATE | RACE TITLE | LOCATION | UCI CODE | PAGE |
|---|---|---|---|---|
| 2–11 July | Giro d'Italia Donne | Italy | 2.Pro W | 316 |
| 3–6 July | Sibiu Cycling Tour | Romania | 2.1 | 326 |
| 14–18 July | Settimana Ciclista Italiana | Italy | 2.1 | 328 |
| 20–24 July | Tour de Wallonie | Belgium | 2.Pro | 331 |
| 24–28 July | Olympic Games | Japan | OG | 334 |
| 25 July | Prueba Villafranca de Ordizia | Spain | 1.1 | 339 |
| 29 July | Vuelta a Castilla y Leon | Spain | 1.1 | 340 |
| 29–31 July | Tour de l'Ain | France | 2.1 | 341 |
| 31 July | Donostia San Sebastián Klasikoa | Spain | 1.UWT | 343 |
| 31 July | Donostia San Sebastián Klasikoa | Spain | 1.WWT | 344 |
| 31 July | Heylen Vastgoed Heistse Pijl | Belgium | 1.1 | 345 |

# GIRO D'ITALIA DONNE

Stage 1 (TTT)
2 July 2021
Fossano–Cuneo
26.7km

As was the case in recent years, the Giro d'Italia Donne began with a team time trial. The first real benchmark on the 26.7km course came from Ceratizit-WNT, who finished in 34:59.02 minutes. Led by Swiss ITT champion Marlen Reusser, Alé BTC Ljubljana improved on that with a time of 34:20.63 minutes, finishing third in the end. FDJ Nouvelle-Aquitaine Futuroscope had a bad day, with Cecilie Uttrup Ludwig crashing early on and Marta Cavalli suffering a puncture halfway through the TTT, resulting in the team losing almost 2 minutes. Trek-Segafredo finished the race with only the minimum four riders together over the line, but despite this they set the new best time in 33:40.82 minutes. When Team SD Worx fell 8 seconds short of that, the US team could celebrate the TTT victory and the leader's jersey for Ruth Winder.

## WEATHER

TEMPERATURE: 27°C
WIND: N 7km/h

## PROFILE

## STAGE RESULTS

| POS | NAME | TEAM | TIME |
|---|---|---|---|
| 1. | Trek-Segafredo | TFS | 33:40 |
| 2. | Team SD Worx | SDW | 0:08 |
| 3. | Alé BTC Ljubljana | ALE | 0:40 |
| 4. | Canyon-SRAM Racing | CSR | 0:46 |
| 5. | Movistar Team Women | MOV | 0:55 |
| 6. | Jumbo-Visma Women Team | JVW | 1:16 |
| 7. | Ceratizit-WNT Pro Cycling | WNT | 1:18 |
| 8. | Team Tibco-Silicon Valley Bank | TIB | 1:19 |
| 9. | Team DSM | DSM | 1:23 |
| 10. | Team BikeExchange | BEX | 1:31 |
| 11. | Liv Racing | LIV | 1:46 |
| 12. | FDJ Nouvelle-Aquitaine Futuroscope | FDJ | 1:46 |
| 13. | A.R. Monex Women's Pro Cycling Team | MNX | 1:58 |
| 14. | BePink | BPK | 2:10 |
| 15. | Isolmant-Premac-Vittoria | SBT | 2:49 |
| 16. | Top Girls Fassa Bortolo | TOP | 3:45 |
| 17. | Arkéa Pro Cycling Team | ARK | 3:48 |
| 18. | Rally Cycling | RLW | 3:54 |
| 19. | Valcar Travel & Service | VAL | 4:01 |
| 20. | Lotto Soudal Ladies | LSL | 4:17 |
| 21. | Aromitalia-Basso Bikes-Vaiano | VAI | 4:26 |
| 22. | Born to Win G20 Ambedo | BTW | 4:27 |
| 23. | Servetto-Makhymo-Beltrami TSA | SER | 4:30 |
| 24. | Bizkaia Durango | BDU | 4:48 |

## GENERAL CLASSIFICATION

| POS | NAME | TEAM | TIME |
|---|---|---|---|
| 1. | R. Winder | TFS | 33:40 |
| 2. | E. van Dijk | TFS | s.t. |
| 3. | E. Longo Borghini | TFS | s.t. |

## YOUNG RIDER

| POS | NAME | TEAM | TIME |
|---|---|---|---|
| 1. | N. Fisher-Black | SDW | 33:48 |
| 2. | E. Norsgaard | MOV | 0:47 |
| 3. | S. Martin | MOV | s.t. |

JULY .PRO WOMEN'S RACE

# GIRO D'ITALIA DONNE
Stage 2
3 July 2021
Boves–Prato Nevoso
100.1km

On the mountain-top finish on the Colle del Prel overlooking the Prato Nevoso ski resort, Team SD Worx put their mark on the race with a clean sweep of the podium. A break of four strong riders went away on the Colle del Morte but was reeled in early on the finishing climb, with *maglia rosa* Ruth Winder herself setting the pace. Niamh Fisher-Black attacked with 10km to go; she and Erica Magnaldi (Ceratizit-WNT) stayed ahead for 2km. Anna van der Breggen then attacked from the peloton, which had been reduced to 15 riders, and soloed to the finish. Her teammate Ashleigh Moolman-Pasio also went solo, followed by Demi Vollering who was caught by Marta Cavalli but beat the Italian in the sprint for third place. Van der Breggen was the new *maglia rosa* with a lead of 3 minutes 31 seconds on anyone not her teammate.

## WEATHER

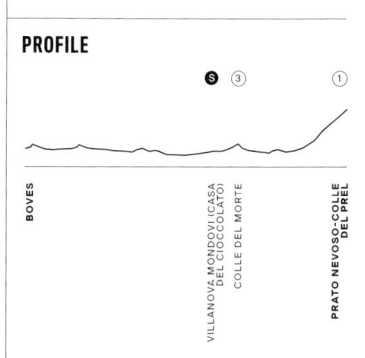

TEMPERATURE: 26°C
WIND: N 9km/h

## PROFILE

## BREAKAWAY
E. Chabbey (CSR), K. Hammes (WNT), S. Bertizzolo (LIV), C. Rivera (DSM)

## STAGE RESULTS

| POS | NAME | TEAM | TIME |
|---|---|---|---|
| 1. | A. van der Breggen | SDW | 2:58:31 |
| 2. | A. Moolman | SDW | 1:22 |
| 3. | D. Vollering | SDW | 1:51 |
| 4. | M. Cavalli | FDJ | 1:53 |
| 5. | E. Magnaldi | WNT | 2:30 |
| 6. | G. Realini | SBT | 2:36 |
| 7. | M. García | ALE | 3:00 |
| 8. | A. Spratt | BEX | 3:05 |
| 9. | T. Guderzo | ALE | 3:26 |
| 10. | J. Labous | DSM | 3:29 |
| 11. | E. Deignan | TFS | s.t. |
| 12. | E. Merino | MNX | s.t. |
| 13. | C. Koppenburg | RLW | 3:55 |
| 14. | N. Fisher-Black | SDW | 4:08 |
| 15. | É. Muzic | FDJ | 4:09 |
| 16. | P. Rooijakkers | LIV | 4:33 |
| 17. | A. Amialiusik | CSR | 5:11 |
| 18. | E. Chabbey | CSR | s.t. |
| 19. | C. U. Ludwig | FDJ | 5:53 |
| 20. | K. Aalerud | MOV | 6:00 |

## GENERAL CLASSIFICATION

| POS | NAME | TEAM | TIME |
|---|---|---|---|
| 1. ↑6 | A. van der Breggen | SDW | 3:32:09 |
| 2. ↑3 | A. Moolman | SDW | 1:26 |
| 3. ↑3 | D. Vollering | SDW | 1:57 |

## QUEEN OF THE MOUNTAINS

| POS | NAME | TEAM | PTS |
|---|---|---|---|
| 1. | A. van der Breggen | SDW | 13 |
| 2. | A. Moolman | SDW | 11 |
| 3. | D. Vollering | SDW | 9 |

## POINTS

| POS | NAME | TEAM | PTS |
|---|---|---|---|
| 1. | A. van der Breggen | SDW | 15 |
| 2. | A. Moolman | SDW | 12 |
| 3. | D. Vollering | SDW | 10 |

## YOUNG RIDER

| POS | NAME | TEAM | TIME |
|---|---|---|---|
| 1. — | N. Fisher-Black | SDW | 3:36:27 |
| 2. ↑9 | G. Realini | SBT | 1:09 |
| 3. ↑1 | É. Muzic | FDJ | 1:39 |

## TRIVIA
» Anna van der Breggen's third Giro stage victory equalled her number of overall Giro titles.

## BONUSES

| TYPE | NAME | TEAM |
|---|---|---|
| QOM 1 | K. Hammes | WNT |
| QOM 2 | A. van der Breggen | SDW |
| Sprint 1 | L. Dixon | TIB |

JULY .PRO WOMEN'S RACE

# GIRO D'ITALIA DONNE
Stage 3
4 July 2021
Casale Monferrato–Ovada
135km

A strong breakaway of four went all the way to the line on this hilly stage. In the rain, no breakaway formed on the flat first half, but things changed in the hilly second half. Six riders made a move on the first classified climb but were quickly brought back. Lucinda Brand (Trek-Segafredo) and Liane Lippert (Team DSM) attacked again on a descent and were joined by Marianne Vos, Elise Chabbey and Mikayla Harvey (Canyon-SRAM) on the next climb. When Harvey lost contact, four riders were left in front. As none of the four was a GC danger, they were given a lead of more than 4 minutes. Vos made it over the final climb with the others, and a headwind in the final discouraged attacks, bringing the group in for a sprint. Brand launched first but was easily passed by Vos, who won her 29th Giro stage.

## WEATHER

TEMPERATURE: 22°C
WIND: S 13km/h

## PROFILE

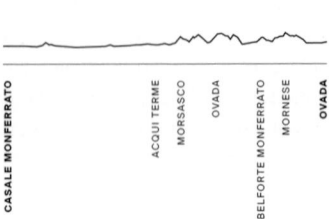

CASALE MONFERRATO — ACQUI TERME — MORSASCO — OVADA — BELFORTE MONFERRATO — MORNESE — OVADA

## BREAKAWAY

L. Brand (TFS), L. Lippert (DSM), M. Vos (JVW), E. Chabbey (CSR)

## STAGE RESULTS

| POS | NAME | TEAM | TIME |
|---|---|---|---|
| 1. | M. Vos | JVW | 3:40:24 |
| 2. | L. Brand | TFS | s.t. |
| 3. | L. Lippert | DSM | s.t. |
| 4. | E. Chabbey | CSR | s.t. |
| 5. | L. Brennauer | WNT | 3:18 |
| 6. | C. Rivera | DSM | s.t. |
| 7. | E. Norsgaard | MOV | s.t. |
| 8. | M. Bastianelli | ALE | s.t. |
| 9. | I. Sanguineti | VAL | s.t. |
| 10. | M. Lach | WNT | s.t. |
| 11. | S. Bertizzolo | LIV | s.t. |
| 12. | A. Ryan | CSR | s.t. |
| 13. | M. Jaskulska | LIV | s.t. |
| 14. | J. Labous | DSM | s.t. |
| 15. | É. Muzic | FDJ | s.t. |
| 16. | A. Spratt | BEX | s.t. |
| 17. | R. Leleivytė | VAI | s.t. |
| 18. | A. Moolman | SDW | s.t. |
| 19. | K. Faulkner | TIB | s.t. |
| 20. | N. Fisher-Black | SDW | 3:23 |

## GENERAL CLASSIFICATION

| POS | NAME | TEAM | TIME |
|---|---|---|---|
| 1. — | A. van der Breggen | SDW | 7:15:56 |
| 2. — | A. Moolman | SDW | 1:21 |
| 3. — | D. Vollering | SDW | 1:57 |

## QUEEN OF THE MOUNTAINS

| POS | NAME | TEAM | PTS |
|---|---|---|---|
| 1. ↑8 | E. Chabbey | CSR | 16 |
| 2. — | L. Brand | TFS | 14 |
| 3. ↓2 | A. van der Breggen | SDW | 13 |

## POINTS

| POS | NAME | TEAM | PTS |
|---|---|---|---|
| 1. — | A. van der Breggen | SDW | 15 |
| 2. — | M. Vos | JVW | 15 |
| 3. ↓1 | A. Moolman | SDW | 12 |

## YOUNG RIDER

| POS | NAME | TEAM | TIME |
|---|---|---|---|
| 1. — | N. Fisher-Black | SDW | 7:20:14 |
| 2. — | G. Realini | SBT | 1:24 |
| 3. — | É. Muzic | FDJ | 1:34 |

## TRIVIA

» This was Vos's 29th career victory at the Italian race.

## BONUSES

| TYPE | NAME | TEAM |
|---|---|---|
| QOM 1 | B. Chapman | FDJ |
| QOM 2 | M. Vos | TJV |
| QOM 3 | E. Chabbey | CSR |
| QOM 4 | E. Chabbey | CSR |
| Sprint 1 | G. Williams | BEX |

JULY .PRO WOMEN'S RACE

# GIRO D'ITALIA DONNE
Stage 4 (ITT)
5 July 2021
Formazza Loc. Fondovalle–Riale Di Formazza
Cascate Del Toce 11.2km

The 11.2km mountain time trial was the next opportunity for SD Worx to increase their advantage on the rest of the peloton, and the team's riders took it with both hands, placing first, second and third on the stage and further cementing their stranglehold on the GC. Starting in the first of three waves, the first benchmark of 28 minutes 49 seconds was set by Sara Casasola (Servetto-Makhymo-Beltrami TSA). In the second wave, this was bettered by Brodie Chapman, but Grace Brown improved on her compatriot's time by over 2 minutes. Most of the GC favourites could not beat Brown's time – only Demi Vollering could go faster than the Australian. Ashleigh Moolman-Pasio fell 24 seconds short of a new best time, but finally *maglia rosa* Anna van der Breggen – one of few riders to use a time trial bike – cut another 1 minute 6 seconds off Vollering's time to win the stage.

## WEATHER

TEMPERATURE: 26°C
WIND: S 7km/h

## PROFILE

FORMAZZA - FONDOVALLE
FORMAZZA-RIALE CASCATA DEL TOCE

## STAGE RESULTS

| POS | NAME | TEAM | TIME |
|---|---|---|---|
| 1. | A. van der Breggen | SDW | 24:57 |
| 2. | D. Vollering | SDW | 1:06 |
| 3. | G. Brown | BEX | 1:17 |
| 4. | A. Moolman | SDW | 1:30 |
| 5. | M. Cavalli | FDJ | 1:55 |
| 6. | J. Labous | DSM | 2:14 |
| 7. | K. Aalerud | MOV | 2:15 |
| 8. | E. Deignan | TFS | 2:22 |
| 9. | G. Realini | SBT | s.t. |
| 10. | E. Longo Borghini | TFS | 2:38 |
| 11. | E. Magnaldi | WNT | 2:45 |
| 12. | L. Thomas | MOV | 2:47 |
| 13. | R. Winder | TFS | 2:51 |
| 14. | L. Stephens | TIB | 2:59 |
| 15. | É. Muzic | FDJ | 3:01 |
| 16. | N. Fisher-Black | SDW | 3:04 |
| 17. | C. Honsinger | TIB | s.t. |
| 18. | P. Rooijakkers | LIV | 3:09 |
| 19. | M. García | ALE | 3:15 |
| 20. | T. Guderzo | ALE | 3:16 |

## GENERAL CLASSIFICATION

| POS | | NAME | TEAM | TIME |
|---|---|---|---|---|
| 1. | – | A. van der Breggen | SDW | 7:40:53 |
| 2. | – | A. Moolman | SDW | 2:51 |
| 3. | – | D. Vollering | SDW | 3:03 |

## QUEEN OF THE MOUNTAINS

| POS | | NAME | TEAM | PTS |
|---|---|---|---|---|
| 1. | – | E. Chabbey | CSR | 16 |
| 2. | – | L. Brand | TFS | 14 |
| 3. | – | A. van der Breggen | SDW | 13 |

## POINTS

| POS | | NAME | TEAM | PTS |
|---|---|---|---|---|
| 1. | – | A. van der Breggen | SDW | 30 |
| 2. | ↑3 | D. Vollering | SDW | 22 |
| 3. | – | A. Moolman | SDW | 20 |

## YOUNG RIDER

| POS | | NAME | TEAM | TIME |
|---|---|---|---|---|
| 1. | – | N. Fisher-Black | SDW | 7:48:15 |
| 2. | – | G. Realini | SBT | 0:42 |
| 3. | – | É. Muzic | FDJ | 1:31 |

## TRIVIA

» This was Anna van der Breggen's 11th time trial victory of her career.

JULY .PRO WOMEN'S RACE

# GIRO D'ITALIA DONNE
Stage 5
6 July 2021
Milano–Carugate
120.1km

After a neutral start in Milan, the stage mainly consisted of four laps of a flat circuit around the finish town of Carugate and was earmarked for the sprinters. A break of six riders went on the second lap and held an advantage of 2 minutes 33, but Team DSM controlled the race and reduced the gap to 38 seconds with 15km left to race. Maria Novolodskaya (A.R. Monex) attacked from the break and held on until she, too, was caught inside 4km to go. After Trek-Segafredo and Canyon-SRAM drove the peloton, Team DSM came to the fore at the kilometre mark with three riders still in front of Lorena Wiebes, and a lead-out from Coryn Rivera meant Wiebes had no trouble holding off Emma Norsgaard and Marianne Vos for her first Giro stage win.

## WEATHER

TEMPERATURE | WIND
30°C | SE 9km/h

## PROFILE

MILANO — CARUGATE — CARUGATE — CARUGATE — CARUGATE

## BREAKAWAY

M. Vitillo (BPK), N. L. Eremita (SBT), S. Zanardi (BPK), G. Vettorello (TOP), F. Piergiovanni (VAL), M. Novolodskaya (MNX)

## STAGE RESULTS

| POS | NAME | TEAM | TIME |
|---|---|---|---|
| 1. | L. Wiebes | DSM | 2:49:15 |
| 2. | E. Norsgaard | MOV | s.t. |
| 3. | M. Vos | JVW | s.t. |
| 4. | L. Brand | TFS | s.t. |
| 5. | M. Bastianelli | ALE | s.t. |
| 6. | M. G. Confalonieri | WNT | s.t. |
| 7. | S. Bertizzolo | LIV | s.t. |
| 8. | E. Gasparrini | VAL | s.t. |
| 9. | M. V. Sperotto | MNX | s.t. |
| 10. | C. Rivera | DSM | s.t. |
| 11. | E. Duval | FDJ | s.t. |
| 12. | I. Sanguineti | VAL | s.t. |
| 13. | A. Trevisi | ALE | s.t. |
| 14. | E. Cecchini | SDW | s.t. |
| 15. | A. Ryan | CSR | s.t. |
| 16. | S. Roy | BEX | s.t. |
| 17. | M. Jaskulska | LIV | s.t. |
| 18. | J. Labous | DSM | s.t. |
| 19. | M. Lach | WNT | s.t. |
| 20. | J. Vandenbulcke | LSL | s.t. |

## GENERAL CLASSIFICATION

| POS | | NAME | TEAM | TIME |
|---|---|---|---|---|
| 1. | — | A. van der Breggen | SDW | 10:30:08 |
| 2. | — | A. Moolman | SDW | 2:51 |
| 3. | — | D. Vollering | SDW | 3:03 |

## QUEEN OF THE MOUNTAINS

| POS | | NAME | TEAM | PTS |
|---|---|---|---|---|
| 1. | — | E. Chabbey | CSR | 16 |
| 2. | — | L. Brand | TFS | 14 |
| 3. | — | A. van der Breggen | SDW | 13 |

## POINTS

| POS | | NAME | TEAM | PTS |
|---|---|---|---|---|
| 1. | — | A. van der Breggen | SDW | 30 |
| 2. | ↑2 | M. Vos | JVW | 25 |
| 3. | ↓1 | D. Vollering | SDW | 22 |

## YOUNG RIDER

| POS | | NAME | TEAM | TIME |
|---|---|---|---|---|
| 1. | — | N. Fisher-Black | SDW | 10:37:30 |
| 2. | — | G. Realini | SBT | 0:42 |
| 3. | — | É. Muzic | FDJ | 1:31 |

## TRIVIA

» This was Lorena Wiebes's first-ever win in Italy.

## BONUSES

| TYPE | NAME | TEAM |
|---|---|---|
| Sprint 1 | L. Brennauer | WNT |
| Sprint 2 | S. Zanardi | BPK |
| Sprint 3 | S. Zanardi | BPK |

JULY .PRO WOMEN'S RACE

# GIRO D'ITALIA DONNE
Stage 6
7 July 2021
Colico–Colico
155km

Doing an almost-complete anticlockwise tour of the shoreline of Lake Como, stage 6 was the longest of the Giro and hillier than the previous stage. Nonetheless, it was raced very fast and decided in a sprint. Elisa Longo Borghini and Ashleigh Moolman-Pasio attacked after 60km. They worked well together and held an advantage of up to 2 minutes 25, but the efforts by Team DSM and Team Jumbo-Visma meant they were caught with 13km to go. Team DSM tried to set up Coryn Rivera, with stage 5 winner Lorena Wiebes leading her out in the sprint, but Emma Norsgaard had the top speed to the line and beat Rivera to win her first Giro stage.

## WEATHER

TEMPERATURE | WIND
27°C | S 7km/h

## PROFILE

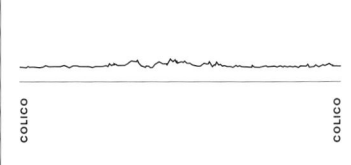

## BREAKAWAY
E. Longo Borghini (TFS), A. Moolman-Pasio (SDW)

## STAGE RESULTS

| POS | NAME | TEAM | TIME |
|---|---|---|---|
| 1. | E. Norsgaard | MOV | 3:41:39 |
| 2. | C. Rivera | DSM | s.t. |
| 3. | M. Vos | JVW | s.t. |
| 4. | M. Bastianelli | ALE | s.t. |
| 5. | L. Brennauer | WNT | s.t. |
| 6. | L. Brand | TFS | s.t. |
| 7. | I. Sanguineti | VAL | s.t. |
| 8. | S. Bertizzolo | LIV | s.t. |
| 9. | M. V. Sperotto | MNX | s.t. |
| 10. | E. Cecchini | SDW | s.t. |
| 11. | A. Ryan | CSR | s.t. |
| 12. | E. Gasparrini | VAL | s.t. |
| 13. | J. Vandenbulcke | LSL | s.t. |
| 14. | E. Duval | FDJ | s.t. |
| 15. | S. Zanardi | BPK | s.t. |
| 16. | L. Wiebes | DSM | s.t. |
| 17. | L. Curinier | ARK | s.t. |
| 18. | E. Chabbey | CSR | s.t. |
| 19. | S. Smulders | LSL | s.t. |
| 20. | J. Korevaar | LIV | s.t. |

## GENERAL CLASSIFICATION

| POS | | NAME | TEAM | TIME |
|---|---|---|---|---|
| 1. | — | A. van der Breggen | SDW | 14:11:47 |
| 2. | — | A. Moolman | SDW | 2:51 |
| 3. | — | D. Vollering | SDW | 3:03 |

## QUEEN OF THE MOUNTAINS

| POS | | NAME | TEAM | PTS |
|---|---|---|---|---|
| 1. | — | E. Chabbey | CSR | 16 |
| 2. | — | L. Brand | TFS | 14 |
| 3. | — | A. van der Breggen | SDW | 13 |

## POINTS

| POS | | NAME | TEAM | PTS |
|---|---|---|---|---|
| 1. | ↑1 | M. Vos | JVW | 35 |
| 2. | ↑4 | E. Norsgaard | MOV | 31 |
| 3. | ↓2 | A. van der Breggen | SDW | 30 |

## YOUNG RIDER

| POS | | NAME | TEAM | TIME |
|---|---|---|---|---|
| 1. | — | N. Fisher-Black | SDW | 14:19:09 |
| 2. | — | G. Realini | SBT | 0:42 |
| 3. | — | É. Muzic | FDJ | 1:31 |

## TRIVIA
» Stage 6 saw Norsgaard claim her sixth win of the season.

JULY .PRO WOMEN'S RACE

# GIRO D'ITALIA DONNE
Stage 7
8 July 2021
Soprazocco Di Gavardo–Puegnago Del Garda
109.6km

This stage mainly consisted of 5.5 laps of a hilly circuit, and Marianne Vos made history when she won her 30th stage in the women's Giro. After an early break was caught, Lucinda Brand set off solo on the second lap. She was caught by a chase group of five with 25km to go, but the peloton reeled them in shortly afterwards. There were many short-lived attacks on the final lap, and in the end it came down to the final climb. Having closed down a move by Tiffany Cromwell, Elisa Longo Borghini then attacked at the kilometre mark, followed by Marianne Vos. Vos sat on the Italian champion's wheel until 500 metres to go, when she accelerated past to win the stage. Longo Borghini just held off race leader Anna van der Breggen for second place. Ⓤ

## WEATHER

TEMPERATURE: 29°C
WIND: E 19km/h

## PROFILE

## BREAKAWAY
M. Vitillo (BPK), R. Markus (JVW), L. Brand (TFS)

## STAGE RESULTS

| POS | NAME | TEAM | TIME |
|---|---|---|---|
| 1. | M. Vos | JVW | 2:48:31 |
| 2. | E. Longo Borghini | TFS | s.t. |
| 3. | A. van der Breggen | SDW | s.t. |
| 4. | D. Vollering | SDW | s.t. |
| 5. | S. Paladin | LIV | s.t. |
| 6. | J. Labous | DSM | s.t. |
| 7. | M. Cavalli | FDJ | s.t. |
| 8. | A. Moolman | SDW | s.t. |
| 9. | I. Sanguineti | VAL | s.t. |
| 10. | M. García | ALE | s.t. |
| 11. | E. Deignan | TFS | s.t. |
| 12. | E. Magnaldi | WNT | s.t. |
| 13. | T. Guderzo | ALE | s.t. |
| 14. | L. Thomas | MOV | s.t. |
| 15. | N. van der Burg | JVW | 0:11 |
| 16. | E. Chabbey | CSR | s.t. |
| 17. | C. Rivera | DSM | 0:13 |
| 18. | S. Smulders | LSL | s.t. |
| 19. | A. Spratt | BEX | 0:15 |
| 20. | A. Amialiusik | CSR | s.t. |

## GENERAL CLASSIFICATION

| POS | NAME | TEAM | TIME |
|---|---|---|---|
| 1. — | A. van der Breggen | SDW | 17:00:14 |
| 2. — | A. Moolman | SDW | 2:55 |
| 3. — | D. Vollering | SDW | 3:07 |

## QUEEN OF THE MOUNTAINS

| POS | NAME | TEAM | PTS |
|---|---|---|---|
| 1. ↑1 | L. Brand | TFS | 32 |
| 2. ↓1 | E. Chabbey | CSR | 20 |
| 3. ↑2 | L. Lippert | DSM | 18 |

## POINTS

| POS | NAME | TEAM | PTS |
|---|---|---|---|
| 1. — | M. Vos | JVW | 50 |
| 2. ↑1 | A. van der Breggen | SDW | 40 |
| 3. ↓1 | E. Norsgaard | MOV | 31 |

## YOUNG RIDER

| POS | NAME | TEAM | TIME |
|---|---|---|---|
| 1. — | N. Fisher-Black | SDW | 17:08:04 |
| 2. — | G. Realini | SBT | 0:37 |
| 3. — | É. Muzic | FDJ | 1:26 |

## TRIVIA
» There were exactly 14 years between Marianne Vos's first and most recent Giro stage wins.

## BONUSES

| TYPE | NAME | TEAM |
|---|---|---|
| QOM 1 | R. Markus | TJV |
| QOM 2 | L. Brand | TFS |
| QOM 3 | L. Brand | TFS |
| QOM 4 | L. Brand | TFS |
| QOM 5 | E. Longo Borghini | TFS |
| Sprint 1 | M. Vitillo | BPK |

JULY .PRO WOMEN'S RACE

# GIRO D'ITALIA DONNE
Stage 8
9 July 2021
San Vendemiano–Mortegliano
129.4km

The peloton that started stage 8 was smaller as Bizkaia Durango and Tibco-SVB withdrew from the race because of Covid-19 positives. Cecilie Uttrup Ludwig also did not start due to injuries she'd suffered on stage 1. On a flat stage, the breakaway only formed after 55km when Born To Win G20 Ambedo teammates Anastasia Carbonari and Natalia Studenikina were joined by Giorgia Vettorello (Top Girls Fassa Bortolo). Their advantage maxed out at 3 minutes 15 with 50km left, but the work by Team DSM and Movistar Team brought this down to 1 minute 33 with 21.8km remaining. Team Jumbo-Visma and Valcar Travel & Service also joined in the chase, and the break was reeled in 6km from the finish. From the wheel of Emma Norsgaard, Coryn Rivera accelerated out of the final turn with 500 metres left to lead out Lorena Wiebes for another sprint victory.

## WEATHER

TEMPERATURE: 27°C
WIND: SE 6km/h

## PROFILE

SAN VENDEMIANO — SAN VITO AL TAGLIAMENTO — MORTEGLIANO — MORTEGLIAINO

## BREAKAWAY
A. Carbonari (BTW), N. Studenikina (BTW), G. Vettorello (TOP)

## STAGE RESULTS

| POS | NAME | TEAM | TIME |
|---|---|---|---|
| 1. | L. Wiebes | DSM | 3:10:01 |
| 2. | E. Norsgaard | MOV | s.t. |
| 3. | M. V. Sperotto | MNX | s.t. |
| 4. | L. Brennauer | WNT | s.t. |
| 5. | M. Vos | JVW | s.t. |
| 6. | M. Bastianelli | ALE | s.t. |
| 7. | E. Cecchini | SDW | s.t. |
| 8. | S. Bertizzolo | LIV | s.t. |
| 9. | I. Sanguineti | VAL | s.t. |
| 10. | L. Brand | TFS | s.t. |
| 11. | S. Zanardi | BPK | s.t. |
| 12. | E. Gasparrini | VAL | s.t. |
| 13. | E. Duval | FDJ | s.t. |
| 14. | C. Rivera | DSM | s.t. |
| 15. | J. Korevaar | LIV | s.t. |
| 16. | L. Jounier | ARK | s.t. |
| 17. | M. Lach | WNT | s.t. |
| 18. | S. Smulders | LSL | s.t. |
| 19. | M. Drummond | BPK | s.t. |
| 20. | A. Ryan | CSR | s.t. |

## GENERAL CLASSIFICATION

| POS | NAME | TEAM | TIME |
|---|---|---|---|
| 1. — | A. van der Breggen | SDW | 20:10:15 |
| 2. — | A. Moolman | SDW | 2:55 |
| 3. — | D. Vollering | SDW | 3:07 |

## QUEEN OF THE MOUNTAINS

| POS | NAME | TEAM | PTS |
|---|---|---|---|
| 1. — | L. Brand | TFS | 32 |
| 2. — | E. Chabbey | CSR | 20 |
| 3. — | L. Lippert | DSM | 18 |

## POINTS

| POS | NAME | TEAM | PTS |
|---|---|---|---|
| 1. — | M. Vos | JVW | 56 |
| 2. ↑1 | E. Norsgaard | MOV | 43 |
| 3. ↓1 | A. van der Breggen | SDW | 40 |

## YOUNG RIDER

| POS | NAME | TEAM | TIME |
|---|---|---|---|
| 1. — | N. Fisher-Black | SDW | 20:18:05 |
| 2. — | G. Realini | SBT | 0:37 |
| 3. — | É. Muzic | FDJ | 1:26 |

## BONUSES

| TYPE | NAME | TEAM |
|---|---|---|
| Sprint 1 | L. Borghesi | VAI |
| Sprint 2 | A. Carbonari | BTW |

JULY .PRO WOMEN'S RACE

# GIRO D'ITALIA DONNE
Stage 9
10 July 2021
Feletto-Umberto–Monte Matajur
122.6km

An early breakaway of three riders fell apart on the category-2 Stregna climb, where Elisa Longo Borghini and Ashleigh Moolman-Pasio attacked from the peloton. Extending their advantage on the flat between the climbs, Longo Borghini and Moolman-Pasio started the 14km climb of the Monte Matajur 2 minutes 18 ahead of the peloton. As the group of favourites came closer, Moolman-Pasio accelerated away from Longo Borghini 8km from the finish. While Longo Borghini was caught by the favourites, the South African climber held on to win her first Giro stage in 11 participations. Her teammates Demi Vollering and Anna van der Breggen crossed the line together, making it another SD Worx 1-2-3.

## WEATHER

TEMPERATURE: 30°C
WIND: E 17km/h

## PROFILE

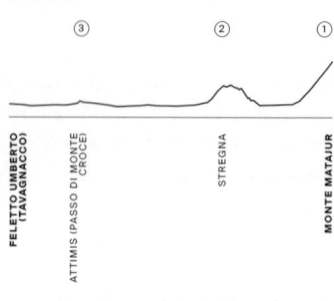

③ ② ①

FELETTO UMBERTO (TAVAGNACCO)
ATTIMIS (PASSO DI MONTE CROCE)
STREGNA
MONTE MATAJUR

## BREAKAWAY

L. Borghesi (VAI), A. Zontone (SER), G. Vettorello (TOP)

## STAGE RESULTS

| POS | NAME | TEAM | TIME |
|---|---|---|---|
| 1. | A. Moolman | SDW | 3:52:35 |
| 2. | D. Vollering | SDW | 1:26 |
| 3. | A. van der Breggen | SDW | s.t. |
| 4. | M. Cavalli | FDJ | 1:39 |
| 5. | E. Deignan | TFS | 2:14 |
| 6. | M. García | ALE | 2:27 |
| 7. | J. Labous | DSM | 2:37 |
| 8. | T. Guderzo | ALE | 2:46 |
| 9. | N. Fisher-Black | SDW | 2:56 |
| 10. | É. Muzic | FDJ | 3:25 |
| 11. | G. Realini | SBT | 3:28 |
| 12. | L. Thomas | MOV | 3:31 |
| 13. | E. Longo Borghini | TFS | 3:41 |
| 14. | E. Merino | MNX | 4:31 |
| 15. | A. Spratt | BEX | 4:53 |
| 16. | B. Chapman | FDJ | 4:58 |
| 17. | S. Stultiens | LIV | 5:41 |
| 18. | E. Chabbey | CSR | s.t. |
| 19. | A. Amialiusik | CSR | 5:50 |
| 20. | M. Novolodskaia | MNX | 6:13 |

## GENERAL CLASSIFICATION

| POS | NAME | TEAM | TIME |
|---|---|---|---|
| 1. – | A. van der Breggen | SDW | 24:04:12 |
| 2. – | A. Moolman | SDW | 1:23 |
| 3. – | D. Vollering | SDW | 3:05 |

## QUEEN OF THE MOUNTAINS

| POS | NAME | TEAM | PTS |
|---|---|---|---|
| 1. – | L. Brand | TFS | 34 |
| 2. ↑4 | A. Moolman | SDW | 31 |
| 3. ↑1 | A. van der Breggen | SDW | 24 |

## POINTS

| POS | NAME | TEAM | PTS |
|---|---|---|---|
| 1. ↑2 | A. van der Breggen | SDW | 50 |
| 2. – | E. Norsgaard | MOV | 43 |
| 3. ↑2 | D. Vollering | SDW | 42 |

## YOUNG RIDER

| POS | NAME | TEAM | TIME |
|---|---|---|---|
| 1. – | N. Fisher-Black | SDW | 24:13:36 |
| 2. – | G. Realini | SBT | 1:09 |
| 3. – | É. Muzic | FDJ | 1:55 |

## TRIVIA

» This was Ashleigh Moolman-Pasio's first victory for SD Worx.

## BONUSES

| TYPE | NAME | TEAM |
|---|---|---|
| QOM 1 | A. Zontone | SER |
| QOM 2 | E. Longo Borghini | TFS |
| QOM 3 | A. Moolman-Pasio | SDW |

JULY .PRO WOMEN'S RACE

# GIRO D'ITALIA DONNE
Stage 10
11 July 2021
Capriva del Friuli–Cormons
113km

The final stage was dominated by a strong breakaway of five, four of whom made it to the finish. Lucinda Brand attacked on the first climb to safeguard her mountain jersey and was joined on the descent by Anna van der Breggen, Lizzie Deignan, Elise Chabbey and Coryn Rivera. *Maglia rosa* Van der Breggen was happy to sit on the wheels and did not contest the sprint in the end. The other four traded turns and had a maximum advantage of just over 2 minutes. Movistar Team and Liv Racing chased in the peloton and reduced this to 1 minute with 15km to go and, after a lot of work, Brand was dropped on the final climb. Rivera and Deignan went head-to-head in the sprint, and Rivera won the stage with a bike throw, dedicating the victory to her late father, a medical worker who had died of Covid-19.

## WEATHER

TEMPERATURE: 31°C
WIND: NW 9km/h

## PROFILE

CAPRIVA DEL FRIULI — SAN FLORIANO DEL COLLIO — RUTTARS — RUTTARS — RUTTARS — CORMONS

## BREAKAWAY

L. Brand (TFS), A. van der Breggen (SDW), E. Deignan (TFS), E. Chabbey (CSR), C. Rivera (DSM)

## STAGE RESULTS

| POS | NAME | TEAM | TIME |
|---|---|---|---|
| 1. | C. Rivera | DSM | 2:56:40 |
| 2. | E. Deignan | TFS | s.t. |
| 3. | E. Chabbey | CSR | 0:03 |
| 4. | A. van der Breggen | SDW | s.t. |
| 5. | E. Norsgaard | MOV | 0:23 |
| 6. | L. Lippert | DSM | s.t. |
| 7. | I. Sanguineti | VAL | s.t. |
| 8. | A. Koster | JVW | s.t. |
| 9. | S. Bertizzolo | LIV | s.t. |
| 10. | A. Ryan | CSR | s.t. |
| 11. | S. Paladin | LIV | s.t. |
| 12. | S. Smulders | LSL | s.t. |
| 13. | D. Vollering | SDW | s.t. |
| 14. | G. Marturano | TOP | s.t. |
| 15. | E. Duval | FDJ | s.t. |
| 16. | L. Brennauer | WNT | s.t. |
| 17. | M. García | ALE | s.t. |
| 18. | D. Silvestri | TOP | s.t. |
| 19. | M. Cavalli | FDJ | s.t. |
| 20. | É. Muzic | FDJ | s.t. |

## GENERAL CLASSIFICATION

| POS | | NAME | TEAM | TIME |
|---|---|---|---|---|
| 1. | — | A. van der Breggen | SDW | 27:00:55 |
| 2. | — | A. Moolman | SDW | 1:43 |
| 3. | — | D. Vollering | SDW | 3:25 |

## QUEEN OF THE MOUNTAINS

| POS | | NAME | TEAM | PTS |
|---|---|---|---|---|
| 1. | — | L. Brand | TFS | 47 |
| 2. | — | A. Moolman | SDW | 31 |
| 3. | — | A. van der Breggen | SDW | 29 |

## POINTS

| POS | | NAME | TEAM | PTS |
|---|---|---|---|---|
| 1. | — | A. van der Breggen | SDW | 58 |
| 2. | — | E. Norsgaard | MOV | 49 |
| 3. | — | D. Vollering | SDW | 42 |

## YOUNG RIDER

| POS | | NAME | TEAM | TIME |
|---|---|---|---|---|
| 1. | — | N. Fisher-Black | SDW | 27:10:39 |
| 2. | — | G. Realini | SBT | 1:09 |
| 3. | — | É. Muzic | FDJ | 1:55 |

## TRIVIA

» This was Van der Breggen's fourth overall victory, just one behind record five-time winner Fabiana Luperini.

## BONUSES

| TYPE | NAME | TEAM |
|---|---|---|
| QOM 1 | L. Brand | TFS |
| QOM 2 | L. Brand | TFS |
| QOM 3 | C. Rivera | DSM |
| QOM 4 | C. Rivera | DSM |

JULY   .1 MEN'S RACE

## SIBIU CYCLING TOUR
Prologue
3 July 2021
Sibiu–Sibiu
2.5km

### WEATHER

| TEMPERATURE | WIND |
|---|---|
| 16°C | NW 17km/h |

### STAGE RESULTS

| POS | NAME | TEAM | TIME |
|---|---|---|---|
| 1. | P. Ackermann | BOH | 3:18 |
| 2. | M. Laas | BOH | 0:03 |
| 3. | R. Stacchiotti | THR | s.t. |
| 4. | M. Walls | BOH | 0:04 |
| 5. | N. Dalla Valle | BCF | 0:05 |
| 6. | T. Wollenberg | PBS | 0:06 |
| 7. | M. Kukrle | EKA | 0:08 |
| 8. | A. Guerin | VBG | s.t. |
| 9. | M. van der Veekens | ABC | 0:09 |
| 10. | K. Camrda | TFA | s.t. |
| 11. | F. Fortin | VBG | s.t. |
| 12. | D. Irvine | TNN | s.t. |
| 13. | L. Meiler | VBG | 0:10 |
| 14. | P. Bernas | MSP | s.t. |
| 15. | D. Crista | NAT | s.t. |
| 16. | A. Toupalik | EKA | s.t. |
| 17. | G. Aleotti | BOH | s.t. |
| 18. | S. Kolb | HAC | 0:11 |
| 19. | A. Kurek | MSP | 0:12 |
| 20. | S. Appel | ABC | s.t. |

### GENERAL CLASSIFICATION

| POS | NAME | TEAM | TIME |
|---|---|---|---|
| 1. | P. Ackermann | BOH | 3:18 |
| 2. | M. Laas | BOH | 0:03 |
| 3. | R. Stacchiotti | THR | s.t. |

### POINTS

| POS | NAME | TEAM | PTS |
|---|---|---|---|
| 1. | P. Ackermann | BOH | 25 |
| 2. | M. Laas | BOH | 20 |
| 3. | R. Stacchiotti | THR | 15 |

### YOUNG RIDER

| POS | NAME | TEAM | TIME |
|---|---|---|---|
| 1. | T. Wollenberg | PBS | 3:24 |
| 2. | K. Camrda | TFA | 0:03 |
| 3. | D. Irvine | TNN | s.t. |

## SIBIU CYCLING TOUR
Stage 1
4 July 2021
Sibiu–Paltinis
177.9km

### WEATHER

| TEMPERATURE | WIND |
|---|---|
| 19°C | NW 15km/h |

### STAGE RESULTS

| POS | NAME | TEAM | TIME |
|---|---|---|---|
| 1. | G. Aleotti | BOH | 4:25:14 |
| 2. | F. Aru | TQA | s.t. |
| 3. | S. Chernetski | GAZ | 0:02 |
| 4. | R. Thalmann | VBG | s.t. |
| 5. | M. Schlegel | EKA | s.t. |
| 6. | R. Zoidl | RSW | 0:13 |
| 7. | J. Rapp | HAC | 0:28 |
| 8. | A. Toupalik | EKA | 0:50 |
| 9. | D. Rebellin | IWM | 0:56 |
| 10. | G. Carboni | BCF | s.t. |
| 11. | J. Otruba | EKA | 1:05 |
| 12. | A. Guerin | VBG | 1:07 |
| 13. | L. Covili | BCF | 1:52 |
| 14. | R. Power | TQA | 1:57 |
| 15. | E. Battaglin | BCF | 1:59 |
| 16. | A. Berlin | GLC | s.t. |
| 17. | K. Camrda | TFA | 2:04 |
| 18. | A. Moreno | VBG | s.t. |
| 19. | M. Canola | GAZ | s.t. |
| 20. | K. Domagalski | MSP | s.t. |

### GENERAL CLASSIFICATION

| POS | NAME | TEAM | TIME |
|---|---|---|---|
| 1. ↑16 | G. Aleotti | BOH | 4:28:32 |
| 2. ↑92 | F. Aru | TQA | 0:17 |
| 3. ↑56 | M. Schlegel | EKA | 0:20 |

### KING OF THE MOUNTAINS

| POS | NAME | TEAM | PTS |
|---|---|---|---|
| 1. | G. Aleotti | BOH | 12 |
| 2. | D. Turek | RSW | 11 |
| 3. | F. Aru | TQA | 8 |

### POINTS

| POS | NAME | TEAM | PTS |
|---|---|---|---|
| 1. — | G. Aleotti | BOH | 25 |
| 2. ↓1 | P. Ackermann | BOH | 25 |
| 3. — | F. Aru | TQA | 20 |

### YOUNG RIDER

| POS | NAME | TEAM | TIME |
|---|---|---|---|
| 1. ↑3 | G. Aleotti | BOH | 4:28:32 |
| 2. — | K. Camrda | TFA | 2:13 |
| 3. ↑4 | K. Vacek | TQA | 2:24 |

JULY .1 MEN'S RACE

## SIBIU CYCLING TOUR
Stage 2
5 July 2021
Sibiu–Bâlea Lac
187.5km

### WEATHER

TEMPERATURE | WIND
24°C | N 13km/h

### STAGE RESULTS

| POS | NAME | TEAM | TIME |
|---|---|---|---|
| 1. | A. Guerin | VBG | 4:50:01 |
| 2. | G. Aleotti | BOH | 0:11 |
| 3. | F. Aru | TQA | s.t. |
| 4. | M. Schlegel | EKA | s.t. |
| 5. | R. Zoidl | RSW | s.t. |
| 6. | S. Chernetski | GAZ | s.t. |
| 7. | J. Rapp | HAC | 0:16 |
| 8. | R. Thalmann | VBG | 0:29 |
| 9. | L. Covili | BCF | 0:35 |
| 10. | E. Battaglin | BCF | 1:06 |
| 11. | E. Dima | GTS | s.t. |
| 12. | A. Berlin | GLC | 1:08 |
| 13. | D. Rebellin | IWM | s.t. |
| 14. | A. Toupalík | EKA | 1:10 |
| 15. | A. Moreno | VBG | s.t. |
| 16. | A. Di Renzo | THR | 1:15 |
| 17. | J. Otruba | EKA | 1:22 |
| 18. | M. Jeannès | ILU | 1:26 |
| 19. | G. Carboni | BCF | 2:08 |
| 20. | N. Cherkasov | GAZ | 2:22 |

### GENERAL CLASSIFICATION

| POS | NAME | TEAM | TIME |
|---|---|---|---|
| 1. — | G. Aleotti | BOH | 9:18:38 |
| 2. — | F. Aru | TQA | 0:19 |
| 3. — | M. Schlegel | EKA | 0:26 |

### KING OF THE MOUNTAINS

| POS | NAME | TEAM | PTS |
|---|---|---|---|
| 1. — | G. Aleotti | BOH | 30 |
| 2. ↑1 | F. Aru | TQA | 24 |
| 3. — | A. Guerin | VBG | 20 |

### POINTS

| POS | NAME | TEAM | PTS |
|---|---|---|---|
| 1. — | G. Aleotti | BOH | 45 |
| 2. ↑1 | F. Aru | TQA | 35 |
| 3. ↑12 | A. Guerin | VBG | 31 |

### YOUNG RIDER

| POS | NAME | TEAM | TIME |
|---|---|---|---|
| 1. — | G. Aleotti | BOH | 9:18:38 |
| 2. ↑2 | M. Weulink | ABC | 5:10 |
| 3. ↓1 | K. Camrda | TFA | 8:52 |

## SIBIU CYCLING TOUR
Stage 3
6 July 2021
Sibiu–Sibiu
205.3km

### WEATHER

TEMPERATURE | WIND
26°C | NW 11km/h

### STAGE RESULTS

| POS | NAME | TEAM | TIME |
|---|---|---|---|
| 1. | P. Ackermann | BOH | 4:26:16 |
| 2. | E. M. Grosu | NAT | 0:02 |
| 3. | M. Walls | BOH | s.t. |
| 4. | A. Toupalík | EKA | s.t. |
| 5. | M. Canola | GAZ | s.t. |
| 6. | R. Stacchiotti | THR | 0:05 |
| 7. | R. Janse Van Rensburg | TQA | s.t. |
| 8. | M. Budzinski | MSP | s.t. |
| 9. | D. Appollonio | AMO | s.t. |
| 10. | F. Burchio | IWM | s.t. |
| 11. | J. Couanon | NIP | s.t. |
| 12. | M. Schlegel | EKA | s.t. |
| 13. | G. Aleotti | BOH | s.t. |
| 14. | A. Iacchi | THR | s.t. |
| 15. | A. Oka | NIP | s.t. |
| 16. | E. Battaglin | BCF | s.t. |
| 17. | M. Stockman | SVL | s.t. |
| 18. | R. Thalmann | VBG | s.t. |
| 19. | J. Hodapp | SVL | s.t. |
| 20. | J. Rapp | HAC | s.t. |

### GENERAL CLASSIFICATION

| POS | NAME | TEAM | TIME |
|---|---|---|---|
| 1. — | G. Aleotti | BOH | 13:44:59 |
| 2. — | F. Aru | TQA | 0:19 |
| 3. — | M. Schlegel | EKA | 0:26 |

### KING OF THE MOUNTAINS

| POS | NAME | TEAM | PTS |
|---|---|---|---|
| 1. ↑3 | D. Turek | RSW | 32 |
| 2. ↓1 | G. Aleotti | BOH | 31 |
| 3. ↓1 | F. Aru | TQA | 26 |

### POINTS

| POS | NAME | TEAM | PTS |
|---|---|---|---|
| 1. ↑3 | P. Ackermann | BOH | 50 |
| 2. ↓1 | G. Aleotti | BOH | 45 |
| 3. ↓1 | F. Aru | TQA | 35 |

### YOUNG RIDER

| POS | NAME | TEAM | TIME |
|---|---|---|---|
| 1. — | G. Aleotti | BOH | 13:44:59 |
| 2. — | M. Weulink | ABC | 5:10 |
| 3. — | K. Camrda | TFA | 8:52 |

JULY .1 MEN'S RACE

# SETTIMANA CICLISTICA ITALIANA
Stage 1
14 July 2021
Alghero–Sassari
155.8km

## WEATHER

TEMPERATURE | WIND
25°C | W 26km/h

## STAGE RESULTS

| POS | NAME | TEAM | TIME |
|---|---|---|---|
| 1. | D. Ulissi | UAD | 3:40:31 |
| 2. | A. Bettiol | NAT | s.t. |
| 3. | G. Aleotti | BOH | s.t. |
| 4. | F. Großschartner | BOH | s.t. |
| 5. | G. Ciccone | NAT | s.t. |
| 6. | S. Vanmarcke | ISN | s.t. |
| 7. | G. Moscon | NAT | s.t. |
| 8. | B. Hermans | ISN | s.t. |
| 9. | I. Zakarin | GAZ | s.t. |
| 10. | D. Villella | MOV | s.t. |
| 11. | J. Irizar | EUS | s.t. |
| 12. | D. Caruso | TBV | s.t. |
| 13. | S. Samitier | MOV | s.t. |
| 14. | F. Masnada | NAT | s.t. |
| 15. | P. Double | MGK | s.t. |
| 16. | A. Zeits | BEX | 0:07 |
| 17. | J. Cepeda Ortiz | ANS | s.t. |
| 18. | M. Padun | TBV | 0:10 |
| 19. | S. Pellaud | ANS | 0:36 |
| 20. | D. Rebellin | IWM | s.t. |

## GENERAL CLASSIFICATION

| POS | NAME | TEAM | TIME |
|---|---|---|---|
| 1. | D. Ulissi | UAD | 3:40:21 |
| 2. | A. Bettiol | NAT | 0:04 |
| 3. | G. Aleotti | BOH | 0:06 |

## KING OF THE MOUNTAINS

| POS | NAME | TEAM | PTS |
|---|---|---|---|
| 1. | S. Pellaud | ANS | 10 |
| 2. | L. Wackermann | EOK | 7 |
| 3. | R. Herregodts | SVB | 6 |

## POINTS

| POS | NAME | TEAM | PTS |
|---|---|---|---|
| 1. | D. Ulissi | UAD | 10 |
| 2. | A. Bettiol | NAT | 8 |
| 3. | G. Aleotti | BOH | 6 |

## YOUNG RIDER

| POS | NAME | TEAM | TIME |
|---|---|---|---|
| 1. | G. Aleotti | BOH | 3:40:27 |
| 2. | J. Cepeda Ortiz | ANS | 0:11 |
| 3. | S. Buitrago | TBV | 0:49 |

# SETTIMANA CICLISTICA ITALIANA
Stage 2
15 July 2021
Sassari–Oristano
185.5km

## WEATHER

TEMPERATURE | WIND
26°C | W 19km/h

## STAGE RESULTS

| POS | NAME | TEAM | TIME |
|---|---|---|---|
| 1. | P. Ackermann | BOH | 4:26:40 |
| 2. | B. Peák | BEX | s.t. |
| 3. | S. Vanmarcke | ISN | s.t. |
| 4. | E. Battaglin | BCF | s.t. |
| 5. | A. Bettiol | NAT | s.t. |
| 6. | M. Bouet | ARK | s.t. |
| 7. | D. Ulissi | UAD | s.t. |
| 8. | M. Louvel | ARK | s.t. |
| 9. | F. Großschartner | BOH | s.t. |
| 10. | G. Garavaglia | IWM | s.t. |
| 11. | M. Canola | GAZ | s.t. |
| 12. | J. Restrepo | ANS | s.t. |
| 13. | E. Prades | DKO | s.t. |
| 14. | A. Fedeli | DKO | s.t. |
| 15. | I. Filosi | GTS | s.t. |
| 16. | A. Zeits | BEX | s.t. |
| 17. | D. Villella | MOV | s.t. |
| 18. | A. Riabushenko | UAD | s.t. |
| 19. | G. Aleotti | BOH | s.t. |
| 20. | R. Herregodts | SVB | s.t. |

## GENERAL CLASSIFICATION

| POS | | NAME | TEAM | TIME |
|---|---|---|---|---|
| 1. | — | D. Ulissi | UAD | 8:07:01 |
| 2. | — | A. Bettiol | NAT | 0:04 |
| 3. | ↑3 | S. Vanmarcke | ISN | 0:06 |

## KING OF THE MOUNTAINS

| POS | | NAME | TEAM | PTS |
|---|---|---|---|---|
| 1. | — | S. Pellaud | ANS | 25 |
| 2. | ↑1 | R. Herregodts | SVB | 17 |
| 3. | — | S. Buitrago | TBV | 12 |

## POINTS

| POS | | NAME | TEAM | PTS |
|---|---|---|---|---|
| 1. | — | D. Ulissi | UAD | 12 |
| 2. | — | A. Bettiol | NAT | 12 |
| 3. | — | P. Ackermann | BOH | 10 |

## YOUNG RIDER

| POS | | NAME | TEAM | TIME |
|---|---|---|---|---|
| 1. | — | G. Aleotti | BOH | 8:07:07 |
| 2. | — | J. Cepeda Ortiz | ANS | 0:11 |
| 3. | — | S. Buitrago | TBV | 0:49 |

JULY .1 MEN'S RACE

## SETTIMANA CICLISTICA ITALIANA
Stage 3
16 July 2021
Oristano–Cagliari
180.9km

## WEATHER

TEMPERATURE   WIND
28°C          NW 28km/h

### STAGE RESULTS

| POS | NAME | TEAM | TIME |
|---|---|---|---|
| 1. | P. Ackermann | BOH | 4:08:34 |
| 2. | J. Milan | TBV | s.t. |
| 3. | R. Barbier | ISN | s.t. |
| 4. | E. Viviani | NAT | s.t. |
| 5. | E. Blikra | UXT | s.t. |
| 6. | L. Pacioni | EOK | s.t. |
| 7. | M. Alonso | EUS | s.t. |
| 8. | F. Fiorelli | BCF | s.t. |
| 9. | M. Malucelli | ANS | s.t. |
| 10. | J. Mareczko | THR | s.t. |
| 11. | D. Appollonio | AMO | s.t. |
| 12. | A. Fedeli | DKO | s.t. |
| 13. | R. Oliveira | UAD | s.t. |
| 14. | F. Burchio | IWM | s.t. |
| 15. | G. Cullaigh | MOV | s.t. |
| 16. | P. Simion | GTS | s.t. |
| 17. | M. Bevilacqua | THR | s.t. |
| 18. | E. Šiškevičius | DKO | s.t. |
| 19. | D. Villella | MOV | s.t. |
| 20. | A. Guardini | GTS | s.t. |

### GENERAL CLASSIFICATION

| POS | NAME | TEAM | TIME |
|---|---|---|---|
| 1. — | D. Ulissi | UAD | 12:15:35 |
| 2. ↑1 | S. Vanmarcke | ISN | 0:06 |
| 3. ↑1 | G. Aleotti | BOH | s.t. |

### KING OF THE MOUNTAINS

| POS | NAME | TEAM | PTS |
|---|---|---|---|
| 1. — | S. Pellaud | ANS | 27 |
| 2. ↑1 | S. Buitrago | TBV | 20 |
| 3. ↓1 | R. Herregodts | SVB | 17 |

### POINTS

| POS | NAME | TEAM | PTS |
|---|---|---|---|
| 1. ↑2 | P. Ackermann | BOH | 20 |
| 2. ↓1 | D. Ulissi | UAD | 12 |
| 3. ↓1 | A. Bettiol | NAT | 12 |

### YOUNG RIDER

| POS | NAME | TEAM | TIME |
|---|---|---|---|
| 1. — | G. Aleotti | BOH | 12:15:41 |
| 2. — | J. Cepeda Ortiz | ANS | 0:53 |
| 3. ↑1 | B. Peák | BEX | 0:57 |

## SETTIMANA CICLISTICA ITALIANA
Stage 4
17 July 2021
Cagliari–Cagliari
168km

## WEATHER

TEMPERATURE   WIND
30°C          N 22km/h

### STAGE RESULTS

| POS | NAME | TEAM | TIME |
|---|---|---|---|
| 1. | D. Ulissi | UAD | 4:03:58 |
| 2. | A. Riabushenko | UAD | s.t. |
| 3. | S. Vanmarcke | ISN | s.t. |
| 4. | E. Šiškevičius | DKO | s.t. |
| 5. | M. Padun | TBV | s.t. |
| 6. | G. Aleotti | BOH | s.t. |
| 7. | J. Abrahamsen | UXT | s.t. |
| 8. | M. Bouet | ARK | s.t. |
| 9. | A. Verwilst | SVB | s.t. |
| 10. | D. Villella | MOV | s.t. |
| 11. | F. Großschartner | BOH | s.t. |
| 12. | T. Kangert | BEX | s.t. |
| 13. | P. Double | MGK | s.t. |
| 14. | B. Hermans | ISN | s.t. |
| 15. | S. Umba | ANS | s.t. |
| 16. | S. Williams | TBV | s.t. |
| 17. | S. Samitier | MOV | s.t. |
| 18. | A. Zeits | BEX | s.t. |
| 19. | I. Zakarin | GAZ | s.t. |
| 20. | T. Grmay | BEX | s.t. |

### GENERAL CLASSIFICATION

| POS | NAME | TEAM | TIME |
|---|---|---|---|
| 1. — | D. Ulissi | UAD | 16:19:23 |
| 2. — | S. Vanmarcke | ISN | 0:12 |
| 3. — | G. Aleotti | BOH | 0:16 |

### KING OF THE MOUNTAINS

| POS | NAME | TEAM | PTS |
|---|---|---|---|
| 1. ↑1 | S. Buitrago | TBV | 33 |
| 2. ↑7 | J. Abrahamsen | UXT | 28 |
| 3. ↓2 | S. Pellaud | ANS | 27 |

### POINTS

| POS | NAME | TEAM | PTS |
|---|---|---|---|
| 1. ↑1 | D. Ulissi | UAD | 22 |
| 2. ↓1 | P. Ackermann | BOH | 20 |
| 3. ↑1 | S. Vanmarcke | ISN | 15 |

### YOUNG RIDER

| POS | NAME | TEAM | TIME |
|---|---|---|---|
| 1. — | G. Aleotti | BOH | 16:19:39 |
| 2. ↑4 | S. Umba | ANS | 1:15 |
| 3. ↑5 | S. Buitrago | TBV | 1:29 |

JULY .1 MEN'S RACE

# SETTIMANA CICLISTICA ITALIANA
Stage 5
18 July 2021
Cagliari–Cagliari
170.2km

## WEATHER

| TEMPERATURE | WIND |
|---|---|
| 33°C | N 28km/h |

## STAGE RESULTS

| POS | NAME | TEAM | TIME |
|---|---|---|---|
| 1. | P. Ackermann | BOH | 4:11:01 |
| 2. | J. Restrepo | ANS | s.t. |
| 3. | S. Vanmarcke | ISN | s.t. |
| 4. | M. Bouet | ARK | s.t. |
| 5. | F. Burchio | IWM | s.t. |
| 6. | M. Canola | GAZ | s.t. |
| 7. | I. Filosi | GTS | s.t. |
| 8. | J. Irizar | EUS | s.t. |
| 9. | G. Garavaglia | IWM | s.t. |
| 10. | G. Cullaigh | MOV | s.t. |
| 11. | A. Fedeli | DKO | s.t. |
| 12. | E. Battaglin | BCF | s.t. |
| 13. | D. Ulissi | UAD | s.t. |
| 14. | S. Williams | TBV | s.t. |
| 15. | L. Wackermann | EOK | s.t. |
| 16. | S. Samitier | MOV | s.t. |
| 17. | F. Großschartner | BOH | s.t. |
| 18. | G. Aleotti | BOH | s.t. |
| 19. | D. Villella | MOV | s.t. |
| 20. | I. Zakarin | GAZ | s.t. |

## GENERAL CLASSIFICATION

| POS | NAME | TEAM | TIME |
|---|---|---|---|
| 1. | — D. Ulissi | UAD | 20:30:24 |
| 2. | — S. Vanmarcke | ISN | 0:08 |
| 3. | — G. Aleotti | BOH | 0:16 |

## KING OF THE MOUNTAINS

| POS | NAME | TEAM | PTS |
|---|---|---|---|
| 1. | — S. Buitrago | TBV | 34 |
| 2. | — J. Abrahamsen | UXT | 28 |
| 3. | — S. Pellaud | ANS | 27 |

## POINTS

| POS | NAME | TEAM | PTS |
|---|---|---|---|
| 1. | ↑1 P. Ackermann | BOH | 30 |
| 2. | ↓1 D. Ulissi | UAD | 22 |
| 3. | — S. Vanmarcke | ISN | 21 |

## YOUNG RIDER

| POS | NAME | TEAM | TIME |
|---|---|---|---|
| 1. | — G. Aleotti | BOH | 20:30:40 |
| 2. | — S. Umba | ANS | 1:15 |
| 3. | — S. Buitrago | TBV | 2:46 |

JULY .PRO MEN'S RACE

# TOUR DE WALLONIE
Stage 1
20 July 2021
Genappe–Héron
185.7km

## WEATHER

TEMPERATURE | WIND
22°C | NE 9km/h

## STAGE RESULTS

| POS | NAME | TEAM | TIME |
|---|---|---|---|
| 1. | D. Groenewegen | TJV | 4:21:36 |
| 2. | H. Hofstetter | ISN | s.t. |
| 3. | G. Vermeersch | AFC | s.t. |
| 4. | A. Kristoff | UAD | s.t. |
| 5. | R. Oliveira | UAD | s.t. |
| 6. | A. Capiot | ARK | s.t. |
| 7. | F. Gaviria | UAD | s.t. |
| 8. | P. Allegaert | COF | s.t. |
| 9. | G. Nizzolo | TQA | s.t. |
| 10. | M. Menten | BWB | s.t. |
| 11. | J. Drizners | HBA | s.t. |
| 12. | L. Mozzato | BBK | s.t. |
| 13. | Q. Simmons | TFS | s.t. |
| 14. | J. Stewart | GFC | s.t. |
| 15. | A. Pasqualon | IWG | s.t. |
| 16. | K. Van Rooy | SVB | s.t. |
| 17. | M. Sarreau | ACT | s.t. |
| 18. | M. Schwarzmann | BOH | s.t. |
| 19. | J. Keukeleire | EFN | s.t. |
| 20. | N. van der Lijke | RIW | s.t. |

## GENERAL CLASSIFICATION

| POS | NAME | TEAM | TIME |
|---|---|---|---|
| 1. | D. Groenewegen | TJV | 4:21:26 |
| 2. | H. Hofstetter | ISN | 0:04 |
| 3. | D. De Bondt | AFC | s.t. |

## KING OF THE MOUNTAINS

| POS | NAME | TEAM | PTS |
|---|---|---|---|
| 1. | T. Paquot | BWB | 12 |
| 2. | S. Dewulf | ACT | 6 |
| 3. | P. Ronhaar | TBL | 6 |

## POINTS

| POS | NAME | TEAM | PTS |
|---|---|---|---|
| 1. | D. Groenewegen | TJV | 25 |
| 2. | H. Hofstetter | ISN | 20 |
| 3. | G. Vermeersch | AFC | 15 |

## YOUNG RIDER

| POS | NAME | TEAM | TIME |
|---|---|---|---|
| 1. | S. Dewulf | ACT | 4:21:34 |
| 2. | T. Paquot | BWB | 0:01 |
| 3. | J. Drizners | HBA | 0:02 |

# TOUR DE WALLONIE
Stage 2
21 July 2021
Zolder–Zolder
120km

## WEATHER

TEMPERATURE | WIND
23°C | NE 15km/h

## STAGE RESULTS

| POS | NAME | TEAM | TIME |
|---|---|---|---|
| 1. | F. Jakobsen | DQT | 2:34:42 |
| 2. | F. Gaviria | UAD | s.t. |
| 3. | A. Capiot | ARK | s.t. |
| 4. | P. Allegaert | COF | s.t. |
| 5. | A. Pasqualon | IWG | s.t. |
| 6. | M. Sarreau | ACT | s.t. |
| 7. | G. Nizzolo | TQA | s.t. |
| 8. | A. Renard | ISN | s.t. |
| 9. | S. Oldani | LTS | s.t. |
| 10. | J. Degenkolb | LTS | s.t. |
| 11. | K. Halvorsen | UXT | s.t. |
| 12. | L. Mozzato | BBK | s.t. |
| 13. | N. Bonifazio | TEN | s.t. |
| 14. | R. Selig | BOH | s.t. |
| 15. | D. Groenewegen | TJV | s.t. |
| 16. | A. M. Richeze | UAD | s.t. |
| 17. | T. Dupont | BWB | s.t. |
| 18. | A. Kristoff | UAD | s.t. |
| 19. | B. Welten | ARK | s.t. |
| 20. | J. Warlop | SVB | s.t. |

## GENERAL CLASSIFICATION

| POS | NAME | TEAM | TIME |
|---|---|---|---|
| 1. — | D. Groenewegen | TJV | 6:56:08 |
| 2. ↑25 | F. Jakobsen | DQT | s.t. |
| 3. ↑10 | F. Gaviria | UAD | 0:04 |

## KING OF THE MOUNTAINS

| POS | NAME | TEAM | PTS |
|---|---|---|---|
| 1. — | T. Paquot | BWB | 12 |
| 2. — | S. Dewulf | ACT | 6 |
| 3. — | P. Ronhaar | TBL | 6 |

## POINTS

| POS | NAME | TEAM | PTS |
|---|---|---|---|
| 1. — | D. Groenewegen | TJV | 25 |
| 2. — | F. Jakobsen | DQT | 25 |
| 3. ↑4 | F. Gaviria | UAD | 24 |

## YOUNG RIDER

| POS | NAME | TEAM | TIME |
|---|---|---|---|
| 1. ↑21 | J. P. López | TFS | 6:56:15 |
| 2. ↓1 | S. Dewulf | ACT | 0:01 |
| 3. ↓1 | T. Paquot | BWB | 0:02 |

JULY · PRO MEN'S RACE

## TOUR DE WALLONIE
Stage 3
22 July 2021
Plombières–Érezée
177km

### WEATHER

TEMPERATURE | WIND
23°C | NW 9km/h

### STAGE RESULTS

| POS | NAME | TEAM | TIME |
|---|---|---|---|
| 1. | Q. Simmons | TFS | 4:07:19 |
| 2. | S. Dewulf | ACT | 0:01 |
| 3. | A. Renard | ISN | 0:13 |
| 4. | F. Barceló | COF | s.t. |
| 5. | P. Eenkhoorn | TJV | s.t. |
| 6. | M. Van Gils | LTS | 0:17 |
| 7. | A. Covi | UAD | 0:25 |
| 8. | T. Wellens | LTS | s.t. |
| 9. | M. Menten | BWB | s.t. |
| 10. | A. Capiot | ARK | s.t. |
| 11. | O. C. Eiking | IWG | s.t. |
| 12. | S. Oldani | LTS | s.t. |
| 13. | D. Claeys | TQA | s.t. |
| 14. | J. Biermans | ISN | s.t. |
| 15. | Q. Hermans | IWG | s.t. |
| 16. | J. P. López | TFS | s.t. |
| 17. | B. Thomas | GFC | s.t. |
| 18. | N. van der Lijke | RIW | s.t. |
| 19. | S. Quinn | HBA | s.t. |
| 20. | K. Van Rooy | SVB | s.t. |

### GENERAL CLASSIFICATION

| POS | | NAME | TEAM | TIME |
|---|---|---|---|---|
| 1. | ↑33 | Q. Simmons | TFS | 11:03:27 |
| 2. | ↑10 | S. Dewulf | ACT | 0:03 |
| 3. | ↑25 | A. Renard | ISN | 0:19 |

### KING OF THE MOUNTAINS

| POS | | NAME | TEAM | PTS |
|---|---|---|---|---|
| 1. | — | F. Vermeersch | LTS | 24 |
| 2. | — | T. Van Asbroeck | ISN | 22 |
| 3. | ↓2 | T. Paquot | BWB | 16 |

### POINTS

| POS | | NAME | TEAM | PTS |
|---|---|---|---|---|
| 1. | — | Q. Simmons | TFS | 25 |
| 2. | — | F. Jakobsen | DQT | 25 |
| 3. | ↓2 | D. Groenewegen | TJV | 25 |

### YOUNG RIDER

| POS | | NAME | TEAM | TIME |
|---|---|---|---|---|
| 1. | ↑7 | Q. Simmons | TFS | 11:03:27 |
| 2. | — | S. Dewulf | ACT | 0:03 |
| 3. | ↑3 | A. Renard | ISN | 0:19 |

## TOUR DE WALLONIE
Stage 4
23 July 2021
Neufchâteau–Fleurus
206km

### WEATHER

TEMPERATURE | WIND
24°C | E 9km/h

### STAGE RESULTS

| POS | NAME | TEAM | TIME |
|---|---|---|---|
| 1. | D. Groenewegen | TJV | 4:55:16 |
| 2. | G. Nizzolo | TQA | s.t. |
| 3. | F. Gaviria | UAD | s.t. |
| 4. | L. Mozzato | BBK | s.t. |
| 5. | Q. Simmons | TFS | s.t. |
| 6. | G. Vermeersch | AFC | s.t. |
| 7. | A. Capiot | ARK | s.t. |
| 8. | S. Oldani | LTS | s.t. |
| 9. | F. Sénéchal | DQT | s.t. |
| 10. | M. Menten | BWB | s.t. |
| 11. | R. Selig | BOH | s.t. |
| 12. | J. Warlop | SVB | s.t. |
| 13. | R. Kamp | PSB | s.t. |
| 14. | T. Van Asbroeck | ISN | s.t. |
| 15. | Q. Hermans | IWG | s.t. |
| 16. | N. van der Lijke | RIW | s.t. |
| 17. | L. Calmejane | ACT | s.t. |
| 18. | J. Stewart | GFC | s.t. |
| 19. | N. Bonifazio | TEN | s.t. |
| 20. | W. Vanhoof | SVB | s.t. |

### GENERAL CLASSIFICATION

| POS | | NAME | TEAM | TIME |
|---|---|---|---|---|
| 1. | — | Q. Simmons | TFS | 15:58:43 |
| 2. | — | S. Dewulf | ACT | 0:03 |
| 3. | — | A. Renard | ISN | 0:19 |

### KING OF THE MOUNTAINS

| POS | | NAME | TEAM | PTS |
|---|---|---|---|---|
| 1. | — | F. Vermeersch | LTS | 32 |
| 2. | — | T. Van Asbroeck | ISN | 26 |
| 3. | ↑14 | A. Gougeard | ACT | 18 |

### POINTS

| POS | | NAME | TEAM | PTS |
|---|---|---|---|---|
| 1. | ↑2 | D. Groenewegen | TJV | 50 |
| 2. | ↑2 | F. Gaviria | UAD | 39 |
| 3. | ↓2 | Q. Simmons | TFS | 33 |

### YOUNG RIDER

| POS | | NAME | TEAM | TIME |
|---|---|---|---|---|
| 1. | — | Q. Simmons | TFS | 15:58:43 |
| 2. | — | S. Dewulf | ACT | 0:03 |
| 3. | — | A. Renard | ISN | 0:19 |

JULY .PRO MEN'S RACE

# TOUR DE WALLONIE

Stage 5
24 July 2021
Dinant–Quaregnon
192.4km

## WEATHER

TEMPERATURE: 21°C
WIND: S 7km/h

## STAGE RESULTS

| POS | NAME | TEAM | TIME |
|---|---|---|---|
| 1. | F. Jakobsen | DQT | 4:32:31 |
| 2. | R. Selig | BOH | s.t. |
| 3. | M. Menten | BWB | s.t. |
| 4. | L. Mozzato | BBK | s.t. |
| 5. | A. Capiot | ARK | s.t. |
| 6. | J. Stewart | GFC | s.t. |
| 7. | A. Kristoff | UAD | s.t. |
| 8. | R. Tiller | UXT | s.t. |
| 9. | N. van der Lijke | RIW | s.t. |
| 10. | S. Oldani | LTS | s.t. |
| 11. | M. Sarreau | ACT | s.t. |
| 12. | H. Hofstetter | ISN | s.t. |
| 13. | R. Kamp | PSB | s.t. |
| 14. | K. Van Rooy | SVB | s.t. |
| 15. | D. Van Gestel | TEN | s.t. |
| 16. | J. Warlop | SVB | s.t. |
| 17. | J. Degenkolb | LTS | s.t. |
| 18. | G. Nizzolo | TQA | s.t. |
| 19. | A. Renard | ISN | s.t. |
| 20. | Q. Simmons | TFS | s.t. |

## GENERAL CLASSIFICATION

| POS | | NAME | TEAM | TIME |
|---|---|---|---|---|
| 1. | — | Q. Simmons | TFS | 20:31:13 |
| 2. | — | S. Dewulf | ACT | 0:04 |
| 3. | — | A. Renard | ISN | 0:20 |

## KING OF THE MOUNTAINS

| POS | | NAME | TEAM | PTS |
|---|---|---|---|---|
| 1. | — | F. Vermeersch | LTS | 32 |
| 2. | — | T. Van Asbroeck | ISN | 26 |
| 3. | — | A. Gougeard | ACT | 18 |

## POINTS

| POS | | NAME | TEAM | PTS |
|---|---|---|---|---|
| 1. | — | D. Groenewegen | TJV | 50 |
| 2. | ↑4 | F. Jakobsen | DQT | 50 |
| 3. | ↓1 | F. Gaviria | UAD | 39 |

## YOUNG RIDER

| POS | | NAME | TEAM | TIME |
|---|---|---|---|---|
| 1. | — | Q. Simmons | TFS | 20:31:13 |
| 2. | — | S. Dewulf | ACT | 0:04 |
| 3. | — | A. Renard | ISN | 0:20 |

## OLYMPIC GAMES MEN'S ROAD RACE

24 July 2021
Musashinonomori Park–Fuji International Speedway
234km

**WEATHER**

TEMPERATURE
33°C

WIND
SE 7km/h

A nine-rider break built up a frighteningly large-sounding 19-minute lead in the sultry heat of the sapping 234km Olympic Road Race. But, with none of the key nations represented, there was always a sense that the central protagonists – including the mighty Belgians, for whom the defending champion Greg van Avermaet was simply a domestique – were waiting for the final climb. Of the 4,543 metres the course would ascend, it was the final Mikuni Pass that provided the launch pad for the first serious and sustained attacks. Unsurprisingly, given that his Tour de France victory was scarcely a week old, it was Tadej Pogačar, in the green of Slovenia, who attacked early. That move prised clear a group of favourites including Wout van Aert, which shrank and swelled but Pogačar's UAE Team Emirates teammate Brandon McNulty chose to attack with 35km remaining. He was joined by Ecuador's Richard Carapaz, and that pairing went clear, establishing a lead of almost a minute. Van Aert then dragged the chase group back to within 15 seconds. But Carapaz, sensing that McNulty was weakening, took off. The Ecuadorian, whose form at the Tour de France had been building as the weeks went on, demonstrated another race-winning quality in taking a major one-day race in style. It was only Ecuador's second ever gold medal at the summer Olympics.

**PROFILE**

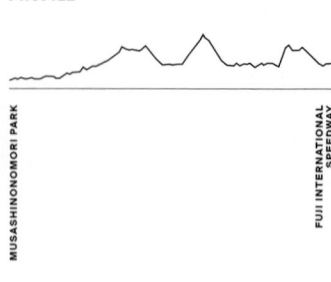

MUSASHINONOMORI PARK — FUJI INTERNATIONAL SPEEDWAY

**BREAKAWAY**

N. Dlamini (RSA), M. Kukrle (CZE), J. Sagan (SVK), P. Tzortzakis (GRE), E. M. Grosu (ROU), A. Sanabria (VEN), P. Daumont (BUR), E. Asadov (AZE)

**TRIVIA**

» Richard Carapaz is the first South American Olympic road race champion.

# RESULTS

| POS | NAME | TEAM | TIME |
|---|---|---|---|
| 1. | R. Carapaz | Ecuador | 6:05:26 |
| 2. | W. van Aert | Belgium | 1:07 |
| 3. | T. Pogačar | Slovenia | s.t. |
| 4. | B. Mollema | Netherlands | s.t. |
| 5. | M. Woods | Canada | s.t. |
| 6. | B. McNulty | United States | s.t. |
| 7. | D. Gaudu | France | s.t. |
| 8. | R. Urán | Colombia | s.t. |
| 9. | A. Yates | Great Britain | s.t. |
| 10. | M. Schachmann | Germany | 1:21 |
| 11. | M. Kwiatkowski | Poland | 1:35 |
| 12. | J. Fuglsang | Denmark | 2:43 |
| 13. | J. Almeida | Portugal | 3:38 |
| 14. | A. Bettiol | Italy | s.t. |
| 15. | D. van Baarle | Netherlands | s.t. |
| 16. | D. Martin | Ireland | s.t. |
| 17. | S. Yates | Great Britain | s.t. |
| 18. | P. Konrad | Austria | s.t. |
| 19. | R. Majka | Poland | 3:40 |
| 20. | G. Moscon | Italy | 3:42 |
| 21. | A. Lutsenko | Kazakhstan | 6:20 |
| 22. | T. Skujiņš | Latvia | s.t. |
| 23. | G. Izagirre | Spain | s.t. |
| 24. | D. Caruso | Italy | s.t. |
| 25. | M. Hirschi | Switzerland | s.t. |
| 26. | G. Bennett | New Zealand | s.t. |
| 27. | G. Martin | France | s.t. |
| 28. | P. Roglič | Slovenia | s.t. |
| 29. | E. Buchmann | Germany | s.t. |
| 30. | H. Pernsteiner | Austria | 7:51 |
| 31. | M. Schär | Switzerland | s.t. |
| 32. | P. Sivakov | ROC | s.t. |
| 33. | K. Neilands | Latvia | 10:12 |
| 34. | M. Hoelgaard | Norway | s.t. |
| 35. | Y. Arashiro | Japan | s.t. |
| 36. | M. Kukrle | Czech Republic | s.t. |
| 37. | K. Geniets | Luxembourg | s.t. |
| 38. | K. Elissonde | France | s.t. |
| 39. | E. Frayre | Mexico | s.t. |
| 40. | S. Küng | Switzerland | s.t. |
| 41. | N. Oliveira | Portugal | s.t. |
| 42. | A. Valverde | Spain | s.t. |
| 43. | J. Polanc | Slovenia | s.t. |
| 44. | T. Dumoulin | Netherlands | s.t. |
| 45. | E. Chaves | Colombia | s.t. |
| 46. | T. Kangert | Estonia | s.t. |
| 47. | J. Narváez | Ecuador | s.t. |
| 48. | R. Porte | Australia | s.t. |
| 49. | R. Evenepoel | Belgium | s.t. |
| 50. | A. Ghebreigzabhier | Eritrea | s.t. |
| 51. | W. Kelderman | Netherlands | s.t. |
| 52. | S. de Bod | South Africa | 11:27 |
| 53. | V. Nibali | Italy | s.t. |
| 54. | N. Arndt | Germany | s.t. |
| 55. | M. Kudus | Eritrea | s.t. |
| 56. | A. Budyak | Ukraine | s.t. |
| 57. | B. Cosnefroy | France | s.t. |
| 58. | T. Benoot | Belgium | s.t. |
| 59. | A. Vlasov | ROC | s.t. |
| 60. | G. Ciccone | Italy | s.t. |
| 61. | T. Foss | Norway | s.t. |
| 62. | Je. Herrada | Spain | s.t. |
| 63. | P. Tzortzakis | Greece | 16:20 |
| 64. | M. Halmuratov | Uzbekistan | s.t. |
| 65. | G. Boivin | Canada | s.t. |
| 66. | A. Riabushenko | Belarus | s.t. |
| 67. | J. Tratnik | Slovenia | s.t. |
| 68. | A. Amador | Costa Rica | s.t. |
| 69. | N. Quintana | Colombia | s.t. |
| 70. | G. Mühlberger | Austria | s.t. |
| 71. | L. Hamilton | Australia | s.t. |
| 72. | L. Durbridge | Australia | s.t. |
| 73. | M. Ries | Luxembourg | s.t. |
| 74. | G. Mäder | Switzerland | s.t. |
| 75. | N. Roche | Ireland | s.t. |
| 76. | E. Dunbar | Ireland | s.t. |
| 77. | M. Vansevenant | Belgium | s.t. |
| 78. | M. Valgren | Denmark | s.t. |
| 79. | I. Izagirre | Spain | s.t. |
| 80. | L. Craddock | United States | s.t. |
| 81. | S. Higuita | Colombia | s.t. |
| 82. | T. H. Johannessen | Norway | 19:46 |
| 83. | A. Leknessund | Norway | s.t. |
| 84. | N. Masuda | Japan | 19:50 |
| 85. | H. Houle | Canada | s.t. |

JULY WOMEN'S OLYMPICS

# OLYMPIC GAMES WOMEN'S ROAD RACE
25 July 2021
Musashinonomori Park–Fuji International Speedway
137km

## WEATHER

TEMPERATURE  WIND
32°C         E 19km/h

## PROFILE

MUSASHINONOMORI PARK — FUJI INTERNATIONAL SPEEDWAY

The only question on most people's lips before the women's road race was which of the quartet of Dutch superstars was going to triumph. After Marianne Vos in London 2012 and Anna van der Breggen in 2016, it seemed likely that Annemiek van Vleuten – denied victory when she crashed in Rio, and having skipped the Giro Rosa in order to prepare for the Games – would be the focus of their efforts. And if she were to fail, they would have considerable reserves in Vos, Van der Breggen and Demi Vollering to draw upon. What happened instead was a wonder of individual brilliance, opportunism and confusion. The unheralded Austrian rider Anna Kiesenhofer – last rider standing from the early breakaway – held off a chase that somehow didn't materialise from the group of favourites until it was too late. This, despite the fact that the Dutch team, unlike any other nation, had all four of their key protagonists in a hesitant and disorganised chase group. No matter, Kiesenhofer rode to a remarkable and historic win, with Van Vleuten crossing the line in second, thinking she had won and unaware that Kiesenhofer was already celebrating. The confusion was blamed in part on the lack of team radios on the race.

## BREAKAWAY

C. Oberholzer (RSA), V. Looser (NAM), O. Shapira (ISR), A. Plichta (POL), A. Kiesenhofer (AUT)

## RESULTS

| POS | NAME | TEAM | TIME |
|---|---|---|---|
| 1. | A. Kiesenhofer | Austria | 3:52:45 |
| 2. | A. van Vleuten | Netherlands | 1:15 |
| 3. | E. Longo Borghini | Italy | 1:29 |
| 4. | L. Kopecky | Belgium | 1:39 |
| 5. | M. Vos | Netherlands | 1:46 |
| 6. | L. Brennauer | Germany | s.t. |
| 7. | C. Rivera | United States | s.t. |
| 8. | M. Cavalli | Italy | s.t. |
| 9. | O. Zabelinskaya | Uzbekistan | s.t. |
| 10. | C. U. Ludwig | Denmark | s.t. |
| 11. | E. Deignan | Great Britain | s.t. |
| 12. | M. García | Spain | s.t. |
| 13. | A. Moolman | South Africa | s.t. |
| 14. | K. Niewiadoma | Poland | s.t. |
| 15. | A. van der Breggen | Netherlands | s.t. |
| 16. | K. A. Canuel | Canada | 2:20 |
| 17. | A. Amialiusik | Belarus | s.t. |
| 18. | M. Lach | Poland | 2:28 |
| 19. | E. Bujak | Slovenia | s.t. |
| 20. | C. Majerus | Luxembourg | s.t. |
| 21. | E. Yonamine | Japan | s.t. |
| 22. | P. A. Patiño | Colombia | 2:30 |
| 23. | L. Lippert | Germany | 2:32 |
| 24. | O. Shapira | Israel | 2:38 |
| 25. | D. Vollering | Netherlands | 2:56 |
| 26. | T. Cromwell | Australia | s.t. |
| 27. | A. Plichta | Poland | 3:13 |
| 28. | A. Santesteban | Spain | 3:19 |
| 29. | L. Thomas | United States | 3:22 |
| 30. | J. Labous | France | s.t. |
| 31. | C. Dygert | United States | 6:06 |
| 32. | A. Jackson | Canada | 7:02 |
| 33. | T. Neumanova | Czech Republic | s.t. |
| 34. | A. Sierra | Cuba | s.t. |
| 35. | R. Leleivytė | Lithuania | s.t. |
| 36. | L. Kirchmann | Canada | s.t. |
| 37. | K. Aalerud | Norway | 7:07 |
| 38. | A. Na | South Korea | 8:23 |
| 39. | T. Dronova-Balabolina | ROC | s.t. |
| 40. | S. Gigante | Australia | s.t. |
| 41. | H. Ludwig | Germany | s.t. |
| 42. | J. Van De Velde | Belgium | s.t. |
| 43. | H. Kaneko | Japan | s.t. |
| 44. | M. Bastianelli | Italy | 9:31 |
| 45. | R. Winder | United States | s.t. |
| 46. | M. Reusser | Switzerland | s.t. |
| 47. | G. Brown | Australia | s.t. |
| 48. | S. Paladin | Italy | 15:55 |

## TRIVIA

» Anna Kiesenhofer has won Austria's first-ever road racing Olympic medal.

JULY    MEN'S OLYMPICS

## OLYMPIC GAMES MEN'S ITT
28 July 2021
Fuji International Speedway–Fuji International Speedway
44.2km

Two laps of a testing 22.1km circuit were made harder by the heat and humidity that had begun to descend on Tokyo. A climb and a descent in the first part of the course were then followed by a rolling finale. Returning to racing after his surprise decision to step away from the sport, 2017 Giro winner Tom Dumoulin reminded the cycling world of his class as he set the best time through every checkpoint. Unfortunately for Dumoulin, Primož Roglič – recovered from the knocks and bruises of the series of falls that had forced him to abandon the Tour de France – was on a simply stunning day. He crushed Dumoulin's time by over a minute, becoming the only rider to go under 56 minutes for the time trial. Gold went to Slovenia, then. Dumoulin picked up silver for the Netherlands. But the battle for bronze was intense: just 2 seconds separated Filippo Ganna of Italy, Switzerland's Stefan Küng and Australia's Rohan Dennis, who pipped them both to finish third.

### WEATHER

TEMPERATURE    WIND
31°C           S 39km/h

### PROFILE

### RESULTS

| POS | NAME | TEAM | TIME |
| --- | --- | --- | --- |
| 1. | P. Roglič | Slovenia | 55:04 |
| 2. | T. Dumoulin | Netherlands | 1:01 |
| 3. | R. Dennis | Australia | 1:04 |
| 4. | S. Küng | Switzerland | s.t. |
| 5. | F. Ganna | Italy | 1:06 |
| 6. | W. van Aert | Belgium | 1:41 |
| 7. | K. Asgreen | Denmark | 1:48 |
| 8. | R. Uràn | Colombia | 2:15 |
| 9. | R. Evenepoel | Belgium | 2:17 |
| 10. | P. Bevin | New Zealand | 2:20 |
| 11. | A. Bettiol | Italy | 2:34 |
| 12. | G. Thomas | Great Britain | 2:42 |
| 13. | H. Houle | Canada | 2:52 |
| 14. | S. de Bod | South Africa | 2:53 |
| 15. | M. Schachmann | Germany | 3:30 |
| 16. | J. Almeida | Portugal | s.t. |
| 17. | R. Cavagna | France | 3:35 |
| 18. | M. Bodnar | Poland | 3:43 |
| 19. | N. Arndt | Germany | 3:45 |
| 20. | A. Vlasov | ROC | 3:51 |
| 21. | N. Oliveira | Portugal | 3:55 |
| 22. | T. Kangert | Estonia | 4:01 |
| 23. | T. Foss | Norway | 4:47 |
| 24. | B. McNulty | United States | 4:54 |
| 25. | G. Bennett | New Zealand | 5:24 |
| 26. | M. Kukrle | Czech Republic | 5:37 |
| 27. | R. Porte | Australia | 5:49 |
| 28. | N. Roche | Ireland | 6:19 |
| 29. | T. Geoghegan Hart | Great Britain | 6:41 |
| 30. | T. Skujiņš | Latvia | 7:01 |
| 31. | P. Konrad | Austria | s.t. |
| 32. | A. Lutsenko | Kazakhstan | 7:17 |
| 33. | A. Ghebreigzabhier | Eritrea | 8:19 |
| 34. | L. Craddock | United States | 8:49 |
| 35. | S. Safarzadeh | Iran | 10:10 |
| 36. | A. Lagab | Algeria | 10:17 |
| 37. | L. Kubiš | Slovakia | 11:21 |
| 38. | A. B. Wais | Refugee Olympic Team | 13:36 |

### TRIVIA

» Tom Dumoulin claimed the silver medal for the second Games in a row, the only two medals the Dutch have ever taken in this discipline.

JULY  WOMEN'S OLYMPICS

## OLYMPIC GAMES WOMEN'S ITT
28 July 2021
Fuji International Speedway–Fuji International Speedway
22.1km

**WEATHER**

TEMPERATURE  WIND
30°C  S 31km/h

The women's race was half the distance of the men's, and presented the Dutch with a clear opportunity to put behind them the difficulties and disappointments of the road race. Already a silver medallist, Van Vleuten crushed the best time of France's Juliette Labous, as the Dutch rider went off sixth from last. She finished her time trial in 30 minutes 13 seconds, and would watch on as a succession of riders tried to dislodge her. Best of all the rest was Switzerland's Marlen Reusser, confirming her growing form of the last couple of years. But there remained the threat of Anna van der Breggen, who took bronze, and the great talent of the American Chloé Dygert, who had suffered a possibly career-ending injury at the World Championships in the autumn of 2020. She could only manage seventh, finishing over 2 minutes down on Van Vleuten, who was a gold medallist at last.

**PROFILE**

FUJI INTERNATIONAL SPEEDWAY — FUJI INTERNATIONAL SPEEDWAY

### RESULTS

| POS | NAME | TEAM | TIME |
|---|---|---|---|
| 1. | A. van Vleuten | Netherlands | 30:13 |
| 2. | M. Reusser | Switzerland | 0:56 |
| 3. | A. van der Breggen | Netherlands | 1:02 |
| 4. | G. Brown | Australia | 1:09 |
| 5. | A. Neben | United States | 1:13 |
| 6. | L. Brennauer | Germany | 1:57 |
| 7. | C. Dygert | United States | 2:16 |
| 8. | A. Moolman | South Africa | 2:24 |
| 9. | J. Labous | France | 2:29 |
| 10. | E. Longo Borghini | Italy | 2:47 |
| 11. | S. Gigante | Australia | 2:48 |
| 12. | L. Kirchmann | Canada | s.t. |
| 13. | L. Klein | Germany | s.t. |
| 14. | K. A. Canuel | Canada | 2:54 |
| 15. | O. Shapira | Israel | 3:02 |
| 16. | A. Amialiusik | Belarus | 3:08 |
| 17. | E. Norsgaard | Denmark | 3:37 |
| 18. | A. Shackley | Great Britain | 4:00 |
| 19. | J. Van De Velde | Belgium | 4:10 |
| 20. | K. Aalerud | Norway | 4:20 |
| 21. | C. Majerus | Luxembourg | 4:21 |
| 22. | E. Yonamine | Japan | s.t. |
| 23. | M. García | Spain | 4:26 |
| 24. | A. Plichta | Poland | 4:43 |
| 25. | M. Alizada | Refugee Olympic Team | 13:51 |

### TRIVIA

» Annemiek van Vleuten's victory helped the Netherlands tie the USA's record of three time trial Olympic titles. The only other nation to have won gold is Russia (at the event's inception at Atlanta 1996).

JULY .1 MEN'S RACE

## PRUEBA VILLAFRANCA DE ORDIZIA

25 July 2021
Ordizia–Ordizia
165.7km

## WEATHER

TEMPERATURE: 23°C
WIND: W 9km/h

## RESULTS

| POS | NAME | TEAM | TIME |
|---|---|---|---|
| 1. | L. L. Sanchez | APT | 3:51:27 |
| 2. | J. Ayuso | UAD | s.t. |
| 3. | R. Adrià | EKP | s.t. |
| 4. | H. Carretero | MOV | s.t. |
| 5. | M. Iturria | EUS | s.t. |
| 6. | O. Rodríguez | APT | 0:08 |
| 7. | G. Serrano | MOV | 0:09 |
| 8. | M. Paluta | GLC | s.t. |
| 9. | J. Simon | TEN | s.t. |
| 10. | A. Delaplace | ARK | s.t. |
| 11. | J. Bol | BBH | s.t. |
| 12. | A. Ropero | EOK | s.t. |
| 13. | J. J. Rojas | MOV | s.t. |
| 14. | Á. Madrazo | BBH | s.t. |
| 15. | D. Rosa | ARK | s.t. |
| 16. | S. R. Martín | CJR | s.t. |
| 17. | U. Cuadrado | EUS | s.t. |
| 18. | G. Mannion | RLY | s.t. |
| 19. | M. Burgaudeau | TEN | s.t. |
| 20. | M. E. Flórez | ARK | s.t. |

JULY   .1 MEN'S RACE

## VUELTA A CASTILLA Y LEON
29 July 2021
León–Ponferrada
181.2km

### WEATHER

TEMPERATURE  
26°C

WIND  
S 9km/h

### RESULTS

| POS | NAME | TEAM | TIME |
|---|---|---|---|
| 1. | M. Louvel | ARK | 4:16:13 |
| 2. | S. Oldani | LTS | 0:44 |
| 3. | M. Moreira | EFP | 1:25 |
| 4. | N. Zukowsky | RLY | 2:01 |
| 5. | A. González | MOV | s.t. |
| 6. | J. Amezqueta | CJR | 2:02 |
| 7. | O. Rodríguez | APT | 2:18 |
| 8. | B. King | RLY | 2:41 |
| 9. | A. Capiot | ARK | s.t. |
| 10. | Á. Jaime | EKP | s.t. |
| 11. | A. Riabushenko | UAD | s.t. |
| 12. | F. Conca | LTS | s.t. |
| 13. | J. Barrenetxea | CJR | 4:54 |
| 14. | G. Serrano | MOV | 5:07 |
| 15. | G. Mannion | RLY | s.t. |
| 16. | C. García | EKP | 5:27 |
| 17. | A. Angulo | EUS | s.t. |
| 18. | D. Rubio | BBH | 7:20 |
| 19. | M. Hollyman | ICA | s.t. |
| 20. | M. Trentin | UAD | 7:22 |

JULY    .1 MEN'S RACE

## TOUR DE L'AIN
Stage 1
29 July 2021
Parc des Oiseaux–Bourg-en-Bresse
141km

## WEATHER

**TEMPERATURE** 24°C  **WIND** N 7km/h

### STAGE RESULTS

| POS | NAME | TEAM | TIME |
|---|---|---|---|
| 1. | A. J. Hodeg | DQT | 3:04:57 |
| 2. | N. Bouhanni | ARK | s.t. |
| 3. | B. Coquard | BBK | s.t. |
| 4. | N. Bonifazio | TEN | s.t. |
| 5. | J. Tesson | AUB | s.t. |
| 6. | R. Minali | IWG | s.t. |
| 7. | F. Vermeersch | LTS | s.t. |
| 8. | E. Morin | COF | s.t. |
| 9. | C. Venturini | ACT | s.t. |
| 10. | D. De Bondt | AFC | s.t. |
| 11. | D. Kowalski | XRL | s.t. |
| 12. | J. Steimle | DQT | s.t. |
| 13. | J. Drucker | COF | s.t. |
| 14. | A. Paret-Peintre | ACT | s.t. |
| 15. | S. Guglielmi | GFC | s.t. |
| 16. | C. Champoussin | ACT | s.t. |
| 17. | G.Garofoli | DSM | s.t. |
| 18. | D. González | CJR | s.t. |
| 19. | G. Zimmermann | IWG | s.t. |
| 20. | M. Skjelmose Jensen | TFS | s.t. |

### GENERAL CLASSIFICATION

| POS | NAME | TEAM | TIME |
|---|---|---|---|
| 1. | A. J. Hodeg | DQT | 3:04:47 |
| 2. | N. Bouhanni | ARK | 0:04 |
| 3. | B. Coquard | BBK | 0:06 |

### KING OF THE MOUNTAINS

| POS | NAME | TEAM | PTS |
|---|---|---|---|
| 1. | A. Tarlton | NAT | 5 |
| 2. | J. Etxeberria | CJR | 3 |
| 3. | A. Duchesne | GFC | 1 |

### POINTS

| POS | NAME | TEAM | PTS |
|---|---|---|---|
| 1. | A. J. Hodeg | DQT | 25 |
| 2. | N. Bouhanni | ARK | 20 |
| 3. | B. Coquard | BBK | 16 |

### YOUNG RIDER

| POS | NAME | TEAM | TIME |
|---|---|---|---|
| 1. | J. Tesson | AUB | 3:04:57 |
| 2. | F. Vermeersch | LTS | s.t. |
| 3. | C. Champoussin | ACT | s.t. |

## TOUR DE L'AIN
Stage 2
30 July 2021
Lagnieu–Saint-Vulbas
136km

## WEATHER

**TEMPERATURE** 25°C  **WIND** SW 7km/h

### STAGE RESULTS

| POS | NAME | TEAM | TIME |
|---|---|---|---|
| 1. | G. Zimmermann | IWG | 3:05:42 |
| 2. | M. Storer | DSM | s.t. |
| 3. | H. Vanhoucke | LTS | s.t. |
| 4. | R. Rochas | COF | s.t. |
| 5. | M. Badilatti | GFC | s.t. |
| 6. | G. Steinhauser | NAT | s.t. |
| 7. | J. M. Díaz | DKO | 0:18 |
| 8. | A. Paret-Peintre | ACT | 0:22 |
| 9. | Q. Simmons | TFS | s.t. |
| 10. | P. Latour | TEN | s.t. |
| 11. | S. Cras | LTS | s.t. |
| 12. | F. Castellarnau | NAT | s.t. |
| 13. | Q. Pacher | BBK | s.t. |
| 14. | R. Molard | GFC | s.t. |
| 15. | O. Le Gac | GFC | s.t. |
| 16. | F. De Tier | AFC | s.t. |
| 17. | A. Bagioli | DQT | s.t. |
| 18. | A. Kron | LTS | s.t. |
| 19. | M. Skjelmose Jensen | TFS | s.t. |
| 20. | S. Chernetski | GAZ | s.t. |

### GENERAL CLASSIFICATION

| POS | NAME | TEAM | TIME |
|---|---|---|---|
| 1. ↑18 | G. Zimmermann | IWG | 6:10:29 |
| 2. ↑95 | M. Storer | DSM | 0:04 |
| 3. ↑44 | H. Vanhoucke | LTS | 0:06 |

### KING OF THE MOUNTAINS

| POS | NAME | TEAM | PTS |
|---|---|---|---|
| 1. — | S. Moniquet | LTS | 15 |
| 2. — | D. Kowalski | XRL | 10 |
| 3. — | R. Rochas | COF | 8 |

### POINTS

| POS | NAME | TEAM | PTS |
|---|---|---|---|
| 1. — | G. Zimmermann | IWG | 25 |
| 2. ↓1 | A. J. Hodeg | DQT | 25 |
| 3. — | M. Storer | DSM | 20 |

### YOUNG RIDER

| POS | NAME | TEAM | TIME |
|---|---|---|---|
| 1. ↑11 | G. Steinhauser | NAT | 6:10:39 |
| 2. ↑1 | C. Champoussin | ACT | 0:22 |
| 3. ↑2 | M. Skjelmose Jensen | TFS | s.t. |

JULY   .1 MEN'S RACE

# TOUR DE L'AIN
Stage 3
31 July 2021
Izernore–Lélex Mont-Jura
125km

## WEATHER

| TEMPERATURE | WIND |
|---|---|
| 22°C | NE 9km/h |

## STAGE RESULTS

| POS | NAME | TEAM | TIME |
|---|---|---|---|
| 1. | M. Storer | DSM | 3:02:46 |
| 2. | A. Bagioli | DQT | 0:43 |
| 3. | M. Skjelmose Jensen | TFS | s.t. |
| 4. | H. Vanhoucke | LTS | s.t. |
| 5. | M. Badilatti | GFC | 0:45 |
| 6. | C. Champoussin | ACT | s.t. |
| 7. | M. Bouet | ARK | 1:23 |
| 8. | O. Le Gac | GFC | s.t. |
| 9. | D. Strakhov | GAZ | s.t. |
| 10. | A. Kron | LTS | s.t. |
| 11. | F. De Tier | AFC | s.t. |
| 12. | S. Cras | LTS | s.t. |
| 13. | J. M. Díaz | DKO | s.t. |
| 14. | M. Chevalier | BBK | s.t. |
| 15. | R. Molard | GFC | s.t. |
| 16. | S. Quinn | HBA | s.t. |
| 17. | A. Delaplace | ARK | s.t. |
| 18. | P. Latour | TEN | s.t. |
| 19. | F. Castellarnau | NAT | s.t. |
| 20. | R. Rochas | COF | s.t. |

## GENERAL CLASSIFICATION

| POS | NAME | TEAM | TIME |
|---|---|---|---|
| 1. ↑1 | M. Storer | DSM | 9:13:09 |
| 2. ↑1 | H. Vanhoucke | LTS | 0:55 |
| 3. ↑3 | M. Badilatti | GFC | 1:01 |

## KING OF THE MOUNTAINS

| POS | NAME | TEAM | PTS |
|---|---|---|---|
| 1. ↑7 | M. Storer | DSM | 20 |
| 2. ↓1 | S. Moniquet | LTS | 15 |
| 3. — | S. Guglielmi | GFC | 13 |

## POINTS

| POS | NAME | TEAM | PTS |
|---|---|---|---|
| 1. ↑2 | M. Storer | DSM | 45 |
| 2. ↑3 | H. Vanhoucke | LTS | 30 |
| 3. ↓2 | G. Zimmermann | IWG | 25 |

## YOUNG RIDER

| POS | NAME | TEAM | TIME |
|---|---|---|---|
| 1. ↑3 | A. Bagioli | DQT | 9:14:24 |
| 2. ↑1 | M. Skjelmose Jensen | TFS | 0:02 |
| 3. ↓1 | C. Champoussin | ACT | 0:08 |

JULY  WORLDTOUR MEN'S RACE

# DONOSTIA SAN SEBASTIAN KLASIKOA
31 July 2021
San Sebastián–San Sebastián
223.5km

## WEATHER

TEMPERATURE   WIND
18°C          NW 4km/h

The first Clásica San Sebastián in two years drew a field packed full of favourites. But while some of the big names were never so much as glimpsed through the pouring rain, the race was lit up by a few young talents who, though far from inexperienced, were yet to make a truly indelible mark on the sport.

The day's breakaway was a hot ticket, and it took a long time for 13 riders to climb out of the peloton. A couple of uneventful hours followed until 22-year-old Javier Romo danced away from the shattered escape on the category-2 Jaizkibel. He led the race for 20km, but the peloton was closing the gap. Mikel Landa sparked the move that swallowed up Romo, attacking with 45km to go. Simon Carr was straight on his wheel, though, and within a kilometre the young climber was on his own. After a solo descent, Carr was joined by teammate Neilson Powless, Matej Mohorič, Mikkel Honoré and Lorenzo Rota, and they hit the final steep climb with over a minute's advantage. After his teammate dropped away, Powless proved strongest on the climb and smartest on the descent, briefly finding himself solo after the others got into trouble on a sketchy corner. Mohorič and Honoré chased back on for the finale, but the Slovenian was forced to lead out the three-up sprint. It was very close, but Powless came up through the middle to snatch it from Mohorič by barely a wheel.

## PROFILE

DONOSTIA-SAN SEBASTIAN — DONOSTIA-SAN SEBASTIAN

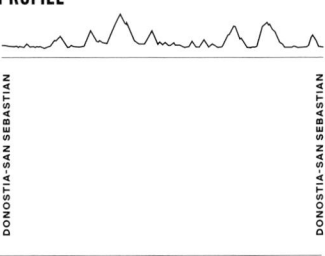

## BREAKAWAY

L. Calmejane (ACT), M. Cherel (ACT), V. Conti (UAD), A. Riabushenko (UAD), J. Jacobs (MOV), J. J. Rojas (MOV), J. Romo (APT), J. Cabot (TEN), J. Murguialday (CJR), J. Barrenetxea (CJR), M. Bizkarra (EUS), T. Grmay (BEX), O. Cabedo (BBH), D. Navarro (BBH), X. Vervloesem (LTS), R. Hardy (ARK)

## RESULTS

| POS | NAME | TEAM | TIME |
|---|---|---|---|
| 1. | N. Powless | EFN | 5:34:31 |
| 2. | M. Mohorič | TBV | s.t. |
| 3. | M. F. Honoré | DQT | s.t. |
| 4. | L. Rota | IWG | s.t. |
| 5. | A. Covi | UAD | 1:04 |
| 6. | J. Alaphilippe | DQT | s.t. |
| 7. | O. C. Eiking | IWG | s.t. |
| 8. | J. Vingegaard | TJV | s.t. |
| 9. | G. Moscon | IGD | s.t. |
| 10. | B. Mollema | TFS | s.t. |
| 11. | G. Serrano | MOV | s.t. |
| 12. | M. Van Gils | LTS | s.t. |
| 13. | M. Padun | TBV | s.t. |
| 14. | G. Ciccone | TFS | s.t. |
| 15. | S. Carr | EFN | 1:08 |
| 16. | E. Bernal | IGD | 1:09 |
| 17. | D. Ulissi | UAD | 1:36 |
| 18. | J. Ayuso | UAD | s.t. |
| 19. | R. Guerreiro | EFN | s.t. |
| 20. | G. Izaguirre | APT | s.t. |

## TRIVIA

» Bauke Mollema is now the active rider with most top-ten results (nine) in the Clásica San Sebastián.

343

JULY — WORLDTOUR WOMEN'S RACE

# DONOSTIA SAN SEBASTIAN KLASIKOA

31 July 2021
San Sebastián–San Sebastián
139.8km

## WEATHER

**TEMPERATURE**
16°C

**WIND**
S 6km/h

Newly crowned Olympic time trial champion Annemiek van Vleuten stole the show at the women's edition of the San Sebastián Classic, launching a phenomenal solo attack to take the victory just three days after her triumph in Tokyo.

With an early start in rainy conditions, the riders set off from La Concha and it wasn't long before the first breakaway of the day established. Giorgia Vettorello (Top Girls Fassa Bortolo) attacked, opened up a gap and hovered around a minute ahead before being swept up by nine more riders. However, as the undulating terrain took its toll, the group was eventually caught with 75km remaining. As the race entered the tough final succession of climbs, local Basque rider Ane Santesteban (BikeExchange), Pauliena Rooijakkers (Liv Racing) and French champion Evita Muzic (FDJ) took control, attacking on the famous Jaizkibel climb before being joined by three more riders following the twisty descent. The move looked to be a threat, as the group held a 2-minute advantage with just 30km remaining. Audrey Cordon-Ragot (Trek-Segafredo) decided her legs were good enough to attack away from the breakaway on the final climb, Murgil-Tontorra, while Movistar had sent their riders to the front and rapidly reduced the escapees' advantage, which set Van Vleuten up perfectly for a final damaging blow. The Olympic champion executed a fierce attack and flew past the fragmented breakaway group, past Cordon-Ragot and to her second WorldTour victory of the season. (LM)

## PROFILE

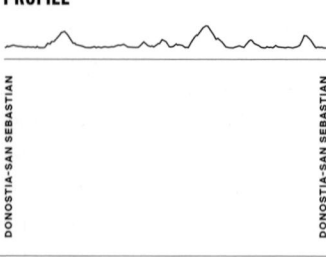

DONOSTIA-SAN SEBASTIAN — DONOSTIA-SAN SEBASTIAN

## BREAKAWAY

E. Muzic (FDJ), P. Rooijakkers (LIV), A. Santesteban (BEX), A. Cordon-Ragot (TFS), O. Baril (MAT), T. Guderzo (ALE)

## RESULTS

| POS | NAME | TEAM | TIME |
|---|---|---|---|
| 1. | A. van Vleuten | MOV | 3:53:37 |
| 2. | R. Winder | TFS | 0:36 |
| 3. | T. Guderzo | ALE | 1:35 |
| 4. | S. Stultiens | LIV | s.t. |
| 5. | É. Muzic | FDJ | s.t. |
| 6. | B. Chapman | FDJ | s.t. |
| 7. | P. Rooijakkers | LIV | 1:38 |
| 8. | A. Cordon-Ragot | TFS | 1:52 |
| 9. | E. Magnaldi | WNT | s.t. |
| 10. | E. van Dijk | TFS | s.t. |
| 11. | J. Korevaar | LIV | 2:00 |
| 12. | J. Ensing | BEX | 2:12 |
| 13. | E. Duval | FDJ | s.t. |
| 14. | U. Pintar | ALE | s.t. |
| 15. | T. Neumanova | WCS | 2:53 |
| 16. | S. Roy | BEX | s.t. |
| 17. | K. Ragusa | MNX | s.t. |
| 18. | M. Jaskulska | LIV | s.t. |
| 19. | S. van Anrooij | TFS | s.t. |
| 20. | V. Guilman | FDJ | s.t. |

## TRIVIA

» 80 hours later, and 10,400km west, Annemiek van Vleuten followed up her Olympic time trial gold with this win.

JULY .1 MEN'S RACE

# HEYLEN VASTGOED HEISTSE PIJL
31 July 2021
Heist-op-den-Berg–Heist-op-den-Berg
192.8km

## WEATHER

TEMPERATURE
19°C

WIND
W 20km/h

## RESULTS

| POS | NAME | TEAM | TIME |
|---|---|---|---|
| 1. | P. Eenkhoorn | TJV | 4:17:07 |
| 2. | Y. Lampaert | DQT | s.t. |
| 3. | J. Rickaert | AFC | 0:01 |
| 4. | B. Van Lerberghe | DQT | 0:12 |
| 5. | J. Debusschere | BBK | s.t. |
| 6. | M. Bostock | DHB | s.t. |
| 7. | B. van Poppel | IWG | s.t. |
| 8. | O. Riesebeek | AFC | 0:21 |
| 9. | R. Townsend | DHB | 0:35 |
| 10. | K. Van Rooy | SVB | 0:41 |
| 11. | J. Scott | DHB | 0:43 |
| 12. | T. Dupont | BWB | 0:49 |
| 13. | L. Bendixen | TCO | s.t. |
| 14. | J. Bouts | BCY | s.t. |
| 15. | T. Devriendt | IWG | s.t. |
| 16. | F. Sénéchal | DQT | s.t. |
| 17. | C. Vermeltfoort | VWE | 0:53 |
| 18. | J. Hesters | BCY | s.t. |
| 19. | T. Roosen | TJV | s.t. |
| 20. | M. Budding | BCY | s.t. |

# OLYMPIC ROAD RACE

It's a long road to the Olympic Games, something that holds true for all athletes, not just the riders who actually take to the tarmac in search of gold every four (or so) years. But what about this journey? A potted history of each medallist in Tokyo from the end of the Rio Games up until them arriving in Japan shows disparate journeys, yet all eventually arrive on the same start line with a chance of glory.

|      | **RICHARD CARAPAZ** | **WOUT VAN AERT** | **TADEJ POGAČAR** |
|------|---------------------|-------------------|--------------------|
| **2017** | Turns pro | Turns pro | |
| **2018** | Takes first pro win | First stage-race victory | Wins Tour de l'Avenir |
| **2019** | Wins Giro d'Italia | Wins first Tour de France stage | Turns pro |
| **2020** | | Wins first Monument | Wins first Tour de France |
| **2021** | First Tour de France podium | Wins three Tour stages | Wins second Tour de France |

|      | **ANNA KIESENHOFER** | **ANNEMIEK VAN VLEUTEN** | **ELISA LONGO BORGHINI** |
|------|----------------------|---------------------------|---------------------------|
| **2017** | Rides for Lotto Soudal Ladies, her last season with a UCI-registered team | Wins La Course. Becomes TT world champion | Wins Strade Bianche and Italian road and TT titles |
| **2018** | | Takes first Giro Rosa title. Defends La Course and world TT title | Takes Mediterranean road race title |
| **2019** | Takes both Austrian road and time trial titles. Fifth in TT at European Championships | Wins Liège–Bastogne–Liège. Defends Giro Rosa title. Becomes world road champion | Joins Trek-Segafredo. Wins Emakumeen Bira |
| **2020** | Retains Austrian TT title. Third overall Tour Cycliste Féminin International de l'Ardèche | Becomes European road champion. Wins second straight Strade Bianche | Reclaims both Italian titles. Wins stage of Giro Rosa |
| **2021** | Wins third straight Austrian TT title, then sixth in road race, her only two road competitions before Tokyo | Wins Tour of Flanders ten years after first win | Wins Trofeo Alfredo Binda. Defends both Italian titles |

THE GALLERY

We consume road racing, by and large, on television. So many races are now televised – and often in their entirety – that we have grown accustomed to the grammar of a bike race on TV: moto 1, moto 2, helicopter, and back to moto 1. And though the moving pictures are extraordinary, sometimes it's the still image that catches our attention and imparts a more concentrated meaning. The following pages will live far, far beyond the span of our memory, and will forever unchangingly reflect the nature of the moment when the shutter clicked.

# 2021 GALLERY

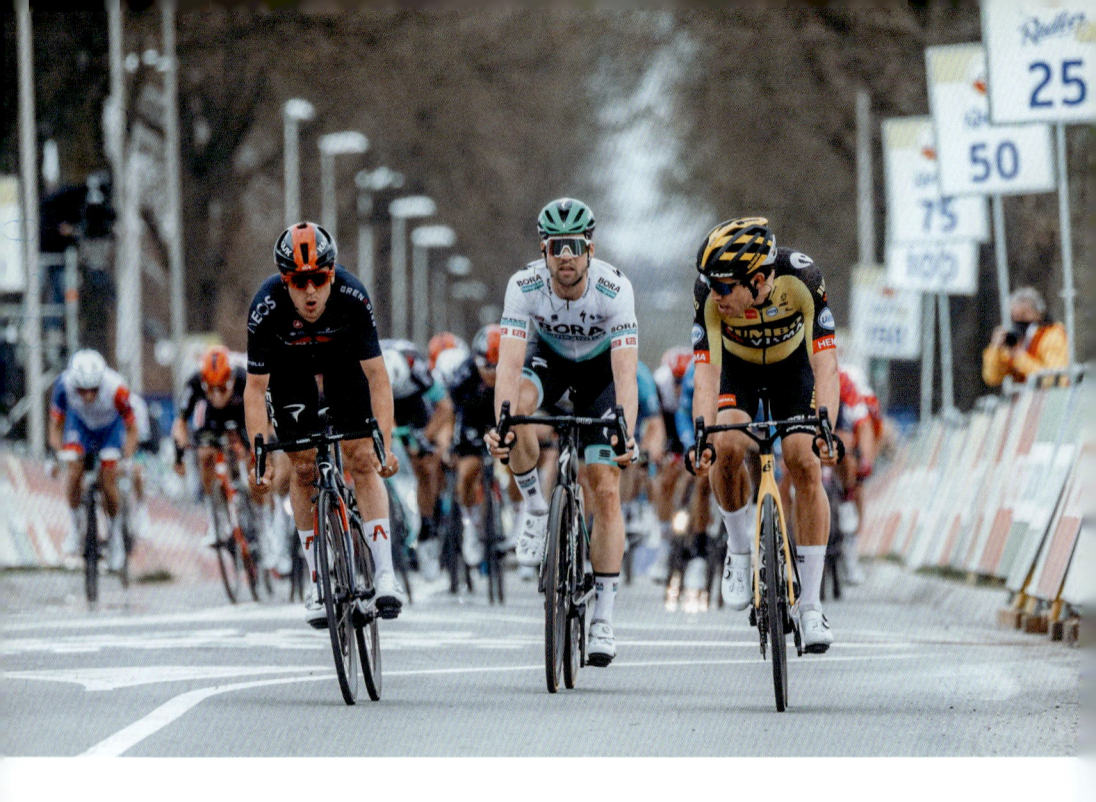

The slimmest of margins separates Tom Pidcock and Wout van Aert across the finish line of the Amstel Gold Race. After a nervy wait, the Belgian is found to have won.

Julian Alaphilippe catches and passes Primož Roglič to win a third Flèche Wallonne title. Pointing to his rainbow bands before wagging his finger across the line, he throws off the curse of his world champion's jersey.

The Giro d'Italia, back in its usual May slot in the calendar.

Egan Bernal grimaces to a first Giro d'Italia stage win and pink jersey on the steep gravel track at Campo Felice.

A resurgent Peter Sagan, winning on stage 10 of the Italian Grand Tour for the second year in a row.

The slow drip of fans returning to the roadsides at bike races continues – this time at Liège–Bastogne–Liège – as the world learns to live with the coronavirus.

The rain reduces roads to mud as Sonny Colbrelli outfoxes Mathieu van der Poel. Paris–Roubaix's return doesn't disappoint.

Lizzie Deignan's accidental solo effort writes her name in the history books as the first female winner of Paris-Roubaix.

Resplendent in the rainbow jersey, Julian Alaphilippe storms to the stage 1 victory and first yellow jersey at the Tour de France.

The Tour de France peloton navigates a crash-filled opening week in Brittany.

One Tour de France stage win was unimaginable, but two... it's even too much for Mark Cavendish.

Mathieu van der Poel carries the yellow jersey throughout the Tour de France's first week, refusing to go down without a fight.

A historic double ascent of Mont Ventoux – bike racing in its purest form.

Tadej Pogačar, playful in his youthfulness, before crushing the dreams of his yellow jersey rivals.

Another penultimate-day time trial at the Tour. This time Tadej Pogačar is in yellow and holds on to it to defend his title.

Julian Alaphilippe bends the World Championships road race to his will, going solo to ensure the rainbow jersey stays on his shoulders for another year.

Tom Pidcock enjoying life at the Vuelta a España, gaining experience of three-week stage racing at his debut Grand Tour.

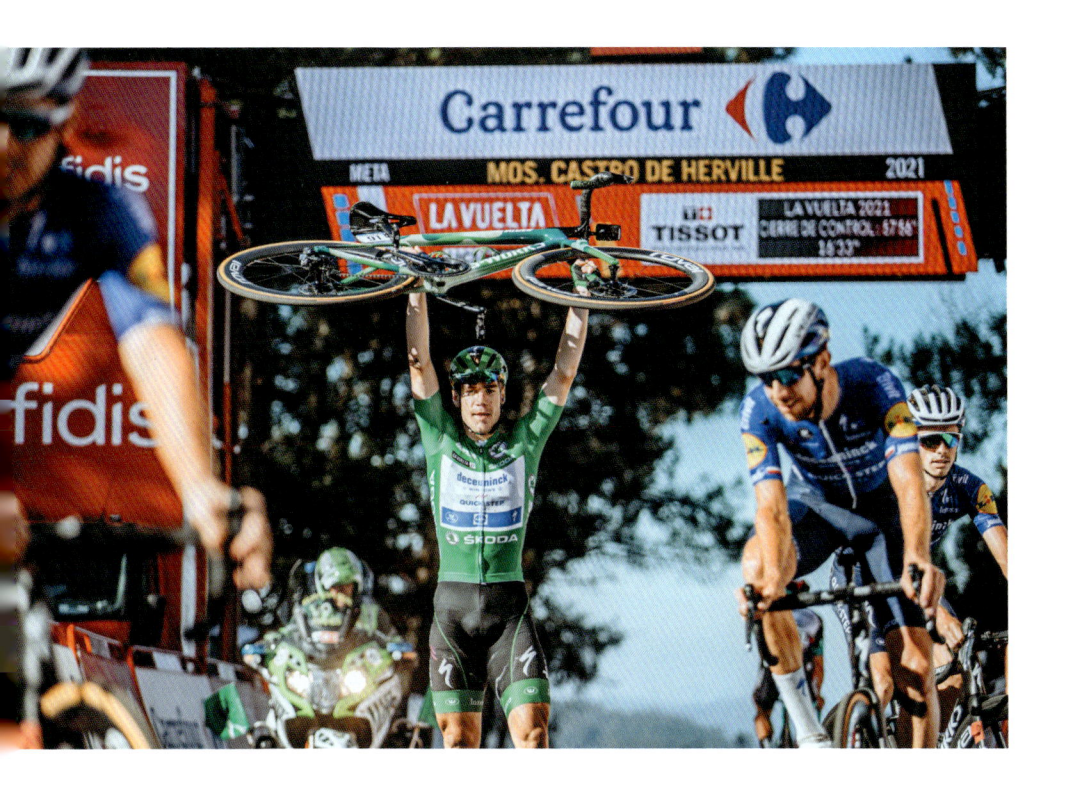

Fabio Jakobsen holds his bike aloft after making it across the finish of stage 20, confirming he will have a green jersey to add to his three Vuelta stage wins – a supreme comeback 12 months on from his horrific crash.

After the disappointment and embarrassment of the road race, Annemiek van Vleuten raises her time trial bike above her head after becoming Olympic champion in the race against the clock.

Egan Bernal wins his second Grand Tour. The Colombian rises to the top once more after a difficult two years since his Tour de France victory.

An image for the ages: one of the greats walks the Roubaix showers, where for so long she wasn't welcome.

Current world champion Anna van der Breggen tracked by former world champion Marianne Vos.

Elisa Longo Borghini opens her account for the season at Trofeo Alfredo Binda.

Annemiek van Vleuten looks to the sky as she signs on at Flèche Wallonne.

The pressure increases and the select group strings out at Flèche Wallonne.

The Giro Donne passes the Duomo in Milan as they roll out for stage 5.

Elisa Longo Borghini in the national champion's jersey at her home race, the Giro Donne.

Demi Vollering takes her first WorldTour and Monument victory. Teammate and world champion Anna van der Breggen celebrates in the background.

Annemiek van Vleuten attacks, soloing to victory at the Tour of Flanders ten years after her first win at this race.

The women's peloton takes on the white Tuscan roads of Strade Bianche.

Men and women combine in the mixed relay event at the World Championships.
The race of truth meets a true celebration of cycling in Bruges.

# AUGUST

With the Tour de France already an increasingly distant memory, within a week of its completion, attention drifted across the time zones to Japan. Ambivalent hosts to the world's visiting Olympians, the Japanese managed nonetheless to stage the delayed 2020 Tokyo Games behind closed doors. After that came races including the Vuelta, restored to the blazing heat of high summer, as the racing fanned across Europe in a proliferation of national week-long stage races for both sexes.

| DATE | RACE TITLE | LOCATION | UCI CODE | PAGE |
| --- | --- | --- | --- | --- |
| 1 August | Circuito de Getxo | Spain | 1.1 | 348 |
| 3–7 August | Vuelta a Burgos | Spain | 2.Pro | 349 |
| 4–15 August | Volta a Portugal | Portugal | 2.1 | 352 |
| 5–8 August | Arctic Race of Norway | Norway | 2.Pro | 358 |
| 5–8 August | Sazka Tour | Czech Republic | 2.1 | 360 |
| 9–15 August | Tour de Pologne | Poland | 2.UWT | 362 |
| 10–14 August | Tour of Denmark | Denmark | 2.Pro | 369 |
| 12–15 August | Ladies Tour of Norway | Norway | 2.WWT | 372 |
| 14 August–5 September | Vuelta a España | Spain | 2.UWT | 376 |
| 15 August | GP Jef Scherens | Belgium | 1.1 | 420 |
| 15 August | La Polynormande | France | 1.1 | 421 |
| 17 August | Egmont Cycling Race | Belgium | 1.1 | 422 |
| 17–20 August | Tour du Limousin | France | 2.1 | 423 |
| 19–22 August | Tour of Norway | Norway | 2.Pro | 425 |
| 20 August | GP Marcel Kint | Belgium | 1.1 | 427 |
| 24–27 August | Tour Poitou-Charentes en Nouvelle Aquitaine | France | 2.1 | 428 |
| 24–29 August | Simac Ladies Tour | Netherlands | 2.WWT | 431 |
| 26 August | Druivenkoers–Overijse | Belgium | 1.1 | 437 |
| 26–29 August | Deutschland Tour | Germany | 2.Pro | 438 |
| 28 August | Brussels Cycling Classic | Belgium | 1.Pro | 440 |
| 29 August | Bretagne Classic – Ouest-France | France | 1.UWT | 441 |
| 30 August | GP de Plouay | France | 1.WWT | 442 |
| 30 August–5 September | Benelux Tour | Belgium & Netherlands | 2.UWT | 443 |
| 31 August–3 September | Paralympic Games | Japan | OG | 450 |
| 31 August–5 September | Turul Romaniei | Romania | 2.1 | 455 |

AUGUST .1 MEN'S RACE

# CIRCUITO DE GETXO
1 August 2021
Bilbao-Getxo
193.5km

## WEATHER

TEMPERATURE  WIND
21°C         NW 15km/h

## RESULTS

| POS | NAME | TEAM | TIME |
|---|---|---|---|
| 1. | G. Nizzolo | TQA | 4:12:24 |
| 2. | G. Aleotti | BOH | s.t. |
| 3. | S. Buitrago | TBV | s.t. |
| 4. | A. González | MOV | 0:12 |
| 5. | I. Schelling | BOH | s.t. |
| 6. | G. Ciccone | TFS | s.t. |
| 7. | A. Covi | UAD | 0:54 |
| 8. | L. L. Sanchez | APT | 1:04 |
| 9. | M. Trentin | UAD | s.t. |
| 10. | A. Soto | EUS | 1:26 |
| 11. | C. Barbero | TQA | 2:50 |
| 12. | Jo. Herrada | COF | 2:54 |
| 13. | V. Albanese | EOK | 2:56 |
| 14. | J. P. López | TFS | 3:05 |
| 15. | J. Hollmann | MOV | 3:07 |
| 16. | J. Ayuso | UAD | s.t. |
| 17. | J. J. Lobato | EUS | s.t. |
| 18. | F. Barceló | COF | 3:10 |
| 19. | M. Paluta | GLC | s.t. |
| 20. | F. Galván | EKP | 3:11 |

AUGUST .PRO MEN'S RACE

## VUELTA A BURGOS
Stage 1
3 August 2021
Burgos (Catedral)–Burgos (El Castillo)
161km

### STAGE RESULTS

| POS | NAME | TEAM | TIME |
|---|---|---|---|
| 1. | E. Planckaert | AFC | 3:34:42 |
| 2. | G. Serrano | MOV | s.t. |
| 3. | V. Albanese | EOK | 0:01 |
| 4. | S. Buitrago | TBV | s.t. |
| 5. | R. Bardet | DSM | 0:03 |
| 6. | R. Stannard | BEX | 0:09 |
| 7. | M. E. Flórez | ARK | s.t. |
| 8. | J. Bol | BBH | s.t. |
| 9. | M. Landa | TBV | s.t. |
| 10. | K. Ledanois | ARK | s.t. |
| 11. | J. Lastra | CJR | s.t. |
| 12. | L. Calmejane | ACT | 0:13 |
| 13. | B. Zwiehoff | BOH | s.t. |
| 14. | G. Bouchard | ACT | s.t. |
| 15. | J. Hänninen | ACT | s.t. |
| 16. | D. de la Cruz | UAD | s.t. |
| 17. | F. Galván | EKP | s.t. |
| 18. | F. Aru | TQA | s.t. |
| 19. | S. Yates | BEX | s.t. |
| 20. | D. Navarro | BBH | s.t. |

### WEATHER

TEMPERATURE 24°C  WIND SW 22km/h

### GENERAL CLASSIFICATION

| POS | NAME | TEAM | TIME |
|---|---|---|---|
| 1. | E. Planckaert | AFC | 3:34:42 |
| 2. | G. Serrano | MOV | s.t. |
| 3. | V. Albanese | EOK | 0:01 |

### KING OF THE MOUNTAINS

| POS | NAME | TEAM | PTS |
|---|---|---|---|
| 1. | E. Planckaert | AFC | 6 |
| 2. | J. Jacobs | MOV | 6 |
| 3. | M. Würst Schmidt | ISN | 4 |

### POINTS

| POS | NAME | TEAM | PTS |
|---|---|---|---|
| 1. | E. Planckaert | AFC | 25 |
| 2. | V. Albanese | EOK | 16 |
| 3. | S. Buitrago | TBV | 14 |

### YOUNG RIDER

| POS | NAME | TEAM | TIME |
|---|---|---|---|
| 1. | S. Buitrago | TBV | 3:34:43 |
| 2. | R. Stannard | BEX | 0:08 |
| 3. | E. A. Rubio | MOV | 0:21 |

## VUELTA A BURGOS
Stage 2
4 August 2021
Tardajos–Briviesca
175km

### STAGE RESULTS

| POS | NAME | TEAM | TIME |
|---|---|---|---|
| 1. | J. S. Molano | UAD | 3:55:39 |
| 2. | A. Dainese | DSM | s.t. |
| 3. | M. Trentin | UAD | s.t. |
| 4. | J. Meeus | BOH | s.t. |
| 5. | J. Aberasturi | CJR | s.t. |
| 6. | R. Janse Van Rensburg | TQA | s.t. |
| 7. | I. Einhorn | ISN | s.t. |
| 8. | C. Lawless | TEN | s.t. |
| 9. | M. Sarreau | ACT | s.t. |
| 10. | G. Serrano | MOV | s.t. |
| 11. | R. Stannard | BEX | s.t. |
| 12. | T. Boudat | ARK | s.t. |
| 13. | E. Planckaert | AFC | s.t. |
| 14. | F. Galván | EKP | s.t. |
| 15. | N. Denz | DSM | s.t. |
| 16. | T. Bayer | AFC | s.t. |
| 17. | J. Jacobs | MOV | s.t. |
| 18. | J. J. Rojas | MOV | s.t. |
| 19. | M. Burghardt | BOH | s.t. |
| 20. | M. Alonso | EUS | s.t. |

### WEATHER

TEMPERATURE 22°C  WIND W 17km/h

### GENERAL CLASSIFICATION

| POS | | NAME | TEAM | TIME |
|---|---|---|---|---|
| 1. | ↑1 | G. Serrano | MOV | 7:30:21 |
| 2. | ↓1 | E. Planckaert | AFC | s.t. |
| 3. | — | V. Albanese | EOK | 0:01 |

### KING OF THE MOUNTAINS

| POS | | NAME | TEAM | PTS |
|---|---|---|---|---|
| 1. | — | E. Planckaert | AFC | 6 |
| 2. | — | J. Jacobs | MOV | 6 |
| 3. | — | M. Würst Schmidt | ISN | 4 |

### POINTS

| POS | | NAME | TEAM | PTS |
|---|---|---|---|---|
| 1. | — | E. Planckaert | AFC | 28 |
| 2. | — | J. S. Molano | UAD | 25 |
| 3. | — | A. Dainese | DSM | 20 |

### YOUNG RIDER

| POS | | NAME | TEAM | TIME |
|---|---|---|---|---|
| 1. | — | S. Buitrago | TBV | 7:30:22 |
| 2. | — | R. Stannard | BEX | 0:08 |
| 3. | — | E. A. Rubio | MOV | 0:21 |

AUGUST .PRO MEN'S RACE

## VUELTA A BURGOS
Stage 3
5 August 2021
Busto de Bureba–Espinosa de los Monteros
173km

### WEATHER

TEMPERATURE: 25°C
WIND: SW 22km/h

### STAGE RESULTS

| POS | NAME | TEAM | TIME |
|---|---|---|---|
| 1. | R. Bardet | DSM | 4:14:14 |
| 2. | D. Pozzovivo | TQA | 0:39 |
| 3. | M. Landa | TBV | s.t. |
| 4. | M. Nieve | BEX | s.t. |
| 5. | T. Bayer | AFC | 0:50 |
| 6. | M. Padun | TBV | s.t. |
| 7. | F. Aru | TQA | s.t. |
| 8. | A. Vlasov | APT | s.t. |
| 9. | D. de la Cruz | UAD | s.t. |
| 10. | O. Rodríguez | APT | s.t. |
| 11. | G. Bouchard | ACT | s.t. |
| 12. | P. Sivakov | IGD | s.t. |
| 13. | E. Bernal | IGD | 0:53 |
| 14. | A. C. Ardila | UAD | 1:20 |
| 15. | R. Adrià | EKP | 1:35 |
| 16. | G. Martín | EUS | s.t. |
| 17. | M. Tusveld | DSM | s.t. |
| 18. | B. Zwiehoff | BOH | s.t. |
| 19. | E. A. Rubio | MOV | s.t. |
| 20. | S. Carr | EFN | s.t. |

### GENERAL CLASSIFICATION

| POS | | NAME | TEAM | TIME |
|---|---|---|---|---|
| 1. | ↑4 | R. Bardet | DSM | 11:44:38 |
| 2. | ↑6 | M. Landa | TBV | 0:45 |
| 3. | ↑23 | D. Pozzovivo | TQA | 0:58 |

### KING OF THE MOUNTAINS

| POS | | NAME | TEAM | PTS |
|---|---|---|---|---|
| 1. | – | R. Bardet | DSM | 30 |
| 2. | – | G. Bouchard | ACT | 25 |
| 3. | – | M. Landa | TBV | 20 |

### POINTS

| POS | | NAME | TEAM | PTS |
|---|---|---|---|---|
| 1. | ↑9 | R. Bardet | DSM | 37 |
| 2. | ↓1 | E. Planckaert | AFC | 28 |
| 3. | ↓1 | J. S. Molano | UAD | 25 |

### YOUNG RIDER

| POS | | NAME | TEAM | TIME |
|---|---|---|---|---|
| 1. | – | S. Buitrago | TBV | 11:46:11 |
| 2. | ↑1 | E. A. Rubio | MOV | 0:21 |
| 3. | ↑2 | A. C. Ardila | UAD | 0:27 |

## VUELTA A BURGOS
Stage 4
6 August 2021
Roa–Aranda de Duero
149km

### WEATHER

TEMPERATURE: 23°C
WIND: SW 15km/h

### STAGE RESULTS

| POS | NAME | TEAM | TIME |
|---|---|---|---|
| 1. | J. S. Molano | UAD | 3:20:28 |
| 2. | J. Aberasturi | CJR | s.t. |
| 3. | V. Albanese | EOK | s.t. |
| 4. | M. Trentin | UAD | s.t. |
| 5. | J. Meeus | BOH | s.t. |
| 6. | M. Sarreau | ACT | s.t. |
| 7. | S. Modolo | AFC | s.t. |
| 8. | G. Serrano | MOV | s.t. |
| 9. | I. Einhorn | ISN | s.t. |
| 10. | J. J. Rojas | MOV | s.t. |
| 11. | A. Dainese | DSM | s.t. |
| 12. | F. Galván | EKP | s.t. |
| 13. | J. Jacobs | MOV | s.t. |
| 14. | A. Petit | TEN | s.t. |
| 15. | T. Boudat | ARK | s.t. |
| 16. | J. Keukeleire | EFN | s.t. |
| 17. | E. Planckaert | AFC | s.t. |
| 18. | C. Canal | BBH | s.t. |
| 19. | M. Alonso | EUS | s.t. |
| 20. | Á. Jaime | EKP | s.t. |

### GENERAL CLASSIFICATION

| POS | | NAME | TEAM | TIME |
|---|---|---|---|---|
| 1. | – | R. Bardet | DSM | 15:05:06 |
| 2. | – | M. Landa | TBV | 0:45 |
| 3. | ↑2 | D. de la Cruz | UAD | 1:00 |

### KING OF THE MOUNTAINS

| POS | | NAME | TEAM | PTS |
|---|---|---|---|---|
| 1. | – | R. Bardet | DSM | 30 |
| 2. | – | G. Bouchard | ACT | 25 |
| 3. | – | M. Landa | TBV | 20 |

### POINTS

| POS | | NAME | TEAM | PTS |
|---|---|---|---|---|
| 1. | ↑2 | J. S. Molano | UAD | 50 |
| 2. | ↓1 | R. Bardet | DSM | 37 |
| 3. | ↑5 | V. Albanese | EOK | 32 |

### YOUNG RIDER

| POS | | NAME | TEAM | TIME |
|---|---|---|---|---|
| 1. | – | S. Buitrago | TBV | 15:06:47 |
| 2. | – | E. A. Rubio | MOV | 0:13 |
| 3. | – | A. C. Ardila | UAD | 0:27 |

## VUELTA A BURGOS
Stage 5
7 August 2021
Comunero de Revenga–Lagunas de Neila
146km

## WEATHER

TEMPERATURE  WIND
20°C          SW 19km/h

### STAGE RESULTS

| POS | NAME | TEAM | TIME |
|---|---|---|---|
| 1. | H. Carthy | EFN | 3:23:53 |
| 2. | E. A. Rubio | MOV | 0:05 |
| 3. | S. Yates | BEX | 0:07 |
| 4. | E. Bernal | IGD | 0:13 |
| 5. | J. Vine | AFC | 0:14 |
| 6. | M. Landa | TBV | 0:16 |
| 7. | S. Buitrago | TBV | 0:29 |
| 8. | F. Aru | TQA | 0:37 |
| 9. | M. Padun | TBV | 0:39 |
| 10. | M. Bizkarra | EUS | 0:43 |
| 11. | A. Yates | IGD | s.t. |
| 12. | P. Sivakov | IGD | s.t. |
| 13. | S. Reichenbach | GFC | 0:46 |
| 14. | C. Rodriguez | IGD | 0:48 |
| 15. | D. de la Cruz | UAD | 0:52 |
| 16. | A. Pedrero | MOV | 1:04 |
| 17. | A. Vlasov | APT | 1:05 |
| 18. | M. Nieve | BEX | 1:10 |
| 19. | D. Caruso | TBV | 1:14 |
| 20. | G. Bouchard | ACT | s.t. |

### GENERAL CLASSIFICATION

| POS | | NAME | TEAM | TIME |
|---|---|---|---|---|
| 1. | ↑1 | M. Landa | TBV | 18:30:00 |
| 2. | ↑2 | F. Aru | TQA | 0:36 |
| 3. | ↑2 | M. Padun | TBV | 0:43 |

### KING OF THE MOUNTAINS

| POS | | NAME | TEAM | PTS |
|---|---|---|---|---|
| 1. | — | R. Bardet | DSM | 30 |
| 2. | — | H. Carthy | EFN | 30 |
| 3. | — | M. Landa | TBV | 30 |

### POINTS

| POS | | NAME | TEAM | PTS |
|---|---|---|---|---|
| 1. | — | J. S. Molano | UAD | 50 |
| 2. | — | R. Bardet | DSM | 37 |
| 3. | ↑7 | M. Landa | TBV | 33 |

### YOUNG RIDER

| POS | | NAME | TEAM | TIME |
|---|---|---|---|---|
| 1. | ↑1 | E. A. Rubio | MOV | 18:30:58 |
| 2. | ↓1 | S. Buitrago | TBV | 0:11 |
| 3. | — | A. C. Ardila | UAD | 1:44 |

AUGUST  .1 MEN'S RACE

## VOLTA A PORTUGAL
Prologue
4 August 2021
Lisboa–Lisboa
5.4km

### WEATHER

| TEMPERATURE | WIND |
|---|---|
| 26°C | N 18km/h |

### STAGE RESULTS

| POS | NAME | TEAM | TIME |
|---|---|---|---|
| 1. | R. Reis | EFP | 6:10 |
| 2. | M. Moreira | EFP | 0:11 |
| 3. | L. G. Mas | MOV | s.t. |
| 4. | D. Lopez | EKP | 0:15 |
| 5. | M. Norsgaard | MOV | 0:17 |
| 6. | S. J. Caldeira | W52 | 0:18 |
| 7. | J. Hollmann | MOV | 0:19 |
| 8. | T. Wirtgen | BWB | s.t. |
| 9. | A. Grigoryev | ATM | 0:20 |
| 10. | G. César Veloso | ATM | s.t. |
| 11. | A. Carvalho | EFP | s.t. |
| 12. | J. Brandão | W52 | 0:21 |
| 13. | O. Aular | CJR | 0:22 |
| 14. | J. Moreno | EFP | s.t. |
| 15. | E. Duarte | ATM | s.t. |
| 16. | J. Rodrigues | W52 | s.t. |
| 17. | O. Peckover | SCB | s.t. |
| 18. | D. Mestre | W52 | 0:23 |
| 19. | A. Trueba | ATM | s.t. |
| 20. | A. M. Marque | ATM | s.t. |

### GENERAL CLASSIFICATION

| POS | NAME | TEAM | TIME |
|---|---|---|---|
| 1. | R. Reis | EFP | 6:10 |
| 2. | M. Moreira | EFP | 0:11 |
| 3. | L. G. Mas | MOV | s.t. |

### YOUNG RIDER

| POS | NAME | TEAM | TIME |
|---|---|---|---|
| 1. | J. Hollmann | MOV | 6:29 |
| 2. | A. Mackellar | ICA | 0:08 |
| 3. | A. González | MOV | 0:09 |

## VOLTA A PORTUGAL
Stage 1
5 August 2021
Torres Vedras–Setúbal
175.8km

### WEATHER

| TEMPERATURE | WIND |
|---|---|
| 27°C | N 14km/h |

### STAGE RESULTS

| POS | NAME | TEAM | TIME |
|---|---|---|---|
| 1. | R. Reis | EFP | 4:12:23 |
| 2. | A. Molenaar | BBH | 0:02 |
| 3. | S. Samitier | MOV | s.t. |
| 4. | L. Gomes | KSU | s.t. |
| 5. | L. Fernandes | RPB | s.t. |
| 6. | R. Silva | CDF | s.t. |
| 7. | K. Molly | BWB | s.t. |
| 8. | O. Aular | CJR | s.t. |
| 9. | C. Fonte | KSU | s.t. |
| 10. | A. Antunes | W52 | s.t. |
| 11. | T. Wirtgen | BWB | s.t. |
| 12. | A. M. Marque | ATM | s.t. |
| 13. | J. F. Parra | EKP | s.t. |
| 14. | J. F. Osorio | BBH | s.t. |
| 15. | T. Antunes | TAV | s.t. |
| 16. | J. Rodrigues | W52 | s.t. |
| 17. | A. Bustamante | KSU | s.t. |
| 18. | D. Mestre | W52 | s.t. |
| 19. | H. Nunes | RPB | s.t. |
| 20. | S. Araiz | EKP | s.t. |

### GENERAL CLASSIFICATION

| POS | | NAME | TEAM | TIME |
|---|---|---|---|---|
| 1. | — | R. Reis | EFP | 4:18:33 |
| 2. | — | M. Moreira | EFP | 0:13 |
| 3. | ↑1 | D. Lopez | EKP | 0:17 |

### KING OF THE MOUNTAINS

| POS | NAME | TEAM | PTS |
|---|---|---|---|
| 1. | H. Nunes | RPB | 10 |
| 2. | C. I. Oyarzún | LLC | 8 |
| 3. | L. Fernandes | RPB | 6 |

### POINTS

| POS | NAME | TEAM | PTS |
|---|---|---|---|
| 1. | R. Reis | EFP | 40 |
| 2. | A. Molenaar | BBH | 32 |
| 3. | S. Samitier | MOV | 28 |

### YOUNG RIDER

| POS | | NAME | TEAM | TIME |
|---|---|---|---|---|
| 1. | — | J. Hollmann | MOV | 4:18:54 |
| 2. | ↑1 | A. González | MOV | 0:09 |
| 3. | ↑3 | A. Molenaar | BBH | 0:10 |

AUGUST  .1 MEN'S RACE

## VOLTA A PORTUGAL
Stage 2
6 August 2021
Ponte de Sor–Castelo Branco
162.1km

### WEATHER

TEMPERATURE: 26°C  
WIND: W 13km/h

### STAGE RESULTS

| POS | NAME | TEAM | TIME |
|---|---|---|---|
| 1. | K. Murphy | RLY | 3:57:49 |
| 2. | J. Brandão | W52 | 0:12 |
| 3. | L. G. Mas | MOV | 0:17 |
| 4. | D. Freitas | RPB | s.t. |
| 5. | L. Gomes | KSU | s.t. |
| 6. | D. Mestre | W52 | s.t. |
| 7. | K. Molly | BWB | s.t. |
| 8. | T. Wirtgen | BWB | s.t. |
| 9. | T. Contte | LLC | s.t. |
| 10. | J. Hollmann | MOV | s.t. |
| 11. | L. Leitão | TAV | s.t. |
| 12. | J. Rodrigues | W52 | s.t. |
| 13. | R. Silva | CDF | s.t. |
| 14. | A. Bustamante | KSU | s.t. |
| 15. | I. Azurmendi | EUS | s.t. |
| 16. | O. Aular | CJR | s.t. |
| 17. | A. Antunes | W52 | s.t. |
| 18. | G. César Veloso | ATM | s.t. |
| 19. | L. Mendonça | EFP | s.t. |
| 20. | V. García de Mateos | CDF | s.t. |

### GENERAL CLASSIFICATION

| POS | | NAME | TEAM | TIME |
|---|---|---|---|---|
| 1. | — | R. Reis | EFP | 8:16:39 |
| 2. | — | M. Moreira | EFP | 0:13 |
| 3. | — | D. Lopez | EKP | 0:17 |

### KING OF THE MOUNTAINS

| POS | | NAME | TEAM | PTS |
|---|---|---|---|---|
| 1. | — | M. Scheulen | LAA | 15 |
| 2. | ↓1 | H. Nunes | RPB | 11 |
| 3. | ↓1 | C. I. Oyarzún | LLC | 8 |

### POINTS

| POS | | NAME | TEAM | PTS |
|---|---|---|---|---|
| 1. | — | K. Murphy | RLY | 45 |
| 2. | ↑2 | L. Gomes | KSU | 44 |
| 3. | ↓2 | R. Reis | EFP | 40 |

### YOUNG RIDER

| POS | | NAME | TEAM | TIME |
|---|---|---|---|---|
| 1. | — | J. Hollmann | MOV | 8:17:00 |
| 2. | — | A. González | MOV | 0:09 |
| 3. | — | A. Molenaar | BBH | 0:10 |

## VOLTA A PORTUGAL
Stage 3
7 August 2021
Sertã–Covilhã (Torre)
170.3km

### WEATHER

TEMPERATURE: 25°C  
WIND: NW 14km/h

### STAGE RESULTS

| POS | NAME | TEAM | TIME |
|---|---|---|---|
| 1. | A. M. Marque | ATM | 4:59:10 |
| 2. | M. Moreira | EFP | 1:03 |
| 3. | A. González | MOV | s.t. |
| 4. | A. Antunes | W52 | 1:12 |
| 5. | G. César Veloso | ATM | s.t. |
| 6. | L. Gomes | KSU | 1:26 |
| 7. | J. Brandão | W52 | 1:33 |
| 8. | L. Fernandes | RPB | 1:36 |
| 9. | F. Figueiredo | EFP | s.t. |
| 10. | J. Rodrigues | W52 | 1:38 |
| 11. | A. Carvalho | EFP | 1:40 |
| 12. | H. Casimiro | KSU | 1:58 |
| 13. | D. Lopez | EKP | 2:01 |
| 14. | R. Vilela | W52 | 2:05 |
| 15. | R. Mestre | W52 | 2:36 |
| 16. | J. Moreno | EFP | 2:39 |
| 17. | T. Antunes | TAV | 2:42 |
| 18. | J. F. Parra | EKP | 2:49 |
| 19. | J. Benta | RPB | 2:53 |
| 20. | A. Cardoso | EFP | 3:07 |

### GENERAL CLASSIFICATION

| POS | | NAME | TEAM | TIME |
|---|---|---|---|---|
| 1. | ↑13 | A. M. Marque | ATM | 13:16:14 |
| 2. | ↑5 | G. César Veloso | ATM | 1:09 |
| 3. | ↑1 | J. Brandão | W52 | 1:26 |

### KING OF THE MOUNTAINS

| POS | | NAME | TEAM | PTS |
|---|---|---|---|---|
| 1. | — | A. M. Marque | ATM | 25 |
| 2. | — | H. Nunes | RPB | 20 |
| 3. | — | M. Moreira | EFP | 20 |

### POINTS

| POS | | NAME | TEAM | PTS |
|---|---|---|---|---|
| 1. | ↑1 | L. Gomes | KSU | 61 |
| 2. | ↓1 | K. Murphy | RLY | 45 |
| 3. | — | R. Reis | EFP | 40 |

### YOUNG RIDER

| POS | | NAME | TEAM | TIME |
|---|---|---|---|---|
| 1. | ↑1 | A. González | MOV | 13:17:42 |
| 2. | ↑3 | P. M. Lopes | KSU | 2:38 |
| 3. | ↑1 | M. Hollyman | ICA | 10:11 |

AUGUST    .1 MEN'S RACE

## VOLTA A PORTUGAL
Stage 4
8 August 2021
Belmonte–Guarda
181.6km

### WEATHER

TEMPERATURE | WIND
23°C | N 11km/h

### STAGE RESULTS

| POS | NAME | TEAM | TIME |
|---|---|---|---|
| 1. | F. Figueiredo | EFP | 4:28:25 |
| 2. | A. Antunes | W52 | s.t. |
| 3. | M. Moreira | EFP | 0:59 |
| 4. | J. Brandão | W52 | 1:03 |
| 5. | A. González | MOV | s.t. |
| 6. | T. Antunes | TAV | 1:08 |
| 7. | D. Freitas | RPB | 1:10 |
| 8. | A. Carvalho | EFP | s.t. |
| 9. | L. Fernandes | RPB | s.t. |
| 10. | H. Casimiro | KSU | s.t. |
| 11. | J. F. Parra | EKP | 1:13 |
| 12. | J. Rodrigues | W52 | 1:15 |
| 13. | V. García de Mateos | CDF | 1:18 |
| 14. | J. Silva | TAV | s.t. |
| 15. | G. Mannion | RLY | 1:21 |
| 16. | A. M. Marque | ATM | s.t. |
| 17. | D. Lopez | EKP | 1:24 |
| 18. | P. M. Lopes | KSU | 1:26 |
| 19. | C. I. Oyarzún | LLC | 1:32 |
| 20. | J. del Pino | LLC | 1:38 |

### GENERAL CLASSIFICATION

| POS | NAME | TEAM | TIME |
|---|---|---|---|
| 2. ↑2 | A. Antunes | W52 | 0:05 |
| 3. ↑7 | F. Figueiredo | EFP | 0:25 |

### KING OF THE MOUNTAINS

| POS | NAME | TEAM | PTS |
|---|---|---|---|
| 1. ↑5 | A. Antunes | W52 | 29 |
| 2. ↑14 | F. Figueiredo | EFP | 25 |
| 3. ↓2 | A. M. Marque | ATM | 25 |

### POINTS

| POS | NAME | TEAM | PTS |
|---|---|---|---|
| 1. — | L. Gomes | KSU | 64 |
| 2. ↑1 | R. Reis | EFP | 51 |
| 3. ↓1 | K. Murphy | RLY | 45 |

### YOUNG RIDER

| POS | NAME | TEAM | TIME |
|---|---|---|---|
| 1. — | A. González | MOV | 17:47:10 |
| 2. — | P. M. Lopes | KSU | 3:01 |
| 3. ↑4 | A. Molenaar | BBH | 29:03 |

## VOLTA A PORTUGAL
Stage 5
10 August 2021
Águeda–Santo Tirso (Nossa Senhora da Assunção)
171.3km

### WEATHER

TEMPERATURE | WIND
21°C | NW 17km/h

### STAGE RESULTS

| POS | NAME | TEAM | TIME |
|---|---|---|---|
| 1. | M. Hollyman | ICA | 4:11:48 |
| 2. | R. Mestre | W52 | 0:35 |
| 3. | T. Contte | LLC | 1:00 |
| 4. | R. Reis | EFP | 1:02 |
| 5. | L. G. Mas | MOV | 1:05 |
| 6. | D. Freitas | RPB | 1:09 |
| 7. | J. A. López-Cózar | BBH | 1:16 |
| 8. | J. Hollmann | MOV | 1:36 |
| 9. | L. Mendonça | EFP | 1:44 |
| 10. | C. Fonte | KSU | 1:47 |
| 11. | A. Peters | SCB | s.t. |
| 12. | K. Swirbul | RLY | 2:01 |
| 13. | K. Molly | BWB | 2:25 |
| 14. | M. Marquez | EKP | 2:37 |
| 15. | J. Macedo | LAA | 3:11 |
| 16. | T. Antunes | TAV | 5:01 |
| 17. | M. Moreira | EFP | 5:04 |
| 18. | A. González | MOV | s.t. |
| 19. | J. Brandão | W52 | 5:07 |
| 20. | H. Casimiro | KSU | s.t. |

### GENERAL CLASSIFICATION

| POS | NAME | TEAM | TIME |
|---|---|---|---|
| 1. ↑15 | D. Freitas | RPB | 22:02:16 |
| 2. ↓1 | A. M. Marque | ATM | 0:42 |
| 3. ↓1 | A. Antunes | W52 | 0:47 |

### KING OF THE MOUNTAINS

| POS | NAME | TEAM | PTS |
|---|---|---|---|
| 1. — | A. Antunes | W52 | 29 |
| 2. ↑1 | A. M. Marque | ATM | 25 |
| 3. ↓1 | F. Figueiredo | EFP | 25 |

### POINTS

| POS | NAME | TEAM | PTS |
|---|---|---|---|
| 1. — | L. Gomes | KSU | 74 |
| 2. — | R. Reis | EFP | 63 |
| 3. — | K. Murphy | RLY | 45 |

### YOUNG RIDER

| POS | NAME | TEAM | TIME |
|---|---|---|---|
| 1. — | A. González | MOV | 22:04:02 |
| 2. — | P. M. Lopes | KSU | 4:25 |
| 3. — | A. Molenaar | BBH | 29:51 |

AUGUST .1 MEN'S RACE

## VOLTA A PORTUGAL
Stage 6
11 August 2021
Viana do Castelo–Fafe
182.4km

### WEATHER

| TEMPERATURE | WIND |
|---|---|
| 20°C | NW 15km/h |

### STAGE RESULTS

| POS | NAME | TEAM | TIME |
|---|---|---|---|
| 1. | B. King | RLY | 4:22:00 |
| 2. | A. Mackellar | ICA | 0:09 |
| 3. | T. Wirtgen | BWB | 0:15 |
| 4. | J. D. Alba | MOV | 0:20 |
| 5. | B. Silva | CDF | 0:24 |
| 6. | R. Campos | LLC | 0:45 |
| 7. | M. Hollyman | ICA | 1:19 |
| 8. | P. Paulinho | TAV | 1:26 |
| 9. | H. Gonçalves | KSU | 1:27 |
| 10. | M. Scheulen | LAA | 1:45 |
| 11. | I. Cantón | BBH | 2:25 |
| 12. | M. Moreira | EFP | 8:11 |
| 13. | T. Antunes | TAV | 8:13 |
| 14. | J. Brandão | W52 | s.t. |
| 15. | A. Antunes | W52 | s.t. |
| 16. | A. Molenaar | BBH | s.t. |
| 17. | A. González | MOV | s.t. |
| 18. | F. Figueiredo | EFP | s.t. |
| 19. | V. García de Mateos | CDF | s.t. |
| 20. | H. Casimiro | KSU | s.t. |

### GENERAL CLASSIFICATION

| POS | | NAME | TEAM | TIME |
|---|---|---|---|---|
| 1. | ↑1 | A. M. Marque | ATM | 26:33:11 |
| 2. | ↑1 | A. Antunes | W52 | 0:05 |
| 3. | ↑1 | F. Figueiredo | EFP | 0:25 |

### KING OF THE MOUNTAINS

| POS | | NAME | TEAM | PTS |
|---|---|---|---|---|
| 1. | ↑7 | B. Silva | CDF | 29 |
| 2. | ↓1 | A. Antunes | W52 | 29 |
| 3. | ↓1 | A. M. Marque | ATM | 25 |

### POINTS

| POS | | NAME | TEAM | PTS |
|---|---|---|---|---|
| 1. | – | L. Gomes | KSU | 74 |
| 2. | – | R. Reis | EFP | 63 |
| 3. | – | B. King | RLY | 46 |

### YOUNG RIDER

| POS | | NAME | TEAM | TIME |
|---|---|---|---|---|
| 1. | – | A. González | MOV | 26:34:15 |
| 2. | – | P. M. Lopes | KSU | 4:30 |
| 3. | – | A. Molenaar | BBH | 29:51 |

## VOLTA A PORTUGAL
Stage 7
12 August 2021
Felgueiras–Bragança
193.2km

### WEATHER

| TEMPERATURE | WIND |
|---|---|
| 29°C | SW 18km/h |

### STAGE RESULTS

| POS | NAME | TEAM | TIME |
|---|---|---|---|
| 1. | R. Reis | EFP | 4:35:30 |
| 2. | B. King | RLY | 0:16 |
| 3. | D. Lopez | EKP | s.t. |
| 4. | J. Silva | TAV | s.t. |
| 5. | A. Moreno | BBH | s.t. |
| 6. | A. Bustamante | KSU | s.t. |
| 7. | P. M. Lopes | KSU | s.t. |
| 8. | J. Moreno | EFP | s.t. |
| 9. | N. Meireles | LLC | s.t. |
| 10. | V. García de Mateos | CDF | s.t. |
| 11. | G. Leaça | LAA | s.t. |
| 12. | R. Campos | LLC | s.t. |
| 13. | J. D. Alba | MOV | s.t. |
| 14. | R. Vilela | W52 | s.t. |
| 15. | J. F. Osorio | BBH | 0:24 |
| 16. | J. A. López-Cózar | BBH | s.t. |
| 17. | I. Moreno | EKP | 0:38 |
| 18. | R. Silva | CDF | 0:46 |
| 19. | L. Mendonça | EFP | 0:52 |
| 20. | R. Mestre | W52 | 1:56 |

### GENERAL CLASSIFICATION

| POS | | NAME | TEAM | TIME |
|---|---|---|---|---|
| 1. | ↑11 | R. Reis | EFP | 31:11:46 |
| 2. | ↓1 | A. M. Marque | ATM | 0:28 |
| 3. | ↓1 | A. Antunes | W52 | 0:33 |

### KING OF THE MOUNTAINS

| POS | | NAME | TEAM | PTS |
|---|---|---|---|---|
| 1. | – | B. Silva | CDF | 29 |
| 2. | – | A. Antunes | W52 | 29 |
| 3. | – | A. M. Marque | ATM | 25 |

### POINTS

| POS | | NAME | TEAM | PTS |
|---|---|---|---|---|
| 1. | ↑1 | R. Reis | EFP | 118 |
| 2. | ↑1 | B. King | RLY | 78 |
| 3. | ↓2 | L. Gomes | KSU | 74 |

### YOUNG RIDER

| POS | | NAME | TEAM | TIME |
|---|---|---|---|---|
| 1. | – | A. González | MOV | 31:13:18 |
| 2. | – | P. M. Lopes | KSU | 1:13 |
| 3. | ↑1 | M. Hollyman | ICA | 32:29 |

AUGUST    .1 MEN'S RACE

## VOLTA A PORTUGAL
Stage 8
13 August 2021
Bragança–Montalegre (Serra do Larouco)
160.7km

### WEATHER
TEMPERATURE: 33°C
WIND: SW 14km/h

### STAGE RESULTS

| POS | NAME | TEAM | TIME |
|---|---|---|---|
| 1. | K. Murphy | RLY | 4:12:06 |
| 2. | J. F. Parra | EKP | 0:13 |
| 3. | H. Casimiro | KSU | 0:25 |
| 4. | G. Goncalves | TAV | 0:54 |
| 5. | A. Moreno | BBH | 0:58 |
| 6. | M. Moreira | EFP | 1:10 |
| 7. | C. Salgueiro | LAA | s.t. |
| 8. | J. Brandão | W52 | 1:14 |
| 9. | F. Figueiredo | EFP | s.t. |
| 10. | A. Antunes | W52 | 1:16 |
| 11. | C. I. Oyarzún | LLC | 1:18 |
| 12. | T. Antunes | TAV | 1:20 |
| 13. | A. M. Marque | ATM | 1:35 |
| 14. | K. Molly | BWB | 1:52 |
| 15. | A. González | MOV | 2:10 |
| 16. | A. Carvalho | EFP | s.t. |
| 17. | J. A. López-Cózar | BBH | 2:17 |
| 18. | J. Rodrigues | W52 | 2:59 |
| 19. | H. Carretero | MOV | 3:52 |
| 20. | R. Campos | LLC | 6:20 |

### GENERAL CLASSIFICATION

| POS | NAME | TEAM | TIME |
|---|---|---|---|
| 1. ↑2 | A. Antunes | W52 | 35:25:41 |
| 2. – | A. M. Marque | ATM | 0:14 |
| 3. ↑3 | F. Figueiredo | EFP | 0:18 |

### KING OF THE MOUNTAINS

| POS | NAME | TEAM | PTS |
|---|---|---|---|
| 1. – | B. Silva | CDF | 46 |
| 2. ↑8 | R. Campos | LLC | 35 |
| 3. ↑5 | R. Silva | CDF | 30 |

### POINTS

| POS | NAME | TEAM | PTS |
|---|---|---|---|
| 1. – | R. Reis | EFP | 118 |
| 2. ↑1 | L. Gomes | KSU | 84 |
| 3. ↓1 | B. King | RLY | 78 |

### YOUNG RIDER

| POS | NAME | TEAM | TIME |
|---|---|---|---|
| 1. – | A. González | MOV | 35:27:34 |
| 2. – | P. M. Lopes | KSU | 26:02 |
| 3. ↑1 | H. Gonçalves | KSU | 52:55 |

---

## VOLTA A PORTUGAL
Stage 9
14 August 2021
Boticas–Mondim de Basto (Senhora da Graça)
145.5km

### WEATHER
TEMPERATURE: 36°C
WIND: W 15km/h

### STAGE RESULTS

| POS | NAME | TEAM | TIME |
|---|---|---|---|
| 1. | M. Moreira | EFP | 3:47:36 |
| 2. | A. Antunes | W52 | 0:08 |
| 3. | J. Brandão | W52 | 0:14 |
| 4. | F. Figueiredo | EFP | 0:45 |
| 5. | J. F. Parra | EKP | 0:56 |
| 6. | A. González | MOV | 1:07 |
| 7. | A. M. Marque | ATM | 1:12 |
| 8. | A. Carvalho | EFP | 3:00 |
| 9. | J. Rodrigues | W52 | 3:13 |
| 10. | C. I. Oyarzún | LLC | 5:46 |
| 11. | A. Cardoso | EFP | 6:21 |
| 12. | R. Vilela | W52 | 6:23 |
| 13. | A. Moreno | BBH | 6:48 |
| 14. | J. del Pino | LLC | 7:02 |
| 15. | L. G. Mas | MOV | 7:11 |
| 16. | G. Leaça | LAA | 7:13 |
| 17. | M. Hollyman | ICA | 7:23 |
| 18. | J. Moreno | EFP | 7:29 |
| 19. | H. Casimiro | KSU | 7:30 |
| 20. | A. Ramalho | LAA | s.t. |

### GENERAL CLASSIFICATION

| POS | NAME | TEAM | TIME |
|---|---|---|---|
| 1. – | A. Antunes | W52 | 39:13:25 |
| 2. ↑2 | M. Moreira | EFP | 0:42 |
| 3. – | F. Figueiredo | EFP | 0:55 |

### KING OF THE MOUNTAINS

| POS | NAME | TEAM | PTS |
|---|---|---|---|
| 1. – | B. Silva | CDF | 57 |
| 2. ↑3 | M. Moreira | EFP | 56 |
| 3. ↑1 | A. Antunes | W52 | 54 |

### POINTS

| POS | NAME | TEAM | PTS |
|---|---|---|---|
| 1. – | R. Reis | EFP | 128 |
| 2. – | L. Gomes | KSU | 84 |
| 3. – | B. King | RLY | 78 |

### YOUNG RIDER

| POS | NAME | TEAM | TIME |
|---|---|---|---|
| 1. – | A. González | MOV | 39:16:17 |
| 2. – | P. M. Lopes | KSU | 52:04 |
| 3. – | H. Gonçalves | KSU | 59:46 |

AUGUST    .1 MEN'S RACE

# VOLTA A PORTUGAL
Stage 10 (ITT)
15 August 2021
Viseu–Viseu
20.3km

## WEATHER

TEMPERATURE  WIND
34°C         W 10km/h

## STAGE RESULTS

| POS | NAME | TEAM | TIME |
|---|---|---|---|
| 1. | R. Reis | EFP | 25:24 |
| 2. | M. Moreira | EFP | 0:12 |
| 3. | J. Hollmann | MOV | 0:41 |
| 4. | A. Antunes | W52 | 0:44 |
| 5. | A. M. Marque | ATM | 0:49 |
| 6. | L. G. Mas | MOV | s.t. |
| 7. | J. Rodrigues | W52 | 0:54 |
| 8. | A. Carvalho | EFP | 0:55 |
| 9. | M. Norsgaard | MOV | 1:01 |
| 10. | R. Mestre | W52 | 1:05 |
| 11. | D. Lopez | EKP | 1:09 |
| 12. | D. Mestre | W52 | 1:10 |
| 13. | R. Britton | RLY | 1:12 |
| 14. | G. César Veloso | ATM | 1:16 |
| 15. | J. Brandão | W52 | s.t. |
| 16. | A. Grigoryev | ATM | 1:22 |
| 17. | G. Mannion | RLY | 1:25 |
| 18. | C. I. Oyarzún | LLC | 1:26 |
| 19. | A. González | MOV | 1:35 |
| 20. | V. García de Mateos | CDF | 1:36 |

## GENERAL CLASSIFICATION

| POS | NAME | TEAM | TIME |
|---|---|---|---|
| 1. — | A. Antunes | W52 | 39:39:33 |
| 2. — | M. Moreira | EFP | 0:10 |
| 3. ↑2 | A. M. Marque | ATM | 1:23 |

## KING OF THE MOUNTAINS

| POS | NAME | TEAM | PTS |
|---|---|---|---|
| 1. — | B. Silva | CDF | 57 |
| 2. — | M. Moreira | EFP | 56 |
| 3. — | A. Antunes | W52 | 54 |

## POINTS

| POS | NAME | TEAM | PTS |
|---|---|---|---|
| 1. — | R. Reis | EFP | 138 |
| 2. — | L. Gomes | KSU | 84 |
| 3. — | B. King | RLY | 78 |

## YOUNG RIDER

| POS | NAME | TEAM | TIME |
|---|---|---|---|
| 1. — | A. González | MOV | 39:43:16 |
| 2. — | P. M. Lopes | KSU | 53:19 |
| 3. ↑1 | M. Hollyman | ICA | 1:01:48 |

AUGUST  .PRO MEN'S RACE

# ARCTIC RACE OF NORWAY
Stage 1
5 August 2021
Tromsø–Tromsø
142.4km

## WEATHER

TEMPERATURE: 12°C
WIND: S 19km/h

## STAGE RESULTS

| POS | NAME | TEAM | TIME |
|---|---|---|---|
| 1. | M. Hoelgaard | UXT | 3:11:29 |
| 2. | A. Kristoff | NAT | 0:02 |
| 3. | B. Coquard | BBK | s.t. |
| 4. | A. Soto | EUS | s.t. |
| 5. | K. Aasvold | TCO | s.t. |
| 6. | A. Angulo | EUS | s.t. |
| 7. | W. Barguil | ARK | s.t. |
| 8. | C. Venturini | ACT | s.t. |
| 9. | A. De Gendt | IWG | s.t. |
| 10. | O. C. Eiking | IWG | s.t. |
| 11. | S. Battistella | APT | s.t. |
| 12. | A. Zingle | COF | s.t. |
| 13. | E. Prades | DKO | s.t. |
| 14. | D. Van Gestel | TEN | s.t. |
| 15. | V. Lafay | COF | s.t. |
| 16. | D. Claeys | TQA | s.t. |
| 17. | F. Felline | APT | s.t. |
| 18. | S. Dewulf | ACT | s.t. |
| 19. | M. Burgaudeau | TEN | s.t. |
| 20. | A. Leknessund | NAT | s.t. |

## GENERAL CLASSIFICATION

| POS | NAME | TEAM | TIME |
|---|---|---|---|
| 1. | M. Hoelgaard | UXT | 3:11:19 |
| 2. | A. Kristoff | NAT | 0:06 |
| 3. | B. Coquard | BBK | 0:08 |

## KING OF THE MOUNTAINS

| POS | NAME | TEAM | PTS |
|---|---|---|---|
| 1. | G. Brussenskiy | APT | 8 |
| 2. | A. Gougeard | ACT | 6 |
| 3. | K. Aasvold | TCO | 3 |

## POINTS

| POS | NAME | TEAM | PTS |
|---|---|---|---|
| 1. | M. Hoelgaard | UXT | 15 |
| 2. | A. Kristoff | NAT | 12 |
| 3. | K. Aasvold | TCO | 9 |

## YOUNG RIDER

| POS | NAME | TEAM | TIME |
|---|---|---|---|
| 1. | S. Battistella | APT | 3:11:29 |
| 2. | A. Zingle | COF | 0:02 |
| 3. | V. Lafay | COF | s.t. |

# ARCTIC RACE OF NORWAY
Stage 2
6 August 2021
Nordkjosbotn–Kilpisjärvi
177.6km

## WEATHER

TEMPERATURE: 23°C
WIND: S 4km/h

## STAGE RESULTS

| POS | NAME | TEAM | TIME |
|---|---|---|---|
| 1. | M. Laas | BOH | 3:56:14 |
| 2. | A. Kristoff | NAT | s.t. |
| 3. | D. van Poppel | IWG | s.t. |
| 4. | R. Barbier | ISN | s.t. |
| 5. | M. Peñalver | BBH | s.t. |
| 6. | A. Marit | SVB | s.t. |
| 7. | T. Devriendt | IWG | s.t. |
| 8. | B. Welten | ARK | s.t. |
| 9. | E. Boasson Hagen | TEN | s.t. |
| 10. | B. Coquard | BBK | s.t. |
| 11. | T. Gudmestad | TCO | s.t. |
| 12. | L. Naesen | ACT | s.t. |
| 13. | D. Van Gestel | TEN | s.t. |
| 14. | L. Coati | TQA | s.t. |
| 15. | Y. Gidich | APT | s.t. |
| 16. | E. M. Grosu | DKO | s.t. |
| 17. | C. Noppe | ARK | s.t. |
| 18. | O. Riesebeek | AFC | s.t. |
| 19. | A. Colman | SVB | s.t. |
| 20. | A. Zingle | COF | s.t. |

## GENERAL CLASSIFICATION

| POS | | NAME | TEAM | TIME |
|---|---|---|---|---|
| 1. | ↑1 | A. Kristoff | NAT | 7:07:33 |
| 2. | ↓1 | M. Hoelgaard | UXT | s.t. |
| 3. | – | B. Coquard | BBK | 0:08 |

## KING OF THE MOUNTAINS

| POS | | NAME | TEAM | PTS |
|---|---|---|---|---|
| 1. | – | F. Dversnes | TCO | 9 |
| 2. | ↓1 | G. Brussenskiy | APT | 8 |
| 3. | ↓1 | A. Gougeard | ACT | 6 |

## POINTS

| POS | | NAME | TEAM | PTS |
|---|---|---|---|---|
| 1. | ↑1 | A. Kristoff | NAT | 24 |
| 2. | ↓1 | M. Hoelgaard | UXT | 15 |
| 3. | – | M. Laas | BOH | 15 |

## YOUNG RIDER

| POS | | NAME | TEAM | TIME |
|---|---|---|---|---|
| 1. | – | S. Battistella | APT | 7:07:43 |
| 2. | – | A. Zingle | COF | 0:02 |
| 3. | ↑3 | A. Leknessund | NAT | s.t. |

AUGUST . PRO MEN'S RACE

## ARCTIC RACE OF NORWAY
Stage 3
7 August 2021
Finnsnes–Målselv
184.5km

## WEATHER

TEMPERATURE  WIND
24°C  E 6km/h

### STAGE RESULTS

| POS | NAME | TEAM | TIME |
|---|---|---|---|
| 1. | B. Hermans | ISN | 4:14:28 |
| 2. | O. C. Eiking | IWG | s.t. |
| 3. | V. Lafay | COF | s.t. |
| 4. | S. Battistella | APT | 0:12 |
| 5. | E. Prades | DKO | 0:19 |
| 6. | K. Aasvold | TCO | s.t. |
| 7. | A. Leknessund | NAT | s.t. |
| 8. | A. Soto | EUS | s.t. |
| 9. | P. Sánchez | BBH | s.t. |
| 10. | T. Træen | UXT | 0:22 |
| 11. | W. Barguil | ARK | s.t. |
| 12. | S. de Bod | APT | 0:24 |
| 13. | J. Eriksson | TCO | 0:26 |
| 14. | P. Vakoč | AFC | 0:41 |
| 15. | T. Sleen | UXT | s.t. |
| 16. | F. Felline | APT | 0:47 |
| 17. | M. Burgaudeau | TEN | 0:53 |
| 18. | L. Wirtgen | BWB | 0:55 |
| 19. | D. Claeys | TQA | 0:57 |
| 20. | A. Livyns | BWB | 0:59 |

### GENERAL CLASSIFICATION

| POS | NAME | TEAM | TIME |
|---|---|---|---|
| 1. ↑25 | B. Hermans | ISN | 11:22:03 |
| 2. ↑23 | O. C. Eiking | IWG | 0:04 |
| 3. ↑17 | V. Lafay | COF | 0:06 |

### KING OF THE MOUNTAINS

| POS | NAME | TEAM | PTS |
|---|---|---|---|
| 1. — | F. Dversnes | TCO | 21 |
| 2. — | G. Brussenskiy | APT | 8 |
| 3. ↑3 | O. C. Eiking | IWG | 6 |

### POINTS

| POS | NAME | TEAM | PTS |
|---|---|---|---|
| 1. — | A. Kristoff | NAT | 24 |
| 2. ↑1 | M. Laas | BOH | 22 |
| 3. — | B. Hermans | ISN | 15 |

### YOUNG RIDER

| POS | NAME | TEAM | TIME |
|---|---|---|---|
| 1. ↑5 | V. Lafay | COF | 11:22:09 |
| 2. ↓1 | S. Battistella | APT | 0:14 |
| 3. — | A. Leknessund | NAT | 0:23 |

## ARCTIC RACE OF NORWAY
Stage 4
8 August 2021
Gratangen–Harstad
163.5km

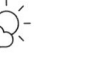

## WEATHER

TEMPERATURE  WIND
18°C  E 24km/h

### STAGE RESULTS

| POS | NAME | TEAM | TIME |
|---|---|---|---|
| 1. | P. Walsleben | AFC | 3:41:40 |
| 2. | N. Terpstra | TEN | s.t. |
| 3. | A. Delettre | DKO | 0:17 |
| 4. | O. C. Eiking | IWG | s.t. |
| 5. | E. N. Resell | UXT | 0:19 |
| 6. | W. Barguil | ARK | s.t. |
| 7. | A. Zingle | COF | s.t. |
| 8. | B. Coquard | BBK | s.t. |
| 9. | V. Lafay | COF | s.t. |
| 10. | P. Vakoč | AFC | s.t. |
| 11. | B. Hermans | ISN | s.t. |
| 12. | M. Hoelgaard | UXT | s.t. |
| 13. | E. Prades | DKO | s.t. |
| 14. | S. Battistella | APT | s.t. |
| 15. | K. Aasvold | TCO | s.t. |
| 16. | M. Burgaudeau | TEN | s.t. |
| 17. | A. Angulo | EUS | s.t. |
| 18. | S. E. Byström | NAT | s.t. |
| 19. | L. Wirtgen | BWB | s.t. |
| 20. | C. Venturini | ACT | s.t. |

### GENERAL CLASSIFICATION

| POS | NAME | TEAM | TIME |
|---|---|---|---|
| 1. — | B. Hermans | ISN | 15:04:02 |
| 2. — | O. C. Eiking | IWG | 0:02 |
| 3. — | V. Lafay | COF | 0:06 |

### KING OF THE MOUNTAINS

| POS | NAME | TEAM | PTS |
|---|---|---|---|
| 1. — | F. Dversnes | TCO | 21 |
| 2. — | N. Terpstra | TEN | 9 |
| 3. ↓1 | G. Brussenskiy | APT | 8 |

### POINTS

| POS | NAME | TEAM | PTS |
|---|---|---|---|
| 1. — | A. Kristoff | NAT | 24 |
| 2. — | M. Laas | BOH | 22 |
| 3. ↑3 | O. C. Eiking | IWG | 20 |

### YOUNG RIDER

| POS | NAME | TEAM | TIME |
|---|---|---|---|
| 1. — | V. Lafay | COF | 15:04:08 |
| 2. — | S. Battistella | APT | 0:14 |
| 3. — | A. Leknessund | NAT | 0:23 |

AUGUST .1 MEN'S RACE

## SAZKA TOUR
Stage 1
5 August 2021
Prostějov–Uničov
150.8km

### WEATHER

TEMPERATURE  WIND
16°C  NW 13km/h

### STAGE RESULTS

| POS | NAME | TEAM | TIME |
|---|---|---|---|
| 1. | J. Huppertz | LKH | 3:34:35 |
| 2. | I. Andersen | UXT | s.t. |
| 3. | T. Lindner | PUS | 0:01 |
| 4. | J. Koch | IWG | 0:15 |
| 5. | D. Neuman | EKA | s.t. |
| 6. | M. Urianstad | UXT | s.t. |
| 7. | M. Kukrle | EKA | s.t. |
| 8. | T. T. Teutenberg | LPC | s.t. |
| 9. | D. Per | ADR | s.t. |
| 10. | S. Janiszewski | VOS | s.t. |
| 11. | T. Sprengers | SVB | s.t. |
| 12. | J. Hugger | LKH | s.t. |
| 13. | L. Dreßler | LKH | s.t. |
| 14. | T. Marsman | MET | s.t. |
| 15. | S. Velasco | GAZ | s.t. |
| 16. | J. Mertens | SVB | s.t. |
| 17. | A. Bajc | RSW | s.t. |
| 18. | J. Bakelants | IWG | s.t. |
| 19. | J. Maas | LPC | s.t. |
| 20. | J. I. Hvideberg | UXT | s.t. |

### GENERAL CLASSIFICATION

| POS | NAME | TEAM | TIME |
|---|---|---|---|
| 1. | J. Huppertz | LKH | 3:34:24 |
| 2. | I. Andersen | UXT | 0:02 |
| 3. | T. Lindner | PUS | 0:06 |

### KING OF THE MOUNTAINS

| POS | NAME | TEAM | PTS |
|---|---|---|---|
| 1. | J. Huppertz | LKH | 9 |
| 2. | I. Andersen | UXT | 9 |
| 3. | T. Lindner | PUS | 6 |

### POINTS

| POS | NAME | TEAM | PTS |
|---|---|---|---|
| 1. | J. Huppertz | LKH | 26 |
| 2. | I. Andersen | UXT | 25 |
| 3. | T. Lindner | PUS | 19 |

### YOUNG RIDER

| POS | NAME | TEAM | TIME |
|---|---|---|---|
| 1. | I. Andersen | UXT | 3:34:26 |
| 2. | T. Lindner | PUS | 0:04 |
| 3. | M. Urianstad | UXT | 0:24 |

## SAZKA TOUR
Stage 2
6 August 2021
Olomouc–Pustevny
203.4km

### WEATHER

TEMPERATURE  WIND
20°C  W 15km/h

### STAGE RESULTS

| POS | NAME | TEAM | TIME |
|---|---|---|---|
| 1. | N. Schultz | BEX | 5:00:28 |
| 2. | F. Zana | BCF | 0:07 |
| 3. | R. Taaramäe | IWG | 0:10 |
| 4. | J. Hirt | IWG | 0:17 |
| 5. | R. Zoidl | RSW | 0:19 |
| 6. | L. Covili | BCF | 0:22 |
| 7. | D. Gabburo | BCF | s.t. |
| 8. | S. Velasco | GAZ | 0:26 |
| 9. | S. Petilli | IWG | 0:28 |
| 10. | F. Van den Bossche | SVB | 0:30 |
| 11. | A. Toupalík | EKA | 0:32 |
| 12. | T. H. Johannessen | UXT | s.t. |
| 13. | M. Kukrle | EKA | 0:34 |
| 14. | A. Garosio | BCF | 0:44 |
| 15. | J. Maas | LPC | 0:46 |
| 16. | E. Zardini | THR | 0:50 |
| 17. | J. Otruba | EKA | 0:51 |
| 18. | D. Turek | RSW | 0:53 |
| 19. | J. Hindsgaul | UXT | s.t. |
| 20. | A. Kuzmin | GAZ | 1:00 |

### GENERAL CLASSIFICATION

| POS | NAME | TEAM | TIME |
|---|---|---|---|
| 1. ↑36 | N. Schultz | BEX | 8:35:18 |
| 2. ↑28 | F. Zana | BCF | 0:07 |
| 3. ↑44 | R. Taaramäe | IWG | 0:10 |

### KING OF THE MOUNTAINS

| POS | NAME | TEAM | PTS |
|---|---|---|---|
| 1. ↑1 | I. Andersen | UXT | 21 |
| 2. — | V. Stojnić | THR | 19 |
| 3. — | D. Per | ADR | 12 |

### POINTS

| POS | NAME | TEAM | PTS |
|---|---|---|---|
| 1. ↑1 | I. Andersen | UXT | 30 |
| 2. ↓1 | J. Huppertz | LKH | 26 |
| 3. — | N. Schultz | BEX | 25 |

### YOUNG RIDER

| POS | NAME | TEAM | TIME |
|---|---|---|---|
| 1. ↑10 | F. Zana | BCF | 8:35:25 |
| 2. ↑11 | F. Van den Bossche | SVB | 0:23 |
| 3. ↑7 | T. H. Johannessen | UXT | 0:25 |

## SAZKA TOUR
Stage 3
7 August 2021
Moravská Třebová–Dlouhé stráně
143.2km

### WEATHER

TEMPERATURE | WIND
25°C | SE 9km/h

### STAGE RESULTS

| POS | NAME | TEAM | TIME |
|---|---|---|---|
| 1. | T. H. Johannessen | UXT | 3:48:41 |
| 2. | F. Zana | BCF | 0:03 |
| 3. | R. Taaramäe | IWG | 0:29 |
| 4. | N. Schultz | BEX | 0:40 |
| 5. | R. Zoidl | RSW | s.t. |
| 6. | L. Covili | BCF | 0:53 |
| 7. | J. Hirt | IWG | 1:12 |
| 8. | A. H. Johannessen | UXT | s.t. |
| 9. | A. Kuzmin | GAZ | 1:18 |
| 10. | D. Gabburo | BCF | s.t. |
| 11. | J. Maas | LPC | 1:39 |
| 12. | J. Hindsgaul | UXT | 1:49 |
| 13. | S. Velasco | GAZ | s.t. |
| 14. | J. Otruba | EKA | 1:52 |
| 15. | S. Petilli | IWG | s.t. |
| 16. | M. Kukrle | EKA | s.t. |
| 17. | K. Hočevar | ADR | 2:22 |
| 18. | A. Toupalík | EKA | s.t. |
| 19. | J. Bárta | EKA | s.t. |
| 20. | N. Cherkasov | GAZ | 2:42 |

### GENERAL CLASSIFICATION

| POS | NAME | TEAM | TIME |
|---|---|---|---|
| 1. ↑1 | F. Zana | BCF | 12:24:09 |
| 2. ↑9 | T. H. Johannessen | UXT | 0:22 |
| 3. — | R. Taaramäe | IWG | 0:29 |

### KING OF THE MOUNTAINS

| POS | NAME | TEAM | PTS |
|---|---|---|---|
| 1. ↑1 | V. Stojnić | THR | 19 |
| 2. ↑1 | D. Per | ADR | 12 |
| 3. — | M. Grabis | VOS | 10 |

### POINTS

| POS | NAME | TEAM | PTS |
|---|---|---|---|
| 1. ↑3 | F. Zana | BCF | 40 |
| 2. ↑1 | N. Schultz | BEX | 39 |
| 3. ↑3 | R. Taaramäe | IWG | 32 |

### YOUNG RIDER

| POS | NAME | TEAM | TIME |
|---|---|---|---|
| 1. — | F. Zana | BCF | 12:24:09 |
| 2. ↑1 | T. H. Johannessen | UXT | 0:22 |
| 3. ↑1 | J. Hindsgaul | UXT | 2:32 |

## SAZKA TOUR
Stage 4
8 August 2021
Šumperk–Šternberk
174.1km

### WEATHER

TEMPERATURE | WIND
23°C | SW 22km/h

### STAGE RESULTS

| POS | NAME | TEAM | TIME |
|---|---|---|---|
| 1. | T. H. Johannessen | UXT | 4:21:18 |
| 2. | F. Zana | BCF | s.t. |
| 3. | A. Toupalík | EKA | 0:04 |
| 4. | J. Maas | LPC | s.t. |
| 5. | D. Gabburo | BCF | 0:05 |
| 6. | J. Otruba | EKA | s.t. |
| 7. | M. Kukrle | EKA | s.t. |
| 8. | J. Bárta | EKA | s.t. |
| 9. | S. Velasco | GAZ | s.t. |
| 10. | R. Taaramäe | IWG | s.t. |
| 11. | N. Schultz | BEX | 0:09 |
| 12. | R. Zoidl | RSW | s.t. |
| 13. | S. Petilli | IWG | s.t. |
| 14. | J. Bakelants | IWG | s.t. |
| 15. | J. Hirt | IWG | s.t. |
| 16. | P. Cieślik | VOS | 0:13 |
| 17. | M. Urianstad | UXT | 0:16 |
| 18. | S. Rekita | VOS | 0:19 |
| 19. | L. Covili | BCF | s.t. |
| 20. | T. Marsman | MET | 0:36 |

### GENERAL CLASSIFICATION

| POS | NAME | TEAM | TIME |
|---|---|---|---|
| 1. — | F. Zana | BCF | 16:45:21 |
| 2. — | T. H. Johannessen | UXT | 0:15 |
| 3. — | R. Taaramäe | IWG | 0:40 |

### KING OF THE MOUNTAINS

| POS | NAME | TEAM | PTS |
|---|---|---|---|
| 1. — | V. Stojnić | THR | 49 |
| 2. ↑8 | T. H. Johannessen | UXT | 18 |
| 3. — | D. Turek | RSW | 17 |

### POINTS

| POS | NAME | TEAM | PTS |
|---|---|---|---|
| 1. — | F. Zana | BCF | 60 |
| 2. ↑2 | T. H. Johannessen | UXT | 59 |
| 3. ↓1 | N. Schultz | BEX | 47 |

### YOUNG RIDER

| POS | NAME | TEAM | TIME |
|---|---|---|---|
| 1. — | F. Zana | BCF | 16:45:21 |
| 2. — | T. H. Johannessen | UXT | 0:15 |
| 3. ↑1 | K. Hočevar | ADR | 4:56 |

AUGUST   WORLDTOUR MEN'S RACE

## TOUR DE POLOGNE
Stage 1
9 August 2021
Lublin–Chełm
216.4km

A year on from the horrifying crash involving Fabio Jakobsen and Dylan Groenewegen, the organisers of the Tour of Poland had a reputation to restore. Gone was the dangerous downhill sprint into Katowice. Instead, stage 1 featured a cobbled uphill sprint to the line in Chełm, a city close to the border with Ukraine that was a place of huge ethnic and religious diversity but whose nature was changed entirely by the devastation of the Second World War. Deceuninck-QuickStep launched Álvaro Hodeg, only to find that Phil Bauhaus of Bahrain Victorious, piloted into position by his compatriot Marcel Sieberg, had timed his effort better. The German won the sprint with relative ease, making Poland the third-consecutive former Eastern Bloc country in which he had raced and won, after two victories in both the Tours of Hungary and Slovenia.

### WEATHER

TEMPERATURE   WIND
23°C          W 11km/h

### PROFILE

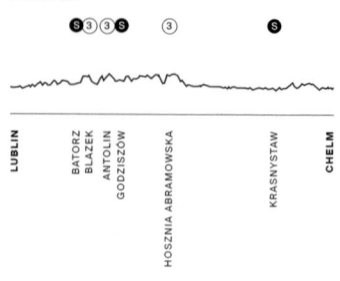

### BREAKAWAY
Y. Fedorov (APT), S. Bennett (TQA), M. Paluta (NAT)

### STAGE RESULTS

| POS | NAME | TEAM | TIME |
|---|---|---|---|
| 1. | P. Bauhaus | TBV | 5:01:24 |
| 2. | A. J. Hodeg | DQT | s.t. |
| 3. | H. Hofstetter | ISN | s.t. |
| 4. | E. Theuns | TFS | s.t. |
| 5. | D. Dekker | TJV | s.t. |
| 6. | D. Smith | BEX | s.t. |
| 7. | J. Rickaert | AFC | s.t. |
| 8. | B. Ghirmay | IWG | s.t. |
| 9. | M. Mohorič | TBV | s.t. |
| 10. | M. Kwiatkowski | IGD | s.t. |
| 11. | D. Ulissi | UAD | s.t. |
| 12. | M. Canola | GAZ | s.t. |
| 13. | J. Almeida | DQT | s.t. |
| 14. | M. F. Honoré | DQT | s.t. |
| 15. | M. Schwarzmann | BOH | s.t. |
| 16. | A. Covi | UAD | s.t. |
| 17. | K. Sbaragli | AFC | s.t. |
| 18. | D. Teuns | TBV | s.t. |
| 19. | J. Stewart | GFC | s.t. |
| 20. | Q. Hermans | IWG | s.t. |

### GENERAL CLASSIFICATION

| POS | NAME | TEAM | TIME |
|---|---|---|---|
| 1. | P. Bauhaus | TBV | 5:01:14 |
| 2. | A. J. Hodeg | DQT | 0:04 |
| 3. | Y. Fedorov | APT | s.t. |

### KING OF THE MOUNTAINS

| POS | NAME | TEAM | PTS |
|---|---|---|---|
| 1. | M. Paluta | NAT | 8 |
| 2. | Y. Fedorov | APT | 5 |
| 3. | Se. Bennett | TQA | 5 |

### POINTS

| POS | NAME | TEAM | PTS |
|---|---|---|---|
| 1. | P. Bauhaus | TBV | 20 |
| 2. | A. J. Hodeg | DQT | 19 |
| 3. | H. Hofstetter | ISN | 18 |

### BONUSES

| TYPE | NAME | TEAM |
|---|---|---|
| KOM 1 | M. Paluta | NAT |
| KOM 2 | Y. Fedorov | APT |
| KOM 3 | M. Paluta | NAT |
| Sprint 1 | Y. Fedorov | APT |
| Sprint 2 | Y. Fedorov | APT |
| Sprint 3 | M. Kwiatkowski | IGD |

### TRIVIA
» This was Phil Bauhaus's sixth victory of the season, three of which have come on opening days of stage races.

AUGUST  WORLDTOUR MEN'S RACE

# TOUR DE POLOGNE
Stage 2
10 August 2021
Zamość–Przemyśl
200.8km

A 200km slog through the regions of Subcarpathia and Lublin ended with a succession of short sharp climbs in the final 40km. The first three of these tore the race apart, as a checklist of some of the strongest riders in the WorldTour went on the attack. Lukas Pöstlberger was the first to go solo, cresting the first two climbs alone. Behind him, the race lead was capitulated by Phil Bauhaus, who found the terrain too tough. After Pöstlberger, Rémi Cavagna tried to go clear but was ridden down. On the final intense, cobbled climb, a trio of riders contested the victory: Matej Mohorič, attempting to keep the leader's jersey with Bahrain Victorious, Diego Ulissi and Deceuninck-QuickStep's João Almeida, who had the sharpest sprint and took the stage as well as the race lead.

## WEATHER

TEMPERATURE  WIND
25°C  SE 6km/h

## PROFILE

ZAMOŚC · KRASNOBRÓD · WOLKA HUSINSKA · JÓZEFÓW · KALWARIA PACLAWSKA · GRUSZOWA · PRZEMYŚL

## BREAKAWAY
N. Stalnov (APT), S. Langeveld (EFN), T. van der Hoorn (IWG), G. Cullaigh (MOV), P. Stosz (NAT)

## STAGE RESULTS

| POS | NAME | TEAM | TIME |
|---|---|---|---|
| 1. | J. Almeida | DQT | 4:41:33 |
| 2. | D. Ulissi | UAD | s.t. |
| 3. | M. Mohorič | TBV | s.t. |
| 4. | M. Kwiatkowski | IGD | 0:04 |
| 5. | M. F. Honoré | DQT | 0:08 |
| 6. | L. Rota | IWG | 0:12 |
| 7. | J. Hindley | DSM | s.t. |
| 8. | G. Aleotti | BOH | s.t. |
| 9. | D. Teuns | TBV | s.t. |
| 10. | T. Wellens | LTS | 0:16 |
| 11. | E. A. Rubio | MOV | s.t. |
| 12. | A. Covi | UAD | 0:21 |
| 13. | C. Berthet | ACT | 0:28 |
| 14. | D. Smith | BEX | s.t. |
| 15. | B. Tulett | AFC | s.t. |
| 16. | Q. Hermans | IWG | 0:30 |
| 17. | D. Nekrasov | GAZ | s.t. |
| 18. | T. Gallopin | ACT | s.t. |
| 19. | R. Fernández | COF | s.t. |
| 20. | P. Eenkhoorn | TJV | 0:35 |

## GENERAL CLASSIFICATION

| POS | | NAME | TEAM | TIME |
|---|---|---|---|---|
| 1. | ↑14 | J. Almeida | DQT | 9:42:47 |
| 2. | ↑4 | M. Mohorič | TBV | 0:04 |
| 3. | ↑10 | D. Ulissi | UAD | s.t. |

## KING OF THE MOUNTAINS

| POS | | NAME | TEAM | PTS |
|---|---|---|---|---|
| 1. | — | M. Paluta | NAT | 8 |
| 2. | — | L. Pöstlberger | BOH | 5 |
| 3. | ↓1 | Y. Fedorov | APT | 5 |

## POINTS

| POS | | NAME | TEAM | PTS |
|---|---|---|---|---|
| 1. | ↑8 | M. Mohorič | TBV | 30 |
| 2. | ↑9 | D. Ulissi | UAD | 29 |
| 3. | ↑10 | J. Almeida | DQT | 28 |

## BONUSES

| TYPE | NAME | TEAM |
|---|---|---|
| KOM 1 | P. Stosz | NAT |
| KOM 2 | L. Pöstlberger | BOH |
| KOM 3 | B. Girmay | IWG |
| Sprint 1 | T. van der Hoorn | IWG |
| Sprint 2 | T. van der Hoorn | IWG |

## TRIVIA
» This was João Almeida's first WorldTour victory. The only other win of his career was the 2021 Portuguese national time trial championships.

AUGUST    WORLDTOUR MEN'S RACE

# TOUR DE POLOGNE
Stage 3
11 August 2021
Sanok–Rzeszów
226.4km

A determined breakaway was only caught with 3km to go on a stage that the sprinters had earmarked as theirs. Of the three riders who survived the breakaway deep into the 226.4km stage, it was Taco van der Hoorn who looked the best, accompanied by Simon Clarke, who also looked strong at times as he attacked and counter-attacked, and Arkéa-Samsic's Łukasz Owsian, riding for the Polish National Team. But, under pressure from Deceuninck-QuickStep, Jumbo-Visma and UAE Team Emirates, the race came back together for the sprint. Fernando Gaviria just caught the 19-year-old Dutchman Olav Kooij on the line to take the victory. It was the Colombian's first win of 2021 and the second time he had prevailed in the finish town of Rzeszów, where he had previously won in his breakthrough year of 2016.

## WEATHER

TEMPERATURE: 24°C
WIND: NW 17km/h

## PROFILE

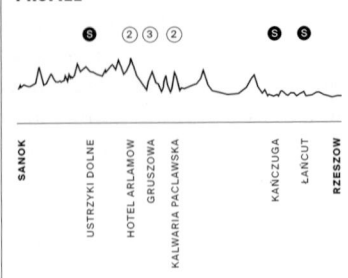

## BREAKAWAY

Ł. Owsian (NAT), L. Taminiaux (AFC), T. van der Hoorn (IWG), A. Konyshev (BEX), F. Conca (LTS), N. Vahtra (ISN), T. Bohli (COF), S. Clarke (TQA), D. Arroyave (EFN), N. Märkl (DSM)

## STAGE RESULTS

| POS | NAME | TEAM | TIME |
|---|---|---|---|
| 1. | F. Gaviria | UAD | 5:18:15 |
| 2. | O. Kooij | TJV | s.t. |
| 3. | P. Bauhaus | TBV | s.t. |
| 4. | M. Kanter | DSM | s.t. |
| 5. | M. Walscheid | TQA | s.t. |
| 6. | J. Rickaert | AFC | s.t. |
| 7. | H. Hofstetter | ISN | s.t. |
| 8. | M. Schwarzmann | BOH | s.t. |
| 9. | M. Kwiatkowski | IGD | s.t. |
| 10. | J. Degenkolb | LTS | s.t. |
| 11. | A. Pasqualon | IWG | s.t. |
| 12. | B. Ghirmay | IWG | s.t. |
| 13. | L. Owen | EFN | s.t. |
| 14. | J. Stewart | GFC | s.t. |
| 15. | D. Dekker | TJV | s.t. |
| 16. | M. Canola | GAZ | s.t. |
| 17. | A. Viviani | COF | s.t. |
| 18. | E. Theuns | TFS | s.t. |
| 19. | D. Ulissi | UAD | s.t. |
| 20. | S. Aniołkowski | NAT | s.t. |

## GENERAL CLASSIFICATION

| POS | NAME | TEAM | TIME |
|---|---|---|---|
| 1. — | J. Almeida | DQT | 15:01:02 |
| 2. ↑1 | D. Ulissi | UAD | 0:04 |
| 3. ↓1 | M. Mohorič | TBV | s.t. |

## KING OF THE MOUNTAINS

| POS | NAME | TEAM | PTS |
|---|---|---|---|
| 1. — | Ł. Owsian | NAT | 13 |
| 2. ↓1 | M. Paluta | NAT | 8 |
| 3. — | D. Arroyave | EFN | 8 |

## POINTS

| POS | NAME | TEAM | PTS |
|---|---|---|---|
| 1. ↑3 | M. Kwiatkowski | IGD | 40 |
| 2. ↑5 | P. Bauhaus | TBV | 38 |
| 3. ↑6 | H. Hofstetter | ISN | 32 |

## BONUSES

| TYPE | NAME | TEAM |
|---|---|---|
| KOM 1 | Ł. Owsian | NAT |
| KOM 2 | Ł. Owsian | NAT |
| KOM 3 | Ł. Owsian | NAT |
| Sprint 1 | T. van der Hoorn | IWG |
| Sprint 2 | T. van der Hoorn | IWG |
| Sprint 3 | N. Vahtra | ISN |

## TRIVIA

» This was Fernando Gaviria's first win of the year. In no other season in his professional career has it taken him so long to get a victory under his belt.

AUGUST    WORLDTOUR MEN'S RACE

# TOUR DE POLOGNE
Stage 4
12 August 2021
Tarnów–Bukovina Resort
159.9km

A first bona fide uphill finish to the spa resort of Bukovina saw a battle for the overall race lead that was dictated by Deceuninck-QuickStep. A powerful breakaway formed early on in the stage and featured, among others, Attila Valter of Groupama-FDJ, who had been one of the discoveries of the Giro d'Italia. But by the time the race reached the foot of the final climb they had been ridden down, and the team of leader João Almeida set a deterrent pace that neutralised any potential attacks. The work done by first Rémi Cavagna and then Mikkel Honoré set Almeida up perfectly for another win, extending his lead once more. It was another notable climb from AG2R Citroën's Andrea Vendrame to finish third. After his Giro stage win, this was further evidence of his emerging and versatile potential.

## WEATHER

TEMPERATURE   WIND
23°C          W 11km/h

## PROFILE

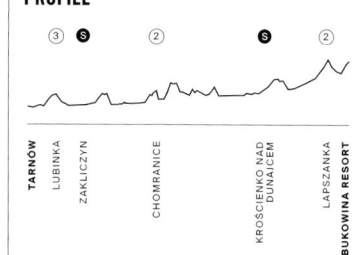

TARNÓW · LUBINKA · ZAKLICZYN · CHOMRANICE · KROSCIENKO NAD DUNAJCEM · LAPSZANKA · BUKOWINA RESORT

## BREAKAWAY
L. Warbasse (ACT), A. Valter (GFC), E. Theuns (TFS), Q. Hermans (IWG), M. Canola (GAZ)

## STAGE RESULTS

| POS | NAME | TEAM | TIME |
|---|---|---|---|
| 1. | J. Almeida | DQT | 3:51:32 |
| 2. | M. Mohorič | TBV | s.t. |
| 3. | A. Vendrame | ACT | s.t. |
| 4. | M. Kwiatkowski | IGD | s.t. |
| 5. | D. Smith | BEX | s.t. |
| 6. | J. Hindley | DSM | s.t. |
| 7. | B. Tulett | AFC | s.t. |
| 8. | D. Ulissi | UAD | s.t. |
| 9. | A. Tiberi | TFS | s.t. |
| 10. | Q. Hermans | IWG | s.t. |
| 11. | B. Ghirmay | IWG | s.t. |
| 12. | T. Wellens | LTS | s.t. |
| 13. | G. Aleotti | BOH | s.t. |
| 14. | P. Eenkhoorn | TJV | s.t. |
| 15. | R. Fernández | COF | s.t. |
| 16. | D. Teuns | TBV | s.t. |
| 17. | E. A. Rubio | MOV | s.t. |
| 18. | D. Nekrasov | GAZ | s.t. |
| 19. | L. Rota | IWG | s.t. |
| 20. | C. Berthet | ACT | s.t. |

## GENERAL CLASSIFICATION

| POS | | NAME | TEAM | TIME |
|---|---|---|---|---|
| 1. | — | J. Almeida | DQT | 18:52:24 |
| 2. | ↑1 | M. Mohorič | TBV | 0:08 |
| 3. | ↓1 | D. Ulissi | UAD | 0:14 |

## KING OF THE MOUNTAINS

| POS | | NAME | TEAM | PTS |
|---|---|---|---|---|
| 1. | — | Ł. Owsian | NAT | 16 |
| 2. | — | M. Paluta | NAT | 8 |
| 3. | — | D. Arroyave | EFN | 8 |

## POINTS

| POS | | NAME | TEAM | PTS |
|---|---|---|---|---|
| 1. | — | M. Kwiatkowski | IGD | 57 |
| 2. | ↑3 | M. Mohorič | TBV | 49 |
| 3. | ↑4 | J. Almeida | DQT | 48 |

## BONUSES

| TYPE | NAME | TEAM |
|---|---|---|
| KOM 1 | L. Owsian | NAT |
| KOM 2 | E. Theuns | TFS |
| KOM 3 | A. Valter | GFC |
| Sprint 1 | Q. Hermans | IWG |
| Sprint 2 | E. Theuns | TFS |

AUGUST    WORLDTOUR MEN'S RACE

# TOUR DE POLOGNE
Stage 5
13 August 2021
Chochołów–Bielsko-Biała
172.8km

The race started at the most western point of the Tour, before reaching back in towards the Silesian city of Bielsko-Biała, where it would finish with an uphill sprint and a closing circuit. The finale was marred by a serious of crashes: one at 1.5km to go, and another one 500 metres later. Those incidents left no more than around a dozen riders to contest a heavily reduced bunch sprint. DSM's Nikias Arndt took the victory, but it was Matej Mohorič who gained the most on GC. By lunging for the line in second place, he picked up a 6-second time bonus to move to within just 2 seconds of João Almeida's yellow jersey. The Portuguese finished just outside the time bonuses, in fourth place.

## WEATHER

TEMPERATURE: 26°C
WIND: SE 11km/h

## PROFILE

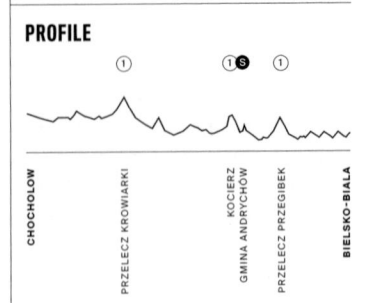

## BREAKAWAY

J. Rickaert (AFC), Y. Fedorov (APT), D. Arroyave (EFN), R. Power (TQA), E. Liepiņš (TFS), L. Owsian (NAT)

## STAGE RESULTS

| POS | NAME | TEAM | TIME |
|---|---|---|---|
| 1. | N. Arndt | DSM | 4:02:20 |
| 2. | M. Mohorič | TBV | s.t. |
| 3. | S. Oldani | LTS | s.t. |
| 4. | J. Almeida | DQT | s.t. |
| 5. | D. Ulissi | UAD | s.t. |
| 6. | Q. Hermans | IWG | s.t. |
| 7. | D. Dekker | TJV | s.t. |
| 8. | J. Stewart | GFC | s.t. |
| 9. | A. Vendrame | ACT | s.t. |
| 10. | M. F. Honoré | DQT | s.t. |
| 11. | M. Kwiatkowski | IGD | s.t. |
| 12. | K. Sbaragli | AFC | s.t. |
| 13. | G. Aleotti | BOH | s.t. |
| 14. | P. Eenkhoorn | TJV | s.t. |
| 15. | T. Wellens | LTS | s.t. |
| 16. | E. A. Rubio | MOV | s.t. |
| 17. | L. Rota | IWG | s.t. |
| 18. | M. Canola | GAZ | s.t. |
| 19. | D. Nekrasov | GAZ | s.t. |
| 20. | D. Villella | MOV | s.t. |

## GENERAL CLASSIFICATION

| POS | NAME | TEAM | TIME |
|---|---|---|---|
| 1. — | J. Almeida | DQT | 22:54:44 |
| 2. — | M. Mohorič | TBV | 0:02 |
| 3. — | D. Ulissi | UAD | 0:14 |

## KING OF THE MOUNTAINS

| POS | NAME | TEAM | PTS |
|---|---|---|---|
| 1. — | Ł. Owsian | NAT | 50 |
| 2. — | E. Liepiņš | TFS | 30 |
| 3. — | J. Rickaert | AFC | 22 |

## POINTS

| POS | NAME | TEAM | PTS |
|---|---|---|---|
| 1. ↑1 | M. Mohorič | TBV | 68 |
| 2. ↓1 | M. Kwiatkowski | IGD | 67 |
| 3. — | J. Almeida | DQT | 65 |

## BONUSES

| TYPE | NAME | TEAM |
|---|---|---|
| KOM 1 | E. Liepiņš | TFS |
| KOM 2 | E. Liepiņš | TFS |
| KOM 3 | L. Owsian | NAT |
| Sprint 1 | D. Arroyave | EFN |

## TRIVIA

» This was Nikias Arndt's first win since 2019.

AUGUST   WORLDTOUR MEN'S RACE

# TOUR DE POLOGNE
Stage 6 (ITT)
14 August 2021
Katowice–Katowice
19.1km

Instead of the highly controversial downhill sprint stage that had been roundly criticised for its dangers and had contributed to the terrible accident involving Fabio Jakobsen in 2020, Katowice hosted a flat 19.1km time trial instead. Rémi Cavagna dislodged Polish time trial champion Maciej Bodnar from the hot seat to post the best time, and then had to watch on while Michal Kwiatkowski and João Almeida completed the course; of the GC riders, those two had perhaps the best time trial pedigree. In the end, Kwiatkowski climbed to third overall, and Matej Mohorič lost a further 18 seconds to Almeida. But the stage victory went to Cavagna. With a single stage remaining, Almeida was almost certain of victory.

## WEATHER

TEMPERATURE: 28°C
WIND: W 13km/h

## PROFILE

KATOWICE – KATOWICE

## STAGE RESULTS

| POS | NAME | TEAM | TIME |
|---|---|---|---|
| 1. | R. Cavagna | DQT | 22:11 |
| 2. | J. Almeida | DQT | 0:13 |
| 3. | M. Bodnar | BOH | 0:16 |
| 4. | M. Bjerg | UAD | 0:18 |
| 5. | M. Kwiatkowski | IGD | s.t. |
| 6. | M. Walscheid | TQA | 0:21 |
| 7. | N. Arndt | DSM | 0:27 |
| 8. | M. F. Honoré | DQT | 0:28 |
| 9. | M. Mohorič | TBV | 0:31 |
| 10. | M. Brändle | ISN | 0:32 |
| 11. | T. Wellens | LTS | 0:34 |
| 12. | A. Amador | IGD | 0:35 |
| 13. | D. Ulissi | UAD | s.t. |
| 14. | M. Sobrero | APT | s.t. |
| 15. | S. Langeveld | EFN | 0:37 |
| 16. | J. van den Berg | EFN | 0:38 |
| 17. | A. De Marchi | ISN | 0:39 |
| 18. | J. van Emden | TJV | 0:43 |
| 19. | C. Quarterman | TFS | 0:46 |
| 20. | J. Hindley | DSM | 0:47 |

## GENERAL CLASSIFICATION

| POS | | NAME | TEAM | TIME |
|---|---|---|---|---|
| 1. | — | J. Almeida | DQT | 23:17:07 |
| 2. | — | M. Mohorič | TBV | 0:20 |
| 3. | ↑1 | M. Kwiatkowski | IGD | 0:27 |

## KING OF THE MOUNTAINS

| POS | | NAME | TEAM | PTS |
|---|---|---|---|---|
| 1. | — | Ł. Owsian | NAT | 50 |
| 2. | — | E. Liepiņš | TFS | 30 |
| 3. | — | J. Rickaert | AFC | 22 |

## POINTS

| POS | | NAME | TEAM | PTS |
|---|---|---|---|---|
| 1. | ↑2 | J. Almeida | DQT | 84 |
| 2. | — | M. Kwiatkowski | IGD | 83 |
| 3. | ↓2 | M. Mohorič | TBV | 80 |

AUGUST   WORLDTOUR MEN'S RACE

# TOUR DE POLOGNE
Stage 7
15 August 2021
Zabrze–Kraków
145.1km

The city of Kraków played host to a breathless finale of the Tour of Poland, with a circuit race that proved successful for the four-man breakaway on the day. Gianni Moscon, Alexis Renard, Matteo Jorgensen and Julius van den Berg somehow managed to thwart the chase and to hold on by 3 seconds to sprint for the win, with the 24-year-old Dutchman Van den Berg getting the better of his breakaway companions to take the first professional win of his career. He later confessed that he had no idea the bunch were as close as they were to catching them. Finishing down in 29th on the stage, João Almeida wrapped up his first-ever GC win, confirming the huge promise that the 23-year-old had shown since his breakthrough ride at the 2020 Giro, and cementing his reputation as one of the most highly prized talents in the peloton.

## WEATHER

**TEMPERATURE**
29°C

**WIND**
W 20km/h

## PROFILE

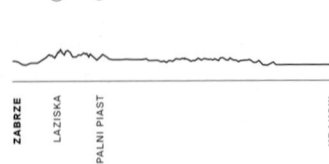

## BREAKAWAY

J. van den Berg (EFN), G. Moscon (IGD),
P. Vanspeybrouck (IWG), A. Reynard (ISN),
M. Jorgenson (MOV)

## STAGE RESULTS

| POS | NAME | TEAM | TIME |
|---|---|---|---|
| 1. | J. van den Berg | EFN | 2:58:46 |
| 2. | A. Renard | ISN | s.t. |
| 3. | M. Jorgenson | MOV | s.t. |
| 4. | G. Moscon | IGD | s.t. |
| 5. | A. J. Hodeg | DQT | 0:03 |
| 6. | F. Gaviria | UAD | s.t. |
| 7. | O. Kooij | TJV | s.t. |
| 8. | J. Degenkolb | LTS | s.t. |
| 9. | P. Bauhaus | TBV | s.t. |
| 10. | L. Taminiaux | AFC | s.t. |
| 11. | H. Hofstetter | ISN | s.t. |
| 12. | M. Kanter | DSM | s.t. |
| 13. | J. Stewart | GFC | s.t. |
| 14. | M. Schwarzmann | BOH | s.t. |
| 15. | A. Konychev | BEX | s.t. |
| 16. | D. Martinelli | APT | s.t. |
| 17. | I. García Cortina | MOV | s.t. |
| 18. | A. Pasqualon | IWG | s.t. |
| 19. | E. Theuns | TFS | s.t. |
| 20. | M. Canola | GAZ | s.t. |

## GENERAL CLASSIFICATION

| POS | NAME | TEAM | TIME |
|---|---|---|---|
| 1. | J. Almeida | DQT | 26:15:56 |
| 2. | M. Mohorič | TBV | 0:20 |
| 3. | M. Kwiatkowski | IGD | 0:27 |

## KING OF THE MOUNTAINS

| POS | NAME | TEAM | PTS |
|---|---|---|---|
| 1. | Ł. Owsian | NAT | 50 |
| 2. | E. Liepiņš | TFS | 30 |
| 3. | J. Rickaert | AFC | 22 |

## POINTS

| POS | NAME | TEAM | PTS |
|---|---|---|---|
| 1. | J. Almeida | DQT | 84 |
| 2. | M. Kwiatkowski | IGD | 83 |
| 3. | M. Mohorič | TBV | 80 |

## BONUSES

| TYPE | NAME | TEAM |
|---|---|---|
| KOM 1 | G. Moscon | IGD |
| Sprint 1 | J. van den Berg | EFN |

## TRIVIA

» Almeida's victory is Deceuninck-Quick-Step's third GC win of the year (after Remco Evenepoel's triumph at the Baloise Belgium Tour and the Tour of Denmark).

AUGUST .1 MEN'S RACE

## TOUR OF DENMARK
Stage 1
10 August 2021
Struer–Esbjerg
175.3km

### WEATHER

TEMPERATURE | WIND
17°C | W 9km/h

### STAGE RESULTS

| POS | NAME | TEAM | TIME |
|---|---|---|---|
| 1. | D. Groenewegen | TJV | 3:47:36 |
| 2. | M. Cavendish | DQT | s.t. |
| 3. | G. Nizzolo | TQA | s.t. |
| 4. | A. de Kleijn | RLY | 0:02 |
| 5. | C. Bol | DSM | s.t. |
| 6. | M. Teunissen | TJV | s.t. |
| 7. | M. Pedersen | TFS | s.t. |
| 8. | T. Van der Sande | LTS | s.t. |
| 9. | J. Steimle | DQT | s.t. |
| 10. | L. Bendixen | NAT | s.t. |
| 11. | Y. Lampaert | DQT | s.t. |
| 12. | M. Menten | BWB | s.t. |
| 13. | G. Thijssen | LTS | s.t. |
| 14. | K. Van Rooy | SVB | s.t. |
| 15. | C. Joyce | RLY | s.t. |
| 16. | J. Warlop | SVB | s.t. |
| 17. | N. Brøchner | TCQ | s.t. |
| 18. | R. Tiller | UXT | s.t. |
| 19. | F. Fiorelli | BCF | s.t. |
| 20. | N. L. N. Broge | BPC | s.t. |

### GENERAL CLASSIFICATION

| POS | NAME | TEAM | TIME |
|---|---|---|---|
| 1. | D. Groenewegen | TJV | 3:47:26 |
| 2. | M. Cavendish | DQT | 0:04 |
| 3. | G. Nizzolo | TQA | 0:06 |

### KING OF THE MOUNTAINS

| POS | NAME | TEAM | PTS |
|---|---|---|---|
| 1. | F. I. Jensen | BPC | 20 |
| 2. | N. Banaszek | MSP | 12 |
| 3. | R. B. Wallin | NAT | 8 |

### POINTS

| POS | NAME | TEAM | PTS |
|---|---|---|---|
| 1. | D. Groenewegen | TJV | 15 |
| 2. | M. Cavendish | DQT | 12 |
| 3. | G. Nizzolo | TQA | 10 |

### YOUNG RIDER

| POS | NAME | TEAM | TIME |
|---|---|---|---|
| 1. | M. A. Nørtoft | RIW | 3:47:38 |
| 2. | M. Skjelmose Jensen | TFS | s.t. |
| 3. | R. Evenepoel | DQT | s.t. |

## TOUR OF DENMARK
Stage 2
11 August 2021
Ribe–Sønderborg
189.6km

### WEATHER

TEMPERATURE | WIND
20°C | W 22km/h

### STAGE RESULTS

| POS | NAME | TEAM | TIME |
|---|---|---|---|
| 1. | M. Pedersen | TFS | 4:02:02 |
| 2. | G. Nizzolo | TQA | s.t. |
| 3. | D. Groenewegen | TJV | s.t. |
| 4. | R. Tiller | UXT | s.t. |
| 5. | J. Steimle | DQT | s.t. |
| 6. | T. Dupont | BWB | s.t. |
| 7. | A. de Kleijn | RLY | s.t. |
| 8. | G. Thijssen | LTS | s.t. |
| 9. | T. Van der Sande | LTS | s.t. |
| 10. | M. Skjelmose Jensen | TFS | s.t. |
| 11. | M. Menten | BWB | s.t. |
| 12. | N. van der Lijke | RIW | s.t. |
| 13. | C. Joyce | RLY | s.t. |
| 14. | L. Bendixen | NAT | s.t. |
| 15. | M. Cavendish | DQT | s.t. |
| 16. | S. Kragh Andersen | DSM | s.t. |
| 17. | M. Teunissen | TJV | s.t. |
| 18. | K. Andersen | TCQ | s.t. |
| 19. | L. Eriksson | RIW | s.t. |
| 20. | R. Evenepoel | DQT | s.t. |

### GENERAL CLASSIFICATION

| POS | NAME | TEAM | TIME |
|---|---|---|---|
| 1. — | D. Groenewegen | TJV | 7:49:24 |
| 2. ↑1 | G. Nizzolo | TQA | 0:04 |
| 3. ↑4 | M. Pedersen | TFS | 0:06 |

### KING OF THE MOUNTAINS

| POS | NAME | TEAM | PTS |
|---|---|---|---|
| 1. ↑2 | R. B. Wallin | NAT | 32 |
| 2. ↓1 | F. I. Jensen | BPC | 20 |
| 3. ↓1 | N. Banaszek | MSP | 12 |

### POINTS

| POS | NAME | TEAM | PTS |
|---|---|---|---|
| 1. — | D. Groenewegen | TJV | 25 |
| 2. ↑1 | G. Nizzolo | TQA | 22 |
| 3. ↑5 | M. Pedersen | TFS | 21 |

### YOUNG RIDER

| POS | NAME | TEAM | TIME |
|---|---|---|---|
| 1. ↑1 | M. Skjelmose Jensen | TFS | 7:49:40 |
| 2. ↑1 | R. Evenepoel | DQT | s.t. |
| 3. ↑2 | A. Puppio | TQA | 0:16 |

AUGUST    .1 MEN'S RACE

## TOUR OF DENMARK
Stage 3
12 August 2021
Tønder–Vejle
219.2km

### WEATHER

TEMPERATURE | WIND
22°C | SW 15km/h

### STAGE RESULTS

| POS | NAME | TEAM | TIME |
|---|---|---|---|
| 1. | R. Evenepoel | DQT | 4:54:44 |
| 2. | T. Van der Sande | LTS | 1:29 |
| 3. | N. van der Lijke | RIW | 1:32 |
| 4. | M. Teunissen | TJV | s.t. |
| 5. | M. Pedersen | TFS | 1:41 |
| 6. | A. Charmig | UXT | 1:54 |
| 7. | M. Skjelmose Jensen | TFS | 3:21 |
| 8. | M. Menten | BWB | s.t. |
| 9. | M. Rahbek | BPC | 3:23 |
| 10. | J. A. Pallesen | TCQ | s.t. |
| 11. | R. Tiller | UXT | s.t. |
| 12. | L. Eriksson | RIW | s.t. |
| 13. | M. Gogl | TQA | s.t. |
| 14. | J. Bernard | TFS | 3:36 |
| 15. | S. Kragh Andersen | DSM | s.t. |
| 16. | P. A. Coté | RLY | s.t. |
| 17. | R. Pluimers | TJV | 3:41 |
| 18. | R. S. Pedersen | NAT | s.t. |
| 19. | J. Steimle | DQT | 4:09 |
| 20. | A. Kamp | TFS | 5:44 |

### GENERAL CLASSIFICATION

| POS | NAME | TEAM | TIME |
|---|---|---|---|
| 1. ↑19 | R. Evenepoel | DQT | 2:44:14 |
| 2. ↑6 | T. Van der Sande | LTS | 1:33 |
| 3. — | M. Pedersen | TFS | 1:36 |

### KING OF THE MOUNTAINS

| POS | NAME | TEAM | PTS |
|---|---|---|---|
| 1. — | R. B. Wallin | NAT | 40 |
| 2. — | F. I. Jensen | BPC | 32 |
| 3. ↑2 | E. Toudal | BPC | 20 |

### POINTS

| POS | NAME | TEAM | PTS |
|---|---|---|---|
| 1. ↑2 | M. Pedersen | TFS | 37 |
| 2. ↓1 | D. Groenewegen | TJV | 25 |
| 3. ↓1 | G. Nizzolo | TQA | 23 |

### YOUNG RIDER

| POS | NAME | TEAM | TIME |
|---|---|---|---|
| 1. ↑1 | R. Evenepoel | DQT | 12:44:14 |
| 2. ↓1 | M. Skjelmose Jensen | TFS | 3:31 |
| 3. ↑11 | R. Pluimers | TJV | 9:33 |

## TOUR OF DENMARK
Stage 4
13 August 2021
Holbæk–Kalundborg
188.4km

### WEATHER

TEMPERATURE | WIND
25°C | SW 22km/h

### STAGE RESULTS

| POS | NAME | TEAM | TIME |
|---|---|---|---|
| 1. | C. Joyce | RLY | 4:22:44 |
| 2. | S. Nielsen | SCC | s.t. |
| 3. | M. Salmon | DSM | s.t. |
| 4. | M. B. Klaris | NAT | s.t. |
| 5. | A. Van Poucke | SVB | s.t. |
| 6. | M. Ø. Kristensen | TCQ | 0:02 |
| 7. | G. Nizzolo | TQA | 0:06 |
| 8. | M. Pedersen | TFS | s.t. |
| 9. | M. Cavendish | DQT | s.t. |
| 10. | M. Mørkøv | DQT | s.t. |
| 11. | C. Bol | DSM | s.t. |
| 12. | M. Menten | BWB | s.t. |
| 13. | A. de Kleijn | RLY | s.t. |
| 14. | K. Van Rooy | SVB | s.t. |
| 15. | M. Teunissen | TJV | s.t. |
| 16. | D. Groenewegen | TJV | s.t. |
| 17. | F. Fiorelli | BCF | s.t. |
| 18. | G. Thijssen | LTS | s.t. |
| 19. | N. van der Lijke | RIW | s.t. |
| 20. | T. Van der Sande | LTS | s.t. |

### GENERAL CLASSIFICATION

| POS | NAME | TEAM | TIME |
|---|---|---|---|
| 1. — | R. Evenepoel | DQT | 7:07:04 |
| 2. — | T. Van der Sande | LTS | 1:33 |
| 3. — | M. Pedersen | TFS | 1:36 |

### KING OF THE MOUNTAINS

| POS | NAME | TEAM | PTS |
|---|---|---|---|
| 1. — | R. B. Wallin | NAT | 40 |
| 2. ↑1 | E. Toudal | BPC | 40 |
| 3. ↓1 | F. I. Jensen | BPC | 32 |

### POINTS

| POS | NAME | TEAM | PTS |
|---|---|---|---|
| 1. — | M. Pedersen | TFS | 42 |
| 2. ↑1 | G. Nizzolo | TQA | 29 |
| 3. ↓1 | D. Groenewegen | TJV | 25 |

### YOUNG RIDER

| POS | NAME | TEAM | TIME |
|---|---|---|---|
| 1. — | R. Evenepoel | DQT | 17:07:04 |
| 2. — | M. Skjelmose Jensen | TFS | 3:43 |
| 3. — | R. Pluimers | TJV | 9:51 |

AUGUST      .1 MEN'S RACE

# TOUR OF DENMARK
Stage 5 (ITT)
14 August 2021
Frederiksberg–Frederiksberg
10.8km

## WEATHER

TEMPERATURE | WIND
20°C | SW 30km/h

## STAGE RESULTS

| POS | NAME | TEAM | TIME |
|---|---|---|---|
| 1. | R. Evenepoel | DQT | 12:13 |
| 2. | S. Kragh Andersen | DSM | 0:01 |
| 3. | M. Pedersen | TFS | 0:06 |
| 4. | E. Affini | TJV | 0:07 |
| 5. | J. Steimle | DQT | 0:14 |
| 6. | M. Teunissen | TJV | 0:20 |
| 7. | M. Skjelmose Jensen | TFS | 0:23 |
| 8. | M. Hulgaard | UXT | 0:28 |
| 9. | M. Cavendish | DQT | 0:31 |
| 10. | A. H. Jørgensen | BPC | 0:33 |
| 11. | T. van Dijke | TJV | 0:34 |
| 12. | F. Muff | TCQ | 0:35 |
| 13. | C. Bol | DSM | 0:36 |
| 14. | N. van der Lijke | RIW | s.t. |
| 15. | M. Mørkøv | DQT | 0:38 |
| 16. | R. Quaade | RIW | 0:39 |
| 17. | A. Stokbro | TQA | 0:42 |
| 18. | T. Roosen | TJV | 0:43 |
| 19. | G. Nizzolo | TQA | 0:44 |
| 20. | P. A. Coté | RLY | s.t. |

## GENERAL CLASSIFICATION

| POS | NAME | TEAM | TIME |
|---|---|---|---|
| 1. — | R. Evenepoel | DQT | 17:19:17 |
| 2. ↑1 | M. Pedersen | TFS | 1:42 |
| 3. ↑2 | M. Teunissen | TJV | 2:00 |

## KING OF THE MOUNTAINS

| POS | NAME | TEAM | PTS |
|---|---|---|---|
| 1. — | R. B. Wallin | NAT | 40 |
| 2. — | E. Toudal | BPC | 40 |
| 3. — | F. I. Jensen | BPC | 32 |

## POINTS

| POS | NAME | TEAM | PTS |
|---|---|---|---|
| 1. — | M. Pedersen | TFS | 52 |
| 2. ↑7 | R. Evenepoel | DQT | 30 |
| 3. ↓1 | G. Nizzolo | TQA | 29 |

## YOUNG RIDER

| POS | NAME | TEAM | TIME |
|---|---|---|---|
| 1. — | R. Evenepoel | DQT | 17:19:17 |
| 2. — | M. Skjelmose Jensen | TFS | 4:06 |
| 3. — | R. Pluimers | TJV | 10:46 |

AUGUST    WORLDTOUR WOMEN'S RACE

# LADIES TOUR OF NORWAY
Stage 1
12 August 2021
Halden–Sarpsborg
141.5km

Covering the rolling hills of Østfold south-east of Oslo, the opening stage finished with three laps of a circuit in Sarpsborg and ended in a close solo victory for Kristen Faulkner (Team Tibco-Silicon Valley Bank), who had been part of a breakaway for 100km. Faulkner had joined the break of five riders to target the mountain points, but Parkhotel Valkenburg's Nina Buijsman was strongest on the day's climbs. From a maximum advantage of 4 minutes 30 seconds, only 20 seconds were left at the start of the finishing circuit when Faulkner left her companions behind. She extended her advantage to a minute again with two laps to go and, as a crash disrupted the chase, Faulkner held off the charging sprinters by about a bike length on the uphill finish to win the stage – her first Women's WorldTour victory – and take the yellow jersey.

## WEATHER

**TEMPERATURE**  19°C
**WIND**  S 26km/h

## PROFILE

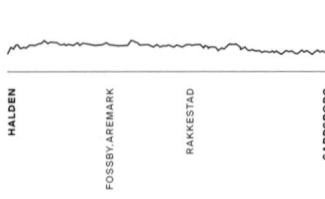

## BREAKAWAY
A. Christian (DRP), N. van Gogh (CCT), N. Buijsman (PHV), K. Faulkner (TIB), T. Jørgensen (NAT)

## STAGE RESULTS

| POS | NAME | TEAM | TIME |
|---|---|---|---|
| 1. | K. Faulkner | TIB | 3:38:15 |
| 2. | S. Andersen | DSM | s.t. |
| 3. | A. Barnes | CSR | s.t. |
| 4. | C. U. Ludwig | FDJ | s.t. |
| 5. | F. Markus | PHV | s.t. |
| 6. | L. Brand | TFS | s.t. |
| 7. | A. van Vleuten | MOV | s.t. |
| 8. | R. Fournier | SDW | s.t. |
| 9. | B. Guarischi | MOV | s.t. |
| 10. | S. Bertizzolo | LIV | s.t. |
| 11. | S. Cant | PLP | s.t. |
| 12. | I. Sanguineti | VAL | s.t. |
| 13. | S. Borgli | FDJ | s.t. |
| 14. | S. Roy | BEX | s.t. |
| 15. | E. Chabbey | CSR | s.t. |
| 16. | J. Labous | DSM | s.t. |
| 17. | E. Moberg | DRP | s.t. |
| 18. | M. García | ALE | s.t. |
| 19. | J. Lowden | DRP | s.t. |
| 20. | N. van der Burg | JVW | s.t. |

## GENERAL CLASSIFICATION

| POS | NAME | TEAM | TIME |
|---|---|---|---|
| 1. | K. Faulkner | TIB | 3:38:05 |
| 2. | S. Andersen | DSM | 0:04 |
| 3. | A. Barnes | CSR | 0:06 |

## QUEEN OF THE MOUNTAINS

| POS | NAME | TEAM | PTS |
|---|---|---|---|
| 1. | N. Buysman | PHV | 7 |
| 2. | A. Christian | DRP | 5 |
| 3. | K. Faulkner | TIB | 5 |

## POINTS

| POS | NAME | TEAM | PTS |
|---|---|---|---|
| 1. | K. Faulkner | TIB | 14 |
| 2. | C. Majerus | SDW | 5 |
| 3. | S. Andersen | DSM | 5 |

## YOUNG RIDER

| POS | NAME | TEAM | TIME |
|---|---|---|---|
| 1. | A. Shackley | SDW | 3:38:15 |
| 2. | M. Bredewold | PHV | s.t. |
| 3. | S. van Anrooij | TFS | s.t. |

## TRIVIA
» This was Kristen Faulkner's debut WorldTour win.

## BONUSES

| TYPE | NAME | TEAM |
|---|---|---|
| Sprint 1 | C. Majerus | SDW |
| Sprint 2 | N. van Gogh | CCT |

AUGUST    WORLDTOUR WOMEN'S RACE

# LADIES TOUR OF NORWAY
Stage 2
13 August 2021
Askim–Mysen
145km

Following in the footsteps of Faulkner, Riejanne Markus (Jumbo-Visma) held off the peloton by 2 seconds after a 45km breakaway to take her first Women's WorldTour victory and the GC lead. On the longest stage of the race, it took over 50km for a breakaway to be allowed to go. Inside the final 50km, Jumbo-Visma forced the pace on a rolling section, splitting the peloton and setting up the attack by Markus, who bridged to the two-rider breakaway. When the sprinters' teams had reduced the gap to only 13 seconds with 24km left, Markus left Audrey Cordon-Ragot (Trek-Segafredo) and Aude Biannic (Movistar Team) behind, eking out a minute again. Despite the chasing efforts by Team DSM in particular, Markus kept a 2-second lead to the line and would start the Queen Stage in the yellow jersey.

## WEATHER

TEMPERATURE    WIND
19°C           S 24km/h

## PROFILE

ASKIM — MYSEN — AMUNDRØD — SKJØNHAUG — MYSEN

## BREAKAWAY
A. Cordon-Ragot (TFS), A. Biannic (MOV)

## STAGE RESULTS

| POS | NAME | TEAM | TIME |
|---|---|---|---|
| 1. | R. Markus | JVW | 3:40:01 |
| 2. | C. Rivera | DSM | 0:02 |
| 3. | A. Jackson | LIV | s.t. |
| 4. | E. Chabbey | CSR | s.t. |
| 5. | S. Cant | PLP | s.t. |
| 6. | L. Brand | TFS | s.t. |
| 7. | S. Roy | BEX | s.t. |
| 8. | E. Gasparrini | VAL | s.t. |
| 9. | S. Borgli | FDJ | s.t. |
| 10. | K. Faulkner | TIB | s.t. |
| 11. | E. Duval | FDJ | s.t. |
| 12. | I. Gaskjenn | HPU | s.t. |
| 13. | C. Majerus | SDW | s.t. |
| 14. | C. U. Ludwig | FDJ | s.t. |
| 15. | A. D. Ysland | HPU | s.t. |
| 16. | H. Barnes | CSR | s.t. |
| 17. | A. van Vleuten | MOV | s.t. |
| 18. | F. Mackaij | DSM | s.t. |
| 19. | M. B. Ottestad | NAT | s.t. |
| 20. | M. Bredewold | PHV | s.t. |

## GENERAL CLASSIFICATION

| POS | NAME | TEAM | TIME |
|---|---|---|---|
| 1. ↑29 | R. Markus | JVW | 7:18:06 |
| 2. ↓1 | K. Faulkner | TIB | 0:02 |
| 3. ↑38 | C. Rivera | DSM | 0:06 |

## QUEEN OF THE MOUNTAINS

| POS | NAME | TEAM | PTS |
|---|---|---|---|
| 1. — | N. Buysman | PHV | 9 |
| 2. — | A. Christian | DRP | 5 |
| 3. — | K. Faulkner | TIB | 5 |

## POINTS

| POS | NAME | TEAM | PTS |
|---|---|---|---|
| 1. — | K. Faulkner | TIB | 18 |
| 2. ↑2 | A. Jackson | LIV | 13 |
| 3. — | R. Markus | JVW | 11 |

## YOUNG RIDER

| POS | NAME | TEAM | TIME |
|---|---|---|---|
| 1. ↑1 | M. Bredewold | PHV | 7:18:16 |
| 2. ↑3 | A. D. Ysland | HPU | s.t. |
| 3. ↑1 | N. Fisher-Black | SDW | s.t. |

## TRIVIA
» This marked Jumbo-Visma's first WorldTour victory that didn't come courtesy of Marianne Vos.

## BONUSES

| TYPE | NAME | TEAM |
|---|---|---|
| QOM 1 | A. Biannic | MOV |
| Sprint 1 | K. Faulkner | TIB |
| Sprint 2 | R. Markus | JVW |

AUGUST　　WORLDTOUR WOMEN'S RACE

# LADIES TOUR OF NORWAY
Stage 3
14 August 2021
Drammen–Norefjell
145km

On the first-ever summit finish of the Ladies Tour of Norway, Annemiek van Vleuten (Movistar Team) lived up to her favourite status and won the stage solo to take the overall lead ahead of the final stage. Brodie Chapman (FDJ Nouvelle-Aquitaine Futuroscope) and Norwegian champion Vita Heine (National Team Norway) formed the break of the day, with several others trying in vain to bridge to the front, and they were caught at the foot of the Norefjell climb. After a first attack by Niamh Fisher-Black (Team SD Worx) and a counter-attack by her teammate Ashleigh Moolman-Pasio, Kristen Faulkner set the pace until the steepest section of the climb. Another move by Moolman-Pasio drew out Van Vleuten, who quickly dropped everyone else and soloed to the finish.

## WEATHER

TEMPERATURE: 19°C
WIND: SW 24km/h

## PROFILE

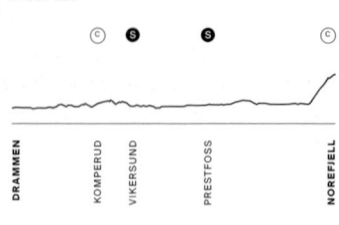

## BREAKAWAY
B. Chapman (FDJ), V. Heine (NAT)

## STAGE RESULTS

| POS | NAME | TEAM | TIME |
|---|---|---|---|
| 1. | A. van Vleuten | MOV | 3:52:17 |
| 2. | A. Moolman | SDW | 0:35 |
| 3. | M. García | ALE | 0:41 |
| 4. | M. Reusser | ALE | 0:44 |
| 5. | C. U. Ludwig | FDJ | 0:48 |
| 6. | K. Faulkner | TIB | 0:50 |
| 7. | R. Neylan | PHV | s.t. |
| 8. | N. Fisher-Black | SDW | 1:01 |
| 9. | L. Brand | TFS | 1:12 |
| 10. | J. Labous | DSM | s.t. |
| 11. | Y. Kastelijn | PLP | 1:14 |
| 12. | L. Kennedy | BEX | s.t. |
| 13. | E. Chabbey | CSR | 1:15 |
| 14. | R. Markus | JVW | s.t. |
| 15. | M. Harvey | CSR | 1:30 |
| 16. | J. Lowden | DRP | s.t. |
| 17. | T. Guderzo | ALE | s.t. |
| 18. | S. van Anrooij | TFS | s.t. |
| 19. | U. Pintar | ALE | s.t. |
| 20. | A. Shackley | SDW | s.t. |

## GENERAL CLASSIFICATION

| POS | NAME | TEAM | TIME |
|---|---|---|---|
| 1. ↑10 | A. van Vleuten | MOV | 11:10:25 |
| 2. ↑14 | A. Moolman | SDW | 0:39 |
| 3. ↑14 | M. García | ALE | 0:47 |

## QUEEN OF THE MOUNTAINS

| POS | NAME | TEAM | PTS |
|---|---|---|---|
| 1. — | N. Buysman | PHV | 13 |
| 2. — | A. Christian | DRP | 5 |
| 3. — | K. Faulkner | TIB | 5 |

## POINTS

| POS | NAME | TEAM | PTS |
|---|---|---|---|
| 1. — | K. Faulkner | TIB | 21 |
| 2. — | A. Jackson | LIV | 19 |
| 3. — | R. Markus | JVW | 11 |

## YOUNG RIDER

| POS | NAME | TEAM | TIME |
|---|---|---|---|
| 1. ↑2 | N. Fisher-Black | SDW | 11:11:36 |
| 2. ↑2 | A. Shackley | SDW | 0:29 |
| 3. ↑4 | S. van Anrooij | TFS | 1:47 |

## TRIVIA
» Annemiek van Vleuten's only other victory in Norway was the TT rainbow jersey in 2017.

## BONUSES

| TYPE | NAME | TEAM |
|---|---|---|
| QOM 1 | N. Buijsman | PHV |
| QOM 2 | A. van Vleuten | MOV |
| Sprint 1 | T. Erath | TIB |
| Sprint 2 | B. Chapman | FDJ |

374

AUGUST  WORLDTOUR WOMEN'S RACE

# LADIES TOUR OF NORWAY
Stage 4
15 August 2021
Drøbak–Halden
141.6km

The final stage came down to the traditional sprint in Halden at the end of a challenging finishing circuit. Chloe Hosking (Trek-Segafredo) won the stage in her first comeback race after a four-and-a-half-month break due to a Covid-19 infection and subsequent pericarditis. The sprinters' teams took no chances and reeled in the break of the day with 20km to go. In the intermediate sprints, Alison Jackson (Liv Racing) took enough points to take the green jersey off Kristen Faulkner. A crash on the finishing circuits brought down Mavi García (Alé BTC Ljubljana), who lost her GC podium place to Faulkner. Team DSM and Valcar Travel & Service closed down all attacks, and on the final lap Lucinda Brand brought her sprinter Hosking to the front of the peloton, from where Hosking launched a long sprint to win the stage.

## WEATHER

**TEMPERATURE**
19°C

**WIND**
S 13km/h

## PROFILE

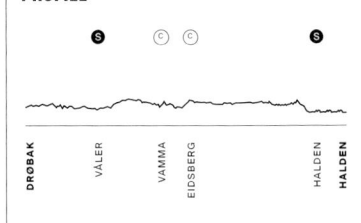

DRØBAK / VALER / VAMMA / EIDSBERG / HALDEN / HALDEN

## BREAKAWAY
R. Ratto (CCT), J. van de Velde (JVW)

## STAGE RESULTS

| POS | NAME | TEAM | TIME |
|---|---|---|---|
| 1. | C. Hosking | TFS | 3:36:06 |
| 2. | C. Rivera | DSM | s.t. |
| 3. | C. Consonni | VAL | s.t. |
| 4. | C. Majerus | SDW | s.t. |
| 5. | S. Roy | BEX | s.t. |
| 6. | E. Chabbey | CSR | s.t. |
| 7. | E. Cecchini | SDW | s.t. |
| 8. | A. Jackson | LIV | s.t. |
| 9. | E. Duval | FDJ | s.t. |
| 10. | E. Moberg | DRP | s.t. |
| 11. | J. Labous | DSM | s.t. |
| 12. | M. Reusser | ALE | s.t. |
| 13. | I. Gaskjenn | HPU | s.t. |
| 14. | C. U. Ludwig | FDJ | s.t. |
| 15. | M. B. Ottestad | NAT | s.t. |
| 16. | A. van Vleuten | MOV | s.t. |
| 17. | I. Sanguineti | VAL | s.t. |
| 18. | A. Moolman | SDW | s.t. |
| 19. | F. Markus | PHV | s.t. |
| 20. | S. Andersen | DSM | s.t. |

## GENERAL CLASSIFICATION

| POS | NAME | TEAM | TIME |
|---|---|---|---|
| 1. — | A. van Vleuten | MOV | 14:46:31 |
| 2. — | A. Moolman | SDW | 0:39 |
| 3. ↑1 | K. Faulkner | TIB | 0:50 |

## QUEEN OF THE MOUNTAINS

| POS | NAME | TEAM | PTS |
|---|---|---|---|
| 1. — | N. Buysman | PHV | 15 |
| 2. ↑11 | J. Van De Velde | JVW | 9 |
| 3. ↓1 | A. Christian | DRP | 6 |

## POINTS

| POS | NAME | TEAM | PTS |
|---|---|---|---|
| 1. ↑1 | A. Jackson | LIV | 25 |
| 2. ↓1 | K. Faulkner | TIB | 24 |
| 3. — | R. Markus | JVW | 11 |

## YOUNG RIDER

| POS | NAME | TEAM | TIME |
|---|---|---|---|
| 1. — | N. Fisher-Black | SDW | 14:47:58 |
| 2. — | A. Shackley | SDW | 0:13 |
| 3. — | S. van Anrooij | TFS | 1:56 |

## TRIVIA
» This was Van Vleuten's tenth GC victory of her career.

## BONUSES

| TYPE | NAME | TEAM |
|---|---|---|
| QOM 1 | J. van de Velde | JVW |
| QOM 2 | J. van de Velde | JVW |
| Sprint 1 | R. Ratto | CCT |
| Sprint 2 | A. Jackson | LIV |

AUGUST    WORLDTOUR MEN'S RACE

# LA VUELTA A ESPAÑA
Stage 1 (ITT)
14 August 2021
Burgos–Burgos
7.1km

## WEATHER

TEMPERATURE
34°C

WIND
SW 26km/h

An opening race against the clock, against the glorious backdrop of Burgos cathedral, on a 7km route around the city looked set to give some initial slim gaps between the contenders for the red jersey. Adam Yates was one of the first riders for the overall to take on the course, setting a decent early benchmark of 8 minutes 52 seconds and explaining he wanted to get back to the hotel as soon as possible since some start times of 8.30pm were 'already past my bedtime'. Movistar's Enric Mas suffered a scare around a corner, but held it upright to go 2 seconds faster than Yates, with Sepp Kuss and Romain Bardet a second quicker still. The Spaniard was the third-last rider out on the road. Giro d'Italia champion Egan Bernal was the penultimate, 9 seconds slower than Yates and also slower than the likes of Steven Kruijswijk, Richard Carapaz and Miguel Ángel López, while Mikel Landa and Hugh Carthy were both slower than Ineos's Colombian co-leader. While a number of the TT specialists had slotted neatly into the top ten, it was all up to Primož Roglič to beat Alex Aranburu's fastest time of 8 minutes 32 and deny the Spaniard an opening-day victory and first leader's jersey. Of course, the Slovenian delivered; he hasn't lost an individual time trial during the previous two Vueltas. He brought his Olympic TT gold-medal form to Europe to lay down a marker as he began his attempt to make it three titles in a row at the Tour of Spain, finishing 6 seconds quicker than Aranburu to give him some early breathing room over his rivals.

## PROFILE

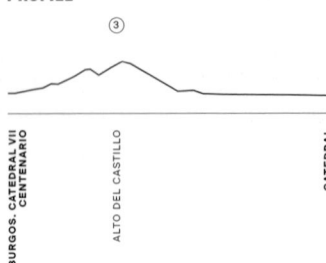

BURGOS. CATEDRAL VII CENTENARIO — ALTO DEL CASTILLO — CATEDRAL

## GENERAL CLASSIFICATION

| POS | NAME | TEAM | TIME |
|---|---|---|---|
| 1. | P. Roglič | TJV | 8:32 |
| 2. | A. Aranburu | APT | 0:06 |
| 3. | J. Tratnik | TBV | 0:08 |
| 4. | T. Scully | EFN | 0:10 |
| 5. | J. Černý | DQT | s.t. |
| 6. | D. van Baarle | IGD | 0:11 |
| 7. | A. Bagioli | DQT | 0:12 |
| 8. | L. Craddock | EFN | 0:13 |
| 9. | M. Matthews | BEX | 0:14 |
| 10. | A. Vlasov | APT | s.t. |

## KING OF THE MOUNTAINS

| POS | NAME | TEAM | PTS |
|---|---|---|---|
| 1. | S. Kuss | TJV | 3 |
| 2. | S. Vanmarcke | ISN | 2 |
| 3. | R. Oliveira | UAD | 1 |

## POINTS

| POS | NAME | TEAM | PTS |
|---|---|---|---|
| 1. | P. Roglič | TJV | 20 |
| 2. | A. Aranburu | APT | 17 |
| 3. | J. Tratnik | TBV | 15 |

## YOUNG RIDER

| POS | NAME | TEAM | TIME |
|---|---|---|---|
| 1. | A. Bagioli | DQT | 8:44 |
| 2. | A. Vlasov | APT | 0:02 |
| 3. | C. Champoussin | ACT | 0:08 |

## TRIVIA
» Primož Roglič has won every time trial he's competed in at the Vuelta (across three editions).

## BONUSES

| TYPE | NAME | TEAM |
|---|---|---|
| KOM 1 | S. Kuss | TJV |

## STAGE RESULTS

| POS | NAME | TEAM | TIME |
|---|---|---|---|
| 1. | P. Roglič | TJV | 8:32 |
| 2. | A. Aranburu | APT | 0:06 |
| 3. | J. Tratnik | TBV | 0:08 |
| 4. | T. Scully | EFN | 0:10 |
| 5. | J. Černý | DQT | s.t. |
| 6. | D. van Baarle | IGD | 0:11 |
| 7. | A. Bagioli | DQT | 0:12 |
| 8. | L. Craddock | EFN | 0:13 |
| 9. | M. Matthews | BEX | 0:14 |
| 10. | A. Vlasov | APT | s.t. |
| 11. | J. Polanc | UAD | 0:15 |
| 12. | S. Kuss | TJV | s.t. |
| 13. | C. Haga | DSM | 0:17 |
| 14. | R. Bardet | DSM | s.t. |
| 15. | E. Mas | MOV | 0:18 |
| 16. | A. Yates | IGD | 0:20 |
| 17. | R. Gibbons | UAD | s.t. |
| 18. | F. Großschartner | BOH | s.t. |
| 19. | C. Champoussin | ACT | s.t. |
| 20. | J. Haig | TBV | 0:21 |
| 21. | M. A. López | MOV | s.t. |
| 22. | D. Caruso | TBV | s.t. |
| 23. | P. Sivakov | IGD | 0:22 |
| 24. | N. Van Hooydonck | TJV | s.t. |
| 25. | M. Schachmann | BOH | s.t. |
| 26. | O. Rodríguez | APT | 0:23 |
| 27. | I. Izagirre | APT | s.t. |
| 28. | M. Tusveld | DSM | s.t. |
| 29. | O. Fraile | APT | s.t. |
| 30. | F. Frison | LTS | s.t. |
| 31. | G. Mäder | TBV | s.t. |
| 32. | N. Oliveira | MOV | 0:24 |
| 33. | D. de la Cruz | UAD | s.t. |
| 34. | G. Izagirre | APT | 0:25 |
| 35. | R. Carapaz | IGD | s.t. |
| 36. | F. Sénéchal | DQT | s.t. |
| 37. | F. Vermeersch | LTS | s.t. |
| 38. | S. Carr | EFN | s.t. |
| 39. | M. Trentin | UAD | 0:26 |
| 40. | S. Kruijswijk | TJV | s.t. |
| 41. | K. Geniets | GFC | s.t. |
| 42. | A. Valverde | MOV | 0:27 |
| 43. | L. L. Sanchez | APT | s.t. |
| 44. | G. Ciccone | TFS | s.t. |
| 45. | C. Hamilton | DSM | s.t. |
| 46. | E. Bernal | IGD | s.t. |
| 47. | A. Démare | GFC | 0:28 |
| 48. | M. Vansevenant | DQT | s.t. |
| 49. | A. Soto | EUS | 0:29 |
| 50. | S. Henao | TQA | s.t. |
| 51. | R. Molard | GFC | s.t. |
| 52. | T. Ludvigsson | GFC | s.t. |
| 53. | D. Touzé | ACT | 0:30 |
| 54. | H. Vanhoucke | LTS | 0:31 |
| 55. | L. Mezgec | BEX | s.t. |
| 56. | J. Jacobs | MOV | s.t. |
| 57. | A. Kron | LTS | s.t. |
| 58. | J. Piccoli | ISN | 0:32 |
| 59. | X. M. Azparren | EUS | s.t. |
| 60. | M. Würst Schmidt | ISN | s.t. |
| 61. | T. Bayer | AFC | 0:33 |
| 62. | H. Carthy | EFN | s.t. |
| 63. | S. Cras | LTS | s.t. |
| 64. | M. Cort | EFN | s.t. |
| 65. | R. Majka | UAD | s.t. |
| 66. | S. Dewulf | ACT | s.t. |
| 67. | K. Elissonde | TFS | s.t. |
| 68. | G. Martin | COF | s.t. |
| 69. | T. Arensman | DSM | 0:34 |
| 70. | Je. Herrada | COF | 0:35 |
| 71. | Z. Štybar | DQT | 0:36 |
| 72. | R. Janse Van Rensburg | TQA | s.t. |
| 73. | J. P. López | TFS | s.t. |
| 74. | T. Pidcock | IGD | s.t. |
| 75. | K. Bouwman | TJV | s.t. |
| 76. | S. Oomen | TJV | s.t. |
| 77. | B. Zwiehoff | BOH | s.t. |
| 78. | D. A. Camargo | EFN | s.t. |
| 79. | J. Keukeleire | EFN | s.t. |
| 80. | N. Schultz | BEX | 0:37 |
| 81. | F. Aru | TQA | s.t. |
| 82. | A. Dainese | DSM | 0:38 |
| 83. | L. Calmejane | ACT | s.t. |
| 84. | D. Howson | BEX | s.t. |
| 85. | W. Poels | TBV | 0:39 |
| 86. | S. Puccio | IGD | s.t. |
| 87. | L. Meintjes | IWG | s.t. |
| 88. | M. Landa | TBV | s.t. |
| 89. | A. Cataford | ISN | s.t. |
| 90. | J. Meeus | BOH | s.t. |
| 91. | P. Gamper | BOH | 0:40 |
| 92. | O. Le Gac | GFC | s.t. |
| 93. | M. Padun | TBV | 0:41 |
| 94. | M. Storer | DSM | s.t. |
| 95. | J. Amezqueta | CJR | s.t. |
| 96. | R. Sinkeldam | GFC | 0:42 |
| 97. | A. Roux | GFC | 0:43 |
| 98. | L. Hamilton | BEX | s.t. |
| 99. | J. Bou | EUS | s.t. |
| 100. | M. Iturria | EUS | s.t. |
| 101. | J. K. Caicedo | EFN | s.t. |
| 102. | G. Bouchard | ACT | 0:44 |
| 103. | R. Stannard | BEX | 0:45 |
| 104. | S. Petilli | IWG | s.t. |
| 105. | S. R. Martín | CJR | 0:46 |
| 106. | D. Rubio | BBH | s.t. |
| 107. | L. Hofstede | TJV | s.t. |
| 108. | J. Narváez | IGD | s.t. |
| 109. | B. Van Lerberghe | DQT | s.t. |
| 110. | A. Kirsch | TFS | s.t. |
| 111. | R. Gesink | TJV | 0:47 |
| 112. | J. S. Molano | UAD | 0:48 |
| 113. | D. Sunderland | TQA | s.t. |
| 114. | J. Dombrowski | UAD | s.t. |
| 115. | G. Martín | EUS | 0:49 |
| 116. | A. Zeits | BEX | s.t. |
| 117. | C. Venturini | ACT | s.t. |
| 118. | R. Taaramäe | IWG | 0:50 |
| 119. | M. Bizkarra | EUS | s.t. |
| 120. | J. Knox | DQT | s.t. |
| 121. | N. Denz | DSM | 0:51 |
| 122. | C. Brown | TQA | s.t. |
| 123. | G. Brambilla | TFS | s.t. |
| 124. | I. Erviti | MOV | s.t. |
| 125. | C. Canal | BBH | 0:52 |
| 126. | C. Benedetti | BOH | s.t. |
| 127. | R. Rochas | COF | s.t. |
| 128. | J. J. Rojas | MOV | 0:53 |
| 129. | J. J. Lobato | EUS | s.t. |
| 130. | O. Lazkano | CJR | 0:54 |
| 131. | F. Jakobsen | DQT | s.t. |
| 132. | B. J. Lindeman | TQA | 0:55 |
| 133. | K. van Melsen | IWG | s.t. |
| 134. | P. Allegaert | COF | s.t. |
| 135. | G. Niv | ISN | s.t. |
| 136. | J. Guarnieri | GFC | s.t. |
| 137. | N. Prodhomme | ACT | s.t. |
| 138. | S. Berwick | ISN | 0:56 |
| 139. | Á. Madrazo | BBH | 0:57 |
| 140. | F. Barceló | COF | s.t. |
| 141. | I. Einhorn | ISN | s.t. |
| 142. | M. Holmes | LTS | s.t. |
| 143. | Jo. Herrada | COF | 0:58 |
| 144. | P. Sánchez | BBH | s.t. |
| 145. | D. Claeys | TQA | s.t. |
| 146. | J. Lastra | CJR | s.t. |
| 147. | O. C. Eiking | IWG | s.t. |
| 148. | E. Morin | COF | s.t. |
| 149. | J. Bol | BBH | 0:59 |
| 150. | J. Vine | AFC | 1:00 |
| 151. | Y. Arashiro | TBV | s.t. |
| 152. | A. Palzer | BOH | 1:02 |
| 153. | A. Cuadros Morata | CJR | s.t. |
| 154. | J. Cepeda Hernández | CJR | 1:04 |
| 155. | M. Nieve | BEX | s.t. |
| 156. | J. Aberasturi | CJR | 1:06 |
| 157. | A. Bagües | CJR | s.t. |
| 158. | S. Moniquet | LTS | s.t. |
| 159. | J. Hirt | IWG | 1:08 |
| 160. | E. Planckaert | AFC | 1:10 |
| 161. | E. Finé | COF | s.t. |
| 162. | C. Verona | MOV | s.t. |
| 163. | L. A. Maté | EUS | 1:12 |
| 164. | Y. Natarov | APT | s.t. |
| 165. | K. Reijnen | TFS | s.t. |
| 166. | R. Minali | IWG | 1:13 |
| 167. | M. Van Gils | LTS | s.t. |
| 168. | S. Thwaites | AFC | s.t. |
| 169. | D. Navarro | BBH | 1:15 |
| 170. | Ó. Cabedo | BBH | s.t. |
| 171. | S. Armée | TQA | s.t. |
| 172. | A. Nibali | TFS | s.t. |
| 173. | R. Oliveira | UAD | 1:17 |
| 174. | M. Cherel | ACT | s.t. |
| 175. | W. Kreder | IWG | 1:18 |
| 176. | D. Cimolai | ISN | 1:21 |
| 177. | S. Modolo | AFC | 1:22 |
| 178. | F. De Tier | AFC | 1:23 |
| 179. | Q. Simmons | TFS | 1:27 |
| 180. | S. Vanmarcke | ISN | s.t. |
| 181. | A. Okamika | BBH | 1:28 |
| 182. | M. Laas | BOH | 1:29 |
| 183. | A. Krieger | AFC | 1:34 |
| 184. | J. Philipsen | AFC | 2:17 |

AUGUST   WORLDTOUR MEN'S RACE

# LA VUELTA A ESPAÑA
Stage 2
15 August 2021
Caleruega–Burgos
166.7km

## WEATHER

**TEMPERATURE**
24°C

**WIND**
NE 22km/h

The first road stage of the Vuelta began with what would become a familiar sight over the next three weeks of racing, as a rider from each of the three Spanish wildcard teams – Burgos-BH, Caja Rural-Seguros RGA and Euskaltel-Euskadi (the orange formation of the latter's return a welcome sight at the race) – plied their trade up the road for their paymasters. But as the temperature hit the mid-thirties, Diego Rubio, Sergio Martín and Xabier Mikel Azparren were rarely allowed enough of an advantage to get them dreaming of any stage-victory heroics. Despite the anticipation of wind before the start, none materialised, resulting in a noticeably calmer beginning to this Grand Tour. A crash 80km from the finish did bring down Alpecin-Fenix's Jay Vine – a graduate of the Zwift Academy – and, although the impact with the tarmac was tangible, he escaped virtually unscathed. As the kilometres ticked down, the breakaway riders fell away one by one, Rubio the last left out on the road, swept up with 20km remaining. Now the sprint teams took over, jostling for position as always, Fabio Jakobsen out-muscling Astana and Aranburu at the intermediate sprint as he looked to pick up some points and bonus seconds to close his small gap to Roglič's red jersey. Then came the rush from the GC teams as they tried to protect their leaders across their finish line of 3km to go (after which crashes wouldn't result in time losses). They were wise to do so: a crash a kilometre out from this safe haven caused the English-speaking trio of Adam Yates, Jack Haig and Hugh Carthy to lose 30 seconds. The teams for the overall then handed back to the sprint trains, with UAE Team Emirates taking control in the closing kilometres, but it was Alpecin-Fenix's Belgian sprinter Jasper Philipsen who came around the left of Juan Sebastián Molano and had enough to keep Michael Matthews and Jakobsen at bay for the stage victory. Aranburu's fifth place denied him the bonus seconds to usurp Roglič. ⓛ

## PROFILE

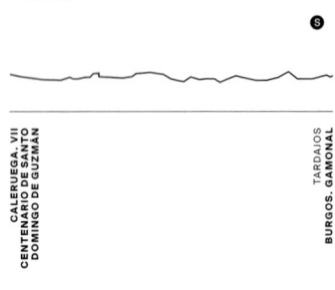

## BREAKAWAY
D. Rubio (BBH), S. Martin (CJR), X. M. Azparren (EUS)

## GENERAL CLASSIFICATION

| POS | NAME | TEAM | TIME |
|---|---|---|---|
| 1. – | P. Roglič | TJV | 4:07:29 |
| 2. – | A. Aranburu | APT | 0:04 |
| 3. ↑6 | M. Matthews | BEX | 0:10 |
| 4. ↑1 | J. Černý | DQT | s.t. |
| 5. ↑1 | D. van Baarle | IGD | 0:11 |
| 6. ↑1 | A. Bagioli | DQT | 0:12 |
| 7. ↑3 | A. Vlasov | APT | 0:14 |
| 8. ↑3 | J. Polanc | UAD | 0:15 |
| 9. ↑3 | S. Kuss | TJV | s.t. |
| 10.↑3 | C. Haga | DSM | 0:17 |

## KING OF THE MOUNTAINS

| POS | NAME | TEAM | PTS |
|---|---|---|---|
| 1. – | S. Kuss | TJV | 3 |
| 2. – | S. Vanmarcke | ISN | 2 |
| 3. – | R. Oliveira | UAD | 1 |

## POINTS

| POS | NAME | TEAM | PTS |
|---|---|---|---|
| 1. – | J. Philipsen | AFC | 50 |
| 2. – | F. Jakobsen | DQT | 50 |
| 3. ↓1 | A. Aranburu | APT | 50 |

## YOUNG RIDER

| POS | NAME | TEAM | TIME |
|---|---|---|---|
| 1. – | A. Bagioli | DQT | 4:07:41 |
| 2. – | A. Vlasov | APT | 0:02 |
| 3. – | C. Champoussin | ACT | 0:08 |

## TRIVIA
» In between his last win at the Tour of Turkey and his victory today, Philipsen has finished in the top four eight times.

## BONUSES

| TYPE | NAME | TEAM |
|---|---|---|
| Sprint 1 | F. Jakobsen | DQT |

## STAGE RESULTS

| POS | NAME | TEAM | TIME |
|---|---|---|---|
| 1. | J. Philipsen | AFC | 3:58:57 |
| 2. | F. Jakobsen | DQT | s.t. |
| 3. | M. Matthews | BEX | s.t. |
| 4. | J. S. Molano | UAD | s.t. |
| 5. | A. Aranburu | APT | s.t. |
| 6. | J. Aberasturi | CJR | s.t. |
| 7. | M. Laas | BOH | s.t. |
| 8. | R. Minali | IWG | s.t. |
| 9. | F. Vermeersch | LTS | s.t. |
| 10. | P. Allegaert | COF | s.t. |
| 11. | A. Soto | EUS | s.t. |
| 12. | A. Dainese | DSM | s.t. |
| 13. | R. Janse Van Rensburg | TQA | s.t. |
| 14. | A. Démare | GFC | s.t. |
| 15. | J. J. Lobato | EUS | s.t. |
| 16. | G. Martín | EUS | s.t. |
| 17. | A. Vlasov | APT | s.t. |
| 18. | C. Venturini | ACT | s.t. |
| 19. | L. Calmejane | ACT | s.t. |
| 20. | M. Trentin | UAD | s.t. |
| 21. | F. Großschartner | BOH | s.t. |
| 22. | J. J. Rojas | MOV | s.t. |
| 23. | G. Ciccone | TFS | s.t. |
| 24. | S. Oomen | TJV | s.t. |
| 25. | M. A. López | MOV | s.t. |
| 26. | I. Einhorn | ISN | s.t. |
| 27. | D. van Baarle | IGD | s.t. |
| 28. | R. Carapaz | IGD | s.t. |
| 29. | E. Bernal | IGD | s.t. |
| 30. | L. Mezgec | BEX | s.t. |
| 31. | N. Van Hooydonck | TJV | s.t. |
| 32. | L. Hofstede | TJV | s.t. |
| 33. | P. Roglič | TJV | s.t. |
| 34. | G. Izaguirre | APT | s.t. |
| 35. | E. Mas | MOV | s.t. |
| 36. | A. Bagioli | DQT | s.t. |
| 37. | R. Stannard | BEX | s.t. |
| 38. | M. Tusveld | DSM | s.t. |
| 39. | B. Van Lerberghe | DQT | s.t. |
| 40. | A. Valverde | MOV | s.t. |
| 41. | R. Bardet | DSM | s.t. |
| 42. | S. Kuss | TJV | s.t. |
| 43. | J. Polanc | UAD | s.t. |
| 44. | I. Erviti | MOV | s.t. |
| 45. | R. Rochas | COF | s.t. |
| 46. | L. L. Sanchez | APT | s.t. |
| 47. | G. Bouchard | ACT | s.t. |
| 48. | C. Champoussin | ACT | s.t. |
| 49. | F. Aru | TQA | s.t. |
| 50. | N. Prodhomme | ACT | s.t. |
| 51. | S. Kruijswijk | TJV | s.t. |
| 52. | C. Benedetti | BOH | s.t. |
| 53. | A. Bagües | CJR | s.t. |
| 54. | C. Haga | DSM | s.t. |
| 55. | G. Mäder | TBV | s.t. |
| 56. | R. Molard | GFC | s.t. |
| 57. | G. Martin | COF | s.t. |
| 58. | M. Vansevenant | DQT | s.t. |
| 59. | M. Landa | TBV | s.t. |
| 60. | I. Izagirre | APT | s.t. |
| 61. | M. Cherel | ACT | s.t. |
| 62. | D. Caruso | TBV | s.t. |
| 63. | J. Černý | DQT | s.t. |
| 64. | T. Bayer | AFC | s.t. |
| 65. | A. Krieger | AFC | s.t. |
| 66. | F. Sénéchal | DQT | s.t. |
| 67. | S. Vanmarcke | ISN | s.t. |
| 68. | W. Kreder | IWG | s.t. |
| 69. | D. Claeys | TQA | s.t. |
| 70. | O. Le Gac | GFC | s.t. |
| 71. | R. Oliveira | UAD | s.t. |
| 72. | R. Sinkeldam | GFC | s.t. |
| 73. | S. Cras | LTS | 0:24 |
| 74. | M. Van Gils | LTS | s.t. |
| 75. | K. Bouwman | TJV | 0:31 |
| 76. | L. Hamilton | BEX | s.t. |
| 77. | A. Yates | IGD | s.t. |
| 78. | J. Guarnieri | GFC | 0:36 |
| 79. | M. Würst Schmidt | ISN | 0:38 |
| 80. | D. Cimolai | ISN | s.t. |
| 81. | S. Carr | EFN | s.t. |
| 82. | A. Palzer | BOH | s.t. |
| 83. | N. Schultz | BEX | s.t. |
| 84. | D. Touzé | ACT | s.t. |
| 85. | J. Tratnik | TBV | s.t. |
| 86. | J. Haig | TBV | s.t. |
| 87. | H. Carthy | EFN | s.t. |
| 88. | G. Brambilla | TFS | s.t. |
| 89. | J. Bol | BBH | s.t. |
| 90. | W. Poels | TBV | s.t. |
| 91. | Jo. Herrada | COF | s.t. |
| 92. | C. Canal | BBH | s.t. |
| 93. | O. C. Eiking | IWG | s.t. |
| 94. | M. Nieve | BEX | s.t. |
| 95. | M. Padun | TBV | s.t. |
| 96. | O. Lazkano | CJR | s.t. |
| 97. | J. Lastra | CJR | s.t. |
| 98. | J. Piccoli | ISN | s.t. |
| 99. | M. Iturria | EUS | s.t. |
| 100. | S. Modolo | AFC | s.t. |
| 101. | J. P. López | TFS | s.t. |
| 102. | J. Vine | AFC | s.t. |
| 103. | J. K. Caicedo | EFN | s.t. |
| 104. | D. Navarro | BBH | s.t. |
| 105. | S. Armée | TQA | s.t. |
| 106. | K. van Melsen | IWG | s.t. |
| 107. | S. Moniquet | LTS | s.t. |
| 108. | J. Amezqueta | CJR | s.t. |
| 109. | L. A. Maté | EUS | s.t. |
| 110. | J. Hirt | IWG | s.t. |
| 111. | F. Barceló | COF | s.t. |
| 112. | E. Finé | COF | s.t. |
| 113. | L. Meintjes | IWG | s.t. |
| 114. | A. Okamika | BBH | s.t. |
| 115. | D. Sunderland | TQA | s.t. |
| 116. | S. Petilli | IWG | s.t. |
| 117. | K. Elissonde | TFS | s.t. |
| 118. | S. Henao | TQA | s.t. |
| 119. | J. Cepeda Hernández | CJR | s.t. |
| 120. | R. Taaramäe | IWG | s.t. |
| 121. | Je. Herrada | COF | s.t. |
| 122. | P. Sánchez | BBH | s.t. |
| 123. | A. Nibali | TFS | s.t. |
| 124. | J. Knox | DQT | 0:50 |
| 125. | F. Frison | LTS | 0:52 |
| 126. | O. Fraile | APT | 1:00 |
| 127. | Z. Štybar | DQT | s.t. |
| 128. | D. de la Cruz | UAD | 1:11 |
| 129. | R. Majka | UAD | s.t. |
| 130. | A. Zeits | BEX | 1:15 |
| 131. | G. Niv | ISN | s.t. |
| 132. | T. Arensman | DSM | s.t. |
| 133. | P. Sivakov | IGD | s.t. |
| 134. | E. Planckaert | AFC | s.t. |
| 135. | J. Keukeleire | EFN | 1:28 |
| 136. | F. De Tier | AFC | 1:31 |
| 137. | Ó. Cabedo | BBH | s.t. |
| 138. | L. Craddock | EFN | 1:36 |
| 139. | M. Cort | EFN | 1:57 |
| 140. | B. J. Lindeman | TQA | 2:10 |
| 141. | Y. Natarov | APT | 2:16 |
| 142. | O. Rodríguez | APT | s.t. |
| 143. | M. Bizkarra | EUS | s.t. |
| 144. | Y. Arashiro | TBV | 0:38 |
| 145. | S. R. Martin | CJR | 2:29 |
| 146. | E. Morin | COF | s.t. |
| 147. | S. Thwaites | AFC | 2:33 |
| 148. | K. Geniets | GFC | 2:35 |
| 149. | M. Schachmann | BOH | s.t. |
| 150. | B. Zwiehoff | BOH | s.t. |
| 151. | C. Verona | MOV | s.t. |
| 152. | R. Gesink | TJV | s.t. |
| 153. | N. Oliveira | MOV | s.t. |
| 154. | J. Jacobs | MOV | s.t. |
| 155. | A. Roux | GFC | s.t. |
| 156. | D. Howson | BEX | s.t. |
| 157. | A. Cuadros Morata | CJR | s.t. |
| 158. | C. Brown | TQA | s.t. |
| 159. | S. Dewulf | ACT | s.t. |
| 160. | D. A. Camargo | EFN | s.t. |
| 161. | S. Puccio | IGD | s.t. |
| 162. | J. Bou | EUS | s.t. |
| 163. | S. Berwick | ISN | s.t. |
| 164. | C. Hamilton | DSM | s.t. |
| 165. | M. Storer | DSM | s.t. |
| 166. | A. Kron | LTS | s.t. |
| 167. | A. Kirsch | TFS | s.t. |
| 168. | T. Ludvigsson | GFC | s.t. |
| 169. | M. Holmes | LTS | s.t. |
| 170. | T. Scully | EFN | s.t. |
| 171. | J. Narváez | IGD | 2:40 |
| 172. | Q. Simmons | TFS | s.t. |
| 173. | J. Dombrowski | UAD | s.t. |
| 174. | H. Vanhoucke | LTS | 3:10 |
| 175. | R. Gibbons | UAD | 0:00 |
| 176. | Á. Madrazo | BBH | 4:11 |
| 177. | K. Reijnen | TFS | s.t. |
| 178. | N. Denz | DSM | 4:13 |
| 179. | T. Pidcock | IGD | 4:16 |
| 180. | X. M. Azparren | EUS | 5:49 |
| 181. | J. Meeus | BOH | 6:19 |
| 182. | D. Rubio | BBH | 7:08 |
| 183. | P. Gamper | BOH | 7:19 |
| 184. | A. Cataford | ISN | 8:27 |

AUGUST   WORLDTOUR MEN'S RACE

## LA VUELTA A ESPAÑA
Stage 3
16 August 2021
Santo Domingo de Silos–Picón Blanco
202.8km

Stage 3 saw 203km culminating in a 7.6km-long, 9.1 per cent average gradient summit finish atop the Picón Blanco. The Vuelta organisers were determined to get GC gaps early this year. A breakaway group struck out, hoping the peloton would allow them to contest the stage honours among themselves. The bunch was slowed by the heat and a headwind as the continued absence of crosswinds on the exposed roads neutered the chance of the GC teams attacking each other. Lilian Calmejane tried to hit out solo before the summit-finish climb but was reeled in as the breakaway group began to go uphill, Joe Dombrowski putting in the first dig, only followed by Rein Taaramäe and Kenny Elissonde. Taaramäe knew he was the inferior climber of the trio, so hit out early and didn't look back, grinding against the gradient to take his second-ever Vuelta stage (the first being ten years ago) and his first Grand Tour leader's jersey. At 34 years old, this was the best day of the Estonian's career. As the peloton began the climb, Bahrain Victorious hit the front in a show of strength, although they relented when it became clear their team leader, Mikel Landa, was one of the riders hurting most from the acceleration. The continued headwind discouraged attacks, and by the summit it was a case of who had managed to hang on and not lose any time. Enric Mas eventually managed to kick clear to take back 3 seconds on Roglič, Bernal, Yates, Landa and Giulio Ciccone, while Hugh Carthy was evidently out of sorts as he finished 21 seconds adrift. Bardet and Aleksandr Vlasov were half a minute in arrears while Richard Carapaz lost more than a minute, the tank perhaps running low after his exploits at the Tour de France and Olympic Games.

### WEATHER

TEMPERATURE  WIND
20°C         NE 30km/h

### PROFILE

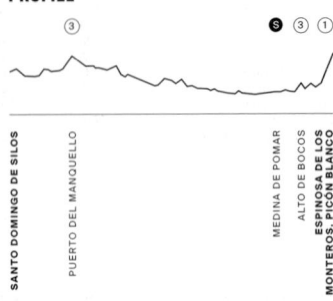

### BREAKAWAY
A. J. Soto (EUS), J. Dombrowski (UAD), L. Calmejane (TEN), K. Elissonde (TFS), R. Taaramäe (IWG), T. Bayer (AFC), J. Amezqueta (CJR), J. Bol (BBH)

### GENERAL CLASSIFICATION

| POS | NAME | TEAM | TIME |
|---|---|---|---|
| 1. ↑96 | R. Taaramäe | IWG | 9:25:44 |
| 2. ↑75 | K. Elissonde | TFS | 0:25 |
| 3. ↓2 | P. Roglič | TJV | 0:30 |
| 4. ↑39 | L. Calmejane | ACT | 0:35 |
| 5. ↑7 | E. Mas | MOV | 0:45 |
| 6. ↑10 | M. A. López | MOV | 0:51 |
| 7. ↑21 | A. Valverde | MOV | 0:57 |
| 8. ↑22 | G. Ciccone | TFS | s.t. |
| 9. ↑22 | E. Bernal | IGD | s.t. |
| 10. ↑34 | M. Landa | TBV | 1:09 |

### KING OF THE MOUNTAINS

| POS | NAME | TEAM | PTS |
|---|---|---|---|
| 1. — | R. Taaramäe | IWG | 10 |
| 2. — | K. Elissonde | TFS | 7 |
| 3. — | J. Dombrowski | UAD | 6 |

### POINTS

| POS | NAME | TEAM | PTS |
|---|---|---|---|
| 1. — | J. Philipsen | AFC | 50 |
| 2. — | F. Jakobsen | DQT | 50 |
| 3. — | A. Aranburu | APT | 50 |

### YOUNG RIDER

| POS | NAME | TEAM | TIME |
|---|---|---|---|
| 1. ↑5 | E. Bernal | IGD | 9:26:41 |
| 2. ↑2 | G. Mäder | TBV | 0:13 |
| 3. ↓1 | A. Vlasov | APT | 0:16 |

### TRIVIA
» This was Rein Taaramäe's third Grand Tour stage win (after stage 14 in the 2011 Vuelta and stage 20 in the 2016 Giro).

### BONUSES

| TYPE | NAME | TEAM |
|---|---|---|
| KOM 1 | K. Elissonde | TFS |
| KOM 2 | T. Bayer | AFC |
| KOM 3 | R. Taaramäe | IWG |
| Sprint 1 | J. Amezqueta | CJR |

## STAGE RESULTS

| POS | NAME | TEAM | TIME |
|---|---|---|---|
| 1. | R. Taaramäe | IWG | 5:16:57 |
| 2. | J. Dombrowski | UAD | 0:21 |
| 3. | K. Elissonde | TFS | 0:36 |
| 4. | L. Calmejane | ACT | 1:16 |
| 5. | E. Mas | MOV | 1:45 |
| 6. | M. A. López | MOV | 1:48 |
| 7. | P. Roglič | TJV | s.t. |
| 8. | A. Yates | IGD | s.t. |
| 9. | M. Landa | TBV | s.t. |
| 10. | G. Ciccone | TFS | s.t. |
| 11. | E. Bernal | IGD | s.t. |
| 12. | A. Valverde | MOV | s.t. |
| 13. | F. Aru | TQA | 1:55 |
| 14. | J. P. López | TFS | 2:00 |
| 15. | D. de la Cruz | UAD | s.t. |
| 16. | G. Mäder | TBV | 2:05 |
| 17. | M. Padun | TBV | 2:09 |
| 18. | Ó. Cabedo | BBH | s.t. |
| 19. | H. Carthy | EFN | s.t. |
| 20. | M. Bizkarra | EUS | 2:12 |
| 21. | S. Carr | EFN | 2:14 |
| 22. | J. Cepeda Hernández | CJR | s.t. |
| 23. | M. Storer | DSM | 2:17 |
| 24. | R. Bardet | DSM | s.t. |
| 25. | A. Vlasov | APT | s.t. |
| 26. | L. Meintjes | IWG | s.t. |
| 27. | D. Caruso | TBV | s.t. |
| 28. | M. Nieve | BEX | s.t. |
| 29. | W. Poels | TBV | s.t. |
| 30. | G. Bouchard | ACT | s.t. |
| 31. | R. Rochas | COF | s.t. |
| 32. | J. K. Caicedo | EFN | 2:32 |
| 33. | A. Soto | EUS | 2:36 |
| 34. | A. Zeits | BEX | 2:42 |
| 35. | M. Vansevenant | DQT | s.t. |
| 36. | J. Polanc | UAD | s.t. |
| 37. | H. Vanhoucke | LTS | 2:46 |
| 38. | R. Carapaz | IGD | 2:48 |
| 39. | J. Amezqueta | CJR | 2:53 |
| 40. | T. Bayer | AFC | 2:57 |
| 41. | F. Großschartner | BOH | 3:15 |
| 42. | J. Knox | DQT | s.t. |
| 43. | J. Haig | TBV | s.t. |
| 44. | G. Martin | COF | s.t. |
| 45. | O. C. Eiking | IWG | 3:19 |
| 46. | M. Tusveld | DSM | 3:23 |
| 47. | G. Brambilla | TFS | 3:27 |
| 48. | B. Zwiehoff | BOH | 3:28 |
| 49. | S. Cras | LTS | 3:31 |
| 50. | G. Martín | EUS | s.t. |
| 51. | R. Majka | UAD | s.t. |
| 52. | J. Lastra | CJR | 3:34 |
| 53. | J. Hirt | IWG | 3:35 |
| 54. | Á. Madrazo | BBH | s.t. |
| 55. | C. Champoussin | ACT | 3:39 |
| 56. | S. Kuss | TJV | 3:43 |
| 57. | R. Molard | GFC | s.t. |
| 58. | D. Navarro | BBH | s.t. |
| 59. | S. Kruijswijk | TJV | s.t. |
| 60. | S. Oomen | TJV | 3:48 |
| 61. | L. L. Sanchez | APT | 4:01 |
| 62. | G. Izaguirre | APT | 4:24 |
| 63. | O. Rodríguez | APT | s.t. |
| 64. | L. A. Maté | EUS | 4:47 |
| 65. | S. Petilli | IWG | s.t. |
| 66. | J. Bol | BBH | 4:50 |
| 67. | G. Niv | ISN | 5:04 |
| 68. | A. Nibali | TFS | 5:54 |
| 69. | A. Bagioli | DQT | s.t. |
| 70. | F. Barceló | COF | 5:58 |
| 71. | A. Roux | GFC | s.t. |
| 72. | C. Hamilton | DSM | 6:26 |
| 73. | N. Schultz | BEX | s.t. |
| 74. | L. Hamilton | BEX | s.t. |
| 75. | P. Sivakov | IGD | s.t. |
| 76. | I. Izaguirre | APT | s.t. |
| 77. | M. Van Gils | LTS | s.t. |
| 78. | S. Henao | TQA | s.t. |
| 79. | M. Würst Schmidt | ISN | 6:42 |
| 80. | A. Okamika | BBH | 6:53 |
| 81. | Y. Natarov | APT | 7:51 |
| 82. | M. Holmes | LTS | 8:16 |
| 83. | C. Verona | MOV | 8:21 |
| 84. | A. Palzer | BOH | 9:48 |
| 85. | Jo. Herrada | COF | s.t. |
| 86. | J. J. Rojas | MOV | s.t. |
| 87. | M. Iturria | EUS | s.t. |
| 88. | Je. Herrada | COF | s.t. |
| 89. | M. Schachmann | BOH | s.t. |
| 90. | D. Touzé | ACT | 9:52 |
| 91. | M. Cherel | ACT | s.t. |
| 92. | T. Ludvigsson | GFC | s.t. |
| 93. | C. Benedetti | BOH | 10:08 |
| 94. | S. Moniquet | LTS | s.t. |
| 95. | N. Prodhomme | ACT | s.t. |
| 96. | P. Sánchez | BBH | s.t. |
| 97. | A. Kron | LTS | s.t. |
| 98. | T. Pidcock | IGD | 10:13 |
| 99. | J. Bou | EUS | s.t. |
| 100. | K. Bouwman | TJV | 10:50 |
| 101. | C. Canal | BBH | 10:56 |
| 102. | K. Geniets | GFC | 11:54 |
| 103. | O. Le Gac | GFC | 12:11 |
| 104. | C. Haga | DSM | 12:51 |
| 105. | T. Arensman | DSM | s.t. |
| 106. | N. Van Hooydonck | TJV | 13:11 |
| 107. | Z. Štybar | DQT | s.t. |
| 108. | R. Gesink | TJV | s.t. |
| 109. | R. Gibbons | UAD | s.t. |
| 110. | W. Kreder | IWG | s.t. |
| 111. | S. Thwaites | AFC | s.t. |
| 112. | C. Venturini | ACT | s.t. |
| 113. | K. van Melsen | IWG | s.t. |
| 114. | E. Finé | COF | s.t. |
| 115. | L. Craddock | EFN | s.t. |
| 116. | J. Keukeleire | EFN | s.t. |
| 117. | N. Oliveira | MOV | s.t. |
| 118. | R. Oliveira | UAD | s.t. |
| 119. | I. Erviti | MOV | s.t. |
| 120. | S. Dewulf | ACT | s.t. |
| 121. | D. Sunderland | TQA | s.t. |
| 122. | S. Armée | TQA | s.t. |
| 123. | F. Sénéchal | DQT | s.t. |
| 124. | C. Brown | TQA | s.t. |
| 125. | D. van Baarle | IGD | s.t. |
| 126. | B. J. Lindeman | TQA | s.t. |
| 127. | S. Berwick | ISN | s.t. |
| 128. | D. A. Camargo | EFN | s.t. |
| 129. | S. Vanmarcke | ISN | 14:31 |
| 130. | D. Claeys | TQA | s.t. |
| 131. | A. Kirsch | TFS | 14:50 |
| 132. | O. Fraile | APT | 14:57 |
| 133. | S. Puccio | IGD | s.t. |
| 134. | X. M. Azparren | EUS | 15:01 |
| 135. | R. Stannard | BEX | 15:43 |
| 136. | D. Howson | BEX | s.t. |
| 137. | J. Tratnik | TBV | s.t. |
| 138. | L. Mezgec | BEX | s.t. |
| 139. | J. Philipsen | AFC | s.t. |
| 140. | E. Planckaert | AFC | s.t. |
| 141. | M. Matthews | BEX | s.t. |
| 142. | J. Narváez | IGD | s.t. |
| 143. | A. Bagües | CJR | s.t. |
| 144. | A. Cuadros Morata | CJR | s.t. |
| 145. | R. Janse Van Rensburg | TQA | s.t. |
| 146. | A. Krieger | AFC | 15:55 |
| 147. | Q. Simmons | TFS | s.t. |
| 148. | M. Cort | EFN | s.t. |
| 149. | F. De Tier | AFC | 16:14 |
| 150. | S. Modolo | AFC | s.t. |
| 151. | J. Piccoli | ISN | 16:17 |
| 152. | R. Sinkeldam | GFC | 16:25 |
| 153. | J. Aberasturi | CJR | s.t. |
| 154. | A. Aranburu | APT | s.t. |
| 155. | J. Vine | AFC | 17:09 |
| 156. | M. Trentin | UAD | 18:38 |
| 157. | J. S. Molano | UAD | s.t. |
| 158. | A. Démare | GFC | s.t. |
| 159. | K. Reijnen | TFS | s.t. |
| 160. | E. Morin | COF | s.t. |
| 161. | P. Gamper | BOH | s.t. |
| 162. | O. Lazkano | CJR | s.t. |
| 163. | B. Van Lerberghe | DQT | 21:38 |
| 164. | P. Allegaert | COF | s.t. |
| 165. | D. Cimolai | ISN | 21:53 |
| 166. | J. Guarnieri | GFC | s.t. |
| 167. | R. Minali | IWG | s.t. |
| 168. | S. R. Martín | CJR | s.t. |
| 169. | N. Denz | DSM | s.t. |
| 170. | J. J. Lobato | EUS | s.t. |
| 171. | T. Scully | EFN | s.t. |
| 172. | A. Dainese | DSM | s.t. |
| 173. | D. Rubio | BBH | s.t. |
| 174. | F. Vermeersch | LTS | s.t. |
| 175. | I. Einhorn | ISN | s.t. |
| 176. | J. Jacobs | MOV | s.t. |
| 177. | J. Jakobsen | DQT | s.t. |
| 178. | L. Hofstede | TJV | s.t. |
| 179. | Y. Arashiro | TBV | s.t. |
| 180. | M. Laas | BOH | s.t. |
| 181. | J. Černý | DQT | s.t. |
| 182. | J. Meeus | BOH | s.t. |

AUGUST    WORLDTOUR MEN'S RACE

## LA VUELTA A ESPAÑA
Stage 4
17 August 2021
El Burgo de Osma–Molina de Aragón
163.9km

A second opportunity for the sprinters on the road to Molina de Aragón but, first, another opportunity of TV time for the Spanish wildcard outfits, which Burgos-BH's Ángel Madrazo and Carlos Canal took in forming the day's break alongside Joan Bou of Euskaltel-Euskadi. (Today was not the day to be inside the Caja Rural bus after they missed the move.) A fairly settled race followed, with a bike change for Primož Roglič one of the only moments of note as Intermarché-Wanty-Gobert Matériaux gladly took up pace-setting duties on the front for the red jersey of Taaramäe. With 20km to go, Groupama-FDJ hit the front for their sprinter Arnaud Démare, which had the effect of bringing the break back with 14km remaining and the GC teams then getting involved, jostling for position as the speed picked up. Ineos's Salvatore Puccio came to the fore to guide Egan Bernal and Adam Yates out of harm's way. Not long after, Taaramäe hit the deck in a crash but within the final 3km so that the leader's jersey would stay on his shoulders for another day. Under the *flamme rouge* and Groupama-FDJ were back in control, Démare with two teammates for company. Fabio Jakobsen won the fight for the Frenchman's wheel as Jasper Philipsen found himself boxed in and Michael Matthews lacked the final kick to compete with the fastest men at the race. Démare opened his sprint, rushing through while Jakobsen waited for the perfect moment before coming past to cross the line first and cap off his comeback from serious injury at the Tour of Poland last year. 'After the crash, I was a long way back, but I'm happy I'm here,' Jakobsen said. 'A lot of time and effort has gone into this by a lot of people, and it's also their victory. I'm talking about all the doctors and surgeons and medical staff in Poland, through to my second family here with the team, and everything in between. It's also their victory. It's also my family's victory, because they're the reason I'm here.' Ⓛ

### TRIVIA
» This was Fabio Jakobsen's first WorldTour win since the opening stage of the 2020 Tour of Poland, the race where he suffered his life-threatening crash.

### WEATHER

TEMPERATURE: 18°C
WIND: NE 30km/h

### PROFILE

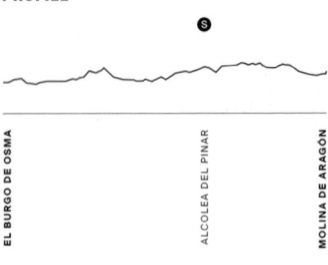

EL BURGO DE OSMA — ALCOLEA DEL PINAR — MOLINA DE ARAGÓN

### BREAKAWAY
C. Canal (BBH), A. Madrazo (BBH), J. Bou (EUS)

### GENERAL CLASSIFICATION

| POS | NAME | TEAM | TIME |
|---|---|---|---|
| 1. — | R. Taaramäe | IWG | 13:08:51 |
| 2. — | K. Elissonde | TFS | 0:25 |
| 3. — | P. Roglič | TJV | 0:30 |
| 4. — | L. Calmejane | ACT | 0:35 |
| 5. — | E. Mas | MOV | 0:45 |
| 6. — | M. A. López | MOV | 0:51 |
| 7. — | A. Valverde | MOV | 0:57 |
| 8. — | G. Ciccone | TFS | s.t. |
| 9. — | E. Bernal | IGD | s.t. |
| 10. — | M. Landa | TBV | 1:09 |

### KING OF THE MOUNTAINS

| POS | NAME | TEAM | PTS |
|---|---|---|---|
| 1. — | R. Taaramäe | IWG | 10 |
| 2. — | K. Elissonde | TFS | 7 |
| 3. — | J. Dombrowski | UAD | 6 |

### POINTS

| POS | NAME | TEAM | PTS |
|---|---|---|---|
| 1. ↑1 | F. Jakobsen | DQT | 100 |
| 2. ↓1 | J. Philipsen | AFC | 68 |
| 3. — | A. Aranburu | APT | 50 |

### YOUNG RIDER

| POS | NAME | TEAM | TIME |
|---|---|---|---|
| 1. — | E. Bernal | IGD | 13:09:48 |
| 2. — | G. Mäder | TBV | 0:13 |
| 3. — | A. Vlasov | APT | 0:16 |

### BONUSES

| TYPE | NAME | TEAM |
|---|---|---|
| Sprint 1 | J. Bou | EUS |

## STAGE RESULTS

| POS | NAME | TEAM | TIME |
|---|---|---|---|
| 1. | F. Jakobsen | DQT | 3:43:07 |
| 2. | A. Démare | GFC | s.t. |
| 3. | M. Cort | EFN | s.t. |
| 4. | A. Dainese | DSM | s.t. |
| 5. | M. Matthews | BEX | s.t. |
| 6. | P. Allegaert | COF | s.t. |
| 7. | J. Meeus | BOH | s.t. |
| 8. | M. Trentin | UAD | s.t. |
| 9. | J. Philipsen | AFC | s.t. |
| 10. | R. Minali | IWG | s.t. |
| 11. | R. Janse Van Rensburg | TQA | s.t. |
| 12. | J. J. Lobato | EUS | s.t. |
| 13. | J. Aberasturi | CJR | s.t. |
| 14. | S. Vanmarcke | ISN | s.t. |
| 15. | R. Oliveira | UAD | s.t. |
| 16. | A. Aranburu | APT | s.t. |
| 17. | A. Soto | EUS | s.t. |
| 18. | J. S. Molano | UAD | s.t. |
| 19. | F. Großschartner | BOH | s.t. |
| 20. | C. Venturini | ACT | s.t. |
| 21. | M. A. López | MOV | s.t. |
| 22. | E. Bernal | IGD | s.t. |
| 23. | G. Mäder | TBV | s.t. |
| 24. | T. Bayer | AFC | s.t. |
| 25. | R. Bardet | DSM | s.t. |
| 26. | J. J. Rojas | MOV | s.t. |
| 27. | R. Rochas | COF | s.t. |
| 28. | G. Ciccone | TFS | s.t. |
| 29. | R. Molard | GFC | s.t. |
| 30. | Q. Simmons | TFS | s.t. |
| 31. | A. Valverde | MOV | s.t. |
| 32. | S. Henao | TQA | s.t. |
| 33. | L. Hofstede | TJV | s.t. |
| 34. | J. Polanc | UAD | s.t. |
| 35. | A. Yates | IGD | s.t. |
| 36. | P. Roglič | TJV | s.t. |
| 37. | G. Martín | EUS | s.t. |
| 38. | G. Izagirre | APT | s.t. |
| 39. | E. Mas | MOV | s.t. |
| 40. | S. Kuss | TJV | s.t. |
| 41. | R. Carapaz | IGD | s.t. |
| 42. | M. Tusveld | DSM | s.t. |
| 43. | O. C. Eiking | IWG | s.t. |
| 44. | R. Gibbons | UAD | s.t. |
| 45. | S. Oomen | TJV | s.t. |
| 46. | K. Elissonde | TFS | s.t. |
| 47. | R. Stannard | BEX | s.t. |
| 48. | A. Vlasov | APT | s.t. |
| 49. | M. Padun | TBV | s.t. |
| 50. | D. de la Cruz | UAD | s.t. |
| 51. | M. Landa | TBV | s.t. |
| 52. | J. Bol | BBH | s.t. |
| 53. | D. Cimolai | ISN | s.t. |
| 54. | S. Modolo | AFC | s.t. |
| 55. | W. Poels | TBV | s.t. |
| 56. | F. Aru | TQA | s.t. |
| 57. | B. J. Lindeman | TQA | s.t. |
| 58. | L. Calmejane | ACT | s.t. |
| 59. | B. Van Lerberghe | DQT | s.t. |
| 60. | D. Caruso | TBV | s.t. |
| 61. | C. Champoussin | ACT | s.t. |
| 62. | Z. Štybar | DQT | s.t. |
| 63. | G. Martin | COF | s.t. |
| 64. | M. Nieve | BEX | s.t. |
| 65. | M. Schachmann | BOH | s.t. |
| 66. | L. Hamilton | BEX | s.t. |
| 67. | S. Cras | LTS | s.t. |
| 68. | J. Keukeleire | EFN | s.t. |
| 69. | L. Mezgec | BEX | s.t. |
| 70. | S. Kruijswijk | TJV | s.t. |
| 71. | A. Bagioli | DQT | s.t. |
| 72. | S. Dewulf | ACT | s.t. |
| 73. | G. Niv | ISN | s.t. |
| 74. | J. Haig | TBV | s.t. |
| 75. | A. Krieger | AFC | s.t. |
| 76. | J. P. López | TFS | s.t. |
| 77. | C. Canal | BBH | s.t. |
| 78. | A. Bagües | CJR | s.t. |
| 79. | D. Sunderland | TQA | s.t. |
| 80. | J. Cepeda Hernández | CJR | s.t. |
| 81. | F. Barceló | COF | s.t. |
| 82. | H. Carthy | EFN | s.t. |
| 83. | F. Vermeersch | LTS | s.t. |
| 84. | J. K. Caicedo | EFN | s.t. |
| 85. | R. Majka | UAD | s.t. |
| 86. | D. Touzé | ACT | s.t. |
| 87. | J. Jacobs | MOV | s.t. |
| 88. | N. Prodhomme | ACT | s.t. |
| 89. | J. Guarnieri | GFC | s.t. |
| 90. | F. Sénéchal | DQT | s.t. |
| 91. | R. Sinkeldam | GFC | s.t. |
| 92. | A. Zeits | BEX | s.t. |
| 93. | L. Meintjes | IWG | s.t. |
| 94. | W. Kreder | IWG | s.t. |
| 95. | M. Würst Schmidt | ISN | s.t. |
| 96. | A. Palzer | BOH | s.t. |
| 97. | G. Bouchard | ACT | s.t. |
| 98. | M. Iturria | EUS | s.t. |
| 99. | J. Dombrowski | UAD | s.t. |
| 100. | J. Lastra | CJR | s.t. |
| 101. | M. Laas | BOH | s.t. |
| 102. | J. Knox | DQT | s.t. |
| 103. | J. Hirt | IWG | s.t. |
| 104. | O. Fraile | APT | s.t. |
| 105. | P. Sánchez | BBH | s.t. |
| 106. | S. Armée | TQA | s.t. |
| 107. | A. Okamika | BBH | s.t. |
| 108. | G. Brambilla | TFS | s.t. |
| 109. | J. Amezqueta | CJR | s.t. |
| 110. | D. van Baarle | IGD | s.t. |
| 111. | M. Van Gils | LTS | s.t. |
| 112. | A. Roux | GFC | s.t. |
| 113. | L. Craddock | EFN | s.t. |
| 114. | D. Claeys | TQA | s.t. |
| 115. | C. Brown | TQA | s.t. |
| 116. | N. Denz | DSM | s.t. |
| 117. | S. Carr | EFN | s.t. |
| 118. | D. Navarro | BBH | s.t. |
| 119. | Á. Madrazo | BBH | s.t. |
| 120. | O. Le Gac | GFC | s.t. |
| 121. | E. Morin | COF | s.t. |
| 122. | N. Schultz | BEX | s.t. |
| 123. | X. M. Azparren | EUS | s.t. |
| 124. | D. Howson | BEX | s.t. |
| 125. | E. Planckaert | AFC | s.t. |
| 126. | Je. Herrada | COF | s.t. |
| 127. | E. Finé | COF | s.t. |
| 128. | Jo. Herrada | COF | s.t. |
| 129. | T. Ludvigsson | GFC | s.t. |
| 130. | S. Moniquet | LTS | s.t. |
| 131. | B. Zwiehoff | BOH | s.t. |
| 132. | J. Narváez | IGD | s.t. |
| 133. | T. Pidcock | IGD | s.t. |
| 134. | I. Erviti | MOV | s.t. |
| 135. | T. Arensman | DSM | s.t. |
| 136. | L. L. Sanchez | APT | s.t. |
| 137. | I. Izagirre | APT | s.t. |
| 138. | S. Berwick | ISN | s.t. |
| 139. | Ó. Cabedo | BBH | s.t. |
| 140. | D. Rubio | BBH | s.t. |
| 141. | Y. Natarov | APT | s.t. |
| 142. | M. Storer | DSM | s.t. |
| 143. | I. Einhorn | ISN | s.t. |
| 144. | K. Bouwman | TJV | s.t. |
| 145. | R. Gesink | TJV | s.t. |
| 146. | H. Vanhoucke | LTS | s.t. |
| 147. | P. Sivakov | IGD | s.t. |
| 148. | C. Benedetti | BOH | s.t. |
| 149. | M. Cherel | ACT | s.t. |
| 150. | M. Bizkarra | EUS | s.t. |
| 151. | O. Rodríguez | APT | s.t. |
| 152. | D. A. Camargo | EFN | s.t. |
| 153. | S. Petilli | IWG | s.t. |
| 154. | N. Oliveira | MOV | s.t. |
| 155. | A. Nibali | TFS | s.t. |
| 156. | Y. Arashiro | TBV | s.t. |
| 157. | J. Piccoli | ISN | s.t. |
| 158. | F. De Tier | AFC | s.t. |
| 159. | S. Puccio | IGD | s.t. |
| 160. | K. Geniets | GFC | s.t. |
| 161. | M. Holmes | LTS | s.t. |
| 162. | J. Bou | EUS | s.t. |
| 163. | A. Cuadros Morata | CJR | s.t. |
| 164. | J. Černý | DQT | s.t. |
| 165. | P. Gamper | BOH | s.t. |
| 166. | K. van Melsen | IWG | s.t. |
| 167. | R. Taaramäe | IWG | s.t. |
| 168. | T. Scully | EFN | s.t. |
| 169. | C. Verona | MOV | s.t. |
| 170. | S. R. Martin | CJR | 2:08 |
| 171. | A. Kirsch | TFS | 0:00 |
| 172. | K. Reijnen | TFS | s.t. |
| 173. | A. Kron | LTS | s.t. |
| 174. | N. Van Hooydonck | TJV | 2:28 |
| 175. | C. Haga | DSM | 2:42 |
| 176. | O. Lazkano | CJR | s.t. |
| 177. | J. Vine | AFC | s.t. |
| 178. | J. Tratnik | TBV | 2:46 |
| 179. | S. Thwaites | AFC | 2:50 |
| 180. | L. A. Maté | EUS | 0:00 |
| 181. | C. Hamilton | DSM | 3:17 |
| 182. | M. Vansevenant | DQT | 3:20 |

AUGUST    WORLDTOUR MEN'S RACE

## LA VUELTA A ESPAÑA
Stage 5
18 August 2021
Tarancón–Albacete
184.4km

A transition stage across central Spain with not a categorised climb to be found? Cue the three riders of the Vuelta-pocalypse – one each from Burgos-BH, Caja Rural and Euskaltel-Euskadi. Xabier Mikel Azparren once again volunteered as sacrificial lamb, this time accompanied by Pelayo Sánchez and Oier Lazkano, plunging into the abyss of the doomed breakaway. They were offered a 7-minute advantage with no resistance, and for 120km everything was still – until the intermediate sprint with 53km to go woke everyone up from their afternoon siestas. Lazkano won the sprint and a bit of pocket money to split between his teammates, while Philipsen edged out Démare in the fight for the minor placings and leftover green-jersey points. As it neared 30km to go, Sánchez was the first to drop from the break, followed 10km later by Azparren, the gap back to the peloton now below a minute and a half. An injection of speed from Deceuninck-QuickStep was then enough to finally bring back Lazkano with 16km to the line, and 5km later a huge crash erupted in the peloton. Mads Würtz Schmidt suffered a touch of wheels, the concertina effect bringing down Rein Taaramäe for the second day in a row, which would wrench the red jersey from his shoulders and onto those of Kenny Elissonde. As many picked themselves up, Romain Bardet was still on the floor, eventually collecting himself and sporting a savaged jersey as he crossed the line 12 and a half minutes down on the peloton. It was full steam ahead for the rest of the bunch, Alpecin-Fenix on the front with 2km left and the other sprint teams trying to muscle in amid the chaos and confusion that often follows a crash in the closing kilometres. Alpecin-Fenix fought through the traffic, dropping Philipsen off with 200 metres to go, and the Belgian unleashed his sprint. Jakobsen was a few wheels back, forced to come past the likes of Reinardt Janse van Rensburg and Alberto Dainese before getting a shot at Philipsen, but it was too late: he already had his hands in the air as he crossed the line. Ⓛ

## WEATHER

TEMPERATURE    WIND
30°C           S 7km/h

## PROFILE

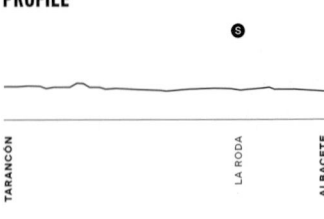

## BREAKAWAY
P. Sanchez (BBH), O. Lazkano (CJR), X. M. Azparren (EUS)

## GENERAL CLASSIFICATION

| POS | NAME | TEAM | TIME |
|---|---|---|---|
| 1. ↑1 | K. Elissonde | TFS | 17:33:57 |
| 2. ↑1 | P. Roglič | TJV | 0:05 |
| 3. ↑1 | L. Calmejane | ACT | 0:10 |
| 4. ↑1 | E. Mas | MOV | 0:20 |
| 5. ↑1 | M. A. López | MOV | 0:26 |
| 6. ↑1 | A. Valverde | MOV | 0:32 |
| 7. ↑1 | G. Ciccone | TFS | s.t. |
| 8. ↑1 | E. Bernal | IGD | s.t. |
| 9. ↑1 | M. Landa | TBV | 0:44 |
| 10.↑1 | G. Mäder | TBV | 0:45 |

## KING OF THE MOUNTAINS

| POS | NAME | TEAM | PTS |
|---|---|---|---|
| 1. – | R. Taaramäe | IWG | 10 |
| 2. – | K. Elissonde | TFS | 7 |
| 3. – | J. Dombrowski | UAD | 6 |

## POINTS

| POS | NAME | TEAM | PTS |
|---|---|---|---|
| 1. ↑1 | J. Philipsen | AFC | 131 |
| 2. ↓1 | F. Jakobsen | DQT | 130 |
| 3. ↑3 | A. Démare | GFC | 50 |

## YOUNG RIDER

| POS | NAME | TEAM | TIME |
|---|---|---|---|
| 1. – | E. Bernal | IGD | 17:34:29 |
| 2. – | G. Mäder | TBV | 0:13 |
| 3. – | A. Vlasov | APT | 0:16 |

## BONUSES

| TYPE | NAME | TEAM |
|---|---|---|
| Sprint 1 | O. Lazkano | CJR |

## STAGE RESULTS

| POS | NAME | TEAM | TIME |
|---|---|---|---|
| 1. | J. Philipsen | AFC | 4:24:41 |
| 2. | F. Jakobsen | DQT | s.t. |
| 3. | A. Dainese | DSM | s.t. |
| 4. | J. S. Molano | UAD | s.t. |
| 5. | P. Allegaert | COF | s.t. |
| 6. | J. Aberasturi | CJR | s.t. |
| 7. | J. Meeus | BOH | s.t. |
| 8. | R. Minali | IWG | s.t. |
| 9. | R. Janse Van Rensburg | TQA | s.t. |
| 10. | A. Démare | GFC | s.t. |
| 11. | D. Touzé | ACT | s.t. |
| 12. | A. Soto | EUS | s.t. |
| 13. | J. Polanc | UAD | s.t. |
| 14. | R. Stannard | BEX | s.t. |
| 15. | G. Martin | EUS | s.t. |
| 16. | J. J. Lobato | EUS | s.t. |
| 17. | L. Calmejane | ACT | s.t. |
| 18. | M. Van Gils | LTS | s.t. |
| 19. | N. Denz | DSM | s.t. |
| 20. | D. Caruso | TBV | s.t. |
| 21. | S. Kuss | TJV | s.t. |
| 22. | R. Molard | GFC | s.t. |
| 23. | K. Elissonde | TFS | s.t. |
| 24. | R. Oliveira | UAD | s.t. |
| 25. | M. Matthews | BEX | s.t. |
| 26. | F. Großschartner | BOH | s.t. |
| 27. | C. Champoussin | ACT | s.t. |
| 28. | A. Valverde | MOV | s.t. |
| 29. | M. Landa | TBV | s.t. |
| 30. | J. Guarnieri | GFC | s.t. |
| 31. | L. Mezgec | BEX | s.t. |
| 32. | L. L. Sanchez | APT | s.t. |
| 33. | S. Modolo | AFC | s.t. |
| 34. | E. Bernal | IGD | s.t. |
| 35. | A. Vlasov | APT | s.t. |
| 36. | A. Zeits | BEX | s.t. |
| 37. | D. van Baarle | IGD | s.t. |
| 38. | N. Van Hooydonck | TJV | s.t. |
| 39. | I. Erviti | MOV | s.t. |
| 40. | S. Cras | LTS | s.t. |
| 41. | S. Oomen | TJV | s.t. |
| 42. | A. Krieger | AFC | s.t. |
| 43. | P. Roglič | TJV | s.t. |
| 44. | M. Laas | BOH | s.t. |
| 45. | A. Bagües | CJR | s.t. |
| 46. | T. Bayer | AFC | s.t. |
| 47. | C. Brown | TQA | s.t. |
| 48. | G. Ciccone | TFS | s.t. |
| 49. | G. Izaguirre | APT | s.t. |
| 50. | A. Yates | IGD | s.t. |
| 51. | R. Carapaz | IGD | s.t. |
| 52. | J. Amezqueta | CJR | s.t. |
| 53. | B. Van Lerberghe | DQT | s.t. |
| 54. | L. A. Maté | EUS | s.t. |
| 55. | G. Mäder | TBV | s.t. |
| 56. | M. Cort | EFN | s.t. |
| 57. | A. Kirsch | TFS | s.t. |
| 58. | L. Hamilton | BEX | s.t. |
| 59. | L. Meintjes | IWG | s.t. |
| 60. | E. Mas | MOV | s.t. |
| 61. | D. de la Cruz | UAD | s.t. |
| 62. | F. Aru | TQA | s.t. |
| 63. | R. Sinkeldam | GFC | s.t. |
| 64. | Y. Natarov | APT | s.t. |
| 65. | J. Haig | TBV | s.t. |
| 66. | M. Schachmann | BOH | s.t. |
| 67. | M. Padun | TBV | s.t. |
| 68. | R. Gesink | TJV | s.t. |
| 69. | N. Oliveira | MOV | s.t. |
| 70. | A. Okamika | BBH | s.t. |
| 71. | N. Schultz | BEX | s.t. |
| 72. | H. Carthy | EFN | s.t. |
| 73. | O. C. Eiking | IWG | s.t. |
| 74. | M. A. López | MOV | s.t. |
| 75. | J. Keukeleire | EFN | s.t. |
| 76. | G. Niv | ISN | s.t. |
| 77. | J. Knox | DQT | s.t. |
| 78. | Ó. Cabedo | BBH | s.t. |
| 79. | W. Poels | TBV | s.t. |
| 80. | D. Navarro | BBH | s.t. |
| 81. | M. Vansevenant | DQT | s.t. |
| 82. | R. Majka | UAD | s.t. |
| 83. | G. Brambilla | TFS | s.t. |
| 84. | M. Iturria | EUS | s.t. |
| 85. | J. Lastra | CJR | s.t. |
| 86. | J. Cepeda Hernández | CJR | s.t. |
| 87. | S. Carr | EFN | s.t. |
| 88. | M. Bizkarra | EUS | s.t. |
| 89. | A. Roux | GFC | s.t. |
| 90. | A. Cuadros Morata | CJR | s.t. |
| 91. | J. Piccoli | ISN | s.t. |
| 92. | P. Sánchez | BBH | s.t. |
| 93. | J. P. López | TFS | s.t. |
| 94. | A. Palzer | BOH | s.t. |
| 95. | D. A. Camargo | EFN | s.t. |
| 96. | Jo. Herrada | COF | s.t. |
| 97. | A. Nibali | TFS | s.t. |
| 98. | R. Gibbons | UAD | 0:20 |
| 99. | S. Berwick | ISN | 0:36 |
| 100. | C. Benedetti | BOH | s.t. |
| 101. | P. Sivakov | IGD | s.t. |
| 102. | P. Gamper | BOH | s.t. |
| 103. | S. Puccio | IGD | s.t. |
| 104. | A. Bagioli | DQT | s.t. |
| 105. | Z. Štybar | DQT | s.t. |
| 106. | E. Planckaert | AFC | 0:44 |
| 107. | W. Kreder | IWG | 0:48 |
| 108. | T. Ludvigsson | GFC | 0:54 |
| 109. | O. Le Gac | GFC | s.t. |
| 110. | D. Howson | BEX | 1:02 |
| 111. | F. De Tier | AFC | 1:08 |
| 112. | J. Černý | DQT | 1:14 |
| 113. | G. Bouchard | ACT | 1:25 |
| 114. | L. Craddock | EFN | s.t. |
| 115. | Á. Madrazo | BBH | 1:27 |
| 116. | T. Pidcock | IGD | 1:30 |
| 117. | J. Narváez | IGD | s.t. |
| 118. | C. Verona | MOV | 1:32 |
| 119. | J. K. Caicedo | EFN | 1:39 |
| 120. | Je. Herrada | COF | 1:40 |
| 121. | S. Thwaites | AFC | 1:51 |
| 122. | S. Dewulf | ACT | 2:08 |
| 123. | G. Martin | COF | s.t. |
| 124. | Y. Arashiro | TBV | s.t. |
| 125. | R. Taaramäe | IWG | 2:21 |
| 126. | J. Hirt | IWG | s.t. |
| 127. | S. Petilli | IWG | s.t. |
| 128. | D. Sunderland | TQA | s.t. |
| 129. | S. Armée | TQA | s.t. |
| 130. | M. Holmes | LTS | s.t. |
| 131. | R. Rochas | COF | s.t. |
| 132. | E. Finé | COF | s.t. |
| 133. | J. Dombrowski | UAD | s.t. |
| 134. | D. Rubio | BBH | s.t. |
| 135. | J. Jacobs | MOV | s.t. |
| 136. | F. Barceló | COF | s.t. |
| 137. | S. Moniquet | LTS | s.t. |
| 138. | J. Bou | EUS | 2:26 |
| 139. | N. Prodhomme | ACT | 2:30 |
| 140. | C. Venturini | ACT | 2:43 |
| 141. | T. Scully | EFN | 3:43 |
| 142. | M. Cherel | ACT | s.t. |
| 143. | F. Sénéchal | DQT | 4:33 |
| 144. | J. Bol | BBH | s.t. |
| 145. | S. R. Martín | CJR | s.t. |
| 146. | J. Tratnik | TBV | s.t. |
| 147. | J. J. Rojas | MOV | s.t. |
| 148. | F. Vermeersch | LTS | s.t. |
| 149. | A. Kron | LTS | s.t. |
| 150. | L. Hofstede | TJV | s.t. |
| 151. | K. Bouwman | TJV | s.t. |
| 152. | S. Kruijswijk | TJV | s.t. |
| 153. | X. M. Azparren | EUS | s.t. |
| 154. | T. Arensman | DSM | 7:00 |
| 155. | C. Haga | DSM | s.t. |
| 156. | M. Tusveld | DSM | s.t. |
| 157. | Q. Simmons | TFS | 7:18 |
| 158. | K. Reijnen | TFS | s.t. |
| 159. | M. Trentin | UAD | 8:30 |
| 160. | J. Vine | AFC | s.t. |
| 161. | O. Rodríguez | APT | s.t. |
| 162. | O. Fraile | APT | s.t. |
| 163. | I. Izaguirre | APT | s.t. |
| 164. | A. Aranburu | APT | s.t. |
| 165. | D. Cimolai | ISN | s.t. |
| 166. | S. Henao | TQA | s.t. |
| 167. | I. Einhorn | ISN | s.t. |
| 168. | O. Lazkano | CJR | s.t. |
| 169. | C. Canal | BBH | s.t. |
| 170. | E. Morin | COF | s.t. |
| 171. | D. Claeys | TQA | s.t. |
| 172. | B. J. Lindeman | TQA | s.t. |
| 173. | M. Storer | DSM | s.t. |
| 174. | H. Vanhoucke | LTS | s.t. |
| 175. | K. van Melsen | IWG | s.t. |
| 176. | K. Geniets | GFC | 9:07 |
| 177. | M. Würst Schmidt | ISN | 11:11 |
| 178. | S. Vanmarcke | ISN | 11:12 |
| 179. | C. Hamilton | DSM | 12:32 |
| 180. | R. Bardet | DSM | s.t. |
| 181. | B. Zwiehoff | BOH | s.t. |
| 182. | M. Nieve | BEX | s.t. |

## TRIVIA

» Before this year Philipsen had never won two stages at the same race; now he's done it twice (after his double at the Tour of Turkey).

AUGUST   WORLDTOUR MEN'S RACE

# LA VUELTA A ESPAÑA
Stage 6
19 August 2021
Requena–Alto de la Montaña de Cullera
158.3km

A five-man group including Ryan Gibbons, Jetse Bol and Magnus Cort finally freed themselves from the clutches of the peloton after 50km of racing. Their gap expanded but was down to 3 minutes with 50km remaining at the intermediate sprint. 20km later, Ineos hit the front and split the peloton as a crosswind blew in from the coast, a 30-man group including Movistar and Jumbo-Visma heading away from the main bunch. Adam Yates was caught behind the front group containing teammates Egan Bernal and Richard Carapaz but made his way back up soon enough, while the peloton featuring the red jersey of Kenny Elissonde took a bit longer, though all was back together under the 25km banner. But when the race was exposed once more to the wind, Movistar put the hammer down. Carthy was caught out, almost getting back before Deceuninck-QuickStep hit the front, meaning the Brit and his EF support squad only returned to the bunch with less than 10km to go. The breakaway was still out front, but only just: 50 seconds with 5km left; at the foot of the finishing climb, 1.9km from the line, it was only 20. Ineos were hot in pursuit, dropping Elissonde as the members of the breakaway made their bids for glory. Cort went 500 metres into the climb, taking Bert-Jan Lindeman with him before dispensing with the Qhubeka man as the pace of the favourites behind slowed momentarily. Michael Matthews sensed it was now or never as Cort still hung on out front, and so the Australian kicked things off properly. Vlasov was straight onto his wheel, with Roglič following, and it looked as if the Slovenian was going to complete the steal, but Cort is no slouch and his sprint was just enough to hold off the Jumbo-Visma man he could see coming with 150 metres still to go. The red jersey was Roglič's consolation prize.

## WEATHER

TEMPERATURE  
30°C

WIND  
SE 15km/h

## PROFILE

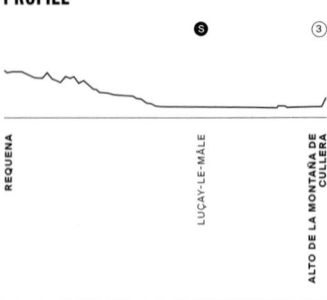

## BREAKAWAY
J. Bou (EUS), R. Gibbons (UAD), J. Bol (BBH), M. Cort (EFN), B. J. Lindeman (TQA)

## GENERAL CLASSIFICATION

| POS | NAME | TEAM | TIME |
|---|---|---|---|
| 1. ↑1 | P. Roglič | TJV | 21:04:49 |
| 2. ↑2 | E. Mas | MOV | 0:25 |
| 3. ↑2 | M. A. López | MOV | 0:36 |
| 4. ↑2 | A. Valverde | MOV | 0:41 |
| 5. ↑3 | E. Bernal | IGD | s.t. |
| 6. ↑5 | A. Vlasov | APT | 0:53 |
| 7. — | G. Ciccone | TFS | 0:58 |
| 8. ↓5 | L. Calmejane | ACT | 1:04 |
| 9. — | M. Landa | TBV | 1:12 |
| 10. ↑2 | F. Aru | TQA | 1:17 |

## KING OF THE MOUNTAINS

| POS | NAME | TEAM | PTS |
|---|---|---|---|
| 1. — | R. Taaramäe | IWG | 10 |
| 2. — | K. Elissonde | TFS | 7 |
| 3. — | J. Dombrowski | UAD | 6 |

## POINTS

| POS | NAME | TEAM | PTS |
|---|---|---|---|
| 1. — | J. Philipsen | AFC | 131 |
| 2. — | F. Jakobsen | DQT | 130 |
| 3. ↑15 | M. Cort | EFN | 67 |

## YOUNG RIDER

| POS | NAME | TEAM | TIME |
|---|---|---|---|
| 1. — | E. Bernal | IGD | 21:05:30 |
| 2. ↑1 | A. Vlasov | APT | 0:12 |
| 3. ↑1 | J. P. López | TFS | 1:24 |

## TRIVIA
» This notched up Cort's fourth Vuelta stage win of his career.

## BONUSES

| TYPE | NAME | TEAM |
|---|---|---|
| KOM 1 | M. Cort | EFN |
| Sprint 1 | J. Bol | BBH |

## STAGE RESULTS

| POS | NAME | TEAM | TIME |
|---|---|---|---|
| 1. | M. Cort | EFN | 3:30:53 |
| 2. | P. Roglič | TJV | s.t. |
| 3. | A. Bagioli | DQT | 0:02 |
| 4. | A. Vlasov | APT | 0:04 |
| 5. | E. Mas | MOV | s.t. |
| 6. | M. Matthews | BEX | 0:06 |
| 7. | E. Bernal | IGD | 0:08 |
| 8. | A. Valverde | MOV | s.t. |
| 9. | M. A. López | MOV | 0:09 |
| 10. | F. Großschartner | BOH | 0:16 |
| 11. | D. de la Cruz | UAD | 0:21 |
| 12. | G. Ciccone | TFS | 0:25 |
| 13. | A. Yates | IGD | s.t. |
| 14. | J. Polanc | UAD | 0:27 |
| 15. | A. Aranburu | APT | s.t. |
| 16. | F. Aru | TQA | s.t. |
| 17. | A. Kron | LTS | s.t. |
| 18. | L. Meintjes | IWG | s.t. |
| 19. | M. Landa | TBV | s.t. |
| 20. | R. Carapaz | IGD | s.t. |
| 21. | C. Champoussin | ACT | s.t. |
| 22. | R. Molard | GFC | s.t. |
| 23. | J. P. López | TFS | 0:33 |
| 24. | M. Storer | DSM | 0:34 |
| 25. | J. Haig | TBV | s.t. |
| 26. | A. Soto | EUS | s.t. |
| 27. | J. Cepeda Hernández | CJR | 0:40 |
| 28. | G. Bouchard | ACT | 0:47 |
| 29. | S. R. Martin | CJR | s.t. |
| 30. | L. Hamilton | BEX | 0:50 |
| 31. | M. Van Gils | LTS | s.t. |
| 32. | G. Martin | COF | s.t. |
| 33. | S. Henao | TQA | s.t. |
| 34. | N. Prodhomme | ACT | 0:53 |
| 35. | T. Bayer | AFC | s.t. |
| 36. | L. Calmejane | ACT | s.t. |
| 37. | L. L. Sanchez | APT | s.t. |
| 38. | M. Padun | TBV | 0:59 |
| 39. | S. Kuss | TJV | 1:00 |
| 40. | J. Bol | BBH | 1:03 |
| 41. | J. K. Caicedo | EFN | 1:09 |
| 42. | M. Vansevenant | DQT | 1:11 |
| 43. | O. C. Eiking | IWG | 1:13 |
| 44. | C. Canal | BBH | 1:14 |
| 45. | S. Kruijswijk | TJV | s.t. |
| 46. | S. Carr | EFN | 1:18 |
| 47. | G. Martín | EUS | 1:21 |
| 48. | W. Poels | TBV | 1:27 |
| 49. | G. Mäder | TBV | s.t. |
| 50. | R. Gibbons | UAD | 1:34 |
| 51. | Á. Madrazo | BBH | 1:47 |
| 52. | B. J. Lindeman | TQA | 1:58 |
| 53. | J. Lastra | CJR | s.t. |
| 54. | J. J. Rojas | MOV | 2:16 |
| 55. | J. Knox | DQT | 2:22 |
| 56. | J. Narváez | IGD | 2:36 |
| 57. | O. Le Gac | GFC | 2:39 |
| 58. | S. Vanmarcke | ISN | 2:50 |
| 59. | H. Carthy | EFN | s.t. |
| 60. | R. Rochas | COF | 2:59 |
| 61. | J. Bou | EUS | 3:12 |
| 62. | Z. Štybar | DQT | 3:30 |
| 63. | G. Izaguirre | APT | 3:52 |
| 64. | I. Izaguirre | APT | s.t. |
| 65. | D. van Baarle | IGD | 4:30 |
| 66. | C. Venturini | ACT | s.t. |
| 67. | K. Elissonde | TFS | s.t. |
| 68. | M. Tusveld | DSM | s.t. |
| 69. | J. Keukeleire | EFN | s.t. |
| 70. | L. Hofstede | TJV | 4:37 |
| 71. | N. Van Hooydonck | TJV | s.t. |
| 72. | S. Dewulf | ACT | s.t. |
| 73. | P. Gamper | BOH | s.t. |
| 74. | E. Planckaert | AFC | s.t. |
| 75. | Y. Arashiro | TBV | 4:59 |
| 76. | A. Bagües | CJR | 5:04 |
| 77. | J. J. Lobato | EUS | s.t. |
| 78. | F. De Tier | AFC | 5:12 |
| 79. | J. Philipsen | AFC | s.t. |
| 80. | L. Mezgec | BEX | s.t. |
| 81. | D. Caruso | TBV | s.t. |
| 82. | I. Erviti | MOV | s.t. |
| 83. | B. Van Lerberghe | DQT | 5:32 |
| 84. | F. Sénéchal | DQT | s.t. |
| 85. | D. Touzé | ACT | 5:36 |
| 86. | M. Cherel | ACT | s.t. |
| 87. | C. Verona | MOV | 5:51 |
| 88. | J. Aberasturi | CJR | 5:58 |
| 89. | D. Claeys | TQA | 6:03 |
| 90. | N. Oliveira | MOV | 6:25 |
| 91. | T. Pidcock | IGD | 6:27 |
| 92. | R. Janse Van Rensburg | TQA | 6:31 |
| 93. | A. Dainese | DSM | s.t. |
| 94. | A. Krieger | AFC | 6:37 |
| 95. | W. Kreder | IWG | 7:25 |

| POS | NAME | TEAM | TIME |
|---|---|---|---|
| 96. | J. Meeus | BOH | s.t. |
| 97. | A. Démare | GFC | 7:41 |
| 98. | R. Sinkeldam | GFC | 7:43 |
| 99. | J. Jacobs | MOV | s.t. |
| 100. | G. Brambilla | TFS | s.t. |
| 101. | R. Gesink | TJV | 7:59 |
| 102. | E. Finé | COF | s.t. |
| 103. | M. Schachmann | BOH | s.t. |
| 104. | N. Denz | DSM | 8:23 |
| 105. | J. Piccoli | ISN | 8:24 |
| 106. | C. Benedetti | BOH | s.t. |
| 107. | K. Geniets | GFC | s.t. |
| 108. | F. Vermeersch | LTS | 8:32 |
| 109. | P. Allegaert | COF | 8:36 |
| 110. | M. Trentin | UAD | s.t. |
| 111. | T. Scully | EFN | 8:43 |
| 112. | X. M. Azparren | EUS | 8:52 |
| 113. | I. Einhorn | ISN | 9:24 |
| 114. | S. Armée | TQA | 9:35 |
| 115. | L. A. Maté | EUS | s.t. |
| 116. | O. Fraile | APT | s.t. |
| 117. | F. Barceló | COF | s.t. |
| 118. | L. Craddock | EFN | s.t. |
| 119. | S. Thwaites | AFC | s.t. |
| 120. | O. Lazkano | CJR | s.t. |
| 121. | J. Amezqueta | CJR | s.t. |
| 122. | N. Schultz | BEX | s.t. |
| 123. | R. Stannard | BEX | s.t. |
| 124. | S. Petilli | IWG | s.t. |
| 125. | R. Minali | IWG | s.t. |
| 126. | O. Rodríguez | APT | s.t. |
| 127. | R. Majka | UAD | s.t. |
| 128. | C. Haga | DSM | s.t. |
| 129. | Ó. Cabedo | BBH | s.t. |
| 130. | G. Niv | ISN | s.t. |
| 131. | D. Rubio | BBH | s.t. |
| 132. | P. Sánchez | BBH | s.t. |
| 133. | D. A. Camargo | EFN | s.t. |
| 134. | R. Oliveira | UAD | s.t. |
| 135. | J. S. Molano | UAD | s.t. |
| 136. | Q. Simmons | TFS | s.t. |
| 137. | K. Reijnen | TFS | s.t. |
| 138. | E. Morin | COF | s.t. |
| 139. | J. Guarnieri | GFC | 9:51 |
| 140. | J. Vine | AFC | 9:53 |
| 141. | T. Ludvigsson | GFC | s.t. |
| 142. | M. Laas | BOH | 10:31 |
| 143. | M. Holmes | LTS | 12:53 |
| 144. | A. Roux | GFC | s.t. |
| 145. | B. Zwiehoff | BOH | s.t. |
| 146. | A. Palzer | BOH | s.t. |
| 147. | P. Sivakov | IGD | s.t. |
| 148. | Jo. Herrada | COF | s.t. |
| 149. | Je. Herrada | COF | s.t. |
| 150. | A. Cuadros Morata | CJR | s.t. |
| 151. | D. Navarro | BBH | s.t. |
| 152. | S. Moniquet | LTS | s.t. |
| 153. | Y. Natarov | APT | s.t. |
| 154. | A. Zeits | BEX | s.t. |
| 155. | S. Oomen | TJV | s.t. |
| 156. | S. Puccio | IGD | s.t. |
| 157. | C. Hamilton | DSM | s.t. |
| 158. | M. Bizkarra | EUS | s.t. |
| 159. | R. Taaramäe | IWG | s.t. |
| 160. | J. Dombrowski | UAD | s.t. |
| 161. | M. Iturria | EUS | s.t. |
| 162. | S. Cras | LTS | s.t. |
| 163. | S. Berwick | ISN | s.t. |
| 164. | K. van Melsen | IWG | s.t. |
| 165. | A. Okamika | BBH | s.t. |
| 166. | T. Arensman | DSM | 13:01 |
| 167. | R. Bardet | DSM | s.t. |
| 168. | D. Sunderland | TQA | s.t. |
| 169. | C. Brown | TQA | s.t. |
| 170. | J. Hirt | IWG | s.t. |
| 171. | H. Vanhoucke | LTS | s.t. |
| 172. | M. Nieve | BEX | s.t. |
| 173. | D. Howson | BEX | s.t. |
| 174. | K. Bouwman | TJV | 13:05 |
| 175. | J. Tratnik | TBV | s.t. |
| 176. | A. Nibali | TFS | s.t. |
| 177. | S. Modolo | AFC | 14:03 |
| 178. | D. Cimolai | ISN | 14:09 |
| 179. | J. Černý | DQT | 14:17 |
| 180. | F. Jakobsen | DQT | s.t. |
| 181. | A. Kirsch | TFS | 15:07 |
| 182. | M. Würst Schmidt | ISN | 20:43 |

AUGUST  WORLDTOUR MEN'S RACE

## LA VUELTA A ESPAÑA
Stage 7
20 August 2021
Gandía–Balcón de Alicante
152km

### WEATHER

TEMPERATURE  WIND
30°C  E 11km/h

### PROFILE

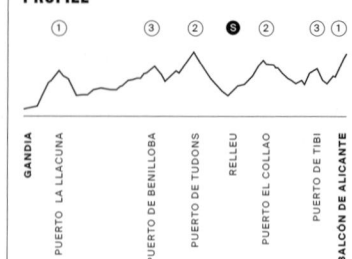

① ③ ② ⓢ ② ③ ①

GANDIA
PUERTO LA LLACUNA
PUERTO DE BENILLOBA
PUERTO DE TUDONS
RELLEU
PUERTO EL COLLAO
PUERTO DE TIBI
BALCÓN DE ALICANTE

The first proper mountain day of this year's Vuelta saw a huge group escape towards the summit of the Puerto la Llacuna, the foot of which arrived after just 7km of racing, with talents such as Sepp Kuss, Jack Haig, Ion Izaguirre and Pavel Sivakov involved. Jumbo-Visma controlled the gap at a manageable 3 minutes behind as Bardet sprinted uphill for KOM points after DSM had thinned out the breakaway, looking to first launch Hamilton and then Michael Storer. Back in the GC group, it was all action too as Movistar's José Joaquín Rojas and Alejandro Valverde attacked, taking Ineos's Yates and Carapaz with them as Jumbo-Visma assumed the chase. Disaster then struck for Valverde, as he slipped on a right-hand bend. The Spaniard valiantly tried to continue before climbing off in tears. His teammate López then combined with Carapaz to test Roglič momentarily, before it all calmed down over the summit of the Puerto El Collao, while up ahead on the descent Lawson Craddock drew out Sivakov and Storer, taking a minute's advantage onto the Puerto de Tibi. Sivakov dropped his chain and was distanced for a moment, before riding back up to Storer. Craddock was then dropped – not overly happy with the lack of empathy from the young rider – but rejoined by the time of the final Balcón de Alicante, though his effort counted for nothing as he fell away when the road went uphill once more and Lotto Soudal's Andreas Kron and Movistar's Carlos Verona bridged across to make it four up front. With 4km to the top, Verona hit out. Storer went with him before dropping the Spaniard and going off up the road alongside Sivakov, who wouldn't stop until the finish line – a breakthrough victory for the DSM rider. In the peloton, Adam Yates' acceleration was marked by Primož Roglič, who also had the likes of Egan Bernal and the Movistar duo of Mas and López for company. Vlasov shipped 13 seconds, while Ciccone, Landa and Carapaz all lost half a minute. Alongside Valverde's abandon, Hugh Carthy also called it a day after struggling through the last few stages.

### GENERAL CLASSIFICATION

| POS | NAME | TEAM | TIME |
|---|---|---|---|
| 1. — | P. Roglič | TJV | 25:18:35 |
| 2. ↑13 | F. Großschartner | BOH | 0:08 |
| 3. ↓1 | E. Mas | MOV | 0:25 |
| 4. ↓1 | M. A. López | MOV | 0:36 |
| 5. ↑7 | J. Polanc | UAD | 0:38 |
| 6. ↓1 | E. Bernal | IGD | 0:41 |
| 7. ↑19 | J. Haig | TBV | 0:57 |
| 8. ↑19 | S. Kuss | TJV | 0:59 |
| 9. ↓3 | A. Vlasov | APT | 1:06 |
| 10.↑1 | A. Yates | IGD | 1:22 |

### KING OF THE MOUNTAINS

| POS | NAME | TEAM | PTS |
|---|---|---|---|
| 1. — | P. Sivakov | IGD | 16 |
| 2. — | M. Storer | DSM | 12 |
| 3. — | J. Haig | TBV | 11 |

### POINTS

| POS | NAME | TEAM | PTS |
|---|---|---|---|
| 1. — | J. Philipsen | AFC | 131 |
| 2. — | F. Jakobsen | DQT | 130 |
| 3. — | M. Cort | EFN | 67 |

### YOUNG RIDER

| POS | NAME | TEAM | TIME |
|---|---|---|---|
| 1. — | E. Bernal | IGD | 25:19:16 |
| 2. — | A. Vlasov | APT | 0:25 |
| 3. ↑1 | G. Mäder | TBV | 2:11 |

### BONUSES

| TYPE | NAME | TEAM |
|---|---|---|
| KOM 1 | J. Haig | TBV |
| KOM 2 | R. Bardet | DSM |
| KOM 3 | J. Polanc | UAD |
| KOM 4 | R. Bardet | DSM |
| KOM 5 | P. Sivakov | IGD |
| KOM 6 | M. Storer | DSM |
| Sprint 1 | M. Trentin | UAD |

### TRIVIA

» After their four Grand Tour stage wins last season, this was DSM's first of 2021.

## STAGE RESULTS

| POS | NAME | TEAM | TIME |
|---|---|---|---|
| 1. | M. Storer | DSM | 4:10:13 |
| 2. | C. Verona | MOV | 0:21 |
| 3. | P. Sivakov | IGD | 0:59 |
| 4. | S. Kuss | TJV | 1:16 |
| 5. | J. Haig | TBV | 1:24 |
| 6. | R. Bardet | DSM | 1:32 |
| 7. | F. Großschartner | BOH | s.t. |
| 8. | A. Kron | LTS | 1:37 |
| 9. | S. Cras | LTS | 2:17 |
| 10. | J. Polanc | UAD | 2:29 |
| 11. | J. Vine | AFC | 2:49 |
| 12. | M. Tusveld | DSM | 2:53 |
| 13. | S. Petilli | IWG | s.t. |
| 14. | Je. Herrada | COF | 3:08 |
| 15. | A. Yates | IGD | 3:33 |
| 16. | P. Roglič | TJV | s.t. |
| 17. | E. Mas | MOV | s.t. |
| 18. | E. Bernal | IGD | s.t. |
| 19. | M. A. López | MOV | s.t. |
| 20. | D. de la Cruz | UAD | s.t. |
| 21. | L. Meintjes | IWG | s.t. |
| 22. | A. Vlasov | APT | 3:46 |
| 23. | G. Martin | COF | 4:03 |
| 24. | G. Ciccone | TFS | s.t. |
| 25. | F. Aru | TQA | s.t. |
| 26. | R. Carapaz | IGD | s.t. |
| 27. | M. Landa | TBV | s.t. |
| 28. | G. Mäder | TBV | 4:12 |
| 29. | D. Caruso | TBV | s.t. |
| 30. | O. C. Eiking | IWG | s.t. |
| 31. | R. Majka | UAD | s.t. |
| 32. | J. P. López | TFS | 4:31 |
| 33. | S. Kruijswijk | TJV | 4:59 |
| 34. | R. Rochas | COF | 5:03 |
| 35. | R. Molard | GFC | 5:45 |
| 36. | L. A. Maté | EUS | 6:13 |
| 37. | S. Dewulf | ACT | 6:24 |
| 38. | C. Champoussin | ACT | s.t. |
| 39. | Ó. Cabedo | BBH | 6:37 |
| 40. | S. Oomen | TJV | 7:17 |
| 41. | B. Zwiehoff | BOH | 8:42 |
| 42. | L. Craddock | EFN | s.t. |
| 43. | L. Calmejane | ACT | 8:53 |
| 44. | L. L. Sanchez | APT | 9:26 |
| 45. | I. Izagirre | APT | s.t. |
| 46. | J. Piccoli | ISN | s.t. |
| 47. | M. Bizkarra | EUS | s.t. |
| 48. | D. Navarro | BBH | s.t. |
| 49. | O. Lazkano | CJR | s.t. |
| 50. | F. De Tier | AFC | 9:58 |
| 51. | D. van Baarle | IGD | 10:31 |
| 52. | C. Hamilton | DSM | 11:18 |
| 53. | H. Vanhoucke | LTS | 11:20 |
| 54. | M. Nieve | BEX | s.t. |
| 55. | G. Brambilla | TFS | s.t. |
| 56. | M. Cherel | ACT | s.t. |
| 57. | S. Henao | TQA | 11:27 |
| 58. | D. A. Camargo | EFN | s.t. |
| 59. | N. Oliveira | MOV | 11:42 |
| 60. | J. Cepeda Hernández | CJR | 11:48 |
| 61. | J. Narváez | IGD | s.t. |
| 62. | S. Moniquet | LTS | 12:47 |
| 63. | J. Dombrowski | UAD | 13:39 |
| 64. | F. Barceló | COF | 14:20 |
| 65. | G. Izagirre | APT | 16:14 |
| 66. | R. Gesink | TJV | s.t. |
| 67. | A. Aranburu | APT | 17:59 |
| 68. | K. Elissonde | TFS | 18:07 |
| 69. | J. J. Rojas | MOV | 20:38 |
| 70. | A. Zeits | BEX | s.t. |
| 71. | J. Bol | BBH | s.t. |
| 72. | C. Haga | DSM | 22:20 |
| 73. | T. Arensman | DSM | s.t. |
| 74. | G. Bouchard | ACT | s.t. |
| 75. | N. Prodhomme | ACT | s.t. |
| 76. | J. Knox | DQT | 22:26 |
| 77. | M. Trentin | UAD | 24:13 |
| 78. | A. Bagioli | DQT | s.t. |
| 79. | M. Vansevenant | DQT | 24:22 |
| 80. | I. Erviti | MOV | 26:29 |
| 81. | Jo. Herrada | COF | s.t. |
| 82. | A. Démare | GFC | s.t. |
| 83. | A. Palzer | BOH | s.t. |
| 84. | A. Roux | GFC | s.t. |
| 85. | J. Keukeleire | EFN | s.t. |
| 86. | N. Schultz | BEX | s.t. |
| 87. | M. Van Gils | LTS | s.t. |
| 88. | S. R. Martín | CJR | s.t. |
| 89. | D. Rubio | BBH | s.t. |
| 90. | G. Martin | EUS | s.t. |
| 91. | C. Venturini | ACT | s.t. |
| 92. | D. Howson | BEX | s.t. |
| 93. | F. Sénéchal | DQT | s.t. |
| 94. | R. Gibbons | UAD | s.t. |
| 95. | E. Finé | COF | s.t. |
| 96. | P. Gamper | BOH | s.t. |
| 97. | S. Vanmarcke | ISN | s.t. |
| 98. | Y. Nataroy | APT | s.t. |
| 99. | S. Carr | EFN | s.t. |
| 100. | E. Planckaert | AFC | s.t. |
| 101. | S. Thwaites | AFC | s.t. |
| 102. | T. Bayer | AFC | s.t. |
| 103. | T. Pidcock | IGD | s.t. |
| 104. | S. Puccio | IGD | s.t. |
| 105. | M. Iturria | EUS | s.t. |
| 106. | J. K. Caicedo | EFN | s.t. |
| 107. | J. Tratnik | TBV | s.t. |
| 108. | W. Poels | TBV | s.t. |
| 109. | B. J. Lindeman | TQA | s.t. |
| 110. | J. Jacobs | MOV | s.t. |
| 111. | M. Padun | TBV | s.t. |
| 112. | M. Holmes | LTS | s.t. |
| 113. | N. Denz | DSM | s.t. |
| 114. | R. Oliveira | UAD | s.t. |
| 115. | F. Vermeersch | LTS | s.t. |
| 116. | L. Hamilton | BEX | s.t. |
| 117. | N. Van Hooydonck | TJV | s.t. |
| 118. | W. Kreder | IWG | s.t. |
| 119. | S. Arméе | TQA | s.t. |
| 120. | C. Benedetti | BOH | s.t. |
| 121. | M. Schachmann | BOH | s.t. |
| 122. | A. Bagües | CJR | s.t. |
| 123. | Á. Madrazo | BBH | s.t. |
| 124. | T. Scully | EFN | s.t. |
| 125. | C. Canal | BBH | s.t. |
| 126. | M. Cort | EFN | s.t. |
| 127. | A. Krieger | AFC | s.t. |
| 128. | Y. Arashiro | TBV | s.t. |
| 129. | K. Geniets | GFC | s.t. |
| 130. | O. Fraile | APT | s.t. |
| 131. | O. Le Gac | GFC | s.t. |
| 132. | G. Niv | ISN | s.t. |
| 133. | J. Bou | EUS | s.t. |
| 134. | A. Okamika | BBH | s.t. |
| 135. | A. Cuadros Morata | CJR | s.t. |
| 136. | T. Ludvigsson | GFC | 26:50 |
| 137. | R. Stannard | BEX | s.t. |
| 138. | M. Matthews | BEX | s.t. |
| 139. | A. Kirsch | TFS | s.t. |
| 140. | C. Brown | TQA | s.t. |
| 141. | J. Lastra | CJR | s.t. |
| 142. | J. Philipsen | AFC | s.t. |
| 143. | Q. Simmons | TFS | s.t. |
| 144. | D. Sunderland | TQA | s.t. |
| 145. | I. Einhorn | ISN | s.t. |
| 146. | K. Reijnen | TFS | s.t. |
| 147. | K. van Melsen | IWG | s.t. |
| 148. | R. Sinkeldam | GFC | s.t. |
| 149. | L. Mezgec | BEX | s.t. |
| 150. | L. Hofstede | TJV | s.t. |
| 151. | K. Bouwman | TJV | s.t. |
| 152. | S. Berwick | ISN | s.t. |
| 153. | D. Claeys | TQA | s.t. |
| 154. | J. Hirt | IWG | 26:57 |
| 155. | R. Taaramäe | IWG | 27:17 |
| 156. | A. Nibali | TFS | s.t. |
| 157. | P. Allegaert | COF | s.t. |
| 158. | D. Touzé | ACT | 27:28 |
| 159. | J. S. Molano | UAD | 28:08 |
| 160. | R. Minali | IWG | s.t. |
| 161. | J. Aberasturi | CJR | 28:12 |
| 162. | Z. Štybar | DQT | 28:28 |
| 163. | X. M. Azparren | EUS | 28:36 |
| 164. | P. Sánchez | BBH | 28:38 |
| 165. | J. J. Lobato | EUS | 28:44 |
| 166. | S. Modolo | AFC | 28:49 |
| 167. | A. Soto | EUS | 29:08 |
| 168. | J. Amezqueta | CJR | s.t. |
| 169. | D. Cimolai | ISN | 29:49 |
| 170. | J. Meeus | BOH | 29:57 |
| 171. | A. Dainese | DSM | s.t. |
| 172. | F. Jakobsen | DQT | 30:01 |
| 173. | B. Van Lerberghe | DQT | s.t. |
| 174. | J. Černý | DQT | s.t. |
| 175. | M. Laas | BOH | s.t. |
| 176. | J. Guarnieri | GFC | s.t. |

## BREAKAWAY

T. Arensman (DSM), C. Hamilton (DSM), M. Storer (DSM), G. Bouchard (ACT), D. Camargo (EFN), H. Vanhoucke (LTS), S. Kuss (TJV), P. Sivakov (IGD), J. Haig (TBV), J. Vine (AFC), K. Elissonde (TFS), J. Polanc (UAD), M. Trentin (UAD), R. Bardet (DSM), M. Tusveld (DSM), N. Oliveira (MOV), C. Verona (MOV), F. Großschartner (BOH), S. Dewulf (ACT), A. Aranburu (APT), G. Izagirre (APT), J. Lastra (CJR), F. Barcelo (COF), Jo. Herrada (COF), L. Craddock (EFN), S. Petilli (IWG), A. Kron (LTS), S. Cras (LTS), A. Zeits (BEX)

AUGUST  WORLDTOUR MEN'S RACE

## LA VUELTA A ESPAÑA
Stage 8
21 August 2021
Santa Pola–La Manga del Mar Menor
173.7km

Another pretty much pan-flat day without classified climbs as the peloton made its way along the Balearic coast to La Manga del Mar Menor. A stage such as this called for one thing and one thing only: a breakaway consisting of a rider from each of the Spanish wildcard outfits, with Ander Okamika representing Burgos-BH, Aritz Bagües of Caja Rural and Euskaltel-Euskadi's Mikel Iturria forming the likeliest of trios. They were only allowed a couple of minutes' leeway – the peloton deciding the breakaways had received their fair share over the past few stages – and after 100km Jasper Philipsen led Arnaud Démare over the intermediate sprint a minute and a half behind the escapees, who had taken the first three placings. It was mostly business as usual: the gap being brought down gradually, and GC teams joining the sprint squads at the front until the 3km banner meant the danger had passed, at which point BikeExchange and Bora-Hansgrohe joined Groupama-FDJ up there. Burgos-BH weren't done for the day just yet, however, Carlos Canal attacking and lasting for 500 metres off the front before being swallowed up as UAE Team Emirates accelerated. The run-in wasn't the cleanest, but Deceuninck-QuickStep's Florian Sénéchal managed to guide Fabio Jakobsen through just in time, pulling off and leaving the Dutchman a run through the middle. As Jakobsen went clear, Dainese and Philipsen followed in his slipstream, but neither was able to find the extra kick to get around, while the likes of Démare had been left in the wind after Sénéchal had pulled away.

### WEATHER
TEMPERATURE 28°C
WIND E 17km/h

### PROFILE

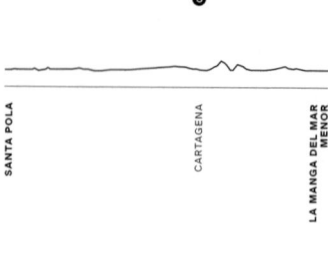

### BREAKAWAY
A. Okamika (BBH), A. Bagües (CJR), M. Iturria (EUS)

### GENERAL CLASSIFICATION

| POS | NAME | TEAM | TIME |
|---|---|---|---|
| 1. — | P. Roglič | TJV | 29:14:40 |
| 2. — | F. Großschartner | BOH | 0:08 |
| 3. — | E. Mas | MOV | 0:25 |
| 4. — | M. A. López | MOV | 0:36 |
| 5. — | J. Polanc | UAD | 0:38 |
| 6. — | E. Bernal | IGD | 0:41 |
| 7. — | J. Haig | TBV | 0:57 |
| 8. — | S. Kuss | TJV | 0:59 |
| 9. — | A. Vlasov | APT | 1:06 |
| 10.— | A. Yates | IGD | 1:22 |

### KING OF THE MOUNTAINS

| POS | NAME | TEAM | PTS |
|---|---|---|---|
| 1. — | P. Sivakov | IGD | 16 |
| 2. — | M. Storer | DSM | 12 |
| 3. — | J. Haig | TBV | 11 |

### POINTS

| POS | NAME | TEAM | PTS |
|---|---|---|---|
| 1. ↑1 | F. Jakobsen | DQT | 180 |
| 2. ↓1 | J. Philipsen | AFC | 164 |
| 3. ↑4 | A. Démare | GFC | 74 |

### YOUNG RIDER

| POS | NAME | TEAM | TIME |
|---|---|---|---|
| 1. — | E. Bernal | IGD | 29:15:21 |
| 2. — | A. Vlasov | APT | 0:25 |
| 3. — | G. Mäder | TBV | 2:11 |

### BONUSES

| TYPE | NAME | TEAM |
|---|---|---|
| Sprint 1 | A. Bagües | CJR |

## STAGE RESULTS

| POS | NAME | TEAM | TIME |
|---|---|---|---|
| 1. | F. Jakobsen | DQT | 3:56:05 |
| 2. | A. Dainese | DSM | s.t. |
| 3. | J. Philipsen | AFC | s.t. |
| 4. | J. Meeus | BOH | s.t. |
| 5. | I. Einhorn | ISN | s.t. |
| 6. | A. Démare | GFC | s.t. |
| 7. | M. Matthews | BEX | s.t. |
| 8. | M. Laas | BOH | s.t. |
| 9. | P. Allegaert | COF | s.t. |
| 10. | J. Aberasturi | CJR | s.t. |
| 11. | A. Soto | EUS | s.t. |
| 12. | R. Minali | IWG | s.t. |
| 13. | C. Venturini | ACT | s.t. |
| 14. | G. Martin | EUS | s.t. |
| 15. | D. Touzé | ACT | s.t. |
| 16. | J. J. Rojas | MOV | s.t. |
| 17. | C. Canal | BBH | s.t. |
| 18. | J. Jacobs | MOV | s.t. |
| 19. | F. Vermeersch | LTS | s.t. |
| 20. | R. Stannard | BEX | s.t. |
| 21. | A. Vlasov | APT | s.t. |
| 22. | J. J. Lobato | EUS | s.t. |
| 23. | J. Guarnieri | GFC | s.t. |
| 24. | J. Haig | TBV | s.t. |
| 25. | J. Tratnik | TBV | s.t. |
| 26. | F. Großschartner | BOH | s.t. |
| 27. | F. Sénéchal | DQT | s.t. |
| 28. | G. Mäder | TBV | s.t. |
| 29. | J. Polanc | UAD | s.t. |
| 30. | O. Lazkano | CJR | s.t. |
| 31. | L. L. Sanchez | APT | s.t. |
| 32. | F. Barceló | COF | s.t. |
| 33. | R. Rochas | COF | s.t. |
| 34. | C. Brown | TQA | s.t. |
| 35. | T. Bayer | AFC | s.t. |
| 36. | S. Cras | LTS | s.t. |
| 37. | K. Reijnen | TFS | s.t. |
| 38. | P. Roglič | TJV | s.t. |
| 39. | A. Zeits | BEX | s.t. |
| 40. | R. Molard | GFC | s.t. |
| 41. | S. Kuss | TJV | s.t. |
| 42. | A. Yates | IGD | s.t. |
| 43. | D. Claeys | TQA | s.t. |
| 44. | E. Mas | MOV | s.t. |
| 45. | G. Ciccone | TFS | s.t. |
| 46. | E. Bernal | IGD | s.t. |
| 47. | L. A. Maté | EUS | s.t. |
| 48. | G. Martin | COF | s.t. |
| 49. | R. Oliveira | UAD | s.t. |
| 50. | D. Rubio | BBH | s.t. |
| 51. | L. Calmejane | ACT | s.t. |
| 52. | L. Meintjes | IWG | s.t. |
| 53. | K. van Melsen | IWG | s.t. |
| 54. | L. Hofstede | TJV | s.t. |
| 55. | C. Benedetti | BOH | s.t. |
| 56. | S. Oomen | TJV | s.t. |
| 57. | R. Carapaz | IGD | s.t. |
| 58. | N. Van Hooydonck | TJV | s.t. |
| 59. | B. Van Lerberghe | DQT | s.t. |
| 60. | M. A. López | MOV | s.t. |
| 61. | N. Denz | DSM | s.t. |
| 62. | N. Oliveira | MOV | s.t. |
| 63. | D. de la Cruz | UAD | s.t. |
| 64. | F. Aru | TQA | s.t. |
| 65. | D. Sunderland | TQA | s.t. |
| 66. | S. Henao | TQA | s.t. |
| 67. | S. Armée | TQA | s.t. |
| 68. | M. Trentin | UAD | s.t. |
| 69. | M. Landa | TBV | s.t. |
| 70. | P. Gamper | BOH | s.t. |
| 71. | D. Caruso | TBV | s.t. |
| 72. | O. C. Eiking | IWG | s.t. |
| 73. | S. Petilli | IWG | s.t. |
| 74. | R. Taaramäe | IWG | s.t. |
| 75. | M. Schachmann | BOH | s.t. |
| 76. | Y. Arashiro | TBV | s.t. |
| 77. | J. Lastra | CJR | s.t. |
| 78. | C. Champoussin | ACT | s.t. |
| 79. | M. Cherel | ACT | s.t. |
| 80. | J. Bol | BBH | s.t. |
| 81. | J. P. López | TFS | s.t. |
| 82. | M. Van Gils | LTS | s.t. |
| 83. | S. Kruijswijk | TJV | s.t. |
| 84. | I. Erviti | MOV | s.t. |
| 85. | G. Izagirre | APT | s.t. |
| 86. | Y. Natarov | APT | s.t. |
| 87. | M. Padun | TBV | s.t. |
| 88. | Á. Madrazo | BBH | s.t. |
| 89. | P. Sánchez | BBH | s.t. |
| 90. | S. Dewulf | ACT | s.t. |
| 91. | Jo. Herrada | COF | s.t. |
| 92. | G. Brambilla | TFS | s.t. |
| 93. | R. Sinkeldam | GFC | s.t. |
| 94. | M. Tusveld | DSM | s.t. |
| 95. | O. Le Gac | GFC | s.t. |
| 96. | J. Cepeda Hernández | CJR | s.t. |
| 97. | R. Gibbons | UAD | s.t. |
| 98. | S. Modolo | AFC | s.t. |
| 99. | N. Prodhomme | ACT | s.t. |
| 100. | F. De Tier | AFC | s.t. |
| 101. | T. Arensman | DSM | s.t. |
| 102. | E. Finé | COF | s.t. |
| 103. | D. Navarro | BBH | s.t. |
| 104. | G. Niv | ISN | s.t. |
| 105. | G. Bouchard | ACT | s.t. |
| 106. | J. Amezqueta | CJR | s.t. |
| 107. | W. Kreder | IWG | s.t. |
| 108. | L. Mezgec | BEX | s.t. |
| 109. | A. Krieger | AFC | s.t. |
| 110. | A. Palzer | BOH | s.t. |
| 111. | B. Zwiehoff | BOH | s.t. |
| 112. | J. S. Molano | UAD | s.t. |
| 113. | R. Majka | UAD | 0:25 |
| 114. | W. Poels | TBV | s.t. |
| 115. | J. Keukeleire | EFN | 0:27 |
| 116. | N. Schultz | BEX | s.t. |
| 117. | A. Bagioli | DQT | 0:30 |
| 118. | J. Knox | DQT | s.t. |
| 119. | A. Okamika | BBH | s.t. |
| 120. | Ó. Cabedo | BBH | s.t. |
| 121. | B. J. Lindeman | TQA | s.t. |
| 122. | R. Gesink | TJV | s.t. |
| 123. | M. Nieve | BEX | s.t. |
| 124. | D. Howson | BEX | s.t. |
| 125. | M. Vansevenant | DQT | s.t. |
| 126. | J. Hirt | IWG | s.t. |
| 127. | J. Dombrowski | UAD | s.t. |
| 128. | O. Fraile | APT | s.t. |
| 129. | S. R. Martin | CJR | s.t. |
| 130. | I. Izagirre | APT | s.t. |
| 131. | K. Elissonde | TFS | s.t. |
| 132. | A. Kirsch | TFS | s.t. |
| 133. | J. Vine | AFC | s.t. |
| 134. | J. K. Caicedo | EFN | s.t. |
| 135. | S. Vanmarcke | ISN | 0:39 |
| 136. | E. Planckaert | AFC | s.t. |
| 137. | T. Pidcock | IGD | 1:09 |
| 138. | Z. Štybar | DQT | 1:21 |
| 139. | A. Roux | GFC | 1:24 |
| 140. | X. M. Azparren | EUS | 1:41 |
| 141. | K. Geniets | GFC | s.t. |
| 142. | J. Narváez | IGD | 2:45 |
| 143. | M. Cort | EFN | 2:56 |
| 144. | A. Kron | LTS | s.t. |
| 145. | M. Holmes | LTS | s.t. |
| 146. | H. Vanhoucke | LTS | s.t. |
| 147. | S. Moniquet | LTS | s.t. |
| 148. | S. Puccio | IGD | s.t. |
| 149. | M. Bizkarra | EUS | s.t. |
| 150. | A. Bagües | CJR | s.t. |
| 151. | M. Storer | DSM | s.t. |
| 152. | T. Scully | EFN | s.t. |
| 153. | Je. Herrada | COF | s.t. |
| 154. | C. Verona | MOV | s.t. |
| 155. | P. Sivakov | IGD | s.t. |
| 156. | S. Berwick | ISN | s.t. |
| 157. | J. Piccoli | ISN | s.t. |
| 158. | A. Nibali | TFS | s.t. |
| 159. | S. Thwaites | AFC | 3:03 |
| 160. | D. van Baarle | IGD | s.t. |
| 161. | Q. Simmons | TFS | 3:05 |
| 162. | J. Černý | DQT | 3:30 |
| 163. | J. Bou | EUS | s.t. |
| 164. | T. Ludvigsson | GFC | s.t. |
| 165. | L. Hamilton | BEX | 0:00 |
| 166. | A. Cuadros Morata | CJR | 3:43 |
| 167. | R. Bardet | DSM | 3:52 |
| 168. | L. Craddock | EFN | 4:11 |
| 169. | M. Iturria | EUS | 4:17 |
| 170. | A. Aranburu | APT | s.t. |
| 171. | D. A. Camargo | EFN | s.t. |
| 172. | K. Bouwman | TJV | 4:24 |
| 173. | C. Hamilton | DSM | 5:55 |
| 174. | C. Haga | DSM | s.t. |
| 175. | S. Carr | EFN | s.t. |

AUGUST   WORLDTOUR MEN'S RACE

# LA VUELTA A ESPAÑA
Stage 9
22 August 2021
Puerto-Lumbreras–Alto de Velefique
188km

An HC summit finish beckoned before the first rest day, providing the hardest stage of the race so far. For 100km no breakaway managed to forge clear but then a group containing Wout Poels and Romain Bardet escaped up the Alto de Cuatro Vientos, Rafał Majka soon leading a counter-attack as more joined from behind to swell their ranks to more than ten riders. Onto the Alto Collado Venta Luisa, and with 13km of the climb left and 70km until the finish line, Bahrain Victorious' Damiano Caruso set off, 2 minutes ahead of the likes of Bardet and Majka by the bottom of the climb. The Italian built his lead on the road up to the base of the Alto de Velefique, taking 3 and a half minutes onto the lower slopes, with the Jumbo-Visma-led peloton a further 2 minutes back and unconcerned by the hunt for glory up ahead. Behind Caruso, Geoffrey Bouchard and Majka pressed on as Bardet dropped his chain, while Sivakov helped shed even more riders from the GC group that only had 40 riders left at the start of the climb. Landa was struggling, Poels and Padun trying to pace him to safety, before Adam Yates hit out with 9km to go. López and Kuss were the first to follow before the Brit's second launch momentarily split the group again, and a third dragged Mas and Roglič clear. Behind, Bernal was unable to respond to the big moves being made. Yates soon paid for his efforts too: Mas and Roglič left him behind, and he joined Bernal, Haig and López in a chase group. Bernal's condition was poor enough that Yates had to ease up further so as not to drop his teammate while Roglič and Mas worked together to heap misery on their rivals. Up ahead and untroubled, Caruso sailed across the line to take another glorious victory in this most remarkable of seasons for the ageing Italian: wins in two Grand Tours and a runner-up spot at his home Giro. Roglič was second across the line a minute later, alongside Mas, with the others nearly 40 seconds adrift.

## TRIVIA

» Of the 15 Grand Tours Damiano Caruso has competed in during his career, he's finally won a stage at the two most recent he's lined up for.

## WEATHER

TEMPERATURE
33°C

WIND
E 16km/h

## PROFILE

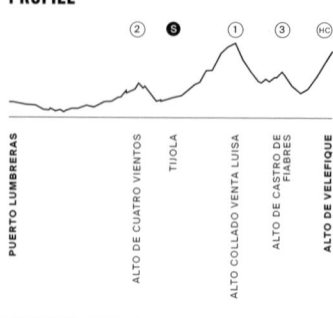

## BREAKAWAY

R. Stannard (BEX), R. Bardet (DSM), R. Majka (UAD), K. Elissonde (TFS), O. Le Gac (GFC), R. Molard (GFC), D. Caruso (TBV), L. Calmejane (ACT), A. Madrazo (BBH), J. Amezqueta (CJR), M. Tusveld (DSM)

## GENERAL CLASSIFICATION

| POS | NAME | TEAM | TIME |
| --- | --- | --- | --- |
| 1. – | P. Roglič | TJV | 34:18:53 |
| 2. ↑1 | E. Mas | MOV | 0:28 |
| 3. ↑1 | M. A. López | MOV | 1:21 |
| 4. ↑3 | J. Haig | TBV | 1:42 |
| 5. ↑1 | E. Bernal | IGD | 1:52 |
| 6. ↑4 | A. Yates | IGD | 2:07 |
| 7. ↑1 | G. Ciccone | TFS | 2:39 |
| 8. – | S. Kuss | TJV | 2:40 |
| 9. ↓7 | F. Großschartner | BOH | 3:25 |
| 10. ↑4 | D. de la Cruz | UAD | 3:55 |

## KING OF THE MOUNTAINS

| POS | NAME | TEAM | PTS |
| --- | --- | --- | --- |
| 1. – | D. Caruso | TBV | 28 |
| 2. ↑2 | R. Bardet | DSM | 22 |
| 3. ↓2 | P. Sivakov | IGD | 16 |

## POINTS

| POS | NAME | TEAM | PTS |
| --- | --- | --- | --- |
| 1. – | F. Jakobsen | DQT | 180 |
| 2. – | J. Philipsen | AFC | 164 |
| 3. – | A. Démare | GFC | 74 |

## YOUNG RIDER

| POS | NAME | TEAM | TIME |
| --- | --- | --- | --- |
| 1. – | E. Bernal | IGD | 34:20:45 |
| 2. – | A. Vlasov | APT | 2:03 |
| 3. – | G. Mäder | TBV | 2:08 |

## BONUSES

| TYPE | NAME | TEAM |
| --- | --- | --- |
| KOM 1 | W. Poels | TBV |
| KOM 2 | D. Caruso | TBV |
| KOM 3 | D. Caruso | TBV |
| KOM 4 | D. Caruso | TBV |
| Sprint 1 | L. Calmejane | ACT |

## STAGE RESULTS

| POS | NAME | TEAM | TIME |
|---|---|---|---|
| 1. | D. Caruso | TBV | 5:03:14 |
| 2. | P. Roglič | TJV | 1:05 |
| 3. | E. Mas | MOV | 1:06 |
| 4. | J. Haig | TBV | 1:44 |
| 5. | M. A. López | MOV | s.t. |
| 6. | A. Yates | IGD | s.t. |
| 7. | G. Mäder | TBV | 2:07 |
| 8. | G. Ciccone | TFS | 2:10 |
| 9. | E. Bernal | IGD | s.t. |
| 10. | D. de la Cruz | UAD | 2:40 |
| 11. | S. Kuss | TJV | s.t. |
| 12. | S. Kruijswijk | TJV | 2:43 |
| 13. | L. Meintjes | IWG | 2:45 |
| 14. | G. Bouchard | ACT | 3:39 |
| 15. | A. Vlasov | APT | 3:48 |
| 16. | F. Aru | TQA | s.t. |
| 17. | J. P. López | TFS | s.t. |
| 18. | C. Verona | MOV | s.t. |
| 19. | M. Nieve | BEX | 3:56 |
| 20. | F. Großschartner | BOH | 4:16 |
| 21. | O. C. Eiking | IWG | 5:04 |
| 22. | M. Padun | TBV | s.t. |
| 23. | M. Landa | TBV | s.t. |
| 24. | G. Martin | COF | s.t. |
| 25. | G. Brambilla | TFS | 6:20 |
| 26. | W. Poels | TBV | 7:56 |
| 27. | J. Polanc | UAD | 8:01 |
| 28. | R. Bardet | DSM | s.t. |
| 29. | R. Majka | UAD | s.t. |
| 30. | J. Piccoli | ISN | 8:32 |
| 31. | R. Carapaz | IGD | 9:08 |
| 32. | J. Bou | EUS | 10:31 |
| 33. | R. Rochas | COF | 10:51 |
| 34. | S. Cras | LTS | 11:07 |
| 35. | N. Schultz | BEX | 12:28 |
| 36. | J. Amezqueta | CJR | s.t. |
| 37. | R. Gibbons | UAD | 13:31 |
| 38. | A. Zeits | BEX | s.t. |
| 39. | M. Bizkarra | EUS | s.t. |
| 40. | S. Oomen | TJV | 14:32 |
| 41. | P. Sivakov | IGD | 14:37 |
| 42. | D. van Baarle | IGD | s.t. |
| 43. | I. Izagirre | APT | s.t. |
| 44. | G. Izagirre | APT | s.t. |
| 45. | S. Henao | TQA | s.t. |
| 46. | M. Tusveld | DSM | 16:49 |
| 47. | K. Bouwman | TJV | s.t. |
| 48. | K. Elissonde | TFS | 20:43 |
| 49. | D. Navarro | BBH | 21:04 |
| 50. | J. Lastra | CJR | s.t. |
| 51. | S. Petilli | IWG | 21:34 |
| 52. | A. Cuadros Morata | CJR | 22:35 |
| 53. | Jo. Herrada | COF | 22:49 |
| 54. | F. Barceló | COF | s.t. |
| 55. | G. Martín | EUS | s.t. |
| 56. | Ó. Cabedo | BBH | s.t. |
| 57. | J. Hirt | IWG | 22:53 |
| 58. | A. Roux | GFC | 23:17 |
| 59. | Y. Natarov | APT | s.t. |
| 60. | Je. Herrada | COF | s.t. |
| 61. | R. Gesink | TJV | s.t. |
| 62. | M. Cherel | ACT | s.t. |
| 63. | I. Erviti | MOV | s.t. |
| 64. | Á. Madrazo | BBH | s.t. |
| 65. | S. Armée | TQA | s.t. |
| 66. | L. Calmejane | ACT | 24:55 |
| 67. | J. J. Rojas | MOV | 26:02 |
| 68. | S. Puccio | IGD | 26:35 |
| 69. | R. Oliveira | UAD | s.t. |
| 70. | C. Hamilton | DSM | 27:07 |
| 71. | J. Tratnik | TBV | s.t. |
| 72. | L. L. Sanchez | APT | 27:46 |
| 73. | J. Narváez | IGD | s.t. |
| 74. | A. Nibali | TFS | s.t. |
| 75. | K. Geniets | GFC | 28:13 |
| 76. | N. Prodhomme | ACT | s.t. |
| 77. | O. Le Gac | GFC | s.t. |
| 78. | C. Canal | BBH | 28:36 |
| 79. | L. A. Maté | EUS | s.t. |
| 80. | X. M. Azparren | EUS | s.t. |
| 81. | E. Finé | COF | s.t. |
| 82. | R. Molard | GFC | s.t. |
| 83. | B. Zwiehoff | BOH | s.t. |
| 84. | P. Gamper | BOH | s.t. |
| 85. | L. Craddock | EFN | s.t. |
| 86. | J. Bol | BBH | s.t. |
| 87. | C. Benedetti | BOH | s.t. |
| 88. | M. Van Gils | LTS | s.t. |
| 89. | J. Knox | DQT | s.t. |
| 90. | J. Keukeleire | EFN | s.t. |
| 91. | M. Iturria | EUS | s.t. |
| 92. | L. Hamilton | BEX | s.t. |
| 93. | C. Champoussin | ACT | s.t. |
| 94. | M. Vansevenant | DQT | s.t. |
| 95. | J. K. Caicedo | EFN | s.t. |
| 96. | D. Howson | BEX | s.t. |
| 97. | G. Niv | ISN | s.t. |
| 98. | N. Oliveira | MOV | s.t. |
| 99. | M. Schachmann | BOH | s.t. |
| 100. | J. Dombrowski | UAD | s.t. |
| 101. | D. Touzé | ACT | 29:00 |
| 102. | S. Dewulf | ACT | s.t. |
| 103. | R. Stannard | BEX | 29:18 |
| 104. | T. Pidcock | IGD | 30:12 |
| 105. | M. Holmes | LTS | 31:45 |
| 106. | M. Cort | EFN | s.t. |
| 107. | H. Vanhoucke | LTS | s.t. |
| 108. | W. Kreder | IWG | s.t. |
| 109. | R. Taaramäe | IWG | s.t. |
| 110. | A. Kron | LTS | 31:52 |
| 111. | L. Hofstede | TJV | 32:52 |
| 112. | S. Soto | EUS | s.t. |
| 113. | O. Fraile | APT | s.t. |
| 114. | T. Bayer | AFC | 32:55 |
| 115. | S. Moniquet | LTS | s.t. |
| 116. | A. Okamika | BBH | s.t. |
| 117. | B. J. Lindeman | TQA | s.t. |
| 118. | S. Modolo | AFC | s.t. |
| 119. | J. Aberasturi | CJR | s.t. |
| 120. | A. Bagües | CJR | s.t. |
| 121. | D. Sunderland | TQA | s.t. |
| 122. | T. Ludvigsson | GFC | s.t. |
| 123. | A. Démare | GFC | s.t. |
| 124. | J. Cepeda Hernández | CJR | s.t. |
| 125. | S. Vanmarcke | ISN | s.t. |
| 126. | S. Berwick | ISN | s.t. |
| 127. | C. Brown | TQA | s.t. |
| 128. | C. Haga | DSM | s.t. |
| 129. | D. A. Camargo | EFN | s.t. |
| 130. | F. Vermeersch | LTS | s.t. |
| 131. | N. Denz | DSM | s.t. |
| 132. | D. Rubio | BBH | s.t. |
| 133. | P. Sánchez | BBH | s.t. |
| 134. | S. Thwaites | AFC | s.t. |
| 135. | M. Storer | DSM | s.t. |
| 136. | C. Venturini | ACT | s.t. |
| 137. | T. Arensman | DSM | s.t. |
| 138. | J. Vine | AFC | s.t. |
| 139. | P. Allegaert | COF | s.t. |
| 140. | E. Planckaert | AFC | s.t. |
| 141. | F. De Tier | AFC | s.t. |
| 142. | D. Claeys | TQA | s.t. |
| 143. | Y. Arashiro | TBV | s.t. |
| 144. | N. Van Hooydonck | TJV | 33:46 |
| 145. | J. Philipsen | AFC | s.t. |
| 146. | T. Scully | EFN | s.t. |
| 147. | Q. Simmons | TFS | s.t. |
| 148. | M. Matthews | BEX | 33:58 |
| 149. | A. Krieger | AFC | 34:38 |
| 150. | M. Trentin | UAD | 34:57 |
| 151. | A. Bagioli | DQT | 38:04 |
| 152. | B. Van Lerberghe | DQT | s.t. |
| 153. | F. Sénéchal | DQT | s.t. |
| 154. | Z. Štybar | DQT | s.t. |
| 155. | J. Meeus | BOH | s.t. |
| 156. | A. Kirsch | TFS | s.t. |
| 157. | K. van Melsen | IWG | s.t. |
| 158. | F. Jakobsen | DQT | s.t. |
| 159. | A. Dainese | DSM | s.t. |
| 160. | R. Minali | IWG | s.t. |
| 161. | R. Sinkeldam | GFC | s.t. |
| 162. | O. Lazkano | CJR | s.t. |
| 163. | A. Aranburu | APT | s.t. |
| 164. | S. Carr | EFN | s.t. |
| 165. | L. Mezgec | BEX | s.t. |
| 166. | J. J. Lobato | EUS | s.t. |
| 167. | A. Palzer | BOH | s.t. |
| 168. | J. Černý | DQT | s.t. |
| 169. | K. Reijnen | TFS | 40:31 |
| 170. | M. Laas | BOH | s.t. |
| 171. | I. Einhorn | ISN | s.t. |

AUGUST  WORLDTOUR MEN'S RACE

# LA VUELTA A ESPAÑA
Stage 10
24 August 2021
Roquetas de Mar–Rincón de la Victoria
189km

A day clearly designed for the breakaway, and 31 riders from a well-rested peloton forced their way into the day's escape, although it took 70km of racing to form. With most teams represented, there was no impetus from anyone, let alone Jumbo-Visma, to control the gap, as it zoomed out to more than 10 minutes, gifting Intermarché's Odd Christian Eiking and Cofidis' Guillaume Martin the virtual one-two in the GC. With 40km to go, as the break neared the category-2 Puerto de Almáchar (10.9km long at 4.9 per cent), Matteo Trentin and Aranburu attacked after the intermediate sprint, taking two more with them before they were brought back at the foot of the climb, Trentin's teammate Rui Oliveira hitting out and splintering the break. Kenny Elissonde was the first to catch and pass the young twin (Rui's brother and teammate Ivo was watching at home on the television), before Storer caught the Frenchman 3.5km from the summit, with Mauri Vansevenant and Clément Champoussin in pursuit. 12 minutes behind, Roglič attacked the GC group, going off alone as no one was able to stick with him. While López, Haig and Mas composed themselves for the chase, and Kuss shadowed their movements, Ineos's Bernal and Yates were assimilated into a larger peloton. Roglič was looking good to take more time on his rivals even if the red jersey was to have a new steward at the end of the day, but on the downhill run to the line he crashed – only down for a few seconds but enough for his chasers to make the catch – yet he still gained more than half a minute on Bernal and Yates. Storer, meanwhile, stayed upright and took a second stage win, while Eiking dropped Martin up the climb to make sure the red jersey would be his at the end of the day – a second for Intermarché this Vuelta.

## WEATHER

TEMPERATURE: 31°C
WIND: E 19km/h

## PROFILE

ROQUETAS DE MAR — TORRE DEL MAR — PUERTO DE ALMÁCHAR — RINCÓN DE LA VICTORIA

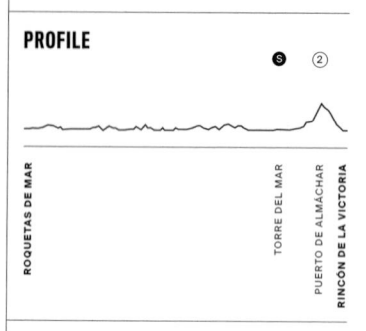

## BREAKAWAY

G. Bouchard (ACT), A. Aranburu (APT), L. L. Sánchez (APT), M. Schachmann (BOH), G. Martin (COF), Jo. Herrada (COF), A. Bagioli (DQT), M. Vansevenant (DQT), M. Cort (EFN), D. Van Baarle (IGD), J. Narváez (IGD), M. Storer (DSM), M. Trentin (UAD), L. Calmejane (ACT), C. Champoussin (ACT), F. De Tier (AFC), C. Benedetti (BOH), J. Lastra (CJR), J. Amezqueta (CJR), X. Azparren (EUS), L. Craddock (EFN), J. Keukeleire (EFN), O. Le Gac (GFC), O. C. Eiking (IWG), G. Vermeersch (AFC), D. Howson (BEX), N. Schultz (BEX), T. Arensman (DSM), M. Tusveld (DSM), R. Oliveira (UAD)

## GENERAL CLASSIFICATION

| POS | NAME | TEAM | TIME |
|---|---|---|---|
| 1. ↑18 | O. C. Eiking | IWG | 38:37:46 |
| 2. ↑18 | G. Martin | COF | 0:58 |
| 3. ↓2 | P. Roglič | TJV | 2:17 |
| 4. ↓2 | E. Mas | MOV | 2:45 |
| 5. ↓2 | M. A. López | MOV | 3:38 |
| 6. ↓2 | J. Haig | TBV | 3:59 |
| 7. ↓2 | E. Bernal | IGD | 4:46 |
| 8. – | S. Kuss | TJV | 4:57 |
| 9. ↓3 | A. Yates | IGD | 5:01 |
| 10. ↓1 | F. Großschartner | BOH | 5:42 |

## KING OF THE MOUNTAINS

| POS | NAME | TEAM | PTS |
|---|---|---|---|
| 1. – | D. Caruso | TBV | 28 |
| 2. – | R. Bardet | DSM | 22 |
| 3. ↑2 | M. Storer | DSM | 17 |

## POINTS

| POS | NAME | TEAM | PTS |
|---|---|---|---|
| 1. – | F. Jakobsen | DQT | 180 |
| 2. – | J. Philipsen | AFC | 164 |
| 3. – | A. Démare | GFC | 74 |

## YOUNG RIDER

| POS | NAME | TEAM | TIME |
|---|---|---|---|
| 1. – | E. Bernal | IGD | 38:42:32 |
| 2. – | A. Vlasov | APT | 1:26 |
| 3. – | G. Mäder | TBV | 2:08 |

## TRIVIA

» A month ago Storer didn't have a professional victory to his name; now he has four.

## BONUSES

| TYPE | NAME | TEAM |
|---|---|---|
| KOM 1 | M. Storer | DSM |
| Sprint 1 | M. Trentin | UAD |

## STAGE RESULTS

| POS | NAME | TEAM | TIME |
|---|---|---|---|
| 1. | M. Storer | DSM | 4:09:21 |
| 2. | M. Vansevenant | DQT | 0:22 |
| 3. | C. Champoussin | ACT | s.t. |
| 4. | D. van Baarle | IGD | s.t. |
| 5. | O. C. Eiking | IWG | s.t. |
| 6. | J. Narváez | IGD | 0:51 |
| 7. | N. Schultz | BEX | s.t. |
| 8. | G. Bouchard | ACT | s.t. |
| 9. | L. Calmejane | ACT | s.t. |
| 10. | K. Elissonde | TFS | s.t. |
| 11. | J. Amezqueta | CJR | s.t. |
| 12. | G. Martin | COF | s.t. |
| 13. | M. Trentin | UAD | 1:32 |
| 14. | F. De Tier | AFC | s.t. |
| 15. | O. Le Gac | GFC | 2:20 |
| 16. | J. Lastra | CJR | 3:00 |
| 17. | D. Howson | BEX | 3:02 |
| 18. | A. Bagioli | DQT | s.t. |
| 19. | Je. Herrada | COF | s.t. |
| 20. | R. Oliveira | UAD | 3:16 |
| 21. | M. Tusveld | DSM | 4:20 |
| 22. | T. Arensman | DSM | 4:54 |
| 23. | M. Schachmann | BOH | 5:17 |
| 24. | C. Benedetti | BOH | s.t. |
| 25. | L. L. Sanchez | APT | s.t. |
| 26. | A. Aranburu | APT | s.t. |
| 27. | M. Cort | EFN | 7:25 |
| 28. | X. M. Azparren | EUS | 8:36 |
| 29. | L. Craddock | EFN | s.t. |
| 30. | J. Keukeleire | EFN | s.t. |
| 31. | F. Vermeersch | LTS | 11:00 |
| 32. | A. Vlasov | APT | 11:49 |
| 33. | M. A. López | MOV | s.t. |
| 34. | S. Kuss | TJV | s.t. |
| 35. | J. Haig | TBV | s.t. |
| 36. | E. Mas | MOV | s.t. |
| 37. | P. Roglič | TJV | s.t. |
| 38. | F. Großschartner | BOH | s.t. |
| 39. | R. Majka | UAD | 12:26 |
| 40. | D. de la Cruz | UAD | s.t. |
| 41. | G. Mäder | TBV | s.t. |
| 42. | A. Yates | IGD | s.t. |
| 43. | E. Bernal | IGD | s.t. |
| 44. | W. Poels | TBV | s.t. |
| 45. | F. Aru | TQA | s.t. |
| 46. | L. Meintjes | IWG | s.t. |
| 47. | G. Ciccone | TFS | 13:03 |
| 48. | R. Rochas | COF | s.t. |
| 49. | M. Nieve | BEX | s.t. |
| 50. | A. Zeits | BEX | s.t. |
| 51. | J. Polanc | UAD | s.t. |
| 52. | S. Oomen | TJV | s.t. |
| 53. | S. Petilli | IWG | s.t. |
| 54. | S. Kruijswijk | TJV | s.t. |
| 55. | J. P. López | TFS | s.t. |
| 56. | B. Zwiehoff | BOH | s.t. |
| 57. | G. Izagirre | APT | s.t. |
| 58. | J. Cepeda Hernández | CJR | s.t. |
| 59. | Ó. Cabedo | BBH | 13:24 |
| 60. | G. Martín | EUS | 14:22 |
| 61. | M. Bizkarra | EUS | s.t. |
| 62. | C. Verona | MOV | s.t. |
| 63. | J. Bol | BBH | 15:58 |
| 64. | P. Sánchez | BBH | s.t. |
| 65. | L. A. Maté | EUS | s.t. |
| 66. | L. Hamilton | BEX | 17:40 |
| 67. | D. Caruso | TBV | 19:04 |
| 68. | R. Molard | GFC | s.t. |
| 69. | J. Hirt | IWG | s.t. |
| 70. | P. Sivakov | IGD | s.t. |
| 71. | J. Dombrowski | UAD | s.t. |
| 72. | S. Henao | TQA | s.t. |
| 73. | G. Brambilla | TFS | s.t. |
| 74. | R. Taaramäe | IWG | 19:08 |
| 75. | P. Gamper | BOH | 19:47 |
| 76. | D. A. Camargo | EFN | s.t. |
| 77. | Á. Madrazo | BBH | s.t. |
| 78. | K. Bouwman | TJV | s.t. |
| 79. | Jo. Herrada | COF | s.t. |
| 80. | I. Izaguirre | APT | 20:59 |
| 81. | A. Palzer | BOH | s.t. |
| 82. | M. Cherel | ACT | s.t. |
| 83. | J. J. Rojas | MOV | s.t. |
| 84. | R. Gibbons | UAD | s.t. |
| 85. | A. Okamika | BBH | s.t. |
| 86. | D. Touzé | ACT | s.t. |
| 87. | R. Carapaz | IGD | s.t. |
| 88. | A. Démare | GFC | 21:41 |
| 89. | J. Piccoli | ISN | s.t. |
| 90. | R. Sinkeldam | GFC | s.t. |
| 91. | C. Brown | TQA | s.t. |
| 92. | O. Lazkano | CJR | s.t. |
| 93. | A. Kirsch | TFS | s.t. |
| 94. | E. Finé | COF | s.t. |
| 95. | C. Hamilton | DSM | s.t. |
| 96. | R. Bardet | DSM | s.t. |
| 97. | D. Sunderland | TQA | s.t. |
| 98. | I. Erviti | MOV | s.t. |
| 99. | S. Armée | TQA | s.t. |
| 100. | C. Haga | DSM | s.t. |
| 101. | N. Oliveira | MOV | s.t. |
| 102. | Y. Arashiro | TBV | s.t. |
| 103. | M. Landa | TBV | s.t. |
| 104. | J. Tratnik | TBV | s.t. |
| 105. | T. Ludvigsson | GFC | s.t. |
| 106. | R. Stannard | BEX | s.t. |
| 107. | F. Barceló | COF | s.t. |
| 108. | Y. Natarov | APT | s.t. |
| 109. | A. Roux | GFC | s.t. |
| 110. | C. Venturini | ACT | s.t. |
| 111. | S. Puccio | IGD | s.t. |
| 112. | A. Nibali | TFS | s.t. |
| 113. | R. Gesink | TJV | s.t. |
| 114. | M. Matthews | BEX | s.t. |
| 115. | D. Rubio | BBH | s.t. |
| 116. | D. Navarro | BBH | s.t. |
| 117. | C. Canal | BBH | s.t. |
| 118. | S. Cras | LTS | s.t. |
| 119. | J. Knox | DQT | s.t. |
| 120. | N. Denz | DSM | s.t. |
| 121. | O. Fraile | APT | s.t. |
| 122. | M. Iturria | EUS | s.t. |
| 123. | W. Kreder | IWG | s.t. |
| 124. | K. van Melsen | IWG | s.t. |
| 125. | A. Cuadros Morata | CJR | s.t. |
| 126. | A. Bagües | CJR | s.t. |
| 127. | T. Scully | EFN | s.t. |
| 128. | M. Padun | TBV | s.t. |
| 129. | Q. Simmons | TFS | s.t. |
| 130. | K. Reijnen | TFS | s.t. |
| 131. | J. K. Caicedo | EFN | s.t. |
| 132. | J. Bou | EUS | 22:59 |
| 133. | J. J. Lobato | EUS | s.t. |
| 134. | L. Hofstede | TJV | s.t. |
| 135. | N. Van Hooydonck | TJV | s.t. |
| 136. | J. Meeus | BOH | s.t. |
| 137. | L. Mezgec | BEX | s.t. |
| 138. | J. Aberasturi | CJR | s.t. |
| 139. | S. Carr | EFN | 24:45 |
| 140. | R. Minali | IWG | 25:24 |
| 141. | B. J. Lindeman | TQA | 25:29 |
| 142. | D. Claeys | TQA | s.t. |
| 143. | G. Niv | ISN | s.t. |
| 144. | J. Černý | DQT | 25:31 |
| 145. | B. Van Lerberghe | DQT | s.t. |
| 146. | S. Moniquet | LTS | s.t. |
| 147. | F. Jakobsen | DQT | s.t. |
| 148. | F. Sénéchal | DQT | s.t. |
| 149. | Z. Štybar | DQT | s.t. |
| 150. | S. Dewulf | ACT | s.t. |
| 151. | S. Thwaites | AFC | s.t. |
| 152. | I. Einhorn | ISN | s.t. |
| 153. | M. Van Gils | LTS | s.t. |
| 154. | E. Planckaert | AFC | s.t. |
| 155. | M. Holmes | LTS | s.t. |
| 156. | T. Bayer | AFC | s.t. |
| 157. | J. Philipsen | AFC | s.t. |
| 158. | A. Dainese | DSM | s.t. |
| 159. | N. Prodhomme | ACT | s.t. |
| 160. | T. Pidcock | IGD | s.t. |
| 161. | A. Kron | LTS | s.t. |
| 162. | A. Krieger | AFC | s.t. |
| 163. | P. Allegaert | COF | s.t. |
| 164. | J. Vine | AFC | s.t. |
| 165. | S. Modolo | AFC | s.t. |
| 166. | K. Geniets | GFC | s.t. |
| 167. | S. Berwick | ISN | s.t. |
| 168. | S. Vanmarcke | ISN | s.t. |
| 169. | A. Soto | EUS | s.t. |
| 170. | M. Laas | BOH | s.t. |
| 171. | H. Vanhoucke | LTS | s.t. |

AUGUST    WORLDTOUR MEN'S RACE

# LA VUELTA A ESPAÑA
Stage 11
25 August 2021
Antequera–Valdepeñas de Jaén
133.6km

Two of week one's animators – Jasper Philipsen and Alex Aranburu – were missing from the start line today (the Belgian coming down with a fever, and the Spaniard finally succumbing to his ailments from a crash). BikeExchange were at the front, patrolling the attacks as they looked to protect the finish for Michael Matthews' chances, but eventually a five-man group containing Magnus Cort unclipped after 20km of racing. The undulating terrain and high speed from the peloton meant the escapees never took out a gap of more than 2 minutes, and when Movistar joined the chase with 30km remaining it came back under a minute. Onto the category-2 Puerto de Locubín and the break fell apart, Cort pushing on as the bunch loomed behind. David de la Cruz hit out 2km from the summit, Jumbo-Visma chasing him and whittling down the peloton to 30 riders, as Eiking tried to keep hold of his red jersey. Cort still held a gap of 20 seconds as he entered Valdepeñas de Jaén but, behind, Steven Kruijswijk and Sepp Kuss were readying Roglič, who led the peloton up the steeper gradient with Enric Mas. Cort was still ahead as Roglič and Mas bided their time but, with 300 metres to go, Roglič opened his sprint, dropped Mas and powered past the Dane, gaining seconds and a psychological victory over his rivals. Eiking hung on for tenth, 11 seconds down, to keep the race lead – at least for the time being.

## WEATHER

TEMPERATURE    WIND
28°C           SE 11km/h

## PROFILE

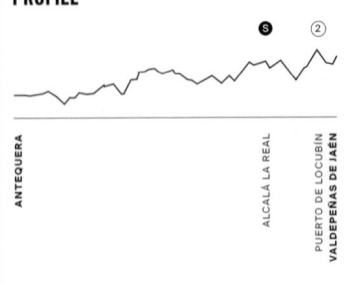

ANTEQUERA — ALCALÁ LA REAL — PUERTO DE LOCUBÍN — VALDEPEÑAS DE JAÉN

## BREAKAWAY
E. Planckaert (AFC), J. Lastra (CJR), M. Cort (EFN), J. Bou (EUS), H. Vanhoucke (LTS)

## GENERAL CLASSIFICATION

| POS | NAME | TEAM | TIME |
|---|---|---|---|
| 1. — | O. C. Eiking | IWG | 41:48:57 |
| 2. — | G. Martin | COF | 0:58 |
| 3. — | P. Roglič | TJV | 1:56 |
| 4. — | E. Mas | MOV | 2:31 |
| 5. — | M. A. López | MOV | 3:28 |
| 6. — | J. Haig | TBV | 3:55 |
| 7. — | E. Bernal | IGD | 4:46 |
| 8. ↑1 | A. Yates | IGD | 4:57 |
| 9. ↓1 | S. Kuss | TJV | 5:03 |
| 10. — | F. Großschartner | BOH | 5:38 |

## KING OF THE MOUNTAINS

| POS | NAME | TEAM | PTS |
|---|---|---|---|
| 1. — | D. Caruso | TBV | 31 |
| 2. — | R. Bardet | DSM | 22 |
| 3. — | M. Storer | DSM | 17 |

## POINTS

| POS | NAME | TEAM | PTS |
|---|---|---|---|
| 1. — | F. Jakobsen | DQT | 180 |
| 2. ↑3 | P. Roglič | TJV | 101 |
| 3. ↑4 | M. Cort | EFN | 84 |

## YOUNG RIDER

| POS | NAME | TEAM | TIME |
|---|---|---|---|
| 1. — | E. Bernal | IGD | 41:53:43 |
| 2. — | A. Vlasov | APT | 1:22 |
| 3. — | G. Mäder | TBV | 2:08 |

## TRIVIA
» Enric Mas has 17 top-ten finishes on Vuelta stages, yet only one stage win.

## BONUSES

| TYPE | NAME | TEAM |
|---|---|---|
| KOM 1 | M. Cort | EFN |
| Sprint 1 | E. Planckaert | AFC |

## STAGE RESULTS

| POS | NAME | TEAM | TIME |
|---|---|---|---|
| 1. | P. Roglič | TJV | 3:11:00 |
| 2. | E. Mas | MOV | 0:03 |
| 3. | M. A. López | MOV | 0:05 |
| 4. | J. Haig | TBV | 0:07 |
| 5. | A. Yates | IGD | s.t. |
| 6. | R. Bardet | DSM | s.t. |
| 7. | F. Großschartner | BOH | s.t. |
| 8. | A. Vlasov | APT | s.t. |
| 9. | E. Bernal | IGD | 0:11 |
| 10. | O. C. Eiking | IWG | s.t. |
| 11. | G. Martin | COF | s.t. |
| 12. | S. Henao | TQA | s.t. |
| 13. | G. Mäder | TBV | s.t. |
| 14. | A. Kron | LTS | 0:17 |
| 15. | S. Kuss | TJV | s.t. |
| 16. | I. Izagirre | APT | 0:20 |
| 17. | G. Ciccone | TFS | 0:23 |
| 18. | L. Meintjes | IWG | s.t. |
| 19. | T. Bayer | AFC | s.t. |
| 20. | J. P. López | TFS | s.t. |
| 21. | R. Rochas | COF | 0:29 |
| 22. | J. Cepeda Hernández | CJR | s.t. |
| 23. | M. Matthews | BEX | 0:34 |
| 24. | D. de la Cruz | UAD | 0:38 |
| 25. | M. Cort | EFN | 0:49 |
| 26. | L. L. Sanchez | APT | s.t. |
| 27. | G. Izagirre | APT | s.t. |
| 28. | S. Kruijswijk | TJV | s.t. |
| 29. | S. Cras | LTS | 1:09 |
| 30. | R. Majka | UAD | s.t. |
| 31. | M. Nieve | BEX | s.t. |
| 32. | C. Verona | MOV | 1:31 |
| 33. | S. Oomen | TJV | 1:59 |
| 34. | D. Caruso | TBV | 2:01 |
| 35. | J. Polanc | UAD | 2:09 |
| 36. | G. Bouchard | ACT | 2:17 |
| 37. | M. Van Gils | LTS | s.t. |
| 38. | N. Prodhomme | ACT | 2:22 |
| 39. | J. Hirt | IWG | 2:51 |
| 40. | D. van Baarle | IGD | s.t. |
| 41. | C. Hamilton | DSM | 2:56 |
| 42. | W. Poels | TBV | s.t. |
| 43. | G. Martin | EUS | 3:00 |
| 44. | D. Navarro | BBH | s.t. |
| 45. | M. Iturria | EUS | 3:03 |
| 46. | A. Zeits | BEX | s.t. |
| 47. | S. Petilli | IWG | s.t. |
| 48. | Ó. Cabedo | BBH | s.t. |
| 49. | J. Amezqueta | CJR | s.t. |
| 50. | L. Mezgec | BEX | 3:23 |
| 51. | G. Brambilla | TFS | 3:31 |
| 52. | K. Geniets | GFC | 3:38 |
| 53. | L. A. Maté | EUS | 6:01 |
| 54. | R. Taaramäe | IWG | s.t. |
| 55. | R. Molard | GFC | s.t. |
| 56. | J. J. Rojas | MOV | 6:09 |
| 57. | F. Sénéchal | DQT | 6:19 |
| 58. | Á. Madrazo | BBH | 6:30 |
| 59. | Y. Natarov | APT | 6:51 |
| 60. | J. Lastra | CJR | 7:07 |
| 61. | N. Schultz | BEX | 7:31 |
| 62. | L. Calmejane | ACT | 7:38 |
| 63. | M. Cherel | ACT | 7:48 |
| 64. | C. Canal | BBH | s.t. |
| 65. | R. Gibbons | UAD | s.t. |
| 66. | J. Keukeleire | EFN | s.t. |
| 67. | J. Dombrowski | UAD | 7:51 |
| 68. | C. Venturini | ACT | 7:53 |
| 69. | B. Zwiehoff | BOH | 8:05 |
| 70. | T. Pidcock | IGD | 8:09 |
| 71. | S. Moniquet | LTS | 8:14 |
| 72. | P. Sivakov | IGD | 9:06 |
| 73. | M. Holmes | LTS | s.t. |
| 74. | P. Sánchez | BBH | 9:08 |
| 75. | H. Vanhoucke | LTS | s.t. |
| 76. | P. Gamper | BOH | s.t. |
| 77. | A. Cuadros Morata | CJR | s.t. |
| 78. | A. Palzer | BOH | s.t. |
| 79. | M. Bizkarra | EUS | s.t. |
| 80. | D. Sunderland | TQA | s.t. |
| 81. | M. Tusveld | DSM | s.t. |
| 82. | Je. Herrada | COF | s.t. |
| 83. | A. Roux | GFC | s.t. |
| 84. | Jo. Herrada | COF | s.t. |
| 85. | I. Erviti | MOV | s.t. |
| 86. | J. K. Caicedo | EFN | 9:24 |
| 87. | J. Piccoli | ISN | s.t. |
| 88. | M. Landa | TBV | 9:25 |
| 89. | D. A. Camargo | EFN | s.t. |
| 90. | S. Dewulf | ACT | 9:27 |
| 91. | O. Le Gac | GFC | s.t. |
| 92. | W. Kreder | IWG | 9:31 |
| 93. | N. Oliveira | MOV | 9:35 |
| 94. | M. Storer | DSM | s.t. |
| 95. | R. Carapaz | IGD | 10:00 |
| 96. | E. Planckaert | AFC | 10:13 |
| 97. | L. Hamilton | BEX | 10:15 |
| 98. | K. Bouwman | TJV | 10:27 |
| 99. | J. Bou | EUS | 11:28 |
| 100. | A. Démare | GFC | 11:31 |
| 101. | R. Sinkeldam | GFC | s.t. |
| 102. | J. Bol | BBH | s.t. |
| 103. | S. Armée | TQA | s.t. |
| 104. | J. Tratnik | TBV | s.t. |
| 105. | M. Padun | TBV | s.t. |
| 106. | Y. Arashiro | TBV | s.t. |
| 107. | F. Aru | TQA | s.t. |
| 108. | C. Haga | DSM | 11:50 |
| 109. | A. Bagioli | DQT | 11:52 |
| 110. | A. Krieger | AFC | s.t. |
| 111. | J. Knox | DQT | s.t. |
| 112. | D. Touzé | ACT | 11:55 |
| 113. | T. Arensman | DSM | 13:27 |
| 114. | N. Denz | DSM | s.t. |
| 115. | M. Trentin | UAD | s.t. |
| 116. | S. Puccio | IGD | s.t. |
| 117. | S. Thwaites | AFC | s.t. |
| 118. | O. Lazkano | CJR | s.t. |
| 119. | D. Rubio | BBH | s.t. |
| 120. | A. Soto | EUS | s.t. |
| 121. | A. Okamika | BBH | s.t. |
| 122. | J. J. Lobato | EUS | s.t. |
| 123. | X. M. Azparren | EUS | s.t. |
| 124. | E. Finé | COF | s.t. |
| 125. | R. Oliveira | UAD | s.t. |
| 126. | F. Barceló | COF | s.t. |
| 127. | O. Fraile | APT | s.t. |
| 128. | T. Ludvigsson | GFC | s.t. |
| 129. | J. Narváez | IGD | s.t. |
| 130. | F. De Tier | AFC | s.t. |
| 131. | A. Bagüés | CJR | s.t. |
| 132. | G. Niv | ISN | s.t. |
| 133. | R. Gesink | TJV | s.t. |
| 134. | C. Benedetti | BOH | 13:38 |
| 135. | K. Elissonde | TFS | s.t. |
| 136. | A. Nibali | TFS | 13:40 |
| 137. | M. Vansevenant | DQT | 13:44 |
| 138. | S. Vanmarcke | ISN | s.t. |
| 139. | L. Craddock | EFN | s.t. |
| 140. | B. J. Lindeman | TQA | 13:49 |
| 141. | K. van Melsen | IWG | s.t. |
| 142. | R. Stannard | BEX | s.t. |
| 143. | D. Claeys | TQA | s.t. |
| 144. | B. Van Lerberghe | DQT | s.t. |
| 145. | F. Jakobsen | DQT | s.t. |
| 146. | P. Allegaert | COF | s.t. |
| 147. | F. Vermeersch | LTS | s.t. |
| 148. | A. Dainese | DSM | s.t. |
| 149. | S. Berwick | ISN | s.t. |
| 150. | Z. Štybar | DQT | s.t. |
| 151. | R. Minali | IWG | s.t. |
| 152. | J. Meeus | BOH | s.t. |
| 153. | N. Van Hooydonck | TJV | 13:56 |
| 154. | J. Aberasturi | CJR | s.t. |
| 155. | L. Hofstede | TJV | s.t. |
| 156. | J. Černý | DQT | s.t. |
| 157. | D. Howson | BEX | s.t. |
| 158. | M. Schachmann | BOH | s.t. |
| 159. | T. Scully | EFN | s.t. |
| 160. | I. Einhorn | ISN | s.t. |
| 161. | Q. Simmons | TFS | s.t. |
| 162. | K. Reijnen | TFS | 14:00 |
| 163. | C. Brown | TQA | s.t. |
| 164. | C. Champoussin | ACT | 14:03 |
| 165. | S. Modolo | AFC | s.t. |
| 166. | J. Vine | AFC | 14:05 |
| 167. | A. Kirsch | TFS | 14:07 |
| 168. | M. Laas | BOH | 14:09 |

AUGUST    WORLDTOUR MEN'S RACE

# LA VUELTA A ESPAÑA
Stage 12
26 August 2021
Jaén–Córdoba
175km

A downhill start out of Jaén saw the peloton still intact after nearly 100km of racing, although that didn't stop some riders trying as the days and breakaway opportunities were already ticking down. But then three riders went clear before being joined by five more. Jetse Bol and Chad Haga were involved, but UAE Team Emirates were watching closely and kept them on a tight leash. Stan Dewulf took the intermediate sprint before the category-3 Alto de San Jerónimo, at which point DSM called Haga back from the break, sensing its futility, while in the peloton a crash brought down Primož Roglič and Adam Yates as well as domestiques from both Ineos and Jumbo-Visma. UAE Team Emirates loaded the pressure as they chased back on, the Slovenian rejoining before the summit and Yates getting back in on the descent. The break's advantage was only 30 seconds at the foot of the Alto del 14%, and soon it was only Maxim Van Gils left out front; when Jonathan Lastra attacked from the peloton, Van Gils' day out was over. As Lastra was pegged back, Giulio Ciccone and Jay Vine took off, followed by Romain Bardet and Sergio Henao. Bardet led over the top as Trentin briefly hit out alongside Ion Izaguirre, testing the waters. This quartet out front were collaborating well, however, and they eked out their gap of half a minute with 7km until just before the *flamme rouge*. BikeExchange and UAE Team Emirates were forced into a frantic chase, and even then Jay Vine was finally brought back in with just 800 metres until the line. After Luka Mezgec had made the catch for Matthews, Jens Keukeleire surged through with Magnus Cort on his wheel. Andrea Bagioli tucked in behind but was unable to pull the Dane back, as Cort was left to take his second stage win this Vuelta.

## TRIVIA
» Magnus Cort becomes the fifth rider in just 12 stages to win two stages at this year's Vuelta.

## WEATHER

TEMPERATURE    WIND
31°C           NE 7km/h

## PROFILE

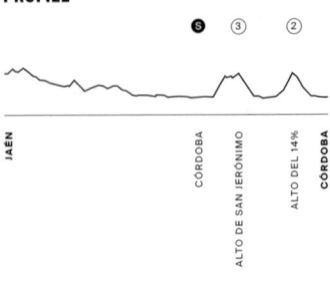

## BREAKAWAY
M. Iturria (EUS), S. Berwick (ISN), S. Armee (TQA), S. Dewulf (ACT), J. Bol (BBH), J. Amezqueta (CJR), M. Van Gils (LTS), C. Haga (DSM)

## GENERAL CLASSIFICATION

| POS | NAME | TEAM | TIME |
|---|---|---|---|
| 1. – | O. C. Eiking | IWG | 45:33:18 |
| 2. – | G. Martin | COF | 0:58 |
| 3. – | P. Roglič | TJV | 1:56 |
| 4. – | E. Mas | MOV | 2:31 |
| 5. – | M. A. López | MOV | 3:28 |
| 6. – | J. Haig | TBV | 3:55 |
| 7. – | E. Bernal | IGD | 4:46 |
| 8. – | A. Yates | IGD | 4:57 |
| 9. – | S. Kuss | TJV | 5:03 |
| 10.– | F. Großschartner | BOH | 5:38 |

## KING OF THE MOUNTAINS

| POS | NAME | TEAM | PTS |
|---|---|---|---|
| 1. – | D. Caruso | TBV | 31 |
| 2. – | R. Bardet | DSM | 27 |
| 3. – | M. Storer | DSM | 17 |

## POINTS

| POS | NAME | TEAM | PTS |
|---|---|---|---|
| 1. – | F. Jakobsen | DQT | 180 |
| 2. ↑1 | M. Cort | EFN | 114 |
| 3. ↓1 | P. Roglič | TJV | 106 |

## YOUNG RIDER

| POS | NAME | TEAM | TIME |
|---|---|---|---|
| 1. – | E. Bernal | IGD | 45:38:04 |
| 2. – | A. Vlasov | APT | 1:22 |
| 3. – | G. Mäder | TBV | 2:08 |

## BONUSES

| TYPE | NAME | TEAM |
|---|---|---|
| KOM 1 | M. Iturria | EUS |
| KOM 2 | R. Bardet | DSM |
| Sprint 1 | S. Dewulf | ACT |

## STAGE RESULTS

| POS | NAME | TEAM | TIME |
|---|---|---|---|
| 1. | M. Cort | EFN | 3:44:21 |
| 2. | A. Bagioli | DQT | s.t. |
| 3. | M. Matthews | BEX | s.t. |
| 4. | M. Trentin | UAD | s.t. |
| 5. | A. Kron | LTS | s.t. |
| 6. | F. Großschartner | BOH | s.t. |
| 7. | A. Soto | EUS | s.t. |
| 8. | A. Roux | GFC | s.t. |
| 9. | G. Brambilla | TFS | s.t. |
| 10. | M. Tusveld | DSM | s.t. |
| 11. | S. Cras | LTS | s.t. |
| 12. | P. Roglič | TJV | s.t. |
| 13. | I. Izaguirre | APT | s.t. |
| 14. | A. Vlasov | APT | s.t. |
| 15. | E. Bernal | IGD | s.t. |
| 16. | R. Rochas | COF | s.t. |
| 17. | R. Molard | GFC | s.t. |
| 18. | M. Cherel | ACT | s.t. |
| 19. | D. de la Cruz | UAD | s.t. |
| 20. | O. C. Eiking | IWG | s.t. |
| 21. | G. Izaguirre | APT | s.t. |
| 22. | J. Haig | TBV | s.t. |
| 23. | L. Meintjes | IWG | s.t. |
| 24. | G. Martin | COF | s.t. |
| 25. | S. Kuss | TJV | s.t. |
| 26. | M. A. López | MOV | s.t. |
| 27. | S. Oomen | TJV | s.t. |
| 28. | G. Mäder | TBV | s.t. |
| 29. | D. Caruso | TBV | s.t. |
| 30. | J. Keukeleire | EFN | s.t. |
| 31. | A. Bagües | CJR | s.t. |
| 32. | J. Piccoli | ISN | s.t. |
| 33. | E. Mas | MOV | s.t. |
| 34. | S. Kruijswijk | TJV | s.t. |
| 35. | A. Yates | IGD | s.t. |
| 36. | G. Ciccone | TFS | s.t. |
| 37. | S. Henao | TQA | s.t. |
| 38. | J. Cepeda Hernández | CJR | s.t. |
| 39. | J. P. López | TFS | s.t. |
| 40. | J. Polanc | UAD | 0:09 |
| 41. | L. Mezgec | BEX | 0:12 |
| 42. | K. Bouwman | TJV | 0:14 |
| 43. | C. Verona | MOV | s.t. |
| 44. | Ó. Cabedo | BBH | 0:16 |
| 45. | S. Moniquet | LTS | s.t. |
| 46. | M. Nieve | BEX | 0:20 |
| 47. | J. Hirt | IWG | s.t. |
| 48. | J. Vine | AFC | 0:32 |
| 49. | N. Schultz | BEX | 0:37 |
| 50. | R. Bardet | DSM | 0:43 |
| 51. | R. Majka | UAD | 1:08 |
| 52. | A. Zeits | BEX | 1:50 |
| 53. | L. Hamilton | BEX | 2:55 |
| 54. | D. Howson | BEX | 3:01 |
| 55. | D. Navarro | BBH | 3:15 |
| 56. | L. A. Maté | EUS | 3:18 |
| 57. | F. Sénéchal | DQT | s.t. |
| 58. | G. Martin | EUS | s.t. |
| 59. | J. Lastra | CJR | s.t. |
| 60. | R. Taaramäe | IWG | 3:21 |
| 61. | Y. Natarov | APT | 5:13 |
| 62. | F. De Tier | AFC | 5:50 |
| 63. | L. Calmejane | ACT | 6:31 |
| 64. | C. Benedetti | BOH | s.t. |
| 65. | G. Bouchard | ACT | 6:57 |
| 66. | C. Champoussin | ACT | s.t. |
| 67. | M. Van Gils | LTS | s.t. |
| 68. | G. Niv | ISN | s.t. |
| 69. | S. Petilli | IWG | s.t. |
| 70. | R. Gibbons | UAD | 8:01 |
| 71. | S. Armée | TQA | s.t. |
| 72. | D. Touzé | ACT | s.t. |
| 73. | A. Démare | GFC | 9:12 |
| 74. | T. Arensman | DSM | s.t. |
| 75. | J. J. Rojas | MOV | s.t. |
| 76. | R. Sinkeldam | GFC | s.t. |
| 77. | N. Denz | DSM | s.t. |
| 78. | Y. Arashiro | TBV | s.t. |
| 79. | J. Bol | BBH | s.t. |
| 80. | O. Le Gac | GFC | s.t. |
| 81. | C. Venturini | ACT | s.t. |
| 82. | N. Van Hooydonck | TJV | s.t. |
| 83. | D. A. Camargo | EFN | s.t. |
| 84. | I. Erviti | MOV | s.t. |
| 85. | S. Dewulf | ACT | s.t. |
| 86. | J. Amezqueta | CJR | s.t. |
| 87. | Z. Štybar | DQT | s.t. |
| 88. | J. Narváez | IGD | s.t. |
| 89. | Jo. Herrada | COF | s.t. |
| 90. | J. K. Caicedo | EFN | s.t. |
| 91. | Je. Herrada | COF | s.t. |
| 92. | L. Craddock | EFN | s.t. |
| 93. | O. Lazkano | CJR | s.t. |
| 94. | M. Landa | TBV | s.t. |
| 95. | K. Elissonde | TFS | s.t. |
| 96. | M. Iturria | EUS | 12:05 |
| 97. | P. Sánchez | BBH | s.t. |
| 98. | E. Planckaert | AFC | s.t. |
| 99. | J. Bou | EUS | s.t. |
| 100. | S. Modolo | AFC | s.t. |
| 101. | R. Oliveira | UAD | s.t. |
| 102. | B. Zwiehoff | BOH | s.t. |
| 103. | W. Poels | TBV | s.t. |
| 104. | S. Berwick | ISN | s.t. |
| 105. | J. Dombrowski | UAD | 12:08 |
| 106. | P. Gamper | BOH | 14:33 |
| 107. | A. Kirsch | TFS | s.t. |
| 108. | M. Holmes | LTS | s.t. |
| 109. | R. Gesink | TJV | s.t. |
| 110. | C. Haga | DSM | s.t. |
| 111. | M. Storer | DSM | s.t. |
| 112. | K. Geniets | GFC | s.t. |
| 113. | T. Scully | EFN | s.t. |
| 114. | J. Tratnik | TBV | s.t. |
| 115. | F. Vermeersch | LTS | s.t. |
| 116. | D. Sunderland | TQA | s.t. |
| 117. | A. Okamika | BBH | s.t. |
| 118. | P. Allegaert | COF | s.t. |
| 119. | D. Rubio | BBH | s.t. |
| 120. | C. Hamilton | DSM | s.t. |
| 121. | R. Stannard | BEX | s.t. |
| 122. | P. Sivakov | IGD | s.t. |
| 123. | M. Bizkarra | EUS | s.t. |
| 124. | B. Van Lerberghe | DQT | s.t. |
| 125. | S. Vanmarcke | ISN | s.t. |
| 126. | F. Aru | TQA | s.t. |
| 127. | B. J. Lindeman | TQA | s.t. |
| 128. | N. Prodhomme | ACT | s.t. |
| 129. | N. Oliveira | MOV | s.t. |
| 130. | J. Aberasturi | CJR | s.t. |
| 131. | X. M. Azparren | EUS | s.t. |
| 132. | A. Krieger | AFC | s.t. |
| 133. | J. Knox | DQT | 14:43 |
| 134. | A. Palzer | BOH | 16:10 |
| 135. | C. Canal | BBH | s.t. |
| 136. | K. van Melsen | IWG | s.t. |
| 137. | E. Finé | COF | s.t. |
| 138. | R. Minali | IWG | s.t. |
| 139. | J. Meeus | BOH | s.t. |
| 140. | J. Černý | DQT | s.t. |
| 141. | T. Ludvigsson | GFC | s.t. |
| 142. | D. Claeys | TQA | s.t. |
| 143. | J. J. Lobato | EUS | s.t. |
| 144. | M. Laas | BOH | s.t. |
| 145. | A. Dainese | DSM | s.t. |
| 146. | I. Einhorn | ISN | s.t. |
| 147. | A. Nibali | TFS | s.t. |
| 148. | W. Kreder | IWG | s.t. |
| 149. | F. Barceló | COF | s.t. |
| 150. | A. Cuadros Morata | CJR | s.t. |
| 151. | M. Vanhoucke | LTS | s.t. |
| 152. | M. Vansevenant | DQT | s.t. |
| 153. | L. Hofstede | TJV | s.t. |
| 154. | F. Jakobsen | DQT | s.t. |
| 155. | T. Pidcock | IGD | s.t. |
| 156. | S. Thwaites | AFC | 17:23 |
| 157. | Q. Simmons | TFS | 22:10 |
| 158. | M. Padun | TBV | s.t. |
| 159. | C. Brown | TQA | s.t. |
| 160. | O. Fraile | APT | s.t. |
| 161. | M. Schachmann | BOH | s.t. |
| 162. | K. Reijnen | TFS | s.t. |
| 163. | S. Puccio | IGD | s.t. |
| 164. | R. Carapaz | IGD | s.t. |
| 165. | Á. Madrazo | BBH | s.t. |
| 166. | L. L. Sanchez | APT | s.t. |
| 167. | D. van Baarle | IGD | s.t. |

AUGUST    WORLDTOUR MEN'S RACE

# LA VUELTA A ESPAÑA
Stage 13
27 August 2021
Belmez–Villanueva de la Serena
203.7km

It had been a few days since a chance for the sprinters, which meant first of all that Diego Rubio, Álvaro Cuadros and Luis Ángel Maté had to get up the road for Burgos-BH, Caja Rural and Euskaltel-Euskadi, respectively. As the trio were allowed TV time off the front – the peloton choosing to spend the majority of the day recovering – the next action came at 60km, when crosswinds briefly split the bunch, but all the GC teams were attentive and it came back together, with Deceuninck-QuickStep taking charge at the front after that. 30km later and the breakaway was brought back, Fabio Jakobsen then taking the intermediate sprint to add to his green-jersey lead. Things appeared set up for the Dutchman to take his third win of this Vuelta – Deceuninck-QuickStep looked to be providing the perfect lead-out to accomplish that, with strength in numbers at the head of proceedings – but then with 2km to go Jakobsen lost the wheel, and Florian Sénéchal received the order on the radio that Jakobsen may have suffered a puncture and the Frenchman could now sprint for stage glory. With Bert Van Lerberghe ahead, Sénéchal waited until a little more than 100 metres from the line before unleashing his sprint. Trentin followed, sure this would be his chance to finally take a win this Tour, but Sénéchal was faster, keeping Trentin at bay and claiming a most unlikely stage victory.

## WEATHER

**TEMPERATURE**
29°C

**WIND**
SW 13km/h

## PROFILE

BELMEZ — DON BENITO — VILLANUEVA DE LA SERENA

## BREAKAWAY
D. Rubio (BBH), L. Á. Maté (EUS), Á. Cuadros (CJR)

## GENERAL CLASSIFICATION

| POS | NAME | TEAM | TIME |
|---|---|---|---|
| 1. | O. C. Eiking | IWG | 50:31:52 |
| 2. | G. Martin | COF | 0:58 |
| 3. | P. Roglič | TJV | 1:56 |
| 4. | E. Mas | MOV | 2:31 |
| 5. | M. A. López | MOV | 3:28 |
| 6. | J. Haig | TBV | 3:55 |
| 7. | E. Bernal | IGD | 4:41 |
| 8. | A. Yates | IGD | 4:57 |
| 9. | S. Kuss | TJV | 5:03 |
| 10. | F. Großschartner | BOH | 5:38 |

## KING OF THE MOUNTAINS

| POS | NAME | TEAM | PTS |
|---|---|---|---|
| 1. | D. Caruso | TBV | 31 |
| 2. | R. Bardet | DSM | 27 |
| 3. | M. Storer | DSM | 17 |

## POINTS

| POS | NAME | TEAM | PTS |
|---|---|---|---|
| 1. | F. Jakobsen | DQT | 200 |
| 2. | M. Cort | EFN | 114 |
| 3. | P. Roglič | TJV | 106 |

## YOUNG RIDER

| POS | NAME | TEAM | TIME |
|---|---|---|---|
| 1. | E. Bernal | IGD | 50:36:33 |
| 2. | A. Vlasov | APT | 1:27 |
| 3. | G. Mäder | TBV | 2:13 |

## TRIVIA
» Florian Sénéchal is the 16th different Deceuninck-QuickStep rider to take a victory this season.

## BONUSES

| TYPE | NAME | TEAM |
|---|---|---|
| Sprint 1 | F. Jakobsen | DQT |

## STAGE RESULTS

| POS | NAME | TEAM | TIME |
|---|---|---|---|
| 1. | F. Sénéchal | DQT | 4:58:23 |
| 2. | M. Trentin | UAD | s.t. |
| 3. | A. Dainese | DSM | 0:02 |
| 4. | L. Mezgec | BEX | 0:03 |
| 5. | S. Dewulf | ACT | s.t. |
| 6. | P. Allegaert | COF | s.t. |
| 7. | I. Einhorn | ISN | s.t. |
| 8. | A. Soto | EUS | s.t. |
| 9. | R. Oliveira | UAD | s.t. |
| 10. | E. Bernal | IGD | 0:06 |
| 11. | A. Krieger | AFC | 0:09 |
| 12. | B. Van Lerberghe | DQT | s.t. |
| 13. | S. Modolo | AFC | 0:11 |
| 14. | R. Minali | IWG | s.t. |
| 15. | J. Aberasturi | CJR | s.t. |
| 16. | N. Denz | DSM | s.t. |
| 17. | J. Meeus | BOH | s.t. |
| 18. | F. Großschartner | BOH | s.t. |
| 19. | A. Yates | IGD | s.t. |
| 20. | M. A. López | MOV | s.t. |
| 21. | J. Haig | TBV | s.t. |
| 22. | O. C. Eiking | IWG | s.t. |
| 23. | S. Kuss | TJV | s.t. |
| 24. | F. Vermeersch | LTS | s.t. |
| 25. | P. Roglič | TJV | s.t. |
| 26. | R. Molard | GFC | s.t. |
| 27. | C. Venturini | ACT | s.t. |
| 28. | E. Mas | MOV | s.t. |
| 29. | G. Izagirre | APT | s.t. |
| 30. | A. Vlasov | APT | s.t. |
| 31. | G. Mäder | TBV | s.t. |
| 32. | N. Van Hooydonck | TJV | s.t. |
| 33. | D. de la Cruz | UAD | s.t. |
| 34. | G. Martin | COF | s.t. |
| 35. | S. Kruijswijk | TJV | s.t. |
| 36. | I. Erviti | MOV | s.t. |
| 37. | S. Oomen | TJV | s.t. |
| 38. | J. Bol | BBH | s.t. |
| 39. | S. Cras | LTS | s.t. |
| 40. | R. Gibbons | UAD | s.t. |
| 41. | R. Sinkeldam | GFC | s.t. |
| 42. | M. Matthews | BEX | s.t. |
| 43. | A. Démare | GFC | s.t. |
| 44. | O. Le Gac | GFC | s.t. |
| 45. | L. Meintjes | IWG | s.t. |
| 46. | G. Ciccone | TFS | s.t. |
| 47. | J. Lastra | CJR | s.t. |
| 48. | A. Zeits | BEX | s.t. |
| 49. | M. Holmes | LTS | s.t. |
| 50. | R. Rochas | COF | s.t. |
| 51. | S. Henao | TQA | s.t. |
| 52. | P. Sánchez | BBH | 0:30 |
| 53. | J. Polanc | UAD | s.t. |
| 54. | J. J. Rojas | MOV | s.t. |
| 55. | R. Stannard | BEX | 0:37 |
| 56. | C. Canal | BBH | s.t. |
| 57. | A. Bagües | CJR | 0:39 |
| 58. | D. Touzé | ACT | s.t. |
| 59. | Y. Natarov | APT | s.t. |
| 60. | Á. Madrazo | BBH | s.t. |
| 61. | Ó. Cabedo | BBH | s.t. |
| 62. | K. Bouwman | TJV | s.t. |
| 63. | A. Roux | GFC | s.t. |
| 64. | G. Bouchard | ACT | s.t. |
| 65. | L. A. Maté | EUS | s.t. |
| 66. | J. P. López | TFS | s.t. |
| 67. | L. Calmejane | ACT | s.t. |
| 68. | M. Cherel | ACT | s.t. |
| 69. | A. Palzer | BOH | s.t. |
| 70. | J. Keukeleire | EFN | s.t. |
| 71. | P. Gamper | BOH | 0:45 |
| 72. | K. Geniets | GFC | s.t. |
| 73. | J. J. Lobato | EUS | s.t. |
| 74. | E. Planckaert | AFC | s.t. |
| 75. | G. Martín | EUS | 0:50 |
| 76. | Z. Štybar | DQT | 0:52 |
| 77. | F. De Tier | AFC | 0:58 |
| 78. | M. Iturria | EUS | s.t. |
| 79. | J. Tratnik | TBV | 1:02 |
| 80. | M. Laas | BOH | 1:05 |
| 81. | A. Okamika | BBH | s.t. |
| 82. | D. Caruso | TBV | s.t. |
| 83. | S. Petilli | IWG | s.t. |
| 84. | R. Taaramäe | IWG | s.t. |
| 85. | D. Sunderland | TQA | s.t. |
| 86. | F. Barceló | COF | s.t. |
| 87. | G. Brambilla | TFS | s.t. |
| 88. | J. Bou | EUS | s.t. |
| 89. | N. Prodhomme | ACT | s.t. |
| 90. | C. Champoussin | ACT | s.t. |
| 91. | C. Benedetti | BOH | s.t. |
| 92. | Y. Arashiro | TBV | s.t. |
| 93. | M. Landa | TBV | s.t. |
| 94. | M. Nieve | BEX | s.t. |
| 95. | G. Niv | ISN | s.t. |
| 96. | J. Dombrowski | UAD | s.t. |
| 97. | O. Lazkano | CJR | s.t. |
| 98. | W. Kreder | IWG | s.t. |
| 99. | A. Kirsch | TFS | s.t. |
| 100. | F. Jakobsen | DQT | s.t. |
| 101. | T. Pidcock | IGD | 1:18 |
| 102. | K. van Melsen | IWG | 1:26 |
| 103. | J. Černý | DQT | 1:36 |
| 104. | R. Bardet | DSM | s.t. |
| 105. | D. Navarro | BBH | 1:39 |
| 106. | N. Schultz | BEX | s.t. |
| 107. | M. Tusveld | DSM | s.t. |
| 108. | B. Zwiehoff | BOH | s.t. |
| 109. | D. Howson | BEX | s.t. |
| 110. | S. Thwaites | AFC | s.t. |
| 111. | J. Amezqueta | CJR | s.t. |
| 112. | M. Van Gils | LTS | s.t. |
| 113. | T. Scully | EFN | s.t. |
| 114. | J. Piccoli | ISN | s.t. |
| 115. | R. Majka | UAD | s.t. |
| 116. | C. Verona | MOV | s.t. |
| 117. | K. Elissonde | TFS | s.t. |
| 118. | M. Padun | TBV | s.t. |
| 119. | T. Ludvigsson | GFC | s.t. |
| 120. | S. Moniquet | LTS | s.t. |
| 121. | Je. Herrada | COF | s.t. |
| 122. | Jo. Herrada | COF | s.t. |
| 123. | S. Armée | TQA | s.t. |
| 124. | D. Claeys | TQA | s.t. |
| 125. | T. Arensman | DSM | s.t. |
| 126. | W. Poels | TBV | s.t. |
| 127. | M. Cort | EFN | s.t. |
| 128. | I. Izagirre | APT | s.t. |
| 129. | J. Hirt | IWG | s.t. |
| 130. | B. J. Lindeman | TQA | s.t. |
| 131. | L. L. Sanchez | APT | s.t. |
| 132. | R. Gesink | TJV | s.t. |
| 133. | P. Sivakov | IGD | s.t. |
| 134. | J. Cepeda Hernández | CJR | s.t. |
| 135. | D. A. Camargo | EFN | s.t. |
| 136. | C. Haga | DSM | s.t. |
| 137. | J. Vine | AFC | s.t. |
| 138. | H. Vanhoucke | LTS | s.t. |
| 139. | D. van Baarle | IGD | s.t. |
| 140. | A. Bagioli | DQT | 1:48 |
| 141. | S. Vanmarcke | ISN | 1:50 |
| 142. | L. Hamilton | BEX | 2:20 |
| 143. | M. Storer | DSM | s.t. |
| 144. | S. Puccio | IGD | s.t. |
| 145. | F. Aru | TQA | s.t. |
| 146. | A. Nibali | TFS | s.t. |
| 147. | M. Vansevenant | DQT | s.t. |
| 148. | S. Berwick | ISN | s.t. |
| 149. | A. Kron | LTS | s.t. |
| 150. | N. Oliveira | MOV | s.t. |
| 151. | L. Craddock | EFN | s.t. |
| 152. | Q. Simmons | TFS | s.t. |
| 153. | K. Reijnen | TFS | s.t. |
| 154. | J. Narváez | IGD | 2:48 |
| 155. | L. Hofstede | TJV | 2:53 |
| 156. | R. Carapaz | IGD | 3:35 |
| 157. | M. Bizkarra | EUS | s.t. |
| 158. | E. Finé | COF | s.t. |
| 159. | J. K. Caicedo | EFN | s.t. |
| 160. | X. M. Azparren | EUS | s.t. |
| 161. | C. Brown | TQA | s.t. |
| 162. | D. Rubio | BBH | s.t. |
| 163. | C. Hamilton | DSM | 3:43 |
| 164. | A. Cuadros Morata | CJR | s.t. |
| 165. | J. Knox | DQT | 4:12 |

AUGUST    WORLDTOUR MEN'S RACE

# LA VUELTA A ESPAÑA
Stage 14
28 August 2021
Don Benito–Pico Villuercas
165.7km

## WEATHER

TEMPERATURE   WIND
27°C          W 13km/h

A win atop the 14.7km Pico Villuercas inspired nearly 20 riders to clip off the front at the start of the day in search of a victory, including Romain Bardet, Jay Vine and Tom Pidcock, while Arnaud Démare's presence was slightly more baffling. The break soon had a gap of more than 7 minutes. Bardet bagged maximum points up the Puerto Berzocana to move to within one point of Damiano Caruso's lead in the KOM competition, then took the jersey on the category-1 Puerto Collado de Ballesteros. The gap was now 10 minutes and the victor would come from this group of escapees. They remained a unit until, with 50km still to race, the road picked up and Matt Holmes attacked then suffered a puncture to lay waste to his efforts, Nicolas Prodhomme and Dani Navarro having joined him and continuing on up the road. Navarro would also soon suffer misfortune, crashing on a corner and taking Sep Vanmarcke with him, the latter's face a picture after the finish when Navarro found him to apologise for the mistake. That left Prodhomme out front alone, at least until 12km to go when Bardet tracked him down. Others also made their way over – including Jay Vine, who had remarkably got back to his feet after a high-speed crash involving his own team car – but, after Bardet's show of strength on the previous climbs, no one was going to catch him when he decided to go, blasting past Prodhomme. Jesús Herrada and Jay Vine finished 44 seconds back, while Pidcock took fourth, another half a minute in arrears. This was not to be a day for the GC proper as the peloton arrived at the finishing climb, although Cofidis piled the pressure on Eiking to try and wrestle the red jersey onto the shoulders of Guillaume Martin, but the Norwegian limited his losses and saved his race lead. Ciccone attempted to ruffle the feathers of the GC contenders but it was López who successfully hit out with 3km remaining, yet his gap only amounted to 4 seconds on the line after Roglič closed him down in the finale.

## PROFILE

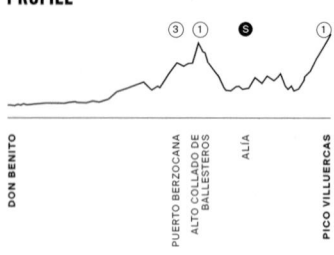

## BREAKAWAY

C. Champoussin (ACT), N. Prodhomme (ACT), J. Vine (AFC), J. Tratnik (TBV), D. Navarro (BBH), A. Bagües (CJR), Jo. Herrada (COF), J. Keukeleire (EFN), X. M. Azparren (EUS), A. Démare (GFC), K. Geniets (GFC), T. Pidcock (IGD), S. Vanmarcke (ISN), M. Holmes (LTS), A. Zeits (BEX), R. Bardet (DSM), D. Sunderland (TQA), R. Gibbons (UAD)

## GENERAL CLASSIFICATION

| POS | NAME | TEAM | TIME |
|---|---|---|---|
| 1. – | O. C. Eiking | IWG | 55:03:17 |
| 2. – | G. Martin | COF | 0:54 |
| 3. – | P. Roglič | TJV | 1:36 |
| 4. – | E. Mas | MOV | 2:11 |
| 5. – | M. A. López | MOV | 3:04 |
| 6. – | J. Haig | TBV | 3:35 |
| 7. – | E. Bernal | IGD | 4:21 |
| 8. – | A. Yates | IGD | 4:49 |
| 9. – | S. Kuss | TJV | 4:59 |
| 10.– | F. Großschartner | BOH | 5:31 |

## KING OF THE MOUNTAINS

| POS | NAME | TEAM | PTS |
|---|---|---|---|
| 1. ↑1 | R. Bardet | DSM | 50 |
| 2. ↓1 | D. Caruso | TBV | 31 |
| 3. – | M. Storer | DSM | 17 |

## POINTS

| POS | NAME | TEAM | PTS |
|---|---|---|---|
| 1. – | F. Jakobsen | DQT | 200 |
| 2. – | M. Cort | EFN | 114 |
| 3. – | P. Roglič | TJV | 106 |

## YOUNG RIDER

| POS | NAME | TEAM | TIME |
|---|---|---|---|
| 1. – | E. Bernal | IGD | 55:07:38 |
| 2. – | A. Vlasov | APT | 1:43 |
| 3. – | G. Mäder | TBV | 2:26 |

## BONUSES

| TYPE | NAME | TEAM |
|---|---|---|
| KOM 1 | R. Bardet | DSM |
| KOM 2 | R. Bardet | DSM |
| KOM 3 | R. Bardet | DSM |
| Sprint 1 | D. Navarro | BBH |

## TRIVIA

» This was Romain Bardet's first WorldTour victory since the 2017 Tour de France.

## STAGE RESULTS

| POS | NAME | TEAM | TIME |
|---|---|---|---|
| 1. | R. Bardet | DSM | 4:20:36 |
| 2. | Je. Herrada | COF | 0:44 |
| 3. | J. Vine | AFC | s.t. |
| 4. | T. Pidcock | IGD | 1:12 |
| 5. | C. Champoussin | ACT | 1:14 |
| 6. | M. Holmes | LTS | 1:16 |
| 7. | A. Zeits | BEX | 1:19 |
| 8. | K. Geniets | GFC | 1:46 |
| 9. | N. Prodhomme | ACT | 2:04 |
| 10. | J. Tratnik | TBV | 2:15 |
| 11. | R. Gibbons | UAD | 2:26 |
| 12. | D. Navarro | BBH | 2:43 |
| 13. | D. Sunderland | TQA | 4:02 |
| 14. | A. Bagües | CJR | 5:39 |
| 15. | A. Démare | GFC | 10:03 |
| 16. | M. A. López | MOV | 10:25 |
| 17. | P. Roglič | TJV | 10:29 |
| 18. | E. Mas | MOV | s.t. |
| 19. | E. Bernal | IGD | s.t. |
| 20. | J. Haig | TBV | s.t. |
| 21. | A. Yates | IGD | 10:41 |
| 22. | F. Großschartner | BOH | 10:42 |
| 23. | G. Mäder | TBV | s.t. |
| 24. | A. Vlasov | APT | 10:45 |
| 25. | G. Ciccone | TFS | s.t. |
| 26. | L. Meintjes | IWG | s.t. |
| 27. | S. Kuss | TJV | s.t. |
| 28. | G. Martin | COF | s.t. |
| 29. | D. de la Cruz | UAD | s.t. |
| 30. | O. C. Eiking | IWG | 10:49 |
| 31. | J. P. López | TFS | 10:54 |
| 32. | R. Taaramäe | IWG | 11:16 |
| 33. | J. Cepeda Hernández | CJR | 11:27 |
| 34. | S. Kruijswijk | TJV | 11:40 |
| 35. | D. Caruso | TBV | s.t. |
| 36. | G. Bouchard | ACT | 11:54 |
| 37. | K. Elissonde | TFS | s.t. |
| 38. | A. Cuadros Morata | CJR | 12:05 |
| 39. | P. Sivakov | IGD | 12:24 |
| 40. | S. Oomen | TJV | s.t. |
| 41. | L. A. Maté | EUS | s.t. |
| 42. | Ó. Cabedo | BBH | 12:37 |
| 43. | R. Majka | UAD | s.t. |
| 44. | C. Verona | MOV | s.t. |
| 45. | J. Hirt | IWG | 12:43 |
| 46. | J. Bou | EUS | 12:53 |
| 47. | G. Martin | EUS | s.t. |
| 48. | Á. Madrazo | BBH | s.t. |
| 49. | S. Henao | TQA | s.t. |
| 50. | J. Keukeleire | EFN | 13:31 |
| 51. | L. Calmejane | ACT | 13:49 |
| 52. | S. Cras | LTS | 13:53 |
| 53. | S. Petilli | IWG | 14:39 |
| 54. | M. Padun | TBV | 15:10 |
| 55. | R. Rochas | COF | 15:20 |
| 56. | K. Bouwman | TJV | 15:39 |
| 57. | M. Cherel | ACT | 16:32 |
| 58. | G. Izaguirre | APT | s.t. |
| 59. | B. Zwiehoff | BOH | s.t. |
| 60. | J. Dombrowski | UAD | 16:36 |
| 61. | O. Lazkano | CJR | 16:55 |
| 62. | J. Polanc | UAD | 17:10 |
| 63. | I. Izaguirre | APT | 17:33 |
| 64. | D. van Baarle | IGD | s.t. |
| 65. | G. Brambilla | TFS | 18:25 |
| 66. | C. Hamilton | DSM | 20:16 |
| 67. | W. Poels | TBV | s.t. |
| 68. | A. Roux | GFC | 20:54 |
| 69. | J. J. Rojas | MOV | 21:16 |
| 70. | M. Landa | TBV | s.t. |
| 71. | R. Molard | GFC | s.t. |
| 72. | Jo. Herrada | COF | s.t. |
| 73. | M. Tusveld | DSM | 22:51 |
| 74. | M. Nieve | BEX | s.t. |
| 75. | J. Amezqueta | CJR | s.t. |
| 76. | R. Gesink | TJV | s.t. |
| 77. | A. Nibali | TFS | s.t. |
| 78. | J. Lastra | CJR | s.t. |
| 79. | F. De Tier | AFC | 23:15 |
| 80. | X. M. Azparren | EUS | 24:07 |
| 81. | M. Iturria | EUS | s.t. |
| 82. | P. Gamper | BOH | s.t. |
| 83. | A. Okamika | BBH | s.t. |
| 84. | S. Armée | TQA | s.t. |
| 85. | M. Bizkarra | EUS | s.t. |
| 86. | G. Niv | ISN | s.t. |
| 87. | Y. Natarov | APT | s.t. |
| 88. | L. L. Sanchez | APT | s.t. |
| 89. | I. Erviti | MOV | s.t. |
| 90. | F. Barceló | COF | s.t. |
| 91. | D. A. Camargo | EFN | s.t. |
| 92. | Y. Arashiro | TBV | s.t. |
| 93. | N. Oliveira | MOV | 24:22 |
| 94. | W. Kreder | IWG | s.t. |
| 95. | S. Vanmarcke | ISN | 24:26 |
| 96. | S. Dewulf | ACT | 25:04 |
| 97. | A. Palzer | BOH | 25:08 |
| 98. | J. Bol | BBH | 25:17 |
| 99. | T. Arensman | DSM | s.t. |
| 100. | P. Sánchez | BBH | s.t. |
| 101. | L. Craddock | EFN | s.t. |
| 102. | C. Haga | DSM | s.t. |
| 103. | E. Finé | COF | s.t. |
| 104. | S. Thwaites | AFC | s.t. |
| 105. | F. Aru | TQA | s.t. |
| 106. | S. Puccio | IGD | s.t. |
| 107. | L. Hofstede | TJV | s.t. |
| 108. | T. Ludvigsson | GFC | s.t. |
| 109. | N. Schultz | BEX | s.t. |
| 110. | L. Hamilton | BEX | s.t. |
| 111. | J. Piccoli | ISN | s.t. |
| 112. | R. Sinkeldam | GFC | s.t. |
| 113. | O. Le Gac | GFC | s.t. |
| 114. | J. Narváez | IGD | s.t. |
| 115. | J. K. Caicedo | EFN | s.t. |
| 116. | H. Vanhoucke | LTS | s.t. |
| 117. | A. Kron | LTS | s.t. |
| 118. | F. Vermeersch | LTS | s.t. |
| 119. | A. Soto | EUS | s.t. |
| 120. | C. Venturini | ACT | s.t. |
| 121. | Q. Simmons | TFS | s.t. |
| 122. | N. Van Hooydonck | TJV | s.t. |
| 123. | D. Touzé | ACT | 25:28 |
| 124. | R. Oliveira | UAD | 27:06 |
| 125. | M. Trentin | UAD | 29:16 |
| 126. | D. Howson | BEX | s.t. |
| 127. | K. van Melsen | IWG | s.t. |
| 128. | P. Allegaert | COF | s.t. |
| 129. | M. Cort | EFN | 29:29 |
| 130. | A. Kirsch | TFS | 29:34 |
| 131. | M. Matthews | BEX | s.t. |
| 132. | M. Vansevenant | DQT | 30:14 |
| 133. | J. Knox | DQT | s.t. |
| 134. | S. Modolo | AFC | 30:16 |
| 135. | F. Jakobsen | DQT | 34:01 |
| 136. | Z. Štybar | DQT | s.t. |
| 137. | F. Sénéchal | DQT | s.t. |
| 138. | R. Minali | IWG | s.t. |
| 139. | R. Stannard | BEX | s.t. |
| 140. | A. Dainese | DSM | s.t. |
| 141. | B. Van Lerberghe | DQT | s.t. |
| 142. | I. Einhorn | ISN | s.t. |
| 143. | T. Scully | EFN | s.t. |
| 144. | K. Reijnen | TFS | s.t. |
| 145. | M. Van Gils | LTS | s.t. |
| 146. | S. Moniquet | LTS | s.t. |
| 147. | B. J. Lindeman | TQA | s.t. |
| 148. | C. Benedetti | BOH | s.t. |
| 149. | A. Bagioli | DQT | s.t. |
| 150. | L. Mezgec | BEX | s.t. |
| 151. | E. Planckaert | AFC | s.t. |
| 152. | J. Černý | DQT | s.t. |
| 153. | D. Rubio | BBH | s.t. |
| 154. | N. Denz | DSM | s.t. |
| 155. | C. Canal | BBH | s.t. |
| 156. | S. Berwick | ISN | s.t. |
| 157. | C. Brown | TQA | s.t. |
| 158. | M. Storer | DSM | s.t. |
| 159. | D. Claeys | TQA | s.t. |
| 160. | J. J. Lobato | EUS | s.t. |
| 161. | A. Krieger | AFC | s.t. |
| 162. | M. Laas | BOH | s.t. |
| 163. | J. Meeus | BOH | s.t. |
| 164. | J. Aberasturi | CJR | s.t. |

AUGUST    WORLDTOUR MEN'S RACE

# LA VUELTA A ESPAÑA
Stage 15
29 August 2021
Navalmoral de la Mata–El Barraco
197.5km

After Richard Carapaz had climbed off the previous day, his teammate Jhonatan Narváez would not make it to the finish today, as Ineos's Vuelta campaign stuttered. But for those still fit and healthy, an upcoming second rest day meant there was no shortage of riders wanting to get into the break on another big mountain stage. Former stage winners Bardet, Storer and Cort all tried to force their way into moves but UAE Team Emirates were closing things down until the right move went, and funnily enough it involved their rider Rafał Majka, who headed up the road in a large group of around 25 that included Fabio Aru and Steven Kruijswijk. Onto the Puerto de Pedro Bernardo with just under 90km still to race, Majka set off alone, not wanting company or passengers. Kruijswijk – probably the most talented climber in the large group that went away – was the lone chaser, reducing his deficit by the top of the Puerto de Mijares from just over 2 minutes to a minute and a half. This didn't seem to overly bother Majka, however, who was unflappable as he turned the pedals, sticking to his tempo with a dogged determination to get the job done. He kept that gap until the finish line, sailing across to take his first victory in four years and pointing to the heavens in memory of his late father, who had died earlier in the year. The group of overall contenders swept up the majority of the breakaway on the category-1 Mijares before the descent down to the category-3 Puerto San Juan di Nava. Yates managed to force his way clear on this final climb but only took a gap of 15 seconds across the line over his rivals, as Eiking led the rest of the GC group over to prolong his stay in red.

## WEATHER

TEMPERATURE: 23°C
WIND: N 4km/h

## PROFILE

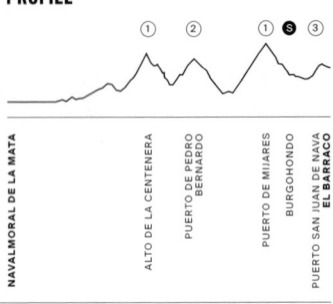

① NAVALMORAL DE LA MATA
② ALTO DE LA CENTENERA
③ PUERTO DE PEDRO BERNARDO
④ PUERTO DE MIJARES
⑤ BURGOHONDO
S PUERTO SAN JUAN DE NAVA
③ EL BARRACO

## BREAKAWAY

R. Majka (UAD), F. Aru (TQA), M. Van Gils (LTS), S. Kruijswijk (TJV), G. Bouchard (ACT), A. Bagioli (DQT), C. Verona (MOV), M. Storer (DSM), S. Cras (LTS), L. Hamilton (BEX), C. Hamilton (DSM), G. Brambilla (TFS)

## GENERAL CLASSIFICATION

| POS | NAME | TEAM | TIME |
|---|---|---|---|
| 1. – | O. C. Eiking | IWG | 59:57:50 |
| 2. – | G. Martin | COF | 0:54 |
| 3. – | P. Roglič | TJV | 1:36 |
| 4. – | E. Mas | MOV | 2:11 |
| 5. – | M. A. López | MOV | 3:04 |
| 6. – | J. Haig | TBV | 3:35 |
| 7. – | E. Bernal | IGD | 4:21 |
| 8. – | A. Yates | IGD | 4:34 |
| 9. – | S. Kuss | TJV | 4:59 |
| 10.– | F. Großschartner | BOH | 5:31 |

## KING OF THE MOUNTAINS

| POS | NAME | TEAM | PTS |
|---|---|---|---|
| 1. – | R. Bardet | DSM | 50 |
| 2. – | D. Caruso | TBV | 31 |
| 3. ↑30 | R. Majka | UAD | 29 |

## POINTS

| POS | NAME | TEAM | PTS |
|---|---|---|---|
| 1. – | F. Jakobsen | DQT | 200 |
| 2. – | M. Cort | EFN | 114 |
| 3. – | P. Roglič | TJV | 108 |

## YOUNG RIDER

| POS | NAME | TEAM | TIME |
|---|---|---|---|
| 1. – | E. Bernal | IGD | 60:02:11 |
| 2. – | A. Vlasov | APT | 1:43 |
| 3. – | G. Mäder | TBV | 2:26 |

## TRIVIA

» This was Rafał Majka's first victory since the 2017 Vuelta.

## BONUSES

| TYPE | NAME | TEAM |
|---|---|---|
| KOM 1 | R. Majka | UAD |
| KOM 2 | R. Majka | UAD |
| KOM 3 | R. Majka | UAD |
| KOM 4 | R. Majka | UAD |
| Sprint 1 | R. Majka | UAD |

## STAGE RESULTS

| POS | NAME | TEAM | TIME |
|---|---|---|---|
| 1. | R. Majka | UAD | 4:51:36 |
| 2. | S. Kruijswijk | TJV | 1:27 |
| 3. | C. Hamilton | DSM | 2:19 |
| 4. | A. Yates | IGD | 2:42 |
| 5. | G. Ciccone | TFS | 2:57 |
| 6. | O. C. Eiking | IWG | s.t. |
| 7. | F. Großschartner | BOH | s.t. |
| 8. | S. Kuss | TJV | s.t. |
| 9. | D. de la Cruz | UAD | s.t. |
| 10. | E. Mas | MOV | s.t. |
| 11. | M. A. López | MOV | s.t. |
| 12. | J. Haig | TBV | s.t. |
| 13. | A. Vlasov | APT | s.t. |
| 14. | P. Roglič | TJV | s.t. |
| 15. | E. Bernal | IGD | s.t. |
| 16. | G. Mäder | TBV | s.t. |
| 17. | G. Martin | COF | s.t. |
| 18. | L. Meintjes | IWG | s.t. |
| 19. | S. Oomen | TJV | 3:03 |
| 20. | R. Rochas | COF | s.t. |
| 21. | S. Henao | TQA | 3:23 |
| 22. | I. Izagirre | APT | s.t. |
| 23. | J. Cepeda Hernández | CJR | s.t. |
| 24. | J. Keukeleire | EFN | 3:57 |
| 25. | S. Cras | LTS | s.t. |
| 26. | C. Champoussin | ACT | s.t. |
| 27. | Ó. Cabedo | BBH | s.t. |
| 28. | J. P. López | TFS | s.t. |
| 29. | R. Molard | GFC | s.t. |
| 30. | M. Landa | TBV | s.t. |
| 31. | S. Petilli | IWG | s.t. |
| 32. | K. Bouwman | TJV | s.t. |
| 33. | R. Gesink | TJV | s.t. |
| 34. | M. Nieve | BEX | 4:02 |
| 35. | C. Verona | MOV | 4:15 |
| 36. | P. Sivakov | IGD | s.t. |
| 37. | G. Bouchard | ACT | 4:25 |
| 38. | G. Izagirre | APT | s.t. |
| 39. | G. Brambilla | TFS | s.t. |
| 40. | M. Storer | DSM | 4:54 |
| 41. | G. Niv | ISN | 5:17 |
| 42. | G. Martin | EUS | s.t. |
| 43. | R. Gibbons | UAD | s.t. |
| 44. | J. Dombrowski | UAD | 5:20 |
| 45. | J. Hirt | IWG | s.t. |
| 46. | Jo. Herrada | COF | 7:37 |
| 47. | D. van Baarle | IGD | 10:26 |
| 48. | S. Puccio | IGD | s.t. |
| 49. | W. Poels | TBV | s.t. |
| 50. | R. Taaramäe | IWG | s.t. |
| 51. | B. Zwiehoff | BOH | s.t. |
| 52. | D. A. Camargo | EFN | s.t. |
| 53. | T. Pidcock | IGD | 10:34 |
| 54. | D. Navarro | BBH | 12:08 |
| 55. | D. Rubio | BBH | 13:28 |
| 56. | M. Tusveld | DSM | s.t. |
| 57. | M. Cherel | ACT | s.t. |
| 58. | I. Erviti | MOV | s.t. |
| 59. | T. Arensman | DSM | s.t. |
| 60. | R. Bardet | DSM | 13:32 |
| 61. | M. Van Gils | LTS | 15:56 |
| 62. | P. Gamper | BOH | 22:28 |
| 63. | M. Iturria | EUS | s.t. |
| 64. | J. Knox | DQT | s.t. |
| 65. | L. Hamilton | BEX | s.t. |
| 66. | A. Roux | GFC | s.t. |
| 67. | J. J. Rojas | MOV | s.t. |
| 68. | E. Finé | COF | s.t. |
| 69. | N. Oliveira | MOV | s.t. |
| 70. | Y. Natarov | APT | s.t. |
| 71. | N. Prodhomme | ACT | s.t. |
| 72. | N. Schultz | BEX | s.t. |
| 73. | C. Benedetti | BOH | s.t. |
| 74. | M. Padun | TBV | s.t. |
| 75. | O. Lazkano | CJR | s.t. |
| 76. | A. Okamika | BBH | s.t. |
| 77. | L. L. Sanchez | APT | s.t. |
| 78. | A. Nibali | TFS | s.t. |
| 79. | J. Amezqueta | CJR | s.t. |
| 80. | Je. Herrada | COF | s.t. |
| 81. | L. Craddock | EFN | s.t. |
| 82. | D. Touzé | ACT | s.t. |
| 83. | F. Aru | TQA | 23:04 |
| 84. | D. Caruso | TBV | s.t. |
| 85. | J. Bol | BBH | s.t. |
| 86. | N. Van Hooydonck | TJV | s.t. |
| 87. | D. Howson | BEX | s.t. |
| 88. | A. Kirsch | TFS | s.t. |
| 89. | T. Ludvigsson | GFC | s.t. |
| 90. | L. A. Maté | EUS | s.t. |
| 91. | D. Claeys | TQA | s.t. |
| 92. | L. Hofstede | TJV | s.t. |
| 93. | K. Elissonde | TFS | 23:08 |
| 94. | J. Lastra | CJR | 24:30 |
| 95. | F. De Tier | AFC | 29:02 |
| 96. | R. Stannard | BEX | s.t. |
| 97. | F. Vermeersch | LTS | s.t. |
| 98. | E. Planckaert | AFC | s.t. |
| 99. | S. Dewulf | ACT | s.t. |
| 100. | R. Oliveira | UAD | s.t. |
| 101. | A. Krieger | AFC | s.t. |
| 102. | L. Mezgec | BEX | s.t. |
| 103. | F. Barceló | COF | s.t. |
| 104. | M. Matthews | BEX | s.t. |
| 105. | N. Denz | DSM | s.t. |
| 106. | F. Sénéchal | DQT | s.t. |
| 107. | L. Calmejane | ACT | s.t. |
| 108. | C. Haga | DSM | s.t. |
| 109. | O. Le Gac | GFC | s.t. |
| 110. | M. Trentin | UAD | s.t. |
| 111. | A. Bagioli | DQT | s.t. |
| 112. | T. Scully | EFN | s.t. |
| 113. | P. Allegaert | COF | s.t. |
| 114. | M. Vansevenant | DQT | s.t. |
| 115. | W. Kreder | IWG | s.t. |
| 116. | K. Geniets | GFC | s.t. |
| 117. | M. Cort | EFN | s.t. |
| 118. | S. Modolo | AFC | s.t. |
| 119. | B. J. Lindeman | TQA | 29:11 |
| 120. | A. Palzer | BOH | 35:47 |
| 121. | Z. Štybar | DQT | s.t. |
| 122. | A. Démare | GFC | s.t. |
| 123. | R. Sinkeldam | GFC | s.t. |
| 124. | A. Zeits | BEX | s.t. |
| 125. | S. Moniquet | LTS | s.t. |
| 126. | Q. Simmons | TFS | s.t. |
| 127. | I. Einhorn | ISN | s.t. |
| 128. | C. Canal | BBH | s.t. |
| 129. | A. Dainese | DSM | s.t. |
| 130. | R. Minali | IWG | s.t. |
| 131. | D. Sunderland | TQA | s.t. |
| 132. | C. Brown | TQA | s.t. |
| 133. | C. Venturini | ACT | s.t. |
| 134. | K. van Melsen | IWG | s.t. |
| 135. | P. Sánchez | BBH | s.t. |
| 136. | J. Meeus | BOH | s.t. |
| 137. | B. Van Lerberghe | DQT | s.t. |
| 138. | J. Černý | DQT | s.t. |
| 139. | F. Jakobsen | DQT | s.t. |
| 140. | J. Vine | AFC | s.t. |
| 141. | J. Aberasturi | CJR | s.t. |
| 142. | M. Laas | BOH | s.t. |
| 143. | J. J. Lobato | EUS | s.t. |
| 144. | A. Bagües | CJR | s.t. |
| 145. | J. Bou | EUS | s.t. |
| 146. | Á. Madrazo | BBH | s.t. |
| 147. | J. Piccoli | ISN | s.t. |
| 148. | J. Tratnik | TBV | s.t. |
| 149. | S. Armée | TQA | s.t. |
| 150. | S. Vanmarcke | ISN | s.t. |
| 151. | S. Berwick | ISN | s.t. |
| 152. | A. Kron | LTS | s.t. |
| 153. | Y. Arashiro | TBV | s.t. |
| 154. | M. Bizkarra | EUS | s.t. |
| 155. | A. Soto | EUS | s.t. |
| 156. | X. M. Azparren | EUS | s.t. |
| 157. | A. Cuadros Morata | CJR | s.t. |
| 158. | M. Holmes | LTS | s.t. |
| 159. | H. Vanhoucke | LTS | s.t. |
| 160. | J. Polanc | UAD | s.t. |
| 161. | S. Thwaites | AFC | 37:22 |

AUGUST   WORLDTOUR MEN'S RACE

## LA VUELTA A ESPAÑA
Stage 16
31 August 2021
Laredo–Santa Cruz de Bezana
180km

A final chance for the sprinters this Vuelta – as long as they could get over the mid-stage Cantabrian hills with the peloton still intact. An early crash brought down Enric Mas and Guillaume Martin before the day's break set off featuring Jetse Bol and Quinn Simmons. The sprint teams rarely afforded them an advantage of more than 2 minutes in the first couple of hours of racing, and at the midway point Ciccone, Vanmarcke and Rudy Molard abandoned due to injuries sustained in the early crash. Next up was the day's only classified climb, the category-3 Alto de Hijas, on which Lotto Soudal's Harm Vanhoucke and Maxim Van Gils attacked, making it across to the breakaway. Another lump in the profile followed, UAE Team Emirates upping the pace and successfully dropping Fabio Jakobsen, whose Deceuninck-QuickStep team dropped back to help. With 50km to go, Jakobsen got back on after chasing from a 30-second deficit, which was also the advantage the break still held up front. The undulating terrain into the finish first cost Simmons his place in the escape group, while Stan Dewulf was the last left out front. As Bora-Hansgrohe and EF Education-Nippo jostled for position heading into the sprint finish, it was Deceuninck-QuickStep who timed it best, coming in late with less than 2km remaining to put Jakobsen and his sprint train on the front. Alpecin-Fenix tried to disrupt things for Sacha Modolo, but Jakobsen played it cool, knowing that even with Trentin on his wheel he had the power to secure a third stage victory. And he did just that – on his 25th birthday, a year on from celebrating his 24th in hospital following the Tour of Poland crash.

### WEATHER

TEMPERATURE  WIND
19°C          S 7km/h

### PROFILE

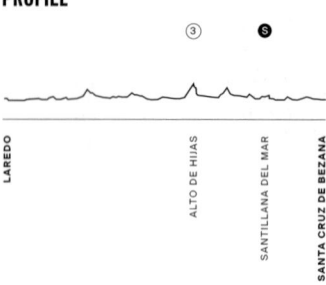

### BREAKAWAY
S. Dewulf (ACT), M. Bizkarra (EUS), D. Claeys (TQA), Q. Simmons (TFS), J. Bol (BBH)

### GENERAL CLASSIFICATION

| POS | NAME | TEAM | TIME |
|---|---|---|---|
| 1. – | O. C. Eiking | IWG | 64:06:47 |
| 2. – | G. Martin | COF | 0:54 |
| 3. – | P. Roglič | TJV | 1:36 |
| 4. – | E. Mas | MOV | 2:11 |
| 5. – | M. A. López | MOV | 3:04 |
| 6. – | J. Haig | TBV | 3:35 |
| 7. – | E. Bernal | IGD | 4:21 |
| 8. – | A. Yates | IGD | 4:34 |
| 9. – | S. Kuss | TJV | 4:59 |
| 10.– | F. Großschartner | BOH | 5:31 |

### KING OF THE MOUNTAINS

| POS | NAME | TEAM | PTS |
|---|---|---|---|
| 1. – | R. Bardet | DSM | 50 |
| 2. – | D. Caruso | TBV | 31 |
| 3. – | R. Majka | UAD | 29 |

### POINTS

| POS | NAME | TEAM | PTS |
|---|---|---|---|
| 1. – | F. Jakobsen | DQT | 250 |
| 2. ↑2 | M. Trentin | UAD | 123 |
| 3. ↓1 | M. Cort | EFN | 114 |

### YOUNG RIDER

| POS | NAME | TEAM | TIME |
|---|---|---|---|
| 1. – | E. Bernal | IGD | 64:11:08 |
| 2. – | A. Vlasov | APT | 1:43 |
| 3. – | G. Mäder | TBV | 2:26 |

### TRIVIA
» This was Deceuninck-QuickStep's ninth Grand Tour stage win of the season – the most since 2018 (when they took 13).

### BONUSES

| TYPE | NAME | TEAM |
|---|---|---|
| KOM 1 | J. Bol | BBH |
| Sprint 1 | J. Bol | BBH |

## STAGE RESULTS

| POS | NAME | TEAM | TIME |
|---|---|---|---|
| 1. | F. Jakobsen | DQT | 4:08:57 |
| 2. | J. Meeus | BOH | s.t. |
| 3. | M. Trentin | UAD | s.t. |
| 4. | M. Matthews | BEX | s.t. |
| 5. | A. Dainese | DSM | s.t. |
| 6. | J. Aberasturi | CJR | s.t. |
| 7. | R. Oliveira | UAD | s.t. |
| 8. | R. Minali | IWG | s.t. |
| 9. | A. Soto | EUS | s.t. |
| 10. | C. Venturini | ACT | s.t. |
| 11. | P. Allegaert | COF | s.t. |
| 12. | F. Vermeersch | LTS | s.t. |
| 13. | S. Modolo | AFC | s.t. |
| 14. | I. Einhorn | ISN | s.t. |
| 15. | C. Canal | BBH | s.t. |
| 16. | A. Démare | GFC | s.t. |
| 17. | J. J. Lobato | EUS | s.t. |
| 18. | R. Gibbons | UAD | s.t. |
| 19. | J. Tratnik | TBV | s.t. |
| 20. | G. Martin | EUS | s.t. |
| 21. | S. Kuss | TJV | s.t. |
| 22. | L. Calmejane | ACT | s.t. |
| 23. | M. Cort | EFN | s.t. |
| 24. | A. Krieger | AFC | s.t. |
| 25. | E. Bernal | IGD | s.t. |
| 26. | J. Haig | TBV | s.t. |
| 27. | T. Pidcock | IGD | s.t. |
| 28. | F. Großschartner | BOH | s.t. |
| 29. | Y. Arashiro | TBV | s.t. |
| 30. | R. Stannard | BEX | s.t. |
| 31. | J. Amezqueta | CJR | s.t. |
| 32. | W. Kreder | IWG | s.t. |
| 33. | I. Erviti | MOV | s.t. |
| 34. | S. Henao | TQA | s.t. |
| 35. | L. Meintjes | IWG | s.t. |
| 36. | S. Cras | LTS | s.t. |
| 37. | G. Izaguirre | APT | s.t. |
| 38. | A. Vlasov | APT | s.t. |
| 39. | P. Roglič | TJV | s.t. |
| 40. | I. Izaguirre | APT | s.t. |
| 41. | S. Oomen | TJV | s.t. |
| 42. | E. Mas | MOV | s.t. |
| 43. | J. J. Rojas | MOV | s.t. |
| 44. | N. Denz | DSM | s.t. |
| 45. | M. Van Gils | LTS | s.t. |
| 46. | O. C. Eiking | IWG | s.t. |
| 47. | A. Yates | IGD | s.t. |
| 48. | D. de la Cruz | UAD | s.t. |
| 49. | G. Martin | COF | s.t. |
| 50. | G. Niv | ISN | s.t. |
| 51. | B. Van Lerberghe | DQT | s.t. |
| 52. | A. Roux | GFC | s.t. |
| 53. | G. Mäder | TBV | s.t. |
| 54. | C. Champoussin | ACT | s.t. |
| 55. | Y. Natarov | APT | s.t. |
| 56. | M. A. López | MOV | s.t. |
| 57. | N. Van Hooydonck | TJV | s.t. |
| 58. | R. Rochas | COF | s.t. |
| 59. | O. Lazkano | CJR | s.t. |
| 60. | K. van Melsen | IWG | s.t. |
| 61. | S. Kruijswijk | TJV | s.t. |
| 62. | K. Bouwman | TJV | s.t. |
| 63. | M. Cherel | ACT | s.t. |
| 64. | J. Bol | BBH | s.t. |
| 65. | S. Petilli | IWG | s.t. |
| 66. | Á. Madrazo | BBH | s.t. |
| 67. | M. Tusveld | DSM | s.t. |
| 68. | Ó. Cabedo | BBH | s.t. |
| 69. | D. Caruso | TBV | s.t. |
| 70. | N. Prodhomme | ACT | s.t. |
| 71. | P. Sánchez | BBH | s.t. |
| 72. | M. Laas | BOH | s.t. |
| 73. | L. A. Maté | EUS | s.t. |
| 74. | J. P. López | TFS | s.t. |
| 75. | S. Armée | TQA | s.t. |
| 76. | C. Benedetti | BOH | s.t. |
| 77. | F. Barceló | COF | s.t. |
| 78. | D. Howson | BEX | s.t. |
| 79. | R. Taaramäe | IWG | s.t. |
| 80. | Jo. Herrada | COF | s.t. |
| 81. | E. Finé | COF | s.t. |
| 82. | P. Gamper | BOH | s.t. |
| 83. | F. De Tier | AFC | s.t. |
| 84. | M. Landa | TBV | s.t. |
| 85. | J. Lastra | CJR | s.t. |
| 86. | L. L. Sanchez | APT | s.t. |
| 87. | M. Iturria | EUS | s.t. |
| 88. | G. Bouchard | ACT | s.t. |
| 89. | J. Cepeda Hernández | CJR | s.t. |
| 90. | M. Nieve | BEX | s.t. |
| 91. | N. Schultz | BEX | 0:26 |
| 92. | F. Sénéchal | DQT | 0:37 |
| 93. | E. Planckaert | AFC | 0:45 |
| 94. | D. Touzé | ACT | s.t. |
| 95. | M. Vansevenant | DQT | 0:49 |
| 96. | L. Mezgec | BEX | s.t. |
| 97. | R. Sinkeldam | GFC | 0:52 |
| 98. | J. Keukeleire | EFN | s.t. |
| 99. | L. Craddock | EFN | s.t. |
| 100. | T. Ludvigsson | GFC | 0:54 |
| 101. | L. Hofstede | TJV | 1:11 |
| 102. | Z. Štybar | DQT | 1:19 |
| 103. | L. Hamilton | BEX | 1:32 |
| 104. | S. Moniquet | LTS | 1:35 |
| 105. | A. Zeits | BEX | s.t. |
| 106. | P. Sivakov | IGD | s.t. |
| 107. | Je. Herrada | COF | s.t. |
| 108. | D. Navarro | BBH | s.t. |
| 109. | J. Dombrowski | UAD | s.t. |
| 110. | A. Bagioli | DQT | s.t. |
| 111. | O. Le Gac | GFC | s.t. |
| 112. | B. Zwiehoff | BOH | 2:05 |
| 113. | A. Palzer | BOH | s.t. |
| 114. | J. Hirt | IWG | s.t. |
| 115. | C. Haga | DSM | 2:26 |
| 116. | W. Poels | TBV | 2:38 |
| 117. | D. van Baarle | IGD | s.t. |
| 118. | G. Brambilla | TFS | s.t. |
| 119. | S. Puccio | IGD | s.t. |
| 120. | J. Polanc | UAD | s.t. |
| 121. | R. Majka | UAD | s.t. |
| 122. | C. Verona | MOV | s.t. |
| 123. | M. Holmes | LTS | s.t. |
| 124. | Q. Simmons | TFS | s.t. |
| 125. | S. Dewulf | ACT | s.t. |
| 126. | A. Kron | LTS | 2:49 |
| 127. | A. Cuadros Morata | CJR | 2:56 |
| 128. | A. Bagües | CJR | s.t. |
| 129. | M. Padun | TBV | s.t. |
| 130. | M. Storer | DSM | s.t. |
| 131. | B. J. Lindeman | TQA | 3:13 |
| 132. | R. Gesink | TJV | 4:03 |
| 133. | J. Piccoli | ISN | s.t. |
| 134. | A. Okamika | BBH | s.t. |
| 135. | T. Scully | EFN | s.t. |
| 136. | C. Hamilton | DSM | s.t. |
| 137. | J. Vine | AFC | s.t. |
| 138. | S. Berwick | ISN | s.t. |
| 139. | T. Arensman | DSM | s.t. |
| 140. | K. Elissonde | TFS | 4:07 |
| 141. | R. Bardet | DSM | s.t. |
| 142. | A. Kirsch | TFS | s.t. |
| 143. | D. Claeys | TQA | s.t. |
| 144. | M. Bizkarra | EUS | s.t. |
| 145. | J. Černý | DQT | 4:28 |
| 146. | S. Thwaites | AFC | 6:32 |
| 147. | D. Sunderland | TQA | s.t. |
| 148. | D. A. Camargo | EFN | s.t. |
| 149. | N. Oliveira | MOV | s.t. |
| 150. | A. Nibali | TFS | s.t. |
| 151. | D. Rubio | BBH | s.t. |
| 152. | J. Bou | EUS | s.t. |
| 153. | X. M. Azparren | EUS | s.t. |
| 154. | J. Knox | DQT | s.t. |
| 155. | F. Aru | TQA | s.t. |
| 156. | H. Vanhoucke | LTS | s.t. |
| 157. | K. Geniets | GFC | s.t. |
| 158. | C. Brown | TQA | 16:19 |

AUGUST  WORLDTOUR MEN'S RACE

# LA VUELTA A ESPAÑA
Stage 17
1 September 2021
Unquera–Lagos de Covadonga
185.8km

## WEATHER

**TEMPERATURE**
21°C

**WIND**
NE 7km/h

A huge day in the mountains, capped off with an HC summit finish at Lagos de Covadonga. While Michael Storer got himself into the day's move and led over the first of two ascents of La Collada Llomena, and Mikel Landa also hit out from the peloton, it soon became clear that the day would be decided by the riders at the top of the GC. The break was brought back by Jumbo-Visma the second time up the climb, before Ineos took over, looking to tee things up for Egan Bernal, with stages already running out if he was going to force his way higher in the overall standings. Race leader Eiking was soon distanced, with Bernal making his move 5km from the top. There was still 60km to race, but Primož Roglič decided to go with the Colombian. On the downhill, Eiking and Vlasov then crashed in the rain; if the Norwegian's red jersey was slipping beforehand, it was surely gone now as Bahrain Victorious led the chase of Roglič and Bernal, who were 2 minutes up the road. At the base of Lagos de Covadonga 40 seconds had been lopped off their lead, and the pace-setting by Wout Poels and Gino Mäder dropped Guillaume Martin – Cofidis' earlier attempts to not let Eiking back into contention now all for nothing as the red jersey slipped from their grasp too. Up ahead, Roglič was determined to show his prowess on this finishing climb, making Bernal suffer and eventually unhitching him with 7.5km left. Attacks behind from López, Mas and Yates brought the Colombian back into the fold, and Roglič eventually crossed the line a minute and a half ahead to reclaim the red jersey, his teammate Sepp Kuss winning the sprint for second in what was a perfect day for Jumbo-Visma.

## PROFILE

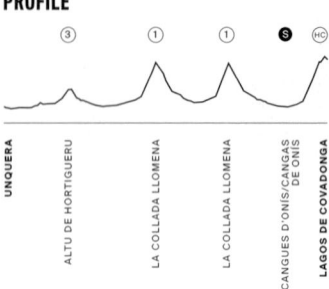

## GENERAL CLASSIFICATION

| POS | NAME | TEAM | TIME |
|---|---|---|---|
| 1. ↑2 | P. Roglič | TJV | 68:42:56 |
| 2. ↑2 | E. Mas | MOV | 2:22 |
| 3. ↑2 | M. A. López | MOV | 3:11 |
| 4. ↑2 | J. Haig | TBV | 3:46 |
| 5. ↓3 | G. Martin | COF | 4:16 |
| 6. ↑1 | E. Bernal | IGD | 4:29 |
| 7. ↑1 | A. Yates | IGD | 4:45 |
| 8. ↑1 | S. Kuss | TJV | 5:04 |
| 9. ↑1 | F. Großschartner | BOH | 6:54 |
| 10. ↑2 | G. Mäder | TBV | 6:58 |

## KING OF THE MOUNTAINS

| POS | NAME | TEAM | PTS |
|---|---|---|---|
| 1. — | R. Bardet | DSM | 51 |
| 2. ↑2 | M. Storer | DSM | 34 |
| 3. ↓1 | D. Caruso | TBV | 33 |

## POINTS

| POS | NAME | TEAM | PTS |
|---|---|---|---|
| 1. — | F. Jakobsen | DQT | 250 |
| 2. ↑4 | P. Roglič | TJV | 145 |
| 3. ↓1 | M. Trentin | UAD | 123 |

## YOUNG RIDER

| POS | NAME | TEAM | TIME |
|---|---|---|---|
| 1. — | E. Bernal | IGD | 68:47:25 |
| 2. ↑1 | G. Mäder | TBV | 2:29 |
| 3. ↑1 | J. P. López | TFS | 10:35 |

## BREAKAWAY

M. Cherel (ACT), J. Vine (AFC), I. Izaguirre (APT), M. Landa (TBV), J. Tratnik (TBV), O. Cabedo (BBH), A. Okamika (BBH), J. Cepeda Hernández (CJR), Je. Herrada (COF), D. A. Camargo (EFN), G. Martin (EUS), O. Le Gac (GFC), D. Van Baarle (IGD), S. Moniquet (LTS), N. Oliveira (MOV), M. Nieve (BEX), C. Hamilton (DSM), M. Storer (DSM), M. Tusveld (DSM), F. Aru (TQA), S. Henao (TQA), A. Nibali (TFS), D. De la Cruz (UAD), M. Trentin (UAD)

## BONUSES

| TYPE | NAME | TEAM |
|---|---|---|
| KOM 1 | J. Polanc | UAD |
| KOM 2 | M. Storer | DSM |
| KOM 3 | E. Bernal | IGD |
| KOM 4 | P. Roglič | TJV |
| Sprint 1 | E. Bernal | IGD |

# STAGE RESULTS

| POS | NAME | TEAM | TIME |
|---|---|---|---|
| 1. | P. Roglič | TJV | 4:34:45 |
| 2. | S. Kuss | TJV | 1:35 |
| 3. | M. A. López | MOV | s.t. |
| 4. | A. Yates | IGD | s.t. |
| 5. | J. Haig | TBV | s.t. |
| 6. | E. Mas | MOV | s.t. |
| 7. | E. Bernal | IGD | s.t. |
| 8. | G. Mäder | TBV | s.t. |
| 9. | L. Meintjes | IWG | 2:29 |
| 10. | C. Champoussin | ACT | 2:44 |
| 11. | S. Kruijswijk | TJV | s.t. |
| 12. | F. Großschartner | BOH | 2:47 |
| 13. | D. de la Cruz | UAD | s.t. |
| 14. | J. Hirt | IWG | 3:43 |
| 15. | G. Martin | COF | 4:46 |
| 16. | F. De Tier | AFC | 5:03 |
| 17. | J. P. López | TFS | 5:20 |
| 18. | W. Poels | TBV | 5:25 |
| 19. | G. Bouchard | ACT | 5:52 |
| 20. | R. Rochas | COF | 5:57 |
| 21. | D. Navarro | BBH | 7:46 |
| 22. | O. Cabedo | BBH | 7:49 |
| 23. | O. C. Eiking | IWG | 9:23 |
| 24. | L. A. Maté | EUS | s.t. |
| 25. | S. Oomen | TJV | 9:41 |
| 26. | M. Nieve | BEX | 11:45 |
| 27. | G. Izagirre | APT | s.t. |
| 28. | G. Brambilla | TFS | s.t. |
| 29. | D. Caruso | TBV | s.t. |
| 30. | G. Martin | EUS | s.t. |
| 31. | K. Bouwman | TJV | s.t. |
| 32. | B. Zwiehoff | BOH | 12:21 |
| 33. | I. Izagirre | APT | 13:08 |
| 34. | S. Henao | TQA | 13:34 |
| 35. | S. Petilli | IWG | s.t. |
| 36. | M. Iturria | EUS | 18:19 |
| 37. | J. Cepeda Hernández | CJR | 18:28 |
| 38. | J. Amezqueta | CJR | 18:59 |
| 39. | A. Okamika | BBH | 20:15 |
| 40. | A. Cuadros Morata | CJR | s.t. |
| 41. | P. Sivakov | IGD | 21:02 |
| 42. | Jo. Herrada | COF | 22:04 |
| 43. | S. Cras | LTS | 22:50 |
| 44. | M. Cherel | ACT | s.t. |
| 45. | M. Bizkarra | EUS | 23:03 |
| 46. | R. Gesink | TJV | 26:32 |
| 47. | A. Zeits | BEX | s.t. |
| 48. | J. J. Rojas | MOV | s.t. |
| 49. | M. Tusveld | DSM | s.t. |
| 50. | T. Arensman | DSM | s.t. |
| 51. | L. Calmejane | ACT | s.t. |
| 52. | Je. Herrada | COF | s.t. |
| 53. | A. Roux | GFC | 26:36 |
| 54. | D. A. Camargo | EFN | 26:38 |
| 55. | J. Dombrowski | UAD | s.t. |
| 56. | R. Majka | UAD | 26:41 |
| 57. | N. Prodhomme | ACT | 26:43 |
| 58. | R. Bardet | DSM | s.t. |
| 59. | R. Taaramäe | IWG | 26:45 |
| 60. | J. Piccoli | ISN | 26:54 |
| 61. | A. Kron | LTS | 28:07 |
| 62. | T. Ludvigsson | GFC | 29:13 |
| 63. | N. Van Hooydonck | TJV | s.t. |
| 64. | M. Storer | DSM | 30:05 |
| 65. | L. Hamilton | BEX | s.t. |
| 66. | J. Polanc | UAD | 32:20 |
| 67. | J. Keukeleire | EFN | 35:13 |
| 68. | D. van Baarle | IGD | s.t. |
| 69. | S. Moniquet | LTS | s.t. |
| 70. | N. Oliveira | MOV | s.t. |
| 71. | O. Le Gac | GFC | s.t. |
| 72. | F. Aru | TQA | s.t. |
| 73. | J. Lastra | CJR | 35:18 |
| 74. | J. Tratnik | TBV | 35:23 |
| 75. | T. Pidcock | IGD | 35:25 |
| 76. | C. Hamilton | DSM | 35:26 |
| 77. | L. Craddock | EFN | s.t. |
| 78. | Y. Natarov | APT | 35:29 |
| 79. | A. Vlasov | APT | s.t. |
| 80. | A. Nibali | TFS | s.t. |
| 81. | Á. Madrazo | BBH | s.t. |
| 82. | A. Palzer | BOH | 36:57 |
| 83. | R. Gibbons | UAD | s.t. |
| 84. | P. Gamper | BOH | 36:59 |
| 85. | M. Matthews | BEX | 37:57 |
| 86. | Q. Simmons | TFS | 38:38 |
| 87. | A. Kirsch | TFS | s.t. |
| 88. | J. Bol | BBH | s.t. |
| 89. | S. Thwaites | AFC | s.t. |
| 90. | W. Kreder | IWG | s.t. |
| 91. | E. Finé | COF | s.t. |
| 92. | K. van Melsen | IWG | s.t. |
| 93. | I. Erviti | MOV | s.t. |
| 94. | C. Canal | BBH | s.t. |
| 95. | M. Holmes | LTS | s.t. |
| 96. | M. Van Gils | LTS | s.t. |
| 97. | N. Schultz | BEX | s.t. |
| 98. | N. Denz | DSM | s.t. |
| 99. | C. Venturini | ACT | s.t. |
| 100. | D. Howson | BEX | s.t. |
| 101. | J. Knox | DQT | s.t. |
| 102. | P. Sánchez | BBH | s.t. |
| 103. | F. Vermeersch | LTS | s.t. |
| 104. | S. Dewulf | ACT | s.t. |
| 105. | X. M. Azparren | EUS | s.t. |
| 106. | D. Sunderland | TQA | s.t. |
| 107. | A. Bagües | CJR | s.t. |
| 108. | Y. Arashiro | TBV | s.t. |
| 109. | C. Haga | DSM | s.t. |
| 110. | F. Barceló | COF | s.t. |
| 111. | M. Padun | TBV | 38:49 |
| 112. | D. Touzé | ACT | s.t. |
| 113. | K. Geniets | GFC | s.t. |
| 114. | S. Berwick | ISN | s.t. |
| 115. | M. Vansevenant | DQT | 38:53 |
| 116. | A. Bagioli | DQT | 38:56 |
| 117. | M. Cort | EFN | 38:59 |
| 118. | S. Modolo | AFC | s.t. |
| 119. | H. Vanhoucke | LTS | 39:06 |
| 120. | J. Vine | AFC | 39:45 |
| 121. | S. Puccio | IGD | 40:23 |
| 122. | R. Sinkeldam | GFC | s.t. |
| 123. | O. Lazkano | CJR | s.t. |
| 124. | C. Verona | MOV | s.t. |
| 125. | J. Aberasturi | CJR | s.t. |
| 126. | B. J. Lindeman | TQA | s.t. |
| 127. | L. Hofstede | TJV | s.t. |
| 128. | T. Scully | EFN | 40:27 |
| 129. | E. Planckaert | AFC | s.t. |
| 130. | D. Rubio | BBH | s.t. |
| 131. | R. Stannard | BEX | 40:35 |
| 132. | M. Trentin | UAD | 40:49 |
| 133. | R. Oliveira | UAD | s.t. |
| 134. | C. Brown | TQA | 40:53 |
| 135. | A. Krieger | AFC | 41:27 |
| 136. | C. Benedetti | BOH | 41:34 |
| 137. | G. Niv | ISN | s.t. |
| 138. | R. Minali | IWG | 42:58 |
| 139. | A. Démare | GFC | s.t. |
| 140. | J. Bou | EUS | 44:58 |
| 141. | A. Soto | EUS | s.t. |
| 142. | J. J. Lobato | EUS | 45:00 |
| 143. | J. Černý | DQT | 45:07 |
| 144. | B. Van Lerberghe | DQT | 45:11 |
| 145. | P. Allegaert | COF | s.t. |
| 146. | J. Meeus | BOH | 45:14 |
| 147. | F. Sénéchal | DQT | 45:16 |
| 148. | A. Dainese | DSM | 45:17 |
| 149. | L. Mezgec | BEX | 45:19 |
| 150. | M. Laas | BOH | s.t. |
| 151. | D. Claeys | TQA | 45:21 |
| 152. | F. Jakobsen | DQT | s.t. |
| 153. | Z. Štybar | DQT | s.t. |

AUGUST   WORLDTOUR MEN'S RACE

# LA VUELTA A ESPAÑA
Stage 18
2 September 2021
Salas–Altu d'El Gamoniteiru
162.6km

The Queen Stage of this year's Spanish Grand Tour culminated atop the formidable Alto d'El Gamoniteiru for the final high-mountain stage of the race. A group of more than 30 riders headed off the front after the flag drop, Storer taking maximum KOM points on the first two climbs, going clear on the second, then staying away and taking 2 and a half minutes onto the penultimate climb as the rest of the move was swallowed up. Bardet struck out as the bunch neared the top to claim as many mountain points as he could before being reeled back in, although he was still usurped in the KOM competition by his DSM teammate. Movistar's tempo at the start of the final climb wasn't strong enough to deter attacks from Geoffrey Bouchard and David de la Cruz – the Spaniard catching and passing the Frenchman – but Storer was still a minute and a half up the road as he went under the 10km banner. De la Cruz dropped Storer with little over 5km to go, but the GC riders were only half a minute behind at this point, De la Cruz looking like the last hope if Spain were to win a stage at their home Grand Tour this year. Bernal then attacked, with Roglič following. López, Mas and Kuss also kept pace, while Haig and Yates dropped, before López made his move a kilometre later and caught De la Cruz as the dropped riders got back in behind. López then made his bid for stage glory inside 3km to go, dropping De la Cruz while Kuss set the pace behind, which was too much for Yates. Roglič then attacked, seated, with 2km remaining, taking Mas and Bernal with him. The Ineos rider tried to make a move once more but was unable to drop his rivals. As López emerged through the clouds to take the stage win, Roglič sprinted in behind, limiting his losses to just 14 seconds, a handful of seconds ahead of both Mas and Bernal.

## TRIVIA
» This was Miguel Ángel López's tenth career victory in Spain.

## WEATHER

TEMPERATURE   WIND
19°C          NW 7km/h

## PROFILE

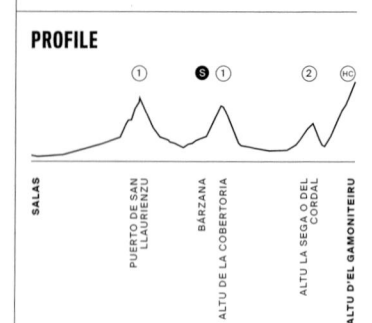

## GENERAL CLASSIFICATION

| POS | NAME | TEAM | TIME |
|---|---|---|---|
| 1. — | P. Roglič | TJV | 73:24:25 |
| 2. — | E. Mas | MOV | 2:30 |
| 3. — | M. A. López | MOV | 2:53 |
| 4. — | J. Haig | TBV | 4:36 |
| 5. ↑1 | E. Bernal | IGD | 4:43 |
| 6. ↑1 | A. Yates | IGD | 5:44 |
| 7. ↑1 | S. Kuss | TJV | 6:02 |
| 8. ↑2 | G. Mäder | TBV | 7:48 |
| 9. ↓4 | G. Martin | COF | 8:31 |
| 10. ↑2 | L. Meintjes | IWG | 9:02 |

## KING OF THE MOUNTAINS

| POS | NAME | TEAM | PTS |
|---|---|---|---|
| 1. ↑1 | M. Storer | DSM | 59 |
| 2. ↓1 | R. Bardet | DSM | 54 |
| 3. ↑1 | P. Roglič | TJV | 48 |

## POINTS

| POS | NAME | TEAM | PTS |
|---|---|---|---|
| 1. — | F. Jakobsen | DQT | 250 |
| 2. — | P. Roglič | TJV | 162 |
| 3. — | M. Trentin | UAD | 123 |

## YOUNG RIDER

| POS | NAME | TEAM | TIME |
|---|---|---|---|
| 1. — | E. Bernal | IGD | 73:29:08 |
| 2. — | G. Mäder | TBV | 3:05 |
| 3. — | J. P. López | TFS | 13:20 |

## BONUSES

| TYPE | NAME | TEAM |
|---|---|---|
| KOM 1 | M. Storer | DSM |
| KOM 2 | M. Storer | DSM |
| KOM 3 | M. Storer | DSM |
| KOM 4 | M. A. López | MOV |
| Sprint 1 | J. Keukeleire | EFN |

## STAGE RESULTS

| POS | NAME | TEAM | TIME |
|---|---|---|---|
| 1. | M. A. López | MOV | 4:41:21 |
| 2. | P. Roglič | TJV | 0:14 |
| 3. | E. Mas | MOV | 0:20 |
| 4. | E. Bernal | IGD | 0:22 |
| 5. | J. Haig | TBV | 0:58 |
| 6. | D. de la Cruz | UAD | s.t. |
| 7. | G. Mäder | TBV | s.t. |
| 8. | L. Meintjes | IWG | s.t. |
| 9. | S. Kuss | TJV | 1:06 |
| 10. | A. Yates | IGD | 1:07 |
| 11. | S. Kruijswijk | TJV | 1:57 |
| 12. | R. Bardet | DSM | 2:49 |
| 13. | J. P. López | TFS | 3:07 |
| 14. | G. Bouchard | ACT | 3:38 |
| 15. | W. Poels | TBV | 3:57 |
| 16. | J. Dombrowski | UAD | 4:01 |
| 17. | Ó. Cabedo | BBH | 4:12 |
| 18. | G. Martin | COF | 4:23 |
| 19. | M. Nieve | BEX | 4:47 |
| 20. | L. A. Maté | EUS | 5:05 |
| 21. | O. C. Eiking | IWG | 5:24 |
| 22. | M. Bizkarra | EUS | 5:27 |
| 23. | A. Zeits | BEX | s.t. |
| 24. | J. Hirt | IWG | 5:33 |
| 25. | D. A. Camargo | EFN | 6:00 |
| 26. | D. Caruso | TBV | 6:22 |
| 27. | F. Großschartner | BOH | 6:49 |
| 28. | S. Cras | LTS | 7:38 |
| 29. | G. Brambilla | TFS | 8:02 |
| 30. | R. Rochas | COF | 8:14 |
| 31. | S. Oomen | TJV | 8:55 |
| 32. | S. Petilli | IWG | s.t. |
| 33. | K. Bouwman | TJV | 9:21 |
| 34. | Á. Madrazo | BBH | s.t. |
| 35. | P. Sivakov | IGD | 10:57 |
| 36. | T. Arensman | DSM | s.t. |
| 37. | M. Storer | DSM | 11:25 |
| 38. | I. Izagirre | APT | 12:11 |
| 39. | M. Iturria | EUS | 12:28 |
| 40. | B. Zwiehoff | BOH | 12:35 |
| 41. | J. Amezqueta | CJR | 12:37 |
| 42. | N. Prodhomme | ACT | 13:59 |
| 43. | C. Champoussin | ACT | s.t. |
| 44. | P. Sánchez | BBH | 14:51 |
| 45. | M. Tusveld | DSM | 16:00 |
| 46. | R. Majka | UAD | 16:07 |
| 47. | R. Gibbons | UAD | s.t. |
| 48. | D. Navarro | BBH | s.t. |
| 49. | K. Geniets | GFC | 16:11 |
| 50. | J. J. Rojas | MOV | 17:34 |
| 51. | L. Hamilton | BEX | 18:15 |
| 52. | J. Cepeda Hernández | CJR | 21:30 |
| 53. | R. Oliveira | UAD | 21:36 |
| 54. | A. Okamika | BBH | 22:43 |
| 55. | A. Palzer | BOH | 25:28 |
| 56. | A. Roux | GFC | 25:32 |
| 57. | J. Vine | AFC | 25:40 |
| 58. | E. Finé | COF | 25:51 |
| 59. | I. Erviti | MOV | 26:01 |
| 60. | R. Gesink | TJV | s.t. |
| 61. | N. Oliveira | MOV | s.t. |
| 62. | G. Izagirre | APT | s.t. |
| 63. | N. Schultz | BEX | s.t. |
| 64. | C. Hamilton | DSM | s.t. |
| 65. | M. Cherel | ACT | s.t. |
| 66. | Jo. Herrada | COF | s.t. |
| 67. | Je. Herrada | COF | s.t. |
| 68. | G. Martín | EUS | s.t. |
| 69. | L. Calmejane | ACT | s.t. |
| 70. | X. M. Azparren | EUS | s.t. |
| 71. | A. Bagües | CJR | s.t. |
| 72. | D. Touzé | ACT | s.t. |
| 73. | R. Taaramäe | IWG | s.t. |
| 74. | J. Piccoli | ISN | s.t. |
| 75. | L. Craddock | EFN | 26:26 |
| 76. | F. Aru | TQA | 26:56 |
| 77. | M. Vansevenant | DQT | 27:07 |
| 78. | J. Keukeleire | EFN | s.t. |
| 79. | S. Dewulf | ACT | 27:14 |
| 80. | Q. Simmons | TFS | s.t. |
| 81. | J. Tratnik | TBV | 28:29 |
| 82. | N. Van Hooydonck | TJV | s.t. |
| 83. | J. Polanc | UAD | s.t. |
| 84. | M. Cort | EFN | 31:28 |
| 85. | A. Kron | LTS | s.t. |
| 86. | T. Ludvigsson | GFC | s.t. |
| 87. | D. Claeys | TQA | 31:39 |
| 88. | C. Haga | DSM | 31:47 |
| 89. | M. Padun | TBV | s.t. |
| 90. | A. Vlasov | APT | s.t. |
| 91. | S. Puccio | IGD | 32:34 |
| 92. | M. Matthews | BEX | 33:12 |
| 93. | E. Planckaert | AFC | 33:42 |
| 94. | J. Bol | BBH | s.t. |
| 95. | G. Niv | ISN | s.t. |
| 96. | F. De Tier | AFC | 33:56 |
| 97. | T. Pidcock | IGD | 34:05 |
| 98. | J. Knox | DQT | s.t. |
| 99. | A. Bagioli | DQT | 35:00 |
| 100. | A. Nibali | TFS | s.t. |
| 101. | C. Canal | BBH | s.t. |
| 102. | O. Le Gac | GFC | 35:25 |
| 103. | C. Venturini | ACT | 36:02 |
| 104. | M. Trentin | UAD | s.t. |
| 105. | P. Gamper | BOH | s.t. |
| 106. | S. Berwick | ISN | s.t. |
| 107. | S. Thwaites | AFC | s.t. |
| 108. | D. Sunderland | TQA | s.t. |
| 109. | A. Cuadros Morata | CJR | s.t. |
| 110. | O. Lazkano | CJR | 36:05 |
| 111. | N. Denz | DSM | s.t. |
| 112. | A. Kirsch | TFS | 37:31 |
| 113. | T. Scully | EFN | s.t. |
| 114. | D. Howson | BEX | s.t. |
| 115. | W. Kreder | IWG | s.t. |
| 116. | A. Soto | EUS | s.t. |
| 117. | K. van Melsen | IWG | s.t. |
| 118. | A. Démare | GFC | s.t. |
| 119. | B. J. Lindeman | TQA | s.t. |
| 120. | C. Benedetti | BOH | s.t. |
| 121. | F. Barceló | COF | s.t. |
| 122. | F. Vermeersch | LTS | s.t. |
| 123. | R. Stannard | BEX | s.t. |
| 124. | L. Mezgec | BEX | s.t. |
| 125. | A. Krieger | AFC | 37:55 |
| 126. | S. Modolo | AFC | 38:23 |
| 127. | J. Bou | EUS | 39:21 |
| 128. | M. Van Gils | LTS | s.t. |
| 129. | Y. Natarov | APT | 39:23 |
| 130. | J. J. Lobato | EUS | s.t. |
| 131. | S. Henao | TQA | s.t. |
| 132. | S. Moniquet | LTS | s.t. |
| 133. | Y. Arashiro | TBV | 39:28 |
| 134. | C. Brown | TQA | 39:33 |
| 135. | R. Sinkeldam | GFC | 39:54 |
| 136. | P. Allegaert | COF | s.t. |
| 137. | H. Vanhoucke | LTS | 39:57 |
| 138. | J. Meeus | BOH | s.t. |
| 139. | A. Dainese | DSM | 40:02 |
| 140. | R. Minali | IWG | s.t. |
| 141. | L. Hofstede | TJV | 40:05 |
| 142. | J. Aberasturi | CJR | 40:12 |
| 143. | B. Van Lerberghe | DQT | 40:54 |
| 144. | Z. Štybar | DQT | s.t. |
| 145. | F. Sénéchal | DQT | s.t. |
| 146. | F. Jakobsen | DQT | s.t. |
| 147. | J. Černý | DQT | s.t. |
| 148. | M. Laas | BOH | s.t. |

## BREAKAWAY

J. Piccoli (ISN), P. Sanchez (BBH), H. Vanhoucke (LTS), B. J. Lindeman (TQA), K. Bouwman (TJV), M. Vansevenant (DQT), M. Cherel (ACT), S. Dewulf (ACT), F. De Tier (AFC), E. Planckaert (AFC), G. Izaguirre (APT), P. Gamper (BOH), Jo. Herrada (COF), J. Keukeleire (EFN), O. Le Gac (GFC), R. Taaramäe (IWG), S. Puccio (IGD), S. Cras (LTS), I. Erviti (MOV), D. Howson (BEX), N. Schultz (BEX), M. Storer (DSM), T. Arensman (DSM), F. Aru (TQA), G. Brambilla (TFS), A. Nibali (TFS), R. Majka (UAD), L. Á. Maté (EUS), G. Martin (EUS), A. Bagues (CJR), C. Canal (BBH), A. Okamika (BBH)

AUGUST  WORLDTOUR MEN'S RACE

## LA VUELTA A ESPAÑA
Stage 19
3 September 2021
Tapia–Monforte de Lemos
191.2km

Mikaël Cherel and Mark Padun were responsible for starting things off before 20 riders headed up the road in a stage that would either be decided by the breakaway or a bunch sprint finish – depending how much will and energy the riders in the bunch still possessed. As Fabio Jakobsen was dropped on the second climb, the chase lost the strength of Deceuninck-QuickStep, while the escape group eked out a 2-minute advantage. Instead, it was BikeExchange and DSM looking to control things on the front of the peloton, while up ahead an attack from Quinn Simmons and Rui Oliveira dropped Fabio Aru as the final days of his career ticked down. Louis Meintjes was brought down in a crash in the bunch with less than 50km to go, the South African forced to abandon the race and his tenth place overall. Simmons went again with 35km left, Oliveira following once more, with Cort, Bagioli, Craddock, Anthony Roux and Kron also making it across not long after. The group of seven only had half a minute over the peloton as they went under the 20km banner, but the downhill run-in to the line would be their ally. Although DSM lent a hand to BikeExchange in the chase, getting the gap down to 20 seconds, it had increased again with 10km remaining. Yet still, with 5km to go, their gap remained, as Lawson Craddock worked on the front to try and set up Magnus Cort, the cohesion of the group remaining all the way up until 200 metres to go such was the precariousness nature of their advantage. Quinn Simmons made his bid for glory, trying to go early and catch the others off guard, but Magnus Cort once more had too much, coming past to take his third stage of the race.

### TRIVIA
» Magnus Cort is the third rider to win three stages at this Vuelta, meaning nearly half of all stage wins were shared between the Dane, Jakobsen and Roglič.

### WEATHER

TEMPERATURE  19°C
WIND  NW 11km/h

### PROFILE

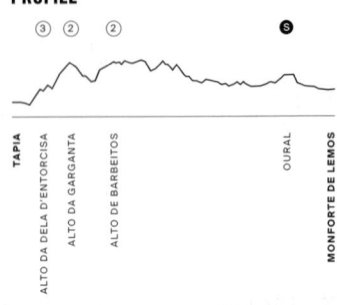

### BREAKAWAY
M. Cherel (ACT), M. Padun (TBV), N. Denz (DSM), A. J. Soto (EUS), D. Touzé (ACT), J. Vine (AFC), P. Sanchez (BBH), J. Amezqueta (CJR), O. Lazkano (CJR), A. Bagioli (DQT), L. Craddock (EFN), M. Cort (EFN), A. Roux (GFC), A. Kron (LTS), R. Stannard (BEX), F. Aru (TQA), Q. Simmons (TFS), R. Oliveira (UAD), J. Polanc (UAD)

### GENERAL CLASSIFICATION
| POS | NAME | TEAM | TIME |
|---|---|---|---|
| 1. — | P. Roglič | TJV | 77:49:37 |
| 2. — | E. Mas | MOV | 2:30 |
| 3. — | M. A. López | MOV | 2:53 |
| 4. — | J. Haig | TBV | 4:36 |
| 5. — | E. Bernal | IGD | 4:43 |
| 6. — | A. Yates | IGD | 5:44 |
| 7. — | S. Kuss | TJV | 6:02 |
| 8. — | G. Mäder | TBV | 7:48 |
| 9. — | G. Martin | COF | 8:31 |
| 10.↑1 | D. de la Cruz | UAD | 9:24 |

### KING OF THE MOUNTAINS
| POS | NAME | TEAM | PTS |
|---|---|---|---|
| 1. — | M. Storer | DSM | 59 |
| 2. — | R. Bardet | DSM | 54 |
| 3. — | P. Roglič | TJV | 48 |

### POINTS
| POS | NAME | TEAM | PTS |
|---|---|---|---|
| 1. — | F. Jakobsen | DQT | 250 |
| 2. — | P. Roglič | TJV | 162 |
| 3. ↑1 | M. Cort | EFN | 144 |

### YOUNG RIDER
| POS | NAME | TEAM | TIME |
|---|---|---|---|
| 1. — | E. Bernal | IGD | 77:54:20 |
| 2. — | G. Mäder | TBV | 3:05 |
| 3. — | J. P. López | TFS | 13:20 |

### BONUSES
| TYPE | NAME | TEAM |
|---|---|---|
| KOM 1 | M. Cort | EFN |
| KOM 2 | F. Aru | TQA |
| KOM 3 | M. Cherel | ACT |
| Sprint 1 | Q. Simmons | TFS |

## STAGE RESULTS

| POS | NAME | TEAM | TIME |
|---|---|---|---|
| 1. | M. Cort | EFN | 4:24:54 |
| 2. | R. Oliveira | UAD | s.t. |
| 3. | Q. Simmons | TFS | s.t. |
| 4. | A. Bagioli | DQT | s.t. |
| 5. | A. Roux | GFC | s.t. |
| 6. | A. Kron | LTS | s.t. |
| 7. | L. Craddock | EFN | 0:05 |
| 8. | A. Dainese | DSM | 0:18 |
| 9. | M. Trentin | UAD | s.t. |
| 10. | A. Krieger | AFC | s.t. |
| 11. | F. Sénéchal | DQT | s.t. |
| 12. | P. Allegaert | COF | s.t. |
| 13. | M. Matthews | BEX | s.t. |
| 14. | A. Démare | GFC | s.t. |
| 15. | A. Kirsch | TFS | s.t. |
| 16. | G. Martín | EUS | s.t. |
| 17. | C. Canal | BBH | s.t. |
| 18. | C. Venturini | ACT | s.t. |
| 19. | J. Bol | BBH | s.t. |
| 20. | X. M. Azparren | EUS | s.t. |
| 21. | T. Pidcock | IGD | s.t. |
| 22. | S. Cras | LTS | s.t. |
| 23. | J. Tratnik | TBV | s.t. |
| 24. | E. Bernal | IGD | s.t. |
| 25. | A. Bagües | CJR | s.t. |
| 26. | M. Van Gils | LTS | s.t. |
| 27. | E. Mas | MOV | s.t. |
| 28. | F. Großschartner | BOH | s.t. |
| 29. | J. Haig | TBV | s.t. |
| 30. | P. Roglič | TJV | s.t. |
| 31. | M. A. López | MOV | s.t. |
| 32. | N. Van Hooydonck | TJV | s.t. |
| 33. | G. Mäder | TBV | s.t. |
| 34. | J. J. Rojas | MOV | s.t. |
| 35. | Y. Natarov | APT | s.t. |
| 36. | D. Caruso | TBV | s.t. |
| 37. | R. Gibbons | UAD | s.t. |
| 38. | N. Oliveira | MOV | s.t. |
| 39. | L. A. Maté | EUS | s.t. |
| 40. | S. Kruijswijk | TJV | s.t. |
| 41. | S. Kuss | TJV | s.t. |
| 42. | S. Oomen | TJV | s.t. |
| 43. | G. Martin | COF | s.t. |
| 44. | G. Izaguirre | APT | s.t. |
| 45. | R. Rochas | COF | s.t. |
| 46. | W. Kreder | IWG | s.t. |
| 47. | C. Brown | TQA | s.t. |
| 48. | D. de la Cruz | UAD | s.t. |
| 49. | J. P. López | TFS | s.t. |
| 50. | F. De Tier | AFC | s.t. |
| 51. | A. Yates | IGD | s.t. |
| 52. | I. Erviti | MOV | s.t. |
| 53. | C. Champoussin | ACT | s.t. |
| 54. | Ó. Cabedo | BBH | s.t. |
| 55. | L. Calmejane | ACT | s.t. |
| 56. | R. Taaramäe | IWG | s.t. |
| 57. | O. C. Eiking | IWG | s.t. |
| 58. | G. Brambilla | TFS | s.t. |
| 59. | F. Barceló | COF | s.t. |
| 60. | S. Petilli | IWG | s.t. |
| 61. | B. Zwiehoff | BOH | s.t. |
| 62. | I. Izaguirre | APT | s.t. |
| 63. | M. Iturria | EUS | s.t. |
| 64. | A. Palzer | BOH | s.t. |
| 65. | J. Amezqueta | CJR | s.t. |
| 66. | O. Le Gac | GFC | s.t. |
| 67. | G. Bouchard | ACT | s.t. |
| 68. | J. Vine | AFC | s.t. |
| 69. | P. Sánchez | BBH | s.t. |
| 70. | Á. Madrazo | BBH | s.t. |
| 71. | S. Puccio | IGD | s.t. |
| 72. | J. Dombrowski | UAD | s.t. |
| 73. | K. Bouwman | TJV | s.t. |
| 74. | M. Bizkarra | EUS | s.t. |
| 75. | S. Moniquet | LTS | s.t. |
| 76. | D. Navarro | BBH | s.t. |
| 77. | W. Poels | TBV | s.t. |
| 78. | J. Cepeda Hernández | CJR | s.t. |
| 79. | M. Cherel | ACT | s.t. |
| 80. | N. Denz | DSM | s.t. |
| 81. | R. Gesink | TJV | s.t. |
| 82. | N. Prodhomme | ACT | s.t. |
| 83. | K. van Melsen | IWG | s.t. |
| 84. | E. Finé | COF | s.t. |
| 85. | Jo. Herrada | COF | s.t. |
| 86. | P. Sivakov | IGD | s.t. |
| 87. | D. Claeys | TQA | 0:39 |
| 88. | J. Keukeleire | EFN | 0:41 |
| 89. | S. Dewulf | ACT | 0:46 |
| 90. | A. Okamika | BBH | 1:04 |
| 91. | M. Tusveld | DSM | 1:19 |
| 92. | J. Polanc | UAD | 1:21 |
| 93. | R. Majka | UAD | s.t. |
| 94. | T. Scully | EFN | s.t. |
| 95. | L. Mezgec | BEX | s.t. |

| POS | NAME | TEAM | TIME |
|---|---|---|---|
| 96. | Je. Herrada | COF | s.t. |
| 97. | J. Hirt | IWG | s.t. |
| 98. | T. Ludvigsson | GFC | 1:25 |
| 99. | K. Geniets | GFC | s.t. |
| 100. | R. Stannard | BEX | 1:42 |
| 101. | D. Touzé | ACT | 1:46 |
| 102. | A. Soto | EUS | 1:57 |
| 103. | J. Bou | EUS | s.t. |
| 104. | M. Padun | TBV | 1:59 |
| 105. | L. Hamilton | BEX | s.t. |
| 106. | D. Sunderland | TQA | s.t. |
| 107. | A. Cuadros Morata | CJR | 2:03 |
| 108. | Y. Arashiro | TBV | s.t. |
| 109. | H. Vanhoucke | LTS | 2:07 |
| 110. | J. Knox | DQT | s.t. |
| 111. | F. Aru | TQA | 2:30 |
| 112. | D. A. Camargo | EFN | s.t. |
| 113. | A. Nibali | TFS | s.t. |
| 114. | M. Nieve | BEX | s.t. |
| 115. | T. Arensman | DSM | 4:02 |
| 116. | C. Haga | DSM | s.t. |
| 117. | M. Storer | DSM | s.t. |
| 118. | N. Schultz | BEX | 4:31 |
| 119. | D. Howson | BEX | s.t. |
| 120. | R. Bardet | DSM | 5:59 |
| 121. | C. Hamilton | DSM | 10:56 |
| 122. | A. Zeits | BEX | s.t. |
| 123. | R. Minali | IWG | 26:26 |
| 124. | E. Planckaert | AFC | s.t. |
| 125. | J. Aberasturi | CJR | s.t. |
| 126. | J. Piccoli | ISN | s.t. |
| 127. | O. Lazkano | CJR | s.t. |
| 128. | B. J. Lindeman | TQA | s.t. |
| 129. | R. Sinkeldam | GFC | s.t. |
| 130. | F. Vermeersch | LTS | s.t. |
| 131. | C. Benedetti | BOH | s.t. |
| 132. | S. Thwaites | AFC | s.t. |
| 133. | A. Vlasov | APT | s.t. |
| 134. | M. Laas | BOH | s.t. |
| 135. | J. J. Lobato | EUS | s.t. |
| 136. | G. Niv | ISN | s.t. |
| 137. | Z. Štybar | DQT | s.t. |
| 138. | M. Vansevenant | DQT | s.t. |
| 139. | P. Gamper | BOH | s.t. |
| 140. | B. Van Lerberghe | DQT | s.t. |
| 141. | L. Hofstede | TJV | s.t. |
| 142. | J. Černý | DQT | s.t. |
| 143. | J. Meeus | BOH | s.t. |
| 144. | S. Berwick | ISN | s.t. |
| 145. | F. Jakobsen | DQT | s.t. |

AUGUST   WORLDTOUR MEN'S RACE

## LA VUELTA A ESPAÑA
Stage 20
4 September 2021
Sanxenxo–Mos. Castro de Herville
202.2km

### WEATHER

TEMPERATURE  WIND
22°C         SW 9km/h

### PROFILE

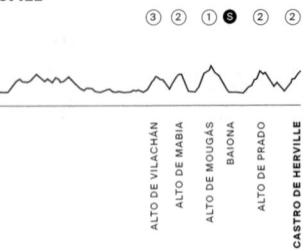

Five classified climbs and 3,200 metres of uphill as a number of familiar faces flung themselves up the road – Bardet, Storer, Gibbons, Padun and Calmejane included. Jumbo-Visma were content to let the gap expand as Storer took the KOM points unchallenged, then Ineos got to work, trimming the GC group down to 30 riders on the Alto de Mabia. Up ahead Trentin attacked, soon followed by Gibbons and Bardet, before Storer and others got back on terms at the foot of the Alto de Mougás, the toughest climb of the day. Ineos worked hard to whittle the GC group down further before Bernal kicked, setting up Yates to make the decisive move of the day. Mäder, Roglič, Mas and Haig chased, as López failed to respond and Bernal sat in his compatriot's wheel. By the summit, the break had 4 minutes and the Yates group nearly 40 seconds on López. Gibbons launched from the escapees on the descent, while Mäder was put to work to extend the Yates group's advantage. Onto the flat and the gap was 3 minutes, with no one willing to help López, and the Colombian soon relenting in helplessness as Padun dropped back to help the Bahrain cause. Onto the final climb and Gibbons' gap was back up to 90 seconds. Yates put in yet another dig, only for Roglič to ride up to his wheel with few qualms. Mas followed, as did Haig after a little while, now 30 seconds behind with 6km to go. Yates persisted but it was Roglič's acceleration that brought Gibbons back. The leading quartet then stuttered, allowing Gibbons and Mikel Bizkarra to come flying back past, but only until each time the GC fight was reignited. Instead, it was Clément Champoussin – from the original breakaway – who snuck up as they slowed, taking the flyer of all flyers to sail past and into the distance for an extraordinary victory. López had given up the chase completely, getting into the team car and abandoning the race in frustration. The fall-out continued past the end of the race.

### BREAKAWAY

M. Trentin (UAD), S. Dewulf (ACT), C. Champoussin (ACT), M. Padun (TBV), Je. Herrada (COF), J. Hirt (IWG), N. Schultz (BEX), R. Bardet (DSM), C. Hamilton (DSM), M. Storer (DSM), F. De Tier (AFC), S. Moniquet (LTS), L. Calmejane (ACT), D. Navarro (BBH), M. Bizkarra (EUS), R. Gibbons (UAD)

### GENERAL CLASSIFICATION

| POS | NAME | TEAM | TIME |
|---|---|---|---|
| 1. – | P. Roglič | TJV | 83:11:27 |
| 2. – | E. Mas | MOV | 2:38 |
| 3. ↑1 | J. Haig | TBV | 4:48 |
| 4. ↑2 | A. Yates | IGD | 5:48 |
| 5. ↑3 | G. Mäder | TBV | 8:14 |
| 6. ↓1 | E. Bernal | IGD | 11:38 |
| 7. – | S. Kuss | TJV | 13:42 |
| 8. ↑1 | G. Martin | COF | 16:11 |
| 9. ↑1 | D. de la Cruz | UAD | 16:19 |
| 10.↑2 | F. Großschartner | BOH | 20:30 |

### KING OF THE MOUNTAINS

| POS | NAME | TEAM | PTS |
|---|---|---|---|
| 1. – | M. Storer | DSM | 80 |
| 2. – | R. Bardet | DSM | 61 |
| 3. – | P. Roglič | TJV | 51 |

### POINTS

| POS | NAME | TEAM | PTS |
|---|---|---|---|
| 1. – | F. Jakobsen | DQT | 250 |
| 2. – | P. Roglič | TJV | 179 |
| 3. ↑1 | M. Trentin | UAD | 145 |

### YOUNG RIDER

| POS | NAME | TEAM | TIME |
|---|---|---|---|
| 1. ↑1 | G. Mäder | TBV | 83:19:41 |
| 2. ↓1 | E. Bernal | IGD | 3:24 |
| 3. – | J. P. López | TFS | 18:04 |

### BONUSES

| TYPE | NAME | TEAM |
|---|---|---|
| KOM 1 | M. Storer | DSM |
| KOM 2 | M. Storer | DSM |
| KOM 3 | M. Storer | DSM |
| KOM 4 | R. Gibbons | UAD |
| KOM 5 | C. Champoussin | ACT |
| Sprint 1 | R. Gibbons | UAD |

### TRIVIA

» This was Clément Champoussin's debut professional victory.

## STAGE RESULTS

| POS | NAME | TEAM | TIME |
|---|---|---|---|
| 1. | C. Champoussin | ACT | 5:21:50 |
| 2. | P. Roglič | TJV | 0:06 |
| 3. | A. Yates | IGD | 0:08 |
| 4. | E. Mas | MOV | s.t. |
| 5. | J. Haig | TBV | 0:12 |
| 6. | C. Hamilton | DSM | 0:16 |
| 7. | M. Bizkarra | EUS | 0:23 |
| 8. | R. Gibbons | UAD | 0:26 |
| 9. | G. Mäder | TBV | s.t. |
| 10. | F. De Tier | AFC | 0:50 |
| 11. | J. Hirt | IWG | 1:05 |
| 12. | L. Calmejane | ACT | 1:09 |
| 13. | S. Moniquet | LTS | 1:13 |
| 14. | S. Dewulf | ACT | 1:15 |
| 15. | N. Schultz | BEX | 1:35 |
| 16. | D. Navarro | BBH | 2:25 |
| 17. | F. Großschartner | BOH | 6:55 |
| 18. | D. de la Cruz | UAD | s.t. |
| 19. | E. Bernal | IGD | s.t. |
| 20. | S. Kruijswijk | TJV | s.t. |
| 21. | A. Cuadros Morata | CJR | 7:31 |
| 22. | O. C. Eiking | IWG | s.t. |
| 23. | M. Padun | TBV | s.t. |
| 24. | L. A. Maté | EUS | s.t. |
| 25. | M. Trentin | UAD | s.t. |
| 26. | D. Caruso | TBV | 7:34 |
| 27. | G. Martin | COF | 7:40 |
| 28. | S. Kuss | TJV | s.t. |
| 29. | R. Majka | UAD | s.t. |
| 30. | S. Cras | LTS | s.t. |
| 31. | A. Soto | EUS | s.t. |
| 32. | J. Dombrowski | UAD | s.t. |
| 33. | S. Oomen | TJV | s.t. |
| 34. | M. Storer | DSM | s.t. |
| 35. | R. Bardet | DSM | s.t. |
| 36. | G. Bouchard | ACT | s.t. |
| 37. | L. Hamilton | BEX | 7:47 |
| 38. | Ó. Cabedo | BBH | 7:49 |
| 39. | J. P. López | TFS | 8:15 |
| 40. | Je. Herrada | COF | 8:20 |
| 41. | G. Brambilla | TFS | 8:30 |
| 42. | R. Rochas | COF | 8:33 |
| 43. | D. Claeys | TQA | 9:33 |
| 44. | M. Cherel | ACT | 11:11 |
| 45. | D. A. Camargo | EFN | 11:21 |
| 46. | W. Poels | TBV | s.t. |
| 47. | G. Izagirre | APT | 14:10 |
| 48. | I. Izagirre | APT | s.t. |
| 49. | Á. Madrazo | BBH | 15:03 |
| 50. | A. Roux | GFC | 16:12 |
| 51. | J. J. Rojas | MOV | 18:21 |
| 52. | P. Sivakov | IGD | s.t. |
| 53. | M. Matthews | BEX | 18:40 |
| 54. | F. Barceló | COF | 22:24 |
| 55. | A. Okamika | BBH | s.t. |
| 56. | Jo. Herrada | COF | s.t. |
| 57. | A. Zeits | BEX | s.t. |
| 58. | I. Erviti | MOV | s.t. |
| 59. | E. Finé | COF | s.t. |
| 60. | J. Amezqueta | CJR | s.t. |
| 61. | T. Arensman | DSM | s.t. |
| 62. | B. Zwiehoff | BOH | s.t. |
| 63. | J. Keukeleire | EFN | s.t. |
| 64. | S. Petilli | IWG | s.t. |
| 65. | M. Tusveld | DSM | s.t. |
| 66. | N. Oliveira | MOV | s.t. |
| 67. | G. Niv | ISN | s.t. |
| 68. | J. Cepeda Hernández | CJR | s.t. |
| 69. | M. Iturria | EUS | s.t. |
| 70. | R. Gesink | TJV | s.t. |
| 71. | K. Bouwman | TJV | s.t. |
| 72. | N. Prodhomme | ACT | 22:29 |
| 73. | G. Martin | EUS | 24:02 |
| 74. | P. Sánchez | BBH | s.t. |
| 75. | N. Van Hooydonck | TJV | 24:44 |
| 76. | J. Polanc | UAD | 24:45 |
| 77. | R. Oliveira | UAD | s.t. |
| 78. | D. Touzé | ACT | s.t. |
| 79. | J. Vine | AFC | 24:49 |
| 80. | F. Aru | TQA | 25:21 |
| 81. | T. Pidcock | IGD | s.t. |
| 82. | A. Palzer | BOH | 27:09 |
| 83. | J. Bol | BBH | s.t. |
| 84. | C. Canal | BBH | s.t. |
| 85. | A. Bagües | CJR | s.t. |
| 86. | S. Puccio | IGD | s.t. |
| 87. | P. Gamper | BOH | s.t. |
| 88. | A. Démare | GFC | s.t. |
| 89. | C. Venturini | ACT | 27:20 |
| 90. | R. Taaramäe | IWG | s.t. |
| 91. | D. Sunderland | TQA | 32:33 |
| 92. | C. Brown | TQA | s.t. |
| 93. | M. Van Gils | LTS | s.t. |
| 94. | O. Le Gac | GFC | s.t. |
| 95. | C. Benedetti | BOH | s.t. |
| 96. | E. Planckaert | AFC | 33:14 |
| 97. | A. Krieger | AFC | 34:17 |
| 98. | A. Kron | LTS | s.t. |
| 99. | F. Vermeersch | LTS | s.t. |
| 100. | C. Haga | DSM | s.t. |
| 101. | M. Nieve | BEX | s.t. |
| 102. | D. Howson | BEX | s.t. |
| 103. | T. Ludvigsson | GFC | s.t. |
| 104. | K. Geniets | GFC | s.t. |
| 105. | A. Kirsch | TFS | s.t. |
| 106. | J. Piccoli | ISN | s.t. |
| 107. | N. Denz | DSM | s.t. |
| 108. | H. Vanhoucke | LTS | s.t. |
| 109. | L. Mezgec | BEX | s.t. |
| 110. | J. Tratnik | TBV | s.t. |
| 111. | A. Nibali | TFS | s.t. |
| 112. | Y. Arashiro | TBV | s.t. |
| 113. | L. Craddock | EFN | s.t. |
| 114. | X. M. Azparren | EUS | 40:17 |
| 115. | J. Bou | EUS | s.t. |
| 116. | K. van Melsen | IWG | s.t. |
| 117. | R. Minali | IWG | s.t. |
| 118. | Y. Natarov | APT | s.t. |
| 119. | R. Sinkeldam | GFC | s.t. |
| 120. | W. Kreder | IWG | s.t. |
| 121. | R. Stannard | BEX | s.t. |
| 122. | B. J. Lindeman | TQA | s.t. |
| 123. | L. Hofstede | TJV | s.t. |
| 124. | S. Thwaites | AFC | s.t. |
| 125. | J. J. Lobato | EUS | s.t. |
| 126. | S. Berwick | ISN | s.t. |
| 127. | P. Allegaert | COF | s.t. |
| 128. | Q. Simmons | TFS | s.t. |
| 129. | J. Aberasturi | CJR | s.t. |
| 130. | T. Scully | EFN | 40:28 |
| 131. | J. Meeus | BOH | 40:29 |
| 132. | A. Dainese | DSM | s.t. |
| 133. | M. Cort | EFN | 40:31 |
| 134. | M. Laas | BOH | s.t. |
| 135. | M. Vansevenant | DQT | 41:13 |
| 136. | F. Sénéchal | DQT | s.t. |
| 137. | A. Bagioli | DQT | s.t. |
| 138. | Z. Štybar | DQT | s.t. |
| 139. | B. Van Lerberghe | DQT | s.t. |
| 140. | F. Jakobsen | DQT | s.t. |
| 141. | J. Černý | DQT | s.t. |
| 142. | J. Knox | DQT | s.t. |

AUGUST    WORLDTOUR MEN'S RACE

## LA VUELTA A ESPAÑA
Stage 21 (ITT)
5 September 2021
Padrón–Santiago de Compostela
33.8km

The final time trial was set to be a coronation for the last rider off the start ramp – the race leader Primož Roglič – and, with no Tadej Pogačar in sight, no Tour de France-esque upset was expected. Deceuninck-QuickStep's Josef Černý was the first off the ramp for a 33.8km lumpy time trial from Padrón to Santiago de Compostela, and posted a strong enough time of 45 minutes 18 seconds to put him into the hot seat for a lengthy stay. That was until one of the stars of this Vuelta, Magnus Cort, came through to beat that time by more than a minute. Fabio Aru finished not long afterwards, putting an end to his professional career, and soon the top ten were on the course. Egan Bernal had too much to do to close the gap to fifth-placed Gino Mäder, the Swiss rider also taking home the white young rider's jersey, while David de la Cruz leapfrogged Guillaume Martin and Sepp Kuss into seventh. Adam Yates's pursuit of Jack Haig's final podium spot looked interesting for a minute, until the Australian composed himself and secured his first-ever Grand Tour top three. Barring disaster, Enric Mas was never going to get close to disturbing Primož Roglič; while the Slovenian did nearly go the wrong way on the course, he would have needed quite a big detour for his red jersey to be in any doubt. As Magnus Cort kept everyone entertained, pulling faces in the hot seat, Roglič caught Mas in the final few hundred metres, blasting past him in a show of dominance that encapsulated his third consecutive Vuelta victory: always in control, never flustered, ready to win. Across the line he was 14 seconds faster than Cort, denying the Dane a fourth stage as he claimed his own fourth stage win. Once again, the Spanish Grand Tour belonged to Roglič.

### WEATHER
TEMPERATURE    WIND
26°C           SE 9km/h

### PROFILE
PADRÓN — SANTIAGO DE COMPOSTELA

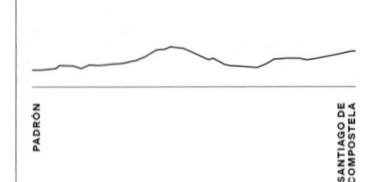

### GENERAL CLASSIFICATION
| POS | | NAME | TEAM | TIME |
|---|---|---|---|---|
| 1. | — | P. Roglič | TJV | 83:55:29 |
| 2. | — | E. Mas | MOV | 4:42 |
| 3. | — | J. Haig | TBV | 7:40 |
| 4. | — | A. Yates | IGD | 9:06 |
| 5. | — | G. Mäder | TBV | 11:33 |
| 6. | — | E. Bernal | IGD | 13:27 |
| 7. | ↑2 | D. de la Cruz | UAD | 18:33 |
| 8. | ↓1 | S. Kuss | TJV | 18:55 |
| 9. | ↓1 | G. Martin | COF | 20:27 |
| 10. | — | F. Großschartner | BOH | 22:22 |

### KING OF THE MOUNTAINS
| POS | | NAME | TEAM | PTS |
|---|---|---|---|---|
| 1. | — | M. Storer | DSM | 80 |
| 2. | — | R. Bardet | DSM | 61 |
| 3. | — | P. Roglič | TJV | 51 |

### POINTS
| POS | | NAME | TEAM | PTS |
|---|---|---|---|---|
| 1. | — | F. Jakobsen | DQT | 250 |
| 2. | — | P. Roglič | TJV | 199 |
| 3. | ↑1 | M. Cort | EFN | 161 |

### TRIVIA
» With this stage victory, Primož Roglič equalled his 2020 Vuelta stage-win haul of four.

### YOUNG RIDER
| POS | | NAME | TEAM | TIME |
|---|---|---|---|---|
| 1. | — | G. Mäder | TBV | 84:07:02 |
| 2. | — | E. Bernal | IGD | 1:54 |
| 3. | — | J. P. López | TFS | 19:48 |

## STAGE RESULTS

| POS | NAME | TEAM | TIME |
|---|---|---|---|
| 1. | P. Roglič | TJV | 44:02 |
| 2. | M. Cort | EFN | 0:14 |
| 3. | T. Arensman | DSM | 0:52 |
| 4. | J. Černý | DQT | 1:16 |
| 5. | C. Haga | DSM | 1:43 |
| 6. | E. Bernal | IGD | 1:49 |
| 7. | F. Großschartner | BOH | 1:52 |
| 8. | S. Kruijswijk | TJV | s.t. |
| 9. | E. Mas | MOV | 2:04 |
| 10. | I. Izagirre | APT | 2:06 |
| 11. | D. de la Cruz | UAD | 2:14 |
| 12. | N. Denz | DSM | 2:17 |
| 13. | L. Craddock | EFN | 2:22 |
| 14. | J. Polanc | UAD | 2:24 |
| 15. | T. Scully | EFN | 2:34 |
| 16. | D. Caruso | TBV | 2:35 |
| 17. | J. Haig | TBV | 2:52 |
| 18. | X. M. Azparren | EUS | 2:54 |
| 19. | M. Storer | DSM | 3:00 |
| 20. | R. Bardet | DSM | s.t. |
| 21. | K. Geniets | GFC | 3:07 |
| 22. | A. Roux | GFC | 3:09 |
| 23. | M. Tusveld | DSM | 3:11 |
| 24. | N. Oliveira | MOV | 3:13 |
| 25. | R. Taaramäe | IWG | 3:15 |
| 26. | R. Majka | UAD | 3:17 |
| 27. | D. A. Camargo | EFN | 3:18 |
| 28. | B. Zwiehoff | BOH | s.t. |
| 29. | A. Yates | IGD | s.t. |
| 30. | W. Poels | TBV | 3:19 |
| 31. | G. Mäder | TBV | s.t. |
| 32. | P. Sivakov | IGD | 3:20 |
| 33. | J. Vine | AFC | s.t. |
| 34. | J. Tratnik | TBV | 3:21 |
| 35. | F. Vermeersch | LTS | 3:22 |
| 36. | M. Matthews | BEX | 3:23 |
| 37. | M. Bizkarra | EUS | 3:24 |
| 38. | Y. Natarov | APT | s.t. |
| 39. | Je. Herrada | COF | 3:41 |
| 40. | R. Gibbons | UAD | 3:44 |
| 41. | N. Van Hooydonck | TJV | 3:47 |
| 42. | S. Cras | LTS | 3:48 |
| 43. | J. Keukeleire | EFN | 3:59 |
| 44. | G. Izagirre | APT | 4:01 |
| 45. | A. Soto | EUS | s.t. |
| 46. | K. Bouwman | TJV | 4:05 |
| 47. | D. Claeys | TQA | 4:06 |
| 48. | C. Brown | TQA | 4:13 |
| 49. | F. Aru | TQA | 4:15 |
| 50. | G. Martin | COF | 4:16 |
| 51. | A. Dainese | DSM | 4:19 |
| 52. | D. Sunderland | TQA | 4:21 |
| 53. | L. Hamilton | BEX | 4:23 |
| 54. | O. C. Eiking | IWG | 4:28 |
| 55. | A. Kirsch | TFS | 4:29 |
| 56. | M. Van Gils | LTS | 4:30 |
| 57. | D. Howson | BEX | 4:31 |
| 58. | D. Touzé | ACT | 4:32 |
| 59. | S. Puccio | IGD | 4:35 |
| 60. | Jo. Herrada | COF | 4:37 |
| 61. | A. Bagioli | DQT | 4:39 |
| 62. | R. Stannard | BEX | 4:41 |
| 63. | A. Krieger | AFC | s.t. |
| 64. | N. Schultz | BEX | 4:43 |
| 65. | T. Pidcock | IGD | s.t. |
| 66. | H. Vanhoucke | LTS | 4:45 |
| 67. | R. Rochas | COF | s.t. |
| 68. | R. Oliveira | UAD | 4:46 |
| 69. | Z. Štybar | DQT | 4:47 |
| 70. | P. Sánchez | BBH | 4:49 |
| 71. | S. Oomen | TJV | s.t. |
| 72. | F. Sénéchal | DQT | 4:55 |
| 73. | M. Iturria | EUS | 4:57 |
| 74. | S. Moniquet | LTS | 5:00 |
| 75. | O. Le Gac | GFC | 5:01 |
| 76. | J. P. López | TFS | 5:03 |
| 77. | R. Gesink | TJV | s.t. |
| 78. | J. Dombrowski | UAD | 5:06 |
| 79. | G. Bouchard | ACT | 5:10 |
| 80. | E. Planckaert | AFC | 5:11 |
| 81. | S. Kuss | TJV | 5:13 |
| 82. | B. J. Lindeman | TQA | 5:17 |
| 83. | L. A. Maté | EUS | 5:19 |
| 84. | A. Palzer | BOH | 5:21 |
| 85. | J. Bol | BBH | s.t. |
| 86. | C. Champoussin | ACT | 5:24 |
| 87. | J. Bou | EUS | 5:29 |
| 88. | T. Ludvigsson | GFC | 5:35 |
| 89. | G. Martín | EUS | 5:38 |
| 90. | M. Vansevenant | DQT | 5:40 |
| 91. | A. Zeits | BEX | 5:41 |
| 92. | C. Hamilton | DSM | 5:42 |
| 93. | C. Benedetti | BOH | 5:45 |
| 94. | A. Kron | LTS | 5:47 |
| 95. | P. Gamper | BOH | 5:48 |
| 96. | S. Dewulf | ACT | 5:49 |
| 97. | S. Thwaites | AFC | 5:50 |
| 98. | C. Canal | BBH | 5:51 |
| 99. | K. van Melsen | IWG | 5:54 |
| 100. | J. Knox | DQT | 5:57 |
| 101. | Ó. Cabedo | BBH | s.t. |
| 102. | G. Niv | ISN | 5:59 |
| 103. | I. Erviti | MOV | 6:00 |
| 104. | A. Démare | GFC | s.t. |
| 105. | J. Meeus | BOH | 6:06 |
| 106. | A. Cuadros Morata | CJR | 6:13 |
| 107. | B. Van Lerberghe | DQT | 6:15 |
| 108. | P. Allegaert | COF | 6:17 |
| 109. | M. Trentin | UAD | s.t. |
| 110. | E. Finé | COF | 6:18 |
| 111. | F. Barceló | COF | 6:19 |
| 112. | G. Brambilla | TFS | 6:20 |
| 113. | J. Piccoli | ISN | 6:22 |
| 114. | F. De Tier | AFC | 6:30 |
| 115. | L. Calmejane | ACT | 6:32 |
| 116. | A. Okamika | BBH | 6:33 |
| 117. | J. J. Rojas | MOV | 6:35 |
| 118. | W. Kreder | IWG | 6:51 |
| 119. | Y. Arashiro | TBV | 6:52 |
| 120. | S. Berwick | ISN | s.t. |
| 121. | R. Sinkeldam | GFC | 6:56 |
| 122. | L. Mezgec | BEX | 6:57 |
| 123. | S. Petilli | IWG | 7:07 |
| 124. | M. Nieve | BEX | 7:08 |
| 125. | J. Hirt | IWG | 7:16 |
| 126. | C. Venturini | ACT | s.t. |
| 127. | J. Amezqueta | CJR | s.t. |
| 128. | M. Cherel | ACT | 7:19 |
| 129. | Q. Simmons | TFS | 7:20 |
| 130. | D. Navarro | BBH | 7:27 |
| 131. | Á. Madrazo | BBH | 7:44 |
| 132. | M. Padun | TBV | 7:49 |
| 133. | J. Aberasturi | CJR | 7:52 |
| 134. | M. Laas | BOH | 7:54 |
| 135. | R. Minali | IWG | 8:01 |
| 136. | L. Hofstede | TJV | 8:17 |
| 137. | N. Prodhomme | ACT | 8:20 |
| 138. | A. Bagües | CJR | 8:21 |
| 139. | J. J. Lobato | EUS | 8:30 |
| 140. | F. Jakobsen | DQT | s.t. |
| 141. | J. Cepeda Hernández | CJR | 8:38 |
| 142. | A. Nibali | TFS | 10:17 |

AUGUST  WORLDTOUR MEN'S RACE

# LA VUELTA A ESPAÑA
Final Classifications

## GENERAL CLASSIFICATION

| POS | NAME | TEAM | TIME |
|---|---|---|---|
| 1. | P. Roglič | TJV | 83:55:29 |
| 2. | E. Mas | MOV | 4:42 |
| 3. | J. Haig | TBV | 7:40 |
| 4. | A. Yates | IGD | 9:06 |
| 5. | G. Mäder | TBV | 11:33 |
| 6. | E. Bernal | IGD | 13:27 |
| 7. | D. de la Cruz | UAD | 18:33 |
| 8. | S. Kuss | TJV | 18:55 |
| 9. | G. Martin | COF | 20:27 |
| 10. | F. Großschartner | BOH | 22:22 |
| 11. | O. C. Eiking | IWG | 25:14 |
| 12. | S. Kruijswijk | TJV | 26:42 |
| 13. | J. P. López | TFS | 31:21 |
| 14. | G. Bouchard | ACT | 49:09 |
| 15. | R. Rochas | COF | 52:32 |
| 16. | C. Champoussin | ACT | 57:29 |
| 17. | D. Caruso | TBV | 1:05:31 |
| 18. | S. Oomen | TJV | 1:09:25 |
| 19. | Ó. Cabedo | BBH | 1:12:43 |
| 20. | S. Cras | LTS | 1:22:06 |
| 21. | R. Majka | UAD | 1:22:14 |
| 22. | G. Brambilla | TFS | 1:22:38 |
| 23. | W. Poels | TBV | 1:34:52 |
| 24. | D. Navarro | BBH | 1:37:26 |
| 25. | R. Bardet | DSM | 1:37:27 |
| 26. | I. Izagirre | APT | 1:37:47 |
| 27. | G. Izagirre | APT | 1:39:03 |
| 28. | J. Hirt | IWG | 1:42:39 |
| 29. | S. Petilli | IWG | 1:45:51 |
| 30. | L. A. Maté | EUS | 1:48:17 |
| 31. | M. Nieve | BEX | 1:56:31 |
| 32. | J. Cepeda Hernández | CJR | 1:58:54 |
| 33. | L. Calmejane | ACT | 2:03:52 |
| 34. | M. Tusveld | DSM | 2:04:06 |
| 35. | P. Sivakov | IGD | 2:04:47 |
| 36. | R. Gibbons | UAD | 2:05:50 |
| 37. | G. Martín | EUS | 2:10:39 |
| 38. | Je. Herrada | COF | 2:16:48 |
| 39. | J. Dombrowski | UAD | 2:17:20 |
| 40. | M. Storer | DSM | 2:22:45 |
| 41. | J. Polanc | UAD | 2:22:55 |
| 42. | K. Bouwman | TJV | 2:24:30 |
| 43. | J. Amezqueta | CJR | 2:25:16 |
| 44. | A. Zeits | BEX | 2:27:52 |
| 45. | M. Cherel | ACT | 2:30:26 |
| 46. | J. Bizkarra | EUS | 2:30:33 |
| 47. | B. Zwiehoff | BOH | 2:32:29 |
| 48. | F. De Tier | AFC | 2:37:18 |
| 49. | N. Schultz | BEX | 2:39:13 |
| 50. | J. Keukeleire | EFN | 2:48:20 |
| 51. | F. Aru | TQA | 2:49:04 |
| 52. | N. Prodhomme | ACT | 2:53:05 |
| 53. | D. A. Camargo | EFN | 2:53:47 |
| 54. | L. Hamilton | BEX | 2:56:47 |
| 55. | R. Taaramäe | IWG | 2:58:46 |
| 56. | J. J. Rojas | MOV | 3:02:19 |
| 57. | Jo. Herrada | COF | 3:05:54 |
| 58. | A. Roux | GFC | 3:07:54 |
| 59. | M. Padun | TBV | 3:09:46 |
| 60. | M. Iturria | EUS | 3:14:26 |
| 61. | T. Arensman | DSM | 3:14:59 |
| 62. | R. Gesink | TJV | 3:15:18 |
| 63. | Á. Madrazo | BBH | 3:15:38 |
| 64. | C. Hamilton | DSM | 3:18:33 |
| 65. | S. Dewulf | ACT | 3:21:21 |
| 66. | I. Erviti | MOV | 3:28:24 |
| 67. | T. Pidcock | IGD | 3:31:54 |
| 68. | A. Kron | LTS | 3:34:35 |
| 69. | L. Craddock | EFN | 3:36:48 |
| 70. | M. Matthews | BEX | 3:39:31 |
| 71. | J. Bol | BBH | 3:39:48 |
| 72. | N. Oliveira | MOV | 3:39:49 |
| 73. | J. Vine | AFC | 3:40:31 |
| 74. | R. Oliveira | UAD | 3:42:10 |
| 75. | A. Okamika | BBH | 3:43:42 |
| 76. | O. Le Gac | GFC | 3:44:56 |
| 77. | M. Cort | EFN | 3:46:48 |
| 78. | A. Cuadros Morata | CJR | 3:46:50 |
| 79. | D. Touzé | ACT | 3:47:28 |
| 80. | M. Trentin | UAD | 3:47:40 |
| 81. | A. Soto | EUS | 3:50:05 |
| 82. | N. Van Hooydonck | TJV | 3:50:19 |
| 83. | S. Moniquet | LTS | 3:52:10 |
| 84. | P. Sánchez | BBH | 3:52:29 |
| 85. | K. Geniets | GFC | 3:52:41 |

| POS | NAME | TEAM | TIME |
|---|---|---|---|
| 86. | J. Piccoli | ISN | 3:52:52 |
| 87. | A. Bagües | CJR | 3:53:02 |
| 88. | M. Van Gils | LTS | 3:53:55 |
| 89. | F. Barceló | COF | 3:55:36 |
| 90. | A. Bagioli | DQT | 3:58:45 |
| 91. | Y. Natarov | APT | 4:02:04 |
| 92. | E. Finé | COF | 4:04:47 |
| 93. | G. Niv | ISN | 4:06:37 |
| 94. | J. Tratnik | TBV | 4:07:22 |
| 95. | D. Howson | BEX | 4:10:16 |
| 96. | A. Démare | GFC | 4:16:42 |
| 97. | C. Venturini | ACT | 4:18:28 |
| 98. | S. Puccio | IGD | 4:18:54 |
| 99. | T. Ludvigsson | GFC | 4:19:24 |
| 100. | J. Knox | DQT | 4:20:47 |
| 101. | M. Vansevenant | DQT | 4:21:19 |
| 102. | A. Palzer | BOH | 4:22:19 |
| 103. | J. Bou | EUS | 4:22:43 |
| 104. | D. Sunderland | TQA | 4:24:21 |
| 105. | D. Claeys | TQA | 4:27:40 |
| 106. | C. Canal | BBH | 4:28:30 |
| 107. | C. Benedetti | BOH | 4:30:10 |
| 108. | A. Nibali | TFS | 4:30:22 |
| 109. | L. Mezgec | BEX | 4:30:30 |
| 110. | W. Kreder | IWG | 4:34:38 |
| 111. | X. M. Azparren | EUS | 4:36:40 |
| 112. | P. Gamper | BOH | 4:38:23 |
| 113. | C. Haga | DSM | 4:38:46 |
| 114. | N. Denz | DSM | 4:42:09 |
| 115. | H. Vanhoucke | LTS | 4:42:31 |
| 116. | Y. Arashiro | TBV | 4:42:59 |
| 117. | A. Krieger | AFC | 4:47:15 |
| 118. | F. Sénéchal | DQT | 4:48:14 |
| 119. | R. Stannard | BEX | 4:48:56 |
| 120. | A. Kirsch | TFS | 4:50:22 |
| 121. | F. Vermeersch | LTS | 4:57:09 |
| 122. | E. Planckaert | AFC | 5:03:10 |
| 123. | P. Allegaert | COF | 5:03:48 |
| 124. | Q. Simmons | TFS | 5:06:02 |
| 125. | T. Scully | EFN | 5:09:47 |
| 126. | K. van Melsen | IWG | 5:10:04 |
| 127. | R. Sinkeldam | GFC | 5:16:27 |
| 128. | L. Hofstede | TJV | 5:20:45 |
| 129. | A. Dainese | DSM | 5:20:50 |
| 130. | C. Brown | TQA | 5:22:42 |
| 131. | B. J. Lindeman | TQA | 5:26:43 |
| 132. | J. Aberasturi | CJR | 5:29:29 |
| 133. | Z. Štybar | DQT | 5:34:14 |
| 134. | S. Thwaites | AFC | 5:36:20 |
| 135. | S. Berwick | ISN | 5:37:10 |
| 136. | J. J. Lobato | EUS | 5:45:39 |
| 137. | B. Van Lerberghe | DQT | 5:48:13 |
| 138. | R. Minali | IWG | 5:50:15 |
| 139. | J. Meeus | BOH | 5:53:36 |
| 140. | M. Laas | BOH | 6:00:28 |
| 141. | F. Jakobsen | DQT | 6:01:24 |
| 142. | J. Černý | DQT | 6:03:50 |

## KING OF THE MOUNTAINS

| POS | NAME | TEAM | PTS |
|---|---|---|---|
| 1. | M. Storer | DSM | 80 |
| 2. | R. Bardet | DSM | 61 |
| 3. | P. Roglič | TJV | 51 |
| 4. | D. Caruso | TBV | 33 |
| 5. | R. Majka | UAD | 33 |
| 6. | J. Haig | TBV | 23 |
| 7. | S. Kuss | TJV | 19 |
| 8. | E. Mas | MOV | 17 |
| 9. | E. Bernal | IGD | 16 |
| 10. | F. Aru | TQA | 16 |

## POINTS

| POS | NAME | TEAM | PTS |
|---|---|---|---|
| 1. | F. Jakobsen | DQT | 250 |
| 2. | P. Roglič | TJV | 199 |
| 3. | M. Cort | EFN | 161 |
| 4. | M. Trentin | UAD | 145 |
| 5. | E. Mas | MOV | 120 |
| 6. | A. Dainese | DSM | 120 |
| 7. | M. Matthews | BEX | 114 |
| 8. | A. Bagioli | DQT | 101 |
| 9. | E. Bernal | IGD | 96 |
| 10. | A. Démare | GFC | 91 |

## YOUNG RIDER

| POS | NAME | TEAM | TIME |
|---|---|---|---|
| 1. | G. Mäder | TBV | 84:07:02 |
| 2. | E. Bernal | IGD | 1:54 |
| 3. | J. P. López | TFS | 19:48 |
| 4. | R. Rochas | COF | 40:59 |
| 5. | C. Champoussin | ACT | 45:56 |
| 6. | S. Cras | LTS | 1:10:33 |
| 7. | J. Cepeda Hernández | CJR | 1:47:21 |
| 8. | P. Sivakov | IGD | 1:53:14 |
| 9. | G. Martin | EUS | 1:59:06 |
| 10. | M. Storer | DSM | 2:11:12 |

## TEAMS

| POS | NAME | TEAM | TIME |
|---|---|---|---|
| 1. | Bahrain Victorious | TBV | 252:19:35 |
| 2. | Jumbo-Visma | TJV | 7:26 |
| 3. | Ineos Grenadiers | IGD | 32:18 |
| 4. | UAE Team Emirates | UAD | 1:05:10 |
| 5. | Intermarché-Wanty-Gobert Matériaux | IWG | 1:15:05 |
| 6. | Movistar Team | MOV | 1:17:16 |
| 7. | AG2R Citroën Team | ACT | 1:43:04 |
| 8. | Cofidis | COF | 2:15:39 |
| 9. | Trek-Segafredo | TFS | 2:38:20 |
| 10. | Team DSM | DSM | 2:59:49 |
| 11. | Euskaltel-Euskadi | EUS | 3:31:29 |
| 12. | Burgos-BH | BBH | 3:49:37 |
| 13. | Astana Premier Tech | APT | 3:49:47 |
| 14. | Team BikeExchange | BEX | 4:00:32 |
| 15. | Caja Rural-Seguros RGA | CJR | 4:52:21 |
| 16. | Bora-Hansgrohe | BOH | 5:11:20 |
| 17. | Lotto Soudal | LTS | 5:53:56 |
| 18. | EF Education-Nippo | EFN | 6:48:08 |
| 19. | Team Qhubeka NextHash | TQA | 7:20:05 |
| 20. | Groupama-FDJ | GFC | 7:28:30 |
| 21. | Alpecin-Fenix | AFC | 8:54:50 |
| 22. | Deceuninck-QuickStep | DQT | 10:47:52 |
| 23. | Israel Start-Up Nation | ISN | 12:17:38 |

## ABANDONS

|  |  |
|---|---|
| Stage 3 | A. Cataford (ISN), F. Frison (LTS) |
| Stage 7 | O. Rodríguez (APT), H. Carthy (EFN), A. Valverde (MOV), E. Morin (COF), M. Würst Schmidt (ISN), R. Janse Van Rensburg (TQA) |
| Stage 8 | D. Cimolai (ISN) |
| Stage 9 | J. Guarnieri (GFC), J. Jacobs (MOV), S. R. Martín (CJR), J. S. Molano (UAD) |
| Stage 11 | S. Carr (EFN), J. Philipsen (AFC), A. Aranburu (APT) |
| Stage 12 | T. Bayer (AFC) |
| Stage 13 | M. Schachmann (BOH), O. Fraile (APT) |
| Stage 14 | R. Carapaz (IGD) |
| Stage 15 | J. Narváez (IGD), K. Reijnen (TFS), J. K. Caicedo (EFN) |
| Stage 16 | R. Molard (GFC), G. Ciccone (TFS), S. Vanmarcke (ISN) |
| Stage 17 | L. L. Sanchez (APT), I. Einhorn (ISN), K. Elissonde (TFS), M. Landa (TBV), S. Armée (TQA) |
| Stage 18 | M. Holmes (LTS), J. Lastra (CJR), D. Rubio (BBH), D. van Baarle (IGD), C. Verona (MOV) |
| Stage 19 | S. Modolo (AFC), L. Meintjes (IWG), S. Henao (TQA) |
| Stage 20 | M. A. López (MOV), O. Lazkano (CJR), A. Vlasov (APT) |

AUGUST  .1 MEN'S RACE

## GP JEF SCHERENS
15 August 2021
Leuven–Leuven
190km

## WEATHER

TEMPERATURE: 26°C
WIND: SW 13km/h

## RESULTS

| POS | NAME | TEAM | TIME |
|---|---|---|---|
| 1. | N. Bonifazio | TEN | 4:28:12 |
| 2. | N. Bouhanni | ARK | s.t. |
| 3. | G. Vermeersch | AFC | s.t. |
| 4. | T. Devriendt | IWG | s.t. |
| 5. | A. Marit | SVB | s.t. |
| 6. | B. Welten | ARK | s.t. |
| 7. | T. Merlier | AFC | s.t. |
| 8. | T. Paquot | BWB | s.t. |
| 9. | J. Reynders | SVB | s.t. |
| 10. | C. Beullens | SVB | s.t. |
| 11. | J. Huppertz | LKH | s.t. |
| 12. | B. Coquard | BBK | 0:04 |
| 13. | D. De Pooter | SEG | s.t. |
| 14. | B. De Backer | BBK | s.t. |
| 15. | H. de Vries | MET | s.t. |
| 16. | L. Teugels | TIS | s.t. |
| 17. | J. Bouts | BCY | s.t. |
| 18. | M. Stockman | SVL | s.t. |
| 19. | S. Culverwell | TRI | s.t. |
| 20. | A. Goeman | TIS | s.t. |

AUGUST   .1 MEN'S RACE

# LA POLY NORMANDE
15 August 2021
Avranches–Saint-Martin-de-Landelles
168.9km

## WEATHER

TEMPERATURE
19°C

WIND
NW 15km/h

## RESULTS

| POS | NAME | TEAM | TIME |
|---|---|---|---|
| 1. | V. Madouas | GFC | 3:49:57 |
| 2. | B. Cosnefroy | ACT | s.t. |
| 3. | A. Perez | COF | s.t. |
| 4. | D. Godon | ACT | 0:09 |
| 5. | R. Hardy | ARK | s.t. |
| 6. | A. Delettre | DKO | s.t. |
| 7. | S. Geschke | COF | 0:16 |
| 8. | A. Brunel | GFC | s.t. |
| 9. | A. Gougeard | ACT | s.t. |
| 10. | A. Delaplace | ARK | 0:19 |
| 11. | J. Tesson | AUB | 1:10 |
| 12. | C. Laporte | COF | s.t. |
| 13. | E. Prades | DKO | s.t. |
| 14. | M. Ladagnous | GFC | s.t. |
| 15. | J. Duval | ACT | s.t. |
| 16. | C. Barthe | BBK | s.t. |
| 17. | V. Retailleau | ACT | s.t. |
| 18. | L. Pithie | GFC | s.t. |
| 19. | J. Leveau | XRL | s.t. |
| 20. | L. Pichon | ARK | s.t. |

AUGUST .1 MEN'S RACE

# EGMONT CYCLING RACE
17 August 2021
Zottegem–Zottegem
192.3km

## WEATHER

TEMPERATURE
16°C

WIND
W 14km/h

## RESULTS

| POS | NAME | TEAM | TIME |
|---|---|---|---|
| 1. | D. van Poppel | IWG | 4:31:51 |
| 2. | N. Bonifazio | TEN | s.t. |
| 3. | L. Mozzato | BBK | s.t. |
| 4. | C. Noppe | ARK | s.t. |
| 5. | J. Reynders | SVB | s.t. |
| 6. | J. Debusschere | BBK | s.t. |
| 7. | T. Dupont | BWB | s.t. |
| 8. | M. Ballerstedt | JVD | s.t. |
| 9. | G. D'heygere | TIS | s.t. |
| 10. | J. Huppertz | LKH | s.t. |
| 11. | J. Warlop | SVB | s.t. |
| 12. | H. de Vries | MET | s.t. |
| 13. | D. Tulett | DHB | s.t. |
| 14. | T. Willems | SVB | s.t. |
| 15. | L. van Belle | JVD | s.t. |
| 16. | L. Hohmann | MET | s.t. |
| 17. | M. Stedman | DHB | s.t. |
| 18. | C. Heiderscheid | LPC | s.t. |
| 19. | V. Broex | MET | s.t. |
| 20. | T. Mein | DHB | s.t. |

## TOUR DU LIMOUSIN

Stage 1
17 August 2021
Isle–Sainte-Feyre
183.3km

### WEATHER

| TEMPERATURE | WIND |
|---|---|
| 16°C | NW 13km/h |

### STAGE RESULTS

| POS | NAME | TEAM | TIME |
|---|---|---|---|
| 1. | C. Laporte | COF | 4:27:55 |
| 2. | D. Godon | ACT | s.t. |
| 3. | T. Paquot | BWB | s.t. |
| 4. | B. Cosnefroy | ACT | s.t. |
| 5. | F. Fiorelli | BCF | s.t. |
| 6. | E. Prades | DKO | s.t. |
| 7. | F. Galván | EKP | s.t. |
| 8. | D. Gabburo | BCF | s.t. |
| 9. | V. Albanese | EOK | s.t. |
| 10. | A. Fedeli | DKO | s.t. |
| 11. | S. Velasco | GAZ | s.t. |
| 12. | V. Madouas | GFC | s.t. |
| 13. | J. Leveau | XRL | s.t. |
| 14. | F. Grellier | TEN | s.t. |
| 15. | F. Maurelet | AUB | s.t. |
| 16. | W. Barguil | ARK | s.t. |
| 17. | M. Burgaudeau | TEN | s.t. |
| 18. | A. Angulo | EUS | s.t. |
| 19. | L. Wirtgen | BWB | s.t. |
| 20. | M. De Witte | XRL | s.t. |

### GENERAL CLASSIFICATION

| POS | NAME | TEAM | TIME |
|---|---|---|---|
| 1. | C. Laporte | COF | 4:27:45 |
| 2. | D. Godon | ACT | 0:04 |
| 3. | T. Paquot | BWB | 0:05 |

### KING OF THE MOUNTAINS

| POS | NAME | TEAM | PTS |
|---|---|---|---|
| 1. | D. Savini | BCF | 4 |
| 2. | T. Juaristi | EUS | 4 |
| 3. | J. Antomarchi | XRL | 4 |

### YOUNG RIDER

| POS | NAME | TEAM | TIME |
|---|---|---|---|
| 1. | D. Godon | ACT | 4:27:49 |
| 2. | T. Paquot | BWB | 0:01 |
| 3. | F. Galván | EKP | 0:06 |

## TOUR DU LIMOUSIN

Stage 2
18 August 2021
Agonac–Payzac
172km

### WEATHER

| TEMPERATURE | WIND |
|---|---|
| 19°C | N 6km/h |

### STAGE RESULTS

| POS | NAME | TEAM | TIME |
|---|---|---|---|
| 1. | D. Godon | ACT | 4:13:02 |
| 2. | W. Barguil | ARK | s.t. |
| 3. | F. Bonnamour | BBK | s.t. |
| 4. | S. Reichenbach | GFC | s.t. |
| 5. | U. Berrade | EKP | s.t. |
| 6. | P. L. Périchon | COF | s.t. |
| 7. | B. Cosnefroy | ACT | 0:37 |
| 8. | R. Adrià | EKP | 0:40 |
| 9. | F. Fiorelli | BCF | 0:45 |
| 10. | A. Perez | COF | s.t. |
| 11. | V. Albanese | EOK | s.t. |
| 12. | F. Galván | EKP | s.t. |
| 13. | S. Velasco | GAZ | s.t. |
| 14. | C. Barthe | BBK | s.t. |
| 15. | J. Simon | TEN | s.t. |
| 16. | L. Wirtgen | BWB | s.t. |
| 17. | C. Laporte | COF | s.t. |
| 18. | A. Fedeli | DKO | s.t. |
| 19. | V. Madouas | GFC | s.t. |
| 20. | A. Angulo | EUS | s.t. |

### GENERAL CLASSIFICATION

| POS | NAME | TEAM | TIME |
|---|---|---|---|
| 1. ↑1 | D. Godon | ACT | 8:40:37 |
| 2. ↑15 | W. Barguil | ARK | 0:14 |
| 3. ↑40 | F. Bonnamour | BBK | 0:16 |

### KING OF THE MOUNTAINS

| POS | NAME | TEAM | PTS |
|---|---|---|---|
| 1. — | D. Savini | BCF | 8 |
| 2. — | F. Bonnamour | BBK | 6 |
| 3. — | S. Reichenbach | GFC | 6 |

### YOUNG RIDER

| POS | NAME | TEAM | TIME |
|---|---|---|---|
| 1. — | D. Godon | ACT | 8:40:37 |
| 2. ↑13 | U. Berrade | EKP | 0:20 |
| 3. ↑6 | R. Adrià | EKP | 1:00 |

AUGUST .1 MEN'S RACE

## TOUR DU LIMOUSIN
Stage 3
19 August 2021
Bugeat – Espace 1000 Sources–Lubersac
184.2km

### WEATHER

TEMPERATURE 17°C
WIND NW 7km/h

### STAGE RESULTS

| POS | NAME | TEAM | TIME |
|---|---|---|---|
| 1. | S. Velasco | GAZ | 4:12:08 |
| 2. | S. Geschke | COF | 0:11 |
| 3. | L. Wackermann | EOK | s.t. |
| 4. | V. Stojnić | THR | s.t. |
| 5. | P. Rolland | BBK | s.t. |
| 6. | J. M. Díaz | DKO | s.t. |
| 7. | A. Angulo | EUS | s.t. |
| 8. | P. Vakoč | AFC | s.t. |
| 9. | D. Gabburo | BCF | s.t. |
| 10. | V. Albanese | EOK | 0:22 |
| 11. | F. Bonnamour | BBK | s.t. |
| 12. | J. Simon | TEN | s.t. |
| 13. | F. Fiorelli | BCF | s.t. |
| 14. | F. Galván | EKP | s.t. |
| 15. | C. Scaroni | GAZ | s.t. |
| 16. | E. Prades | DKO | s.t. |
| 17. | M. Urruty | XRL | s.t. |
| 18. | A. Delettre | DKO | s.t. |
| 19. | W. Barguil | ARK | s.t. |
| 20. | A. Fedeli | DKO | s.t. |

### GENERAL CLASSIFICATION

| POS | | NAME | TEAM | TIME |
|---|---|---|---|---|
| 1. | – | D. Godon | ACT | 12:53:07 |
| 2. | – | W. Barguil | ARK | 0:14 |
| 3. | – | F. Bonnamour | BBK | s.t. |

### KING OF THE MOUNTAINS

| POS | | NAME | TEAM | PTS |
|---|---|---|---|---|
| 1. | ↑7 | T. Pinot | GFC | 14 |
| 2. | ↑5 | B. Cosnefroy | ACT | 10 |
| 3. | ↑9 | V. Lafay | COF | 10 |

### YOUNG RIDER

| POS | | NAME | TEAM | TIME |
|---|---|---|---|---|
| 1. | – | D. Godon | ACT | 12:53:07 |
| 2. | – | U. Berrade | EKP | 0:20 |
| 3. | – | R. Adrià | EKP | 1:00 |

## TOUR DU LIMOUSIN
Stage 4
20 August 2021
Sauviat-sur-Vige–Limoges
169.7km

### WEATHER

TEMPERATURE 21°C
WIND S 7km/h

### STAGE RESULTS

| POS | NAME | TEAM | TIME |
|---|---|---|---|
| 1. | E. Fetter | EOK | 4:07:14 |
| 2. | V. Albanese | EOK | s.t. |
| 3. | V. Madouas | GFC | s.t. |
| 4. | P. Vakoč | AFC | s.t. |
| 5. | L. Manzin | TEN | s.t. |
| 6. | A. Perez | COF | s.t. |
| 7. | R. Adrià | EKP | s.t. |
| 8. | R. Mertz | BWB | s.t. |
| 9. | F. Maurelet | AUB | s.t. |
| 10. | M. Burgaudeau | TEN | s.t. |
| 11. | A. Delettre | DKO | s.t. |
| 12. | S. Reichenbach | GFC | s.t. |
| 13. | W. Barguil | ARK | s.t. |
| 14. | S. Velasco | GAZ | s.t. |
| 15. | E. Prades | DKO | s.t. |
| 16. | A. Angulo | EUS | s.t. |
| 17. | L. Wirtgen | BWB | s.t. |
| 18. | J. Janssens | AFC | s.t. |
| 19. | U. Cuadrado | EUS | s.t. |
| 20. | U. Berrade | EKP | s.t. |

### GENERAL CLASSIFICATION

| POS | | NAME | TEAM | TIME |
|---|---|---|---|---|
| 1. | ↑1 | W. Barguil | ARK | 17:00:35 |
| 2. | ↑1 | F. Bonnamour | BBK | s.t. |
| 3. | ↑1 | P. L. Périchon | COF | 0:06 |

### KING OF THE MOUNTAINS

| POS | | NAME | TEAM | PTS |
|---|---|---|---|---|
| 1. | – | D. Bais | EOK | 18 |
| 2. | ↓1 | T. Pinot | GFC | 14 |
| 3. | ↓1 | B. Cosnefroy | ACT | 10 |

### YOUNG RIDER

| POS | | NAME | TEAM | TIME |
|---|---|---|---|---|
| 1. | ↑1 | U. Berrade | EKP | 17:00:41 |
| 2. | ↑2 | V. Albanese | EOK | 0:39 |
| 3. | – | R. Adrià | EKP | 0:40 |

AUGUST .PRO MEN'S RACE

## TOUR OF NORWAY
Stage 1
19 August 2021
Egersund–Sokndal (Kroheia)
150.8km

### WEATHER

TEMPERATURE | WIND
16°C | NW 35km/h

### STAGE RESULTS

| POS | NAME | TEAM | TIME |
|---|---|---|---|
| 1. | E. Hayter | IGD | 3:44:30 |
| 2. | I. Schelling | BOH | 0:01 |
| 3. | T. Træen | UXT | 0:11 |
| 4. | M. Skjelmose Jensen | TFS | 0:13 |
| 5. | J. Shaw | RWC | s.t. |
| 6. | F. Ganna | IGD | s.t. |
| 7. | M. Teunissen | TJV | s.t. |
| 8. | K. Aasvold | TCO | s.t. |
| 9. | M. Hoelgaard | UXT | s.t. |
| 10. | L. Eriksson | RIW | s.t. |
| 11. | G. Bennett | TJV | 0:16 |
| 12. | R. Combaud | DSM | 0:21 |
| 13. | S. E. Byström | UAD | s.t. |
| 14. | A. Leknessund | DSM | s.t. |
| 15. | A. Berlin | GLC | 0:24 |
| 16. | M. Donovan | DSM | s.t. |
| 17. | W. Vanhoof | SVB | 0:26 |
| 18. | F. Dversnes | TCO | s.t. |
| 19. | J. Schultz | RIW | s.t. |
| 20. | L. Basso | IGD | s.t. |

### GENERAL CLASSIFICATION

| POS | NAME | TEAM | TIME |
|---|---|---|---|
| 1. | E. Hayter | IGD | 3:44:20 |
| 2. | I. Schelling | BOH | 0:05 |
| 3. | T. Træen | UXT | 0:17 |

### KING OF THE MOUNTAINS

| POS | NAME | TEAM | PTS |
|---|---|---|---|
| 1. | E. Hayter | IGD | 6 |
| 2. | A. Charmig | UXT | 6 |
| 3. | I. Schelling | BOH | 5 |

### POINTS

| POS | NAME | TEAM | PTS |
|---|---|---|---|
| 1. | E. Hayter | IGD | 15 |
| 2. | I. Schelling | BOH | 14 |
| 3. | T. Træen | UXT | 13 |

### YOUNG RIDER

| POS | NAME | TEAM | TIME |
|---|---|---|---|
| 1. | M. Skjelmose Jensen | TFS | 3:44:43 |
| 2. | A. Leknessund | DSM | 0:08 |
| 3. | M. Donovan | DSM | 0:11 |

## TOUR OF NORWAY
Stage 2
20 August 2021
Sirdal (Tjørhomfjellet)–Sirdal (Fidjeland)
185.3km

### WEATHER

TEMPERATURE | WIND
16°C | NW 25km/h

### STAGE RESULTS

| POS | NAME | TEAM | TIME |
|---|---|---|---|
| 1. | E. Hayter | IGD | 4:16:32 |
| 2. | T. Van der Sande | LTS | s.t. |
| 3. | M. Teunissen | TJV | s.t. |
| 4. | I. Schelling | BOH | s.t. |
| 5. | S. E. Byström | UAD | s.t. |
| 6. | K. Aasvold | TCO | s.t. |
| 7. | J. Shaw | RWC | s.t. |
| 8. | M. Hoelgaard | UXT | s.t. |
| 9. | L. Eriksson | RIW | s.t. |
| 10. | N. van der Lijke | RIW | s.t. |
| 11. | J. A. Pallesen | TCQ | s.t. |
| 12. | A. Skaarseth | UXT | s.t. |
| 13. | C. Beullens | SVB | s.t. |
| 14. | M. Skjelmose Jensen | TFS | s.t. |
| 15. | M. Weulink | ABC | s.t. |
| 16. | A. Van Poucke | SVB | s.t. |
| 17. | R. Combaud | DSM | s.t. |
| 18. | M. Ø. Kristensen | TCQ | s.t. |
| 19. | G. Bennett | TJV | 0:08 |
| 20. | T. Træen | UXT | s.t. |

### GENERAL CLASSIFICATION

| POS | NAME | TEAM | TIME |
|---|---|---|---|
| 1. — | E. Hayter | IGD | 8:00:42 |
| 2. — | I. Schelling | BOH | 0:15 |
| 3. ↑4 | M. Teunissen | TJV | 0:29 |

### KING OF THE MOUNTAINS

| POS | NAME | TEAM | PTS |
|---|---|---|---|
| 1. ↑1 | A. Charmig | UXT | 16 |
| 2. — | E. S. Iwersen | BPC | 8 |
| 3. ↓2 | E. Hayter | IGD | 6 |

### POINTS

| POS | NAME | TEAM | PTS |
|---|---|---|---|
| 1. — | E. Hayter | IGD | 30 |
| 2. — | I. Schelling | BOH | 26 |
| 3. ↑4 | M. Teunissen | TJV | 22 |

### YOUNG RIDER

| POS | NAME | TEAM | TIME |
|---|---|---|---|
| 1. — | M. Skjelmose Jensen | TFS | 8:01:15 |
| 2. — | A. Leknessund | DSM | 0:17 |
| 3. — | M. Donovan | DSM | 0:20 |

AUGUST .PRO MEN'S RACE

## TOUR OF NORWAY
Stage 3
21 August 2021
Jørpeland–Jørpeland
159.9km

## WEATHER

TEMPERATURE | WIND
16°C | W 19km/h

### STAGE RESULTS

| POS | NAME | TEAM | TIME |
|---|---|---|---|
| 1. | M. Pedersen | TFS | 3:49:02 |
| 2. | A. Kristoff | UAD | s.t. |
| 3. | M. Teunissen | TJV | s.t. |
| 4. | M. Hoelgaard | UXT | s.t. |
| 5. | E. Hayter | IGD | s.t. |
| 6. | K. Aasvold | TCO | s.t. |
| 7. | T. Van der Sande | LTS | s.t. |
| 8. | N. Politt | BOH | s.t. |
| 9. | C. Beullens | SVB | s.t. |
| 10. | I. Schelling | BOH | s.t. |
| 11. | J. Shaw | RWC | s.t. |
| 12. | N. van der Lijke | RIW | s.t. |
| 13. | R. Combaud | DSM | s.t. |
| 14. | J. A. Pallesen | TCQ | s.t. |
| 15. | J. Kench | BSC | s.t. |
| 16. | L. Eriksson | RIW | s.t. |
| 17. | M. Skjelmose Jensen | TFS | s.t. |
| 18. | M. Rahbek | BPC | s.t. |
| 19. | K. Magnusson | RIW | s.t. |
| 20. | A. Skaarseth | UXT | s.t. |

### GENERAL CLASSIFICATION

| POS | NAME | TEAM | TIME |
|---|---|---|---|
| 1. — | E. Hayter | IGD | 11:49:44 |
| 2. — | I. Schelling | BOH | 0:15 |
| 3. — | M. Teunissen | TJV | 0:25 |

### KING OF THE MOUNTAINS

| POS | NAME | TEAM | PTS |
|---|---|---|---|
| 1. — | A. Charmig | UXT | 22 |
| 2. — | M. Rahbek | BPC | 9 |
| 3. ↓1 | E. S. Iwersen | BPC | 8 |

### POINTS

| POS | NAME | TEAM | PTS |
|---|---|---|---|
| 1. — | E. Hayter | IGD | 41 |
| 2. ↑1 | M. Teunissen | TJV | 35 |
| 3. ↓1 | I. Schelling | BOH | 32 |

### YOUNG RIDER

| POS | NAME | TEAM | TIME |
|---|---|---|---|
| 1. — | M. Skjelmose Jensen | TFS | 11:50:17 |
| 2. — | A. Leknessund | DSM | 0:17 |
| 3. — | M. Donovan | DSM | 0:20 |

## TOUR OF NORWAY
Stage 4
22 August 2021
Hinna Park–Stavanger
156.5km

## WEATHER

TEMPERATURE | WIND
18°C | W 15km/h

### STAGE RESULTS

| POS | NAME | TEAM | TIME |
|---|---|---|---|
| 1. | M. Walls | BOH | 3:25:16 |
| 2. | M. Pedersen | TFS | s.t. |
| 3. | D. Hoelgaard | UXT | s.t. |
| 4. | M. Teunissen | TJV | s.t. |
| 5. | T. Van der Sande | LTS | s.t. |
| 6. | A. Kristoff | UAD | s.t. |
| 7. | N. L. N. Broge | BPC | s.t. |
| 8. | M. Hoelgaard | UXT | s.t. |
| 9. | N. van der Lijke | RIW | s.t. |
| 10. | C. Beullens | SVB | s.t. |
| 11. | L. Bendixen | TCO | s.t. |
| 12. | S. E. Bystrøm | UAD | s.t. |
| 13. | M. Skjelmose Jensen | TFS | s.t. |
| 14. | J. Shaw | RWC | s.t. |
| 15. | L. Eriksson | RIW | s.t. |
| 16. | W. Vanhoof | SVB | s.t. |
| 17. | K. Aasvold | TCO | s.t. |
| 18. | K. Magnusson | RIW | s.t. |
| 19. | O. Hjemsæter | TCO | s.t. |
| 20. | R. Combaud | DSM | s.t. |

### GENERAL CLASSIFICATION

| POS | NAME | TEAM | TIME |
|---|---|---|---|
| 1. — | E. Hayter | IGD | 15:15:00 |
| 2. — | I. Schelling | BOH | 0:15 |
| 3. — | M. Teunissen | TJV | 0:25 |

### KING OF THE MOUNTAINS

| POS | NAME | TEAM | PTS |
|---|---|---|---|
| 1. — | A. Charmig | UXT | 22 |
| 2. ↑5 | O. Hjemsæter | TCO | 14 |
| 3. — | N. L. N. Broge | BPC | 12 |

### POINTS

| POS | NAME | TEAM | PTS |
|---|---|---|---|
| 1. ↑1 | M. Teunissen | TJV | 47 |
| 2. ↓1 | E. Hayter | IGD | 41 |
| 3. ↑2 | M. Hoelgaard | UXT | 35 |

### YOUNG RIDER

| POS | NAME | TEAM | TIME |
|---|---|---|---|
| 1. — | M. Skjelmose Jensen | TFS | 15:15:33 |
| 2. ↑1 | M. Donovan | DSM | 0:20 |
| 3. ↑1 | J. Kench | BSC | 0:47 |

AUGUST    .1 MEN'S RACE

# GP MARCEL KINT
20 August 2021
Zwevegem–Kortrijk
196.3km

## WEATHER

TEMPERATURE: 19°C
WIND: W 11km/h

## RESULTS

| POS | NAME | TEAM | TIME |
|---|---|---|---|
| 1. | A. J. Hodeg | DQT | 4:23:39 |
| 2. | T. Merlier | AFC | s.t. |
| 3. | D. van Poppel | IWG | s.t. |
| 4. | B. Welten | ARK | s.t. |
| 5. | J. Reynders | SVB | s.t. |
| 6. | L. Mozzato | BBK | s.t. |
| 7. | J. Hesters | BCY | s.t. |
| 8. | J. Warlop | SVB | s.t. |
| 9. | S. Archbold | DQT | 0:03 |
| 10. | M. Mayrhofer | DDS | 0:05 |
| 11. | V. Broex | MET | s.t. |
| 12. | S. Flynn | SEG | s.t. |
| 13. | R. Tiller | UXT | s.t. |
| 14. | R. Christensen | DHB | s.t. |
| 15. | B. van der Kooij | VWE | s.t. |
| 16. | K. Van Rooy | SVB | s.t. |
| 17. | A. De Decker | TIS | s.t. |
| 18. | R. Apers | SVB | s.t. |
| 19. | W. Krul | SEG | s.t. |
| 20. | J. Bouts | BCY | s.t. |

AUGUST    .1 MEN'S RACE

## TOUR POITOU-CHARENTES EN NOUVELLE AQUITAINE
Stage 1
24 August 2021
Pons–Parthenay
197.3km

### WEATHER

TEMPERATURE    WIND
22°C    NE 22km/h

### STAGE RESULTS

| POS | NAME | TEAM | TIME |
|---|---|---|---|
| 1. | E. Viviani | COF | 5:01:31 |
| 2. | S. Consonni | COF | s.t. |
| 3. | M. Sarreau | ACT | s.t. |
| 4. | E. M. Grosu | DKO | s.t. |
| 5. | T. Dupont | BWB | s.t. |
| 6. | E. Vermeulen | XRL | s.t. |
| 7. | H. Hofstetter | ISN | s.t. |
| 8. | C. Joyce | RLY | s.t. |
| 9. | C. Swift | ARK | s.t. |
| 10. | L. Wackermann | EOK | s.t. |
| 11. | D. Rajović | DKO | s.t. |
| 12. | A. Zingle | COF | s.t. |
| 13. | T. Boudat | ARK | s.t. |
| 14. | F. Bonnamour | BBK | s.t. |
| 15. | T. Gallopin | ACT | s.t. |
| 16. | M. Urianstad | UXT | s.t. |
| 17. | A. Paret-Peintre | ACT | s.t. |
| 18. | A. Jensen | DKO | s.t. |
| 19. | M. Belletti | EOK | s.t. |
| 20. | M. Malucelli | ANS | s.t. |

### GENERAL CLASSIFICATION

| POS | NAME | TEAM | TIME |
|---|---|---|---|
| 1. | E. Viviani | COF | 5:01:21 |
| 2. | S. Consonni | COF | 0:04 |
| 3. | M. Sarreau | ACT | 0:06 |

### KING OF THE MOUNTAINS

| POS | NAME | TEAM | PTS |
|---|---|---|---|
| 1. | R. J. Skivild | UXT | 16 |
| 2. | M. Viel | ANS | 3 |
| 3. | T. Denis | XRL | 3 |

### POINTS

| POS | NAME | TEAM | PTS |
|---|---|---|---|
| 1. | E. Viviani | COF | 25 |
| 2. | S. Consonni | COF | 20 |
| 3. | M. Sarreau | ACT | 16 |

### YOUNG RIDER

| POS | NAME | TEAM | TIME |
|---|---|---|---|
| 1. | D. Rajović | DKO | 5:01:31 |
| 2. | A. Zingle | COF | s.t. |
| 3. | M. Urianstad | UXT | s.t. |

## TOUR POITOU-CHARENTES EN NOUVELLE AQUITAINE
Stage 2
25 August 2021
Parthenay–Ruffec
191.6km

### WEATHER

TEMPERATURE    WIND
24°C    NE 28km/h

### STAGE RESULTS

| POS | NAME | TEAM | TIME |
|---|---|---|---|
| 1. | J. Tesson | AUB | 4:27:00 |
| 2. | E. Viviani | COF | s.t. |
| 3. | S. De Bie | BWB | s.t. |
| 4. | A. Turgis | TEN | s.t. |
| 5. | M. Sarreau | ACT | s.t. |
| 6. | C. Joyce | RLY | s.t. |
| 7. | D. Rajović | DKO | s.t. |
| 8. | T. Boudat | ARK | s.t. |
| 9. | M. Belletti | EOK | s.t. |
| 10. | C. Swift | ARK | s.t. |
| 11. | F. Bonnamour | BBK | s.t. |
| 12. | A. Angulo | EUS | s.t. |
| 13. | S. Consonni | COF | s.t. |
| 14. | P. A. Coté | RLY | s.t. |
| 15. | G. Lonardi | BCF | s.t. |
| 16. | M. Malucelli | ANS | s.t. |
| 17. | N. Venchiarutti | ANS | s.t. |
| 18. | R. Cardis | AUB | s.t. |
| 19. | A. Boileau | BBK | s.t. |
| 20. | A. Delaplace | ARK | s.t. |

### GENERAL CLASSIFICATION

| POS | NAME | TEAM | TIME |
|---|---|---|---|
| 1. | — E. Viviani | COF | 9:28:15 |
| 2. | ↑28 J. Tesson | AUB | 0:06 |
| 3. | ↓1 S. Consonni | COF | 0:10 |

### KING OF THE MOUNTAINS

| POS | NAME | TEAM | PTS |
|---|---|---|---|
| 1. | — R. J. Skivild | UXT | 16 |
| 2. | — S. Rivi | EOK | 8 |
| 3. | — T. Juaristi | EUS | 4 |

### POINTS

| POS | NAME | TEAM | PTS |
|---|---|---|---|
| 1. | — E. Viviani | COF | 45 |
| 2. | ↑1 M. Sarreau | ACT | 28 |
| 3. | — J. Tesson | AUB | 25 |

### YOUNG RIDER

| POS | NAME | TEAM | TIME |
|---|---|---|---|
| 1. | ↑8 J. Tesson | AUB | 9:28:21 |
| 2. | ↓1 D. Rajović | DKO | 0:10 |
| 3. | ↑3 P. Penhoët | GFC | 0:17 |

AUGUST    .1 MEN'S RACE

## TOUR POITOU-CHARENTES EN NOUVELLE AQUITAINE
Stage 3
26 August 2021
Moncontour–Loudun
109.6km

### WEATHER

TEMPERATURE    WIND
17°C           NE 13km/h

### STAGE RESULTS

| POS | NAME | TEAM | TIME |
|---|---|---|---|
| 1. | E. Viviani | COF | 2:22:49 |
| 2. | T. Dupont | BWB | s.t. |
| 3. | S. Consonni | COF | s.t. |
| 4. | R. Cardis | AUB | s.t. |
| 5. | M. Malucelli | ANS | s.t. |
| 6. | T. Boudat | ARK | s.t. |
| 7. | M. Sarreau | ACT | s.t. |
| 8. | H. Hofstetter | ISN | s.t. |
| 9. | J. Tesson | AUB | s.t. |
| 10. | E. Vermeulen | XRL | s.t. |
| 11. | P. Penhoët | GFC | s.t. |
| 12. | P. A. Coté | RLY | s.t. |
| 13. | N. Venchiarutti | ANS | s.t. |
| 14. | C. Joyce | RLY | s.t. |
| 15. | A. Turgis | TEN | s.t. |
| 16. | N. Dalla Valle | BCF | s.t. |
| 17. | M. Hulgaard | UXT | s.t. |
| 18. | C. Swift | ARK | s.t. |
| 19. | P. Miquel | EKP | s.t. |
| 20. | L. Wackermann | EOK | s.t. |

### GENERAL CLASSIFICATION

| POS | | NAME | TEAM | TIME |
|---|---|---|---|---|
| 1. | — | E. Viviani | COF | 11:50:58 |
| 2. | — | J. Tesson | AUB | 0:12 |
| 3. | — | S. Consonni | COF | 0:14 |

### KING OF THE MOUNTAINS

| POS | | NAME | TEAM | PTS |
|---|---|---|---|---|
| 1. | — | R. J. Skivild | UXT | 20 |
| 2. | — | S. Rivi | EOK | 8 |
| 3. | — | A. Gougeard | ACT | 8 |

### POINTS

| POS | | NAME | TEAM | PTS |
|---|---|---|---|---|
| 1. | — | E. Viviani | COF | 70 |
| 2. | ↑2 | S. Consonni | COF | 39 |
| 3. | ↓1 | M. Sarreau | ACT | 37 |

### YOUNG RIDER

| POS | | NAME | TEAM | TIME |
|---|---|---|---|---|
| 1. | — | J. Tesson | AUB | 11:51:10 |
| 2. | — | D. Rajović | DKO | 0:10 |
| 3. | — | P. Penhoët | GFC | 0:17 |

---

## TOUR POITOU-CHARENTES EN NOUVELLE AQUITAINE
Stage 4 (ITT)
27 August 2021
Monts-sur-Guesnes–Loudun
23.5km

### WEATHER

TEMPERATURE    WIND
20°C           NE 19km/h

### STAGE RESULTS

| POS | NAME | TEAM | TIME |
|---|---|---|---|
| 1. | B. Hermans | ISN | 27:55 |
| 2. | J. Archibald | EOK | 0:01 |
| 3. | B. Armirail | GFC | 0:07 |
| 4. | P. Latour | TEN | 0:10 |
| 5. | M. Hulgaard | UXT | 0:15 |
| 6. | A. De Marchi | ISN | 0:19 |
| 7. | T. Pinot | GFC | 0:21 |
| 8. | A. Brunel | GFC | 0:24 |
| 9. | C. Swift | ARK | 0:26 |
| 10. | T. Guernalec | ARK | s.t. |
| 11. | P. A. Coté | RLY | 0:43 |
| 12. | S. Rossetto | AUB | 0:51 |
| 13. | C. Davy | GFC | 0:52 |
| 14. | A. Turgis | TEN | 0:53 |
| 15. | A. Delaplace | ARK | 1:02 |
| 16. | A. Nych | GAZ | 1:04 |
| 17. | F. Bonnamour | BBK | 1:07 |
| 18. | A. Riou | ARK | 1:12 |
| 19. | D. Strakhov | GAZ | s.t. |
| 20. | A. Paret-Peintre | ACT | 1:14 |

### GENERAL CLASSIFICATION

| POS | | NAME | TEAM | TIME |
|---|---|---|---|---|
| 1. | ↑4 | C. Swift | ARK | 12:19:40 |
| 2. | ↑19 | B. Armirail | GFC | 0:10 |
| 3. | ↑17 | M. Hulgaard | UXT | 0:18 |

### KING OF THE MOUNTAINS

| POS | | NAME | TEAM | PTS |
|---|---|---|---|---|
| 1. | — | R. J. Skivild | UXT | 20 |
| 2. | — | S. Rivi | EOK | 8 |
| 3. | — | A. Gougeard | ACT | 8 |

### POINTS

| POS | | NAME | TEAM | PTS |
|---|---|---|---|---|
| 1. | — | E. Viviani | COF | 70 |
| 2. | — | S. Consonni | COF | 39 |
| 3. | — | M. Sarreau | ACT | 37 |

### YOUNG RIDER

| POS | | NAME | TEAM | TIME |
|---|---|---|---|---|
| 1. | ↑4 | M. Hulgaard | UXT | 12:19:58 |
| 2. | ↑7 | T. Guernalec | ARK | 0:35 |
| 3. | ↑8 | P. A. Coté | RLY | 1:00 |

AUGUST    .1 MEN'S RACE

# TOUR POITOU-CHARENTES EN NOUVELLE AQUITAINE
Stage 5
28 August 2021
Villefagnan–Poitiers
164.6km

## WEATHER

TEMPERATURE: 22°C    WIND: N 24km/h

## STAGE RESULTS

| POS | NAME | TEAM | TIME |
|---|---|---|---|
| 1. | C. Carisey | DKO | 3:41:47 |
| 2. | S. Ravanelli | ANS | 0:03 |
| 3. | R. Carpenter | RLY | s.t. |
| 4. | J. Trarieux | DKO | s.t. |
| 5. | S. Consonni | COF | s.t. |
| 6. | A. Zingle | COF | s.t. |
| 7. | F. Bonnamour | BBK | s.t. |
| 8. | T. Dupont | BWB | s.t. |
| 9. | D. Kowalski | XRL | s.t. |
| 10. | N. Tesfatsion | ANS | s.t. |
| 11. | S. Velasco | GAZ | s.t. |
| 12. | A. Nych | GAZ | s.t. |
| 13. | A. Brunel | GFC | s.t. |
| 14. | A. Angulo | EUS | s.t. |
| 15. | R. Cardis | AUB | s.t. |
| 16. | M. Belletti | EOK | s.t. |
| 17. | A. Turgis | TEN | s.t. |
| 18. | P. A. Coté | RLY | s.t. |
| 19. | H. Hofstetter | ISN | s.t. |
| 20. | M. Hulgaard | UXT | s.t. |

## GENERAL CLASSIFICATION

| POS | NAME | TEAM | TIME |
|---|---|---|---|
| 1. — | C. Swift | ARK | 16:01:28 |
| 2. — | B. Armirail | GFC | 0:12 |
| 3. — | M. Hulgaard | UXT | 0:20 |

## KING OF THE MOUNTAINS

| POS | NAME | TEAM | PTS |
|---|---|---|---|
| 1. — | R. J. Skivild | UXT | 20 |
| 2. — | I. Ruiz | EKP | 12 |
| 3. ↓1 | S. Rivi | EOK | 8 |

## POINTS

| POS | NAME | TEAM | PTS |
|---|---|---|---|
| 1. ↑1 | S. Consonni | COF | 51 |
| 2. ↑3 | T. Dupont | BWB | 40 |
| 3. — | C. Carisey | DKO | 25 |

## YOUNG RIDER

| POS | NAME | TEAM | TIME |
|---|---|---|---|
| 1. — | M. Hulgaard | UXT | 16:01:48 |
| 2. ↑1 | P. A. Coté | RLY | 1:00 |
| 3. ↑1 | A. Paret-Peintre | ACT | 1:03 |

AUGUST    WORLDTOUR WOMEN'S RACE

# SIMAC LADIES TOUR
Prologue
24 August 2021
Ede–Ede
2.4km

The 12th event on the 2021 Women's WorldTour calendar, the Simac Ladies Tour (formerly known as Boels Ladies Tour), started with a lung-busting, short and intense 2.4km prologue around the town of Ede, with local Dutch riders dominating the standings. In her first race since the Tokyo Olympic Games, highly decorated all-rounder Marianne Vos (Jumbo-Visma) beat numerous time trial specialists to take the stage victory, blasting around the flat but technical course with a time of 3 minutes and 1 second. Despite the twists and turns, the 34-year-old was able to maintain an incredible pace, averaging 47.7kmph, to beat former World Time Trial champion Ellen van Dijk by 5 seconds and Cecilie Uttrup Ludwig by 6 seconds to move into the race lead.

## WEATHER

TEMPERATURE
21°C

WIND
NE 13km/h

## PROFILE

## STAGE RESULTS

| POS | NAME | TEAM | TIME |
|---|---|---|---|
| 1. | M. Vos | JVW | 3:01 |
| 2. | E. van Dijk | TFS | 0:05 |
| 3. | C. U. Ludwig | FDJ | 0:06 |
| 4. | L. Uneken | SDW | s.t. |
| 5. | L. Wiebes | DSM | 0:07 |
| 6. | C. Majerus | SDW | s.t. |
| 7. | E. Balsamo | VAL | 0:08 |
| 8. | L. Klein | CSR | s.t. |
| 9. | B. Guarischi | MOV | s.t. |
| 10. | C. Kool | NXG | s.t. |
| 11. | C. van den Broek-Blaak | SDW | 0:09 |
| 12. | A. Koster | JVW | s.t. |
| 13. | P. Georgi | DSM | s.t. |
| 14. | A. Barnes | CSR | 0:10 |
| 15. | A. Pieters | SDW | s.t. |
| 16. | K. Swinkels | JVW | 0:11 |
| 17. | C. Copponi | FDJ | s.t. |
| 18. | M. Reusser | ALE | s.t. |
| 19. | E. Norsgaard | MOV | s.t. |
| 20. | L. Nooijen | PHV | s.t. |

## GENERAL CLASSIFICATION

| POS | NAME | TEAM | TIME |
|---|---|---|---|
| 1. | M. Vos | JVW | 3:01 |
| 2. | E. van Dijk | TFS | 0:05 |
| 3. | C. U. Ludwig | FDJ | 0:06 |

## POINTS

| POS | NAME | TEAM | PTS |
|---|---|---|---|
| 1. | M. Vos | JVW | 25 |
| 2. | E. van Dijk | TFS | 20 |
| 3. | C. U. Ludwig | FDJ | 16 |

## YOUNG RIDER

| POS | NAME | TEAM | TIME |
|---|---|---|---|
| 1. | L. Uneken | SDW | 3:07 |
| 2. | L. Wiebes | DSM | 0:01 |
| 3. | C. Kool | NXG | 0:02 |

## TRIVIA

» Five Dutchwomen made the top ten today, all from different teams.

AUGUST  WORLDTOUR WOMEN'S RACE

# SIMAC LADIES TOUR
Stage 1
25 August 2021
Zwolle–Hardenberg
134.4km

The first road stage of the Simac Ladies Tour saw the breakaway prevail as American rider Alison Jackson (Liv Racing) outsprinted Maëlle Grossetête (FDJ Nouvelle-Aquitaine Futuroscope) to take the stage honours. Over typical Dutch terrain, Jackson initiated a surprise early move with 107km of racing remaining. The Canadian rider dangled ahead of the bunch, riding solo for 8km before being joined by Grossetête and Nina Buijsman (Parkhotel Valkenburg). The trio then opened up a gap of over 2 minutes and as they entered the final 15km, despite a hard chase from sprinters' teams Movistar, Canyon-SRAM and Team DSM, their gap remained over a minute. After losing Buijsman, the peloton was closing in and had the leading duo in their sights with just 3km to go. Leaving it too late, the sprinters missed their opportunity and Jackson took her first-ever WorldTour victory. (LM)

## WEATHER

TEMPERATURE: 18°C
WIND: NW 19km/h

## PROFILE

ZWOLLE — LEMELERBERG — HARDENBERG — HARDENBERG

## BREAKAWAY
A. Jackson (LIV), M. Grossetête (FDJ), N. Buijsman (PHV)

## STAGE RESULTS

| POS | NAME | TEAM | TIME |
|---|---|---|---|
| 1. | A. Jackson | LIV | 3:18:20 |
| 2. | M. Grossetête | FDJ | s.t. |
| 3. | L. Wiebes | DSM | 0:04 |
| 4. | M. Vos | JVW | s.t. |
| 5. | C. Kool | NXG | s.t. |
| 6. | B. Guarischi | MOV | s.t. |
| 7. | E. Norsgaard | MOV | s.t. |
| 8. | E. Balsamo | VAL | s.t. |
| 9. | M. Bastianelli | ALE | s.t. |
| 10. | L. Uneken | SDW | s.t. |
| 11. | A. van der Hulst | PHV | s.t. |
| 12. | V. Guazzini | VAL | s.t. |
| 13. | C. Copponi | FDJ | s.t. |
| 14. | E. Duval | FDJ | s.t. |
| 15. | A. Pieters | SDW | s.t. |
| 16. | K. Wild | WNT | s.t. |
| 17. | D. Hengeveld | GKT | s.t. |
| 18. | K. Niewiadoma | CSR | s.t. |
| 19. | C. Hosking | TFS | s.t. |
| 20. | A. Barnes | CSR | s.t. |

## GENERAL CLASSIFICATION

| POS | | NAME | TEAM | TIME |
|---|---|---|---|---|
| 1. | ↑39 | A. Jackson | LIV | 3:21:25 |
| 2. | ↓1 | M. Vos | JVW | s.t. |
| 3. | ↑2 | L. Wiebes | DSM | 0:03 |

## QUEEN OF THE MOUNTAINS

| POS | NAME | TEAM | PTS |
|---|---|---|---|
| 1. | A. Jackson | LIV | 5 |
| 2. | N. Buysman | PHV | 3 |
| 3. | G. Rodríguez | MOV | 1 |

## POINTS

| POS | | NAME | TEAM | PTS |
|---|---|---|---|---|
| 1. | — | M. Vos | JVW | 39 |
| 2. | ↑3 | L. Wiebes | DSM | 28 |
| 3. | — | A. Jackson | LIV | 25 |

## YOUNG RIDER

| POS | | NAME | TEAM | TIME |
|---|---|---|---|---|
| 1. | ↑1 | L. Wiebes | DSM | 3:21:28 |
| 2. | ↓1 | L. Uneken | SDW | 0:03 |
| 3. | — | C. Kool | NXG | 0:05 |

## BONUSES

| TYPE | NAME | TEAM |
|---|---|---|
| QOM 1 | A. Jackson | LIV |
| Sprint 1 | M. Grossetête | FDJ |

AUGUST    WORLDTOUR WOMEN'S RACE

# SIMAC LADIES TOUR
Stage 2 (ITT)
26 August 2021
Gennep–Gennep
17km

The third day of the Simac Ladies Tour was a 17km race against the clock on a flat, out-and-back course, which saw Swiss champion and Olympic silver medallist Marlen Reusser (Alé BTC Ljubljana) take a convincing victory over former World Time Trial champion Ellen van Dijk (Trek-Segafredo). The first half provided a fast time due to a strong tailwind before the riders turned and faced a challenging headwind on their return. With large time gaps at the finish line, the day caused a significant shake-up to the General Classification standings, as Reusser moved into the overall race lead, and the two previous days' leaders, Marianne Vos and Alison Jackson, dropped down to 10th and 20th positions respectively. ⓜ

## WEATHER

TEMPERATURE | WIND
18°C | NW 11km/h

## PROFILE

GENNEP — GENNEP

## STAGE RESULTS

| POS | NAME | TEAM | TIME |
|---|---|---|---|
| 1. | M. Reusser | ALE | 20:41 |
| 2. | E. van Dijk | TFS | 0:18 |
| 3. | C. van den Broek-Blaak | SDW | 0:41 |
| 4. | L. Klein | CSR | 0:50 |
| 5. | E. Norsgaard | MOV | 1:01 |
| 6. | D. Vollering | SDW | 1:18 |
| 7. | S. Roy | BEX | 1:28 |
| 8. | J. Leth | WNT | s.t. |
| 9. | A. Barnes | CSR | 1:30 |
| 10. | A. Koster | JVW | 1:31 |
| 11. | V. Guazzini | VAL | 1:37 |
| 12. | K. Niewiadoma | CSR | 1:39 |
| 13. | C. U. Ludwig | FDJ | 1:41 |
| 14. | P. Georgi | DSM | 1:42 |
| 15. | F. Brausse | WNT | 1:43 |
| 16. | M. Vos | JVW | 1:45 |
| 17. | H. Barnes | CSR | s.t. |
| 18. | K. Wild | WNT | 1:46 |
| 19. | B. Chapman | FDJ | s.t. |
| 20. | M. G. Confalonieri | WNT | 1:50 |

## GENERAL CLASSIFICATION

| POS | NAME | TEAM | TIME |
|---|---|---|---|
| 1. ↑19 | M. Reusser | ALE | 3:42:17 |
| 2. ↑2 | E. van Dijk | TFS | 0:12 |
| 3. ↑10 | C. van den Broek-Blaak | SDW | 0:39 |

## QUEEN OF THE MOUNTAINS

| POS | NAME | TEAM | PTS |
|---|---|---|---|
| 1. — | A. Jackson | LIV | 5 |
| 2. — | N. Buysman | PHV | 3 |
| 3. — | G. Rodriguez | MOV | 1 |

## POINTS

| POS | NAME | TEAM | PTS |
|---|---|---|---|
| 1. ↑3 | E. van Dijk | TFS | 40 |
| 2. ↓1 | M. Vos | JVW | 39 |
| 3. ↓1 | L. Wiebes | DSM | 28 |

## YOUNG RIDER

| POS | NAME | TEAM | TIME |
|---|---|---|---|
| 1. ↑5 | E. Norsgaard | MOV | 3:43:18 |
| 2. ↑5 | V. Guazzini | VAL | 0:36 |
| 3. ↑1 | P. Georgi | DSM | 0:39 |

AUGUST  WORLDTOUR WOMEN'S RACE

# SIMAC LADIES TOUR
Stage 3
27 August 2021
Stramproy–Weert
125.9km

21-year-old Lonneke Uneken (SD Worx) claimed her first WorldTour stage-race victory, after a dramatic finale that saw a huge crash in the peloton 5km from the finish. On the narrow, twisty Dutch roads the front of the bunch was strung out with SD Worx and DSM setting a blistering pace until Lorena Wiebes (DSM) clipped a ridge on the side of the tarmac road, instantly catapulting herself over the bars, which caused a large collision as riders dropped like dominoes. Six SD Worx and DSM riders who were sitting towards the front managed to miss the pile-up and decided to charge on ahead, opening up a gap while riders behind them scrambled to find their bikes. Despite being caught behind the crash, Marlen Reusser was able to maintain her race lead by 10 seconds over Chantal van den Broek-Blaak (SD Worx). GM

## WEATHER

TEMPERATURE: 18°C
WIND: NW 13km/h

## PROFILE

## BREAKAWAY
Q. Ton (GKT), H. Nilsson (LSL)

## STAGE RESULTS

| POS | NAME | TEAM | TIME |
|---|---|---|---|
| 1. | L. Uneken | SDW | 2:52:41 |
| 2. | S. Andersen | DSM | s.t. |
| 3. | P. Georgi | DSM | s.t. |
| 4. | C. van den Broek-Blaak | SDW | s.t. |
| 5. | A. Pieters | SDW | s.t. |
| 6. | D. Vollering | SDW | s.t. |
| 7. | M. Bastianelli | ALE | 0:14 |
| 8. | M. Vos | JVW | s.t. |
| 9. | C. Consonni | VAL | 0:29 |
| 10. | A. Dideriksen | TFS | s.t. |
| 11. | A. Jackson | LIV | s.t. |
| 12. | E. van Dijk | TFS | s.t. |
| 13. | A. van der Hulst | PHV | s.t. |
| 14. | M. G. Confalonieri | WNT | s.t. |
| 15. | D. Braam | LSL | s.t. |
| 16. | M. Jaskulska | LIV | s.t. |
| 17. | A. Koster | JVW | s.t. |
| 18. | M. Grossetête | FDJ | s.t. |
| 19. | M. Reusser | ALE | s.t. |
| 20. | L. Klein | CSR | s.t. |

## GENERAL CLASSIFICATION

| POS | NAME | TEAM | TIME |
|---|---|---|---|
| 1. — | M. Reusser | ALE | 6:35:27 |
| 2. ↑1 | C. van den Broek-Blaak | SDW | 0:10 |
| 3. ↓1 | E. van Dijk | TFS | 0:12 |

## QUEEN OF THE MOUNTAINS

| POS | NAME | TEAM | PTS |
|---|---|---|---|
| 1. — | A. Jackson | LIV | 5 |
| 2. — | N. Buysman | PHV | 3 |
| 3. — | M. Grossetête | FDJ | 1 |

## POINTS

| POS | NAME | TEAM | PTS |
|---|---|---|---|
| 1. ↑1 | M. Vos | JVW | 47 |
| 2. ↑8 | L. Uneken | SDW | 45 |
| 3. ↓2 | E. van Dijk | TFS | 44 |

## YOUNG RIDER

| POS | NAME | TEAM | TIME |
|---|---|---|---|
| 1. ↑2 | P. Georgi | DSM | 6:36:34 |
| 2. — | V. Guazzini | VAL | 0:30 |
| 3. ↑4 | M. Jaskulska | LIV | 1:01 |

## BONUSES

| TYPE | NAME | TEAM |
|---|---|---|
| Sprint 1 | S. Persico | VAL |

AUGUST  WORLDTOUR MEN'S RACE

# SIMAC LADIES TOUR
Stage 4
28 August 2021
Geleen–Sweikhuizen
148.9km

On a stage consisting of eight hilly 18.5km laps, Marianne Vos took her second stage victory after outsprinting Katarzyna Niewiadoma (Canyon-SRAM) and Chantal van den Broek-Blaak. Anouska Koster (Jumbo-Visma) caught the bunch by surprise with an early solo attack with 120km remaining and the Dutch rider managed to quickly open a gap of over 2 minutes despite the tough wet and windy conditions. A dangerous group of 11 riders then broke away inside 45km, before Niewiadoma forced the race-winning move, launching away with 30km remaining and taking Vos and Van den Broek-Blaak for company. Koster was then swallowed up and it came down to a battle between the trio. Niewiadoma tried various attacks but it was Vos who showed the speed to win, with compatriot Van den Broek-Blaak successfully moving into the overall race lead, jumping ahead of Marlen Reusser by 20 seconds. (LM)

## WEATHER

TEMPERATURE: 17°C
WIND: N 20km/h

## PROFILE

## BREAKAWAY
A. Koster (JVW)

## STAGE RESULTS

| POS | NAME | TEAM | TIME |
|---|---|---|---|
| 1. | M. Vos | JVW | 4:15:08 |
| 2. | K. Niewiadoma | CSR | 0:02 |
| 3. | C. van den Broek-Blaak | SDW | s.t. |
| 4. | A. Pieters | SDW | 0:17 |
| 5. | D. Vollering | SDW | s.t. |
| 6. | M. Bastianelli | ALE | s.t. |
| 7. | A. Jackson | LIV | s.t. |
| 8. | P. Georgi | DSM | 0:19 |
| 9. | E. Duval | FDJ | s.t. |
| 10. | E. Harris | CSR | 0:21 |
| 11. | E. van Dijk | TFS | s.t. |
| 12. | M. Reusser | ALE | 0:23 |
| 13. | S. Smulders | LSL | 0:26 |
| 14. | M. Bredewold | PHV | 0:28 |
| 15. | J. Korevaar | LIV | 0:35 |
| 16. | H. Barnes | CSR | 0:41 |
| 17. | H. Nilsson | LSL | 1:11 |
| 18. | J. Borgström | NXG | 1:29 |
| 19. | N. Buysman | PHV | 1:30 |
| 20. | A. van der Hulst | PHV | 1:42 |

## GENERAL CLASSIFICATION

| POS | NAME | TEAM | TIME |
|---|---|---|---|
| 1. ↑1 | C. van den Broek-Blaak | SDW | 10:50:38 |
| 2. ↓1 | M. Reusser | ALE | 0:20 |
| 3. – | E. van Dijk | TFS | 0:30 |

## QUEEN OF THE MOUNTAINS

| POS | NAME | TEAM | PTS |
|---|---|---|---|
| 1. – | A. Jackson | LIV | 19 |
| 2. – | C. van den Broek-Blaak | SDW | 5 |
| 3. – | J. Korevaar | LIV | 3 |

## POINTS

| POS | NAME | TEAM | PTS |
|---|---|---|---|
| 1. – | M. Vos | JVW | 72 |
| 2. ↑2 | C. van den Broek-Blaak | SDW | 51 |
| 3. – | E. van Dijk | TFS | 49 |

## YOUNG RIDER

| POS | NAME | TEAM | TIME |
|---|---|---|---|
| 1. – | P. Georgi | DSM | 10:52:01 |
| 2. ↑3 | M. Bredewold | PHV | 1:27 |
| 3. ↑6 | S. Smulders | LSL | 2:08 |

## TRIVIA
» Compared to yesterday's stage, 28 fewer riders were in the race, nine failed to take the start and 19 didn't finish today's stage.

## BONUSES

| TYPE | NAME | TEAM |
|---|---|---|
| QOM 1 | A. Jackson | LIV |
| QOM 2 | A. Koster | JVW |
| QOM 3 | A. Koster | JVW |
| QOM 4 | A. Koster | JVW |
| QOM 5 | C. van den Broek-Blaak | SDW |
| Sprint 1 | C. van den Broek-Blaak | SDW |
| Sprint 2 | A. Koster | JVW |

AUGUST    WORLDTOUR MEN'S RACE

# SIMAC LADIES TOUR
Stage 5
29 August 2021
Arnhem–Arnhem
150.3km

Marianne Vos stamped her dominance on the five-day race, claiming the final stage victory by outsprinting Alice Barnes (Canyon-SRAM) and Amy Pieters (SD Worx) in tough rainy conditions. The day began with only 57 riders taking to the start line after the previous day's crash and a positive case of Covid-19 that forced the Ceratizit-WNT team to withdraw. The riders took on 19 laps of a hilly 7.8km circuit and, despite numerous attempts, it wasn't until 60km to go that a breakaway was finally able to establish itself. A group of five riders got away by over 2 minutes but, with SD Worx working to keep them on a tight leash and then Canyon-SRAM providing additional help, all the escapees were swept up with just 3km left. Amalie Dideriksen (Trek-Segafredo) opened up the sprint but Vos stole the show and took her third win of the Women's WorldTour. Chantal van den Broek-Blaak secured the overall victory. (LM)

## WEATHER

TEMPERATURE: 16°C
WIND: NW 11km/h

## PROFILE

ARNHEM – ZIJPENDAALSEWEG – ZIJPENDAALSEWEG – ZIJPENDAALSEWEG – ZIJPENDAALSEWEG – ZIJPENDAALSEWEG – ARNHEM

## BREAKAWAY

T. Worrack (TFS), E. Harris (CSR), T. Campbell (BEX), N. Buijsman (PHV), J. Korevaar (LIV)

## STAGE RESULTS

| POS | NAME | TEAM | TIME |
|---|---|---|---|
| 1. | M. Vos | JVW | 3:55:58 |
| 2. | A. Barnes | CSR | s.t. |
| 3. | A. Pieters | SDW | s.t. |
| 4. | A. Dideriksen | TFS | s.t. |
| 5. | A. Jackson | LIV | s.t. |
| 6. | P. Georgi | DSM | s.t. |
| 7. | A. González | MOV | s.t. |
| 8. | M. Reusser | ALE | s.t. |
| 9. | C. Copponi | FDJ | s.t. |
| 10. | E. van Dijk | TFS | 0:03 |
| 11. | C. van den Broek-Blaak | SDW | s.t. |
| 12. | E. Balsamo | VAL | s.t. |
| 13. | A. van der Hulst | PHV | s.t. |
| 14. | K. Niewiadoma | CSR | s.t. |
| 15. | S. Smulders | LSL | s.t. |
| 16. | E. Duval | FDJ | s.t. |
| 17. | M. Bastianelli | ALE | s.t. |
| 18. | S. Andersen | DSM | s.t. |
| 19. | L. Klein | CSR | s.t. |
| 20. | D. Braam | LSL | s.t. |

## GENERAL CLASSIFICATION

| POS | NAME | TEAM | TIME |
|---|---|---|---|
| 1. — | C. van den Broek-Blaak | SDW | 14:46:39 |
| 2. — | M. Reusser | ALE | 0:17 |
| 3. — | E. van Dijk | TFS | 0:30 |

## QUEEN OF THE MOUNTAINS

| POS | NAME | TEAM | PTS |
|---|---|---|---|
| 1. — | A. Koster | JVW | 29 |
| 2. ↓1 | A. Jackson | LIV | 19 |
| 3. ↓1 | C. van den Broek-Blaak | SDW | 5 |

## POINTS

| POS | NAME | TEAM | PTS |
|---|---|---|---|
| 1. — | M. Vos | JVW | 97 |
| 2. — | C. van den Broek-Blaak | SDW | 56 |
| 3. — | E. van Dijk | TFS | 55 |

## YOUNG RIDER

| POS | NAME | TEAM | TIME |
|---|---|---|---|
| 1. — | P. Georgi | DSM | 14:47:59 |
| 2. — | M. Bredewold | PHV | 1:30 |
| 3. — | S. Smulders | LSL | 2:11 |

## TRIVIA

» This was win number 238 for Marianne Vos.

## BONUSES

| TYPE | NAME | TEAM |
|---|---|---|
| QOM 1 | A. Koster | JVW |
| QOM 2 | K. Niewiadoma | CSR |
| QOM 3 | A. Koster | JVW |
| QOM 4 | N. Buijsman | PHV |
| QOM 5 | N. Buijsman | PHV |

AUGUST .1 MEN'S RACE

## DRUIVENKOERS-OVERIJSE

26 August 2021
Overijse–Overijse
192km

## WEATHER

TEMPERATURE
17°C

WIND
NW 17km/h

## RESULTS

| POS | NAME | TEAM | TIME |
| --- | --- | --- | --- |
| 1. | R. Evenepoel | DQT | 4:15:55 |
| 2. | M. F. Honoré | DQT | 0:40 |
| 3. | A. De Gendt | IWG | 0:53 |
| 4. | K. Asgreen | DQT | 0:55 |
| 5. | B. Welten | ARK | s.t. |
| 6. | G. Vermeersch | AFC | s.t. |
| 7. | B. Ghirmay | IWG | s.t. |
| 8. | L. Rex | BWB | s.t. |
| 9. | P. Gilbert | LTS | s.t. |
| 10. | M. Hirschi | UAD | s.t. |
| 11. | N. van der Lijke | RIW | s.t. |
| 12. | C. Noppe | ARK | 0:58 |
| 13. | J. Alaphilippe | DQT | s.t. |
| 14. | P. Serry | DQT | 1:01 |
| 15. | L. Eriksson | RIW | s.t. |
| 16. | X. Meurisse | AFC | 1:08 |
| 17. | J. I. Hvideberg | UXT | 1:27 |
| 18. | T. Wellens | LTS | s.t. |
| 19. | C. Beullens | SVB | 1:29 |
| 20. | R. Townsend | DHB | 1:38 |

AUGUST .PRO MEN'S RACE

# DEUTSCHLAND TOUR
Stage 1
26 August 2021
Stralsund–Schwerin
191.4km

## WEATHER

TEMPERATURE: 15°C
WIND: NW 26km/h

## STAGE RESULTS

| POS | NAME | TEAM | TIME |
|---|---|---|---|
| 1. | P. Ackermann | BOH | 4:07:01 |
| 2. | P. Bauhaus | TBV | s.t. |
| 3. | M. Haller | TBV | s.t. |
| 4. | Y. Lampaert | DQT | s.t. |
| 5. | J. Steimle | DQT | s.t. |
| 6. | D. Van der Poel | AFC | s.t. |
| 7. | L. Mozzato | BBK | s.t. |
| 8. | J. Reynders | SVB | s.t. |
| 9. | M. Canola | GAZ | s.t. |
| 10. | K. Heiduk | LKH | s.t. |
| 11. | N. Märkl | DSM | s.t. |
| 12. | J. Koch | IWG | s.t. |
| 13. | S. Mora | MOV | s.t. |
| 14. | S. E. Byström | UAD | s.t. |
| 15. | L. Naesen | ACT | s.t. |
| 16. | M. Jorgenson | MOV | s.t. |
| 17. | R. Apers | SVB | s.t. |
| 18. | R. Cavagna | DQT | s.t. |
| 19. | K. Halvorsen | UXT | s.t. |
| 20. | A. Verwilst | SVB | s.t. |

## GENERAL CLASSIFICATION

| POS | NAME | TEAM | TIME |
|---|---|---|---|
| 1. | P. Ackermann | BOH | 4:06:51 |
| 2. | P. Bauhaus | TBV | 0:04 |
| 3. | M. Haller | TBV | 0:06 |

## KING OF THE MOUNTAINS

| POS | NAME | TEAM | PTS |
|---|---|---|---|
| 1. | R. Jägeler | PUS | 3 |
| 2. | J. Huppertz | LKH | 2 |
| 3. | A. Colman | SVB | 1 |

## POINTS

| POS | NAME | TEAM | PTS |
|---|---|---|---|
| 1. | P. Ackermann | BOH | 15 |
| 2. | P. Bauhaus | TBV | 12 |
| 3. | M. Haller | TBV | 9 |

## YOUNG RIDER

| POS | NAME | TEAM | TIME |
|---|---|---|---|
| 1. | J. Knolle | SVL | 4:07:00 |
| 2. | J. Steimle | DQT | 0:01 |
| 3. | L. Mozzato | BBK | s.t. |

# DEUTSCHLAND TOUR
Stage 2
27 August 2021
Sangerhausen–Ilmenau
180.6km

## WEATHER

TEMPERATURE: 32°C
WIND: NW 17km/h

## STAGE RESULTS

| POS | NAME | TEAM | TIME |
|---|---|---|---|
| 1. | A. Kristoff | UAD | 4:24:12 |
| 2. | P. Bauhaus | TBV | s.t. |
| 3. | P. Ackermann | BOH | s.t. |
| 4. | J. Steimle | DQT | 0:02 |
| 5. | S. E. Byström | UAD | s.t. |
| 6. | R. Tiller | UXT | s.t. |
| 7. | J. Koch | IWG | s.t. |
| 8. | M. Jorgenson | MOV | s.t. |
| 9. | L. Mozzato | BBK | s.t. |
| 10. | Y. Lampaert | DQT | s.t. |
| 11. | J. Degenkolb | NAT | s.t. |
| 12. | C. Berthet | ACT | s.t. |
| 13. | A. Skaarseth | UXT | s.t. |
| 14. | M. Haller | TBV | s.t. |
| 15. | J. Huppertz | LKH | s.t. |
| 16. | J. Almeida | DQT | s.t. |
| 17. | T. Lindner | PUS | s.t. |
| 18. | N. Politt | BOH | s.t. |
| 19. | D. Teuns | TBV | s.t. |
| 20. | G. Zimmermann | IWG | s.t. |

## GENERAL CLASSIFICATION

| POS | NAME | TEAM | TIME |
|---|---|---|---|
| 1. — | P. Ackermann | BOH | 8:30:59 |
| 2. — | P. Bauhaus | TBV | 0:02 |
| 3. ↑102 | A. Kristoff | UAD | 0:04 |

## KING OF THE MOUNTAINS

| POS | NAME | TEAM | PTS |
|---|---|---|---|
| 1. — | K. Murphy | RLY | 5 |
| 2. — | L. Vervaeke | AFC | 5 |
| 3. ↓2 | R. Jägeler | PUS | 3 |

## POINTS

| POS | NAME | TEAM | PTS |
|---|---|---|---|
| 1. — | P. Ackermann | BOH | 24 |
| 2. — | P. Bauhaus | TBV | 24 |
| 3. — | A. Kristoff | UAD | 15 |

## YOUNG RIDER

| POS | NAME | TEAM | TIME |
|---|---|---|---|
| 1. ↑40 | G. Zimmermann | IWG | 8:31:12 |
| 2. — | J. Steimle | DQT | 0:03 |
| 3. — | L. Mozzato | BBK | s.t. |

AUGUST  .PRO MEN'S RACE

## DEUTSCHLAND TOUR
Stage 3
28 August 2021
Ilmenau–Erlangen
193.9km

### WEATHER

TEMPERATURE  WIND
15°C  N 6km/h

### STAGE RESULTS

| POS | NAME | TEAM | TIME |
|---|---|---|---|
| 1. | N. Politt | BOH | 4:25:15 |
| 2. | D. Teuns | TBV | 0:11 |
| 3. | A. Greipel | ISN | 0:12 |
| 4. | P. Ackermann | BOH | s.t. |
| 5. | J. Degenkolb | NAT | s.t. |
| 6. | M. Cavendish | DQT | s.t. |
| 7. | M. Mayrhofer | DSM | s.t. |
| 8. | A. Kristoff | UAD | s.t. |
| 9. | S. Mora | MOV | s.t. |
| 10. | J. Hodapp | SVL | s.t. |
| 11. | J. Koch | IWG | s.t. |
| 12. | N. Märkl | DSM | s.t. |
| 13. | L. Naesen | ACT | s.t. |
| 14. | L. Mozzato | BBK | s.t. |
| 15. | M. Canola | GAZ | s.t. |
| 16. | S. De Pestel | SVB | s.t. |
| 17. | P. Bauhaus | TBV | s.t. |
| 18. | F. Galván | EKP | s.t. |
| 19. | J. Reynders | SVB | s.t. |
| 20. | P. Benz | NAT | s.t. |

### GENERAL CLASSIFICATION

| POS | | NAME | TEAM | TIME |
|---|---|---|---|---|
| 1. | ↑6 | N. Politt | BOH | 12:56:18 |
| 2. | ↓1 | P. Ackermann | BOH | 0:08 |
| 3. | ↓1 | P. Bauhaus | TBV | 0:10 |

### KING OF THE MOUNTAINS

| POS | | NAME | TEAM | PTS |
|---|---|---|---|---|
| 1. | ↑1 | L. Vervaeke | AFC | 7 |
| 2. | ↓1 | K. Murphy | RLY | 5 |
| 3. | ↑4 | J. Peter | NAT | 4 |

### POINTS

| POS | | NAME | TEAM | PTS |
|---|---|---|---|---|
| 1. | — | P. Ackermann | BOH | 31 |
| 2. | — | P. Bauhaus | TBV | 24 |
| 3. | — | A. Kristoff | UAD | 18 |

### YOUNG RIDER

| POS | | NAME | TEAM | TIME |
|---|---|---|---|---|
| 1. | — | G. Zimmermann | IWG | 12:56:37 |
| 2. | ↑1 | L. Mozzato | BBK | 0:05 |
| 3. | ↑5 | N. Märkl | DSM | s.t. |

## DEUTSCHLAND TOUR
Stage 4
29 August 2021
Erlangen–Nürnberg
156.3km

### WEATHER

TEMPERATURE  WIND
16°C  W 15km/h

### STAGE RESULTS

| POS | NAME | TEAM | TIME |
|---|---|---|---|
| 1. | A. Kristoff | UAD | 3:33:25 |
| 2. | P. Ackermann | BOH | s.t. |
| 3. | L. Mozzato | BBK | s.t. |
| 4. | R. Tiller | UXT | s.t. |
| 5. | F. Galván | EKP | s.t. |
| 6. | M. Haller | TBV | s.t. |
| 7. | J. Steimle | DQT | s.t. |
| 8. | V. Retailleau | ACT | s.t. |
| 9. | J. Degenkolb | NAT | s.t. |
| 10. | J. Koch | IWG | s.t. |
| 11. | J. Hollmann | MOV | s.t. |
| 12. | M. Meisen | AFC | s.t. |
| 13. | T. Lindner | PUS | s.t. |
| 14. | F. Van den Bossche | SVB | s.t. |
| 15. | N. Politt | BOH | s.t. |
| 16. | B. Tulett | AFC | s.t. |
| 17. | F. Dversnes | GAZ | s.t. |
| 18. | J. Rutsch | NAT | s.t. |
| 19. | R. Adrià | EKP | s.t. |
| 20. | M. Canola | GAZ | s.t. |

### GENERAL CLASSIFICATION

| POS | | NAME | TEAM | TIME |
|---|---|---|---|---|
| 1. | — | N. Politt | BOH | 16:29:41 |
| 2. | — | P. Ackermann | BOH | 0:04 |
| 3. | ↑1 | A. Kristoff | UAD | s.t. |

### KING OF THE MOUNTAINS

| POS | | NAME | TEAM | PTS |
|---|---|---|---|---|
| 1. | — | L. Vervaeke | AFC | 10 |
| 2. | — | D. Cataldo | MOV | 10 |
| 3. | — | J. Wolf | BAI | 8 |

### POINTS

| POS | | NAME | TEAM | PTS |
|---|---|---|---|---|
| 1. | — | P. Ackermann | BOH | 46 |
| 2. | ↑1 | A. Kristoff | UAD | 33 |
| 3. | ↑2 | J. Steimle | DQT | 17 |

### YOUNG RIDER

| POS | | NAME | TEAM | TIME |
|---|---|---|---|---|
| 1. | — | G. Zimmermann | IWG | 16:30:00 |
| 2. | — | L. Mozzato | BBK | 0:03 |
| 3. | ↑2 | J. Steimle | DQT | 0:07 |

AUGUST .PRO MEN'S RACE

# BRUSSELS CYCLING CLASSIC
28 August 2021
Brussels–Brussels
205.3km

## WEATHER

TEMPERATURE
19°C

WIND
N 19km/h

## RESULTS

| POS | NAME | TEAM | TIME |
|---|---|---|---|
| 1. | R. Evenepoel | DQT | 4:28:30 |
| 2. | A. De Gendt | IWG | 0:50 |
| 3. | T. Van der Sande | LTS | 2:13 |
| 4. | P. Gilbert | LTS | s.t. |
| 5. | M. Hirschi | UAD | s.t. |
| 6. | B. McNulty | UAD | s.t. |
| 7. | T. Merlier | AFC | 2:16 |
| 8. | D. van Poppel | IWG | s.t. |
| 9. | J. Lecroq | BBK | s.t. |
| 10. | F. Gaviria | UAD | s.t. |
| 11. | M. Budding | BCY | s.t. |
| 12. | M. Walscheid | TQA | s.t. |
| 13. | V. Campenaerts | TQA | s.t. |
| 14. | B. Welten | ARK | s.t. |
| 15. | K. Van Rooy | SVB | s.t. |
| 16. | G. Thijssen | LTS | s.t. |
| 17. | J. Drucker | COF | s.t. |
| 18. | R. Mertz | BWB | s.t. |
| 19. | C. Beullens | SVB | s.t. |
| 20. | K. Sbaragli | AFC | s.t. |

AUGUST    WORLDTOUR MEN'S RACE

# BRETAGNE CLASSIC – OUEST-FRANCE
29 August 2021
Plouay–Plouay
251km

## WEATHER

**TEMPERATURE**
20°C

**WIND**
NE 22km/h

## PROFILE

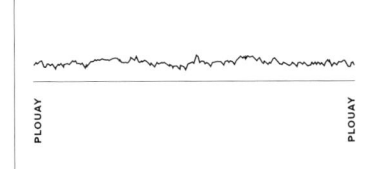

PLOUAY — PLOUAY

## BREAKAWAY

A. De Marchi (ISN), A. Gougeard (ACT), Q. Hermans (IWG), S. Grignard (LTS)

With 251km of distinctly jagged terrain, this had all the hallmarks of a one-day battle of spring Classic proportions. Four riders eased away from the peloton early on, entering a holding pattern for several hours before Deceuninck-QuickStep's harbinger of change, Tim Declercq, moved to the front with about 75km to go. Sébastian Grignard and Alexis Gougeard had been dropped from the breakaway, leaving only Quinten Hermans and Alessandro De Marchi with an advantage now just under 5 minutes. Declercq's singular effort cut swathes out of the gap and set up the inevitable attack on the gravel climb of Saoutalarin. Julian Alaphilippe was the first to put the hammer down, taking teammate Mikkel Honoré, along with Benoît Cosnefroy and Tadej Pogačar. As the quartet drove into the gap, Pogačar's lack of racing – and abundance of post-Tour celebrations – caught up with him after he visibly struggled for 15km, leaving three to chase down the remains of the breakaway. Attacks continued in the peloton behind, but their advantage held into the last 10km. Accelerations from both Frenchmen, tempers flaring, saw Honoré dropped, but the Dane was back on the front to lead under the *flamme rouge*. The dangerously outnumbered Cosnefroy found himself wedged between the Deceuninck riders on the finishing straight, but he was ready to respond when Alaphilippe launched his sprint. Against all the odds, Cosnefroy had the lasting power to reach the line first, taking a defiant maiden WorldTour victory.

## RESULTS

| POS | NAME | TEAM | TIME |
|---|---|---|---|
| 1. | B. Cosnefroy | ACT | 5:59:56 |
| 2. | J. Alaphilippe | DQT | s.t. |
| 3. | M. F. Honoré | DQT | 0:03 |
| 4. | E. Hayter | IGD | 0:13 |
| 5. | C. Swift | ARK | s.t. |
| 6. | F. Bonnamour | BBK | s.t. |
| 7. | J. Stuyven | TFS | s.t. |
| 8. | V. Madouas | GFC | s.t. |
| 9. | Q. Pacher | BBK | 0:16 |
| 10. | G. Nizzolo | TQA | 0:17 |
| 11. | H. Hofstetter | ISN | s.t. |
| 12. | D. Ballerini | DQT | s.t. |
| 13. | G. Aleotti | BOH | s.t. |
| 14. | A. Paret-Peintre | ACT | s.t. |
| 15. | J. Simon | TEN | s.t. |
| 16. | D. Godon | ACT | s.t. |
| 17. | L. Pichon | ARK | s.t. |
| 18. | G. Serrano | MOV | s.t. |
| 19. | B. Hermans | ISN | s.t. |
| 20. | W. Barguil | ARK | s.t. |

## TRIVIA

» This was the first time Cosnefroy has ever won a race Alaphilippe has competed in; the world champion has won five that featured his compatriot.

AUGUST    WORLDTOUR WOMEN'S RACE

# GP DE PLOUAY

30 August 2021
Plouay–Plouay
150.5km

The 20th edition of GP Plouay was raced over 11 local laps of a tough 13.68km circuit, with the peloton tackling three climbs per lap, the first of which reached sections of 19 per cent gradients. The race began with various attacks flying but with no significant breakaways able to establish until around 70km to go, when Alena Amialiusik (Canyon-SRAM) and Jade Wiel (FDJ Nouvelle-Aquitaine Futuroscope) snapped the elastic and quickly stretched their lead out to almost 3 minutes. A chasing group of eight riders went in pursuit but, with three laps remaining, the chasers were caught as Amialiusik dropped Wiel. Once the race entered the final two laps, it was Team DSM and Trek-Segafredo who took up the chase, before Tokyo Olympic bronze medallist, Elisa Longo Borghini, attacked with 25.6km left. Mavi García (Alé BTC Ljubljana) bridged across shortly after, and the pair were able to draw back Amialiusik. It looked as though the podium had been decided; however, with 15km to go, the peloton hadn't given up and Ashleigh Moolman-Pasio (SD Worx) drew the leading trio back in, opening up the race once again. The race-winning move eventually came with 10km remaining as four riders – Longo Borghini, Taitana Guderzo (Alé BTC Ljubljana), Liane Lippert (Team DSM) and Erica Magnaldi (Ceratizit-WNT Pro Cycling) – broke free. But, not content with settling for a sprint finish, Longo Borghini immediately attacked 7km from the line and held on by just 12 seconds to take a spectacular solo victory. (JM)

## WEATHER

**TEMPERATURE**
19°C

**WIND**
NE 24km/h

## PROFILE

PLOUAY — PLOUAY

## BREAKAWAY

J. Wiel (FDJ), A. Amialiusik (CSR)

## RESULTS

| POS | NAME | TEAM | TIME |
|---|---|---|---|
| 1. | E. Longo Borghini | TFS | 4:06:02 |
| 2. | G. Verhulst | ARK | 0:12 |
| 3. | K. Faulkner | TIB | s.t. |
| 4. | S. Bertizzolo | LIV | s.t. |
| 5. | E. Muzic | FDJ | s.t. |
| 6. | E. Bujak | ALE | s.t. |
| 7. | E. Deignan | TFS | s.t. |
| 8. | C. Rivera | DSM | s.t. |
| 9. | A. Moolman | SDW | s.t. |
| 10. | A. Henderson | JVW | s.t. |
| 11. | S. Persico | VAL | s.t. |
| 12. | N. Fisher-Black | SDW | s.t. |
| 13. | E. Chabbey | CSR | s.t. |
| 14. | I. Grangier | SRC | s.t. |
| 15. | E. Magnaldi | WNT | s.t. |
| 16. | A. Smith | TIB | s.t. |
| 17. | U. Pintar | ALE | s.t. |
| 18. | T. Guderzo | ALE | s.t. |
| 19. | R. Neylan | PHV | s.t. |
| 20. | A. Shackley | SDW | s.t. |

## TRIVIA

» This marked Longo Borghini's first victory outside of Italy since Emakumeen Bira in May 2019.

AUGUST   WORLDTOUR MEN'S RACE

# BENELUX TOUR
Stage 1
30 August 2021
Surhuisterveen–Dokkum
169.6km

The first stage of the newly named Benelux Tour (formerly the BinckBank Tour, and before that the Eneco Tour) was ridden over a pan-flat 169.6km and duly ended in a sprint. Alpecin-Fenix's extremely consistent Belgian Tim Merlier beat Phil Bauhaus into second, the German having left his national Tour in Germany a day early in order to line up in Belgium. But it was a relatively small group that came together to the line, after crosswinds had created echelons. Race favourite Remco Evenepoel had found himself in the front group, but suffered a broken wheel, which he blamed squarely on Gianni Vermeersch of Alpecin-Fenix after the two had collided. The subsequent ponderous wheel change by the neutral service mechanic left Evenepoel furious, frustrated and 57 seconds down on GC in the second group over the line. (NR)

## WEATHER

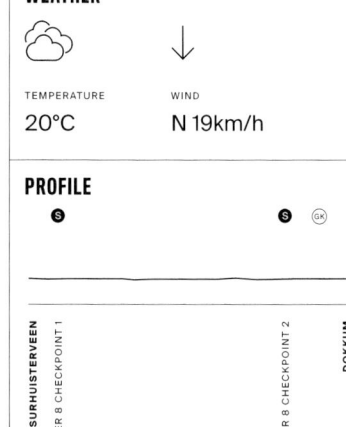

TEMPERATURE: 20°C
WIND: N 19km/h

## PROFILE

## BREAKAWAY
L. Durbridge (BEX), G. Boivin (ISN), L. Owen (EFN), L. Robert (BWB), J. Duval (ACT), A. Livyns (BWB), W. Vanhoof (SVB)

## STAGE RESULTS

| POS | NAME | TEAM | TIME |
| --- | --- | --- | --- |
| 1. | T. Merlier | AFC | 3:32:20 |
| 2. | P. Bauhaus | TBV | s.t. |
| 3. | A. J. Hodeg | DQT | s.t. |
| 4. | F. Gaviria | UAD | s.t. |
| 5. | D. van Poppel | IWG | s.t. |
| 6. | M. Pedersen | TFS | s.t. |
| 7. | M. Walscheid | TQA | s.t. |
| 8. | S. Aniołkowski | BWB | s.t. |
| 9. | M. Teunissen | TJV | s.t. |
| 10. | C. Laporte | COF | s.t. |
| 11. | T. Van der Sande | LTS | s.t. |
| 12. | R. Kluge | LTS | s.t. |
| 13. | O. Naesen | ACT | s.t. |
| 14. | M. Mohorič | TBV | s.t. |
| 15. | S. Küng | GFC | s.t. |
| 16. | N. Arndt | DSM | s.t. |
| 17. | V. Campenaerts | TQA | s.t. |
| 18. | W. Kelderman | BOH | s.t. |
| 19. | C. Bol | DSM | s.t. |
| 20. | S. Colbrelli | TBV | s.t. |

## GENERAL CLASSIFICATION

| POS | NAME | TEAM | TIME |
| --- | --- | --- | --- |
| 1. | T. Merlier | AFC | 3:32:10 |
| 2. | P. Bauhaus | TBV | 0:04 |
| 3. | A. J. Hodeg | DQT | 0:06 |

## POINTS

| POS | NAME | TEAM | PTS |
| --- | --- | --- | --- |
| 1. | T. Merlier | AFC | 30 |
| 2. | P. Bauhaus | TBV | 25 |
| 3. | A. J. Hodeg | DQT | 22 |

## BONUSES

| TYPE | NAME | TEAM |
| --- | --- | --- |
| Sprint 1 | A. Livyns | BWB |
| Sprint 2 | A. Livyns | BWB |

AUGUST  WORLDTOUR MEN'S RACE

# BENELUX TOUR
Stage 2 (ITT)
31 August 2021
Lelystad–Lelystad
11.1km

A time trial provided the opportunity for Remco Evenepoel and others to start to claw back time lost in the crosswinds of stage 1. But the young Belgian woke up sick, couldn't eat in the morning, and finished the race off the pace in 18th place. Instead it was Swiss rider Stefan Bissegger who took victory, once again confirming his place in the very top order of the world time trialling scene with the third WorldTour win of his breakthrough year. In Edoardo Affini and European champion Stefan Küng, Bissegger once again prevailed against a high-calibre field to take the race lead. This achievement was made all the more remarkable when he subsequently divulged that he'd been driven into by a car on a training ride the previous Friday. (NB)

## WEATHER

TEMPERATURE  WIND
20°C         S 37km/h

## PROFILE

LELYSTAD — LELYSTAD

## STAGE RESULTS

| POS | NAME | TEAM | TIME |
|---|---|---|---|
| 1. | S. Bissegger | EFN | 12:08 |
| 2. | E. Affini | TJV | 0:15 |
| 3. | S. Küng | GFC | 0:20 |
| 4. | K. Asgreen | DQT | 0:21 |
| 5. | M. Walscheid | TQA | 0:22 |
| 6. | T. Dumoulin | TJV | 0:23 |
| 7. | S. Kragh Andersen | DSM | 0:24 |
| 8. | V. Campenaerts | TQA | 0:26 |
| 9. | C. Laporte | COF | 0:29 |
| 10. | B. McNulty | UAD | 0:31 |
| 11. | J. van Emden | TJV | 0:32 |
| 12. | S. Langeveld | EFN | 0:35 |
| 13. | B. Thomas | GFC | 0:36 |
| 14. | M. Sobrero | APT | s.t. |
| 15. | F. Wright | TBV | 0:38 |
| 16. | L. Durbridge | BEX | 0:39 |
| 17. | R. Herregodts | SVB | s.t. |
| 18. | R. Evenepoel | DQT | s.t. |
| 19. | M. Mohorič | TBV | 0:40 |
| 20. | H. Houle | APT | 0:44 |

## GENERAL CLASSIFICATION

| POS |  | NAME | TEAM | TIME |
|---|---|---|---|---|
| 1. | ↑24 | S. Bissegger | EFN | 3:44:28 |
| 2. | ↑7 | K. Asgreen | DQT | 0:19 |
| 3. | ↑16 | S. Küng | GFC | 0:20 |

## POINTS

| POS |  | NAME | TEAM | PTS |
|---|---|---|---|---|
| 1. | – | S. Bissegger | EFN | 30 |
| 2. | ↓1 | T. Merlier | AFC | 30 |
| 3. | ↑4 | M. Walscheid | TQA | 30 |

## TRIVIA

» Head-to-head in time trials versus his third-place compatriot Stefan Küng, Bissegger has come out on top three times compared to Küng's five better placings.

444

AUGUST  WORLDTOUR MEN'S RACE

# BENELUX TOUR
Stage 3
1 September 2021
Essen–Hoogerheide
168.3km

Five varied riders managed to stave off the chase by the sprinters' teams to contest victory on a day in which race leader Stefan Bissegger managed to stay out of trouble. And, on an another day in which Odd Christian Eiking continued his prolonged spell in the Vuelta's red jersey, Intermarché-Wanty-Gobert enjoyed further success when their Giro stage winner Taco van der Hoorn took a second win of 2021. Unlike his solo victory in Italy, this one was earned by outsprinting his breakaway companions. And yet there were similarities. The chase by the sprinters' teams was slightly disrupted by mechanical incidents affecting both Kasper Asgreen and Caleb Ewan, meaning that the joint efforts of both Deceuninck-QuickStep and Lotto Soudal stalled as they waited for key riders to get back on. In the end, the margin of victory for the lead group was a narrow, but emphatic, 4 seconds.

## WEATHER

TEMPERATURE: 16°C
WIND: N 7km/h

## PROFILE

ESSEN — ESSEN — RIJZENDE WEG — HOOGERHEIDE

## BREAKAWAY
T. van der Hoorn (IWG), M. Norsgaard (MOV), L. Durbridge (BEX), S. Battistella (APT), T. Willems (SVB), A. Livyns (BWB)

## STAGE RESULTS

| POS | NAME | TEAM | TIME |
|---|---|---|---|
| 1. | T. van der Hoorn | IWG | 3:40:23 |
| 2. | M. Norsgaard | MOV | s.t. |
| 3. | L. Durbridge | BEX | s.t. |
| 4. | S. Battistella | APT | s.t. |
| 5. | T. Willems | SVB | s.t. |
| 6. | P. Sagan | BOH | 0:04 |
| 7. | P. Bauhaus | TBV | s.t. |
| 8. | D. van Poppel | IWG | s.t. |
| 9. | C. Ewan | LTS | s.t. |
| 10. | M. Pedersen | TFS | s.t. |
| 11. | M. Teunissen | TJV | s.t. |
| 12. | T. Van Asbroeck | ISN | s.t. |
| 13. | F. Gaviria | UAD | s.t. |
| 14. | J. Stuyven | TFS | s.t. |
| 15. | R. Janse Van Rensburg | TQA | s.t. |
| 16. | S. Colbrelli | TBV | s.t. |
| 17. | M. Mohorič | TBV | s.t. |
| 18. | I. García Cortina | MOV | s.t. |
| 19. | T. Van der Sande | LTS | s.t. |
| 20. | S. Aniołkowski | BWB | s.t. |

## GENERAL CLASSIFICATION

| POS | | NAME | TEAM | TIME |
|---|---|---|---|---|
| 1. | — | S. Bissegger | EFN | 7:24:55 |
| 2. | — | K. Asgreen | DQT | 0:19 |
| 3. | — | S. Küng | GFC | 0:20 |

## POINTS

| POS | | NAME | TEAM | PTS |
|---|---|---|---|---|
| 1. | ↑4 | P. Bauhaus | TBV | 38 |
| 2. | ↓1 | S. Bissegger | EFN | 30 |
| 3. | ↓1 | T. Merlier | AFC | 30 |

## BONUSES

| TYPE | NAME | TEAM |
|---|---|---|
| Sprint 1 | T. Willems | SVB |
| Sprint 2 | T. Willems | SVB |

## TRIVIA
» Of Taco van der Hoorn's five career victories, three of them have come on stage 3 of stage races.

AUGUST    WORLDTOUR MEN'S RACE

# BENELUX TOUR
Stage 4
2 September 2021
Aalter–Ardooie
166.1km

A huge crash just after the flag dropped set the tone for a day that proved to be more hectic than many might have anticipated. The organisers briefly halted the race as riders sought the attention of medics and remounted. Later on, when a three-man breakaway was caught 50km from the line as the race entered the closing circuit, it opened the bunch up to repeated and successive attack from small groups. Then came the 'Golden Kilometre', for which the Benelux Tour is renowned, with three successive bonus sprints all within 1,000 metres. Remco Evenepoel led out GC rider Kasper Asgreen, who took two of the three and closed his deficit to Stefan Bissegger from 19 seconds to 13 by the end of the day. The stage was eventually decided by a bunch sprint, in which Mads Pedersen struck out first only to find Tim Merlier overhauling him to take a second victory at the race.

## WEATHER

TEMPERATURE  WIND
18°C         NE 14km/h

## PROFILE

## BREAKAWAY
A. Livyns (BWB), T. Sprengers (SVB), S. Bewley (BEX)

## STAGE RESULTS

| POS | NAME | TEAM | TIME |
|---|---|---|---|
| 1. | T. Merlier | AFC | 3:36:29 |
| 2. | M. Pedersen | TFS | s.t. |
| 3. | D. van Poppel | IWG | s.t. |
| 4. | P. Sagan | BOH | s.t. |
| 5. | C. Laporte | COF | s.t. |
| 6. | P. Bauhaus | TBV | s.t. |
| 7. | F. Gaviria | UAD | s.t. |
| 8. | M. Walscheid | TQA | s.t. |
| 9. | D. Groenewegen | TJV | s.t. |
| 10. | F. Lienhard | GFC | s.t. |
| 11. | L. G. Mas | MOV | s.t. |
| 12. | T. Van Asbroeck | ISN | s.t. |
| 13. | K. Van Rooy | SVB | s.t. |
| 14. | A. J. Hodeg | DQT | s.t. |
| 15. | V. Campenaerts | TQA | s.t. |
| 16. | J. Stewart | GFC | s.t. |
| 17. | I. García Cortina | MOV | s.t. |
| 18. | L. Rex | BWB | s.t. |
| 19. | S. Bissegger | EFN | s.t. |
| 20. | J. Drucker | COF | s.t. |

## GENERAL CLASSIFICATION

| POS | NAME | TEAM | TIME |
|---|---|---|---|
| 1. — | S. Bissegger | EFN | 11:01:24 |
| 2. — | K. Asgreen | DQT | 0:13 |
| 3. ↑1 | L. Durbridge | BEX | 0:20 |

## POINTS

| POS | NAME | TEAM | PTS |
|---|---|---|---|
| 1. ↑2 | T. Merlier | AFC | 60 |
| 2. ↓1 | P. Bauhaus | TBV | 53 |
| 3. ↑3 | D. van Poppel | IWG | 51 |

## BONUSES

| TYPE | NAME | TEAM |
|---|---|---|
| Sprint 1 | T. Sprengers | SVB |
| Sprint 2 | T. Sprengers | SVB |

## TRIVIA
» Of Tim Merlier's 18 career victories, half of them have been in 2021.

AUGUST    WORLDTOUR MEN'S RACE

# BENELUX TOUR
Stage 5
3 September 2021
Riemst–Bilzen
192km

All change in the General Classification after both Stefan Bissegger and Kasper Asgreen fell away, and the race lead passed to Stefan Küng. Bissegger lost the wheels on the last lap of the testing final circuit and slipped out of contention. Asgreen suffered from mechanical misfortune. Having attacked on the Kleiberg, the Dane had ridden clear before having to stop at the side of the road to remount his chain and adjust his gears. His subsequent, unsuccessful chase back on yielded a 43-second time loss at the end of the day and saw him drop to 13th on GC, 35 seconds down on Stefan Küng who finished in the bunch. The stage win was contested once again by the sprinters, with Caleb Ewan prevailing. It was the Australian's first victory since his high-speed crash at the Tour de France.

## WEATHER

TEMPERATURE   WIND
24°C          NE 15km/h

## PROFILE

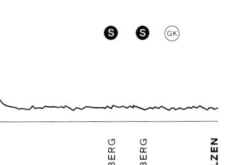

RIEMST — SLINGERBERG — LETENBERG — BILZEN

## BREAKAWAY

H. Houle (APT), J. Bauer (BEX), C. Pedersen (DSM)

## STAGE RESULTS

| POS | NAME | TEAM | TIME |
|---|---|---|---|
| 1. | C. Ewan | LTS | 4:26:24 |
| 2. | S. Colbrelli | TBV | s.t. |
| 3. | D. van Poppel | IWG | s.t. |
| 4. | P. Sagan | BOH | s.t. |
| 5. | J. Stuyven | TFS | s.t. |
| 6. | T. Merlier | AFC | s.t. |
| 7. | M. Teunissen | TJV | s.t. |
| 8. | M. Mohorič | TBV | s.t. |
| 9. | C. Laporte | COF | s.t. |
| 10. | O. Naesen | ACT | s.t. |
| 11. | M. Menten | BWB | s.t. |
| 12. | A. Renard | ISN | s.t. |
| 13. | J. Stewart | GFC | s.t. |
| 14. | T. Benoot | DSM | s.t. |
| 15. | N. Arndt | DSM | s.t. |
| 16. | L. Pöstlberger | BOH | s.t. |
| 17. | S. Küng | GFC | s.t. |
| 18. | B. Swift | IGD | s.t. |
| 19. | A. Stokbro | TQA | s.t. |
| 20. | M. Hirschi | UAD | s.t. |

## GENERAL CLASSIFICATION

| POS | NAME | TEAM | TIME |
|---|---|---|---|
| 1. ↑3 | S. Küng | GFC | 15:28:08 |
| 2. ↑1 | L. Durbridge | BEX | 0:02 |
| 3. ↑3 | C. Laporte | COF | 0:06 |

## POINTS

| POS | NAME | TEAM | PTS |
|---|---|---|---|
| 1. — | T. Merlier | AFC | 75 |
| 2. ↑1 | D. van Poppel | IWG | 73 |
| 3. ↑4 | P. Sagan | BOH | 53 |

## BONUSES

| TYPE | NAME | TEAM |
|---|---|---|
| Sprint 1 | J. Bauer | BEX |
| Sprint 2 | J. Bauer | BEX |

## TRIVIA

» Before joining Lotto Soudal, Caleb Ewan had never taken a victory in Belgium; since signing in 2019 he's won six times.

AUGUST   WORLDTOUR MEN'S RACE

# BENELUX TOUR
Stage 6
4 September 2021
Ottignies-Louvain-la-Neuve–Houffalize
207.6km

The Côte Bois des Moines provided the springboard for Sonny Colbrelli to seize control of the Benelux Tour as the race switched languages and entered hilly French-speaking terrain more usually associated with the Ardennes Classics, where the Italian has historically enjoyed success. A two-up attack from Colbrelli and his Bahrain Victorious teammate Matej Mohorič spelled the end of Geraint Thomas's day in a two-man breakaway. However, the definitive move of the day came elsewhere – at 25km to go – and meant that Colbrelli scooped up all 9 bonus seconds on the Golden Kilometre without having to exert himself in a sprint. The chase group failed to cooperate, which allowed Colbrelli to build a race-winning lead. Mohorič's second place capped a perfect day for one of the outstanding teams of 2021.

## WEATHER

TEMPERATURE: 23°C
WIND: NE 15km/h

## PROFILE

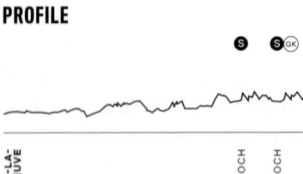

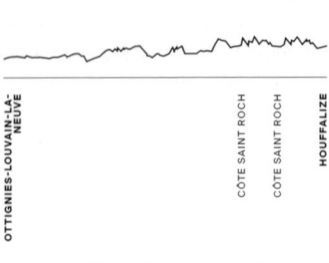

## BREAKAWAY
J. Rickaert (AFC), G. Thomas (IGD)

## STAGE RESULTS

| POS | NAME | TEAM | TIME |
|---|---|---|---|
| 1. | S. Colbrelli | TBV | 4:55:27 |
| 2. | M. Mohorič | TBV | 0:42 |
| 3. | J. Stuyven | TFS | s.t. |
| 4. | T. Benoot | DSM | s.t. |
| 5. | V. Campenaerts | TQA | s.t. |
| 6. | T. Wellens | LTS | s.t. |
| 7. | M. Hirschi | UAD | s.t. |
| 8. | T. Dumoulin | TJV | s.t. |
| 9. | N. Arndt | DSM | 1:02 |
| 10. | G. Vermeersch | AFC | s.t. |
| 11. | F. Wright | TBV | s.t. |
| 12. | M. Teunissen | TJV | s.t. |
| 13. | G. Moscon | IGD | s.t. |
| 14. | D. Villella | MOV | s.t. |
| 15. | B. McNulty | UAD | s.t. |
| 16. | M. Würst Schmidt | ISN | s.t. |
| 17. | L. Owen | EFN | s.t. |
| 18. | S. Battistella | APT | s.t. |
| 19. | K. Asgreen | DQT | s.t. |
| 20. | L. Durbridge | BEX | s.t. |

## GENERAL CLASSIFICATION

| POS | NAME | TEAM | TIME |
|---|---|---|---|
| 1. ↑4 | S. Colbrelli | TBV | 20:23:30 |
| 2. ↑4 | M. Mohorič | TBV | 0:51 |
| 3. ↑1 | V. Campenaerts | TQA | 0:53 |

## POINTS

| POS | NAME | TEAM | PTS |
|---|---|---|---|
| 1. – | T. Merlier | AFC | 75 |
| 2. – | D. van Poppel | IWG | 73 |
| 3. ↑8 | S. Colbrelli | TBV | 55 |

## BONUSES

| TYPE | NAME | TEAM |
|---|---|---|
| Sprint 1 | G. Thomas | IGD |
| Sprint 2 | M. Mohorič | TBV |

## TRIVIA

» Sonny Colbrelli has now won stages at three different WorldTour races this year.

448

AUGUST    WORLDTOUR MEN'S RACE

# BENELUX TOUR
Stage 7
5 September 2021
Namur–Geraardsbergen
177.9km

Bahrain Victorious produced another masterclass in race tactics over the final stage, which included multiple ascents of the famous Muur van Geraardsbergen. Sitting in first and second place on GC, they managed somehow to repeat the previous day's feat of taking the first two places over the line, only this time swapping their order. Matej Mohorič attacked and went clear on the foot of the Muur at the beginning on the final lap, and the race didn't see him again. The chase group formed, re-formed, was attacked by Tom Dumoulin, and countered by the Italian race leader. But Mohorič had the stage sewn up – winning with an 11-second gap over Colbrelli in second – just as Colbrelli had the race won for his second career GC victory (after he'd won the Tour du Limousin in 2015).

## WEATHER

TEMPERATURE  WIND
24°C         NE 6km/h

## PROFILE

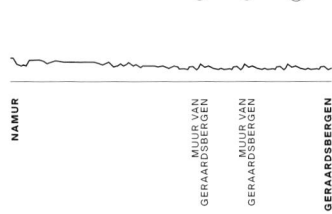

## BREAKAWAY

O. Riesebeek (AFC), D. Devenyns (DQT), P. Gilbert (LTS), T. Van der Sande (LTS), H. Houle (APT), D. Oss (BOH), J. Biermans (ISN), B. Peák (BEX), C. Pedersen (DSM), R. Janse van Rensburg (TQA), T. Skujiņš (TFS)

## STAGE RESULTS

| POS | NAME | TEAM | TIME |
|---|---|---|---|
| 1. | M. Mohorič | TBV | 3:50:56 |
| 2. | S. Colbrelli | TBV | 0:11 |
| 3. | T. Dumoulin | TJV | 0:15 |
| 4. | C. Laporte | COF | 0:22 |
| 5. | F. Wright | TBV | s.t. |
| 6. | D. van Poppel | IWG | 0:24 |
| 7. | T. Van Asbroeck | ISN | s.t. |
| 8. | G. Van Avermaet | ACT | s.t. |
| 9. | T. Benoot | DSM | s.t. |
| 10. | P. Sagan | BOH | s.t. |
| 11. | J. Stuyven | TFS | s.t. |
| 12. | M. Würst Schmidt | ISN | s.t. |
| 13. | T. Wellens | LTS | s.t. |
| 14. | K. Van Rooy | SVB | s.t. |
| 15. | G. Vermeersch | AFC | s.t. |
| 16. | M. Teunissen | TJV | s.t. |
| 17. | M. Hirschi | UAD | s.t. |
| 18. | A. Amador | IGD | s.t. |
| 19. | S. Küng | GFC | s.t. |
| 20. | L. Robeet | BWB | s.t. |

## GENERAL CLASSIFICATION

| POS | | NAME | TEAM | TIME |
|---|---|---|---|---|
| 1. | — | S. Colbrelli | TBV | 24:14:29 |
| 2. | — | M. Mohorič | TBV | 0:29 |
| 3. | — | V. Campenaerts | TQA | 1:14 |

## POINTS

| POS | | NAME | TEAM | PTS |
|---|---|---|---|---|
| 1. | ↑1 | D. van Poppel | IWG | 88 |
| 2. | ↑1 | S. Colbrelli | TBV | 80 |
| 3. | ↓2 | T. Merlier | AFC | 75 |

## BONUSES

| TYPE | NAME | TEAM |
|---|---|---|
| Sprint 1 | M. Mohorič | TBV |
| Sprint 2 | M. Mohorič | TBV |

## PARALYMPIC GAMES
31 August – 3 September 2021
Fuji International Speedway

Dame Sarah Storey became Britain's most successful Paralympian of all time after winning a rain-soaked C4-5 women's road race to complete a hattrick of gold medals at Tokyo 2020. It was the 17th gold medal of her Paralympic career, taking the 43-year-old clear of swimmer Mike Kenny's total of 16. Heavy rain made life difficult during the race but suited Storey, who beat compatriot Crystal Lane-Wright to the line, making it a British one-two, just as they had in the time trial. A smiling Lane-Wright called time on her career immediately but Storey shows no sign of slowing down 29 years after her first appearance at the Games in the swimming pool. As well as winning both road events, Storey also lowered her own world record in the individual pursuit on the track and went on to catch – you've guessed it – Crystal Lane-Wright in the final.

Ireland enjoyed a double gold-medal success on the road as Katie-George Dunlevy piloted by Eve McCrystal won both of the Women's B races for the visually impaired. Their second gold medal was secured in the road race with a searing late attack that took them 7 seconds clear of the British tandem of Sophie Unwin piloted by Jenny Holl. Earlier in the week Dunlevy had successfully defended her time trial crown and left Tokyo with three medals, having won silver on the track in the B individual pursuit.

The most exciting finish of all came in the men's handcycling H5 road race, where Dutchman Mitch Valize caught Frenchman Loïc Vergnaud on the line to win by centimetres after closing a considerable gap in a thrilling chase down the finishing straight at the end of 79.2km of racing.

This was the first time the road cycling events had ever been televised at a Paralympic Games and, while having several races on the circuit at the same time did occasionally appear a little chaotic, it nonetheless provided a valuable window for the sport. (SB)

---

31 August 2021
Fuji International Speedway–Fuji International Speedway

### WEATHER

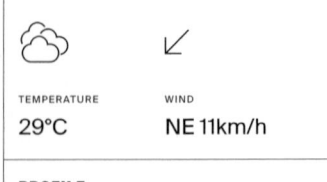

| TEMPERATURE | WIND |
|---|---|
| 29°C | NE 11km/h |

### PROFILE

### MEN'S C2 ITT 24km

| POS | NAME | TEAM | TIME |
|---|---|---|---|
| 1. | D. Hicks | Australia | 34:40 |
| 2. | E. Vromant | Belgium | 1:32 |
| 3. | A. Leaute | France | 2:27 |

### MEN'S C1 ITT 16km

| POS | NAME | TEAM | TIME |
|---|---|---|---|
| 1. | M. Astashov | RPC | 24:53 |
| 2. | A. Keith | United States | 0:02 |
| 3. | M. Teuber | Germany | 0:05 |

### MEN'S H5 ITT 24km

| POS | NAME | TEAM | TIME |
|---|---|---|---|
| 1. | M. Valize | Netherlands | 38:13 |
| 2. | L. Vergnaud | France | 1:02 |
| 3. | G. O'Reilly | Ireland | 1:24 |

### MEN'S H4 ITT 24km

| POS | NAME | TEAM | TIME |
|---|---|---|---|
| 1. | J. Plat | Netherlands | 37:29 |
| 2. | T. Fruehwirth | Austria | 1:02 |
| 3. | A. Gritsch | Austria | 2:30 |

### MEN'S H3 ITT 24km

| POS | NAME | TEAM | TIME |
|---|---|---|---|
| 1. | W. Ablinger | Austria | 43:39 |
| 2. | V. Merklein | Germany | 0:02 |
| 3. | L. M. García-Marquina | Spain | 0:10 |

### MEN'S H2 ITT 16km

| POS | NAME | TEAM | TIME |
|---|---|---|---|
| 1. | S. Garrote Muñoz | Spain | 31:24 |
| 2. | L. Mazzone | Italy | s.t. |
| 3. | F. Jounny | France | 1:18 |

## MEN'S H1 ITT 16km

| POS | NAME | TEAM | TIME |
|---|---|---|---|
| 1. | P. du Preez | South Africa | 43:49 |
| 2. | F. Cornegliani | Italy | 1:56 |
| 3. | M. Hordies | Belgium | 3:12 |

## MEN'S B ITT 32km

| POS | NAME | TEAM | TIME |
|---|---|---|---|
| 1. | A. Lloveras, Pilot: C. Ermenault | France | 41:54 |
| 2. | V. ter Schure, Pilot: T. Fransen | Netherlands | 0:06 |
| 3. | C. Venge Balboa, Pilot: N. M. Infante | Spain | 0:58 |

## MEN'S C5 ITT 32km

| POS | NAME | TEAM | TIME |
|---|---|---|---|
| 1. | D. A. Gebru | Netherlands | 42:46 |
| 2. | Y. Dementyev | Ukraine | 0:33 |
| 3. | A. Donohoe | Australia | 0:50 |

## MEN'S C4 ITT 32km

| POS | NAME | TEAM | TIME |
|---|---|---|---|
| 1. | P. Kuril | Slovakia | 45:47 |
| 2. | J. Metelka | Slovakia | 0:18 |
| 3. | G. Peasgood | Great Britain | 0:22 |

## MEN'S C3 ITT 24km

| POS | NAME | TEAM | TIME |
|---|---|---|---|
| 1. | B. Watson | Great Britain | 35:01 |
| 2. | S. Warias | Germany | 0:57 |
| 3. | M. Schindler | Germany | 1:17 |

## MEN'S T1-2 ITT 16km

| POS | NAME | TEAM | TIME |
|---|---|---|---|
| 1. | C. Jianxin | China | 25:00 |
| 2. | G. Farroni | Italy | 2:50 |
| 3. | T. Celen | Belgium | 5:44 |

## WOMEN'S C5 ITT 24km

| POS | NAME | TEAM | TIME |
|---|---|---|---|
| 1. | S. Storey | Great Britain | 36:09 |
| 2. | C. Lane-Wright | Great Britain | 1:32 |
| 3. | K. Brachtendorf | Germany | 2:26 |

## WOMEN'S C4 ITT 24km

| POS | NAME | TEAM | TIME |
|---|---|---|---|
| 1. | S. Morelli | United States | 39.34 |
| 2. | E. Petricola | Australia | 0:09 |
| 3. | M. Lemon | Australia | 1:41 |

## WOMEN'S C1-3 ITT 16km

| POS | NAME | TEAM | TIME |
|---|---|---|---|
| 1. | K. Sugiura | Japan | 25:56 |
| 2. | A. Beck | Sweden | 0:22 |
| 3. | P. Greco | Australia | 0:42 |

## WOMEN'S H4-5 ITT 24km

|   |   |   | Results |
|---|---|---|---|
| 1. | O. Masters | United States | 45:40 |
| 2. | S. Bianbian | China | 1:47 |
| 3. | J. Jansen | Netherlands | 3:06 |

## WOMEN'S H1-3 ITT 16km

| POS | NAME | TEAM | TIME |
|---|---|---|---|
| 1. | A. Zeyen | Germany | 32:47 |
| 2. | F. Porcellato | Italy | 0:44 |
| 3. | R. Kaluza | Poland | 1:03 |

## WOMEN'S B ITT 32km

| POS | NAME | TEAM | TIME |
|---|---|---|---|
| 1. | K. G. Dunlevy, Pilot: E. McCrystal | Ireland | 47:32.07 |
| 2. | L. Fachie, Pilot: C. Hall | Great Britain | 1:00 |
| 3. | L. Jannering, Pilot: A. Svärdström | Sweden | 2:04 |

## WOMEN'S T1-2 ITT 16km

| POS | NAME | TEAM | TIME |
|---|---|---|---|
| 1. | J. Majunke | Germany | 36:06 |
| 2. | C. Cooke | Australia | 0:32 |
| 3. | A. Droeck-Käser | Germany | 0:48 |

## PARALYMPIC GAMES
1 September 2021
Fuji International Speedway–Fuji International Speedway

### WEATHER

TEMPERATURE  
23°C

WIND  
NE 20km/h

### PROFILE

FUJI INTERNATIONAL SPEEDWAY — FUJI INTERNATIONAL SPEEDWAY

#### MEN'S H5 ROAD RACE 79.2km

| POS | NAME | TEAM | TIME |
|---|---|---|---|
| 1. | M. Valize | Netherlands | 2:24:30 |
| 2. | L. Vergnaud | France | s.t. |
| 3. | T. de Vries | Netherlands | 0:06 |

#### MEN'S H1-2 ROAD RACE 52.8km

| POS | NAME | TEAM | TIME |
|---|---|---|---|
| 1. | F. Jouanny | France | 1:49:36 |
| 2. | L. Mazzone | Italy | 4:07 |
| 3. | S. Garrote | Spain | 5:00 |

#### MEN'S H4 ROAD RACE 79.2km

| POS | NAME | TEAM | TIME |
|---|---|---|---|
| 1. | J. Plat | Netherlands | 2:15:13 |
| 2. | T. Frühwirth | Austria | 5:43 |
| 3. | A. Gritsch | Austria | 7:25 |

#### MEN'S H3 ROAD RACE 79.2km

| POS | NAME | TEAM | TIME |
|---|---|---|---|
| 1. | R. Kuzentsov | RPC | 2:34:35 |
| 2. | H. Frei | Switzerland | s.t. |
| 3. | W. Ablinger | Austria | 0:31 |

#### WOMEN'S H5 ROAD RACE 26.4km

| POS | NAME | TEAM | TIME |
|---|---|---|---|
| 1. | O. Masters | United States | 2:23:39 |
| 2. | S. Bianbian | China | 3:11 |
| 3. | K. Aere | Italy | 4:32 |

#### WOMEN'S H1-4 ROAD RACE 26.4km

| POS | NAME | TEAM | TIME |
|---|---|---|---|
| 1. | J. Jansen | Netherlands | 56:15 |
| 2. | A. Zeyen | Germany | 0:06 |
| 3. | A. Dana | United States | 0:09 |

AUGUST  PARALYMPIC GAMES

## PARALYMPIC GAMES
2 September 2021
Fuji International Speedway–Fuji International Speedway

**WEATHER**

TEMPERATURE
21°C

WIND
N 19km/h

### MEN'S C1-3 ROAD RACE 79.2km

| POS | NAME | TEAM | TIME |
|---|---|---|---|
| 1. | B. Watson | Great Britain | 2:04:23 |
| 2. | F. Graham | Great Britain | 1:20 |
| 3. | A. Léauté | France | 6:43 |

### MEN'S T1-2 ROAD RACE 26.4km

| POS | NAME | TEAM | TIME |
|---|---|---|---|
| 1. | C. Jianxin | China | 51:07 |
| 2. | T. Celen | Belgium | 1:08 |
| 3. | J. J. Betancourt Quiroga | Columbia | 1:34 |

### WOMEN'S C4-5 ROAD RACE 79.2km

| POS | NAME | TEAM | TIME |
|---|---|---|---|
| 1. | S. Storey | Great Britain | 2:21:51 |
| 2. | C. Lane-Wright | Great Britain | 0:07 |
| 3. | M. Patouillet | France | 1:58 |

### WOMEN'S T1-2 ROAD RACE 26.4km

| POS | NAME | TEAM | TIME |
|---|---|---|---|
| 1. | J. Majunke | Germany | 1:00:58 |
| 2. | A. Dreock-Käser | Germany | 2:42 |
| 3. | J. Walsh | United States | 4:50 |

### MIXED H1-5 ROAD RACE 24.3km

| POS | NAME | TEAM | TIME |
|---|---|---|---|
| 1. | P. Cecchetto, L. Mazzone, D. Colombari | Italy | 52:32 |
| 2. | R. Tarsim, F. Jouanny, L. Vergnaud | France | 0:31 |
| 3. | R. Pinney, A. Dana, A. de los Santos | United States | 0:39 |

**PROFILE**

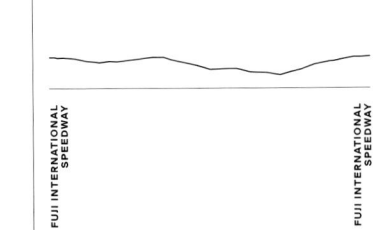

FUJI INTERNATIONAL SPEEDWAY — FUJI INTERNATIONAL SPEEDWAY

## PARALYMPIC GAMES
3 September 2021
Fuji International Speedway–Fuji International Speedway

**WEATHER**

TEMPERATURE
21°C

WIND
N 17km/h

### MEN'S C4-5 ROAD RACE 92.4km

| POS | NAME | TEAM | TIME |
|---|---|---|---|
| 1. | K. Le Cunff | France | 2:14:49 |
| 2. | Y. Dementyev | Ukraine | 0:22 |
| 3. | D. Abraham | Netherlands | 0:31 |

### MEN'S B ROAD RACE 118.8km

| POS | NAME | TEAM | TIME |
|---|---|---|---|
| 1. | V. ter Schure, Pilot: T. Fransen | Netherlands | 2:59:13 |
| 2. | T. Bangma, Pilot: P. Bos | Netherlands | 5:48 |
| 3. | A. Lloveras, Pilot: C. Ermenault | France | 7:01 |

### WOMEN'S C1-3 ROAD RACE 39.6km

| POS | NAME | TEAM | TIME |
|---|---|---|---|
| 1. | K. Sugiura | Japan | 1:12:55 |
| 2. | A. Beck | Sweden | 0:16 |
| 3. | P. Greco | Australia | s.t. |

### WOMEN'S B ROAD RACE 92.4km

| POS | NAME | TEAM | TIME |
|---|---|---|---|
| 1. | K. G. Dunlevy, Pilot: E. McCrystal | Ireland | 2:35:53 |
| 2. | S. Unwin, Pilot: J. Holl | Great Britain | 0:07 |
| 3. | L. Jannering, Pilot: A. Svärdström | Sweden | s.t. |

**PROFILE**

AUGUST  .1 MEN'S RACE

# TURUL ROMANIEI

Prologue
31 August 2021
Timișoara–Timișoara
4km

## WEATHER

TEMPERATURE | WIND
25°C | W 24km/h

## STAGE RESULTS

| POS | NAME | TEAM | TIME |
|---|---|---|---|
| 1. | J. Pelikán | ANS | 4:51 |
| 2. | D. Crista | NAT | 0:02 |
| 3. | J. Wolf | BAI | 0:05 |
| 4. | T. Pawlak | MSP | 0:08 |
| 5. | A. Banaszek | MSP | 0:09 |
| 6. | N. Banaszek | MSP | s.t. |
| 7. | A. Hoehn | WGC | 0:10 |
| 8. | S. Tvetcov | WGC | s.t. |
| 9. | A. Banaszek | MSP | s.t. |
| 10. | M. Heming | PBS | s.t. |
| 11. | J. Kaczmarek | MSP | s.t. |
| 12. | F. Burchio | IWM | 0:11 |
| 13. | M. Boguslawski | MSP | s.t. |
| 14. | N. Vinokurov | VAM | s.t. |
| 15. | P. Stosz | VOS | 0:12 |
| 16. | E. Dima | GTS | 0:13 |
| 17. | T. Kalojíros | CAT | s.t. |
| 18. | E. Sepúlveda | ANS | s.t. |
| 19. | M. Bilyi | AZT | 0:14 |
| 20. | S. Rekita | VOS | 0:15 |

## GENERAL CLASSIFICATION

| POS | NAME | TEAM | TIME |
|---|---|---|---|
| 1. | J. Pelikán | ANS | 4:51 |
| 2. | D. Crista | NAT | 0:02 |
| 3. | J. Wolf | BAI | 0:05 |

## POINTS

| POS | NAME | TEAM | PTS |
|---|---|---|---|
| 1. | J. Pelikán | ANS | 25 |
| 2. | D. Crista | NAT | 20 |
| 3. | J. Wolf | BAI | 15 |

## YOUNG RIDER

| POS | NAME | TEAM | TIME |
|---|---|---|---|
| 1. | M. Heming | PBS | 5:01 |
| 2. | N. Vinokurov | VAM | 0:01 |
| 3. | M. Bilyi | AZT | 0:04 |

# TURUL ROMANIEI

Stage 1
1 September 2021
Timișoara–Deva
201.5km

## WEATHER

TEMPERATURE | WIND
19°C | NW 20km/h

## STAGE RESULTS

| POS | NAME | TEAM | TIME |
|---|---|---|---|
| 1. | P. Stosz | VOS | 4:33:15 |
| 2. | L. Carstensen | BAI | s.t. |
| 3. | D. Rajović | NAT | s.t. |
| 4. | E. M. Grosu | NAT | s.t. |
| 5. | A. Banaszek | MSP | s.t. |
| 6. | K. Ross | WGC | s.t. |
| 7. | A. Guardini | GTS | s.t. |
| 8. | D. Smarzaro | AZT | s.t. |
| 9. | C. Rocchetta | ANS | s.t. |
| 10. | E. Onesti | GTS | s.t. |
| 11. | M. Paterski | VOS | s.t. |
| 12. | P. Szostka | NAT | s.t. |
| 13. | J. Rumac | ANS | s.t. |
| 14. | K. J. Yustre | GTS | s.t. |
| 15. | N. Banaszek | MSP | s.t. |
| 16. | M. Bilyi | AZT | s.t. |
| 17. | J. Lino | BAI | s.t. |
| 18. | T. Kalojíros | CAT | s.t. |
| 19. | N. Holler | BAI | s.t. |
| 20. | J. Kaczmarek | MSP | s.t. |

## GENERAL CLASSIFICATION

| POS | NAME | TEAM | TIME |
|---|---|---|---|
| 1. ↑1 | D. Crista | NAT | 4:37:59 |
| 2. ↓1 | J. Pelikán | ANS | 0:07 |
| 3. ↑12 | P. Stosz | VOS | 0:09 |

## KING OF THE MOUNTAINS

| POS | NAME | TEAM | PTS |
|---|---|---|---|
| 1. | D. Crista | NAT | 6 |
| 2. | S. Klisurić | NAT | 4 |
| 3. | I. Filosi | GTS | 2 |

## POINTS

| POS | NAME | TEAM | PTS |
|---|---|---|---|
| 1. ↑1 | D. Crista | NAT | 38 |
| 2. ↓1 | J. Pelikán | ANS | 25 |
| 3. — | P. Stosz | VOS | 25 |

## YOUNG RIDER

| POS | NAME | TEAM | TIME |
|---|---|---|---|
| 1. — | M. Heming | PBS | 4:38:14 |
| 2. — | N. Vinokurov | VAM | 0:03 |
| 3. — | M. Bilyi | AZT | 0:06 |

AUGUST  .1 MEN'S RACE

## TURUL ROMANIEI
Stage 2
2 September 2021
Deva–Păltiniș
154.9km

### WEATHER

TEMPERATURE  WIND
18°C  NW 13km/h

### STAGE RESULTS

| POS | NAME | TEAM | TIME |
|---|---|---|---|
| 1. | D. Muñoz | ANS | 3:43:51 |
| 2. | S. Rekita | VOS | s.t. |
| 3. | S. Tvetcov | WGC | s.t. |
| 4. | J. Kaczmarek | MSP | s.t. |
| 5. | E. Sepúlveda | ANS | s.t. |
| 6. | J. Wolf | BAI | 0:02 |
| 7. | D. Rebellin | IWM | 0:06 |
| 8. | M. Paterski | VOS | 0:55 |
| 9. | M. Bilyi | AZT | s.t. |
| 10. | J. Lino | BAI | 0:56 |
| 11. | A. Bisolti | ANS | 1:08 |
| 12. | T. Budzinski | MSP | s.t. |
| 13. | K. J. Yustre | GTS | 1:11 |
| 14. | E. Dima | GTS | 1:14 |
| 15. | M. Grabis | VOS | 1:46 |
| 16. | J. Rumac | ANS | s.t. |
| 17. | L. Quartucci | AZT | s.t. |
| 18. | M. Podlaski | NAT | s.t. |
| 19. | A. Sowinski | NAT | s.t. |
| 20. | A. Hoehn | WGC | 1:55 |

### GENERAL CLASSIFICATION

| POS | NAME | TEAM | TIME |
|---|---|---|---|
| 1. ↑10 | S. Tvetcov | WGC | 8:22:03 |
| 2. ↑10 | J. Kaczmarek | MSP | s.t. |
| 3. ↑1 | J. Wolf | BAI | s.t. |

### KING OF THE MOUNTAINS

| POS | NAME | TEAM | PTS |
|---|---|---|---|
| 1. — | J. Kaczmarek | MSP | 21 |
| 2. — | D. Muñoz | ANS | 20 |
| 3. — | S. Rekita | VOS | 18 |

### POINTS

| POS | NAME | TEAM | PTS |
|---|---|---|---|
| 1. — | D. Crista | NAT | 38 |
| 2. ↑7 | E. M. Grosu | NAT | 30 |
| 3. — | D. Muñoz | ANS | 25 |

### YOUNG RIDER

| POS | NAME | TEAM | TIME |
|---|---|---|---|
| 1. ↑2 | M. Bilyi | AZT | 8:23:06 |
| 2. ↑5 | L. Quartucci | AZT | 0:58 |
| 3. ↑1 | E. Bergstrom Frisk | BAI | 2:56 |

## TURUL ROMANIEI
Stage 3
3 September 2021
Sibiu–Poiana Brașov
187km

### WEATHER

TEMPERATURE  WIND
20°C  NE 7km/h

### STAGE RESULTS

| POS | NAME | TEAM | TIME |
|---|---|---|---|
| 1. | E. Dima | GTS | 4:24:35 |
| 2. | P. Stosz | VOS | 0:02 |
| 3. | E. Sepúlveda | ANS | s.t. |
| 4. | D. Muñoz | ANS | s.t. |
| 5. | J. Kaczmarek | MSP | s.t. |
| 6. | D. Rebellin | IWM | s.t. |
| 7. | S. Rekita | VOS | s.t. |
| 8. | N. Vinokurov | VAM | s.t. |
| 9. | G. Garavaglia | IWM | s.t. |
| 10. | K. J. Yustre | GTS | s.t. |
| 11. | S. Tvetcov | WGC | 0:06 |
| 12. | V. Filutás | GTS | 0:08 |
| 13. | A. Sowinski | NAT | s.t. |
| 14. | M. Bilyi | AZT | s.t. |
| 15. | A. Bisolti | ANS | s.t. |
| 16. | D. Pronskiy | VAM | 0:13 |
| 17. | E. Bergstrom Frisk | BAI | s.t. |
| 18. | J. Lino | BAI | s.t. |
| 19. | M. Grabis | VOS | s.t. |
| 20. | A. Van Engelen | BAI | s.t. |

### GENERAL CLASSIFICATION

| POS | NAME | TEAM | TIME |
|---|---|---|---|
| 1. ↑1 | J. Kaczmarek | MSP | 12:46:38 |
| 2. ↑2 | S. Rekita | VOS | 0:05 |
| 3. ↑2 | E. Sepúlveda | ANS | s.t. |

### KING OF THE MOUNTAINS

| POS | NAME | TEAM | PTS |
|---|---|---|---|
| 1. — | J. Kaczmarek | MSP | 25 |
| 2. — | D. Muñoz | ANS | 22 |
| 3. ↑4 | M. Paterski | VOS | 21 |

### POINTS

| POS | NAME | TEAM | PTS |
|---|---|---|---|
| 1. ↑3 | P. Stosz | VOS | 45 |
| 2. ↓1 | D. Crista | NAT | 38 |
| 3. — | D. Muñoz | ANS | 37 |

### YOUNG RIDER

| POS | NAME | TEAM | TIME |
|---|---|---|---|
| 1. — | M. Bilyi | AZT | 12:47:49 |
| 2. — | L. Quartucci | AZT | 1:14 |
| 3. — | E. Bergstrom Frisk | BAI | 3:01 |

## TURUL ROMANIEI

Stage 4
4 September 2021
Brasov–Bucharest
159.3km

### WEATHER

TEMPERATURE: 19°C
WIND: N 13km/h

### STAGE RESULTS

| POS | NAME | TEAM | TIME |
|---|---|---|---|
| 1. | D. Babor | SKC | 3:19:19 |
| 2. | D. Smarzaro | AZT | s.t. |
| 3. | L. Quartucci | AZT | s.t. |
| 4. | A. Banaszek | MSP | s.t. |
| 5. | E. M. Grosu | NAT | s.t. |
| 6. | T. Wollenberg | PBS | s.t. |
| 7. | I. Filosi | GTS | s.t. |
| 8. | D. Rajović | NAT | s.t. |
| 9. | P. Stosz | VOS | s.t. |
| 10. | A. Guardini | GTS | s.t. |
| 11. | M. Heming | PBS | s.t. |
| 12. | A. N. Marcu | NAT | s.t. |
| 13. | R. Bobbo | IWM | s.t. |
| 14. | R. Holec | SKC | s.t. |
| 15. | F. Zandri | IWM | s.t. |
| 16. | J. Stöhr | CAT | s.t. |
| 17. | M. Bilyi | AZT | s.t. |
| 18. | M. Paterski | VOS | s.t. |
| 19. | J. Kaczmarek | MSP | s.t. |
| 20. | A. Semenov | VAM | s.t. |

### GENERAL CLASSIFICATION

| POS | NAME | TEAM | TIME |
|---|---|---|---|
| 1. — | J. Kaczmarek | MSP | 16:05:57 |
| 2. ↑2 | S. Tvetcov | WGC | 0:04 |
| 3. ↓1 | S. Rekita | VOS | 0:05 |

### KING OF THE MOUNTAINS

| POS | NAME | TEAM | PTS |
|---|---|---|---|
| 1. ↑2 | M. Paterski | VOS | 27 |
| 2. ↓1 | J. Kaczmarek | MSP | 25 |
| 3. ↓1 | D. Muñoz | ANS | 22 |

### POINTS

| POS | NAME | TEAM | PTS |
|---|---|---|---|
| 1. — | P. Stosz | VOS | 51 |
| 2. ↑2 | E. M. Grosu | NAT | 51 |
| 3. ↓1 | D. Crista | NAT | 38 |

### YOUNG RIDER

| POS | NAME | TEAM | TIME |
|---|---|---|---|
| 1. — | M. Bilyi | AZT | 16:07:08 |
| 2. — | L. Quartucci | AZT | 1:10 |
| 3. — | E. Bergstrom Frisk | BAI | 3:01 |

## TURUL ROMANIEI

Stage 5
5 September 2021
Bucharest–Bucharest
116km

### WEATHER

TEMPERATURE: 24°C
WIND: NE 22km/h

### STAGE RESULTS

| POS | NAME | TEAM | TIME |
|---|---|---|---|
| 1. | P. Stosz | VOS | 2:15:22 |
| 2. | D. Smarzaro | NAT | s.t. |
| 3. | E. M. Grosu | NAT | s.t. |
| 4. | A. Guardini | GTS | s.t. |
| 5. | C. Rocchetta | ANS | s.t. |
| 6. | A. Banaszek | MSP | s.t. |
| 7. | T. Wollenberg | PBS | s.t. |
| 8. | P. Szostka | NAT | s.t. |
| 9. | L. Carstensen | BAI | s.t. |
| 10. | T. Kalojíros | CAT | s.t. |
| 11. | A. Sowinski | NAT | s.t. |
| 12. | D. Smarzaro | AZT | s.t. |
| 13. | N. Vinokurov | VAM | s.t. |
| 14. | R. Bobbo | IWM | s.t. |
| 15. | A. Semenov | VAM | s.t. |
| 16. | D. Veselinović | NAT | s.t. |
| 17. | A. Małkowski | NAT | s.t. |
| 18. | J. Stöhr | CAT | s.t. |
| 19. | K. Ross | WGC | s.t. |
| 20. | A. Hoehn | WGC | s.t. |

### GENERAL CLASSIFICATION

| POS | NAME | TEAM | TIME |
|---|---|---|---|
| 1. — | J. Kaczmarek | MSP | 18:21:19 |
| 2. — | S. Tvetcov | WGC | 0:04 |
| 3. — | S. Rekita | VOS | 0:05 |

### KING OF THE MOUNTAINS

| POS | NAME | TEAM | PTS |
|---|---|---|---|
| 1. — | M. Paterski | VOS | 27 |
| 2. — | J. Kaczmarek | MSP | 25 |
| 3. — | D. Muñoz | ANS | 22 |

### POINTS

| POS | NAME | TEAM | PTS |
|---|---|---|---|
| 1. — | P. Stosz | VOS | 76 |
| 2. — | E. M. Grosu | NAT | 66 |
| 3. — | D. Crista | NAT | 50 |

### YOUNG RIDER

| POS | NAME | TEAM | TIME |
|---|---|---|---|
| 1. — | M. Bilyi | AZT | 18:22:30 |
| 2. — | L. Quartucci | AZT | 1:08 |
| 3. — | E. Bergstrom Frisk | BAI | 3:01 |

# A PILGRIM'S PROGRESS

BY DANIEL FRIEBE

Burgos sits on the northern tidemark of what Spaniards call their *Meseta Central* or 'Central Plateau', the spires of its gothic cathedral rising to greet approaching visitors out of an oversized saucer of beige flatlands. The birthplace of El Cid, the home of Spain's most prized blood sausage, the cradle of General Franco's fascist regime. Despite other distinctions or claims to infamy, the city has not hosted the start of a Vuelta a España until this year. What the organisers have christened the *Vuelta de las Catedrales* rolls out from the very front step of the burgaleses' proudest landmark at the end of a scorching, topaz-skied afternoon on the middle weekend of August – and instantly pairs an ancient backdrop with a modern-day cycling tradition: Primož Roglič in the leader's jersey, as sure and snug as a bishop in his cassock.

The Slovenian is attempting to become only the second rider in the Vuelta's history to win three consecutive editions, after Tony Rominger in the mid-1990s. The Vuelta is an 89-year-old institution, a now self-confident paean to a sublime canvas of coastline, mountains and other landlocked wonders – and yet it is not usually classed among races that can define a career. Nothing, though, about Roglič's journey to this point has obeyed a familiar logic or timetable – from the ski-jumping to the transformation of his public persona in the last year. The modern Vuelta indeed almost allegorises his trajectory, with its stomach-lurching, theme-park stage profiles and perennial promise of redemption. If Roglič's entire cycling career is itself a wildly successful Plan B – undertaken because, as he has said, 'I realised I would never be the world's best ski-jumper' – the Vuelta has become his favourite indemnity. More importantly – or just romantically – the 2020 edition reinforced, or perhaps indulged is a better word, our childlike belief in plotlines generally only found in fairy stories and sport-showbusiness, particularly the fable of dire misfortune followed by happily-ever-after.

This year, too, Roglič has decided to defend his Vuelta title only because of disaster at the Tour de France. 'When things go wrong I try to look at things neutrally, not positively,' he said before the Tour – an almost seminal Roglič-ism. After his crashes in France and eventual withdrawal after a week of racing, the approach has allowed him to reset, regroup and win gold in the Olympic time trial in Tokyo. What presents itself as an infuriating commitment to non-committal in the first week of Vuelta – the daily refrain of 'We'll see, huh?' or 'I don't know, huh,' delivered in the same playful baritone, mixed zone after mixed zone – is therefore not the vapid cliché it seems. Rather, we are hearing the same sincere and neutral voice with which Primož Roglič addresses himself every morning, readying himself for the day. It tells him that we really *will* see, that he really *doesn't* know, least of all in a sport as cruel as cycling has sometimes been to him in the last couple of years, in a race as unpredictable as this.

That fickleness reveals itself as early as day three, when Rein Taaramäe takes Roglič's *maillot rojo* on the Picón Blanco. It is a choreographed move by Jumbo-Visma, designed to discharge or at least defer responsibility, but it is still something of a surprise when Taaramäe wins from a large break. The Estonian is 34 years old, with a much richer palmarès than most probably realise, including another stage win at the Vuelta exactly ten years ago. There was also a 2015 *annus mirabilis*, when he triumphed precisely here, at the Vuelta a Burgos, and much closer to home, in the Arctic Race of Norway. Taaramäe has an intriguing alias – Vader, inherited from an arctic fox in an Estonian literary classic, not a *Star Wars* über-baddie – and soft, downturned eyes offering a window into a gentle soul. Thirteen years ago, aged 22, he announced himself as the closest thing pro cycling then had to the Pogačar of the day – which in truth wasn't very close at all – by escaping to a seemingly certain victory on the stage to Xorret de Catí, only to vaporise in the final 3km. I ask him to relive the moment on the morning of stage 4, and he laughs: 'I hadn't even read the road book… I was so young, so naive.' Now neither of those things, he is under no illusions about how long the 'dream' might last. But, as Roglič keeps saying, 'We'll see, huh?'

That afternoon – Rein's first in red – is also a journey into a Spain that time has forgotten. Before Covid, the last (and, in fact, still ongoing) pandemic in this part of the country was called 'depopulation'. Stage 4 finishes in Molina de Aragón, a Moorish *taifa* before the Reconquista. Media outlets from all over the world have made what at first seems like a dubious claim: that the area surrounding the town is 'Europe's biggest population desert' with its 1.6 inhabitants per square kilometre. Census data suggests only parts of Lapland are as devoid of human life. The day of the biggest thing to happen to Molina in years is no doubt the worst time to get a sense of the problem, but the entrance to the town before and the exit in the evening – over the scorched prairies of what even locals refer to as *La España vacía* or 'Empty Spain' – offer some clues. Against the backdrop of a wider exodus from rural areas all across southern Europe, here especially it is frankly not hard to imagine why young people are fleeing. The temperature today edges 40 degrees, which is not uncommon in summer, but in winter it frequently dips to 10 below zero. This accounts for another nickname you won't find in the tourist pamphlet: 'the Spanish Siberia'. In some of the neighbouring villages, where today we see cries for help – work, subsidies, hope – scrawled on cardboard banners and bedsheets, there isn't a single inhabitant under the age of 18.

One thing the Vuelta's flying visit does bring Molina is a beautiful, poignant storyline. It is a year and 12 days since Fabio Jakobsen's horrifying crash at the Tour of Poland, and today his comeback seems complete as he wins in a Grand Tour for the first time since the final stage of the 2019 Vuelta in Madrid. Again it is Deceuninck-QuickStep, and again it is a sprinter back from oblivion, but the celebration is more restrained, less tearful than the one we witnessed in Fougères after the first of Mark Cavendish's four stage wins at the Tour. Jakobsen has said repeatedly that he now wishes to put the whole nightmare behind him. For months that was also what one of his lead-out men today, Florian Sénéchal, wanted to do. The Frenchman was the first to attend to Jakobsen in Poland – and indeed his quick thinking, propping his teammate's head and tongue in a safe position, may even have saved his life. Sénéchal had to have therapy to get over the trauma of what he saw that day, which may also explain why his is a measured, mindful joy. He says the ordeal has taught him that 'If you stay as mentally strong as Fabio, you can achieve anything.'

There are already many subscribers to that credo in the pro peloton, although to Primož Roglič it may seem a little too like wishful thinking. For now, as the race continues south-west towards the Costa Blanca, Roglič appears in unusually relaxed, even cavalier mood. His belly laughs in the morning mixed zone are one of the few sounds that can be heard above the deafening PA system or this year's looping official Vuelta anthem, '1932', a raspy, upbeat ode to more innocent times by Burgos's answer to Mumford & Sons, La M.O.D.A. Speaking of popular culture, Roglič's frivolity does not extend to an appraisal of the fly-on-the-wall documentary about the Movistar team that, even several months after the release of season two, is still a popular subject of conversation. 'Ach, I don't know, huh…' he says, rather confusingly, when asked whether he's at least familiar with the series. Finally he concedes that he 'might' have caught season one. He then sounds genuinely grateful for the recommendation of the even juicier latest instalment.

He may want to gather as much intel as he can, for the Movistar pair of Enric Mas and Miguel Ángel 'Superman' López have staked their claim as his most troublesome opponents. Last year it was Richard Carapaz who pushed him to the dying metres of the final mountain stage. One head of the latest Ineos Grenadiers Grand-Tour Hydra, this year the Olympic road race gold medallist is already out of contention after a week. Meanwhile Egan Bernal and Adam Yates seem a paler imitation of the Movistar chimera, which has suffered its own decapitation – of Alejandro Valverde, the victim of a crash and broken collarbone on stage 7 to the Balcón de Alicante.

The first true test of climbing comes at the Alto de Velefique. This glorious, hairpinned helter-skelter soars out of the dustbowl where some of the most famous scenes in Sergio Leone's Spaghetti Westerns were filmed. Damiano Caruso takes the stage in a long solo break while, behind him, Mas and Roglič ride clear, leaving López to mark and meddle with anyone who gives chase. The move restores Roglič to the red jersey, or it to him. Mas comes next, just 28 seconds down, Superman third, less than a minute further back. 'We have to plan to beat Roglič,' Mas will say when the race pauses in Almería the following day. Roglič replies, 'We'll see, huh?'

The next day the race sets out on its journey to Rincón de la Victoria from adjacent to the Mediterranean but submerged in a manmade sea – the *Mar de Plástico* or 'Sea of Plastic' to the west of Almería. This astonishing, visible-from-space, 30,000 hectare expanse of commercial greenhouses reportedly supplies enough fruit and vegetables to feed 500 million Europeans but is also nowadays decried as an environmental disaster and a hive of modern-day slavery. Many of the workers come from Africa, desperate, undocumented, and find themselves living in the shanties we glimpse tucked between the enormous hothouses. The growers who pay them a few Euros an hour supply major Northern European supermarkets. What some don't provide is access to running water, electricity or sanitation. The workers possess one 'luxury': bikes, though it's a jarring contrast when we see the Vuelta peloton off in Roquetas de Mar then a few moments later are driving through echelons of much darker-skinned, much slower-moving men on steel rather than carbon fibre. The smile on some of their lips nonetheless tells us these may be the best moments of their day.

Down the coast towards Malaga, the technicolour, million-dollar cycling we know has resumed with the latest exhibit of Roglič hyperrealism – a sort of shoulder-shrugging, now almost hedonistic resignation to the universe's kinks and caprices. With a break down the road – way down the road – he attacks, apparently on a whim, on the category-2 Puerto de Almáchar 20km from the line. He immediately opens up half a minute before misjudging a bend and skidding off the road – a karaoke cover of his crashes in Paris–Nice this spring, the 2020 Dauphiné or the stage to Como that may have cost him the 2019 Giro. After remounting, he returns to the group of his GC rivals like a runaway teenager sheepishly going back to the family home, and it's no time losses, all laughs and 'All good, huh' when he's crossed the line. The stage has been won by Michael Storer, his second successful breakaway of the Vuelta, and Roglič is also pleased to have given up the red jersey to Odd Christian Eiking of Intermarché-Wanty-Gobert Matériaux. Eiking has made headlines at the Vuelta once before – when his erstwhile team, FDJ, denied him the honour of finishing the 2017 race because he had allegedly got drunk the night before.

Mas, Yates, Bernal and the surprising Jack Haig start the next day with hopes pinned on a groggy Roglič but instead get a sobering reality check. It comes in the form a prototypical 'Roglification': a poker-faced mass cull in which the coup de grâce is delivered late, in the closing metres, almost apologetically, as though to preserve the victims' dignity. The valiant Mas follows him almost to the line, but more seconds have been lost. Mas and Movistar believe their chance could come in Extremadura and the Sierra de Gredos on the third weekend, where the climbs will be longer. That, though, reeks of an optimism that Roglič won't need – or that he won't entertain – and so it proves. Thus week two ends with Eiking still in red and the Slovenian dream-crusher lying in wait.

The race is now heading north to where a different Spain begins – greener, multilingual, denser in other more and less tangible ways. Carlos Arribas of *El País* provides reading material for the long decampment with a timely homage to the late José María 'El Chava' Jiménez, whose hometown, El Barraco, hosted the stage 15 finish. Arribas's article contains details that are made even more gut-wrenching by the mental jigsaw I've pieced together the previous day, waiting for the peloton to arrive on the Calle José María Jiménez, outside his old house and directly opposite one now owned by his sister and her husband, the 2008 Tour winner Carlos Sastre. Arribas writes that on the weekend when he died – when his body gave out, at 32, after several years of assorted excesses – El Chava was supposed to be packing to go skiing in Switzerland. His wife had booked the trip in the hope that it would bring some light relief after his months in a psychiatric clinic. Not that at least superficial levity, or humour, was ever something he lacked, as former friends and colleagues have reminded me over the weekend. Another journalist, José Carlos Carábias, tells me that his last conversation with Jiménez occurred shortly before he died, and focused on his regular visits to Burger King to buy fellow patients at his clinic their lunches. 'He said they needed some fun in their life, and those burgers were a little glimpse of fun and normality…'

The Vuelta will be decided on the Asturian mountains – where 'El Chava' often dazzled in the 1990s – if not at the Lagos de Covadonga on stage 17 then the following day at El Gamoniteiru. In the event, it is the first half of the double-bill that gives us a stage to savour and also the near-certainty that Roglič will complete his historic treble. Riding like a man who has nothing left to lose, Egan Bernal strikes out for glory on the Collada Llomena, 60km from the Lagos. Riding like a man who thinks he won't lose but is prepared to find out, Roglič follows Bernal and goes with him to the final climb. Had Bernal not fallen ill with Covid after the Giro and lost vital training weeks, this may have been the defining duel of the Vuelta. Instead, even here it turns into a mismatch, with Roglič powering away to not his most characteristic but maybe his most memorable victory.

With a lead of over 2 minutes and a 33km time trial still to come, it would take something heroic – or a comic-book hero – to stop him now. Alas, it won't be Superman, for all that the Colombian brings Movistar their first stage win of the race on El Gamoniteiru. At this point he also lies third on General Classification, 35 seconds clear of Jack Haig. The last road stage of the Vuelta in southwest Galicia, though, will become a study in partnership dynamics – of harmony between Haig and the other GC revelation of the race, Gino Mäder, and dysfunction between López and Mas or at least López and Movistar. The race blows apart on the eucalyptus-cloaked hills overlooking the Atlantic, again ignited by Bernal, and Mäder and Haig suddenly find themselves closing in, respectively, on the white jersey and López's third place overall. López is stranded in the second group, already in free-fall down the virtual General Classification, when word reaches the Movistar staff members waiting a few yards from me at the finish that he has simply climbed off his bike. There will be no pictures for over an hour. Barely any details will crackle over race radio or even Movistar's own intercom if Mas is to believed. But the rumour, as much as it seems odd to refer to a mid-race occurrence in a globally televised event as such, turns out to be true. 'Some kind of psychological crisis,' is teammate José Joaquín Rojas's fag-packet diagnosis when he arrives in the mixed zone. A failure to look at things neutrally when they began to go south would be another explanation – presumably Primož Roglič's.

The following evening the Vuelta ends its voyage, its odyssey, why not its pilgrimage, in the shadow of Santiago de Compostela's magnificent cathedral. This is also where around 300 people every day finish their 'Camino de Santiago' – now one of the world's most popular spiritual or religious journeys, an 800km walk from the French Pyrenees in its most common iteration. The pilgrims are easy to spot, with their wooden poles, scallop shells hanging from their rucksacks – a symbol of the Camino – and their gaunt but contented faces. I notice three resting, reflecting on the cathedral steps – two students from northern Italy and their friend from Greece. 'It starts as an adventure but becomes more of a spiritual journey,' they tell me. 'I've proven to myself that I can do anything now,' one of them adds.

All of which to Primož Roglič probably sounds like forgivable hubris. After three weeks of the future tense – his least favourite – finally in Santiago he can conjugate verbs in the past. 'It was super nice, huh?' Another Vuelta that went according to plan – just his latest, tentatively, modestly made Plan B.

# SEPTEMBER

With all three Grand Tours almost done, and as the heat of another record-breaking summer started to dissipate across Europe, space opened up in the calendar for a smattering of one-day as well as shorter national stage races. The women's peloton raced in Spain, before many of the best in the world headed off to Trento, where the European Championships would be disputed. And then to Leuven for the much-anticipated World Championships. Disruption from Covid was starting to feel like a receding memory, at least for now.

| DATE | RACE TITLE | LOCATION | UCI CODE | PAGE |
| --- | --- | --- | --- | --- |
| 2–5 September | Ceratizit Challenge | Spain | 2.WWT | 464 |
| 3 September | Classic Grand Besançon Doubs | France | 1.1 | 468 |
| 4 September | Tour du Jura | France | 1.1 | 469 |
| 5 September | Tour du Doubs | France | 1.1 | 470 |
| 5–12 September | Tour of Britain | Great Britain | 2.Pro | 471 |
| 8–12 September | European Championships | Italy | CC | 475 |
| 12 September | GP de Fourmies | France | 1.Pro | 479 |
| 12 September | Antwerp Port Epic | Belgium | 1.1 | 480 |
| 14–18 September | Tour de Luxembourg | Luxembourg | 2.Pro | 481 |
| 15 September | GP de Wallonie | Belgium | 1.Pro | 484 |
| 15 September | Giro della Toscana | Italy | 1.1 | 485 |
| 15–19 September | Tour de Slovaquie | Slovakia | 2.1 | 486 |
| 16 September | Coppa Sabatini | Italy | 1.Pro | 489 |
| 17 September | Kampioenschap van Vlaanderen | Belgium | 1.1 | 490 |
| 18 September | Primus Classic | Belgium | 1.Pro | 491 |
| 18 September | Memorial Marco Pantani | Italy | 1.1 | 492 |
| 19 September | Eschborn–Frankfurt | Germany | 1.UWT | 493 |
| 19 September | Trofeo Matteotti | Italy | 1.1 | 494 |
| 19 September | Gooikse Pijl | Belgium | 1.1 | 495 |
| 19 September | GP d'Isbergues | France | 1.1 | 496 |
| 19–26 September | World Championships | Belgium | CM | 497 |
| 21 September | GP de Denain | France | 1.Pro | 504 |
| 23 September | Omloop van het Houtland Middelkerke-Lichtervelde | Belgium | 1.1 | 505 |
| 26 September | Paris–Chauny | France | 1.1 | 506 |
| 28 September–1 October | Giro di Sicilia | Italy | 2.1 | 507 |
| 28 September–3 October | Cro Race | Croatia | 2.1 | 509 |
| 29 September | 80° Eurométropole Tour | Belgium | 1.Pro | 512 |

SEPTEMBER  WORLDTOUR WOMEN'S RACE

## CERATIZIT CHALLENGE
Stage 1
2 September 2021
Estación Invernal Cabeza de Manzaneda–A Rua
118.7km

Olympic time trial silver medallist Marlen Reusser (Alé BTC Ljubljana) stole the show on the opening stage of the Ceratizit Challenge, which had extended to four days for the 2021 edition. It began with an unusual 15km descent that naturally caused splits in the peloton and, at 60km from the line, Reusser, Pauliena Rooijakkers (Liv Racing), Elise Chabbey (Canyon-SRAM), Lucy Kennedy (BikeExchange) and Erica Magnaldi (Ceratizit-WNT) successfully attacked before shortly being joined by Coryn Rivera (DSM). Kennedy and Magnaldi didn't last long and dropped off the pace, leaving the four riders to battle on ahead. SD Worx had missed the move and began chasing but it was clear the quartet would survive to the line. With 5km to go, the leaders began to attack but it was the power of Reusser than shone, as she successfully broke away with 2.2km left and held on for victory. (LM)

### WEATHER

TEMPERATURE  
22°C

WIND  
N 11km/h

### PROFILE

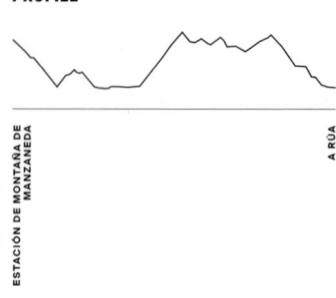

ESTACIÓN DE MONTAÑA DE MANZANEDA — A RUA

### BREAKAWAY
P. Rooijakkers (LIV), M. Reusser (ALE), E. Chabbey (CSR), L. Kennedy (BEX), E. Magnaldi (WNT), C. Rivera (DSM)

### STAGE RESULTS

| POS | NAME | TEAM | TIME |
|---|---|---|---|
| 1. | M. Reusser | ALE | 3:07:46 |
| 2. | C. Rivera | DSM | 0:22 |
| 3. | E. Chabbey | CSR | s.t. |
| 4. | P. Rooijakkers | LIV | s.t. |
| 5. | E. Balsamo | VAL | 1:48 |
| 6. | A. Henderson | JVW | s.t. |
| 7. | L. Kopecky | LIV | s.t. |
| 8. | A. Jackson | LIV | s.t. |
| 9. | M. Le Net | FDJ | s.t. |
| 10. | F. Mackaij | DSM | s.t. |
| 11. | E. Bujak | ALE | s.t. |
| 12. | M. Drummond | BPK | s.t. |
| 13. | T. Guderzo | ALE | s.t. |
| 14. | R. Markus | JVW | s.t. |
| 15. | V. Guazzini | VAL | s.t. |
| 16. | E. Longo Borghini | TFS | s.t. |
| 17. | E. Pirrone | VAL | s.t. |
| 18. | J. Ensing | BEX | s.t. |
| 19. | K. B. Vas | SDW | s.t. |
| 20. | K. Niewiadoma | CSR | s.t. |

### GENERAL CLASSIFICATION

| POS | NAME | TEAM | TIME |
|---|---|---|---|
| 1. | M. Reusser | ALE | 3:07:36 |
| 2. | C. Rivera | DSM | 0:26 |
| 3. | E. Chabbey | CSR | 0:28 |

### POINTS

| POS | NAME | TEAM | PTS |
|---|---|---|---|
| 1. | M. Reusser | ALE | 25 |
| 2. | C. Rivera | DSM | 20 |
| 3. | E. Chabbey | CSR | 16 |

### TRIVIA
» A week ago Marlen Reusser had never won a WorldTour race; now she's won two.

SEPTEMBER    WORLDTOUR WOMEN'S RACE

## CERATIZIT CHALLENGE
Stage 2 (ITT)
3 September 2021
Estación Invernal Cabeza de Manzaneda–Estación Invernal Cabeza de Manzaneda
7.3km

**WEATHER**

TEMPERATURE
24°C

WIND
E 11km/h

**PROFILE**

19-year-old Shirin van Anrooij (Trek-Segafredo) was the first rider to set a tough benchmark time on the 7.3km uphill time trial event, blasting up the climb to stop the clock with an impressive time of 21 minutes 18 seconds. Anrooijn then waited in the hot seat as the other riders completed the distance, with most opting for road bikes on a course that featured 484 metres of altitude gain. Olympic time trial champion Annemiek van Vleuten began as the race favourite and rode as expected, obliterating Anrooij's time by stopping the clock with a blistering time of 19 minutes 8 seconds. The Dutch powerhouse held on for the stage win, with stage 1 winner Marlen Reusser having to settle for second place but retaining her overall race lead by 1 minute 36 seconds over second-placed Pauliena Rooijakkers.

### STAGE RESULTS

| POS | NAME | TEAM | TIME |
|---|---|---|---|
| 1. | A. van Vleuten | MOV | 19:08 |
| 2. | M. Reusser | ALE | 0:20 |
| 3. | M. Cavalli | FDJ | 0:28 |
| 4. | K. Faulkner | TIB | 0:48 |
| 5. | L. Thomas | MOV | 0:59 |
| 6. | J. Labous | DSM | 1:00 |
| 7. | L. Lippert | DSM | 1:15 |
| 8. | K. Niewiadoma | CSR | 1:20 |
| 9. | U. Žigart | BEX | 1:23 |
| 10. | P. Rooijakkers | LIV | 1:24 |
| 11. | A. Moolman | SDW | 1:26 |
| 12. | A. Amialiusik | CSR | 1:27 |
| 13. | T. Wiles | TFS | 1:29 |
| 14. | A. Kraak | JVW | 1:31 |
| 15. | A. Smith | TIB | 1:33 |
| 16. | E. van Dijk | TFS | s.t. |
| 17. | E. Longo Borghini | TFS | 1:35 |
| 18. | E. Magnaldi | WNT | 1:36 |
| 19. | C. Rivera | DSM | 1:38 |
| 20. | E. Chabbey | CSR | 1:39 |

### GENERAL CLASSIFICATION

| POS | NAME | TEAM | TIME |
|---|---|---|---|
| 1. — | M. Reusser | ALE | 3:27:03 |
| 2. ↑2 | P. Rooijakkers | LIV | 1:36 |
| 3. ↑27 | A. van Vleuten | MOV | 1:39 |

### POINTS

| POS | NAME | TEAM | PTS |
|---|---|---|---|
| 1. — | M. Reusser | ALE | 25 |
| 2. — | C. Rivera | DSM | 20 |
| 3. — | E. Chabbey | CSR | 16 |

SEPTEMBER  WORLDTOUR WOMEN'S RACE

# CERATIZIT CHALLENGE
Stage 3
4 September 2021
Estación Invernal Cabeza de Manzaneda–Pereiro de Aguiar
107.9km

## WEATHER

TEMPERATURE  
25°C

WIND  
NW 7km/h

## PROFILE

ESTACIÓN DE MONTAÑA DE MANZANEDA

PEREIRO DE AGUIAR

Full of confidence after her stage 2 victory, Annemiek van Vleuten dominated the third stage, cementing her authority on the event by creating the race-winning move with 60km remaining. She took with her Elisa Longo Borghini (Trek-Segafredo), Katarzyna Niewiadoma (Canyon-SRAM) and Kata Blanka Vas (SD Worx), and the quartet opened up a lead of 1 minute 35 seconds before Van Vleuten broke away solo with 50km still to race. Having won events before with long-range attacks, Van Vleuten put her head down and continued to increase her advantage over the field, eventually crossing the line 2 minutes 41 seconds ahead of her nearest rival to take the stage victory and move into a convincing overall lead. Behind, her original breakaway companions battled it out for the minor placings, with Liane Lippert taking second place ahead of Niewiadoma.

## BREAKAWAY

A. van Vleuten (MOV), E. Longo Borghini (TFS), K. Niewiadoma (CSR), K. B. Vas (SDW)

## STAGE RESULTS

| POS | NAME | TEAM | TIME |
|---|---|---|---|
| 1. | A. van Vleuten | MOV | 2:41:53 |
| 2. | L. Lippert | DSM | 2:48 |
| 3. | K. Niewiadoma | CSR | s.t. |
| 4. | E. Longo Borghini | TFS | 2:51 |
| 5. | F. Mackaij | DSM | 2:55 |
| 6. | K. B. Vas | SDW | 3:01 |
| 7. | E. Chabbey | CSR | s.t. |
| 8. | M. Cavalli | FDJ | s.t. |
| 9. | M. Reusser | ALE | 3:03 |
| 10. | E. Balsamo | VAL | 7:13 |
| 11. | A. Henderson | JVW | s.t. |
| 12. | L. Kopecky | LIV | s.t. |
| 13. | I. Gaskjenn | HPU | s.t. |
| 14. | S. Zanardi | BPK | s.t. |
| 15. | E. van Dijk | TFS | s.t. |
| 16. | A. Santesteban | BEX | s.t. |
| 17. | V. Guilman | FDJ | s.t. |
| 18. | É. Muzic | FDJ | s.t. |
| 19. | L. Brennauer | WNT | s.t. |
| 20. | M. García | ALE | s.t. |

## GENERAL CLASSIFICATION

| POS | | NAME | TEAM | TIME |
|---|---|---|---|---|
| 1. | ↑2 | A. van Vleuten | MOV | 6:10:25 |
| 2. | ↓1 | M. Reusser | ALE | 1:34 |
| 3. | ↑2 | E. Chabbey | CSR | 3:20 |

## POINTS

| POS | | NAME | TEAM | PTS |
|---|---|---|---|---|
| 1. | – | M. Reusser | ALE | 32 |
| 2. | – | A. van Vleuten | MOV | 25 |
| 3. | – | E. Chabbey | CSR | 25 |

## TRIVIA

» Today and yesterday's stage wins were Van Vleuten's first at the Madrid Challenge.

SEPTEMBER   WORLDTOUR WOMEN'S RACE

# CERATIZIT CHALLENGE
Stage 4
5 September 2021
As Pontes–Santiago de Compostela
107.4km

Like the previous road stages, it wasn't until around 50km from the finish when the day's breakaway established itself and a large group got away. The group was never given much freedom from the peloton and began to fragment over the undulating terrain as they approached the final 30km. Leah Thomas (Movistar) decided to make a move with 10km to go and was able to increase her advantage out to 50 seconds while Liv Racing did most of the chasing behind. It was touch and go as to whether the American rider could hold on solo and, as she began the final drag to the line, the chasers closed in, with Belgian sprinter Lotte Kopecky (Liv Racing) flying past to take the victory ahead of Elisa Longo Borghini. The final-stage standings didn't impact the overall classification, and Annemiek van Vleuten secured the title ahead of Marlen Reusser.

## WEATHER

**TEMPERATURE**
27°C

**WIND**
NE 4km/h

## PROFILE

AS PONTES — SANTIAGO DE COMPOSTELA

## BREAKAWAY

A. van der Breggen (SDW), L. Thomas (MOV), S. Martín (MOV), A. Dideriksen (TFS), S. Borgli (FDJ), S. Bertizzolo (LIV), U. Pintar (ALE), A. Amialiusik (CSR), H. Ludwig (CSR), A. Kraak (JVW), J. Ensing (BEX), K. Hammes (WNT), M. Jasinska (WCS)

## STAGE RESULTS

| POS | NAME | TEAM | TIME |
|---|---|---|---|
| 1. | L. Kopecky | LIV | 2:29:37 |
| 2. | E. Longo Borghini | TFS | s.t. |
| 3. | A. Henderson | JVW | 0:04 |
| 4. | K. B. Vas | SDW | 0:06 |
| 5. | S. Zanardi | BPK | s.t. |
| 6. | E. Balsamo | VAL | s.t. |
| 7. | K. Niewiadoma | CSR | s.t. |
| 8. | L. Lippert | DSM | 0:08 |
| 9. | F. Mackaij | DSM | s.t. |
| 10. | R. Markus | JVW | s.t. |
| 11. | M. Cavalli | FDJ | s.t. |
| 12. | E. Chabbey | CSR | s.t. |
| 13. | E. van Dijk | TFS | s.t. |
| 14. | A. Santesteban | BEX | s.t. |
| 15. | I. Gaskjenn | HPU | 0:12 |
| 16. | L. Thomas | MOV | s.t. |
| 17. | S. Alonso | BDU | 0:13 |
| 18. | A. Moolman | SDW | s.t. |
| 19. | É. Muzic | FDJ | 0:16 |
| 20. | E. Magnaldi | WNT | s.t. |

## GENERAL CLASSIFICATION

| POS | | NAME | TEAM | TIME |
|---|---|---|---|---|
| 1. | — | A. van Vleuten | MOV | 8:40:18 |
| 2. | — | M. Reusser | ALE | 1:34 |
| 3. | — | E. Chabbey | CSR | 3:12 |

## POINTS

| POS | | NAME | TEAM | PTS |
|---|---|---|---|---|
| 1. | ↑10 | L. Kopecky | LIV | 38 |
| 2. | ↑7 | E. Longo Borghini | TFS | 34 |
| 3. | ↓2 | M. Reusser | ALE | 32 |

## TRIVIA

» Only four of Kopecky's 15 career victories haven't been in her Belgian homeland: one in Italy, one in Germany and now two in Spain.

SEPTEMBER .1 MEN'S RACE

## CLASSIC GRAND BESANÇON DOUBS
3 September 2021
Besançon–Marchaux
172.5km

## WEATHER

TEMPERATURE: 23°C
WIND: SW 4km/h

## RESULTS

| POS | NAME | TEAM | TIME |
| --- | --- | --- | --- |
| 1. | B. Ghirmay | IWG | 4:10:20 |
| 2. | A. Vendrame | ACT | s.t. |
| 3. | A. Zingle | COF | s.t. |
| 4. | N. Quintana | ARK | s.t. |
| 5. | T. Pinot | GFC | s.t. |
| 6. | L. Chirico | ANS | 0:35 |
| 7. | D. Nekrasov | GAZ | 0:37 |
| 8. | M. Louvel | ARK | 0:45 |
| 9. | A. Maldonado | AUB | s.t. |
| 10. | T. Paquot | BWB | s.t. |
| 11. | D. Godon | ACT | s.t. |
| 12. | P. L. Périchon | COF | s.t. |
| 13. | J. Simon | TEN | s.t. |
| 14. | S. Velasco | GAZ | s.t. |
| 15. | B. Planckaert | IWG | s.t. |
| 16. | M. Urruty | XRL | s.t. |
| 17. | A. Delettre | DKO | s.t. |
| 18. | N. Tesfatsion | ANS | s.t. |
| 19. | P. A. Coté | RLY | s.t. |
| 20. | C. Scaroni | GAZ | s.t. |

SEPTEMBER .1 MEN'S RACE

## TOUR DU JURA
4 September 2021
Lons-le-Saunier–Lons-le-Saunier
181.7km

## WEATHER

TEMPERATURE
23°C

WIND
W 4km/h

## RESULTS

| POS | NAME | TEAM | TIME |
|---|---|---|---|
| 1. | B. Cosnefroy | ACT | 4:21:33 |
| 2. | S. Velasco | GAZ | s.t. |
| 3. | V. Madouas | GFC | s.t. |
| 4. | N. Quintana | ARK | s.t. |
| 5. | D. Gaudu | GFC | 0:03 |
| 6. | A. Zingle | NAT | 0:09 |
| 7. | B. Ghirmay | IWG | 0:23 |
| 8. | F. Bonnamour | BBK | s.t. |
| 9. | L. Wirtgen | BWB | s.t. |
| 10. | A. Vendrame | ACT | s.t. |
| 11. | L. Chirico | ANS | s.t. |
| 12. | S. Schönberger | BBK | s.t. |
| 13. | R. Thalmann | VBG | s.t. |
| 14. | R. Seigle | GFC | s.t. |
| 15. | D. Peyskens | BWB | s.t. |
| 16. | T. Pinot | GFC | s.t. |
| 17. | S. Reichenbach | GFC | s.t. |
| 18. | D. Nekrasov | GAZ | s.t. |
| 19. | M. Urruty | XRL | 0:29 |
| 20. | C. Scaroni | GAZ | s.t. |

SEPTEMBER .1 MEN'S RACE

## TOUR DU DOUBS
5 September 2021
Morteau–Pontarlier
201km

## WEATHER

TEMPERATURE: 24°C
WIND: SW 9km/h

## RESULTS

| POS | NAME | TEAM | TIME |
|---|---|---|---|
| 1. | D. Godon | ACT | 4:55:07 |
| 2. | B. Ghirmay | IWG | s.t. |
| 3. | T. Paquot | BWB | s.t. |
| 4. | N. Tesfatsion | ANS | s.t. |
| 5. | V. Madouas | GFC | s.t. |
| 6. | N. Quintana | ARK | s.t. |
| 7. | J. Simon | TEN | s.t. |
| 8. | R. Mertz | BWB | s.t. |
| 9. | P. L. Périchon | COF | s.t. |
| 10. | R. Thalmann | VBG | s.t. |
| 11. | V. Lafay | COF | s.t. |
| 12. | B. Cosnefroy | ACT | 0:02 |
| 13. | T. Pinot | GFC | s.t. |
| 14. | F. Bonnamour | BBK | s.t. |
| 15. | A. Maldonado | AUB | s.t. |
| 16. | S. Reichenbach | GFC | s.t. |
| 17. | É. Gesbert | ARK | s.t. |
| 18. | A. Paret-Peintre | ACT | 0:09 |
| 19. | P. A. Coté | RLY | 0:18 |
| 20. | L. Wirtgen | BWB | s.t. |

SEPTEMBER .PRO MEN'S RACE

## TOUR OF BRITAIN
Stage 1
5 September 2021
Penzance–Bodmin
180.8km

### WEATHER

TEMPERATURE | WIND
18°C | E 20km/h

### STAGE RESULTS

| POS | NAME | TEAM | TIME |
|---|---|---|---|
| 1. | W. van Aert | TJV | 4:33:36 |
| 2. | N. Eekhoff | DSM | s.t. |
| 3. | G. Serrano | MOV | s.t. |
| 4. | E. Hayter | IGD | s.t. |
| 5. | R. Townsend | DHB | s.t. |
| 6. | M. Woods | ISN | s.t. |
| 7. | G. Nizzolo | TQA | s.t. |
| 8. | J. Alaphilippe | DQT | s.t. |
| 9. | X. Meurisse | AFC | s.t. |
| 10. | K. Sbaragli | AFC | s.t. |
| 11. | R. Donaldson | NAT | s.t. |
| 12. | J. Shaw | RWC | s.t. |
| 13. | M. F. Honoré | DQT | s.t. |
| 14. | M. Jorgenson | MOV | s.t. |
| 15. | C. Swift | ARK | s.t. |
| 16. | D. Martin | ISN | s.t. |
| 17. | M. Kwiatkowski | IGD | s.t. |
| 18. | S. Clarke | TQA | s.t. |
| 19. | A. Peters | SCB | s.t. |
| 20. | M. Donovan | DSM | s.t. |

### GENERAL CLASSIFICATION

| POS | NAME | TEAM | TIME |
|---|---|---|---|
| 1. | W. van Aert | TJV | 4:33:26 |
| 2. | N. Eekhoff | DSM | 0:04 |
| 3. | G. Serrano | MOV | 0:06 |

### KING OF THE MOUNTAINS

| POS | NAME | TEAM | PTS |
|---|---|---|---|
| 1. | J. Scott | DHB | 9 |
| 2. | N. Dlamini | TQA | 8 |
| 3. | M. Walker | TRI | 8 |

### POINTS

| POS | NAME | TEAM | PTS |
|---|---|---|---|
| 1. | W. van Aert | TJV | 15 |
| 2. | N. Eekhoff | DSM | 14 |
| 3. | G. Serrano | MOV | 13 |

## TOUR OF BRITAIN
Stage 2
6 September 2021
Sherford–Exeter
183.9km

### WEATHER

TEMPERATURE | WIND
25°C | SW 6km/h

### STAGE RESULTS

| POS | NAME | TEAM | TIME |
|---|---|---|---|
| 1. | R. Carpenter | RLY | 4:45:56 |
| 2. | E. Hayter | IGD | 0:33 |
| 3. | A. Peters | SCB | s.t. |
| 4. | M. Kanter | DSM | s.t. |
| 5. | J. Alaphilippe | DQT | s.t. |
| 6. | R. Townsend | DHB | s.t. |
| 7. | M. F. Honoré | DQT | s.t. |
| 8. | E. Vernon | NAT | s.t. |
| 9. | K. Sbaragli | AFC | s.t. |
| 10. | G. Nizzolo | TQA | s.t. |
| 11. | J. Shaw | RWC | s.t. |
| 12. | C. Joyce | RLY | s.t. |
| 13. | M. Paluta | GLC | s.t. |
| 14. | M. Gibson | RWC | s.t. |
| 15. | G. Serrano | MOV | s.t. |
| 16. | M. Woods | ISN | s.t. |
| 17. | R. Donaldson | NAT | s.t. |
| 18. | X. Meurisse | AFC | s.t. |
| 19. | M. Stedman | DHB | s.t. |
| 20. | S. Clarke | TQA | s.t. |

### GENERAL CLASSIFICATION

| POS | NAME | TEAM | TIME |
|---|---|---|---|
| 1. ↑35 | R. Carpenter | RLY | 9:19:33 |
| 2. ↓1 | W. van Aert | TJV | 0:22 |
| 3. ↑1 | E. Hayter | IGD | 0:26 |

### KING OF THE MOUNTAINS

| POS | NAME | TEAM | PTS |
|---|---|---|---|
| 1. — | J. Scott | DHB | 27 |
| 2. — | R. Carpenter | RLY | 15 |
| 3. — | N. Sessler | GLC | 12 |

### POINTS

| POS | NAME | TEAM | PTS |
|---|---|---|---|
| 1. ↑3 | E. Hayter | IGD | 26 |
| 2. ↑3 | R. Townsend | DHB | 21 |
| 3. ↑5 | J. Alaphilippe | DQT | 19 |

SEPTEMBER .PRO MEN'S RACE

# TOUR OF BRITAIN
Stage 3 (TTT)
7 September 2021
Llandeilo–National Botanic Garden of Wales
18.2km

## WEATHER

TEMPERATURE | WIND
27°C | E 15km/h

## STAGE RESULTS

| POS | NAME | TEAM | TIME |
|---|---|---|---|
| 1. | Ineos Grenadiers | IGD | 20:22 |
| 2. | Deceuninck-QuickStep | DQT | 0:17 |
| 3. | Jumbo-Visma | TJV | 0:20 |
| 4. | Israel Start-Up Nation | ISN | 0:43 |
| 5. | Alpecin-Fenix | AFC | 0:57 |
| 6. | Team DSM | DSM | 0:57 |
| 7. | Movistar Team | MOV | 1:08 |
| 8. | Ribble Weldtite Pro Cycling | RWC | 1:09 |
| 9. | Trinity Racing | TRI | 1:24 |
| 10. | Team Arkéa-Samsic | ARK | 1:28 |
| 11. | Rally Cycling | RLY | 1:32 |
| 12. | Great Britain | NAT | 1:57 |
| 13. | Canyon dhb SunGod | DHB | 2:02 |
| 14. | Team Qhubeka NextHash | TQA | 2:21 |
| 15. | Caja Rural-Seguros RGA | CJR | 2:25 |
| 16. | Saint Piran | SPC | 2:32 |
| 17. | SwiftCarbon Pro Cycling | SCB | 2:38 |
| 18. | Global 6 Cycling | GLC | 2:56 |

## GENERAL CLASSIFICATION

| POS | NAME | TEAM | TIME |
|---|---|---|---|
| 1. ↑2 | E. Hayter | IGD | 9:40:21 |
| 2. ↑20 | R. Dennis | IGD | 0:06 |
| 3. ↓1 | W. van Aert | TJV | 0:16 |

## KING OF THE MOUNTAINS

| POS | NAME | TEAM | PTS |
|---|---|---|---|
| 1. – | J. Scott | DHB | 27 |
| 2. – | R. Carpenter | RLY | 15 |
| 3. – | N. Sessler | GLC | 12 |

## POINTS

| POS | NAME | TEAM | PTS |
|---|---|---|---|
| 1. – | E. Hayter | IGD | 26 |
| 2. – | R. Townsend | DHB | 21 |
| 3. – | J. Alaphilippe | DQT | 19 |

# TOUR OF BRITAIN
Stage 4
8 September 2021
Aberaeron–Great Orme, Llandudno
210km

## WEATHER

TEMPERATURE | WIND
23°C | E 11km/h

## STAGE RESULTS

| POS | NAME | TEAM | TIME |
|---|---|---|---|
| 1. | W. van Aert | TJV | 5:04:22 |
| 2. | J. Alaphilippe | DQT | s.t. |
| 3. | M. Woods | ISN | 0:01 |
| 4. | M. F. Honoré | DQT | 0:04 |
| 5. | E. Hayter | IGD | 0:08 |
| 6. | D. Martin | ISN | 0:13 |
| 7. | K. Sbaragli | AFC | 0:16 |
| 8. | S. Clarke | TQA | s.t. |
| 9. | S. R. Martín | CJR | 0:27 |
| 10. | N. Roche | DSM | 0:29 |
| 11. | M. Stedman | DHB | s.t. |
| 12. | C. Rodriguez | IGD | s.t. |
| 13. | M. Bouet | ARK | 0:35 |
| 14. | M. Donovan | DSM | 0:37 |
| 15. | O. Stockwell | NAT | 0:41 |
| 16. | X. Meurisse | AFC | s.t. |
| 17. | J. Nicolau | CJR | s.t. |
| 18. | C. Swift | ARK | 0:44 |
| 19. | G. Mannion | RLY | s.t. |
| 20. | R. Dennis | IGD | s.t. |

## GENERAL CLASSIFICATION

| POS | NAME | TEAM | TIME |
|---|---|---|---|
| 1. ↑2 | W. van Aert | TJV | 14:44:49 |
| 2. ↓1 | E. Hayter | IGD | 0:02 |
| 3. ↑1 | J. Alaphilippe | DQT | 0:11 |

## KING OF THE MOUNTAINS

| POS | NAME | TEAM | PTS |
|---|---|---|---|
| 1. – | J. Scott | DHB | 43 |
| 2. ↑1 | N. Sessler | GLC | 25 |
| 3. ↓1 | R. Carpenter | RLY | 15 |

## POINTS

| POS | NAME | TEAM | PTS |
|---|---|---|---|
| 1. – | E. Hayter | IGD | 37 |
| 2. ↑1 | J. Alaphilippe | DQT | 33 |
| 3. ↑1 | W. van Aert | TJV | 30 |

SEPTEMBER .PRO MEN'S RACE

## TOUR OF BRITAIN
Stage 5
9 September 2021
Alderley Park–Warrington
152.2km

### WEATHER

TEMPERATURE | WIND
22°C | SW 7km/h

### STAGE RESULTS

| POS | NAME | TEAM | TIME |
|---|---|---|---|
| 1. | E. Hayter | IGD | 3:33:01 |
| 2. | G. Nizzolo | TQA | s.t. |
| 3. | D. McLay | ARK | s.t. |
| 4. | L. Lamperti | TRI | s.t. |
| 5. | M. Cavendish | DQT | s.t. |
| 6. | C. Joyce | RLY | s.t. |
| 7. | M. Paluta | GLC | s.t. |
| 8. | J. Alaphilippe | DQT | s.t. |
| 9. | G. Serrano | MOV | s.t. |
| 10. | K. Sbaragli | AFC | s.t. |
| 11. | R. Britton | NAT | s.t. |
| 12. | M. Bouet | ARK | s.t. |
| 13. | Ł. Owsian | ARK | s.t. |
| 14. | S. R. Martín | CJR | s.t. |
| 15. | M. Kwiatkowski | IGD | s.t. |
| 16. | C. Barbero | TQA | s.t. |
| 17. | M. Gibson | RWC | s.t. |
| 18. | X. Meurisse | AFC | s.t. |
| 19. | J. Shaw | RWC | s.t. |
| 20. | D. González | CJR | s.t. |

### GENERAL CLASSIFICATION

| POS | NAME | TEAM | TIME |
|---|---|---|---|
| 1. ↑1 | E. Hayter | IGD | 18:17:42 |
| 2. ↓1 | W. van Aert | TJV | 0:08 |
| 3. — | J. Alaphilippe | DQT | 0:19 |

### KING OF THE MOUNTAINS

| POS | NAME | TEAM | PTS |
|---|---|---|---|
| 1. — | J. Scott | DHB | 57 |
| 2. — | N. Sessler | GLC | 25 |
| 3. — | R. Carpenter | RLY | 16 |

### POINTS

| POS | NAME | TEAM | PTS |
|---|---|---|---|
| 1. — | E. Hayter | IGD | 52 |
| 2. — | J. Alaphilippe | DQT | 41 |
| 3. — | W. van Aert | TJV | 30 |

## TOUR OF BRITAIN
Stage 6
10 September 2021
Carlisle–Gateshead
198km

### WEATHER

TEMPERATURE | WIND
20°C | W 7km/h

### STAGE RESULTS

| POS | NAME | TEAM | TIME |
|---|---|---|---|
| 1. | W. van Aert | TJV | 4:35:56 |
| 2. | E. Hayter | IGD | s.t. |
| 3. | J. Alaphilippe | DQT | s.t. |
| 4. | G. Serrano | MOV | s.t. |
| 5. | J. Shaw | RWC | s.t. |
| 6. | M. Woods | ISN | s.t. |
| 7. | D. Martin | ISN | s.t. |
| 8. | M. F. Honoré | DQT | s.t. |
| 9. | M. Jorgenson | MOV | 0:04 |
| 10. | C. Rodriguez | IGD | s.t. |
| 11. | C. Barbero | TQA | 0:10 |
| 12. | C. Swift | ARK | s.t. |
| 13. | Y. Lampaert | DQT | s.t. |
| 14. | G. Mannion | RLY | s.t. |
| 15. | M. Stedman | DHB | s.t. |
| 16. | K. Sbaragli | AFC | s.t. |
| 17. | X. Meurisse | AFC | s.t. |
| 18. | M. Kwiatkowski | IGD | s.t. |
| 19. | R. Dennis | IGD | s.t. |
| 20. | S. R. Martín | CJR | s.t. |

### GENERAL CLASSIFICATION

| POS | NAME | TEAM | TIME |
|---|---|---|---|
| 1. — | E. Hayter | IGD | 22:53:32 |
| 2. — | W. van Aert | TJV | 0:04 |
| 3. — | J. Alaphilippe | DQT | 0:21 |

### KING OF THE MOUNTAINS

| POS | NAME | TEAM | PTS |
|---|---|---|---|
| 1. — | J. Scott | DHB | 66 |
| 2. — | R. Townsend | DHB | 30 |
| 3. ↓1 | N. Sessler | GLC | 28 |

### POINTS

| POS | NAME | TEAM | PTS |
|---|---|---|---|
| 1. — | E. Hayter | IGD | 66 |
| 2. — | J. Alaphilippe | DQT | 54 |
| 3. — | W. van Aert | TJV | 45 |

SEPTEMBER .PRO MEN'S RACE

# TOUR OF BRITAIN
Stage 7
11 September 2021
Hawick–Edinburgh
194.8km

## WEATHER

TEMPERATURE  WIND
18°C  W 26km/h

## STAGE RESULTS

| POS | NAME | TEAM | TIME |
|---|---|---|---|
| 1. | Y. Lampaert | DQT | 4:39:09 |
| 2. | M. Jorgenson | MOV | s.t. |
| 3. | M. Gibson | RWC | s.t. |
| 4. | D. Ballerini | DQT | 0:35 |
| 5. | P. Eenkhoorn | TJV | 0:41 |
| 6. | E. Hayter | IGD | 1:51 |
| 7. | W. van Aert | TJV | s.t. |
| 8. | M. Kanter | DSM | s.t. |
| 9. | R. Dennis | IGD | s.t. |
| 10. | K. Sbaragli | AFC | s.t. |
| 11. | T. Mein | DHB | s.t. |
| 12. | J. Alaphilippe | DQT | s.t. |
| 13. | M. Cavendish | DQT | s.t. |
| 14. | G. Serrano | MOV | s.t. |
| 15. | G. Cullaigh | MOV | s.t. |
| 16. | M. Paluta | GLC | s.t. |
| 17. | R. Christensen | DHB | s.t. |
| 18. | M. F. Honoré | DQT | s.t. |
| 19. | C. Swift | ARK | s.t. |
| 20. | C. Rodriguez | IGD | s.t. |

## GENERAL CLASSIFICATION

| POS | NAME | TEAM | TIME |
|---|---|---|---|
| 1. — | E. Hayter | IGD | 27:34:32 |
| 2. — | W. van Aert | TJV | 0:04 |
| 3. — | J. Alaphilippe | DQT | 0:21 |

## KING OF THE MOUNTAINS

| POS | NAME | TEAM | PTS |
|---|---|---|---|
| 1. — | J. Scott | DHB | 66 |
| 2. — | R. Townsend | DHB | 30 |
| 3. — | N. Sessler | GLC | 28 |

## POINTS

| POS | NAME | TEAM | PTS |
|---|---|---|---|
| 1. — | E. Hayter | IGD | 76 |
| 2. — | J. Alaphilippe | DQT | 58 |
| 3. — | W. van Aert | TJV | 54 |

# TOUR OF BRITAIN
Stage 8
12 September 2021
Stonehaven–Aberdeen
173km

## WEATHER

TEMPERATURE  WIND
14°C  N 19km/h

## STAGE RESULTS

| POS | NAME | TEAM | TIME |
|---|---|---|---|
| 1. | W. van Aert | TJV | 4:07:56 |
| 2. | A. Greipel | ISN | s.t. |
| 3. | M. Cavendish | DQT | s.t. |
| 4. | C. Joyce | RLY | s.t. |
| 5. | M. Kanter | DSM | s.t. |
| 6. | R. Townsend | DHB | s.t. |
| 7. | M. Gibson | RWC | s.t. |
| 8. | O. Peckover | SCB | s.t. |
| 9. | M. Bostock | DHB | s.t. |
| 10. | G. Cullaigh | MOV | s.t. |
| 11. | E. Hayter | IGD | s.t. |
| 12. | R. Britton | NAT | s.t. |
| 13. | D. González | CJR | s.t. |
| 14. | T. Mazzone | SPC | s.t. |
| 15. | A. Peters | SCB | s.t. |
| 16. | C. Barbero | TQA | s.t. |
| 17. | D. McLay | ARK | s.t. |
| 18. | T. Mein | DHB | s.t. |
| 19. | R. Christensen | DHB | s.t. |
| 20. | N. Zukowsky | RLY | s.t. |

## GENERAL CLASSIFICATION

| POS | NAME | TEAM | TIME |
|---|---|---|---|
| 1. ↑1 | W. van Aert | TJV | 31:42:22 |
| 2. ↓1 | E. Hayter | IGD | 0:06 |
| 3. — | J. Alaphilippe | DQT | 0:27 |

## KING OF THE MOUNTAINS

| POS | NAME | TEAM | PTS |
|---|---|---|---|
| 1. — | J. Scott | DHB | 66 |
| 2. ↑1 | N. Sessler | GLC | 32 |
| 3. ↓1 | R. Townsend | DHB | 30 |

## POINTS

| POS | NAME | TEAM | PTS |
|---|---|---|---|
| 1. — | E. Hayter | IGD | 81 |
| 2. ↑1 | W. van Aert | TJV | 69 |
| 3. ↓1 | J. Alaphilippe | DQT | 58 |

## EUROPEAN CHAMPIONSHIPS WOMEN'S ITT

9 September 2021
Trento–Trento
22.4km

### WEATHER

TEMPERATURE: 22°C
WIND: S 2km/h

### RESULTS

| POS | NAME | TEAM | TIME |
|---|---|---|---|
| 1. | M. Reusser | Switzerland | 27:13 |
| 2. | E. van Dijk | Netherlands | 0:19 |
| 3. | L. Brennauer | Germany | 1:02 |
| 4. | L. Klein | Germany | 1:22 |
| 5. | R. Markus | Netherlands | 1:43 |
| 6. | V. Kononenko | Ukraine | 1:52 |
| 7. | A. Kiesenhofer | Austria | 2:00 |
| 8. | V. Bussi | Italy | 2:09 |
| 9. | S. Van de Vel | Belgium | 2:13 |
| 10. | E. Norsgaard | Denmark | 2:18 |
| 11. | N. Eklund | Sweden | 2:25 |
| 12. | A. Amialiusik | Belarus | 2:28 |
| 13. | A. S. Duyck | Belgium | 2:30 |
| 14. | A. Nerlo | Poland | 2:32 |
| 15. | A. Cordon-Ragot | France | 2:36 |
| 16. | K. Aalerud | Norway | 2:39 |
| 17. | T. Dronova-Balabolina | Russia | 2:40 |
| 18. | O. Shapira | Israel | 2:42 |
| 19. | K. Karasiewicz | Poland | 2:49 |
| 20. | E. Chabbey | Switzerland | 2:50 |

SEPTEMBER   EUROPEAN CHAMPIONSHIPS

# EUROPEAN CHAMPIONSHIPS MEN'S ITT
9 September 2021
Trento–Trento
22.4km

## WEATHER

**TEMPERATURE**
29°C

**WIND**
S 7km/h

## RESULTS

| POS | NAME | TEAM | TIME |
|---|---|---|---|
| 1. | S. Küng | Switzerland | 24:29 |
| 2. | F. Ganna | Italy | 0:08 |
| 3. | R. Evenepoel | Belgium | 0:15 |
| 4. | S. Bissegger | Switzerland | 0:23 |
| 5. | M. Walscheid | Germany | 0:38 |
| 6. | E. Affini | Italy | 0:39 |
| 7. | K. Asgreen | Denmark | 0:52 |
| 8. | M. Bodnar | Poland | 1:04 |
| 9. | R. Cavagna | France | 1:06 |
| 10. | J. Almeida | Portugal | 1:17 |
| 11. | J. van Emden | Netherlands | s.t. |
| 12. | T. Pogačar | Slovenia | 1:21 |
| 13. | R. Herregodts | Belgium | 1:30 |
| 14. | R. Reis | Portugal | 1:34 |
| 15. | B. Armirail | France | 1:35 |
| 16. | M. Heidemann | Germany | 1:38 |
| 17. | J. Bárta | Czech Republic | 1:51 |
| 18. | R. Mullen | Ireland | 2:10 |
| 19. | A. Nych | Russia | s.t. |
| 20. | F. Ritzinger | Austria | 2:12 |

## EUROPEAN CHAMPIONSHIPS WOMEN'S ROAD RACE

11 September 2021
Trento–Trento
107.2km

### WEATHER

**TEMPERATURE**
29°C

**WIND**
S 4km/h

### RESULTS

| POS | NAME | TEAM | TIME |
| --- | --- | --- | --- |
| 1. | E. van Dijk | Netherlands | 2:50:35 |
| 2. | L. Lippert | Germany | 1:18 |
| 3. | R. Leleivytė | Lithuania | s.t. |
| 4. | K. Niewiadoma | Poland | s.t. |
| 5. | D. Vollering | Netherlands | s.t. |
| 6. | M. Cavalli | Italy | s.t. |
| 7. | M. Reusser | Switzerland | s.t. |
| 8. | A. Amialiusik | Belarus | s.t. |
| 9. | A. van Vleuten | Netherlands | 1:21 |
| 10. | E. Balsamo | Italy | 2:29 |
| 11. | L. Brennauer | Germany | s.t. |
| 12. | F. Mackaij | Netherlands | s.t. |
| 13. | E. Bujak | Slovenia | s.t. |
| 14. | L. Kopecky | Belgium | s.t. |
| 15. | E. Chabbey | Switzerland | s.t. |
| 16. | A. Pieters | Netherlands | s.t. |
| 17. | R. Markus | Netherlands | s.t. |
| 18. | J. Labous | France | s.t. |
| 19. | E. Merino | Spain | s.t. |
| 20. | K. Hammes | Germany | s.t. |

SEPTEMBER  EUROPEAN CHAMPIONSHIPS

# EUROPEAN CHAMPIONSHIPS MEN'S ROAD RACE
12 September 2021
Trento–Trento
179.2km

**WEATHER**

TEMPERATURE  WIND
28°C  S 6km/h

## RESULTS

| POS | NAME | TEAM | TIME |
| --- | --- | --- | --- |
| 1. | S. Colbrelli | Italy | 4:19:45 |
| 2. | R. Evenepoel | Belgium | s.t. |
| 3. | B. Cosnefroy | France | 1:30 |
| 4. | M. Trentin | Italy | 1:44 |
| 5. | T. Pogačar | Slovenia | s.t. |
| 6. | M. Hirschi | Switzerland | s.t. |
| 7. | M. Hoelgaard | Norway | s.t. |
| 8. | B. Hermans | Belgium | 1:46 |
| 9. | P. Sivakov | Russia | 1:49 |
| 10. | V. Campenaerts | Belgium | 5:41 |
| 11. | S. Dewulf | Belgium | 5:49 |
| 12. | R. Bardet | France | s.t. |
| 13. | M. Mohorič | Slovenia | 5:50 |
| 14. | J. Almeida | Portugal | 6:00 |
| 15. | D. Ulissi | Italy | s.t. |
| 16. | S. Geschke | Germany | s.t. |
| 17. | B. Mollema | Netherlands | 6:15 |
| 18. | R. Costa | Portugal | 9:13 |
| 19. | K. Bouwman | Netherlands | s.t. |
| 20. | M. Kukrle | Czech Republic | s.t. |

SEPTEMBER  .PRO MEN'S RACE

## GP DE FOURMIES
12 September 2021
Fourmies–Fourmies
197.6km

## WEATHER

TEMPERATURE
18°C

WIND
W 13km/h

### RESULTS

| POS | NAME | TEAM | TIME |
| --- | --- | --- | --- |
| 1. | E. Viviani | COF | 4:23:12 |
| 2. | P. Ackermann | BOH | s.t. |
| 3. | F. Gaviria | UAD | s.t. |
| 4. | H. Hofstetter | ISN | s.t. |
| 5. | G. Thijssen | LTS | s.t. |
| 6. | J. Degenkolb | LTS | s.t. |
| 7. | A. J. Hodeg | DQT | s.t. |
| 8. | J. Tesson | AUB | s.t. |
| 9. | M. Louvel | ARK | s.t. |
| 10. | B. Planckaert | IWG | s.t. |
| 11. | S. Aniołkowski | BWB | s.t. |
| 12. | B. Ghirmay | IWG | s.t. |
| 13. | C. Russo | ARK | s.t. |
| 14. | L. Naesen | ACT | s.t. |
| 15. | N. Vandepitte | BWB | s.t. |
| 16. | M. Moschetti | TFS | s.t. |
| 17. | F. Maitre | TEN | s.t. |
| 18. | J. Mareczko | THR | s.t. |
| 19. | E. Vermeulen | XRL | s.t. |
| 20. | C. Barthe | BBK | s.t. |

SEPTEMBER .1 MEN'S RACE

# ANTWERP PORT EPIC
12 September 2021
Antwerp–Antwerp
183.4km

## WEATHER

**TEMPERATURE**
19°C

**WIND**
W 11km/h

## RESULTS

| POS | NAME | TEAM | TIME |
|---|---|---|---|
| 1. | M. van der Poel | AFC | 4:12:03 |
| 2. | T. van der Hoorn | IWG | 0:01 |
| 3. | T. Merlier | AFC | 1:14 |
| 4. | D. van Poppel | IWG | s.t. |
| 5. | R. Tiller | UXT | s.t. |
| 6. | P. Havik | BCY | s.t. |
| 7. | L. Robeet | BWB | s.t. |
| 8. | T. Joseph | TIS | s.t. |
| 9. | D. De Bondt | AFC | 1:19 |
| 10. | T. Benoot | DSM | 1:30 |
| 11. | K. Van Rooy | SVB | s.t. |
| 12. | B. De Backer | BBK | s.t. |
| 13. | J. Rickaert | AFC | 1:43 |
| 14. | C. van Uden | DSM | 2:50 |
| 15. | C. Stewart | BSC | s.t. |
| 16. | T. L. Andresen | DDS | 2:51 |
| 17. | C. Beullens | SVB | 5:09 |
| 18. | W. Vanhoof | SVB | s.t. |
| 19. | A. Skaarseth | UXT | 5:10 |
| 20. | T. Dupont | BWB | s.t. |

SEPTEMBER .PRO MEN'S RACE

## TOUR DE LUXEMBOURG
Stage 1
14 September 2021
Luxembourg-City–Luxembourg-City
140km

### STAGE RESULTS

| POS | NAME | TEAM | TIME |
|---|---|---|---|
| 1. | J. Almeida | DQT | 3:16:09 |
| 2. | B. Mollema | TFS | s.t. |
| 3. | M. Hirschi | UAD | s.t. |
| 4. | C. Champoussin | ACT | s.t. |
| 5. | N. Quintana | ARK | s.t. |
| 6. | Je. Herrada | COF | s.t. |
| 7. | D. Gaudu | GFC | s.t. |
| 8. | A. Vendrame | ACT | s.t. |
| 9. | T. Pinot | GFC | s.t. |
| 10. | K. Goossens | LTS | s.t. |
| 11. | J. Bol | BBH | s.t. |
| 12. | P. Latour | TEN | s.t. |
| 13. | L. Wirtgen | BWB | s.t. |
| 14. | O. Lazkano | CJR | s.t. |
| 15. | P. Vakoč | AFC | s.t. |
| 16. | E. Prades | DKO | s.t. |
| 17. | E. Chaves | BEX | s.t. |
| 18. | D. de la Cruz | UAD | s.t. |
| 19. | D. Formolo | UAD | s.t. |
| 20. | F. Bonnamour | BBK | s.t. |

### WEATHER

TEMPERATURE    WIND
18°C           S 6km/h

### GENERAL CLASSIFICATION

| POS | NAME | TEAM | TIME |
|---|---|---|---|
| 1. | J. Almeida | DQT | 3:15:59 |
| 2. | B. Mollema | TFS | 0:04 |
| 3. | M. Hirschi | UAD | 0:06 |

### KING OF THE MOUNTAINS

| POS | NAME | TEAM | PTS |
|---|---|---|---|
| 1. | K. Molly | BWB | 10 |
| 2. | S. Schönberger | BBK | 8 |
| 3. | E. Oronte | RLY | 4 |

### POINTS

| POS | NAME | TEAM | PTS |
|---|---|---|---|
| 1. | J. Almeida | DQT | 20 |
| 2. | B. Mollema | TFS | 16 |
| 3. | M. Hirschi | UAD | 13 |

### YOUNG RIDER

| POS | NAME | TEAM | TIME |
|---|---|---|---|
| 1. | J. Almeida | DQT | 3:15:59 |
| 2. | M. Hirschi | UAD | 0:06 |
| 3. | C. Champoussin | ACT | 0:10 |

---

## TOUR DE LUXEMBOURG
Stage 2
15 September 2021
Steinfort–Eschdorf
186.1km

### STAGE RESULTS

| POS | NAME | TEAM | TIME |
|---|---|---|---|
| 1. | M. Hirschi | UAD | 4:45:12 |
| 2. | J. Almeida | DQT | 0:08 |
| 3. | D. Gaudu | GFC | s.t. |
| 4. | D. Formolo | UAD | s.t. |
| 5. | D. de la Cruz | UAD | s.t. |
| 6. | T. Pinot | GFC | s.t. |
| 7. | P. Latour | TEN | 0:20 |
| 8. | S. Reichenbach | GFC | s.t. |
| 9. | N. Quintana | ARK | s.t. |
| 10. | C. Champoussin | ACT | s.t. |
| 11. | Je. Herrada | COF | s.t. |
| 12. | B. Mollema | TFS | 0:26 |
| 13. | F. Bonnamour | BBK | s.t. |
| 14. | V. Nibali | TFS | s.t. |
| 15. | A. Valter | GFC | 0:41 |
| 16. | O. Lazkano | CJR | s.t. |
| 17. | T. Træen | UXT | s.t. |
| 18. | K. Goossens | LTS | s.t. |
| 19. | P. Vakoč | AFC | s.t. |
| 20. | M. Cattaneo | DQT | s.t. |

### WEATHER

TEMPERATURE    WIND
19°C           SW 15km/h

### GENERAL CLASSIFICATION

| POS | | NAME | TEAM | TIME |
|---|---|---|---|---|
| 1. | ↑2 | M. Hirschi | UAD | 8:01:06 |
| 2. | ↓1 | J. Almeida | DQT | 0:04 |
| 3. | ↑4 | D. Gaudu | GFC | 0:19 |

### KING OF THE MOUNTAINS

| POS | | NAME | TEAM | PTS |
|---|---|---|---|---|
| 1. | — | K. Molly | BWB | 29 |
| 2. | — | S. Schönberger | BBK | 20 |
| 3. | — | A. de Vos | RLY | 5 |

### POINTS

| POS | | NAME | TEAM | PTS |
|---|---|---|---|---|
| 1. | — | J. Almeida | DQT | 36 |
| 2. | ↑1 | M. Hirschi | UAD | 33 |
| 3. | ↑4 | D. Gaudu | GFC | 18 |

### YOUNG RIDER

| POS | | NAME | TEAM | TIME |
|---|---|---|---|---|
| 1. | ↑1 | M. Hirschi | UAD | 8:01:06 |
| 2. | ↓1 | J. Almeida | DQT | 0:04 |
| 3. | ↑1 | D. Gaudu | GFC | 0:19 |

SEPTEMBER .PRO MEN'S RACE

## TOUR DE LUXEMBOURG
Stage 3
16 September 2021
Mondorf-les-Bains–Mamer
189.3km

### WEATHER

| TEMPERATURE | WIND |
|---|---|
| 16°C | N 9km/h |

### STAGE RESULTS

| POS | NAME | TEAM | TIME |
|---|---|---|---|
| 1. | S. Modolo | AFC | 4:17:47 |
| 2. | B. Cosnefroy | ACT | s.t. |
| 3. | E. M. Grosu | DKO | s.t. |
| 4. | E. Boasson Hagen | TEN | s.t. |
| 5. | A. Vendrame | ACT | s.t. |
| 6. | C. Champoussin | ACT | s.t. |
| 7. | A. Marit | SVB | s.t. |
| 8. | F. Bonnamour | BBK | s.t. |
| 9. | M. Peñalver | BBH | s.t. |
| 10. | A. de Kleijn | RLY | s.t. |
| 11. | J. Trarieux | DKO | s.t. |
| 12. | B. Coquard | BBK | s.t. |
| 13. | J. Mareczko | THR | s.t. |
| 14. | R. Stacchiotti | THR | s.t. |
| 15. | C. Barthe | BBK | s.t. |
| 16. | M. Hoelgaard | UXT | s.t. |
| 17. | K. Van Rooy | SVB | s.t. |
| 18. | T. T. Teutenberg | LPC | s.t. |
| 19. | A. Van Poucke | SVB | s.t. |
| 20. | J. Almeida | DQT | s.t. |

### GENERAL CLASSIFICATION

| POS | | NAME | TEAM | TIME |
|---|---|---|---|---|
| 1. | – | M. Hirschi | UAD | 12:18:53 |
| 2. | – | J. Almeida | DQT | 0:04 |
| 3. | – | D. Gaudu | GFC | 0:19 |

### KING OF THE MOUNTAINS

| POS | | NAME | TEAM | PTS |
|---|---|---|---|---|
| 1. | – | K. Molly | BWB | 29 |
| 2. | – | S. Schönberger | BBK | 20 |
| 3. | – | K. Van Rooy | SVB | 8 |

### POINTS

| POS | | NAME | TEAM | PTS |
|---|---|---|---|---|
| 1. | – | J. Almeida | DQT | 36 |
| 2. | – | M. Hirschi | UAD | 33 |
| 3. | – | S. Modolo | AFC | 20 |

### YOUNG RIDER

| POS | | NAME | TEAM | TIME |
|---|---|---|---|---|
| 1. | – | M. Hirschi | UAD | 12:18:53 |
| 2. | – | J. Almeida | DQT | 0:04 |
| 3. | – | D. Gaudu | GFC | 0:19 |

## TOUR DE LUXEMBOURG
Stage 4 (ITT)
17 September 2021
Dudelange–Dudelange
25.4km

### WEATHER

| TEMPERATURE | WIND |
|---|---|
| 19°C | SE 9km/h |

### STAGE RESULTS

| POS | NAME | TEAM | TIME |
|---|---|---|---|
| 1. | M. Cattaneo | DQT | 30:53 |
| 2. | J. Almeida | DQT | 0:02 |
| 3. | M. Skjelmose Jensen | TFS | 0:26 |
| 4. | D. de la Cruz | UAD | 0:35 |
| 5. | P. Latour | TEN | 0:38 |
| 6. | M. Hirschi | UAD | 0:49 |
| 7. | J. Bauer | BEX | 0:50 |
| 8. | H. Sweeny | LTS | 0:55 |
| 9. | A. Tiberi | TFS | s.t. |
| 10. | V. Nibali | TFS | 0:57 |
| 11. | B. Armirail | GFC | 1:00 |
| 12. | K. Goossens | LTS | 1:04 |
| 13. | T. Pinot | GFC | s.t. |
| 14. | F. Frison | LTS | 1:05 |
| 15. | Je. Herrada | COF | 1:08 |
| 16. | B. O'Connor | ACT | s.t. |
| 17. | F. Masnada | DQT | s.t. |
| 18. | D. Gaudu | GFC | s.t. |
| 19. | M. Hulgaard | UXT | 1:09 |
| 20. | A. Perez | COF | 1:15 |

### GENERAL CLASSIFICATION

| POS | | NAME | TEAM | TIME |
|---|---|---|---|---|
| 1. | ↑1 | J. Almeida | DQT | 12:49:51 |
| 2. | ↓1 | M. Hirschi | UAD | 0:43 |
| 3. | ↑16 | M. Cattaneo | DQT | 0:50 |

### KING OF THE MOUNTAINS

| POS | | NAME | TEAM | PTS |
|---|---|---|---|---|
| 1. | – | K. Molly | BWB | 29 |
| 2. | – | S. Schönberger | BBK | 20 |
| 3. | – | K. Van Rooy | SVB | 8 |

### POINTS

| POS | | NAME | TEAM | PTS |
|---|---|---|---|---|
| 1. | – | J. Almeida | DQT | 52 |
| 2. | – | M. Hirschi | UAD | 40 |
| 3. | – | M. Cattaneo | DQT | 20 |

### YOUNG RIDER

| POS | | NAME | TEAM | TIME |
|---|---|---|---|---|
| 1. | ↑1 | J. Almeida | DQT | 12:49:51 |
| 2. | ↓1 | M. Hirschi | UAD | 0:43 |
| 3. | – | D. Gaudu | GFC | 1:21 |

SEPTEMBER .PRO MEN'S RACE

# TOUR DE LUXEMBOURG
Stage 5
18 September 2021
Mersch–Luxembourg-City
183.7km

## WEATHER

TEMPERATURE | WIND
19°C | E 11km/h

## STAGE RESULTS

| POS | NAME | TEAM | TIME |
|---|---|---|---|
| 1. | D. Gaudu | GFC | 4:30:59 |
| 2. | J. Almeida | DQT | s.t. |
| 3. | P. Latour | TEN | s.t. |
| 4. | M. Hirschi | UAD | s.t. |
| 5. | B. Cosnefroy | ACT | s.t. |
| 6. | A. Kirsch | TFS | s.t. |
| 7. | F. Masnada | DQT | s.t. |
| 8. | C. Champoussin | ACT | s.t. |
| 9. | Je. Herrada | COF | s.t. |
| 10. | O. Lazkano | CJR | s.t. |
| 11. | N. Quintana | ARK | s.t. |
| 12. | J. Bauer | BEX | s.t. |
| 13. | T. Pinot | GFC | s.t. |
| 14. | F. Bonnamour | BBK | 0:11 |
| 15. | M. Hoelgaard | UXT | s.t. |
| 16. | D. Fernández | DKO | s.t. |
| 17. | A. Valter | GFC | s.t. |
| 18. | M. Cattaneo | DQT | s.t. |
| 19. | F. Barceló | COF | s.t. |
| 20. | K. Goossens | LTS | s.t. |

## GENERAL CLASSIFICATION

| POS | NAME | TEAM | TIME |
|---|---|---|---|
| 1. — | J. Almeida | DQT | 17:20:44 |
| 2. — | M. Hirschi | UAD | 0:46 |
| 3. — | M. Cattaneo | DQT | 1:05 |

## KING OF THE MOUNTAINS

| POS | NAME | TEAM | PTS |
|---|---|---|---|
| 1. — | K. Molly | BWB | 42 |
| 2. — | S. Schönberger | BBK | 20 |
| 3. — | K. Van Rooy | SVB | 8 |

## POINTS

| POS | NAME | TEAM | PTS |
|---|---|---|---|
| 1. — | J. Almeida | DQT | 68 |
| 2. — | M. Hirschi | UAD | 51 |
| 3. ↑4 | D. Gaudu | GFC | 38 |

## YOUNG RIDER

| POS | NAME | TEAM | TIME |
|---|---|---|---|
| 1. — | J. Almeida | DQT | 17:20:44 |
| 2. — | M. Hirschi | UAD | 0:46 |
| 3. — | D. Gaudu | GFC | 1:17 |

SEPTEMBER .PRO MEN'S RACE

# GP DE WALLONIE
15 September 2021
Aywaille–Citadelle de Namur
208.1km

## WEATHER

TEMPERATURE
19°C

WIND
W 7km/h

## RESULTS

| POS | NAME | TEAM | TIME |
|---|---|---|---|
| 1. | C. Laporte | COF | 4:59:57 |
| 2. | W. Barguil | ARK | s.t. |
| 3. | T. Van der Sande | LTS | s.t. |
| 4. | D. Godon | ACT | s.t. |
| 5. | G. Vermeersch | AFC | s.t. |
| 6. | R. Tiller | UXT | s.t. |
| 7. | P. Konrad | BOH | s.t. |
| 8. | T. Van Asbroeck | ISN | s.t. |
| 9. | T. Benoot | DSM | s.t. |
| 10. | D. Claeys | TQA | s.t. |
| 11. | L. Teugels | TIS | s.t. |
| 12. | A. Paret-Peintre | ACT | s.t. |
| 13. | B. Hermans | ISN | s.t. |
| 14. | J. Simon | TEN | s.t. |
| 15. | L. Calmejane | ACT | s.t. |
| 16. | A. De Gendt | IWG | s.t. |
| 17. | T. Ferasse | BBK | s.t. |
| 18. | M. Menten | BWB | s.t. |
| 19. | M. Van Gils | LTS | s.t. |
| 20. | L. Eriksson | RIW | s.t. |

SEPTEMBER .1 MEN'S RACE

# GIRO DELLA TOSCANA

15 September 2021
Pontedera–Pontedera
191.6km

## WEATHER

TEMPERATURE  
26°C

WIND  
S 19km/h

## RESULTS

| POS | NAME | TEAM | TIME |
|---|---|---|---|
| 1. | M. Valgren | EFN | 4:33:37 |
| 2. | A. De Marchi | NAT | 1:13 |
| 3. | D. Ulissi | UAD | 1:18 |
| 4. | L. Rota | IWG | s.t. |
| 5. | D. Villella | MOV | s.t. |
| 6. | M. Canola | GAZ | s.t. |
| 7. | S. Chernetski | GAZ | s.t. |
| 8. | G. Moscon | IGD | s.t. |
| 9. | S. Higuita | EFN | s.t. |
| 10. | S. Battistella | APT | s.t. |
| 11. | G. Martín | EUS | s.t. |
| 12. | S. Williams | TBV | s.t. |
| 13. | D. Muñoz | ANS | s.t. |
| 14. | C. Scaroni | GAZ | s.t. |
| 15. | A. Geniez | TEN | s.t. |
| 16. | L. Fortunato | EOK | s.t. |
| 17. | N. Powless | EFN | s.t. |
| 18. | L. Wackermann | EOK | s.t. |
| 19. | R. Majka | UAD | 1:26 |
| 20. | T. Geoghegan Hart | IGD | 1:58 |

SEPTEMBER .1 MEN'S RACE

## TOUR DE SLOVAQUIE
Prologue
15 September 2021
Košice–Košice
1.6km

### WEATHER

TEMPERATURE: 25°C
WIND: SW 11km/h

### STAGE RESULTS

| POS | NAME | TEAM | TIME |
|---|---|---|---|
| 1. | K. Groves | BEX | 1:50 |
| 2. | J. Steimle | DQT | s.t. |
| 3. | M. Boguslawski | MSP | 0:01 |
| 4. | C. Bol | DSM | s.t. |
| 5. | A. J. Hodeg | DQT | s.t. |
| 6. | C. Pedersen | DSM | s.t. |
| 7. | M. Bodnar | BOH | 0:02 |
| 8. | F. Rodenberg | UXT | s.t. |
| 9. | J. Osborne | DQT | s.t. |
| 10. | P. Sagan | BOH | 0:03 |
| 11. | I. Einhorn | ISN | s.t. |
| 12. | S. Archbold | DQT | s.t. |
| 13. | J. Johansen | UXT | s.t. |
| 14. | A. Kurek | MSP | s.t. |
| 15. | L. Heinschke | DSM | s.t. |
| 16. | A. Lutsenko | APT | 0:04 |
| 17. | F. Dversnes | GAZ | s.t. |
| 18. | M. Hepburn | BEX | s.t. |
| 19. | S. Steels | DQT | s.t. |
| 20. | E. Baška | BOH | s.t. |

### GENERAL CLASSIFICATION

| POS | NAME | TEAM | TIME |
|---|---|---|---|
| 1. | K. Groves | BEX | 1:50 |
| 2. | J. Steimle | DQT | s.t. |
| 3. | M. Boguslawski | MSP | 0:01 |

### YOUNG RIDER

| POS | NAME | TEAM | TIME |
|---|---|---|---|
| 1. | J. Johansen | UXT | 1:53 |
| 2. | L. Heinschke | DSM | s.t. |
| 3. | R. Carretta | CTF | 0:01 |

## TOUR DE SLOVAQUIE
Stage 1
16 September 2021
Košice–Košice
158.4km

### WEATHER

TEMPERATURE: 23°C
WIND: E 7km/h

### STAGE RESULTS

| POS | NAME | TEAM | TIME |
|---|---|---|---|
| 1. | A. J. Hodeg | DQT | 3:34:38 |
| 2. | P. Sagan | BOH | s.t. |
| 3. | R. Janse Van Rensburg | TQA | s.t. |
| 4. | C. Bol | DSM | s.t. |
| 5. | M. Mørkøv | DQT | s.t. |
| 6. | I. Einhorn | ISN | s.t. |
| 7. | L. Coati | TQA | s.t. |
| 8. | D. Neuman | EKA | s.t. |
| 9. | N. Vahtra | ISN | s.t. |
| 10. | F. Galván | EKP | s.t. |
| 11. | G. Lonardi | BCF | s.t. |
| 12. | M. Štoček | TFA | s.t. |
| 13. | K. Groves | BEX | s.t. |
| 14. | N. Dalla Valle | BCF | s.t. |
| 15. | J. Kaczmarek | MSP | s.t. |
| 16. | A. Toupalík | EKA | s.t. |
| 17. | D. Martinelli | APT | s.t. |
| 18. | L. Kubiš | DKB | s.t. |
| 19. | A. Stokbro | TQA | s.t. |
| 20. | R. Carretta | CTF | s.t. |

### GENERAL CLASSIFICATION

| POS | | NAME | TEAM | TIME |
|---|---|---|---|---|
| 1. | ↑4 | A. J. Hodeg | DQT | 3:36:19 |
| 2. | ↑8 | P. Sagan | BOH | 0:06 |
| 3. | ↑40 | E. Lunder | GAZ | 0:08 |

### KING OF THE MOUNTAINS

| POS | NAME | TEAM | PTS |
|---|---|---|---|
| 1. | A. Garosio | BCF | 10 |
| 2. | T. Budzinski | MSP | 8 |
| 3. | G. Petrelli | CTF | 6 |

### POINTS

| POS | NAME | TEAM | PTS |
|---|---|---|---|
| 1. | E. Lunder | GAZ | 16 |
| 2. | A. J. Hodeg | DQT | 15 |
| 3. | R. Adrià | EKP | 12 |

### YOUNG RIDER

| POS | | NAME | TEAM | TIME |
|---|---|---|---|---|
| 1. | ↑10 | E. Lunder | GAZ | 7:12:46 |
| 2. | — | L. Heinschke | DSM | 0:04 |
| 3. | — | R. Carretta | CTF | 0:05 |

## TOUR DE SLOVAQUIE

Stage 2
17 September 2021
Spišské Podhradie–Dolný Kubín
179.7km

### WEATHER

TEMPERATURE: 15°C
WIND: SW 9km/h

### STAGE RESULTS

| POS | NAME | TEAM | TIME |
|---|---|---|---|
| 1. | J. Steimle | DQT | 4:18:30 |
| 2. | P. Sagan | BOH | s.t. |
| 3. | A. J. Hodeg | DQT | s.t. |
| 4. | L. Kubiš | DKB | s.t. |
| 5. | F. Galván | EKP | s.t. |
| 6. | G. Glivar | ADR | s.t. |
| 7. | F. Felline | APT | s.t. |
| 8. | A. Lutsenko | APT | s.t. |
| 9. | M. Štoček | TFA | s.t. |
| 10. | I. Andersen | UXT | s.t. |
| 11. | A. Puppio | TQA | s.t. |
| 12. | A. Peron | TNN | s.t. |
| 13. | M. Zahálka | EKA | s.t. |
| 14. | A. Stokbro | TQA | s.t. |
| 15. | M. Maestri | BCF | s.t. |
| 16. | E. Lunder | GAZ | s.t. |
| 17. | G. Brussenskiy | APT | s.t. |
| 18. | N. Märkl | DSM | s.t. |
| 19. | M. Budzinski | MSP | s.t. |
| 20. | D. Nekrasov | GAZ | s.t. |

### GENERAL CLASSIFICATION

| POS | NAME | TEAM | TIME |
|---|---|---|---|
| 1. — | A. J. Hodeg | DQT | 7:54:45 |
| 2. ↑4 | J. Steimle | DQT | 0:03 |
| 3. ↓1 | P. Sagan | BOH | 0:04 |

### KING OF THE MOUNTAINS

| POS | NAME | TEAM | PTS |
|---|---|---|---|
| 1. — | A. Garosio | BCF | 28 |
| 2. — | F. Dversnes | GAZ | 10 |
| 3. ↓1 | T. Budzinski | MSP | 8 |

### POINTS

| POS | NAME | TEAM | PTS |
|---|---|---|---|
| 1. ↑1 | A. J. Hodeg | DQT | 25 |
| 2. ↑2 | P. Sagan | BOH | 24 |
| 3. ↓2 | E. Lunder | GAZ | 16 |

### YOUNG RIDER

| POS | NAME | TEAM | TIME |
|---|---|---|---|
| 1. — | E. Lunder | GAZ | 7:54:57 |
| 2. ↑2 | I. Andersen | UXT | 0:03 |
| 3. ↓1 | L. Heinschke | DSM | 0:04 |

## TOUR DE SLOVAQUIE

Stage 3
18 September 2021
Dolný Kubín–Považská Bystrica
193.2km

### WEATHER

TEMPERATURE: 14°C
WIND: W 4km/h

### STAGE RESULTS

| POS | NAME | TEAM | TIME |
|---|---|---|---|
| 1. | K. Halvorsen | UXT | 4:28:47 |
| 2. | K. Groves | BEX | s.t. |
| 3. | P. Sagan | BOH | s.t. |
| 4. | A. J. Hodeg | DQT | s.t. |
| 5. | A. Puppio | TQA | s.t. |
| 6. | G. Lonardi | BCF | s.t. |
| 7. | I. Einhorn | ISN | s.t. |
| 8. | M. Mørkøv | DQT | s.t. |
| 9. | A. Toupalík | EKA | s.t. |
| 10. | D. Neuman | EKA | s.t. |
| 11. | E. Zanoncello | BCF | s.t. |
| 12. | J. Steimle | DQT | s.t. |
| 13. | N. Dalla Valle | BCF | s.t. |
| 14. | T. Bárta | TFA | s.t. |
| 15. | D. Martinelli | APT | s.t. |
| 16. | F. Galván | EKP | s.t. |
| 17. | A. Peron | TNN | s.t. |
| 18. | N. Vahtra | ISN | s.t. |
| 19. | R. Carretta | CTF | s.t. |
| 20. | C. Bol | DSM | s.t. |

### GENERAL CLASSIFICATION

| POS | NAME | TEAM | TIME |
|---|---|---|---|
| 1. ↑2 | P. Sagan | BOH | 12:23:30 |
| 2. ↓1 | A. J. Hodeg | DQT | 0:02 |
| 3. ↓1 | J. Steimle | DQT | 0:05 |

### KING OF THE MOUNTAINS

| POS | NAME | TEAM | PTS |
|---|---|---|---|
| 1. — | A. Garosio | BCF | 37 |
| 2. — | R. Adrià | EKP | 16 |
| 3. — | T. Budzinski | MSP | 13 |

### POINTS

| POS | NAME | TEAM | PTS |
|---|---|---|---|
| 1. ↑1 | P. Sagan | BOH | 38 |
| 2. ↓1 | A. J. Hodeg | DQT | 34 |
| 3. ↑4 | R. Adrià | EKP | 18 |

### YOUNG RIDER

| POS | NAME | TEAM | TIME |
|---|---|---|---|
| 1. — | E. Lunder | GAZ | 12:23:44 |
| 2. — | I. Andersen | UXT | 0:03 |
| 3. — | L. Heinschke | DSM | 0:04 |

# TOUR DE SLOVAQUIE

Stage 4
19 September 2021
Trenčianske Teplice–Trnava
159.2km

## WEATHER

TEMPERATURE: 15°C
WIND: N 22km/h

## STAGE RESULTS

| POS | NAME | TEAM | TIME |
|---|---|---|---|
| 1. | I. Einhorn | ISN | 3:27:40 |
| 2. | P. Sagan | BOH | s.t. |
| 3. | C. Bol | DSM | s.t. |
| 4. | J. Steimle | DQT | s.t. |
| 5. | K. Groves | BEX | s.t. |
| 6. | F. Felline | APT | s.t. |
| 7. | A. Konychev | BEX | s.t. |
| 8. | A. Stokbro | TQA | s.t. |
| 9. | A. Lutsenko | APT | s.t. |
| 10. | J. Kaczmarek | MSP | s.t. |
| 11. | A. Toupalík | EKA | s.t. |
| 12. | R. Adrià | EKP | s.t. |
| 13. | G. Petrelli | CTF | s.t. |
| 14. | I. Andersen | UXT | s.t. |
| 15. | D. Pozzovivo | TQA | s.t. |
| 16. | D. Strakhov | GAZ | s.t. |
| 17. | C. Pedersen | DSM | s.t. |
| 18. | D. Sunderland | TQA | s.t. |
| 19. | M. Kukrle | EKA | s.t. |
| 20. | C. Juul-Jensen | BEX | s.t. |

## GENERAL CLASSIFICATION

| POS | NAME | TEAM | TIME |
|---|---|---|---|
| 1. — | P. Sagan | BOH | 15:51:00 |
| 2. ↑1 | J. Steimle | DQT | 0:11 |
| 3. ↑5 | C. Bol | DSM | 0:17 |

## KING OF THE MOUNTAINS

| POS | NAME | TEAM | PTS |
|---|---|---|---|
| 1. — | A. Garosio | BCF | 37 |
| 2. — | R. Adrià | EKP | 16 |
| 3. — | T. Budzinski | MSP | 13 |

## POINTS

| POS | NAME | TEAM | PTS |
|---|---|---|---|
| 1. — | P. Sagan | BOH | 58 |
| 2. — | A. J. Hodeg | DQT | 34 |
| 3. ↑4 | J. Steimle | DQT | 32 |

## YOUNG RIDER

| POS | NAME | TEAM | TIME |
|---|---|---|---|
| 1. ↑1 | I. Andersen | UXT | 15:51:24 |
| 2. ↑3 | N. Märkl | DSM | 0:06 |
| 3. ↑12 | G. Petrelli | CTF | 1:09 |

## COPPA SABATINI

16 September 2021
Peccioli–Peccioli
210.8km

### WEATHER

TEMPERATURE: 27°C
WIND: S 22km/h

### RESULTS

| POS | NAME | TEAM | TIME |
|---|---|---|---|
| 1. | M. Valgren | EFN | 5:14:20 |
| 2. | S. Colbrelli | TBV | 0:03 |
| 3. | M. Burgaudeau | TEN | 0:06 |
| 4. | F. Baroncini | NAT | 0:09 |
| 5. | L. Rota | IWG | 0:11 |
| 6. | N. Powless | EFN | 0:17 |
| 7. | G. Moscon | IGD | 0:33 |
| 8. | A. Pedrero | MOV | 0:40 |
| 9. | A. Okamika | BBH | 1:25 |
| 10. | R. Guerreiro | EFN | 1:31 |
| 11. | D. Villella | MOV | 1:38 |
| 12. | S. Higuita | EFN | s.t. |
| 13. | A. Covi | UAD | s.t. |
| 14. | V. Albanese | EOK | s.t. |
| 15. | L. Chirico | ANS | s.t. |
| 16. | T. Geoghegan Hart | IGD | s.t. |
| 17. | A. Angulo | EUS | s.t. |
| 18. | D. Teuns | TBV | s.t. |
| 19. | S. Velasco | GAZ | s.t. |
| 20. | K. Sbaragli | NAT | s.t. |

SEPTEMBER .1 MEN'S RACE

## KAMPIOENSCHAP VAN VLAANDEREN
17 September 2021
Koolskamp–Koolskamp
195.3km

### WEATHER

TEMPERATURE: 19°C
WIND: SW 7km/h

### RESULTS

| POS | NAME | TEAM | TIME |
|---|---|---|---|
| 1. | J. Philipsen | AFC | 4:11:14 |
| 2. | D. Groenewegen | TJV | s.t. |
| 3. | M. Laas | BOH | s.t. |
| 4. | M. Moschetti | TFS | s.t. |
| 5. | N. Bonifazio | TEN | s.t. |
| 6. | B. Planckaert | IWG | s.t. |
| 7. | W. Krul | SEG | s.t. |
| 8. | M. Pluto | ABC | s.t. |
| 9. | N. Vandepitte | BWB | s.t. |
| 10. | S. Aniołkowski | BWB | s.t. |
| 11. | O. Kooij | TJV | s.t. |
| 12. | M. Picoux | XRL | s.t. |
| 13. | C. Stewart | BSC | s.t. |
| 14. | L. Taminiaux | AFC | s.t. |
| 15. | M. Van Staeyen | EVO | s.t. |
| 16. | G. D'heygere | TIS | s.t. |
| 17. | J. Plowright | BLN | s.t. |
| 18. | G. Nizzolo | TQA | s.t. |
| 19. | G. Thijssen | LTS | s.t. |
| 20. | C. Joyce | RLY | s.t. |

SEPTEMBER .PRO MEN'S RACE

# PRIMUS CLASSIC
18 September 2021
Brakel–Haacht
197.7km

## WEATHER

**TEMPERATURE**
22°C

**WIND**
SE 11km/h

## RESULTS

| POS | NAME | TEAM | TIME |
|---|---|---|---|
| 1. | F. Sénéchal | DQT | 4:34:05 |
| 2. | T. Van der Sande | LTS | s.t. |
| 3. | J. Stuyven | TFS | s.t. |
| 4. | M. F. Honoré | DQT | s.t. |
| 5. | S. Clarke | TQA | 0:04 |
| 6. | Y. Lampaert | DQT | s.t. |
| 7. | Z. Štybar | DQT | 1:00 |
| 8. | M. van der Poel | AFC | s.t. |
| 9. | G. Nizzolo | TQA | s.t. |
| 10. | D. Ballerini | DQT | s.t. |
| 11. | M. Louvel | ARK | s.t. |
| 12. | S. Dewulf | ACT | s.t. |
| 13. | H. Hofstetter | ISN | s.t. |
| 14. | S. Consonni | COF | s.t. |
| 15. | G. Aleotti | BOH | s.t. |
| 16. | O. Naesen | ACT | s.t. |
| 17. | M. Urianstad | UXT | s.t. |
| 18. | L. Naesen | ACT | s.t. |
| 19. | T. Van Asbroeck | ISN | s.t. |
| 20. | M. Gogl | TQA | s.t. |

SEPTEMBER .1 MEN'S RACE

# MEMORIAL MARCO PANTANI

18 September 2021
Castrocaro Terme e Terra del Sole–Cesenatico
190.7km

## WEATHER

**TEMPERATURE**
27°C

**WIND**
E 6km/h

## RESULTS

| POS | NAME | TEAM | TIME |
|---|---|---|---|
| 1. | S. Colbrelli | TBV | 4:50:29 |
| 2. | V. Albanese | EOK | s.t. |
| 3. | A. Aranburu | APT | s.t. |
| 4. | M. Trentin | UAD | s.t. |
| 5. | G. Martín | EUS | s.t. |
| 6. | K. Sbaragli | NAT | s.t. |
| 7. | D. Villella | MOV | s.t. |
| 8. | M. Burgaudeau | TEN | s.t. |
| 9. | T. Geoghegan Hart | IGD | s.t. |
| 10. | M. Bais | ANS | s.t. |
| 11. | S. Ravanelli | ANS | s.t. |
| 12. | V. Ferron | TEN | s.t. |
| 13. | D. Ulissi | UAD | s.t. |
| 14. | D. Gabburo | BCF | s.t. |
| 15. | M. Kudus | APT | 0:04 |
| 16. | A. Angulo | EUS | 0:07 |
| 17. | E. A. Rubio | MOV | s.t. |
| 18. | H. Pernsteiner | TBV | 0:11 |
| 19. | A. Piccolo | NAT | 0:15 |
| 20. | F. Doubey | TEN | 0:21 |

SEPTEMBER   WORLDTOUR MEN'S RACE

# ESCHBORN–FRANKFURT

19 September 2021
Eschborn–Frankfurt-am-Main
187.4km

## WEATHER

**TEMPERATURE**
18°C

**WIND**
NE 19km/h

## PROFILE

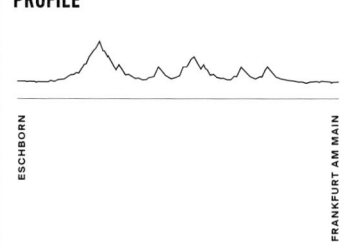

ESCHBORN — FRANKFURT AM MAIN

Eschborn–Frankfurt has ended in a bunch sprint more often than not in recent decades, and despite aggressive racing in the Taunus Hills, there was no stopping the German semi-Classic from following its established formula in 2021. A five-man breakaway escaped a few kilometres outside Eschborn and quickly found an advantage of over 6 minutes. After a fairly predictable 100km, only Luke Durbridge, Mathias Norsgaard and Simone Velasco remained at the front, with their gap dipping to around a minute. The final act began on the penultimate climb of the Mammolshainer Stich when Team BikeExchange initiated a volley of attacks from the peloton. The lift in pace put an end to the breakaway and saw a group of around 15 ride away from the bunch for the last climb. But their gap never exceeded a minute and the peloton chased them down on the flat 30km run-in. Only Georg Zimmermann (Intermarché-Wanty-Gobert Matériaux) and Cristian Scaroni (Gazprom-RusVelo) resisted the catch, and the sprint teams were content to dangle the pair out front until just inside 10km to go. The inevitable bunch sprint played out in front of the Alte Oper concert hall after three finishing laps, and it was John Degenkolb who made the first big acceleration in his home race. However, the in-form Jasper Philipsen was unmatched in the final gallop to the line, surging around the German to take victory at his first appearance. Four-time winner Alexander Kristoff settled for third.

## BREAKAWAY

M. Matthews (BEX), M. Teunissen (TJV), B. Hermans (ISN), L. Vervaeke (AFC), D. Teuns (TBV), G. Zimmerman (IWG), S. Oomen (TJV), C. Scaroni (GAZ), S. Velasco (GAZ), M. Fabbro (BOH), G. Brambilla (TFS), L. Durbridge (BEX), D. Touzé (ACT), L. Hamilton (BEX), S. Geschke (COF)

## RESULTS

| POS | NAME | TEAM | TIME |
|---|---|---|---|
| 1. | J. Philipsen | AFC | 4:28:03 |
| 2. | J. Degenkolb | LTS | s.t. |
| 3. | A. Kristoff | UAD | s.t. |
| 4. | A. Pasqualon | IWG | s.t. |
| 5. | P. Ackermann | BOH | s.t. |
| 6. | I. García Cortina | MOV | s.t. |
| 7. | C. Laporte | COF | s.t. |
| 8. | M. Teunissen | TJV | s.t. |
| 9. | M. Matthews | BEX | s.t. |
| 10. | F. Wright | TBV | s.t. |
| 11. | A. Skaarseth | UXT | s.t. |
| 12. | C. Beullens | SVB | s.t. |
| 13. | C. Swift | ARK | s.t. |
| 14. | A. Van Poucke | SVB | s.t. |
| 15. | M. Chevalier | BBK | s.t. |
| 16. | C. Gautier | BBK | s.l. |
| 17. | D. Touzé | ACT | s.t. |
| 18. | G. Van Avermaet | ACT | s.t. |
| 19. | L. Rota | IWG | s.t. |
| 20. | O. Goldstein | ISN | s.t. |

## TRIVIA

» There hasn't been a Belgian winner since 1992 (Frank Van Den Abeele), but in the previous 31 editions Belgium won 17 editions of the one-day race.

SEPTEMBER .1 MEN'S RACE

# TROFEO MATTEOTTI
19 September 2021
Pescara–Pescara
195km

## WEATHER

TEMPERATURE: 28°C
WIND: E 22km/h

## RESULTS

| POS | NAME | TEAM | TIME |
|---|---|---|---|
| 1. | M. Trentin | UAD | 4:40:15 |
| 2. | J. Restrepo | ANS | 0:21 |
| 3. | V. Ferron | TEN | s.t. |
| 4. | D. Villella | MOV | 0:51 |
| 5. | M. Govekar | TIR | 0:55 |
| 6. | S. Battistella | NAT | s.t. |
| 7. | S. Zoccarato | BCF | s.t. |
| 8. | S. Rivi | EOK | 2:59 |
| 9. | M. Bais | ANS | s.t. |
| 10. | F. Engelhardt | TIR | s.t. |
| 11. | A. Geniez | TEN | 3:19 |
| 12. | L. Colnaghi | BCF | 3:29 |
| 13. | K. Sbaragli | NAT | s.t. |
| 14. | A. Angulo | EUS | s.t. |
| 15. | P. Totò | AMO | s.t. |
| 16. | D. Orrico | THR | s.t. |
| 17. | G. Martín | EUS | s.t. |
| 18. | G. Garavaglia | IWM | s.t. |
| 19. | A. Riabushenko | UAD | s.t. |
| 20. | M. Baseggio | GEF | s.t. |

SEPTEMBER .1 MEN'S RACE

## GOOIKSE PIJL
19 September 2021
Halle–Gooik
199km

## WEATHER

TEMPERATURE: 20°C
WIND: NE 7km/h

### RESULTS

| POS | NAME | TEAM | TIME |
|---|---|---|---|
| 1. | F. Jakobsen | DQT | 4:21:48 |
| 2. | D. van Poppel | IWG | s.t. |
| 3. | J. Meeus | BOH | s.t. |
| 4. | A. Marit | SVB | s.t. |
| 5. | H. Hofstetter | ISN | s.t. |
| 6. | R. Barbier | ISN | s.t. |
| 7. | T. Van Asbroeck | ISN | s.t. |
| 8. | L. Taminiaux | AFC | s.t. |
| 9. | B. van der Kooij | VWE | s.t. |
| 10. | K. Aasvold | TCO | s.t. |
| 11. | W. Krul | SEG | s.t. |
| 12. | P. Stosz | VOS | s.t. |
| 13. | G. D'heygere | TIS | s.t. |
| 14. | L. Mudgway | BSC | s.t. |
| 15. | M. Van Staeyen | EVO | s.t. |
| 16. | S. Dehairs | AFC | s.t. |
| 17. | T. de Jong | VWE | s.t. |
| 18. | J. Reynders | SVB | s.t. |
| 19. | D. De Maeght | BWB | s.t. |
| 20. | S. Flynn | SEG | s.t. |

SEPTEMBER .1 MEN'S RACE

# GP D'ISBERGUES
19 September 2021
Isbergues–Isbergues
199.3km

## WEATHER

**TEMPERATURE**
22°C

**WIND**
NE 4km/h

## RESULTS

| POS | NAME | TEAM | TIME |
|---|---|---|---|
| 1. | E. Viviani | COF | 4:26:51 |
| 2. | T. Merlier | AFC | s.t. |
| 3. | A. Dainese | DSM | s.t. |
| 4. | B. Welten | ARK | s.t. |
| 5. | A. Démare | GFC | s.t. |
| 6. | J. Lecroq | BBK | s.t. |
| 7. | R. Cardis | AUB | s.t. |
| 8. | L. Naesen | ACT | s.t. |
| 9. | R. Minali | IWG | s.t. |
| 10. | G. Nizzolo | TQA | s.t. |
| 11. | B. Planckaert | IWG | s.t. |
| 12. | A. Renard | NAT | s.t. |
| 13. | J. Tesson | AUB | s.t. |
| 14. | M. Moschetti | TFS | s.t. |
| 15. | C. Noppe | ARK | s.t. |
| 16. | P. Penhoët | NAT | s.t. |
| 17. | S. Consonni | COF | s.t. |
| 18. | D. Godon | ACT | s.t. |
| 19. | L. Mozzato | BBK | s.t. |
| 20. | M. De Witte | XRL | s.t. |

SEPTEMBER  WORLD CHAMPIONSHIPS

## WORLD CHAMPIONSHIPS MEN'S ITT
19 September 2021
Knokke-Heist–Bruges
43.3km

### WEATHER

TEMPERATURE: 20°C
WIND: E 7km/h

### PROFILE

KNOKKE-HEIST — BRUGES

It was quite a feat of timing in his preparations which saw Filippo Ganna win the World Time Trial championship for the second time in a row. Only ten days previously, he had raced the European Championships in Trento, finishing 8 seconds behind Stefan Küng in the time trial and failing to finish the road race. Here, on the opening day of racing in Flanders, and over a course nearly twice as long, he reaped the benefit of a very short training camp between the two championships. In unusually benign conditions for late September in Belgium, Ganna delivered a duel with Wout van Aert that kept the host nation on the edge of its seat, and ultimately disappointed. Belgium has yet to win this race in its history, and only three Belgian men have ever won medals – Victor Campenaerts being the first to do so, with his bronze in 2018. The other two are Remco Evenepoel and Wout van Aert, who filled the podium places. Van Aert was just 6 seconds off Ganna's 54.37 kmph pace, but Evenepoel finished fully 44 seconds down in third place. Kasper Asgreen was only 2 seconds slower than Evenepoel, in fourth. With the race finishing in Bruges, the lifting of Covid restrictions on crowds in Belgium and the consequent noisy and considerable support lent the race a very welcome sense of normality.

### RESULTS

| POS | NAME | TEAM | TIME |
|---|---|---|---|
| 1. | F. Ganna | Italy | 47:47 |
| 2. | W. van Aert | Belgium | 0:06 |
| 3. | R. Evenepoel | Belgium | 0:44 |
| 4. | K. Asgreen | Denmark | 0:46 |
| 5. | S. Küng | Switzerland | 1:07 |
| 6. | T. Martin | Germany | 1:18 |
| 7. | S. Bissegger | Switzerland | 1:26 |
| 8. | E. Hayter | Great Britain | 1:27 |
| 9. | E. Affini | Italy | 1:49 |
| 10. | T. Pogačar | Slovenia | 1:53 |
| 11. | M. Walscheid | Germany | 1:54 |
| 12. | J. van Emden | Netherlands | s.t. |
| 13. | N. Oliveira | Portugal | 1:55 |
| 14. | R. Cavagna | France | 1:59 |
| 15. | J. Tratnik | Slovenia | 2:04 |
| 16. | D. Bigham | Great Britain | 2:11 |
| 17. | M. Bjerg | Denmark | 2:16 |
| 18. | L. Craddock | United States | 2:37 |
| 19. | R. Gibbons | South Africa | s.t. |
| 20. | H. Houle | Canada | 3:03 |
| 21. | M. Sobrero | Italy | 3:06 |
| 22. | B. McNulty | United States | 3:09 |
| 23. | T. Scully | New Zealand | 3:10 |
| 24. | M. Kwiatkowski | Poland | s.t. |
| 25. | C. Rodriguez | Spain | 3:24 |
| 26. | A. Leknessund | Norway | 3:27 |
| 27. | B. Thomas | France | 3:28 |
| 28. | A. Miltiadis | Cyprus | 3:30 |
| 29. | B. Peák | Hungary | 3:33 |
| 30. | R. Reis | Portugal | 3:35 |
| 31. | D. Gruzdev | Kazakhstan | 3:59 |
| 32. | J. Černý | Czech Republic | 4:00 |
| 33. | R. Mullen | Ireland | 4:12 |
| 34. | R. Urán | Colombia | 4:18 |
| 35. | O. Ilić | Serbia | 4:19 |
| 36. | D. Fominykh | Kazakhstan | 5:02 |
| 37. | F. Ritzinger | Austria | 5:08 |
| 38. | P. Rikunov | Russia | 5:10 |
| 39. | M. Christie | Ireland | 5:20 |
| 40. | M. Kononenko | Ukraine | 5:47 |
| 41. | C. R. Jurado | Panama | 6:10 |
| 42. | V. Lašinis | Lithuania | 6:25 |
| 43. | M. Halmuratov | Uzbekistan | 6:29 |
| 44. | F. Archibold | Panama | 6:48 |
| 45. | R. Kuba | Slovakia | 7:53 |
| 46. | R. Ö. Ágústsson | Iceland | 8:08 |
| 47. | N. Jaser | Syria | 8:20 |
| 48. | S. Sirironnachai | Thailand | 8:35 |
| 49. | S. Gyurov | Bulgaria | 9:12 |
| 50. | A. Sunnatov | Uzbekistan | 10:43 |
| 51. | F. Alkhater | Qatar | 10:57 |
| 52. | A. Jawaid | Pakistan | 11:06 |
| 53. | L. Tchambaz | Algeria | 11:43 |
| 54. | K. Amjad | Pakistan | 13:20 |
| 55. | C. Symonds | Ghana | 18:09 |

### TRIVIA

» Ganna is the second back-to-back winner (after Rohan Dennis in 2018 and 2019). Since 2019 the Belgians have also won the silver medal every time.

SEPTEMBER  WORLD CHAMPIONSHIPS

# WORLD CHAMPIONSHIPS WOMEN'S ITT
20 September 2021
Knokke-Heist–Bruges
30.3km

## WEATHER

| TEMPERATURE | WIND |
|---|---|
| 18°C | NE 15km/h |

## PROFILE

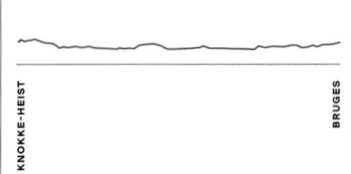

KNOKKE-HEIST — BRUGES

In a year of comeback stories, this was another. Ellen van Dijk – 34-year-old Dutch stalwart of the peloton, and the winner of this event once already in her long career (in 2013) – had to produce the ride of her life to get the better of newly crowned European TT champion Marlen Reusser, and Van Dijk's compatriot Annemiek van Vleuten who produced, in her words, the highest average power numbers she'd ever achieved. It was some race. Van Dijk went off early, had briefly to circumnavigate a rogue moped that appeared on the course, and set comfortably the best time. But Reusser – the silver medallist from 2020 – bettered her time at both of the checkpoints, only to fade over the final third of the course and finish 10 seconds off the pace. For Van Dijk, it was a remarkable double. Only nine days previously, she had soloed to victory in the European Championship road race, and had begun to feel as if her form was starting to return after she'd contracted Covid in March. That infection had called an early halt to her spring Classics campaign, and had also resulted in her missing out on selection for the Olympics. But, in late September, her tearful press conference was testament to what it meant to her to win a second world title. (NB)

## RESULTS

| POS | NAME | TEAM | TIME |
|---|---|---|---|
| 1. | E. van Dijk | Netherlands | 36:05 |
| 2. | M. Reusser | Switzerland | 0:10 |
| 3. | A. van Vleuten | Netherlands | 0:24 |
| 4. | A. Neben | United States | 1:24 |
| 5. | L. Brennauer | Germany | 1:29 |
| 6. | J. Labous | France | 1:47 |
| 7. | L. Klein | Germany | 1:52 |
| 8. | J. Lowden | Great Britain | 1:59 |
| 9. | R. Markus | Netherlands | s.t. |
| 10. | A. Amialiusik | Belarus | 2:19 |
| 11. | L. Kirchmann | Canada | 2:34 |
| 12. | E. Norsgaard | Denmark | 2:43 |
| 13. | K. A. Canuel | Canada | 2:48 |
| 14. | L. Thomas | United States | 2:50 |
| 15. | V. Kononenko | Ukraine | s.t. |
| 16. | A. Cordon-Ragot | France | 2:56 |
| 17. | A. Kiesenhofer | Austria | s.t. |
| 18. | N. Eklund | Sweden | 2:57 |
| 19. | E. Bujak | Slovenia | 2:59 |
| 20. | K. Karasiewicz | Poland | 3:04 |
| 21. | M. Jaskulska | Poland | 3:06 |
| 22. | J. Van De Velde | Belgium | 3:07 |
| 23. | O. Shapira | Israel | 3:15 |
| 24. | V. Guazzini | Italy | 3:17 |
| 25. | P. Georgi | Great Britain | 3:18 |
| 26. | G. Solovei | Ukraine | 3:30 |
| 27. | K. Aalerud | Norway | 3:31 |
| 28. | D. Rožlapa | Latvia | 3:38 |
| 29. | E. Pirrone | Italy | 4:08 |
| 30. | S. Van de Vel | Belgium | s.t. |
| 31. | R. Koerner | Denmark | s.t. |
| 32. | R. Gafinovitz | Israel | 4:19 |
| 33. | T. Dronova-Balabolina | Russia | 4:22 |
| 34. | L. M. Hernández | Colombia | s.t. |
| 35. | Z. Isasi | Spain | 4:31 |
| 36. | F. Yapura | Argentina | 4:33 |
| 37. | A. E. Bjornsdóttir | Iceland | 4:54 |
| 38. | F. Janse van Rensburg | South Africa | 5:16 |
| 39. | Y. Kuskova | Uzbekistan | 5:19 |
| 40. | H. Preen | South Africa | 5:36 |
| 41. | D. Campos | Portugal | 5:47 |
| 42. | L. Colmenares | Colombia | 6:15 |
| 43. | P. Somrat | Thailand | 6:44 |
| 44. | B. K. Gunnarsdóttir | Iceland | 7:07 |
| 45. | L. Roland | Argentina | 7:39 |
| 46. | A. Tesfalem | Eritrea | 8:43 |
| 47. | D. Ingabire | Rwanda | 9:12 |
| 48. | K. Malik | Pakistan | 14:49 |
| 49. | A. Jan | Pakistan | 15:44 |

## TRIVIA

» The Dutch have now claimed two medals in the women's time trial in each of the previous five women's TT events at the Worlds.

498

# MVDP v WVA

The rivalry between Mathieu van der Poel and Wout van Aert is one that is already well storied. Both have taken huge wins in careers that are really only just getting started at WorldTour level, and this summer at the Tour de France they took turns in dominating the biggest bike race on the planet. More often than not, it seems they're both competing at the pointy end, and the data backs this up. The statistics from a comparison of their head-to-head results illustrate just how dominant the pair are.

Number of road races the pair have raced together since their first, the 2014 Ronde van Limburg

**46**

Van der Poel has finished higher in 28 of the races the two have ridden

**28 v 18**

Of the 46 races, 15 have been won by either rider, Van der Poel taking nine and Van Aert winning six

**9 v 6**

No. of races abandoned by either rider when both on the start line (this year's TdF and the 2017 Baloise Belgium Tour)

**2**

Chances of either rider finishing in the top ten of a race when they're both on the start line

**78%**

Number of times both riders have been on the podium

**8**

Number of times they've finished 1-2 (Van der Poel has won twice)

**3**

Major victories

1 X RONDE VAN VLAANDEREN
1 X BINCKBANK TOUR
2 X AMSTEL GOLD RACE
2 X STRADE BIANCHE
1 X DWARS DOOR VLAANDEREN
5 X STAGE TIRRENO-ADRIATICO
7 X STAGE TOUR DE FRANCE
1 X TOUR OF BRITAIN
1 X MILANO-SANREMO
1 X GENT-WEVELGEM
3 X STAGE CRITÉRIUM DU DAUPHINÉ
1 X TOUR OF DENMARK

SEPTEMBER  WORLD CHAMPIONSHIPS

## WORLD CHAMPIONSHIPS WOMEN'S ROAD RACE
25 September 2021
Antwerp–Leuven
157.7km

### WEATHER

**TEMPERATURE**
20°C

**WIND**
SE 7km/h

### PROFILE

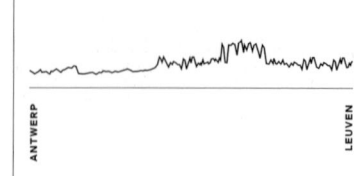

ANTWERP — LEUVEN

### BREAKAWAY
U. Bravek (SLO), F. Yapura (ARG)

The mighty Dutch had everything to lose, and everything to gain from this race. Having swapped most major honours among themselves for the previous few years, it felt like a matter of simply determining which 'van' or 'vos' would win. But, if the trajectory of 2021 had taught us anything, it was that the dominant team is not preordained to succeed, despite their numerical and physical advantages; there is always a way to disrupt the natural order. Perhaps the most telling of the various moments in the race was the inability of Annemiek van Vleuten to deliver a decisive blow. On a couple of occasions, the Olympic silver medallist attacked the front of a bunch from which the defending champion, Anna van der Breggen, had already been dropped. But rather than riding away, a succession of rivals from from a variety of nations (Italy, Denmark, etc) were able to follow her wheel and stifle her aggression. The closer to the finish line in Leuven, the more apparent it became that a diminished, elite group would be contesting some sort of a reduced sprint. The Dutch then went into their 'Plan Vos'. Banking on Marianne Vos's prodigious sprint, they stopped attacking and allowed Italy to take the race to the line. Elisa Longo Borghini produced another astonishingly strong ride to take her compatriot Elisa Balsamo close enough to the finish line to hold off – and ultimately convincingly beat – Vos for a wildly unexpected and emotional win. Vos, beaten within a few metres of victory, was uncharacteristically emotional in defeat. But Balsamo had never known success on anything approaching this scale.

### TRIVIA
» Elisa Balsamo is the first non-Dutch winner since 2016.

## RESULTS

| POS | NAME | TEAM | TIME |
|---|---|---|---|
| 1. | E. Balsamo | Italy | 3:52:27 |
| 2. | M. Vos | Netherlands | s.t. |
| 3. | K. Niewiadoma | Poland | 0:01 |
| 4. | K. B. Vas | Hungary | s.t. |
| 5. | A. Sierra | Cuba | s.t. |
| 6. | A. Jackson | Canada | s.t. |
| 7. | D. Vollering | Netherlands | s.t. |
| 8. | C. U. Ludwig | Denmark | s.t. |
| 9. | L. Brennauer | Germany | s.t. |
| 10. | C. Rivera | United States | s.t. |
| 11. | A. Moolman | South Africa | s.t. |
| 12. | A. Amialiusik | Belarus | s.t. |
| 13. | E. Chabbey | Switzerland | s.t. |
| 14. | E. Deignan | Great Britain | s.t. |
| 15. | S. Frei | Switzerland | s.t. |
| 16. | L. Kopecky | Belgium | s.t. |
| 17. | E. Longo Borghini | Italy | s.t. |
| 18. | E. van Dijk | Netherlands | 0:08 |
| 19. | A. van Vleuten | Netherlands | s.t. |
| 20. | M. Cavalli | Italy | 0:15 |
| 21. | R. Winder | United States | 0:17 |
| 22. | M. Bastianelli | Italy | s.t. |
| 23. | M. G. Confalonieri | Italy | 0:29 |
| 24. | R. Neylan | Australia | 0:45 |
| 25. | A. Henderson | Great Britain | 0:49 |
| 26. | E. Harris | New Zealand | s.t. |
| 27. | A. Cordon-Ragot | France | s.t. |
| 28. | Š. Kern | Slovenia | 0:50 |
| 29. | M. García | Spain | s.t. |
| 30. | A. Pieters | Netherlands | s.t. |
| 31. | K. A. Canuel | Canada | s.t. |
| 32. | C. van den Broek-Blaak | Netherlands | s.t. |
| 33. | C. Majerus | Luxembourg | s.t. |
| 34. | J. D'hoore | Belgium | 1:21 |
| 35. | P. Georgi | Great Britain | s.t. |
| 36. | L. Brand | Netherlands | 3:01 |
| 37. | F. Koch | Germany | 3:29 |
| 38. | S. Roy | Australia | 3:31 |
| 39. | A. Santesteban | Spain | s.t. |
| 40. | A. Shackley | Great Britain | s.t. |
| 41. | T. Cromwell | Australia | s.t. |
| 42. | P. A. Patiño | Colombia | s.t. |
| 43. | H. Nilsson | Sweden | s.t. |
| 44. | O. Shapira | Israel | s.t. |
| 45. | A. Biannic | France | 3:34 |
| 46. | J. Labous | France | s.t. |
| 47. | A. D. Ysland | Norway | 6:23 |
| 48. | J. Vandenbulcke | Belgium | 7:31 |
| 49. | E. Duval | France | s.t. |
| 50. | É. Muzic | France | s.t. |
| 51. | K. Kumiega | Poland | s.t. |
| 52. | K. Faulkner | United States | 8:22 |
| 53. | M. Lach | Poland | 8:50 |
| 54. | R. Leleivytė | Lithuania | s.t. |
| 55. | E. Merino | Spain | 8:55 |
| 56. | L. Thomas | United States | 9:13 |
| 57. | G. Solovei | Ukraine | s.t. |
| 58. | E. Bujak | Slovenia | s.t. |
| 59. | S. Bossuyt | Belgium | s.t. |
| 60. | J. Machačová | Czech Republic | s.t. |
| 61. | H. Preen | South Africa | s.t. |
| 62. | N. Rüegg | Switzerland | s.t. |
| 63. | L. Kirchmann | Canada | s.t. |
| 64. | M. Drummond | New Zealand | s.t. |
| 65. | A. Diderihsen | Denmark | s.t. |
| 66. | L. Klein | Germany | s.t. |
| 67. | S. Rijkes | Austria | s.t. |
| 68. | M. Jaskulska | Poland | s.t. |
| 69. | S. Martin | Spain | s.t. |
| 70. | A. Kolesava | Belarus | s.t. |
| 71. | T. Wiles | United States | s.t. |
| 72. | A. Nerlo | Poland | s.t. |
| 73. | N. Eklund | Sweden | s.t. |
| 74. | K. Hammes | Germany | s.t. |
| 75. | S. Andersen | Norway | s.t. |
| 76. | V. Demey | Belgium | s.t. |
| 77. | L. Oyarbide | Spain | s.t. |
| 78. | I. Gaskjenn | Norway | s.t. |
| 79. | J. Leth | Denmark | s.t. |
| 80. | S. Borgli | Norway | s.t. |
| 81. | S. Gutiérrez | Spain | s.t. |
| 82. | E. Norsgaard | Denmark | s.t. |
| 83. | K. Aalerud | Norway | s.t. |
| 84. | A. Barnes | Great Britain | s.t. |
| 85. | E. Yonamine | Japan | s.t. |
| 86. | R. Gafinovitz | Israel | s.t. |
| 87. | R. Kasper | Germany | 9:25 |
| 88. | L. L. Teutenberg | Germany | s.t. |
| 89. | A. van der Breggen | Netherlands | 9:30 |
| 90. | M. Reusser | Switzerland | s.t. |
| 91. | N. Fisher-Black | New Zealand | s.t. |
| 92. | L. Hanson | Australia | s.t. |
| 93. | A. Spratt | Australia | s.t. |
| 94. | V. Guazzini | Italy | s.t. |
| 95. | E. Cecchini | Italy | s.t. |
| 96. | M. Jensen | Denmark | 13:21 |
| 97. | K. Karasiewicz | Poland | s.t. |
| 98. | D. Peñuela | Colombia | s.t. |
| 99. | L. Y. Salazar | Mexico | s.t. |
| 100. | P. Somrat | Thailand | s.t. |
| 101. | J. Borgström | Sweden | s.t. |
| 102. | T. Holmsgaard | Denmark | s.t. |
| 103. | D. Campos | Portugal | s.t. |
| 104. | C. Schweinberger | Austria | s.t. |
| 105. | C. Baur | Switzerland | s.t. |
| 106. | L. Stephens | United States | s.t. |
| 107. | V. Kononenko | Ukraine | s.t. |
| 108. | D. Rožlapa | Latvia | s.t. |
| 109. | R. Fournier | France | s.t. |
| 110. | J. Erić | Serbia | s.t. |
| 111. | J. Allen | Australia | s.t. |
| 112. | F. Janse van Rensburg | South Africa | 18:47 |
| 113. | Y. Biriukova | Ukraine | s.t. |
| 114. | Y. Kuskova | Uzbekistan | s.t. |
| 115. | I. Češulienė | Lithuania | s.t. |
| 116. | N. Berton | Luxembourg | 22:01 |
| 117. | L. Colmenares | Colombia | s.t. |

SEPTEMBER

SEPTEMBER  WORLD CHAMPIONSHIPS

## WORLD CHAMPIONSHIPS MEN'S ROAD RACE
26 September 2021
Antwerp–Leuven
268.3km

### WEATHER

**TEMPERATURE**
21°C

**WIND**
S 11km/h

### PROFILE

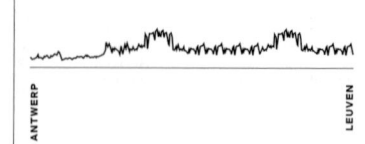

ANTWERP — LEUVEN

### BREAKAWAY
R. Townsend (IRE), J. T. Hernandez (COL), J. Burbano (ECU), P. Kochetkov (RCF), P. Gamper (AUT), O. Nisu (EST), K. Magnusson (SWE), J. Sainbayar (MNG)

One more day of late-summer sunshine in Flanders, as Belgium expected with unusual belief that Wout van Aert would be crowned their first World Champion in a decade. It wasn't to be. Despite the wild exhortations of a sun-kissed crowd wielding Flandrian signs into the warm autumn air, and despite the extraordinary contribution of Remco Evenepoel, who tried for over 100km in one attack after another to rip up the race and put it beyond the reach of the other nations, there was one rider who was once again unanswerable. Julian Alaphilippe was a constant, waspish presence at the front of a group of favourites that he knew he dare not take to the line. So, having attacked and attacked, he attacked once more; this time with 17km to go on the wheel of his excellent French teammate Valentin Madouas. Once the Breton could do no more, Alaphilippe soloed and was not seen again. The chase quartet soon gave up heart, and the prestige duo of Van der Poel and Van Aert were stranded and breathless in the third group. By 10km to go, it was done. The Frenchman had earned his rainbow bands in a vacuum in 2020, at a deserted motor track in Italy. Now, he doubled up in front of the most knowledgeable and fervent supporters in the world. Though he had torn up the team's tactics, he had proven once again that his spirit of improvisation and risk is unmatched in the world.

### TRIVIA
» Julian Alaphilippe is the first Frenchman to claim the rainbow jersey twice.

## RESULTS

| POS | NAME | TEAM | TIME |
|---|---|---|---|
| 1. | J. Alaphilippe | France | 5:56:34 |
| 2. | D. van Baarle | Netherlands | 0:32 |
| 3. | M. Valgren | Denmark | s.t. |
| 4. | J. Stuyven | Belgium | s.t. |
| 5. | N. Powless | United States | s.t. |
| 6. | T. Pidcock | Great Britain | 0:49 |
| 7. | Z. Štybar | Czech Republic | 1:06 |
| 8. | M. van der Poel | Netherlands | 1:18 |
| 9. | F. Sénéchal | France | s.t. |
| 10. | S. Colbrelli | Italy | s.t. |
| 11. | W. van Aert | Belgium | s.t. |
| 12. | M. Hoelgaard | Norway | s.t. |
| 13. | V. Madouas | France | s.t. |
| 14. | M. Mohorič | Slovenia | 4:00 |
| 15. | G. Nizzolo | Italy | 4:05 |
| 16. | N. Politt | Germany | 5:25 |
| 17. | G. Boivin | Canada | s.t. |
| 18. | J. Polanc | Slovenia | s.t. |
| 19. | B. Cosnefroy | France | 5:30 |
| 20. | V. Campenaerts | Belgium | s.t. |
| 21. | A. Kristoff | Norway | 6:27 |
| 22. | M. Teunissen | Netherlands | s.t. |
| 23. | I. García Cortina | Spain | s.t. |
| 24. | D. Ulissi | Italy | s.t. |
| 25. | M. Matthews | Australia | s.t. |
| 26. | P. Sagan | Slovakia | s.t. |
| 27. | D. Teuns | Belgium | s.t. |
| 28. | S. Schönberger | Austria | s.t. |
| 29. | B. Mollema | Netherlands | s.t. |
| 30. | L. Mezgec | Slovenia | s.t. |
| 31. | T. Benoot | Belgium | s.t. |
| 32. | P. Vakoč | Czech Republic | s.t. |
| 33. | S. E. Bystrøm | Norway | s.t. |
| 34. | V. S. Laengen | Norway | s.t. |
| 35. | E. Hayter | Great Britain | s.t. |
| 36. | M. Kwiatkowski | Poland | s.t. |
| 37. | T. Pogačar | Slovenia | s.t. |
| 38. | P. Gamper | Austria | s.t. |
| 39. | R. Oliveira | Portugal | s.t. |
| 40. | A. Nych | Russia | 6:31 |
| 41. | S. Küng | Switzerland | s.t. |
| 42. | G. Izaguirre | Spain | s.t. |
| 43. | I. Erviti | Spain | s.t. |
| 44. | G. Serrano | Spain | s.t. |
| 45. | S. Dillier | Switzerland | s.t. |
| 46. | C. Benedetti | Poland | s.t. |
| 47. | J. Almeida | Portugal | s.t. |
| 48. | P. Roglič | Slovenia | s.t. |
| 49. | Y. Arashiro | Japan | s.t. |
| 50. | M. Kudus | Eritrea | s.t. |
| 51. | R. Tiller | Norway | s.t. |
| 52. | E. Liepiņš | Latvia | s.t. |
| 53. | C. Rodriguez | Spain | 6:39 |
| 54. | M. Gogl | Austria | 6:40 |
| 55. | N. Oliveira | Portugal | s.t. |
| 56. | A. Démare | France | 6:48 |
| 57. | L. Craddock | United States | 6:49 |
| 58. | G. Moscon | Italy | 6:52 |
| 59. | R. Adrià | Spain | 7:04 |
| 60. | T. Skujiņš | Latvia | 7:07 |
| 61. | Y. Lampaert | Belgium | 7:22 |
| 62. | R. Evenepoel | Belgium | s.t. |
| 63. | F. Lienhard | Switzerland | 15:43 |
| 64. | E. Chaves | Colombia | s.t. |
| 65. | N. Soto | Colombia | 17:18 |
| 66. | P. Eenkhoorn | Netherlands | s.t. |
| 67. | N. Arndt | Germany | s.t. |
| 68. | G. Zimmermann | Germany | s.t. |

SEPTEMBER .PRO MEN'S RACE

# GP DE DENAIN

21 September 2021
Denain–Denain
200.3km

## WEATHER

**TEMPERATURE**
18°C

**WIND**
NE 15km/h

## RESULTS

| POS | NAME | TEAM | TIME |
| --- | --- | --- | --- |
| 1. | J. Philipsen | AFC | 4:40:44 |
| 2. | J. Meeus | BOH | s.t. |
| 3. | B. Swift | IGD | s.t. |
| 4. | H. Hofstetter | ISN | s.t. |
| 5. | T. Van Asbroeck | ISN | s.t. |
| 6. | A. Démare | GFC | s.t. |
| 7. | K. Van Rooy | SVB | s.t. |
| 8. | B. Planckaert | IWG | s.t. |
| 9. | P. Allegaert | COF | s.t. |
| 10. | J. Debusschere | BBK | s.t. |
| 11. | J. Reynders | SVB | s.t. |
| 12. | A. Jensen | DKO | s.t. |
| 13. | B. Welten | ARK | s.t. |
| 14. | N. Zukowsky | RLY | s.t. |
| 15. | A. De Gendt | IWG | s.t. |
| 16. | S. Leroux | XRL | s.t. |
| 17. | E. N. Resell | UXT | s.t. |
| 18. | T. Wirtgen | BWB | s.t. |
| 19. | L. Robeet | BWB | s.t. |
| 20. | D. Rajović | DKO | s.t. |

SEPTEMBER .1 MEN'S RACE

## OMLOOP VAN HET HOUTLAND MIDDELKERKE–LICHTERVELDE

23 September 2021

Middelkerke–Lichtervelde

190km

### WEATHER

TEMPERATURE
18°C

WIND
W 30km/h

### RESULTS

| POS | NAME | TEAM | TIME |
|---|---|---|---|
| 1. | T. van der Hoorn | IWG | 3:57:19 |
| 2. | D. van Poppel | IWG | 0:04 |
| 3. | G. Thijssen | LTS | s.t. |
| 4. | T. Dupont | BWB | s.t. |
| 5. | A. Dainese | DSM | s.t. |
| 6. | A. de Kleijn | RLY | s.t. |
| 7. | C. Stewart | BSC | s.t. |
| 8. | A. Marit | SVB | s.t. |
| 9. | G. D'heygere | TIS | s.t. |
| 10. | E. Blikra | UXT | s.t. |
| 11. | S. Aniołkowski | BWB | s.t. |
| 12. | S. Flynn | SEG | s.t. |
| 13. | M. Van Staeyen | EVO | s.t. |
| 14. | T. Joseph | TIS | s.t. |
| 15. | S. De Bie | BWB | s.t. |
| 16. | S. Siemons | EVO | s.t. |
| 17. | V. Broex | MET | s.t. |
| 18. | M. Zijlaard | SEG | s.t. |
| 19. | J. W. van Schip | BCY | s.t. |
| 20. | D. De Bondt | AFC | s.t. |

SEPTEMBER .1 MEN'S RACE

# PARIS–CHAUNY
26 September 2021
Margny-lès-Compiègne–Chauny
205.3km

## WEATHER

TEMPERATURE: 21°C
WIND: SW 19km/h

## RESULTS

| POS | NAME | TEAM | TIME |
|---|---|---|---|
| 1. | J. Philipsen | AFC | 4:30:38 |
| 2. | A. Dainese | DSM | s.t. |
| 3. | A. Pasqualon | IWG | s.t. |
| 4. | N. Bouhanni | ARK | s.t. |
| 5. | A. de Kleijn | RLY | s.t. |
| 6. | J. Tesson | AUB | s.t. |
| 7. | A. Banaszek | MSP | s.t. |
| 8. | L. Naesen | ACT | s.t. |
| 9. | C. Barthe | BBK | s.t. |
| 10. | G. D'heygere | TIS | s.t. |
| 11. | B. Welten | ARK | s.t. |
| 12. | R. Cardis | AUB | s.t. |
| 13. | L. Rex | BWB | s.t. |
| 14. | L. Teugels | TIS | 0:05 |
| 15. | J. Kaczmarek | MSP | s.t. |
| 16. | N. Eekhoff | DSM | s.t. |
| 17. | M. Urruty | XRL | 0:09 |
| 18. | G. Soupe | TEN | 0:10 |
| 19. | J. Castrique | BWB | s.t. |
| 20. | N. Vandepitte | BWB | 0:11 |

SEPTEMBER .1 MEN'S RACE

## GIRO DI SICILIA
Stage 1
28 September 2021
Avola–Licata
179km

### STAGE RESULTS

| POS | NAME | TEAM | TIME |
|---|---|---|---|
| 1. | J. S. Molano | UAD | 4:37:21 |
| 2. | V. Albanese | EOK | s.t. |
| 3. | A. M. Richeze | UAD | s.t. |
| 4. | M. Moschetti | TFS | s.t. |
| 5. | F. Fiorelli | BCF | s.t. |
| 6. | J. Mareczko | THR | s.t. |
| 7. | A. Guardini | GTS | s.t. |
| 8. | M. Belletti | EOK | s.t. |
| 9. | F. Di Felice | MGK | s.t. |
| 10. | J. Restrepo | ANS | s.t. |
| 11. | D. Cima | GAZ | s.t. |
| 12. | L. Colnaghi | BCF | s.t. |
| 13. | M. Gazzoli | CPK | s.t. |
| 14. | D. González | CJR | s.t. |
| 15. | K. Vermaerke | DSM | s.t. |
| 16. | S. Velasco | GAZ | s.t. |
| 17. | M. Frapporti | EOK | s.t. |
| 18. | J. J. Rojas | MOV | s.t. |
| 19. | N. Nesi | AZT | s.t. |
| 20. | R. Bardet | DSM | s.t. |

### WEATHER

TEMPERATURE: 28°C
WIND: W 20km/h

### GENERAL CLASSIFICATION

| POS | NAME | TEAM | TIME |
|---|---|---|---|
| 1. | J. S. Molano | UAD | 4:37:11 |
| 2. | V. Albanese | EOK | 0:04 |
| 3. | A. M. Richeze | UAD | 0:06 |

### KING OF THE MOUNTAINS

| POS | NAME | TEAM | PTS |
|---|---|---|---|
| 1. | C. E. Chrétien | RLY | 5 |
| 2. | M. Zurlo | ZEF | 3 |
| 3. | J. Cortese | MGK | 2 |

### POINTS

| POS | NAME | TEAM | PTS |
|---|---|---|---|
| 1. | J. S. Molano | UAD | 12 |
| 2. | V. Albanese | EOK | 10 |
| 3. | A. M. Richeze | UAD | 8 |

### YOUNG RIDER

| POS | NAME | TEAM | TIME |
|---|---|---|---|
| 1. | V. Albanese | EOK | 4:37:15 |
| 2. | M. Zurlo | ZEF | 0:03 |
| 3. | C. E. Chrétien | RLY | 0:04 |

---

## GIRO DI SICILIA
Stage 2
29 September 2021
Selinunte–Mondello
173km

### STAGE RESULTS

| POS | NAME | TEAM | TIME |
|---|---|---|---|
| 1. | J. S. Molano | UAD | 4:25:41 |
| 2. | M. Moschetti | TFS | s.t. |
| 3. | J. Mareczko | THR | s.t. |
| 4. | E. Onesti | GTS | s.t. |
| 5. | M. Belletti | EOK | s.t. |
| 6. | F. Carollo | MGK | s.t. |
| 7. | S. Zambelli | ANS | s.t. |
| 8. | N. Nesi | AZT | s.t. |
| 9. | O. Goldstein | ISN | s.t. |
| 10. | M. Bais | ANS | s.t. |
| 11. | L. Colnaghi | BCF | s.t. |
| 12. | D. González | CJR | s.t. |
| 13. | A. Guardini | GTS | s.t. |
| 14. | J. Aranburu | EUS | s.t. |
| 15. | P. Simion | GTS | s.t. |
| 16. | F. Di Felice | MGK | s.t. |
| 17. | A. M. Richeze | UAD | s.t. |
| 18. | C. Scaroni | GAZ | s.t. |
| 19. | A. Serrano | CJR | s.t. |
| 20. | M. Skjelmose Jensen | TFS | s.t. |

### WEATHER

TEMPERATURE: 27°C
WIND: NW 13km/h

### GENERAL CLASSIFICATION

| POS | NAME | TEAM | TIME |
|---|---|---|---|
| 1. — | J. S. Molano | UAD | 9:02:42 |
| 2. ↑6 | M. Moschetti | TFS | 0:14 |
| 3. ↓1 | V. Albanese | EOK | s.t. |

### KING OF THE MOUNTAINS

| POS | NAME | TEAM | PTS |
|---|---|---|---|
| 1. — | S. Gandin | ZEF | 8 |
| 2. — | T. Juaristi | EUS | 8 |
| 3. ↓2 | C. E. Chrétien | RLY | 5 |

### POINTS

| POS | NAME | TEAM | PTS |
|---|---|---|---|
| 1. — | J. S. Molano | UAD | 24 |
| 2. ↑2 | M. Moschetti | TFS | 17 |
| 3. ↑4 | J. Mareczko | THR | 13 |

### YOUNG RIDER

| POS | NAME | TEAM | TIME |
|---|---|---|---|
| 1. ↑4 | M. Moschetti | TFS | 9:02:56 |
| 2. ↓1 | V. Albanese | EOK | s.t. |
| 3. ↓1 | M. Zurlo | ZEF | 0:03 |

SEPTEMBER .1 MEN'S RACE

## GIRO DI SICILIA
Stage 3
30 September 2021
Termini Imerese–Caronia
180km

### STAGE RESULTS

| POS | NAME | TEAM | TIME |
|---|---|---|---|
| 1. | A. Valverde | MOV | 4:42:29 |
| 2. | A. Covi | UAD | s.t. |
| 3. | J. Restrepo | ANS | s.t. |
| 4. | S. Velasco | GAZ | s.t. |
| 5. | R. Bardet | DSM | s.t. |
| 6. | C. Scaroni | GAZ | s.t. |
| 7. | L. Fortunato | EOK | s.t. |
| 8. | B. McNulty | UAD | s.t. |
| 9. | A. Martinelli | CPK | s.t. |
| 10. | N. Eg | TFS | s.t. |
| 11. | V. Nibali | TFS | s.t. |
| 12. | M. Bais | ANS | s.t. |
| 13. | K. Murphy | RLY | s.t. |
| 14. | T. Arensman | DSM | s.t. |
| 15. | D. Gabburo | BCF | s.t. |
| 16. | O. Goldstein | ISN | 0:10 |
| 17. | J. Cepeda Ortiz | ANS | s.t. |
| 18. | S. R. Martín | CJR | s.t. |
| 19. | D. Villella | MOV | s.t. |
| 20. | S. Ravanelli | ANS | s.t. |

### WEATHER

TEMPERATURE: 25°C
WIND: N 17km/h

### GENERAL CLASSIFICATION

| POS | NAME | TEAM | TIME |
|---|---|---|---|
| 1. ↑54 | A. Valverde | MOV | 13:45:18 |
| 2. ↑66 | A. Covi | UAD | 0:07 |
| 3. ↑22 | J. Restrepo | ANS | 0:09 |

### KING OF THE MOUNTAINS

| POS | NAME | TEAM | PTS |
|---|---|---|---|
| 1. — | B. King | RLY | 30 |
| 2. — | A. Valverde | MOV | 20 |
| 3. — | C. Scaroni | GAZ | 20 |

### POINTS

| POS | NAME | TEAM | PTS |
|---|---|---|---|
| 1. — | J. S. Molano | UAD | 24 |
| 2. ↑21 | A. Valverde | MOV | 18 |
| 3. ↓1 | M. Moschetti | TFS | 17 |

### YOUNG RIDER

| POS | NAME | TEAM | TIME |
|---|---|---|---|
| 1. ↑38 | A. Covi | UAD | 13:45:25 |
| 2. ↑10 | M. Bais | ANS | 0:06 |
| 3. ↑16 | A. Martinelli | CPK | s.t. |

## GIRO DI SICILIA
Stage 4
1 October 2021
Sant'Agata di Militello–Mascali
180km

### STAGE RESULTS

| POS | NAME | TEAM | TIME |
|---|---|---|---|
| 1. | V. Nibali | TFS | 4:24:29 |
| 2. | S. Ravanelli | ANS | 0:49 |
| 3. | A. Covi | UAD | s.t. |
| 4. | R. Bardet | DSM | s.t. |
| 5. | J. Restrepo | ANS | s.t. |
| 6. | A. Valverde | MOV | s.t. |
| 7. | S. Velasco | GAZ | s.t. |
| 8. | L. Fortunato | EOK | s.t. |
| 9. | T. Arensman | DSM | s.t. |
| 10. | D. de la Cruz | UAD | s.t. |
| 11. | D. Villella | MOV | s.t. |
| 12. | N. Eg | TFS | s.t. |
| 13. | A. Nibali | TFS | s.t. |
| 14. | M. Bizkarra | EUS | s.t. |
| 15. | M. Bais | ANS | 2:09 |
| 16. | J. Piccoli | ISN | s.t. |
| 17. | E. Sepúlveda | ANS | s.t. |
| 18. | O. Goldstein | ISN | 3:02 |
| 19. | M. Tizza | AMO | s.t. |
| 20. | D. Gabburo | BCF | s.t. |

### WEATHER

TEMPERATURE: 26°C
WIND: E 22km/h

### GENERAL CLASSIFICATION

| POS | NAME | TEAM | TIME |
|---|---|---|---|
| 1. ↑9 | V. Nibali | TFS | 18:09:50 |
| 2. ↓1 | A. Valverde | MOV | 0:46 |
| 3. ↓1 | A. Covi | UAD | 0:49 |

### KING OF THE MOUNTAINS

| POS | NAME | TEAM | PTS |
|---|---|---|---|
| 1. ↑2 | C. Scaroni | GAZ | 45 |
| 2. — | A. Valverde | MOV | 32 |
| 3. ↓2 | B. King | RLY | 30 |

### POINTS

| POS | NAME | TEAM | PTS |
|---|---|---|---|
| 1. — | J. S. Molano | UAD | 24 |
| 2. — | A. Valverde | MOV | 23 |
| 3. ↑2 | A. Covi | UAD | 18 |

### YOUNG RIDER

| POS | NAME | TEAM | TIME |
|---|---|---|---|
| 1. — | A. Covi | UAD | 18:10:39 |
| 2. ↑3 | T. Arensman | DSM | 0:10 |
| 3. ↑3 | L. Fortunato | EOK | s.t. |

SEPTEMBER .1 MEN'S RACE

## CRO RACE
Stage 1
28 September 2021
Osijek–Varaždin
237km

### STAGE RESULTS

| POS | NAME | TEAM | TIME |
|---|---|---|---|
| 1. | P. Bauhaus | TBV | 5:52:06 |
| 2. | O. Kooij | TJV | s.t. |
| 3. | K. Halvorsen | UXT | s.t. |
| 4. | A. Angulo | EUS | s.t. |
| 5. | M. van Dijke | TJV | s.t. |
| 6. | I. Einhorn | ISN | s.t. |
| 7. | M. Aschenbrenner | PUS | s.t. |
| 8. | G. Martín | EUS | s.t. |
| 9. | M. Menten | BWB | s.t. |
| 10. | D. Per | ADR | s.t. |
| 11. | S. Janiszewski | VOS | s.t. |
| 12. | A. Skaarseth | UXT | s.t. |
| 13. | R. Carretta | CTF | s.t. |
| 14. | J. Rumac | ANS | s.t. |
| 15. | D. Auer | WSA | s.t. |
| 16. | R. Thalmann | VBG | s.t. |
| 17. | A. Peron | TNN | s.t. |
| 18. | J. Kaczmarek | MSP | s.t. |
| 19. | N. Buratti | CTF | s.t. |
| 20. | S. Oomen | TJV | s.t. |

### WEATHER

TEMPERATURE: 20°C
WIND: W 11km/h

### GENERAL CLASSIFICATION

| POS | NAME | TEAM | TIME |
|---|---|---|---|
| 1. | P. Bauhaus | TBV | 5:51:56 |
| 2. | O. Kooij | TJV | 0:04 |
| 3. | K. Halvorsen | UXT | 0:05 |

### KING OF THE MOUNTAINS

| POS | NAME | TEAM | PTS |
|---|---|---|---|
| 1. | M. Boguslawski | MSP | 3 |
| 2. | F. Miholjević | CTF | 2 |
| 3. | P. Franczak | VOS | 1 |

### POINTS

| POS | NAME | TEAM | PTS |
|---|---|---|---|
| 1. | P. Bauhaus | TBV | 25 |
| 2. | O. Kooij | TJV | 20 |
| 3. | K. Halvorsen | UXT | 17 |

### YOUNG RIDER

| POS | NAME | TEAM | TIME |
|---|---|---|---|
| 1. | O. Kooij | TJV | 5:52:00 |
| 2. | F. Miholjević | CTF | 0:03 |
| 3. | M. van Dijke | TJV | 0:06 |

---

## CRO RACE
Stage 2
29 September 2021
Slunj–Otočac
187km

### STAGE RESULTS

| POS | NAME | TEAM | TIME |
|---|---|---|---|
| 1. | O. Kooij | TJV | 4:22:07 |
| 2. | I. Einhorn | ISN | s.t. |
| 3. | K. Groves | BEX | s.t. |
| 4. | J. Aberasturi | CJR | s.t. |
| 5. | D. Auer | WSA | s.t. |
| 6. | L. Marchiori | ANS | s.t. |
| 7. | M. Menten | BWB | s.t. |
| 8. | A. Angulo | EUS | s.t. |
| 9. | G. Martín | EUS | s.t. |
| 10. | K. Halvorsen | UXT | s.t. |
| 11. | C. Rocchetta | ANS | s.t. |
| 12. | P. Bauhaus | TBV | s.t. |
| 13. | V. Götzinger | WSA | s.t. |
| 14. | M. Paterski | VOS | s.t. |
| 15. | Ž. Grošelj | RSW | s.t. |
| 16. | D. Peyskens | BWB | s.t. |
| 17. | D. Per | ADR | s.t. |
| 18. | M. Aschenbrenner | PUS | s.t. |
| 19. | A. Peron | TNN | s.t. |
| 20. | N. Buratti | CTF | s.t. |

### WEATHER

TEMPERATURE: 21°C
WIND: E 4km/h

### GENERAL CLASSIFICATION

| POS | NAME | TEAM | TIME |
|---|---|---|---|
| 1. ↑1 | O. Kooij | TJV | 10:13:57 |
| 2. ↓1 | P. Bauhaus | TBV | 0:06 |
| 3. ↑9 | I. Einhorn | ISN | 0:10 |

### KING OF THE MOUNTAINS

| POS | NAME | TEAM | PTS |
|---|---|---|---|
| 1. — | M. Budzinski | MSP | 10 |
| 2. — | J. Castrillo | EKP | 6 |
| 3. — | D. Röber | PUS | 4 |

### POINTS

| POS | NAME | TEAM | PTS |
|---|---|---|---|
| 1. ↑1 | O. Kooij | TJV | 45 |
| 2. ↑4 | I. Einhorn | ISN | 30 |
| 3. ↓2 | P. Bauhaus | TBV | 29 |

### YOUNG RIDER

| POS | NAME | TEAM | TIME |
|---|---|---|---|
| 1. — | O. Kooij | TJV | 10:13:57 |
| 2. — | F. Miholjević | CTF | 0:13 |
| 3. ↑9 | S. Novikov | EKP | 0:14 |

SEPTEMBER .1 MEN'S RACE

# CRO RACE
Stage 3
30 September 2021
Primošten–Makarska
167km

## WEATHER

TEMPERATURE | WIND
28°C | NE 11km/h

## STAGE RESULTS

| POS | NAME | TEAM | TIME |
|---|---|---|---|
| 1. | M. Menten | BWB | 3:58:33 |
| 2. | M. van Dijke | TJV | s.t. |
| 3. | A. Skaarseth | UXT | s.t. |
| 4. | J. Rumac | ANS | s.t. |
| 5. | S. Williams | TBV | s.t. |
| 6. | M. Hoelgaard | UXT | s.t. |
| 7. | A. Bajc | RSW | s.t. |
| 8. | C. Stüssi | VBG | s.t. |
| 9. | A. Angulo | EUS | s.t. |
| 10. | R. Thalmann | VBG | s.t. |
| 11. | K. Groves | BEX | s.t. |
| 12. | J. Kaczmarek | MSP | s.t. |
| 13. | G. Martín | EUS | s.t. |
| 14. | A. Charmig | UXT | s.t. |
| 15. | M. Paterski | VOS | s.t. |
| 16. | M. Friedrich | RSW | s.t. |
| 17. | G. Glivar | ADR | s.t. |
| 18. | L. Wirtgen | BWB | s.t. |
| 19. | Ž. Grošelj | RSW | s.t. |
| 20. | K. Molly | BWB | s.t. |

## GENERAL CLASSIFICATION

| POS | NAME | TEAM | TIME |
|---|---|---|---|
| 1. ↑16 | M. Menten | BWB | 14:12:34 |
| 2. ↑8 | A. Skaarseth | UXT | 0:03 |
| 3. ↑19 | M. van Dijke | TJV | 0:06 |

## KING OF THE MOUNTAINS

| POS | NAME | TEAM | PTS |
|---|---|---|---|
| 1. — | T. Træen | UXT | 12 |
| 2. ↓1 | M. Budzinski | MSP | 10 |
| 3. — | S. Oomen | TJV | 8 |

## POINTS

| POS | NAME | TEAM | PTS |
|---|---|---|---|
| 1. — | O. Kooij | TJV | 45 |
| 2. ↑4 | M. Menten | BWB | 44 |
| 3. ↑8 | M. van Dijke | TJV | 32 |

## YOUNG RIDER

| POS | NAME | TEAM | TIME |
|---|---|---|---|
| 1. ↑5 | M. van Dijke | TJV | 14:12:40 |
| 2. ↑2 | D. Röber | PUS | 0:04 |
| 3. ↑13 | G. Glivar | ADR | 0:06 |

# CRO RACE
Stage 4
1 October 2021
Zadar–Crikvenica
197km

## WEATHER

TEMPERATURE | WIND
23°C | W 7km/h

## STAGE RESULTS

| POS | NAME | TEAM | TIME |
|---|---|---|---|
| 1. | O. Kooij | TJV | 4:49:16 |
| 2. | K. Groves | BEX | s.t. |
| 3. | J. Rumac | ANS | s.t. |
| 4. | M. Paterski | VOS | s.t. |
| 5. | I. Einhorn | ISN | s.t. |
| 6. | A. Angulo | EUS | s.t. |
| 7. | P. Brożyna | MSP | s.t. |
| 8. | R. Carretta | CTF | s.t. |
| 9. | S. Williams | TBV | s.t. |
| 10. | G. Martín | EUS | s.t. |
| 11. | J. Kaczmarek | MSP | s.t. |
| 12. | U. Berrade | EKP | s.t. |
| 13. | A. Dowsett | ISN | s.t. |
| 14. | M. Paasschens | BWB | s.t. |
| 15. | J. F. Parra | EKP | s.t. |
| 16. | A. Skaarseth | UXT | s.t. |
| 17. | A. Peron | TNN | s.t. |
| 18. | F. Miholjević | CTF | s.t. |
| 19. | S. Oomen | TJV | s.t. |
| 20. | D. Peyskens | BWB | s.t. |

## GENERAL CLASSIFICATION

| POS | NAME | TEAM | TIME |
|---|---|---|---|
| 1. ↑1 | A. Skaarseth | UXT | 19:01:50 |
| 2. ↓1 | M. Menten | BWB | s.t. |
| 3. — | M. van Dijke | TJV | 0:06 |

## KING OF THE MOUNTAINS

| POS | NAME | TEAM | PTS |
|---|---|---|---|
| 1. — | T. Træen | UXT | 15 |
| 2. — | M. Budzinski | MSP | 10 |
| 3. — | S. Oomen | TJV | 8 |

## POINTS

| POS | NAME | TEAM | PTS |
|---|---|---|---|
| 1. — | O. Kooij | TJV | 70 |
| 2. — | M. Menten | BWB | 44 |
| 3. ↑1 | I. Einhorn | ISN | 42 |

## YOUNG RIDER

| POS | NAME | TEAM | TIME |
|---|---|---|---|
| 1. — | M. van Dijke | TJV | 19:01:56 |
| 2. — | D. Röber | PUS | 0:04 |
| 3. ↑1 | M. Messner | WSA | 0:06 |

SEPTEMBER .1 MEN'S RACE

## CRO RACE
Stage 5
2 October 2021
Rabac/Labin–Opatija
137.5km

### STAGE RESULTS

| POS | NAME | TEAM | TIME |
|---|---|---|---|
| 1. | S. Williams | TBV | 3:20:35 |
| 2. | M. Hoelgaard | UXT | 0:10 |
| 3. | M. van Dijke | TJV | s.t. |
| 4. | G. Martín | EUS | s.t. |
| 5. | A. Guerin | VBG | s.t. |
| 6. | J. Nicolau | CJR | s.t. |
| 7. | U. Berrade | EKP | s.t. |
| 8. | R. Thalmann | VBG | s.t. |
| 9. | J. F. Parra | EKP | s.t. |
| 10. | S. Buitrago | TBV | s.t. |
| 11. | O. Lazkano | CJR | s.t. |
| 12. | C. F. Hagen | ISN | s.t. |
| 13. | H. Pernsteiner | TBV | s.t. |
| 14. | S. Yates | BEX | s.t. |
| 15. | R. Zoidl | RSW | 0:16 |
| 16. | A. Zeits | BEX | 0:20 |
| 17. | S. Oomen | TJV | s.t. |
| 18. | T. Træen | UXT | 2:04 |
| 19. | D. Röber | PUS | 4:06 |
| 20. | F. Miholjević | CTF | 4:24 |

## WEATHER

TEMPERATURE  WIND
22°C         SE 4km/h

### GENERAL CLASSIFICATION

| POS | NAME | TEAM | TIME |
|---|---|---|---|
| 1. ↑8 | S. Williams | TBV | 22:22:20 |
| 2. ↑1 | M. van Dijke | TJV | 0:17 |
| 3. ↑2 | M. Hoelgaard | UXT | 0:18 |

### KING OF THE MOUNTAINS

| POS | NAME | TEAM | PTS |
|---|---|---|---|
| 1. — | S. Yates | BEX | 30 |
| 2. — | S. Williams | TBV | 25 |
| 3. ↓2 | T. Træen | UXT | 23 |

### POINTS

| POS | NAME | TEAM | PTS |
|---|---|---|---|
| 1. — | O. Kooij | TJV | 70 |
| 2. ↑10 | S. Williams | TBV | 55 |
| 3. ↑4 | M. van Dijke | TJV | 48 |

### YOUNG RIDER

| POS | NAME | TEAM | TIME |
|---|---|---|---|
| 1. — | M. van Dijke | TJV | 22:22:37 |
| 2. ↑5 | O. Lazkano | CJR | 2:01 |
| 3. ↑5 | S. Buitrago | TBV | 2:03 |

## CRO RACE
Stage 6
3 October 2021
Samobor–Zagreb
156.5km

### STAGE RESULTS

| POS | NAME | TEAM | TIME |
|---|---|---|---|
| 1. | T. van Dijke | TJV | 3:23:03 |
| 2. | S. Williams | TBV | s.t. |
| 3. | M. Hoelgaard | UXT | s.t. |
| 4. | K. Groves | BEX | 0:05 |
| 5. | J. Aberasturi | CJR | s.t. |
| 6. | M. Menten | BWB | s.t. |
| 7. | O. Kooij | TJV | s.t. |
| 8. | A. Peron | TNN | s.t. |
| 9. | G. Martín | EUS | s.t. |
| 10. | J. Kaczmarek | MSP | s.t. |
| 11. | R. Thalmann | VBG | s.t. |
| 12. | J. Nicolau | CJR | s.t. |
| 13. | S. Janiszewski | VOS | s.t. |
| 14. | D. Per | ADR | s.t. |
| 15. | C. F. Hagen | ISN | s.t. |
| 16. | A. Guerin | VBG | s.t. |
| 17. | U. Berrade | EKP | s.t. |
| 18. | S. Oomen | TJV | s.t. |
| 19. | A. Angulo | EUS | s.t. |
| 20. | M. Paasschens | BWB | s.t. |

## WEATHER

TEMPERATURE  WIND
24°C         SW 20km/h

### GENERAL CLASSIFICATION

| POS | NAME | TEAM | TIME |
|---|---|---|---|
| 1. | S. Williams | TBV | 25:45:17 |
| 2. | M. Hoelgaard | UXT | 0:17 |
| 3. | M. van Dijke | TJV | 0:28 |

### KING OF THE MOUNTAINS

| POS | NAME | TEAM | PTS |
|---|---|---|---|
| 1. — | S. Yates | BEX | 30 |
| 2. — | S. Williams | TBV | 25 |
| 3. — | T. Træen | UXT | 23 |

### POINTS

| POS | NAME | TEAM | PTS |
|---|---|---|---|
| 1. — | O. Kooij | TJV | 79 |
| 2. — | S. Williams | TBV | 75 |
| 3. ↑6 | M. Hoelgaard | UXT | 56 |

### YOUNG RIDER

| POS | NAME | TEAM | TIME |
|---|---|---|---|
| 1. — | M. van Dijke | TJV | 25:45:45 |
| 2. ↑2 | D. Röber | PUS | 4:22 |
| 3. ↑2 | G. Glivar | ADR | 4:42 |

SEPTEMBER .PRO MEN'S RACE

# 80° EUROMÉTROPOLE TOUR
29 September 2021
La Louvière–Tournai
177.6km

## WEATHER

TEMPERATURE: 13°C
WIND: W 20km/h

## RESULTS

| POS | NAME | TEAM | TIME |
|---|---|---|---|
| 1. | F. Jakobsen | DQT | 4:08:32 |
| 2. | J. Meeus | BOH | s.t. |
| 3. | M. Pedersen | TFS | s.t. |
| 4. | D. van Poppel | IWG | s.t. |
| 5. | H. Hofstetter | ISN | s.t. |
| 6. | N. Bouhanni | ARK | s.t. |
| 7. | K. Van Rooy | SVB | s.t. |
| 8. | L. Mozzato | BBK | s.t. |
| 9. | R. Janse Van Rensburg | TQA | s.t. |
| 10. | S. Leroux | XRL | s.t. |
| 11. | D. De Bondt | AFC | s.t. |
| 12. | P. Allegaert | COF | s.t. |
| 13. | L. Robeet | BWB | s.t. |
| 14. | A. Capiot | ARK | s.t. |
| 15. | T. Van der Sande | LTS | s.t. |
| 16. | X. Meurisse | AFC | s.t. |
| 17. | D. Strakhov | GAZ | s.t. |
| 18. | S. E. Bystrøm | UAD | s.t. |
| 19. | S. Vanmarcke | ISN | s.t. |
| 20. | J. Biermans | ISN | 0:03 |

# OCTOBER

The most notable race in the final month of the season was Paris–Roubaix, uprooted from the spring for the first time in its 125-year history. Its late running – the first edition since 2019 – was a reminder of the scarring the race calendar had suffered over two consecutive years due to the Covid pandemic. The addition of the first-ever women's edition of the race pointed the way to a brighter future. Meanwhile in Italy, the calendar featured a proliferation of autumn races, including the year's final Monument, Il Lombardia.

| DATE | RACE TITLE | LOCATION | UCI CODE | PAGE |
|---|---|---|---|---|
| 1 October | Route Adélie de Vitré | France | 1.1 | 514 |
| 2 October | Paris–Roubaix | France | 1.WWT | 515 |
| 2 October | Giro dell'Emilia | Italy | 1.Pro | 516 |
| 2 October | Classic Loire Atlantique | France | 1.1 | 517 |
| 3 October | Paris–Roubaix | France | 1.UWT | 518 |
| 3 October | Münsterland Giro | Germany | 1.Pro | 520 |
| 4 October | Coppa Bernocchi | Italy | 1.Pro | 521 |
| 4–9 October | Women's Tour | Great Britain | 2.WWT | 522 |
| 5 October | Tre Valli Varesine | Italy | 1.Pro | 528 |
| 5 October | Binche–Chimay–Binche | Belgium | 1.1 | 529 |
| 6 October | Milano–Torino | Italy | 1.Pro | 530 |
| 7 October | Gran Piemonte | Italy | 1.Pro | 531 |
| 7 October | Paris–Bourges | France | 1.1 | 532 |
| 9 October | Il Lombardia | Italy | 1.UWT | 534 |
| 9 October | Tour de Vendée | France | 1.1 | 536 |
| 10 October | Paris–Tours | France | 1.Pro | 537 |
| 11 October | Coppa Agostini | Italy | 1.1 | 538 |
| 13 October | Giro del Veneto | Italy | 1.1 | 539 |
| 16 October | GP de Plumelec-Morbihan | France | 1.Pro | 542 |
| 17 October | Boucles de l'Aulne | France | 1.1 | 543 |
| 17 October | Chrono des Nations | France | 1.1 | 544 |
| 17 October | Veneto Classic | Italy | 1.1 | 545 |
| 23 October | Ronde van Drenthe | Netherlands | 1.WWT | 546 |
| 24 October | Ronde van Drenthe | Netherlands | 1.1 | 547 |

OCTOBER .1 MEN'S RACE

## ROUTE ADÉLIE DE VITRÉ
1 October 2021
Vitré–Vitré
197.8km

## WEATHER

TEMPERATURE
16°C

WIND
S 22km/h

## RESULTS

| POS | NAME | TEAM | TIME |
|---|---|---|---|
| 1. | A. de Kleijn | RLY | 4:44:23 |
| 2. | E. Morin | COF | 0:02 |
| 3. | J. Tesson | AUB | s.t. |
| 4. | E. Reinders | RIW | 0:04 |
| 5. | B. Ghirmay | IWG | s.t. |
| 6. | Á. Fuentes | BBH | s.t. |
| 7. | J. Reynders | SVB | s.t. |
| 8. | A. Zingle | COF | s.t. |
| 9. | C. Barthe | BBK | s.t. |
| 10. | T. Kongstad | RIW | s.t. |
| 11. | A. Krieger | AFC | s.t. |
| 12. | T. Sprengers | SVB | s.t. |
| 13. | E. Vermeulen | XRL | s.t. |
| 14. | L. Manzin | TEN | s.t. |
| 15. | J. Bakelants | IWG | s.t. |
| 16. | Á. Jaime | EKP | s.t. |
| 17. | R. Cardis | AUB | s.t. |
| 18. | W. Vanhoof | SVB | s.t. |
| 19. | S. Siemons | EVO | s.t. |
| 20. | M. Louvel | ARK | s.t. |

OCTOBER   WORLDTOUR WOMEN'S RACE

## PARIS–ROUBAIX
2 October 2021
Denain–Roubaix
116.4km

**WEATHER**

TEMPERATURE   WIND
15°C          S 20km/h

**PROFILE**

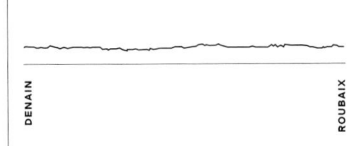

DENAIN — ROUBAIX

**BREAKAWAY**

E. Moberg (DRP), N. Steigenga (DVE), E. Pirrone (VAL)

It is hard to overstate the importance of this race. First run in 1896, it had taken 125 years for parity of opportunity to reach the cobbled farm tracks of northern France. Postponed from Covid-cancelled 2020, and delayed by a further six months, the anticipation leading up to this event was huge. More perhaps than any other race in the calendar, Paris–Roubaix has been mythologised as a brute test of courage and strength. The contention that these properties were incompatible with women's racing could no longer be sustained. And by the time eventual winner Lizzie Deignan – soloing with poise, power and great skill for upwards of 80km – was seen somehow keeping her bike upright as her rear wheel slewed capriciously in thick mud covering cobblestones, all such doubts were consigned to the dustbin of sexism. Deignan's victory – tactically unplanned – was a ride of massive character that garnered unequivocal praise from across the cycling world. The great Marianne Vos (and what a rivalry those two continue to display!) could only roll in a distant second, having powered away from the chasing group at the moment Ellen van Dijk and a number of others fell like skittles on the treacherous road behind her. But Deignan was untouchable. She raced without wearing gloves and by the time she crossed the line in Roubaix – the first woman in history to do so – her bar tape was soaked with blood. The race may not have been close, but it was dripping with significance. In the end, it was another leap of great importance in the accelerating trajectory of women's racing. Another dinosaur slayed.

**RESULTS**

| POS | NAME | TEAM | TIME |
|---|---|---|---|
| 1. | E. Deignan | TFS | 2:56:07 |
| 2. | M. Vos | JVW | 1:17 |
| 3. | E. Longo Borghini | TFS | 1:47 |
| 4. | L. Brennauer | WNT | 1:51 |
| 5. | M. Bastianelli | ALE | 2:10 |
| 6. | E. Norsgaard | MOV | s.t. |
| 7. | F. Koch | DSM | s.t. |
| 8. | A. Cordon-Ragot | TFS | s.t. |
| 9. | M. Cavalli | FDJ | s.t. |
| 10. | C. van den Broek-Blaak | SDW | s.t. |
| 11. | C. Majerus | SDW | 3:03 |
| 12. | L. Thomas | MOV | s.t. |
| 13. | M. van't Geloof | DRP | s.t. |
| 14. | A. Pieters | SDW | 4:26 |
| 15. | L. Kopecky | LIV | 4:33 |
| 16. | C. U. Ludwig | FDJ | s.t. |
| 17. | T. Beekhuis | JVW | 4:36 |
| 18. | R. Kasper | JVW | 4:41 |
| 19. | M. Martins | DRP | 5:55 |
| 20. | L. Jounier | ARK | s.t. |

**TRIVIA**

» Lizzie Deignan has now won all the Monuments open to her: Flanders in 2016, Liège in 2020 and now Roubaix. There is currently no women's Milan–Sanremo or Il Lombardia.

OCTOBER . PRO MEN'S RACE

# GIRO DELL'EMILIA
2 October 2021
Casalecchio di Reno–San Luca
195.3km

## WEATHER

TEMPERATURE
22°C

WIND
NE 13km/h

## RESULTS

| POS | NAME | TEAM | TIME |
|---|---|---|---|
| 1. | P. Roglič | TJV | 4:54:26 |
| 2. | J. Almeida | DQT | 0:03 |
| 3. | M. Woods | ISN | 0:05 |
| 4. | A. Yates | IGD | 0:10 |
| 5. | R. Evenepoel | DQT | 0:28 |
| 6. | D. Martin | ISN | 1:23 |
| 7. | B. Mollema | TFS | 1:45 |
| 8. | D. Ulissi | UAD | 1:46 |
| 9. | B. Hermans | ISN | 1:50 |
| 10. | N. Quintana | ARK | 1:59 |
| 11. | A. De Marchi | ISN | 2:05 |
| 12. | J. Vingegaard | TJV | 2:09 |
| 13. | C. Scaroni | GAZ | s.t. |
| 14. | D. Pozzovivo | TQA | 2:11 |
| 15. | S. Kruijswijk | TJV | 2:15 |
| 16. | S. Cras | LTS | 2:23 |
| 17. | P. Sivakov | IGD | 2:46 |
| 18. | C. Champoussin | ACT | 3:08 |
| 19. | G. Aleotti | BOH | 3:59 |
| 20. | N. Powless | EFN | 4:23 |

OCTOBER .1 MEN'S RACE

## CLASSIC LOIRE ATLANTIQUE
2 October 2021
La Haye-Fouassière–La Haye-Fouassière
182.8km

## WEATHER

TEMPERATURE
17°C

WIND
S 31km/h

### RESULTS

| POS | NAME | TEAM | TIME |
|---|---|---|---|
| 1. | A. Riou | ARK | 4:29:30 |
| 2. | V. Madouas | GFC | s.t. |
| 3. | D. Godon | ACT | s.t. |
| 4. | M. Scotson | GFC | s.t. |
| 5. | L. Calmejane | ACT | 0:03 |
| 6. | P. A. Coté | RLY | 0:07 |
| 7. | M. Burgaudeau | TEN | 0:09 |
| 8. | A. Delettre | DKO | 0:17 |
| 9. | A. Delaplace | ARK | s.t. |
| 10. | A. Okamika | BBH | 1:32 |
| 11. | A. de Vos | RLY | 1:49 |
| 12. | S. Leroux | XRL | s.t. |
| 13. | L. Pichon | ARK | s.t. |
| 14. | C. Barthe | BBK | s.t. |
| 15. | J. Bakelants | IWG | s.t. |
| 16. | A. Krieger | AFC | s.t. |
| 17. | R. Adrià | EKP | s.t. |
| 18. | N. Prodhomme | ACT | 1:52 |
| 19. | T. Kongstad | RIW | 2:36 |
| 20. | J. Reynders | SVB | s.t. |

OCTOBER    WORLDTOUR MEN'S RACE

# PARIS–ROUBAIX
3 October 2021
Compiègne–Roubaix
257.7km

## WEATHER

TEMPERATURE  
12°C

WIND  
W 30km/h

## PROFILE

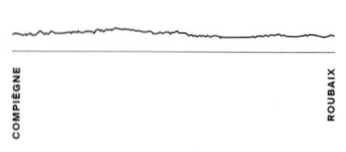

COMPIÈGNE — ROUBAIX

## BREAKAWAY

F. Vermeersch (LTS), H. Sweeny (LTS), T. van der Sande (LTS), D. Oss (BOH), D. Ballerini (DQT), T. Declercq (DQT), E. Affini (TJV), T. Roosen (TJV), N. Van Hooydonck (TJV), T. van Asbroeck (ISN), J. Philipsen (AFC), T. Skujiņš (TFS), M. Haller (TBV), F. Wright (TBV), G. Van Avermaet (ACT), S. Bissegger (EFN), A. Carvalho (COF), V. S. Laengen (UAD), G. Moscon (IGD), L. Rowe (IGD), F. Maître (TEN), L. Durbridge (BEX), R. Stannard (BEX), E. Siskevicius (DKO), N. Eekhoff (DSM), M. Walscheid (TQA), I. Erviti (MOV), M. Jorgensen (MOV), L. Mozzato (BBK)

Italy, continuing their summer of success on the track and the road (not to mention the football pitch), were one of the prime animating forces behind a historic edition of Paris–Roubaix, raced in appalling weather conditions. The rain was every bit as bad as many might have dreaded and many more might have hoped for, watching in their millions from the comfort of their homes as this unique edition played out in the middle of an autumnal storm. Puddles encroached from the side of some of the more rutted sectors, almost meeting at the crown of the road at certain points. Gianni Moscon – often saddled with a hipster's outsider status following a promising fifth place in 2017 – built up a solo advantage that looked at one point as if it might be sufficient as a group behind splintered, blew up, formed, fell apart and generally slid around on the cobbles. With 30km to go, he punctured and lost half his lead. Then, 4km later, he fell and suddenly a chase group nearly had him. Despite that, he took a slender lead onto the Carrefour de l'Arbre, where Mathieu van der Poel, Sonny Colbrelli and Florian Vermeersch – all debutants on the race – accelerated to snuff out any lingering hopes he might have had. With Moscon eventually dropped, the three riders made it to the velodrome together, caked in mud from head to toe. Colbrelli outsprinted Vermeersch to the line for a win that left him gasping in disbelief as the Italian and European champion rounded off the greatest win of his career. For a race that began in 1896, this was an edition that will never be forgotten.

## TRIVIA

» Colbrelli is the first Italian winner since Andrea Tafi in 1999.

# RESULTS

| POS | NAME | TEAM | TIME |
|---|---|---|---|
| 1. | S. Colbrelli | TBV | 6:01:57 |
| 2. | F. Vermeersch | LTS | s.t. |
| 3. | M. van der Poel | AFC | s.t. |
| 4. | G. Moscon | IGD | 0:44 |
| 5. | Y. Lampaert | DQT | 1:16 |
| 6. | C. Laporte | COF | s.t. |
| 7. | W. van Aert | TJV | s.t. |
| 8. | T. Van Asbroeck | ISN | s.t. |
| 9. | G. Boivin | ISN | s.t. |
| 10. | H. Haussler | TBV | s.t. |
| 11. | J. Rutsch | EFN | s.t. |
| 12. | M. Walscheid | TQA | 3:17 |
| 13. | A. Turgis | TEN | s.t. |
| 14. | A. Kristoff | UAD | 4:40 |
| 15. | G. Vermeersch | AFC | s.t. |
| 16. | S. Langeveld | EFN | 4:45 |
| 17. | M. Haller | TBV | 6:21 |
| 18. | A. Capiot | ARK | s.t. |
| 19. | B. Planckaert | IWG | s.t. |
| 20. | L. Mozzato | BBK | s.t. |
| 21. | L. Rex | BWB | s.t. |
| 22. | N. Van Hooydonck | TJV | s.t. |
| 23. | S. Vanmarcke | ISN | s.t. |
| 24. | S. Kragh Andersen | DSM | 6:26 |
| 25. | J. Stuyven | TFS | s.t. |
| 26. | Z. Štybar | DQT | s.t. |
| 27. | I. García Cortina | MOV | 7:14 |
| 28. | C. Swift | ARK | 7:22 |
| 29. | P. Gilbert | LTS | 7:26 |
| 30. | E. Boasson Hagen | TEN | 8:37 |
| 31. | D. Van Gestel | TEN | s.t. |
| 32. | G. Van Avermaet | ACT | 9:23 |
| 33. | E. Šiškevičius | DKO | s.t. |
| 34. | A. Démare | GFC | s.t. |
| 35. | C. Davy | GFC | s.t. |
| 36. | L. Robeet | BWB | s.t. |
| 37. | T. Van der Sande | LTS | 9:26 |
| 38. | B. De Backer | BBK | 9:29 |
| 39. | H. Sweeny | LTS | 10:03 |
| 40. | T. van der Hoorn | IWG | 10:52 |
| 41. | J. Philipsen | AFC | s.t. |
| 42. | B. Welten | ARK | s.t. |
| 43. | J. Drucker | COF | s.t. |
| 44. | T. Skujiņš | TFS | 11:06 |
| 45. | J. Rickaert | AFC | 11:11 |
| 46. | N. Eekhoff | DSM | 12:24 |
| 47. | J. Biermans | ISN | s.t. |
| 48. | T. Merlier | AFC | s.t. |
| 49. | S. Dillier | AFC | s.t. |
| 50. | C. Bol | DSM | s.t. |
| 51. | F. Wright | TBV | s.t. |
| 52. | O. Naesen | ACT | s.t. |
| 53. | J. Degenkolb | LTS | s.t. |
| 54. | L. Durbridge | BEX | s.t. |
| 55. | S. Clarke | TQA | s.t. |
| 56. | B. Van Lerberghe | DQT | s.t. |
| 57. | P. Sagan | BOH | s.t. |
| 58. | S. Dewulf | ACT | s.t. |
| 59. | C. Lemoine | BBK | 12:28 |
| 60. | M. Gołaś | IGD | 12:32 |
| 61. | J. van den Berg | EFN | 12:37 |
| 62. | S. Bissegger | EFN | s.t. |
| 63. | T. Roosen | TJV | 13:19 |
| 64. | A. Livyns | BWB | 16:21 |
| 65. | M. Jorgenson | MOV | 16:25 |
| 66. | J. Bauer | BEX | 17:59 |
| 67. | L. Rowe | IGD | 20:28 |
| 68. | K. Asgreen | DQT | s.t. |
| 69. | T. Declercq | DQT | s.t. |
| 70. | M. Kwiatkowski | IGD | s.t. |
| 71. | F. Sénéchal | DQT | s.t. |
| 72. | T. Bohli | COF | s.t. |
| 73. | C. Russo | ARK | s.t. |
| 74. | J. Sagan | BOH | s.t. |
| 75. | L. Naesen | ACT | s.t. |
| 76. | A. Petit | TEN | s.t. |
| 77. | M. Schachmann | BOH | s.t. |
| 78. | M. Bjerg | UAD | s.t. |
| 79. | C. Juul-Jensen | BEX | s.t. |
| 80. | T. Scully | EFN | s.t. |
| 81. | D. Groenewegen | TJV | s.t. |
| 82. | E. Affini | TJV | 22:50 |
| 83. | R. Stannard | BEX | 22:53 |
| 84. | S. Sajnok | COF | 23:04 |
| 85. | M. Teunissen | TJV | 24:33 |
| 86. | M. Norsgaard | MOV | 26:09 |
| 87. | P. Allegaert | COF | 26:14 |
| 88. | R. Janse Van Rensburg | TQA | 26:18 |
| 89. | J. Meeus | BOH | 27:22 |
| 90. | R. Barbier | ISN | 28:36 |
| 91. | C. Noppe | ARK | s.t. |
| 92. | T. Dupont | BWB | s.t. |
| 93. | E. Finé | COF | s.t. |
| 94. | F. Frison | LTS | s.t. |
| 95. | L. G. Mas | MOV | s.t. |
| 96. | E. Liepiņš | TFS | 28:46 |

OCTOBER

OCTOBER .PRO MEN'S RACE

# MÜNSTERLAND GIRO
3 October 2021
Enschede–Munster
188.5km

## WEATHER

TEMPERATURE
19°C

WIND
S 26km/h

## RESULTS

| POS | NAME | TEAM | TIME |
|---|---|---|---|
| 1. | M. Cavendish | DQT | 4:11:52 |
| 2. | A. Renard | ISN | s.t. |
| 3. | M. Hulgaard | UXT | s.t. |
| 4. | J. Černý | DQT | 0:06 |
| 5. | N. Märkl | DSM | 0:09 |
| 6. | R. Herregodts | SVB | 0:12 |
| 7. | A. Janssen | ABC | s.t. |
| 8. | A. J. Hodeg | DQT | 0:58 |
| 9. | P. Ackermann | BOH | 1:21 |
| 10. | A. Greipel | ISN | 1:33 |
| 11. | G. Zimmermann | IWG | 1:39 |
| 12. | D. De Bondt | AFC | 1:45 |
| 13. | S. Steels | DQT | 1:46 |
| 14. | N. Denz | DSM | s.t. |
| 15. | M. Urianstad | UXT | s.t. |
| 16. | A. Van Poucke | SVB | 1:50 |
| 17. | A. Tarlton | LKH | 1:58 |
| 18. | A. Schillinger | BOH | 2:06 |
| 19. | R. Selig | BOH | 2:08 |
| 20. | I. Keisse | DQT | 2:11 |

OCTOBER .PRO MEN'S RACE

## COPPA BERNOCCHI
4 October 2021
Legnano–Legnano
197.1km

## WEATHER

TEMPERATURE
18°C

WIND
SE 20km/h

## RESULTS

| POS | NAME | TEAM | TIME |
|---|---|---|---|
| 1. | R. Evenepoel | DQT | 4:26:13 |
| 2. | A. Covi | UAD | 1:49 |
| 3. | F. Masnada | DQT | 1:50 |
| 4. | S. Battistella | APT | 2:25 |
| 5. | T. Pinot | GFC | 2:26 |
| 6. | A. Puppio | TQA | 2:55 |
| 7. | J. S. Molano | UAD | 8:27 |
| 8. | F. Fiorelli | BCF | s.t. |
| 9. | N. Bonifazio | TEN | s.t. |
| 10. | E. Viviani | COF | s.t. |
| 11. | J. Mosca | TFS | s.t. |
| 12. | A. Stokbro | TQA | s.t. |
| 13. | V. Albanese | EOK | s.t. |
| 14. | M. Walls | BOH | s.t. |
| 15. | D. González | CJR | s.t. |
| 16. | J. J. Rojas | MOV | s.t. |
| 17. | E. Hayter | IGD | s.t. |
| 18. | S. Consonni | COF | s.t. |
| 19. | N. Schultz | BEX | s.t. |
| 20. | F. Tagliani | ANS | s.t. |

OCTOBER  WORLDTOUR WOMEN'S RACE

# WOMEN'S TOUR
Stage 1
4 October 2021
Bicester–Banbury
147.7km

The 2021 edition of the Women's Tour was initially set to take place in June, but conditions surrounding Covid-19 meant the six-day event was rescheduled for autumn and became the final stage-race event of the season for the women's WorldTour peloton. Despite numerous attacks early on in the opening stage, riders weren't given much freedom and no significant breakaway groups were able to establish. Nina Kessler (Tibco-SVB) asserted dominance in the sprint competition, collecting maximum points in both intermediate sprints, while Janneke Ensing (Team BikeExchange) took the first mountain classification points, after a short spell out front. As the peloton entered Banbury for a local finishing lap it was clear that teams wanted a sprint finish, and Marta Bastianelli (Alé BTC Ljubljana) avoided a late crash to take the victory ahead of Chloe Hosking (Trek-Segafredo) and Clara Copponi (FDJ Nouvelle-Aquitaine Futuroscope).

## WEATHER

TEMPERATURE  WIND
15°C  SW 20km/h

## PROFILE

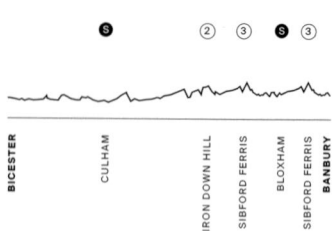

BICESTER — CULHAM — IRON DOWN HILL — SIBFORD FERRIS — BLOXHAM — SIBFORD FERRIS — BANBURY

## BREAKAWAY
J. Ensing (BEX)

## STAGE RESULTS

| POS | NAME | TEAM | TIME |
|---|---|---|---|
| 1. | M. Bastianelli | ALE | 3:44:41 |
| 2. | C. Hosking | TFS | s.t. |
| 3. | C. Copponi | FDJ | s.t. |
| 4. | S. Gutiérrez | MOV | s.t. |
| 5. | E. Cecchini | SDW | s.t. |
| 6. | H. Barnes | CSR | s.t. |
| 7. | S. Bertizzolo | LIV | s.t. |
| 8. | J. Nelson | HPU | s.t. |
| 9. | A. Pieters | SDW | s.t. |
| 10. | L. Kirchmann | DSM | s.t. |
| 11. | S. Roy | BEX | s.t. |
| 12. | J. Labous | DSM | s.t. |
| 13. | C. Majerus | SDW | s.t. |
| 14. | D. Vollering | SDW | s.t. |
| 15. | C. van den Broek-Blaak | SDW | s.t. |
| 16. | E. Duval | FDJ | s.t. |
| 17. | E. Chabbey | CSR | s.t. |
| 18. | A. Biannic | MOV | s.t. |
| 19. | N. Kessler | TIB | s.t. |
| 20. | E. Bujak | ALE | s.t. |

## GENERAL CLASSIFICATION

| POS | NAME | TEAM | TIME |
|---|---|---|---|
| 1. | M. Bastianelli | ALE | 3:44:31 |
| 2. | C. Hosking | TFS | 0:04 |
| 3. | N. Kessler | TIB | s.t. |

## QUEEN OF THE MOUNTAINS

| POS | NAME | TEAM | PTS |
|---|---|---|---|
| 1. | D. Vollering | SDW | 7 |
| 2. | J. Ensing | BEX | 6 |
| 3. | A. Jackson | LIV | 5 |

## POINTS

| POS | NAME | TEAM | PTS |
|---|---|---|---|
| 1. | M. Bastianelli | ALE | 15 |
| 2. | C. Hosking | TFS | 12 |
| 3. | C. Copponi | FDJ | 9 |

## TRIVIA
» This was Marta Bastianelli's second-ever win in Britain. Her first was at the 2018 European Championships in Glasgow.

## BONUSES

| TYPE | NAME | TEAM |
|---|---|---|
| QOM 1 | J. Ensing | BEX |
| QOM 2 | C. Consonni | VAL |
| QOM 3 | D. Vollering | SDW |
| Sprint 1 | N. Kessler | TIB |
| Sprint 2 | N. Kessler | TIB |

OCTOBER    WORLDTOUR WOMEN'S RACE

## WOMEN'S TOUR
Stage 2
5 October 2021
Walsall–Walsall
102.2km

The second stage was raced on a circuit that saw the peloton covering ten laps of a 10km route with the Barr Beacon climb to tackle each time.
In cold and rainy conditions, it proved to be a race of attrition, with riders constantly dropping off the back but no real breakaway groups establishing ahead. Nina Kessler took more points in the intermediate sprints to retain her lead in the sprint classification, while Elise Chabbey (Canyon-SRAM) snatched top points on the day's first mountains classification sprint, jumping ahead of Demi Vollering (SD Worx) in the standings. It wasn't until the final lap that a group of ten riders broke free on the lower slopes of the climb, and Amy Pieters (SD Worx) then powered to victory ahead of Clara Copponi and Sheyla Gutiérrez (Movistar). After third place on stage 1, Copponi moved into the race lead ahead of Pieters. (LM)

### WEATHER
TEMPERATURE  WIND
13°C         W 33km/h

### PROFILE

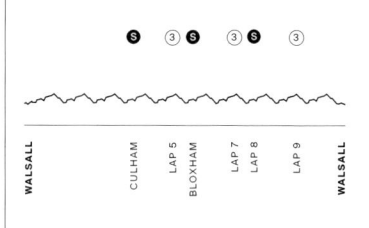

### BREAKAWAY
E. Harris (CSR), S. Gutiérrez (MOV), C. Majerus (SDW), L. Lippert (DSM), C. Hosking (TFS), A. van der Hulst (PHV), M. Grossetête (FDJ), T. Campbell (BEX)

### STAGE RESULTS

| POS | NAME | TEAM | TIME |
|---|---|---|---|
| 1. | A. Pieters | SDW | 2:38:03 |
| 2. | C. Copponi | FDJ | s.t. |
| 3. | S. Gutiérrez | MOV | s.t. |
| 4. | A. Cordon-Ragot | TFS | s.t. |
| 5. | P. Georgi | DSM | s.t. |
| 6. | E. Chabbey | CSR | s.t. |
| 7. | M. Boogaard | ALE | s.t. |
| 8. | A. Biannic | MOV | s.t. |
| 9. | J. Labous | DSM | s.t. |
| 10. | D. Vollering | SDW | s.t. |
| 11. | L. Wiebes | DSM | 0:42 |
| 12. | C. Hosking | TFS | s.t. |
| 13. | A. van der Hulst | PHV | s.t. |
| 14. | J. Nelson | HPU | s.t. |
| 15. | J. Erić | MOV | s.t. |
| 16. | S. Bertizzolo | LIV | s.t. |
| 17. | E. Duval | FDJ | s.t. |
| 18. | E. Cecchini | SDW | s.t. |
| 19. | L. Kirchmann | DSM | s.t. |
| 20. | M. Grossetête | FDJ | s.t. |

### GENERAL CLASSIFICATION

| POS | NAME | TEAM | TIME |
|---|---|---|---|
| 1. ↑3 | C. Copponi | FDJ | 6:22:34 |
| 2. ↑11 | A. Pieters | SDW | s.t. |
| 3. ↑5 | S. Gutiérrez | MOV | 0:06 |

### QUEEN OF THE MOUNTAINS

| POS | NAME | TEAM | PTS |
|---|---|---|---|
| 1. ↑3 | E. Chabbey | CSR | 10 |
| 2. ↓1 | D. Vollering | SDW | 9 |
| 3. ↓1 | J. Ensing | BEX | 6 |

### POINTS

| POS | NAME | TEAM | PTS |
|---|---|---|---|
| 1. ↑2 | C. Copponi | FDJ | 21 |
| 2. ↑7 | A. Pieters | SDW | 17 |
| 3. ↑1 | S. Gutiérrez | MOV | 16 |

### TRIVIA
» This was Pieters' fourth career stage win in this race.

### BONUSES

| TYPE | NAME | TEAM |
|---|---|---|
| QOM 1 | E. Chabbey | CSR |
| QOM 2 | E. Chabbey | CSR |
| QOM 3 | E. Harris | CSR |
| Sprint 1 | N. Kessler | TIB |
| Sprint 2 | S. Bertizzolo | LIV |
| Sprint 3 | N. Kessler | TIB |

OCTOBER   WORLDTOUR WOMEN'S RACE

# WOMEN'S TOUR
Stage 3 (ITT)
6 October 2021
Atherstone–Atherstone
16.6km

For the first time in the race's history an individual time trial stage took place, but – unlike a traditional British ITT – this stage was over 10 miles long and not held on a typical out-and-back circuit route. Demi Vollering obliterated the field, completing the 10.3 miles/16.6km distance 1 minute 4 seconds faster than her nearest rival, Joss Lowden (Drops Le Col), who had broken the world hour record on the track just six days prior. Vollering shone on the rolling course, powering on despite a harsh north-westerly crosswind and strong headwind for the final 1.5km. Race leader Clara Copponi finished the day in 11th place, dropping to third place overall and allowing Vollering to move into the race lead ahead of Juliette Labous (Team DSM).

## WEATHER

| TEMPERATURE | WIND |
|---|---|
| 15°C | NW 17km/h |

## PROFILE

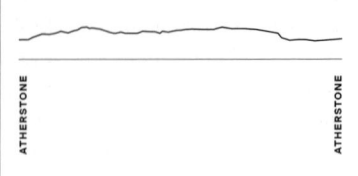

## STAGE RESULTS

| POS | NAME | TEAM | TIME |
|---|---|---|---|
| 1. | D. Vollering | SDW | 23:18 |
| 2. | J. Lowden | DRP | 1:04 |
| 3. | L. Kirchmann | DSM | 1:05 |
| 4. | A. Barnes | CSR | 1:08 |
| 5. | J. Labous | DSM | s.t. |
| 6. | C. van den Broek-Blaak | SDW | 1:09 |
| 7. | A. Smith | TIB | 1:20 |
| 8. | V. Ewers | TIB | 1:21 |
| 9. | A. Shackley | SDW | 1:25 |
| 10. | H. Barnes | CSR | 1:27 |
| 11. | C. Copponi | FDJ | 1:28 |
| 12. | A. Pieters | SDW | 1:31 |
| 13. | A. Biannic | MOV | 1:32 |
| 14. | C. Majerus | SDW | 1:34 |
| 15. | E. Harris | CSR | 1:46 |
| 16. | S. Roy | BEX | 1:49 |
| 17. | P. Georgi | DSM | 1:52 |
| 18. | E. Chabbey | CSR | 1:53 |
| 19. | L. Stephens | TIB | 2:05 |
| 20. | J. Ensing | BEX | 2:08 |

## GENERAL CLASSIFICATION

| POS | | NAME | TEAM | TIME |
|---|---|---|---|---|
| 1. | ↑3 | D. Vollering | SDW | 6:46:01 |
| 2. | ↑3 | J. Labous | DSM | 1:09 |
| 3. | ↓2 | C. Copponi | FDJ | 1:19 |

## QUEEN OF THE MOUNTAINS

| POS | | NAME | TEAM | PTS |
|---|---|---|---|---|
| 1. | — | E. Chabbey | CSR | 10 |
| 2. | — | D. Vollering | SDW | 9 |
| 3. | — | J. Ensing | BEX | 6 |

## POINTS

| POS | | NAME | TEAM | PTS |
|---|---|---|---|---|
| 1. | — | C. Copponi | FDJ | 21 |
| 2. | — | A. Pieters | SDW | 17 |
| 3. | ↑13 | D. Vollering | SDW | 16 |

## TRIVIA

» This was Vollering's second-ever professional victory against the clock. The first was her debut win in the prologue at Festival Elsy Jacobs.

OCTOBER    WORLDTOUR WOMEN'S RACE

# WOMEN'S TOUR
Stage 4
7 October 2021
Shoeburyness–Southend-on-Sea
117.8km

On a flat and fast fourth stage, no breakaway groups were able to establish themselves as the peloton covered 40km in the first hour of racing. Midway through the stage, Janneke Ensing jumped away solo and swept up the first intermediate sprint points, but shortly afterwards the Dutch rider returned to the peloton. Next it was Lourdes Oyarbide (Movistar) who tried her luck, riding away from the peloton and opening an advantage of 1 minute, but as the race entered the final 40km the Spaniard also returned to the peloton. Lorena Wiebes (Team DSM) then decided to test her legs and sprinted to victory in the second intermediate sprint. The move didn't affect Nina Kessler, who was able to hold on to the sprint classification lead. On the seafront finish Wiebes bided her time, launching late and passing Chiara Consonni to take the victory, while Chloe Hosking settled for third.

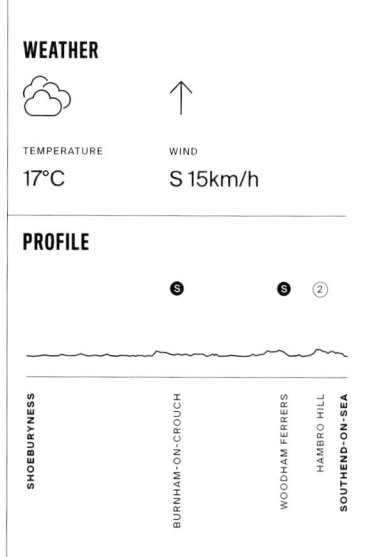

## WEATHER

TEMPERATURE  WIND
17°C         S 15km/h

## PROFILE

SHOEBURYNESS — BURNHAM-ON-CROUCH — WOODHAM FERRERS — HAMBRO HILL — SOUTHEND-ON-SEA

## BREAKAWAY

J. Ensing (BEX), L. Oyarbide (MOV)

## STAGE RESULTS

| POS | NAME | TEAM | TIME |
|---|---|---|---|
| 1. | L. Wiebes | DSM | 2:54:43 |
| 2. | C. Consonni | VAL | s.t. |
| 3. | C. Hosking | TFS | s.t. |
| 4. | S. Gutiérrez | MOV | s.t. |
| 5. | M. van't Geloof | DRP | s.t. |
| 6. | S. Bertizzolo | LIV | s.t. |
| 7. | S. Roy | BEX | s.t. |
| 8. | A. Barnes | CSR | s.t. |
| 9. | M. Bastianelli | ALE | s.t. |
| 10. | A. Pieters | SDW | s.t. |
| 11. | J. Nelson | HPU | s.t. |
| 12. | C. Copponi | FDJ | s.t. |
| 13. | A. van der Hulst | PHV | s.t. |
| 14. | A. Biannic | MOV | s.t. |
| 15. | N. Kessler | TIB | s.t. |
| 16. | A. González | MOV | s.t. |
| 17. | L. Kirchmann | DSM | s.t. |
| 18. | E. Bujak | ALE | s.t. |
| 19. | E. Balsamo | VAL | s.t. |
| 20. | E. Chabbey | CSR | s.t. |

## GENERAL CLASSIFICATION

| POS | | NAME | TEAM | TIME |
|---|---|---|---|---|
| 1. | — | D. Vollering | SDW | 9:40:44 |
| 2. | — | J. Labous | DSM | 1:09 |
| 3. | — | C. Copponi | FDJ | 1:19 |

## QUEEN OF THE MOUNTAINS

| POS | | NAME | TEAM | PTS |
|---|---|---|---|---|
| 1. | — | E. Chabbey | CSR | 16 |
| 2. | — | D. Vollering | SDW | 9 |
| 3. | ↑3 | A. Santesteban | BEX | 7 |

## POINTS

| POS | | NAME | TEAM | PTS |
|---|---|---|---|---|
| 1. | ↑3 | S. Gutiérrez | MOV | 23 |
| 2. | ↓1 | C. Copponi | FDJ | 21 |
| 3. | ↑4 | C. Hosking | TFS | 21 |

## BONUSES

| TYPE | NAME | TEAM |
|---|---|---|
| QOM 1 | E. Chabbey | CSR |
| Sprint 1 | J. Ensing | BEX |
| Sprint 2 | L. Wiebes | DSM |

OCTOBER　　WORLDTOUR WOMEN'S RACE

# WOMEN'S TOUR
Stage 5
8 October 2021
Colchester–Clacton
95.4km

## WEATHER

TEMPERATURE　　WIND
16°C　　SE 11km/h

## PROFILE

COLCHESTER · TENPENNY HILL · HOLLAND-ON-SEA · MISTLEY MANNINGTREE · TENPENNY HILL · CLACTON-ON-SEA

The overall classification contenders were put under pressure on the fifth stage after a local British rider Hayley Simmonds (CAMS-Basso Bikes) made a brave move, riding herself into the virtual lead for several kilometres. The day began with Simmonds attacking and riding away from the peloton shortly after the start flag was dropped and, with no real concerted chase behind, the 33-year-old opened a gap of 4 minutes 30 seconds after 50km of racing. Connie Hayes (AWOL O'Shea) tried to bridge across but was unable to make the junction and quickly returned to the peloton. A trio of chasers – Sarah Roy, Ane Santesteban (Team BikeExchange) and Elise Chabbey (Canyon-SRAM) – then followed but were also unsuccessful in closing the gap. After a hard chase from Team DSM and SD Worx, Simmonds was finally reeled back in with 16km left before Wiebes launched to a convincing second consecutive victory.

## BREAKAWAY

H. Simmonds (CAT)

## STAGE RESULTS

| POS | NAME | TEAM | TIME |
|---|---|---|---|
| 1. | M. Bastianelli | ALE | 3:44:41 |
| 2. | C. Hosking | TFS | s.t. |
| 3. | C. Copponi | FDJ | s.t. |
| 4. | S. Gutiérrez | MOV | s.t. |
| 5. | E. Cecchini | SDW | s.t. |
| 6. | H. Barnes | CSR | s.t. |
| 7. | S. Bertizzolo | LIV | s.t. |
| 8. | J. Nelson | HPU | s.t. |
| 9. | A. Pieters | SDW | s.t. |
| 10. | L. Kirchmann | DSM | s.t. |
| 11. | S. Roy | BEX | s.t. |
| 12. | J. Labous | DSM | s.t. |
| 13. | C. Majerus | SDW | s.t. |
| 14. | D. Vollering | SDW | s.t. |
| 15. | C. van den Broek-Blaak | SDW | s.t. |
| 16. | E. Duval | FDJ | s.t. |
| 17. | E. Chabbey | CSR | s.t. |
| 18. | A. Biannic | MOV | s.t. |
| 19. | N. Kessler | TIB | s.t. |
| 20. | E. Bujak | ALE | s.t. |

## GENERAL CLASSIFICATION

| POS | | NAME | TEAM | TIME |
|---|---|---|---|---|
| 1. | – | D. Vollering | SDW | 12:00:37 |
| 2. | – | J. Labous | DSM | 1:09 |
| 3. | – | C. Copponi | FDJ | 1:16 |

## QUEEN OF THE MOUNTAINS

| POS | | NAME | TEAM | PTS |
|---|---|---|---|---|
| 1. | – | E. Chabbey | CSR | 20 |
| 2. | – | D. Vollering | SDW | 9 |
| 3. | – | A. Santesteban | BEX | 8 |

## POINTS

| POS | | NAME | TEAM | PTS |
|---|---|---|---|---|
| 1. | ↑6 | L. Wiebes | DSM | 30 |
| 2. | ↑1 | C. Hosking | TFS | 28 |
| 3. | ↓1 | C. Copponi | FDJ | 27 |

## TRIVIA

» At the age of just 22 Lorena Wiebes has already taken 35 professional victories.

## BONUSES

| TYPE | NAME | TEAM |
|---|---|---|
| QOM 1 | H. Simmonds | CAT |
| QOM 2 | H. Simmonds | CAT |
| QOM 3 | A. Towers | DRP |
| Sprint 1 | H. Simmonds | CAT |
| Sprint 2 | H. Simmonds | CAT |

OCTOBER    WORLDTOUR WOMEN'S RACE

# WOMEN'S TOUR
Stage 6
9 October 2021
Haverhill–Felixstowe
155.3km

Only a few weeks after winning the World Championship road race, Elisa Balsamo (Valcar Travel & Service) sprinted to the final stage victory in Felixstowe after a breakaway group of five riders was caught with 14.5km to go. Having launched from the peloton at different times, the group of five escapees came together with 77km remaining and opened up a lead of over 3 minutes. With one last sprint opportunity up for grabs, the leaders didn't survive to the line as Balsamo showed her speed and flew past Wiebes in the final metres to deny the Dutch rider a hattrick of victories. After her ITT win on stage 3, Demi Vollering was able to secure the overall General Classification victory with a convincing advantage over second-placed Juliette Labous (Team DSM). Clara Copponi, in third, took the prize for the best-placed Under-23 rider.

## WEATHER

**TEMPERATURE**
15°C

**WIND**
NW 19km/h

## PROFILE

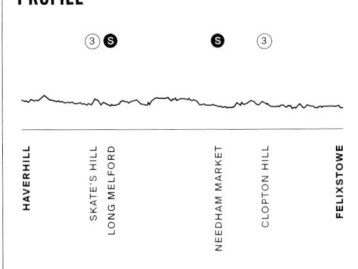

HAVERHILL · SKATE'S HILL / LONG MELFORD · NEEDHAM MARKET · CLOPTON HILL · FELIXSTOWE

## BREAKAWAY
E. Bujak (ALE), D. Christmas (DRP), A. Santesteban (BEX), V. Ewers (TIB), S. Bertizzolo (LIV)

## STAGE RESULTS

| POS | NAME | TEAM | TIME |
|---|---|---|---|
| 1. | E. Balsamo | VAL | 3:53:51 |
| 2. | L. Wiebes | DSM | s.t. |
| 3. | C. Hosking | TFS | s.t. |
| 4. | S. Gutiérrez | MOV | s.t. |
| 5. | A. van der Hulst | PHV | s.t. |
| 6. | C. Copponi | FDJ | s.t. |
| 7. | M. van't Geloof | DRP | s.t. |
| 8. | S. Roy | BEX | s.t. |
| 9. | M. Bastianelli | ALE | s.t. |
| 10. | A. Barnes | CSR | s.t. |
| 11. | J. Nelson | HPU | s.t. |
| 12. | A. Pieters | SDW | s.t. |
| 13. | E. Chabbey | CSR | s.t. |
| 14. | J. Labous | DSM | s.t. |
| 15. | P. Georgi | DSM | s.t. |
| 16. | L. Kirchmann | DSM | s.t. |
| 17. | C. Consonni | VAL | s.t. |
| 18. | A. Biannic | MOV | s.t. |
| 19. | M. Boogaard | ALE | s.t. |
| 20. | C. Majerus | SDW | s.t. |

## GENERAL CLASSIFICATION

| POS | | NAME | TEAM | TIME |
|---|---|---|---|---|
| 1. | — | D. Vollering | SDW | 15:54:38 |
| 2. | — | J. Labous | DSM | 1:02 |
| 3. | — | C. Copponi | FDJ | 1:05 |

## QUEEN OF THE MOUNTAINS

| POS | | NAME | TEAM | PTS |
|---|---|---|---|---|
| 1. | — | E. Chabbey | CSR | 20 |
| 2. | ↑1 | A. Santesteban | BEX | 14 |
| 3. | ↓1 | D. Vollering | SDW | 11 |

## POINTS

| POS | | NAME | TEAM | PTS |
|---|---|---|---|---|
| 1. | — | L. Wiebes | DSM | 42 |
| 2. | — | C. Hosking | TFS | 37 |
| 3. | ↑1 | S. Gutiérrez | MOV | 33 |

## TRIVIA
» When finishing first and second, Balsamo has won four times to Wiebes' five.

## BONUSES

| TYPE | NAME | TEAM |
|---|---|---|
| QOM 1 | A. Santesteban | BEX |
| QOM 2 | A. Santesteban | BEX |
| Sprint 1 | L. Wiebes | DSM |
| Sprint 2 | E. Bujak | ALE |

OCTOBER .PRO MEN'S RACE

## TRE VALLI VARESINE
5 October 2021
Busto Arsizio–Varese
196.7km

### WEATHER

TEMPERATURE  WIND
17°C         E 6km/h

### RESULTS

| POS | NAME | TEAM | TIME |
|---|---|---|---|
| 1. | A. De Marchi | ISN | 4:47:04 |
| 2. | D. Formolo | UAD | s.t. |
| 3. | T. Pogačar | UAD | 0:38 |
| 4. | B. Cosnefroy | ACT | s.t. |
| 5. | A. Kron | LTS | s.t. |
| 6. | S. Higuita | EFN | s.t. |
| 7. | L. Rota | IWG | s.t. |
| 8. | D. Gaudu | GFC | s.t. |
| 9. | A. Covi | UAD | s.t. |
| 10. | A. Paret-Peintre | ACT | s.t. |
| 11. | N. Oliveira | MOV | s.t. |
| 12. | G. Martin | COF | s.t. |
| 13. | M. Hirschi | UAD | 0:42 |
| 14. | A. Lutsenko | APT | 0:49 |
| 15. | C. Berthet | ACT | s.t. |
| 16. | J. Restrepo | ANS | s.t. |
| 17. | V. Nibali | TFS | s.t. |
| 18. | P. Latour | TEN | s.t. |
| 19. | S. Ravanelli | ANS | s.t. |
| 20. | M. Bais | ANS | s.t. |

OCTOBER    .1 MEN'S RACE

# BINCHE-CHIMAY-BINCHE
5 October 2021
Binche–Binche
198.6km

## WEATHER

TEMPERATURE | WIND
12°C | S 26km/h

## RESULTS

| POS | NAME | TEAM | TIME |
|---|---|---|---|
| 1. | D. van Poppel | IWG | 4:44:45 |
| 2. | R. Tiller | UXT | 0:03 |
| 3. | L. Taminiaux | AFC | 0:05 |
| 4. | H. Hofstetter | ISN | 0:07 |
| 5. | S. Dewulf | ACT | s.t. |
| 6. | C. Noppe | ARK | s.t. |
| 7. | M. Menten | BWB | s.t. |
| 8. | D. Hoole | TFS | s.t. |
| 9. | D. Groenewegen | TJV | s.t. |
| 10. | A. Pasqualon | IWG | s.t. |
| 11. | V. Stokke | DDS | s.t. |
| 12. | L. Mozzato | BBK | s.t. |
| 13. | N. Vahtra | ISN | s.t. |
| 14. | G. Van Hoecke | ACT | s.t. |
| 15. | M. Cavendish | DQT | s.t. |
| 16. | A. Riou | ARK | s.t. |
| 17. | J. Steimle | DQT | 0:13 |
| 18. | J. Reynders | SVB | s.t. |
| 19. | J. Fouché | BSC | s.t. |
| 20. | F. Dauphin | BBK | s.t. |

OCTOBER    .PRO MEN'S RACE

# MILANO-TORINO
6 October 2021
Magenta–Torino
190km

## WEATHER

TEMPERATURE: 19°C
WIND: E 26km/h

## RESULTS

| POS | NAME | TEAM | TIME |
|-----|------|------|------|
| 1. | P. Roglič | TJV | 4:17:41 |
| 2. | A. Yates | IGD | 0:12 |
| 3. | J. Almeida | DQT | 0:35 |
| 4. | T. Pogačar | UAD | s.t. |
| 5. | M. Woods | ISN | 0:48 |
| 6. | D. Gaudu | GFC | s.t. |
| 7. | D. Ulissi | UAD | s.t. |
| 8. | F. Masnada | DQT | s.t. |
| 9. | N. Quintana | ARK | s.t. |
| 10. | A. Valverde | MOV | 0:56 |
| 11. | B. Hermans | ISN | s.t. |
| 12. | A. Vlasov | APT | s.t. |
| 13. | M. Fabbro | BOH | s.t. |
| 14. | R. Taaramäe | IWG | s.t. |
| 15. | M. Storer | DSM | 1:27 |
| 16. | M. Bizkarra | EUS | 1:50 |
| 17. | P. Sivakov | IGD | 2:01 |
| 18. | D. Pozzovivo | TQA | 2:05 |
| 19. | M. Vansevenant | DQT | 2:30 |
| 20. | C. Champoussin | ACT | 2:35 |

OCTOBER .PRO MEN'S RACE

## GRAN PIEMONTE
7 October 2021
Rocca Canavese–Borgosesia
168km

## WEATHER

| TEMPERATURE | WIND |
|---|---|
| 20°C | S 9km/h |

## RESULTS

| POS | NAME | TEAM | TIME |
|---|---|---|---|
| 1. | M. Walls | BOH | 3:34:47 |
| 2. | G. Nizzolo | TQA | s.t. |
| 3. | O. Kooij | TJV | s.t. |
| 4. | M. Trentin | UAD | s.t. |
| 5. | B. Ghirmay | IWG | s.t. |
| 6. | J. Mareczko | THR | s.t. |
| 7. | R. Minali | IWG | s.t. |
| 8. | A. de Kleijn | RLY | s.t. |
| 9. | A. Capiot | ARK | s.t. |
| 10. | S. Oldani | LTS | s.t. |
| 11. | E. Hayter | IGD | s.t. |
| 12. | S. Consonni | COF | s.t. |
| 13. | M. Moschetti | TFS | s.t. |
| 14. | A. Aranburu | APT | s.t. |
| 15. | A. M. Richeze | UAD | s.t. |
| 16. | J. J. Rojas | MOV | s.t. |
| 17. | D. Gabburo | BCF | s.t. |
| 18. | G. Serrano | MOV | s.t. |
| 19. | S. Colbrelli | TBV | s.t. |
| 20. | C. Joyce | RLY | s.t. |

OCTOBER .1 MEN'S RACE

## PARIS-BOURGES
7 October 2021
Gien–Bourges
198km

## WEATHER

**TEMPERATURE**
16°C

**WIND**
NE 7km/h

## RESULTS

| POS | NAME | TEAM | TIME |
|---|---|---|---|
| 1. | J. Meeus | BOH | 4:20:58 |
| 2. | A. Démare | GFC | s.t. |
| 3. | N. Bonifazio | TEN | s.t. |
| 4. | P. Allegaert | COF | s.t. |
| 5. | B. Coquard | BBK | s.t. |
| 6. | D. McLay | ARK | s.t. |
| 7. | D. van Poppel | IWG | s.t. |
| 8. | J. Tesson | AUB | s.t. |
| 9. | M. Menten | BWB | s.t. |
| 10. | A. Jensen | DKO | s.t. |
| 11. | J. Rickaert | AFC | s.t. |
| 12. | A. Marit | SVB | s.t. |
| 13. | C. Russo | ARK | s.t. |
| 14. | S. Leroux | XRL | s.t. |
| 15. | Á. Fuentes | BBH | s.t. |
| 16. | F. Galván | EKP | s.t. |
| 17. | T. Bayer | AFC | s.t. |
| 18. | P. L. Périchon | COF | s.t. |
| 19. | B. Font | EVO | s.t. |
| 20. | E. Boasson Hagen | TEN | s.t. |

# PARIS-ROUBAIX PRIZE MONEY

While seeing the women's peloton take on the cobbles of Paris–Roubaix for the first time was a moment to cherish, some of the statistics behind the racing show there is a lot more to do. On the current prize money being offered, a female rider would have to win the Hell of the North 20 times to equal what a male rider takes home for winning it just once.

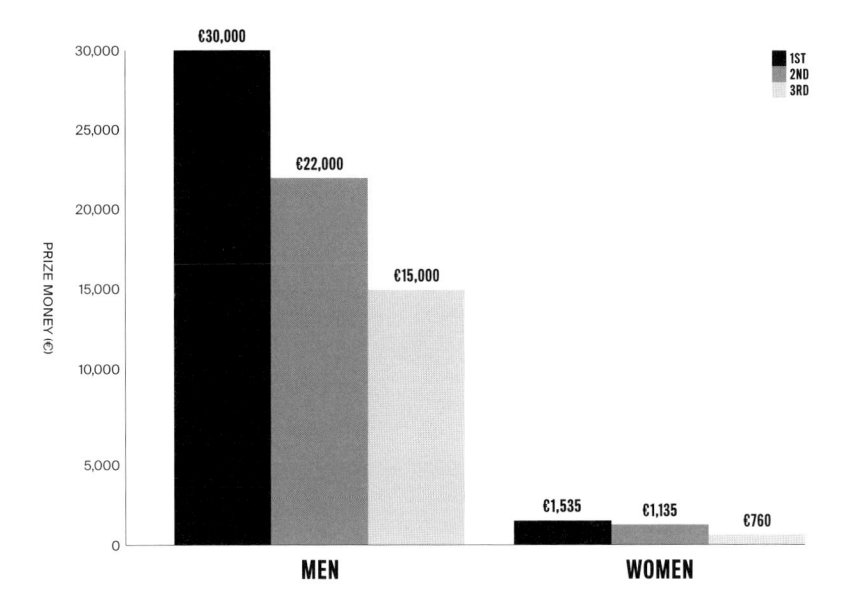

OCTOBER    WORLDTOUR MEN'S RACE

# IL LOMBARDIA
9 October 2021
Como–Bergamo
239km

## WEATHER

TEMPERATURE    WIND
15°C           S 6km/h

## PROFILE

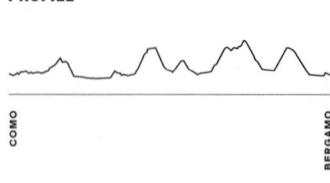

COMO — BERGAMO

## BREAKAWAY

J. Bakelants (IWG), D. Novak (TBV), C. Hamilton (DSM), A. Ghebreigzabhier (TFS), T. Champion (COF), A. Garosio (BCF), D. Orrico (THR), M. Bais (ANS), V. Campenaerts (TQA), T. Wellens (LTS)

Tadej Pogačar made his debut in the season's final Monument uncertain of his form but determined to enjoy himself just as he had a few days earlier when finishing third at the Tre Valli Varesine after a 120km breakaway. Climbing the penultimate climb of the Passo di Ganda with 36km remaining, the young Tour de France champion decided to make hay once again, jumping clear of his rivals, who waited for each other to respond. Ultimately, the only rider who did commit to chasing Pogačar was Deceuninck-QuickStep domestique Fausto Masnada, given the task of defending the hopes of world champion Julian Alaphilippe but also highly motivated by the finish being in his home city of Bergamo. The Italian's back-of-the-hand knowledge of the descent off the Ganda enabled him to reel in Pogačar as the pair reached the flatlands approaching Bergamo. When Masnada then refused to collaborate with his rival because of his commitment to Alaphilippe, Pogačar gave a rueful shake of the head and pressed on. With their lead fluctuating between 20 and 45 seconds, the pair crossed the final climb on the very outskirts of Bergamo, Masnada still hitched on to Pogačar's rear wheel until he tried to jump the UAE leader with 3km remaining. The Slovenian quickly subdued that attack, then took up the pacemaking once again, staying at it into the last 200 metres, when he delivered a sprint flourish that left Masnada trailing. It made him just the third rider (after Fausto Coppi and Eddy Merckx) to win the Tour and two Monuments in the same season.

## TRIVIA

» Tadej Pogačar joins Eddy Merckx, Fausto Coppi and Bernard Hinault in a select group of riders to have won the Tour de France and Il Lombardia in the same season. Of that foursome, Pogačar and Merckx have also won Liège–Bastogne–Liège in the same season, Merckx doing it two years in a row.

# RESULTS

| POS | NAME | TEAM | TIME |
|---|---|---|---|
| 1. | T. Pogačar | UAD | 6:01:39 |
| 2. | F. Masnada | DQT | s.t. |
| 3. | A. Yates | IGD | 0:51 |
| 4. | P. Roglič | TJV | s.t. |
| 5. | A. Valverde | MOV | s.t. |
| 6. | J. Alaphilippe | DQT | s.t. |
| 7. | D. Gaudu | GFC | s.t. |
| 8. | R. Bardet | DSM | s.t. |
| 9. | M. Woods | ISN | s.t. |
| 10. | S. Higuita | EFN | 2:25 |
| 11. | N. Quintana | ARK | s.t. |
| 12. | A. Valter | GFC | s.t. |
| 13. | V. Nibali | TFS | s.t. |
| 14. | J. Vingegaard | TJV | s.t. |
| 15. | L. Fortunato | EOK | s.t. |
| 16. | N. Oliveira | MOV | s.t. |
| 17. | P. Sivakov | IGD | 2:35 |
| 18. | M. Nieve | BEX | 2:49 |
| 19. | R. Evenepoel | DQT | 3:13 |
| 20. | B. Mollema | TFS | 3:23 |
| 21. | B. Tulett | AFC | s.t. |
| 22. | D. Villella | MOV | 3:33 |
| 23. | D. Ulissi | UAD | s.t. |
| 24. | R. Majka | UAD | s.t. |
| 25. | M. Storer | DSM | s.t. |
| 26. | A. Ghebreigzabhier | TFS | 4:28 |
| 27. | T. Skujiņš | TFS | 5:22 |
| 28. | L. Rota | IWG | s.t. |
| 29. | T. Benoot | DSM | s.t. |
| 30. | D. Pozzovivo | TQA | s.t. |
| 31. | L. Warbasse | ACT | s.t. |
| 32. | G. Bouchard | ACT | 5:36 |
| 33. | H. Vanhoucke | LTS | s.t. |
| 34. | A. Paret-Peintre | ACT | s.t. |
| 35. | M. Badilatti | GFC | s.t. |
| 36. | M. Hirschi | UAD | s.t. |
| 37. | D. Teuns | TBV | s.t. |
| 38. | D. Martin | ISN | s.t. |
| 39. | A. Vlasov | APT | 5:56 |
| 40. | J. Almeida | DQT | 6:56 |
| 41. | F. Großschartner | BOH | 7:05 |
| 42. | S. Petilli | IWG | 8:18 |
| 43. | S. Kruijswijk | TJV | 8:23 |
| 44. | G. Martin | COF | s.t. |
| 45. | D. Cataldo | MOV | s.t. |
| 46. | C. Berthet | ACT | 8:37 |
| 47. | K. Sbaragli | AFC | s.t. |
| 48. | A. Zeits | BEX | s.t. |
| 49. | A. Garosio | BCF | s.t. |
| 50. | T. Pinot | GFC | s.t. |
| 51. | N. Powless | EFN | 11:06 |
| 52. | J. J. Rojas | MOV | s.t. |
| 53. | O. C. Eiking | IWG | s.t. |
| 54. | J. Bakelants | IWG | s.t. |
| 55. | P. Konrad | BOH | 11:09 |
| 56. | R. Urán | EFN | s.t. |
| 57. | T. Geoghegan Hart | IGD | s.t. |
| 58. | M. Bouet | ARK | s.t. |
| 59. | N. Schultz | BEX | s.t. |
| 60. | S. Reichenbach | GFC | s.t. |
| 61. | M. Christian | EOK | s.t. |
| 62. | C. Champoussin | ACT | s.t. |
| 63. | J. Castroviejo | IGD | s.t. |
| 64. | C. Hamilton | DSM | s.t. |
| 65. | B. McNulty | UAD | 11:44 |
| 66. | S. Ravanelli | ANS | 14:19 |
| 67. | M. Bais | ANS | 14:36 |
| 68. | M. Fabbro | BOH | s.t. |
| 69. | D. Formolo | UAD | s.t. |
| 70. | A. Bagioli | DQT | 14:42 |
| 71. | D. Orrico | THR | 15:33 |
| 72. | E. Zardini | THR | 16:24 |
| 73. | R. Hollenstein | ISN | 17:13 |
| 74. | L. Vervaeke | AFC | s.t. |
| 75. | R. Taaramäe | IWG | s.t. |
| 76. | D. Quintana | ARK | s.t. |
| 77. | D. Novak | TBV | s.t. |
| 78. | S. Cras | LTS | s.t. |
| 79. | L. Covili | BCF | 19:02 |
| 80. | S. Oomen | TJV | 19:06 |
| 81. | E. Ravasi | EOK | 19:28 |
| 82. | T. Wellens | LTS | 19:38 |
| 83. | A. Tiberi | TFS | 19:58 |
| 84. | K. Colleoni | BEX | 20:21 |
| 85. | G. Bennett | TJV | 20:47 |
| 86. | S. Yates | BEX | s.t. |
| 87. | E. Dunbar | IGD | s.t. |
| 88. | T. Arensman | DSM | 21:38 |
| 89. | M. Donovan | DSM | s.t. |
| 90. | T. Champion | COF | s.t. |
| 91. | K. Bouwman | TJV | s.t. |
| 92. | R. Fernández | COF | s.t. |
| 93. | S. Geschke | COF | s.t. |
| 94. | E. Sepúlveda | ANS | s.t. |
| 95. | D. Gabburo | BCF | s.t. |
| 96. | D. Savini | BCF | s.t. |
| 97. | H. Pernsteiner | TBV | s.t. |
| 98. | B. Swift | IGD | s.t. |
| 99. | V. Campenaerts | TQA | s.t. |
| 100. | D. Howson | BEX | 27:59 |
| 101. | S. Buitrago | TBV | s.t. |
| 102. | G. Serrano | MOV | s.t. |
| 103. | T. Marczyński | LTS | 28:37 |
| 104. | C. Juul-Jensen | BEX | s.t. |
| 105. | A. Monaco | BCF | s.t. |
| 106. | W. Barta | EFN | s.t. |
| 107. | A. Leknessund | DSM | s.t. |

OCTOBER  .1 MEN'S RACE

# TOUR DE VENDÉE
9 October 2021
Les Herbiers–La Roche-sur-Yon
199.8km

## WEATHER

TEMPERATURE  WIND
19°C  NE 15km/h

## RESULTS

| POS | NAME | TEAM | TIME |
|---|---|---|---|
| 1. | B. Welten | ARK | 4:39:25 |
| 2. | E. Prades | DKO | s.t. |
| 3. | S. Schönberger | BBK | s.t. |
| 4. | G. Vermeersch | AFC | s.t. |
| 5. | P. L. Périchon | COF | s.t. |
| 6. | E. Boasson Hagen | TEN | s.t. |
| 7. | T. Ferasse | BBK | s.t. |
| 8. | A. Zingle | COF | s.t. |
| 9. | M. Peñalver | BBH | s.t. |
| 10. | D. Godon | ACT | s.t. |
| 11. | A. Balmer | GFC | s.t. |
| 12. | L. De Vreese | AFC | s.t. |
| 13. | L. van den Berg | GFC | s.t. |
| 14. | V. Ferron | TEN | s.t. |
| 15. | L. Pichon | ARK | s.t. |
| 16. | A. Guerin | VBG | s.t. |
| 17. | I. Konovalovas | GFC | s.t. |
| 18. | A. Vendrame | ACT | s.t. |
| 19. | L. Calmejane | ACT | 0:07 |
| 20. | M. Marquez | EKP | s.t. |

OCTOBER .PRO MEN'S RACE

## PARIS–TOURS

10 October 2021
Chartres–Tours
212.3km

## WEATHER

| TEMPERATURE | WIND |
|---|---|
| 15°C | NE 17km/h |

### RESULTS

| POS | NAME | TEAM | TIME |
|---|---|---|---|
| 1. | A. Démare | GFC | 4:33:07 |
| 2. | F. Bonnamour | BBK | s.t. |
| 3. | J. Stuyven | TFS | s.t. |
| 4. | S. Dewulf | ACT | 0:03 |
| 5. | D. van Poppel | IWG | 0:40 |
| 6. | B. Coquard | BBK | s.t. |
| 7. | A. Marit | SVB | s.t. |
| 8. | A. Pasqualon | IWG | s.t. |
| 9. | J. Trarieux | DKO | s.t. |
| 10. | A. Capiot | ARK | s.t. |
| 11. | G. Van Hoecke | ACT | s.t. |
| 12. | J. Philipsen | AFC | s.t. |
| 13. | S. Leroux | XRL | s.t. |
| 14. | V. Tabellion | XRL | s.t. |
| 15. | P. Allegaert | COF | s.t. |
| 16. | A. Turgis | TEN | s.t. |
| 17. | U. Berrade | EKP | s.t. |
| 18. | M. Louvel | ARK | s.t. |
| 19. | R. Adrià | EKP | s.t. |
| 20. | J. van Emden | TJV | s.t. |

OCTOBER    .1 MEN'S RACE

## COPPA AGOSTONI
11 October 2021
Lissone–Lissone
180km

## WEATHER

TEMPERATURE
18°C

WIND
SW 7km/h

## RESULTS

| POS | NAME | TEAM | TIME |
|---|---|---|---|
| 1. | A. Lutsenko | APT | 4:19:44 |
| 2. | M. Trentin | UAD | s.t. |
| 3. | A. Covi | UAD | 0:12 |
| 4. | S. Velasco | GAZ | s.t. |
| 5. | V. Albanese | EOK | s.t. |
| 6. | K. Sbaragli | AFC | s.t. |
| 7. | L. Rota | IWG | s.t. |
| 8. | B. Tulett | AFC | s.t. |
| 9. | A. Valverde | MOV | s.t. |
| 10. | M. Bais | ANS | s.t. |
| 11. | A. Garosio | BCF | s.t. |
| 12. | O. C. Eiking | IWG | s.t. |
| 13. | S. Ravanelli | ANS | s.t. |
| 14. | B. Hermans | ISN | s.t. |
| 15. | R. Rochas | COF | s.t. |
| 16. | L. Fortunato | EOK | s.t. |
| 17. | G. Martin | COF | s.t. |
| 18. | X. Meurisse | AFC | 0:21 |
| 19. | R. Taaramäe | IWG | s.t. |
| 20. | L. Vervaeke | AFC | 0:31 |

OCTOBER .1 MEN'S RACE

# GIRO DEL VENETO

13 October 2021
Cittadella–Padova
168.8km

## WEATHER

TEMPERATURE
18°C

WIND
E 15km/h

## RESULTS

| POS | NAME | TEAM | TIME |
|---|---|---|---|
| 1. | X. Meurisse | AFC | 3:54:11 |
| 2. | M. Trentin | UAD | s.t. |
| 3. | A. Dainese | NAT | s.t. |
| 4. | S. Consonni | COF | s.t. |
| 5. | A. Covi | UAD | s.t. |
| 6. | V. Albanese | EOK | s.t. |
| 7. | J. Restrepo | ANS | s.t. |
| 8. | A. Pasqualon | IWG | s.t. |
| 9. | S. Velasco | GAZ | s.t. |
| 10. | D. Orrico | THR | s.t. |
| 11. | G. Carboni | BCF | s.t. |
| 12. | L. Chirico | ANS | s.t. |
| 13. | K. Sbaragli | AFC | s.t. |
| 14. | D. Gabburo | BCF | s.t. |
| 15. | M. Tizza | AMO | s.t. |
| 16. | M. Bais | ANS | s.t. |
| 17. | A. Lutsenko | APT | s.t. |
| 18. | O. C. Eiking | IWG | s.t. |
| 19. | S. Ravanelli | ANS | s.t. |
| 20. | A. Tolio | ZEF | s.t. |

## POGAČAR v OTHER POST-WAR MULTIPLE TOUR WINNERS

When Tadej Pogačar won the stage 5 time trial at the 2021 Tour de France, confirming that his 2020 form was still intact, the conversation turned to how many yellow jerseys the 22-year-old would go on to win. The Slovenian has so far made two appearances and claimed two victories, but how does that stand up against the other winners of multiple Tours in the post-war era? Each rider's Tour career presents its own signature, and Pogačar's could end up being a rather boring one if he finishes on the top step of the podium every year.

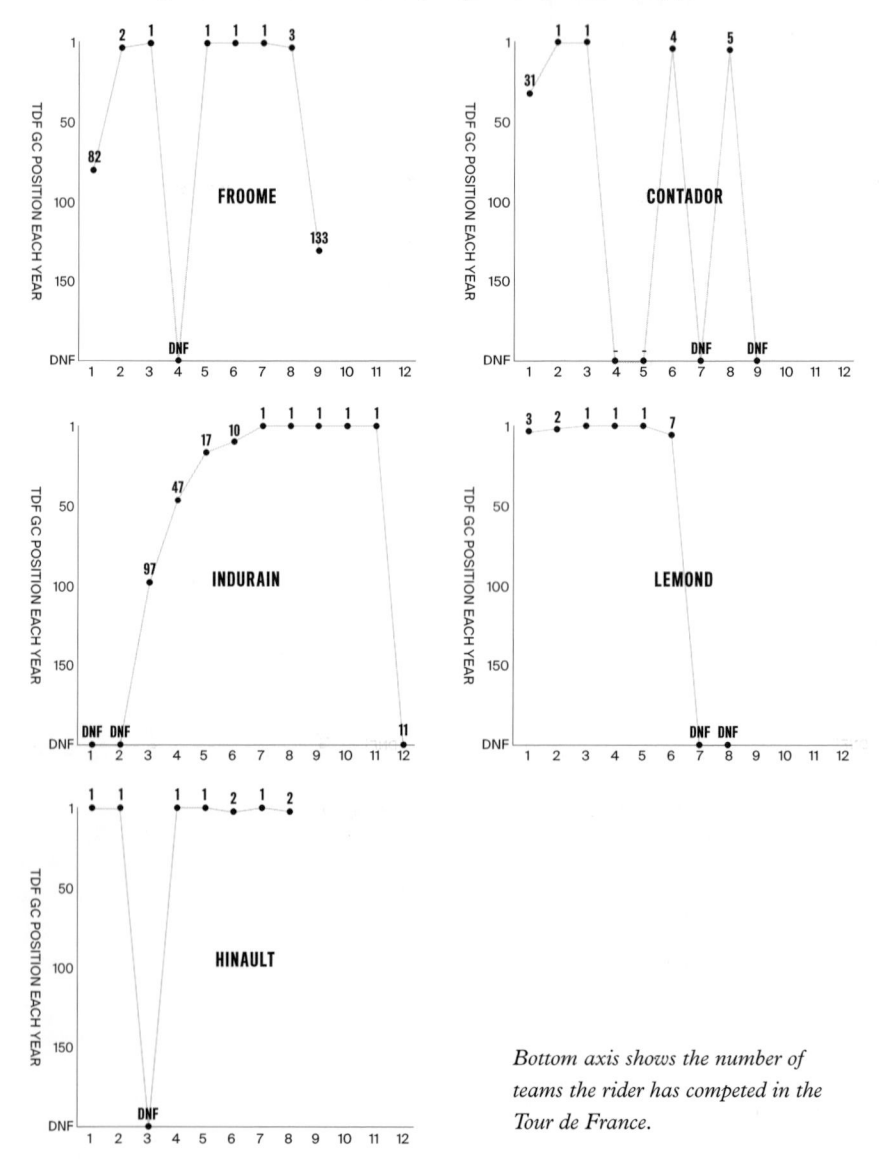

*Bottom axis shows the number of teams the rider has competed in the Tour de France.*

541

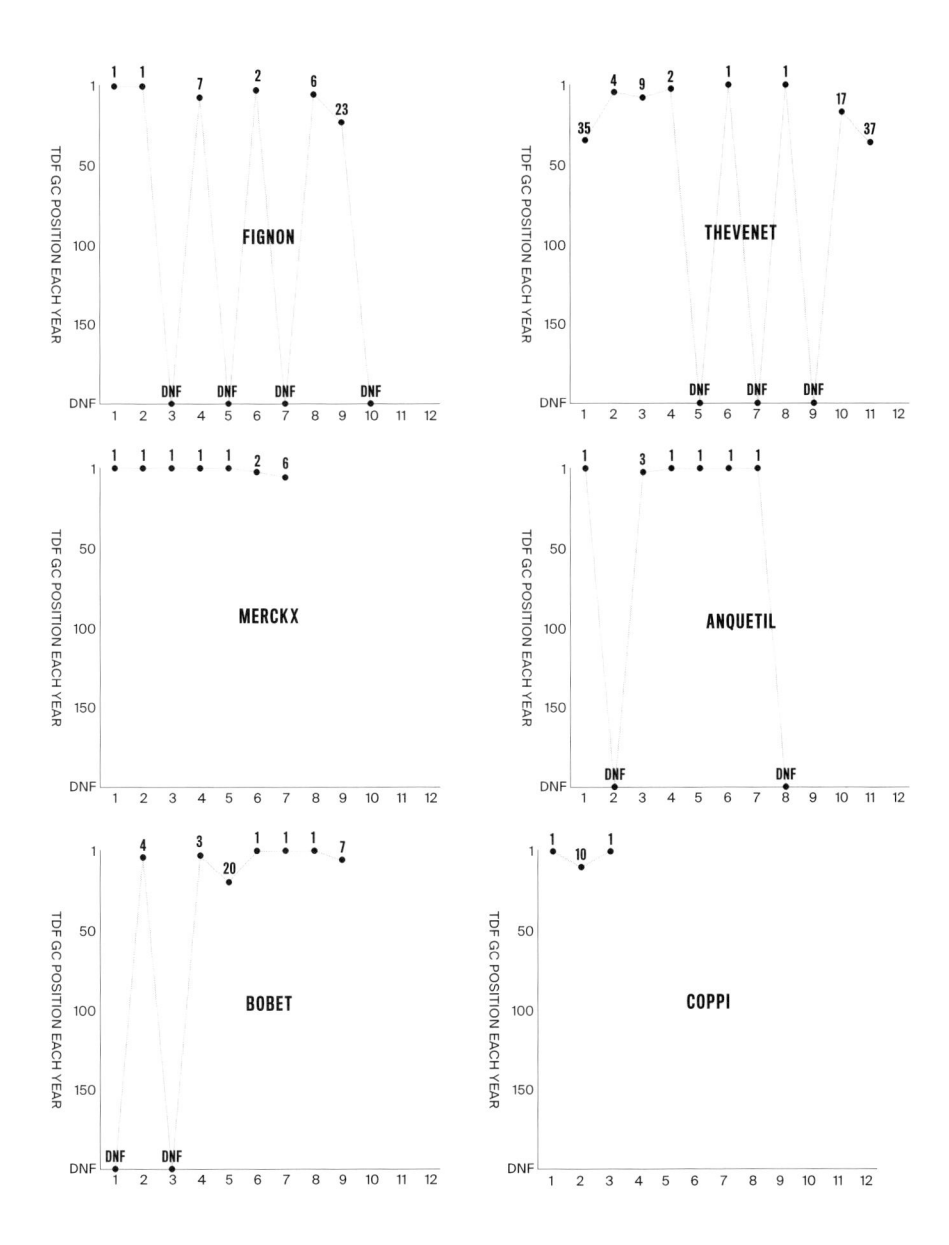

OCTOBER .PRO MEN'S RACE

## GP DU PLUMELEC-MORBIHAN
16 October 2021
Grand-Champ–Grand-Champ
176.9km

## WEATHER

TEMPERATURE  WIND
16°C  SE 15km/h

## RESULTS

| POS | NAME | TEAM | TIME |
|---|---|---|---|
| 1. | A. Marit | SVB | 3:51:40 |
| 2. | B. Coquard | BBK | s.t. |
| 3. | E. Viviani | COF | s.t. |
| 4. | J. Tesson | AUB | s.t. |
| 5. | D. Godon | ACT | s.t. |
| 6. | M. Peñalver | BBH | s.t. |
| 7. | T. Cotard | NAT | s.t. |
| 8. | R. Cardis | AUB | s.t. |
| 9. | A. Goeman | TIS | s.t. |
| 10. | L. Calmejane | ACT | s.t. |
| 11. | K. Van Rooy | SVB | s.t. |
| 12. | J. Simon | TEN | s.t. |
| 13. | M. De Witte | XRL | s.t. |
| 14. | N. Mahoudo | NAT | s.t. |
| 15. | S. Siemons | EVO | s.t. |
| 16. | M. Louvel | ARK | s.t. |
| 17. | G. De Wilde | SVB | s.t. |
| 18. | L. Teugels | TIS | s.t. |
| 19. | A. Riou | ARK | s.t. |
| 20. | S. Leroux | XRL | s.t. |

OCTOBER  .1 MEN'S RACE

# BOUCLES DE L'AULNE

17 October 2021
Châteaulin–Châteaulin
177.6km

## WEATHER

TEMPERATURE
16°C

WIND
S 13km/h

## RESULTS

| POS | NAME | TEAM | TIME |
|---|---|---|---|
| 1. | S. Dewulf | ACT | 4:11:03 |
| 2. | V. Madouas | GFC | 0:36 |
| 3. | M. Burgaudeau | TEN | s.t. |
| 4. | L. Pichon | ARK | s.t. |
| 5. | T. Træen | UXT | s.t. |
| 6. | S. Schönberger | BBK | s.t. |
| 7. | P. L. Périchon | COF | s.t. |
| 8. | J. I. Hvideberg | UXT | 0:42 |
| 9. | V. Ferron | TEN | 0:54 |
| 10. | R. Cardis | AUB | 1:00 |
| 11. | J. Antomarchi | XRL | 2:10 |
| 12. | T. Willems | SVB | 3:30 |
| 13. | A. Vuillermoz | TEN | 3:31 |
| 14. | S. Guglielmi | GFC | 3:32 |
| 15. | A. Zingle | COF | s.t. |
| 16. | E. Finé | COF | s.t. |
| 17. | J. Simon | TEN | s.t. |
| 18. | O. Le Gac | GFC | s.t. |
| 19. | F. Grellier | TEN | s.t. |
| 20. | L. Teugels | TIS | s.t. |

OCTOBER .1 MEN'S RACE

# CHRONO DES NATIONS

17 October 2021
Les Herbiers–Les Herbiers
44.5km

## WEATHER

**TEMPERATURE**
17°C

**WIND**
SE 11km/h

## RESULTS

| POS | NAME | TEAM | TIME |
|---|---|---|---|
| 1. | S. Küng | GFC | 51:47 |
| 2. | M. T. Madsen | BPC | 0:36 |
| 3. | A. De Marchi | ISN | 1:16 |
| 4. | A. Gate | BSC | 1:22 |
| 5. | R. Evenepoel | DQT | s.t. |
| 6. | R. Herregodts | SVB | 1:28 |
| 7. | F. Muff | TCQ | 1:32 |
| 8. | P. Latour | TEN | 1:44 |
| 9. | J. Wolf | BAI | 1:49 |
| 10. | M. Heidemann | LPC | 2:03 |
| 11. | S. Rossetto | AUB | 2:18 |
| 12. | R. Taaramäe | IWG | 2:22 |
| 13. | A. Delaplace | ARK | 2:27 |
| 14. | F. Ritzinger | NAT | 3:24 |
| 15. | J. Braun | SVL | 3:34 |
| 16. | I. Keisse | DQT | 3:39 |
| 17. | O. Ilić | NAT | 3:59 |
| 18. | T. Thill | XSU | 5:10 |
| 19. | M. Paasschens | BWB | 5:28 |
| 20. | P. Tzortzakis | KPT | 5:48 |

OCTOBER  .1 MEN'S RACE

## VENETO CLASSIC
17 October 2021
Venezia–Bassano Del Grappa
206.5km

## WEATHER

TEMPERATURE
18°C

WIND
SE 9km/h

### RESULTS

| POS | NAME | TEAM | TIME |
| --- | --- | --- | --- |
| 1. | S. Battistella | APT | 5:01:49 |
| 2. | M. Hirschi | UAD | 0:06 |
| 3. | J. Restrepo | ANS | s.t. |
| 4. | A. Lutsenko | APT | s.t. |
| 5. | R. Rochas | COF | 0:10 |
| 6. | D. Ulissi | UAD | 0:27 |
| 7. | L. Rota | IWG | s.t. |
| 8. | G. Martin | COF | 0:29 |
| 9. | A. Piccolo | NAT | 0:55 |
| 10. | C. Scaroni | GAZ | s.t. |
| 11. | V. Albanese | EOK | 1:37 |
| 12. | A. Dainese | NAT | 1:39 |
| 13. | A. Pasqualon | IWG | s.t. |
| 14. | E. Battaglin | BCF | s.t. |
| 15. | S. Velasco | GAZ | s.t. |
| 16. | D. Gabburo | BCF | s.t. |
| 17. | A. Garosio | BCF | s.t. |
| 18. | M. Trentin | UAD | s.t. |
| 19. | D. Orrico | THR | s.t. |
| 20. | M. Bais | ANS | s.t. |

OCTOBER    WORLDTOUR WOMEN'S RACE

# RONDE VAN DRENTHE
23 October 2021
Assen–Hoogeveen
159.1km

## WEATHER

TEMPERATURE
12°C

WIND
SW 19km/h

## PROFILE

ASSEN — HOOGEVEEN

The final race on the 2021 Women's WorldTour calendar took place in an unfamiliar October slot, after being postponed due to the Covid-19 pandemic. The lengthy 159.1km event saw Team DSM dominating the final, with four of its riders making it into the winning seven-strong move that established itself just 14km from the finish. As the day began, Lieke Nooijen (Parkhotel Valkenburg) rode away solo, opening a lead of over 3 minutes before being joined by Janneke Ensing (Team BikeExchange), who was riding on the offensive in the final professional race of her career. After a mechanical issue for Nooijen and the pace picking up in the peloton, the two leaders didn't last long and returned to the bunch with 85km remaining. More attacks came over the cobbles, then Kirstie van Haaften (Parkhotel Valkenburg) and Margaux Vigie (Valcar Travel & Service) jumped away and opened a 1-minute lead. However, Team DSM were alert to the danger and increased the pace in the bunch, reeling them back in. Further attacks followed but it wasn't until the final ascent of the short, steep VAMberg that the select group of seven riders managed to break away. By the time the leaders arrived at the finish line in Hoogeveen, their advantage was over a minute, with Team DSM riding with strength in numbers and delivering Lorena Wiebes to the victory. Despite not starting, Annemiek van Vleuten (Movistar Team) had enough points to secure the overall win in the WorldTour classification. (LM)

## BREAKAWAY

L. Nooijen (PHV), J. Ensing (BEX)

## RESULTS

| POS | NAME | TEAM | TIME |
|---|---|---|---|
| 1. | L. Wiebes | DSM | 4:07:34 |
| 2. | E. Cecchini | SDW | s.t. |
| 3. | E. Gasparrini | VAL | s.t. |
| 4. | E. Chabbey | CSR | s.t. |
| 5. | F. Mackaij | DSM | s.t. |
| 6. | P. Georgi | DSM | s.t. |
| 7. | F. Koch | DSM | 0:06 |
| 8. | S. Andersen | DSM | 1:15 |
| 9. | C. Consonni | VAL | s.t. |
| 10. | N. Kessler | TIB | s.t. |
| 11. | A. Jackson | LIV | s.t. |
| 12. | A. van der Hulst | PHV | s.t. |
| 13. | S. Roy | BEX | s.t. |
| 14. | C. Kool | NXG | s.t. |
| 15. | R. Kasper | JVW | s.t. |
| 16. | M. Bredewold | PHV | s.t. |
| 17. | A. Cordon-Ragot | TFS | s.t. |
| 18. | E. Harris | CSR | s.t. |
| 19. | L. Uneken | SDW | 1:21 |
| 20. | A. Barnes | CSR | s.t. |

## TRIVIA

» While Wiebes has won 13 races this year, it took her until October to claim a WorldTour victory, taking three in one month.

OCTOBER   .1 MEN'S RACE

# RONDE VAN DRENTHE
24 October 2021
Assen–Hoogeveen
188.5km

## WEATHER

**TEMPERATURE**
12°C

**WIND**
S 15km/h

## RESULTS

| POS | NAME | TEAM | TIME |
|---|---|---|---|
| 1. | R. Herregodts | SVB | 4:22:07 |
| 2. | A. Pasqualon | IWG | 0:13 |
| 3. | D. Groenewegen | JVD | s.t. |
| 4. | C. Vermeltfoort | VWE | s.t. |
| 5. | A. Marit | SVB | s.t. |
| 6. | T. de Jong | VWE | s.t. |
| 7. | T. Willems | SVB | s.t. |
| 8. | N. Eekhoff | DSM | s.t. |
| 9. | J. Knolle | SVL | s.t. |
| 10. | V. Broex | MET | s.t. |
| 11. | N. van der Lijke | RIW | s.t. |
| 12. | J. Huppertz | LKH | s.t. |
| 13. | K. Van Rooy | SVB | s.t. |
| 14. | T. van der Hoorn | IWG | s.t. |
| 15. | S. Flynn | SEG | s.t. |
| 16. | C. Desal | BWB | s.t. |
| 17. | D. De Maeght | BWB | s.t. |
| 18. | D. Neuman | EKA | s.t. |
| 19. | J. Bouts | BCY | s.t. |
| 20. | J. Eyskens | EVO | s.t. |

# NATIONAL CHAMPIONS

An almost full programme of National Championships (with the odd exception) returned to its rightful place in June. The weekend before the Tour de France once again saw the coronation of dozens of new national champions, just in time for many of the men to take their newly stitched jerseys to the Tour. The road races retain eccentric individual characteristics, given their nature. For example, in France Groupama-FDJ started the men's race with 15 riders and still failed to win the race. And the Czech and Slovak races were held together, one peloton racing as a reminder of the way things were before the dissolution of Czechoslovakia.

# MEN'S ROAD RACE NATIONAL CHAMPIONS 2021

|  |  |
|---|---|
| Albania | 1. Y. Sefa / 2. K. Sota / 3. D. Bardhi |
| Algeria | 1. A. Lagab / 2. E. K. Sassane / 3. A. Mansouri |
| Australia | 1. C. Meyer / 2. K. O'Brien / 3. S. Bowden |
| Austria | 1. P. Konrad / 2. M. Haller / 3. P. Gamper |
| Azerbaijan | 1. M. Mikayilzade / 2. S. Jabrayilov / 3. S. Eyvazov |
| Belarus | 1. S. Bazhkou / 2. M Grinkevich / 3. Y. Sobal |
| Belgium | 1. W. van Aert / 2. E. Theuns / 3. R. Evenepoel |
| Belize | 1. J. Williams / 2. O. Quiroz / 3. S. Codd |
| Bermuda | 1. D. Mayho / 2. C. White / 3. K. Hopkins |
| Bulgaria | 1. S. Gyurov / 2. M. Papanov / 3. P. Balabanov |
| Burkina Faso | 1. P. Daumont / 2. B. Nikiema / 3. S. Kone |
| Canada | 1. G. Boivin / 2. A. Duchesne / 3. D. Gee |
| Chile | 1. J. L. Rodriguez / 2. A. Paredes / 3. F. Kotsakis |
| Colombia | 1. A. Cala / 2. M. T. Suesca / 3. L. M. Martinez |
| Croatia | 1. V. Potočki / 2. F. Miholjević / 3. F. Kvasina |
| Czech Republic | 1. M. Kukrle / 2. D. Neuman / 3. D. Turek |
| Denmark | 1. M. Würtz Schmidt / 2. F. Wandahl / 3. M. Norsgaard |
| Ecuador | 1. J. A. Cepeda / 2. B. Guamá / 3. S. Navarrete |
| El Salvador | 1. C. Alvergue / 2. J. D. Joya / 3. A. V. Orellana |
| Eritrea | 1. D. Yemane / 2. M. Kudus / 3. M. Eyob |
| Estonia | 1. M. Räim / 2. K. P. Lauk / 3. A. Jakin |
| Ethiopia | 1. H. Hailu / 2. A. Abdureazak / 3. A. Belachew |
| Finland | 1. J. Henttala / 2. U. I. Peltonen / 3. A. J. Juntunen |
| France | 1. R. Cavagna / 2. R. Molard / 3. D. Touzé |
| Georgia | 1. N. Sitchinava / 2. G. Suvadzoglu / 3. G. Kochakidze |
| Germany | 1. M. Schachmann / 2. J. Koch / 3. G. Zimmerman |
| Great Britain | 1. B. Swift / 2. F. Wright / 3. E. Hayter |
| Greece | 1. G. Boutopoulos / 2. N. Drakos / 3. P. Christopoulos-Cheller |
| Guatemala | 1. A. Julajuj / 2. S. G. Chumil / 3. F. O. Toc |
| Hungary | 1. V. Filutás / 2. Z. Istlstekker / 3. G. Orosz |
| Iran | 1. S. Safarzadeh / 2. M. Ganjkhanlou / 3. M. Rezaei |
| Ireland | 1. R. Mullen / 2. D. Feeley / 3. C. McDunphy |
| Israel | 1. V. Logionov / 2. S. Abu-Fares / 3. I. Einhorn |
| Italy | 1. S. Colbrelli / 2. F. Masnada / 3. S. Zoccarato |
| Kazakhstan | 1. Y. Federov / 2. Y. Gidich / 3. A. Zakharov |
| Kosovo | 1. A. Delija / 2. E. Misini / 3. A. Ymeri |
| Latvia | 1. T. Skujiņš / 2. A. Flaksis / 3. M. Bogdanovics |
| Libenon | 1. J. Alahmad / 2. A. Salloum / 3. N. Elkadi |
| Lithuania | 1. I. Konovalovas / 2. A. Mikutis / 3. E. Šiškevičius |
| Luxembourg | 1. K. Geniets / 2. J. Drucker / 3. L. Bettendorff |
| Mauritius | 1. A. Mayer / 2. Y. Lincoln / 3. T. Desvaux De Marigny |
| Mexico | 1. E. Frayre / 2. O. Garibay / 3. F. A. De Luna |
| Moldova | 1. A. Sobennicov / 2. C. Raileanu / 3. N. Bumbu |
| Mongolia | 1. E. Bolor-Erdene / 2. M. Erdensuren / 3. G. Bat-Orshikh |
| Montenegro | 1. S. Milonjić / 2. F. Krgović / 3. M. Dašić |
| Namibia | 1. D. Coetzee / 2. T. De Lange / 3. I. Cuff |
| Netherlands | 1. T. Roosen / 2. S. Bax / 3. O. Riesebeek |
| New Zealand | 1. G. Bennett / 2. M. Torckler / 3. R. Christensen |
| North Macedonia | 1. P. Dimevski / 2. K. Vanchevski / 3. M. Memedi |
| Norway | 1. T. Foss / 2. A. Skaarseth / 3. K. Aasvold |
| Panama | 1. F. Archibold / 2. C. R. Jurado / 3. A. A. Strah |
| Poland | 1. M. Paterski / 2. A. Banaszek / 3. L. Owsian |
| Portugal | 1. J. C. P. Neves Fernandes / 2. R. Oliveira / 3. G. Goncalves |
| Puerto Rico | 1. A. González / 2. E. N. Reyes / 3. G. Pérez |
| Romania | 1. S. Tvetcov / 2. E. M. Grosu / 3. D. Crista |
| Russia | 1. A. Nych / 2. I. Zakarin / 3. I. Rovny |
| Serbia | 1. D. Rajović / 2. S. Stefanović / 3. V. Stojnić |
| Slovakia | 1. P. Sagan / 2. M. Štoček / 3. L. Kubiš |
| Slovenia | 1. M. Mohorič / 2. J. Polanc / 3. L. Mezgec |
| South Africa | 1. M. O. Pritzen / 2. W. Smit / 3. N. Dlamini |
| South Korea | 1. K. G. Jang / 2. D. Choi / 3. D. Joo |
| Spain | 1. O. Fraile / 2. J. Herrada / 3. A. Aranburu |
| Sweden | 1. V. Hillerström Rundh / 2. R. Larsen / 3. L. Eriksson |
| Switzerland | 1. S. Dillier / 2. S. Pellaud / 3. J. Jacobs |
| Thailand | 1. S. Sirironnachai / 2. P. Chawchiangkwang / 3. T. Chaiyasombat |
| Turkey | 1. O. Balkan / 2. B. Özgür / 3. A. Örken |
| Ukraine | 1. A. Ponomar / 2. A. Budyak / 3. A. Kulyk |
| UAE | 1. Y. Mirza / 2. A. Al Mansoori / 3. K. Mayouf |

NATIONAL CHAMPIONS

| | | |
|---|---|---|
| USA | 1. | J. Rosskopf |
| | 2. | B. Bookwalter |
| | 3. | K. Murphy |
| Uruguay | 1. | R. Asconeguy |
| | 2. | A. S. Maldonado |
| | 3. | P. D. Pintos |
| Uzbekistan | 1. | D. Evdokimov |
| | 2. | B. Rakhimbaev |
| | 3. | A. Sunnatov |
| Venezuela | 1. | L. Gomez |
| | 2. | Á. Pulgar |
| | 3. | R. Sierra |

# MEN'S TIME TRIAL NATIONAL CHAMPIONS 2021

|  |  |
|---|---|
| Albania | 1. Y. Sefa<br>2. O. Velia<br>3. D. Bardhi |
| Algeria | 1. H. Mansouri<br>2. S. Badlis<br>3. S. Benganif |
| Australia | 1. L. Plapp<br>2. L. Durbridge<br>3. K. O'Brien |
| Austria | 1. M. Brändle<br>2. F. Ritzinger<br>3. M. Wildauer |
| Azerbaijan | 1. M. Mikayilzade<br>2. S. Jabrayilov<br>3. A. Abdulazizli |
| Belarus | 1. Y. Karaliok<br>2. S. Bazhkou<br>3. Y. Sobal |
| Belgium | 1. Y. Lampaert<br>2. R. Evenepoel<br>3. V. Campenaerts |
| Belize | 1. O. Quiroz<br>2. E. Trapp<br>3. J. Fuller |
| Bulgaria | 1. P. Dimitrov<br>2. S. Gyurov<br>3. N. Genov |
| Canada | 1. H. Houle<br>2. A. Cowan<br>3. D. Gee |
| Chile | 1. J. L. Rodriguez<br>2. A. Paredes<br>3. J. Lira |
| Colombia | 1. W. Vargas<br>2. D. A. Camargo<br>3. A. C. Ardila |
| Croatia | 1. T. Stojanov<br>2. L. Marenzi<br>3. J. Bugarija |
| Czech Republic | 1. J. Černy<br>2. J. Bárta<br>3. A. Toupalík |
| Denmark | 1. K. Asgreen<br>2. M. Bjerg<br>3. M. T. Madsen |
| Ecuador | 1. J. Montenegro<br>2. S. Navarrete<br>3. L. S. Novoa |
| El Salvador | 1. R. E. Monroy<br>2. A. V. Orellana<br>3. B. F. Mendoza |
| Eritrea | 1. M. Kudus<br>2. M. Debesay<br>3. D. Yemane |
| Estonia | 1. R. Taaramäe<br>2. N. Vahtra<br>3. A. Mirzojev |
| Ethiopia | 1. H. Hailu<br>2. A. Abdureazak<br>3. A. Kider |
| Finland | 1. M. Hietajärvi<br>2. U. I. Peltonen<br>3. M. Auvinen |
| France | 1. B. Thomas<br>2. B. Armirail<br>3. A. Brunel |
| Georgia | 1. N. Sitchinava<br>2. V. Mamulashvili<br>3. G. Suvadzoglu |
| Germany | 1. T. Martin<br>2. M. Heidemann<br>3. M. Walscheid |
| Great Britain | 1. E. Hayter<br>2. D. Bigham<br>3. J. Shaw |
| Greece | 1. P. Tzortzakis<br>2. A. Mengoulas<br>3. D. Christakos |
| Guatemala | 1. M. Rodas<br>2. F. O .Toc<br>3. G. Toc |
| Hungary | 1. E. Fetter<br>2. A. Valter<br>3. J. Pelikán |
| Iran | 1. B. Ariyan<br>2. M. Rezvani<br>3. S. Safarzadeh |
| Ireland | 1. R. Mullen<br>2. N. Roche<br>3. M. Christie |
| Israel | 1. O. Goldstein<br>2. V. Logionov<br>3. G. Sagiv |
| Italy | 1. M. Sobrero<br>2. E. Affini<br>3. M. Cattaneo |
| Kazakhstan | 1. D. Fominykh<br>2. Y. Fedorov<br>3. Y. Natarov |
| Kosovo | 1. A. Delija<br>2. A. Ymeri<br>3. E. Misini |
| Latvia | 1. T. Skujiņš<br>2. E. Liepiņš<br>3. A. Vosekalns |
| Libenon | 1. K. Chehade<br>2. J. Alahmad<br>3. A. Zoobi |
| Lithuania | 1. E. Šiškevičius<br>2. A. Mikutis<br>3. V. Lašinis |
| Luxembourg | 1. K. Geniets<br>2. M. Ries<br>3. A. Kirsch |
| Mauritius | 1. C. Rougier-Lagane<br>2. Y. Lincoln<br>3. A. Mayer |
| Mexico | 1. I. D. J. Prado<br>2. O. Aguilera<br>3. M. Zamora |
| Moldova | 1. C. Raileanu<br>2. A. Vrabii<br>3. A. Garibian |
| Mongolia | 1. M. E. Batmunkh<br>2. E. Bolor-Erdene<br>3. T. B. Batsaikhan |
| Montenegro | 1. G. Cerovic<br>2. A. Radunović<br>3. D. Vukčević |
| Namibia | 1. D. Coetzee<br>2. H. Neumann<br>3. E. Masckernzy |
| Netherlands | 1. T. Dumoulin<br>2. S. Langeveld<br>3. K. Bouwman |
| New Zealand | 1. A. Gate<br>2. G. Bennett<br>3. M. Vink |
| North Macedonia | 1. A. Petrovski<br>2. D. Jakimovski<br>3. M. Nacevski |
| Norway | 1. T. Foss<br>2. S. Wærenskjold<br>3. A. Leknessund |
| Panama | 1. C. R. Jurado<br>2. F. Archibold<br>3. B. Espinoza Serrano |
| Poland | 1. M. Bodnar<br>2. F. Maciejuk<br>3. Ł. Wiśniowski |
| Portugal | 1. J. Almeida<br>2. R. Reis<br>3. J. C. P. Neves Fernandes |
| Puerto Rico | 1. A. González<br>2. E. N. Reyes<br>3. R. Morales |
| Romania | 1. S. Tvetcov<br>2. D. Crista<br>3. E. Dima |
| Russia | 1. A. Vlasov<br>2. A. Ovechkin<br>3. V. Duyunov |
| Serbia | 1. O. Ilić<br>2. S. Klisurić<br>3. D. Veselinović |
| Singapore | 1. B. K. Yeo<br>2. Z. Y. D. Lim<br>3. T. K. C. Sim |
| Slovakia | 1. R. Kuba<br>2. L. Kubiš<br>3. J. A. Cully |
| Slovenia | 1. J. Tratnik<br>2. J. Polanc<br>3. T. Pogačar |
| South Africa | 1. R. Gibbons<br>2. M. Beers<br>3. K. Main |
| South Korea | 1. S. Choi<br>2. K. Min<br>3. D. Shin |
| Spain | 1. I. Izagirre<br>2. D. de la Cruz<br>3. C. Rodriguez |
| Sweden | 1. H. Forssell<br>2. J. Ahlsson<br>3. T. Ludvigsson |
| Switzerland | 1. S. Küng<br>2. M. Hirschi<br>3. T. Schir |
| Thailand | 1. P. Chawchiangkwang<br>2. S. Sirironnachai<br>3. P. Ladngern |
| Turkey | 1. A. Örken<br>2. O. Tiryaki<br>3. M. Sayar |
| Ukraine | 1. M. Kononenko<br>2. O. Golovash<br>3. V. Gryniv |
| UAE | 1. Y. Mirza<br>2. A. Al Mansoori<br>3. J. A. Qambar |
| USA | 1. L. Craddock<br>2. C. Haga<br>3. T. van Garderen |
| Uzbekistan | 1. M. Halmuratov<br>2. A. Fomovskiy<br>3. B. Rakhimbaev |
| Venezuela | 1. J. J. Rujano<br>2. E. Viloria<br>3. J. A. Díaz |

# WOMEN'S ROAD RACE NATIONAL CHAMPIONS 2021

| | | | | | |
|---|---|---|---|---|---|
| Algeria | 1. Y. Elmeddah<br>2. N. Y. Bouzenzen<br>3. T. L. Kasmi | Germany | 1. L. Brennauer<br>2. L. Lippert<br>3. R. Bauernfeind | Puerto Rico | 1. D. Cariño<br>2. C. Sánchez<br>3. V. Bracero |
| Australia | 1. S. Roy<br>2. G. Brown<br>3. L. Hanson | Great Britain | 1. P. Georgi<br>2. J. Nelson<br>3. J. Lowden | Romania | 1. G. Ungureanu<br>2. M. Stan<br>3. M. Muresan |
| Austria | 1. K. Schweinberger<br>2. V. Eberhardt<br>3. C. Schweinberger | Greece | 1. V. Fasoi<br>2. S. Liodaki<br>3. E. M. Karousou | Russia | 1. S. Krylova<br>2. D. Fomina<br>3. T. Dronova-Balabolina |
| Azerbaijan | 1. A. Khankishiyeva<br>2. N. Valiyeva<br>3. M. Isgandarova | Guatemala | 1. J. G. Soto<br>2. C. E. Lee<br>3. V. Gomez Fuentes | Serbia | 1. J. Erić<br>2. S. Počuča<br>3. M. Urošević |
| Belarus | 1. T. Sharakova<br>2. H. Tserakh<br>3. A. Abramenko | Hungary | 1. K. B. Vas<br>2. B. Benko<br>3. Z. Szabó | Slovakia | 1. T. Medvedová<br>2. R. Paulechová<br>3. N. Jenčušová |
| Belgium | 1. L. Kopecky<br>2. J. Van de Velde<br>3. A. Castrique | Iran | 1. S. Yazdani<br>2. M. Dehghan<br>3. F. Abdollahi | Slovenia | 1. E. Bujak<br>2. U. Pintar<br>3. Š. Kern |
| Belize | 1. A. Thompson<br>2. K. Cattouse<br>3. N. Gallego | Ireland | 1. I. Cotter<br>2. M. Armitage<br>3. L. Kelly | South Africa | 1. H. Preen<br>2. C. Oberholzer<br>3. F. Janse van Rensburg |
| Bermuda | 1. C. Conyers<br>2. N. Mitchell<br>3. K. Smith | Israel | 1. O. Shapira<br>2. R. Gafinovitz<br>3. N. Maoz | South Korea | 1. E. Lee<br>2. S. Jang<br>3. Y. Lee |
| Bulgaria | 1. P. Minkova<br>2. V. Danova<br>3. M. Garalieva | Italy | 1. E. Longo Borghini<br>2. T. Guderzo<br>3. I. Sanguineti | Spain | 1. M. García<br>2. A. Santesteban<br>3. S. Martin |
| Burkina Faso | 1. A. Bamogo<br>2. L. Lamoussa<br>3. C. Bilgo | Kazakhstan | 1. M. Umutzhanova<br>2. F. Potapova<br>3. R. Sultanova | Sweden | 1. C. Winell<br>2. H. Johansson<br>3. A. Nessmar |
| Canada | 1. A. Jackson<br>2. M. Rochette<br>3. S. Poidevin | Latvia | 1. L. Svarinska<br>2. D. Rožlapa<br>3. L. Laizane | Switzerland | 1. M. Reusser<br>2. E. Chabbey<br>3. N. Rüegg |
| Chile | 1. A. V. Villalón<br>2. P. C. Villalon Sanchez<br>3. K. Vallejos | Lithuania | 1. I. Češuliene<br>2. A. Gedraitytė<br>3. O. Baleišytė | Thailand | 1. S. Nuntana<br>2. P. Somrat<br>3. C. Nontasin |
| Colombia | 1. Y. L. Colmenares<br>2. P. A. Patiño<br>3. D. Peñuela | Luxembourg | 1. C. Majerus<br>2. S. Margue<br>3. M. Berg | Turkey | 1. A. Bekar<br>2. E. Kurkcu<br>3. E. Bayram |
| Croatia | 1. M. Perinović<br>2. M. Radotić<br>3. M. Marukić | Mauritius | 1. R. Lamusse<br>2. L. De Marigny-Lagesse<br>3. C. Halbwachs | Ukraine | 1. O. Shekel<br>2. V. Kononenko<br>3. O. Sharga |
| Czech Republic | 1. T. Neumanova<br>2. N. Bajgerová<br>3. N. Nosková | Mexico | 1. L. Y. Salazar<br>2. M. A. Gaxiola<br>3. K. Martinez | USA | 1. L. Stephens<br>2. C. Rivera<br>3. V. Ewers |
| Denmark | 1. A. Dideriksen<br>2. E. Norsgaard<br>3. C. Uttrup Ludwig | Mongolia | 1. T. Solongo<br>2. E. Gantogtokh<br>3. A. Jinjilbadam | Uruguay | 1. A. Fernánde<br>2. F. Giordano<br>3. F. Granizal |
| Ecuador | 1. M. M. Nuñez<br>2. D. A. Jimenez<br>3. N. P. Narvaez | Namibia | 1. V. Looser<br>2. G. Raith<br>3. R. Dreyer | Uzbekistan | 1. Y. Kuskova<br>2. N. Kozieva<br>3. S. Abdullaeva |
| El Salvador | 1. I. Diaz<br>2. K. Umaña<br>3. X. Estrada | Netherlands | 1. A. Pieters<br>2. N. van der Burg<br>3. K. Swinkels | Venezuela | 1. W. Moreno<br>2. K. Clement<br>3. M. Briceño Jimenez |
| Eritrea | 1. B. Ghebremeskel<br>2. A. Dawit<br>3. A. Tesfalem | New Zealand | 1. G. Williams<br>2. K. McCarthy<br>3. S. Lucas | | |
| Estonia | 1. A. G. Tuisk<br>2. M. I. Möttus<br>3. L. Ehrberg | Norway | 1. V. Heine<br>2. E. Moberg<br>3. I. Gåskjenn | | |
| Ethiopia | 1. T. Tesfay<br>2. S. T. Watango<br>3. E. Tafese | Panama | 1. W. Ducruex<br>2. A. Von Chong<br>3. Y. Cubilla | | |
| Finland | 1. A. Gröndahl<br>2. M. M. Kangas<br>3. M. Helmi | Poland | 1. K. Karasiewicz<br>2. D. Pikulik<br>3. D. Wlodarczyk | | |
| France | 1. É. Muzic<br>2. A. Cordon-Ragot<br>3. G. Verhulst | Portugal | 1. M. Martins<br>2. D. Campos<br>3. D. Pereira | | |

## WOMEN'S TIME TRIAL NATIONAL CHAMPIONS 2021

|  |  |  |  |  |  |
|---|---|---|---|---|---|
| Algeria | 1. Y. Elmeddah<br>2. N. Y. Bouzenzen<br>3. T. L. Kasmi | Greece | 1. E. M. Tsavari<br>2. A. Milaki<br>3. A. Chatzistyli | Singapore | 1. Y. Luo<br>2. C. W. S. Tan<br>3. S. Tan |
| Australia | 1. S. Gigante<br>2. G. Brown<br>3. N. Frain | Guatemala | 1. J. G. Soto<br>2. C. E. Lee<br>3. V. Gomez Fuentes | Slovakia | 1. N. Jenčušová<br>2. J. Stevkova<br>3. N. Čorbová |
| Austria | 1. A. Kiesenhofer<br>2. G. Erharter<br>3. C. Schweinberger | Hungary | 1. K. B. Vas<br>2. B. Benko<br>3. D. Jordán | Slovenia | 1. E. Bujak<br>2. U. Pintar<br>3. U. Žigart |
| Azerbaijan | 1. A. Khankishiyeva<br>2. N. Valiyeva<br>3. M. Isgandarova | Iran | 1. M. Dehghan<br>2. S. Yazdani<br>3. S. Siyahian | South Africa | 1. C. Lill<br>2. C. Oberholzer<br>3. Z. Rossouw |
| Belarus | 1. T. Sharakova<br>2. H. Tserakh<br>3. M. Zueva | Ireland | 1. J. Patterson<br>2. E. McCrystal<br>3. L. Kelly | South Korea | 1. J. Shin<br>2. Y. Lee<br>3. S. Jang |
| Belgium | 1. L. Kopeky<br>2. J. Van de Velde<br>3. J. De Wilde | Italy | 1. E. Longo Borghini<br>2. S. Paladin<br>3. T. Guderzo | Spain | 1. M. García<br>2. S. Martin<br>3. L. Oyarbide |
| Belize | 1. N. Gallego<br>2. K. Cattouse<br>3. A. Thompson | Kazakhstan | 1. R. Sultanova<br>2. M. Kuzmina<br>3. A. Solovyeva | Sweden | 1. N. Eklund<br>2. E. Granqvist<br>3. H. Nilsson |
| Bulgaria | 1. I. Kostadinova<br>2. P. Minkova<br>3. V. Danova | Latvia | 1. D. Rožlapa<br>2. L. Laizane<br>3. L. Svarinska | Switzerland | 1. M. Reusser<br>2. M. Maurer<br>3. F. Buri |
| Canada | 1. A. Jackson<br>2. M. S. Blais<br>3. G. Ellsay | Lithuania | 1. I. Češulienė<br>2. V. Senkutė<br>3. O. Baleišytė | Thailand | 1. P. Somrat<br>2. S. Nuntana<br>3. K. Chairin |
| Chile | 1. A. V. Villalón<br>2. P. C. Villalon Sanchez<br>3. S. Subercaseaux | Luxembourg | 1. C. Majerus<br>2. C. Coljon<br>3. M. Berg | Turkey | 1. E. Bayram<br>2. A. Bekar<br>3. B. Hepkaradeniz |
| Colombia | 1. S. Guluma<br>2. A. Sanabria<br>3. A. Fagua | Mexico | 1. A. Barraza<br>2. V. Leal<br>3. A. M. Hernández | Ukraine | 1. V. Kononenko<br>2. G. Solovei<br>3. O. Shekel |
| Croatia | 1. M. Radotić<br>2. M. Marukić<br>3. A. Musa | Mongolia | 1. A. Jinjiibadam<br>2. T. Solongo<br>3. S. Ariuntsengel | USA | 1. C. Dygert<br>2. A. Neben<br>3. L. Thomas |
| Czech Republic | 1. N. Nosková<br>2. J. Machačová<br>3. N. Flašarová | Namibia | 1. V. Looser<br>2. R. Dreyer<br>3. C. Liebenberg | Uzbekistan | 1. Y. Kuskova<br>2. A. Kulikova<br>3. E. Golotina |
| Denmark | 1. E. Norsgaard<br>2. L. Holm Houbak<br>3. C. Uttrup Ludwig | Netherlands | 1. A. van der Breggen<br>2. E. Van Dijk<br>3. L. Brand | Venezuela | 1. W. Moreno<br>2. A. Luque De Briceño<br>3. K. Clemant |
| Ecuador | 1. M. M. Nuñez<br>2. A. E. Ortega<br>3. N. P. Narvaez | New Zealand | 1. G. Williams<br>2. J. Nielsen<br>3. B. Macgregor | | |
| El Salvador | 1. K. Umaña<br>2. G. Cárcamo<br>3. W. Paez | Norway | 1. K. Aalerud<br>2. V. Heine<br>3. M. B. Ottestad | | |
| Eritrea | 1. A. Tesfalem<br>2. D. Fitsum<br>3. B. Fessehaye | Panama | 1. C. M. Mata<br>2. W. Ducruex<br>3. A. S. Rodríguez Morales | | |
| Estonia | 1. M. I. Mõttus<br>2. K. Reinpõld<br>3. A. G. Tuisk | Poland | 1. K. Karasiewicz<br>2. A. Nerlo<br>3. M. Jaskulska | | |
| Ethiopia | 1. T. Tesfay<br>2. S. T. Watango<br>3. E. Tafese | Portugal | 1. D. Campos<br>2. A. Caramelo<br>3. L. Domingues Jesus | | |
| Finland | 1. T. Pohjalainen<br>2. M. M. Kangas<br>3. M. Tuliniemi | Puerto Rico | 1. D. Cariño<br>2. K. Marrero<br>3. A. Acevedo | | |
| France | 1. A. Cordon-Ragot<br>2. J. Labous<br>3. C. Kerbaol | Romania | 1. M. Muresan<br>2. M. E. Stancu<br>3. G. Ungureanu | | |
| Germany | 1. L. Brennauer<br>2. L. Klein<br>3. H. Ludwig | Russia | 1. T. Dronova-Balabolina<br>2. N. Studenikina<br>3. T. Antoshina | | |
| Great Britain | 1. A. Henderson<br>2. J. Lowden<br>3. L. Dixon | Serbia | 1. S. Počuča<br>2. M. Urošević<br>3. I. Vilim | | |

# SHAKING MY CONFIDENCE

BY CECILIE UTTRUP LUDWIG

*Cecilie Uttrup Ludwig is one of the most talented and engaging riders in the women's peloton. After racing La Course in 2018, and then the Tour of Flanders in 2019, she became well known across the world for giving post-race interviews on television that were brimming over with her love for the sport and her excitement at participating. Her default setting is searing honesty. Yet this enthusiasm can belie the fact that the Dane is a very serious athlete and belongs squarely in the small group of elite racers who routinely contest victory in the biggest races. However, going into 2021, she had yet to win a WorldTour race. That was about to change, but the journey to victory would be intense.*

---

In January we had a team camp in Spain, in Cambrils. It's one of those places that is a bit like a black hole. If there's any wind around, it finds Cambrils. Every time we're there, you step out of the front door of the hotel and it's like a hurricane. I mean, it's unbelievable! But it was good training, although not on a TT bike; that would be scary.

After three weeks off the bike, I always feel like: 'Holy crap, I'm in such a shit state! It's so lucky that I am not racing for months.' But I also feel that it's so important from the mental side to really put the bike aside. Because then, when I get back on the bike, I'm super-hungry for training and preparing. I always think: 'Next year I want to be even better. I want to train harder.'

I was supposed to make my season's debut in Valencia. I always like to start there; it's in Spain, quite close to where Girona is, the weather is normally OK and it's a stage race so you can get into the rhythm of doing some hard racing. Then, a few weeks before the race, they cancelled it. I couldn't help wondering if this was just the start of it – that all the next races would be cancelled too. But I was hopeful that the Belgian races would go ahead; after all, they'd held the Cyclocross World Championships there in January, so I always thought that Omloop Het Nieuwsblad would happen. What a tough start, though. I mean, right in at the deep end!

I was pretty calm on the morning before the race. Normally you're so nervous before the first race of the season, worrying about your form compared to your competitors. But I knew there was nothing more that I could do; there was no more time for training. Now was the time to go out and play and hope for the best. But then when we drove into the big warehouse for the race presentation, it really struck home: 'Shit's getting real.' And that's when it hit me, and I started to get nervous.

It's always a nervy start to Omloop. I remember thinking: 'Wow, this is actually really nice weather for Belgium.' It was 10 degrees and no rain, but for the first hour I was quite cold because the speed wasn't so high. The break went and then we just trundled along.

When the break had about three minutes, we got stopped at a level crossing because a train had to pass. And straight away, every girl threw their bike into the gutter: it was time to pee! Everyone started peeing, and I thought to myself: 'Now I think about it, I need to as well.' But in Belgium the barriers don't stay down for long. The train zoomed past, and less than 30 seconds later the barriers went up just as I was sitting there with my arse in the ditch. Half the peloton was crouching down peeing. Then the motorbikes pulled away and they restarted the race and I was still sitting there! It was actually pretty difficult to get all the clothing back on again with the radio and all the rest of it. We managed to get back on, but they hadn't stopped the breakaway, so suddenly they had five minutes.

Then it was full speed ahead. Everyone was fighting for position onto the Molenberg at around 80km. I had an OK position coming onto the climb: not right at the very front but not too bad. Over the top, SD Worx put the whole team onto the front into the crosswind and the peloton split completely. I managed to stay in the front group, but lots of the favourites – like Lizzie Deignan and Annemiek van Vleuten – were behind. That was a huge moment in the race. Suddenly we were only about 30 riders and we still had more than 50km to go. From that moment on, the final phase of the race began. SD Worx had the numbers and so they kept attacking and counter-attacking. That was when Demi Vollering went.

We reached the Muur. I just love riding the Muur. I get goosebumps even writing about it. It's always a big test of how everything feels. It's a matter of who can survive to the top. I remember we caught Demi just near to the top. Then, at the bottom of the Bosberg, Anna van der Breggen just went. I wasn't on her wheel, but even though I wasn't all that well positioned I started passing riders, right up to Lotte Kopecky. And I remember we were so freaking close to Anna but – arrgh! – we couldn't quite make it up to her. And from that point on, she just rode away.

The chase never really got organised. One rider would do a big pull and then drop back and it would stop. If three, four or five teams had worked together we could have reeled her in. There was a headwind, so we could have done it together, but instead it was every girl for themselves. It was messy, and we couldn't catch Anna.

It wasn't the result that we wanted, but on the other hand it was the first race of the year, and the first with our new teammate Marta Cavalli. I was satisfied with my form and determined to look for the positives from the race so that we could use them in the next races. That way we would grow as a team. I was actually pretty happy.

The following Tuesday I flew to Bologna and met up with the team on the Wednesday morning. I just love, love, love being in Tuscany. I was so excited about the food because it's always so good.

I love the Italians. The whole thing is so 'me' because I am also a girl with a bit of a temper and a lot of emotion, and they're the same in Italy so I really feel at home. I must have some southern blood in me.

Siena is mega-special and Strade Bianche is an epic race – probably one of the most beautiful races in the calendar – and everyone wants to win it. I was the leader on the day. I was going pretty well, and I no longer could feel the sore throat I'd woken up with. But nevertheless I told my teammates not to ride for me. A leader needs to be able to say when they're not feeling 100 per cent. The worst thing is if a whole team works for you and then you get dropped and say to them afterwards that you weren't feeling great. I needed to be honest with them.

After sector five, Canyon started to attack and everything went bananas. There was a bit of wind and it split us into two groups and then we regathered. Then there was attack and counter-attack and it was pretty hectic. Normally in that part of the race there's 20km of nothing before the final, so everyone was a bit caught off guard.

We all knew that Annemiek always goes on gravel sector seven, and obviously she did again. I wanted to do everything to hang on, which I did, together with Kasia Niewiadoma and Demi Vollering, I think. That took us across to the breakaway, at which point we all eased off and nothing much happened, which allowed the group to grow to about 20. SD Worx had four of them. It was hard because we were so outnumbered. Elisa Longo Borghini went about 6km out. I felt I could have bridged to her, but I was sure that SD Worx would bring her back. I mean, you can't go with everything.

When you come into Siena, it's just such an epic finish that you get that extra adrenaline kick. On the final climb I wanted to give it my all, which I did. I surprised myself a bit. I actually felt OK. I passed two riders, including Annemiek, and I thought: '*What?!* What is happening?!' But then I did exactly what I did two years ago again: I stopped pedalling as I turned right, and she came past me full gas in the last three metres. Seriously, the exact same thing as happened two years previously. I was fourth then too, and Marta Bastianelli came past me and I finished fifth. And that's just stupid. I mean, just stupid. I had to learn from that mistake and obviously I didn't.

SD Worx were going to be a problem for the races to come. We needed teams to gather together and get organised against them. They were the next nut to crack. I didn't know how but I knew that we would. Somehow.

———

Trofeo Alfredo Binda was a nice race but super-hard. I wasn't quite able to follow Elisa Longo Borghini when she attacked, and I knew that, coming into the sprint, it was going to be hard to beat Marianne Vos. But it was nice to get a podium for the team. They had been working really hard for me and it was nice to give something back. I also felt like we were getting closer to cracking the SD Worx nut. We were starting to show that they were not unbeatable.

I was really excited for Flanders, which is always one of the highlights of my year. It was a slightly different course heading into Kanarieberg, which is normally where the final starts. I actually felt really good. But when I think back to it, I remember how I fucked up on the Paterberg. I'm sorry for the language, but this is the truth! Grace Brown had attacked, and then Annemiek, and I had gone with her. Then we got to the Paterberg and I was suddenly out in the gutter. I couldn't get back in again. I just dropped like a sack of potatoes from the group and ended up last rider. I got so angry as I had to chase back on.

The teamwork trying to get Annemiek back wasn't that great. We could see her all the time but couldn't get her back. We'd ride hard and then everyone would stop and look at each other. Unfortunately this is a big problem in women's cycling at the moment. As it develops it will get better and better, but it's not as organised as the men's peloton. Of course, the structure in men's racing is a bit more professional, but you can see when you watch women's cycling that – even though it's getting more organised and professional – we are still a bit behind. I don't feel like we have any 'patrons'. There are very experienced riders like Anna van der Breggen and Marianne Vos who've been around for ever, but they don't have a big mouth. They just *know* what to do, when to get on the front, like they are in the military. They don't scream orders at anyone; we just follow their lead. Not like dogs, of course, but we still take their lead because they are the legends that they are.

A lot of the spring races played out in the same way. I was up there in the top ten in so many races. I proved time and time again that I have the legs to be up there with the world's best, but I was not quite making it. Every time. After the Flèche Wallonne, where I finished eighth, I was devastated. That had been one of my main goals since I'd come second the previous year. I had been targeting that race particularly for so long, but I had a meltdown. When Annemiek attacked on the climb before the Mur de Huy I'd felt really good. Then on the final climb, when I needed to finish the job and when Anna attacked, I just failed. To get eighth when I had expected so much more was heart-breaking. In my eyes I had failed badly and I was devastated. It was a bitter pill to swallow.

For weeks I was a little sad and frustrated, wondering to myself: 'What the fuck is it that I am doing wrong? Why is it that I am always up there but never actually fighting for the win?' It was a big question mark. That is why being an athlete is so hard sometimes. You train so hard. You eat so well. You sleep so well. And then you come to a race and wonder why it is that it's not going your way.

After that, I said to myself: 'Well, Cile, you're back to square one. You're going to race Liège–Bastogne–Liège with the mindset that you have nothing to lose. You must race your bike how you love to. You must race like you want to race.'

I was so tired of being up there but not getting the result from the race that I wanted. Then it all culminated at Liège. I almost get emotional just thinking about it. It was such a release, and it was so much fun to be right up there and not just hanging on. I was actually able to animate the race – attacking, doing what I love about racing.

In all of the other races I felt as if I had this unfulfilled potential. I know that I didn't succeed at Liège, and I know that in the end I got the same placing as in the other races – and if you just saw the result you might think that I'd been racing the same way – but the feeling afterwards was like night and day. The fact that I hadn't succeeded didn't matter to me. The fact that I reminded myself why I love racing was such a victory for me.

After that I went home on a small break back to Denmark. I took that good feeling with me. I was hungry for more, wanting more, instead of going on vacation a little bit unsatisfied. I was at the point where I didn't feel I needed to prove again and again that I can be up there. Perhaps I needed to risk everything, knowing that I could get dropped and finish, like, 15th or 40th or 60th. Liège was the point where I said to myself: 'You need to fucking do something! Stop playing safe. Go out there and really risk it.'

I didn't think I needed to change anything in my training programme, and there was nothing wrong with the form I was in, but there was definitely something I needed to change – maybe the *way* I was riding. I felt as if this was the turning point in my career. I figured out that if I raced like I had done in Liège, eventually a victory had to come my way. Maybe nine times out of ten I would still not succeed, but it *would* come. I was super-hungry for the next races.

---

Cycling is so much in the head. It's not just about who has the best legs and who's best on the bike. I wanted to become the best bike rider in the world. In order to do that, I realised I needed to work on the mental side of the sport. I needed to understand what was happening to me at those key times in the race. If I couldn't do this, I'd never fulfil my potential and become the best rider I could be.

I called everyone: my coach, my family, and everyone I knew in cycling who might be able to recommend a good mental coach. From that moment I started to work with quite a few different coaches and I began the process. We talked about me as a person, what happens in the races and what thoughts go through my head. And it was *such* a relief and an inspiration. It was such an interesting process and I was excited by it. Every day I would focus on the things I needed to do.

I am my worst enemy. A lot of the pressure, I put on myself. But the reason I am honest and open to talking about this is because I think it's important. Too few people talk about the mental side of the sport. Now that, in my own environment, I have been honest and admitted to what I am going through and that we are not all perfect, a lot of people have told me that they are also struggling a bit. When I have told people about my work with a mental coach, I have been really surprised by the feedback and the number of people who have responded to it. I think there is still a bit of a taboo around the subject.

Then came the one-day races in Spain. In the first two I had really shit legs and didn't do very well. Then in Durango, I raced a bit like Liège and had some fun. It was a wet race but it was one of the best days that I can remember this year: I raced with my heart. I knew that I needed a 30-second gap over Anna and Annemiek going onto the last climb, which is exactly what I had. (Those two are the benchmark; you measure yourself against them, and to become one of the best riders in the world you sometimes have to beat them.) But then they caught me and they gapped me a little bit, but I could see them all the time just a little bit ahead, only about ten seconds. And I didn't give up, I just kept on fighting. I caught them with 200 metres to go, but that was it: I was finished and they left me. Still, it was such a good feeling, and it was the first step on the journey.

Then we raced Burgos. On stage three everything just clicked into place. There were four climbs towards the end of the race. I thought: 'Why wait until the last climb? Because that would be the smartest thing to do? Because SD Worx had such a strong team there? No! Let's just go out there. This is what I want. This is how I want to race, how I see myself as a rider.' So I attacked on the first of the four climbs and went clear with Niamh Fisher-Black and Pauliena Rooijakkers, but we didn't work very well together and we got caught on the second or third climb. Then my teammate

Evita Muzic attacked. All year I had been watching Evita grow as a rider, but this was also a new step for her to be attacking and to be animating the race. She was the same kind of rider as me, so I had been coaching her on the radio and telling her, 'When I get caught you counter-attack!' She was a bit afraid but I was so happy that she had the balls to attack. And then she went solo with Sabrina Stultiens. Our little FDJ team! A small team like ours, animating the race? What were the other teams doing?

I think she got caught with 5km to go, and I thought: 'OK!' I had just been following the race but I knew, coming into the final climb, I had to be on Anna van der Breggen's wheel. Period. And that was what I did. I didn't think too much.

Grace Brown pulled the whole time on the front but started to slow with about 400 metres to go. I pulled alongside Anna and I looked around. I so wanted to start my sprint but it was still a long way uphill. It was too early! I could feel the others coming back. We passed the 200 metre sign and still it was too early. Then Kasia Niewiadoma went and I followed her wheel, but I still had an extra kick and I went around her. I was still wondering when the others were going to come past me, but they didn't and I suddenly realised I was going to win.

It was really special. All the big names, they were all there. It meant a lot to me but I think it also meant a lot to the team, because they knew how hard we had all worked at it. For so long people had told me that my first win was bound to come soon. It was a relief and it felt so good that we had finally done it.

I had always imagined that I would celebrate my first WorldTour win with a big salute, but I only had time for a sad little fist pump! But it was just the best feeling ever.

# TEAMS

Every team, whether in the men's or women's peloton, is either in a process of building, declining or simply clinging on to its budget by its fingertips in a sport that relies almost entirely on the goodwill of brands seeking association with success. Every year the names morph as the jerseys change design; new sponsors are brought on board, old ones withdraw and the circus somehow carries on. But, ultimately, it's about the riders. What they achieve on the road will determine their individual fate and will have a significant bearing on the viability of each and every team's future.

TEAMS     MEN'S WORLDTOUR

# AG2R CITROËN

**2021 SEASON REVIEW**

Stage wins at each of the Grand Tours this year will mark it as a successful season for the French outfit, Andrea Vendrame victorious at his home Giro d'Italia before Ben O'Connor followed suit at the Tour and Clément Champoussin stole a march on the big boys at the Vuelta a España to take victory. Reinforcements named Greg Van Avermaet and Bob Jungels came with the promise of turning the AG2R squad into a Classics powerhouse, but very little evidence of that was produced in the spring. Ⓡ

**2021 VICTORIES**

| | | |
|---|---|---|
| GP Cycliste la Marseillaise | 1.1 | A. Paret-Peintre |
| Giro d'Italia – stage 12 | 2.UWT | A. Vendrame |
| Tour du Finistère | 1.1 | B. Cosnefroy |
| La Route d'Occitanie – stage 1 | 2.1 | A. Vendrame |
| Paris–Camembert | 1.1 | D. Godon |
| Tour de France – stage 9 | WT | B. O'Connor |
| Tour du Limousin – stage 2 | 2.1 | D. Godon |
| Bretagne Classic - Ouest-France | 1.UWT | B. Cosnefroy |
| Tour du Jura Cycliste | 1.1 | B. Cosnefroy |
| Vuelta a España – stage 20 | 2.UWT | C. Champoussin |
| Tour du Doubs | 1.1 | D. Godon |
| Boucles de l'Aulne | 1.1 | S. Dewulf |

**TEAM INFORMATION**

| | |
|---|---|
| UCI CODE | ACT |
| UCI STATUS | MEN'S WORLDTOUR |
| COUNTRY | FRANCE |
| FOUNDED | 2000 |

**TEAM NAME HISTORY**

| | |
|---|---|
| 1992–1996 | CHAZAL |
| 1997–1999 | CASINO-AG2R PRÉVOYANCE |
| 2000–2007 | AG2R PRÉVOYANCE |
| 2008–2020 | AG2R LA MONDIALE |
| 2021 | AG2R CITROËN |

**TEAM MANAGER**

VINCENT LAVENU

**2021 NEW RIDERS**

GREG VAN AVERMAET, BOB JUNGELS, LILIAN CALMEJANE, MARC SARREAU, MICHAEL SCHÄR, BEN O'CONNOR, GIJS VAN HOECKE, DAMIEN TOUZÉ, STAN DEWULF, NICOLAS PRODHOMME, CLÉMENT BERTHET

**2021 STAGIAIRES**

THOMAS DELPHIS, PAUL LAPEIRA, VALENTIN RETAILLEAU

**EQUIPMENT**

| | |
|---|---|
| BIKE | BMC |

## RIDER PROFILES

### BENOÎT COSNEFROY

France
17.10.95
Years Pro 4
Years On Team 4
Grand Tour Apps 3
Wins 12
UCI Ranking 42

There's hardly a tougher way to take your first WorldTour win than by outfoxing the world champion, Julian Alaphilippe. The pair's escape quartet was completed by Honoré and Pogačar – and not every rider can say they beat a QuickStep duo and the Tour champion. Cosnefroy also won at the Tour du Finistère, Tour du Jura and Tour du Doubs.

### BEN O'CONNOR

Australia
25.11.95
Years Pro 5
Years On Team 1
Grand Tour Apps 5
Wins 5
UCI Ranking 40

The Australian thanked his new French team for picking him up from the precarious-looking situation at NTT in the biggest way possible: a stage win at the Tour de France. The 25-year-old was dogged in his effort up to Tignes, catapulting himself into second on GC before holding on for fourth overall.

---

**CLÉMENT BERTHET**
France
02.08.1997
Years Pro 1
Years On Team 1
Grand Tour Apps 0
Wins 0
UCI Ranking 612

**FRANÇOIS BIDARD**
France
19.03.92
Years Pro 6
Years On Team 6
Grand Tour Apps 7
Wins 0
UCI Ranking 1951

**GEOFFREY BOUCHARD**
France
01.04.92
Years Pro 3
Years On Team 3
Grand Tour Apps 4
Wins 0
UCI Ranking 156

**LILIAN CALMEJANE**
France
06.12.92
Years Pro 6
Years On Team 1
Grand Tour Apps 6
Wins 12
UCI Ranking 366

**CLÉMENT CHAMPOUSSIN**
France
29.05.1998
Years Pro 2
Years On Team 2
Grand Tour Apps 3
Wins 1
UCI Ranking 122

**MIKAËL CHEREL**
France
17.03.86
Years Pro 15
Years On Team 11
Grand Tour Apps 15
Wins 0
UCI Ranking 1359

**STAN DEWULF**
Belgium
20.12.97
Years Pro 3
Years On Team 1
Grand Tour Apps 0
Wins 1
UCI Ranking 117

**JULIEN DUVAL**
France
27.05.90
Years Pro 5
Years On Team 5
Grand Tour Apps 2
Wins 0
UCI Ranking 1565

**MATHIAS FRANK**
Switzerland
09.12.86
Years Pro 14
Years On Team 5
Grand Tour Apps 13
Wins 7
UCI Ranking 887

**TONY GALLOPIN**
France
24.05.88
Years Pro 12
Years On Team 4
Grand Tour Apps 14
Wins 12
UCI Ranking 980

**BEN GASTAUER**
Luxembourg
14.11.87
Years Pro 12
Years On Team 12
Grand Tour Apps 13
Wins 2
UCI Ranking –

**DORIAN GODON**
France
25.05.96
Years Pro 5
Years On Team 3
Grand Tour Apps 3
Wins 6
UCI Ranking 59

**ALEXIS GOUGEARD**
France
05.03.93
Years Pro 8
Years On Team 8
Grand Tour Apps 6
Wins 11
UCI Ranking 1100

**JAAKKO HÄNNINEN**
Finland
16.04.97
Years Pro 2
Years On Team 2
Grand Tour Apps 1
Wins 0
UCI Ranking 846

**ANTHONY JULIEN**
France
05.03.1998
Years Pro 1
Years On Team 1
Grand Tour Apps 0
Wins 0
UCI Ranking 1512

**BOB JUNGELS**
Luxembourg
22.09.92
Years Pro 9
Years On Team 1
Grand Tour Apps 8
Wins 23
UCI Ranking 811

**LAWRENCE NAESEN**
Belgium
28.08.1992
Years Pro 4
Years On Team 1
Grand Tour Apps 1
Wins 0
UCI Ranking 504

**OLIVER NAESEN**
Belgium
16.09.90
Years Pro 7
Years On Team 5
Grand Tour Apps 6
Wins 5
UCI Ranking 143

**AURÉLIEN PARET-PEINTRE**
France
27.02.96
Years Pro 3
Years On Team 3
Grand Tour Apps 2
Wins 1
UCI Ranking 81

**NANS PETERS**
France
12.03.94
Years Pro 5
Years On Team 5
Grand Tour Apps 5
Wins 2
UCI Ranking 1139

**NICOLAS PRODHOMME**
France
01.02.1997
Years Pro 1
Years On Team 1
Grand Tour Apps 1
Wins 0
UCI Ranking 896

**MARC SARREAU**
France
10.06.93
Years Pro 7
Years On Team 1
Grand Tour Apps 3
Wins 12
UCI Ranking 211

**MICHAEL SCHÄR**
Switzerland
29.09.86
Years Pro 16
Years On Team 1
Grand Tour Apps 13
Wins 2
UCI Ranking 846

**DAMIEN TOUZÉ**
France
07.07.96
Years Pro 3
Years On Team 1
Grand Tour Apps 2
Wins 0
UCI Ranking 411

**GREG VAN AVERMAET**
Belgium
17.05.85
Years Pro 15
Years On Team 1
Grand Tour Apps 12
Wins 41
UCI Ranking 58

**GIJS VAN HOECKE**
Belgium
12.11.91
Years Pro 10
Years On Team 1
Grand Tour Apps 1
Wins 0
UCI Ranking 584

**ANDREA VENDRAME**
Italy
20.07.94
Years Pro 5
Years On Team 2
Grand Tour Apps 4
Wins 4
UCI Ranking 164

**CLÉMENT VENTURINI**
France
16.10.93
Years Pro 8
Years On Team 4
Grand Tour Apps 4
Wins 4
UCI Ranking 587

**LARRY WARBASSE**
United States
28.06.90
Years Pro 9
Years On Team 3
Grand Tour Apps 8
Wins 2
UCI Ranking 796

TEAMS    MEN'S WORLDTOUR

# ASTANA PREMIER TECH

**2021 SEASON REVIEW**

An eventful year for Astana – but when isn't it? This year the drama circled around the power struggle behind the scenes, with the Canadian Premier Tech side ousting Alexander Vinokourov before the man synonymous with Astana was later reinstated and Premier Tech were announced to be departing at the end of the season. You get the sense these disturbances affected results on the road. Two stages of the Itzulia Basque Country and a stage of the Dauphiné were all the squad really had to show for the year, with 11 total victories even fewer than they achieved during the 2020 Covid season. Ⓛ

**TEAM INFORMATION**

| | |
|---|---|
| UCI CODE | **APT** |
| UCI STATUS | **MEN'S WORLDTOUR** |
| COUNTRY | **KAZAKHSTAN** |
| FOUNDED | **2006** |

**TEAM NAME HISTORY**

| | |
|---|---|
| 2006 | **ASTANA-WÜRTH TEAM** |
| 2007–2010 | **ASTANA** |
| 2011 | **PRO TEAM ASTANA** |
| 2012–2020 | **ASTANA PRO TEAM** |
| 2021 | **ASTANA PREMIER TECH** |

**TEAM MANAGER**

**ALEXANDER VINOKOUROV**

**2021 NEW RIDERS**

**SAMUELE BATTISTELLA, STEFAN DE BOD, MATTEO SOBRERO, BENJAMIN PERRY, YEVGENIY FEDOROV, JAVIER ROMO, GLEB BRUSSENSKIY, ANDREA PICCOLO**

**EQUIPMENT**

| | |
|---|---|
| BIKE | **WILLIER** |

**2021 VICTORIES**

| | | |
|---|---|---|
| Itzulia Basque Country – stage 2 | 2.UWT | A. Aranburu |
| Itzulia Basque Country – stage 4 | 2.UWT | I. Izaguirre |
| Critérium du Dauphiné – stage 4 (ITT) | 2.UWT | A. Lutsenko |
| National Championships Russia – ITT | NC | A. Vlasov |
| National Championships Spain – ITT | NC | I. Izaguirre |
| National Championships Italy – ITT | NC | M. Sobrero |
| National Championships Kazakhstan – RR | NC | Y. Fedorov |
| National Championships Spain – RR | NC | O. Fraile |
| National Championships Eritrea – ITT | NC | M. Kudus |
| Prueba Villafranca de Ordiziako | 1.1 | L. L. Sánchez |
| National Championships – ITT | NC | H. Houle |
| Coppa Agostini | 1.1 | A. Lutsenko |
| Veneto Classic | 1.1 | S. Battistella |

RIDER PROFILES

## ALEKSANDR VLASOV
Russia
23.04.96
Years Pro 4
Years On Team 2
Grand Tour Apps 4
Wins 6
UCI Ranking 35

Vlasov secured his first Grand Tour top ten and the biggest step so far to delivering on his promise with fourth overall at the Giro d'Italia. At the Vuelta he was hovering around the top ten before a crash on stage 17 saw him plummet down the rankings, eventually calling it quits before the start of stage 20.

## ALEXEY LUTSENKO
Kazakhstan
07.09.92
Years Pro 9
Years On Team 9
Grand Tour Apps 9
Wins 29
UCI Ranking 39

While Lutsenko didn't reach the heights of his 2020 Tour de France stage win this year, the stage-4 time trial victory at the Dauphiné saw him come close to overall victory, losing the race lead to Richie Porte by 17 seconds on the penultimate day. At the Tour de France, he rode to seventh place, the first Grand Tour top ten of his career.

### ALEX ARANBURU
Spain
19.09.95
Years Pro 5
Years On Team 2
Grand Tour Apps 5
Wins 4
UCI Ranking 94

### SAMUELE BATTISTELLA
Italy
14.11.98
Years Pro 2
Years On Team 1
Grand Tour Apps 1
Wins 1
UCI Ranking 159

### MANUELE BOARO
Italy
12.03.87
Years Pro 11
Years On Team 3
Grand Tour Apps 11
Wins 3
UCI Ranking 2293

### GLEB BRUSSENSKIY
Kazakhstan
18.04.2000
Years Pro 1
Years On Team 1
Grand Tour Apps 0
Wins 0
UCI Ranking 2255

### RODRIGO CONTRERAS
Colombia
02.06.94
Years Pro 6
Years On Team 3
Grand Tour Apps 1
Wins 1
UCI Ranking 1171

### STEFAN DE BOD
South Africa
17.11.96
Years Pro 3
Years On Team 1
Grand Tour Apps 2
Wins 1
UCI Ranking 433

### YEGENIY FEDOROV
Kazakhstan
06.02.2000
Years Pro 1
Years On Team 1
Grand Tour Apps 0
Wins 3
UCI Ranking 483

### FABIO FELLINE
Italy
29.03.90
Years Pro 12
Years On Team 2
Grand Tour Apps 12
Wins 14
UCI Ranking 571

### OMAR FRAILE
Spain
17.07.90
Years Pro 9
Years On Team 4
Grand Tour Apps 13
Wins 7
UCI Ranking 306

### JAKOB FUGLSANG
Denmark
22.03.85
Years Pro 13
Years On Team 9
Grand Tour Apps 16
Wins 26
UCI Ranking 97

### YEVGENIY GIDICH
Kazakhstan
19.05.96
Years Pro 4
Years On Team 4
Grand Tour Apps 0
Wins 8
UCI Ranking 599

### JONAS GREGAARD
Denmark
30.07.96
Years Pro 3
Years On Team 3
Grand Tour Apps 1
Wins 0
UCI Ranking —

### DMITRIY GRUZDEV
Kazakhstan
13.03.86
Years Pro 10
Years On Team 10
Grand Tour Apps 8
Wins 8
UCI Ranking —

### HUGO HOULE
Canada
27.09.90
Years Pro 11
Years On Team 4
Grand Tour Apps 6
Wins 2
UCI Ranking 351

### GORKA IZAGUIRRE
Spain
07.10.87
Years Pro 12
Years On Team 3
Grand Tour Apps 16
Wins 9
UCI Ranking 452

### ION IZAGUIRRE
Spain
04.02.89
Years Pro 11
Years On Team 3
Grand Tour Apps 14
Wins 15
UCI Ranking 55

### MERHAWI KUDUS
Eritrea
23.01.94
Years Pro 8
Years On Team 1
Grand Tour Apps 7
Wins 5
UCI Ranking 224

### DAVIDE MARTINELLI
Italy
31.05.93
Years Pro 6
Years On Team 1
Grand Tour Apps 1
Wins 2
UCI Ranking 2296

### YURIY NATAROV
Kazakhstan
28.12.96
Years Pro 3
Years On Team 3
Grand Tour Apps 1
Wins 1
UCI Ranking 682

### BENJAMIN PERRY
Canada
07.03.94
Years Pro 1
Years On Team 1
Grand Tour Apps 0
Wins 1
UCI Ranking 2257

### ANDREA PICCOLO
Italy
23.03.2001
Years Pro 1
Years On Team 1
Grand Tour Apps 0
Wins 0
UCI Ranking 629

### VADIM PRONSKIY
Kazakhstan
04.06.98
Years Pro 2
Years On Team 2
Grand Tour Apps 1
Wins 0
UCI Ranking 525

### ÓSCAR RODRÍGUEZ
Spain
06.05.95
Years Pro 4
Years On Team 2
Grand Tour Apps 4
Wins 1
UCI Rankings 214

### JAVIER ROMO
Spain
06.01.99
Years Pro 1
Years On Team 1
Grand Tour Apps 0
Wins 0
UCI Ranking 467

### LUIS LEÓN SÁNCHEZ
Spain
24.11.83
Years Pro 18
Years On Team 7
Grand Tour Apps 26
Wins 47
UCI Ranking 150

### MATTEO SOBRERO
Italy
14.05.97
Years Pro 2
Years On Team 1
Grand Tour Apps 2
Wins 1
UCI Ranking 218

### NIKITA STALNOV
Kazakhstan
14.09.91
Years Pro 5
Years On Team 5
Grand Tour Apps 2
Wins 1
UCI Ranking 2882

### HAROLD TEJADA
Colombia
27.04.97
Years Pro 2
Years On Team 2
Grand Tour Apps 2
Wins 0
UCI Ranking 1172

### ARTYOM ZAKHAROV
Kazakhstan
27.10.91
Years Pro 6
Years On Team 6
Grand Tour Apps 0
Wins 1
UCI Ranking 651

TEAMS     MEN'S WORLDTOUR

# BAHRAIN VICTORIOUS

**2021 SEASON REVIEW**

Many doubted a name change to include a goal of all competitive cycling teams would work out, but miracles do happen. A haul of 16 WorldTour victories – including stage wins at all three Grand Tours, where they rode at times imperiously – was capped off when Sonny Colbrelli poured his sensational form onto the muddy cobbles of northern France to win Paris–Roubaix. Their season wasn't without contention, though, with the team hotel raided at the Tour de France, riders insisting they had 'nothing to hide', and Matej Mohorič putting his fingers to his lips as he crossed the finish line to take his second stage win – the team's third – of the race. ⒶL

**2021 VICTORIES**

| | | |
|---|---|---|
| Tour de la Provence – stage 4 | 2.Pro | P. Bauhaus |
| Tour of the Alps – stage 4 | 2.Pro | P. Bilbao |
| Tour de Romandie – stage 2 | 2.UWT | S. Colbrelli |
| Tour de Hongrie – stage 1 | 2.1 | P. Bauhaus |
| Giro d'Italia – stage 6 | 2.UWT | G. Mäder |
| Tour de Hongrie – stage 3 | 2.1 | P. Bauhaus |
| Giro d'Italia – stage 20 | 2.UWT | D. Caruso |
| Critérium du Dauphiné – stage 3 | 2.UWT | S. Colbrelli |
| Critérium du Dauphiné – stage 7 | 2.UWT | M. Padun |
| Critérium du Dauphiné – stage 8 | 2.UWT | M. Padun |
| Tour of Slovenia – stage 1 | 2.Pro | P. Bauhaus |
| Tour of Slovenia – stage 5 | 2.Pro | P. Bauhaus |
| Tour de Suisse – stage 8 | 2.UWT | G. Mäder |
| National Championships Slovenia – ITT | NC | J. Tratnik |
| National Championships Slovenia – RR | NC | M. Mohorič |
| National Championships Italy – RR | NC | S. Colbrelli |
| Tour de France – stage 7 | 2.UWT | M. Mohorič |
| Tour de France – stage 8 | 2.UWT | D. Teuns |
| Tour de France – stage 19 | 2.UWT | M. Mohorič |
| Vuelta a Burgos | 2.Pro | M. Landa |
| Tour de Pologne – stage 1 | 2.UWT | P. Bauhaus |
| Vuelta a España – stage 9 | 2.UWT | D. Caruso |
| Benelux Tour – stage 6 | 2.UWT | S. Colbrelli |
| Benelux Tour – stage 7 | 2.UWT | M. Mohorič |
| Benelux Tour | 2.UWT | S. Colbrelli |
| Memorial Marco Pantani | 1.1 | S. Colbrelli |
| Cro Race – stage 1 | 2.1 | P. Bauhaus |
| Cro Race – stage 5 | 2.1 | S. Williams |
| Cro Race | 2.1 | S. Williams |
| Paris–Roubaix | 1.UWT | S. Colbrelli |

**TEAM INFORMATION**

| | |
|---|---|
| UCI CODE | **TBV** |
| UCI STATUS | **MEN'S WORLDTOUR** |
| COUNTRY | **BAHRAIN** |
| FOUNDED | **2017** |

**TEAM NAME HISTORY**

| | |
|---|---|
| 2017–2018 | **BAHRAIN MERIDA PRO CYCLING TEAM** |
| 2019 | **BAHRAIN MERIDA** |
| 2020 | **BAHRAIN-MCLAREN** |
| 2021 | **BAHRAIN VICTORIOUS** |

**TEAM MANAGER**

**MILAN ERŽEN**

**2021 NEW RIDERS**

**JACK HAIG, GINO MÄDER, JONATHAN MILAN, AHMED MADAN**

**EQUIPMENT**

| | |
|---|---|
| BIKE | **MERIDA** |

## RIDER PROFILES

### SONNY COLBRELLI
Italy
17.05.90
Years Pro 11
Years On Team 5
Grand Tour Apps 10
Wins 34
UCI Ranking 6

Colbrelli started the season with a top ten at Milan–Sanremo and a stage win at the Tour de Romandie and Dauphiné. Then overall victory at the Benelux Tour gave way to playing a distraught Evenepoel like a fiddle in Trento to claim the European champion's jersey. At Roubaix he yet again cleverly made the moves that mattered before easing past Vermeersch in the velodrome.

### MATEJ MOHORIČ
Slovenia
19.10.94
Years Pro 8
Years On Team 4
Grand Tour Apps 10
Wins 15
UCI Ranking 12

A scary head-over-heels crash on a descent at the Giro ended his first Grand Tour of the year but he claimed the Slovenian national champion's jersey (his first victory since 2019), then two magnificent solo stage victories at the Tour de France. Stunning performances were overshadowed by the raid on his team's hotel as well as the finger-on-lips celebration after his stage 19 win.

### YUKIYA ARASHIRO
Japan
22.09.84
Years Pro 13
Years On Team 5
Grand Tour Apps 15
Wins 7
UCI Ranking 1418

### PHIL BAUHAUS
Germany
08.07.94
Years Pro 7
Years On Team 3
Grand Tour Apps 2
Wins 17
UCI Ranking 283

### PELLO BILBAO
Spain
25.02.90
Years Pro 11
Years On Team 2
Grand Tour Apps 13
Wins 11
UCI Ranking 66

### SANTIAGO BUITRAGO
Colombia
26.09.99
Years Pro 2
Years On Team 2
Grand Tour Apps 1
Wins 0
UCI Ranking 326

### EROS CAPECCHI
Italy
13.06.86
Years Pro 16
Years On Team 2
Grand Tour Apps 19
Wins 4
UCI Ranking –

### DAMIANO CARUSO
Italy
12.10.87
Years Pro 13
Years On Team 2
Grand Tour Apps 15
Wins 4
UCI Ranking 37

### SCOTT DAVIES
Great Britain
05.08.95
Years Pro 4
Years On Team 2
Grand Tour Apps 2
Wins 0
UCI Ranking –

### CHUN KAI FENG
Taiwan
02.11.88
Years Pro 9
Years On Team 5
Grand Tour Apps 0
Wins 6
UCI Ranking –

### JACK HAIG
Australia
06.09.93
Years Pro 6
Years On Team 1
Grand Tour Apps 8
Wins 2
UCI Ranking 42

### MARCO HALLER
Austria
01.04.91
Years Pro 10
Years On Team 2
Grand Tour Apps 8
Wins 4
UCI Ranking 229

### HEINRICH HAUSSLER
Australia
25.02.84
Years Pro 18
Years On Team 5
Grand Tour Apps 12
Wins 22
UCI Ranking 175

### KEVIN INKELAAR
Netherlands
08.07.97
Years Pro 2
Years On Team 2
Grand Tour Apps 1
Wins 0
UCI Ranking –

### MIKEL LANDA
Spain
13.12.89
Years Pro 11
Years On Team 2
Grand Tour Apps 16
Wins 16
UCI Ranking 63

### AHMED MADAN
Bahrain
25.08.2000
Years Pro 1
Years On Team 1
Grand Tour Apps 0
Wins 0
UCI Ranking –

### GINO MÄDER
Switzerland
04.01.97
Years Pro 3
Years On Team 1
Grand Tour Apps 3
Wins 3
UCI Ranking 79

### JONATHAN MILAN
Italy
01.10.2000
Years Pro 1
Years On Team 1
Grand Tour Apps 0
Wins 0
UCI Ranking 2082

### DOMEN NOVAK
Slovenia
12.07.95
Years Pro 5
Years On Team 5
Grand Tour Apps 12
Wins 1
UCI Ranking –

### MARK PADUN
Ukraine
06.07.96
Years Pro 4
Years On Team 4
Grand Tour Apps 4
Wins 6
UCI Ranking 199

### HERMANN PERNSTEINER
Austria
07.08.90
Years Pro 4
Years On Team 4
Grand Tour Apps 3
Wins 0
UCI Ranking 496

### WOUT POELS
Netherlands
01.10.87
Years Pro 13
Years On Team 1
Grand Tour Apps 18
Wins 19
UCI Ranking 204

### MARCEL SIEBERG
Germany
30.04.82
Years Pro 16
Years On Team 3
Grand Tour Apps 11
Wins 2
UCI Ranking –

### DYLAN TEUNS
Belgium
01.03.92
Years Pro 7
Years On Team 3
Grand Tour Apps 6
Wins 12
UCI Ranking 112

### JAN TRATNIK
Slovenia
23.02.90
Years Pro 11
Years On Team 3
Grand Tour Apps 5
Wins 10
UCI Ranking 330

### RAFAEL VALLS
Spain
25.06.87
Years Pro 12
Years On Team 3
Grand Tour Apps 11
Wins 4
UCI Ranking –

### STEPHEN WILLIAMS
Great Britain
09.06.96
Years Pro 3
Years On Team 3
Grand Tour Apps 1
Wins 2
UCI Ranking 332

### FRED WRIGHT
Great Britain
13.06.99
Years Pro 2
Years On Team 2
Grand Tour Apps 2
Wins 0
UCI Ranking 362

TEAMS    MEN'S WORLDTOUR

# BORA–HANSGROHE

**2021 SEASON REVIEW**

A successful season for the German outfit, with victories spread across a balanced squad. Things weren't quiet behind the scenes either, with the bosses reportedly looking at buying the entire Deceuninck-QuickStep set-up in order to acquire the services of Remco Evenepoel, while the planned return of sprinter Sam Bennett to Bora-Hansgrohe also caused consternation. Meanwhile, Peter Sagan was announced to be departing at the end of the season. There were two stage wins at the Tour de France, Max Schachmann defending his Paris–Nice victory, as well as a smattering of other WorldTour wins. It will be a changing of the guard this off-season, with Pascal Ackermann also out the door as the team makes room for the likes of Aleksandr Vlasov, Sergio Higuita and Jai Hindley.

## TEAM INFORMATION

| UCI CODE | BOH |
| UCI STATUS | MEN'S WORLDTOUR |
| COUNTRY | GERMANY |
| FOUNDED | 2010 |

**TEAM NAME HISTORY**

| 2010–2012 | TEAM NETAPP |
| 2013–2014 | TEAM NETAPP-ENDURA |
| 2015–2016 | BORA-ARGON 18 |
| 2017–2021 | BORA-HANSGROHE |

**TEAM MANAGER**

RALPH DENK

**2021 NEW RIDERS**

WILCO KELDERMAN, NILS POLITT, JORDI MEEUS, GIOVANNI ALEOTTI, MATTHEW WALLS, BEN ZWIEHOFF, ANTON PALZER, FREDERIK WANDAHL

**EQUIPMENT**

| BIKE | SPECIALIZED |

**2021 VICTORIES**

| Paris–Nice | 2.UWT | Max Schachmann |
| Volta Ciclista a Catalunya – stage 5 | 2.UWT | L. Kämna |
| Volta Ciclista a Catalunya – stage 6 | 2.UWT | P. Sagan |
| Tour of the Alps – stage 5 | 2.Pro | F. Großschartner |
| Tour de Romandie – stage 1 | 2.UWT | P. Sagan |
| Tour de Hongrie – stage 2 | 2.1 | J. Meeus |
| Giro d'Italia – stage 10 | 2.UWT | P. Sagan |
| Critérium du Dauphiné – stage 2 | 2.UWT | L. Pöstlberger |
| GP des Kantons Aargau | 1.1 | I. Schelling |
| National Championships Poland – ITT | NC | M. Bodnar |
| National Championships Germany – RR | NC | M. Schachmann |
| National Championships Slovakia – RR | NC | P. Sagan |
| National Championships Austria – RR | NC | P. Konrad |
| Sibiu Cycling Tour – prologue | 2.1 | P. Ackermann |
| Sibiu Cycling Tour – stage 1 | 2.1 | G. Aleotti |
| Sibiu Cycling Tour | 2.1 | G. Aleotti |
| Tour de France – stage 12 | 2.UWT | N. Politt |
| Tour de France – stage 16 | 2.UWT | P. Konrad |
| Settimana Ciclista Italiana – stage 2 | 2.1 | P. Ackermann |
| Settimana Ciclista Italiana – stage 3 | 2.1 | P. Ackermann |
| Settimana Ciclista Italiana – stage 5 | 2.1 | P. Ackermann |
| Arctic Race of Norway – stage 2 | 2.Pro | M. Laas |
| Tour of Norway – stage 4 | 2.Pro | M. Walls |
| Deutschland Tour – stage 1 | 2.Pro | P. Ackermann |
| Deutschland Tour – stage 3 | 2.Pro | N. Politt |
| Deutschland Tour | 2.Pro | N. Politt |
| Tour de Slovaquie | 2.1 | P. Sagan |
| Gran Piemonte | 1.Pro | M. Walls |
| Paris–Bourges | 1.1 | J. Meeus |

RIDER PROFILES

## PETER SAGAN

Slovakia
26.01.90
Years Pro 12
Years On Team 5
Grand Tour Apps 16
Wins 119
UCI Ranking 57

No Monuments and rainbow jersey this year, but most riders would take his 2021 haul no questions asked. He bagged stage wins at the Volta Ciclista a Catalunya and Tour de Romandie, before winning the stage-10 sprint at the Giro and going on to successfully battle for the green jersey. The cherry on top was overall victory at his home Tour of Slovakia.

## NILS POLITT

Germany
06.03.94
Years Pro 6
Years On Team 1
Grand Tour Apps 5
Wins 4
UCI Ranking 83

Before this season he had only one professional win to his name: a stage of the Deutschland Tour in 2018. But on stage 12 of the Tour he got himself into the breakaway and went solo over the final 10km to claim a huge victory. A month later he took his second Deutschland Tour stage with another late solo escape, also sealing the overall victory.

### PASCAL ACKERMANN
Germany
17.01.94
Years Pro 5
Years On Team 5
Grand Tour Apps 2
Wins 36
UCI Ranking 50

### GIOVANNI ALEOTTI
Italy
25.05.99
Years Pro 1
Years On Team 1
Grand Tour Apps 1
Wins 2
UCI Ranking 139

### ERIK BAŠKA
Slovakia
12.01.94
Years Pro 6
Years On Team 5
Grand Tour Apps 0
Wins 1
UCI Ranking 905

### CESARE BENEDETTI
Poland
03.08.81
Years Pro 11
Years On Team 12
Grand Tour Apps 10
Wins 1
UCI Ranking 1787

### MACIEJ BODNAR
Poland
07.03.85
Years Pro 14
Years On Team 5
Grand Tour Apps 14
Wins 11
UCI Ranking 510

### EMANUEL BUCHMANN
Germany
18.11.92
Years Pro 7
Years On Team 7
Grand Tour Apps 9
Wins 4
UCI Ranking 362

### MARCUS BURGHARDT
Germany
30.06.83
Years Pro 18
Years On Team 5
Grand Tour Apps 15
Wins 7
UCI Ranking 538

### MATTEO FABBRO
Italy
10.04.95
Years Pro 4
Years On Team 2
Grand Tour Apps 3
Wins 0
UCI Ranking 174

### PATRICK GAMPER
Austria
18.02.97
Years Pro 2
Years On Team 2
Grand Tour Apps 2
Wins 0
UCI Ranking 587

### FELIX GROßSCHARTNER
Austria
23.12.93
Years Pro 6
Years On Team 4
Grand Tour Apps 7
Wins 4
UCI Ranking 238

### LENNARD KÄMNA
Germany
09.09.96
Years Pro 6
Years On Team 2
Grand Tour Apps 3
Wins 3
UCI Ranking 837

### WILCO KELDERMAN
Netherlands
25.03.91
Years Pro 10
Years On Team 1
Grand Tour Apps 12
Wins 4
UCI Ranking 47

### PATRICK KONRAD
Austria
13.10.91
Years Pro 7
Years On Team 7
Grand Tour Apps 7
Wins 3
UCI Ranking 90

### MARTIN LAAS
Estonia
15.09.93
Years Pro 6
Years On Team 2
Grand Tour Apps 2
Wins 14
UCI Ranking 189

### JORDI MEEUS
Belgium
01.07.98
Years Pro 1
Years On Team 1
Grand Tour Apps 1
Wins 5
UCI Ranking 87

### DANIEL OSS
Italy
13.01.87
Years Pro 13
Years On Team 4
Grand Tour Apps 14
Wins 2
UCI Ranking 1565

### ANTON PALZER
Germany
11.03.93
Years Pro 1
Years On Team 1
Grand Tour Apps 1
Wins 0
UCI Ranking 1711

### LUKAS PÖSTLBERGER
Austria
10.01.92
Years Pro 6
Years On Team 6
Grand Tour Apps 6
Wins 5
UCI Ranking 405

### JURAJ SAGAN
Slovakia
23.12.88
Years Pro 11
Years On Team 5
Grand Tour Apps 1
Wins 4
UCI Ranking 2082

### MAXIMILIAN SCHACHMANN
Germany
09.01.94
Years Pro 5
Years On Team 3
Grand Tour Apps 4
Wins 13
UCI Ranking 22

### IDE SCHELLING
Netherlands
06.02.98
Years Pro 2
Years On Team 2
Grand Tour Apps 2
Wins 1
UCI Ranking 96

### ANDREAS SCHILLINGER
Germany
13.07.83
Years Pro 11
Years On Team 12
Grand Tour Apps 7
Wins 0
UCI Ranking 2082

### MICHAEL SCHWARZMANN
Germany
07.01.91
Years Pro 11
Years On Team 12
Grand Tour Apps 5
Wins 1
UCI Ranking 1951

### RÜDIGER SELIG
Germany
19.02.89
Years Pro 10
Years On Team 6
Grand Tour Apps 6
Wins 3
UCI Ranking 1553

### MATTHEW WALLS
Great Britain
20.04.98
Years Pro 1
Years On Team 1
Grand Tour Apps 0
Wins 2
UCI Ranking 272

### FREDERIK WANDAHL
Denmark
09.05.01
Years Pro 1
Years On Team 1
Grand Tour Apps 0
Wins 0
UCI Ranking 686

### BEN ZWIEHOFF
Germany
22.02.94
Years Pro 1
Years On Team 1
Grand Tour Apps 1
Wins 0
UCI Ranking 1064

TEAMS

TEAMS    MEN'S WORLDTOUR

# COFIDIS

### 2021 SEASON REVIEW

Cofidis' second year at WorldTour level would always struggle to be worse than their first – just two wins during the Covid year – although their sophomore effort only just reached double digits, with most wins on home roads and at 1.1 and 1.2 level. Victor Lafay's Giro d'Italia stage win was their sole WT victory, although top tens at two Grand Tours will give hope that they're heading in the right direction. Christophe Laporte's sixth at Paris–Roubaix was impressive but the team will lose his services to Jumbo-Visma next year. Ⓐ

### 2021 VICTORIES

| | | |
|---|---|---|
| Etoile de Bessèges – stage 1 | 2.1 | C. Laporte |
| Cholet - Pays de la Loire | 1.1 | E. Viviani |
| Circuit de Wallonie | 1.1 | C. Laporte |
| Trofeo Serra de Tramuntana | 1.1 | Je. Herrada |
| Giro d'Italia | 2.UWT | V. Lafay |
| Mercan'Tour Classic Alpes-Maritimes | 1.1 | G. Martin |
| Tour du Limousin – stage 1 | 2.1 | C. Laporte |
| Tour Poitou–Charentes en Nouvelle Aquitaine – stage 1 | 2.1 | E. Viviani |
| Tour Poitou–Charentes en Nouvelle Aquitaine – stage 3 | 2.1 | E. Viviani |
| GP de Fourmies | 1.Pro | E. Viviani |
| GP de Wallonie | 1.Pro | C. Laporte |
| GP d'Isbergues | 1.1 | E. Viviani |

### TEAM INFORMATION

| | |
|---|---|
| UCI CODE | COF |
| UCI STATUS | MEN'S WORLDTOUR |
| COUNTRY | FRANCE |
| FOUNDED | 1997 |

### TEAM NAME HISTORY

| | |
|---|---|
| 1997-2003 | COFIDIS |
| 2004-2008 | COFIDIS, LE CRÉDIT PAR TÉLÉPHONE |
| 2009-2012 | COFIDIS, LE CRÉDIT EN LIGNE |
| 2013-2021 | COFIDIS, SOLUTIONS CREDITS |

### TEAM MANAGER

**CÉDRIC VASSEUR**

### 2021 NEW RIDERS

**JEMPY DRUCKER, SIMON GESCHKE, JELLE WALLAYS, RUBÉN FERNÁNDEZ, TOM BOHLI, SZYMON SAJNOK, RÉMY ROCHAS, ANDRE CARVALHO, THOMAS CHAMPION**

### 2021 STAGIAIRES

**JACQUES LEBRETON, HUGO TOUMIRE, AXEL ZINGLE**

### EQUIPMENT

| | |
|---|---|
| BIKE | DE ROSA |

570

## RIDER PROFILES

### GUILLAUME MARTIN
France
09.06.93
Years Pro 6
Years On Team 2
Grand Tour Apps 7
Wins 7
UCI Ranking 49

His first Grand Tour top ten, at the Tour de France, was followed up by his second at the Vuelta. You don't win any prizes for coming eighth and ninth, respectively, but it will ensure his position as Cofidis' out-and-out leader for another season. It seems he's on the right trajectory to fulfilling his status as a French Grand Tour hope.

### ELIA VIVIANI
Italy
07.02.89
Years Pro 12
Years On Team 2
Grand Tour Apps 13
Wins 85
UCI Ranking 68

Another season in which he struggled to show the form of his Deceuninck-QuickStep days, but at least he won this season – seven times, albeit not at the races that truly mattered to a rider of his calibre. Continuing to combine track and road, he took bronze in the men's Omnium in Tokyo.

### PIET ALLEGAERT
Belgium
20.01.95
Years Pro 5
Years On Team 2
Grand Tour Apps 1
Wins 1
UCI Ranking 141

### FERNANDO BARCELÓ
Spain
06.01.96
Years Pro 4
Years On Team 2
Grand Tour Apps 3
Wins 0
UCI Ranking 430

### NATNAEL BERHANE
Eritrea
05.01.91
Years Pro 9
Years On Team 3
Grand Tour Apps 8
Wins 9
UCI Ranking –

### TOM BOHLI
Switzerland
17.01.94
Years Pro 6
Years On Team 1
Grand Tour Apps 1
Wins 1
UCI Ranking 1951

### ANDRE CARVALHO
Portugal
31.10.97
Years Pro 1
Years On Team 1
Grand Tour Apps 0
Wins 0
UCI Ranking 1787

### THOMAS CHAMPION
France
08.09.99
Years Pro 1
Years On Team 1
Grand Tour Apps 0
Wins 0
UCI Ranking 2664

### SIMONE CONSONNI
Italy
12.09.94
Years Pro 5
Years On Team 2
Grand Tour Apps 5
Wins 1
UCI Ranking 248

### JEMPY DRUCKER
Luxembourg
03.09.86
Years Pro 11
Years On Team 1
Grand Tour Apps 4
Wins 6
UCI Ranking 567

### NICOLAS EDET
France
02.12.87
Years Pro 11
Years On Team 11
Grand Tour Apps 13
Wins 2
UCI Ranking 1273

### RUBÉN FERNÁNDEZ
Spain
01.03.91
Years Pro 9
Years On Team 1
Grand Tour Apps 5
Wins 0
UCI Ranking 430

### EDDY FINÉ
France
20.11.97
Years Pro 2
Years On Team 2
Grand Tour Apps 1
Wins 0
UCI Ranking 1999

### SIMON GESCHKE
Germany
13.03.86
Years Pro 13
Years On Team 1
Grand Tour Apps 16
Wins 3
UCI Ranking 536

### NATHAN HAAS
Australia
12.03.89
Years Pro 10
Years On Team 2
Grand Tour Apps 7
Wins 7
UCI Ranking 1297

### JÉSUS HERRADA
Spain
26.07.90
Years Pro 11
Years On Team 4
Grand Tour Apps 11
Wins 16
UCI Ranking 98

### JOSÉ HERRADA
Spain
01.10.85
Years Pro 14
Years On Team 4
Grand Tour Apps 13
Wins 2
UCI Ranking 1067

### VICTOR LAFAY
France
17.01.96
Years Pro 4
Years On Team 4
Grand Tour Apps 2
Wins 1
UCI Ranking 158

### CHRISTOPHE LAPORTE
France
11.12.92
Years Pro 8
Years On Team 8
Grand Tour Apps 7
Wins 21
UCI Ranking 41

### EMMANUEL MORIN
France
13.03.95
Years Pro 3
Years On Team 3
Grand Tour Apps 2
Wins 0
UCI Ranking 609

### ANTHONY PEREZ
France
22.04.91
Years Pro 6
Years On Team 6
Grand Tour Apps 5
Wins 3
UCI Ranking 418

### PIERRE-LUC PÉRICHON
France
04.01.87
Years Pro 9
Years On Team 3
Grand Tour Apps 7
Wins 2
UCI Ranking 209

### RÉMY ROCHAS
France
18.05.96
Years Pro 3
Years On Team 1
Grand Tour Apps 2
Wins 0
UCI Ranking 293

### FABIO SABATINI
Italy
18.02.85
Years Pro 16
Years On Team 2
Grand Tour Apps 21
Wins 0
UCI Ranking –

### KENNETH VANBILSEN
Belgium
01.06.90
Years Pro 9
Years On Team 7
Grand Tour Apps 4
Wins 2
UCI Ranking –

### ATTILIO VIVIANI
Italy
18.10.24
Years Pro 2
Years On Team 2
Grand Tour Apps 1
Wins 2
UCI Ranking 1951

### JELLE WALLAYS
Belgium
11.05.89
Years Pro 11
Years On Team 1
Grand Tour Apps 5
Wins 8
UCI Ranking 1251

TEAMS  MEN'S WORLDTOUR

# DECEUNINCK–QUICKSTEP

**2021 SEASON REVIEW**

Deceuninck-QuickStep could hardly write a better script for professional road cycling if they tried. Scintillating victories, heroes and villains, heroic comebacks – the Belgian outfit had it all. Fabio Jakobsen's return from horrific injury to win at WorldTour level once more was juxtaposed with the comedown of Sam Bennett's dreamy 2020, the Irishman on the receiving end of boss Patrick Lefevere's vitriol in the press. The ageing Belgian made nearly as many headlines as his riders – an impressive feat – as he courted scandal frequently. Remco Evenepoel got back on track, returning to winning ways and possibly the hungriest wolf in their self-ordained pack. More than 60 victories, including nine Grand Tour stages and a Monument, is somehow par for the course for this sensational team.

## TEAM INFORMATION

| | |
|---|---|
| UCI CODE | **DQT** |
| UCI STATUS | **MEN'S WORLDTOUR** |
| COUNTRY | **BELGIUM** |
| FOUNDED | **1999** |

**TEAM NAME HISTORY**

| | |
|---|---|
| 1999-2002 | **MAPEI-QUICKSTEP** |
| 2003-2004 | **QUICKSTEP-DAVITAMON** |
| 2005-2010 | **QUICKSTEP-INNERGETIC** |
| 2011 | **QUICKSTEP CYCLING TEAM** |
| 2012-2014 | **OMEGA PHARMA-QUICK-STEP** |
| 2015-2016 | **ETIXX-QUICKSTEP** |
| 2017-2018 | **QUICK-STEP FLOORS** |
| 2019-2021 | **DECEUNINCK-QUICKSTEP** |

**TEAM MANAGER**

**PATRICK LEFEVERE**

**2021 NEW RIDERS**

**MARK CAVENDISH, JOSEF ČERNÝ**

**2021 STAGIAIRES**

**JASON OSBORNE, STAN VAN TRICHT**

**EQUIPMENT**

| | |
|---|---|
| BIKE | **SPECIALIZED** |

## 2021 VICTORIES

| | | |
|---|---|---|
| Tour de la Provence – stage 1 | 2.Pro | D. Ballerini |
| Tour de la Provence – stage 2 | 2.Pro | D. Ballerini |
| UAE Tour – stage 4 | 2.UWT | S. Bennett |
| UAE Tour – stage 6 | 2.UWT | S. Bennett |
| Omloop Het Nieuwsblad ME | 1.UWT | D. Ballerini |
| La Drôme Classic | 1.Pro | A. Bagioli |
| GP Industria & Artigianato | 1.Pro | M. Vansevenant |
| Paris-Nice – stage 1 | 2.UWT | S. Bennett |
| Tirreno-Adriatico – stage 2 | 2.UWT | J. Alaphilippe |
| Paris-Nice – stage 5 | 2.UWT | S. Bennett |
| Brugge-De Panne | 1.UWT | S. Bennett |
| E3 Classic | 1.UWT | K. Asgreen |
| Settimana Internazionale Coppi e Bartali – stage 5 | 2.1 | M. F. Honoré |
| Tour of Flanders | 1.UWT | K. Asgreen |
| Itzulia Basque Country – stage 5 | 2.UWT | M. F. Honoré |
| Presidential Cycling Tour of Turkey – stage 2 | 2.Pro | M. Cavendish |
| Presidential Cycling Tour of Turkey – stage 3 | 2.Pro | M. Cavendish |
| Presidential Cycling Tour of Turkey – stage 4 | 2.Pro | M. Cavendish |
| Presidential Cycling Tour of Turkey – stage 8 | 2.Pro | M. Cavendish |
| La Flèche Wallonne | 1.UWT | J. Alaphilippe |
| Tour de Romandie – stage 5 (ITT) | 2.UWT | R. Cavagna |
| Volta ao Algarve – stage 1 | 2.Pro | S. Bennett |
| Volta ao Algarve – stage 3 | 2.Pro | S. Bennett |
| Volta ao Algarve – stage 4 (ITT) | 2.Pro | K. Asgreen |
| Baloise Belgium Tour – stage 2 (ITT) | 2.Pro | R. Evenepoel |
| Baloise Belgium Tour | 2.Pro | R. Evenepoel |
| Baloise Belgium Tour – stage 5 | 2.Pro | M. Cavendish |
| National Championships Belgium – ITT | NC | Y. Lampaert |
| National Championships Denmark – ITT | NC | K. Asgreen |
| National Championships Czech Republic – ITT | NC | J. Černý |
| National Championships Portugal – ITT | NC | J. Almeida |
| National Championships France – RR | NC | R. Cavagna |
| Tour de France – stage 1 | 2.UWT | J. Alaphilippe |
| Tour de France – stage 4 | 2.UWT | M. Cavendish |
| Tour de France – stage 6 | 2.UWT | M. Cavendish |
| Tour de France – stage 10 | 2.UWT | M. Cavendish |
| Tour de France – stage 13 | 2.UWT | M. Cavendish |
| Tour de Wallonie – stage 2 | 2.Pro | F. Jakobsen |
| Tour de Wallonie – stage 5 | 2.Pro | F. Jakobsen |
| Tour de l'Ain – stage 1 | 2.1 | Á. J. Hodeg |
| Tour de Pologne – stage 2 | 2.UWT | J. Almeida |
| Tour of Denmark – stage 3 | 2.Pro | R. Evenepoel |
| Tour de Pologne – stage 4 | 2.UWT | J. Almeida |
| Tour of Denmark – stage 5 (ITT) | 2.Pro | R. Evenepoel |
| Tour of Denmark | 2.Pro | R. Evenepoel |
| Tour de Pologne | 2.UWT | J. Almeida |
| Vuelta a España – stage 4 | 2.UWT | F. Jakobsen |
| GP Marcel Kint | 1.1 | Á. J. Hodeg |

**2021 VICTORIES (CONT)**

| | | |
|---|---|---|
| Vuelta a España – stage 8 | 2.UWT | F. Jakobsen |
| Druivenkoers-Overijse | 1.1 | R. Evenepoel |
| Vuelta a España – stage 13 | 2.UWT | F. Sénéchal |
| Brussels Cycling Classic | 1.Pro | R. Evenepoel |
| Vuelta a España – stage 16 | 2.UWT | F. Jakobsen |
| Tour of Britain – stage 7 | 2.Pro | Y. Lampaert |
| Tour de Luxembourg – stage 1 | 2.Pro | J. Almeida |
| Tour of Slovakia – stage 1 | 2.1 | Á. J. Hodeg |
| Tour de Luxembourg – stage 4 (ITT) | 2.Pro | M. Cattaneo |
| Tour of Slovakia – stage 2 | 2.1 | J. Steimle |
| Tour de Luxembourg | 2.Pro | J. Almeida |
| Primus Classic | 1.Pro | F. Sénéchal |
| Gooikse Pijl | 1.1 | F. Jakobsen |
| Eurométropole Tour | 1.Pro | F. Jakobsen |
| Münsterland Giro | 1.Pro | M. Cavendish |
| Coppa Bernocchi | 1.Pro | R. Evenepoel |

RIDER PROFILES

## MARK CAVENDISH

Great Britain
21.05.85
Years Pro 15
Years On Team 1
Grand Tour Apps 20
Wins 156
UCI Ranking 32

The whispers of a return to form in Turkey gave way to a Tour de France participation no one saw coming, let alone four stage wins and a green jersey. Cav was back: combative, sprinting, winning, all emotion and speed. Equalling Merckx's record, which he was recalcitrant to engage with, it was a sporting comeback for the ages.

## JULIAN ALAPHILIPPE

France
11.06.92
Years Pro 8
Years On Team 8
Grand Tour Apps 6
Wins 37
UCI Ranking 4

Liège was the one he really wanted but he was bested by Pogačar. He arrived at the Tour de France with fire in his belly, and claimed stage 1 and the first yellow jersey while in the rainbow bands. Nobody was prepared for his unrelenting defence of the world title in Flanders, as he made it two solo Worlds wins in a row.

### JOÃO ALMEIDA
Portugal
05.08.98
Years Pro 4
Years On Team 2
Grand Tour Apps 2
Wins 6
UCI Ranking 9

### SHANE ARCHBOLD
New Zealand
02.02.89
Years Pro 8
Years On Team 2
Grand Tour Apps 2
Wins 2
UCI Ranking 1087

### KASPER ASGREEN
Denmark
08.02.95
Years Pro 4
Years On Team 4
Grand Tour Apps 4
Wins 10
UCI Ranking 23

### ANDREA BAGIOLI
Italy
23.03.99
Years Pro 2
Years On Team 2
Grand Tour Apps 2
Wins 3
UCI Ranking 173

### DAVIDE BALLERINI
Italy
21.09.94
Years Pro 5
Years On Team 2
Grand Tour Apps 3
Wins 8
UCI Ranking 126

### SAM BENNETT
Ireland
16.10.90
Years Pro 8
Years On Team 2
Grand Tour Apps 7
Wins 56
UCI Ranking 80

### MATTIA CATTANEO
Italy
25.10.90
Years Pro 9
Years On Team 2
Grand Tour Apps 8
Wins 3
UCI Ranking 101

### RÉMI CAVAGNA
France
10.08.95
Years Pro 5
Years On Team 5
Grand Tour Apps 5
Wins 8
UCI Ranking 163

### JOSEF ČERNÝ
Czech Republic
11.05.93
Years Pro 9
Years On Team 1
Grand Tour Apps 3
Wins 8
UCI Ranking 330

### TIM DECLERCQ
Belgium
21.03.89
Years Pro 10
Years On Team 5
Grand Tour Apps 5
Wins 0
UCI Ranking 1760

### DRIES DEVENYNS
Belgium
22.07.83
Years Pro 15
Years On Team 5
Grand Tour Apps 12
Wins 7
UCI Ranking 1129

### REMCO EVENEPOEL
Belgium
25.01.00
Years Pro 3
Years On Team 3
Grand Tour Apps 1
Wins 22
UCI Ranking 14

### IAN GARRISON
United States
14.04.98
Years Pro 4
Years On Team 2
Grand Tour Apps 1
Wins 1
UCI Ranking 2883

### ÁLVARO JOSÉ HODEG
Colombia
16.09.96
Years Pro 4
Years On Team 4
Grand Tour Apps 1
Wins 15
UCI Ranking 217

### MIKKEL FRØLICH HONORÉ
Denmark
21.01.97
Years Pro 3
Years On Team 3
Grand Tour Apps 3
Wins 2
UCI Ranking 27

### FABIO JAKOBSEN
Netherlands
31.08.96
Years Pro 4
Years On Team 4
Grand Tour Apps 2
Wins 25
UCI Ranking 61

### ILJO KEISSE
Belgium
21.12.82
Years Pro 17
Years On Team 12
Grand Tour Apps 8
Wins 5
UCI Ranking 1951

### JAMES KNOX
Great Britain
04.11.95
Years Pro 4
Years On Team 4
Grand Tour Apps 5
Wins 0
UCI Ranking 424

### YVES LAMPAERT
Belgium
10.04.91
Years Pro 9
Years On Team 7
Grand Tour Apps 4
Wins 13
UCI Ranking 45

### FAUSTO MASNADA
Italy
06.11.93
Years Pro 5
Years On Team 2
Grand Tour Apps 4
Wins 5
UCI Ranking 48

### MICHAEL MØRKOV
Denmark
30.04.85
Years Pro 13
Years On Team 4
Grand Tour Apps 13
Wins 5
UCI Ranking 326

### FLORIAN SÉNÉCHAL
France
10.07.93
Years Pro 8
Years On Team 4
Grand Tour Apps 6
Wins 4
UCI Ranking 31

### PIETER SERRY
Belgium
21.11.88
Years Pro 11
Years On Team 9
Grand Tour Apps 12
Wins 0
UCI Ranking 1160

### STIJN STEELS
Belgium
21.08.89
Years Pro 9
Years On Team 2
Grand Tour Apps 0
Wins 0
UCI Ranking 1418

### JANNIK STEIMLE
Germany
04.04.96
Years Pro 2
Years On Team 2
Grand Tour Apps 1
Wins 6
UCI Ranking 421

### ZDENEK ŠTYBAR
Czech Republic
11.12.85
Years Pro 11
Years On Team 11
Grand Tour Apps 9
Wins 18
UCI Ranking 128

### BERT VAN LERBERGHE
Belgium
29.09.92
Years Pro 7
Years On Team 2
Grand Tour Apps 1
Wins 0
UCI Ranking 380

### MAURI VANSEVENANT
Belgium
01.06.99
Years Pro 2
Years On Team 2
Grand Tour Apps 2
Wins 1
UCI Ranking 119

TEAMS

TEAMS  MEN'S WORLDTOUR

# EF EDUCATION-NIPPO

**2021 SEASON REVIEW**

Rigoberto Úran's Tour de France podium bid fell apart in the final few days, while Hugh Carthy's return to the Vuelta a España after his third place in 2020 was cut short early by illness. A string of WorldTour wins made for a decent year, Alberto Bettiol winning at the Giro, and Neilson Powless in San Sebastian. Magnus Cort did his best impression of Wout van Aert at the Spanish Grand Tour, winning in a multitude of ways, while Michael Valgren peaked late to win a couple of Italian one-dayers before his bronze medal at the World Championships. Next year sees a number of intriguing names join the ranks: Esteban Chaves, Owain Doull, Odd Christian Eiking and the young Irishman Ben Healy. ⓙⓛ

**2021 VICTORIES**

| | | |
|---|---|---|
| Paris-Nice – stage 3 (ITT) | 2.UWT | S. Bissegger |
| Paris-Nice – stage 8 | 2.UWT | M. Cort |
| Giro d'Italia – stage 18 | 2.UWT | A. Bettiol |
| Tour de Suisse – stage 4 | 2.UWT | S. Bissegger |
| Tour de Suisse – stage 7 (ITT) | 2.UWT | R. Úran |
| La Route d'Occitanie – stage 4 | 2.1 | M. Cort |
| National Championships United States – ITT | NC | L. Craddock |
| Donostia San Sebastian Klasikoa | 1.UWT | N. Powless |
| Vuelta a Burgos – stage 5 | 2.Pro | H. Carthy |
| Tour de Pologne – stage 7 | 2.UWT | J. van den Berg |
| Vuelta a España – stage 6 | 2.UWT | M. Cort |
| Vuelta a España – stage 12 | 2.UWT | M. Cort |
| Benelux Tour – stage 2 (ITT) | 2.UWT | S. Bissegger |
| Vuelta a España – stage 19 | 2.UWT | M. Cort |
| Giro della Toscana | 1.1 | M. Valgren |
| Coppa Sabatini | 1.Pro | M. Valgren |

**TEAM INFORMATION**

| | |
|---|---|
| UCI CODE | **EFN** |
| UCI STATUS | **MEN'S WORLDTOUR** |
| COUNTRY | **UNITED STATES** |
| FOUNDED | **2005** |

**TEAM NAME HISTORY**

| | |
|---|---|
| 2005-2006 | **TEAM TIAA-CREF** |
| 2007 | **TEAM SLIPSTREAM** |
| 2008 | **TEAM GARMIN-CHIPOTLE** |
| 2009 | **TEAM GARMIN-SLIPSTREAM** |
| 2010 | **TEAM GARMIN-TRANSITIONS** |
| 2011 | **TEAM GARMIN-CERVÉLO** |
| 2012-2014 | **GARMIN SHARP** |
| 2015 | **TEAM CANNONDALE-GARMIN** |
| 2016-2017 | **CANNONDALE-DRAPAC PRO CYCLING TEAM** |
| 2018 | **TEAM EF EDUCATION FIRST-DRAPAC P/B CANNONDALE** |
| 2019 | **EF EDUCATION FIRST** |
| 2020 | **EF PRO CYCLING** |
| 2021 | **EF EDUCATION-NIPPO** |

**TEAM MANAGER**

**JONATHAN VAUGHTERS**

**2021 NEW RIDERS**

**MICHAEL VALGREN, JULIEN EL FARES, FUMIYUKI BEPPU, HIDETO NAKANE, SIMON CARR, WILL BARTA, DIEGO ANDRÉS CAMARGO, DANIEL ARROYAVE**

**EQUIPMENT**

| | |
|---|---|
| BIKE | **CANNONDALE** |

RIDER PROFILES

## MAGNUS CORT

Denmark
16.01.93
Years Pro 7
Years On Team 2
Grand Tour Apps 7
Wins 21
UCI Ranking 107

Victory on the final stage of Paris–Nice opened his season account relatively early but the Vuelta was where he showed what he was capable of. A late surge to deny Roglič on stage 6, bunch-sprint victor a week later before breakaway heroics on the penultimate road stage, and only the Slovenian overall winner could stop him making it four in the final time trial.

## LACHLAN MORTON

Australia
02.01.92
Years Pro 9
Years On Team 3
Grand Tour Apps 2
Wins 5
UCI Ranking 1787

According to the stat sheet the Australian rider had a rather anaemic year but, while most of the world was watching the Tour de France, Morton was riding the entire race – including transfers between stages – by himself in his charity 'Alt Tour'. The 29-year-old beat the peloton to Paris with days to spare, resplendent in sandals after succumbing to trench foot.

### DANIEL ARROYAVE
Colombia
19.06.000
Years Pro 1
Years On Team 1
Grand Tour Apps 0
Wins 0
UCI Ranking —

### WILL BARTA
United States
04.01.96
Years Pro 4
Years On Team 1
Grand Tour Apps 2
Wins 0
UCI Ranking 1565

### FUMIYUKI BEPPU
Japan
10.04.83
Years Pro 17
Years On Team 1
Grand Tour Apps 6
Wins 6
UCI Ranking —

### ALBERTO BETTIOL
Italy
29.10.93
Years Pro 8
Years On Team 7
Grand Tour Apps 5
Wins 3
UCI Ranking 275

### STEFAN BISSEGGER
Switzerland
13.09.98
Years Pro 1
Years On Team 1
Grand Tour Apps 1
Wins 3
UCI Ranking 127

### JONATHAN KLEVER CAICEDO
Ecuador
28.04.93
Years Pro 3
Years On Team 3
Grand Tour Apps 4
Wins 4
UCI Ranking 1393

### DIEGO ANDRÉS CAMARGO
Colombia
03.05.98
Years Pro 1
Years On Team 1
Grand Tour Apps 0
Wins 0
UCI Ranking 1021

### SIMON CARR
Great Britain
29.08.98
Years Pro 2
Years On Team 1
Grand Tour Apps 1
Wins 1
UCI Ranking 371

### HUGH CARTHY
Great Britain
09.07.94
Years Pro 7
Years On Team 5
Grand Tour Apps 9
Wins 7
UCI Ranking 103

### LAWSON CRADDOCK
United States
20.02.92
Years Pro 8
Years On Team 6
Grand Tour Apps 7
Wins 1
UCI Ranking 483

### MITCHELL DOCKER
Australia
02.10.86
Years Pro 15
Years On Team 4
Grand Tour Apps 9
Wins 2
UCI Ranking —

### JULIEN EL FARES
France
01.06.85
Years Pro 14
Years On Team 1
Grand Tour Apps 4
Wins 3
UCI Ranking 804

### RUBEN GUERREIRO
Portugal
06.07.94
Years Pro 5
Years On Team 2
Grand Tour Apps 4
Wins 2
UCI Ranking 301

### SERGIO HIGUITA
Colombia
01.08.97
Years Pro 5
Years On Team 3
Grand Tour Apps 3
Wins 4
UCI Ranking 157

### MORENO HOFLAND
Netherlands
31.08.91
Years Pro 9
Years On Team 3
Grand Tour Apps 4
Wins 13
UCI Ranking —

### ALEX HOWES
United States
01.01.88
Years Pro 10
Years On Team 10
Grand Tour Apps 5
Wins 4
UCI Ranking 2296

### JENS KEUKELEIRE
Belgium
23.11.88
Years Pro 12
Years On Team 2
Grand Tour Apps 11
Wins 11
UCI Ranking 1512

### SEBASTIAN LANGEVELD
Netherlands
17.01.85
Years Pro 16
Years On Team 8
Grand Tour Apps 9
Wins 7
UCI Ranking 1036

### HIDETO NAKANE
Japan
02.05.90
Years Pro 5
Years On Team 1
Grand Tour Apps 0
Wins 1
UCI Ranking 637

### LOGAN OWEN
United States
25.03.95
Years Pro 4
Years On Team 4
Grand Tour Apps 2
Wins 2
UCI Ranking 955

### NEILSON POWLESS
United States
03.09.96
Years Pro 4
Years On Team 2
Grand Tour Apps 3
Wins 1
UCI Ranking 52

### JONAS RUTSCH
Germany
24.01.98
Years Pro 2
Years On Team 2
Grand Tour Apps 1
Wins 0
UCI Ranking 497

### TOM SCULLY
New Zealand
14.01.90
Years Pro 6
Years On Team 6
Grand Tour Apps 5
Wins 2
UCI Ranking 1753

### RIGOBERTO URÁN
Colombia
26.01.87
Years Pro 16
Years On Team 6
Grand Tour Apps 20
Wins 14
UCI Ranking 62

### MICHAEL VALGREN
Denmark
07.02.92
Years Pro 8
Years On Team 1
Grand Tour Apps 9
Wins 8
UCI Ranking 60

### JULIUS VAN DEN BERG
Netherlands
23.10.96
Years Pro 4
Years On Team 4
Grand Tour Apps 2
Wins 1
UCI Ranking 776

### TEJAY VAN GARDEREN
United States
12.08.88
Years Pro 12
Years On Team 3
Grand Tour Apps 17
Wins 16
UCI Ranking 1369

### JAMES WHELAN
Australia
11.07.96
Years Pro 3
Years On Team 3
Grand Tour Apps 1
Wins 0
UCI Ranking 1139

TEAMS  MEN'S WORLDTOUR

# GROUPAMA-FDJ

**2021 SEASON REVIEW**

Another year where the squad tried to do their best without Thibaut Pinot performing at the height of his powers, but his absence could not be avoided. While the Frenchman started to make promising steps in the right direction towards the end of the season, it was up to the likes of Démare, Küng and Gaudu to deliver victories, although a properly big one evaded the French squad and no Grand Tour stage wins will be a disappointment for Marc Madiot and co.

**2021 VICTORIES**

| | | |
|---|---|---|
| Faun-Ardèche Classic | 1.Pro | D. Gaudu |
| Trophée Harmonie Mutuelle | 1.1 | A. Démare |
| Itzulia Basque Country – stage 6 | 2.UWT | D. Gaudu |
| Volta a la Comunitat Valenciana – stage 1 | 2. Pro | M. Scotson |
| Volta a la Comunitat Valenciana – stage 2 | 2. Pro | A. Démare |
| Volta a la Comunitat Valenciana – stage 4 (ITT) | 2. Pro | S. Küng |
| Volta a la Comunitat Valenciana – stage 5 | 2. Pro | A. Démare |
| Volta a la Comunitat Valenciana | 2. Pro | S. Küng |
| Boucles de la Mayenne – stage 2 | 2.Pro | A. Démare |
| Boucles de la Mayenne – stage 3 | 2.Pro | A. Démare |
| Boucles de la Mayenne – stage 4 | 2.Pro | A. Démare |
| Boucles de la Mayenne | 2.Pro | A. Démare |
| Tour de Suisse – stage 1 (ITT) | 2.UWT | S. Küng |
| La Route d'Occitanie – stage 2 | 2.1 | A. Démare |
| National Championships Switzerland – ITT | NC | S. Küng |
| National Championships France – ITT | NC | B. Thomas |
| National Championships Luxembourg – ITT | NC | K. Geniets |
| National Championships Lithuania – RR | NC | I. Konovalovas |
| National Championships Luxembourg – RR | NC | K. Geniets |
| La Polynormande | 1.1 | V. Madouas |
| Tour de Luxembourg – stage 5 | 2.Pro | D. Gaudu |
| Paris-Tours | 1.Pro | A. Démare |
| Chrono des Nations | 1.1 | S. Küng |

**TEAM INFORMATION**

| | |
|---|---|
| UCI CODE | **GFC** |
| UCI STATUS | **MEN'S WORLDTOUR** |
| COUNTRY | **FRANCE** |
| FOUNDED | **1997** |

**TEAM NAME HISTORY**

| | |
|---|---|
| 1997-2002 | **LA FRANÇAISE DES JEUX** |
| 2003-2004 | **FDJEUX.COM** |
| 2005-2010 | **LA FRANÇAISE DES JEUX** |
| 2010-2011 | **FDJ** |
| 2012 | **FDJ-BIGMAT** |
| 2013-2014 | **FDJ.FR** |
| 2015-2017 | **FDJ** |
| 2018-2021 | **GROUPAMA-FDJ** |

**TEAM MANAGER**

**MARC MADIOT**

**2021 NEW RIDERS**

**ATTILA VALTER, MATTEO BADILATTI, LARS VAN DEN BERG, CLÉMENT DAVY**

**EQUIPMENT**

| | |
|---|---|
| BIKE | **LAPIERRE** |

**RIDER PROFILES**

## STEFAN KÜNG

Switzerland
16.11.93
Years Pro 7
Years On Team 3
Grand Tour Apps 7
Wins 22
UCI Ranking 26

The overall victory at the Volta a la Comunitat Valenciana gave way to the opening time trial win at his home Tour de Suisse then Pogačar denied him ITT victory on stage 5 at the Tour. He finished fifth at the Worlds ITT, and in cruel fourth at the Olympics ITT. The European time trial champion title will provide some consolation.

## DAVID GAUDU

France
10.10.96
Years Pro 5
Years On Team 5
Grand Tour Apps 5
Wins 7
UCI Ranking 16

While not recreating his achievement of two Grand Tour stage wins and eighth overall at the 2020 Vuelta, the 25-year-old continues to progress. He claimed a stage win at the Tours of both the Basque Country and Luxembourg. Narrowly missing out on top ten at the Tour de France, his 11th place was backed up by a hatful of top-ten finishes.

---

**BRUNO ARMIRAIL**
France
11.04.94
Years Pro 4
Years On Team 4
Grand Tour Apps 3
Wins 0
UCI Ranking 306

**MATTEO BADILATTI**
Switzerland
30.07.92
Years Pro 3
Years On Team 1
Grand Tour Apps 2
Wins 0
UCI Ranking 403

**WILLIAM BONNET**
France
25.06.82
Years Pro 16
Years On Team 11
Grand Tour Apps 18
Wins 4
UCI Ranking –

**ALEXYS BRUNEL**
France
10.10.98
Years Pro 2
Years On Team 2
Grand Tour Apps 0
Wins 1
UCI Ranking 846

**CLÉMENT DAVY**
France
17.07.98
Years Pro 1
Years On Team 1
Grand Tour Apps 0
Wins 0
UCI Ranking 1522

**MICKAËL DELAGE**
France
06.08.85
Years Pro 17
Years On Team 11
Grand Tour Apps 17
Wins 2
UCI Ranking –

**ARNAUD DÉMARE**
France
26.08.91
Years Pro 10
Years On Team 10
Grand Tour Apps 10
Wins 84
UCI Ranking 51

**ANTOINE DUCHESNE**
Canada
12.09.91
Years Pro 8
Years On Team 8
Grand Tour Apps 4
Wins 1
UCI Ranking 686

**KEVIN GENIETS**
Luxembourg
09.01.97
Years Pro 3
Years On Team 3
Grand Tour Apps 1
Wins 3
UCI Ranking 224

**JACOPO GUARNIERI**
Italy
14.08.87
Years Pro 14
Years On Team 5
Grand Tour Apps 10
Wins 4
UCI Ranking –

**SIMON GUGLIELMI**
France
01.07.97
Years Pro 2
Years On Team 2
Grand Tour Apps 2
Wins 0
UCI Ranking 1553

**IGNATAS KONOVALOVAS**
Lithuania
08.12.85
Years Pro 14
Years On Team 6
Grand Tour Apps 11
Wins 12
UCI Ranking 538

**MATTHIEU LADAGNOUS**
France
12.12.84
Years Pro 16
Years On Team 16
Grand Tour Apps 14
Wins 11
UCI Ranking 1951

**OLIVIER LE GAC**
France
27.08.93
Years Pro 8
Years On Team 8
Grand Tour Apps 7
Wins 1
UCI Ranking 428

**FABIAN LIENHARD**
Switzerland
03.09.93
Years Pro 4
Years On Team 2
Grand Tour Apps 0
Wins 0
UCI Ranking 1418

**TOBIAS LUDVIGSSON**
Sweden
22.02.91
Years Pro 10
Years On Team 5
Grand Tour Apps 12
Wins 5
UCI Ranking 811

**VALENTIN MADOUAS**
France
12.07.96
Years Pro 4
Years On Team 4
Grand Tour Apps 3
Wins 2
UCI Ranking 71

**RUDY MOLARD**
France
17.09.89
Years Pro 10
Years On Team 5
Grand Tour Apps 12
Wins 2
UCI Ranking 277

**THIBAUT PINOT**
France
29.05.90
Years Pro 12
Years On Team 12
Grand Tour Apps 14
Wins 31
UCI Ranking 243

**SÉBASTIEN REICHENBACH**
Switzerland
28.05.89
Years Pro 9
Years On Team 6
Grand Tour Apps 8
Wins 2
UCI Ranking 326

**ANTHONY ROUX**
France
18.04.87
Years Pro 14
Years On Team 14
Grand Tour Apps 14
Wins 2
UCI Ranking –

**MILES SCOTSON**
Australia
18.01.94
Years Pro 5
Years On Team 3
Grand Tour Apps 3
Wins 16
UCI Ranking 440

**ROMAIN SEIGLE**
France
11.10.94
Years Pro 4
Years On Team 4
Grand Tour Apps 3
Wins 0
UCI Ranking 1021

**RAMON SINKELDAM**
Netherlands
09.02.89
Years Pro 10
Years On Team 4
Grand Tour Apps 9
Wins 7
UCI Ranking 2296

**JAKE STEWART**
Great Britain
02.10.99
Years Pro 2
Years On Team 2
Grand Tour Apps 0
Wins 0
UCI Ranking 142

**BENJAMIN THOMAS**
France
12.09.95
Years Pro 4
Years On Team 4
Grand Tour Apps 3
Wins 4
UCI Ranking 424

**ATTILA VALTER**
Hungary
12.06.98
Years Pro 2
Years On Team 1
Grand Tour Apps 2
Wins 3
UCI Ranking 240

**LARS VAN DEN BERG**
Netherlands
07.07.98
Years Pro 1
Years On Team 1
Grand Tour Apps 1
Wins 0
UCI Ranking 723

TEAMS   MEN'S WORLDTOUR

# INEOS GRENADIERS

**2021 SEASON REVIEW**

Victories at the Tour de Romandie, Giro d'Italia, Dauphiné and Tour de Suisse hinted that the Ineos pre-Tadej Pogačar were back. But we all know the British squad are judged primarily on the Tour de France, given their proclivity for taking home the yellow jersey. Geraint Thomas succumbed to crashes and, while Richard Carapaz's third place was well earned, the gap between them and Pogačar will provide real cause for concern. Rumours swirl over Egan Bernal's happiness at the team as well as Dave Brailsford's continued presence, yet the evolution of Tom Pidcock and Ethan Hayter give hope for the future. In fact, the latter is the only rider to have taken a victory since June.

**TEAM INFORMATION**

| UCI CODE | **IGD** |
|---|---|
| UCI STATUS | **MEN'S WORLDTOUR** |
| COUNTRY | **UNITED KINGDOM** |
| FOUNDED | **2010** |

**TEAM NAME HISTORY**

| 2010-2013 | **SKY PROCYCLING** |
|---|---|
| 2014-2018 | **TEAM SKY** |
| 2019 | **TEAM INEOS** |
| 2020-2021 | **INEOS GRENADIERS** |

**TEAM MANAGER**

**DAVID BRAILSFORD**

**2021 NEW RIDERS**

**RICHIE PORTE, ADAM YATES, DANIEL FELIPE MARTÍNEZ, LAURENS DE PLUS, THOMAS PIDCOCK**

**2021 STAGIAIRES**

**LUKE PLAPP**

**EQUIPMENT**

BIKE   **PINARELLO**

**2021 VICTORIES**

| Etoile de Bessèges – stage 4 | 2.1 | F. Ganna |
|---|---|---|
| Etoile de Bessèges – stage 5 (ITT) | 2.1 | F. Ganna |
| Tour de la Provence – stage 3 | 2.Pro | I. Sosa |
| Tour de la Provence | 2.Pro | I. Sosa |
| UAE Tour – stage 2 (ITT) | 2.UWT | F. Ganna |
| Volta Ciclista a Catalunya – stage 2 (ITT) | 2.UWT | R. Dennis |
| Volta Ciclista a Catalunya – stage 3 | 2.UWT | A. Yates |
| Settimana Internazionale Coppi e Bartali – stage 3 | 2.1 | E. Hayter |
| Volta Ciclista a Catalunya | 2.UWT | A. Yates |
| Dwars door Vlaanderen | 1.UWT | D. van Baarle |
| De Brabntse Pijl | 1.Pro | T. Pidcock |
| Tour of the Alps – stage 1 | 2.Pro | G. Moscon |
| Tour of the Alps – stage 3 | 2.Pro | G. Moscon |
| Tour de Romandie – prologue | 2.UWT | R. Dennis |
| Tour de Romandie | 2.UWT | G. Thomas |
| Volta ao Algarve – stage 2 | 2.Pro | E. Hayter |
| Giro d'Italia – stage 1 (ITT) | 2.UWT | F. Ganna |
| Giro d'Italia – stage 9 | 2.UWT | E. Bernal |
| Vuelta a Andalucia – stage 2 | 2.Pro | E. Hayter |
| Vuelta a Andalucia – stage 5 | 2.Pro | E. Hayter |
| Giro d'Italia – stage 16 | 2.UWT | E. Bernal |
| Giro d'Italia – stage 21 | 2.UWT | F. Ganna |
| Giro d'Italia | 2.UWT | E. Bernal |
| Critérium du Dauphiné – stage 5 | 2.UWT | G. Thomas |
| Critérium du Dauphiné | 2.UWT | R. Porte |
| Tour de Suisse – stage 5 | 2.UWT | R. Carapaz |
| Tour de Suisse | 2.UWT | R. Carapaz |
| GP Città di Lugano | 1.1 | G. Moscon |
| Tour of Norway – stage 1 | 2.Pro | E. Hayter |
| Tour of Norway – stage 2 | 2.Pro | E. Hayter |
| Tour of Norway | 2.Pro | E. Hayter |
| Tour of Britain – stage 3 (TTT) | 2.Pro | TTT |
| Tour of Britain – stage 5 | 2.Pro | E. Hayter |
| National Championships Great Britain – ITT | NC | E. Hayter |
| National Championships Great Britain – RR | NC | B. Swift |

RIDER PROFILES

## EGAN BERNAL

Colombia
13.01.97
Years Pro 6
Years On Team 4
Grand Tour Apps 5
Wins 19
UCI Ranking 5

The Colombian looked reinvigorated at the beginning of the year, a surprise third in Strade Bianche, and at the Giro d'Italia he got back to his Grand Tour best, winning his first pink jersey with a little help from Dani Martínez. He couldn't follow it up at the Vuelta, finishing sixth and a fair way off the podium places, let alone the red jersey.

## RICHARD CARAPAZ

Ecuador
29.05.93
Years Pro 5
Years On Team 2
Grand Tour Apps 8
Wins 12
UCI Ranking 10

Victory at the Tour de Suisse led into a Tour de France where he ended up being the only option for Ineos, completing the Pogačar/Vingegaard trio in the final week to secure a podium finish. Gold in the Olympic Games followed, with a canny solo move towards the finish, but at the Vuelta he paid for his efforts and climbed off after two weeks.

### ANDREY AMADOR
Costa Rica
29.08.86
Years Pro 13
Years On Team 2
Grand Tour Apps 17
Wins 2
UCI Ranking 1932

### LEONARDO BASSO
Italy
25.12.93
Years Pro 4
Years On Team 4
Grand Tour Apps 0
Wins 0
UCI Ranking 2257

### JONATHAN CASTROVIEJO
Spain
27.04.87
Years Pro 12
Years On Team 4
Grand Tour Apps 14
Wins 10
UCI Ranking 811

### LAURENS DE PLUS
Belgium
04.09.95
Years Pro 6
Years On Team 1
Grand Tour Apps 4
Wins 1
UCI Ranking 955

### ROHAN DENNIS
Australia
28.05.90
Years Pro 9
Years On Team 2
Grand Tour Apps 10
Wins 30
UCI Ranking 132

### OWAIN DOULL
Great Britain
02.05.93
Years Pro 5
Years On Team 5
Grand Tour Apps 1
Wins 2
UCI Ranking 621

### EDDIE DUNBAR
Ireland
01.09.96
Years Pro 4
Years On Team 4
Grand Tour Apps 1
Wins 0
UCI Ranking 489

### FILIPPO GANNA
Italy
25.07.96
Years Pro 5
Years On Team 3
Grand Tour Apps 2
Wins 16
UCI Ranking 53

### TAO GEOGHEGAN HART
Great Britain
30.03.95
Years Pro 5
Years On Team 5
Grand Tour Apps 5
Wins 5
UCI Ranking 332

### MICHAŁ GOŁAŚ
Poland
29.04.84
Years Pro 15
Years On Team 6
Grand Tour Apps 9
Wins 2
UCI Ranking 608

### ETHAN HAYTER
Great Britain
18.09.98
Years Pro 2
Years On Team 2
Grand Tour Apps 0
Wins 10
UCI Ranking 28

### SEBASTIÁN HENAO
Colombia
05.08.93
Years Pro 8
Years On Team 8
Grand Tour Apps 6
Wins 0
UCI Ranking 767

### MICHAŁ KWIATKOWSKI
Poland
02.06.90
Years Pro 11
Years On Team 6
Grand Tour Apps 11
Wins 28
UCI Ranking 93

### DANIEL FELIPE MARTÍNEZ
Colombia
25.04.96
Years Pro 7
Years On Team 1
Grand Tour Apps 7
Wins 7
UCI Ranking 146

### GIANNI MOSCON
Italy
20.04.94
Years Pro 6
Years On Team 6
Grand Tour Apps 4
Wins 11
UCI Ranking 77

### JHONATAN NARVÁEZ
Ecuador
04.03.97
Years Pro 4
Years On Team 3
Grand Tour Apps 2
Wins 4
UCI Ranking 666

### THOMAS PIDCOCK
Great Britain
30.07.99
Years Pro 1
Years On Team 1
Grand Tour Apps 0
Wins 1
UCI Ranking 33

### RICHIE PORTE
Australia
30.01.85
Years Pro 12
Years On Team 1
Grand Tour Apps 16
Wins 33
UCI Ranking 29

### SALVATORE PUCCIO
Italy
31.08.89
Years Pro 10
Years On Team 10
Grand Tour Apps 15
Wins 0
UCI Ranking —

### BRANDON RIVERA
Colombia
21.03.96
Years Pro 2
Years On Team 2
Grand Tour Apps 1
Wins 1
UCI Ranking 2664

### CARLOS RODRIGUEZ
Spain
02.02.01
Years Pro 2
Years On Team 2
Grand Tour Apps 0
Wins 0
UCI Ranking 155

### LUKE ROWE
Great Britain
10.03.90
Years Pro 10
Years On Team 10
Grand Tour Apps 9
Wins 2
UCI Ranking 1711

### PAVEL SIVAKOV
Russia
11.07.97
Years Pro 4
Years On Team 4
Grand Tour Apps 5
Wins 3
UCI Ranking 162

### IVÁN RAMIRO SOSA
Colombia
31.10.97
Years Pro 5
Years On Team 3
Grand Tour Apps 2
Wins 13
UCI Ranking 284

### BEN SWIFT
Great Britain
05.11.87
Years Pro 13
Years On Team 3
Grand Tour Apps 7
Wins 15
UCI Ranking 245

### GERAINT THOMAS
Great Britain
25.05.86
Years Pro 15
Years On Team 12
Grand Tour Apps 16
Wins 24
UCI Ranking 34

### DYLAN VAN BAARLE
Netherlands
21.05.92
Years Pro 8
Years On Team 4
Grand Tour Apps 10
Wins 5
UCI Ranking 38

### CAMERON WURF
Australia
03.08.83
Years Pro 9
Years On Team 2
Grand Tour Apps 4
Wins 0
UCI Ranking —

### ADAM YATES
Great Britain
07.08.92
Years Pro 8
Years On Team 1
Grand Tour Apps 10
Wins 16
UCI Ranking 8

TEAMS    MEN'S WORLDTOUR

# INTERMARCHÉ–WANTY–GOBERT MATÉRIAUX

**2021 SEASON REVIEW**

A first year at WorldTour level is always a tricky one, and often the Belgian squad were dismissed as just being there to make up the numbers. But Intermarché often had other plans and, with breakaway stage victories in the Giro d'Italia and Vuelta a España, claimed a greater haul than a lot of the more established top-tier outfits have to look back on at the end of this season. ®

**2021 VICTORIES**

| Race | Cat | Rider |
|---|---|---|
| Giro d'Italia – stage 3 | 2.UWT | T. van der Hoorn |
| National Championships Estonia – ITT | NC | R. Taaramäe |
| Tour de l'Ain – stage 2 | 2.1 | G. Zimmerman |
| Vuelta a España – stage 3 | 2.UWT | R. Taaramäe |
| Egmont Cycling Race | 1.1 | D. Van Poppel |
| Benelux Tour – stage 3 | 2.UWT | T. van der Hoorn |
| Classic Grand Besançon Doubs | 1.1 | B. Ghirmay |
| Omloop van het Houtland Middelkerke -Lichtervelde | 1.1 | T. van der Hoorn |
| Binche–Chimay–Binche | 1.1 | D. Van Poppel |
| Paris–Mantes | 1.2 | M. Jarnet |

**TEAM INFORMATION**

| | |
|---|---|
| UCI CODE | IWG |
| UCI STATUS | MEN'S WORLDTOUR |
| COUNTRY | BELGIUM |
| FOUNDED | 2009 |

**TEAM NAME HISTORY**

| | |
|---|---|
| 2009 | WILLEMS VERANDAS |
| 2010 | VERANDAS WILLEMS |
| 2011 | VERANDA'S WILLEMS-ACCENT |
| 2012 | ACCENT.JOBS-WILLEMS VERANDA'S |
| 2013 | ACCENT.JOBS-WANTY |
| 2014–2018 | WANTY-GROUPE GOBERT |
| 2019 | WANTY-GOBERT CYCLING TEAM |
| 2020 | CIRCUS-WANTY GOBERT |
| 2021 | INTERMARCHÉ-WANTY-GOBERT MATÉRIAUX |

**TEAM MANAGER**

JEAN FRANCOIS BOURLART

**2021 NEW RIDERS**

REIN TAARAMÄE, BAPTISTE PLANCKAERT, LOUIS MEINTJES, JAN HIRT, TACO VAN DER HOORN, LORENZO ROTA, JONAS KOCH, RICCARDO MINALI, BINIAM GHIRMAY HAILU, GEORG ZIMMERMAN

**2021 STAGIAIRES**

STIJN DAEMEN, DRIES DE POOTER, MAXIME JARNET

**EQUIPMENT**

| | |
|---|---|
| BIKE | CUBE |

## RIDER PROFILES

### TACO VAN DER HOORN
Netherlands
04.12.93
Years Pro 5
Years On Team 1
Grand Tour Apps 1
Wins 6
UCI Ranking 151

Some would say Taco van der Hoorn is already a winner by virtue of his fantastic name, but the way in which he stole a march from an unsuspecting peloton on stage 3 of the Giro d'Italia made his breakaway effort one of the rides of the year. He would follow it up with another stage 3 win, this time at the Benelux Tour.

### REIN TAARAMÄE
Estonia
24.04.87
Years Pro 14
Years On Team 1
Grand Tour Apps 15
Wins 19
UCI Ranking 187

Ten years after his first Vuelta stage win, the 34-year-old Estonian outlasted his breakaway companions to take the honours on the third day, wearing the *maillot jaune* only for two days in the end, but it was a career-defining moment nonetheless for a member of the peloton in the twilight of his riding days.

---

**JAN BAKELANTS**
Belgium
14.02.86
Years Pro 12
Years On Team 2
Grand Tour Apps 14
Wins 6
UCI Ranking 726

**JEREMY BELLICAUD**
France
08.06.98
Years Pro 2
Years On Team 2
Grand Tour Apps 0
Wins 0
UCI Ranking 1088

**AIMÉ DE GENDT**
Belgium
17.06.94
Years Pro 6
Years On Team 3
Grand Tour Apps 1
Wins 1
UCI Ranking 194

**JASPER DE PLUS**
Belgium
11.06.97
Years Pro 2
Years On Team 2
Grand Tour Apps 0
Wins 0
UCI Ranking 2296

**LUDWIG DE WINTER**
Belgium
31.12.92
Years Pro 5
Years On Team 3
Grand Tour Apps 0
Wins 0
UCI Ranking –

**THEO DELACROIX**
France
21.02.99
Years Pro 2
Years On Team 2
Grand Tour Apps 0
Wins 0
UCI Ranking –

**TOM DEVRIENDT**
Belgium
29.10.91
Years Pro 7
Years On Team 7
Grand Tour Apps 0
Wins 2
UCI Ranking 576

**ODD CHRISTIAN EIKING**
Norway
28.12.94
Years Pro 7
Years On Team 4
Grand Tour Apps 4
Wins 3
UCI Ranking 100

**ALEXANDER EVANS**
Australia
28.01.97
Years Pro 2
Years On Team 2
Grand Tour Apps 0
Wins 0
UCI Ranking –

**BINIAM GHIRMAY**
Eritrea
02.04.00
Years Pro 2
Years On Team 1
Grand Tour Apps 0
Wins 5
UCI Ranking 75

**QUINTEN HERMANS**
Belgium
29.07.95
Years Pro 2
Years On Team 2
Grand Tour Apps 1
Wins 1
UCI Ranking 318

**JAN HIRT**
Czech Republic
21.01.91
Years Pro 7
Years On Team 1
Grand Tour Apps 8
Wins 2
UCI Ranking 596

**JONAS KOCH**
Germany
25.06.93
Years Pro 6
Years On Team 1
Grand Tour Apps 2
Wins 0
UCI Ranking 418

**WESLEY KREDER**
Netherlands
04.11.90
Years Pro 10
Years On Team 5
Grand Tour Apps 2
Wins 2
UCI Ranking 1711

**MAURITS LAMMERTINK**
Netherlands
31.08.90
Years Pro 9
Years On Team 2
Grand Tour Apps 4
Wins 3
UCI Ranking 796

**LOUIS MEINTJES**
South Africa
21.02.92
Years Pro 9
Years On Team 1
Grand Tour Apps 13
Wins 4
UCI Ranking 341

**RICCARDO MINALI**
Italy
19.04.95
Years Pro 5
Years On Team 1
Grand Tour Apps 1
Wins 2
UCI Ranking 429

**ANDREA PASQUALON**
Italy
02.01.88
Years Pro 11
Years On Team 5
Grand Tour Apps 4
Wins 8
UCI Ranking 105

**SIMONE PETILLI**
Italy
04.05.93
Years Pro 6
Years On Team 2
Grand Tour Apps 5
Wins 0
UCI Ranking 455

**BAPTISTE PLANCKAERT**
Belgium
28.09.88
Years Pro 12
Years On Team 1
Grand Tour Apps 1
Wins 4
UCI Ranking 167

**LORENZO ROTA**
Italy
23.05.95
Years Pro 6
Years On Team 1
Grand Tour Apps 4
Wins 0
UCI Ranking 89

**CORNÉ VAN KESSEL**
Netherlands
07.08.91
Years Pro 2
Years On Team 2
Grand Tour Apps 0
Wins 0
UCI Ranking 1787

**KÉVIN VAN MELSEN**
Belgium
01.04.87
Years Pro 11
Years On Team 12
Grand Tour Apps 2
Wins 0
UCI Ranking 2082

**BOY VAN POPPEL**
Netherlands
18.01.88
Years Pro 11
Years On Team 5
Grand Tour Apps 7
Wins 1
UCI Ranking 341

**DANNY VAN POPPEL**
Netherlands
36.07.93
Years Pro 9
Years On Team 2
Grand Tour Apps 6
Wins 18
UCI Ranking 30

**PIETER VANSPEYBROUCK**
Belgium
10.02.87
Years Pro 14
Years On Team 5
Grand Tour Apps 1
Wins 1
UCI Ranking 2296

**LOÏC VLIEGEN**
Belgium
20.12.93
Years Pro 7
Years On Team 3
Grand Tour Apps 3
Wins 3
UCI Ranking 1067

**GEORG ZIMMERMAN**
Germany
11.10.97
Years Pro 2
Years On Team 1
Grand Tour Apps 2
Wins 1
UCI Ranking 206

TEAMS   MEN'S WORLDTOUR

# ISRAEL START-UP NATION

**2021 SEASON REVIEW**

A year marked by heavyweight new arrivals Chris Froome, Michael Woods, Sep Vanmarcke and Daryl Impey. Martin secured a Grand Tour stage win at the Giro but couldn't follow it up at the Tour, while Michael Woods and Mads Würtz Schmidt took WorldTour wins at the Tour de Romandie and Tirreno–Adriatico. André Greipel also returned to winning ways in what would be his final season of a magnificent career. ⓘ

**TEAM INFORMATION**

| | |
|---|---|
| UCI CODE | **ISN** |
| UCI STATUS | **MEN'S WORLDTOUR** |
| COUNTRY | **ISRAEL** |
| FOUNDED | **2015** |

**TEAM NAME HISTORY**

| | |
|---|---|
| 2015-2016 | **CYCLING ACADEMY TEAM** |
| 2017-2019 | **ISRAEL CYCLING ACADEMY** |
| 2020-2021 | **ISRAEL START-UP NATION** |

**TEAM MANAGER**

**KJELL CARLSTRÖM**

**2021 VICTORIES**

| | | |
|---|---|---|
| Tour des Alpes Maritimes et du Var – stage 2 | 2.1 | M. Woods |
| Tirreno–Adriatico – stage 6 | 2.UWT | M. Würtz Schmidt |
| Settimana Internazionale Coppi e Bartali – stage 1b (TTT) | 2.1 | TTT |
| Tour de Romandie – stage 4 | 2.UWT | M. Woods |
| Trofeo Alcudia | 1.1 | A. Greipel |
| Vuelta a Andalucia – stage 4 | 2.Pro | A. Greipel |
| Giro d'Italia – stage 17 | 2.UWT | D. Martin |
| National Championships Israel – ITT | NC | O. Goldstein |
| National Championships Austria – ITT | NC | M. Brändle |
| National Championships Denmark – RR | NC | M. Würtz Schmidt |
| Giro dell'Appennino | 1.1 | B. Hermans |
| Arctic Race of Norway – stage 3 | 2.Pro | B. Hermans |
| Arctic Race of Norway | 2.Pro | B. Hermans |
| Tour Poitou–Charentes en Nouvelle Aquitaine – stage 4 (ITT) | 2.1 | B. Hermans |
| National Championships Canada – RR | NC | G. Boivin |
| Tour of Slovakia – stage 4 | 2.1 | I. Einhorn |
| Tre Valli Varesine | 1.Pro | A. De Marchi |

**2021 NEW RIDERS**

**CHRIS FROOME, SEP VANMARCKE, DARYL IMPEY, MICHAEL WOODS, ALESSANDRO DE MARCHI, PATRICK BEVIN, CARL FREDERIK HAGEN, SEBASTIAN BERWICK, TAJ JONES**

**EQUIPMENT**

| | |
|---|---|
| BIKE | **FACTOR** |

## RIDER PROFILES

### DAN MARTIN
Ireland
20.08.86
Years Pro 14
Years On Team 2
Grand Tour Apps 19
Wins 22
UCI Ranking 123

Along with Greipel, this would be Martin's final season as a professional cyclist. He finished it on a high, and on his own terms after the Covid-blighted 2020, winning a Giro stage and being competitive at the business end of things in the hunt for stages at the Tour de France and among the overall contenders at the Tour of Britain.

### CHRIS FROOME
Great Britain
20.05.85
Years Pro 14
Years On Team 1
Grand Tour Apps 19
Wins 46
UCI Ranking 2296

Another difficult season for Froome, who hoped to race himself into form in time for his Tour de France return but rarely broke the top 100 on the stage over the three weeks. He persisted, however, no matter the amount of criticism or the number of times the TV cameras followed him dropping off the back of the bunch.

---

### RUDY BARBIER
France
18.12.92
Years Pro 5
Years On Team 3
Grand Tour Apps 1
Wins 6
UCI Ranking 615

### SEBASTIAN BERWICK
Australia
15.12.99
Years Pro 1
Years On Team 1
Grand Tour Apps 1
Wins 0
UCI Ranking 2082

### PATRICK BEVIN
New Zealand
15.02.91
Years Pro 6
Years On Team 1
Grand Tour Apps 6
Wins 6
UCI Ranking 463

### JENTHE BIERMANS
Belgium
30.10.95
Years Pro 5
Years On Team 2
Grand Tour Apps 1
Wins 0
UCI Ranking 380

### GUILLAUME BOIVIN
Canada
25.05.89
Years Pro 11
Years On Team 6
Grand Tour Apps 5
Wins 5
UCI Ranking 268

### MATTHIAS BRÄNDLE
Austria
07.12.89
Years Pro 13
Years On Team 3
Grand Tour Apps 8
Wins 18
UCI Ranking 887

### ALEXANDER CATAFORD
Canada
01.09.93
Years Pro 5
Years On Team 3
Grand Tour Apps 2
Wins 0
UCI Ranking —

### DAVIDE CIMOLAI
Italy
13.08.89
Years Pro 12
Years On Team 3
Grand Tour Apps 10
Wins 9
UCI Ranking 386

### ALESSANDRO DE MARCHI
Italy
19.05.86
Years Pro 11
Years On Team 1
Grand Tour Apps 14
Wins 6
UCI Ranking 106

### ALEX DOWSETT
Great Britain
03.10.88
Years Pro 11
Years On Team 2
Grand Tour Apps 6
Wins 15
UCI Ranking 954

### ITAMAR EINHORN
Israel
20.09.97
Years Pro 3
Years On Team 3
Grand Tour Apps 1
Wins 1
UCI Ranking 615

### OMER GOLDSTEIN
Israel
13.08.96
Years Pro 4
Years On Team 4
Grand Tour Apps 2
Wins 3
UCI Ranking 726

### ANDRÉ GREIPEL
Germany
16.07.82
Years Pro 16
Years On Team 2
Grand Tour Apps 19
Wins 158
UCI Ranking 285

### CARL FREDRIK HAGEN
Norway
26.09.91
Years Pro 3
Years On Team 1
Grand Tour Apps 2
Wins 0
UCI Ranking 1584

### BEN HERMANS
Belgium
08.06.86
Years Pro 13
Years On Team 4
Grand Tour Apps 7
Wins 19
UCI Ranking 56

### HUGO HOFSTETTER
France
13.02.94
Years Pro 6
Years On Team 1
Grand Tour Apps 1
Wins 2
UCI Ranking 83

### RETO HOLLENSTEIN
Switzerland
22.08.85
Years Pro 10
Years On Team 2
Grand Tour Apps 9
Wins 0
UCI Ranking 1711

### DARYL IMPEY
South Africa
06.12.84
Years Pro 14
Years On Team 1
Grand Tour Apps 10
Wins 29
UCI Ranking 310

### TAJ JONES
Australia
26.07.00
Years Pro 1
Years On Team 1
Grand Tour Apps 0
Wins 1
UCI Ranking 2652

### KRISTS NEILANDS
Latvia
18.08.94
Years Pro 5
Years On Team 5
Grand Tour Apps 4
Wins 9
UCI Ranking 355

### GUY NIV
Israel
08.03.94
Years Pro 4
Years On Team 4
Grand Tour Apps 5
Wins 1
UCI Ranking 1951

### JAMES PICCOLI
Canada
05.09.91
Years Pro 2
Years On Team 2
Grand Tour Apps 2
Wins 2
UCI Ranking 376

### ALEXIS RENARD
France
01.06.99
Years Pro 2
Years On Team 2
Grand Tour Apps 1
Wins 0
UCI Ranking 195

### GUY SAGIV
Israel
05.12.94
Years Pro 5
Years On Team 6
Grand Tour Apps 2
Wins 5
UCI Ranking 1762

### NORMAN VAHTRA
Estonia
23.11.96
Years Pro 2
Years On Team 2
Grand Tour Apps 0
Wins 1
UCI Ranking 717

### TOM VAN ASBROECK
Belgium
19.04.90
Years Pro 10
Years On Team 3
Grand Tour Apps 5
Wins 4
UCI Ranking 114

### SEP VANMARCKE
Belgium
28.07.88
Years Pro 13
Years On Team 1
Grand Tour Apps 7
Wins 8
UCI Ranking 99

### MICHAEL WOODS
Canada
12.10.86
Years Pro 6
Years On Team 1
Grand Tour Apps 7
Wins 8
UCI Ranking 13

### MADS WÜRTZ SCHMIDT
Denmark
31.03.94
Years Pro 5
Years On Team 2
Grand Tour Apps 3
Wins 4
UCI Ranking 215

### RICK ZABEL
Germany
07.12.93
Years Pro 8
Years On Team 2
Grand Tour Apps 7
Wins 2
UCI Ranking 1369

# LOTTO SOUDAL

### 2021 SEASON REVIEW

Only a dozen wins for the Belgian team as Philippe Gilbert, John Degenkolb and Tim Wellens struggled to make a dent, while Caleb Ewan provided most of the victories. There will be changes next year as long-time team managers Marc Sergeant and Herman Frison depart the squad and in comes Cherie Pridham, personally selected by the team's riders. Ⓡ

### 2021 VICTORIES

| | | |
|---|---|---|
| Etoile de Bessèges – stage 3 | 2.1 | T. Wellens |
| Etoile de Bessèges | 2.1 | T. Wellens |
| UAE Tour – stage 7 | 2.UWT | C. Ewan |
| Volta Ciclista a Catalunya – stage 1 | 2.UWT | A. Kron |
| Volta Ciclista a Catalunya – stage 7 | 2.UWT | T. De Gendt |
| Giro d'Italia – stage 5 | 2.UWT | C. Ewan |
| Giro d'Italia – stage 7 | 2.UWT | C. Ewan |
| Critérium du Dauphiné – stage 1 | 2.UWT | B. Van Moer |
| Baloise Belgium Tour – stage 3 | 2.Pro | C. Ewan |
| Tour de Suisse – stage 6 | 2.UWT | A. Kron |
| Baloise Belgium Tour – stage 4 | 2.Pro | C. Ewan |
| Benelux Tour – stage 5 | 2.UWT | C. Ewan |

## TEAM INFORMATION

| | |
|---|---|
| UCI CODE | LTS |
| UCI STATUS | MEN'S WORLDTOUR |
| COUNTRY | BELGIUM |
| FOUNDED | 1985 |

### TEAM NAME HISTORY

| | |
|---|---|
| 1985 | LOTTO |
| 1986 | LOTTO-EMERXIL-MERCKX |
| 1987 | LOTTO-MERCKX |
| 1988 | LOTTO-EDDY MERCKX |
| 1989 | LOTTO |
| 1990–1991 | LOTTO-SUPER CLUB |
| 1992 | LOTTO-MAVIC |
| 1993 | LOTTO-CALOI |
| 1994 | LOTTO-VETTA-CALOI |
| 1995–1996 | LOTTO-ISOGLASS |
| 1997–1999 | LOTTO-MOBISTAR |
| 2000–2002 | LOTTO-ADECCO |
| 2003–2004 | LOTTO-DOMO |
| 2005–2006 | DAVITAMON-LOTTO |
| 2007 | PREDICTOR-LOTTO |
| 2008–2009 | SILENCE-LOTTO |
| 2010–2011 | OMEGA PHARMA-LOTTO |
| 2012–2014 | LOTTO BELISOL TEAM |
| 2015–2021 | LOTTO SOUDAL |

### TEAM MANAGER

**JOHN LELANGUE**

### 2021 NEW RIDERS

**ANDREAS KRON, KAMIL MAŁECKI, HARRY SWEENY, MAXIM VAN GILS, SYLVAIN MONIQUET, FILIPPO CONCA, XANDRES VERVLOESEM, VIKTOR VERSCHAEVE, SÉBASTIEN GRIGNARD**

### EQUIPMENT

| | |
|---|---|
| BIKE | RIDLEY |

RIDER PROFILES

### CALEB EWAN
Australia
11.07.94
Years Pro 8
Years On Team 3
Grand Tour Apps 8
Wins 52
UCI Ranking 72

The Australian sprinter's stated goal for the year was to win stages at all three Grand Tours and, after a spritely start at the UAE Tour, he hit the ground running at the Giro, winning two stages in the opening week. But a race-ending crash in the finale of stage 3 of the Tour put paid to the dream for this year at least.

### THOMAS DE GENDT
Belgium
06.11.86
Years Pro 13
Years On Team 7
Grand Tour Apps 21
Wins 16
UCI Ranking 905

A beautiful outfoxing of Matej Mohorič on the run-in to Barcelona opened De Gendt's account in Catalunya, yet the Belgian seemed mystified at the Tour de France, where the elevated form of his rivals left him despondent and he didn't make his usual cameos in breakaways.

### FILIPPO CONCA
Italy
22.09.98
Years Pro 1
Years On Team 1
Grand Tour Apps 0
Wins 0
UCI Ranking 1359

### STEFF CRAS
Belgium
13.02.96
Years Pro 4
Years On Team 2
Grand Tour Apps 3
Wins 0
UCI Ranking 800

### JASPER DE BUYST
Belgium
24.11.93
Years Pro 9
Years On Team 7
Grand Tour Apps 8
Wins 5
UCI Ranking 536

### JOHN DEGENKOLB
Germany
07.01.89
Years Pro 11
Years On Team 2
Grand Tour Apps 14
Wins 48
UCI Ranking 104

### FREDERIK FRISON
Belgium
28.07.92
Years Pro 6
Years On Team 6
Grand Tour Apps 3
Wins 0
UCI Ranking 1400

### PHILIPPE GILBERT
Belgium
05.07.82
Years Pro 19
Years On Team 3
Grand Tour Apps 24
Wins 78
UCI Ranking 165

### KOBE GOOSSENS
Belgium
29.04.96
Years Pro 2
Years On Team 2
Grand Tour Apps 2
Wins 0
UCI Ranking 805

### SÉBASTIEN GRIGNARD
Belgium
29.04.99
Years Pro 1
Years On Team 1
Grand Tour Apps 0
Wins 0
UCI Ranking 2296

### MATTHEW HOLMES
Great Britain
08.12.93
Years Pro 2
Years On Team 2
Grand Tour Apps 2
Wins 1
UCI Ranking —

### ROGER KLUGE
Germany
05.02.86
Years Pro 12
Years On Team 3
Grand Tour Apps 9
Wins 5
UCI Ranking —

### ANDREAS KRON
Denmark
01.06.98
Years Pro 3
Years On Team 1
Grand Tour Apps 1
Wins 3
UCI Ranking 244

### TOMASZ MARCZYŃSKI
Poland
06.03.84
Years Pro 15
Years On Team 5
Grand Tour Apps 8
Wins 8
UCI Ranking —

### KAMIL MALECKI
Poland
02.01.96
Years Pro 7
Years On Team 1
Grand Tour Apps 1
Wins 0
UCI Ranking 2296

### SYLVAIN MONIQUET
Belgium
14.01.98
Years Pro 1
Years On Team 1
Grand Tour Apps 1
Wins 0
UCI Ranking —

### STEFANO OLDANI
Italy
10.01.98
Years Pro 2
Years On Team 2
Grand Tour Apps 2
Wins 0
UCI Ranking 371

### HARRY SWEENY
Australia
09.07.98
Years Pro 1
Years On Team 1
Grand Tour Apps 1
Wins 0
UCI Ranking 880

### GERBEN THIJSSEN
Belgium
21.06.98
Years Pro 3
Years On Team 3
Grand Tour Apps 1
Wins 0
UCI Ranking 378

### TOSH VAN DER SANDE
Belgium
28.11.90
Years Pro 10
Years On Team 10
Grand Tour Apps 10
Wins 2
UCI Ranking 73

### MAXIM VAN GILS
Belgium
25.11.99
Years Pro 1
Years On Team 1
Grand Tour Apps 1
Wins 0
UCI Ranking 446

### BRENT VAN MOER
Belgium
12.01.98
Years Pro 3
Years On Team 3
Grand Tour Apps 2
Wins 0
UCI Ranking 587

### HARM VANHOUCKE
Belgium
17.06.97
Years Pro 4
Years On Team 4
Grand Tour Apps 4
Wins 0
UCI Ranking 278

### FLORIAN VERMEERSCH
Belgium
12.03.99
Years Pro 2
Years On Team 2
Grand Tour Apps 1
Wins 0
UCI Ranking 110

### VIKTOR VERSCHAEVE
Belgium
03.08.98
Years Pro 1
Years On Team 1
Grand Tour Apps 0
Wins 0
UCI Ranking —

### XANDRES VERVLOESEM
Belgium
13.05.00
Years Pro 1
Years On Team 1
Grand Tour Apps 0
Wins 0
UCI Ranking 2652

### TIM WELLENS
Belgium
10.05.91
Years Pro 10
Years On Team 10
Grand Tour Apps 7
Wins 32
UCI Ranking 65

TEAMS  MEN'S WORLDTOUR

# MOVISTAR TEAM

**2021 SEASON REVIEW**

Yet another bizarre year for the Spanish team. Alejandro Valverde continued to chip in with victories alongside the recently arrived Miguel Ángel López. Enric Mas managed sixth overall at the Tour de France ahead of the team's home Grand Tour, their most important race. Mas rode consistently to cement second place on GC but the headlines were stolen by now former teammate Miguel Ángel López: the Colombian won the mountainous stage 18 as the Movistar duo locked in the two podium spots behind Roglič, before abandoning in frustration on stage 20 after he missed a split in the GC group, sacrificing his third place overall. Less than a month later Movistar had terminated his contract. Fans can only hope a third instalment of the team's Netflix documentary series is on its way.

**2021 VICTORIES**

| Race | Cat. | Rider |
|---|---|---|
| GP Miguel Indurian | 1.Pro | A. Valverde |
| Volta a la Comunitat Valenciana – stage 3 | 2.Pro | E. Mas |
| Tour de Romandie – stage 3 | 2.UWT | M. Soler |
| Vuelta Asturias – stage 2 | 2.1 | H. Carretero |
| Vuelta a Andalucia – stage 1 | 2.Pro | G. Serrano |
| Vuelta a Andalucia – stage 3 | 2.Pro | M. Á. López |
| Vuelta a Andalucia | 2.Pro | M. Á. López |
| Critérium du Dauphiné – stage 6 | 2.UWT | A. Valverde |
| Mont Ventoux Dénivelé Challenge | 1.1 | M. Á. López |
| La Route d'Occitanie – stage 3 | 2.1 | A. Pedrero |
| La Route d'Occitanie | 2.1 | A. Pedrero |
| National Championships Puerto Rico – ITT | NC | A. González |
| National Championships Puerto Rico – RR | NC | A. González |
| Vuelta a España – stage 18 | 2.UWT | M. Á. López |
| Giro di Sicilia – stage 3 | 2.1 | A. Valverde |

**TEAM INFORMATION**

| | |
|---|---|
| UCI CODE | MOV |
| UCI STATUS | MEN'S WORLDTOUR |
| COUNTRY | SPAIN |
| FOUNDED | 1980 |

**TEAM NAME HISTORY**

| | |
|---|---|
| 1980 | REYNOLDS-BENOTTO |
| 1981–1982 | REYNOLDS-GALLI |
| 1983–1986 | REYNOLDS |
| 1987 | REYNOLDS-SEUR |
| 1988 | REYNOLDS |
| 1989 | REYNOLDS-BANESTO |
| 1990–2000 | BANESTO |
| 2001–2003 | IBANESTO.COM |
| 2004 | ILLES BALEARS-BANESTO |
| 2005 | ILLES BALEARS-CAISSE D'EPARGNE |
| 2006 | CAISSE D'EPARGNE-ILLES BALEARS |
| 2007–2010 | CAISSE D'EPARGNE |
| 2011–2021 | MOVISTAR TEAM |

**TEAM MANAGER**

EUSEBIO UNZUÉ

**2021 NEW RIDERS**

MIGUEL ÁNGEL LÓPEZ, GREGOR MÜHLBERGER, IVÁN GARCÍA CORTINA, GONZALO SERRANO, ABNER GONZÁLEZ

**EQUIPMENT**

| | |
|---|---|
| BIKE | CANYON |

**RIDER PROFILES**

## MIGUEL ÁNGEL LÓPEZ

Colombia
04.02.94
Years Pro 7
Years On Team 1
Grand Tour Apps 10
Wins 21
UCI Ranking 91

Before the Vuelta a España episode, López was one of the few shining lights at Movistar, with victory at the Vuelta a Andalucia and the Mont Ventoux Challenge. He then rode the Tour de France, abandoning before stage 19, but his brief stay at Movistar will always be remembered for stage 20 of the Spanish Grand Tour.

## ENRIC MAS

Spain
07.01.95
Years Pro 5
Years On Team 2
Grand Tour Apps 7
Wins 5
UCI Ranking 25

Sixth at the Tour de France and second at the Vuelta are a good return for the 26-year-old, the only problem being he never looked liked winning either Grand Tour. Unassuming yet clearly with the legs to hang with the best, Mas will still need to find another level if he's to live up to the Movistar leaders that have come before him.

### JUAN DIEGO ALBA
Colombia
11.09.97
Years Pro 2
Years On Team 2
Grand Tour Apps 0
Wins 0
UCI Ranking 2082

### JORGE ARCAS
Spain
08.07.92
Years Pro 6
Years On Team 6
Grand Tour Apps 4
Wins 0
UCI Ranking 1787

### HÉCTOR CARRETERO
Spain
28.05.95
Years Pro 5
Years On Team 5
Grand Tour Apps 2
Wins 1
UCI Ranking 424

### DARIO CATALDO
Italy
17.03.85
Years Pro 15
Years On Team 2
Grand Tour Apps 23
Wins 5
UCI Ranking 980

### GABRIEL CULLAIGH
Great Britain
08.04.96
Years Pro 2
Years On Team 2
Grand Tour Apps 0
Wins 0
UCI Ranking 504

### IÑIGO ELOSEGUI
Spain
06.03.98
Years Pro 2
Years On Team 2
Grand Tour Apps 0
Wins 0
UCI Ranking –

### IMANOL ERVITI
Spain
15.11.83
Years Pro 17
Years On Team 17
Grand Tour Apps 27
Wins 3
UCI Ranking 651

### IVÁN GARCÍA CORTINA
Spain
20.11.95
Years Pro 5
Years On Team 1
Grand Tour Apps 4
Wins 2
UCI Ranking 190

### ABNER GONZÁLEZ
Puerto Rico
09.10.00
Years Pro 1
Years On Team 1
Grand Tour Apps 0
Wins 3
UCI Ranking 242

### JURI HOLLMANN
Germany
30.08.99
Years Pro 2
Years On Team 2
Grand Tour Apps 0
Wins 0
UCI Ranking 1251

### JOHAN JACOBS
Switzerland
01.03.97
Years Pro 2
Years On Team 2
Grand Tour Apps 1
Wins 0
UCI Ranking 668

### MATTEO JORGENSEN
United States
01.07.99
Years Pro 2
Years On Team 2
Grand Tour Apps 1
Wins 0
UCI Ranking 418

### LLUÍS MAS
Spain
15.10.89
Years Pro 8
Years On Team 3
Grand Tour Apps 6
Wins 1
UCI Ranking 707

### SEBASTIÁN MORA
Spain
19.02.88
Years Pro 3
Years On Team 2
Grand Tour Apps 0
Wins 0
UCI Ranking 2296

### GREGOR MÜHLBERGER
Austria
04.04.94
Years Pro 6
Years On Team 1
Grand Tour Apps 6
Wins 6
UCI Ranking 1139

### MATHIAS NORSGAARD
Denmark
05.05.97
Years Pro 3
Years On Team 2
Grand Tour Apps 0
Wins 0
UCI Ranking –

### NELSON OLIVEIRA
Portugal
06.03.89
Years Pro 12
Years On Team 6
Grand Tour Apps 15
Wins 6
UCI Ranking 176

### ANTONIO PEDRERO
Spain
23.10.91
Years Pro 6
Years On Team 6
Grand Tour Apps 6
Wins 0
UCI Ranking 203

### JOSÉ JOAQUÍN ROJAS
Spain
08.06.85
Years Pro 16
Years On Team 15
Grand Tour Apps 19
Wins 10
UCI Ranking 525

### EINER RUBIO
Colombia
22.0.2.98
Years Pro 2
Years On Team 2
Grand Tour Apps 2
Wins 0
UCI Ranking 367

### SERGIO SAMITIER
Spain
31.08.95
Years Pro 4
Years On Team 2
Grand Tour Apps 2
Wins 0
UCI Ranking 1009

### GONZALO SERRANO
Spain
17.08.94
Years Pro 4
Years On Team 1
Grand Tour Apps 2
Wins 2
UCI Ranking 131

### MARC SOLER
Spain
22.11.93
Years Pro 7
Years On Team 7
Grand Tour Apps 8
Wins 5
UCI Ranking 147

### ALBERT TORRES
Spain
26.04.90
Years Pro 2
Years On Team 2
Grand Tour Apps 2
Wins 0
UCI Ranking –

### ALEJANDRO VALVERDE
Spain
25.04.80
Years Pro 20
Years On Team 17
Grand Tour Apps 30
Wins 130
UCI Ranking 11

### CARLOS VERONA
Spain
04.11.92
Years Pro 9
Years On Team 3
Grand Tour Apps 10
Wins 0
UCI Ranking 596

### DAVIDE VILLELLA
Italy
27.06.91
Years Pro 8
Years On Team 2
Grand Tour Apps 11
Wins 3
UCI Ranking 222

TEAMS    MEN'S WORLDTOUR

# TEAM BIKEEXCHANGE

## 2021 SEASON REVIEW

With the twins split up – Adam having left for Ineos – Simon Yates would mostly carry the team. A Giro stage and podium finish were the highlights of an otherwise uninspiring season of performances at Grand Tours. Esteban Chaves looked resurgent at times, taking the squad's only other WorldTour victory, at the Volta Ciclista a Catalunya, yet he's off to EF for next year. The return of Michael Matthews was much celebrated but yielded few results, try as they might to deliver their rider a victory.

## 2021 VICTORIES

| | | |
|---|---|---|
| National Championships Australia – RR | NC | C. Meyer |
| Volta Ciclista a Catalunya – stage 4 | 2.UWT | E. Chaves |
| Tour of the Alps – stage 2 | 2.Pro | S. Yates |
| Tour of the Alps | 2.Pro | S. Yates |
| Tour de Hongrie – stage 4 | 2.1 | D. Howson |
| Tour de Hongrie | 2.1 | D. Howson |
| Giro d'Italia – stage 19 | 2.UWT | S. Yates |
| Sazka Tour – stage 2 | 2.1 | N. Schultz |
| Tour of Slovakia – prologue | 2.1 | K. Groves |

## TEAM INFORMATION

| | |
|---|---|
| UCI CODE | **BEX** |
| UCI STATUS | **MEN'S WORLDTOUR** |
| COUNTRY | **AUSTRALIA** |
| FOUNDED | **2012** |

## TEAM NAME HISTORY

| | |
|---|---|
| 2012-2015 | **ORICA GREENEDGE** |
| 2016 | **ORICA-BIKEEXCHANGE** |
| 2017 | **ORICA-SCOTT** |
| 2018-2020 | **MITCHELTON-SCOTT** |
| 2021 | **TEAM BIKEEXCHANGE** |

## TEAM MANAGER

**MATT WHITE**

## 2021 NEW RIDERS

**MICHAEL MATTHEWS, TANEL KANGERT, AMUND GRØNDAHL JANSEN, KEVIN COLLEONI**

## 2021 STAGIAIRES

**CHOON HUAT GOH, KELLAND O'BRIEN**

## EQUIPMENT

| | |
|---|---|
| BIKE | **SCOTT** |

RIDER PROFILES

## SIMON YATES

Great Britain
07.08.92
Years Pro 8
Years On Team 8
Grand Tour Apps 12
Wins 23
UCI Ranking 36

Overall victory at the Tour of the Alps confirmed Yates' form ahead of the Giro, and had he been more consistent he could have mounted a proper challenge to Bernal's grip on the pink jersey. He did achieve his first Grand Tour stage win since 2019, however, and third overall was his highest placing since the Vuelta he won in 2018.

## MICHAEL MATTHEWS

Australia
26.09.90
Years Pro 11
Years On Team 1
Grand Tour Apps 12
Wins 37
UCI Ranking 44

His form looked promising in the spring Classics, with numerous top tens. He came close more times at both the Tour and Vuelta than he will probably care to look back on, often just lacking that extra edge or final kick to best the plethora of fast and punchy finishers present in the peloton.

### JACK BAUER
New Zealand
07.04.85
Years Pro 10
Years On Team 4
Grand Tour Apps 8
Wins 6
UCI Ranking 805

### SAM BEWLEY
New Zealand
22.07.87
Years Pro 12
Years On Team 10
Grand Tour Apps 9
Wins 0
UCI Ranking —

### BRENT BOOKWALTER
United States
16.02.84
Years Pro 14
Years On Team 8
Grand Tour Apps 11
Wins 3
UCI Ranking 651

### ESTEBAN CHAVES
Colombia
17.01.90
Years Pro 11
Years On Team 8
Grand Tour Apps 13
Wins 16
UCI Ranking 92

### KEVIN COLLEONI
Italy
11.11.99
Years Pro 1
Years On Team 1
Grand Tour Apps 0
Wins 0
UCI Ranking 1711

### LUKE DURBRIDGE
Australia
09.04.91
Years Pro 10
Years On Team 10
Grand Tour Apps 11
Wins 13
UCI Ranking 256

### ALEX EDMONDSON
Australia
22.12.93
Years Pro 6
Years On Team 6
Grand Tour Apps 3
Wins 1
UCI Ranking 1787

### TSGABU GRMAY
Ethiopia
25.08.91
Years Pro 9
Years On Team 3
Grand Tour Apps 8
Wins 11
UCI Ranking 375

### KADEN GROVES
Australia
23.12.98
Years Pro 3
Years On Team 3
Grand Tour Apps 0
Wins 6
UCI Ranking 1139

### LUCAS HAMILTON
Australia
12.02.96
Years Pro 4
Years On Team 4
Grand Tour Apps 4
Wins 4
UCI Ranking 125

### MICHAEL HEPBURN
Australia
17.08.91
Years Pro 10
Years On Team 10
Grand Tour Apps 8
Wins 3
UCI Ranking —

### DAMIEN HOWSON
Australia
13.08.92
Years Pro 8
Years On Team 8
Grand Tour Apps 9
Wins 6
UCI Ranking 347

### AMUND GRØNDAHL JANSEN
Norway
11.02.94
Years Pro 5
Years On Team 1
Grand Tour Apps 4
Wins 2
UCI Ranking 980

### CHRISTOPHER JUUL-JENSEN
Denmark
06.07.89
Years Pro 10
Years On Team 6
Grand Tour Apps 11
Wins 3
UCI Ranking —

### TANEL KANGERT
Estonia
11.03.87
Years Pro 13
Years On Team 1
Grand Tour Apps 17
Wins 11
UCI Ranking 408

### ALEXANDER KONYCHEV
Italy
25.07.98
Years Pro 2
Years On Team 2
Grand Tour Apps 0
Wins 0
UCI Ranking 854

### CAMERON MEYER
Australia
11.01.88
Years Pro 13
Years On Team 5
Grand Tour Apps 10
Wins 12
UCI Ranking 554

### LUKA MEZGEC
Slovenia
27.06.88
Years Pro 9
Years On Team 6
Grand Tour Apps 11
Wins 19
UCI Ranking 455

### MIKEL NIEVE
Spain
26.05.84
Years Pro 13
Years On Team 4
Grand Tour Apps 22
Wins 5
UCI Ranking 567

### BARNABÁS PEÁK
Hungary
29.11.98
Years Pro 2
Years On Team 2
Grand Tour Apps 0
Wins 3
UCI Ranking 1273

### NICK SCHULTZ
Australia
13.09.94
Years Pro 5
Years On Team 3
Grand Tour Apps 6
Wins 2
UCI Ranking 254

### CALLUM SCOTSON
Australia
10.08.96
Years Pro 3
Years On Team 3
Grand Tour Apps 2
Wins 0
UCI Ranking —

### DION SMITH
New Zealand
03.03.93
Years Pro 6
Years On Team 3
Grand Tour Apps 4
Wins 1
UCI Ranking 629

### ROBERT STANNARD
Australia
16.09.98
Years Pro 4
Years On Team 3
Grand Tour Apps 2
Wins 0
UCI Ranking 390

### ANDREY ZEITS
Kazakhstan
14.12.86
Years Pro 13
Years On Team 2
Grand Tour Apps 19
Wins 1
UCI Ranking 811

TEAMS    MEN'S WORLDTOUR

# TEAM DSM

## 2021 SEASON REVIEW

The brain drain at DSM left the squad slightly depleted at the start of the year, with Marc Hirschi's late transfer to UAE providing a shock to jolt everyone awake in the new year. Achieving only half the wins they did in the Covid-blighted 2020 will feel like a step back, and the team didn't manage to replicate the tactical nous displayed at last year's Tour. Three Vuelta stage wins will have gone some way to rescuing their season but, with Roche retiring and Australians Hindley and Storer off, the team must hope the youth they are promoting into the ranks will cut the mustard.

## 2021 VICTORIES

| | | |
|---|---|---|
| Paris–Nice – stage 2 | 2.UWT | C. Bol |
| Tour de l'Ain – stage 3 | 2.1 | M. Storer |
| Tour de l'Ain | 2.1 | M. Storer |
| Vuelta a Burgos – stage 3 | 2.Pro | R. Bardet |
| Tour de Pologne – stage 5 | 2.UWT | N. Arndt |
| Vuelta a España – stage 7 | 2.UWT | M. Storer |
| Vuelta a España – stage 10 | 2.UWT | M. Storer |
| Vuelta a España – stage 14 | 2.UWT | R. Bardet |

## TEAM INFORMATION

| | |
|---|---|
| UCI CODE | DSM |
| UCI STATUS | MEN'S WORLDTOUR |
| COUNTRY | GERMANY |
| FOUNDED | 2005 |

## TEAM NAME HISTORY

| | |
|---|---|
| 2005 | SHIMANO-MEMORY CORP |
| 2006–2011 | SKIL-SHIMANO |
| 2012 | ARGOS-SHIMANO |
| 2013 | TEAM ARGOS-SHIMANO |
| 2014 | TEAM GIANT-SHIMANO |
| 2015–2016 | TEAM GIANT-ALPECIN |
| 2017–2020 | TEAM SUNWEB |
| 2021 | TEAM DSM |

## TEAM MANAGER

IWAN SPEKENBRINK

## 2021 NEW RIDERS

ROMAIN BARDET, ROMAIN COMBAUD, ANDREAS LEKNESSUND, NIKLAS MÄRKL, KEVIN VERMAERKE, MARCO BRENNER

## EQUIPMENT

| | |
|---|---|
| BIKE | SCOTT |

## RIDER PROFILES

### ROMAIN BARDET
France
09.11.90
Years Pro 10
Years On Team 1
Grand Tour Apps 11
Wins 9
UCI Ranking 54

Arriving at DSM in need of a fresh start, he did what he hadn't done since 2018: win a bike race. Seventh overall in the Giro, coming close to a stage victory, he then got his win at the Vuelta a Burgos before adding another at the Vuelta a España atop the Pico Villuercas.

### MICHAEL STORER
Australia
28.02.97
Years Pro 4
Years On Team 4
Grand Tour Apps 5
Wins 4
UCI Ranking 120

The baby-faced 24-year-old Australian won the Tour de l'Ain in commanding fashion before taking on what is already his fourth Vuelta. Stage wins on days seven and ten, outlasting breakaway companions on both occasions, saw him then contest the polka dot mountain's jersey, claiming it ahead of teammate Bardet.

---

**THYMEN ARENSMAN**
Netherlands
04.12.99
Years Pro 2
Years On Team 2
Grand Tour Apps 2
Wins 0
UCI Ranking 411

**NIKIAS ARNDT**
Germany
18.11.91
Years Pro 9
Years On Team 9
Grand Tour Apps 11
Wins 0
UCI Ranking 233

**TIESJ BENOOT**
Belgium
11.03.94
Years Pro 7
Years On Team 2
Grand Tour Apps 6
Wins 3
UCI Ranking 74

**CEES BOL**
Netherlands
27.07.95
Years Pro 3
Years On Team 3
Grand Tour Apps 3
Wins 5
UCI Ranking 287

**MARCO BRENNER**
Germany
27.08.02
Years Pro 1
Years On Team 1
Grand Tour Apps 0
Wins 0
UCI Ranking 1553

**ROMAIN COMBAUD**
France
01.04.91
Years Pro 6
Years On Team 1
Grand Tour Apps 0
Wins 0
UCI Ranking 970

**ALBERTO DAINESE**
Italy
25.03.98
Years Pro 2
Years On Team 2
Grand Tour Apps 1
Wins 2
UCI Ranking 153

**NICO DENZ**
Germany
15.02.94
Years Pro 7
Years On Team 2
Grand Tour Apps 6
Wins 2
UCI Ranking 1273

**MARK DONOVAN**
Great Britain
03.04.99
Years Pro 2
Years On Team 2
Grand Tour Apps 2
Wins 0
UCI Ranking 576

**NILS EEKHOFF**
Netherlands
23.01.98
Years Pro 2
Years On Team 2
Grand Tour Apps 2
Wins 0
UCI Ranking 497

**FELIX GALL**
Austria
27.02.98
Years Pro 2
Years On Team 2
Grand Tour Apps 0
Wins 0
UCI Ranking 1025

**CHAD HAGA**
United States
26.08.88
Years Pro 8
Years On Team 8
Grand Tour Apps 12
Wins 2
UCI Ranking 761

**CHRIS HAMILTON**
Australia
18.05.95
Years Pro 5
Years On Team 5
Grand Tour Apps 6
Wins 0
UCI Ranking 475

**JAI HINDLEY**
Australia
05.05.96
Years Pro 4
Years On Team 4
Grand Tour Apps 4
Wins 6
UCI Ranking 347

**MAX KANTER**
Germany
22.10.97
Years Pro 3
Years On Team 3
Grand Tour Apps 2
Wins 0
UCI Ranking –

**ASBJORN KRAGH ANDERSEN**
Denmark
09.04.92
Years Pro 6
Years On Team 3
Grand Tour Apps 0
Wins 2
UCI Ranking –

**SØREN KRAGH ANDERSEN**
Denmark
10.08.94
Years Pro 6
Years On Team 6
Grand Tour Apps 5
Wins 8
UCI Ranking 323

**ANDREAS LEKNESSUND**
Norway
21.05.99
Years Pro 2
Years On Team 1
Grand Tour Apps 0
Wins 2
UCI Ranking 321

**NIKLAS MÄRKL**
Germany
03.03.99
Years Pro 1
Years On Team 1
Grand Tour Apps 0
Wins 0
UCI Ranking 475

**JORIS NIEUWENHUIS**
Netherlands
11.02.96
Years Pro 3
Years On Team 3
Grand Tour Apps 2
Wins 0
UCI Ranking 2257

**CASPER PEDERSEN**
Denmark
15.03.96
Years Pro 4
Years On Team 3
Grand Tour Apps 3
Wins 2
UCI Ranking 712

**NICOLAS ROCHE**
Ireland
03.07.84
Years Pro 17
Years On Team 3
Grand Tour Apps 24
Wins 12
UCI Ranking 471

**MARTIN SALMON**
Germany
29.10.97
Years Pro 2
Years On Team 2
Grand Tour Apps 1
Wins 0
UCI Ranking 2082

**FLORIAN STORK**
Germany
27.04.97
Years Pro 3
Years On Team 3
Grand Tour Apps 0
Wins 0
UCI Ranking –

**JASHA SÜTTERLIN**
Germany
04.11.92
Years Pro 8
Years On Team 2
Grand Tour Apps 5
Wins 1
UCI Ranking 1951

**MARTIJN TUSVELD**
Netherlands
09.09.93
Years Pro 5
Years On Team 4
Grand Tour Apps 4
Wins 0
UCI Ranking 599

**ILAN VAN WILDER**
Belgium
14.05.00
Years Pro 2
Years On Team 2
Grand Tour Apps 1
Wins 0
UCI Ranking 572

**KEVIN VERMAERKE**
United States
16.10.00
Years Pro 1
Years on Team 1
Grand Tour Apps 0
Wins 0
UCI Ranking 1762

TEAMS

TEAMS    MEN'S WORLDTOUR

# TEAM JUMBO-VISMA

## 2021 SEASON REVIEW

Nearly half a century of wins for the Dutch outfit who continue to go from strength to strength. Jonas Vingegaard was the latest revelation and a surprise runner-up at the Tour de France. Roglič continued to vacuum up victories, apart from the Tour one he and the team so desperately seek, before going on to claim his third Vuelta in a row, by now the redemption arc of the Slovenian's past two seasons. Dylan Groenewegen served out his suspension for the Jakobsen crash and started winning bike races again, while Tom Dumoulin took a break from cycling before also making a comeback – a big moment for the sport to have such a high-profile athlete take a leave of absence in aid of their mental health. Ⓛ

## 2021 VICTORIES

| | | |
|---|---|---|
| National Championships New Zealand – RR | NC | G. Bennett |
| UAE Tour – stage 5 | 2.UWT | J. Vingegaard |
| Paris–Nice – stage 4 | 2.UWT | P. Roglič |
| Tirreno–Adriatico – stage 1 | 2.UWT | W. van Aert |
| Paris–Nice – stage 6 | 2.UWT | P. Roglič |
| Paris–Nice – stage 7 | 2.UWT | P. Roglič |
| Tirreno–Adriatico – stage 7 (ITT) | 2.UWT | W. van Aert |
| Settimana Internazionale Coppi e Bartali – stage 2 | 2.1 | J. Vingegaard |
| Settimana Internazionale Coppi e Bartali – stage 4 | 2.1 | J. Vingegaard |
| Settimana Internazionale Coppi e Bartali | 2.1 | J. Vingegaard |
| Gent–Wevelgem | 1.UWT | W. van Aert |
| Itzulia Basque Country – stage 1 (ITT) | 2.UWT | P. Roglič |
| Itzulia Basque Country | 2.UWT | P. Roglič |
| Amstel Gold Race | 1.UWT | W. van Aert |
| National Championships Netherlands – ITT | NC | T. Dumoulin |
| National Championships Norway – ITT | NC | T. Foss |
| National Championships Germany – ITT | NC | T. Martin |
| National Championships Belgium – RR | NC | W. van Aert |
| National Championships Netherlands – RR | NC | T. Roosen |
| National Championships Norway – RR | NC | T. Foss |
| Tour de France – stage 11 | 2.UWT | W. van Aert |
| Tour de France – stage 15 | 2.UWT | S. Kuss |
| Tour de France – stage 20 (ITT) | 2.UWT | W. van Aert |
| Tour de France – stage 21 | 2.UWT | W. van Aert |
| Tour de Wallonie – stage 1 | 2.Pro | D. Groenewegen |
| Tour de Wallonie – stage 4 | 2.Pro | D. Groenewegen |
| Heylen Vastgoed Heistse Pijl | 1.1 | P. Eenkhorn |
| Tour of Denmark – stage 1 | 1.Pro | D. Groenewegen |
| Vuelta a España – stage 1 (ITT) | 2.UWT | P. Roglič |
| Vuelta a España – stage 11 | 2.UWT | P. Roglič |
| Vuelta a España – stage 17 | 2.UWT | P. Roglič |
| Vuelta a España – stage 21 (ITT) | 2.UWT | P. Roglič |
| Vuelta a España | 2.UWT | P. Roglič |
| Tour of Britain – stage 1 | 2.Pro | W. van Aert |
| Tour of Britain – stage 4 | 2.Pro | W. van Aert |
| Tour of Britain – stage 6 | 2.Pro | W. van Aert |
| Tour of Britain – stage 8 | 2.Pro | W. van Aert |
| Tour of Britain | 2.Pro | W. van Aert |
| Cro Race – stage 2 | 2.1 | O. Kooij |
| Cro Race – stage 4 | 2.1 | O. Kooij |
| Giro dell'Emilia | 1.Pro | P. Roglič |
| Cro Race – stage 6 | 2.1 | T. van Dijke |
| Milano–Torino | 1.Pro | P. Roglič |

## TEAM INFORMATION

| | |
|---|---|
| UCI CODE | TJV |
| UCI STATUS | MEN'S WORLDTOUR |
| COUNTRY | NETHERLANDS |
| FOUNDED | 1990 |

## TEAM NAME HISTORY

| | |
|---|---|
| 1990–1992 | BUCKLER-COLNAGO-DECCA |
| 1993–1994 | WORDPERFECT-COLNAGO-DECCA |
| 1995 | NOVELL SOFTWARE-DECCA |
| 1996–2010 | RABOBANK PROTEAM |
| 2011–2012 | RABOBANK CYCLING TEAM |
| 2013–2014 | BELKIN-PRO CYCLING TEAM |
| 2015–2018 | TEAM LOTTONL-JUMBO |
| 2019–2021 | TEAM JUMBO-VISMA |

## TEAM MANAGER

**RICHARD PLUGGE**

## 2021 NEW RIDERS

**SAM OOMEN, EDOARDO AFFINI, NATHAN VAN HOOYDONCK, OLAV KOOIJ, DAVID DEKKER, MICK VAN DIJKE, GIJS LEEMREIZE**

## EQUIPMENT

| | |
|---|---|
| BIKE | **CERVÉLO** |

RIDER PROFILES

## WOUT VAN AERT

Belgium
15.09.94
Years Pro 5
Years On Team 3
Grand Tour Apps 3
Wins 30
UCI Ranking 2

A trio of Tour wins across differing terrain confirmed his all-encompassing powers. A successful season by all accounts: victorious at Amstel Gold, Gent–Wevelgem and the Tour of Britain, while near-misses in the Tokyo road race and Flanders Worlds time trial saw him saddled with silver once more. By Roubaix his engine was finally running on empty.

## PRIMOŽ ROGLIČ

Slovenia
29.10.89
Years Pro 6
Years On Team 6
Grand Tour Apps 9
Wins 60
UCI Ranking 3

Brought down more than once in the Tour's crash-marred opening week, his yellow jersey hopes were shattered once again. He bounced back at the Vuelta, however, taking his third title in a row. A Paris–Nice implosion was rectified with victory in the Basque Country, while Tokyo time trial gold added a nice flair to his ever-expanding palmarès.

### EDOARDO AFFINI
Italy
24.06.96
Years Pro 3
Years On Team 1
Grand Tour Apps 2
Wins 2
UCI Ranking 198

### GEORGE BENNETT
New Zealand
07.04.90
Years Pro 10
Years On Team 7
Grand Tour Apps 14
Wins 3
UCI Ranking 167

### KOEN BOUWMAN
Netherlands
02.12.93
Years Pro 6
Years On Team 6
Grand Tour Apps 7
Wins 1
UCI Ranking 205

### DAVID DEKKER
Netherlands
02.02.98
Years Pro 1
Years On Team 1
Grand Tour Apps 1
Wins 0
UCI Ranking 1021

### TOM DUMOULIN
Netherlands
11.11.90
Years Pro 10
Years On Team 2
Grand Tour Apps 13
Wins 22
UCI Ranking 149

### PASCAL EENKHOORN
Netherlands
08.02.97
Years Pro 4
Years On Team 4
Grand Tour Apps 0
Wins 4
UCI Ranking 241

### TOBIAS FOSS
Norway
25.05.97
Years Pro 2
Years On Team 2
Grand Tour Apps 2
Wins 2
UCI Ranking 154

### ROBERT GESINK
Netherlands
31.05.86
Years Pro 15
Years On Team 15
Grand Tour Apps 20
Wins 13
UCI Ranking 1088

### DYLAN GROENEWEGEN
Netherlands
21.06.93
Years Pro 7
Years On Team 6
Grand Tour Apps 5
Wins 56
UCI Ranking 206

### CHRIS HARPER
Australia
23.11.94
Years Pro 2
Years On Team 2
Grand Tour Apps 1
Wins 3
UCI Ranking 315

### LENNARD HOFSTEDE
Netherlands
29.12.94
Years Pro 5
Years On Team 3
Grand Tour Apps 5
Wins 0
UCI Ranking —

### OLAV KOOIJ
Netherlands
17.10.01
Years Pro 1
Years On Team 1
Grand Tour Apps 0
Wins 3
UCI Ranking 169

### STEVEN KRUIJSWIJK
Netherlands
07.06.87
Years Pro 12
Years On Team 12
Grand Tour Apps 20
Wins 2
UCI Ranking 256

### SEPP KUSS
United States
13.09.94
Years Pro 4
Years On Team 4
Grand Tour Apps 7
Wins 7
UCI Ranking 115

### GIJS LEEMREIZE
Netherlands
23.10.99
Years Pro 1
Years On Team 1
Grand Tour Apps 1
Wins 0
UCI Ranking 530

### PAUL MARTENS
Germany
26.10.83
Years Pro 16
Years On Team 14
Grand Tour Apps 12
Wins 7
UCI Ranking —

### TONY MARTIN
Germany
23.04.85
Years Pro 16
Years On Team 3
Grand Tour Apps 21
Wins 67
UCI Ranking 256

### SAM OOMEN
Netherlands
15.08.95
Years Pro 6
Years On Team 1
Grand Tour Apps 5
Wins 2
UCI Ranking 272

### CHRISTOPH PFINGSTEN
Germany
20.11.87
Years Pro 7
Years On Team 2
Grand Tour Apps 4
Wins 0
UCI Ranking 1418

### TIMO ROOSEN
Netherlands
11.01.93
Years Pro 7
Years On Team 7
Grand Tour Apps 4
Wins 3
UCI Ranking 421

### MIKE TEUNISSEN
Netherlands
25.08.92
Years Pro 7
Years On Team 3
Grand Tour Apps 5
Wins 6
UCI Ranking 130

### ANTWAN TOLHOEK
Netherlands
29.04.94
Years Pro 6
Years On Team 5
Grand Tour Apps 4
Wins 1
UCI Ranking 312

### MICK VAN DIJKE
Netherlands
15.03.00
Years Pro 1
Years On Team 1
Grand Tour Apps 0
Wins 0
UCI Ranking 193

### JOS VAN EMDEN
Netherlands
18.02.85
Years Pro 14
Years On Team 14
Grand Tour Apps 13
Wins 13
UCI Ranking 450

### NATHAN VAN HOOYDONCK
Belgium
12.10.95
Years Pro 5
Years On Team 1
Grand Tour Apps 2
Wins 0
UCI Ranking 335

### JONAS VINGEGAARD
Denmark
10.12.96
Years Pro 3
Years On Team 3
Grand Tour Apps 2
Wins 5
UCI Ranking 18

### MAARTEN WYNANTS
Belgium
13.05.82
Years Pro 17
Years On Team 11
Grand Tour Apps 8
Wins 0
UCI Ranking 1787

TEAMS    MEN'S WORLDTOUR

# TEAM QHUBEKA NEXTHASH

### 2021 SEASON REVIEW

Once again, the team's future seemed to hang by a thread for the entire year. Assos were replaced midway through the year by mysterious blockchain finance company NextHash in a five-year deal, but months later the squad was struggling to pay riders' wages before being encouraged to find other teams for 2022. Despite only registering five wins for the season, three at the Giro d'Italia is a good return for a team of their size, as Mauro Schimd, Giacomo Nizzolo and Victor Campenaerts all won in the space of five days. ®

### 2021 VICTORIES

| | | |
|---|---|---|
| Clasica de Almeria | 1.Pro | G. Nizzolo |
| Giro d'Italia – stage 11 | 2.UWT | M. Schmid |
| Giro d'Italia – stage 13 | 2.UWT | G. Nizzolo |
| Giro d'Italia – stage 15 | 2.UWT | V. Campenaerts |
| Circuito de Getxo | 1.1 | G. Nizzolo |

### TEAM INFORMATION

| | |
|---|---|
| UCI CODE | TQA |
| UCI STATUS | MEN'S WORLDTOUR |
| COUNTRY | SOUTH AFRICA |
| FOUNDED | 2008 |

### TEAM NAME HISTORY

| | |
|---|---|
| 2008-2010 | MTN ENERGADE ROAD TEAM |
| 2011-2012 | TEAM MTN QHUBEKA |
| 2013-2015 | MTN-QHUBEKA |
| 2016-2019 | TEAM DIMENSION DATA |
| 2020 | NTT PRO CYCLING |
| 2021 | TEAM QHUBEKA ASSOS |
| 2021 | TEAM QHUBEKA NEXTHASH |

### TEAM MANAGER

**DOUGLAS RYDER**

### 2021 NEW RIDERS

**SERGIO HENAO, FABIO ARU, SIMON CLARKE, DIMITRI CLAEYS, MATTEO PELUCCHI, SANDER ARMÉE, BERT-JAN LINDEMAN, ROBERT POWER, LASSE NORMAN HANSEN, ŁUKASZ WISNIOWSKI, KILIAN FRANKINY, EMIL VINJEBO, SEAN BENNETT, MAURO SCHMID, HARRY TANFIELD, CONNOR BROWN, KAREL VACEK**

### EQUIPMENT

| | |
|---|---|
| BIKE | BMC |

RIDER PROFILES

## NIC DLAMINI

South Africa
12.08.95
Years Pro 4
Years On Team 4
Grand Tour Apps 3
Wins 0
UCI Ranking 811

Nic Dlamini made history when he became the first black South African rider to line up at the Tour de France, with worldwide media attention retelling the story of his harsh upbringing in a township. But his Tour story was made when he refused to give up after crashing on the Tignes summit-finish stage, crossing the line 40 minutes outside the time cut.

## GIACOMO NIZZOLO

Italy
30.01.89
Years Pro 11
Years On Team 3
Grand Tour Apps 11
Wins 28
UCI Ranking 21

Turning up to the Giro with a Covid-19 form printed on his helmet put a light twist on the continued difficulty of international travel across the world, and he finally won a stage at the race in his eighth participation. He also bagged victory at the Clasica de Almeira and again in Spain at the Circuito de Getxo.

### SANDER ARMÉE
Belgium
10.12.85
Years Pro 12
Years On Team 1
Grand Tour Apps 10
Wins 2
UCI Ranking 1522

### FABIO ARU
Italy
03.07.90
Years Pro 10
Years On Team 1
Grand Tour Apps 14
Wins 9
UCI Ranking 186

### CARLOS BARBERO
Spain
29.04.91
Years Pro 7
Years On Team 2
Grand Tour Apps 3
Wins 0
UCI Ranking 905

### SEAN BENNETT
United States
31.03.96
Years Pro 4
Years On Team 1
Grand Tour Apps 3
Wins 0
UCI Ranking 1172

### CONNOR BROWN
New Zealand
06.08.98
Years Pro 1
Years On Team 1
Grand Tour Apps 1
Wins 0
UCI Ranking —

### VICTOR CAMPENAERTS
Belgium
28.10.91
Years Pro 8
Years On Team 2
Grand Tour Apps 8
Wins 8
UCI Ranking 111

### DIMITRI CLAEYS
Belgium
18.06.87
Years Pro 8
Years On Team 1
Grand Tour Apps 3
Wins 5
UCI Ranking 310

### SIMON CLARKE
Australia
18.07.86
Years Pro 13
Years On Team 1
Grand Tour Apps 15
Wins 6
UCI Ranking 218

### KILIAN FRANKINY
Switzerland
26.01.94
Years Pro 5
Years On Team 1
Grand Tour Apps 5
Wins 0
UCI Ranking 1512

### MICHAEL GOGL
Denmark
07.02.95
Years Pro 7
Years On Team 2
Grand Tour Apps 6
Wins 0
UCI Ranking 250

### LASSE NORMAN HANSEN
Denmark
11.02.92
Years Pro 8
Years On Team 1
Grand Tour Apps 1
Wins 4
UCI Ranking 2082

### SERGIO HENAO
Colombia
10.12.87
Years Pro 10
Years On Team 1
Grand Tour Apps 14
Wins 8
UCI Ranking 433

### REINARDT JANSE VAN RENSBURG
South Africa
03.02.89
Years Pro 9
Years On Team 7
Grand Tour Apps 8
Wins 9
UCI Ranking 368

### BERT-JAN LINDEMAN
Netherlands
16.06.89
Years Pro 10
Years On Team 1
Grand Tour Apps 9
Wins 4
UCI Ranking —

### MATTEO PELUCCHI
Italy
21.01.89
Years Pro 11
Years On Team 1
Grand Tour Apps 5
Wins 16
UCI Ranking —

### ROBERT POWER
Australia
11.05.95
Years Pro 6
Years On Team 1
Grand Tour Apps 3
Wins 2
UCI Ranking 970

### DOMENICO POZZOVIVO
Italy
30.11.82
Years Pro 17
Years On Team 2
Grand Tour Apps 21
Wins 13
UCI Ranking 236

### MAURO SCHMID
Switzerland
04.12.99
Years Pro 1
Years On Team 1
Grand Tour Apps 1
Wins 1
UCI Ranking 319

### ANDREAS STOKBRO
Denmark
08.04.97
Years Pro 3
Years On Team 2
Grand Tour Apps 0
Wins 0
UCI Ranking 980

### DYLAN SUNDERLAND
Australia
26.02.96
Years Pro 2
Years On Team 2
Grand Tour Apps 2
Wins 0
UCI Ranking 2028

### HARRY TANFIELD
Great Britain
17.11.94
Years Pro 3
Years On Team 1
Grand Tour Apps 1
Wins 1
UCI Ranking 905

### JAY THOMSON
South Africa
12.04.86
Years Pro 9
Years On Team 10
Grand Tour Apps 4
Wins 4
UCI Ranking —

### KAREL VACEK
Czech Republic
09.09.00
Years Pro 1
Years On Team 1
Grand Tour Apps 0
Wins 0
UCI Ranking —

### EMIL VINJEBO
Denmark
24.03.94
Years Pro 3
Years On Team 1
Grand Tour Apps 0
Wins 0
UCI Ranking 2296

### MAX WALSCHEID
Germany
13.06.93
Years Pro 6
Years On Team 2
Grand Tour Apps 5
Wins 11
UCI Ranking 135

### ŁUKASZ WIŚNIOWSKI
Poland
07.12.91
Years Pro 7
Years On Team 1
Grand Tour Apps 4
Wins 0
UCI Ranking 1009

TEAMS   MEN'S WORLDTOUR

# TREK-SEGAFREDO

**2021 SEASON REVIEW**

19 victories was a modest return for Trek-Segafredo, who would have hoped for more top-level wins. Stuyven's Milan–Sanremo victory and Bauke Mollema's Tour de France stage were the shining highlights. Elsewhere Quinn Simmons stuck to racing and won the Tour de Wallonie while Mads Pedersen won stages at Scandinavian races, as well as Kuurne–Brussels–Kuurne.

**2021 VICTORIES**

| Race | Cat | Rider |
|---|---|---|
| Tour des Alpes Maritimes et du Var – stage 1 | 2.1 | B. Mollema |
| Tour des Alpes Maritimes et du Var – stage 3 | 2.1 | G. Brambilla |
| Tour des Alpes Maritimes et du Var | 2.1 | G. Brambilla |
| Kuurne–Bruxelles–Kuurne | 1.Pro | M. Pedersen |
| Trofeo Laigueglia | 1.Pro | B. Mollema |
| Milan–Sanremo | 1.UWT | J. Stuyven |
| Per Sempre Alfredo | 1.1 | M. Moschetti |
| Tour de Hongrie – stage 5 | 2.1 | E. Theuns |
| National Championships Latvia – ITT | NC | T. Skujiņš |
| National Championships Latvia – RR | NC | T. Skujiņš |
| Tour de France – stage 14 | 2.UWT | B. Mollema |
| Tour de Wallonie – stage 3 | 2.Pro | Q. Simmons |
| Tour de Wallonie | 2.Pro | Q. Simmons |
| Tour of Denmark – stage 2 | 2.Pro | M. Pedersen |
| Tour of Norway – stage 3 | 2.Pro | M. Pedersen |
| National Championships Ireland – ITT | NC | R. Mullen |
| Giro di Sicilia 2.1 – stage 4 | 2.1 | V. Nibali |
| Giro di Sicilia 2.1 | 2.1 | V. Nibali |
| National Championships Ireland – RR | NC | R. Mullen |

**TEAM INFORMATION**

| | |
|---|---|
| UCI CODE | **TFS** |
| UCI STATUS | **MEN'S WORLDTOUR** |
| COUNTRY | **UNITED STATES** |
| FOUNDED | **2011** |

**TEAM NAME HISTORY**

| | |
|---|---|
| 2011 | **LEOPARD TREK** |
| 2012 | **RADIOSHACK-NISSAN** |
| 2013 | **RADIOSHACK-LEOPARD** |
| 2014-2015 | **TREK FACTORY RACING** |
| 2016-2021 | **TREK-SEGAFREDO** |

**TEAM MANAGER**

**LUCA GUERCILENA**

**2021 NEW RIDERS**

**AMANUEL GHEBREIGZABHIER, MATTIAS SKJELMOSE JENSEN, ANTONIO TIBERI, JAKOB EGHOLM**

**2021 STAGIAIRES**

**FILIPPO BARONCINI, ASBJØRN HELLEMOSE, DAAN HOOLE**

**EQUIPMENT**

| | |
|---|---|
| BIKE | **TREK** |

RIDER PROFILES

## BAUKE MOLLEMA

Netherlands
26.11.86
Years Pro 14
Years On Team 7
Grand Tour Apps 19
Wins 17
UCI Ranking 20

A stage win evaded him at the Giro, but after third on the Tour's Ventoux stage, he got his victory three days later with a 40km solo effort. In Tokyo he was just edged out by Pogačar in the RR sprint finish, missing out on bronze by one place, but he picked up silver and bronze in the Worlds and European mixed relay TT events.

## JASPER STUYVEN

Belgium
17.04.92
Years Pro 8
Years On Team 8
Grand Tour Apps 8
Wins 9
UCI Ranking 17

He was a surprise winner of Milan–Sanremo, with eyes drawn to Van Aert, Van der Poel and Ewan on the run-in, before taking fourth at the Tour of Flanders. The pain of second on stage 7 at the Tour was compounded by fourth in the Worlds road race, outsprinted by Van Baarle and Valgren on his home roads of Leuven.

### JULIEN BERNARD
France
17.03.92
Years Pro 6
Years On Team 6
Grand Tour Apps 7
Wins 1
UCI Ranking 493

### GIANLUCA BRAMBILLA
Italy
22.08.87
Years Pro 12
Years On Team 4
Grand Tour Apps 16
Wins 6
UCI Ranking 199

### GIULIO CICCONE
Italy
20.12.94
Years Pro 6
Years On Team 3
Grand Tour Apps 8
Wins 6
UCI Ranking 178

### NICOLA CONCI
Italy
05.01.97
Years Pro 4
Years On Team 4
Grand Tour Apps 3
Wins 0
UCI Ranking 1129

### KOEN DE KORT
Netherlands
08.09.82
Years Pro 17
Years On Team 5
Grand Tour Apps 18
Wins 2
UCI Ranking –

### NIKLAS EG
Denmark
06.01.95
Years Pro 4
Years On Team 4
Grand Tour Apps 4
Wins 0
UCI Ranking 668

### JAKOB EGHOLM
Denmark
27.04.98
Years Pro 1
Years On Team 1
Grand Tour Apps 0
Wins 0
UCI Ranking –

### KENNY ELISSONDE
France
22.07.91
Years Pro 10
Years On Team 2
Grand Tour Apps 11
Wins 2
UCI Ranking 299

### AMANUEL GHEBREIGZABHIER
Eritrea
17.08.94
Years Pro 4
Years On Team 1
Grand Tour Apps 5
Wins 3
UCI Ranking 520

### ALEXANDER KAMP
Denmark
14.12.93
Years Pro 3
Years On Team 2
Grand Tour Apps 1
Wins 3
UCI Ranking 1584

### ALEX KIRSCH
Luxembourg
12.06.92
Years Pro 7
Years On Team 3
Grand Tour Apps 2
Wins 0
UCI Ranking 686

### EMĪLS LIEPIŅŠ
Latvia
29.10.92
Years Pro 3
Years On Team 2
Grand Tour Apps 1
Wins 2
UCI Ranking 637

### JUAN PEDRO LÓPEZ
Spain
31.07.97
Years Pro 2
Years On Team 2
Grand Tour Apps 2
Wins 0
UCI Ranking 542

### JACOPO MOSCA
Italy
29.08.93
Years Pro 5
Years On Team 3
Grand Tour Apps 4
Wins 3
UCI Ranking 726

### MATTEO MOSCHETTI
Italy
14.08.96
Years Pro 3
Years On Team 3
Grand Tour Apps 3
Wins 5
UCI Ranking 255

### RYAN MULLEN
Ireland
07.08.94
Years Pro 6
Years On Team 4
Grand Tour Apps 1
Wins 9
UCI Ranking 415

### ANTONIO NIBALI
Italy
23.09.92
Years Pro 7
Years On Team 2
Grand Tour Apps 5
Wins 1
UCI Ranking 1418

### VINCENZO NIBALI
Italy
14.11.84
Years Pro 17
Years On Team 2
Grand Tour Apps 25
Wins 54
UCI Ranking 134

### MADS PEDERSEN
Denmark
18.12.95
Years Pro 7
Years On Team 5
Grand Tour Apps 4
Wins 18
UCI Ranking 75

### CHARLIE QUARTERMAN
Great Britain
06.09.98
Years Pro 2
Years On Team 2
Grand Tour Apps 0
Wins 3
UCI Ranking 2296

### KIEL REIJNEN
United States
01.06.86
Years Pro 11
Years On Team 6
Grand Tour Apps 4
Wins 5
UCI Ranking –

### MICHEL RIES
Luxembourg
11.03.98
Years Pro 2
Years On Team 2
Grand Tour Apps 1
Wins 0
UCI Ranking 651

### QUINN SIMMONS
United States
08.05.01
Years Pro 2
Years On Team 2
Grand Tour Apps 1
Wins 2
UCI Ranking 218

### MATTIAS SKJELMOSE JENSEN
Denmark
26.09.00
Years Pro 1
Years On Team 1
Grand Tour Apps 0
Wins 0
UCI Ranking 170

### TOMS SKUJIŅŠ
Latvia
15.06.91
Years Pro 6
Years On Team 4
Grand Tour Apps 5
Wins 10
UCI Ranking 145

### EDWARD THEUNS
Belgium
30.04.91
Years Pro 8
Years On Team 6
Grand Tour Apps 6
Wins 9
UCI Ranking 278

### ANTONIO TIBERI
Italy
24.06.01
Years Pro 1
Years On Team 1
Grand Tour Apps 0
Wins 0
UCI Ranking 584

# UAE TEAM EMIRATES

### 2021 SEASON REVIEW

A squad bolstered by the likes of Rafał Majka, Marc Hirschi and Matteo Trentin continued their upward trend towards becoming one of the more powerful squads in the WorldTour. Yet Tadej Pogačar still faced relentless questioning as to the strength of his Tour squad despite the young Slovenian suffocating the life out of the GC race. The team's star was responsible for the majority of their victories this year, although Fernando Gaviria managed a WorldTour win in Poland, Joe Dombrowski won stage 4 of the Giro, while Majka took a stage of the Vuelta. Hirschi's late surprise signing set mouths watering yet the Swiss struggled, eventually taking his first win for his new employers in Luxembourg. Next year the arrivals of João Almeida, Pascal Ackermann, George Bennett and Marc Soler will make them even more formidable as UAE look to shore up the generational talent of Pogačar.

### TEAM INFORMATION

| UCI CODE | UAD |
|---|---|
| UCI STATUS | MEN'S WORLDTOUR |
| COUNTRY | UNITED ARAB EMIRATES |
| FOUNDED | 1999 |

### TEAM NAME HISTORY

| 1999 | LAMPRE-DAIKIN-COLNAGO |
|---|---|
| 2000-2002 | LAMPRE-DAIKIN |
| 2003-2004 | LAMPRE |
| 2005 | LAMPRE-CAFFITA |
| 2006-2007 | LAMPRE-FONDITAL |
| 2008 | LAMPRE |
| 2009 | LAMPRE-NGC |
| 2010 | LAMPRE-FARNESE VINI |
| 2011-2012 | LAMPRE-ISD |
| 2013-2016 | LAMPRE-MERIDA |
| 2017-2021 | UAE TEAM EMIRATES |

### TEAM MANAGER

MATXIN FERNANDEZ

### 2021 NEW RIDERS

RAFAŁ MAJKA, MATTEO TRENTIN, MARC HIRSCHI, RYAN GIBBONS, JUAN AYUSO, FINN FISHER-BLACK

### 2021 STAGIAIRES

FELIX GROSS

### EQUIPMENT

| BIKE | COLNAGO |
|---|---|

### 2021 VICTORIES

| | | |
|---|---|---|
| UAE Tour – stage 3 | 2.UWT | T. Pogačar |
| UAE Tour | 2.UWT | T. Pogačar |
| National Championships UAE – Road Race | NC | Y. Mirza |
| Tirreno–Adriatico – stage 4 | 2.UWT | T. Pogačar |
| Tirreno–Adriatico | 2.UWT | T. Pogačar |
| National Championships South Africa – ITT | NC | R. Gibbons |
| National Championships UAE – ITT | NC | Y. Mirza |
| Itzulia Basque Country – stage 3 | 2.UWT | T. Pogačar |
| Liège–Bastogne–Liège | 1.UWT | T. Pogačar |
| Giro d'Italia – stage 4 | 2.UWT | J. Dombrowski |
| Trofeo Calvia | 1.1 | R. Gibbons |
| Tour of Slovenia – stage 2 | 2.Pro | T. Pogačar |
| Tour of Slovenia – stage 4 | 2.Pro | D. Ulissi |
| Tour of Slovenia | 2.Pro | T. Pogačar |
| Tour de France – stage 5 (ITT) | 2.UWT | T. Pogačar |
| Settimana Ciclista Italiana – stage 1 | 2.1 | D. Ulissi |
| Tour de France – stage 17 | 2.UWT | T. Pogačar |
| Tour de France – stage 18 | 2.UWT | T. Pogačar |
| Settimana Ciclista Italiana – stage 4 | 2.1 | D. Ulissi |
| Tour de France | 2.UWT | T. Pogačar |
| Settimana Ciclista Italiana | 2.1 | D. Ulissi |
| Vuelta a Burgos – stage 2 | 2.Pro | J. S. Molano |
| Vuelta a Burgos – stage 4 | 2.Pro | J. S. Molano |
| Tour de Pologne – stage 3 | 2.UWT | F. Gaviria |
| Deutschland Tour – stage 4 | 2.Pro | A. Kristoff |
| Tour de Luxembourg – stage 2 | 2.Pro | M. Hirschi |
| Trofeo Matteotti | 1.1 | M. Trentin |
| Giro di Sicilia – stage 1 | 2.1 | J. S. Molano |
| Giro di Sicilia – stage 2 | 2.1 | J. S. Molano |
| Il Lombardia | 1.UWT | T. Pogačar |

## RIDER PROFILES

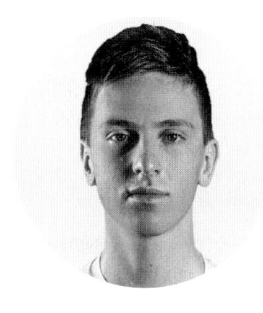

### TADEJ POGAČAR
Slovenia
21.09.98
Years Pro 3
Years On Team 3
Grand Tour Apps 3
Wins 30
UCI Ranking 1

Victories at the UAE Tour and Tirreno–Adriatico came before his debut Monument win in Liège. Yet all roads led to his Tour defence: assured and rarely in danger, he blew away his competition in the mountains and in the time trials. No one could get close. Bronze in the Olympics road race was a nice addition a week after celebration on the Champs-Élysées.

### MATTEO TRENTIN
Italy
02.08.89
Years Pro 11
Years On Team 1
Grand Tour Apps 11
Wins 26
UCI Ranking 24

He took top tens at Omloop Het Nieuwsblad, Kuurne–Brussels–Kuurne and Gent–Wevelgem, before coming close three times in Vuelta bunch sprints. A victory finally came at Trofeo Matteotti but, for how strong the Italian looked throughout the season, he would have wanted more to show for it.

---

**ANDRÉS CAMILO ARDILA**
Colombia
02.06.99
Years Pro 2
Years On Team 2
Grand Tour Apps 0
Wins 0
UCI Ranking 1273

**JUAN AYUSO**
Spain
16.09.02
Years Pro 1
Years On Team 1
Grand Tour Apps 0
Wins 0
UCI Ranking 197

**MIKKEL BJERG**
Denmark
03.11.98
Years Pro 4
Years On Team 2
Grand Tour Apps 2
Wins 0
UCI Ranking 396

**SVEN ERIK BYSTRØM**
Norway
21.01.92
Years Pro 7
Years On Team 4
Grand Tour Apps 4
Wins 1
UCI Ranking 297

**VALERIO CONTI**
Italy
30.03.93
Years Pro 8
Years On Team 8
Grand Tour Apps 11
Wins 4
UCI Ranking 371

**RUI COSTA**
Portugal
05.10.86
Years Pro 15
Years On Team 8
Grand Tour Apps 13
Wins 27
UCI Ranking 184

**ALESSANDRO COVI**
Italy
28.09.98
Years Pro 2
Years On Team 2
Grand Tour Apps 0
Wins 0
UCI Ranking 83

**DAVID DE LA CRUZ**
Spain
06.05.89
Years Pro 9
Years On Team 2
Grand Tour Apps 13
Wins 5
UCI Ranking 124

**JOE DOMBROWSKI**
United States
12.05.91
Years Pro 9
Years On Team 2
Grand Tour Apps 10
Wins 4
UCI Ranking 355

**FINN FISHER-BLACK**
New Zealand
21.12.01
Years Pro 1
Years On Team 1
Grand Tour Apps 0
Wins 0
UCI Ranking 265

**DAVIDE FORMOLO**
Italy
25.10.92
Years Pro 8
Years On Team 2
Grand Tour Apps 12
Wins 4
UCI Ranking 178

**FERNANDO GAVIRIA**
Colombia
19.08.94
Years Pro 6
Years On Team 3
Grand Tour Apps 6
Wins 47
UCI Ranking 185

**RYAN GIBBONS**
South Africa
13.08.94
Years Pro 5
Years On Team 1
Grand Tour Apps 6
Wins 8
UCI Ranking 82

**MARC HIRSCHI**
Switzerland
24.08.98
Years Pro 3
Years On Team 1
Grand Tour Apps 2
Wins 3
UCI Ranking 67

**ALEXANDER KRISTOFF**
Norway
05.07.87
Years Pro 12
Years On Team 4
Grand Tour Apps 10
Wins 81
UCI Ranking 69

**VEGARD STAKE LAENGEN**
Norway
07.02.89
Years Pro 10
Years On Team 5
Grand Tour Apps 8
Wins 1
UCI Ranking 637

**RAFAŁ MAJKA**
Poland
12.09.89
Years Pro 11
Years On Team 1
Grand Tour Apps 19
Wins 12
UCI Ranking 206

**MARCO MARCATO**
Italy
11.02.84
Years Pro 16
Years On Team 5
Grand Tour Apps 12
Wins 5
UCI Ranking 2028

**BRANDON MCNULTY**
United States
02.04.98
Years Pro 4
Years On Team 2
Grand Tour Apps 2
Wins 2
UCI Ranking 138

**YOUSIF MIRZA**
United Arab Emirates
08.10.88
Years Pro 5
Years On Team 5
Grand Tour Apps 0
Wins 4
UCI Ranking 686

**JUAN SEBASTIÁN MOLANO**
Colombia
04.11.94
Years Pro 7
Years On Team 3
Grand Tour Apps 6
Wins 17
UCI Ranking 378

**CRISTIAN CAMILO MUÑOZ**
Colombia
20.03.96
Years Pro 3
Years On Team 3
Grand Tour Apps 0
Wins 0
UCI Ranking 1297

**IVO OLIVEIRA**
Portugal
05.09.96
Years Pro 3
Years On Team 3
Grand Tour Apps 1
Wins 1
UCI Ranking –

**RUI OLIVEIRA**
Portugal
05.09.96
Years Pro 4
Years On Team 3
Grand Tour Apps 2
Wins 0
UCI Ranking 392

**JAN POLANC**
Slovenia
06.05.92
Years Pro 9
Years On Team 9
Grand Tour Apps 9
Wins 3
UCI Ranking 238

**ALEXANDR RIABUSHENKO**
Belarus
12.10.95
Years Pro 4
Years On Team 4
Grand Tour Apps 1
Wins 1
UCI Ranking 1067

**MAXIMILIANO RICHEZE**
Argentina
07.03.83
Years Pro 16
Years On Team 2
Grand Tour Apps 15
Wins 17
UCI Ranking 1400

**OLIVIERO TROIA**
Italy
01.09.94
Years Pro 5
Years On Team 5
Grand Tour Apps 2
Wins 0
UCI Ranking –

**DIEGO ULISSI**
Italy
15.07.89
Years Pro 11
Years On Team 11
Grand Tour Apps 11
Wins 42
UCI Ranking 46

TEAMS    WOMEN'S WORLDTOUR

# ALÉ BTC LJUBLJANA

**2021 SEASON REVIEW**

The team's new signing Reusser had a breakthrough season, winning the European ITT title and silver in the Olympic time trial next to many other Classics and time trial results – but Reusser will move to SD Worx for 2022. García performed well in hilly Classics and stage races, winning the Spanish championships and Giro dell'Emilia and finishing sixth in the Trofeo Binda and Amstel Gold Race, fifth in Flèche Wallonne and Giro Donne, and second in the Tour de l'Ardèche and Setmana Valenciana. Bastianelli continued to play a big role in the team with top-ten results in the Omloop Het Nieuwsblad, Gent–Wevelgem and Paris–Roubaix, also sprinting to stage victories in the Tour de Suisse, Tour de l'Ardèche and Women's Tour. Chursina won stage 2 of the Vuelta a Burgos from a breakaway, Bujak won the Slovenian ITT and road race championships. For 2022, the team will merge with men's team UAE Team Emirates.

**TEAM INFORMATION**

| UCI CODE | **ALE** |
|---|---|
| UCI STATUS | **WOMEN'S WORLDTOUR** |
| COUNTRY | **ITALY** |
| FOUNDED | **2011** |

**TEAM NAME HISTORY**

| 2011 | **CIPOLLINI-GIORDANA** |
|---|---|
| 2012 | **CIPOLLINI-GIAMBENINI-GAUSS** |
| 2013 | **CIPOLLINI-GIORDANA** |
| 2014–2019 | **ALE CIPOLLINI** |
| 2020–2021 | **ALÉ BTC LJUBLJANA** |

**TEAM MANAGER**

**FORTUNATO LAQUANITI**

**2021 NEW RIDERS**

**MARLEN REUSSER, LAURA TOMASI, SOPHIE WRIGHT**

**EQUIPMENT**

| BIKE | **CIPOLLINI** |
|---|---|

**2021 VICTORIES**

| Vuelta a Burgos Feminas – stage 2 | 2.WWT | A. Chursina |
|---|---|---|
| Tour de Suisse Women – stage 2 | 2.1 | M. Bastianelli |
| National Championships Switzerland – ITT | NC | M. Reusser |
| National Championships Slovenia – ITT | NC | E. Bujak |
| National Championships Spain – ITT | NC | M. García |
| National Championships Spain – RR | NC | M. García |
| National Championships Slovenia – RR | NC | E. Bujak |
| National Championships Switzerland – RR | NC | M. Reusser |
| La Périgord Ladies | 1.2 | M. Bastianelli |
| Simac Ladies Tour – stage 2 (ITT) | 2.WWT | M. Reusser |
| Ceratizit Challenge – stage 1 | 2.WWT | M. Reusser |
| Tour de l'Ardèche – stage 5 | 2.1 | M. Bastianelli |
| Giro dell'Emilia | 1.Pro | M. García |
| The Women's Tour – stage 1 | 2.WWT | M. Bastianelli |
| Chrono des Nations | 1.1 | M. Reusser |

## RIDER PROFILES

**MARLEN REUSSER**
Switzerland
20.09.91
Years Pro 3
Years On Team 1
Wins 12
UCI Ranking 6

After a ninth place in the Tour of Flanders, she was third in the Tour de Suisse, won the Swiss ITT and RR championships, and took silver in the Olympic ITT. A fourth place in the Ladies Tour of Norway was followed by second places in the Simac Ladies Tour, Ceratizit Challenge and World ITT Championships as well as the European ITT title.

**MARGARITA VICTORIA GARCÍA**
Spain
02.01.84
Years Pro 7
Years On Team 2
Wins 9
UCI Ranking 17

After top-ten results in Trofeo Binda, Amstel Gold Race and Flèche Wallonne, top-20s in Strade Bianche and Liège–Bastogne–Liège, and second overall in the Setmana Valenciana, she won the Spanish ITT and RR championships before finishing fifth in the Giro Donne. 12th in the Olympic road race, García then won the Giro dell'Emilia and was runner-up in the Tour de l'Ardèche and Tre Valli Varesine.

**MARTA BASTIANELLI**
Italy
30.04.87
Years Pro 14
Years On Team 7
Wins 35
UCI Ranking 25

**MAAIKE BOOGAARD**
Netherlands
24.08.98
Years Pro 5
Years On Team 5
Wins 0
UCI Ranking 234

**EUGENIA BUJAK**
Slovenia
25.06.89
Years Pro 8
Years On Team 8
Wins 12
UCI Ranking 53

**ANASTASIIA CHURSINA**
Russia
07.04.95
Years Pro 4
Years On Team 4
Wins 5
UCI Ranking 103

**TATIANI GUDERZO**
Italy
22.08.84
Years Pro 17
Years On Team 2
Wins 14
UCI Ranking 45

**ALESSIA PATUELLI**
Italy
22.12.02
Years Pro 1
Years On Team 1
Wins 0
UCI Ranking —

**URSA PINTAR**
Slovenia
03.10.85
Years Pro 8
Years On Team 8
Wins 3
UCI Ranking 114

**LAURA TOMASI**
Italy
01.07.99
Years Pro 4
Years On Team 1
Wins 0
UCI Ranking 202

**ANNA TREVISI**
Italy
08.05.92
Years Pro 10
Years On Team 6
Wins 0
UCI Ranking 297

**SOPHIE WRIGHT**
Great Britain
15.03.99
Years Pro 4
Years On Team 1
Wins 0
UCI Ranking 590

# A.R. MONEX WOMEN'S PRO CYCLING TEAM

**2021 SEASON REVIEW**

Their absolute leader was Sierra, who combined a strong sprint with resilience in the hills and mountains to achieve top results across the board with six victories, including Tre Valli Varesine and a stage of the Tour de l'Ardèche. Novolodskaya was the team's best finisher in the Ardennes Classics and won Madison bronze in the Olympics. Merino was eighth in the GP Ciudad de Eibar, 13th in Durango-Durango and finished 17th overall in the Giro Donne. Sperotto reached the top ten on three stages of the Giro Donne and finished eighth in Tre Valli Varesine. Ragusa finished 13th in the Trofeo Binda, 14th in Gent–Wevelgem and 18th in Brugge–De Panne and reached the top ten in the Giro dell'Emilia and Tre Valli Varesine. Salazar won the Mexican championships, participated in the Olympics, and finished fourth in the Pan-American Championships.

## TEAM INFORMATION

| UCI CODE | MNX |
| --- | --- |
| UCI STATUS | UCI WOMEN'S CONTINENTAL TEAM |
| COUNTRY | ITALY |
| FOUNDED | 2015 |

**TEAM NAME HISTORY**

| 2015 | ASTANA-ACCA DUE O |
| --- | --- |
| 2016-2020 | ASTANA WOMEN'S TEAM |
| 2021 | A.R. MONEX WOMEN'S PRO CYCLING TEAM |

**TEAM MANAGER**

ZULFIA ZABIROVA / MAURIZIO FABRETTO

**2021 NEW RIDERS**

MARIA NOVOLODSKAYA, EIDER MERINO, MARIA JOSE VARGAS, ANDREA RAMIREZ, MARIA VITTORIA SPEROTTO, ARIADNA GUTIERREZ, MARIIA MILIAEVA, EMMA FAORO, JULIETA LLEDIAS, MARIA PIA CHIATTO, GAIA BENZI

**EQUIPMENT**

| BIKE | LIV |
| --- | --- |

## 2021 VICTORIES

| | | |
| --- | --- | --- |
| Navarra Women's Elite Classics | 1.1 | A. Sierra |
| National Championships Mexico – RR | NC | L. Y. Salazar |
| Premondiale Giro Toscana – prologue | 2.2 | A. Sierra |
| Premondiale Giro Toscana – stage 1 | 2.2 | A. Sierra |
| Premondiale Giro Toscana | 2.2 | A. Sierra |
| Tour de l'Ardèche – stage 1 | 2.1 | A. Sierra |
| Tre Valli Varesine | 1.2 | A. Sierra |

## RIDER PROFILES

### ARLENIS SIERRA
Cuba
07.12.92
Years Pro 5
Years On Team 5
Wins 43
UCI Ranking 26

The Cuban all-rounder had top-20 results in the spring at Brugge–De Panne, Gent–Wevelgem, Scheldeprijs and Brabantse Pijl. She won the Navarra Classic and placed sixth in Durango-Durango before winning two stages and the overall at the Giro Toscana, the first stage of the Tour de l'Ardèche, and Tre Valli Varesine. She was fifth in the World Championships and runner-up in the Giro dell'Emilia.

### MARIA NOVOLODSKAYA
Russia
28.07.99
Years Pro 4
Years On Team 1
Wins 2
UCI Ranking 113

The 22-year-old Russian achieved top-25 results in the spring Classics Trofeo Binda, Gent–Wevelgem, Scheldeprijs, Amstel Gold Race, Flèche Wallonne and Liège–Bastogne–Liège. Her Giro Donne breakaways were not successful, but she won Madison bronze at the Tokyo Olympics, was eighth in the Giro Toscana and tenth in the Under-23 European ITT championships.

---

**GAIA BENZI**
Italy
20.12.99
Years Pro 1
Years On Team 1
Wins 0
UCI Ranking —

**MARIA PIA CHIATTO**
Italy
13.05.02
Years Pro 1
Years On Team 1
Wins 0
UCI Ranking —

**EMMA FAORO**
Italy
21.03.02
Years Pro 1
Years On Team 1
Wins 0
UCI Ranking —

**ARIADNA GUTIERREZ**
Mexico
22.08.91
Years Pro 4
Years On Team 1
Wins 0
UCI Ranking 544

**JULIETA LLEDIAS**
Mexico
16.04.01
Years Pro 2
Years On Team 1
Wins 0
UCI Ranking —

**EIDER MERINO**
Spain
02.08.94
Years Pro 9
Years On Team 1
Wins 2
UCI Ranking 148

**MARIIA MILIAEVA**
Russia
16.07.01
Years Pro 2
Years On Team 1
Wins 0
UCI Ranking —

**KATIA RAGUSA**
Italy
19.05.97
Years Pro 6
Years On Team 2
Wins 0
UCI Ranking 122

**ANDREA RAMIREZ**
Mexico
25.09.99
Years Pro 1
Years On Team 1
Wins 5
UCI Ranking 455

**LIZBETH YARELI SALAZAR**
Mexico
08.12.96
Years Pro 4
Years On Team 3
Wins 2
UCI Ranking 96

**MARIA VITTORIA SPEROTTO**
Italy
20.11.96
Years Pro 6
Years On Team 1
Wins 1
UCI Ranking 654

**JADE TEOLIS**
France
12.01.02
Years Pro 1
Years On Team 1
Wins 0
UCI Ranking 856

**MARIA JOSE VARGAS**
Costa Rica
15.02.96
Years Pro 4
Years On Team 1
Wins 6
UCI Ranking 155

TEAMS     WOMEN'S WORLDTOUR

# CANYON-SRAM RACING

**2021 SEASON REVIEW**

Harvey performed well and finished fifth in the Tour de Suisse as well as 15th in the Ladies Tour of Norway and La Course but was overshadowed by Chabbey who often received leadership duties over Harvey and placed even higher. Niewiadoma remained winless throughout the year, but a runner-up place in Flèche Wallonne and third place in the World Championships showed that she was close to victory. Dygert focused on recovering from her late-2020 leg fracture. She won the US time trial championships, won the bronze medal with the US pursuit team, and finished seventh in the Olympic ITT. Alice Barnes won a stage in the Setmana Valenciana, was close to a sprint victory on several other occasions, and placed seventh in the Women's Tour thanks to her time trial abilities. Klein won two stages and the GC of the Baloise Ladies Tour, was part of the German squad that won team pursuit gold in Tokyo, and also won the mixed relay World Championships. Shapira became Israeli road race champion. Amialiusik won a stage and finished fifth overall in the Lotto Belgium Tour and represented her country with top-20 placings in the Olympics and European and World Championships. ⓒⓀ

**TEAM INFORMATION**

| UCI CODE | **CSR** |
|---|---|
| UCI STATUS | **WOMEN'S WORLDTOUR** |
| COUNTRY | **GERMANY** |
| FOUNDED | **2003** |

**TEAM NAME HISTORY**

| 2016-2021 | **CANYON-SRAM RACING** |

**TEAM MANAGER**

**RONNY LAUKE**

**2021 NEW RIDERS**

**CHLOE DYGERT, ELISE CHABBEY, MIKAYLA HARVEY, NEVE BRADBURY**

**EQUIPMENT**

| BIKE | **CANYON** |

**2021 VICTORIES**

| Setmana Ciclista Valenciana – stage 3 | 2.1 | A. Barnes |
| Tour de Suisse – stage 1 | 2.1 | E. Chabbey |
| National Championships United States – ITT | NC | C. Dygert |
| National Championships Israel – RR | NC | O. Shapira |
| Lotto Belgium Tour – stage 2 | 2.1 | A. Amialiusik |
| Baloise Ladies Tour – prologue | 2.1 | L. Klein |
| Baloise Ladies Tour – stage 2b (ITT) | 2.1 | L. Klein |
| Baloise Ladies Tour | 2.1 | L. Klein |

### KATARZYNA NIEWIADOMA

Poland
29.09.94
| | |
|---|---|
| Years Pro | 8 |
| Years On Team | 4 |
| Wins | 18 |
| UCI Ranking | 7 |

Runner-up in Dwars door Vlaanderen and Flèche Wallonne and fourth in Trofeo Binda and Liège–Bastogne–Liège, she finished tenth in the Amstel Gold Race and Vuelta a Burgos. A sixth place in La Course was followed by 14th in the Olympic road race, 13th in the Simac Ladies Tour, sixth in the Ceratizit Challenge, fourth in the European Championships and bronze at the World Championships.

### ELISE CHABBEY

Switzerland
24.04.93
| | |
|---|---|
| Years Pro | 4 |
| Years On Team | 1 |
| Wins | 2 |
| UCI Ranking | 19 |

She came to the fore with a second place on stage 1 of the Vuelta a Burgos. In the Giro Donne, she finished tenth, followed by 11th in the Ladies Tour of Norway, 13th at the GP de Plouay, third in the Ceratizit Challenge, a 15th place in the European and 13th in the World Championships, and ninth overall in the Women's Tour.

| ALENA AMIALIUSIK | ALICE BARNES | HANNAH BARNES | NEVE BRADBURY | TIFFANY CROMWELL | CHLOE DYGERT |
|---|---|---|---|---|---|
| Belarus | Great Britain | Great Britain | Australia | Australia | United States |
| 06.02.89 | 17.07.95 | 04.05.93 | 11.04.02 | 06.07.88 | 01.01.97 |
| Years Pro 9 | Years Pro 6 | Years Pro 8 | Years Pro 1 | Years Pro 11 | Years Pro 6 |
| Years On Team 7 | Years On Team 4 | Years On Team 6 | Years On Team 1 | Years On Team 8 | Years On Team 1 |
| Wins 23 | Wins 5 | Wins 12 | Wins 0 | Wins 6 | Wins 18 |
| UCI Ranking 72 | UCI Ranking 46 | UCI Ranking 95 | UCI Ranking 476 | UCI Ranking 108 | UCI Ranking 141 |

| ELLA HARRIS | MIKAYLA HARVEY | LISA KLEIN | HANNAH LUDWIG | ALEXIS RYAN | OMER SHAPIRA |
|---|---|---|---|---|---|
| New Zealand | New Zealand | Germany | Germany | United States | Israel |
| 18.07.98 | 07.09.98 | 15.07.96 | 15.02.00 | 18.08.94 | 09.09.94 |
| Years Pro 3 | Years Pro 5 | Years Pro 7 | Years Pro 3 | Years Pro 8 | Years Pro 5 |
| Years On Team 3 | Years On Team 1 | Years On Team 4 | Years On Team 3 | Years On Team 6 | Years On Team 3 |
| Wins 1 | Wins 1 | Wins 13 | Wins 0 | Wins 2 | Wins 6 |
| UCI Ranking 157 | UCI Ranking 83 | UCI Ranking 34 | UCI Ranking 103 | UCI Ranking 134 | UCI Ranking 110 |

# CERATIZIT–WNT PRO CYCLING

**2021 SEASON REVIEW**

Winning German, European and World Championships and Olympic gold on the road and track, Brennauer had an excellent season where she also was runner-up in Gent–Wevelgem and the Healthy Ageing Tour, third in the Tour of Flanders, fourth in Paris–Roubaix, fifth in the World ITT Championships, sixth in the Olympic road race and time trial and ninth in the World Road Race Championships. Magnaldi showed her abilities in hilly Classics and stage races, finishing ninth in the Clásica San Sebastián, 13th in the Giro Donne and Flèche Wallonne, 14th in the Amstel Gold Race and 16th in the Ceratizit Challenge. Confalonieri mixed up the sprints with a fifth place in the Flanders Diamond Tour, sixth in the GP d'Isbergues and GP Oetingen, and seventh in the Nokere Koerse and finished third overall in the Festival Elsy Jacobs. Lach won La Picto-Charentaise and placed fourth in La Périgord, ninth in the GP d'Isbergues and 18th in the Olympic road race. Hammes finished 11th in the Thüringen Ladies Tour, where she also won the mountain jersey. Wild finished sixth in Brugge–De Panne but otherwise focused on the Olympics, where she won bronze in the Omnium.

**TEAM INFORMATION**

| | |
|---|---|
| UCI CODE | WNT |
| UCI STATUS | UCI WOMEN'S CONTINENTAL |
| COUNTRY | GERMANY |
| FOUNDED | 2016 |

**TEAM NAME HISTORY**

| | |
|---|---|
| 2016 | TEAM WNT |
| 2017 | TEAM WNT PRO CYCLING |
| 2018-2019 | WNT ROTOR PRO CYCLING |
| 2020-2021 | CERATIZIT-WNT PRO CYCLING |

**TEAM MANAGER**

CLAUDE SUN

**2021 NEW RIDERS**

LOTTA HENTTALA, ELIZABETH BANKS, MARTA LACH

**EQUIPMENT**

BIKE — ORBEA

**2021 VICTORIES**

| | | |
|---|---|---|
| National Championships Germany – ITT | NC | L. Brennauer |
| National Championships Germany – RR | NC | L. Brennauer |
| La Picto-Charentaise | 1.2 | M. Lach |

RIDER PROFILES

## LISA BRENNAUER

Germany
08.06.88
| | |
|---|---|
| Years Pro | 12 |
| Years On Team | 3 |
| Wins | 41 |
| UCI Ranking | 10 |

She finished on the podium in Gent–Wevelgem and the Tour of Flanders before winning the German ITT and RR championships. In the Olympics, she finished sixth in the ITT and road race and won gold with the German pursuit team. She won the mixed relay world title, finished fourth in Paris–Roubaix and finally won the European team and individual pursuit championships.

## ERICA MAGNALDI

Italy
24.08.92
| | |
|---|---|
| Years Pro | 4 |
| Years On Team | 3 |
| Wins | 1 |
| UCI Ranking | 56 |

The Italian climber reached the top 20 of the Trofeo Binda, Amstel Gold Race, Flèche Wallonne and Liège–Bastogne–Liège, then finished ninth in the two-stage Tour de Suisse and 13th in the Giro Donne. Her best result was a ninth place in the Clásica San Sebastián, followed by top-20 placings in the GP de Plouay and Ceratizit Challenge.

---

**LAURA ASENCIO**
France
14.05.98
| | |
|---|---|
| Years Pro | 3 |
| Years On Team | 3 |
| Wins | 0 |
| UCI Ranking | 554 |

**ELIZABETH BANKS**
Great Britain
07.11.90
| | |
|---|---|
| Years Pro | 3 |
| Years On Team | 1 |
| Wins | 2 |
| UCI Ranking | – |

**FRANZISKA BRAUSSE**
Germany
20.11.98
| | |
|---|---|
| Years Pro | 4 |
| Years On Team | 3 |
| Wins | 0 |
| UCI Ranking | 856 |

**MARIA GIULIA CONFALONIERI**
Italy
30.03.93
| | |
|---|---|
| Years Pro | 10 |
| Years On Team | 2 |
| Wins | 0 |
| UCI Ranking | 67 |

**KATHRIN HAMMES**
Germany
09.01.89
| | |
|---|---|
| Years Pro | 7 |
| Years On Team | 3 |
| Wins | 2 |
| UCI Ranking | 172 |

**LOTTA HENTTALA**
Finland
28.06.89
| | |
|---|---|
| Years Pro | 8 |
| Years On Team | 1 |
| Wins | 25 |
| UCI Ranking | – |

**MARTA LACH**
Poland
26.05.97
| | |
|---|---|
| Years Pro | 3 |
| Years On Team | 1 |
| Wins | 3 |
| UCI Ranking | 127 |

**JULIE LETH**
Denmark
13.07.92
| | |
|---|---|
| Years Pro | 11 |
| Years On Team | 2 |
| Wins | 3 |
| UCI Ranking | 175 |

**SARAH RIJKES**
Austria
02.04.91
| | |
|---|---|
| Years Pro | 9 |
| Years On Team | 3 |
| Wins | 1 |
| UCI Ranking | 296 |

**LEA LIN TEUTENBERG**
Germany
02.07.99
| | |
|---|---|
| Years Pro | 4 |
| Years On Team | 4 |
| Wins | 0 |
| UCI Ranking | – |

**LARA VIECELI**
Italy
16.07.93
| | |
|---|---|
| Years Pro | 9 |
| Years On Team | 3 |
| Wins | 1 |
| UCI Ranking | 747 |

**KIRSTEN WILD**
Netherlands
15.10.82
| | |
|---|---|
| Years Pro | 18 |
| Years On Team | 3 |
| Wins | 109 |
| UCI Ranking | 154 |

# FDJ NOUVELLE-AQUITAINE FUTUROSCOPE

**2021 SEASON REVIEW**

Uttrup Ludwig and Cavalli brought home a host of top results, although crashes and punctures in the opening TTT thwarted an even better Giro Donne overall result. Uttrup Ludwig took her first Women's WorldTour victory when she won a stage of the Vuelta a Burgos. When the team's two big names were unavailable, Fahlin or Borgli took over, achieving top-ten results in Gent–Wevelgem, Dwars door Vlaanderen and Brabantse Pijl as well as the Thüringen Ladies Tour. The young French riders, Grossetête, Le Net, Wiel and Copponi, continued to develop while supporting their teammates but also had the chance to go for results themselves. Copponi was fifth in the GP d'Isbergues, finished on the overall podium of the Women's Tour, and competed in the Olympics where she finished fifth in the Madison with Le Net who also placed eighth in the Lotto Belgium Tour. Muzic won the French road race championships, placed fifth in the GP de Plouay and was second in the Women's WorldTour Under-23 ranking. Grossetête was 14th in the Healthy Ageing Tour, eighth in the Ronde de Mouscron, and second on a stage of the Simac Ladies Tour. Wiel's best result was fifth in La Picto-Charentaise.

## TEAM INFORMATION

| | |
|---|---|
| UCI CODE | **FDJ** |
| UCI STATUS | **WOMEN'S WORLDTOUR** |
| COUNTRY | **FRANCE** |
| FOUNDED | **2008** |

**TEAM NAME HISTORY**

| | |
|---|---|
| 2008–2013 | **VIENNE FUTUROSCOPE** |
| 2014–2016 | **POITOU-CHARENTES. FUTUROSCOPE.86** |
| 2017–2021 | **FDJ NOUVELLE-AQUITAINE FUTUROSCOPE** |

**TEAM MANAGER**

**NICOLAS MAIRE**

**2021 NEW RIDERS**

**MARTA CAVALLI**

**EQUIPMENT**

| | |
|---|---|
| BIKE | **LAPIERRE** |

**2021 VICTORIES**

| | | |
|---|---|---|
| Vuelta a Burgos Feminas – stage 3 | 2.WWT | C. Uttrup Ludwig |
| National Championships France – RR | NC | É. Muzic |

## RIDER PROFILES

### CECILIE UTTRUP LUDWIG

Denmark
23.08.95
Years Pro 8
Years On Team 2
Wins 10
UCI Ranking 9

After a spring with fifth in Strade Bianche, third in Trofeo Binda and top-ten results in the Tour of Flanders, Amstel Gold Race, Flèche Wallonne and Liège–Bastogne–Liège, she won a stage and finished fourth overall in the Vuelta a Burgos. Runner-up in La Course, she placed tenth in the Olympic road race, fifth in the Ladies Tour of Norway and eighth at the World Championships.

### MARTA CAVALLI

Italy
18.03.98
Years Pro 5
Years On Team 1
Wins 2
UCI Ranking 18

She was in the top ten in the Omloop Het Nieuwsblad, Strade Bianche, Tour of Flanders, Olympic road race, and Paris–Roubaix, 13th in La Course, and 14th in Liège–Bastogne–Liège and the Thüringen Ladies Tour. After a sixth place overall in the Giro Donne and fourth in the Ceratizit Challenge, she was part of the Italian team that won the mixed relay European Championships.

---

**STINE BORGLI**
Norway
04.07.90
Years Pro 3
Years On Team 3
Wins 1
UCI Ranking 327

**BRODIE CHAPMAN**
Australia
09.04.91
Years Pro 4
Years On Team 2
Wins 8
UCI Ranking 114

**CLARA COPPONI**
France
12.01.99
Years Pro 3
Years On Team 3
Wins 0
UCI Ranking 64

**EUGÉNIE DUVAL**
France
03.05.93
Years Pro 7
Years On Team 7
Wins 0
UCI Ranking 128

**EMILIA FAHLIN**
Sweden
24.10.88
Years Pro 15
Years On Team 3
Wins 16
UCI Ranking 54

**MAËLLE GROSSETÊTE**
France
10.04.98
Years Pro 4
Years On Team 4
Wins 0
UCI Ranking 230

**VICTORIE GUILMAN**
France
25.03.96
Years Pro 6
Years On Team 6
Wins 0
UCI Ranking 202

**LAUREN KITCHEN**
Australia
21.11.90
Years Pro 10
Years On Team 4
Wins 6
UCI Ranking —

**MARIE LE NET**
France
25.01.00
Years Pro 3
Years On Team 3
Wins 0
UCI Ranking 146

**ÉVITA MUZIC**
France
26.05.99
Years Pro 4
Years On Team 4
Wins 2
UCI Ranking 36

**JADE WIEL**
France
02.04.00
Years Pro 4
Years On Team 3
Wins 1
UCI Ranking 422

# JUMBO-VISMA WOMEN TEAM

**2021 SEASON REVIEW**

Built around superstar Marianne Vos, this newly formed team had its share of success with Vos winning, among others, Gent–Wevelgem and the Amstel Gold Race. Henderson was an excellent super-domestique for Vos in the Classics and also got results of her own as she won Kreiz Breizh, was third in the Baloise Ladies Tour and tenth in the GP de Plouay and Healthy Ageing Tour. Riejanne Markus won stage 2 of the Ladies Tour of Norway with a solo breakaway, wearing the leader's jersey for a day and finishing seventh overall. She also placed ninth in the Festival Elsy Jacobs and the World ITT Championships, 12th in the Omloop Het Nieuwsblad and Liège–Bastogne–Liège and 15th in the Ceratizit Challenge. Koster finished sixth overall in the Festival Elsy Jacobs and Trophée des Grimpeuses and won the hills jersey at the Simac Ladies Tour. Swinkels was fourth in the Festival Elsy Jacobs and stood on the podium of the Dutch championships together with Van den Burg. Van den Bos finished fifth in Dwars door de Westhoek and 12th in the Baloise Ladies Tour, while Beekhuis was eighth in the Healthy Ageing Tour and 17th in Paris–Roubaix.

## TEAM INFORMATION

| | |
|---|---|
| UCI CODE | JVW |
| UCI STATUS | UCI WOMEN'S CONTINENTAL |
| COUNTRY | NETHERLANDS |
| FOUNDED | 2021 |

**TEAM NAME HISTORY**

| | |
|---|---|
| 2021 | TEAM JUMBO-VISMA WOMEN |

**TEAM MANAGER**

ESRA TROMP

**2021 NEW RIDERS**

MARIANNE VOS, ANOUSKA KOSTER, RIEJANNE MARKUS, ROMY KASPER, JIP VAN DEN BOS, PERNILLE MATHIESEN, ANNA HENDERSON, JULIE VAN DE VELDE, KARLIJN SWINKELS, AAFKE SOET, NANCY VAN DER BURG, TEUNTJE BEEKHUIS, AMBER KRAAK

**EQUIPMENT**

| | |
|---|---|
| BIKE | CERVÉLO |

## 2021 VICTORIES

| | | |
|---|---|---|
| Gent-Wevelgem | 1.WWT | M. Vos |
| Amstel Gold Race | 1.WWT | M. Vos |
| Giro Donne – stage 3 | 2.Pro | M. Vos |
| Giro Donne – stage 7 | 2.Pro | M. Vos |
| Tour de Belle Isle en Terre – stage 1 | 2.2 | A. Henderson |
| Tour de Belle Isle en Terre – stage 2 | 2.2 | A. Henderson |
| Tour de Belle Isle en Terre | 2.2 | A. Henderson |
| Laides Tour of Norway – stage 2 | 2.WWT | R. Markus |
| Simac Ladies Tour – prologue | 2.WWT | M. Vos |
| Simac Ladies Tour – stage 4 | 2.WWT | M. Vos |
| Simac Ladies Tour – stage 5 | 2.WWT | M. Vos |
| National Championships Great Britain – ITT | NC | A. Henderson |

RIDER PROFILES

## MARIANNE VOS

Netherlands
13.05.87
Years Pro 16
Years On Team 1
Wins 238
UCI Ranking 3

Vos won Gent–Wevelgem and the Amstel Gold Race and reached the podium in Trofeo Binda and La Course. After two stage victories in the Giro Donne, she placed fifth in the Olympic road race and won three stages of the Simac Ladies Tour, placing fourth overall. Her road season ended with runner-up places in the World Championships and Paris–Roubaix.

## ANNA HENDERSON

Great Britain
14.11.98
Years Pro 2
Years On Team 1
Wins 4
UCI Ranking 44

Starting with 20th place in the Omloop Het Nieuwsblad and top-ten results in Le Samyn and Healthy Ageing Tour, the 22-year-old Briton had a breakthrough season. She finished 17th in La Course, third in the Baloise Ladies Tour and won both stages and the GC of the Kreiz Breizh. Her biggest stand-alone result was a tenth place in the GP de Plouay.

### TEUNTJE BEEKHUIS
Netherlands
18.08.95
Years Pro 4
Years On Team 1
Wins 0
UCI Ranking 226

### ROMY KASPER
Germany
05.05.88
Years Pro 14
Years On Team 1
Wins 2
UCI Ranking 168

### ANOUSKA KOSTER
Netherlands
20.08.93
Years Pro 10
Years On Team 1
Wins 7
UCI Ranking 96

### AMBER KRAAK
Netherlands
29.07.94
Years Pro 1
Years On Team 1
Wins 0
UCI Ranking 587

### RIEJANNE MARKUS
Netherlands
01.09.94
Years Pro 8
Years On Team 1
Wins 5
UCI Ranking 49

### PERNILLE MATHIESEN
Denmark
05.10.97
Years Pro 6
Years On Team 1
Wins 1
UCI Ranking —

### AAFKE SOET
Netherlands
23.11.97
Years Pro 5
Years On Team 1
Wins 1
UCI Ranking —

### KARLIJN SWINKELS
Netherlands
28.10.98
Years Pro 5
Years On Team 1
Wins 1
UCI Ranking 100

### JULIE VAN DE VELDE
Belgium
02.06.93
Years Pro 5
Years On Team 1
Wins 1
UCI Ranking 170

### JIP VAN DEN BOS
Netherlands
12.04.96
Years Pro 7
Years On Team 1
Wins 1
UCI Ranking 289

### NANCY VAN DER BURG
Netherlands
18.05.92
Years Pro 4
Years On Team 1
Wins 0
UCI Ranking 190

TEAMS

# LIV RACING

**2021 SEASON REVIEW**

The team signed only two new riders, in Kopecky and Jackson, and both were an immediate hit – so much so that Kopecky will move on to SD Worx while Jackson extended her contract. The Belgian ITT and road race champion took eight victories, including the defence of both national titles, and never finished outside the top 20, but lost out on an Olympic medal in the Madison. Jackson had an excellent second half of the season. After participating in the Olympic Games, she took home the points jersey in the Ladies Tour of Norway, won stage 1 of the Simac Ladies Tour from a breakaway on her way to eighth overall, won the Canadian ITT and road race championships, and finished sixth in the World Championships. Paladin finished fifth in the Trofeo Binda and Amstel Gold Race and on a Giro Donne stage, seventh in La Course, 11th in Liège–Bastogne–Liège and 14th in Strade Bianche. Bertizzolo was often just behind Paladin, placing eighth in the Trofeo Binda, tenth in La Course and 15th in Strade Bianche, but also finished fourth in the GP de Plouay. Stultiens was fourth in the Clásica San Sebastián and 18th in Flèche Wallonne.

**2021 VICTORIES**

| | | |
|---|---|---|
| Le Samyn | 1.1 | L. Kopecky |
| National Championships Belgium – ITT | NC | L. Kopecky |
| National Championships Belgium – RR | NC | L. Kopecky |
| Simac Ladies Tour – stage 1 | 2.WWT | A. Jackson |
| Ceratizit Challenge – stage 4 | 2.WWT | L. Kopecky |
| National Championships Canada – ITT | NC | A. Jackson |
| National Championships Canada – RR | NC | A. Jackson |
| La Classique Morbihan | 1.1 | S. Bertizzolo |

**TEAM INFORMATION**

| | |
|---|---|
| UCI CODE | LIV |
| UCI STATUS | WOMEN'S WORLDTOUR |
| COUNTRY | NETHERLANDS |
| FOUNDED | 2006 |

**TEAM NAME HISTORY**

| | |
|---|---|
| 2006 | TEAM DSB-BALLAST NEDAM |
| 2007 | TEAM DSB BANK |
| 2008 | DSB BANK LADIES CYCLING-TEAM |
| 2009 | DSB BANK-NEDERLAND BLOEIT |
| 2010-2011 | NEDERLAND BLOEIT |
| 2012 | RABOBANK WOMEN TEAM |
| 2013 | RABOBANK-LIV GIANT |
| 2014-2016 | RABOBANK-LIV WOMAN CYCLING TEAM |
| 2017 | WM3 ENERGIE |
| 2018 | WAOWDEALS PRO CYCLING |
| 2019-2020 | CCC LIV |
| 2021 | LIV RACING |

**TEAM MANAGER**

**LARS BOOM**

**2021 NEW RIDERS**

**LOTTE KOPECKY, ALISON JACKSON**

**2021 STAGIAIRES**

**AYESHA MCGOWAN**

**EQUIPMENT**

| | |
|---|---|
| BIKE | LIV |

RIDER PROFILES

## LOTTE KOPECKY

Belgium
10.11.95
Years Pro 10
Years On Team 1
Wins 16
UCI Ranking 8

After winning Le Samyn, she was fourth in Brugge–De Panne and runner-up in Gent–Wevelgem. Second in the Thüringen Ladies Tour, where she also won a stage, she won the Belgian ITT and RR championships as well as a stage and GC of the Lotto Belgium Tour. Tenth in the Olympic Madison, Kopecky then won a stage each of the Ceratizit Challenge and Trophée des Grimpeuses.

## PAULIENA ROOIJAKKERS

Netherlands
12.05.93
Years Pro 10
Years On Team 4
Wins 1
UCI Ranking 47

She achieved her best results in stage races and hilly Classics. After top-ten places in the Brabantse Pijl, Emakumeen Nafarroako, and Durango-Durango, the 28-year-old climber finished ninth in the Vuelta a Burgos. A seventh place in the Clásica San Sebastián was followed by tenth in the Ceratizit Challenge. Finally Rooijakkers was fourth in the Tour de l'Ardèche, where she won the mountain and combination classifications.

| | | | | | |
|---|---|---|---|---|---|
| **SOFIA BERTIZZOLO** | **VALERIE DEMEY** | **ALISON JACKSON** | **MARTA JASKULSKA** | **JEANNE KOREVAAR** | **EVY KUIJPERS** |
| Italy | Belgium | Canada | Poland | Netherlands | Netherlands |
| 21.08.97 | 17.01.94 | 14.12.88 | 25.03.00 | 24.09.96 | 15.02.95 |
| Years Pro 6 | Years Pro 6 | Years Pro 7 | Years Pro 2 | Years Pro 7 | Years Pro 8 |
| Years On Team 2 | Years On Team 3 | Years On Team 1 | Years On Team 2 | Years On Team 7 | Years On Team 3 |
| Wins 1 | Wins 0 | Wins 7 | Wins 0 | Wins 1 | Wins 0 |
| UCI Ranking 30 | UCI Ranking 178 | UCI Ranking 31 | UCI Ranking 168 | UCI Ranking 86 | UCI Ranking 844 |

| | |
|---|---|
| **SORAYA PALADIN** | **SABRINA STULTIENS** |
| Italy | Netherlands |
| 04.05.93 | 08.07.93 |
| Years Pro 8 | Years Pro 10 |
| Years On Team 2 | Years On Team 4 |
| Wins 7 | Wins 1 |
| UCI Ranking 33 | UCI Ranking 74 |

TEAMS    WOMEN'S WORLDTOUR

# MOVISTAR TEAM WOMEN

**2021 SEASON REVIEW**

The Spanish team often united behind its new signing, Van Vleuten, and the Dutchwoman repaid their faith with 12 victories. At the end of the season, she led the Women's WorldTour and the World Ranking. Norsgaard got her breakthrough as a sprinter and also established herself as a rider for the time trials and Classics. When neither of the two were present, leadership fell to Thomas, Biannic or Erić. The latter was runner-up in the Ronde de Mouscron and won the Serbian RR championships, while Biannic showed her tactical nous with 11th at Brugge–De Panne and her time trial abilities with fifth overall at the Women's Tour. Thomas was fourth in the Brabantse Pijl, 11th in La Course and 16th in the Giro Donne and won a stage and the GC of the Tour de l'Ardèche.

**TEAM INFORMATION**

| | |
|---|---|
| UCI CODE | **MOV** |
| UCI STATUS | **WOMEN'S WORLDTOUR** |
| COUNTRY | **SPAIN** |
| FOUNDED | **2018** |

**TEAM NAME HISTORY**

| | |
|---|---|
| 2018-2021 | **MOVISTAR TEAM** |

**TEAM MANAGER**

**JORGE SANZ**

**2021 NEW RIDERS**

**ANNEMIEK VAN VLEUTEN, LEAH THOMAS, EMMA NORSGAARD, SARA MARTIN**

**EQUIPMENT**

| | |
|---|---|
| BIKE | **CANYON** |

**2021 VICTORIES**

| | | |
|---|---|---|
| Dwars door Vlaanderen | 1.1 | A. van Vleuten |
| Tour of Flanders | 1.WWT | A. van Vleuten |
| Ceratizit Festival Elsy Jacobs – stage 1 | 2.Pro | E. Norsgaard |
| Ceratizit Festival Elsy Jacobs – stage 2 | 2.Pro | E. Norsgaard |
| Ceratizit Festival Elsy Jacobs | 2.Pro | E. Norsgaard |
| Setmana Ciclista Valenciana – stage 1 | 2.1 | A. van Vleuten |
| Setmana Ciclista Valenciana | 2.1 | A. van Vleuten |
| Emakumeen Nafarroako | 1.1 | A. van Vleuten |
| Thüringen Ladies Tour – stage 1 | 2.Pro | E. Norsgaard |
| National Championships Denmark – ITT | NC | E. Norsgaard |
| National Championships Norway – ITT | NC | K. Aalerud |
| National Championships Serbia – RR | NC | J. Erić |
| Giro Donne – stage 6 | 2.Pro | E. Norsgaard |
| Donostia San Sebastian Klasikoa | 1.WWT | A. van Vleuten |
| Ladies Tour of Norway – stage 3 | 2.WWT | A. van Vleuten |
| Ladies Tour of Norway | 2.WWT | A. van Vleuten |
| Ceratizit Challenge – stage 2 | 2.WWT | A. van Vleuten |
| Ceratizit Challenge – stage 3 | 2.WWT | A. van Vleuten |
| Ceratizit Challenge | 2.WWT | A. van Vleuten |
| Tour de l'Ardèche – stage 2 | 2.1 | L. Thomas |
| Tour de l'Ardèche | 2.1 | L. Thomas |

RIDER PROFILES

## ANNEMIEK VAN VLEUTEN

Netherlands
08.10.82
Years Pro 14
Years On Team 1
Wins 86
UCI Ranking 1

Despite turning 39 this season, she had a very successful season where she went from victory to victory – from Dwars door Vlaanderen and the Tour of Flanders via the Setmana Valenciana and Emakumeen Nafarroako to silver in the Olympic Road Race and the coveted gold in the Olympic ITT, followed by the Clásica San Sebastián, Ladies Tour of Norway and Ceratizit Challenge.

## EMMA NORSGAARD

Denmark
26.07.99
Years Pro 4
Years On Team 1
Wins 9
UCI Ranking 11

She chased a victory for most of the spring campaign, finishing runner-up in Omloop Het Nieuwsblad, Le Samyn, Brugge–De Panne and Scheldeprijs before winning two stages and the GC at the Festival Elsy Jacobs. Later, she won stages of the Thüringen Ladies Tour and Giro Donne as well as the Danish ITT championships and finished sixth in Paris–Roubaix.

### KATRINE AALERUD
Norway
04.12.94
Years Pro 5
Years On Team 2
Wins 2
UCI Ranking 51

### AUDE BIANNIC
France
27.03.91
Years Pro 9
Years On Team 4
Wins 3
UCI Ranking 89

### JELENA ERIĆ
Serbia
15.01.96
Years Pro 7
Years On Team 2
Wins 3
UCI Ranking 93

### ALICIA GONZÁLEZ
Spain
27.05.95
Years Pro 8
Years On Team 4
Wins 0
UCI Ranking 548

### BARBARA GUARISCHI
Italy
02.10.90
Years Pro 13
Years On Team 2
Wins 6
UCI Ranking 99

### SHEYLA GUTIÉRREZ
Spain
01.01.94
Years Pro 9
Years On Team 3
Wins 9
UCI Ranking 105

### SARA MARTIN
Spain
22.03.99
Years Pro 4
Years On Team 1
Wins 0
UCI Ranking 117

### LOURDES OYARBIDE
Spain
08.04.94
Years Pro 9
Years On Team 4
Wins 3
UCI Ranking 164

### PAULA PATIÑO
Colombia
29.03.97
Years Pro 3
Years On Team 3
Wins 2
UCI Ranking 180

### GLORIA RODRÍGUEZ
Spain
06.03.92
Years Pro 9
Years On Team 4
Wins 0
UCI Ranking –

### ALBA TERUEL
Spain
17.08.96
Years Pro 7
Years On Team 4
Wins 0
UCI Ranking 843

### LEAH THOMAS
United States
30.05.89
Years Pro 7
Years On Team 1
Wins 10
UCI Ranking 40

TEAMS    WOMEN'S WORLDTOUR

# PARKHOTEL VALKENBURG

**2021 SEASON REVIEW**

Without their previous leaders Wiebes and Vollering, and with many other riders also having left, it was a new-look team that had to find its place in the peloton this season. Buijsman won a stage of the Tour de Feminin and the mountain jersey of the Ladies Tour of Norway and finished sixth in Tre Valli Varesine, seventh in the GP Fourmies and 11th in the Giro dell'Emilia. Van der Hulst also stepped up, her best results being podium places in the GP d'Isbergues, GP Eco-Struct, and Flanders Diamond Tour. Raaijmakers won stage 1 and the GC of the Watersley Challenge and the Under-23 jersey in the Trophée des Grimpeuses and finished sixth in the GP Fourmies. Gerritse also won a stage of the Watersley Challenge, where she placed fourth overall, and was fifth in the Dutch road race championships. Bredewold won a stage and the Under-23 jersey in the Baloise Ladies Tour and finished tenth in the Lotto Belgium Tour and 11th in the Simac Ladies Tour. Mid-season transfer Neylan finished sixth in the Ladies Tour of Norway and seventh in the Trophée des Grimpeuses and stood on the podium of the GP Fourmies, Giro dell'Emilia and Tre Valli Varesine. (UK)

**TEAM INFORMATION**

| UCI CODE | **PHV** |
| UCI STATUS | **UCI WOMEN'S CONTINENTAL** |
| COUNTRY | **NETHERLANDS** |
| FOUNDED | **2014** |

**TEAM NAME HISTORY**

| 2014-2016 | **PARKHOTEL VALKENBURG** |
| 2017 | **PARKHOTEL VALKENBURG-DESTIL CYCLING TEAM** |
| 2018 | **PARKHOTEL VALKENBURG CYCLING TEAM** |
| 2019-2021 | **PARKHOTEL VALKENBURG** |

**TEAM MANAGER**

**RAYMOND ROL**

**2021 NEW RIDERS**

**RACHEL NEYLAN, MISCHA BREDEWOLD, KIRSTIE VAN HAAFTEN, PIEN LIMPENS, FEMKE GERRITSE, LIEKE NOOIJEN, SOFIE VAN ROOIJEN, JULIA VAN BOKHOVEN, LEONIE BOS**

**EQUIPMENT**

| BIKE | **FACTOR** |

**2021 VICTORIES**

| Tour de Feminin – stage 2 | 2.2 | N. Buijsman |
| Baloise Ladies Tour – stage 1 | 2.1 | M. Bredewold |
| Watersley Challenge – stage 1 | 2.2 | M. Raaijmakers |
| Watersley Challenge – stage 3 | 2.2 | F. Gerritse |
| Watersley Challenge | 2.2 | M. Raaijmakers |

RIDER PROFILES

### AMBER VAN DER HULST
Netherlands
21.09.99
Years Pro 2
Years On Team 2
Wins 0
UCI Ranking 65

Placing well throughout the season, she was third in the GP Eco-Struct, Flanders Diamond Tour and GP d'Isbergues, fourth in the Omloop van de Westhoek, and ninth in Le Samyn, Dwars door het Hageland and the stage races Healthy Ageing Tour and Lotto Belgium Tour. A good performance in the Simac Ladies Tour brought her a 15th place overall in the Dutch stage race.

### MISCHA BREDEWOLD
Netherlands
20.06.00
Years Pro 1
Years On Team 1
Wins 1
UCI Ranking 98

In her first season on a UCI team, she wore the Baloise Ladies Tour leader's jersey for two days after winning stage 1, finishing fourth overall and winning the Under-23 jersey. She also placed tenth in the Lotto Belgium Tour, was the best Under-23 rider in the Tour of Flanders, and finished 11th overall and runner-up of the Under-23 ranking in the Simac Ladies Tour.

### LEONIE BOS
Netherlands
03.02.01
Years Pro 1
Years On Team 1
Wins 0
UCI Ranking —

### NINA BUIJSMAN
Netherlands
16.11.97
Years Pro 5
Years On Team 5
Wins 2
UCI Ranking 155

### BELLE DE GAST
Netherlands
04.02.91
Years Pro 4
Years On Team 4
Wins 0
UCI Ranking 722

### FEMKE GERRITSE
Netherlands
14.05.01
Years Pro 1
Year On Team 1
Wins 0
UCI Ranking 347

### PIEN LIMPENS
Netherlands
24.02.01
Years Pro 1
Years On Team 1
Wins 0
UCI Ranking 650

### FEMKE MARKUS
Netherlands
17.11.96
Years Pro 3
Years On Team 3
Wins 0
UCI Ranking 157

### RACHEL NEYLAN
Australia
09.03.82
Years Pro 11
Years On Team 1
Wins 4
UCI Ranking 65

### LIEKE NOOIJEN
Netherlands
20.07.01
Years Pro 1
Years On Team 1
Wins 0
UCI Ranking 369

### MARIT RAAIJMAKERS
Netherlands
02.06.99
Years Pro 4
Years On Team 4
Wins 0
UCI Ranking 460

### SYLVIE SWINKELS
Netherlands
31.07.00
Years Pro 4
Years On Team 4
Wins 2
UCI Ranking —

### JULIA VAN BOKHOVEN
Netherlands
01.04.01
Years Pro 3
Years On Team 3
Wins 0
UCI Ranking 487

### KIRSTIE VAN HAAFTEN
Netherlands
21.01.99
Years Pro 3
Years On Team 1
Wins 0
UCI Ranking 596

### SOFIE VAN ROOIJEN
Netherlands
13.07.02
Years Pro 1
Years On Team 1
Wins 0
UCI Ranking 940

# SD WORX

### 2021 SEASON REVIEW

With Van der Breggen and D'hoore retiring at the end of 2021 and Van den Broek-Blaak after the 2022 spring campaign, the team needed a changing of the guard – and achieved it with Vollering taking over as the team's most successful rider, finishing second in the Women's WorldTour. Fisher-Black, Uneken and Vas also stepped up: Uneken won stages of the Healthy Ageing Tour, Baloise Ladies Tour and Simac Ladies Tour, while Vas won the Hungarian championships, was ninth in the Ceratizit Challenge and fourth in the World Championships. Fisher-Black won the Under-23 jerseys in the Vuelta a Burgos, Giro Donne and Ladies Tour of Norway and the Women's WorldTour Under-23 classification. Moolman-Pasio won a stage of the Giro Donne and was part of a 1-2-3 at the Italian stage race that was won by Van der Breggen with Vollering in third. Van den Broek-Blaak won the Simac Ladies Tour overall, while Pieters won the Dutch championships, Nokere Koerse and a stage of the Women's Tour.

### TEAM INFORMATION

| | |
|---|---|
| UCI CODE | **SDW** |
| UCI STATUS | **WOMEN'S WORLDTOUR** |
| COUNTRY | **NETHERLANDS** |
| FOUNDED | **2010** |

### TEAM NAME HISTORY

| | |
|---|---|
| 2010-2011 | **DOLMANS LANDSCAPING TEAM** |
| 2012 | **DOLMANS-BOELS CYCLING TEAM** |
| 2013-2020 | **BOELS DOLMANS CYCLING TEAM** |
| 2021 | **SD WORX** |

### TEAM MANAGER

**DANNY STAM**

### 2021 NEW RIDERS

**ASHLEIGH MOOLMAN-PASIO, ELENA CECCHINI, DEMI VOLLERING, ROXANE FOURNIER, NIKOLA NOSKOVÁ, NIAMH FISHER-BLACK, KATA BLANKA VAS, ANNA SHACKLEY**

### EQUIPMENT

| | |
|---|---|
| BIKE | **SPECIALIZED** |

### 2021 VICTORIES

| Race | Class | Rider |
|---|---|---|
| Omloop Het Nieuwsblad | 1.Pro | A. van der Breggen |
| Strade Bianche | 1.WWT | C. van den Broek-Blaak |
| Healthy Ageing Tour – stage 1 | 2.1 | J. D'hoore |
| Healthy Ageing Tour – stage 3 | 2.1 | L. Uneken |
| Danilith Nokere Koerse | 1.Pro | A. Pieters |
| Omloop van de Westhoek | 1.1 | C. Majerus |
| Flèche Wallonne | 1.WWT | A. van der Breggen |
| Liège-Bastogne-Liège | 1.WWT | D. Vollering |
| GP Ciudad de Eibar | 1.1 | A. van der Breggen |
| Durango-Durango Emakumeen Saria | 1.1 | A. van der Breggen |
| Vuelta a Burgos – stage 4 | 2.WWT | A. van der Breggen |
| Vuelta a Burgos | 2.WWT | A. van der Breggen |
| Dwars door het Hageland | 1.2 | C. van den Broek-Blaak |
| National Championships Netherlands – ITT | NC | A. van der Breggen |
| National Championships Hungary – ITT | NC | K. B. Vas |
| National Championships Czech Republic – ITT | NC | N. Nosková |
| National Championships Luxembourg – ITT | NC | C. Majerus |
| National Championships Netherlands – RR | NC | A. Pieters |
| National Championships Luxembourg – RR | NC | C. Majerus |
| National Championships Hungary – RR | NC | K. B. Vas |
| La Course | 1.WWT | D. Vollering |
| Giro Donne – stage 2 | 2.Pro | A. van der Breggen |
| Giro Donne – stage 4 (ITT) | 2.Pro | A. van der Breggen |
| Giro Donne – stage 9 | 2.Pro | A. Moolman-Pasio |
| Giro Donne | 2.Pro | A. van der Breggen |
| Baloise Ladies Tour – stage 3 | 2.1 | L. Uneken |
| Simac Ladies Tour – stage 3 | 2.WWT | L. Uneken |
| Simac Ladies Tour | 2.WWT | C. van den Broek-Blaak |
| The Women's Tour – stage 2 | 2.WWT | A. Pieters |
| The Women's Tour – stage 3 (ITT) | 2.WWT | D. Vollering |
| The Women's Tour | 2.WWT | D. Vollering |
| Drenthe Acht van Westerveld | 1.2 | C. van den Broek-Blaak |

RIDER PROFILES

## ANNA VAN DER BREGGEN

Netherlands
18.04.90
Years Pro 10
Years On Team 5
Wins 62
UCI Ranking 5

In her final season before retirement, the 31-year-old won the Flèche Wallonne for the seventh consecutive time as well as the Omloop Het Nieuwsblad, the Vuelta a Burgos plus one stage and the Giro Donne plus two stages. She also won the Dutch ITT championships, took bronze in the Olympic ITT and helped her teammates to victories in Strade Bianche and Liège–Bastogne–Liège.

## DEMI VOLLERING

Netherlands
15.11.96
Years Pro 3
Years On Team 1
Wins 6
UCI Ranking 4

In a season when she never finished outside the top 25, she won Liège–Bastogne–Liège, La Course and the Women's Tour, was runner-up in the Amstel Gold Race and Brabantse Pijl, finished third in the Vuelta a Burgos and Giro Donne, and fifth in the Simac Ladies Tour. Additionally, she was in the top ten of the Strade Bianche, Tour of Flanders and the European and World Championships.

### KAROL-ANN CANUEL
Canada
18.04.88
Years Pro 12
Years On Team 6
Wins 6
UCI Ranking 137

### ELENA CECCHINI
Italy
25.05.92
Years Pro 11
Years On Team 1
Wins 12
UCI Ranking 48

### JOLIEN D'HOORE
Belgium
14.03.90
Years Pro 14
Years On Team 3
Wins 48
UCI Ranking 41

### NIAMH FISHER-BLACK
New Zealand
12.08.00
Years Pro 3
Years On Team 1
Wins 2
UCI Ranking 63

### ROXANE FOURNIER
France
07.11.91
Years Pro 12
Years on Team 1
Wins 9
UCI Ranking 395

### CHRISTINE MAJERUS
Luxembourg
25.02.87
Years Pro 14
Years On Team 8
Wins 39
UCI Ranking 35

### ASHLEIGH MOOLMAN-PASIO
South Africa
09.12.85
Years Pro 10
Years On Team 1
Wins 42
UCI Ranking 16

### NIKOLA NOSKOVÁ
Czech Republic
01.07.97
Years Pro 5
Years On Team 1
Wins 5
UCI Ranking 184

### AMY PIETERS
Netherlands
01.06.91
Years Pro 9
Years On Team 5
Wins 17
UCI Ranking 15

### ANNA SHACKLEY
Great Britain
17.05.01
Years Pro 1
Years On Team 1
Wins 0
UCI Ranking 87

### LONNEKE UNEKEN
Netherlands
02.03.00
Years Pro 3
Years On Team 2
Wins 3
UCI Ranking 82

### CHANTAL VAN DEN BROEK-BLAAK
Netherlands
22.10.89
Years Pro 9
Years On Team 7
Wins 26
UCI Ranking 21

### KATA BLANKA VAS
Hungary
03.09.01
Years Pro 2
Years On Team 1
Wins 3
UCI Ranking 43

TEAMS    WOMEN'S WORLDTOUR

# TEAM BIKEEXCHANGE

**2021 SEASON REVIEW**

With Van Vleuten gone, the Australian team could not replicate previous seasons' success. The team's biggest results were Brown's victories in Brugge–De Panne and on stage 1 of the Vuelta a Burgos, but she suffered a season-ending shoulder injury in August. Spratt had some good results, including fourth in the Amstel Gold Race, ninth in Flèche Wallonne and tenth in Liège–Bastogne–Liège, but could not perform to her best and was eventually diagnosed with iliac artery endofibrosis. In her last season before retirement, Kennedy finished second in the Santos Festival of Cycling, then reached the top 20 in the Amstel Gold Race and Flèche Wallonne before finishing 15th overall in the Tour de l'Ardèche. In the same race, Campbell won a stage, and Santesteban finished third overall. Santesteban also was runner-up in the Spanish championships, placed in the top ten in three Spanish one-day races and was 18th in Liège–Bastogne–Liège and the Vuelta a Burgos as well as 19th in the Brabantse Pijl. Williams won the New Zealand ITT and road race titles, while Roy became the Australian champion then finished eighth in Gent–Wevelgem and seventh in the Scheldeprijs, 23rd in Paris–Roubaix and 15th overall in the Women's Tour. (JK)

**TEAM INFORMATION**

| | |
|---|---|
| UCI CODE | **BEX** |
| UCI STATUS | **WOMEN'S WORLDTOUR** |
| COUNTRY | **AUSTRALIA** |
| FOUNDED | **2012** |

**TEAM NAME HISTORY**

| | |
|---|---|
| 2012–2016 | **ORICA-AIS** |
| 2017 | **ORICA-SCOTT** |
| 2018–2020 | **MITCHELTON-SCOTT** |
| 2021 | **TEAM BIKEEXCHANGE** |

**TEAM MANAGER**

**GENE BATES**

**2021 NEW RIDERS**

**ANE SANTESTEBAN, ARIANNA FIDANZA, TENIEL CAMPBELL, URŠKA ŽIGART**

**EQUIPMENT**

| | |
|---|---|
| BIKE | **BIANCHI** |

**2021 VICTORIES**

| | | |
|---|---|---|
| National Championships Australia – RR | NC | S. Roy |
| National Championships New Zealand – ITT | NC | G. Williams |
| National Championships New Zealand – RR | NC | G. Williams |
| Brugge–De Panne | 1.WWT | G. Brown |
| Setmana Ciclista Valenciana – stage 4 | 2.1 | U. Žigart |
| Vuelta a Burgos – stage 1 | 2.WWT | G. Brown |
| Tour de l'Ardèche – stage 6 | 2.1 | T. Campbell |

RIDER PROFILES

## GRACE BROWN

Australia
07.07.92
Years Pro 4
Years On Team 3
Wins 6
UCI Ranking 14

She had her best season to date, triumphing in Brugge–De Panne with a solo attack and winning stage 1 of the Vuelta a Burgos, where she finished seventh overall. She was third in the Tour of Flanders and fifth in La Course and missed an Olympic ITT medal by just 7 seconds before she had to end her season early due to a shoulder injury.

## AMANDA SPRATT

Australia
17.09.87
Years Pro 10
Years On Team 10
Wins 21
UCI Ranking 50

The diagnosis of iliac artery endofibrosis in October explained why she was off her best all year. Nevertheless, Spratt finished in the top ten of the Ardennes Classics and the top 20 of the Omloop Het Nieuwsblad, Strade Bianche and La Course. She was 14th in the Vuelta a Burgos and in the same position in the Giro Donne when she had to abandon after a crash.

### JESSICA ALLEN
Australia
17.04.93
Years Pro 9
Years On Team 6
Wins 1
UCI Ranking —

### TENIEL CAMPBELL
Trinidad & Tobago
23.09.97
Years Pro 3
Years On Team 1
Wins 6
UCI Ranking 120

### JANNEKE ENSING
Netherlands
21.09.86
Years Pro 13
Years On Team 2
Wins 3
UCI Ranking 139

### ARIANNA FIDANZA
Italy
06.01.95
Years Pro 8
Years On Team 1
Wins 2
UCI Ranking 192

### LUCY KENNEDY
Australia
11.07.88
Years Pro 4
Years On Team 4
Wins 8
UCI Ranking 227

### SARAH ROY
Australia
27.02.86
Years Pro 9
Years On Team 7
Wins 7
UCI Ranking 57

### ANE SANTESTEBAN
Spain
12.12.90
Years Pro 10
Years On Team 1
Wins 1
UCI Ranking 61

### MONIEK TENNIGLO
Netherlands
02.05.88
Years Pro 8
Years On Team 1
Wins 0
UCI Ranking —

### GEORGIA WILLIAMS
New Zealand
25.08.93
Years Pro 9
Years On Team 5
Wins 5
UCI Ranking 145

### URŠKA ŽIGART
Slovenia
04.12.96
Years Pro 7
Years On Team 1
Wins 2
UCI Ranking 179

TEAMS    WOMEN'S WORLDTOUR

# TEAM DSM

## 2021 SEASON REVIEW

The young squad often rode in support of Wiebes, who established herself as the strongest sprinter in the women's peloton with 12 victories. Labous brought results in stage races like the Giro Donne, Ladies Tour of Norway and Women's Tour as well as the hilly spring Classics. Lippert was runner-up in the European and German championships, finished fourth overall in the Thüringen Ladies Tour, fifth in the Ceratizit Challenge and eighth in La Course. Georgi won the GP Fourmies and the Under-23 classification in the Simac Ladies Tour, where she finished sixth overall, and placed eighth in the Women's Tour. Mackaij won stage 2 and the overall classification of the Trophée des Grimpeuses, was runner-up in Kreiz Breizh, and finished eighth in the Ceratizit Challenge, tenth in the Trofeo Binda and 17th in the Tour of Flanders. Rivera won the final stage of the Giro Donne and placed seventh in the Olympic road race, eighth in the GP de Plouay and tenth in the World Championships. Kirchmann was second overall in the Festival Elsy Jacobs and sixth in the Women's Tour.

## TEAM INFORMATION

| UCI CODE | **DSM** |
|---|---|
| UCI STATUS | **WOMEN'S WORLDTOUR** |
| COUNTRY | **NETHERLANDS** |
| FOUNDED | **2010** |

## TEAM NAME HISTORY

| 2010 | **SKIL-ARGOS** |
|---|---|
| 2011 | **SKIL-KOGA** |
| 2012 | **SKIL-ARGOS** |
| 2013 | **ARGOS-SHIMANO** |
| 2014 | **TEAM GIANT-SHIMANO** |
| 2015-2016 | **TEAM LIV-PLANTUR** |
| 2017-2020 | **TEAM SUNWEB** |
| 2021 | **TEAM DSM** |

## TEAM MANAGER

**HANS TIMMERMANS**

## 2021 NEW RIDERS

**ESMÉE PEPERKAMP, MEGAN JASTRAB**

## EQUIPMENT

| BIKE | **CERVÉLO** |
|---|---|

## 2021 VICTORIES

| | | |
|---|---|---|
| Scheldeprijs | 1.1 | L. Wiebes |
| Ceratizit Festival Elsy Jacobs – prologue | 2.Pro | L. Wiebes |
| GP Eco-Struct | 1.2 | L. Wiebes |
| Thüringen Ladies Tour – stage 2 | 2.Pro | L. Wiebes |
| Thüringen Ladies Tour – stage 6 | 2.Pro | L. Wiebes |
| Dwars door de Westhoek | 1.1 | L. Wiebes |
| Flanders Diamond Tour | 1.1 | L. Wiebes |
| Lotto Belgium Tour – stage 1 | 2.1 | L. Wiebes |
| Giro Donne – stage 5 | 2.Pro | L. Wiebes |
| Giro Donne – stage 8 | 2.Pro | L. Wiebes |
| Giro Donne – stage 10 | 2.Pro | C. Rivera |
| La Choralis Fourmies | 1.2 | P. Georgi |
| Trophée des Grimpeuses – stage 2 | 2.2 | F. Mackaij |
| Trophée des Grimpeuses | 2.2 | F. Mackaij |
| The Women's Tour – stage 4 | 2.WWT | L. Wiebes |
| The Women's Tour – stage 5 | 2.WWT | L. Wiebes |
| National Championships Great Britain – RR | NC | P. Georgi |
| Ronde van Drenthe | 1.WWT | L. Wiebes |

RIDER PROFILES

## LORENA WIEBES

Netherlands
17.03.99
Years Pro 4
Years On Team 2
Wins 36
UCI Ranking 20

She collected a host of victories from spring to autumn, focusing almost entirely on sprint races. This paid off with wins in the Scheldeprijs, the Festival Elsy Jacobs prologue, GP Eco-Struct, two stages of the Thüringen Ladies Tour, Dwars door de Westhoek, Flanders Diamond Tour, a stage of the Lotto Belgium Tour and two stages each of the Giro Donne and Women's Tour.

## JULIETTE LABOUS

France
04.11.98
Years Pro 5
Years On Team 5
Wins 2
UCI Ranking 23

The young Frenchwoman finished 16th in the Amstel Gold Race, sixth in the Flèche Wallonne, tenth in the Festival Elsy Jacobs and 18th in La Course. In stage races, she was seventh in the Giro Donne, eighth in the Ladies Tour of Norway, and runner-up in the Women's Tour. In between, she was ninth in the Olympic ITT and sixth in the World ITT Championships.

**SUSANNE ANDERSEN**
Norway
23.07.98
Years Pro 6
Years On Team 3
Wins 0
UCI Ranking 70

**PFEIFFER GEORGI**
Great Britain
27.09.00
Years Pro 3
Years On Team 3
Wins 2
UCI Ranking 38

**MEGAN JASTRAB**
United States
29.01.02
Years Pro 1
Years On Team 1
Wins 0
UCI Ranking 664

**LEAH KIRCHMANN**
Canada
30.06.90
Years Pro 9
Years On Team 6
Wins 12
UCI Ranking 60

**FRANZISKA KOCH**
Germany
13.07.00
Years Pro 3
Years On Team 3
Wins 1
UCI Ranking 81

**LIANE LIPPERT**
Germany
13.01.98
Years Pro 5
Years On Team 5
Wins 4
UCI Ranking 27

**FLOORTJE MACKAIJ**
Netherlands
18.10.95
Years Pro 9
Years On Team 9
Wins 8
UCI Ranking 42

**WILMA OLAUSSON**
Sweden
09.04.01
Years Pro 2
Years On Team 2
Wins 0
UCI Ranking 747

**ESMÉE PEPERKAMP**
Netherlands
23.07.97
Years Pro 1
Years On Team 1
Wins 0
UCI Ranking 931

**CORYN RIVERA**
United States
26.08.92
Years Pro 8
Years On Team 5
Wins 20
UCI Ranking 37

**JULIA SOEK**
Netherlands
12.12.90
Years Pro 9
Years On Team 8
Wins 1
UCI Ranking —

TEAMS    WOMEN'S WORLDTOUR

# TEAM TIBCO–SILICON VALLEY BANK

**2021 SEASON REVIEW**

Faulkner was the team's biggest revelation with a string of top results, somewhat outshining Stephens who won the US road race championships. Third in the US championships, Ewers was a mid-season addition to the team and went on to finish second at the Joe Martin Stage Race, finishing on the podium in every single stage, and fifth in the Tour de l'Ardèche. Yonamine was diagnosed with iliac artery endofibrosis but managed the injury in order to start at her home Olympics, where she finished 21st in the road race and 22nd in the time trial. Kessler won the sprints jersey at the Women's Tour. In her first senior season, Smith finished 16th in the GP de Plouay and Women's Tour and 17th in the GP Eco-Struct and Ceratizit Challenge. Gigante dominated the Santos Festival of Cycling with two stage wins and the overall victory, then took the Australian ITT title. In a promising spring campaign, she placed 11th in Dwars door Vlaanderen but sustained heavy injuries in a Flèche Wallonne crash. She recovered to participate in the Olympics, where she was 11th in the time trial.

**TEAM INFORMATION**

| UCI CODE | TIB |
| UCI STATUS | UCI WOMEN'S CONTINENTAL |
| COUNTRY | UNITED STATES |
| FOUNDED | 2007 |

**TEAM NAME HISTORY**

| 2007–2009 | TEAM TIBCO |
| 2010–2014 | TEAM TIBCO-TO THE TOP |
| 2015–2021 | TEAM TIBCO-SVB |

**TEAM MANAGER**

LINDA JACKSON

**2021 NEW RIDERS**

EVA BUURMAN, ERI YONAMINE, TANJA ERATH, VERONICA EWERS, EMMA LANGLEY, NICOLE FRAIN, ABI SMITH, CLARA HONSINGER, MADDY WARD

**EQUIPMENT**

| BIKE | CANNONDALE |

**2021 VICTORIES**

| National Championships Australia – ITT | NC | S. Gigante |
| National Championships United States – RR | NC | L. Stephens |
| Ladies Tour of Norway – stage 1 | 2.WWT | K. Faulkner |
| Joe Martin Stage Race – stage 2 | 2.2 | E. Langley |
| Joe Martin Stage Race – stage 3 (ITT) | 2.2 | E. Langley |

RIDER PROFILES

## KRISTEN FAULKNER

United States
18.12.92
| | |
|---|---|
| Years Pro | 2 |
| Years On Team | 2 |
| Wins | 2 |
| UCI Ranking | 24 |

In her first full pro season, Faulkner broke through with seventh in Gent–Wevelgem, tenth in the Tour of Flanders and top-20 results in Strade Bianche, Amstel Gold Race and Flèche Wallonne. After a solo victory on stage 1 of the Ladies Tour of Norway, she was sixth on the stage-3 summit finish and finished third on GC, then third at the GP de Plouay.

## LAUREN STEPHENS

United States
28.12.86
| | |
|---|---|
| Years Pro | 9 |
| Years On Team | 9 |
| Wins | 13 |
| UCI Ranking | 91 |

After a spring campaign with a tenth place in Gent–Wevelgem and top 20s in Trofeo Binda and Brabantse Pijl, she won the US national championships for the first time. In the second half of the season, she supported her teammates at the Joe Martin Stage Race and Tour de l'Ardèche while winning or finishing on the podium in various gravel races in between.

### EVA BUURMAN
Netherlands
07.09.94
| | |
|---|---|
| Years Pro | 6 |
| Years On Team | 1 |
| Wins | 0 |
| UCI Ranking | 856 |

### LEAH DIXON
Great Britain
26.08.91
| | |
|---|---|
| Years Pro | 3 |
| Years On Team | 3 |
| Wins | 0 |
| UCI Ranking | 587 |

### TANJA ERATH
Germany
07.10.89
| | |
|---|---|
| Years Pro | 4 |
| Years On Team | 1 |
| Wins | 0 |
| UCI Ranking | 475 |

### VERONICA EWERS
United States
01.09.94
| | |
|---|---|
| Years Pro | 1 |
| Years On Team | 1 |
| Wins | 0 |
| UCI Ranking | 111 |

### NICOLE FRAIN
Australia
24.08.92
| | |
|---|---|
| Years Pro | 1 |
| Years On Team | 1 |
| Wins | 0 |
| UCI Ranking | 494 |

### SARAH GIGANTE
Australia
06.10.00
| | |
|---|---|
| Years Pro | 2 |
| Years On Team | 2 |
| Wins | 3 |
| UCI Ranking | 123 |

### CLARA HONSINGER
United States
05.06.97
| | |
|---|---|
| Years Pro | 1 |
| Years On Team | 1 |
| Wins | 0 |
| UCI Ranking | 542 |

### NINA KESSLER
Netherlands
04.07.88
| | |
|---|---|
| Years Pro | 12 |
| Years On Team | 3 |
| Wins | 3 |
| UCI Ranking | 210 |

### EMMA LANGLEY
United States
23.11.95
| | |
|---|---|
| Years Pro | 2 |
| Years On Team | 1 |
| Wins | 2 |
| UCI Ranking | 431 |

### EMILY NEWSOM
United States
04.09.83
| | |
|---|---|
| Years Pro | 4 |
| Years On Team | 4 |
| Wins | 0 |
| UCI Ranking | 821 |

### DIANA PEÑUELA
Colombia
08.09.86
| | |
|---|---|
| Years Pro | 6 |
| Years On Team | 2 |
| Wins | 3 |
| UCI Ranking | 294 |

### ABI SMITH
Great Britain
01.04.02
| | |
|---|---|
| Years Pro | 1 |
| Years On Team | 1 |
| Wins | 0 |
| UCI Ranking | 207 |

### MADDY WARD
United States
25.07.94
| | |
|---|---|
| Years Pro | 1 |
| Years On Team | 1 |
| Wins | 0 |
| UCI Ranking | — |

### ERI YONAMINE
Japan
25.04.91
| | |
|---|---|
| Years Pro | 6 |
| Years On Team | 1 |
| Wins | 11 |
| UCI Ranking | 395 |

# TREK–SEGAFREDO WOMEN

**2021 SEASON REVIEW**

Hosking had to sit out for months due to a Covid-19 infection, then sprinted to a stage win in the Ladies Tour of Norway and followed this up with a stage in the Tour de l'Ardèche and good placings in the Women's Tour. After winning the World Cyclocross Championships, Brand won two stages and the GC of the Thüringen Ladies Tour, was part of the TTT-winning squad at the Giro Donne, where she took home the mountain jersey, and won a stage of the Tour de l'Ardèche. Deignan finished fourth overall in the Giro Donne, won the Tour de Suisse and made history as the first winner of the women's Paris–Roubaix. In her final season, Ruth Winder won the Brabantse Pijl and a stage in the Tour de l'Ardèche. Cordon-Ragot became the French ITT champion, while Dideriksen won the Danish road race title.

**TEAM INFORMATION**

| | |
|---|---|
| UCI CODE | TFS |
| UCI STATUS | WOMEN'S WORLDTOUR |
| COUNTRY | UNITED STATES |
| FOUNDED | 2020 |

**TEAM NAME HISTORY**

| | |
|---|---|
| 2019-2021 | TREK-SEGAFREDO WOMEN |

**TEAM MANAGER**

INA-YOKO TEUTENBERG

**2021 NEW RIDERS**

CHLOE HOSKING, AMALIE DIDERIKSEN

**EQUIPMENT**

| | |
|---|---|
| BIKE | TREK |

**2021 VICTORIES**

| | | |
|---|---|---|
| Healthy Ageing Tour – stage 2 (ITT) | 2.1 | E. van Dijk |
| Healthy Ageing Tour | 2.1 | E. van Dijk |
| Trofeo Alfredo Binda | 1.WWT | E. Longo Borghini |
| Brabantse Pijl | 1.1 | R. Winder |
| Thüringen Ladies Tour – stage 3 | 2.Pro | L. Brand |
| Thüringen Ladies Tour – stage 5 | 2.Pro | L. Brand |
| Thüringen Ladies Tour | 2.Pro | L. Brand |
| Tour de Suisse | 2.1 | E. Deignan |
| National Championships France – ITT | NC | A. Cordon-Ragot |
| National Championships Italy – ITT | NC | E. Longo Borghini |
| National Championships Denmark – RR | NC | A. Dideriksen |
| National Championships Italy – RR | NC | E. Longo Borghini |
| Lotto Belgium Tour – prologue | 2.1 | E. van Dijk |
| Giro Donne– stage 1 (TTT) | 2.Pro | TTT |
| Ladies Tour of Norway – stage 4 | 2.WWT | C. Hosking |
| GP de Plouay | 1.WWT | E. Longo Borghini |
| Tour de l'Ardèche – stage 3 | 2.1 | C. Hosking |
| Tour de l'Ardèche – stage 4 | 2.1 | R. Winder |
| Tour de l'Ardèche – stage 7 | 2.1 | L. Brand |
| Paris–Roubaix | 1.WWT | E. Deignan |

RIDER PROFILES

### ELISA LONGO BORGHINI

Italy
10.12.91
Years Pro 11
Years On Team 3
Wins 29
UCI Ranking 2

In her most successful season, she won the Trofeo Binda and GP de Plouay, finished on the podium at Strade Bianche, Flèche Wallonne, Liège–Bastogne–Liège and Paris–Roubaix, and won Olympic road race bronze. She also defended the Italian ITT and RR titles, won the mixed relay European Championships and achieved top-ten results in a string of other races.

### ELLEN VAN DIJK

Netherlands
11.02.87
Years Pro 16
Years On Team 3
Wins 57
UCI Ranking 13

She won the Healthy Ageing Tour, was runner-up in the Lotto Belgium Tour and third in the Simac Ladies Tour – all due to her time trial abilities. Runner-up in the European ITT Championships, Van Dijk then won the road race and the World ITT Championships. Finally, she placed tenth in Strade Bianche and the Clásica San Sebastián.

---

**ELYNOR BÄCKSTEDT**
Great Britain
06.12.01
Years Pro 2
Years On Team 2
Wins 0
UCI Ranking 739

**LUCINDA BRAND**
Netherlands
02.07.89
Years Pro 9
Years On Team 2
Wins 21
UCI Ranking 29

**AUDREY CORDON-RAGOT**
France
22.09.89
Years Pro 14
Years On Team 3
Wins 16
UCI Ranking 62

**ELIZABETH DEIGNAN**
Great Britain
18.12.88
Years Pro 15
Years On Team 3
Wins 43
UCI Ranking 22

**AMALIE DIDERIKSEN**
Denmark
24.05.96
Years Pro 7
Years On Team 1
Wins 13
UCI Ranking 101

**LAURETTA HANSON**
Australia
29.10.94
Years Pro 6
Years On Team 3
Wins 1
UCI Ranking 160

**CHLOE HOSKING**
Australia
01.10.90
Years Pro 12
Years On Team 1
Wins 39
UCI Ranking 59

**LETIZIA PATERNOSTER**
Italy
22.07.99
Years Pro 4
Years On Team 3
Wins 4
UCI Ranking 1079

**SHIRIN VAN ANROOIJ**
Netherlands
05.02.02
Years Pro 1
Years On Team 1
Wins 0
UCI Ranking 128

**TAYLER WILES**
United States
20.07.89
Years Pro 9
Years On Team 3
Wins 8
UCI Ranking 125

**RUTH WINDER**
United States
09.07.93
Years Pro 8
Years On Team 3
Wins 17
UCI Ranking 28

**TRIXI WORRACK**
Germany
28.09.81
Years Pro 18
Years On Team 3
Wins 47
UCI Ranking —

TEAMS    WOMEN'S WORLDTOUR

# VALCAR TRAVEL & SERVICE

### 2021 SEASON REVIEW

As a team that prides itself on developing talents, the Italian squad lost Campbell and Cavalli before the 2021 season and has to let Balsamo go after this year too – but the 23-year-old sprinter had a parting gift as she won the World Championships and then went on to sprint to victory on stage 6 of the Women's Tour wearing her new rainbow jersey. Consonni won the Ronde de Mouscron and Vuelta CV Feminas and achieved several other top-ten places, including podium places on stages of the Ladies Tour of Norway and Women's Tour. Guazzini, Alzini and Balsamo were part of the Italian pursuit team that finished sixth in the Olympics. Guazzini also was fourth in Dwars door Vlaanderen and 12th in the Brabantse Pijl and won the Under-23 European ITT Championships where Pirrone finished third. Malcotti was the team's strongest card in hilly Classics, finishing fourth in Tre Valli Varesine, eighth in the Giro dell'Emilia and 12th in the Under-23 European RR Championships. Sanguineti was third in the Italian road race championships and eighth in Dwars door het Hageland. Italian cyclocross champion Arzuffi mainly did stage races in her road season, finishing 16th in the Ladies Tour of Norway.

### TEAM INFORMATION

| UCI CODE | VAL |
| --- | --- |
| UCI STATUS | UCI WOMEN'S CONTINENTAL |
| COUNTRY | ITALY |
| FOUNDED | 2017 |

### TEAM NAME HISTORY

| 2017-2018 | VALCAR PBM |
| --- | --- |
| 2019 | VALCAR CYLANCE CYCLING |
| 2020-2021 | VALCAR TRAVEL & SERVICE |

### TEAM MANAGER

DAVIDE ARZENI

### 2021 NEW RIDERS

ALICE MARIA ARZUFFI,
ELEONORA CAMILLA GASPARRINI,
ELIZABETH STANNARD,
MATILDE BERTOLINI

### EQUIPMENT

| BIKE | CANNONDALE |
| --- | --- |

### 2021 VICTORIES

| GP Oetingen | 1.2 | E. Balsamo |
| Ronde de Mouscron | 1.1 | C. Consonni |
| Vuelta CV Feminas | 1.1 | C. Consonni |
| The Women's Tour – stage 6 | 2.WWT | E. Balsamo |
| GP du Morbihan | 1.1 | C. Consonni |

RIDER PROFILES

### ELISA BALSAMO
Italy
27.02.98
Years Pro 5
Years On Team 5
Wins 10
UCI Ranking 12

The young Italian sprinter won the GP Oetingen, finished on the podium in the Scheldeprijs and Brabantse Pijl, and achieved top-ten results in Trofeo Binda, Brugge–De Panne and Gent–Wevelgem. She had a disappointing Olympic track campaign without any medals. Runner-up in the GP d'Isbergues, she then sprinted to the world title and won the final stage of the Women's Tour in the rainbow jersey.

### CHIARA CONSONNI
Italy
24.06.99
Years Pro 4
Years On Team 4
Wins 4
UCI Ranking 38

Another sprint talent, Consonni won the Ronde de Mouscron and Vuelta CV Feminas in April. Later, she was runner-up in the Flanders Diamond Tour and on stage 4 of the Women's Tour. She also placed third on the final stage of the Ladies Tour of Norway as well as ninth on stage 3 of the Simac Ladies Tour.

### MARTINA ALZINI
Italy
10.02.97
Years Pro 6
Years On Team 2
Wins 0
UCI Ranking 222

### ALICE MARIA ARZUFFI
Italy
19.11.94
Years Pro 9
Years On Team 1
Wins 0
UCI Ranking 423

### MATILDE BERTOLINI
Italy
24.09.02
Years Pro 1
Years On Team 1
Wins 0
UCI Ranking –

### ELEONORA CAMILLA GASPARRINI
Italy
25.03.02
Years Pro 1
Years On Team 1
Wins 0
UCI Ranking 68

### VITTORIA GUAZZINI
Italy
26.12.00
Years Pro 3
Years On Team 3
Wins 0
UCI Ranking 139

### SILVIA MAGRI
Italy
17.10.00
Years Pro 3
Years On Team 2
Wins 0
UCI Ranking 255

### BARBARA MALCOTTI
Italy
19.02.00
Years Pro 3
Years On Team 3
Wins 0
UCI Ranking 160

### SILVIA PERSICO
Italy
25.07.97
Years Pro 5
Years On Team 5
Wins 0
UCI Ranking 130

### FEDERICA DAMIANA PIERGIOVANNI
Italy
30.07.01
Year Pro 2
Years On Team 2
Wins 0
UCI Ranking 344

### ELENA PIRRONE
Italy
21.02.99
Years Pro 4
Years On Team 3
Wins 0
UCI Ranking 300

### SILVIA POLLICINI
Italy
31.12.98
Years Pro 5
Years On Team 5
Wins 0
UCI Ranking 825

### ILARIA SANGUINETI
Italy
15.04.94
Years Pro 9
Years On Team 4
Wins 3
UCI Ranking 187

### ELIZABETH STANNARD
Australia
27.05.97
Years Pro 1
Years On Team 1
Wins 0
UCI Ranking 399

### MIRIAM VECE
Italy
16.03.97
Years Pro 5
Years On Team 5
Wins 0
UCI Ranking –

### MARGAUX VIGIE
France
21.07.95
Years Pro 2
Years On Team 2
Wins 0
UCI Ranking 664

TEAMS  MEN'S PRO CONTINENTAL

# ALPECIN–FENIX

## 2021 VICTORIES

| | | |
|---|---|---|
| UAE Tour – stage 1 | 2.UWT | M. van der Poel |
| Le Samyn | 1.1 | T. Merlier |
| Strade Bianche | 1.UWT | M. van der Poel |
| GP Jean-Pierre Monseré | 1.1 | T. Merlier |
| Tirreno–Adriatico – stage 3 | 2.UWT | M. van der Poel |
| Tirreno–Adriatico – stage 5 | 2.UWT | M. van der Poel |
| Bredene Koksijde Classic | 1.Pro | T. Merlier |
| Scheldeprijs | 1.Pro | J. Philipsen |
| Presidential Cycling Tour of Turkey – stage 6 | 2.Pro | J. Philipsen |
| Presidential Cycling Tour of Turkey – stage 7 | 2.Pro | J. Philipsen |
| Giro d'Italia – stage 2 | 2.UWT | T. Merlier |
| Ronde van Limburg | 1.1 | T. Merlier |
| Tour de Suisse – stage 2 | 2.UWT | M. van der Poel |
| Tour de Suisse – stage 3 | 2.UWT | M. van der Poel |
| National Championships Austria Under-23 – ITT | NC | T. Bayer |
| National Championships Switzerland – RR | NC | S. Dillier |
| Tour de France – stage 2 | 2.UWT | M. van der Poel |
| Tour de France – stage 3 | 2.UWT | T. Merlier |
| Vuelta a Burgos – stage 1 | 2.Pro | E. Planckaert |
| Arctic Race of Norway – stage 4 | 2.Pro | P. Walsleben |
| Vuelta a España – stage 2 | 2.UWT | J. Philipsen |
| Vuelta a España – stage 5 | 2.UWT | J. Philipsen |
| Benelux Tour – stage 1 | 2.UWT | T. Merlier |
| Benelux Tour – stage 4 | 2.UWT | T. Merlier |
| Antwerp Port Epic | 1.1 | M. van der Poel |
| Tour de Luxembourg – stage 3 | 2.Pro | S. Modolo |
| Kampioenschap van Vlaanderen | 1.1 | J. Philipsen |
| Eschborn-Frankfurt | 1.UWT | J. Philipsen |
| GP de Denain | 1.Pro | J. Philipsen |
| Paris–Chauny | 1.1 | J. Philipsen |
| Giro del Veneto | 1.1 | X. Meurisse |

## TEAM INFORMATION

| | |
|---|---|
| UCI CODE | AFC |
| UCI STATUS | MEN'S PROTEAM |
| COUNTRY | BELGIUM |
| FOUNDED | 2009 |

### TEAM NAME HISTORY

| | |
|---|---|
| 2009–2015 | BKCP-POWERPLUS |
| 2016–2017 | BEOBANK-CORENDON |
| 2018–2019 | CORENDON-CIRCUS |
| 2020–2021 | ALPECIN-FENIX |

### TEAM MANAGER

CHRISTOPH ROODHOOFT

### 2021 NEW RIDERS

JASPER PHILIPSEN, SILVAN DILLIER, XANDRO MEURISSE, JULIEN VERMOTE, LAURENS DE VREESE, EDWARD PLANCKAERT, LIONEL TAMINIAUX, JAY VINE, TOBIAS BAYER, EDWARD ANDERSON

### EQUIPMENT

BIKE  CANYON

## RIDERS

**EDWARD ANDERSON**
United States
18.04.98
Years Pro 1
Years On Team 1
Grand Tour Apps 0
Wins 0
UCI Ranking —

**TOBIAS BAYER**
Austria
17.11.99
Years Pro 1
Years On Team 1
Grand Tour Apps 1
Wins 0
UCI Ranking 303

**DRIES DE BONDT**
Belgium
04.07.91
Years Pro 5
Years On Team 3
Grand Tour Apps 1
Wins 5
UCI Ranking 368

**FLORIS DE TIER**
Belgium
20.01.92
Years Pro 7
Years On Team 2
Grand Tour Apps 3
Wins 0
UCI Ranking —

**LAURENS DE VREESE**
Belgium
29.09.88
Years Pro 11
Years On Team 1
Grand Tour Apps 8
Wins 0
UCI Ranking 1568

**SILVAN DILLIER**
Switzerland
03.08.90
Years Pro 8
Years On Team 1
Grand Tour Apps 7
Wins 8
UCI Ranking 334

**ROY JANS**
Belgium
15.09.90
Years Pro 9
Years On Team 3
Grand Tour Apps 0
Wins 3
UCI Ranking —

**JIMMY JANSSENS**
Belgium
30.05.89
Years Pro 3
Years On Team 3
Grand Tour Apps 1
Wins 0
UCI Ranking 1956

**ALEXANDER KRIEGER**
Germany
28.11.91
Years Pro 2
Years On Team 2
Grand Tour Apps 2
Wins 0
UCI Ranking 1371

**SENNE LEYSEN**
Belgium
18.03.96
Years Pro 4
Years On Team 2
Grand Tour Apps 1
Wins 0
UCI Ranking 2005

**MARCEL MEISEN**
Germany
08.01.89
Years Pro 3
Years On Team 4
Grand Tour Apps 0
Wins 1
UCI Ranking 905

**TIM MERLIER**
Belgium
30.10.92
Years Pro 5
Years On Team 3
Grand Tour Apps 2
Wins 18
UCI Ranking 19

**XANDRO MEURISSE**
Belgium
31.01.92
Years Pro 5
Years On Team 1
Grand Tour Apps 2
Wins 5
UCI Ranking 281

**SACHA MODOLO**
Italy
19.06.87
Years Pro 12
Years On Team 2
Grand Tour Apps 12
Wins 47
UCI Ranking —

**JASPER PHILIPSEN**
Belgium
02.03.98
Years Pro 4
Years On Team 1
Grand Tour Apps 4
Wins 14
UCI Ranking 15

TEAMS    MEN'S PRO CONTINENTAL

**RIDERS (CONT)**

### EDWARD PLANCKAERT
Belgium
01.02.95
| | |
|---|---|
| Years Pro | 5 |
| Years On Team | 5 |
| Grand Tour Apps | 1 |
| Wins | 1 |
| UCI Ranking | 1028 |

### ALEXANDER RICHARDSON
Great Britain
30.04.90
| | |
|---|---|
| Years Pro | 2 |
| Years On Team | 2 |
| Grand Tour Apps | 0 |
| Wins | 0 |
| UCI Ranking | — |

### JONAS RICKAERT
Belgium
07.02.94
| | |
|---|---|
| Years Pro | 8 |
| Years On Team | 3 |
| Grand Tour Apps | 1 |
| Wins | 1 |
| UCI Ranking | 245 |

### OSCAR RIESEBEEK
Netherlands
23.12.92
| | |
|---|---|
| Years Pro | 5 |
| Years On Team | 2 |
| Grand Tour Apps | 1 |
| Wins | 0 |
| UCI Ranking | 250 |

### KRISTIAN SBARAGLI
Italy
08.05.90
| | |
|---|---|
| Years Pro | 9 |
| Years On Team | 2 |
| Grand Tour Apps | 8 |
| Wins | 1 |
| UCI Ranking | 165 |

### DIETHER SWEECK
Belgium
17.12.93
| | |
|---|---|
| Years Pro | 1 |
| Years On Team | 1 |
| Grand Tour Apps | 0 |
| Wins | 0 |
| UCI Ranking | — |

### LIONEL TAMINIAUX
Belgium
21.05.96
| | |
|---|---|
| Years Pro | 3 |
| Years On Team | 1 |
| Grand Tour Apps | 0 |
| Wins | 1 |
| UCI Ranking | 497 |

### SCOTT THWAITES
Great Britain
12.02.90
| | |
|---|---|
| Years Pro | 9 |
| Years On Team | 2 |
| Grand Tour Apps | 3 |
| Wins | 0 |
| UCI Ranking | 2087 |

### BEN TULETT
Great Britain
26.08.01
| | |
|---|---|
| Years Pro | 2 |
| Years On Team | 2 |
| Grand Tour Apps | 0 |
| Wins | 0 |
| UCI Ranking | 271 |

### PETR VAKOC
Czech Republic
11.07.92
| | |
|---|---|
| Years Pro | 8 |
| Years On Team | 2 |
| Grand Tour Apps | 3 |
| Wins | 7 |
| UCI Ranking | 668 |

### DAVID VAN DER POEL
Netherlands
15.06.92
| | |
|---|---|
| Years Pro | 3 |
| Years On Team | 11 |
| Grand Tour Apps | 0 |
| Wins | 0 |
| UCI Ranking | 1956 |

### MATHIEU VAN DER POEL
Netherlands
19.01.95
| | |
|---|---|
| Years Pro | 3 |
| Years On Team | 8 |
| Grand Tour Apps | 1 |
| Wins | 35 |
| UCI Ranking | 7 |

### OTTO VERGAERDE
Belgium
15.07.94
| | |
|---|---|
| Years Pro | 8 |
| Years On Team | 3 |
| Grand Tour Apps | 0 |
| Wins | 0 |
| UCI Ranking | — |

### GIANNI VERMEERSCH
Belgium
19.11.92
| | |
|---|---|
| Years Pro | 3 |
| Years On Team | 5 |
| Grand Tour Apps | 1 |
| Wins | 2 |
| UCI Ranking | 78 |

### JULIEN VERMOTE
Belgium
26.07.89
| | |
|---|---|
| Years Pro | 11 |
| Years On Team | 1 |
| Grand Tour Apps | 7 |
| Wins | 3 |
| UCI Ranking | — |

### LOUIS VERVAEKE
Belgium
06.10.93
| | |
|---|---|
| Years Pro | 8 |
| Years On Team | 2 |
| Grand Tour Apps | 5 |
| Wins | 0 |
| UCI Ranking | 767 |

### JAY VINE
Australia
16.11.95
| | |
|---|---|
| Years Pro | 1 |
| Years On Team | 1 |
| Grand Tour Apps | 1 |
| Wins | 0 |
| UCI Ranking | 397 |

### PHILIPP WALSLEBEN
Germany
19.11.87
| | |
|---|---|
| Years Pro | 3 |
| Years On Team | 11 |
| Grand Tour Apps | 0 |
| Wins | 2 |
| UCI Ranking | 295 |

TEAMS   MEN'S PRO CONTINENTAL

# ANDRONI GIOCATTOLI-SIDERMEC

## 2021 VICTORIES

| | | |
|---|---|---|
| Vuelta al Tachira – stage 1 | 2.2 | M. Malucelli |
| Vuelta al Tachira – stage 8 | 2.2 | S. Pellaud |
| Tour du Rwanda – stage 7 (ITT) | 2.1 | J. Restrepo |
| National Championships Ecuador – RR | NC | J. A. Cepeda |
| National Championships Ukraine – RR | NC | A. Ponomar |
| Tour Alsace – stage 3 | 2.2 | S. Umba |
| Le Tour de Savoie Mont Blanc – stage 1 | 2.2 | S. Umba |
| Le Tour de Savoie Mont Blanc – stage 2 | 2.2 | J. A. Cepeda |
| Le Tour de Savoie Mont Blanc | 2.2 | J. A. Cepeda |
| Turul Romaniei – prologue | 2.1 | J. Pelikán |
| Turul Romaniei – stage 2 | 2.1 | D. Muñoz |
| Le Tour de Bretagne Cycliste – stage 5 | 2.2 | L. Marchiori |

## RIDERS

**MATTIA BAIS**
Italy
19.10.96
Years Pro 2
Years On Team 2
Grand Tour Apps 1
Wins 0
UCI Ranking 523

**ALESSANDRO BISOLTI**
Italy
07.03.85
Years Pro 15
Years On Team 4
Grand Tour Apps 4
Wins 0
UCI Ranking 1420

**JEFFERSON ALEXANDER CEPEDA**
Ecuador
16.06.98
Years Pro 2
Years On Team 2
Grand Tour Apps 0
Wins 3
UCI Ranking 269

**LUCA CHIRICO**
Italy
16.07.92
Years Pro 7
Years On Team 2
Grand Tour Apps 2
Wins 0
UCI Ranking 471

**ŽIGA JERMAN**
Slovenia
26.06.98
Years Pro 1
Years On Team 1
Grand Tour Apps 0
Wins 0
UCI Ranking 1068

**MATTEO MALUCELLI**
Italy
20.10.93
Years Pro 5
Years On Team 1
Grand Tour Apps 0
Wins 4
UCI Ranking 1140

**LEONARDO MARCHIORI**
Italy
13.06.98
Years Pro 1
Years On Team 1
Grand Tour Apps 0
Wins 0
UCI Ranking 1037

**DANIEL MUÑOZ**
Colombia
21.11.96
Years Pro 3
Years On Team 3
Grand Tour Apps 0
Wins 3
UCI Ranking 516

**JÁNOS PELIKÁN**
Hungary
19.04.95
Years Pro 2
Years On Team 2
Grand Tour Apps 0
Wins 4
UCI Ranking 1037

**SIMON PELLAUD**
Switzerland
06.11.92
Years Pro 7
Years On Team 2
Grand Tour Apps 4
Wins 1
UCI Ranking 392

**ANDRII PONOMAR**
Ukraine
05.09.02
Years Pro 0
Years On Team 0
Grand Tour Apps 1
Wins 1
UCI Ranking 560

**SIMONE RAVANELLI**
Italy
04.07.95
Years Pro 2
Years On Team 2
Grand Tour Apps 2
Wins 0
UCI Ranking 761

**JHONATAN RESTREPO**
Colombia
28.11.94
Years Pro 6
Years On Team 2
Grand Tour Apps 3
Wins 5
UCI Ranking 182

**JOSIP RUMAC**
Croatia
26.10.94
Years Pro 3
Years On Team 3
Grand Tour Apps 1
Wins 6
UCI Ranking 1515

**EDUARDO SEPÚLVEDA**
Argentina
13.06.91
Years Pro 9
Years On Team 1
Grand Tour Apps 6
Wins 3
UCI Ranking 232

**FILIPPO TAGLIANI**
Italy
14.08.95
Years Pro 1
Years On Team 1
Grand Tour Apps 1
Wins 0
UCI Ranking 905

**NATNEAL TESFATSION**
Eritrea
23.05.99
Years Pro 1
Years On Team 1
Grand Tour Apps 1
Wins 0
UCI Ranking 459

**SANTIAGO UMBA**
Colombia
20.11.02
Years Pro 1
Years On Team 1
Grand Tour Apps 0
Wins 0
UCI Ranking 551

**NICOLA VENCHIARUTTI**
Italy
07.10.98
Years Pro 2
Years On Team 2
Grand Tour Apps 1
Wins 0
UCI Ranking 2033

**MATTIA VIEL**
Italy
22.04.95
Years Pro 3
Years On Team 3
Grand Tour Apps 0
Wins 0
UCI Ranking —

**MARTÍ VIGO**
Spain
22.12.97
Years Pro 1
Years On Team 1
Grand Tour Apps 0
Wins 0
UCI Ranking —

## TEAM INFORMATION

| | |
|---|---|
| UCI CODE | ANS |
| UCI STATUS | MEN'S PROTEAM |
| COUNTRY | ITALY |
| FOUNDED | 1981 |

## TEAM NAME HISTORY

| | |
|---|---|
| 1997–1998 | KROSS-SELLE ITALIA |
| 1999 | SELLE ITALIA |
| 2000 | AGUARDIENTE NECTAR-SELLE ITALIA 2000 |
| 2001 | SELLE ITALIA-PACIFIC |
| 2002 | COLOMBIA-SELLE ITALIA |
| 2003 | COLOMBIA-SELLE ITALIA |
| 2004–2005 | COLOMBIA-SELLE ITALIA |
| 2006 | SELLE ITALIA-SERRAMENTI DIQUIGIOVANNI |
| 2007–2009 | SERRAMENTI PVC DIQUIGIOVANNI-ANDRONI GIOCATTOLI |
| 2010–2011 | ANDRONI GIOCATTOLI-SERRAMENTI PVC DIQUIGIOVANNI |
| 2012–2014 | ANDRONI GIOCATTOLI-VENEZUELA |
| 2015–2016 | ANDRONI GIOCATTOLI-SIDERMEC |
| 2017 | ANDRONI-SIDERMEC-BOTTECCHIA |
| 2018–2021 | ANDRONI GIOCATTOLI-SIDERMEC |

## TEAM MANAGER

**GIANNI SAVIO**

## 2021 NEW RIDERS

**EDUARDO SEPÚLVEDA, MATTEO MALUCELLI, NATNEAL TESFATSION, ŽIGA JERMAN, FILIPPO TAGLIANI, SANTIAGO UMBA, ANDRII PONOMAR, LEONARDO MARCHIORI, MARTÍ VIGO**

## 2021 STAGIAIRES

**CRISTIAN ROCCHETTA, MANUELE TAROZZI, SAMUELE ZAMBELLI**

## EQUIPMENT

| | |
|---|---|
| BIKE | BOTTECCHIA |

TEAMS  MEN'S PRO CONTINENTAL

# B&B HOTELS P/B KTM

## 2021 VICTORIES

| | | |
|---|---|---|
| Tour du Rwanda – stage 2 | 2.1 | A. Boileau |
| Tour du Rwanda – stage 3 | 2.1 | A. Boileau |
| Tour du Rwanda – stage 5 | 2.1 | A. Boileau |
| Tour du Rwanda – stage 6 | 2.1 | P. Rolland |
| Le Tour de Savoie Mont Blanc – prologue | 2.2 | M. Chevalier |
| Le Tour de Savoie Mont Blanc – stage 3 | 2.2 | A. Boileau |

## TEAM INFORMATION

| | |
|---|---|
| UCI CODE | BBK |
| UCI STATUS | MEN'S PROTEAM |
| COUNTRY | FRANCE |
| FOUNDED | 2018 |

## TEAM NAME HISTORY

| | |
|---|---|
| 2018 | VITAL CONCEPT CYCLING CLUB |
| 2019 | VITAL CONCEPT-B&B HOTELS |
| 2020 | B&B HOTELS - VITAL CONCEPT P/B KTM |
| 2021 | B&B HOTELS P/B KTM |

## TEAM MANAGER

JÉRÔME PINEAU

## 2021 NEW RIDERS

JONATHAN HIVERT, CYRIL LEMOINE, ELIOT LIETAER, FRANCK BONNAMOUR, QUENTIN JAUREGUI, NICOLA BAGIOLI, THIBAULT FERASSE

## 2021 STAGIAIRES

FLORIAN DAUPHIN, ADRIEN LAGRÉE, AXEL LAURANCE

## EQUIPMENT

| | |
|---|---|
| BIKE | KTM |

## RIDERS

**FREDERIK BACKAERT**
Belgium
13.03.90
Years Pro 8
Years On Team 2
Grand Tour Apps 2
Wins 1
UCI Ranking 2087

**ALAN BOILEAU**
France
25.06.99
Years Pro 1
Years On Team 1
Grand Tour Apps 0
Wins 3
UCI Ranking 497

**MAXIME CHEVALIER**
France
16.05.99
Years Pro 2
Years On Team 2
Grand Tour Apps 0
Wins 0
UCI Ranking 510

**JENS DEBUSSCHERE**
Belgium
28.08.89
Years Pro 11
Years On Team 2
Grand Tour Apps 8
Wins 15
UCI Ranking 455

**JONATHAN HIVERT**
France
23.03.85
Years Pro 16
Years On Team 1
Grand Tour Apps 4
Wins 17
UCI Ranking 644

**ELIOT LIETAER**
Belgium
15.08.90
Years Pro 10
Years On Team 1
Grand Tour Apps 0
Wins 1
UCI Ranking 551

**KÉVIN REZA**
France
18.05.88
Years Pro 11
Years On Team 4
Grand Tour Apps 6
Wins 0
UCI Ranking —

**NICOLA BAGIOLI**
Italy
19.02.95
Years Pro 5
Years On Team 1
Grand Tours 1
Wins 0
UCI Ranking —

**FRANCK BONNAMOUR**
France
20.06.95
Years Pro 6
Years On Team 1
Grand Tour Apps 1
Wins 0
UCI Ranking 109

**BRYAN COQUARD**
France
25.04.92
Years Pro 9
Years On Team 4
Grand Tour Apps 5
Wins 45
UCI Ranking 113

**THIBAULT FERASSE**
France
12.09.94
Years Pro 1
Years On Team 1
Grand Tour Apps 0
Wins 1
UCI Ranking 572

**QUENTIN JAUREGUI**
France
22.04.94
Years Pro 7
Years On Team 1
Grand Tour Apps 5
Wins 1
UCI Ranking —

**JULIEN MORICE**
France
20.07.91
Years Pro 7
Years On Team 1
Grand Tour Apps 1
Wins 1
UCI Ranking —

**PIERRE ROLLAND**
France
10.10.86
Years Pro 15
Years On Team 3
Grand Tour Apps 18
Wins 12
UCI Ranking 1089

**CYRIL BARTHE**
France
14.02.96
Years Pro 4
Years On Team 2
Grand Tour Apps 3
Wins 0
UCI Ranking 443

**MAXIME CAM**
France
09.07.92
Years Pro 7
Years On Team 3
Grand Tour Apps 0
Wins 0
UCI Ranking 2302

**BERT DE BACKER**
Belgium
02.04.84
Years Pro 13
Years On Team 4
Grand Tour Apps 4
Wins 1
UCI Ranking 1173

**CYRIL GAUTIER**
France
26.09.87
Years Pro 13
Years On Team 3
Grand Tour Apps 11
Wins 5
UCI Ranking 726

**JÉRÉMY LECROQ**
France
07.04.95
Years Pro 4
Years On Team 4
Grand Tour Apps 0
Wins 0
UCI Ranking 303

**LUCA MOZZATO**
Italy
15.02.98
Years Pro 2
Years On Team 2
Grand Tour Apps 0
Wins 0
UCI Ranking 120

**SEBASTIAN SCHÖNBERGER**
Austria
14.05.94
Years Pro 4
Years On Team 2
Grand Tour Apps 0
Wins 0
UCI Ranking 390

**CYRIL LEMOINE**
France
03.03.83
Years Pro 17
Years On Team 1
Grand Tour Apps 10
Wins 0
UCI Ranking 668

**QUENTIN PACHER**
France
06.01.92
Years Pro 6
Years On Team 4
Grand Tour Apps 2
Wins 0
UCI Ranking 306

**JONAS VAN GENECHTEN**
Belgium
16.09.86
Years Pro 10
Years On Team 4
Grand Tour Apps 2
Wins 8
UCI Ranking —

TEAMS    MEN'S PRO CONTINENTAL

# BARDIANI CSF FAIZANE

### 2021 VICTORIES

| | | | |
|---|---|---|---|
| GP Alanya | 1.2 | D. Gabburo | |
| Trofej Poreč | 1.2 | F. Fiorelli | |
| Istrian Spring Trophy – stage 2 | 2.2 | F. Zana | |
| GP Slovenian Istria | 1.2 | M. Maestri | |
| GP Slovenia | 1.2 | M. Maestri | |
| Tour of Bulgaria – stage 1 | 2.2 | G. Lonardi | |
| Sazka Tour | 2.1 | F. Zana | |

### RIDERS

**ENRICO BATTAGLIN**
Italy
17.11.89
Years Pro 10
Years On Team 1
Grand Tour Apps 12
Wins 4
UCI Ranking 542

**LUCA COVILI**
Italy
10.02.97
Years Pro 3
Years On Team 3
Grand Tour Apps 2
Wins 0
UCI Ranking 567

**DAVIDE GABBURO**
Italy
01.04.93
Years Pro 3
Years On Team 2
Grand Tour Apps 1
Wins 0
UCI Ranking 415

**MIRCO MAESTRI**
Italy
26.10.91
Years Pro 6
Years On Team 6
Grand Tour Apps 4
Wins 1
UCI Ranking 629

**ALESSANDRO MONACO**
Italy
04.02.98
Years Pro 2
Years On Team 2
Grand Tour Apps 0
Wins 0
UCI Ranking 1004

**TOMAS TRAININI**
Italy
23.09.01
Years Pro 1
Years On Team 1
Grand Tour Apps 0
Wins 0
UCI Ranking —

**ENRICO ZANONCELLO**
Italy
02.08.97
Years Pro 1
Years On Team 1
Grand Tour Apps 0
Wins 0
UCI Ranking 1420

**JOHNATAN CAÑAVERAL**
Colombia
02.11.96
Years Pro 1
Years On Team 1
Grand Tour Apps 0
Wins 0
UCI Ranking —

**NICOLAS DALLA VALLE**
Italy
13.09.97
Years Pro 2
Years On Team 2
Grand Tour Apps 0
Wins 0
UCI Ranking 2672

**ANDREA GAROSIO**
Italy
06.12.93
Years Pro 3
Years On Team 1
Grand Tour Apps 1
Wins 0
UCI Ranking 629

**UMBERTO MARENGO**
Italy
21.07.92
Years Pro 3
Years On Team 1
Grand Tour Apps 1
Wins 1
UCI Ranking 1587

**DANIEL SAVINI**
Italy
26.09.97
Years Pro 4
Years On Team 4
Grand Tour Apps 0
Wins 0
UCI Ranking 968

**GIOVANNI VISCONTI**
Italy
13.01.83
Years Pro 17
Years On Team 1
Grand Tour Apps 15
Wins 34
UCI Ranking 1937

**SAMUELE ZOCCARATO**
Italy
09.01.98
Years Pro 1
Years On Team 1
Grand Tour Apps 0
Wins 0
UCI Ranking 648

**GIOVANNI CARBONI**
Italy
31.08.95
Years Pro 4
Years On Team 4
Grand Tour Apps 3
Wins 0
UCI Ranking 343

**FILIPPO FIORELLI**
Italy
19.11.94
Years Pro 2
Years On Team 2
Grand Tour Apps 2
Wins 0
UCI Ranking 249

**GIOVANNI LONARDI**
Italy
09.11.96
Years Pro 2
Years On Team 2
Grand Tour Apps 2
Wins 3
UCI Ranking 554

**FABIO MAZZUCCO**
Italy
14.04.99
Years Pro 2
Years On Team 2
Grand Tour Apps 1
Wins 0
UCI Ranking —

**ALESSANDRO TONELLI**
Italy
29.05.92
Years Pro 7
Years On Team 7
Grand Tour Apps 2
Wins 1
UCI Ranking 1101

**FILIPPO ZANA**
Italy
18.03.99
Years Pro 2
Years On Team 2
Grand Tour Apps 2
Wins 1
UCI Ranking 133

### TEAM INFORMATION

| | |
|---|---|
| UCI CODE | BCF |
| UCI STATUS | MEN'S PROTEAM |
| COUNTRY | ITALY |
| FOUNDED | 1982 |

### TEAM NAME HISTORY

| | |
|---|---|
| 1982-1983 | TERMOLAN |
| 1984-1986 | SANTINI |
| 1987-1989 | SELCA |
| 1990 | ITALBONIFICA |
| 1991 | ITALBONIFICA-NAVIGARE |
| 1992 | ITALBONIFICA |
| 1993-1995 | NAVIGARE-BLUE STORM |
| 1996-1998 | SCRIGNO-GAERNE |
| 1999 | NAVIGARE-GAERNE |
| 2000-2003 | PANARIA-FIORDO |
| 2004 | CERAMICA PANARIA-MARGRES |
| 2005-2007 | CERAMICA PANARIA-NAVIGARE |
| 2008-2009 | CSF GROUP-NAVIGARE |
| 2010-2011 | COLNAGO-CSF INOX |
| 2012 | COLNAGO CSF BARDIANI |
| 2013 | BARDIANI VALVOLE-CSF INOX |
| 2014-2019 | BARDIANI CSF |
| 2020-2021 | BARDIANI CSF FAIZANE |

### TEAM MANAGER

**ROBERTO REVERBERI**

### 2021 NEW RIDERS

**GIOVANNI VISCONTI, ENRICO BATTAGLIN, DAVIDE GABBURO, KEVIN RIVERA, UMBERTO MARENGO, ANDREA GAROSIO, JONATHAN CAÑAVERAL, SAMUELE ZOCCARATO, ENRICO ZANONCELLO, TOMAS TRAININI**

### 2021 STAGIAIRES

**LUCA COLNAGHI, FILIPPO MAGLI, JURI ZANOTTI**

### EQUIPMENT

| | |
|---|---|
| BIKE | CIPOLLINI |

TEAMS    MEN'S PRO CONTINENTAL

# BINGOAL PAUWELS SAUCES

### 2021 VICTORIES

| Etoile de Bessèges – stage 2 | 2.1 | T. Dupont |
| Danilith Nokere Koerse | 1.Pro | L. Robeet |
| Cro Race – stage 3 | 2.1 | M. Menten |

### RIDERS

**STANISŁAW ANIOŁKOWSKI**
Poland
20.01.97
Years Pro 1
Years On Team 1
Grand Tour Apps 0
Wins 3
UCI Ranking 227

**JONAS CASTRIQUE**
Belgium
13.01.97
Years Pro 2
Years On Team 2
Grand Tour Apps 0
Wins 0
UCI Ranking 2302

**SEAN DE BIE**
Belgium
03.10.91
Years Pro 8
Years On Team 2
Grand Tour Apps 2
Wins 0
UCI Ranking 587

**TIMOTHY DUPONT**
Belgium
01.11.87
Years Pro 5
Years On Team 1
Grand Tour Apps 1
Wins 7
UCI Ranking 137

**LAURENS HUYS**
Belgium
24.09.98
Years Pro 2
Years On Team 2
Grand Tour Apps 0
Wins 0
UCI Ranking 668

**ARJEN LIVYNS**
Belgium
01.09.1994
Years Pro 4
Years On Team 2
Grand Tour Apps 0
Wins 0
UCI Ranking 483

**MILAN MENTEN**
Belgium
31.10.96
Years Pro 4
Years On Team 1
Grand Tour Apps 0
Wins 1
UCI Ranking 192

**RÉMY MERTZ**
Belgium
17.07.95
Years Pro 5
Years On Team 1
Grand Tour Apps 2
Wins 0
UCI Ranking 446

**KENNY MOLLY**
Belgium
24.12.96
Years Pro 5
Years On Team 4
Grand Tour Apps 0
Wins 0
UCI Ranking 2302

**MATHIJS PAASSCHENS**
Netherlands
18.03.96
Years Pro 3
Years On Team 3
Grand Tour Apps 0
Wins 0
UCI Ranking 1706

**TOM PAQUOT**
Belgium
22.09.99
Years Pro 1
Years On Team 1
Grand Tour Apps 0
Wins 0
UCI Ranking 433

**DIMITRI PEYSKENS**
Belgium
26.11.91
Years Pro 5
Years On Team 5
Grand Tour Apps 0
Wins 0
UCI Ranking 1587

**LAURENZ REX**
Belgium
15.12.99
Years Pro 1
Years On Team 1
Grand Tour Apps 0
Wins 0
UCI Ranking 726

**LUDOVIC ROBEET**
Belgium
22.05.94
Years Pro 5
Years On Team 5
Grand Tour Apps 0
Wins 2
UCI Ranking 234

**JOEL SUTER**
Switzerland
25.10.98
Years Pro 2
Years On Team 2
Grand Tour Apps 0
Wins 0
UCI Ranking 854

**BORIS VALLÉE**
Belgium
03.06.93
Years Pro 8
Years On Team 2
Grand Tour Apps 0
Wins 2
UCI Ranking —

**JELLE VANENDERT**
Belgium
19.02.85
Years Pro 15
Years On Team 2
Grand Tour Apps 10
Wins 2
UCI Ranking 1402

**QUENTIN VENNER**
Belgium
15.06.98
Years Pro 1
Years On Team 1
Grand Tour Apps 0
Wins 0
UCI Ranking —

**LUC WIRTGEN**
Luxembourg
07.07.98
Years Pro 2
Years On Team 2
Grand Tour Apps 0
Wins 0
UCI Ranking 503

**TOM WIRTGEN**
Luxembourg
04.03.96
Years Pro 3
Years On Team 3
Grand Tour Apps 0
Wins 0
UCI Ranking 1556

### TEAM INFORMATION

| UCI CODE | BWB |
| UCI STATUS | MEN'S PROTEAM |
| COUNTRY | BELGIUM |
| FOUNDED | 2011 |

### TEAM NAME HISTORY

| 2011-2016 | WALLONIE-BRUXELLES |
| 2017 | WB VERANCLASSIC AQUA PROTECT |
| 2018 | WB AQUA PROTECT VERANCLASSIC |
| 2019 | WALLONIE BRUXELLES |
| 2020-2021 | BINGOAL - WALLONIE BRUXELLES |
| 2021 | BINGOAL PAUWELS SAUCES |

### TEAM MANAGER

**CHRISTOPHE BRANDT**

### 2021 NEW RIDERS

**TIMOTHY DUPONT, MILAN MENTEN, STANISŁAW ANIOŁKOWSKI, RÉMY MERTZ, TOM PAQUOT, LAURENZ REX, QUENTIN VENNER**

### 2021 STAGIAIRES

**DORIAN DE MAEGHT, CERIEL DESAL**

### EQUIPMENT

BIKE    **DE ROSA**

TEAMS   MEN'S PRO CONTINENTAL

# BURGOS-BH

### 2021 VICTORIES

None

### RIDERS

**MARIO APARICIO**
Spain
23.04.00
Years Pro 1
Years On Team 1
Grand Tour Apps 0
Wins 0
UCI Ranking —

**EDWIN ÁVILA**
Colombia
21.11.89
Years Pro 9
Years On Team 1
Grand Tour Apps 2
Wins 9
UCI Ranking —

**JETSE BOL**
Netherlands
08.09.89
Years Pro 12
Years On Team 4
Grand Tour Apps 6
Wins 0
UCI Ranking 887

**ÓSCAR CABEDO**
Spain
12.11.94
Years Pro 4
Years On Team 4
Grand Tour Apps 4
Wins 0
UCI Ranking 1004

**CARLOS CANAL**
Spain
28.06.01
Years Pro 2
Years On Team 2
Grand Tour Apps 1
Wins 0
UCI Ranking 1037

**ISAAC CANTÓN**
Spain
13.06.96
Years Pro 2
Years On Team 2
Grand Tour Apps 0
Wins 0
UCI Ranking —

**JESÚS EZQUERRA**
Spain
30.11.90
Years Pro 4
Years On Team 4
Grand Tour Apps 3
Wins 1
UCI Ranking 748

**ÁNGEL FUENTES**
Spain
05.11.96
Years Pro 3
Years On Team 3
Grand Tour Apps 0
Wins 0
UCI Ranking 842

**VICTOR LANGELLOTTI**
Monaco
07.06.95
Years Pro 4
Years On Team 4
Grand Tour Apps 0
Wins 0
UCI Ranking 2033

**JUAN ANOTNIO LÓPEZ-CÓZAR**
Spain
20.08.94
Years Pro 3
Years On Team 1
Grand Tour Apps 0
Wins 0
UCI Ranking 1956

**ÁNGEL MADRAZO**
Spain
30.07.88
Years Pro 13
Years On Team 3
Grand Tour Apps 6
Wins 3
UCI Ranking 542

**ALEX MOLENAAR**
Netherlands
13.07.99
Years Pro 2
Years On Team 2
Grand Tour Apps 1
Wins 0
UCI Ranking 1525

**GABRIEL MULLER**
France
04.12.85
Years Pro 1
Years On Team 1
Grand Tour Apps 0
Wins 0
UCI Ranking —

**DANIEL NAVARRO**
Spain
18.07.83
Years Pro 17
Years On Team 1
Grand Tour Apps 21
Wins 4
UCI Ranking 651

**ANDER OKAMIKA**
Spain
02.04.93
Years Pro 1
Years On Team 1
Grand Tour Apps 1
Wins 0
UCI Ranking 576

**FELIPE ORTS**
Spain
01.04.95
Years Pro 1
Years On Team 1
Grand Tour Apps 0
Wins 0
UCI Ranking 2302

**JUAN FELIPE OSORIO**
Colombia
30.01.95
Years Pro 5
Years On Team 2
Grand Tour Apps 2
Wins 0
UCI Ranking —

**MANUEL PEÑALVER**
Spain
10.12.98
Years Pro 3
Years On Team 3
Grand Tour Apps 0
Wins 1
UCI Ranking 561

**DIEGO RUBIO**
Spain
13.06.91
Years Pro 6
Years On Team 4
Grand Tour Apps 4
Wins 0
UCI Ranking 525

**PELAYO SÁNCHEZ**
Spain
27.03.00
Years Pro 0
Years On Team 0
Grand Tour Apps 1
Wins 0
UCI Ranking 1525

**WILLIE SMIT**
South Africa
29.12.92
Years Pro 4
Years On Team 2
Grand Tour Apps 2
Wins 1
UCI Ranking 576

### TEAM INFORMATION

| | |
|---|---|
| UCI CODE | **BBH** |
| UCI STATUS | **MEN'S PROTEAM** |
| COUNTRY | **SPAIN** |
| FOUNDED | **2008** |

### TEAM NAME HISTORY

| | |
|---|---|
| 2008 | **BURGOS MONUMENTAL** |
| 2009 | **BURGOS MONUMENTAL-CASTILLA Y LEON** |
| 2010-2011 | **BURGOS 2016-CASTILLA Y LEON** |
| 2012-2013 | **BURGOS BH-CASTILLA Y LEON** |
| 2014-2021 | **BURGOS-BH** |

### TEAM MANAGER

**JULIO IZQUIERDO**

### 2021 NEW RIDERS

**DANIEL NAVARRO, EDWIN ÁVILA, JUAN ANTONIO LÓPEZ-CÓZAR, ANDER OKAMIKA, PELAYO SÁNCHEZ, MARIO APARICIO, FELIPE ORTS, GABRIEL MULLER**

### 2021 STAGIAIRES

**RODRIGO ALVAREZ, SANTIAGO MESA, ADRIÀ MORENO**

### EQUIPMENT

| | |
|---|---|
| BIKE | **BH** |

TEAMS    MEN'S PRO CONTINENTAL

# CAJA RURAL-SEGUROS RGA

## 2021 VICTORIES

| Tour of Slovenia – stage 3 | 2.Pro | J. Aberasturi |
|---|---|---|

## TEAM INFORMATION

| UCI CODE | **CJR** |
|---|---|
| UCI STATUS | **MEN'S PROTEAM** |
| COUNTRY | **SPAIN** |
| FOUNDED | **2005** |

## TEAM NAME HISTORY

| 2005-2012 | **CAJA RURAL** |
|---|---|
| 2013-2021 | **CAJA RURAL-SEGUROS RGA** |

## TEAM MANAGER

**JUAN MANUEL HERNÁNDEZ**

## 2021 NEW RIDERS

**JOKIN MURGUIALDAY, JON BARRENETXEA**

## 2021 STAGIAIRES

**PABLO GARCIA FRANCES, YESID ALBEIRO PIRA, ALBERTO SERRANO**

## EQUIPMENT

| BIKE | **GUERCIOTTI** |
|---|---|

## RIDERS

### JON ABERASTURI
Spain
28.03.89
Years Pro 9
Years On Team 3
Grand Tour Apps 4
Wins 15
UCI Ranking 211

### JULEN AMEZQUETA
Spain
12.08.93
Years Pro 6
Years On Team 4
Grand Tour Apps 2
Wins 0
UCI Ranking 231

### ORLUIS AULAR
Venezuela
05.11.96
Years Pro 2
Years On Team 2
Grand Tour Apps 0
Wins 1
UCI Ranking 1010

### ARITZ BAGÜES
Spain
19.08.89
Years Pro 4
Years On Team 2
Grand Tour Apps 4
Wins 0
UCI Ranking 2302

### JON BARRENETXEA
Spain
20.04.00
Years Pro 1
Years On Team 1
Grand Tour Apps 0
Wins 0
UCI Ranking 2263

### JUAN FERNANDO CALLE
Colombia
18.07.99
Years Pro 2
Years On Team 2
Grand Tour Apps 0
Wins 0
UCI Ranking —

### JEFFERSON ALVEIRO CEPEDA
Ecuador
02.03.96
Years Pro 3
Years On Team 3
Grand Tour Apps 2
Wins 4
UCI Ranking 1173

### ÁLVARO CUADROS
Spain
12.04.95
Years Pro 4
Years On Team 4
Grand Tour Apps 1
Wins 0
UCI Ranking —

### JOSU ETXEBERRIA
Spain
09.09.00
Years Pro 1
Years On Team 1
Grand Tour Apps 0
Wins 0
UCI Ranking 2302

### JHOJAN GARCÍA
Colombia
10.01.98
Years Pro 5
Years On Team 2
Grand Tour Apps 1
Wins 0
UCI Ranking 347

### DAVID GONZÁLEZ
Spain
21.02.96
Years Pro 3
Years On Team 3
Grand Tour Apps 0
Wins 0
UCI Ranking 1173

### JON IRISARRI
Spain
09.11.95
Years Pro 5
Years On Team 5
Grand Tour Apps 0
Wins 0
UCI Ranking —

### JONATHAN LASTRA
Spain
03.06.93
Years Pro 6
Years On Team 6
Grand Tour Apps 4
Wins 0
UCI Ranking 151

### OIER LAZKANO
Spain
07.11.99
Years Pro 2
Years On Team 2
Grand Tour Apps 1
Wins 1
UCI Ranking 1791

### SERGIO ROMAN MARTÍN
Spain
13.12.96
Years Pro 2
Years On Team 2
Grand Tour Apps 1
Wins 0
UCI Ranking 1161

### JOKIN MURGUIALDAY
Spain
19.03.00
Years Pro 1
Years On Team 1
Grand Tour Apps 0
Wins 0
UCI Ranking 1556

### JOEL NICOLAU
Spain
23.12.97
Years Pro 3
Years On Team 3
Grand Tour Apps 0
Wins 0
UCI Ranking 1068

### ALEJANDRO OSORIO
Colombia
28.05.98
Years Pro 3
Years On Team 2
Grand Tour Apps 0
Wins 0
UCI Ranking 761

### HÉCTOR SÁEZ
Spain
06.11.93
Years Pro 7
Years On Team 2
Grand Tour Apps 4
Wins 1
UCI Ranking —

### CARMELO URBANO
Spain
03.02.97
Years Pro 2
Years On Team 2
Grand Tour Apps 0
Wins 0
UCI Ranking —

TEAMS    MEN'S PRO CONTINENTAL

# DELKO

## 2021 VICTORIES

| | | |
|---|---|---|
| Presidential Cycling Tour of Turkey – stage 5 | 2.Pro | J. M. Díaz |
| Presidential Cycling Tour of Turkey | 2.Pro | J. M. Díaz |
| National Championships Lithuania – ITT | NC | E. Šiškevičius |
| National Championships Serbia – RR | NC | D. Rajović |
| Tour Poitou–Charentes en Nouvelle Aquitaine – stage 5 | 2.1 | C. Carisey |

## RIDERS

**PIERRE BARBIER**
France
25.09.97
Years Pro 2
Years On Team 2
Grand Tour Apps 0
Wins 0
UCI Ranking 383

**CLÉMENT CARISEY**
France
23.03.92
Years Pro 2
Years On Team 1
Grand Tour Apps 0
Wins 1
UCI Ranking 1022

**LUCAS DE ROSSI**
France
16.08.95
Years Pro 4
Years On Team 4
Grand Tour Apps 0
Wins 0
UCI Ranking —

**YAKOB DEBESAY**
Eritrea
28.06.99
Years Pro 1
Years On Team 1
Grand Tour Apps 0
Wins 1
UCI Ranking —

**ALEXANDRE DELETTRE**
France
25.10.97
Years Pro 1
Years On Team 1
Grand Tour Apps 0
Wins 0
UCI Ranking 463

**JOSÉ MANUEL DÍAZ**
Spain
18.01.95
Years Pro 5
Years On Team 2
Grand Tour Apps 0
Wins 3
UCI Ranking 181

**ALESSANDRO FEDELI**
Italy
02.03.96
Years Pro 3
Years On Team 3
Grand Tour Apps 0
Wins 0
UCI Ranking 1140

**DELIO FERNÁNDEZ**
Spain
17.02.86
Years Pro 14
Years On Team 3
Grand Tour Apps 2
Wins 4
UCI Ranking 599

**IURI FILOSI**
Italy
17.01.92
Years Pro 5
Years On Team 2
Grand Tour Apps 1
Wins 1
UCI Ranking 2296

**MAURO FINETTO**
Italy
10.05.85
Years Pro 14
Years On Team 5
Grand Tour Apps 3
Wins 10
UCI Ranking 832

**JOSÉ GONÇALVES**
Portugal
13.02.89
Years Pro 7
Years On Team 2
Grand Tour Apps 7
Wins 9
UCI Ranking 1420

**EDUARD MICHAEL GROSU**
Romania
04.09.92
Years Pro 7
Years On Team 3
Grand Tour Apps 2
Wins 17
UCI Ranking 439

**MULU KINFE HAILEMICHAEL**
Ethiopia
12.06.99
Years Pro 2
Years On Team 2
Grand Tour Apps 0
Wins 1
UCI Ranking —

**AUGUST JENSEN**
Norway
29.08.91
Years Pro 4
Years On Team 1
Grand Tour Apps 0
Wins 1
UCI Ranking 896

**JUSTIN JULES**
France
20.09.86
Years Pro 5
Years On Team 2
Grand Tour Apps 0
Wins 7
UCI Ranking —

**MATHIAS LE TURNIER**
France
14.03.95
Years Pro 5
Years On Team 5
Grand Tour Apps 2
Wins 0
UCI Ranking —

**ATSUSHI OKA**
Japan
03.09.95
Years Pro 2
Years On Team 2
Grand Tour Apps 0
Wins 1
UCI Ranking 854

**EDUARD PRADES**
Spain
09.08.87
Years Pro 7
Years On Team 1
Grand Tour Apps 2
Wins 8
UCI Ranking 360

**DUSAN RAJOVIC**
Serbia
19.11.97
Years Pro 2
Years On Team 2
Grand Tour Apps 0
Wins 9
UCI Ranking 751

**EVALDAS ŠIŠKEVIČIUS**
Lithuania
30.12.88
Years Pro 9
Years On Team 8
Grand Tour Apps 0
Wins 4
UCI Ranking 312

**JULIEN TRARIEUX**
France
19.08.92
Years Pro 4
Years On Team 4
Grand Tour Apps 0
Wins 0
UCI Ranking 761

## TEAM INFORMATION

| | |
|---|---|
| UCI CODE | **DKO** |
| UCI STATUS | **MEN'S PROTEAM** |
| COUNTRY | **FRANCE** |
| FOUNDED | **2011** |

## TEAM NAME HISTORY

| | |
|---|---|
| 2011–2013 | **LA POMME MARSEILLE** |
| 2014 | **TEAM LA POMME MARSEILLE 13** |
| 2015 | **TEAM MARSEILLE 13 KTM** |
| 2016–2018 | **DELKO MARSEILLE PROVENCE KTM** |
| 2019 | **DELKO MARSEILLE PROVENCE** |
| 2020 | **NIPPO DELKO ONE PROVENCE** |
| 2021 | **DELKO** |

## TEAM MANAGER

**PHILIPPE LANNES**

## 2021 NEW RIDERS

**EDUARD PRADES, AUGUST JENSEN, MATHIAS LE TURNIER, YAKOB DEBESAY, CLÉMENT CARISEY, CLÉMENT BERTHET**

## EQUIPMENT

| | |
|---|---|
| BIKE | **LOOK** |

TEAMS    MEN'S PRO CONTINENTAL

# EOLO-KOMETA

### 2021 VICTORIES

| Giro d'Italia – stage 14 | 2.UWT | L. Fortunato |
| Adriatica Ionica Race – stage 2 | 2.1 | L. Fortunato |
| Adriatica Ionica Race | 2.1 | L. Fortunato |
| National Championships Hungary – ITT | NC | E. Fetter |
| Tour du Limousin – stage 4 | 2.1 | E. Fetter |

### RIDERS

**VINCENZO ALBANESE**
Italy
12.11.96
Years Pro 5
Years On Team 1
Grand Tour Apps 2
Wins 1
UCI Ranking 228

**MANUEL BELLETTI**
Italy
14.10.85
Years Pro 14
Years On Team 1
Grand Tour Apps 10
Wins 19
UCI Ranking 2087

**ALESSANDRO FANCELLU**
Italy
24.04.00
Years Pro 1
Years On Team 1
Grand Tour Apps 0
Wins 0
UCI Ranking –

**MATTIA FRAPPORTI**
Italy
02.07.94
Years Pro 5
Years On Team 1
Grand Tour Apps 0
Wins 0
UCI Ranking –

**ARTURO GRÁVALOS**
Spain
02.03.98
Years Pro 1
Years On Team 1
Grand Tour Apps 0
Wins 0
UCI Ranking –

**SAMUELE RIVI**
Italy
11.05.98
Years Pro 1
Years On Team 1
Grand Tour Apps 1
Wins 0
UCI Ranking 1101

**DANIEL VIEGAS**
Portugal
05.01.98
Years Pro 1
Years On Team 3
Grand Tour Apps 0
Wins 0
UCI Ranking –

**JOHN ARCHIBALD**
Great Britain
14.11.90
Years Pro 1
Years On Team 1
Grand Tour Apps 0
Wins 0
UCI Ranking 845

**MARK CHRISTIAN**
Great Britain
20.11.90
Years Pro 5
Years On Team 1
Grand Tour Apps 2
Wins 0
UCI Ranking 1937

**ERIK FETTER**
Hungary
05.04.00
Years Pro 1
Years On Team 1
Grand Tour Apps 0
Wins 2
UCI Ranking 430

**SERGIO GARCÍA**
Spain
11.06.99
Years Pro 1
Years On Team 1
Grand Tour Apps 0
Wins 0
UCI Ranking –

**LUCA PACIONI**
Italy
13.08.93
Years Pro 6
Years On Team 1
Grand Tour Apps 0
Wins 4
UCI Ranking 1715

**ALEJANDRO ROPERO**
Spain
17.04.98
Years Pro 1
Years On Team 2
Grand Tour Apps 0
Wins 0
UCI Ranking 1253

**LUCA WACKERMANN**
Italy
13.03.92
Years Pro 9
Years On Team 1
Grand Tour Apps 1
Wins 4
UCI Ranking 1766

**DAVIDE BAIS**
Italy
02.04.98
Years Pro 1
Years On Team 1
Grand Tour Apps 0
Wins 0
UCI Ranking 2263

**MÁRTON DINA**
Hungary
11.04.96
Years Pro 1
Years On Team 1
Grand Tour Apps 1
Wins 0
UCI Ranking 2302

**LORENZO FORTUNATO**
Italy
09.05.96
Years Pro 3
Years On Team 1
Grand Tour Apps 1
Wins 3
UCI Ranking 160

**FRANCESCO GAVAZZI**
Italy
01.08.84
Years Pro 15
Years On Team 1
Grand Tour Apps 9
Wins 13
UCI Ranking 726

**EDWARD RAVASI**
Italy
05.06.94
Years Pro 5
Years On Team 1
Grand Tour Apps 3
Wins 0
UCI Ranking 1253

**DIEGO PABLO SEVILLA**
Spain
04.03.96
Years Pro 1
Years On Team 4
Grand Tour Apps 0
Wins 0
UCI Ranking –

### TEAM INFORMATION

| UCI CODE | **EOK** |
| UCI STATUS | **MEN'S PROTEAM** |
| COUNTRY | **ITALY** |
| FOUNDED | **2018** |

### TEAM NAME HISTORY

| 2018 | **POLARTEC-KOMETA** |
| 2019 | **KOMETA CYCLING TEAM** |
| 2020 | **KOMETA XSTRA CYCLING TEAM** |
| 2021 | **EOLO-KOMETA** |

### TEAM MANAGER

**FÉLIX GARCÍA CASAS**

### 2021 NEW RIDERS

**FRANCESCO GAVAZZI, MANUEL BELLETTI, LUCA WACKERMANN, LUCA PACIONI, VINCENZO ALBANESE, LORENZO FORTUNATO, EDWARD RAVASI, MARK CHRISTIAN, MATTIA FRAPPORTI, ALESSANDRO FANCELLU, SAMUELE RIVI, JOHN ARCHIBALD, DAVIDE BAIS**

### 2021 STAGIAIRES

**VICENTE HERNAIZ, DAVID MARTIN, DAVIDE PIGANZOLI**

### EQUIPMENT

| BIKE | **AURUM** |

TEAMS    MEN'S PRO CONTINENTAL

# EQUIPO KERN PHARMA

### 2021 VICTORIES

| | | | |
|---|---|---|---|
| Volta ao Alentejo – stage 6 | 2.2 | E. Sanz |
| Tour Alsace – stage 4 | 2.2 | J. F. Parra |
| Tour Alsace | 2.2 | J. F. Parra |

### RIDERS

**ROGER ADRIÀ**
Spain
18.04.98
Years Pro 1
Years On Team 2
Grand Tour Apps 0
Wins 0
UCI Ranking 229

**JON AGIRRE**
Spain
10.09.97
Years Pro 1
Years On Team 2
Grand Tour Apps 0
Wins 0
UCI Ranking 1089

**SERGIO ARAIZ**
Spain
29.04.98
Years Pro 1
Years On Team 2
Grand Tour Apps 0
Wins 0
UCI Ranking —

**IGOR ARRIETA**
Spain
08.12.02
Years Pro 1
Years On Team 1
Grand Tour Apps 0
Wins 0
UCI Ranking 1284

**URKO BERRADE**
Spain
08.11.97
Years Pro 3
Years On Team 2
Grand Tour Apps 0
Wins 0
UCI Ranking 451

**JAIME CASTRILLO**
Spain
13.03.96
Years Pro 4
Years On Team 2
Grand Tour Apps 0
Wins 0
UCI Ranking 2033

**FRANCISCO GALVÁN**
Spain
01.12.97
Years Pro 1
Years On Team 2
Grand Tour Apps 0
Wins 0
UCI Ranking 594

**CARLOS GARCÍA PIERNA**
Spain
23.07.99
Years Pro 1
Years On Team 1
Grand Tour Apps 0
Wins 0
UCI Ranking 2033

**RAÚL GARCÍA PIERNA**
Spain
23.02.01
Years Pro 1
Years On Team 1
Grand Tour Apps 0
Wins 0
UCI Ranking 1159

**ÁLEX JAIME**
Spain
29.09.98
Years Pro 1
Years On Team 1
Grand Tour Apps 0
Wins 0
UCI Ranking 1253

**DIEGO LOPEZ**
Spain
09.12.97
Years Pro 2
Years on Team 1
Grand Tour Apps 0
Wins 0
UCI Ranking 970

**JORDI LÓPEZ**
Spain
14.08.98
Years Pro 1
Years on Team 1
Grand Tour Apps 0
Wins 0
UCI Ranking 651

**MARTI MARQUEZ**
Spain
09.02.96
Years Pro 1
Years On Team 2
Grand Tour Apps 0
Wins 0
UCI Ranking 1140

**DANIEL ALEJANDRO MENDEZ**
Colombia
02.06.00
Years Pro 1
Years On Team 2
Grand Tour Apps 0
Wins 0
UCI Ranking 2302

**IVAN MORENO**
Spain
27.05.96
Years Pro 1
Years On Team 2
Grand Tour Apps 0
Wins 0
UCI Ranking 1371

**SAVVA NOVIKOV**
Russia
27.07.99
Years Pro 1
Years on Team 1
Grand Tour Apps 0
Wins 3
UCI Ranking 832

**JOSÉ FÉLIX PARRA**
Spain
16.01.97
Years Pro 1
Years on Team 2
Grand Tour Apps 0
Wins 2
UCI Ranking 355

**VOJTĚCH ŘEPA**
Czech Republic
14.08.00
Years Pro 1
Years On Team 1
Grand Tour Apps 0
Wins 0
UCI Ranking 2302

**IBON RUIZ**
Spain
30.01.99
Years Pro 1
Years On Team 2
Grand Tour Apps 0
Wins 0
UCI Ranking —

**ENRIQUE SANZ**
Spain
11.09.89
Years Pro 11
Years On Team 2
Grand Tour Apps 0
Wins 5
UCI Ranking 887

**DANN VAN DER TUUK**
Netherlands
05.11.99
Years Pro 1
Years On Team 1
Grand Tour Apps 0
Wins 0
UCI Ranking 2263

### TEAM INFORMATION

| | |
|---|---|
| UCI CODE | EKP |
| UCI STATUS | MEN'S PROTEAM |
| COUNTRY | SPAIN |
| FOUNDED | 2020 |

### TEAM NAME HISTORY

2020-2021    EQUIPO KERN PHARMA

### TEAM MANAGER

JUAN JOSÉ OROZ

### 2021 NEW RIDERS

SAVVA NOVIKOV, DIEGO LOPEZ, VOJTĚCH ŘEPA, ÁLEX JAIME, RAÚL PIERNA GARCÍA, CARLOS PIERNA GARCÍA, DANNY VAN DER TUUK, IGOR ARRIETA

### 2021 STAGIAIRES

IVÁN COBO, PAU MIQUEL

### EQUIPMENT

BIKE    GIANT

TEAMS   MEN'S PRO CONTINENTAL

# EUSKALTEL-EUSKADI

## 2021 VICTORIES

| Vuelta a Murcia | 1.1 | A.J. Soto |
| Volta ao Alentejo – stage 1 | 2.2 | J. J. Lobato |

## RIDERS

**MIKEL ALONSO**
Spain
23.09.96
Years Pro 2
Years On Team 4
Grand Tour Apps 0
Wins 0
UCI Ranking 2087

**MIKEL ARISTI**
Spain
28.05.93
Years Pro 6
Years On Team 2
Grand Tour Apps 0
Wins 3
UCI Ranking 471

**IKER BALLARIN**
Spain
04.05.97
Years Pro 2
Years On Team 2
Grand Tour Apps 0
Wins 0
UCI Ranking —

**GARIKOITZ BRAVO**
Spain
31.07.89
Years Pro 11
Years On Team 2
Grand Tour Apps 1
Wins 0
UCI Ranking 1371

**JULIEN IRIZAR**
Spain
26.03.95
Years Pro 4
Years On Team 2
Grand Tour Apps 0
Wins 0
UCI Ranking 1937

**JUAN JOSÉ LOBATO**
Spain
30.12.88
Years Pro 11
Years On Team 2
Grand Tour Apps 7
Wins 15
UCI Ranking 811

**ANTONIO JESUS SOTO**
Spain
24.12.94
Years Pro 2
Years On Team 3
Grand Tour Apps 1
Wins 0
UCI Ranking 493

**ANTONIO ANGULO**
Spain
18.02.92
Years Pro 2
Years On Team 2
Grand Tour Apps 0
Wins 0
UCI Ranking 708

**XABIER MIKEL AZPARREN**
Spain
25.02.99
Years Pro 1
Years On Team 1
Grand Tour Apps 1
Wins 0
UCI Ranking 1703

**MIKEL BIZKARRA**
Spain
21.08.89
Years Pro 4
Years On Team 1
Grand Tour Apps 3
Wins 1
UCI Ranking 482

**UNAI CUADRADO**
Spain
26.09.97
Years Pro 2
Years On Team 3
Grand Tour Apps 0
Wins 0
UCI Ranking 1253

**MIKEL ITURRIA**
Spain
16.03.92
Years Pro 4
Years On Team 2
Grand Tour Apps 3
Wins 1
UCI Ranking 403

**GOTZON MARTÍN**
Spain
15.02.96
Years Pro 2
Years On Team 4
Grand Tour Apps 1
Wins 0
UCI Ranking 337

**DZMITRY ZHYHUNOU**
Belarus
10.07.96
Years Pro 2
Years On Team 3
Grand Tour Apps 0
Wins 0
UCI Ranking —

**JOKIN ARANBURU**
Spain
14.02.97
Years Pro 2
Years On Team 3
Grand Tour Apps 0
Wins 0
UCI Ranking —

**IBAI AZURMENDI**
Spain
11.06.96
Years Pro 2
Years On Team 4
Grand Tour Apps 0
Wins 0
UCI Ranking —

**JOAN BOU**
Spain
16.01.97
Years Pro 4
Years On Team 2
Grand Tour Apps 1
Wins 0
UCI Ranking 1068

**PEIO GOIKOETXEA**
Spain
14.02.92
Years Pro 2
Years On Team 4
Grand Tour Apps 0
Wins 0
UCI Ranking —

**TXOMIN JUARISTI**
Spain
20.07.95
Years Pro 2
Years On Team 4
Grand Tour Apps 0
Wins 0
UCI Ranking 2302

**LUIS ÁNGEL MATÉ**
Spain
23.03.84
Years Pro 14
Years On Team 1
Grand Tour Apps 16
Wins 2
UCI Ranking 515

## TEAM INFORMATION

| UCI CODE | EUS |
| UCI STATUS | MEN'S PROTEAM |
| COUNTRY | SPAIN |
| FOUNDED | 2018 |

## TEAM NAME HISTORY

| 2018-2019 | FUNDACIÓN EUSKADI |
| 2020-2021 | EUSKALTEL-EUSKADI |

## TEAM MANAGER

**JORGE AZANZA**

## 2021 NEW RIDERS

**LUIS ÁNGEL MATÉ,
MIKEL XABIER AZPARREN**

## 2021 STAGIAIRES

**ASIER EXTEBERRIA, UNAI IRIBAR**

## EQUIPMENT

| BIKE | **ORBEA** |

TEAMS    MEN'S PRO CONTINENTAL

# GAZPROM-RUSVELO

### 2021 VICTORIES

| | | |
|---|---|---|
| National Championships Russia – RR | NC | A. Nych |
| Tour du Limousin – stage 3 | 2.1 | S. Velasco |
| Tour of South Bohemia – stage 4 | 2.2 | D. Cima |

### RIDERS

**IGOR BOEV**
Russia
22.11.89
Years Pro 9
Years On Team 9
Grand Tour Apps 0
Wins 0
UCI Ranking —

**MARCO CANOLA**
Italy
26.12.88
Years Pro 10
Years On Team 2
Grand Tour Apps 3
Wins 9
UCI Ranking 440

**NIKOLAY CHERKASOV**
Russia
26.09.96
Years Pro 4
Years On Team 4
Grand Tour Apps 0
Wins 0
UCI Ranking 1937

**SERGEI CHERNETSKI**
Russia
09.04.90
Years Pro 9
Years On Team 2
Grand Tour Apps 4
Wins 5
UCI Ranking 487

**DAMIANO CIMA**
Italy
13.09.93
Years Pro 4
Years On Team 1
Grand Tour Apps 1
Wins 3
UCI Ranking 644

**IMERIO CIMA**
Italy
29.10.97
Years Pro 4
Years On Team 2
Grand Tour Apps 0
Wins 0
UCI Ranking —

**PAVEL KOCHETKOV**
Russia
07.03.86
Years Pro 9
Years On Team 2
Grand Tour Apps 9
Wins 1
UCI Ranking 2025

**ROMAN KREUZIGER**
Czech Republic
06.05.86
Years Pro 16
Years On Team 1
Grand Tour Apps 18
Wins 15
UCI Ranking 1956

**ANTON KUZMIN**
Kazakhstan
20.11.96
Years Pro 2
Years On Team 2
Grand Tour Apps 0
Wins 0
UCI Ranking 1140

**VIACHESLAV KUZNETSOV**
Russia
24.06.89
Years Pro 9
Years On Team 2
Grand Tour Apps 5
Wins 0
UCI Ranking 1420

**DENIS NEKRASOV**
Russia
19.02.97
Years Pro 3
Years On Team 3
Grand Tour Apps 0
Wins 0
UCI Ranking 726

**ARTEM NYCH**
Russia
21.03.95
Years Pro 7
Years On Team 7
Grand Tour Apps 0
Wins 1
UCI Ranking 323

**PETR RIKUNOV**
Russia
24.02.97
Years Pro 3
Years On Team 3
Grand Tour Apps 0
Wins 0
UCI Ranking 1274

**IVAN ROVNY**
Russia
30.09.87
Years Pro 15
Years On Team 5
Grand Tour Apps 9
Wins 1
UCI Ranking 811

**CRISTIAN SCARONI**
Italy
16.10.97
Years Pro 2
Years On Team 2
Grand Tour Apps 0
Wins 0
UCI Ranking 717

**EVGENY SHALUNOV**
Russia
08.01.92
Years Pro 10
Years On Team 6
Grand Tour Apps 1
Wins 4
UCI Ranking —

**DMITRY STRAKHOV**
Russia
17.05.95
Years Pro 3
Years On Team 2
Grand Tour Apps 1
Wins 3
UCI Ranking 981

**MATHIAS VACEK**
Czech Republic
12.06.02
Years Pro 1
Years On Team 1
Grand Tour Apps 0
Wins 0
UCI Ranking 837

**SIMONE VELASCO**
Italy
02.12.95
Years Pro 6
Years On Team 2
Grand Tour Apps 0
Wins 3
UCI Ranking 136

**ILNUR ZAKARIN**
Russia
15.09.89
Years Pro 9
Years On Team 1
Grand Tour Apps 11
Wins 8
UCI Ranking 321

### TEAM INFORMATION

| | |
|---|---|
| UCI CODE | GAZ |
| UCI STATUS | MEN'S PROTEAM |
| COUNTRY | RUSSIA |
| FOUNDED | 2012 |

### TEAM NAME HISTORY

| | |
|---|---|
| 2012-2015 | RUSVELO |
| 2016-2021 | GAZPROM-RUSVELO |

### TEAM MANAGER

**RENAT KHAMIDULIN**

### 2021 NEW RIDERS

**ROMAN KREUZIGER, ILNUR ZAKARIN, PAVEL KOCHETKOV, MATHIAS VACEK**

### 2021 STAGIAIRES

**FREDERIK DVERSNES, RICCARDO LUCCA, EIRIK LUNDER**

### EQUIPMENT

| | |
|---|---|
| BIKE | COLNAGO |

TEAMS   MEN'S PRO CONTINENTAL

# RALLY UHC CYCLING

### 2021 VICTORIES

| Presidential Cycling Tour of Turkey – stage 1 | 2.Pro | A. de Kleijn |
| National Championships United States – RR | NC | J. Rosskopf |
| Volta a Portugal – stage 2 | 2.1 | K. Murphy |
| Volta a Portugal – stage 6 | 2.1 | B. King |
| Volta a Portugal – stage 8 | 2.1 | K. Murphy |
| Tour of Denmark – stage 4 | 2.Pro | C. Joyce |
| Tour of Britain – stage 2 | 2.Pro | R. Carpenter |
| Route Adélie de Vitré | 1.1 | A. de Kleijn |

### RIDERS

**STEPHEN BASSETT**
United States
27.03.95
Years Pro 2
Years On Team 2
Grand Tour Apps 0
Wins 0
UCI Ranking 1791

**ROB BRITTON**
Canada
22.09.84
Years Pro 4
Years On Team 6
Grand Tour Apps 0
Wins 3
UCI Ranking —

**NATHAN BROWN**
United States
07.07.91
Years Pro 8
Years On Team 2
Grand Tour Apps 6
Wins 0
UCI Ranking —

**ROBIN CARPENTER**
United States
20.06.92
Years Pro 4
Years On Team 4
Grand Tour Apps 0
Wins 5
UCI Ranking 1089

**PIER-ANDRÉ CÔTÉ**
Canada
24.04.97
Years Pro 3
Years On Team 3
Grand Tour Apps 0
Wins 0
UCI Ranking 446

**MATTEO DAL-CIN**
Canada
14.01.91
Years Pro 4
Years On Team 5
Grand Tour Apps 0
Wins 1
UCI Ranking —

**ARVID DE KLEIJN**
Netherlands
21.03.94
Years Pro 2
Years On Team 1
Grand Tour Apps 0
Wins 4
UCI Ranking 224

**ADAM DE VOS**
Canada
21.10.93
Years Pro 4
Years On Team 4
Grand Tour Apps 0
Wins 2
UCI Ranking 1402

**COLIN JOYCE**
United States
06.08.94
Years Pro 4
Years On Team 5
Grand Tour Apps 0
Wins 3
UCI Ranking 971

**BEN KING**
United States
22.03.89
Years Pro 11
Years On Team 1
Grand Tour Apps 8
Wins 6
UCI Ranking 1101

**GAVIN MANNION**
United States
24.08.91
Years Pro 6
Years On Team 3
Grand Tour Apps 0
Wins 2
UCI Ranking 767

**KYLE MURPHY**
United States
05.10.91
Years Pro 4
Years On Team 4
Grand Tour Apps 0
Wins 2
UCI Ranking 668

**EMERSON ORONTE**
United States
29.01.90
Years Pro 4
Years On Team 6
Grand Tour Apps 0
Wins 0
UCI Ranking —

**JOEY ROSSKOPF**
United States
05.09.89
Years Pro 11
Years On Team 1
Grand Tour Apps 6
Wins 5
UCI Ranking 452

**MAGNUS SHEFFIELD**
United States
19.04.02
Years Pro 1
Years On Team 1
Grand Tour Apps 0
Wins 0
UCI Ranking 1172

**KEEGAN SWIRBUL**
United States
02.09.95
Years Pro 1
Years On Team 1
Grand Tour Apps 0
Wins 0
UCI Ranking 2087

**NICKOLAS ZUKOWSKY**
Canada
03.06.98
Years Pro 2
Years On Team 2
Grand Tour Apps 0
Wins 0
UCI Ranking 615

### TEAM INFORMATION

| UCI CODE | RLY |
| UCI STATUS | MEN'S PROTEAM |
| COUNTRY | UNITED STATES |
| FOUNDED | 2007 |

### TEAM NAME HISTORY

| 2007-2009 | KELLY BENEFIT STRATEGIES / MEDIFAST |
| 2010 | KELLY BENEFIT STRATEGIES |
| 2011 | KELLY BENEFIT STRATEGIES-OPTUMHEALTH |
| 2012-2015 | OPTUM P/B KELLY BENEFIT STRATEGIES |
| 2016-2018 | RALLY CYCLING |
| 2019 | RALLY UHC CYCLING |
| 2020-2021 | RALLY CYCLING |

### TEAM MANAGER

**ERIC WOHLBERG**

### 2021 NEW RIDERS

**JOEY ROSSKOPF, BEN KING, ARVID DE KLEIJN, KEEGAN SWIRBUL, MAGNUS SHEFFIELD**

### 2021 STAGIAIRES

**CHARLES-ÉTIENNE CHRÉTIEN, RAPHAEL PARISELLA, RILEY SHEEHAN**

### EQUIPMENT

BIKE   **FELT**

TEAMS     MEN'S PRO CONTINENTAL

# SPORT VLAANDEREN-BALOISE

### 2021 VICTORIES

| | | | |
|---|---|---|---|
| Baloise Belgium Tour – stage 1 | | 2.Pro | R. Ghys |
| Ronde van Drenthe | | 1.1 | R. Herregodts |

### RIDERS

**RUBEN APERS**
Belgium
25.08.98
Years Pro 1
Years On Team 1
Grand Tour Apps 0
Wins 0
UCI Ranking 1766

**CÉDRIC BEULLENS**
Belgium
27.01.97
Years Pro 2
Years On Team 2
Grand Tour Apps 0
Wins 0
UCI Ranking 629

**ALEX COLMAN**
Belgium
22.07.98
Years Pro 1
Years On Team 1
Grand Tour Apps 0
Wins 0
UCI Ranking —

**KENNY DE KETELE**
Belgium
05.06.85
Years Pro 12
Years On Team 12
Grand Tour Apps 0
Wins 0
UCI Ranking —

**SANDER DE PESTEL**
Belgium
11.10.98
Years Pro 2
Years On Team 2
Grand Tour Apps 0
Wins 0
UCI Ranking —

**LINDSAY DE VYLDER**
Belgium
30.05.95
Years Pro 5
Years On Team 5
Grand Tour Apps 0
Wins 0
UCI Ranking 1402

**GILLES DE WILDE**
Belgium
12.10.99
Years Pro 2
Years On Team 2
Grand Tour Apps 0
Wins 0
UCI Ranking 2033

**ROBBE GHYS**
Belgium
11.01.97
Years Pro 4
Years On Team 4
Grand Tour Apps 0
Wins 1
UCI Ranking 1420

**RUNE HERREGODTS**
Belgium
27.07.98
Years Pro 1
Years On Team 1
Grand Tour Apps 0
Wins 1
UCI Ranking 161

**ARNE MARIT**
Belgium
21.01.99
Years Pro 1
Years On Team 1
Grand Tour Apps 0
Wins 0
UCI Ranking 118

**JULIAN MERTENS**
Belgium
06.10.97
Years Pro 2
Years On Team 2
Grand Tour Apps 0
Wins 0
UCI Ranking 2302

**JENS REYNDERS**
Belgium
25.05.98
Years Pro 1
Years On Team 1
Grand Tour Apps 0
Wins 0
UCI Ranking 300

**THOMAS SPRENGERS**
Belgium
05.02.90
Years Pro 9
Years On Team 9
Grand Tour Apps 0
Wins 0
UCI Ranking 1085

**FABIO VAN DEN BOSSCHE**
Belgium
21.09.00
Years Pro 2
Years On Team 2
Grand Tour Apps 0
Wins 0
UCI Ranking 767

**AARON VAN POUCKE**
Belgium
04.04.98
Years Pro 3
Years On Team 3
Grand Tour Apps 0
Wins 0
UCI Ranking 1010

**KENNETH VAN ROOY**
Belgium
08.10.93
Years Pro 6
Years On Team 6
Grand Tour Apps 0
Wins 0
UCI Ranking 259

**WARD VANHOOF**
Belgium
18.04.99
Years Pro 1
Years On Team 1
Grand Tour Apps 0
Wins 0
UCI Ranking 1140

**AARON VERWILST**
Belgium
02.05.97
Years Pro 4
Years On Team 4
Grand Tour Apps 0
Wins 0
UCI Ranking 2302

**JORDI WARLOP**
Belgium
04.06.96
Years Pro 4
Years On Team 4
Grand Tour Apps 0
Wins 0
UCI Ranking 338

**SASHA WEEMAES**
Belgium
09.02.98
Years Pro 4
Years On Team 4
Grand Tour Apps 0
Wins 0
UCI Ranking 726

**THIMO WILLEMS**
Belgium
09.02.96
Years Pro 3
Years On Team 3
Grand Tour Apps 0
Wins 0
UCI Ranking 708

### TEAM INFORMATION

| | |
|---|---|
| UCI CODE | SVB |
| UCI STATUS | MEN'S PROTEAM |
| COUNTRY | BELGIUM |
| FOUNDED | 2003 |

### TEAM NAME HISTORY

| | |
|---|---|
| 2003 | MARLUX-WINCOR NIXDORF |
| 2004 | CHOCOLADE JACQUES-WINCOR NIXDORF |
| 2005 | CHOCOLADE JACQUES-T INTERIM |
| 2006-2008 | CHOCOLADE JACQUES / TOPSPORT VLAANDEREN |
| 2009-2012 | TOPSPORT VLAANDEREN-MERCATOR |
| 2013-2016 | TOPSPORT VLAANDEREN-BALOISE |
| 2017-2021 | SPORT VLAANDEREN-BALOISE |

### TEAM MANAGER

**CHRISTOPHE SERCU**

### 2021 NEW RIDERS

**ARNE MARIT, RUNE HERREGODTS, JENS REYNDERS, ALEX COLMAN, WARD VANHOOF, RUBEN APERS**

### EQUIPMENT

| | |
|---|---|
| BIKE | MERCKX |

TEAMS    MEN'S PRO CONTINENTAL

# TEAM ARKÉA-SAMSIC

## 2021 VICTORIES

| | | |
|---|---|---|
| Vuelta Asturias – stage 1 | 2.1 | N. Quintana |
| Vuelta Asturias | 2.1 | N. Quintana |
| Volta ao Algarve – stage 5 | 2.Pro | É. Gesbert |
| Trofeo Andratx | 1.1 | W. Anacona |
| Tro-Bro Léon | 1.Pro | C. Swift |
| Vuelta a Castilla y Leon | 1.1 | M. Louvel |
| Tour du Limousin | 2.1 | W. Barguil |
| Tour Poitou–Charentes en Nouvelle Aquitaine | 2.1 | C. Swift |
| Classic Loire Atlantique | 1.1 | A. Riou |
| Tour de Vendée | 1.1 | B. Welten |

## TEAM INFORMATION

| | |
|---|---|
| UCI CODE | **ARK** |
| UCI STATUS | **MEN'S PROTEAM** |
| COUNTRY | **FRANCE** |
| FOUNDED | **2005** |

### TEAM NAME HISTORY

| | |
|---|---|
| 2005-2006 | **BRETAGNE-JEAN FLOC'H** |
| 2007-2008 | **BRETAGNE ARMOR LUX** |
| 2009-2012 | **BRETAGNE SCHULLER** |
| 2013-2015 | **BRETAGNE-SÉCHÉ ENVIRONNEMENT** |
| 2016 | **FORTUNEO-VITAL CONCEPT** |
| 2017 | **FORTUNEO-OSCARO** |
| 2018 | **TEAM FORTUNEO-SAMSIC** |
| 2019-2021 | **TEAM ARKÉA-SAMSIC** |

### TEAM MANAGER

**EMMANUEL HUBERT**

### 2021 NEW RIDERS

**AMAURY CAPIOT, MIGUEL EDUARDO FLÓREZ, MARKUS PAJUR**

### 2021 STAGIAIRES

**MATHIS LE BERRE, KEVIN VAUQUELIN, YANNIS VOISARD**

### EQUIPMENT

| | |
|---|---|
| BIKE | **CANYON** |

## RIDERS

**WINNER ANACONA**
Colombia
11.08.88
Years Pro 10
Years On Team 2
Grand Tour Apps 9
Wins 4
UCI Ranking 459

**WARREN BARGUIL**
France
28.10.91
Years Pro 9
Years On Team 4
Grand Tour Apps 11
Wins 6
UCI Ranking 70

**THOMAS BOUDAT**
France
24.02.94
Years Pro 7
Years On Team 2
Grand Tour Apps 2
Wins 5
UCI Ranking 387

**MAXIME BOUET**
France
03.11.86
Years Pro 14
Years On Team 5
Grand Tour Apps 14
Wins 5
UCI Ranking 510

**NACER BOUHANNI**
France
25.07.90
Years Pro 11
Years On Team 2
Grand Tour Apps 10
Wins 69
UCI Ranking 128

**AMAURY CAPIOT**
Belgium
25.06.93
Years Pro 7
Years On Team 1
Grand Tour Apps 0
Wins 0
UCI Ranking 170

**BENJAMIN DECLERQ**
Belgium
04.02.94
Years Pro 5
Years On Team 2
Grand Tours 0
Wins 0
UCI Ranking 1525

**ANTHONY DELAPLACE**
France
11.09.89
Years Pro 13
Years On Team 8
Grand Tour Apps 8
Wins 1
UCI Ranking 235

**MIGUEL EDUARDO FLÓREZ**
Colombia
21.02.96
Years Pro 5
Years On Team 1
Grand Tour Apps 1
Wins 1
UCI Ranking 1715

**ÉLIE GESBERT**
France
01.07.95
Years Pro 6
Years On Team 6
Grand Tour Apps 4
Wins 2
UCI Ranking 188

**DONAVAN GRONDIN**
France
26.09.00
Years Pro 2
Years On Team 2
Grand Tour Apps 0
Wins 0
UCI Ranking 1715

**THIBAULT GUERNALEC**
France
31.07.97
Years Pro 4
Years On Team 4
Grand Tour Apps 0
Wins 0
UCI Ranking 666

**ROMAIN HARDY**
France
24.08.88
Years Pro 11
Years On Team 5
Grand Tour Apps 5
Wins 2
UCI Ranking 411

**KÉVIN LEDANOIS**
France
13.07.93
Years Pro 7
Years On Team 7
Grand Tour Apps 3
Wins 0
UCI Ranking 1101

**MATIS LOUVEL**
France
19.07.99
Years Pro 2
Years On Team 2
Grand Tour Apps 0
Wins 1
UCI Ranking 223

**DANIEL MCLAY**
Great Britain
03.01.92
Years Pro 7
Years On Team 2
Grand Tour Apps 3
Wins 10
UCI Ranking 216

**CHRISTOPHE NOPPE**
Belgium
29.11.94
Years Pro 5
Years On Team 2
Grand Tour Apps 0
Wins 0
UCI Ranking 489

**ŁUKASZ OWSIAN**
Poland
24.02.90
Years Pro 9
Years On Team 2
Grand Tour Apps 3
Wins 0
UCI Ranking 981

**MARKUS PAJUR**
Estonia
23.09.00
Years Pro 1
Years on Team 1
Grand Tour Apps 0
Wins 0
UCI Ranking 751

**LAURENT PICHON**
France
19.07.86
Years Pro 11
Years On Team 5
Grand Tour Apps 6
Wins 3
UCI Ranking 542

**DAYER QUINTANA**
Colombia
10.08.92
Years Pro 8
Years On Team 2
Grand Tour Apps 3
Wins 3
UCI Ranking 2302

**NAIRO QUINTANA**
Colombia
04.02.90
Years Pro 11
Years On Team 2
Grand Tour Apps 16
Wins 47
UCI Ranking 64

**ALAN RIOU**
France
02.04.97
Years Pro 3
Years On Team 3
Grand Tour Apps 0
Wins 1
UCI Ranking 347

**DIEGO ROSA**
Italy
27.03.89
Years Pro 9
Years On Team 1
Grand Tour Apps 8
Wins 0
UCI Ranking 1395

**CLÉMENT RUSSO**
France
20.01.95
Years Pro 4
Years On Team 4
Grand Tour Apps 2
Wins 1
UCI Ranking 326

**CONNOR SWIFT**
Great Britain
30.10.95
Years Pro 3
Years On Team 3
Grand Tour Apps 2
Wins 3
UCI Ranking 88

**BRAM WELTEN**
Netherlands
29.03.97
Years Pro 4
Years On Team 4
Grand Tour Apps 0
Wins 1
UCI Ranking 102

TEAMS     MEN'S PRO CONTINENTAL

# TEAM NOVO NORDISK

## 2021 VICTORIES

| National Championships Finland – RR | NC | J. Henttala |
|---|---|---|

### TEAM INFORMATION

| UCI CODE | **TNN** |
|---|---|
| UCI STATUS | **MEN'S PROTEAM** |
| COUNTRY | **UNITED STATES** |
| FOUNDED | **2008** |

### TEAM NAME HISTORY

| 2008-2010 | **TEAM TYPE 1** |
|---|---|
| 2011-2012 | **TEAM TYPE 1-SANOFI** |
| 2013-2021 | **TEAM NOVO NORDISK** |

### TEAM MANAGER

**VASSILI DAVIDENKO**

### 2021 NEW RIDERS

**LUCAS DAUGE, LOGAN PHIPPEN**

### EQUIPMENT

| BIKE | **COLNAGO** |
|---|---|

## RIDERS

**HAMISH BEADLE**
New Zealand
02.04.98
| Years Pro | 2 |
| Years On Team | 2 |
| Grand Tour Apps | 0 |
| Wins | 0 |
| UCI Ranking | — |

**OLIVER BEHRINGER**
Switzerland
20.03.96
| Years Pro | 3 |
| Years On Team | 3 |
| Grand Tour Apps | 0 |
| Wins | 0 |
| UCI Ranking | — |

**MEHDI BENHAMOUDA**
France
02.01.95
| Years Pro | 6 |
| Years On Team | 6 |
| Grand Tour Apps | 0 |
| Wins | 0 |
| UCI Ranking | — |

**SAM BRAND**
Great Britain
27.02.91
| Years Pro | 4 |
| Years On Team | 4 |
| Grand Tour Apps | 0 |
| Wins | 0 |
| UCI Ranking | — |

**STEPHEN CLANCY**
Ireland
19.07.92
| Years Pro | 9 |
| Years On Team | 9 |
| Grand Tour Apps | 0 |
| Wins | 0 |
| UCI Ranking | — |

**LUCAS DAUGE**
France
28.12.96
| Years Pro | 1 |
| Years On Team | 1 |
| Grand Tour Apps | 0 |
| Wins | 0 |
| UCI Ranking | — |

**GERD DE KEIJZER**
Netherlands
18.01.94
| Years Pro | 5 |
| Years On Team | 5 |
| Grand Tour Apps | 0 |
| Wins | 0 |
| UCI Ranking | — |

**JOONAS HENTTALA**
Finland
17.09.91
| Years Pro | 9 |
| Years On Team | 9 |
| Grand Tour Apps | 0 |
| Wins | 1 |
| UCI Ranking | 905 |

**DECLAN IRVINE**
Australia
11.03.99
| Years Pro | 3 |
| Years On Team | 3 |
| Grand Tour Apps | 0 |
| Wins | 0 |
| UCI Ranking | — |

**BRIAN KAMSTRA**
Netherlands
05.07.93
| Years Pro | 6 |
| Years On Team | 6 |
| Grand Tour Apps | 0 |
| Wins | 0 |
| UCI Ranking | — |

**PÉTER KUSZTOR**
Hungary
27.12.84
| Years Pro | 3 |
| Years On Team | 3 |
| Grand Tour Apps | 0 |
| Wins | 3 |
| UCI Ranking | — |

**DAVID LOZANO**
Spain
21.12.88
| Years Pro | 9 |
| Years On Team | 9 |
| Grand Tour Apps | 0 |
| Wins | 0 |
| UCI Ranking | 1937 |

**SAMUEL MUNDAY**
Australia
04.03.98
| Years Pro | 3 |
| Years On Team | 3 |
| Grand Tour Apps | 0 |
| Wins | 0 |
| UCI Ranking | — |

**ANDREA PERON**
Italy
28.10.88
| Years Pro | 9 |
| Years On Team | 9 |
| Grand Tour Apps | 0 |
| Wins | 0 |
| UCI Ranking | 1956 |

**LOGAN PHIPPEN**
United States
10.05.92
| Years Pro | 1 |
| Years On Team | 1 |
| Grand Tour Apps | 0 |
| Wins | 0 |
| UCI Ranking | — |

**CHARLES PLANET**
France
30.10.93
| Years Pro | 8 |
| Years On Team | 8 |
| Grand Tour Apps | 0 |
| Wins | 0 |
| UCI Ranking | — |

**UMBERTO POLI**
Italy
27.08.96
| Years Pro | 5 |
| Years On Team | 5 |
| Grand Tour Apps | 0 |
| Wins | 0 |
| UCI Ranking | — |

TEAMS  MEN'S PRO CONTINENTAL

# TOTALENERGIES

## 2021 VICTORIES

| | | | |
|---|---|---|---|
| GP Valencia | 1.2 | L. Manzin | |
| Vuelta Asturias – stage 3 | 2.1 | P. Latour | |
| Tour du Rwanda – stage 4 | 2.1 | V. Ferron | |
| Tour du Rwanda – stage 8 | 2.1 | C. Rodríguez | |
| Tour du Rwanda | 2.1 | C. Rodríguez | |
| GP Jef Scherens | 1.1 | N. Bonifazio | |

## RIDERS

**EDVALD BOASSON HAGEN**
Norway
17.05.87
Years Pro 14
Years On Team 1
Grand Tour Apps 15
Wins 81
UCI Ranking 887

**LEONARDO BONIFAZIO**
Italy
20.03.91
Years Pro 2
Years On Team 2
Grand Tour Apps 0
Wins 0
UCI Ranking —

**NICCOLÒ BONIFAZIO**
Italy
29.10.93
Years Pro 8
Years On Team 3
Grand Tour Apps 4
Wins 19
UCI Ranking 140

**MATHIEU BURGAUDEAU**
France
17.11.98
Years Pro 3
Years On Team 3
Grand Tour Apps 1
Wins 0
UCI Ranking 199

**JÉRÉMY CABOT**
France
24.07.91
Years Pro 2
Years On Team 2
Grand Tour Apps 1
Wins 0
UCI Ranking 615

**JÉRÔME COUSIN**
France
05.06.89
Years Pro 11
Years On Team 4
Grand Tour Apps 7
Wins 2
UCI Ranking —

**VÍCTOR DE LA PARTE**
Spain
22.06.86
Years Pro 11
Years On Team 1
Grand Tour Apps 6
Wins 4
UCI Ranking 489

**FABIEN DOUBEY**
France
21.10.93
Years Pro 5
Years On Team 5
Grand Tour Apps 1
Wins 0
UCI Ranking 1956

**VALENTIN FERRON**
France
08.02.98
Years Pro 2
Years On Team 2
Grand Tour Apps 1
Wins 1
UCI Ranking 436

**MARLON GAILLARD**
France
09.05.96
Years Pro 2
Years On Team 2
Grand Tour Apps 0
Wins 0
UCI Ranking 2302

**DAMIEN GAUDIN**
France
20.08.86
Years Pro 14
Years On Team 4
Grand Tour Apps 5
Wins 6
UCI Ranking 411

**ALEXANDRE GENIEZ**
France
16.04.88
Years Pro 12
Years On Team 1
Grand Tour Apps 14
Wins 15
UCI Ranking 1285

**FABIEN GRELLIER**
France
31.10.94
Years Pro 6
Years On Team 6
Grand Tour Apps 3
Wins 0
UCI Ranking 1706

**PIERRE LATOUR**
France
12.10.93
Years Pro 7
Years On Team 1
Grand Tour Apps 6
Wins 5
UCI Ranking 148

**CHRIS LAWLESS**
Great Britain
04.11.95
Years Pro 4
Years On Team 4
Grand Tour Apps 0
Wins 2
UCI Ranking —

**FLORIAN MAITRE**
France
03.09.96
Years Pro 2
Years On Team 2
Grand Tour Apps 0
Wins 0
UCI Ranking 1299

**LORRENZO MANZIN**
France
26.07.94
Years Pro 7
Years on Team 2
Grand Tour Apps 4
Wins 5
UCI Ranking 355

**PAUL OURSELIN**
France
13.04.94
Years Pro 5
Years On Team 5
Grand Tour Apps 2
Wins 0
UCI Ranking —

**ADRIEN PETIT**
France
26.09.90
Years Pro 11
Years On Team 6
Grand Tour Apps 4
Wins 9
UCI Ranking 2033

**CRISTIÁN RODRÍGUEZ**
Spain
03.03.95
Years Pro 6
Years On Team 1
Grand Tour Apps 5
Wins 2
UCI Ranking 209

**ROMAIN SICARD**
France
01.01.88
Years Pro 12
Years On Team 8
Grand Tour Apps 13
Wins 1
UCI Ranking —

**JULIEN SIMON**
France
04.10.85
Years Pro 14
Years On Team 2
Grand Tour Apps 10
Wins 10
UCI Ranking 176

**GEOFFREY SOUPE**
France
22.03.88
Years Pro 11
Years On Team 2
Grand Tour Apps 7
Wins 1
UCI Ranking 1956

**NIKI TERPSTRA**
Netherlands
18.05.84
Years Pro 15
Years On Team 3
Grand Tour Apps 15
Wins 22
UCI Ranking 1275

**ANTHONY TURGIS**
France
16.05.94
Years Pro 7
Years On Team 3
Grand Tour Apps 5
Wins 6
UCI Ranking 86

**DRIES VAN GESTEL**
Belgium
30.09.94
Years Pro 6
Years On Team 2
Grand Tour Apps 0
Wins 1
UCI Ranking 387

**ALEXIS VUILLERMOZ**
France
01.06.88
Years Pro 9
Years On Team 1
Grand Tour Apps 9
Wins 8
UCI Ranking 468

## TEAM INFORMATION

| | |
|---|---|
| UCI CODE | **TEN** |
| UCI STATUS | **MEN'S PROTEAM** |
| COUNTRY | **FRANCE** |
| FOUNDED | **2005** |

### TEAM NAME HISTORY

| | |
|---|---|
| 2005-2008 | **BOUYGUES TELECOM** |
| 2009 | **BBOX BOUYGUES TELEKOM** |
| 2010 | **BBOX BOUYGUES TELECOM** |
| 2011-2015 | **TEAM EUROPCAR** |
| 2016-2018 | **DIRECT ENERGIE** |
| 2019-2020 | **TEAM TOTAL DIRECT ENERGIE** |
| 2021 | **TOTALENERGIES** |

### TEAM MANAGER

**JEAN-RENÉ BERNAUDEAU**

### 2021 NEW RIDERS

**EDVALD BOASSON HAGEN, ALEXIS VUILLERMOZ, PIERRE LATOUR, ALEXANDRE GENIEZ, VÍCTOR DE LA PARTE, CHRIS LAWLESS, CRISTIÁN RODRÍGUEZ, FABIEN DOUBEY**

### 2021 STAGIAIRES

**THOMAS BONNET, EMILIEN JEANNIERE, ALAN JOUSSEAUME**

### EQUIPMENT

| | |
|---|---|
| BIKE | **WILIER** |

TEAMS   MEN'S PRO CONTINENTAL

# UNO-X PRO CYCLING TEAM

## 2021 VICTORIES

| | | |
|---|---|---|
| Tour de la Mirabelle – prologue | 2.2 | I. Andersen |
| Tour de la Mirabelle – stage 3 | 2.2 | I. Andersen |
| Tour de la Mirabelle | 2.2 | I. Andersen |
| Tour of Funen | 1.2 | N. Larsen |
| Dwars door het Hageland | 1.Pro | R. Tiller |
| Arctic Race of Norway – stage 1 | 2.Pro | M. Hoelgaard |
| Sazka Tour – stage 3 | 2.1 | T. H. Johannessen |
| Sazka Tour – stage 4 | 2.1 | T. H. Johannessen |
| Tour of Slovakia | 2.1 | K. Halvorsen |
| Lillehammer GP | 1.2 | I. Andersen |
| Paris–Tours Espoirs | 1.2U | J. I. Hvideberg |

## TEAM INFORMATION

| | |
|---|---|
| UCI CODE | UXT |
| UCI STATUS | MEN'S PROTEAM |
| COUNTRY | NORWAY |
| FOUNDED | 2010 |

## TEAM NAME HISTORY

| | |
|---|---|
| 2010-2011 | TEAM RINGERIKS-KRAFT |
| 2012-2013 | TEAM RINGERIKS KRAFT LOOK |
| 2013-2016 | TEAM RINGERIKS-KRAFT |
| 2017 | UNO-X HYDROGEN DEVELOPMENT TEAM |
| 2018-2019 | UNO-X NORWEGIAN DEVELOPMENT TEAM |
| 2020-2021 | UNO-X PRO CYCLING TEAM |

## TEAM MANAGER

JENS HAUGLAND

## 2021 NEW RIDERS

KRISTOFFER HALVORSEN, RASMUS TILLER, SØREN WÆRENSKJOLD

## EQUIPMENT

| | |
|---|---|
| BIKE | DARE |

## RIDERS

**JONAS ABRAHAMSEN**
Norway
20.09.95
Years Pro 2
Years On Team 7
Grand Tour Apps 0
Wins 0
UCI Ranking 2898

**IDAR ANDERSEN**
Norway
30.04.99
Years Pro 2
Years on Team 4
Grand Tour Apps 0
Wins 0
UCI Ranking 343

**ERLEND BLIKRA**
Norway
11.01.97
Years Pro 2
Years On Team 2
Grand Tour Apps 0
Wins 0
UCI Ranking 1064

**KRISTOFFER HALVORSEN**
Norway
13.04.96
Years Pro 4
Years On Team 1
Grand Tour Apps 0
Wins 5
UCI Ranking 195

**JACOB HINDSGAUL MADSEN**
Denmark
14.07.00
Years Pro 2
Years On Team 2
Grand Tour Apps 0
Wins 0
UCI Ranking 1037

**DANIEL HOELGAARD**
Norway
01.07.93
Years Pro 6
Years On Team 2
Grand Tour Apps 1
Wins 0
UCI Ranking 2087

**MARKUS HOELGAARD**
Norway
04.10.94
Years Pro 2
Years On Team 3
Grand Tour Apps 0
Wins 2
UCI Ranking 108

**MORTEN HULGAARD**
Denmark
23.08.98
Years Pro 2
Years On Team 2
Grand Tour Apps 0
Wins 0
UCI Ranking 292

**JONAS IVERSBY HVIDEBERG**
Norway
09.02.1999
Years Pro 2
Years On Team 4
Grand Tour Apps 0
Wins 0
UCI Ranking 685

**JULIUS JOHANSEN**
Denmark
13.09.99
Years Pro 2
Years On Team 2
Grand Tour Apps 0
Wins 0
UCI Ranking —

**KRISTIAN KULSET**
Norway
01.10.95
Years Pro 2
Years On Team 6
Grand Tour Apps 0
Wins 0
UCI Ranking —

**SINDRE KULSET**
Norway
07.08.98
Years Pro 2
Years On Team 4
Grand Tour Apps 0
Wins 0
UCI Ranking —

**NIKLAS LARSEN**
Denmark
22.03.97
Years Pro 2
Years On Team 2
Grand Tour Apps 0
Wins 1
UCI Ranking 686

**JOHAN PRICE-PEJTERSEN**
Denmark
26.05.99
Years Pro 2
Years On Team 2
Grand Tour Apps 0
Wins 0
UCI Ranking 291

**ERIK NORDSAETER RESELL**
Norway
28.09.96
Years Pro 2
Years On Team 5
Grand Tour Apps 0
Wins 0
UCI Ranking 637

**FREDERIK RODENBERG**
Denmark
22.01.98
Years Pro 2
Years On Team 2
Grand Tour Apps 0
Wins 0
UCI Ranking —

**LARS SAUGSTAD**
Norway
28.05.97
Years Pro 2
Years On Team 5
Grand Tour Apps 0
Wins 0
UCI Ranking 1586

**ANDERS SKAARSETH**
Norway
07.05.95
Years Pro 2
Years On Team 3
Grand Tour Apps 0
Wins 0
UCI Ranking 387

**IVER SKAARSETH**
Norway
15.03.98
Years Pro 2
Years On Team 4
Grand Tour Apps 0
Wins 0
UCI Ranking 2898

**TORJUS SLEEN**
Norway
30.03.97
Years Pro 2
Years On Team 5
Grand Tour Apps 0
Wins 0
UCI Ranking 2672

**RASMUS TILLER**
Norway
28.07.96
Years Pro 3
Years On Team 1
Grand Tour Apps 1
Wins 2
UCI Ranking 95

**TORSTEIN TRAEEN**
Norway
16.07.95
Years Pro 2
Years On Team 7
Grand Tour Apps 0
Wins 0
UCI Ranking 397

**MARTIN URIANSTAD**
Norway
06.02.99
Years Pro 2
Years On Team 3
Grand Tour Apps 0
Wins 0
UCI Ranking 1285

**SØREN WÆRENSKJOLD**
Norway
12.03.00
Years Pro 1
Years On Team 1
Grand Tour Apps 0
Wins 0
UCI Ranking 276

**SYVER WAERSTED**
Norway
08.08.96
Years Pro 2
Years On Team 5
Grand Tour Apps 0
Wins 0
UCI Ranking 2087

TEAMS   MEN'S PRO CONTINENTAL

# VINI ZABÙ

### 2021 VICTORIES

| Trofej Umag | 1.2 | J. Mareczko |
| Settimana Internazionale Coppi e Bartali – stage 1a | 2.1 | J. Mareczko |

### RIDERS

**ANDREA BARTOLOZZI**
Italy
03.05.99
Years Pro 2
Years On Team 2
Grand Tour Apps 0
Wins 0
UCI Ranking —

**SIMONE BEVILACQUA**
Italy
22.02.97
Years Pro 4
Years On Team 4
Grand Tour Apps 1
Wins 1
UCI Ranking 2672

**ROBERTO CARLOS GONZÁLEZ**
Panama
21.05.94
Years Pro 3
Years On Team 3
Grand Tour Apps 0
Wins 0
UCI Ranking 951

**JAKUB MARECZKO**
Italy
30.04.94
Years Pro 7
Years On Team 1
Grand Tour Apps 5
Wins 44
UCI Ranking 408

**JAN PETELIN**
Luxembourg
02.07.96
Years Pro 2
Years On Team 2
Grand Tour Apps 0
Wins 0
UCI Ranking 2087

**VELJKO STOJNIC**
Serbia
04.02.99
Years Pro 2
Years On Team 2
Grand Tour Apps 0
Wins 2
UCI Ranking 1371

**ETIENNE VAN EMPEL**
Netherlands
14.04.94
Years Pro 7
Years On Team 3
Grand Tour Apps 1
Wins 0
UCI Ranking —

**LIAM BERTAZZO**
Italy
17.02.92
Years Pro 7
Years On Team 6
Grand Tour Apps 2
Wins 2
UCI Ranking —

**ANDREA DI RENZO**
Italy
24.01.95
Years Pro 2
Years On Team 2
Grand Tour Apps 0
Wins 0
UCI Ranking 2302

**KAMIL GRADEK**
Poland
17.09.90
Years Pro 6
Years On Team 1
Grand Tour Apps 2
Wins 3
UCI Ranking 1766

**DAVIDE ORRICO**
Italy
17.02.90
Years Pro 1
Years On Team 1
Grand Tour Apps 0
Wins 0
UCI Ranking 887

**JOAB SCHNEITER**
Switzerland
06.08.98
Years Pro 1
Years On Team 1
Grand Tour Apps 0
Wins 0
UCI Ranking —

**LEONARDO TORTOMASI**
Italy
21.01.94
Years Pro 2
Years On Team 2
Grand Tour Apps 0
Wins 0
UCI Ranking —

**EDOARDO ZARDINI**
Italy
02.11.89
Years Pro 9
Years On Team 4
Grand Tour Apps 5
Wins 2
UCI Ranking 1791

**MATTIA BEVILACQUA**
Italy
17.06.98
Years Pro 2
Years On Team 2
Grand Tour Apps 0
Wins 0
UCI Ranking —

**MARCO FRAPPORTI**
Italy
30.03.85
Years Pro 14
Years On Team 2
Grand Tour Apps 7
Wins 4
UCI Ranking —

**ALESSANDRO IACCHI**
Italy
26.05.99
Years Pro 2
Years On Team 2
Grand Tour Apps 0
Wins 0
UCI Ranking —

**DANIEL PEARSON**
Great Britain
26.02.94
Years Pro 5
Years On Team 1
Grand Tour Apps 0
Wins 0
UCI Ranking 2302

**RICCARDO STACCHIOTTI**
Italy
08.11.91
Years Pro 9
Years On Team 2
Grand Tour Apps 2
Wins 4
UCI Ranking 2302

**WOUT VAN ELZAKKER**
Netherlands
14.11.98
Years Pro 1
Years On Team 1
Grand Tour Apps 0
Wins 0
UCI Ranking —

### TEAM INFORMATION

| UCI CODE | **THR** |
| UCI STATUS | **MEN'S PROTEAM** |
| COUNTRY | **ITALY** |
| FOUNDED | **2009** |

### TEAM NAME HISTORY

| 2009 | **ISD CYCLING TEAM** |
| 2010 | **ISD-NERI** |
| 2011–2012 | **FARNESE VINI-NERI-SOTTOLI** |
| 2013 | **VINI FANTINI** |
| 2014 | **NERI SOTTOLI** |
| 2015 | **SOUTHEAST** |
| 2016 | **WILIER-SOUTHEAST** |
| 2017–2018 | **WILIER TRIESTINA-SELLE ITALIA** |
| 2019 | **NERI SOTTOLI-SELLE ITALIA-KTM** |
| 2020 | **VINI ZABÙ BRADO KTM** |
| 2021 | **VINI ZABÙ** |

### TEAM MANAGER

**LUCA SCINTO**

### 2021 NEW RIDERS

**JAKUB MARECZKO, KAMIL GRADEK, DANIEL PEARSON, DAVIDE ORRICO, JOAB SCHNEITER, WOUT VAN ELZAKKER**

### 2021 STAGIAIRES

**GREGORIO FERRI, GIULIO MASOTTO, RICARDO TOSIN**

### EQUIPMENT

| BIKE | **CORRATEC** |

TEAMS  FINAL RANKINGS

# MEN'S WORLDTOUR

## INDIVIDUAL FINAL RANKINGS

| POS | NAME | TEAM | PTS |
|---|---|---|---|
| 1. | T. Pogačar | UAD | 5363 |
| 2. | W. van Aert | TJV | 4382 |
| 3. | P. Roglič | TJV | 3924 |
| 4. | J. Alaphilippe | DQT | 3104.67 |
| 5. | E. Bernal | IGD | 2576 |
| 6. | S. Colbrelli | TBV | 2553 |
| 7. | M. van der Poel | AFC | 2461 |
| 8. | A. Yates | IGD | 2251 |
| 9. | J. Almeida | DQT | 2219 |
| 10. | R. Carapaz | IGD | 2018 |
| 11. | A. Valverde | MOV | 1981 |
| 12. | M. Mohorič | TBV | 1897 |
| 13. | M. Woods | ISN | 1893 |
| 14. | R. Evenepoel | DQT | 1799 |
| 15. | J. Philipsen | AFC | 1777 |
| 16. | D. Gaudu | GFC | 1773 |
| 17. | J. Stuyven | TFS | 1771 |
| 18. | J. Vingegaard | TJV | 1730 |
| 19. | T. Merlier | AFC | 1703 |
| 20. | B. Mollema | TFS | 1620.66 |
| 21. | G. Nizzolo | TQA | 1607 |
| 22. | M. Schachmann | BOH | 1579 |
| 23. | K. Asgreen | DQT | 1553 |
| 24. | M. Trentin | UAD | 1535 |
| 25. | E. Mas | MOV | 1533 |
| 26. | S. Küng | GFC | 1463 |
| 27. | M. F. Honoré | DQT | 1419.27 |
| 28. | E. Hayter | IGD | 1335.33 |
| 29. | R. Porte | IGD | 1303.33 |
| 30. | D. van Poppel | IWG | 1291 |
| 31. | F. Senechal | DQT | 1288 |
| 32. | M. Cavendish | DQT | 1280.27 |
| 33. | T. Pidcock | IGD | 1275 |
| 34. | G. Thomas | IGD | 1268 |
| 35. | A. Vlasov | APT | 1241 |
| 36. | S. Yates | BEX | 1239 |
| 37. | D. Caruso | TBV | 1238 |
| 38. | D. van Baarle | IGD | 1235 |
| 39. | A. Lutsenko | APT | 1230 |
| 40. | B. O'Connor | ACT | 1227 |
| 41. | C. Laporte | COF | 1219 |
| 42. | J. Haig | TBV | 1131 |
| 42. | B. Cosnefroy | ACT | 1131 |
| 44. | M. Matthews | BEX | 1087 |
| 45. | Y. Lampaert | DQT | 1080 |
| 46. | D. Ulissi | UAD | 1074 |
| 47. | W. Kelderman | BOH | 1070 |
| 48. | F. Masnada | DQT | 1053 |
| 49. | G. Martin | COF | 1038 |
| 50. | P. Ackermann | BOH | 1027 |
| 51. | A. Démare | GFC | 1014 |
| 52. | N. Powless | EFN | 986 |
| 53. | F. Ganna | IGD | 981 |
| 54. | R. Bardet | DSM | 974 |
| 55. | I. Izagirre | APT | 953 |
| 56. | B. Hermans | ISN | 931.33 |
| 57. | P. Sagan | BOH | 923 |
| 58. | G. Van Avermaet | ACT | 906 |
| 59. | J. Godon | ACT | 900 |
| 60. | M. Valgren | EFN | 877 |
| 61. | F. Jakobsen | DQT | 845 |
| 62. | R. Urán | EFN | 835 |
| 63. | M. Landa | TBV | 833 |
| 64. | N. Quintana | ARK | 827 |
| 65. | T. Wellens | LTS | 826 |
| 66. | P. Bilbao | TBV | 819 |
| 67. | M. Hirschi | UAD | 814 |
| 68. | E. Viviani | COF | 810 |
| 69. | A. Kristoff | UAD | 805 |
| 70. | W. Barguil | ARK | 804 |
| 71. | V. Madouas | GFC | 768 |
| 72. | C. Ewan | LTS | 766 |
| 73. | T. Van der Sande | LTS | 756 |
| 74. | T. Benoot | DSM | 754 |
| 75. | M. Pedersen | TFS | 746 |
| 75. | B. Ghirmay | IWG | 746 |
| 77. | G. Moscon | IGD | 741 |
| 78. | G. Vermeersch | AFC | 739 |
| 79. | G. Mäder | TBV | 736 |
| 80. | S. Bennett | DQT | 735 |
| 81. | A. Paret-Peintre | ACT | 732 |
| 82. | R. Gibbons | UAD | 730.66 |
| 83. | N. Politt | BOH | 727 |
| 83. | H. Hofstetter | ISN | 727 |
| 83. | A. Covi | UAD | 727 |
| 86. | A. Turgis | TEN | 725 |
| 87. | J. Meeus | BOH | 723 |

| POS | NAME | TEAM | PTS |
|---|---|---|---|
| 88. | C. Swift | ARK | 710 |
| 89. | L. Rota | IWG | 706 |
| 90. | P. Konrad | BOH | 705 |
| 91. | M. A. López | MOV | 704 |
| 92. | E. Chaves | BEX | 703 |
| 93. | M. Kwiatkowski | IGD | 702.33 |
| 94. | A. Aranburu | APT | 702 |
| 95. | R. Tiller | UXT | 687 |
| 96. | I. Schelling | BOH | 663 |
| 97. | J. Fuglsang | APT | 660 |
| 98. | Je. Herrada | COF | 650 |
| 99. | S. Vanmarcke | ISN | 645 |
| 100. | O. C. Eiking | IWG | 643 |
| 101. | M. Cattaneo | DQT | 639 |
| 102. | B. Welten | ARK | 623 |
| 103. | H. Carthy | EFN | 602 |
| 104. | J. Degenkolb | LTS | 594 |
| 105. | A. Pasqualon | IWG | 588 |
| 106. | A. De Marchi | ISN | 577.33 |
| 107. | M. Cort | EFN | 571.33 |
| 108. | M. Hoelgaard | UXT | 571 |
| 109. | F. Bonnamour | BBK | 566 |
| 110. | F. Vermeersch | LTS | 564 |
| 111. | V. Campenaerts | TQA | 559.33 |
| 112. | D. Teuns | TBV | 558 |
| 113. | B. Coquard | BBK | 557 |
| 114. | T. Van Asbroeck | ISN | 552 |
| 115. | S. Kuss | TJV | 550 |
| 115. | F. Baroncini | CPK | 550 |
| 117. | S. Dewulf | ACT | 547 |
| 118. | A. Marit | SVB | 535 |
| 119. | M. Vansevenant | DQT | 530.6 |
| 120. | M. Storer | DSM | 526 |
| 120. | L. Mozzato | BBK | 526 |
| 122. | C. Champoussin | ACT | 522 |
| 123. | D. Martin | ISN | 513 |
| 124. | D. de la Cruz | UAD | 508 |
| 125. | L. Hamilton | BEX | 490 |
| 126. | D. Ballerini | DQT | 486.67 |
| 127. | S. Bissegger | EFN | 481 |
| 128. | Z. Štybar | DQT | 480 |
| 128. | N. Bouhanni | ARK | 480 |
| 130. | M. Teunissen | TJV | 478 |
| 131. | G. Serrano | MOV | 472 |
| 132. | R. Dennis | IGD | 471.33 |
| 133. | F. Zana | BCF | 471 |
| 134. | V. Nibali | TFS | 467 |
| 135. | M. Walscheid | TQA | 465.33 |
| 136. | S. Velasco | GAZ | 463 |
| 137. | T. Dupont | BWB | 461 |
| 138. | B. McNulty | UAD | 456 |
| 139. | G. Aleotti | BOH | 455 |
| 140. | N. Bonifazio | TEN | 454 |
| 141. | P. Allegaert | COF | 441 |
| 142. | J. Stewart | GFC | 431 |
| 143. | O. Naesen | ACT | 425 |
| 143. | J. Tesson | AUB | 425 |
| 145. | T. Skujiņš | TFS | 424 |
| 146. | D. F. Martínez | IGD | 420 |
| 147. | M. Soler | MOV | 415 |
| 148. | P. Latour | TEN | 411 |
| 149. | T. Dumoulin | TJV | 408 |
| 150. | L. L. Sanchez | APT | 405 |

TEAMS    FINAL RANKINGS

# MEN'S WORLDTOUR

## TEAM FINAL RANKINGS

| POS | NAME | TEAM | PTS |
|---|---|---|---|
| 1. | Deceuninck-QuickStep | DQT | 15641.21 |
| 2. | Ineos Grenadiers | IGD | 14998.66 |
| 3. | Jumbo-Visma | TJV | 12914.67 |
| 4. | UAE Team Emirates | UAD | 12355.66 |
| 5. | Bahrain Victorious | TBV | 10429 |
| 6. | Alpecin-Fenix | AFC | 8251 |
| 7. | Bora-Hansgrohe | BOH | 8222 |
| 8. | AG2R Citroën Team | ACT | 7151 |
| 9. | Groupama-FDJ | GFC | 6715 |
| 10. | Israel Start-Up Nation | ISN | 6704.66 |
| 11. | Movistar Team | MOV | 6656 |
| 12. | Trek-Segafredo | TFS | 6593.66 |
| 13. | Astana Premier Tech | APT | 6469 |
| 14. | Intermarché-Wanty-Gobert Matériaux | IWG | 5571 |
| 15. | Cofidis | COF | 5481 |
| 16. | EF Education-Nippo | EFN | 5362.33 |
| 17. | Team Arkéa-Samsic | ARK | 5000 |
| 18. | Lotto Soudal | LTS | 4704 |
| 19. | Team BikeExchange | BEX | 4686.33 |
| 20. | Team Qhubeka NextHash | TQA | 4368.66 |
| 21. | Team DSM | DSM | 3887 |
| 22. | TotalEnergies | TEN | 3192 |
| 23. | Uno-X Pro Cycling Team | UXT | 2848.17 |
| 24. | B&B Hotels p/b KTM | BBK | 2726 |
| 25. | Bingoal Pauwels Sauces | BWB | 2037 |

TEAMS    FINAL RANKINGS

# WOMEN'S WORLDTOUR

## INDIVIDUAL FINAL RANKINGS

| POS | NAME | TEAM | PTS |
|---|---|---|---|
| 1. | A. van Vleuten | MOV | 5053.33 |
| 2. | E. Longo Borghini | TFS | 3485 |
| 3. | M. Vos | JVW | 3378 |
| 4. | D. Vollering | SDW | 3343.33 |
| 5. | A. van der Breggen | SDW | 2732 |
| 6. | M. Reusser | ALE | 2364 |
| 7. | K. Niewiadoma | CSR | 2223 |
| 8. | L. Kopecky | LIV | 2152.33 |
| 9. | C. Ludwig | FDJ | 2140 |
| 10. | L. Brennauer | WNT | 1969 |
| 11. | E. Norsgaard | MOV | 1800.33 |
| 12. | E. Balsamo | VAL | 1744 |
| 13. | E. van Dijk | TFS | 1641.33 |
| 14. | G. Brown | BEX | 1636 |
| 15. | A. Pieters | SDW | 1508.33 |
| 16. | A. Moolman-Pasio | SDW | 1455 |
| 17. | M. García | ALE | 1443 |
| 18. | M. Cavalli | FDJ | 1433 |
| 19. | E. Chabbey | CSR | 1432 |
| 20. | L. Wiebes | DSM | 1428 |
| 21. | C. van den Broek-Blaak | SDW | 1242 |
| 22. | E. Deignan | TFS | 1195 |
| 23. | J. Labous | DSM | 1134 |
| 24. | K. Faulkner | TIB | 987 |
| 25. | M. Bastianelli | ALE | 953 |
| 26. | A. Sierra | MNX | 950 |
| 27. | L. Lippert | DSM | 895 |
| 28. | R. Winder | TFS | 892 |
| 29. | L. Brand | TFS | 827 |
| 30. | S. Bertizzolo | LIV | 796 |
| 31. | A. Jackson | LIV | 792 |
| 32. | A. Kiesenhofer | – | 785 |
| 33. | S. Paladin | LIV | 747 |
| 34. | L. Klein | CSR | 738 |
| 35. | C. Majerus | SDW | 734 |
| 36. | E. Muzic | FDJ | 727 |
| 37. | C. Rivera | DSM | 725 |
| 38. | P. Georgi | DSM | 720 |
| 38. | C. Consonni | VAL | 720 |
| 40. | L. Thomas | MOV | 708 |
| 41. | J. D'hoore | SDW | 692.33 |
| 42. | F. Mackaij | DSM | 688.33 |
| 43. | K. B. Vas | SDW | 683 |
| 44. | A. Henderson | JVW | 622.67 |
| 45. | T. Guderzo | ALE | 604 |
| 46. | A. Barnes | CSR | 585.67 |
| 47. | P. Rooijakkers | LIV | 585 |
| 48. | E. Cecchini | SDW | 584 |
| 49. | R. Markus | JVW | 577.33 |
| 50. | A. Spratt | BEX | 552 |
| 51. | K. Aalerud | MOV | 542 |
| 52. | L. Verhulst | ARK | 535 |
| 53. | E. Bujak | ALE | 521 |
| 54. | E. Fahlin | FDJ | 491 |
| 55. | C. Oberholzer | – | 465.83 |
| 56. | E. Magnaldi | WNT | 465 |
| 57. | S. Roy | BEX | 458 |
| 58. | J. Lowden | DRP | 455.67 |
| 59. | C. Hosking | TFS | 453 |
| 60. | L. Kirchmann | DSM | 447 |
| 61. | A. Santesteban | BEX | 443 |
| 62. | A. Cordon-Ragot | TFS | 441 |
| 63. | N. Fisher-Black | SDW | 439 |
| 64. | C. Copponi | FDJ | 422 |
| 65. | R. Neylan | PHV | 415 |
| 65. | A. van der Hulst | PHV | 415 |
| 67. | M. G. Confalonieri | WNT | 406 |
| 68. | E. Gasparrini | VAL | 401 |
| 69. | L. M. Hernández | – | 391 |
| 70. | S. Andersen | DSM | 377 |
| 71. | S. Zanardi | BPK | 376 |
| 72. | A. Amialiusik | CSR | 374 |
| 73. | H. Preen | – | 340.83 |
| 74. | S. Stultiens | LIV | 339 |
| 75. | A. Neben | CGS | 325 |
| 76. | T. Dronova | CGS | 313.67 |
| 77. | F. Janse van Rensburg | WCC | 310.83 |
| 78. | C. Koppenburg | RLW | 309 |
| 79. | R. Leleivyte | VAI | 308 |
| 80. | T. De Jong | CCT | 302 |
| 81. | F. Koch | DSM | 301 |
| 82. | L. Uneken | SDW | 299 |
| 83. | M. Harvey | CSR | 293 |
| 84. | M. Kröger | HPU | 291.33 |
| 85. | O. Zabelinskaya | CGS | 291 |
| 86. | J. Korevaar | LIV | 288 |
| 87. | A. Shackley | SDW | 279 |

| POS | NAME | TEAM | PTS |
|---|---|---|---|
| 88. | C. Kool | NXG | 273 |
| 89. | A. Biannic | MOV | 272 |
| 90. | V. Looser | ILP | 265 |
| 91. | L. Stephens | TIB | 260 |
| 91. | L. Jounier | ARK | 260 |
| 93. | J. Erić | MOV | 247 |
| 94. | A. V. Villalón | – | 246 |
| 95. | H. Barnes | CSR | 245 |
| 96. | A. Koster | JVW | 241 |
| 96. | L. Y. Salazar | MNX | 241 |
| 98. | M. Bredewold | PHV | 231 |
| 99. | B. Guarischi | MOV | 229 |
| 100. | K. Swinkels | JVW | 226 |
| 101. | A. Dideriksen | TFS | 224.33 |
| 102. | O. Shekel | – | 221 |
| 103. | A. Chursina | ALE | 217 |
| 103. | H. Ludwig | CSR | 217 |
| 105. | S. Gutiérrez | MOV | 216 |
| 106. | V. Kononenko | CCM | 205 |
| 106. | J. Joseph | – | 205 |
| 108. | T. Cromwell | CSR | 202 |
| 108. | D. Silvestri | TOP | 202 |
| 110. | O. Shapira | CSR | 201 |
| 111. | P. Muñoz Grandon | – | 200 |
| 111. | V. Ewers | TIB | 200 |
| 113. | M. Novolodskaia | MNX | 199 |
| 114. | U. Pintar | ALE | 196 |
| 114. | B. Chapman | FDJ | 196 |
| 116. | T. Neumanová | WCS | 192 |
| 117. | S. Martin | MOV | 188.33 |
| 118. | Š. Kern | MAT | 187 |
| 119. | M. Nunez | – | 180 |
| 120. | T. Campbell | BEX | 179 |
| 121. | E. Moberg | DRP | 178 |
| 122. | K. Ragusa | MNX | 177 |
| 123. | S. Gigante | TIB | 176 |
| 124. | M. van't Geloof | DRP | 175 |
| 125. | T. Wiles | TFS | 173 |
| 126. | K. Karasiewicz | – | 171.67 |
| 127. | M. Lach | WNT | 171 |
| 128. | E. Duval | FDJ | 169 |
| 128. | S. van Anrooij | TFS | 169 |
| 130. | V. Persico | VAL | 168 |
| 131. | M. Mena | – | 164 |
| 132. | Y. L. Comenares | – | 163 |
| 133. | S. Bossuyt | NXG | 162.33 |
| 134. | A. Ryan | CSR | 161 |
| 135. | V. Heine | MAT | 160 |
| 135. | D. Rozlapa | – | 160 |
| 137. | K. A. Canuel | SDW | 158 |
| 137. | I. Česulienė | VAI | 158 |
| 139. | J. Ensing | BEX | 157 |
| 139. | V. Guazzini | VAL | 157 |
| 141. | C. Dygert | CSR | 155 |
| 141. | M. Martins | DRP | 155 |
| 143. | K. Schweinberger | DVE | 153.33 |
| 143. | C. Schweinberger | DVE | 153.33 |
| 145. | G. Williams | BEX | 153 |
| 146. | M. Le Net | FDJ | 152 |
| 147. | K. Montoya | CCM | 150 |
| 148. | E. Merino | MNX | 148 |
| 149. | D. Ingabire | – | 147.08 |
| 150. | I. Grangier | SRC | 147 |

TEAMS   FINAL RANKINGS

# WOMEN'S WORLDTOUR

## TEAM FINAL RANKINGS

| POS | NAME | TEAM | PTS |
|---|---|---|---|
| 1. | Team SD Worx | SDW | 12389.99 |
| 2. | Trek-Segafredo | TFS | 9158.66 |
| 3. | Movistar Team Women | MOV | 9067.66 |
| 4. | Team DSM | DSM | 6414.33 |
| 5. | Alé BTC Ljubljana | ALE | 6396 |
| 6 | Canyon-SRAM Racing | CSR | 6107.67 |
| 7. | Liv Racing | LIV | 5834.33 |
| 8. | FDJ Nouvelle-Aquitaine Futuroscope | FDJ | 5730 |
| 9. | Jumbo-Visma Women Team | JVW | 5413 |
| 10. | Team BikeExchange | BEX | 3695 |
| 11. | Valcar Travel & Service | VAL | 3525 |
| 12. | Ceratizit-WNT Pro Cycling | WNT | 3472.66 |
| 13. | Team Tibco-Silicon Valley Bank | TIB | 1869 |
| 14. | A.R. Monex Women's Pro Cycling Team | MNX | 1799 |
| 15. | Parkhotel Valkenburg | PHV | 1454 |
| 16. | Drops Le Col s/b Tempur | DRP | 1094.67 |
| 17. | Cogeas Mettler Pro Cycling Team | CGS | 1044.67 |
| 18. | Arkéa Pro Cycling Team | ARK | 974 |
| 19. | WCC Team | WCC | 866.98 |
| 20. | BePink | BPK | 746 |
| 21. | Aromitalia-Basso Bikes-Vaiano | VAI | 688 |
| 22. | Rally Cycling | RLW | 614 |
| 23. | Stade Rochelais Charente-Maritime Women Cycling | SRC | 592 |
| 24. | NXTG Racing | NXG | 552.33 |
| 25. | Team Coop-Hitec Products | HPU | 551.33 |

# WOMEN'S WORLDTOUR TOTAL POINTS

It would be a surprise if the Dutch didn't top a table detailing success in the Women's WorldTour, and a totalling of the sprint points at all WWT stage races falls in line accordingly. Marianne Vos just pips young upstart Demi Vollering and, although Annemiek van Vleuten has the most WorldTour wins in this list, she only ranks tenth for the points she's accumulated.

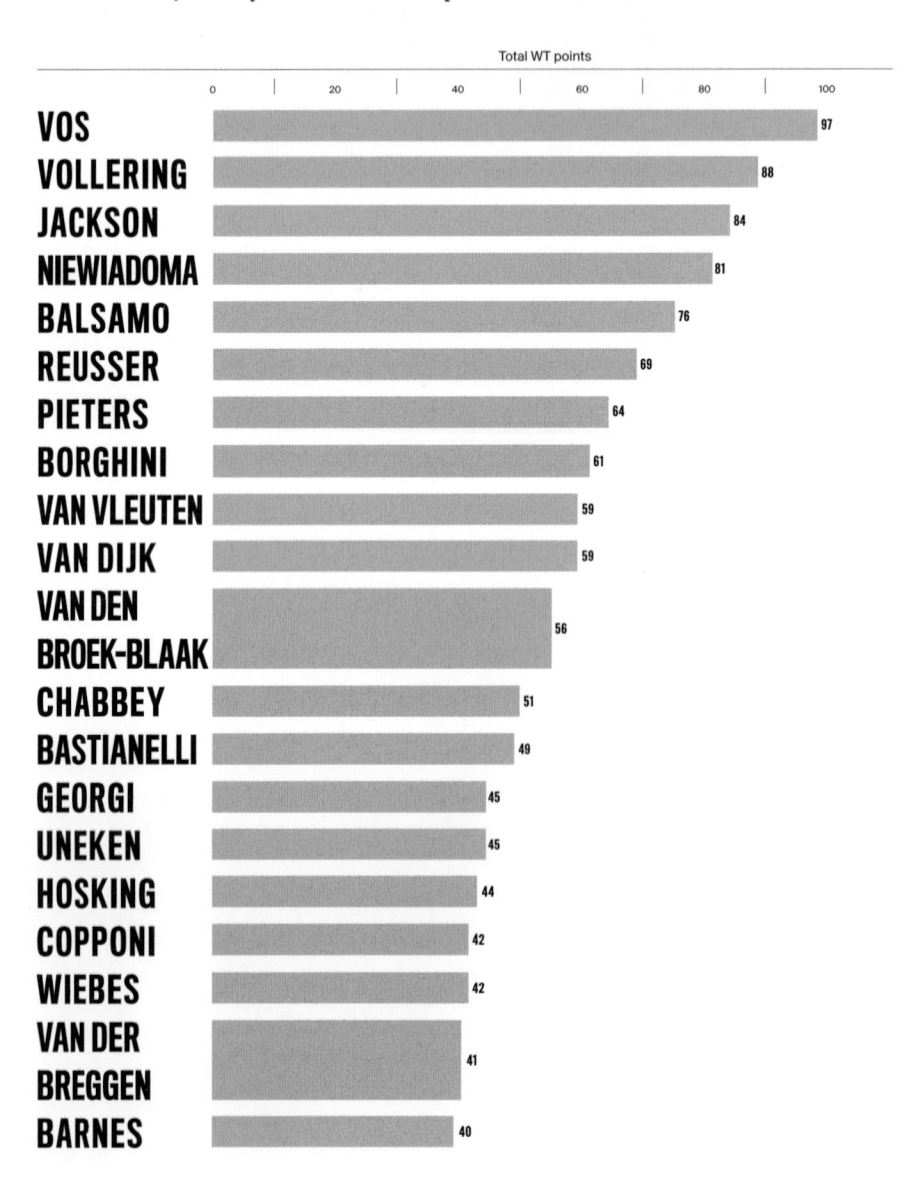

Total WT points

| Rider | Points |
|---|---|
| VOS | 97 |
| VOLLERING | 88 |
| JACKSON | 84 |
| NIEWIADOMA | 81 |
| BALSAMO | 76 |
| REUSSER | 69 |
| PIETERS | 64 |
| BORGHINI | 61 |
| VAN VLEUTEN | 59 |
| VAN DIJK | 59 |
| VAN DEN BROEK-BLAAK | 56 |
| CHABBEY | 51 |
| BASTIANELLI | 49 |
| GEORGI | 45 |
| UNEKEN | 45 |
| HOSKING | 44 |
| COPPONI | 42 |
| WIEBES | 42 |
| VAN DER BREGGEN | 41 |
| BARNES | 40 |

# HISTORICAL RESULTS

Races aren't simply born whole. They evolve, sometimes from small beginnings to take up ever more prominence in the calendar, swelling in importance and attracting the very biggest names. The Vuelta, for example, has not always drawn the same calibre of Tour de France winners and top GC candidates that it would now routinely attract. Other races remain something of a national affair, churning out a worthy succession of home-grown winners, and stubbornly holding out against the crashing waves of globalisation in the sport. Some races have been won repeatedly by one rider, like Sean Kelly's astonishing dominance of Paris–Nice. But each race has a different story to tell over time. The decades flit across the page, each subsequent year acting like an unbroken chain linking the present with the long and rich past of a sport that is in love like few other sports are with its own lineage.

MEN'S HISTORICAL RESULTS

# LIÈGE-BASTOGNE-LIÈGE

## RESULTS BY YEAR

| YEAR | 1ST | 2ND | 3RD |
|---|---|---|---|
| 2021 | T. Pogačar | J. Alaphilppe | D. Gaudu |
| 2020 | P. Roglič | M. Hirschi | T. Pogačar |
| 2019 | J. Fuglsang | D. Formolo | M. Schachmann |
| 2018 | B. Jungels | M. Woods | R. Bardet |
| 2017 | A. Valverde | D. Martin | M. Kwiatkowski |
| 2016 | W. Poels | M. Albasini | R. Costa |
| 2015 | A. Valverde | J. Alaphilippe | J. Rodriguez |
| 2014 | S. Gerrans | A. Valverde | M. Kwiatkowski |
| 2013 | D. Martin | J. Rodriguez | A. Valverde |
| 2012 | M. Iglinskiy | V. Nibali | E. Gasparotto |
| 2011 | P. Gilbert | F. Schleck | A. Schleck |
| 2010 | A. Vinokourov | A. Kolobnev | P. Gilbert |
| 2009 | A. Schleck | J. Rodriguez | D. Rebellin |
| 2008 | A. Valverde | D. Rebellin | F. Schleck |
| 2007 | D. Di Luca | A. Valverde | F. Schleck |
| 2006 | A. Valverde | P. Bettini | D. Cunego |
| 2005 | A. Vinokourov | J. Voigt | P. Bettini |
| 2004 | D. Rebellin | M. Boogerd | A. Vinokourov |
| 2003 | T. Hamilton | I. Mayo | M. Boogerd |
| 2002 | P. Bettini | S. Garzelli | I. Basso |
| 2001 | O. Camenzind | D. Rebellin | D. Etxebarria |
| 2000 | P. Bettini | D. Etxebarria | D. Rebellin |
| 1999 | F. Vandenbroucke | M. Boogerd | M. Den Bakker |
| 1998 | M. Bartoli | L. Jalabert | R. Massi |
| 1997 | M. Bartoli | L. Jalabert | G. Colombo |
| 1996 | P. Richard | L. Armstrong | M. Gianetti |
| 1995 | M. Gianetti | G. Bugno | M. Bartoli |
| 1994 | Y. Berzin | L. Armstrong | G. Furlan |
| 1993 | R. Sorensen | T. Rominger | M. Fondriest |
| 1992 | D. De Wolf | S. Rooks | J. F. Bernard |
| 1991 | M. Argentin | C. Criquielion | R. Sorensen |
| 1990 | E. Van Lancker | J. C. Leclercq | S. Rooks |
| 1989 | S. Kelly | F. Philipot | P. Anderson |
| 1988 | A. van der Poel | M. Dernies | R. Millar |
| 1987 | M. Argentin | S. Roche | C. Criquielion |
| 1986 | M. Argentin | A. van der Poel | D. E. Pedersen |
| 1985 | M. Argentin | C. Criquielion | S. Roche |
| 1984 | S. Kelly | P. Anderson | G. Lemond |
| 1983 | S. Rooks | G. Saronni | P. Jules |
| 1982 | S. Contini | F. De Wolf | S. Mutter |
| 1981 | J. Fuchs | S. Mutter | L. Peeters |
| 1980 | B. Hinault | H. Kuiper | R. Claes |
| 1979 | D. Thurau | B. Hinault | D. Willems |
| 1978 | J. Bruyere | D. Thurau | F. Moser |
| 1977 | B. Hinault | A. Dierickx | D. Thurau |
| 1976 | J. Bruyere | F. Maertens | F. Verbeeck |
| 1975 | E. Merckx | B. Thevenet | W. Godefroot |
| 1974 | G. Pintens | W. Planckaert | W. Panizza |
| 1973 | E. Merckx | F. Verbeeck | W. Godefroot |
| 1972 | E. Merckx | W. Schepers | H. Van Springel |
| 1971 | E. Merckx | G. Pintens | F. Verbeeck |
| 1970 | R. De Vlaeminck | F. Verbeeck | E. Merckx |
| 1969 | E. Merckx | V. Van Schil | B. Hoban |
| 1968 | V. Van Sweevelt | W. Godefroot | R. Poulidor |
| 1967 | W. Godefroot | E. Merckx | W. Monty |
| 1966 | J. Anquetil | V. Van Schil | W. In 't Ven |
| 1965 | C. Preziosi | V. Adorni | M. Vandenbossche |
| 1964 | W. Bocklant | G. Vanconingsloo | V. Adorni |
| 1963 | F. Melckenbeeck | P. Cerami | V. Adorni |
| 1962 | J. Planckaert | R. Wolfshohl | C. Colette |
| 1961 | R. Van Looy | M. Rohrbach | A. Desmet |
| 1960 | A. Geldermans | P. Everaert | J. Planckaert |
| 1959 | A. De Bruyne | F. Schoubben | F. De Mulder |
| 1958 | A. De Bruyne | J. Zagers | J. Theuns |
| 1957 | G. Derycke/ F. Schoubben | N/A | M. Buys |
| 1956 | A. De Bruyne | R. Van Genechten | A. Close |
| 1955 | S. Ockers | R. Impanis | J. Brankart |
| 1954 | M. Ernzer | R. Impanis | F. Kubler |
| 1953 | A. De Hertog | M. Diot | R. Remy |
| 1952 | F. Kubler | H. Van Kerckhove | J. Robic |
| 1951 | F. Kubler | G. Derycke | W. Wagtmans |
| 1950 | P. Depredomme | J. Bogaerts | E. Van Dijck |
| 1949 | C. Danguillaume | A. Verschueren | R. Gyselinck |
| 1948 | M. Mollin | R. Impanis | L. Caput |
| 1947 | R. Depoorter | R. Impanis | F. Mathieu |
| 1946 | P. Depredomme | A. Hendrickx | T. Verstraeten |
| 1945 | J. Engels | E. Van Dijck | J. Moerenhout |
| 1943 | R. Depoorter | J. Didden | S. Ockers |
| 1939 | A. Ritserveldt | C. Van Overberghe | E. Vissers |
| 1938 | A. Deloor | M. Kint | F. Vervaecke |
| 1937 | E. Meulenberg | G. Deloor | J. Heernaert |
| 1936 | A. Beckaert | G. Levae | J. Horemans |
| 1935 | A. Schepers | F. Bonduel | L. Hardiquest |
| 1934 | T. Herckenrath | M. Cardynaels | J. Moerenhout |
| 1933 | F. Gardier | R. Dewolf | A. Bolly |
| 1932 | M. Houyoux | L. Roosemont | G. Lambrechts |

## RIDER RESULTS

| WINS | RIDER |
|---|---|
| 5 | E. Merckx |
| 4 | M. Argentin, A. Valverde |
| 3 | A. De Bruyne, L. Houa, A. Schepers |
| 2 | M. Bartoli, P. Bettini, J. Bruyere, R. Depoorter, P. Depredomme, B. Hinault, S. Kelly, F. Kubler, L. Mottiat, R. Vermandel, A. Vinokourov |

| PODIUMS | RIDER |
|---|---|
| 7 | E. Merckx, A. Valverde |
| 5 | D. Rebellin |
| 4 | M. Argentin, P. Bettini, W. Godefroot, R. Impanis, F. Verbeeck |
| 3 | V. Adorni, M. Bartoli, M. Boogerd, C. Criquielion, A. De Bruyne, B. Hinault, L. Houa, F. Kubler, M. Raes, J. Rodriguez, S. Rooks, A. Schepers, F. Schleck, D. Thurau, A. Vinokourov |
| 2 | J. Alaphilppe, P. Anderson, L. Armstrong, J. Bruyere, J. Coomans, R. Depoorter, P. Depredomme, G. Derycke, D. Etxebarria, F. Gardier, M. Gianetti, P. Gilbert, M. Houyoux, L. Jalabert, S. Kelly, M. Kwiatkowski, D. Martin, J. Moerenhout, L. Mottiat, S. Mutter, S. Ockers, G. Pintens, J. Planckaert, T. Pogačar, L. Rasquinet, S. Roche, J. Rossius, A. Schleck, F. Schoubben, J. Siquet, R. Sorensen, A. van der Poel, E. Van Dijck, V. Van Schil, R. Vermandel |

## COUNTRY RESULTS

| WINS | COUNTRY |
|---|---|
| 60 | Belgium |
| 12 | Italy |
| 6 | Switzerland |
| 4 | France, Netherlands, Spain |
| 3 | Ireland, Kazakhstan, Luxembourg |
| 2 | Denmark, Germany, Slovenia |
| 1 | Australia, Russia, United States |

| PODIUMS | COUNTRY |
|---|---|
| 174 | Belgium |
| 36 | Italy |
| 25 | France |
| 14 | Netherlands |
| 13 | Spain, Switzerland |
| 7 | Germany, Luxembourg |
| 6 | Ireland |
| 4 | Kazakhstan, United States |
| 3 | Australia, Denmark, Slovenia |
| 2 | Poland, Russia, United Kingdom |
| 1 | Canada, Norway, Portugal |

MEN'S HISTORICAL RESULTS

## RESULTS BY YEAR (CONT.)

| YEAR | 1ST | 2ND | 3RD |
|---|---|---|---|
| 1931 | A. Schepers | M. Houyoux | J. Deschepper |
| 1930 | H. Buse | G. Laloup | F. Gardier |
| 1929 | A. Schepers | G. Hombroeckx | M. Raes |
| 1928 | E. Mottard | M. Raes | E. Van Belle |
| 1927 | M. Raes | J. Hans | J. Siquet |
| 1926 | D. Smets | J. Siquet | A. Macar |
| 1925 | G. Ronsse | G. Van Slembrouck | L. Eelen |
| 1924 | R. Vermandel | A. Benoit | J. Matton |
| 1923 | R. Vermandel | J. Rossius | F. Sellier |
| 1922 | L. Mottiat | A. Jordens | L. Seret |
| 1921 | L. Mottiat | M. Lacour | J. Rossius |
| 1920 | L. Scieur | L. Buysse | J. Coomans |
| 1919 | L. Devos | H. Hanlet | A. Claerhout |
| 1913 | M. Moritz | A. Fonson | H. Noel |
| 1912 | O. Verschoore | J. Coomans | A. Blaise |
| 1911 | J. Vandaele | A. Lenoir | V. Kraenen |
| 1909 | V. Fastre | E. Charlier | P. Deman |
| 1908 | A. Trousselier | A. Lauwers | H. Dubois |
| 1894 | L. Houa | L. Rasquinet | R. Nulens |
| 1893 | L. Houa | M. Borisowski | C. Collette |
| 1892 | L. Houa | L. Lhoest | L. Rasquinet |

MEN'S HISTORICAL RESULTS

# PARIS-ROUBAIX

## RESULTS BY YEAR

| YEAR | 1ST | 2ND | 3RD |
|---|---|---|---|
| 2021 | S. Colbrelli | F. Vermeersch | M. van der Poel |
| 2020 | Race cancelled | | |
| 2019 | P. Gilbert | N. Politt | Y. Lampaert |
| 2018 | P. Sagan | S. Dillier | N. Terpstra |
| 2017 | G. Van Avermaet | Z. Stybar | S. Langeveld |
| 2016 | M. Hayman | T. Boonen | I. Stannard |
| 2015 | J. Degenkolb | Z. Stybar | G. Van Avermaet |
| 2014 | N. Terpstra | J. Degenkolb | F. Cancellara |
| 2013 | F. Cancellara | S. Vanmarcke | N. Terpstra |
| 2012 | T. Boonen | S. Turgot | A. Ballan |
| 2011 | J. Vansummeren | F. Cancellara | M. Tjallingii |
| 2010 | F. Cancellara | T. Hushovd | J. A. Flecha |
| 2009 | T. Boonen | F. Pozzato | T. Hushovd |
| 2008 | T. Boonen | F. Cancellara | A. Ballan |
| 2007 | S. O'Grady | J. A. Flecha | S. Wesemann |
| 2006 | F. Cancellara | T. Boonen | A. Ballan |
| 2005 | T. Boonen | G. Hincapie | J. A. Flecha |
| 2004 | M. Backstedt | T. Hoffman | R. Hammond |
| 2003 | P. Van Petegem | D. Pieri | V. Ekimov |
| 2002 | J. Museeuw | S. Wesemann | T. Boonen |
| 2001 | S. Knaven | J. Museeuw | R. Vainsteins |
| 2000 | J. Museeuw | P. Van Petegem | E. Zabel |
| 1999 | A. Tafi | W. Peeters | T. Steels |
| 1998 | F. Ballerini | A. Tafi | W. Peeters |
| 1997 | F. Guesdon | J. Planckaert | J. Museeuw |
| 1996 | J. Museeuw | G. Bortolami | A. Tafi |
| 1995 | F. Ballerini | A. Tchmil | J. Museeuw |
| 1994 | A. Tchmil | F. Baldato | F. Ballerini |
| 1993 | G. Duclos Lassalle | F. Ballerini | O. Ludwig |
| 1992 | G. Duclos Lassalle | O. Ludwig | J. Capiot |
| 1991 | M. Madiot | J. C. Colotti | C. Bomans |
| 1990 | E. Planckaert | S. Bauer | E. Van Hooydonck |
| 1989 | J. M. Wampers | D. De Wolf | E. Van Hooydonck |
| 1988 | D. Demol | T. Wegmuller | L. Fignon |
| 1987 | E. Vanderaerden | P. Versluys | R. Dhaenens |
| 1986 | S. Kelly | R. Dhaenens | A. van der Poel |
| 1985 | M. Madiot | B. Wojtinek | S. Kelly |
| 1984 | S. Kelly | R. Rogiers | A. Bondue |
| 1983 | H. Kuiper | G. Duclos Lassalle | F. Moser |
| 1982 | J. Raas | Y. Bertin | G. Braun |
| 1981 | B. Hinault | R. De Vlaeminck | F. Moser |
| 1980 | F. Moser | G. Duclos Lassalle | D. Thurau |
| 1979 | F. Moser | R. De Vlaeminck | H. Kuiper |
| 1978 | F. Moser | R. De Vlaeminck | J. Raas |
| 1977 | R. De Vlaeminck | W. Teirlinck | F. Maertens |
| 1976 | M. Demeyer | F. Moser | R. De Vlaeminck |
| 1975 | R. De Vlaeminck | E. Merckx | A. Dierickx |
| 1974 | R. De Vlaeminck | F. Moser | M. Demeyer |
| 1973 | E. Merckx | W. Godefroot | R. Rosiers |
| 1972 | R. De Vlaeminck | A. Dierickx | B. Hoban |
| 1971 | R. Rosiers | H. Van Springel | M. Basso |
| 1970 | E. Merckx | R. De Vlaeminck | E. Leman |
| 1969 | W. Godefroot | E. Merckx | W. Vekemans |
| 1968 | E. Merckx | H. Van Springel | W. Godefroot |
| 1967 | J. Janssen | R. Van Looy | R. Altig |
| 1966 | F. Gimondi | J. Janssen | G. Desmet |
| 1965 | R. Van Looy | W. Sels | W. Vannitsen |
| 1964 | P. Post | B. Beheyt | Y. Molenaers |
| 1963 | E. Daems | R. Van Looy | J. Janssen |
| 1962 | R. Van Looy | E. Daems | F. Schoubben |
| 1961 | R. Van Looy | M. Janssens | R. Vanderveken |
| 1960 | P. Cerami | T. Sabbadini | M. Poblet |
| 1959 | N. Fore | G. Desmet | M. Janssens |
| 1958 | L. Vandaele | M. Poblet | R. Van Looy |
| 1957 | A. De Bruyne | R. Van Steenbergen | L. Vandaele |
| 1956 | L. Bobet | A. De Bruyne | J. Forestier |
| 1955 | J. Forestier | F. Coppi | L. Bobet |
| 1954 | R. Impanis | S. Ockers | M. Ryckaert |
| 1953 | G. Derycke | D. Piazza | W. Wagtmans |
| 1952 | R. Van Steenbergen | F. Coppi | A. Mahe |
| 1951 | A. Bevilacqua | L. Bobet | R. Van Steenbergen |
| 1950 | F. Coppi | M. Diot | F. Magni |
| 1949 | S. Coppi/A. Mahe | N/A | G. Martin/F. Leenen /I.-J. Moujica |
| 1948 | R. Van Steenbergen | E. Idee | G. Claes |
| 1947 | G. Claes | A. Verschueren | L. Thietard |
| 1946 | G. Claes | L. Gauthier | L. Vlaemynck |
| 1945 | P. Maye | L. Teisseire | K. Piot |
| 1944 | M. De Simpelaere | J. Rossi | L. Thietard |
| 1943 | M. Kint | J. Lowie | L. Thietard |
| 1939 | E. Masson | M. Kint | R. Lapebie |
| 1938 | L. Storme | L. Hardiquest | M. Van Houtte |
| 1937 | J. Rossi | A. Hendrickx | N. Declercq |
| 1936 | G. Speicher | R. Maes | G. Rebry |
| 1935 | G. Rebry | A. Leducq | J. Aerts |
| 1934 | G. Rebry | J. Wauters | F. Bonduel |
| 1933 | S. Maes | J. Vervaecke | L. Le Calvez |

## RIDER RESULTS

| WINS | RIDER |
|---|---|
| 4 | T. Boonen, R. De Vlaeminck |
| 3 | F. Cancellara, O. Lapize, E. Merckx, F. Moser, J. Museeuw, G. Rebry, R. Van Looy |
| 2 | H. Aucouturier, F. Ballerini, G. Claes, C. Crupelandt, G. Duclos-Lassalle, M. Garin, S. Kelly, L. Lesna, M. Madiot, H. Pelissier, R. Van Steenbergen |

| PODIUMS | RIDER |
|---|---|
| 9 | R. De Vlaeminck |
| 7 | T. Boonen, F. Moser |
| 6 | F. Cancellara, J. Museeuw, R. Van Looy |
| 5 | E. Merckx, G. Rebry |
| 4 | F. Ballerini, G. Duclos-Lassalle, M. Garin, G. Ronsse, L. Troussellier, C. Van Hauwaert, R. Van Steenbergen |
| 3 | J. A. Flecha, A. Ballan, L. Bobet, G. Claes, F. Coppi, C. Crupelandt, A. Garin, W. Godefroot, J. Janssen, S. Kelly, O. Lapize, F. Sellier, A. Tafi, N. Terpstra, L. Thietard |
| 2 | H. Aucouturier, E. Christophe, H. Cornet, E. Daems, A. De Bruyne, J. Degenkolb, M. Demeyer, G. Desmet, R. Dhaenens, A. Dierickx, F. Faber, J. Fischer, J. Forestier, T. Hushovd, M. Janssens, M. Kint, H. Kuiper, A. Leducq, L. Lesna, O. Ludwig, M. Madiot, A. Mahe, C. Meunier, W. Peeters, C. Pelissier, H. Pelissier, M. Poblet, R. Pottier, J. Raas, R. Rosiers, J. Rossi, Z. Štybar, A. Tchmil, G. Van Avermaet, L. Vandaele, J. Van Hevel, E. Van Hooydonck, P. Van Petegem, H. Van Springel, J. Vervaecke, E. Wattelier, S. Wesemann |

## COUNTRY RESULTS

| WINS | COUNTRY |
|---|---|
| 58 | Belgium |
| 30 | France |
| 12 | Italy |
| 6 | Netherlands |
| 4 | Switzerland |
| 2 | Australia, Germany, Ireland |
| 1 | Luxembourg, Slovakia, Sweden |

| PODIUMS | COUNTRY |
|---|---|
| 161 | Belgium |
| 92 | France |
| 34 | Italy |
| 19 | Netherlands |
| 12 | Germany, Switzerland |
| 5 | Spain |
| 3 | Ireland, United Kingdom |
| 2 | Australia, Czech Republic, Luxembourg, Norway |
| 1 | Canada, Denmark, Latvia, Russia, Slovakia, Sweden, United States |

MEN'S HISTORICAL RESULTS

## RESULTS BY YEAR (CONT.)

| YEAR | 1ST | 2ND | 3RD |
|---|---|---|---|
| 1932 | R. Gijssels | G. Ronsse | H. Sieronski |
| 1931 | G. Rebry | C. Pelissier | E. Decroix |
| 1930 | J. Vervaecke | J. Marechal | A. Magne |
| 1929 | C. Meunier | G. Ronsse | A. Deolet |
| 1928 | A. Leducq | G. Ronsse | C. Meunier |
| 1927 | G. Ronsse | J. Curtel | C. Pelissier |
| 1926 | J. Delbecque | G. Van Slembrouck | G. Rebry |
| 1925 | F. Sellier | P. Bestetti | J. Van Hevel |
| 1924 | J. Van Hevel | M. Ville | F. Sellier |
| 1923 | H. Suter | R. Vermandel | F. Sellier |
| 1922 | A. Dejonghe | J. Rossius | E. Masson |
| 1921 | H. Pelissier | F. Pelissier | L. Scieur |
| 1920 | P. Deman | E. Christophe | L. Buysse |
| 1919 | H. Pelissier | P. Thys | H. Barthelemy |
| 1914 | C. Crupelandt | L. Luguet | L. Mottiat |
| 1913 | F. Faber | C. Deruyter | C. Crupelandt |
| 1912 | C. Crupelandt | G. Garrigou | M. Leturgie |
| 1911 | O. Lapize | A. Charpiot | C. Van Hauwaert |
| 1910 | O. Lapize | C. Van Hauwaert | E. Christophe |
| 1909 | O. Lapize | L. Trousselier | J. Masselis |
| 1908 | C. Van Hauwaert | G. Lorgeou | F. Faber |
| 1907 | G. Passerieu | C. Van Hauwaert | L. Trousselier |
| 1906 | H. Cornet | M. Cadolle | R. Pottier |
| 1905 | L. Trousselier | R. Pottier | H. Cornet |
| 1904 | H. Aucouturier | C. Garin | L. Pothier |
| 1903 | H. Aucouturier | C. Chapperon | L. Trousselier |
| 1902 | L. Lesna | E. Wattelier | A. Garin |
| 1901 | L. Lesna | A. Garin | L. Itsweire |
| 1900 | E. Bouhours | J. Fischer | M. Garin |
| 1899 | A. Champion | P. Bor | A. Garin |
| 1898 | M. Garin | A. Stephane | E. Wattelier |
| 1897 | M. Garin | M. Cordang | M. Frederick |
| 1896 | J. Fischer | C. Meyer | M. Garin |

HISTORICAL RESULTS

659

MEN'S HISTORICAL RESULTS

# TOUR DE FRANCE

## RESULTS BY YEAR

| YEAR | 1ST | 2ND | 3RD |
|---|---|---|---|
| 2021 | T. Pogačar | J. Vingegaard | R. Carapaz |
| 2020 | T. Pogačar | P. Roglič | R. Porte |
| 2019 | E. Bernal | G. Thomas | S. Kruijswijk |
| 2018 | G. Thomas | T. Dumoulin | C. Froome |
| 2017 | C. Froome | R. Urán | R. Bardet |
| 2016 | C. Froome | R. Bardet | N. Quintana |
| 2015 | C. Froome | N. Quintana | A. Valverde |
| 2014 | V. Nibali | J. C. Peraud | T. Pinot |
| 2013 | C. Froome | N. Quintana | J. Rodriguez |
| 2012 | B. Wiggins | C. Froome | V. Nibali |
| 2011 | C. Evans | A. Schleck | F. Schleck |
| 2010 | A. Schleck | S. Sanchez | J. Van den Broeck |
| 2009 | A. Contador | A. Schleck | L. Armstrong* |
| 2008 | C. Sastre | C. Evans | D. Menchov |
| 2007 | A. Contador | C. Evans | C. Sastre |
| 2006 | O. Pereiro | A. Kloden | C. Sastre |
| 2005 | L. Armstrong* | I. Basso | J. Ullrich |
| 2004 | L. Armstrong* | A. Kloden | I. Basso |
| 2003 | L. Armstrong* | J. Ullrich | A. Vinokourov |
| 2002 | L. Armstrong* | J. Beloki | R. Rumsas |
| 2001 | L. Armstrong* | J. Ullrich | J. Beloki |
| 2000 | L. Armstrong* | J. Ullrich | J. Beloki |
| 1999 | L. Armstrong* | A. Zulle | F. Escartin |
| 1998 | M. Pantani | J. Ullrich | B. Julich |
| 1997 | J. Ullrich | R. Virenque | M. Pantani |
| 1996 | B. Riis | J. Ullrich | R. Virenque |
| 1995 | M. Indurain | A. Zulle | B. Riis |
| 1994 | M. Indurain | P. Ugrumov | M. Pantani |
| 1993 | M. Indurain | T. Rominger | Z. Jaskula |
| 1992 | M. Indurain | C. Chiappucci | G. Bugno |
| 1991 | M. Indurain | G. Bugno | C. Chiappucci |
| 1990 | G. Lemond | C. Chiappucci | E. Breukink |
| 1989 | G. Lemond | L. Fignon | P. Delgado |
| 1988 | P. Delgado | S. Rooks | F. E. Parra |
| 1987 | S. Roche | P. Delgado | J. F. Bernard |
| 1986 | G. Lemond | B. Hinault | U. Zimmermann |
| 1985 | B. Hinault | G. Lemond | S. Roche |
| 1984 | L. Fignon | B. Hinault | G. Lemond |
| 1983 | L. Fignon | A. Arroyo | P. Winnen |
| 1982 | B. Hinault | J. Zoetemelk | J. van der Velde |
| 1981 | B. Hinault | L. Van Impe | R. Alban |
| 1980 | J. Zoetemelk | H. Kuiper | R. Martin |
| 1979 | B. Hinault | J. Zoetemelk | J. Agostinho |
| 1978 | B. Hinault | J. Zoetemelk | J. Agostinho |
| 1977 | B. Thevenet | H. Kuiper | L. Van Impe |
| 1976 | L. Van Impe | J. Zoetemelk | R. Poulidor |
| 1975 | B. Thevenet | E. Merckx | L. Van Impe |
| 1974 | E. Merckx | R. Poulidor | V. Lopez |
| 1973 | L. Ocana | B. Thevenet | J. M. Fuente |
| 1972 | E. Merckx | F. Gimondi | R. Poulidor |
| 1971 | E. Merckx | J. Zoetemelk | L. Van Impe |
| 1970 | E. Merckx | J. Zoetemelk | G. Pettersson |
| 1969 | E. Merckx | R. Pingeon | R. Poulidor |
| 1968 | J. Janssen | H. Van Springel | F. Bracke |
| 1967 | R. Pingeon | J. Jimenez | F. Balmamion |
| 1966 | L. Aimar | J. Janssen | R. Poulidor |
| 1965 | F. Gimondi | R. Poulidor | G. Motta |
| 1964 | J. Anquetil | R. Poulidor | F. Bahamontes |
| 1963 | J. Anquetil | F. Bahamontes | J. Perez |
| 1962 | J. Anquetil | J. Planckaert | R. Poulidor |
| 1961 | J. Anquetil | G. Carlesi | C. Gaul |
| 1960 | G. Nencini | G. Battistini | J. Adriaensens |
| 1959 | F. Bahamontes | H. Anglade | J. Anquetil |
| 1958 | C. Gaul | V. Favero | R. Geminiani |
| 1957 | J. Anquetil | M. Janssens | A. Christian |
| 1956 | R. Walkowiak | G. Bauvin | J. Adriaensens |
| 1955 | L. Bobet | J. Brankart | C. Gaul |
| 1954 | L. Bobet | F. Kubler | F. Schar |
| 1953 | L. Bobet | J. Mallejac | G. Astrua |
| 1952 | F. Coppi | S. Ockers | B. Ruiz |
| 1951 | H. Koblet | R. Geminiani | L. Lazarides |
| 1950 | F. Kubler | S. Ockers | L. Bobet |
| 1949 | F. Coppi | G. Bartali | J. Marinelli |
| 1948 | G. Bartali | B. Schotte | G. Lapebie |
| 1947 | J. Robic | E. Fachleitner | P. Brambilla |
| 1939 | S. Maes | R. Vietto | L. Vlaemynck |
| 1938 | G. Bartali | F. Vervaecke | V. Cosson |
| 1937 | R. Lapebie | M. Vicini | L. Amberg |
| 1936 | S. Maes | A. Magne | F. Vervaecke |
| 1935 | R. Maes | A. Morelli | F. Vervaecke |
| 1934 | A. Magne | G. Martano | R. Lapebie |
| 1933 | G. Speicher | L. Guerra | G. Martano |
| 1932 | A. Leducq | K. Stoepel | F. Camusso |
| 1931 | A. Magne | J. Demuysere | A. Pesenti |
| 1930 | A. Leducq | L. Guerra | A. Magne |
| 1929 | M. De Waele | G. Pancera | J. Demuysere |
| 1928 | N. Frantz | A. Leducq | M. De Waele |

## RIDER RESULTS

| WINS | RIDER |
|---|---|
| 5 | J. Anquetil, B. Hinault, M. Indurain, E. Merckx |
| 4 | C. Froome |
| 3 | L. Bobet, G. Lemond, P. Thys |
| 2 | G. Bartali, O. Bottecchia, A. Contador, F. Coppi, L. Fignon, N. Frantz, A. Magne, F. Lambot, A. Leducq, S. Maes, A. Magne, L. Petit Breton, T. Pogačar, B. Thevenet |

| PODIUMS | RIDER |
|---|---|
| 8 | R. Poulidor |
| 7 | B. Hinault, J. Ullrich, J. Zoetemelk |
| 6 | J. Anquetil, C. Froome, G. Garrigou, E. Merckx |
| 5 | M. Indurain, G. Lemond, L. Van Impe |
| 4 | J. Alavoine, L. Bobet, N. Frantz, A. Magne |
| 3 | F. Bahamontes, G. Bartali, J. Beloki, O. Bottecchia, L. Buysse, C. Chiappucci, A. Contador, M. De Waele, P. Delgado, C. Evans, F. Faber, L. Fignon, C. Gaul, F. Lambot, A. Leducq, M. Pantani, N. Quintana, C. Sastre, A. Schleck, B. Thevenet, P. Thys, F. Vervaecke |
| 2 | J. Adriaensens, J. Agostinho, B. Aimo, J. B. Dortignacq, R. Bardet, I. Basso, G. Bugno, E. Christophe, F. Coppi, J. Demuysere, M. Garin, R. Geminiani, E. Georget, F. Gimondi, L. Guerra, H. Heusghem, J. Janssen, A. Kloden, F. Kubler, H. Kuiper, R. Lapebie, S. Maes, G. Martano, V. Nibali, S. Ockers, G. Passerieu, H. Pelissier, L. Petit Breton, R. Pingeon, T. Pogačar, L. Pothier, B. Riis, S. Roche, G. Thomas, L. Trousselier, R. Virenque, A. Zulle |

## COUNTRY RESULTS

| WINS | COUNTRY |
|---|---|
| 36 | France |
| 18 | Belgium |
| 12 | Spain |
| 10 | Italy |
| 6 | United Kingdom |
| 5 | Luxembourg |
| 3 | United States |
| 2 | Netherlands, Slovenia, Switzerland |
| 1 | Australia, Colombia, Denmark, Germany, Ireland |

| PODIUMS | COUNTRY |
|---|---|
| 101 | France |
| 51 | Belgium |
| 40 | Italy |
| 31 | Spain |
| 17 | Netherlands |
| 13 | Luxembourg |
| 11 | Germany |
| 9 | Switzerland, United Kingdom |
| 7 | United States |
| 6 | Colombia |
| 4 | Australia |
| 3 | Denmark, Slovenia |
| 2 | Ireland, Portugal |
| 1 | Austria, Ecuador, Kazakhstan, Latvia, Lithuania, Poland, Russia, Sweden |

## RESULTS BY YEAR (CONT.)

| YEAR | 1ST | 2ND | 3RD |
|---|---|---|---|
| 1927 | N. Frantz | M. De Waele | J. Vervaecke |
| 1926 | L. Buysse | N. Frantz | B. Aimo |
| 1925 | O. Bottecchia | L. Buysse | B. Aimo |
| 1924 | O. Bottecchia | N. Frantz | L. Buysse |
| 1923 | H. Pelissier | O. Bottecchia | R. Bellenger |
| 1922 | F. Lambot | J. Alavoine | F. Sellier |
| 1921 | L. Scieur | H. Heusghem | H. Barthelemy |
| 1920 | P. Thys | H. Heusghem | F. Lambot |
| 1919 | F. Lambot | J. Alavoine | E. Christophe |
| 1914 | P. Thys | H. Pelissier | J. Alavoine |
| 1913 | P. Thys | G. Garrigou | M. Buysse |
| 1912 | O. Defraye | E. Christophe | G. Garrigou |
| 1911 | G. Garrigou | P. Duboc | E. Georget |
| 1910 | O. Lapize | F. Faber | G. Garrigou |
| 1909 | F. Faber | G. Garrigou | J. Alavoine |
| 1908 | L. Petit Breton | F. Faber | G. Passerieu |
| 1907 | L. Petit Breton | G. Garrigou | E. Georget |
| 1906 | R. Pottier | G. Passerieu | L. Trousselier |
| 1905 | L. Trousselier | H. Aucouturier | J. B. Dortignacq |
| 1904 | H. Cornet | J. B. Dortignacq | A. Catteau |
| 1903 | M. Garin | L. Pothier | F. Augereau |

MEN'S HISTORICAL RESULTS

# IL LOMBARDIA

## RESULTS BY YEAR

| YEAR | 1ST | 2ND | 3RD |
|---|---|---|---|
| 2021 | T. Pogačar | F. Masnada | A. Yates |
| 2020 | J. Fuglsang | G. Bennett | A. Vlasov |
| 2019 | B. Mollema | A. Valverde | E. Bernal |
| 2018 | T. Pinot | V. Nibali | D. Teuns |
| 2017 | V. Nibali | J. Alaphilippe | G. Moscon |
| 2016 | E. Chaves | D. Rosa | R. Urán |
| 2015 | V. Nibali | D. Moreno | T. Pinot |
| 2014 | D. Martin | A. Valverde | R. Costa |
| 2013 | J. Rodriguez | A. Valverde | R. Majka |
| 2012 | J. Rodriguez | S. Sanchez | R. Urán |
| 2011 | O. Zaugg | D. Martin | J. Rodriguez |
| 2010 | P. Gilbert | M. Scarponi | P. Lastras |
| 2009 | P. Gilbert | S. Sanchez | A. Kolobnev |
| 2008 | D. Cunego | J. Brajkovic | R. Urán |
| 2007 | D. Cunego | R. Ricco | S. Sanchez |
| 2006 | P. Bettini | S. Sanchez | F. Wegmann |
| 2005 | P. Bettini | G. Simoni | F. Schleck |
| 2004 | D. Cunego | M. Boogerd | I. Basso |
| 2003 | M. Bartoli | A. Lopeboselli | D. Frigo |
| 2002 | M. Bartoli | D. Rebellin | O. Camenzind |
| 2001 | D. Di Luca | G. Figueras | M. Boogerd |
| 2000 | R. Rumsas | F. Casagrande | N. Axelsson |
| 1999 | M. Celestino | D. Di Luca | E. Mazzoleni |
| 1998 | O. Camenzind | M. Boogerd | F. Puttini |
| 1997 | L. Jalabert | P. Lanfranchi | F. Casagrande |
| 1996 | A. Tafi | F. Jeker | A. Merckx |
| 1995 | G. Faresin | D. Nardello | M. Bartoli |
| 1994 | V. Bobrik | C. Chiappucci | P. Richard |
| 1993 | P. Richard | G. Furlan | M. Sciandri |
| 1992 | T. Rominger | C. Chiappucci | D. Cassani |
| 1991 | S. Kelly | M. Gayant | F. Ballerini |
| 1990 | G. Delion | P. Richard | C. Mottet |
| 1989 | T. Rominger | G. Delion | L. Roosen |
| 1988 | C. Mottet | G. Bugno | M. Lejarreta |
| 1987 | M. Argentin | E. Van Lancker | M. Madiot |
| 1986 | G. Baronchelli | S. Kelly | P. Anderson |
| 1985 | S. Kelly | A. Van Der Poel | C. Mottet |
| 1984 | B. Hinault | L. Peeters | T. Van Vliet |
| 1983 | S. Kelly | G. Lemond | A. Van Der Poel |
| 1982 | G. Saronni | P. Jules | F. Moser |
| 1981 | H. Kuiper | M. Argentin | A. Chinetti |
| 1980 | F. De Wolf | A. Chinetti | L. Peeters |
| 1979 | B. Hinault | S. Contini | G. Battaglin |
| 1978 | F. Moser | B. Johansson | B. Hinault |
| 1977 | G. Baronchelli | J. L. Vandenbroucke | F. Bitossi |
| 1976 | R. De Vlaeminck | B. Thevenet | W. Panizza |
| 1975 | F. Moser | E. Paolini | A. Chinetti |
| 1974 | R. De Vlaeminck | E. Merckx | T. Conti |
| 1973 | F. Gimondi | R. De Vlaeminck | H. Van Springel |
| 1972 | E. Merckx | C. Guimard | F. Gimondi |
| 1971 | E. Merckx | F. Bitossi | F. Verbeeck |
| 1970 | F. Bitossi | F. Gimondi | G. Motta |
| 1969 | J. P. Monsere | H. Van Springel | F. Bitossi |
| 1968 | H. Van Springel | F. Bitossi | E. Merckx |
| 1967 | F. Bitossi | F. Gimondi | R. Poulidor |
| 1966 | F. Gimondi | E. Merckx | R. Poulidor |
| 1965 | T. Simpson | G. Karstens | J. Stablinski |
| 1964 | G. Motta | C. Preziosi | J. Hoevenaers |
| 1963 | J. De Roo | A. Durante | M. Dancelli |
| 1962 | J. De Roo | L. Trape | A. Cerato |
| 1961 | V. Taccone | I. Massignan | R. Fontona |
| 1960 | E. Daems | D. Ronchini | M. Fontana |
| 1959 | R. Van Looy | W. Vannitsen | M. Poblet |
| 1958 | N. Defilippis | M. Poblet | M. Van Aerde |
| 1957 | D. Ronchini | B. Monti | A. Cestari |
| 1956 | A. Darrigade | F. Coppi | F. Magni |
| 1955 | C. Maule | A. De Bruyne | A. Conterno |
| 1954 | F. Coppi | F. Magni | M. De Rossi |
| 1953 | B. Landi | P. Cerami | P. Molineris |
| 1952 | G. Minardi | N. Defilippis | A. Padovan |
| 1951 | L. Bobet | G. Minardi | F. Coppi |
| 1950 | R. Soldani | A. Bevilacqua | F. Coppi |
| 1949 | F. Coppi | F. Kubler | N. Logli |
| 1948 | F. Coppi | A. Leoni | F. Schar |
| 1947 | F. Coppi | G. Bartali | I. De Zan |
| 1946 | F. Coppi | L. Casola | M. Motta |
| 1945 | M. Ricci | A. Bini | G. Bartali |
| 1942 | A. Bini | G. Bartali | Q. Toccacelli |
| 1941 | M. Ricci | C. Cinelli | S. Canavesi |
| 1940 | G. Bartali | O. Bailo | C. Cinelli |
| 1939 | G. Bartali | A. Leoni | S. Crippa |
| 1938 | C. Cinelli | G. Bartali | O. Bailo |
| 1937 | A. Bini | G. Bartali | A. Landi |
| 1936 | G. Bartali | D. Marabelli | L. Barral |
| 1935 | E. Mollo | A. Bini | G. Bartali |
| 1934 | L. Guerra | M. Cipriani | D. Piemontesi |
| 1933 | D. Piemontesi | L. Barral | P. Rimoldi |

## RIDER RESULTS

| WINS | RIDER |
|---|---|
| 5 | F. Coppi |
| 4 | A. Binda |
| 3 | G. Bartali, G. Belloni, D. Cunego, |
|   | C. Girardengo, S. Kelly, H. Pelissier |
| 2 | G. Baronchelli, M. Bartoli, P. Bettini, |
|   | A. Bini, F. Bitossi, G. Brunero, J. De Roo, |
|   | R. De Vlaeminck, P. Gilbert, F. Gimondi, |
|   | B. Hinault, E. Merckx, F. Moser, V. Nibali, |
|   | M. Ricci, J. Rodriguez, T. Rominger |

| PODIUMS | RIDER |
|---|---|
| 9 | G. Bartali |
| 8 | F. Coppi |
| 6 | G. Belloni, F. Bitossi |
| 5 | A. Binda, L. Ganna, F. Gimondi, E. Merckx |
| 4 | A. Bini, C. Girardengo, S. Kelly, H. Pelissier, |
|   | S. Sanchez |
| 3 | M. Bartoli, M. Boogerd, G. Brunero, |
|   | A. Chinetti, C. Cinelli, D. Cunego, R. De |
|   | Vlaeminck, B. Hinault, F. Moser, C. Mottet, |
|   | A. Negrini, V. Nibali, D. Piemontesi, |
|   | P. Richard, J. Rodriguez, R. Urán, |
|   | A. Valverde, H. Van Springel |
| 2 | M. Argentin, G. Azzini, O. Bailo, |
|   | G. Baronchelli, L. Barral, P. Bettini, |
|   | M. Brocco, O. Camenzind, F. Casagrande, |
|   | C. Chiappucci, J. De Roo, N. Defilippis, |
|   | G. Delion, D. Di Luca, P. Fossati, C. Galetti, |
|   | F. Gay, G. Gerbi, P. Gilbert, L. Guerra, |
|   | A. Leoni, P. Linari, F. Magni, M. Mara, |
|   | D. Martin, G. Micheletto, G. Minardi, |
|   | G. Motta, L. Peeters, M. Poblet, |
|   | R. Poulidor, M. Ricci, T. Rominger, |
|   | D. Ronchini, A. Sivocci, L. Torricelli, |
|   | E. Vallazza, A. Van Der Poel |

## COUNTRY RESULTS

| WINS | COUNTRY |
|---|---|
| 69 | Italy |
| 12 | Belgium, France |
| 5 | Switzerland |
| 4 | Ireland, Netherlands |
| 2 | Spain |
| 1 | Colombia, Denmark, Lithuania, |
|   | Luxembourg, Russia, Slovenia, |
|   | United Kingdom |

| PODIUMS | COUNTRY |
|---|---|
| 210 | Italy |
| 33 | France |
| 32 | Belgium |
| 15 | Spain |
| 13 | Switzerland |
| 11 | Netherlands |
| 6 | Ireland |
| 5 | Colombia |
| 3 | Russia, United Kingdom |
| 2 | Luxembourg, Slovenia, Sweden |
| 1 | Australia, Denmark, Germany, Lithuania, |
|   | New Zealand, Poland, Portugal, |
|   | United States |

## RESULTS BY YEAR (CONT.)

| YEAR | 1ST | 2ND | 3RD |
|---|---|---|---|
| 1932 | A. Negrini | D. Piemontesi | R. Bertoni |
| 1931 | A. Binda | M. Mara | G. Firpo |
| 1930 | M. Mara | A. Binda | L. Guerra |
| 1929 | P. Fossati | A. Zanaga | R. Di Paco |
| 1928 | G. Belloni | A. Grandi | P. Fossati |
| 1927 | A. Binda | A. Piccin | A. Negrini |
| 1926 | A. Binda | A. Negrini | E. Vallazza |
| 1925 | A. Binda | B. Giuntelli | E. Vallazza |
| 1924 | G. Brunero | C. Girardengo | P. Linari |
| 1923 | G. Brunero | P. Linari | F. Gay |
| 1922 | C. Girardengo | G. Azzini | B. Aimo |
| 1921 | C. Girardengo | G. Belloni | F. Gay |
| 1920 | H. Pelissier | G. Brunero | G. Belloni |
| 1919 | C. Girardengo | G. Belloni | H. Suter |
| 1918 | G. Belloni | A. Sivocci | C. Galetti |
| 1917 | P. Thys | H. Pelissier | L. Torricelli |
| 1916 | L. Torricelli | C. Bertarelli | A. Sivocci |
| 1915 | G. Belloni | P. Ferrari | G. Caravaglia |
| 1914 | L. Bordin | G. Azzini | P. Piacco |
| 1913 | H. Pelissier | M. Brocco | M. Godivier |
| 1912 | C. Oriani | E. Verde | M. Brocco |
| 1911 | H. Pelissier | G. Micheletto | C. Van Hauwaert |
| 1910 | G. Micheletto | L. Ganna | L. Bailo |
| 1909 | G. Cuniolo | O. Beaugendre | L. Trousselier |
| 1908 | F. Faber | L. Ganna | G. Gerbi |
| 1907 | G. Garrigou | E. Azzini | L. Ganna |
| 1906 | C. Brambilla | C. Galetti | L. Ganna |
| 1905 | G. Gerbi | G. Rossignoli | L. Ganna |

MEN'S HISTORICAL RESULTS

# MILAN-SANREMO

## RESULTS BY YEAR

| YEAR | 1ST | 2ND | 3RD |
|---|---|---|---|
| 2021 | J. Stuyven | C. Ewan | W. van Aert |
| 2020 | W. van Aert | J. Alaphilippe | M. Matthews |
| 2019 | J. Alaphilippe | O. Naesen | M. Kwiatkowski |
| 2018 | V. Nibali | C. Ewan | A. Demare |
| 2017 | M. Kwiatkowski | P. Sagan | J. Alaphilippe |
| 2016 | A. Demare | B. Swift | J. Roelandts |
| 2015 | J. Degenkolb | A. Kristoff | M. Matthews |
| 2014 | A. Kristoff | F. Cancellara | B. Swift |
| 2013 | G. Ciolek | P. Sagan | F. Cancellara |
| 2012 | S. Gerrans | F. Cancellara | V. Nibali |
| 2011 | M. Goss | F. Cancellara | P. Gilbert |
| 2010 | O. Freire | T. Boonen | A. Petacchi |
| 2009 | M. Cavendish | H. Haussler | T. Hushovd |
| 2008 | F. Cancellara | F. Pozzato | P. Gilbert |
| 2007 | O. Freire | A. Davis | T. Boonen |
| 2006 | F. Pozzato | A. Petacchi | L. Paolini |
| 2005 | A. Petacchi | D. Hondo | T. Hushovd |
| 2004 | O. Freire | E. Zabel | S. O'Grady |
| 2003 | P. Bettini | M. Celestino | L. Paolini |
| 2002 | M. Cipollini | F. Rodriguez | M. Zberg |
| 2001 | E. Zabel | M. Cipollini | R. Vainsteins |
| 2000 | E. Zabel | F. Baldato | O. Freire |
| 1999 | A. Tchmil | E. Zabel | Z. Spruch |
| 1998 | E. Zabel | E. Magnien | F. Moncassin |
| 1997 | E. Zabel | A. Elli | B. Conte |
| 1996 | G. Colombo | A. Gontsjenkov | M. Coppolillo |
| 1995 | L. Jalabert | M. Fondriest | S. Zanini |
| 1994 | G. Furlan | M. Cipollini | A. Baffi |
| 1993 | M. Fondriest | L. Gelfi | M. Sciandri |
| 1992 | S. Kelly | M. Argentin | J. Museeuw |
| 1991 | C. Chiappucci | R. Sorensen | E. Vanderaerden |
| 1990 | G. Bugno | R. Golz | G. Delion |
| 1989 | L. Fignon | F. Maassen | A. Baffi |
| 1988 | L. Fignon | M. Fondriest | S. Rooks |
| 1987 | E. Machler | E. Vanderaerden | G. Bontempi |
| 1986 | S. Kelly | G. Lemond | M. Beccia |
| 1985 | H. Kuiper | T. van Vliet | S. Ricco |
| 1984 | F. Moser | S. Kelly | E. Vanderaerden |
| 1983 | G. Saronni | G. Bontempi | J. Raas |
| 1982 | M. Gomez | A. Bondue | M. Argentin |
| 1981 | F. De Wolf | R. De Vlaeminck | J. Bossis |
| 1980 | P. Gavazzi | G. Saronni | J. Raas |
| 1979 | R. De Vlaeminck | G. Saronni | K. Knudsen |
| 1978 | R. De Vlaeminck | G. Saronni | A. Antonini |
| 1977 | J. Raas | R. De Vlaeminck | W. Wesemael |
| 1976 | E. Merckx | W. Panizza | M. Laurent |
| 1975 | E. Merckx | F. Moser | G. Sibille |
| 1974 | F. Gimondi | E. Leman | R. De Vlaeminck |
| 1973 | R. De Vlaeminck | W. Francioni | F. Gimondi |
| 1972 | E. Merckx | G. Motta | M. Basso |
| 1971 | E. Merckx | F. Gimondi | G. Pettersson |
| 1970 | M. Dancelli | G. Karstens | E. Leman |
| 1969 | E. Merckx | R. De Vlaeminck | M. Basso |
| 1968 | R. Altig | C. Grosskost | A. Durante |
| 1967 | E. Merckx | G. Motta | F. Bitossi |
| 1966 | E. Merckx | A. Durante | H. Van Springel |
| 1965 | A. Den Hartog | V. Adorni | F. Balmamion |
| 1964 | T. Simpson | R. Poulidor | W. Bocklant |
| 1963 | J. Groussard | R. Wolfshohl | W. Schroeders |
| 1962 | E. Daems | Y. Molenaers | L. Proost |
| 1961 | R. Poulidor | R. Van Looy | R. Benedetti |
| 1960 | R. Privat | J. Graczyk | Y. Molenaers |
| 1959 | M. Poblet | R. Van Steenbergen | L. Vandaele |
| 1958 | R. Van Looy | M. Poblet | A. Darrigade |
| 1957 | M. Poblet | A. De Bruyne | B. Robinson |
| 1956 | A. De Bruyne | F. Magni | J. Planckaert |
| 1955 | G. Derycke | B. Gauthier | J. Bobet |
| 1954 | R. Van Steenbergen | F. Anastasi | G. Favero |
| 1953 | L. Petrucci | G. Minardi | V. Ollivier |
| 1952 | L. Petrucci | G. Minardi | S. Blusson |
| 1951 | L. Bobet | P. Barbotin | L. Petrucci |
| 1950 | G. Bartali | N. Logli | O. Conte |
| 1949 | F. Coppi | V. Ortelli | F. Magni |
| 1948 | F. Coppi | V. Rossello | F. Camellini |
| 1947 | G. Bartali | E. Cecchi | S. Maggini |
| 1946 | F. Coppi | L. Teisseire | M. Ricci |
| 1943 | C. Cinelli | G. Servadei | Q. Toccacelli |
| 1942 | A. Leoni | A. Bevilacqua | P. Favalli |
| 1941 | P. Favalli | M. Ricci | P. Chiappini |
| 1940 | G. Bartali | P. Rimoldi | A. Bini |
| 1939 | G. Bartali | A. Bini | O. Bailo |
| 1938 | G. Olmo | P. Favalli | A. Bovet |
| 1937 | C. Del Cancia | P. Favalli | M. Cimatti |
| 1936 | A. Varetto | C. Romanatti | O. Bizzi |
| 1935 | G. Olmo | L. Guerra | M. Cipriani |
| 1934 | J. Demuysere | G. Cazzulani | F. Camusso |
| 1933 | L. Guerra | A. Bovet | P. Rimoldi |

## RIDER RESULTS

| WINS | RIDER |
|---|---|
| 7 | E. Merckx |
| 6 | C. Girardengo |
| 4 | G. Bartali, E. Zabel |
| 3 | F. Coppi, R. De Vlaeminck, O. Freire |
| 2 | G. Belloni, A. Binda, L. Fignon, S. Kelly, G. Olmo, L. Petrucci, M. Poblet |

| PODIUMS | RIDER |
|---|---|
| 11 | C. Girardengo |
| 7 | R. De Vlaeminck, E. Merckx |
| 6 | E. Zabel |
| 5 | G. Belloni, A. Binda, F. Cancellara |
| 4 | G. Bartali, G. Brunero, P. Favalli, O. Freire, G. Saronni |
| 3 | J. Alaphilippe, A. Bovet, M. Cipollini, F. Coppi, M. Fondriest, L. Ganna, G. Garrigou, F. Gimondi, A. Gremo, L. Guerra, S. Kelly, A. Petacchi, L. Petrucci, D. Piemontesi, M. Poblet, J. Raas, E. Vanderaerden |
| 2 | U. Agostoni, M. Argentin, G. Azzini, A. Baffi, M. Basso, A. Bini, G. Bontempi, T. Boonen, P. Caimmi, E. Corlaita, A. De Bruyne, A. Démare, A. Durante, C. Ewan, L. Fignon, P. Gilbert, T. Hushovd, A. Kristoff, M. Kwiatkowski, E. Leman, P. Linari,F. Magni, M. Mara, M. Matthews, G. Minardi, Y. Molenaers, F. Moser, G. Motta, V. Nibali, G. Olmo, L. Paolini, H. Pelissier, R. Poulidor, F. Pozzato, M. Ricci, P. Rimoldi, P. Sagan, B. Swift, W. van Aert, R. Van Looy, R. Van Steenbergen |

## COUNTRY RESULTS

| WINS | COUNTRY |
|---|---|
| 51 | Italy |
| 22 | Belgium |
| 14 | France |
| 7 | Germany |
| 5 | Spain |
| 3 | Netherlands |
| 2 | Australia, Ireland, Switzerland, United Kingdom |
| 1 | Norway, Poland |

| PODIUMS | COUNTRY |
|---|---|
| 172 | Italy |
| 54 | Belgium |
| 41 | France |
| 12 | Germany |
| 9 | Australia, Netherlands |
| 7 | Spain, Switzerland |
| 6 | United Kingdom |
| 5 | Norway |
| 3 | Ireland, Poland |
| 2 | Slovakia, United States |
| 1 | Denmark, Latvia, Russia, Sweden |

MEN'S HISTORICAL RESULTS

## RESULTS BY YEAR (CONT.)

| YEAR | 1ST | 2ND | 3RD |
|---|---|---|---|
| 1932 | A. Bovet | A. Binda | M. Mara |
| 1931 | A. Binda | L. Guerra | D. Piemontesi |
| 1930 | M. Mara | P. Caimmi | D. Piemontesi |
| 1929 | A. Binda | L. Frascarelli | P. Caimmi |
| 1928 | C. Girardengo | A. Binda | G. Brunero |
| 1927 | P. Chiesi | A. Binda | D. Piemontesi |
| 1926 | C. Girardengo | N. Ciaccheri | E. Picchiottino |
| 1925 | C. Girardengo | G. Brunero | P. Linari |
| 1924 | P. Linari | G. Belloni | C. Girardengo |
| 1923 | C. Girardengo | G. Belloni | G. Azzini |
| 1922 | G. Brunero | C. Girardengo | B. Aimo |
| 1921 | C. Girardengo | G. Brunero | G. Azzini |
| 1920 | G. Belloni | H. Pelissier | C. Girardengo |
| 1919 | A. Gremo | C. Girardengo | G. Oliveri |
| 1918 | C. Girardengo | G. Belloni | U. Agostoni |
| 1917 | G. Belloni | C. Girardengo | A. Gremo |
| 1915 | E. Corlaita | L. Lucotti | A. Gremo |
| 1914 | U. Agostoni | C. Galetti | C. Crupelandt |
| 1913 | O. Defraye | L. Mottiat | E. Corlaita |
| 1912 | H. Pelissier | G. Garrigou | J. Masselis |
| 1911 | G. Garrigou | L. Trousselier | L. Ganna |
| 1910 | E. Christophe | G. Cocchi | G. Marchese |
| 1909 | L. Ganna | E. Georget | G. Cuniolo |
| 1908 | C. Van Hauwaert | L. Ganna | A. Pottier |
| 1907 | L. Petit Breton | G. Garrigou | G. Gerbi |

MEN'S HISTORICAL RESULTS

# GIRO D'ITALIA

## RESULTS BY YEAR

| YEAR | 1ST | 2ND | 3RD |
|---|---|---|---|
| 2021 | E. Bernal | D. Caruso | S. Yates |
| 2020 | T. Geoghegan Hart | J. Hindley | W. Kelderman |
| 2019 | R. Carapaz | V. Nibali | P. Roglič |
| 2018 | C. Froome | T. Dumoulin | M. A. López |
| 2017 | T. Dumoulin | N. Quintana | V. Nibali |
| 2016 | V. Nibali | E. Chaves | A. Valverde |
| 2015 | A. Contador | F. Aru | M. Landa |
| 2014 | N. Quintana | R. Urán | F. Aru |
| 2013 | V. Nibali | R. Urán | C. Evans |
| 2012 | R. Hesjedal | J. Rodriguez | T. De Gendt |
| 2011 | M. Scarponi | V. Nibali | J. Gadret |
| 2010 | I. Basso | D. Arroyo | V. Nibali |
| 2009 | D. Menchov | C. Sastre | I. Basso |
| 2008 | A. Contador | R. Ricco | M. Bruseghin |
| 2007 | D. Di Luca | A. Schleck | E. Mazzoleni |
| 2006 | I. Basso | J. E. Gutierrez | G. Simoni |
| 2005 | P. Savoldelli | G. Simoni | J. H. Rujano |
| 2004 | D. Cunego | S. Honchar | G. Simoni |
| 2003 | G. Simoni | S. Garzelli | Y. Popovych |
| 2002 | P. Savoldelli | T. Hamilton | P. Caucchioli |
| 2001 | G. Simoni | A. Olano | U. Osa |
| 2000 | S. Garzelli | F. Casagrande | G. Simoni |
| 1999 | I. Gotti | P. Savoldelli | G. Simoni |
| 1998 | M. Pantani | P. Tonkov | G. Guerini |
| 1997 | I. Gotti | P. Tonkov | G. Guerini |
| 1996 | P. Tonkov | E. Zaina | A. Olano |
| 1995 | T. Rominger | Y. Berzin | P. Ugrumov |
| 1994 | Y. Berzin | M. Pantani | M. Indurain |
| 1993 | M. Indurain | P. Ugrumov | C. Chiappucci |
| 1992 | M. Indurain | C. Chiappucci | F. Chioccioli |
| 1991 | F. Chioccioli | C. Chiappucci | M. Lelli |
| 1990 | G. Bugno | C. Mottet | M. Giovannetti |
| 1989 | L. Fignon | F. Giupponi | A. Hampsten |
| 1988 | A. Hampsten | E. Breukink | U. Zimmermann |
| 1987 | S. Roche | R. Millar | E. Breukink |
| 1986 | R. Visentini | G. Saronni | F. Moser |
| 1985 | B. Hinault | F. Moser | G. Lemond |
| 1984 | F. Moser | L. Fignon | M. Argentin |
| 1983 | G. Saronni | R. Visentini | A. Fernandez |
| 1982 | B. Hinault | T. Prim | S. Contini |
| 1981 | G. Battaglin | T. Prim | G. Saronni |
| 1980 | B. Hinault | W. Panizza | G. Battaglin |
| 1979 | G. Saronni | F. Moser | B. Johansson |
| 1978 | J. De Muynck | G. Baronchelli | F. Moser |
| 1977 | M. Pollentier | F. Moser | G. Baronchelli |
| 1976 | F. Gimondi | J. De Muynck | F. Bertoglio |
| 1975 | F. Bertoglio | F. Galdos | F. Gimondi |
| 1974 | E. Merckx | G. Baronchelli | F. Gimondi |
| 1973 | E. Merckx | F. Gimondi | G. Battaglin |
| 1972 | E. Merckx | J. M. Fuente | F. Galdos |
| 1971 | G. Pettersson | H. Van Springel | U. Colombo |
| 1970 | E. Merckx | F. Gimondi | M. Vandenbossche |
| 1969 | F. Gimondi | C. Michelotto | I. Zilioli |
| 1968 | E. Merckx | V. Adorni | F. Gimondi |
| 1967 | F. Gimondi | F. Balmamion | J. Anquetil |
| 1966 | G. Motta | I. Zilioli | J. Anquetil |
| 1965 | V. Adorni | I. Zilioli | F. Gimondi |
| 1964 | J. Anquetil | I. Zilioli | G. De Rosso |
| 1963 | F. Balmamion | V. Adorni | G. Zancanaro |
| 1962 | F. Balmamion | I. Massignan | N. Defilippis |
| 1961 | A. Pambianco | J. Anquetil | A. Suarez |
| 1960 | J. Anquetil | G. Nencini | C. Gaul |
| 1959 | C. Gaul | J. Anquetil | D. Ronchini |
| 1958 | E. Baldini | J. Brankart | C. Gaul |
| 1957 | G. Nencini | L. Bobet | E. Baldini |
| 1956 | C. Gaul | F. Magni | A. Coletto |
| 1955 | F. Magni | F. Coppi | G. Nencini |
| 1954 | C. Clerici | H. Koblet | N. Assirelli |
| 1953 | F. Coppi | H. Koblet | P. Fornara |
| 1952 | F. Coppi | F. Magni | F. Kubler |
| 1951 | F. Magni | R. Van Steenbergen | F. Kubler |
| 1950 | H. Koblet | G. Bartali | A. Martini |
| 1949 | F. Coppi | G. Bartali | G. Cottur |
| 1948 | F. Magni | E. Cecchi | G. Cottur |
| 1947 | F. Coppi | G. Bartali | G. Bresci |
| 1946 | G. Bartali | F. Coppi | V. Ortelli |
| 1940 | F. Coppi | E. Mollo | G. Cottur |
| 1939 | G. Valetti | G. Bartali | M. Vicini |
| 1938 | G. Valetti | E. Cecchi | S. Canavesi |
| 1937 | G. Bartali | G. Valetti | E. Mollo |
| 1936 | G. Bartali | G. Olmo | S. Canavesi |
| 1935 | V. Bergamaschi | G. Martano | G. Olmo |
| 1934 | L. Guerra | F. Camusso | G. Cazzulani |
| 1933 | A. Binda | J. Demuysere | D. Piemontesi |
| 1932 | A. Pesenti | J. Demuysere | R. Bertoni |
| 1931 | F. Camusso | L. Giacobbe | L. Marchisio |
| 1930 | L. Marchisio | L. Giacobbe | A. Grandi |

## RIDER RESULTS

| WINS | RIDER |
|---|---|
| 5 | A. Binda, F. Coppi, E. Merckx |
| 3 | G. Bartali, G. Brunero, A. Contador, F. Gimondi, B. Hinault, F. Magni |
| 2 | J. Anquetil, F. Balmamion, I. Basso, C. Galetti, C. Gaul, C. Girardengo, I. Gotti, M. Indurain, V. Nibali, G. Saronni, P. Savoldelli, G. Simoni, G. Valetti |

| PODIUMS | RIDER |
|---|---|
| 9 | F. Gimondi |
| 7 | G. Bartali, F. Coppi, G. Simoni |
| 6 | J. Anquetil, A. Binda, G. Brunero, F. Moser, V. Nibali |
| 5 | F. Magni, E. Merckx |
| 4 | B. Aimo, C. Gaul, G. Saronni, I. Zilioli |
| 3 | V. Adorni, F. Balmamion, G. Baronchelli, I. Basso, G. Battaglin, G. Belloni, C. Chiappucci, A. Contador, G. Cottur, C. Galetti, C. Girardengo, B. Hinault, M. Indurain, H. Koblet, G. Nencini, P. Savoldelli, P. Tonkov, G. Valetti |
| 2 | F. Aru, E. Baldini, F. Bertoglio, Y. Berzin, E. Breukink, F. Camusso, S. Canavesi, E. Cecchi, F. Chioccioli, J. De Muynck, J. Demuysere, T. Dumoulin, G. Enrici, L. Fignon, F. Galdos, L. Ganna, S. Garzelli, G. Giacobbe, I. Gotti, G. Guerini, A. Hampsten, F. Kubler, L. Marchisio, E. Mollo, A. Olano, G. Olmo, M. Pantani, E. Pavesi, D. Piemontesi, T. Prim, N. Quintana, G. Rossignoli, P. Ugrumov, R. Urán, R. Visentini |

## COUNTRY RESULTS

| WINS | COUNTRY |
|---|---|
| 69 | Italy |
| 7 | Belgium |
| 6 | France |
| 4 | Spain |
| 3 | Russia, Switzerland |
| 2 | Luxembourg, United Kingdom |
| 1 | Colombia, Canada, Ecuador, Ireland, Netherlands, Sweden, United States |

| PODIUMS | COUNTRY |
|---|---|
| 209 | Italy |
| 19 | Spain |
| 16 | Belgium |
| 15 | France |
| 8 | Switzerland |
| 7 | Colombia |
| 6 | Russia |
| 5 | Colombia, Luxembourg, Netherlands |
| 4 | Sweden, United Kingdom, United States |
| 2 | Australia, Latvia, Ukraine |
| 1 | Canada, Ecuador, Ireland, Slovenia, Venezuela |

## RESULTS BY YEAR (CONT.)

| YEAR | 1ST | 2ND | 3RD |
|---|---|---|---|
| 1929 | A. Binda | D. Piemontesi | L. Frascarelli |
| 1928 | A. Binda | G. Pancera | B. Aimo |
| 1927 | A. Binda | G. Brunero | A. Negrini |
| 1926 | G. Brunero | A. Binda | A. Bresciani |
| 1925 | A. Binda | C. Girardengo | G. Brunero |
| 1924 | G. Enrici | F. Gay | A. Gabrielli |
| 1923 | C. Girardengo | G. Brunero | B. Aimo |
| 1922 | G. Brunero | B. Aimo | G. Enrici |
| 1921 | G. Brunero | G. Belloni | B. Aimo |
| 1920 | G. Belloni | A. Gremo | J. Alavoine |
| 1919 | C. Girardengo | G. Belloni | M. Buysse |
| 1914 | A. Calzolari | P. Albini | L. Lucotti |
| 1913 | C. Oriani | E. Pavesi | G. Azzini |
| 1912 | Atala-Dunlop | Peugeot | Gerbi |
| 1911 | C. Galetti | G. Rossignoli | G. Gerbi |
| 1910 | C. Galetti | E. Pavesi | L. Ganna |
| 1909 | L. Ganna | C. Galetti | G. Rossignoli |

# VOLTA CICLISTA A CATALUNYA

## RESULTS BY YEAR

| YEAR | 1ST | 2ND | 3RD |
|---|---|---|---|
| 2021 | A. Yates | R. Porte | G. Thomas |
| 2020 | Race cancelled | | |
| 2019 | M. A. Lopez | A. Yates | E. Bernal |
| 2018 | A. Valverde | N. Quintana | P. Latour |
| 2017 | A. Valverde | A. Contador | M. Soler |
| 2016 | N. Quintana | A. Contador | D. Martin |
| 2015 | R. Porte | A. Valverde | D. Pozzovivo |
| 2014 | J. Rodriguez | A. Contador | T. van Garderen |
| 2013 | D. Martin | J. Rodriguez | M. Scarponi |
| 2012 | M. Albasini | S. Sanchez | J. Van den Broeck |
| 2011 | M. Scarponi | D. Martin | C. Horner |
| 2010 | J. Rodriguez | X. Tondo | R. Taaramae |
| 2009 | A. Valverde | D. Martin | H. Zubeldia |
| 2008 | G. C. Veloso | R. Urán | R. Pauriol |
| 2007 | V. Karpets | M. Rogers | D. Menchov |
| 2006 | D. Canada | S. Botero | C. Moreau |
| 2005 | Y. Popovych | L. Piepoli | D. Moncoutie |
| 2004 | M. A. Martin | V. Karpets | R. Laiseka |
| 2003 | J. A. Pecharroman | R. Heras | K. Gil |
| 2002 | R. Heras | A. Garmendia | L. Perez |
| 2001 | J. Beloki | I. Gonzalez De Galdeano | F. Escartin |
| 2000 | J. M. Jimenez | O. Sevilla | L. Piepoli |
| 1999 | M. Beltran | R. Heras | J. M. Jimenez |
| 1998 | H. Buenahora | G. Totschnig | F. Escartin |
| 1997 | F. Escartin | A. L. Casero | M. Zarrabeitia |
| 1996 | A. Zulle | P. Jonker | M. Fincato |
| 1995 | L. Jalabert | M. Mauri | J. Montoya |
| 1994 | C. Chiappucci | F. Escartin | P. Delgado |
| 1993 | A. Mejia | M. Fondriest | A. Martin |
| 1992 | M. Indurain | T. Rominger | A. Martin |
| 1991 | M. Indurain | P. Delgado | A. Zulle |
| 1990 | L. Cubino | M. Lejarreta | P. Delgado |
| 1989 | M. Lejarreta | P. Delgado | A. Pino |
| 1988 | M. Indurain | L. Cubino | M. Lejarreta |
| 1987 | A. Pino | A. Arroyo | I. Gaston |
| 1986 | S. Kelly | A. Pino | C. Mottet |
| 1985 | R. Millar | S. Kelly | J. Gorospe |
| 1984 | S. Kelly | P. Munoz | A. Arroyo |
| 1983 | J. Recio | F. Ruperez | J. Thallmann |
| 1982 | A. Fernandez | P. Munoz | J. Gorospe |
| 1981 | F. Ruperez | S. Demierre | M. Lejarreta |
| 1980 | M. Lejarreta | J. van der Velde | V. Belda |
| 1979 | V. Belda | P. Vilardebo | C. Jourdan |
| 1978 | F. Moser | F. Galdos | P. Torres |
| 1977 | F. Maertens | J. De Muynck | J. Zoetemelk |
| 1976 | E. Martinez | R. De Witte | A. Tamames |
| 1975 | F. Bertoglio | M. Laurent | J. Martins |
| 1974 | B. Thevenet | A. Oliva | D. Perurena |
| 1973 | D. Perurena | J. Manzaneque | A. Martos |
| 1972 | F. Gimondi | J. A. Gonzalez | A. Martos |
| 1971 | L. Ocana | B. Labourdette | D. Perurena |
| 1970 | F. Bitossi | F. Galdos | B. Labourdette |
| 1969 | M. Diaz | F. Bitossi | J. Manzaneque |
| 1968 | E. Merckx | F. Gimondi | G. Ferretti |
| 1967 | J. Anquetil | A. Gomez | R. Hagmann |
| 1966 | A. Den Hartog | J. Anquetil | P. Gutty |
| 1965 | J. Gomez | C. Echevarria | R. Poggiali |
| 1964 | J. Carrara | P. Fabbri | J. M. Errandonea |
| 1963 | J. Novales | A. Soler | A. Suarez |
| 1962 | A. Karmany | M. Martin | G. Garcia |
| 1961 | H. Duez | J. J. Nicolau | J. M. Menendez |
| 1960 | M. Poblet | J. Perez | E. Cruz |
| 1959 | S. Botella | F. Manzaneque | J. Herrero |
| 1958 | R. Van Genechten | G. Mas | A. Utset |
| 1957 | J. Lorono | S. Botella | R. Marigil |
| 1956 | A. Utset | V. Iturat | F. Masip |
| 1955 | J. Gomez | G. Company | E. Rodriguez |
| 1954 | W. Serena | A. Sant | M. Poblet |
| 1953 | S. Botella | F. Masip | J. Serra |
| 1952 | M. Poblet | A. Grosso | J. Gil |
| 1951 | P. Volpi | F. Masip | M. Rodriguez |
| 1950 | A. Gelabert | J. Serra | F. Masip |
| 1949 | E. Rol | M. Poblet | R. Desbats |
| 1948 | E. Rodriguez | G. Bresci | E. Cecchi |
| 1947 | E. Rodriguez | M. Gual | G. Aeschlimann |
| 1946 | J. Berrendero | G. Weilemann | B. Capo |
| 1945 | B. Ruiz | J. Gimeno | R. Zimmermann |
| 1944 | M. Casas | D. Langarica | V. Miro |
| 1943 | J. Berrendero | V. Miro | A. Destrieux |
| 1942 | F. Ezquerra | J. Berrendero | D. Chafer |
| 1941 | F. A. Andres | A. Canais | J. Campana |
| 1940 | C. Didier | M. Clemens | M. Canardo |
| 1939 | M. Canardo | D. Chafer | F. Trueba |
| 1936 | M. Canardo | F. Bonduel | J. Gimeno |
| 1935 | M. Canardo | F. Ezquerra | J. Huts |
| 1934 | B. Rogora | A. Deloor | A. Sella |
| 1933 | A. Bovet | A. Morelli | A. Dignef |

## RIDER RESULTS

| WINS | RIDER |
|---|---|
| 7 | M. Canardo |
| 3 | M. Indurain, A. Valverde |
| 2 | J. Berrendero, S. Botella, V. Fontan, J. Gomez, S. Kelly, M. Lejarreta, M. Mucio, M. Poblet, E. Rodriguez, J. Rodriguez |

| PODIUMS | RIDER |
|---|---|
| 11 | M. Canardo |
| 5 | M. Lejarreta |
| 4 | P. Delgado, F. Escartin, D. Martin, F. Masip, M. Mucio, M. Poblet, A. Valverde |
| 3 | J. Berrendero, S. Botella, A. Contador, R. Heras, M. Indurain, S. Kelly, D. Perurena, A. Pino, E. Rodriguez, J. Rodriguez |
| 2 | J. Anquetil, A. Arroyo, V. Belda, F. Bitossi, D. Chafer, A. Crespo, L. Cubino, F. Ezquerra, V. Fontan, F. Galdos, J. Gimeno, F. Gimondi, J. Gomez, J. Gorospe, J. Janer, V. Karpets, B. Labourdette, J. Magdalena, J. Manzaneque, J. Maria Jimenez, A. Martin, A. Martos, V. Miro, T. Monteys, P. Munoz Machin, J. Nat, J. Pelletier, L. Piepoli, R. Porte, N. Quintana, F. Ruperez, M. Scarponi, J. Serra, A. Utset, A. Yates, A. Zulle |

## COUNTRY RESULTS

| WINS | COUNTRY |
|---|---|
| 60 | Spain |
| 11 | Italy |
| 10 | France |
| 4 | Colombia |
| 3 | Belgium, Ireland |
| 2 | Switzerland, United Kingdom |
| 1 | Australia, Luxembourg, Netherlands, Russia, Ukraine |

| PODIUMS | COUNTRY |
|---|---|
| 185 | Spain |
| 29 | Italy |
| 28 | France |
| 11 | Belgium |
| 10 | Switzerland |
| 8 | Colombia, Ireland |
| 5 | Australia |
| 3 | Netherlands, Russia, United Kingdom |
| 2 | Luxembourg, United States |
| 1 | Austria, Estonia, Portugal, Ukraine |

## RESULTS BY YEAR (CONT.)

| YEAR | 1ST | 2ND | 3RD |
|---|---|---|---|
| 1932 | M. Canardo | D. Piemontesi | I. Figueras |
| 1931 | S. Cardona | M. Canardo | A. Simoni |
| 1930 | M. Canardo | M. Maurel | R. Montero |
| 1929 | M. Canardo | J. Aerts | A. Bresciani |
| 1928 | M. Canardo | M. Mucio | J. Borras |
| 1927 | V. Fontan | M. Canardo | G. Cuvelier |
| 1926 | V. Fontan | M. Mucio | M. Canardo |
| 1925 | M. Mucio | J. Janer | T. Monteys |
| 1924 | M. Mucio | T. Monteys | V. Otero |
| 1923 | M. Ville | J. Pelletier | J. Nat |
| 1920 | J. Pelletier | J. Nat | J. Janer |
| 1913 | J. Marti | A. Crespo | G. Anton |
| 1912 | J. Magdalena | J. Marti | A. Crespo |
| 1911 | S. Masdeu | J. Magdalena | V. Blanco |

# MEN'S HISTORICAL RESULTS

# TOUR OF FLANDERS

## RESULTS BY YEAR

| YEAR | 1ST | 2ND | 3RD |
|---|---|---|---|
| 2021 | K. Asgreen | M. van der Poel | G. Van Avermaet |
| 2020 | M. van der Poel | W. van Aert | A. Kristoff |
| 2019 | A. Bettiol | K. Asgreen | A. Kristoff |
| 2018 | N. Terpstra | M. Pedersen | P. Gilbert |
| 2017 | P. Gilbert | G. Van Avermaet | N. Terpstra |
| 2016 | P. Sagan | F. Cancellara | S. Vanmarcke |
| 2015 | A. Kristoff | N. Terpstra | G. Van Avermaet |
| 2014 | F. Cancellara | G. Van Avermaet | S. Vanmarcke |
| 2013 | F. Cancellara | P. Sagan | J. Roelandts |
| 2012 | T. Boonen | F. Pozzato | A. Ballan |
| 2011 | N. Nuyens | S. Chavanel | F. Cancellara |
| 2010 | F. Cancellara | T. Boonen | P. Gilbert |
| 2009 | S. Devolder | H. Haussler | P. Gilbert |
| 2008 | S. Devolder | N. Nuyens | J. A. Flecha |
| 2007 | A. Ballan | L. Hoste | L. Paolini |
| 2006 | T. Boonen | L. Hoste | G. Hincapie |
| 2005 | T. Boonen | A. Klier | P. Van Petegem |
| 2004 | S. Wesemann | L. Hoste | D. Bruylandts |
| 2003 | P. Van Petegem | F. Vandenbroucke | S. O'Grady |
| 2002 | A. Tafi | J. Museeuw | P. Van Petegem |
| 2001 | G. Bortolami | E. Dekker | D. Zanette |
| 2000 | A. Tchmil | D. Pieri | R. Vainsteins |
| 1999 | P. Van Petegem | F. Vandenbroucke | J. Museeuw |
| 1998 | J. Museeuw | S. Zanini | A. Tchmil |
| 1997 | R. Sorensen | F. Moncassin | F. Ballerini |
| 1996 | M. Bartoli | F. Baldato | J. Museeuw |
| 1995 | J. Museeuw | F. Baldato | A. Tchmil |
| 1994 | G. Bugno | J. Museeuw | A. Tchmil |
| 1993 | J. Museeuw | F. Maassen | D. Bottaro |
| 1992 | J. Durand | T. Wegmuller | E. Van Hooydonck |
| 1991 | E. Van Hooydonck | J. Museeuw | R. Sorensen |
| 1990 | M. Argentin | R. Dhaenens | J. Talen |
| 1989 | E. Van Hooydonck | H. Frison | D. O. Lauritzen |
| 1988 | E. Planckaert | P. Anderson | A. van der Poel |
| 1987 | C. Criquielion | S. Kelly | E. Vanderaerden |
| 1986 | A. van der Poel | S. Kelly | J. P. Vandenbrande |
| 1985 | E. Vanderaerden | P. Anderson | H. Kuiper |
| 1984 | J. Lammerts | S. Kelly | J. L. Vandenbroucke |
| 1983 | J. Raas | L. Peeters | M. Sergeant |
| 1982 | R. Martens | E. Planckaert | R. Pevenage |
| 1981 | H. Kuiper | F. Pirard | J. Raas |
| 1980 | M. Pollentier | F. Moser | J. Raas |
| 1979 | J. Raas | M. Demeyer | D. Willems |
| 1978 | W. Godefroot | M. Pollentier | G. Braun |
| 1977 | R. De Vlaeminck | W. Godefroot | J. Raas |
| 1976 | W. Planckaert | F. Moser | M. Demeyer |
| 1975 | E. Merckx | F. Verbeeck | M. Demeyer |
| 1974 | C. Bal | F. Verbeeck | E. Merckx |
| 1973 | E. Leman | F. Maertens | E. Merckx |
| 1972 | E. Leman | A. Dierickx | F. Verbeeck |
| 1971 | E. Dolman | F. Kerremans | C. Guimard |
| 1970 | E. Leman | W. Godefroot | E. Merckx |
| 1969 | E. Merckx | F. Gimondi | M. Basso |
| 1968 | W. Godefroot | G. Reybroeck | R. Altig |
| 1967 | D. Zandegu | N. Fore | E. Merckx |
| 1966 | W. Sels | A. Durante | G. Vandenberghe |
| 1965 | J. De Roo | W. Sels | G. Vanconingsloo |
| 1964 | R. Altig | B. Beheyt | J. De Roo |
| 1963 | N. Fore | F. Melckenbeeck | T. Simpson |
| 1962 | R. Van Looy | M. Van Aerde | N. Kerckhove |
| 1961 | T. Simpson | N. Defilippis | J. De Haan |
| 1960 | A. De Cabooter | J. Graczyk | R. Van Looy |
| 1959 | R. Van Looy | F. Schoubben | G. Desmet |
| 1958 | G. Derycke | W. Truye | A. Conterno |
| 1957 | A. De Bruyne | J. Planckaert | N. Kerckhove |
| 1956 | J. Forestier | S. Ockers | L. Vandaele |
| 1955 | L. Bobet | H. Koblet | R. Van Steenbergen |
| 1954 | R. Impanis | F. Mahe | A. Van Den Brande |
| 1953 | W. Van Est | D. Keteleer | B. Gauthier |
| 1952 | R. Decock | L. Petrucci | B. Schotte |
| 1951 | F. Magni | B. Gauthier | A. Redolfi |
| 1950 | F. Magni | B. Schotte | L. Caput |
| 1949 | F. Magni | V. Ollivier | B. Schotte |
| 1948 | B. Schotte | A. Ramon | M. Ryckaert |
| 1947 | E. Faignaert | R. Desmet | R. Renders |
| 1946 | R. Van Steenbergen | L. Thietard | B. Schotte |
| 1945 | S. Grysolle | A. Sercu | J. Moerenhout |
| 1944 | R. Van Steenbergen | B. Schotte | J. Moerenhout |
| 1943 | A. Buysse | A. Sercu | C. Beeckman |
| 1942 | B. Schotte | G. Claes | R. Van Eenaeme |
| 1941 | A. Buysse | G. Van Overloop | O. Van Den Meerschaut |
| 1940 | A. Buysse | G. Christiaens | B. Schotte |
| 1939 | K. Kaers | R. Maes | E. Vissers |
| 1938 | E. De Caluwe | S. Maes | M. Kint |
| 1937 | M. D'Hooghe | H. Deltour | L. Hardiquest |
| 1936 | L. Hardiquest | E. De Caluwe | F. Neuville |
| 1935 | L. Duerloo | E. Meulenberg | C. Leemans |

## RIDER RESULTS

| WINS | RIDER |
|---|---|
| 3 | T. Boonen, A. Buysse, F. Cancellara, E. Leman, F. Magni, J. Museeuw |
| 2 | G. Debaets, S. Devolder, R. Gijssels, W. Godefroot, E. Merckx, J. Raas, B. Schotte, E. Van Hooydonck, R. Van Looy, P. Van Petegem, R. Van Steenbergen |

| PODIUMS | RIDER |
|---|---|
| 8 | J. Museeuw, B. Schotte |
| 6 | E. Merckx |
| 5 | F. Cancellara, W. Godefroot |
| 4 | T. Boonen, P. Gilbert, J. Raas, A. Tchmil, G. Van Avermaet, P. Van Petegem |
| 3 | A. Buysse, M. Demeyer, R. Gijssels, L. Hoste, S. Kelly, A. Kristoff, E. Leman, F. Magni, N. Terpstra, J. Van Hevel, E. Van Hooydonck, R. Van Looy, R. Van Steenbergen, F. Verbeeck |
| 2 | R. Altig, P. Anderson, K. Asgreen, F. Baldato, A. Ballan, E. De Caluwe, J. De Roo, G. Debaets, A. Dejonghe, S. Devolder, N. Fore, B. Gauthier, A. Haemerlinck, L. Hardiquest, N. Kerckhove, H. Kuiper, J. Moerenhout, F. Moser, N. Nuyens, E. Planckaert, M. Pollentier, P. Sagan, A. Schepers, W. Sels, A. Sercu, T. Simpson, R. Sorensen, A. van der Poel, M. van der Poel, H. Van Lerberghe, G. Van Slembrouck, F. Vandenbroucke, E. Vanderaerden, S. Vanmarcke, R. Vermandel |

## COUNTRY RESULTS

| WINS | COUNTRY |
|---|---|
| 69 | Belgium |
| 11 | Italy, Netherlands |
| 4 | Switzerland |
| 3 | France |
| 2 | Denmark, Germany |
| 1 | Norway, Slovakia, United Kingdom |

| PODIUMS | COUNTRY |
|---|---|
| 209 | Belgium |
| 29 | Italy |
| 26 | Netherlands |
| 15 | France |
| 9 | Switzerland |
| 5 | Denmark |
| 4 | Australia, Germany, Norway |
| 3 | Ireland |
| 2 | Slovakia, United Kingdom |
| 1 | Latvia, Spain, United States |

MEN'S HISTORICAL RESULTS

## RESULTS BY YEAR (CONT.)

| YEAR | 1ST | 2ND | 3RD |
|---|---|---|---|
| 1934 | G. Rebry | A. Schepers | F. Vervaecke |
| 1933 | A. Schepers | L. Tommies | R. Gijssels |
| 1932 | R. Gijssels | A. Deloor | A. Haemerlinck |
| 1931 | R. Gijssels | C. Bogaert | J. Aerts |
| 1930 | F. Bonduel | A. Dossche | E. Joly |
| 1929 | J. Dervaes | G. Ronsse | A. Haemerlinck |
| 1928 | J. Mertens | A. Mortelmans | L. Delannoy |
| 1927 | G. Debaets | G. Van Slembrouck | M. De Waele |
| 1926 | D. Verschueren | G. Van Slembrouck | R. Decorte |
| 1925 | J. Delbecque | J. Pe | H. Martin |
| 1924 | G. Debaets | R. Vermandel | F. Sellier |
| 1923 | H. Suter | C. Deruyter | A. Dejonghe |
| 1922 | L. Devos | J. Brunier | F. Pelissier |
| 1921 | R. Vermandel | J. Van Hevel | L. Budts |
| 1920 | J. Van Hevel | A. Dejonghe | A. Van Hecke |
| 1919 | H. Van Lerberghe | L. Buysse | J. Van Hevel |
| 1914 | M. Buysse | H. Van Lerberghe | P. Van De Velde |
| 1913 | P. Deman | J. Vandaele | V. Doms |

# ITZULIA BASQUE COUNTRY

## RESULTS BY YEAR

| YEAR | 1ST | 2ND | 3RD |
|---|---|---|---|
| 2021 | P. Roglič | J. Vingegaard | T. Pogačar |
| 2020 | Race cancelled | | |
| 2019 | I. Izaguirre | D. Martin | E. Buchmann |
| 2018 | P. Roglič | M. Landa | I. Izaguirre |
| 2017 | A. Valverde | A. Contador | I. Izaguirre |
| 2016 | A. Contador | S. Henao | N. Quintana |
| 2015 | J. Rodriguez | S. Henao | I. Izaguirre |
| 2014 | A. Contador | M. Kwiatkowski | J. C. Peraud |
| 2013 | N. Quintana | R. Porte | S. Henao |
| 2012 | S. Sanchez | J. Rodriguez | B. Mollema |
| 2011 | A. Kloden | C. Horner | R. Gesink |
| 2010 | C. Horner | B. Intxausti | J. Rodriguez |
| 2009 | A. Contador | A. Colom | S. Sanchez |
| 2008 | A. Contador | C. Evans | T. Dekker |
| 2007 | J. J. Cobo | A. Vicioso | S. Sanchez |
| 2006 | J. A. Gomez | A. Valverde | A. Colom |
| 2005 | D. Di Luca | D. Rebellin | A. Contador |
| 2004 | D. Menchov | I. Mayo | D. Etxebarria |
| 2003 | I. Mayo | T. Hamilton | S. Sanchez |
| 2002 | A. Osa | D. Etxebarria | G. Bayarri |
| 2001 | R. Rumsas | J. A. Martinez | M. A. Serrano |
| 2000 | A. Kloden | D. Di Luca | L. Jalabert |
| 1999 | L. Jalabert | W. Belli | D. Rebellin |
| 1998 | I. Cuesta | L. Jalabert | A. Zulle |
| 1997 | A. Zulle | L. Jalabert | M. Pantani |
| 1996 | F. Casagrande | P. Herve | A. Olano |
| 1995 | A. Zulle | L. Jalabert | T. Rominger |
| 1994 | T. Rominger | Y. Berzin | C. Chiappucci |
| 1993 | T. Rominger | R. Sorensen | A. Zulle |
| 1992 | T. Rominger | R. Alcala | M. Zarrabeitia |
| 1991 | C. Chiappucci | J. Bruyneel | P. Ugrumov |
| 1990 | J. Gorospe | R. Golz | M. Indurain |
| 1989 | S. Roche | F. Echave | J. Blanco |
| 1988 | E. Breukink | L. Suykerbuyk | J. Gorospe |
| 1987 | S. Kelly | R. Golz | J. Gorospe |
| 1986 | S. Kelly | M. Rossi | F. Echave |
| 1985 | P. Ruiz | G. Lemond | M. Lejarreta |
| 1984 | S. Kelly | F. Ruperez | M. Lejarreta |
| 1983 | J. Gorospe | R. Visentini | M. Lejarreta |
| 1982 | J. L. Laguia | J. Gorospe | F. Moser |
| 1981 | S. Contini | M. Beccia | M. Lejarreta |
| 1980 | A. Fernandez | M. M. Lasa | M. Lejarreta |
| 1979 | G. Battaglin | V. Belda | M. M. Lasa |
| 1978 | J. A. Gonzalez | J. Enrique | J. Nazabal |
| 1977 | J. A. Gonzalez | P. Wellens | J. P. Baert |
| 1976 | G. Baronchelli | J. F. Elorriaga | J. Agostinho |
| 1975 | J. A. Gonzalez | J. Manzaneque | A. Tamames |
| 1974 | M. M. Lasa | J. Manzaneque | L. Ocana |
| 1973 | L. Ocana | J. A. Gonzalez | D. Perurena |
| 1972 | J. A. Gonzalez | J. Manzaneque | J. Esperanza |
| 1971 | L. Ocana | R. Poulidor | M. M. Lasa |
| 1970 | L. P. Santamarina | J. Aranzabal | A. Gandarias |
| 1969 | J. Anquetil | F. Gabica | M. Diaz |
| 1935 | G. Bartali | D. Gianello | J. Berrendero |
| 1930 | M. Canardo | A. Magne | J. Aerts |
| 1929 | M. De Waele | M. Bidot | N. Frantz |
| 1928 | M. De Waele | A. Leducq | M. Canardo |
| 1927 | V. Fontan | A. Leducq | L. Buysse |
| 1926 | N. Frantz | O. Bottecchia | V. Fontan |
| 1925 | A. Verdyck | J. Pe | M. Bidot |
| 1924 | F. Pelissier | H. Pelissier | C. Lacquehay |

## RIDER RESULTS

| WINS | RIDER |
|---|---|
| 4 | J. A. Gonzalez, A. Contador |
| 3 | S. Kelly, T. Rominger |
| 2 | M. De Waele, J. Gorospe, A. Kloden, L. Ocaña, A. Zulle |

| PODIUMS | RIDER |
|---|---|
| 6 | A. Contador |
| 5 | J. A. Gonzalez, J. Gorospe, L. Jalabert, M. Lejarreta |
| 4 | I. Izaguirre, M. Maria Lasa, T. Rominger, S. Sanchez, A. Zulle |
| 3 | S. Kelly, S. Henao, J. Manzaneque, L. Ocaña, J. Rodriguez |
| 2 | M. Bidot, M. Canardo, C. Chiappucci, A. Colom, M. De Waele, D. Di Luca, F. Echave, D. Etxebarria, V. Fontan, N. Frantz, R. Golz, C. Horner, A. Kloden, A. Leducq, I. Mayo, N. Quintana, D. Rebellin, P. Roglič, A. Valverde |

## COUNTRY RESULTS

| WINS | COUNTRY |
|---|---|
| 27 | Spain |
| 7 | Italy |
| 5 | Switzerland |
| 4 | France, Ireland |
| 3 | Belgium |
| 2 | Germany, Slovenia |
| 1 | Colombia, Lithuania, Luxembourg, Netherlands, Russia, United States |

| PODIUMS | COUNTRY |
|---|---|
| 85 | Spain |
| 20 | France |
| 18 | Italy |
| 9 | Belgium |
| 8 | Switzerland |
| 5 | Colombia, Germany, Ireland, Netherlands |
| 4 | United States |
| 3 | Slovenia |
| 2 | Australia, Denmark, Luxembourg, Russia |
| 1 | Latvia, Lithuania, Mexico, Poland, Portugal |

# WORLD CHAMPIONSHIPS MEN'S ROAD RACE

## RESULTS BY YEAR

| YEAR | 1ST | 2ND | 3RD |
|---|---|---|---|
| 2021 | J. Alaphilppe | D. van Baarle | M. Valgren |
| 2020 | J. Alaphilippe | W. van Aert | M. Hirschi |
| 2019 | M. Pedersen | M. Trentin | S. Küng |
| 2018 | A. Valverde | R. Bardet | M. Woods |
| 2017 | P. Sagan | A. Kristoff | M. Matthews |
| 2016 | P. Sagan | M. Cavendish | T. Boonen |
| 2015 | P. Sagan | M. Matthews | R. Navardauskas |
| 2014 | M. Kwiatkowski | S. Gerrans | A. Valverde |
| 2013 | R. Costa | J. Rodriguez | A. Valverde |
| 2012 | P. Gilbert | E. Boasson Hagen | A. Valverde |
| 2011 | M. Cavendish | M. Goss | A. Greipel |
| 2010 | T. Hushovd | M. Breschel | A. Davis |
| 2009 | C. Evans | A. Kolobnev | J. Rodriguez |
| 2008 | A. Ballan | D. Cunego | M. Breschel |
| 2007 | P. Bettini | A. Kolobnev | S. Schumacher |
| 2006 | P. Bettini | E. Zabel | A. Valverde |
| 2005 | T. Boonen | A. Valverde | A. Geslin |
| 2004 | O. Freire | E. Zabel | L. Paolini |
| 2003 | I. Astarloa | A. Valverde | P. Van Petegem |
| 2002 | M. Cipollini | R. McEwen | E. Zabel |
| 2001 | O. Freire | P. Bettini | A. Hauptman |
| 2000 | R. Vainsteins | Z. Spruch | O. Freire |
| 1999 | O. Freire | M. Zberg | J. C. Robin |
| 1998 | O. Camenzind | P. Van Petegem | M. Bartoli |
| 1997 | L. Brochard | B. Hamburger | L. van Bon |
| 1996 | J. Museeuw | M. Gianetti | M. Bartoli |
| 1995 | A. Olano | M. Indurain | M. Pantani |
| 1994 | L. Leblanc | C. Chiappucci | R. Virenque |
| 1993 | L. Armstrong | M. Indurain | O. Ludwig |
| 1992 | G. Bugno | L. Jalabert | D. Konishev |
| 1991 | G. Bugno | S. Rooks | M. Indurain |
| 1990 | R. Dhaenens | D. De Wolf | G. Bugno |
| 1989 | G. Lemond | D. Konishev | S. Kelly |
| 1988 | M. Fondriest | M. Gayant | J. Fernandez |
| 1987 | S. Roche | M. Argentin | J. Fernandez |
| 1986 | M. Argentin | C. Mottet | G. Saronni |
| 1985 | J. Zoetemelk | G. Lemond | M. Argentin |
| 1984 | C. Criquielion | C. Corti | S. Bauer |
| 1983 | G. Lemond | A. van der Poel | S. Roche |
| 1982 | G. Saronni | G. Lemond | S. Kelly |
| 1981 | F. Maertens | G. Saronni | B. Hinault |
| 1980 | B. Hinault | G. Baronchelli | J. Fernandez |
| 1979 | J. Raas | D. Thurau | J. R. Bernaudeau |
| 1978 | G. Knetemann | F. Moser | J. Marcussen |
| 1977 | F. Moser | D. Thurau | F. Bitossi |
| 1976 | F. Maertens | F. Moser | T. Conti |
| 1975 | H. Kuiper | R. De Vlaeminck | J. P. Danguillaume |
| 1974 | E. Merckx | R. Poulidor | M. Martinez |
| 1973 | F. Gimondi | F. Maertens | L. Ocana |
| 1972 | M. Basso | F. Bitossi | C. Guimard |
| 1971 | E. Merckx | F. Gimondi | C. Guimard |
| 1970 | J. P. Monsere | L. Mortensen | F. Gimondi |
| 1969 | H. Ottenbros | J. Stevens | M. Dancelli |
| 1968 | V. Adorni | H. Van Springel | M. Dancelli |
| 1967 | E. Merckx | J. Janssen | R. Saez |
| 1966 | R. Altig | J. Anquetil | R. Poulidor |
| 1965 | T. Simpson | R. Altig | R. Swerts |
| 1964 | J. Janssen | V. Adorni | R. Poulidor |
| 1963 | B. Beheyt | R. Van Looy | J. De Haan |
| 1962 | J. Stablinski | S. Elliott | J. Hoevenaers |
| 1961 | R. Van Looy | N. Defilippis | R. Poulidor |
| 1960 | R. Van Looy | A. Darrigade | P. Cerami |
| 1959 | A. Darrigade | M. Gismondi | N. Fore |
| 1958 | E. Baldini | L. Bobet | A. Darrigade |
| 1957 | R. Van Steenbergen | L. Bobet | A. Darrigade |
| 1956 | R. Van Steenbergen | R. Van Looy | G. Schulte |
| 1955 | S. Ockers | J. P. Schmitz | G. Derycke |
| 1954 | L. Bobet | F. Schar | C. Gaul |
| 1953 | F. Coppi | G. Derycke | S. Ockers |
| 1952 | H. Muller | G. Weilemann | L. Hormann |
| 1951 | F. Kubler | F. Magni | A. Bevilacqua |
| 1950 | B. Schotte | T. Middelkamp | F. Kubler |
| 1949 | R. Van Steenbergen | F. Kubler | F. Coppi |
| 1948 | B. Schotte | A. Lazarides | L. Teisseire |
| 1947 | T. Middelkamp | A. Sercu | J. Janssen |
| 1946 | H. Knecht | M. Kint | R. Van Steenbergen |
| 1938 | M. Kint | P. Egli | L. Amberg |
| 1937 | E. Meulenberg | E. Kijewski | P. Egli |
| 1936 | A. Magne | A. Bini | T. Middelkamp |
| 1935 | J. Aerts | L. Montero | G. Danneels |
| 1934 | K. Kaers | L. Guerra | G. Danneels |
| 1933 | G. Speicher | A. Magne | M. Valentijn |
| 1932 | A. Binda | R. Bertoni | N. Frantz |
| 1931 | L. Guerra | F. Le Drogo | A. Buechi |
| 1930 | A. Binda | L. Guerra | G. Ronsse |
| 1929 | G. Ronsse | N. Frantz | A. Binda |
| 1928 | G. Ronsse | H. Nebe | B. Wolke |
| 1927 | A. Binda | C. Girardengo | D. Piemontesi |

## RIDER RESULTS

| WINS | RIDER |
|---|---|
| 3 | A. Binda, O. Freire, E. Merckx, P. Sagan, R. Van Steenbergen |
| 2 | J. Alaphilippe, P. Bettini, G. Bugno, G. Lemond, F. Maertens, G. Ronsse, B. Schotte, R. Van Looy |

| PODIUMS | RIDER |
|---|---|
| 7 | A. Valverde |
| 4 | A. Binda, A. Darrigade, O. Freire, G. Lemond, R. Poulidor, R. Van Looy, R. Van Steenbergen |
| 3 | M. Argentin, P. Bettini, L. Bobet, G. Bugno, J. Fernandez, F. Gimondi, L. Guerra, M. Indurain, J. Janssen, F. Kubler, F. Maertens, E. Merckx, T. Middelkamp, F. Moser, G. Ronsse, P. Sagan, G. Saronni, E. Zabel |
| 2 | V. Adorni, J. Alaphilippe, R. Altig, M. Bartoli, F. Bitossi, T. Boonen, M. Breschel, M. Cavendish, F. Coppi, M. Dancelli, G. Danneels, G. Derycke, P. Egli, N. Frantz, C. Guimard, B. Hinault, S. Kelly, M. Kint, A. Kolobnev, D. Konishev, A. Magne, M. Matthews, S. Ockers, S. Roche, J. Rodriguez, B. Schotte, D. Thurau, P. Van Petegem |

## COUNTRY RESULTS

| WINS | COUNTRY |
|---|---|
| 26 | Belgium |
| 19 | Italy |
| 10 | France |
| 7 | Netherlands |
| 6 | Spain |
| 3 | Slovakia, Switzerland, United States |
| 2 | Germany, United Kingdom |
| 1 | Australia, Denmark, Ireland, Latvia, Norway, Poland, Portugal |

| PODIUMS | COUNTRY |
|---|---|
| 56 | Italy |
| 49 | Belgium |
| 36 | France |
| 24 | Spain |
| 18 | Netherlands |
| 15 | Germany, Switzerland |
| 7 | Australia, Denmark |
| 5 | Ireland, United States |
| 4 | Luxembourg, Russia |
| 3 | Norway, Slovakia, United Kingdom |
| 2 | Canada, Poland |
| 1 | Latvia, Lithuania, Portugal, Slovenia |

MEN'S HISTORICAL RESULTS

# BRETAGNE CLASSIC – OUEST-FRANCE

## RESULTS BY YEAR

| YEAR | 1ST | 2ND | 3RD |
|---|---|---|---|
| 2021 | B. Cosnefroy | J. Alaphilippe | M. F. Honoré |
| 2020 | M. Matthews | L. Mezgec | F. Sénéchal |
| 2019 | S. Vanmarcke | T. Benoot | J. Haig |
| 2018 | O. Naesen | M. Valgren | T. Wellens |
| 2017 | E. Viviani | A. Kristoff | S. Colbrelli |
| 2016 | O. Naesen | A. Bettiol | A. Kristoff |
| 2015 | A. Kristoff | S. Ponzi | R. Navardauskas |
| 2014 | S. Chavanel | A. Fedi | A. Vichot |
| 2013 | F. Pozzato | G. Nizzolo | S. Dumoulin |
| 2012 | E. Boasson Hagen | R. Costa | H. Haussler |
| 2011 | G. Bole | S. Gerrans | T. Voeckler |
| 2010 | M. Goss | T. Farrar | Y. Offredo |
| 2009 | S. Gerrans | P. Fedrigo | P. Martens |
| 2008 | P. Fedrigo | A. Ballan | D. Garcia |
| 2007 | T. Voeckler | T. Hushovd | D. Di Luca |
| 2006 | V. Nibali | J. A. Flecha | M. Mori |
| 2005 | G. Hincapie | A. Usov | D. Rebellin |
| 2004 | D. Rous | S. Baguet | G. Trentin |
| 2003 | A. Flickinger | A. Geslin | N. Jalabert |
| 2002 | J. Hunt | S. O Grady | B. Cooke |
| 2001 | N. Mattan | P. Halgand | P. Jonker |
| 2000 | M. Bartoli | N. Mattan | W. Beneteau |
| 1999 | C. Mengin | M. Zberg | S. Ivanov |
| 1998 | P. Herve | L. Dierckxsens | S. Heulot |
| 1997 | A. Ferrigato | S. Barbero | C. Horner |
| 1996 | F. Vandenbroucke | L. Brochard | A. Tchmil |
| 1995 | R. Jaermann | L. Madouas | C. Henn |
| 1994 | A. Tchmil | R. Virenque | J. Heppner |
| 1993 | T. Claveyrolat | J. F. Bernard | T. Laurent |
| 1992 | R. Pensec | S. Baguet | T. Claveyrolat |
| 1991 | A. De Las Cuevas | A. Kappes | M. Arroyo |
| 1990 | B. Cornillet | M. Gayant | T. Wegmuller |
| 1989 | J. C. Colotti | B. Cornillet | G. Delion |
| 1988 | L. Leblanc | C. Mottet | P. Esnault |
| 1987 | G. Duclos Lassalle | J. C. Bagot | F. Brun |
| 1986 | M. Gayant | S. Kelly | S. Lilholt |
| 1985 | E. Guyot | R. Matthijs | M. Madiot |
| 1984 | S. Kelly | F. Vichot | E. Caritoux |
| 1983 | P. Bazzo | M. Madiot | S. Roche |
| 1982 | F. Castaing | R. Clere | D. Vanoverschelde |
| 1981 | G. Duclos Lassalle | D. Arnaud | J. Martin |
| 1980 | P. Friou | J. Bossis | B. Becaas |
| 1979 | F. Pirard | J. Chassang | Y. Bertin |
| 1978 | P. R. Villemiane | J. Zoetemelk | M. Tinazzi |
| 1977 | J. Bossis | R. Legeay | C. Seznec |
| 1976 | J. Bossis | P. Perret | P. R. Villemiane |
| 1975 | C. Guimard | J. L. Danguillaume | G. Santy |
| 1974 | R. Martin | J. Botherel | C. Aiguesparses |
| 1973 | J. C. Largeau | G. Bellone | G. Sibille |
| 1972 | R. Bouloux | G. Besnard | E. Mattioda |
| 1971 | J. P. Danguillaume | J. Gestraud | R. Delisle |
| 1970 | J. Marcarini | R. Bouloux | R. Berland |
| 1969 | J. Jourden | F. Goasduff | L. P. Ménard |
| 1968 | J. Jourden | J. C. Lebaube | A. Zimmermann |
| 1967 | F. Hamon | G. Chappe | M. Morin |
| 1966 | C. Mazeaud | J. Bourles | P. Le Mellec |
| 1965 | F. Goasduff | H. Niel | J. L. Jagueneau |
| 1964 | J. Bourles | H. Ferrer | J. Gainche |
| 1963 | F. Picot | P. Le Mellec | F. Delort |
| 1962 | J. Gainche | G. Groussard | J. Morvan |
| 1961 | F. Picot | E. Le Bigault | M. Bleneau |
| 1960 | H. Ferrer | A. Foucher | J. Velly |
| 1959 | E. Crenn | J. Gainche | F. Le Buhotel |
| 1958 | J. Gainche | A. Ruffet | F. Picot |
| 1957 | I. Vitre | J. Morvan | J. Groussard |
| 1956 | V. Huot | R. Fournier | J. Morvan |
| 1955 | J. J. Petit Jean | J. Dupont | J. Le Cadet |
| 1954 | U. Anzile | J. Le Guilly | J. Gadras |
| 1953 | S. Blusson | L. Gillet | R. Scardin |
| 1952 | E. Guerinel | F. Mahe | J. Bobet |
| 1951 | E. Guerinel | G. Butteux | J. Erussard |
| 1950 | A. Audaire | A. Ruffet | G. Mercier |
| 1949 | A. Audaire | G. Butteux | R. Haugustaine |
| 1948 | E. Tassin | F. Chretien | R. Louviot |
| 1947 | R. Louviot | A. Bourlon | R. Chupin |
| 1946 | A. Le Strat | R. Chupin | P. Cogan |
| 1945 | E. Tassin | C. Taeron | F. Gouyette |
| 1938 | P. Cloarec | R. Tanneveau | J. M. Goasmat |
| 1937 | J. M. Goasmat | R. Oubron | A. Fournier |
| 1936 | P. Cogan | F. Lucas | J. Le Dilly |
| 1935 | J. Le Dilly | E. Le Gallo | R. Drouet |
| 1934 | L. Tulot | J. Keriel | R. Durin |
| 1933 | P. Bono | R. Louviot | J. Grujon |
| 1932 | P. Bono | P. Le Drogo | F. Le Drogo |
| 1931 | F. Fave | P. Le Doare | A. Godinat |

## RIDER RESULTS

| WINS | RIDER |
|---|---|
| 2 | A. Audaire, P. Bono, J. Bossis, G. Duclos Lassalle, J. Gainche, E. Guérinel, J. Jourden, O. Naesen, F. Picot, E. Tassin |

| PODIUMS | RIDER |
|---|---|
| 4 | J. Gainche |
| 3 | J. Bossis, A. Kristoff, R. Louviot, J. Morvan, F. Picot |
| 2 | A. Audaire, S. Baguet, P. Bono, R. Bouloux, J. Bourles, G. Butteux, R. Chupin, T. Claveyrolat, P. Cogan, B. Cornillet, G. Duclos Lassalle, P. Fedrigo, H. Ferrer, M. Gayant, S. Gerrans, J. F. Goasduff, M. Goasmat, G. Groussard, E. Guerinel, J. Jourden, S. Kelly, J. Le Dilly, P. Le Mellec, R. Martin, M. Madiot, N. Mattan, O. Naesen, A. Ruffet, E. Tassin, A. Tchmil, P. R. Villemiane, T. Voeckler |

## COUNTRY RESULTS

| WINS | COUNTRY |
|---|---|
| 63 | France |
| 6 | Belgium |
| 5 | Italy |
| 3 | Australia |
| 2 | Norway |
| 1 | Ireland, Netherlands, Slovenia, Switzerland, United Kingdom, United States |

| PODIUMS | COUNTRY |
|---|---|
| 181 | France |
| 16 | Belgium, Italy |
| 9 | Australia |
| 5 | Norway |
| 4 | Germany |
| 3 | Denmark, Ireland, Switzerland, United States |
| 2 | Slovenia, Spain |
| 1 | Belarus, Lithuania, Mexico, Portugal, Russia, United Kingdom |

MEN'S HISTORICAL RESULTS

# PARIS–NICE

## RESULTS BY YEAR

| YEAR | 1ST | 2ND | 3RD |
|---|---|---|---|
| 2021 | M. Schachmann | A. Vlasov | I. Izaguirre |
| 2020 | M. Schachmann | T. Benoot | S. Higuita |
| 2019 | E. Bernal | N. Quintana | M. Kwiatkowski |
| 2018 | M. Soler | S. Yates | G. Izaguirre |
| 2017 | S. Henao | A. Contador | D. Martin |
| 2016 | G. Thomas | A. Contador | R. Porte |
| 2015 | R. Porte | M. Kwiatkowski | S. Spilak |
| 2014 | C. Betancur | R. Costa | A. Vichot |
| 2013 | R. Porte | A. Talansky | J. C. Peraud |
| 2012 | B. Wiggins | L. Westra | A. Valverde |
| 2011 | T. Martin | A. Kloden | B. Wiggins |
| 2010 | A. Contador | L. L. Sanchez | R. Kreuziger |
| 2009 | L. L. Sanchez | F. Schleck | S. Chavanel |
| 2008 | D. Rebellin | R. Nocentini | Y. Popovych |
| 2007 | A. Contador | D. Rebellin | L. L. Sanchez |
| 2006 | F. Landis | F. J. Vila | A. Colom |
| 2005 | B. Julich | A. Valverde | C. Zaballa |
| 2004 | J. Jaksche | D. Rebellin | B. Julich |
| 2003 | A. Vinokourov | M. Zarrabeitia | D. Rebellin |
| 2002 | A. Vinokourov | S. Casar | L. Jalabert |
| 2001 | D. Frigo | R. Rumsas | P. Van Petegem |
| 2000 | A. Kloden | L. Brochard | F. Mancebo |
| 1999 | M. Boogerd | M. Zberg | S. Botero |
| 1998 | F. Vandenbroucke | L. Jalabert | M. Garcia |
| 1997 | L. Jalabert | L. Dufaux | S. Blanco |
| 1996 | L. Jalabert | L. Armstrong | C. Boardman |
| 1995 | L. Jalabert | V. Bobrik | A. Zulle |
| 1994 | T. Rominger | J. Montoya | V. Ekimov |
| 1993 | A. Zulle | L. Bezault | P. Lance |
| 1992 | J. F. Bernard | T. Rominger | M. Indurain |
| 1991 | T. Rominger | L. Jalabert | M. Gayant |
| 1990 | M. Indurain | S. Roche | L. Leblanc |
| 1989 | M. Indurain | S. Roche | M. Madiot |
| 1988 | S. Kelly | R. Pensec | J. Gorospe |
| 1987 | S. Kelly | J. F. Bernard | L. Fignon |
| 1986 | S. Kelly | U. Zimmermann | G. Lemond |
| 1985 | S. Kelly | S. Roche | F. Vichot |
| 1984 | S. Kelly | S. Roche | B. Hinault |
| 1983 | S. Kelly | J. M. Grezet | S. Rooks |
| 1982 | S. Kelly | G. Duclos Lassalle | J. L. Vandenbroucke |
| 1981 | S. Roche | A. van Der Poel | F. De Wolf |
| 1980 | G. Duclos Lassalle | S. Mutter | G. Knetemann |
| 1979 | J. Zoetemelk | S. A. Nilsson | G. Knetemann |
| 1978 | G. Knetemann | B. Hinault | J. Zoetemelk |
| 1977 | F. Maertens | G. Knetemann | J. L. Vandenbroucke |
| 1976 | M. Laurent | H. Kuiper | L. Ocana |
| 1975 | J. Zoetemelk | E. Merckx | G. Knetemann |
| 1974 | J. Zoetemelk | A. Santy | E. Merckx |
| 1973 | R. Poulidor | J. Zoetemelk | E. Merckx |
| 1972 | R. Poulidor | E. Merckx | L. Ocana |
| 1971 | E. Merckx | G. Pettersson | L. Ocana |
| 1970 | E. Merckx | L. Ocana | J. Janssen |
| 1969 | E. Merckx | R. Poulidor | J. Anquetil |
| 1968 | R. Wolfshohl | F. Bracke | J. L. Bodin |
| 1967 | T. Simpson | B. Guyot | R. Wolfshohl |
| 1966 | J. Anquetil | R. Poulidor | V. Adorni |
| 1965 | J. Anquetil | R. Altig | I. Zilioli |
| 1964 | J. Janssen | J. C. Annaert | J. Forestier |
| 1963 | J. Anquetil | R. Altig | R. Van Looy |
| 1962 | J. Planckaert | T. Simpson | R. Wolfshohl |
| 1961 | J. Anquetil | J. Groussard | J. Planckaert |
| 1960 | R. Impanis | F. Mahe | R. Cazala |
| 1959 | J. Graczyk | G. Saint | P. Baffi |
| 1958 | A. De Bruyne | P. Fornara | G. Derycke |
| 1957 | J. Anquetil | D. Keteleer | J. Brankart |
| 1956 | A. De Bruyne | P. Barbotin | F. Mahe |
| 1955 | J. Bobet | P. Molineris | B. Gauthier |
| 1954 | R. Impanis | N. Lauredi | F. Anastasi |
| 1953 | J. P. Munch | R. Walkowiak | R. Bertaz |
| 1952 | L. Bobet | D. Zampini | R. Impanis |
| 1951 | R. Decock | L. Teisseire | K. Piot |
| 1946 | F. Camellini | M. De Muer | F. Bonduel |
| 1939 | M. Archambaud | F. Bonduel | G. Desmet |
| 1938 | J. Lowie | A. Disseaux | A. van Schendel |
| 1937 | R. Lapebie | S. Marcaillou | A. van Schendel |
| 1936 | M. Archambaud | J. Fontenay | A. Deloor |
| 1935 | R. Vietto | A. Dignef | R. Lesueur |
| 1934 | G. Rebry | R. Lapebie | M. Archambaud |
| 1933 | A. Schepers | L. Hardiquest | B. Faure |

## RIDER RESULTS

| WINS | RIDER |
|---|---|
| 7 | S. Kelly |
| 5 | J. Anquetil |
| 3 | L. Jalabert, E. Merckx, J. Zoetemelk |
| 2 | M. Archambaud, A. Contador, A. De Bruyne, R. Impanis, M. Indurain, R. Porte, R. Poulidor, T. Rominger, M. Schachmann, A. Vinokourov |

| PODIUMS | RIDER |
|---|---|
| 7 | S. Kelly, E. Merckx |
| 6 | J. Anquetil, L. Jalabert |
| 5 | G. Knetemann, S. Roche, J. Zoetemelk |
| 4 | A. Contador, L. Ocaña, R. Poulidor, D. Rebellin |
| 3 | M. Archambaud, R. Impanis, M. Indurain, L. L. Sanchez, R. Porte, T. Rominger, R. Wolfshohl |
| 2 | R. Altig, F. Bonduel, A. De Bruyne, G. Duclos-Lassalle, J. Francois Bernard, B. Hinault, J. Janssen, B. Julich, A. Kloden, M. Kwiatkowski, R. Lapebie, J. L. Vandenbroucke, F. Mahe, J. Planckaert, M. Schachmann, T. Simpson, A. van Schendel, A. Valverde, A. Vinokourov, B. Wiggins, A. Zulle |

## COUNTRY RESULTS

| WINS | COUNTRY |
|---|---|
| 21 | France |
| 14 | Belgium |
| 8 | Ireland |
| 6 | Germany, Netherlands, Spain |
| 3 | Colombia, Italy, Switzerland, United Kingdom |
| 2 | Australia,, Kazakhstan, United States |

| PODIUMS | COUNTRY |
|---|---|
| 70 | France |
| 37 | Belgium |
| 27 | Spain |
| 19 | Netherlands |
| 13 | Ireland |
| 12 | Italy |
| 11 | Germany |
| 10 | Switzerland |
| 7 | United Kingdom |
| 6 | Colombia, United States |
| 3 | Australia, Russia |
| 2 | Kazakhstan, Poland, Sweden |
| 1 | Czech Republic, Lithuania, Luxembourg, Portugal, Slovenia, Ukraine |

MEN'S HISTORICAL RESULTS

# TOUR DE SUISSE

## RESULTS BY YEAR

| YEAR | 1ST | 2ND | 3RD |
|---|---|---|---|
| 2021 | R. Carapaz | R. Urán | J. Fuglsang |
| 2020 | Race cancelled | | |
| 2019 | E. Bernal | R. Dennis | P. Konrad |
| 2018 | R. Porte | J. Fuglsang | N. Quintana |
| 2017 | S. Spilak | D. Caruso | S. Kruijswijk |
| 2016 | M. A. López | I. Izaguirre | W. Barguil |
| 2015 | S. Spilak | G. Thomas | T. Dumoulin |
| 2014 | R. Costa | M. Frank | B. Mollema |
| 2013 | R. Costa | B. Mollema | R. Kreuziger |
| 2012 | R. Costa | F. Schleck | L. Leipheimer |
| 2011 | L. Leipheimer | D. Cunego | S. Kruijswijk |
| 2010 | F. Schleck | L. Armstrong | J. Fuglsang |
| 2009 | F. Cancellara | T. Martin | R. Kreuziger |
| 2008 | R. Kreuziger | A. Kloden | I. Anton |
| 2007 | V. Karpets | K. Kirchen | S. Devolder |
| 2006 | J. Ullrich | K. Gil | J. Jaksche |
| 2005 | A. Gonzalez | M. Rogers | J. Ullrich |
| 2004 | J. Ullrich | F. Jeker | D. Cioni |
| 2003 | A. Vinokourov | G. Guerini | O. Pereiro |
| 2002 | A. Zulle | P. Wadecki | N. Fritsch |
| 2001 | L. Armstrong | G. Simoni | W. Belli |
| 2000 | O. Camenzind | D. Frigo | W. Belli |
| 1999 | F. Casagrande | L. Jalabert | G. Simoni |
| 1998 | S. Garzelli | B. Zberg | W. Belli |
| 1997 | C. Agnolutto | O. Camenzind | J. Ullrich |
| 1996 | P. Luttenberger | G. Faresin | G. Bugno |
| 1995 | P. Tonkov | A. Zulle | Z. Jaskula |
| 1994 | P. Richard | V. Pulnikov | G. Pierobon |
| 1993 | M. Saligari | R. Jaermann | F. Escartin |
| 1992 | G. Furlan | G. Bugno | F. Jeker |
| 1991 | L. Roosen | P. Richard | A. Hampsten |
| 1990 | S. Kelly | R. Millar | A. Hampsten |
| 1989 | B. Breu | D. Steiger | J. Muller |
| 1988 | H. Wechselberger | S. Bauer | A. Da Silva |
| 1987 | A. Hampsten | P. Winnen | F. E. Parra |
| 1986 | A. Hampsten | R. Millar | G. Lemond |
| 1985 | P. Anderson | N. Ruttimann | G. Winterberg |
| 1984 | U. Zimmermann | A. Da Silva | G. Zadrobilek |
| 1983 | S. Kelly | P. Winnen | J. M. Grezet |
| 1982 | G. Saronni | T. De Rooy | G. Van Calster |
| 1981 | B. Breu | J. Fuchs | L. Natale |
| 1980 | M. Beccia | J. Fuchs | J. Zoetemelk |
| 1979 | W. Wesemael | R. Pevenage | L. Mazzantini |
| 1978 | P. Wellens | U. Sutter | J. Fuchs |
| 1977 | M. Pollentier | L. Van Impe | B. Pronk |
| 1976 | H. Kuiper | M. Pollentier | J. Pesarrodona |
| 1975 | R. De Vlaeminck | E. Merckx | L. Pfenninger |
| 1974 | E. Merckx | G. Pettersson | L. Pfenninger |
| 1973 | J. M. Fuente | D. Giuliani | W. Panizza |
| 1972 | L. Pfenninger | R. Pingeon | M. Dancelli |
| 1971 | G. Pintens | L. Pfenninger | U. Colombo |
| 1970 | R. Poggiali | L. Pfenninger | P. Mori |
| 1969 | V. Adorni | A. Gonzalez | B. Vifian |
| 1968 | L. Pfenninger | R. Hagmann | H. Van Springel |
| 1967 | G. Motta | R. Maurer | L. P. Santamarina |
| 1966 | A. Portalupi | C. Chiappano | R. Zollinger |
| 1965 | F. Bitossi | J. Huysmans | M. Mugnaini |
| 1964 | R. Maurer | F. Balmamion | I. Zilioli |
| 1963 | G. Fezzardi | R. Maurer | A. Moresi |
| 1962 | H. Junkermann | F. Balmamion | A. Moser |
| 1961 | A. Moresi | H. Couvreur | A. Ruegg |
| 1960 | A. Ruegg | K. Gimmi | R. Strehler |
| 1959 | H. Junkermann | H. Anglade | F. Bahamontes |
| 1958 | P. Fornara | H. Junkermann | A. Catalano |
| 1957 | P. Fornara | E. Sorgeloos | A. Moresi |
| 1956 | R. Graf | F. Schar | J. Planckaert |
| 1955 | H. Koblet | S. Ockers | C. Clerici |
| 1954 | P. Fornara | A. Coletto | G. Astrua |
| 1953 | H. Koblet | F. Schar | D. Barozzi |
| 1952 | P. Fornara | F. Kubler | C. Clerici |
| 1951 | F. Kubler | H. Koblet | A. Martini |
| 1950 | H. Koblet | J. Goldschmit | A. Ronconi |
| 1949 | G. Weilemann | G. Aeschlimann | E. Stettler |
| 1948 | F. Kubler | G. Bresci | H. Sommer |
| 1947 | G. Bartali | G. Bresci | S. Ockers |
| 1946 | G. Bartali | J. Wagner | A. Ronconi |
| 1942 | F. Kubler | W. Kern | F. Stocker |
| 1941 | J. Wagner | W. Buchwalder | F. Kubler |
| 1939 | R. Zimmermann | M. Bolliger | C. Didier |
| 1938 | G. Valetti | A. Mersch | S. Canavesi |
| 1937 | K. Litschi | L. Amberg | W. Blattmann |
| 1936 | H. Garnier | G. Deloor | L. Amberg |
| 1935 | G. Rinaldi | L. Amberg | H. Garnier |
| 1934 | L. Geyer | L. Level | F. Camusso |
| 1933 | M. Bulla | A. Buechi | G. Rinaldi |

## RIDER RESULTS

| WINS | RIDER |
|---|---|
| 4 | P. Fornara |
| 3 | R. Costa, H. Koblet, F. Kubler |
| 2 | G. Bartali, B. Breu, A. Hampsten, H. Junkermann, S. Kelly, L. Pfenninger, S. Špilak, J. Ullrich |

| PODIUMS | RIDER |
|---|---|
| 6 | L. Pfenninger |
| 5 | F. Kubler |
| 4 | P. Fornara, A. Hampsten, H. Koblet, J. Ullrich |
| 3 | L. Amberg, W. Belli, R. Costa, J. Fuchs, J. Fuglsang, H. Junkermann, R. Kreuziger, R. Maurer, A. Moresi |
| 2 | L. Armstrong, F. Balmamion, G. Bartali, G. Bresci, B. Breu, G. Bugno, O. Camenzind, C. Clerici, A. Da Silva, H. Garnier, F. Jeker, S. Kelly, S. Kruijswijk, L. Leipheimer, E. Merckx, R. Millar, B. Mollema, S. Ockers, M. Pollentier, P. Richard, G. Rinaldi, A. Ronconi, A. Ruegg, F. Schar, F. Schleck, G. Simoni, S. Špilak, J. Wagner, P. Winnen, A. Zulle |

## COUNTRY RESULTS

| WINS | COUNTRY |
|---|---|
| 22 | Switzerland |
| 20 | Italy |
| 8 | Belgium |
| 5 | Germany |
| 4 | United States |
| 3 | Austria, Portugal |
| 2 | Australia, Colombia, France, Ireland, Russia, Slovenia, Spain |
| 1 | Czech Republic, Ecuador, Kazakhstan, Luxembourg, Netherlands |

| PODIUMS | COUNTRY |
|---|---|
| 71 | Switzerland |
| 60 | Italy |
| 23 | Belgium |
| 12 | Germany |
| 11 | Netherlands, Spain |
| 9 | France, United States |
| 6 | Luxembourg |
| 5 | Colombia, Portugal |
| 4 | Australia, Austria |
| 3 | Czech Republic, Denmark, United Kingdom |
| 2 | Ireland, Poland, Russia, Slovenia |
| 1 | Canada, Ecuador, Kazakhstan, Sweden, Ukraine |

MEN'S HISTORICAL RESULTS

# GENT-WEVELGEM

## RESULTS BY YEAR

| YEAR | 1ST | 2ND | 3RD |
|---|---|---|---|
| 2021 | W. van Aert | G. Nizzolo | M. Trentin |
| 2020 | M. Pedersen | F. Sénéchal | M. Trentin |
| 2019 | A. Kristoff | J. Degenkolb | O. Naesen |
| 2018 | P. Sagan | E. Viviani | A. Demare |
| 2017 | G. Van Avermaet | J. Keukeleire | P. Sagan |
| 2016 | P. Sagan | S. Vanmarcke | V. Kuznetsov |
| 2015 | L. Paolini | N. Terpstra | G. Thomas |
| 2014 | J. Degenkolb | A. Demare | P. Sagan |
| 2013 | P. Sagan | B. Bozic | G. Van Avermaet |
| 2012 | T. Boonen | P. Sagan | M. Breschel |
| 2011 | T. Boonen | D. Bennati | T. Farrar |
| 2010 | B. Eisel | S. Vanmarcke | P. Gilbert |
| 2009 | E. Boasson Hagen | A. Kuchynski | M. Goss |
| 2008 | O. Freire | A. Clerc | W. Weylandt |
| 2007 | M. Burghardt | R. Hammond | O. Freire |
| 2006 | T. Hushovd | D. Kopp | A. Petacchi |
| 2005 | N. Mattan | J. A. Flecha | D. Bennati |
| 2004 | T. Boonen | M. Backstedt | J. Kirsipuu |
| 2003 | A. Klier | H. Vogels | T. Boonen |
| 2002 | M. Cipollini | F. Rodriguez | G. Hincapie |
| 2001 | G. Hincapie | L. van Bon | S. Wesemann |
| 2000 | G. Van Bondt | P. Van Petegem | J. Museeuw |
| 1999 | T. Steels | Z. Spruch | T. Hoffman |
| 1998 | F. Vandenbroucke | L. Michaelsen | N. Mattan |
| 1997 | P. Gaumont | A. Tchmil | J. Capiot |
| 1996 | T. Steels | G. Lombardi | F. Baldato |
| 1995 | L. Michaelsen | M. Fondriest | L. Roosen |
| 1994 | W. Peeters | F. Ballerini | J. Museeuw |
| 1993 | M. Cipollini | E. Vanderaerden | D. Abduzhaparov |
| 1992 | M. Cipollini | J. Capiot | A. Baffi |
| 1991 | D. Abduzhaparov | M. Cipollini | O. Ludwig |
| 1990 | H. Frison | J. Museeuw | F. Ballerini |
| 1989 | G. Solleveld | S. Yates | R. Sorensen |
| 1988 | S. Kelly | G. Bugno | R. Kiefel |
| 1987 | T. van Vliet | E. De Wilde | H. Frison |
| 1986 | G. Bontempi | T. Poels | J. M. Wampers |
| 1985 | E. Vanderaerden | P. Anderson | R. Dhaenens |
| 1984 | G. Bontempi | E. Vanderaerden | P. Gavazzi |
| 1983 | L. van Vliet | J. Raas | F. Hoste |
| 1982 | F. Hoste | E. Vanhaerens | F. De Wolf |
| 1981 | J. Raas | R. De Vlaeminck | F. De Wolf |
| 1980 | H. Lubberding | F. De Wolf | P. van Katwijk |
| 1979 | F. Moser | R. De Vlaeminck | J. Raas |
| 1978 | F. Van Den Haute | W. Planckaert | F. Moser |
| 1977 | B. Hinault | V. Algeri | P. van Katwijk |
| 1976 | F. Maertens | R. Van Linden | F. Verbeeck |
| 1975 | F. Maertens | F. Verbeeck | R. Van Linden |
| 1974 | B. Hoban | E. Merckx | R. De Vlaeminck |
| 1973 | E. Merckx | F. Verbeeck | W. Planckaert |
| 1972 | R. Swerts | F. Gimondi | E. Merckx |
| 1971 | G. Pintens | R. De Vlaeminck | G. Karstens |
| 1970 | E. Merckx | W. Vekemans | W. Godefroot |
| 1969 | W. Vekemans | R. De Vlaeminck | E. De Vlaeminck |
| 1968 | W. Godefroot | W. Van Neste | F. Gimondi |
| 1967 | E. Merckx | J. Janssen | W. Sels |
| 1966 | H. Van Springel | N. Vanclooster | P. L. Jensen |
| 1965 | N. Depauw | B. Van de Kerckhove | G. Desmet |
| 1964 | J. Anquetil | Y. Molenaers | R. Van Looy |
| 1963 | B. Beheyt | T. Simpson | M. Van Aerde |
| 1962 | R. Van Looy | F. Schoubben | A. Desmet |
| 1961 | F. Aerenhouts | R. Impanis | Y. Molenaers |
| 1960 | F. Aerenhouts | F. De Mulder | J. Planckaert |
| 1959 | L. Vandaele | J. Hoevenaers | J. Anquetil |
| 1958 | N. Fore | R. Van Looy | A. De Bruyne |
| 1957 | R. Van Looy | A. Noyelle | L. Mathys |
| 1956 | R. Van Looy | R. Van Genechten | D. Keteleer |
| 1955 | B. Schotte | D. Keteleer | R. Impanis |
| 1954 | R. Graf | F. Kubler | E. Sterckx |
| 1953 | R. Impanis | W. Van Est | G. Derycke |
| 1952 | R. Impanis | M. Blomme | A. De Hertog |
| 1951 | A. Rosseel | R. Jonckheere | L. Van Brabant |
| 1950 | B. Schotte | A. Decin | A. Declercq |
| 1949 | M. Kint | A. Declercq | A. Decin |
| 1948 | V. Ollivier | A. Ramon | H. Couvreur |
| 1947 | M. De Simpelaere | R. Beyens | L. Vlaemynck |
| 1946 | E. Sterckx | M. De Simpelaere | M. Remue |
| 1945 | R. Van Eenaeme | M. Van Herzele | A. Declercq |
| 1939 | A. Declercq | F. Van Hellemont | A. Van Laecke |
| 1938 | H. Godart | E. Delathouwer | G. Van Cauwenberghe |
| 1937 | R. Van Eenaeme | A. Ritserveldt | A. Hallaert |
| 1936 | R. Van Eenaeme | J. Somers | G. Denys |
| 1935 | A. Depreitere | J. Dufromont | K. Catrysse |
| 1934 | G. Van Belle | M. Vandenberghe | J. Dufromont |

## RIDER RESULTS

| WINS | RIDER |
|---|---|
| 3 | T. Boonen, M. Cipollini, E. Merckx, P. Sagan, R. Van Eenaeme, R. Van Looy |
| 2 | F. Aerenhouts, G. Bontempi, R. Impanis, F. Maertens, B. Schotte, T. Steels |

| PODIUMS | RIDER |
|---|---|
| 6 | P. Sagan |
| 5 | R. De Vlaeminck, E. Merckx, R. Van Looy |
| 4 | T. Boonen, M. Cipollini, A. Declercq, R. Impanis |
| 3 | F. De Wolf, J. Museeuw, J. Raas, R. Van Eenaeme, E. Vanderaerden, F. Verbeeck |
| 2 | D. Abduzhaparov, F. Aerenhouts, J. Anquetil, F. Ballerini, D. Bennati, G. Bontempi, J. Capiot, M. De Simpelaere, A. Decin, J. Degenkolb, A. Démare, J. Dufromont, O. Freire, H. Frison, F. Gimondi, W. Godefroot, G. Hincapie, F. Hoste, D. Keteleer, F. Maertens, N. Mattan, L. Michaelsen, Y. Molenaers, F. Moser, W. Planckaert, B. Schotte, T. Steels, E. Sterckx, M. Trentin, G. Van Avermaet, P. van Katwijk, R. Van Linden, S. Vanmarcke, W. Vekemans |

## COUNTRY RESULTS

| WINS | COUNTRY |
|---|---|
| 50 | Belgium |
| 7 | Italy |
| 5 | Netherlands |
| 3 | France, Germany, Norway, Slovakia |
| 2 | Denmark |
| 1 | Austria, Ireland, Spain, Switzerland, United Kingdom, United States, Uzbekistan |

| PODIUMS | COUNTRY |
|---|---|
| 148 | Belgium |
| 27 | Italy |
| 16 | Netherlands |
| 7 | France |
| 6 | Denmark, Germany, Slovakia |
| 5 | United Kingdom, United States |
| 4 | Switzerland |
| 3 | Australia, Norway, Spain |
| 2 | Uzbekistan |
| 1 | Austria, Belarus, Estonia, Ireland, Poland, Russia, Slovenia, Sweden |

MEN'S HISTORICAL RESULTS

# VUELTA A ESPAÑA

## RESULTS BY YEAR

| YEAR | 1ST | 2ND | 3RD |
|---|---|---|---|
| 2021 | P. Roglič | E. Mas | J. Haig |
| 2020 | P. Roglič | R. Carapaz | H. Carthy |
| 2019 | P. Roglič | A. Valverde | T. Pogačar |
| 2018 | S. Yates | E. Mas | M. A. López |
| 2017 | C. Froome | V. Nibali | I. Zakarin |
| 2016 | N. Quintana | C. Froome | E. Chaves |
| 2015 | F. Aru | J. Rodriguez | R. Majka |
| 2014 | A. Contador | C. Froome | A. Valverde |
| 2013 | C. Horner | V. Nibali | A. Valverde |
| 2012 | A. Contador | A. Valverde | J. Rodriguez |
| 2011 | J. J. Cobo | C. Froome | B. Wiggins |
| 2010 | V. Nibali | P. Velits | J. Rodriguez |
| 2009 | A. Valverde | S. Sanchez | C. Evans |
| 2008 | A. Contador | L. Leipheimer | C. Sastre |
| 2007 | D. Menchov | C. Sastre | S. Sanchez |
| 2006 | A. Vinokourov | A. Valverde | A. Kashechkin |
| 2005 | R. Heras | D. Menchov | C. Sastre |
| 2004 | R. Heras | S. Perez | F. Mancebo |
| 2003 | R. Heras | I. N. Vega | A. Valverde |
| 2002 | A. Gonzalez Jimenez | R. Heras | J. Beloki |
| 2001 | A. L. Casero | O. Sevilla | L. Leipheimer |
| 2000 | R. Heras | A. L. Casero | P. Tonkov |
| 1999 | J. Ullrich | I. Gonzalez De Galdeano | R. Heras |
| 1998 | A. Olano | F. Escartin | J. M. Jimenez |
| 1997 | A. Zulle | F. Escartin | L. Dufaux |
| 1996 | A. Zulle | L. Dufaux | T. Rominger |
| 1995 | L. Jalabert | A. Olano | J. Bruyneel |
| 1994 | T. Rominger | M. Zarrabeitia | P. Delgado |
| 1993 | T. Rominger | A. Zulle | L. Cubino |
| 1992 | T. Rominger | J. Montoya | P. Delgado |
| 1991 | M. Mauri | M. Indurain | M. Lejarreta |
| 1990 | M. Giovannetti | P. Delgado | A. Fuerte |
| 1989 | P. Delgado | F. E. Parra | O. J. Vargas |
| 1988 | S. Kelly | R. Dietzen | A. Fuerte |
| 1987 | L. A. Herrera | R. Dietzen | L. Fignon |
| 1986 | A. Pino | R. Millar | S. Kelly |
| 1985 | P. Delgado | R. Millar | F. Rodriguez |
| 1984 | E. Caritoux | A. Fernandez | R. Dietzen |
| 1983 | B. Hinault | M. Lejarreta | A. Fernandez |
| 1982 | M. Lejarreta | M. Pollentier | S. A. Nilsson |
| 1981 | G. Battaglin | P. Munoz | V. Belda |
| 1980 | F. Ruperez | P. Torres | C. Criquielion |
| 1979 | J. Zoetemelk | F. Galdos | M. Pollentier |
| 1978 | B. Hinault | J. Pesarrodona | J. R. Bernaudeau |
| 1977 | F. Maertens | M. M. Lasa | K. P. Thaler |
| 1976 | J. Pesarrodona | L. Ocana | J. Nazabal |
| 1975 | A. Tamames | D. Perurena | M. M. Lasa |
| 1974 | J. M. Fuente | J. Agostinho | M. M. Lasa |
| 1973 | E. Merckx | L. Ocana | B. Thevenet |
| 1972 | J. M. Fuente | M. M. Lasa | A. Tamames |
| 1971 | F. Bracke | W. David | L. Ocana |
| 1970 | L. Ocana | A. Tamames | H. Van Springel |
| 1969 | R. Pingeon | L. Ocana | R. Wagtmans |
| 1968 | F. Gimondi | J. Perez | E. Velez |
| 1967 | J. Janssen | J. P. Ducasse | A. Gonzalez |
| 1966 | F. Gabica | E. Velez | C. Echevarria |
| 1965 | R. Wolfshohl | R. Poulidor | R. Van Looy |
| 1964 | R. Poulidor | L. Otano | J. Perez |
| 1963 | J. Anquetil | J. M. Colmenarejo | M. Pacheco |
| 1962 | R. Altig | J. Perez | S. Elliott |
| 1961 | A. Soler | F. Mahe | J. Perez |
| 1960 | F. De Mulder | A. Desmet | M. Pacheco |
| 1959 | A. Suarez | J. Segu | R. Van Looy |
| 1958 | J. Stablinski | P. Fornara | F. Manzaneque |
| 1957 | J. Lorono | F. Bahamontes | B. Ruiz |
| 1956 | A. Conterno | J. Lorono | R. Impanis |
| 1955 | J. Dotto | A. Jimenez | R. Geminiani |
| 1950 | E. Rodriguez | M. Rodriguez | J. Serra |
| 1948 | B. Ruiz | E. Rodriguez | B. Capo |
| 1947 | E. Van Dijck | M. Costa | D. Rodriguez |
| 1946 | D. Langarica | J. Berrendero | J. Lambrichs |
| 1945 | D. Rodriguez | J. Berrendero | J. Gimeno |
| 1942 | J. Berrendero | D. Chafer | F. A. Andres |
| 1941 | J. Berrendero | F. Trueba | J. Jabardo |
| 1936 | G. Deloor | A. Deloor | A. Bertola |
| 1935 | G. Deloor | M. Canardo | A. Dignef |

## RIDER RESULTS

| WINS | RIDER |
|---|---|
| 4 | R. Heras |
| 3 | A. Contador, P. Roglič, T. Rominger |
| 2 | J. Berrendero, P. Delgado, G. Deloor, J. M. Fuente, B. Hinault, A. Zulle |

| PODIUMS | RIDER |
|---|---|
| 7 | A. Valverde |
| 6 | R. Heras |
| 5 | P. Delgado, L. Ocaña |
| 4 | J. Berrendero, C. Froome, M. Maria Lasa, J. Perez, T. Rominger |
| 3 | A. Contador, R. Dietzen, M. Lejarreta, V. Nibali, J. Rodriguez, P. Roglič, C. Sastre, A. Tamames, A. Zulle |
| 2 | A. L. Casero, G. Deloor, L. Dufaux, F. Escartin, A. Fernandez, J. M. Fuente, A. Fuerte, B. Hinault, S. Kelly, L. Leipheimer, J. Lorono, E. Mas, D. Menchov, R. Millar, A. Olano, M. Pacheco, J. Pesarrodona, M. Pollentier, R. Poulidor, E. Rodriguez, D. Rodriguez, B. Ruiz, S. Sanchez, R. Van Looy, E. Velez |

## COUNTRY RESULTS

| WINS | COUNTRY |
|---|---|
| 33 | Spain |
| 9 | France |
| 7 | Belgium |
| 6 | Italy |
| 5 | Switzerland |
| 3 | Germany, Slovenia |
| 2 | Colombia, Netherlands, United Kingdom |
| 1 | Ireland, Kazakhstan, Russia, United States |

| PODIUMS | COUNTRY |
|---|---|
| 125 | Spain |
| 19 | Belgium |
| 16 | France |
| 10 | Italy |
| 9 | Switzerland, United Kingdom |
| 7 | Colombia, Germany |
| 4 | Netherlands, Russia, Slovenia |
| 3 | Ireland, United States |
| 2 | Australia, Kazakhstan |
| 1 | Ecuador, Poland, Portugal, Sweden |

MEN'S HISTORICAL RESULTS

# FLÈCHE WALLONNE

## RESULTS BY YEAR

| YEAR | 1ST | 2ND | 3RD |
|---|---|---|---|
| 2021 | J. Alaphilippe | P. Roglič | A. Valverde |
| 2020 | M. Hirschi | B. Cosnefroy | M. Woods |
| 2019 | J. Alaphilippe | J. Fuglsang | D. Ulissi |
| 2018 | J. Alaphilippe | A. Valverde | J. Vanendert |
| 2017 | A. Valverde | D. Martin | D. Teuns |
| 2016 | A. Valverde | J. Alaphilippe | D. Martin |
| 2015 | A. Valverde | J. Alaphilippe | M. Albasini |
| 2014 | A. Valverde | D. Martin | M. Kwiatkowski |
| 2013 | D. Moreno | S. Henao | C. Betancur |
| 2012 | J. Rodriguez | M. Albasini | P. Gilbert |
| 2011 | P. Gilbert | J. Rodriguez | S. Sanchez |
| 2010 | C. Evans | J. Rodriguez | A. Contador |
| 2009 | D. Rebellin | A. Schleck | D. Cunego |
| 2008 | K. Kirchen | C. Evans | D. Cunego |
| 2007 | D. Rebellin | A. Valverde | D. Di Luca |
| 2006 | A. Valverde | S. Sanchez | K. Kroon |
| 2005 | D. Di Luca | K. Kirchen | D. Rebellin |
| 2004 | D. Rebellin | D. Di Luca | M. Kessler |
| 2003 | I. Astarloa | A. Osa | A. Shefer |
| 2002 | M. Aerts | U. Etxebarria | M. Bartoli |
| 2001 | R. Verbrugghe | I. Basso | J. Jaksche |
| 2000 | F. Casagrande | R. Verbrugghe | L. Jalabert |
| 1999 | M. Bartoli | M. Den Bakker | M. Aerts |
| 1998 | B. Hamburger | F. Vandenbroucke | A. Elli |
| 1997 | L. Jalabert | L. Leblanc | A. Zulle |
| 1996 | L. Armstrong | D. Rous | M. Fondriest |
| 1995 | L. Jalabert | M. Fondriest | Y. Berzin |
| 1994 | M. Argentin | G. Furlan | Y. Berzin |
| 1993 | M. Fondriest | G. Rue | C. Chiappucci |
| 1992 | G. Furlan | G. Rue | D. Cassani |
| 1991 | M. Argentin | C. Criquielion | C. Chiappucci |
| 1990 | M. Argentin | J. C. Leclercq | G. J. Theunisse |
| 1989 | C. Criquielion | S. Rooks | W. Van Eynde |
| 1988 | R. Golz | M. Argentin | S. Rooks |
| 1987 | J. C. Leclercq | C. Criquielion | R. Golz |
| 1986 | L. Fignon | J. C. Leclercq | C. Criquielion |
| 1985 | C. Criquielion | M. Argentin | L. Fignon |
| 1984 | K. Andersen | W. Tackaert | H. Nieuwdorp |
| 1983 | B. Hinault | R. Bittinger | H. Seiz |
| 1982 | M. Beccia | J. Wilmann | P. Haghedooren |
| 1981 | D. Willems | A. van der Poel | G. Van Calster |
| 1980 | G. Saronni | S. A. Nilsson | B. Hinault |
| 1979 | B. Hinault | G. Saronni | B. Johansson |
| 1978 | M. Laurent | G. Baronchelli | D. Thurau |
| 1977 | F. Moser | G. Saronni | H. Van Springel |
| 1976 | J. Zoetemelk | F. Verbeeck | F. Maertens |
| 1975 | A. Dierickx | F. Verbeeck | E. Merckx |
| 1974 | F. Verbeeck | R. De Vlaeminck | E. Leman |
| 1973 | A. Dierickx | E. Merckx | F. Verbeeck |
| 1972 | E. Merckx | R. Poulidor | W. Van Neste |
| 1971 | R. De Vlaeminck | F. Verbeeck | J. De Schoenmaecker |
| 1970 | E. Merckx | G. Pintens | E. De Vlaeminck |
| 1969 | J. Huysmans | E. De Vlaeminck | E. Leman |
| 1968 | R. Van Looy | J. Samyn | J. Janssen |
| 1967 | E. Merckx | R. Post | W. Bocklant |
| 1966 | M. Dancelli | L. Aimar | R. Altig |
| 1965 | R. Poggiali | F. Gimondi | T. Simpson |
| 1964 | G. Desmet | J. Janssen | P. Post |
| 1963 | R. Poulidor | J. Janssen | P. Post |
| 1962 | H. Dewolf | P. Cerami | H. Junkermann |
| 1961 | W. Vannitsen | J. Graczyk | F. Aerenhouts |
| 1960 | P. Cerami | P. Beuffeuil | C. Goossens |
| 1959 | J. Hoevenaers | M. Janssens | F. Schoubben |
| 1958 | R. Van Steenbergen | J. Planckaert | P. Everaert |
| 1957 | R. Impanis | R. Privat | V. Wartel |
| 1956 | R. Van Genechten | S. Ranucci | A. Vlayen |
| 1955 | S. Ockers | A. Van Den Brande | S. Bober |
| 1954 | G. Derycke | F. Kubler | J. De Valck |
| 1953 | S. Ockers | F. Kubler | L. Petrucci |
| 1952 | F. Kubler | S. Ockers | R. Impanis |
| 1951 | F. Kubler | G. Bartali | J. Robic |
| 1950 | F. Coppi | R. Impanis | J. Storms |
| 1949 | R. Van Steenbergen | E. Peeters | F. Coppi |
| 1948 | F. Camellini | B. Schotte | C. Beeckman |
| 1947 | E. Sterckx | M. De Simpelaere | G. Van Overloop |
| 1946 | D. Keteleer | R. Walschot | E. Van Dijck |
| 1945 | M. Kint | L. Vlaemynck | A. Maelbrancke |
| 1944 | M. Kint | B. Schotte | M. Quertinmont |
| 1943 | M. Kint | G. Claes | D. Keteleer |
| 1942 | K. Thijs | F. Bonduel | J. Geus |
| 1941 | S. Grysolle | G. Van Overloop | J. Geus |
| 1939 | E. Delathouwer | H. Syen | A. Perikel |
| 1938 | E. Masson | S. Maes | C. Dubois |
| 1937 | A. Braeckeveldt | M. Kint | A. Perikel |
| 1936 | P. De Meersman | A. Verniers | C. Michielsen |

## RIDER RESULTS

| WINS | RIDER |
|---|---|
| 5 | A. Valverde |
| 3 | J. Alaphilippe, M. Argentin, M. Kint, E. Merckx, D. Rebellin |
| 2 | C. Criquielion, A. Dierickx, B. Hinault, L. Jalabert, F. Kubler, S. Ockers, R. Van Steenbergen |

| PODIUMS | RIDER |
|---|---|
| 8 | A. Valverde |
| 5 | J. Alaphilippe, M. Argentin, C. Criquielion, E. Merckx, F. Verbeeck |
| 4 | M. Kint, F. Kubler, D. Rebellin |
| 3 | J. C. Leclercq, D. Di Luca, M. Fondriest, B. Hinault, R. Impanis, L. Jalabert, J. Janssen, D. Martin, S. Ockers, P. Post, J. Rodriguez, G. Saronni |
| 2 | M. Aerts, M. Albasini, M. Bartoli, Y. Berzin, P. Cerami, C. Chiappucci, F. Coppi, D. Cunego, R. De Vlaeminck, E. De Vlaeminck, A. Dierickx, C. Evans, L. Fignon, G. Furlan, J. Geus, P. Gilbert, R. Golz, D. Keteleer, K. Kirchen, E. Leman, A. Perikel, R. Poulidor, S. Rooks, G. Rue, S. Sanchez, B. Schotte, G. Van Overloop, R. Van Steenbergen, R. Verbrugghe |

## COUNTRY RESULTS

| WINS | COUNTRY |
|---|---|
| 38 | Belgium |
| 18 | Italy |
| 11 | France |
| 8 | Spain |
| 3 | Switzerland |
| 2 | Denmark |
| 1 | Australia, Germany, Luxembourg, Netherlands, United States |

| PODIUMS | COUNTRY |
|---|---|
| 106 | Belgium |
| 43 | Italy |
| 33 | France |
| 17 | Spain |
| 15 | Netherlands |
| 9 | Switzerland |
| 7 | Germany |
| 3 | Denmark, Ireland, Luxembourg |
| 2 | Australia, Colombia, Russia, Sweden |
| 1 | Canada, Kazakhstan, Norway, Poland, Slovenia, United Kingdom, United States, Venezuela |

# DWARS DOOR VLAANDEREN

## RESULTS BY YEAR

| YEAR | 1ST | 2ND | 3RD |
|---|---|---|---|
| 2021 | D. van Baarle | C. Laporte | T. Merlier |
| 2020 | Race cancelled | | |
| 2019 | M. van der Poel | A. Turgis | B. Jungels |
| 2018 | Y. Lampaert | M. Teunissen | S. Vanmarcke |
| 2017 | Y. Lampaert | P. Gilbert | A. Lutsenko |
| 2016 | J. Debusschere | B. Coquard | E. Theuns |
| 2015 | J. Wallays | E. Theuns | D. van Baarle |
| 2014 | N. Terpstra | T. Farrar | B. Bozic |
| 2013 | O. Gatto | B. Bozic | M. Hayman |
| 2012 | N. Terpstra | S. Chavanel | K. De Kort |
| 2011 | N. Nuyens | G. Thomas | T. Farrar |
| 2010 | M. Breschel | B. Leukemans | N. Terpstra |
| 2009 | K. Van Impe | N. Eeckhout | T. Boonen |
| 2008 | S. Chavanel | S. De Jongh | N. Eeckhout |
| 2007 | T. Boonen | N. Eeckhout | S. O'Grady |
| 2006 | F. Veuchelen | J. Hunt | L. Mondory |
| 2005 | N. Eeckhout | R. Hammond | G. Balducci |
| 2004 | L. Capelle | J. Kirsipuu | R. Hammond |
| 2003 | R. McEwen | B. Cooke | M. van Heeswijk |
| 2002 | B. Cooke | L. Bodrogi | J. Planckaert |
| 2001 | N. Eeckhout | W. Peeters | A. Piziks |
| 2000 | T. Hoffman | P. Van Petegem | L. Michaelsen |
| 1999 | J. Museeuw | M. Vanhaecke | C. Peers |
| 1998 | T. Steels | J. Capiot | A. Tchmil |
| 1997 | A. Tchmil | L. Auger | H. De Clercq |
| 1996 | T. Hoffman | E. Van Hooydonck | B. Holm Sorensen |
| 1995 | J. Nijdam | T. Steels | A. Baffi |
| 1994 | C. Bomans | M. Sergeant | L. Willems |
| 1993 | J. Museeuw | F. Ballerini | J. Planckaert |
| 1992 | O. Ludwig | M. Zanoli | J. P. Heynderickx |
| 1991 | E. Vanderaerden | U. Raab | R. Stumpf |
| 1990 | E. Van Hooydonck | A. van der Poel | M. Sergeant |
| 1989 | D. De Wolf | T. De Rooy | J. Museeuw |
| 1988 | J. Talen | F. De Wolf | N. Verhoeven |
| 1987 | J. Nijdam | H. Frison | S. Kelly |
| 1986 | E. Vanderaerden | A. van der Poel | P. Stevenhaagen |
| 1985 | E. Planckaert | E. Vanderaerden | J. Lieckens |
| 1984 | W. Planckaert | R. Matthijs | M. Sergeant |
| 1983 | E. De Wilde | J. Raas | E. Vanderaerden |
| 1982 | J. Raas | J. L. Vandenbroucke | E. Vanhaerens |
| 1981 | F. Hoste | C. Priem | G. Van Gestel |
| 1980 | J. Van Der Meer | J. Raas | G. Van Sweevelt |
| 1979 | G. Van Roosbroeck | W. Planckaert | J. Raas |
| 1978 | A. J. Schipper | F. Hoste | G. Van Sweevelt |
| 1977 | W. Planckaert | E. Leman | M. Demeyer |
| 1976 | W. Planckaert | M. Demeyer | W. Planckaert |
| 1975 | C. Priem | T. Tabak | R. Swerts |
| 1974 | L. Verreydt | R. De Witte | R. Pijnen |
| 1973 | R. Loysch | J. Abelshausen | F. Maertens |
| 1972 | M. Demeyer | N. Vantyghem | E. Verstraeten |
| 1970 | D. Van Ryckeghem | E. Leman | F. Verbeeck |
| 1969 | E. Leman | A. Van Vlierberghe | W. Van Neste |
| 1968 | W. Godefroot | W. Monty | B. Van de Kerckhove |
| 1967 | D. Van Ryckeghem | G. Vandenberghe | J. Spruyt |
| 1966 | W. Godefroot | W. Bocklant | P. Post |
| 1965 | A. Hermans | J. Haelterman | R. De Breucker |
| 1964 | P. Van Est | E. Vercauteren | J. Dewit |
| 1963 | C. Roman | D. Puschel | R. Seneca |
| 1962 | M. Van Geneugden | P. Rentmeester | P. Van Est |
| 1961 | M. Meuleman | R. Van Wynsberghe | L. Vandaele |
| 1960 | A. De Cabooter | E. Sorgeloos | J. Schepens |
| 1959 | R. Baens | L. Proost | B. Schotte |
| 1958 | A. Vlayen | N. Van Tieghem | E. Heyvaert |
| 1957 | N. Fore | M. Van Aerde | A. Noyelle |
| 1956 | L. Demunster | F. Schoubben | A. Rosseel |
| 1955 | B. Schotte | A. De Bruyne | A. Van Den Brande |
| 1954 | G. Derycke | B. Schotte | F. Rondele |
| 1953 | B. Schotte | A. Voorting | M. De Mulder |
| 1952 | A. Maelbrancke | L. Wouters | K. Debaere |
| 1951 | R. Impanis | M. Hendrickx | A. Rosseel |
| 1950 | A. Rosseel | E. Vanderveken | J. Depoorter |
| 1949 | R. Impanis | L. Van Brabant | M. Mollin |
| 1948 | A. Rosseel | F. Mathieu | R. Desmet |
| 1947 | A. Sercu | J. Van Dycke | E. Masson |
| 1946 | M. De Simpelaere | N. Callens | B. Schotte |
| 1945 | R. Van Steenbergen | B. Schotte | N. Callens |

## RIDER RESULTS

| WINS | RIDER |
|---|---|
| 3 | W. Planckaert |
| 2 | N. Eeckhout, W. Godefroot, T. Hoffman, R. Impanis, Y. Lampaert, J. Museeuw, J. Nijdam, A. Rosseel, B. Schotte, N. Terpstra, D. Van Ryckeghem, E. Vanderaerden |

| PODIUMS | RIDER |
|---|---|
| 6 | B. Schotte |
| 5 | N. Eeckhout, W. Planckaert |
| 4 | J. Raas, A. Rosseel, E. Vanderaerden |
| 3 | M. Demeyer, E. Leman, J. Museeuw, M. Sergeant, N. Terpstra |
| 2 | T. Boonen, B. Bozic, N. Callens, S. Chavanel, B. Cooke, T. Farrar, W. Godefroot, R. Hammond, T. Hoffman, F. Hoste, R. Impanis, Y. Lampaert, J. Nijdam, J. Planckaert, C. Priem, T. Steels, A. Tchmil, E. Theuns, D. van Baarle, A. van der Poel, P. Van Est, E. Van Hooydonck, D. Van Ryckeghem, G. Van Sweevelt |

## COUNTRY RESULTS

| WINS | COUNTRY |
|---|---|
| 55 | Belgium |
| 14 | Netherlands |
| 2 | Australia |
| 1 | Denmark, France, Germany, Italy |

| Podiums | Country |
|---|---|
| 152 | Belgium |
| 36 | Netherlands |
| 8 | France |
| 5 | Australia |
| 4 | Germany, Italy, United Kingdom |
| 3 | Denmark |
| 2 | Slovenia, United States |
| 1 | Estonia, Ireland, Kazakhstan, Latvia, Luxemburg |

# OMLOOP HET NIEUWSBLAD

## RESULTS BY YEAR

| YEAR | 1ST | 2ND | 3RD |
|---|---|---|---|
| 2021 | D. Ballerini | J. Stewart | S. Vanmarcke |
| 2020 | J. Stuyven | Y. Lampaert | S. Kragh Andersen |
| 2019 | Z. Štybar | G. Van Avermaet | T. Wellens |
| 2018 | M. Valgren | L. Wisniowski | S. Vanmarcke |
| 2017 | G. Van Avermaet | P. Sagan | S. Vanmarcke |
| 2016 | G. Van Avermaet | P. Sagan | T. Benoot |
| 2015 | I. Stannard | N. Terpstra | T. Boonen |
| 2014 | I. Stannard | G. Van Avermaet | E. Boasson Hagen |
| 2013 | L. Paolini | S. Vandenbergh | S. Vandousselaere |
| 2012 | S. Vanmarcke | T. Boonen | J. A. Flecha |
| 2011 | S. Langeveld | J. A. Flecha | M. Hayman |
| 2010 | J. A. Flecha | H. Haussler | T. Farrar |
| 2009 | T. Hushovd | K. Ista | J. A. Flecha |
| 2008 | P. Gilbert | N. Nuyens | T. Hushovd |
| 2007 | F. Pozzato | J. A. Flecha | T. Boonen |
| 2006 | P. Gilbert | B. De Waele | L. van Bon |
| 2005 | N. Nuyens | T. Boonen | S. De Jongh |
| 2003 | J. Museeuw | M. van Heeswijk | P. Bettini |
| 2002 | P. Van Petegem | F. Hoj | M. Vanhaecke |
| 2001 | M. Bartoli | H. Van Dyck | M. Pronk |
| 2000 | J. Museeuw | S. Wesemann | S. Knaven |
| 1999 | F. Vandenbroucke | W. Peeters | T. Steels |
| 1998 | P. Van Petegem | G. Bortolami | A. Tchmil |
| 1997 | P. Van Petegem | T. Steels | J. Capiot |
| 1996 | T. Steels | H. Redant | O. Ludwig |
| 1995 | F. Ballerini | E. Van Hooydonck | A. Tchmil |
| 1994 | W. Nelissen | F. Moncassin | A. Kappes |
| 1993 | W. Nelissen | O. Ludwig | E. Vanderaerden |
| 1992 | J. Capiot | P. Pieters | E. Vanderaerden |
| 1991 | A. Kappes | C. Bomans | E. Van Hooydonck |
| 1990 | J. Capiot | E. Van Hooydonck | E. De Wilde |
| 1989 | E. De Wilde | S. Kelly | R. Stumpf |
| 1988 | R. Van Holen | J. Lammerts | J. Talen |
| 1987 | T. van Vliet | S. Rooks | J. Goessens |
| 1985 | E. Planckaert | J. Hanegraaf | J. Lieckens |
| 1984 | E. Planckaert | J. L. Vandenbroucke | L. Peeters |
| 1983 | F. De Wolf | J. Raas | L. Colyn |
| 1982 | F. De Wolf | G. Jones | S. Kelly |
| 1981 | J. Raas | G. Duclos Lassalle | J. L. Vandenbroucke |
| 1980 | J. Bruyere | W. Planckaert | S. Kelly |
| 1979 | R. De Vlaeminck | J. Raas | F. Hoste |
| 1978 | F. Maertens | F. van Katwijk | J. Raas |
| 1977 | F. Maertens | J. Raas | L. Peeters |
| 1976 | W. Peeters | H. Kuiper | P. Sercu |
| 1975 | J. Bruyere | P. Sercu | J. De Cauwer |
| 1974 | J. Bruyere | P. Sercu | R. Van Linden |
| 1973 | E. Merckx | R. De Vlaeminck | A. Van Vlierberghe |
| 1972 | F. Verbeeck | A. Dierickx | E. Merckx |
| 1971 | E. Merckx | R. Rosiers | N. Vantyghem |
| 1970 | F. Verbeeck | R. Rosiers | A. Dierickx |
| 1969 | R. De Vlaeminck | D. Van Ryckeghem | V. Van Sweevelt |
| 1968 | H. Van Springel | R. Wolfshohl | B. Van de Kerckhove |
| 1967 | W. Vekemans | J. Spruyt | W. Sels |
| 1966 | J. De Roo | W. Godefroot | E. Merckx |
| 1965 | N. Depauw | M. Van Den Bogaert | J. van der Vleuten |
| 1964 | F. Melckenbeeck | A. De Cabooter | Y. Molenaers |
| 1963 | R. Van Meenen | L. Janssens | J. B. Claes |
| 1962 | R. De Middeleir | J. B. Claes | R. De Coninck |
| 1961 | A. De Cabooter | F. Schoubben | G. Decraeye |
| 1959 | S. Elliott | A. De Bruyne | T. Dingens |
| 1958 | J. Planckaert | R. Van Looy | R. De Corte |
| 1957 | N. Kerckhove | P. Cerami | L. Vandaele |
| 1956 | E. Sterckx | B. Schotte | L. Schaeken |
| 1955 | L. Anthonis | A. Rosseel | A. Vlayen |
| 1954 | K. Debaere | R. De Corte | J. De Valck |
| 1953 | E. Sterckx | M. Mollin | M. Ryckaert |
| 1952 | E. Sterckx | R. Impanis | A. Declercq |
| 1951 | J. Bogaerts | L. Van Brabant | R. Impanis |
| 1950 | A. Declercq | M. Meersman | B. Schotte |
| 1949 | A. Declercq | F. Leenen | M. Mollin |
| 1948 | S. Grysolle | F. Coppi | M. Hendrickx |
| 1947 | A. Sercu | E. Faignaert | A. Buysse |
| 1946 | A. Pieters | M. Ryckaert | E. Thoma |
| 1945 | J. Bogaerts | M. De Simpelaere | R. Van Eenaeme |

## RIDER RESULTS

| WINS | RIDER |
|---|---|
| 3 | J. Bruyere, E. Sterckx, P. Van Petegem |
| 2 | J. Bogaerts, J. Capiot, R. De Vlaeminck, F. De Wolf, A. Declercq, P. Gilbert, F. Maertens, E. Merckx, J. Museeuw, W. Nelissen, E. Planckaert, I. Stannard, G. Van Avermaet, F. Verbeeck |

| PODIUMS | RIDER |
|---|---|
| 5 | J. A. Flecha, J. Raas |
| 4 | T. Boonen, E. Merckx, G. Van Avermaet, S. Vanmarcke |
| 3 | J. Bruyere, J. Capiot, R. De Vlaeminck, A. Declercq, S. Kelly, P. Sercu, T. Steels, E. Sterckx, E. Van Hooydonck, P. Van Petegem |
| 2 | J. B. Claes, J. Bogaerts, A. De Cabooter, R. De Corte, E. De Wilde, F. De Wolf, A. Dierickx, P. Gilbert, T. Hushovd, R. Impanis, A. Kappes, J. L. Vandenbroucke, O. Ludwig, F. Maertens, M. Mollin, J. Museeuw, W. Nelissen, N. Nuyens, W. Peeters, L. Peeters, E. Planckaert, R. Rosiers, M. Ryckaert, P. Sagan, B. Schotte, I. Stannard, A. Tchmil, E. Vanderaerden, F. Verbeeck |

## COUNTRY RESULTS

| WINS | COUNTRY |
|---|---|
| 57 | Belgium |
| 5 | Italy |
| 4 | Netherlands |
| 2 | Denmark, United Kingdom |
| 1 | Czech Republic, Germany, Ireland, Norway, Spain |

| PODIUMS | COUNTRY |
|---|---|
| 157 | Belgium |
| 22 | Netherlands |
| 8 | Italy |
| 6 | Germany |
| 5 | Spain |
| 4 | Ireland, United Kingdom |
| 3 | Denmark, Norway |
| 2 | Australia, France, Slovakia |
| 1 | Czech Republic, Poland, Switzerland, United States |

# CRITÉRIUM DU DAUPHINÉ

## RESULTS BY YEAR

| YEAR | 1ST | 2ND | 3RD |
|---|---|---|---|
| 2021 | R. Porte | A. Lutsenko | G. Thomas |
| 2020 | D. F. Martínez | T. Pinot | G. Martin |
| 2019 | J. Fuglsang | T. Van Garderen | E. Buchmann |
| 2018 | G. Thomas | A. Yates | R. Bardet |
| 2017 | J. Fuglsang | R. Porte | D. Martin |
| 2016 | C. Froome | R. Bardet | D. Martin |
| 2015 | C. Froome | T. van Garderen | R. Costa |
| 2014 | A. Talansky | A. Contador | J. Van den Broeck |
| 2013 | C. Froome | R. Porte | D. Moreno |
| 2012 | B. Wiggins | M. Rogers | C. Evans |
| 2011 | B. Wiggins | C. Evans | A. Vinokourov |
| 2010 | J. Brajkovic | A. Contador | T. van Garderen |
| 2009 | A. Valverde | C. Evans | A. Contador |
| 2008 | A. Valverde | C. Evans | L. Leipheimer |
| 2007 | C. Moreau | C. Evans | A. Kashechkin |
| 2006 | L. Leipheimer | C. Moreau | B. Kohl |
| 2005 | I. Landaluze | S. Botero | L. Leipheimer |
| 2004 | I. Mayo | T. Hamilton | O. Sevilla |
| 2003 | L. Armstrong | I. Mayo | D. Millar |
| 2002 | L. Armstrong | F. Landis | C. Moreau |
| 2001 | C. Moreau | P. Tonkov | B. Salmon |
| 2000 | T. Hamilton | H. Zubeldia | L. Armstrong |
| 1999 | A. Vinokourov | J. Vaughters | W. Belli |
| 1998 | A. De Las Cuevas | M. A. Pena | A. Teteriouk |
| 1997 | U. Bolts | A. Olano | J. C. Robin |
| 1996 | M. Indurain | T. Rominger | R. Virenque |
| 1995 | M. Indurain | C. Boardman | V. Aparicio |
| 1994 | L. Dufaux | R. Pensec | A. Kasputis |
| 1993 | L. Dufaux | O. Rincon | E. Boyer |
| 1992 | C. Mottet | L. Leblanc | G. Bugno |
| 1991 | L. A. Herrera | L. Cubino | T. Rominger |
| 1990 | R. Millar | T. Claveyrolat | A. Mejia |
| 1989 | C. Mottet | R. Millar | T. Claveyrolat |
| 1988 | L. A. Herrera | N. Ruttimann | C. Mottet |
| 1987 | C. Mottet | O. Cardenas | R. Pensec |
| 1986 | U. Zimmermann | R. Pensec | J. Zoetemelk |
| 1985 | P. Anderson | S. Rooks | P. Bazzo |
| 1984 | M. A. Ramirez | B. Hinault | G. Lemond |
| 1983 | G. Lemond | R. Millar | R. Alban |
| 1982 | M. Laurent | J. R. Bernaudeau | P. Simon |
| 1981 | B. Hinault | J. Agostinho | G. Lemond |
| 1980 | J. van der Velde | R. Martin | J. Agostinho |
| 1979 | B. Hinault | H. Lubberding | F. Galdos |
| 1978 | M. Pollentier | M. Martinez | F. Galdos |
| 1977 | B. Hinault | B. Thevenet | L. Van Impe |
| 1976 | B. Thevenet | V. Lopez | R. Delisle |
| 1975 | B. Thevenet | F. Moser | J. Zoetemelk |
| 1974 | A. Santy | R. Poulidor | J. P. Danguillaume |
| 1973 | L. Ocana | B. Thevenet | J. Zoetemelk |
| 1972 | L. Ocana | B. Thevenet | L. Van Impe |
| 1971 | E. Merckx | L. Ocana | B. Thevenet |
| 1970 | L. Ocana | R. Pingeon | H. Van Springel |
| 1969 | R. Poulidor | F. Bracke | R. Pingeon |
| 1966 | R. Poulidor | C. Echevarria | F. Gabica |
| 1965 | J. Anquetil | R. Poulidor | K. H. Kunde |
| 1964 | V. Uriona | R. Poulidor | E. Martin |
| 1963 | J. Anquetil | J. Perez | F. Manzaneque |
| 1962 | R. Mastrotto | H. Junkermann | R. Poulidor |
| 1961 | B. Robinson | R. Mastrotto | F. Mahe |
| 1960 | J. Dotto | R. Mastrotto | G. Thielin |
| 1959 | H. Anglade | R. Mastrotto | R. Riviere |
| 1958 | L. Rostollan | F. Pipelin | J. P. Schmitz |
| 1957 | M. Rohrbach | R. Privat | J. P. Schmitz |
| 1956 | A. Close | A. Rolland | F. Picot |
| 1955 | L. Bobet | R. Walkowiak | M. De Mulder |
| 1954 | N. Lauredi | J. P. Schmitz | P. Molineris |
| 1953 | L. Teisseire | C. Gaul | J. Robic |
| 1952 | J. Dotto | N. Lauredi | J. Le Guilly |
| 1951 | N. Lauredi | A. Rolland | L. Lazarides |
| 1950 | N. Lauredi | A. Lazarides | J. B. Diederich |
| 1949 | L. Lazarides | J. Robic | F. Camellini |
| 1948 | E. Fachleitner | P. Giguet | J. Robic |
| 1947 | E. Klabinski | G. Sciardis | F. Camellini |

## RIDER RESULTS

| WINS | RIDER |
|---|---|
| 3 | C. Froome, B. Hinault, N. Lauredi, C. Mottet, L. Ocaña |
| 2 | L. A. Herrera, J. Anquetil, L. Armstrong, J. Dotto, L. Dufaux, J. Fuglsang, M. Indurain, C. Moreau, R. Poulidor, B. Thevenet, A. Valverde, B. Wiggins |

| PODIUMS | RIDER |
|---|---|
| 6 | R. Poulidor, B. Thevenet |
| 5 | C. Evans |
| 4 | B. Hinault, N. Lauredi, R. Mastrotto, C. Moreau, C. Mottet, L. Ocaña |
| 3 | L. Armstrong, A. Contador, C. Froome, L. Leipheimer, G. Lemond, R. Millar, R. Pensec, J. Pierre Schmitz, R. Porte, J. Robic, T. Van Garderen, J. Zoetemelk |
| 2 | J. Agostinho, L. A. Herrera, J. Anquetil, R. Bardet, F. Camellini, T. Claveyrolat, J. Dotto, L. Dufaux, J. Fuglsang, F. Galdos, T. Hamilton, M. Indurain, L. Lazarides, D. Martin, I. Mayo, R. Pingeon, A. Rolland, T. Rominger, G. Thomas, A. Valverde, L. Van Impe, A. Vinokourov, B. Wiggins |

## COUNTRY RESULTS

| WINS | COUNTRY |
|---|---|
| 30 | France |
| 10 | Spain |
| 8 | United Kingdom |
| 6 | United States |
| 4 | Colombia |
| 3 | Belgium, Switzerland |
| 2 | Australia, Denmark |
| 1 | Germany, Kazakhstan, Netherlands, Poland, Slovenia |

| PODIUMS | COUNTRY |
|---|---|
| 88 | France |
| 30 | Spain |
| 17 | United States |
| 14 | United Kingdom |
| 10 | Australia |
| 9 | Belgium |
| 8 | Colombia |
| 6 | Netherlands, Switzerland |
| 5 | Italy, Kazakhstan, Luxembourg |
| 4 | Germany |
| 3 | Portugal |
| 2 | Denmark, Ireland |
| 1 | Austria, Lithuania, Poland, Russia, Slovenia |

MEN'S HISTORICAL RESULTS

# TOUR DE ROMANDIE

## RESULTS BY YEAR

| YEAR | 1ST | 2ND | 3RD |
|---|---|---|---|
| 2021 | G. Thomas | R. Porte | F. Masnada |
| 2020 | Race cancelled | | |
| 2019 | P. Roglič | R. Costa | G. Thomas |
| 2018 | P. Roglič | E. Bernal | R. Porte |
| 2017 | R. Porte | S. Yates | P. Roglič |
| 2016 | N. Quintana | T. Pinot | I. Izaguirre |
| 2015 | I. Zakarin | S. Spilak | C. Froome |
| 2014 | C. Froome | S. Spilak | R. Costa |
| 2013 | C. Froome | S. Spilak | R. Costa |
| 2012 | B. Wiggins | A. Talansky | R. Costa |
| 2011 | C. Evans | T. Martin | A. Vinokourov |
| 2010 | S. Spilak | D. Menchov | M. Rogers |
| 2009 | R. Kreuziger | V. Karpets | R. Taaramae |
| 2008 | A. Kloden | R. Kreuziger | M. Pinotti |
| 2007 | T. Dekker | P. Savoldelli | A. Kashechkin |
| 2006 | C. Evans | A. Contador | A. Valverde |
| 2005 | S. Botero | D. Cunego | D. Menchov |
| 2004 | T. Hamilton | F. Jeker | L. Piepoli |
| 2003 | T. Hamilton | L. Dufaux | F. Perez |
| 2002 | D. Frigo | A. Zulle | C. Evans |
| 2001 | D. Frigo | F. Garcia | W. Belli |
| 2000 | P. Savoldelli | J. Beloki | L. Dufaux |
| 1999 | L. Jalabert | B. Zberg | W. Belli |
| 1998 | L. Dufaux | A. Zulle | F. Casagrande |
| 1997 | P. Tonkov | C. Boardman | B. Zberg |
| 1996 | A. Olano | A. Gontsjenkov | G. Guerini |
| 1995 | T. Rominger | P. Ugrumov | F. Casagrande |
| 1994 | P. Richard | A. De Las Cuevas | A. Hampsten |
| 1993 | P. Richard | C. Chiappucci | A. Hampsten |
| 1992 | A. Hampsten | M. Indurain | C. Mottet |
| 1991 | T. Rominger | R. Millar | M. Carter |
| 1990 | C. Mottet | R. Millar | L. Roosen |
| 1989 | P. Anderson | G. Delion | R. Millar |
| 1988 | G. Veldscholten | T. Rominger | U. Zimmermann |
| 1987 | S. Roche | J. C. Leclercq | R. Pensec |
| 1986 | C. Criquielion | J. F. Bernard | B. Cornillet |
| 1985 | J. Muller | A. Da Silva | T. Prim |
| 1984 | S. Roche | J. M. Grezet | N. Ruttimann |
| 1983 | S. Roche | P. Anderson | T. Prim |
| 1982 | J. Wilmann | T. Prim | S. Contini |
| 1981 | T. Prim | G. Saronni | P. Winnen |
| 1980 | B. Hinault | S. Contini | G. Saronni |
| 1979 | G. Saronni | G. Baronchelli | H. Lubberding |
| 1978 | J. van der Velde | H. Kuiper | J. De Muynck |
| 1977 | G. Baronchelli | J. Zoetemelk | K. Knudsen |
| 1976 | J. De Muynck | R. De Vlaeminck | E. Merckx |
| 1975 | F. Galdos | J. Fuchs | K. Knudsen |
| 1974 | J. Zoetemelk | W. Panizza | F. Den Hertog |
| 1973 | W. David | L. Van Impe | M. Pollentier |
| 1972 | B. Thevenet | L. Van Impe | R. Delisle |
| 1971 | G. Motta | A. Salutini | W. Vannitsen |
| 1970 | G. Pettersson | D. Boifava | J. Zoetemelk |
| 1969 | F. Gimondi | V. Adorni | A. Houbrechts |
| 1968 | E. Merckx | R. Delisle | R. Hagmann |
| 1967 | V. Adorni | L. Pfenninger | A. Desmet |
| 1966 | G. Motta | R. Delisle | R. Maurer |
| 1965 | V. Adorni | R. Maurer | R. Hagmann |
| 1964 | R. Maurer | H. Zilverberg | G. Nencini |
| 1963 | W. Bocklant | F. Bahamontes | G. De Rosso |
| 1962 | G. De Rosso | F. Cribiori | J. Novales |
| 1961 | L. Rostollan | G. Fezzardi | I. Massignan |
| 1960 | L. Rostollan | E. Delberghe | J. Hoevenaers |
| 1959 | K. Gimmi | R. Graf | A. Ruegg |
| 1958 | G. Bauvin | P. Cerami | G. Pettinati |
| 1957 | J. Forestier | G. Carlesi | H. Koblet |
| 1956 | P. Fornara | C. Clerici | R. Strehler |
| 1955 | R. Strehler | H. Koblet | M. Schellenberg |
| 1954 | J. Forestier | P. Fornara | C. Clerici |
| 1953 | H. Koblet | P. Fornara | L. Bobet |
| 1952 | W. Wagtmans | H. Koblet | R. Impanis |
| 1951 | F. Kubler | H. Koblet | F. Schar |
| 1950 | E. Fachleitner | H. Koblet | K. Piot |
| 1949 | G. Bartali | F. Kubler | S. Simonini |
| 1948 | F. Kubler | J. Goldschmit | M. Clemens |
| 1947 | D. Keteleer | G. Bartali | F. Kubler |

## RIDER RESULTS

| WINS | RIDER |
|---|---|
| 3 | S. Roche |
| 2 | V. Adorni, C. Evans, J. Forestier, D. Frigo, C. Froome, T. Hamilton, F. Kubler, G. Motta, P. Richard, T. Rominger, L. Rostollan |

| PODIUMS | RIDER |
|---|---|
| 6 | H. Koblet |
| 4 | R. Costa, F. Kubler, T. Prim, S. Špilak |
| 3 | V. Adorni, R. Delisle, L. Dufaux, C. Evans, P. Fornara, C. Froome, A. Hampsten, R. Maurer, R. Millar, R. Porte, S. Roche, P. Roglič, T. Rominger, G. Saronni, J. Zoetemelk |
| 2 | P. Anderson, G. Baronchelli, G. Bartali, W. Belli, F. Casagrande, C. Clerici, S. Contini, J. De Muynck, G. De Rosso, J. Forestier, D. Frigo, R. Hagmann, T. Hamilton, K. Knudsen, R. Kreuziger, D. Menchov, E. Merckx, G. Motta, C. Mottet, P. Richard, L. Rostollan, P. Savoldelli, R. Strehler, G. Thomas, L. Van Impe, B. Zberg, A. Zulle |

## COUNTRY RESULTS

| WINS | COUNTRY |
|---|---|
| 13 | Italy |
| 12 | Switzerland |
| 10 | France |
| 6 | Belgium |
| 5 | Netherlands |
| 4 | Australia, United Kingdom |
| 3 | Ireland, Slovenia, United States |
| 2 | Colombia, Russia, Spain, Sweden |
| 1 | Czech Republic, Germany, Norway |

| PODIUMS | COUNTRY |
|---|---|
| 44 | Italy |
| 43 | Switzerland |
| 24 | France |
| 19 | Belgium |
| 12 | Netherlands |
| 11 | United Kingdom |
| 10 | Spain |
| 8 | Australia |
| 7 | Russia, United States |
| 6 | Slovenia |
| 5 | Portugal, Sweden |
| 3 | Colombia, Ireland, Norway |
| 2 | Czech Republic, Germany, Kazakhstan, Luxembourg |
| 1 | Estonia, Latvia |

# BENELUX TOUR

## RESULTS BY YEAR

| YEAR | 1ST | 2ND | 3RD |
|---|---|---|---|
| 2021 | S. Colbrelli | M. Mohorič | V. Campenaerts |
| 2020 | M. van der Poel | S. Kragh Andersen | S. Küng |
| 2019 | L. De Plus | O. Naesen | T. Wellens |
| 2018 | M. Mohorič | M. Matthews | T. Wellens |
| 2017 | T. Dumoulin | T. Wellens | J. Stuyven |
| 2016 | N. Terpstra | O. Naesen | P. Sagan |
| 2015 | T. Wellens | G. Van Avermaet | W. Kelderman |
| 2014 | T. Wellens | L. Boom | T. Dumoulin |
| 2013 | Z. Stybar | T. Dumoulin | A. Grivko |
| 2012 | L. Boom | S. Chavanel | N. Terpstra |
| 2011 | E. Boasson Hagen | P. Gilbert | D. Millar |
| 2010 | T. Martin | K. Moerenhout | E. Boasson Hagen |
| 2009 | E. Boasson Hagen | S. Chavanel | S. Langeveld |
| 2008 | I. Gutierrez | S. Rosseler | M. Rogers |
| 2007 | I. Gutierrez | D. Millar | G. Larsson |
| 2006 | S. Schumacher | G. Hincapie | V. Nibali |
| 2005 | B. Julich | E. Dekker | L. Hoste |
| 2004 | E. Dekker | V. Ekimov | M. Wauters |
| 2003 | V. Ekimov | B. McGee | S. Honchar |
| 2002 | K. Kirchen | E. Dekker | V. Hugo Pena |
| 2001 | L. van Bon | E. Dekker | S. Honchar |
| 2000 | E. Dekker | R. Hunter | S. Knaven |
| 1999 | S. Honchar | E. Dekker | D. Casey |
| 1998 | R. Sorensen | V. Ekimov | P. Van Petegem |
| 1997 | E. Dekker | P. Meinert Nielsen | J. Ullrich |
| 1996 | R. Sorensen | L. Armstrong | V. Ekimov |
| 1995 | J. Nijdam | V. Ekimov | F. Vanzella |
| 1994 | J. Skibby | D. Abduzhaparov | D. Bottaro |
| 1993 | E. Breukink | J. Nijdam | O. Ludwig |
| 1992 | J. Nijdam | T. Marie | L. Bezault |
| 1991 | F. Maassen | O. Ludwig | E. Schurer |
| 1990 | J. Nijdam | E. Breukink | T. Marie |
| 1989 | L. Fignon | T. Marie | E. Schurer |
| 1988 | T. Marie | E. Breukink | P. Stevenhaagen |
| 1987 | T. van Vliet | M. Sergeant | A. van der Poel |
| 1986 | G. Knetemann | G. Solleveld | P. Pieters |
| 1985 | E. Vanderaerden | T. De Rooy | A. Van Houwelingen |
| 1984 | J. Lammerts | J. Lammertink | G. J. Theunisse |
| 1983 | A. Van Houwelingen | J. Broers | H. Frison |
| 1982 | B. Oosterbosch | J. Raas | G. Knetemann |
| 1981 | G. Knetemann | H. Kuiper | R. Martens |
| 1980 | G. Knetemann | L. Delcroix | G. Verlinden |
| 1979 | J. Raas | G. Knetemann | D. Willems |
| 1978 | J. van der Velde | E. Van Der Helst | R. Pevenage |
| 1977 | B. Pronk | S. Kelly | R. Pevenage |
| 1976 | G. Knetemann | L. Peeters | J. Jacobs |
| 1975 | J. Zoetemelk | F. Verbeeck | G. Vianen |
| 1965 | J. Janssen | B. Maliepaard | J. Huysmans |
| 1963 | L. Van Kreuningen | L. Van De Ven | T. Nijs |
| 1961 | D. Enthoven | H. Zilverberg | J. Captein |
| 1960 | P. Post | R. Baens | C. Niesten |
| 1958 | P. Van Est | P. Post | L. Van Den Brand |
| 1957 | R. Van Looy | W. Van Est | P. Van Den Brekel |
| 1956 | R. Van Looy | G. Carlesi | W. Van Est |
| 1955 | P. Haan | W. Van Est | H. Van Breenen |
| 1954 | W. Van Est | G. Schulte | G. Voorting |
| 1952 | W. Van Est | W. Wagtmans | G. Voorting |
| 1951 | J. Bogaerts | J. Van Staeyen | J. De Feyter |
| 1950 | H. Lakeman | J. Depoorter | N. Callens |
| 1949 | G. Schulte | D. Keteleer | B. Schellingerhoudt |
| 1948 | E. Rogiers | J. Goldschmit | A. Vooren |

## RIDER RESULTS

| WINS | RIDER |
|---|---|
| 4 | G. Knetemann |
| 3 | E. Dekker, J. Nijdam |
| 2 | E. Boasson Hagen, I. Gutierrez, R. Sorensen, W. Van Est, R. Van Looy, T. Wellens |

| PODIUMS | RIDER |
|---|---|
| 7 | E. Dekker |
| 6 | G. Knetemann |
| 5 | V. Ekimov, W. Van Est, T. Wellens |
| 4 | T. Marie, J. Nijdam |
| 3 | E. Boasson Hagen, E. Breukink, T. Dumoulin, S. Honchar |
| 2 | L. Boom, S. Chavanel, I. Gutierrez, O. Ludwig, D. Millar, M. Mohorič, R. Pevenage, P. Post, J. Raas, G. Schulte, E. Schurer, R. Sorensen, N. Terpstra, A. Van Houwelingen, R. Van Looy, G. Voorting |

## COUNTRY RESULTS

| WINS | COUNTRY |
|---|---|
| 35 | Netherlands |
| 8 | Belgium |
| 3 | Denmark |
| 2 | France, Germany, Norway, Spain |
| 1 | Czech Republic, Italy, Luxembourg, Russia, Slovenia, Ukraine, United States |

| PODIUMS | COUNTRY |
|---|---|
| 84 | Netherlands |
| 41 | Belgium |
| 8 | France |
| 5 | Denmark, Germany, Italy, Russia |
| 4 | Ukraine, United States |
| 3 | Australia, Norway |
| 2 | Luxembourg, Slovenia, Spain, United Kingdom |
| 1 | Colombia, Czech Republic, Ireland, Slovakia, South Africa, Sweden, Switzerland, Uzbekistan |

MEN'S HISTORICAL RESULTS

# E3 CLASSIC

## RESULTS BY YEAR

| YEAR | 1ST | 2ND | 3RD |
|---|---|---|---|
| 2021 | K. Asgreen | F. Sénéchal | M. van der Poel |
| 2020 | Race cancelled | | |
| 2019 | Z. Štybar | W. van Aert | G. Van Avermaet |
| 2018 | N. Terpstra | P. Gilbert | G. Van Avermaet |
| 2017 | G. Van Avermaet | P. Gilbert | O. Naesen |
| 2016 | M. Kwiatkowski | P. Sagan | I. Stannard |
| 2015 | G. Thomas | Z. Štybar | M. Trentin |
| 2014 | P. Sagan | N. Terpstra | G. Thomas |
| 2013 | F. Cancellara | P. Sagan | D. Oss |
| 2012 | T. Boonen | O. Freire | B. Eisel |
| 2011 | F. Cancellara | J. Roelandts | V. Gusev |
| 2010 | F. Cancellara | T. Boonen | J. A. Flecha |
| 2009 | F. Pozzato | T. Boonen | M. Iglinskiy |
| 2008 | K. A. Arvesen | D. Kopp | G. Van Avermaet |
| 2007 | T. Boonen | F. Cancellara | M. Burghardt |
| 2006 | T. Boonen | A. Ballan | A. Vierhouten |
| 2005 | T. Boonen | A. Klier | P. Van Petegem |
| 2004 | T. Boonen | J. Kirsipuu | A. Nauduzs |
| 2003 | S. De Jongh | S. Wesemann | S. Devolder |
| 2002 | D. Pieri | J. Planckaert | J. Museeuw |
| 2001 | A. Tchmil | S. Wesemann | M. Hvastija |
| 2000 | S. Ivanov | G. Van Bondt | C. Peers |
| 1999 | P. Van Petegem | A. Tchmil | F. Vandenbroucke |
| 1998 | J. Museeuw | M. Bartoli | M. Celestino |
| 1997 | H. Van Dyck | P. Fornaciari | B. Holm Sorensen |
| 1996 | C. Bomans | P. Van Petegem | W. Nelissen |
| 1995 | B. Leysen | S. Wesemann | C. Bomans |
| 1994 | A. Tchmil | V. Ekimov | S. Martinello |
| 1993 | M. Cipollini | O. Ludwig | J. Nijdam |
| 1992 | J. Museeuw | W. Veenstra | E. Vanderaerden |
| 1991 | O. Ludwig | P. Anderson | U. Raab |
| 1990 | S. Lilholt | F. Roscioli | A. van der Poel |
| 1989 | E. Planckaert | A. van der Poel | M. Sergeant |
| 1988 | G. Bontempi | A. Peiper | E. Planckaert |
| 1987 | E. Planckaert | J. Nijdam | M. Sergeant |
| 1986 | E. Vanderaerden | F. Pirard | J. Lammertink |
| 1985 | P. Anderson | J. Lieckens | E. Planckaert |
| 1984 | B. Oosterbosch | E. Planckaert | L. van Vliet |
| 1983 | W. Tackaert | B. Oosterbosch | J. Jonckers |
| 1982 | J. Bogaert | R. De Vlaeminck | D. Willems |
| 1981 | J. Raas | L. Delcroix | F. De Wolf |
| 1980 | J. Raas | S. Kelly | R. Van Linden |
| 1979 | J. Raas | F. Hoste | M. Pollentier |
| 1978 | F. Maertens | J. Raas | R. De Witte |
| 1977 | D. Thurau | P. Sercu | E. De Vlaeminck |
| 1976 | W. Planckaert | W. Godefroot | D. Verplancke |
| 1975 | F. Verbeeck | F. Maertens | C. Bal |
| 1974 | H. Van Springel | F. Maertens | F. Verbeeck |
| 1973 | W. In 't Ven | A. Van Vlierberghe | W. Planckaert |
| 1972 | H. Hutsebaut | E. Merckx | W. Godefroot |
| 1971 | R. De Vlaeminck | G. Pintens | E. Merckx |
| 1970 | D. Van Ryckeghem | R. De Vlaeminck | R. Rosiers |
| 1969 | R. Van Looy | G. Vanconingsloo | W. Vekemans |
| 1968 | J. Deboever | J. Huysmans | H. Van Springel |
| 1967 | W. Bocklandt | J. Huysmans | A. Desmet |
| 1966 | R. Van Looy | W. Bocklandt | J. Spruyt |
| 1965 | R. Van Looy | G. Vanconingsloo | R. Thysen |
| 1964 | R. Van Looy | N. Kerckhove | E. Sorgeloos |
| 1963 | N. Fore | P. Post | J. Planckaert |
| 1962 | A. Messelis | L. Schaeken | F. Demulder |
| 1961 | A. De Cabooter | F. Aerenhoudts | A. Noyelle |
| 1960 | D. Doom | O. Vanderlinden | P. Oelibrandt |
| 1959 | N. Kerckhove | J. Zagers | N. Van Tieghem |
| 1958 | A. Desmet | L. Demunster | B. Schotte |

## RIDER RESULTS

| WINS | RIDER |
|---|---|
| 5 | T. Boonen |
| 4 | R. Van Looy |
| 3 | F. Cancellara, J. Raas |
| 2 | J. Museeuw, E. Planckaert, A. Tchmil |

| PODIUMS | RIDER |
|---|---|
| 7 | T. Boonen |
| 5 | E. Planckaert |
| 4 | F. Cancellara, J. Raas, G. Van Avermaet, R. Van Looy |
| 3 | R. De Vlaeminck, F. Maertens, J. Museeuw, P. Sagan, A. Tchmil, P. Van Petegem, S. Wesemann |
| 2 | P. Anderson, W. Bocklandt, C. Bomans, A. Desmet, P. Gilbert, W. Godefroot, J. Huysmans, N. Kerckhove, O. Ludwig, E. Merckx, J. Nijdam, B. Oosterbosch, W. Planckaert, J. Planckaert, M. Sergeant, Z. Štybar, N. Terpstra, G. Thomas, A. van der Poel, H. Van Springel, G. Vanconingsloo, E. Vanderaerden, F. Verbeeck |

## COUNTRY RESULTS

| WINS | COUNTRY |
|---|---|
| 39 | Belgium |
| 6 | Netherlands |
| 4 | Italy |
| 3 | Switzerland |
| 2 | Denmark, Germany |
| 1 | Australia, Czech Republic, Norway, Poland, Russia, Slovakia, United Kingdom |

| PODIUMS | COUNTRY |
|---|---|
| 114 | Belgium |
| 21 | Netherlands |
| 12 | Italy |
| 7 | Germany, Switzerland |
| 3 | Australia, Denmark, Russia, Slovakia, United Kingdom |
| 2 | Czech Republic, Spain |
| 1 | Austria, Estonia, France, Ireland, Kazakhstan, Latvia, Norway, Poland, Slovenia |

MEN'S HISTORICAL RESULTS

# ESCHBORN-FRANKFURT

## RESULTS BY YEAR

| YEAR | 1ST | 2ND | 3RD |
|---|---|---|---|
| 2021 | J. Philipsen | J. Degenkolb | A. Kristoff |
| 2020 | Race cancelled | | |
| 2019 | P. Ackermann | J. Degenkolb | A. Kristoff |
| 2018 | A. Kristoff | M. Matthews | O. Naesen |
| 2017 | A. Kristoff | R. Zabel | J. Degenkolb |
| 2016 | A. Kristoff | M. Richeze | S. Bennett |
| 2014 | A. Kristoff | J. Degenkolb | J. Baugnies |
| 2013 | S. Spilak | M. Moser | A. Greipel |
| 2012 | M. Moser | D. Nerz | S. Firsanov |
| 2011 | J. Degenkolb | J. Baugnies | M. Matthews |
| 2010 | F. Wegmann | G. Verheyen | B. Scheirlinckx |
| 2009 | F. Wegmann | K. Kroon | C. Knees |
| 2008 | K. Kroon | D. Rebellin | M. A. Ardila |
| 2007 | P. Sinkewitz | K. A. Arvesen | D. Cataldo |
| 2006 | S. Garzelli | G. Ciolek | D. Hondo |
| 2005 | E. Zabel | A. A. Borrajo | M. Zberg |
| 2004 | K. Kroon | D. Hondo | J. Coenen |
| 2003 | D. Rebellin | E. Zabel | I. Astarloa |
| 2002 | E. Zabel | J. Planckaert | S. Ivanov |
| 2001 | M. Zberg | D. Rebellin | K. Van De Wouwer |
| 2000 | K. Hundertmarck | M. Tosatto | J. Heppner |
| 1999 | E. Zabel | L. van Bon | A. Ongarato |
| 1998 | F. Baldato | N. Bo Larsen | S. Garzelli |
| 1997 | M. Bartoli | B. Riis | M. Gianetti |
| 1996 | B. Zberg | J. Heppner | R. Sorensen |
| 1995 | F. Frattini | J. Heppner | M. Podenzana |
| 1994 | O. Ludwig | A. Kappes | E. Magnien |
| 1993 | R. Sorensen | M. Sciandri | E. Bouwmans |
| 1992 | F. Van Den Abbeele | C. Chiappucci | F. Maassen |
| 1991 | J. Bruyneel | J. Museeuw | M. Earley |
| 1990 | T. Wegmuller | J. Wynants | P. Winnen |
| 1989 | J. M. Wampers | M. Gayant | C. Chiappucci |
| 1988 | M. Dernies | R. Sorensen | G. Mantovani |
| 1987 | D. O. Lauritzen | P. Stevenhaagen | H. Lubberding |
| 1986 | J. M. Wampers | S. Bauer | M. Wilson |
| 1985 | P. Anderson | J. Lammerts | R. Golz |
| 1984 | P. Anderson | E. Vanderaerden | S. Kelly |
| 1983 | L. Peeters | L. van Vliet | L. Colyn |
| 1982 | L. Peeters | J. Wilmann | S. Kelly |
| 1981 | J. Jacobs | D. Thurau | D. Willems |
| 1980 | G. Baronchelli | F. Moser | F. De Wolf |
| 1979 | D. Willems | H. Lubberding | G. Braun |
| 1978 | G. Braun | R. Pevenage | H. Kuiper |
| 1977 | G. Knetemann | D. Thurau | F. Verbeeck |
| 1976 | F. Maertens | F. Verbeeck | R. De Vlaeminck |
| 1975 | R. Schuiten | F. Verbeeck | W. Godefroot |
| 1974 | W. Godefroot | E. Merckx | F. Verbeeck |
| 1973 | G. Pintens | J. Tschan | F. Maertens |
| 1972 | G. Bellone | E. Merckx | N. Vantyghem |
| 1971 | E. Merckx | J. De Schoenmaecker | L. Aimar |
| 1970 | R. Altig | J. Zoetemelk | O. Crepaldi |
| 1969 | G. Pintens | M. Dancelli | H. Van Springel |
| 1968 | E. Beugels | V. Van Sweevelt | H. Van Springel |
| 1967 | D. Van Ryckeghem | W. Planckaert | G. Vanconingsloo |
| 1966 | B. Hoban | W. Godefroot | W. Planckaert |
| 1965 | J. Stablinski | F. Verbeeck | G. Vanconingsloo |
| 1964 | C. Roman | F. Mahe | Y. Molenaers |
| 1963 | H. Junkermann | R. Altig | J. Stablinski |
| 1962 | A. Desmet | H. Zilverberg | R. Van Looy |

## RIDER RESULTS

| WINS | RIDER |
|---|---|
| 4 | A. Kristoff |
| 3 | E. Zabel |
| 2 | P. Anderson, K. Kroon, J. M. Wampers, L. Peeters, G. Pintens, F. Wegmann |

| PODIUMS | RIDER |
|---|---|
| 6 | A. Kristoff |
| 5 | J. Degenkolb, F. Verbeeck |
| 4 | E. Zabel |
| 3 | W. Godefroot, J. Heppner, K. Kroon, E. Merckx, D. Rebellin, R. Sorensen |
| 2 | R. Altig, P. Anderson, J. Baugnies, G. Braun, C. Chiappucci, S. Garzelli, D. Hondo, S. Kelly, H. Lubberding, F. Maertens, J. M. Wampers, M. Matthews, M. Moser, L. Peeters, G. Pintens, W. Planckaert, J. Stablinski, D. Thurau, H. Van Springel, G. Vanconingsloo, F. Wegmann, D. Willems, M. Zberg |

## COUNTRY RESULTS

| WINS | COUNTRY |
|---|---|
| 18 | Belgium |
| 13 | Germany |
| 7 | Italy |
| 5 | Netherlands, Norway |
| 3 | Switzerland |
| 2 | Australia, France |
| 1 | Denmark, Slovenia, United Kingdom |

| PODIUMS | COUNTRY |
|---|---|
| 55 | Belgium |
| 35 | Germany |
| 21 | Italy |
| 18 | Netherlands |
| 9 | Norway |
| 7 | France |
| 5 | Australia, Denmark, Switzerland |
| 4 | Ireland |
| 2 | Argentina, Russia, United Kingdom |
| 1 | Canada, Colombia, Slovenia, Spain |

MEN'S HISTORICAL RESULTS

# AMSTEL GOLD RACE

## RESULTS BY YEAR

| YEAR | 1ST | 2ND | 3RD |
|---|---|---|---|
| 2021 | W. van Aert | T. Pidcock | M. Schachmann |
| 2020 | Race cancelled | | |
| 2019 | M. van der Poel | S. Clarke | J. Fuglsang |
| 2018 | M. Valgren | R. Kreuziger | E. Gasparotto |
| 2017 | P. Gilbert | M. Kwiatkowski | M. Albasini |
| 2016 | E. Gasparotto | M. Valgren | S. Colbrelli |
| 2015 | M. Kwiatkowski | A. Valverde | M. Matthews |
| 2014 | P. Gilbert | J. Vanendert | S. Gerrans |
| 2013 | R. Kreuziger | A. Valverde | S. Gerrans |
| 2012 | E. Gasparotto | J. Vanendert | P. Sagan |
| 2011 | P. Gilbert | J. Rodriguez | S. Gerrans |
| 2010 | P. Gilbert | R. Hesjedal | E. Gasparotto |
| 2009 | S. Ivanov | K. Kroon | R. Gesink |
| 2008 | D. Cunego | F. Schleck | A. Valverde |
| 2007 | S. Schumacher | D. Rebellin | D. Di Luca |
| 2006 | F. Schleck | S. Wesemann | K. Kroon |
| 2005 | D. Di Luca | M. Celestino | D. Rebellin |
| 2004 | D. Rebellin | M. Boogerd | P. Bettini |
| 2003 | A. Vinokourov | M. Boogerd | D. Di Luca |
| 2002 | M. Bartoli | S. Ivanov | M. Boogerd |
| 2001 | E. Dekker | L. Armstrong | S. Baguet |
| 2000 | E. Zabel | M. Boogerd | M. Zberg |
| 1999 | M. Boogerd | L. Armstrong | G. Missaglia |
| 1998 | R. Jaermann | M. Den Bakker | M. Bartoli |
| 1997 | B. Riis | A. Tafi | B. Zberg |
| 1996 | S. Zanini | M. Bettin | J. Museeuw |
| 1995 | M. Gianetti | D. Cassani | B. Zberg |
| 1994 | J. Museeuw | B. Cenghialta | M. Saligari |
| 1993 | R. Jaermann | G. Bugno | J. Heppner |
| 1992 | O. Ludwig | J. Museeuw | D. Konishev |
| 1991 | F. Maassen | M. Fondriest | D. De Wolf |
| 1990 | A. van der Poel | L. Roosen | J. Nijdam |
| 1989 | E. Van Lancker | C. Criquielion | S. Bauer |
| 1988 | J. Nijdam | S. Rooks | C. Criquielion |
| 1987 | J. Zoetemelk | S. Rooks | M. Elliott |
| 1986 | S. Rooks | J. Zoetemelk | R. Van Holen |
| 1985 | G. Knetemann | J. Lieckens | J. Broers |
| 1984 | J. Hanegraaf | K. Andersen | P. Versluys |
| 1983 | P. Anderson | J. Bogaert | J. Raas |
| 1982 | J. Raas | S. Roche | G. Braun |
| 1981 | B. Hinault | R. De Vlaeminck | F. De Wolf |
| 1980 | J. Raas | F. De Wolf | S. Kelly |
| 1979 | J. Raas | H. Lubberding | S. A. Nilsson |
| 1978 | J. Raas | F. Moser | J. Zoetemelk |
| 1977 | J. Raas | G. Knetemann | H. Kuiper |
| 1976 | F. Maertens | J. Raas | L. Leman |
| 1975 | E. Merckx | F. Maertens | J. Bruyere |
| 1974 | G. Knetemann | W. Planckaert | W. Godefroot |
| 1973 | E. Merckx | F. Verbeeck | H. Van Springel |
| 1972 | W. Planckaert | W. De Geest | J. Zoetemelk |
| 1971 | F. Verbeeck | G. Karstens | R. Rosiers |
| 1970 | G. Pintens | W. Van Neste | A. Dierickx |
| 1969 | G. Reybroeck | J. Huysmans | E. Merckx |
| 1968 | H. Steevens | R. Rosiers | D. Van Ryckeghem |
| 1967 | A. Den Hartog | C. Lute | H. Steevens |
| 1966 | J. Stablinski | B. Van de Kerckhove | J. Hugens |

## RIDER RESULTS

| WINS | RIDER |
|---|---|
| 5 | J. Raas |
| 4 | P. Gilbert |
| 2 | E. Gasparotto, R. Jaermann, G. Knetemann, E. Merckx |

| PODIUMS | RIDER |
|---|---|
| 7 | J. Raas |
| 5 | M. Boogerd |
| 4 | E. Gasparotto, P. Gilbert, J. Zoetemelk |
| 3 | D. Di Luca, S. Gerrans, G. Knetemann, E. Merckx, J. Museeuw, D. Rebellin, S. Rooks, A. Valverde |
| 2 | L. Armstrong, M. Bartoli, C. Criquielion, F. De Wolf, S. Ivanov, R. Jaermann, R. Kreuziger, K. Kroon, M. Kwiatkowski, F. Maertens, J. Nijdam, W. Planckaert, R. Rosiers, F. Schleck, H. Steevens, M. Valgren Andersen, J. Vanendert, F. Verbeeck, B. Zberg |

## COUNTRY RESULTS

| WINS | COUNTRY |
|---|---|
| 18 | Netherlands |
| 14 | Belgium |
| 7 | Italy |
| 3 | Germany, Switzerland |
| 2 | Denmark, France |
| 1 | Australia, Czech Republic, Kazakhstan, Luxembourg, Poland, Russia |

| PODIUMS | COUNTRY |
|---|---|
| 46 | Belgium |
| 42 | Netherlands |
| 26 | Italy |
| 8 | Switzerland |
| 6 | Australia, Germany |
| 5 | Denmark |
| 4 | Spain |
| 3 | Russia |
| 2 | Canada, Czech Republic, France, Ireland, Luxembourg, Poland, United Kingdom, United States |
| 1 | Kazakhstan, Slovakia, Sweden |

MEN'S HISTORICAL RESULTS

# TIRRENO–ADRIATICO

## RESULTS BY YEAR

| YEAR | 1ST | 2ND | 3RD |
|---|---|---|---|
| 2021 | T. Pogačar | W. van Aert | M. Landa |
| 2020 | S. Yates | G. Thomas | R. Majka |
| 2019 | P. Roglič | A. Yates | J. Fuglsang |
| 2018 | M. Kwiatkowski | D. Caruso | G. Thomas |
| 2017 | N. Quintana | R. Dennis | T. Pinot |
| 2016 | G. Van Avermaet | P. Sagan | B. Jungels |
| 2015 | N. Quintana | B. Mollema | R. Urán |
| 2014 | A. Contador | N. Quintana | R. Kreuziger |
| 2013 | V. Nibali | C. Froome | A. Contador |
| 2012 | V. Nibali | C. Horner | R. Kreuziger |
| 2011 | C. Evans | R. Gesink | M. Scarponi |
| 2010 | S. Garzelli | M. Scarponi | C. Evans |
| 2009 | M. Scarponi | S. Garzelli | A. Kloden |
| 2008 | F. Cancellara | E. Gasparotto | T. Lofkvist |
| 2007 | A. Kloden | K. Kirchen | A. Vinokourov |
| 2006 | T. Dekker | J. Jaksche | A. Ballan |
| 2005 | O. Freire | A. Petacchi | F. Guidi |
| 2004 | P. Bettini | O. Freire | E. Zabel |
| 2003 | F. Pozzato | D. Di Luca | R. Marzoli |
| 2002 | E. Dekker | D. Di Luca | O. Freire |
| 2001 | D. Rebellin | G. Colombo | M. Boogerd |
| 2000 | A. Olano | J. Hruska | J. C. Dominguez |
| 1999 | M. Bartoli | D. Rebellin | S. Garzelli |
| 1998 | R. Jaermann | F. Ballerini | J. Heppner |
| 1997 | R. Petito | G. Pianegonda | B. Zberg |
| 1996 | F. Casagrande | A. Gontsjenkov | G. Pianegonda |
| 1995 | S. Colage | M. Fondriest | D. Konishev |
| 1994 | G. Furlan | Y. Berzin | S. Colage |
| 1993 | M. Fondriest | A. Tchmil | S. Della Santa |
| 1992 | R. Sorensen | R. Alcala | F. Jeker |
| 1991 | H. Diaz | F. Ghiotto | R. Alcala |
| 1990 | T. Rominger | Z. Jaskula | G. Delion |
| 1989 | T. Rominger | R. Golz | C. Mottet |
| 1988 | E. Machler | T. Rominger | R. Sorensen |
| 1987 | R. Sorensen | G. Calcaterra | T. Rominger |
| 1986 | L. Rabottini | F. Moser | G. Petito |
| 1985 | J. Zoetemelk | A. Da Silva | S. Mutter |
| 1984 | T. Prim | E. Machler | R. Visentini |
| 1983 | R. Visentini | G. Knetemann | F. Moser |
| 1982 | G. Saronni | G. Knetemann | G. Lemond |
| 1981 | F. Moser | R. Gradi | M. Amadori |
| 1980 | F. Moser | F. De Wolf | D. Morandi |
| 1979 | K. Knudsen | G. Saronni | G. Battaglin |
| 1978 | G. Saronni | K. Knudsen | F. Moser |
| 1977 | R. De Vlaeminck | F. Moser | G. Saronni |
| 1976 | R. De Vlaeminck | E. Merckx | G. Baronchelli |
| 1975 | R. De Vlaeminck | K. Knudsen | W. Panizza |
| 1974 | R. De Vlaeminck | K. Knudsen | S. Fraccaro |
| 1973 | R. De Vlaeminck | F. Verbeeck | G. Pettersson |
| 1972 | R. De Vlaeminck | J. Fuchs | T. Pettersson |
| 1971 | I. Zilioli | G. Pintens | M. Bergamo |
| 1970 | A. Houbrechts | I. Zilioli | F. Gimondi |
| 1969 | C. Chiappano | A. Van Vlierberghe | G. Fezzardi |
| 1968 | C. Michelotto | I. Zilioli | R. Altig |
| 1967 | F. Bitossi | C. Preziosi | V. Taccone |
| 1966 | D. Zandegu | V. Taccone | R. Maurer |

## RIDER RESULTS

| WINS | RIDER |
|---|---|
| 6 | R. De Vlaeminck |
| 2 | F. Moser, V. Nibali, N. Quintana, T. Rominger, G. Saronni, R. Sorensen |

| PODIUMS | RIDER |
|---|---|
| 6 | R. De Vlaeminck, F. Moser |
| 4 | K. Knudsen, T. Rominger, G. Saronni |
| 3 | O. Freire, S. Garzelli, N. Quintana, M. Scarponi, R. Sorensen, I. Zilioli |
| 2 | R. Alcala, S. Colage, A. Contador, D. Di Luca, C. Evans, M. Fondriest, A. Kloden, G. Knetemann, R. Kreuziger, E. Machler, V. Nibali, G. Pianegonda, D. Rebellin, V. Taccone, G. Thomas, R. Visentini |

## COUNTRY RESULTS

| WINS | COUNTRY |
|---|---|
| 24 | Italy |
| 8 | Belgium |
| 5 | Switzerland |
| 4 | Spain |
| 3 | Netherlands |
| 2 | Colombia, Denmark, Slovenia |
| 1 | Australia, Germany, Norway, Poland, Sweden, United Kingdom |

| PODIUMS | COUNTRY |
|---|---|
| 69 | Italy |
| 15 | Belgium |
| 13 | Switzerland |
| 9 | Spain |
| 8 | Netherlands |
| 7 | Germany |
| 4 | Australia, Colombia, Denmark, Norway, Sweden, United Kingdom |
| 3 | Czech Republic, France, Poland, Russia |
| 2 | Luxembourg, Mexico, Slovenia, United States |
| 1 | Kazakhstan, Portugal, Slovakia |

MEN'S HISTORICAL RESULTS

# BRUGGE–DE PANNE

## RESULTS BY YEAR

| YEAR | 1ST | 2ND | 3RD |
|---|---|---|---|
| 2021 | S. Bennett | J. Philipsen | P. Ackermann |
| 2020 | Y. Lampaert | T. Declerq | T. Merlier |
| 2019 | D. Groenewegen | F. Gaviria | E. Viviani |
| 2018 | E. Viviani | P. Ackermann | J. Philipsen |
| 2017 | P. Gilbert | M. Brändle | A. Kristoff |
| 2016 | L. Westra | A. Kristoff | A. Lutsenko |
| 2015 | A. Kristoff | S. Devolder | B. Wiggins |
| 2014 | G. Van Keirsbulck | L. Durbridge | G. Steegmans |
| 2013 | S. Chavanel | A. Kristoff | N. Terpstra |
| 2012 | S. Chavanel | L. Westra | M. Bodnar |
| 2011 | S. Rosseler | L. Westra | M. Kwiatkowski |
| 2010 | D. Millar | A. Grivko | L. Paolini |
| 2009 | F. Willems | J. Posthuma | T. Leezer |
| 2008 | J. Posthuma | M. Quinziato | E. Gasparotto |
| 2007 | A. Ballan | J. Posthuma | B. Roesems |
| 2006 | L. Hoste | B. Eisel | L. L. Sanchez |
| 2005 | S. Devolder | A. Ballan | N. Mattan |
| 2004 | G. Hincapie | D. Hondo | G. Löwik |
| 2003 | R. Belohvoščiks | G. Bortolami | P. Van Petegem |
| 2002 | P. Van Petegem | S. Zanini | G. Hincapie |
| 2001 | N. Mattan | E. Dekker | V. Ekimov |
| 2000 | V. Ekimov | R. Vainšteins | S. Ivanov |
| 1999 | P. Van Petegem | F. Vandenbroucke | D. Zanette |
| 1998 | M. Bartoli | E. Magnien | V. Ekimov |
| 1997 | J. Museeuw | C. Bomans | M. Milesi |
| 1996 | V. Ekimov | W. Peeters | O. Ludwig |
| 1995 | M. Bartoli | R. Sørensen | G. Bortolami |
| 1994 | F. Roscioli | D. Abduzhaparov | F. Maassen |
| 1993 | E. Vanderaerden | F. Maassen | E. Van Hooydonck |
| 1992 | F. Maassen | V. Ekimov | T. Marie |
| 1991 | J. Nijdam | F. Maassen | M. Sciandri |
| 1990 | E. Nijboer | J. Museeuw | G. Solleveld |
| 1989 | E. Vanderaerden | J. Nijdam | A. Peiper |
| 1988 | E. Vanderaerden | A. Peiper | F. Maassen |
| 1987 | E. Vanderaerden | S. Kelly | J. L. Vandenbroucke |
| 1986 | E. Vanderaerden | S. Kelly | J. L. Vandenbroucke |
| 1985 | J. L. Vandenbroucke | S. Kelly | A. Van Der Poel |
| 1984 | B. Oosterbosch | E. Vanderaerden | F. Van Den Haute |
| 1983 | C. Priem | E. De Wilde | M. Pollentier |
| 1982 | G. Knetemann | D. Willems | J. L. Vandenbroucke |
| 1981 | J. Bogaert | A. Dierickx | J. Jacobs |
| 1980 | S. Kelly | G. Van Roosbroeck | E. Van Der Helst |
| 1979 | G. Van Roosbroeck | M. Renier | G. Van Calster |
| 1978 | G. Van Sweevelt | J. Jacobs | C. Priem |
| 1977 | R. Rosiers | Y. Bertin | G. Van Sweevelt |

## RIDER RESULTS

| WINS | RIDER |
|---|---|
| 5 | E. Vanderaerden |
| 2 | M. Bartoli, S. Chavanel, V. Ekimov, P. Van Petegem |

| PODIUMS | RIDER |
|---|---|
| 6 | E. Vanderaerden |
| 5 | V. Ekimov |
| 4 | S. Kelly, A. Kristoff, F. Maassen, J. L. Vandenbroucke |
| 3 | J. Posthuma, P. Van Petegem, L. Westra |
| 2 | P. Ackermann, A. Ballan, M. Bartoli, S. Chavanel, S. Devolder, G. Hincapie, J. Jacobs, N. Mattan, J. Museeuw, J. Nijdam, A. Peiper, J. Philipsen, C. Priem, G. Van Roosbroeck, G. Van Sweevelt, E. Viviani |

## COUNTRY RESULTS

| WINS | COUNTRY |
|---|---|
| 22 | Belgium |
| 9 | Netherlands |
| 4 | Italy |
| 2 | France, Ireland, Russia |
| 1 | Norway, United Kingdom, United States |

| PODIUMS | COUNTRY |
|---|---|
| 30 | Belgium |
| 16 | Netherlands |
| 11 | Italy |
| 4 | Germany, Ireland |
| 3 | Australia, France, Norway, Russia |
| 2 | Austria, Poland, United Kingdom, United States |

# DONOSTIA SAN SEBASTIAN KLASIKOA

## RESULTS BY YEAR

| YEAR | 1ST | 2ND | 3RD |
|---|---|---|---|
| 2021 | N. Powless | M. Mohorič | M. F. Honoré |
| 2020 | Race cancelled | | |
| 2019 | R. Evenepoel | G. Van Avermaet | M. Hirschi |
| 2018 | J. Alaphilippe | B. Mollema | A. Roux |
| 2017 | M. Kwiatkowski | T. Gallopin | B. Mollema |
| 2016 | B. Mollema | T. Gallopin | A. Valverde |
| 2015 | A. Yates | P. Gilbert | A. Valverde |
| 2014 | A. Valverde | B. Mollema | J. Rodriguez |
| 2013 | T. Gallopin | A. Valverde | R. Kreuziger |
| 2012 | L. L. Sanchez | S. Gerrans | G. Meersman |
| 2011 | P. Gilbert | G. Van Avermaet | J. Rodriguez |
| 2010 | L. L. Sanchez | A. Vinokourov | C. Sastre |
| 2009 | R. Kreuziger | M. Delage | P. Velits |
| 2008 | A. Valverde | A. Kolobnev | D. Rebellin |
| 2007 | J. M. Garate | A. Valverde | A. Ballan |
| 2006 | X. Florencio | S. Garzelli | A. Kashechkin |
| 2005 | C. Zaballa | J. Rodriguez | E. Mazzoleni |
| 2004 | M. A. Martin | P. Bettini | D. Rebellin |
| 2003 | P. Bettini | I. Basso | D. Di Luca |
| 2002 | L. Jalabert | I. Astarloa | G. Missaglia |
| 2001 | L. Jalabert | F. Casagrande | D. Rebellin |
| 2000 | E. Dekker | A. Tchmil | R. Vainsteins |
| 1999 | F. Casagrande | R. Verbrugghe | G. Figueras |
| 1998 | F. Casagrande | A. Merckx | L. Piepoli |
| 1997 | D. Rebellin | A. Gontsjenkov | S. Colage |
| 1996 | U. Bolts | S. Cattai | M. Podenzana |
| 1995 | L. Armstrong | S. Della Santa | J. Museeuw |
| 1994 | A. De Las Cuevas | L. Armstrong | S. Della Santa |
| 1993 | C. Chiappucci | G. Faresin | A. Volpi |
| 1992 | R. Alcala | C. Chiappucci | E. Bouwmans |
| 1991 | G. Bugno | P. Delgado | M. Fondriest |
| 1990 | M. Indurain | L. Jalabert | S. Kelly |
| 1989 | G. Zadrobilek | F. J. Antequera | T. Rominger |
| 1988 | G. J. Theunisse | E. A. Aja | S. Rooks |
| 1987 | M. Lejarreta | A. Arroyo | F. Echave |
| 1986 | I. Gaston | M. Lejarreta | J. Fernandez |
| 1985 | A. van der Poel | I. Gaston | J. Fernandez |
| 1984 | N. Ruttimann | R. Dietzen | C. Prieto |
| 1983 | C. Criquielion | A. Coll | R. Dietzen |
| 1982 | M. Lejarreta | J. Rodriguez | P. Delgado |
| 1981 | M. Lejarreta | G. Jones | F. Ruperez |

## RIDER RESULTS

| WINS | RIDER |
|---|---|
| 3 | M. Lejarreta |
| 2 | F. Casagrande, L. Jalabert, L. L. Sanchez, A. Valverde |

| PODIUMS | RIDER |
|---|---|
| 6 | A. Valverde |
| 4 | M. Lejarreta, B. Mollema, D. Rebellin |
| 3 | F. Casagrande, T. Gallopin, L. Jalabert, J. Rodriguez |
| 2 | L. Armstrong, C. Barredo, P. Bettini, C. Chiappucci, P. Delgado, S. Della Santa, R. Dietzen, J. Fernandez, I. Gaston, P. Gilbert, R. Kreuziger, L. L. Sanchez, G. Van Avermaet |

## COUNTRY RESULTS

| WINS | COUNTRY |
|---|---|
| 13 | Spain |
| 6 | Italy |
| 5 | France |
| 4 | Netherlands |
| 3 | Belgium |
| 2 | United States |
| 1 | Austria, Germany, Mexico, Poland, Switzerland, United Kingdom |

| PODIUMS | COUNTRY |
|---|---|
| 37 | Spain |
| 28 | Italy |
| 11 | France |
| 10 | Belgium |
| 9 | Netherlands |
| 3 | Germany, Switzerland, United States |
| 2 | Kazakhstan, Russia, United Kingdom |
| 1 | Australia, Austria, Czech Republic, Denmark, Ireland, Latvia, Mexico, Poland, Slovakia, Slovenia |

MEN'S HISTORICAL RESULTS

# WORLD CHAMPIONSHIPS MEN'S ITT

## RESULTS BY YEAR

| YEAR | 1ST | 2ND | 3RD |
|---|---|---|---|
| 2021 | F. Ganna | W. van Aert | R. Evenepoel |
| 2020 | F. Ganna | W. van Aert | S. Küng |
| 2019 | R. Dennis | R. Evenepoel | F. Ganna |
| 2018 | R. Dennis | T. Dumoulin | V. Campenaerts |
| 2017 | T. Dumoulin | P. Roglič | C. Froome |
| 2016 | T. Martin | V. Kiryienka | J. Castroviejo |
| 2015 | V. Kiryienka | A. Malori | J. Coppel |
| 2014 | B. Wiggins | T. Martin | T. Dumoulin |
| 2013 | T. Martin | B. Wiggins | F. Cancellara |
| 2012 | T. Martin | T. Phinney | V. Kiryienka |
| 2011 | T. Martin | B. Wiggins | F. Cancellara |
| 2010 | F. Cancellara | D. Millar | T. Martin |
| 2009 | F. Cancellara | G. Larsson | T. Martin |
| 2008 | B. Grabsch | S. Tuft | D. Zabriskie |
| 2007 | F. Cancellara | L. Bodrogi | S. Clement |
| 2006 | F. Cancellara | D. Zabriskie | A. Vinokourov |
| 2005 | M. Rogers | I. Gutierrez | F. Cancellara |
| 2004 | M. Rogers | M. Rich | A. Vinokourov |
| 2003 | M. Rogers | U. Peschel | M. Rich |
| 2002 | S. Botero | M. Rich | I. Gonzalez De Galdeano |
| 2001 | J. Ullrich | D. Millar | S. Botero |
| 2000 | S. Honchar | M. Rich | L. Bodrogi |
| 1999 | J. Ullrich | M. Andersson | C. Boardman |
| 1998 | A. Olano | M. Mauri | S. Honchar |
| 1997 | L. Jalabert | S. Honchar | C. Boardman |
| 1996 | A. Zulle | C. Boardman | T. Rominger |
| 1995 | M. Indurain | A. Olano | U. Peschel |
| 1994 | C. Boardman | A. Chiurato | J. Ullrich |

## RIDER RESULTS

| WINS | RIDER |
|---|---|
| 4 | F. Cancellara, T. Martin |
| 3 | M. Rogers |
| 2 | R. Dennis, F. Ganna, J. Ullrich |

| PODIUMS | RIDER |
|---|---|
| 7 | F. Cancellara, T. Martin |
| 4 | C. Boardman, M. Rich |
| 3 | T. Dumoulin, F. Ganna, S. Honchar, V. Kiryienka, M. Rogers, J. Ullrich, B. Wiggins |
| 2 | L. Bodrogi, S. Botero, R. Dennis, R. Evenepoel, D. Millar, A. Olano, U. Peschel, W. van Aert, A. Vinokourov, D. Zabriskie |

## COUNTRY RESULTS

| WINS | COUNTRY |
|---|---|
| 7 | Germany |
| 5 | Australia, Switzerland |
| 2 | Italy, Spain, United Kingdom |
| 1 | Belarus, Colombia, France, Netherlands, Ukraine |

| PODIUMS | COUNTRY |
|---|---|
| 17 | Germany |
| 10 | Switzerland, United Kingdom |
| 7 | Spain |
| 5 | Australia, Belgium, Italy |
| 4 | France, Netherlands |
| 3 | Belarus, Ukraine, United States |
| 2 | Colombia, Kazakhstan, Sweden |
| 1 | Canada, Slovenia |

# CYCLASSICS HAMBURG

## RESULTS BY YEAR

| YEAR | 1ST | 2ND | 3RD |
|---|---|---|---|
| 2021 | Race cancelled | | |
| 2020 | Race cancelled | | |
| 2019 | E. Viviani | C. Ewan | G. Nizzolo |
| 2018 | E. Viviani | A. Demare | A. Kristoff |
| 2017 | E. Viviani | A. Demare | D. Groenewegen |
| 2016 | C. Ewan | J. Degenkolb | G. Nizzolo |
| 2015 | A. Greipel | A. Kristoff | G. Nizzolo |
| 2014 | A. Kristoff | G. Nizzolo | S. Gerrans |
| 2013 | J. Degenkolb | A. Greipel | A. Kristoff |
| 2012 | A. Demare | A. Greipel | G. Nizzolo |
| 2011 | E. Boasson Hagen | G. Ciolek | B. Bozic |
| 2010 | T. Farrar | E. Boasson Hagen | A. Greipel |
| 2009 | T. Farrar | M. Breschel | G. Ciolek |
| 2008 | R. McEwen | M. Renshaw | A. Davis |
| 2007 | A. Ballan | O. Freire | G. Ciolek |
| 2006 | O. Freire | E. Zabel | F. Pozzato |
| 2005 | F. Pozzato | L. Paolini | A. Davis |
| 2004 | S. O'Grady | P. Bettini | I. Astarloa |
| 2003 | P. Bettini | D. Rebellin | J. Ullrich |
| 2002 | J. Museeuw | I. Astarloa | D. Rebellin |
| 2001 | E. Zabel | R. Vainsteins | E. Dekker |
| 2000 | G. Missaglia | F. Casagrande | F. Baldato |
| 1999 | M. Celestino | R. Schweda | R. Vainsteins |
| 1998 | L. van Bon | M. Bartoli | L. Dierckxsens |
| 1997 | J. Ullrich | W. Peeters | J. Heppner |
| 1996 | R. Brasi | B. Dietz | S. Rein |

## RIDER RESULTS

| WINS | RIDER |
|---|---|
| 3 | E. Viviani |
| 2 | T. Farrar |

| PODIUMS | RIDER |
|---|---|
| 5 | G. Nizzolo |
| 4 | A. Greipel, A. Kristoff |
| 3 | G. Ciolek, A. Démare |
| 2 | I. Astarloa, P. Bettini, E. Boasson Hagen, A. Davis, J. Degenkolb, C. Ewan, T. Farrar, O. Freire, F. Pozzato, D. Rebellin, J. Ullrich, R. Vainsteins, E. Viviani, E. Zabel |

## COUNTRY RESULTS

| WINS | COUNTRY |
|---|---|
| 9 | Italy |
| 4 | Germany |
| 3 | Australia |
| 2 | Norway, United States |
| 1 | Belgium, France, Netherlands, Spain |

| PODIUMS | COUNTRY |
|---|---|
| 22 | Italy |
| 17 | Germany |
| 8 | Australia |
| 6 | Norway |
| 4 | Spain |
| 3 | Belgium, France, Netherlands |
| 2 | Latvia, United States |
| 1 | Denmark, Slovenia |

# TOUR DE POLOGNE

## RESULTS BY YEAR

| YEAR | 1ST | 2ND | 3RD |
|---|---|---|---|
| 2021 | J. Almeida | M. Mohorič | M. Kwiatkowski |
| 2020 | R. Evenepoel | J. Fuglsang | S. Yates |
| 2019 | P. Sivakov | J. Hindley | D. Ulissi |
| 2018 | M. Kwiatkowski | S. Yates | T. Pinot |
| 2017 | D. Teuns | R. Majka | W. Poels |
| 2016 | T. Wellens | F. Felline | A. Bettiol |
| 2015 | I. Izaguirre | B. De Clercq | B. Hermans |
| 2014 | R. Majka | I. Izaguirre | B. Intxausti |
| 2013 | P. Weening | I. Izaguirre | C. Riblon |
| 2012 | M. Moser | M. Kwiatkowski | S. Henao |
| 2011 | P. Sagan | D. Martin | M. Marcato |
| 2010 | D. Martin | G. Bole | B. Mollema |
| 2009 | A. Ballan | D. Moreno | E. Boasson Hagen |
| 2008 | J. Voigt | L. Y. Bak | F. Pellizotti |
| 2007 | J. Vansummeren | R. Gesink | K. Kirchen |
| 2006 | S. Schumacher | C. Evans | A. Ballan |
| 2005 | K. Kirchen | P. Weening | T. Dekker |
| 2004 | O. Sosenka | H. Sabido | F. Pellizotti |
| 2003 | C. Zamana | A. Noe | D. Bruylandts |
| 2002 | L. Brochard | T. Brozyna | M. Rutkiewicz |
| 2001 | O. Sosenka | J. Voigt | P. Przydzial |
| 2000 | P. Przydzial | P. Wadecki | S. Ivanov |
| 1999 | T. Brozyna | C. Zamana | J. Voigt |
| 1998 | S. Ivanov | J. Durand | F. Malberti |
| 1997 | R. Jaermann | Z. Jaskula | S. Sviben |

## RIDER RESULTS

| WINS | RIDER |
|---|---|
| 2 | O. Sosenka |

| PODIUMS | RIDER |
|---|---|
| 3 | I. Izaguirre, M. Kwiatkowski, J. Voigt |
| 2 | A. Ballan, T. Brozyna, M. Fondriest, S. Ivanov, K. Kirchen, R. Majka, D. Martin, A. Noe, F. Pellizotti, P. Przydzial, O. Sosenka, P. Weening, S. Yates, C. Zamana |

## COUNTRY RESULTS

| WINS | COUNTRY |
|---|---|
| 5 | Poland |
| 4 | Belgium |
| 2 | Czech Republic, Germany, Italy, Russia |
| 1 | France, Ireland, Luxembourg, Netherlands, Portugal, Slovakia, Spain, Switzerland |

| PODIUMS | COUNTRY |
|---|---|
| 14 | Poland |
| 11 | Italy |
| 7 | Belgium |
| 6 | Netherlands |
| 5 | Spain |
| 4 | France, Germany |
| 3 | Russia, Slovenia |
| 2 | Australia, Czech Republic, Denmark, Ireland, Luxembourg, Portugal, United Kingdom |
| 1 | Colombia, Norway, Slovakia, Switzerland |

# TOUR DOWN UNDER

## RESULTS BY YEAR

| YEAR | 1ST | 2ND | 3RD |
|---|---|---|---|
| 2021 | Race cancelled | | |
| 2020 | R. Porte | D. Ulissi | S. Geschke |
| 2019 | D. Impey | R. Porte | W. Poels |
| 2018 | D. Impey | R. Porte | T. J. Slagter |
| 2017 | R. Porte | E. Chaves | J. McCarthy |
| 2016 | S. Gerrans | R. Porte | S. Henao |
| 2015 | R. Dennis | R. Porte | C. Evans |
| 2014 | S. Gerrans | C. Evans | D. Ulissi |
| 2013 | T. J. Slagter | J. Moreno | G. Thomas |
| 2012 | S. Gerrans | A. Valverde | T. Machado |
| 2011 | C. Meyer | M. Goss | B. Swift |
| 2010 | A. Greipel | L. L. Sanchez | G. Henderson |
| 2009 | A. Davis | S. O'Grady | J. J. Rojas |
| 2008 | A. Greipel | A. Davis | J. J. Rojas |
| 2007 | M. Elmiger | K. Menzies | L. Y. Bak |
| 2006 | S. Gerrans | L. L. Sanchez | R. McEwen |
| 2005 | L. L. Sanchez | A. Davis | S. O'Grady |
| 2004 | P. Jonker | R. McEwen | B. Cooke |
| 2003 | M. Astarloza | L. Kristensen | S. O'Grady |
| 2002 | M. Rogers | A. Botcharov | P. Jonker |
| 2001 | S. O'Grady | K. Hundertmarck | F. Sacchi |
| 2000 | G. Maignan | S. O'Grady | S. Wesemann |
| 1999 | S. O'Grady | J. Skibby | M. Backstedt |

## RIDER RESULTS

| WINS | RIDER |
|---|---|
| 4 | S. Gerrans |
| 2 | A. Greipel, D. Impey, S. O'Grady, R. Porte |

| PODIUMS | RIDER |
|---|---|
| 6 | S. O'Grady, R. Porte |
| 4 | S. Gerrans |
| 3 | A. Davis, L. L. Sanchez |
| 2 | C. Evans, A. Greipel, T. J. Slagter, J. J. Rojas, P. Jonker, R. McEwen, D. Ulissi |

## COUNTRY RESULTS

| WINS | COUNTRY |
|---|---|
| 13 | Australia |
| 2 | Germany, South Africa, Spain |
| 1 | France, Netherlands, Switzerland |

| PODIUMS | COUNTRY |
|---|---|
| 32 | Australia |
| 8 | Spain |
| 4 | Germany |
| 3 | Denmark, Italy, Netherlands |
| 2 | Colombia, South Africa, Switzerland, United Kingdom |
| 1 | France, New Zealand, Portugal, Russia, Sweden |

MEN'S HISTORICAL RESULTS

# STRADE BIANCHE

## RESULTS BY YEAR

| YEAR | 1ST | 2ND | 3RD |
|---|---|---|---|
| 2021 | M. van der Poel | J. Alaphilippe | E. Bernal |
| 2020 | W. van Aert | D. Formolo | M. Schachmann |
| 2019 | J. Alaphilippe | J. Fuglsang | W. van Aert |
| 2018 | T. Benoot | R. Bardet | W. van Aert |
| 2017 | M. Kwiatkowski | G. Van Avermaet | T. Wellens |
| 2016 | F. Cancellara | Z. Stybar | G. Brambilla |
| 2015 | Z. Stybar | G. Van Avermaet | A. Valverde |
| 2014 | M. Kwiatkowski | P. Sagan | A. Valverde |
| 2013 | M. Moser | P. Sagan | R. Nocentini |
| 2012 | F. Cancellara | M. Iglinskiy | O. Gatto |
| 2011 | P. Gilbert | A. Ballan | D. Cunego |
| 2010 | M. Iglinskiy | T. Lofkvist | M. Rogers |
| 2009 | T. Lofkvist | F. Wegmann | M. Elmiger |
| 2008 | F. Cancellara | A. Ballan | L. Gerdemann |
| 2007 | A. Kolobnev | M. Ljungqvist | M. Khalilov |

## RIDER RESULTS

| WINS | RIDER |
|---|---|
| 3 | F. Cancellara |
| 2 | M. Kwiatkowski |

| PODIUMS | RIDER |
|---|---|
| 3 | F. Cancellara, W. van Aert |
| 2 | J. Alaphilippe, A. Ballan, M. Iglinskiy, M. Kwiatkowski, T. Lofkvist, P. Sagan, Z. Štybar, A. Valverde, G. Van Avermaet |

## COUNTRY RESULTS

| WINS | COUNTRY |
|---|---|
| 3 | Belgium, Switzerland |
| 2 | Poland |
| 1 | Czech Republic, France, Italy, Kazakhstan, Netherlands, Russia, Sweden |

| PODIUMS | COUNTRY |
|---|---|
| 8 | Belgium, Italy |
| 4 | Switzerland |
| 3 | France, Germany, Sweden |
| 2 | Czech Republic, Kazakhstan, Poland, Slovakia, Spain |
| 1 | Australia, Colombia, Denmark, Italy, Netherlands, Russia, Ukraine |

# GP CYCLISTE DE QUÉBEC

## RESULTS BY YEAR

| YEAR | 1ST | 2ND | 3RD |
|---|---|---|---|
| 2021 | Race cancelled | | |
| 2020 | Race cancelled | | |
| 2019 | M. Matthews | P. Sagan | G. Van Avermaet |
| 2018 | M. Matthews | G. Van Avermaet | J. Stuyven |
| 2017 | P. Sagan | G. Van Avermaet | M. Matthews |
| 2016 | P. Sagan | G. Van Avermaet | A. Roux |
| 2015 | R. Urán | M. Matthews | A. Kristoff |
| 2014 | S. Gerrans | T. Dumoulin | R. Navardauskas |
| 2013 | R. Gesink | A. Vichot | G. Van Avermaet |
| 2012 | S. Gerrans | G. Van Avermaet | R. Costa |
| 2011 | P. Gilbert | R. Gesink | R. Urán |
| 2010 | T. Voeckler | E. Boasson Hagen | R. Gesink |

## RIDER RESULTS

| WINS | RIDER |
|---|---|
| 2 | S. Gerrans, M. Matthews, P. Sagan |

| PODIUMS | RIDER |
|---|---|
| 6 | G. Van Avermaet |
| 4 | M. Matthews |
| 3 | R. Gesink, P. Sagan |
| 2 | S. Gerrans, R. Urán |

## COUNTRY RESULTS

| WINS | COUNTRY |
|---|---|
| 4 | Australia |
| 2 | Slovakia |
| 1 | Belgium, Colombia, France, Netherlands |

| PODIUMS | COUNTRY |
|---|---|
| 8 | Belgium |
| 6 | Australia |
| 4 | Netherlands |
| 3 | France, Slovakia |
| 2 | Colombia, Norway |
| 1 | Lithuania, Portugal |

MEN'S HISTORICAL RESULTS

# GP CYCLISTE DE MONTRÉAL

## RESULTS BY YEAR

| YEAR | 1ST | 2ND | 3RD |
|---|---|---|---|
| 2021 | Race cancelled | | |
| 2020 | Race cancelled | | |
| 2019 | G. Van Avermaet | D. Ulissi | I. García |
| 2018 | M. Matthews | S. Colbrelli | G. Van Avermaet |
| 2017 | D. Ulissi | Je. Herrada | T. J. Slagter |
| 2016 | G. Van Avermaet | P. Sagan | D. Ulissi |
| 2015 | T. Wellens | A. Yates | R. Costa |
| 2014 | S. Gerrans | R. Costa | T. Gallopin |
| 2013 | P. Sagan | S. Ponzi | R. Hesjedal |
| 2012 | L. P. Nordhaug | M. Moser | A. Kolobnev |
| 2011 | R. Costa | P. Fedrigo | P. Gilbert |
| 2010 | R. Gesink | P. Sagan | R. Hesjedal |

## RIDER RESULTS

| WINS | RIDER |
|---|---|
| 2 | G. Van Avermaet |

| PODIUMS | RIDER |
|---|---|
| 3 | R. Costa, P. Sagan, D. Ulissi, G. Van Avermaet |
| 2 | R. Hesjedal |

## COUNTRY RESULTS

| WINS | COUNTRY |
|---|---|
| 3 | Belgium |
| 2 | Australia |
| 1 | Italy, Netherlands, Norway, Portugal, Slovakia |

| PODIUMS | COUNTRY |
|---|---|
| 6 | Italy |
| 5 | Belgium |
| 3 | Portugal, Slovakia |
| 2 | Australia, Canada, France, Netherlands, Spain |
| 1 | Norway, Russia, United Kingdom |

# UAE TOUR

## RESULTS BY YEAR

| YEAR | 1ST | 2ND | 3RD |
|---|---|---|---|
| 2021 | T. Pogačar | A. Yates | J. Almeida |
| 2020 | A. Yates | T. Pogačar | A. Lutsenko |
| 2019 | P. Roglič | A. Valverde | D. Gaudu |
| 2018 | A. Valverde | W. Kelderman | M. A. López |
| 2017 | R. Costa | I. Zakarin | T. Dumoulin |
| 2016 | T. Kangert | N. Roche | D. Ulissi |
| 2015 | E. Chaves | F. Aru | W. Poels |

## RIDER RESULTS

| WINS | RIDER |
|---|---|
| | No riders have won this race more than once. |

| PODIUMS | RIDER |
|---|---|
| 2 | T. Pogačar, A. Valverde, A. Yates |

## COUNTRY RESULTS

| WINS | COUNTRY |
|---|---|
| 2 | Slovenia |
| 1 | Colombia, Estonia, Portugal, Spain, United Kingdom |

| PODIUMS | COUNTRY |
|---|---|
| 3 | Netherlands, Slovenia |
| 2 | Colombia, Italy, Portugal, Spain, United Kingdom |
| 1 | Estonia, France, Ireland, Kazakhstan, Russia |

MEN'S HISTORICAL RESULTS

# CADEL EVANS GREAT OCEAN ROAD RACE

## RESULTS BY YEAR

| YEAR | 1ST | 2ND | 3RD |
|---|---|---|---|
| 2021 | Race cancelled | | |
| 2020 | D. Devenyns | P. Sivakov | D. Impey |
| 2019 | E. Viviani | C. Ewan | D. Impey |
| 2018 | J. McCarthy | E. Viviani | D. Impey |
| 2017 | N. Arndt | S. Gerrans | C. Meyer |
| 2016 | P. Kennaugh | L. Howard | N. Bonifazio |
| 2015 | G. Meersman | S. Clarke | N. Haas |

## RIDER RESULTS

| WINS | RIDER |
|---|---|
| | No riders have won this race more than once. |

| PODIUMS | RIDER |
|---|---|
| 3 | D. Impey |
| 2 | E. Viviani |

## COUNTRY RESULTS

| WINS | COUNTRY |
|---|---|
| 2 | Belgium |
| 1 | Australia, Germany, Italy, United Kingdom |

| PODIUMS | COUNTRY |
|---|---|
| 7 | Australia |
| 3 | Italy, South Africa |
| 2 | Belgium |
| 1 | Germany, Russia, United Kingdom |

# TOUR OF GUANGXI

## RESULTS BY YEAR

| YEAR | 1ST | 2ND | 3RD |
|---|---|---|---|
| 2021 | Race cancelled | | |
| 2020 | Race cancelled | | |
| 2019 | E. Mas | D. F. Martínez | D. Rosa |
| 2018 | G. Moscon | F. Großschartner | S. Chernetskiy |
| 2017 | T. Wellens | B. Mollema | N. Roche |

## RIDER RESULTS

| WINS | RIDER |
|---|---|
| | No riders have won this race more than once. |

| PODIUMS | RIDER |
|---|---|
| | No riders have finished on the podium of this race more than once. |

## COUNTRY RESULTS

| WINS | COUNTRY |
|---|---|
| 1 | Belgium, Italy, Spain |

| PODIUMS | COUNTRY |
|---|---|
| 2 | Italy |
| 1 | Austria, Belgium, Colombia, Ireland, Netherlands, Russia, Spain |

# DUTCH DOMINANCE OF THE WOMEN'S WORLDTOUR

The Dutch seem to win a lot, and this year the data backs that up more than ever. In the Women's WorldTour, 78 per cent of races were won by a Dutch rider – the highest percentage since the WWT's inception. The inaugural year of 2016 saw the lowest, with a 'mere' 29 per cent of races won by women from the Netherlands.

■ % OF DUTCH WWT WINNERS
% OF NON-DUTCH WINNERS

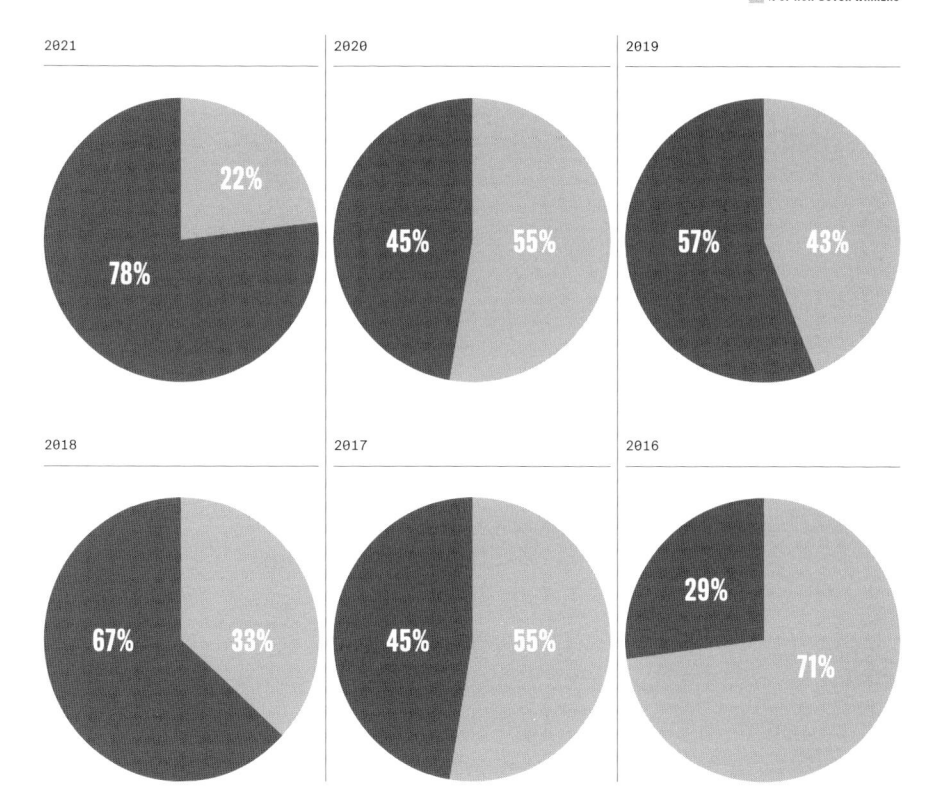

**2021**: 78% / 22%
**2020**: 45% / 55%
**2019**: 57% / 43%
**2018**: 67% / 33%
**2017**: 45% / 55%
**2016**: 29% / 71%

WOMEN'S HISTORICAL RESULTS

# WORLD CHAMPIONSHIPS WOMEN'S ROAD RACE

## RESULTS BY YEAR

| YEAR | 1ST | 2ND | 3RD |
|---|---|---|---|
| 2021 | E. Balsamo | M. Vos | K. Niewiadoma |
| 2020 | A. van der Breggen | A. van Vleuten | E. Longo Borghini |
| 2019 | A. van Vleuten | A. van der Breggen | A. Spratt |
| 2018 | A. van der Breggen | A. Spratt | T. Guderzo |
| 2017 | C. van den Broek-Blaak | K. Garfoot | A. Dideriksen |
| 2016 | A. Dideriksen | K. Wild | L. Lepistö |
| 2015 | E. Deignan | A. van der Breggen | M. Guarnier |
| 2014 | P. Ferrand Prevot | L. Brennauer | E. Johansson |
| 2013 | M. Vos | E. Johansson | R. Ratto |
| 2012 | M. Vos | R. Neylan | E. Longo Borghini |
| 2011 | G. Bronzini | M. Vos | I. Y. Teutenberg |
| 2010 | G. Bronzini | M. Vos | E. Johansson |
| 2009 | T. Guderzo | M. Vos | N. Cantele |
| 2008 | N. Cooke | M. Vos | J. Arndt |
| 2007 | M. Bastianelli | M. Vos | G. Bronzini |
| 2006 | M. Vos | T. Worrack | N. Cooke |
| 2005 | R. Schleicher | N. Cooke | O. Wood |
| 2004 | J. Arndt | T. Guderzo | A. Valen De Vries |
| 2003 | S. Ljungskog | M. Melchers | N. Cooke |
| 2002 | S. Ljungskog | N. Brandli | J. Somarriba |
| 2001 | R. Polikeviciute | E. Pucinskaite | J. Longo |
| 2000 | Z. Stahurskaya | C. Beltman | M. Lindberg |
| 1999 | E. Pucinskaite | A. Millward | D. Ziliute |
| 1998 | D. Ziliute | L. Zijlaard van Moorsel | H. Kupfernagel |
| 1997 | A. Cappellotto | E. Tadich | C. Marsal |
| 1996 | B. Heeb | R. Polikeviciute | L. Jackson |
| 1995 | J. Longo | C. Marsal | E. Pucinskaite |
| 1994 | M. Valen | P. Maegerman | J. Golay |
| 1993 | L. Zijlaard van Moorsel | J. Longo | L. Charameda |
| 1991 | L. Zijlaard van Moorsel | I. Thompson | A. Sydor |
| 1990 | C. Marsal | R. Matthes | L. Seghezzi |
| 1989 | J. Longo | C. Marsal | M. Canins |
| 1987 | J. Longo | H. Hage | C. Meijer |
| 1986 | J. Longo | J. Parks | A. Jakovleva |
| 1985 | J. Longo | M. Canins | S. Schumacher |
| 1983 | M. Berglund | R. Twigg | M. Canins |
| 1982 | M. Jones | M. Canins | G. Sierens |
| 1981 | U. Enzenauer | J. Longo | C. Carpenter Phinney |
| 1980 | B. Heiden | T. Jahre | M. Jones |
| 1979 | P. De Bruin | J. De Smet | B. Habetz |
| 1978 | B. Habetz | K. Hage | E. Lorenzon |
| 1977 | J. Bost | C. Carpenter Phinney | M. Brinkhof Nieuwenhuis |
| 1976 | K. Hage | L. Bissoli | Y. Reynders |
| 1975 | T. Fopma | G. Gambillon | K. Hage |
| 1974 | G. Gambillon | B. Tsaune | K. Hage |
| 1973 | N. Van Den Broeck | K. Hage | V. Rebrovskaia |
| 1972 | G. Gambillon | L. Zadorojnaya | A. Konkina |
| 1971 | A. Konkina | M. Tartagni | K. Hage |
| 1970 | A. Konkina | M. Tartagni | R. Obodovskaya |
| 1969 | A. McElmury | B. Swinnerton | N. Trofimova |
| 1968 | K. Hage | B. Tsaune | M. Tartagni |
| 1967 | B. Burton | L. Zadorojnaya | A. Konkina |
| 1966 | Y. Reynders | K. Hage | A. Puronen |
| 1965 | E. Kleinhans Eicholz | Y. Reynders | A. Puronen |
| 1964 | E. Sonka | G. Yudina | R. Sels |
| 1963 | Y. Reynders | R. Sels | A. Puronen |
| 1962 | M. R. Gaillard | Y. Reynders | M. T. Naessens |
| 1961 | Y. Reynders | B. Burton | E. Jacobs |
| 1960 | B. Burton | R. Sels | E. Kleinhans Eicholz |
| 1959 | Y. Reynders | A. Puronen | V. Gorbatcheva |
| 1958 | E. Jacobs | T. Novikova | M. Lukshina |

## RIDER RESULTS

| WINS | RIDER |
|---|---|
| 5 | J. Longo |
| 4 | Y. Reynders |
| 3 | M. Vos |
| 2 | G. Bronzini, B. Burton, G. Gambillon, K. Hage, A. Konkina, S. Ljungskog, A. van der Breggen, L. Zijlaard van Moorsel |

| PODIUMS | RIDER |
|---|---|
| 9 | M. Vos |
| 8 | K. Hage, J. Longo |
| 7 | Y. Reynders |
| 4 | M. Canins, N. Cooke, A. Konkina, C. Marsal, A. Puronen, A. van der Breggen |
| 3 | G. Bronzini, B. Burton, G. Gambillon, T. Guderzo, E. Johansson, E. Pucinskaite, R. Sels, M. Tartagni, L. Zijlaard van Moorsel |
| 2 | J. Arndt, C. Carpenter Phinney, A. Dideriksen, B. Habetz, E. Jacobs, M. Jones, E. Kleinhans Eicholz, S. Ljungskog, E. Longo Borghini, R. Polikeviciute, B. Tsaune, A. van Vleuten, L. Zadorojnaya, D. Ziliute |

## COUNTRY RESULTS

| WINS | COUNTRY |
|---|---|
| 13 | Netherlands |
| 10 | France |
| 6 | Belgium, Italy |
| 5 | Germany, United Kingdom |
| 3 | Lithuania, Sweden |
| 2 | Russia, United States |
| 1 | Belarus, Denmark, Latvia, Luxembourg, Norway, Switzerland |

| PODIUMS | COUNTRY |
|---|---|
| 35 | Netherlands |
| 23 | Italy |
| 20 | Russia |
| 17 | France |
| 16 | Belgium |
| 13 | Germany |
| 11 | United Kingdom, United States |
| 8 | Sweden |
| 7 | Australia, Lithuania |
| 2 | Canada, Denmark, Luxembourg, Norway, Switzerland |
| 1 | Belarus, Finland, Latvia, Poland, Spain |

WOMEN'S HISTORICAL RESULTS

# TROFEO BINDA

## RESULTS BY YEAR

| YEAR | 1ST | 2ND | 3RD |
|---|---|---|---|
| 2021 | E. Longo Borghini | M. Vos | C. U. Ludwig |
| 2020 | Race cancelled | | |
| 2019 | M. Vos | A. Spratt | C. U. Ludwig |
| 2018 | K. Niewiadoma | C. van den Broek-Blaak | M. Vos |
| 2017 | C. Rivera | A. Sierra | C. U. Ludwig |
| 2016 | E. Deignan | M. Guarnier | J. Neff |
| 2015 | E. Deignan | P. Ferrand Prevot | A. van der Breggen |
| 2014 | E. Johansson | E. Deignan | A. Amialiusik |
| 2013 | E. Longo Borghini | E. Johansson | E. van Dijk |
| 2012 | M. Vos | T. Guderzo | T. Worrack |
| 2011 | E. Pooley | E. Johansson | A. van Vleuten |
| 2010 | M. Vos | M. Bras | E. Johansson |
| 2009 | M. Vos | E. Johansson | K. Armstrong |
| 2008 | E. Pooley | S. De Goede | D. Ziliute |
| 2007 | N. Cooke | G. Bronzini | M. Corazza |
| 2006 | R. Schleicher | D. Ziliute | K. Longhin |
| 2005 | N. Cooke | K. Longhin | M. Oki |
| 2004 | O. Wood | O. Gollan | N. Cantele |
| 2003 | D. Ziliute | V. Karpenko | A. Wright |
| 2002 | S. Stolbova | R. Schleicher | Z. Stahurskaya |
| 2001 | N. Brandli | N. Cantele | D. Ziliute |
| 2000 | F. Luperini | P. Sundstedt | F. Lecourtois |
| 1999 | F. Lecourtois | M. Holden | P. Sundstedt |
| 1996 | V. Cappellotto | I. Chiappa | D. Ziliute |
| 1995 | V. Cappellotto | A. Cappellotto | I. Chiappa |
| 1994 | F. Luperini | L. Pizzolotto | K. Longhin |
| 1993 | R. Ferrero | M. Calliope | L. Pizzolotto |
| 1992 | M. Canins | M. P. Turcutto | M. Calliope |
| 1991 | M. P. Turcutto | | |
| 1990 | M. Canins | | |
| 1989 | E. Fanton | | |
| 1988 | E. Fanton | | |
| 1987 | R. Galbiati | | |
| 1986 | S. Carmine | | |
| 1985 | M. Canins | M. Mosole | E. Menuzzo |
| 1984 | M. Canins | | |
| 1983 | M. Tommasi | | |
| 1982 | L. Pizzolotto | | |
| 1981 | E. Menuzzo | | |
| 1980 | F. Galli | | |
| 1979 | A. Morlacchi | | |
| 1978 | E. Menuzzo | | |
| 1977 | N. Castelli | | |
| 1976 | M. Tartagni | | |
| 1975 | N. Van Den Broeck | | |
| 1974 | G. Micheloni | | |

## RIDER RESULTS

| WINS | RIDER |
|---|---|
| 4 | M. Canins, M. Vos |
| 2 | V. Cappellotto, N. Cooke, E. Deignan, E. Fanton, F. Luperini, E. Menuzzo, E. Pooley |

| PODIUMS | RIDER |
|---|---|
| 6 | M. Vos |
| 5 | E. Johansson, D. Ziliute |
| 4 | M. Canins |
| 3 | E. Deignan, K. Longhin, C. U. Ludwig, E. Menuzzo, L. Pizzolotto |
| 2 | M. Calliope, N. Cantele, V. Cappellotto, I. Chiappa, N. Cooke, E. Fanton, F. Lecourtois, E. Longo Borghini, F. Luperini, M. P. Turcutto, E. Pooley, R. Schleicher, P. Sundstedt |

## COUNTRY RESULTS

| WINS | COUNTRY |
|---|---|
| 24 | Italy |
| 6 | United Kingdom |
| 4 | Netherlands |
| 2 | Switzerland |
| 1 | Australia, Belgium, France, Germany, Lithuania, Poland, Russia, Sweden, United States |

| PODIUMS | COUNTRY |
|---|---|
| 42 | Italy |
| 12 | Netherlands |
| 7 | United Kingdom |
| 5 | Lithuania, Sweden |
| 4 | Australia, United States |
| 3 | Denmark, France, Germany, Switzerland |
| 2 | Belarus, Finland |
| 1 | Belgium, Cuba, Japan, Poland, Russia, Ukraine |

# WOMEN'S HISTORICAL RESULTS

# GIRO ROSA

## RESULTS BY YEAR

| YEAR | 1ST | 2ND | 3RD |
|---|---|---|---|
| 2021 | A. van der Breggen | A. Moolman-Pasio | D. Vollering |
| 2020 | A. van der Breggen | K. Niewiadoma | E. Longo Borghini |
| 2019 | A. van Vleuten | A. van der Breggen | A. Spratt |
| 2018 | A. van Vleuten | A. Moolman-Pasio | A. Spratt |
| 2017 | A. van der Breggen | E. Longo Borghini | A. van Vleuten |
| 2016 | M. Guarnier | E. Stevens | A. van der Breggen |
| 2015 | A. van der Breggen | M. Abbott | M. Guarnier |
| 2014 | M. Vos | P. Ferrand Prevot | A. van der Breggen |
| 2013 | M. Abbott | T. Guderzo | C. Lichtenberg |
| 2012 | M. Vos | E. Pooley | E. Stevens |
| 2011 | M. Vos | E. Pooley | J. Arndt |
| 2010 | M. Abbott | J. Arndt | T. Guderzo |
| 2009 | C. Lichtenberg | M. Abbott | N. Brandli |
| 2008 | F. Luperini | A. Neben | C. Lichtenberg |
| 2007 | E. Pucinskaite | N. Brandli | M. I. Moreno |
| 2006 | E. Pucinskaite | N. Brandli | S. Ljungskog |
| 2005 | N. Brandli | J. Somarriba | E. Pucinskaite |
| 2004 | N. Cooke | F. Luperini | P. Doppmann |
| 2003 | N. Brandli | E. Pucinskaite | J. Somarriba |
| 2002 | S. Stolbova | Z. Stahurskaya | D. Ziliute |
| 2001 | N. Brandli | D. Ziliute | E. Pucinskaite |
| 2000 | J. Somarriba | A. Cappellotto | V. Polkhanova |
| 1999 | J. Somarriba | S. Stolbova | D. Veronesi |
| 1998 | F. Luperini | L. Jackson | B. Heeb |
| 1997 | F. Luperini | L. Jackson | E. Pucinskaite |
| 1996 | F. Luperini | A. Cappellotto | I. Chiappa |
| 1995 | F. Luperini | L. Zberg | R. Bonanomi |
| 1994 | M. Fanini | K. Watt | L. Zberg |
| 1993 | L. Ilavska | L. Zberg | I. Chiappa |
| 1990 | C. Marsal | M. Canins | K. Watt |
| 1989 | R. Bonanomi | A. Koliaseva | T. Vikstedt Nyman |
| 1988 | M. Canins | E. Hepple | P. Rossner |

## RIDER RESULTS

| WINS | RIDER |
|---|---|
| 5 | F. Luperini |
| 4 | A. van der Breggen |
| 3 | N. Brandli, M. Vos |
| 2 | M. Abbott, E. Pucinskaite, J. Somarriba, A. van Vleuten |

| PODIUMS | RIDER |
|---|---|
| 7 | A. van der Breggen |
| 6 | N. Brandli, F. Luperini, E. Pucinskaite |
| 4 | M. Abbott, J. Somarriba |
| 3 | C. Lichtenberg, A. van Vleuten, M. Vos, L. Zberg |
| 2 | J. Arndt, R. Bonanomi, M. Canins, A. Cappellotto, I. Chiappa, M. Guarnier, T. Guderzo, L. Jackson, A. Moolman-Pasio, E. Pooley, A. Spratt, E. Stevens, S. Stolbova, K. Watt, D. Ziliute |

## COUNTRY RESULTS

| WINS | COUNTRY |
|---|---|
| 9 | Netherlands |
| 8 | Italy |
| 3 | Switzerland, United States |
| 2 | Lithuania, Spain |
| 1 | France, Germany, Russia, Slovakia, United Kingdom |

| PODIUMS | COUNTRY |
|---|---|
| 19 | Italy |
| 14 | Netherlands |
| 11 | Switzerland |
| 9 | United States |
| 8 | Lithuania |
| 6 | Germany |
| 5 | Australia, Spain |
| 4 | Russia |
| 3 | United Kingdom |
| 2 | Canada, France, South Africa |
| 1 | Belarus, Finland, Poland, San Marino, Slovakia, Sweden |

# WORLD CHAMPIONSHIPS WOMEN'S ITT

## RESULTS BY YEAR

| YEAR | 1ST | 2ND | 3RD |
|---|---|---|---|
| 2021 | E. van Dijk | M. Reusser | A. van Vleuten |
| 2020 | A. van der Breggen | M. Reusser | E. van Dijk |
| 2019 | C. Dygert | A. van der Breggen | A. van Vleuten |
| 2018 | A. van Vleuten | A. van der Breggen | E. van Dijk |
| 2017 | A. van Vleuten | A. van der Breggen | K. Garfoot |
| 2016 | A. Neben | E. van Dijk | K. Garfoot |
| 2015 | L. Villumsen | A. van der Breggen | L. Brennauer |
| 2014 | L. Brennauer | A. Solovey | E. Stevens |
| 2013 | E. van Dijk | L. Villumsen | C. Small |
| 2012 | J. Arndt | E. Stevens | L. Villumsen |
| 2011 | J. Arndt | L. Villumsen | E. Pooley |
| 2010 | E. Pooley | J. Arndt | L. Villumsen |
| 2009 | K. Armstrong | N. Cantele | L. Villumsen |
| 2008 | A. Neben | C. Soeder | J. Arndt |
| 2007 | H. Kupfernagel | K. Armstrong | C. Soeder |
| 2006 | K. Armstrong | K. Thurig | C. Thornburn |
| 2005 | K. Thurig | J. Somarriba | K. Armstrong |
| 2004 | K. Thurig | J. Arndt | Z. Zabirova |
| 2003 | J. Somarriba | J. Arndt | Z. Zabirova |
| 2002 | Z. Zabirova | N. Brandli | K. Thurig |
| 2001 | J. Longo | N. Brandli | D. Ruano |
| 2000 | M. Holden | J. Longo | R. Polikeviciute |
| 1999 | L. Zijlaard van Moorsel | A. Millward | E. Pucinskaite |
| 1998 | L. Zijlaard van Moorsel | Z. Zabirova | H. Kupfernagel |
| 1997 | J. Longo | Z. Zabirova | J. Arndt |
| 1996 | J. Longo | C. Marsal | A. Cappellotto |
| 1995 | J. Longo | C. Hughes | K. Watt |
| 1994 | K. Kurreck | A. Samplonius | J. Longo |

## RIDER RESULTS

| WINS | RIDER |
|---|---|
| 4 | J. Longo |
| 2 | K. Armstrong, J. Arndt, A. Neben, K. Thurig, E. van Dijk, A. van Vleuten, L. Zijlaard van Moorsel |

| PODIUMS | RIDER |
|---|---|
| 7 | J. Arndt |
| 6 | J. Longo, L. Villumsen |
| 5 | Z. Zabirova, A. van der Breggen, E. van Dijk |
| 4 | K. Armstrong, K. Thurig, A. van Vleuten |
| 2 | N. Brandli, L. Brennauer, K. Garfoot, H. Kupfernagel, A. Neben, E. Pooley, M. Reusser, C. Soeder, J. Somarriba, E. Stevens, L. Zijlaard van Moorsel |

## COUNTRY RESULTS

| WINS | COUNTRY |
|---|---|
| 7 | Netherlands, United States |
| 4 | France, Germany |
| 2 | Switzerland |
| 1 | Kazakhstan, New Zealand, Spain, United Kingdom |

| PODIUMS | COUNTRY |
|---|---|
| 16 | Netherlands |
| 13 | United States |
| 11 | Germany |
| 8 | Switzerland |
| 7 | France |
| 6 | New Zealand |
| 5 | Kazakhstan |
| 4 | Australia |
| 3 | Spain |
| 2 | Austria, Canada, Italy, Lithuania, United Kingdom |

WOMEN'S HISTORICAL RESULTS

# SIMAC LADIES TOUR

## RESULTS BY YEAR

| YEAR | 1ST | 2ND | 3RD |
|---|---|---|---|
| 2021 | C. van den Broek-Blaak | M. Reusser | E. van Dijk |
| 2020 | Race cancelled | | |
| 2019 | C. Majerus | L. Wiebes | L. Klein |
| 2018 | A. van Vleuten | E. van Dijk | A. van der Breggen |
| 2017 | A. van Vleuten | A. van der Breggen | E. van Dijk |
| 2016 | C. van den Broek-Blaak | E. van Dijk | A. Amialiusik |
| 2015 | L. Brennauer | L. Brand | E. van Dijk |
| 2014 | E. Stevens | L. Brennauer | E. van Dijk |
| 2013 | E. van Dijk | A. van Vleuten | E. Deignan |
| 2012 | M. Vos | E. Stevens | J. Arndt |
| 2011 | M. Vos | E. Johansson | K. Wild |
| 2010 | M. Vos | K. Wild | E. van Dijk |
| 2009 | M. Vos | K. Wild | I. Y. Teutenberg |
| 2008 | C. Becker | I. Y. Teutenberg | I. Van De Broek |
| 2007 | K. Armstrong | J. Arndt | L. Villumsen |
| 2006 | S. Ljungskog | T. Worrack | J. Arndt |
| 2005 | T. Hennes | S. Ljungskog | M. Melchers |
| 2004 | M. Melchers | T. Worrack | S. van Alebeek |
| 2003 | S. Ljungskog | T. Worrack | O. Zabelinskaya |
| 2002 | D. Mansveld | M. Melchers | A. Grimberg |
| 2001 | P. Rossner | D. Ziliute | D. Mansveld |
| 2000 | M. Melchers | I. Y. Teutenberg | S. Ljungskog |
| 1999 | L. Zijlaard van Moorsel | J. Arndt | S. Ljungskog |
| 1998 | E. van Rooy-Vink | L. Zijlaard van Moorsel | I. Bollerud |

## RIDER RESULTS

| WINS | RIDER |
|---|---|
| 4 | M. Vos |
| 2 | S. Ljungskog, M. Melchers, C. van den Broek-Blaak, A. van Vleuten |

| PODIUMS | RIDER |
|---|---|
| 8 | E. van Dijk |
| 5 | S. Ljungskog |
| 4 | J. Arndt, M. Melchers, M. Vos |
| 3 | A. van Vleuten, K. Wild, T. Worrack, I. Y. Teutenberg |
| 2 | L. Brennauer, D. Mansveld, E. Stevens, C. van den Broek-Blaak, A. van der Breggen, L. Zijlaard van Moorsel |

## COUNTRY RESULTS

| WINS | COUNTRY |
|---|---|
| 14 | Netherlands |
| 4 | Germany |
| 2 | Sweden, United States |
| 1 | Luxembourg |

| PODIUMS | COUNTRY |
|---|---|
| 36 | Netherlands |
| 16 | Germany |
| 6 | Sweden |
| 3 | United States |
| 1 | Belarus, Lithuania, Luxembourg, New Zealand, Norway, Switzerland, United Kingdom, Uzbekistan |

WOMEN'S HISTORICAL RESULTS

# FLÈCHE WALLONNE

## RESULTS BY YEAR

| YEAR | 1ST | 2ND | 3RD |
|---|---|---|---|
| 2021 | A. van der Breggen | K. Niewiadoma | E. Longo Borghini |
| 2020 | A. van der Breggen | C. U. Ludwig | D. Vollering |
| 2019 | A. van der Breggen | A. van Vleuten | A. Langvad |
| 2018 | A. van der Breggen | A. Moolman-Pasio | M. Guarnier |
| 2017 | A. van der Breggen | E. Deignan | K. Niewiadoma |
| 2016 | A. van der Breggen | E. Stevens | M. Guarnier |
| 2015 | A. van der Breggen | A. van Vleuten | M. Guarnier |
| 2014 | P. Ferrand Prevot | E. Deignan | E. Longo Borghini |
| 2013 | M. Vos | E. Longo Borghini | A. Moolman-Pasio |
| 2012 | E. Stevens | M. Vos | L. Villumsen |
| 2011 | M. Vos | E. Johansson | J. Arndt |
| 2010 | E. Pooley | N. Cooke | E. Johansson |
| 2009 | M. Vos | E. Johansson | C. Lichtenberg |
| 2008 | M. Vos | M. Bastianelli | J. Arndt |
| 2007 | M. Vos | N. Cooke | J. Arndt |
| 2006 | N. Cooke | J. Arndt | T. Worrack |
| 2005 | N. Cooke | O. Wood | J. Arndt |
| 2004 | S. Huguet | H. Kupfernagel | E. Pucinskaite |
| 2003 | N. Cooke | S. Palmer Komar | O. Wood |
| 2002 | F. Luperini | L. Bessette | P. Doppmann |
| 2001 | F. Luperini | A. Millward | T. Worrack |
| 2000 | G. Jeanson | P. Sundstedt | F. Lecourtois |
| 1999 | H. Kupfernagel | E. Pucinskaite | C. Pieters |
| 1998 | F. Luperini | P. Sundstedt | C. Marsal |

## RIDER RESULTS

| WINS | RIDER |
|---|---|
| 7 | A. van der Breggen |
| 5 | M. Vos |
| 3 | N. Cooke, F. Luperini |

| PODIUMS | RIDER |
|---|---|
| 7 | A. van der Breggen |
| 6 | M. Vos |
| 5 | J. Arndt, N. Cooke |
| 3 | M. Guarnier, E. Johansson, E. Longo Borghini, F. Luperini |
| 2 | E. Deignan, H. Kupfernagel, A. Moolman-Pasio, K. Niewiadoma, E. Pucinskaite, E. Stevens, P. Sundstedt, A. van Vleuten, O. Wood, T. Worrack |

## COUNTRY RESULTS

| WINS | COUNTRY |
|---|---|
| 12 | Netherlands |
| 4 | United Kingdom |
| 3 | Italy |
| 2 | France |
| 1 | Canada, Germany, United States |

| PODIUMS | COUNTRY |
|---|---|
| 16 | Netherlands |
| 10 | Germany |
| 8 | United Kingdom |
| 7 | Italy |
| 5 | United States |
| 4 | France |
| 3 | Australia, Canada, Sweden |
| 2 | Denmark, Finland, Lithuania, Poland, South Africa |
| 1 | Belgium, New Zealand, Switzerland |

WOMEN'S HISTORICAL RESULTS

# AMSTEL GOLD RACE

## RESULTS BY YEAR

| YEAR | 1ST | 2ND | 3RD |
|---|---|---|---|
| 2021 | M. Vos | D. Vollering | A. van Vleuten |
| 2020 | Race cancelled | | |
| 2019 | K. Niewiadoma | A. van Vleuten | M. Vos |
| 2018 | C. van den Broek-Blaak | L. Brand | A. Spratt |
| 2017 | A. van der Breggen | E. Deignan | A. van Vleuten/ K. Niewiadoma |
| 2003 | N. Cooke | O. Gollan | E. Pucinskaite |
| 2002 | L. Zijlaard van Moorsel | M. Melchers | K. Bates |
| 2001 | D. Mansveld | M. Melchers | L. Zijlaard van Moorsel |

## RIDER RESULTS

| WINS | RIDER |
|---|---|
| | No riders have won this race more than once. |

| PODIUMS | RIDER |
|---|---|
| 3 | A. van Vleuten |
| 2 | M. Melchers, K. Niewiadoma, M. Vos, L. Zijlaard van Moorsel |

## COUNTRY RESULTS

| WINS | COUNTRY |
|---|---|
| 5 | Netherlands |
| 1 | Poland, United Kingdom |

| PODIUMS | COUNTRY |
|---|---|
| 14 | Netherlands |
| 3 | Australia |
| 2 | Poland, United Kingdom |
| 1 | Lithuania |

WOMEN'S HISTORICAL RESULTS

# GP DE PLOUAY

## RESULTS BY YEAR

| YEAR | 1ST | 2ND | 3RD |
|---|---|---|---|
| 2021 | E. Longo Borghini | G. Verhulst | K. Faulkner |
| 2020 | E. Deignan | E. Banks | C. Consonni |
| 2019 | A. van der Breggen | C. Rivera | A. Pieters |
| 2018 | A. Pieters | C. Rivera | C. Rivera |
| 2017 | E. Deignan | M. Vos | S. Roy |
| 2016 | E. Bujak | P. Ferrand Prevot | J. Numainville |
| 2015 | E. Deignan | E. Cecchini | P. Ferrand Prevot |
| 2014 | L. Brand | E. Johansson | P. Ferrand Prevot |
| 2013 | M. Vos | M. Vos | A. van der Breggen |
| 2012 | M. Vos | E. Johansson | E. Longo Borghini |
| 2011 | A. van Vleuten | T. Cromwell | M. Vos |
| 2010 | E. Pooley | E. Stevens | E. Johansson |
| 2009 | E. Pooley | M. Vos | E. Johansson |
| 2008 | F. Luperini | M. Vos | S. De Goede |
| 2007 | N. Cantele | L. Keller | M. Bastianelli |
| 2006 | N. Brandli | N. Cooke | N. Cooke |
| 2005 | N. Cantele | G. Bronzini | M. Holler |
| 2004 | E. Pucinskaite | E. Pucinskaite | O. Wood |
| 2003 | N. Cooke | M. Melchers | M. Melchers |
| 2002 | R. Schleicher | J. Arndt | S. Ljungskog |
|  |  | P. Rossner |  |

## RIDER RESULTS

| WINS | RIDER |
|---|---|
| 3 | E. Deignan |
| 2 | N. Cantele, E. Pooley, M. Vos |

| PODIUMS | RIDER |
|---|---|
| 7 | M. Vos |
| 4 | E. Johansson |
| 3 | N. Cooke, E. Deignan, P. Ferrand Prevot |
| 2 | N. Cantele, E. Longo Borghini, M. Melchers, A. Pieters, E. Pooley, E. Pucinskaite, C. Rivera, A. van der Breggen |

## COUNTRY RESULTS

| WINS | COUNTRY |
|---|---|
| 6 | Netherlands, United Kingdom |
| 4 | Italy |
| 1 | Germany, Lithuania, Slovenia, Switzerland |

| PODIUMS | COUNTRY |
|---|---|
| 16 | Netherlands |
| 9 | Italy, United Kingdom |
| 6 | Sweden |
| 4 | France, Germany, United States |
| 3 | Australia |
| 2 | Lithuania |
| 1 | Canada, Slovenia, Switzerland |

WOMEN'S HISTORICAL RESULTS

# TOUR OF FLANDERS

## RESULTS BY YEAR

| YEAR | 1ST | 2ND | 3RD |
|------|-----|-----|-----|
| 2021 | A. van Vleuten | L. Brennauer | G. Brown |
| 2020 | C. van den Broek-Blaak | A. Pieters | L. Kopecky |
| 2019 | M. Bastianelli | A. van Vleuten | C. U. Ludwig |
| 2018 | A. van der Breggen | A. Pieters | A. van Vleuten |
| 2017 | C. Rivera | G. Elvin | C. van den Broek-Blaak |
| 2016 | E. Deignan | E. Johansson | C. van den Broek-Blaak |
| 2015 | E. Longo Borghini | J. D'hoore | A. van der Breggen |
| 2014 | E. van Dijk | E. Deignan | E. Johansson |
| 2013 | M. Vos | E. van Dijk | E. Johansson |
| 2012 | J. Arndt | K. Armstrong | J. Numainville |
| 2011 | A. van Vleuten | T. Antoshina | M. Vos |
| 2010 | G. Verbeke | M. Vos | K. Wild |
| 2009 | I. Y. Teutenberg | K. Wild | E. Johansson |
| 2008 | J. Arndt | K. Armstrong | K. Wild |
| 2007 | N. Cooke | Z. Zabirova | M. Vos |
| 2006 | M. Melchers | C. Soeder | L. Gunnewijk |
| 2005 | M. Melchers | S. Ljungskog | M. Baccaille |
| 2004 | Z. Zabirova | T. Worrack | L. Zijlaard van Moorsel |

## RIDER RESULTS

| WINS | RIDER |
|------|-------|
| 2 | J. Arndt, M. Melchers, A. van Vleuten |

| PODIUMS | RIDER |
|---------|-------|
| 4 | E. Johansson, A. van Vleuten, M. Vos |
| 3 | K. Wild, C. van den Broek-Blaak |
| 2 | K. Armstrong, J. Arndt, E. Deignan, M. Melchers, A. van der Breggen, E. van Dijk, Z. Zabirova |

## COUNTRY RESULTS

| WINS | COUNTRY |
|------|---------|
| 8 | Netherlands |
| 3 | Germany |
| 2 | Italy, United Kingdom |
| 1 | Belgium, Kazakhstan, United States |

| PODIUMS | COUNTRY |
|---------|---------|
| 24 | Netherlands |
| 5 | Germany, Sweden |
| 3 | Belgium, Italy, United Kingdom, United States |
| 2 | Australia, Kazakhstan |
| 1 | Austria, Canada, Denmark, Russia |

WOMEN'S HISTORICAL RESULTS

# VÅRGÅRDA ROAD RACE

## RESULTS BY YEAR

| YEAR | 1ST | 2ND | 3RD |
|---|---|---|---|
| 2021 | Race cancelled | | |
| 2020 | Race cancelled | | |
| 2019 | M. Bastianelli | M. Vos | L. Wiebes |
| 2018 | M. Vos | K. Wild | L. Lepistö |
| 2017 | L. Lepistö | M. Vos | L. Kirchmann |
| 2016 | E. Fahlin | L. Lepistö | C. van den Broek-Blaak |
| 2015 | J. D'hoore | G. Bronzini | L. Brennauer |
| 2014 | C. van den Broek-Blaak | A. Pieters | R. Knetemann |
| 2013 | M. Vos | E. Johansson | A. Pieters |
| 2012 | I. Slappendel | H. Kupfernagel | M. Vos |
| 2011 | A. van Vleuten | E. van Dijk | N. Cooke |
| 2010 | K. Wild | A. Visser | E. Johansson |
| 2009 | M. Vos | K. Wild | E. Johansson |
| 2008 | K. Kelley Seehafer | K. Anderson | C. Becker |
| 2007 | C. Beltman | K. Thurig | N. Cantele |
| 2006 | S. Ljungskog | N. Cooke | M. Holler |

## RIDER RESULTS

| WINS | RIDER |
|---|---|
| 3 | M. Vos |

| PODIUMS | RIDER |
|---|---|
| 6 | M. Vos |
| 3 | E. Johansson, L. Lepistö, K. Wild |
| 2 | N. Cooke, A. Pieters, C. van den Broek-Blaak |

## COUNTRY RESULTS

| WINS | COUNTRY |
|---|---|
| 8 | Netherlands |
| 2 | Sweden |
| 1 | Belgium, Finland, United States |

| PODIUMS | COUNTRY |
|---|---|
| 20 | Netherlands |
| 6 | Sweden |
| 3 | Finland, Germany, Italy |
| 2 | United Kingdom, United States |
| 1 | Belgium, Canada, Switzerland |

WOMEN'S HISTORICAL RESULTS

# RONDE VAN DRENTHE

## RESULTS BY YEAR

| YEAR | 1ST | 2ND | 3RD |
|---|---|---|---|
| 2021 | L. Wiebes | E. Cecchini | E. Gasparrini |
| 2020 | Race cancelled | | |
| 2019 | M. Bastianelli | C. van den Broek-Blaak | E. van Dijk |
| 2018 | A. Pieters | A. Ryan | C. Hosking |
| 2017 | A. Dideriksen | E. Cecchini | L. Brand |
| 2016 | C. van den Broek-Blaak | G. Elvin | T. Worrack |
| 2015 | J. D'hoore | A. Pieters | E. van Dijk |
| 2014 | E. Deignan | A. van der Breggen | S. Olds |
| 2013 | M. Vos | E. van Dijk | E. Johansson |
| 2012 | M. Vos | K. Wild | E. Johansson |
| 2011 | M. Vos | K. Wild | G. Bronzini |
| 2010 | L. Gunnewijk | A. van Vleuten | G. Bronzini |
| 2009 | E. Johansson | L. Gunnewijk | C. van den Broek-Blaak |
| 2008 | C. Beltman | M. Vos | I. Y. Teutenberg |
| 2007 | A. Visser | E. Touffet | M. Vos |

## RIDER RESULTS

| WINS | RIDER |
|---|---|
| 3 | M. Vos |

| PODIUMS | RIDER |
|---|---|
| 5 | M. Vos |
| 3 | E. Johansson, C. van den Broek-Blaak, E. van Dijk |
| 2 | G. Bronzini, E. Cecchini, L. Gunnewijk, A. Pieters, K. Wild |

## COUNTRY RESULTS

| WINS | COUNTRY |
|---|---|
| 9 | Netherlands |
| 1 | Belgium, Denmark, Italy, Sweden, United Kingdom |

| PODIUMS | COUNTRY |
|---|---|
| 23 | Netherlands |
| 6 | Italy |
| 3 | Sweden |
| 2 | Australia, Germany, United States |
| 1 | Belgium, Denmark, France, United Kingdom |

WOMEN'S HISTORICAL RESULTS

# TOUR OF CHONGMING ISLAND

## RESULTS BY YEAR

| YEAR | 1ST | 2ND | 3RD |
|---|---|---|---|
| 2021 | Race cancelled | | |
| 2020 | Race cancelled | | |
| 2019 | L. Wiebes | J. Maneephan | L. Kopecky |
| 2018 | C. Becker | S. Malseed | A. Iakovenko |
| 2017 | J. D'hoore | K. Wild | C. Hosking |
| 2016 | C. Hosking | T. Y. Huang | L. Kirchmann |
| 2015 | K. Wild | R. Fournier | A. Cucinotta |
| 2014 | K. Wild | S. Olds | G. Bronzini |
| 2013 | A. Edmondson | C. Hosking | L. Garner |
| 2012 | M. Hoskins | M. Baccaille | L. De Vocht |
| 2011 | I. Y. Teutenberg | A. van Vleuten | M. Baccaille |
| 2010 | I. Y. Teutenberg | K. Wild | R. Gilmore |
| 2009 | C. Hosking | M. Johrend | N. Zhao |
| 2008 | M. Li | L. Meng | H. Sha |
| 2007 | M. Li | E. van Dijk | B. Goss |

## RIDER RESULTS

| WINS | RIDER |
|---|---|
| 2 | C. Hosking, M. Li, K. Wild, I. Y. Teutenberg |

| PODIUMS | RIDER |
|---|---|
| 4 | C. Hosking , K. Wild |
| 2 | M. Bacaille, M. Li, I. Y. Teutenberg |

## COUNTRY RESULTS

| WINS | COUNTRY |
|---|---|
| 4 | Australia |
| 3 | Germany, Netherlands |
| 2 | China |
| 1 | Belgium |

| PODIUMS | COUNTRY |
|---|---|
| 9 | Australia |
| 7 | Netherlands |
| 5 | China |
| 4 | Germany, Italy |
| 3 | Belgium |
| 1 | Canada, France, Russia, Taiwan, Thailand, United Kingdom, United States |

WOMEN'S HISTORICAL RESULTS

# GENT-WEVELGEM

## RESULTS BY YEAR

| YEAR | 1ST | 2ND | 3RD |
|---|---|---|---|
| 2021 | M. Vos | L. Kopecky | L. Brennauer |
| 2020 | J. D'hoore | L. Kopecky | L. Brennauer |
| 2019 | K. Wild | L. Wiebes | L. Paternoster |
| 2018 | M. Bastianelli | J. D'hoore | L. Klein |
| 2017 | L. Lepistö | J. D'hoore | C. Rivera |
| 2016 | C. van den Broek-Blaak | L. Brennauer | L. Brand |
| 2015 | F. Mackaij | J. Ensing | C. Hosking |
| 2014 | L. Hall | J. Ensing | V. Koedooder |
| 2013 | K. Wild | S. Van Paassen | K. Druyts |
| 2012 | E. Deignan | I. Slappendel | J. Daams |

## RIDER RESULTS

| WINS | RIDER |
|---|---|
| | No riders have won this race more than once. |

| PODIUMS | RIDER |
|---|---|
| 3 | L. Brennauer, J. D'hoore |
| 2 | J. Ensing, L. Kopecky |

## COUNTRY RESULTS

| WINS | COUNTRY |
|---|---|
| 5 | Netherlands |
| 1 | Belgium, Finland, Italy, United Kingdom, United States |

| PODIUMS | COUNTRY |
|---|---|
| 12 | Netherlands |
| 7 | Belgium |
| 4 | Germany |
| 2 | Italy, United Kingdom, United States |
| 1 | Australia, Finland |

WOMEN'S HISTORICAL RESULTS

# LA COURSE

## RESULTS BY YEAR

| YEAR | 1ST | 2ND | 3RD |
|---|---|---|---|
| 2021 | D. Vollering | C. U. Ludwig | M. Vos |
| 2020 | E. Deignan | M. Vos | D. Vollering |
| 2019 | M. Vos | L. Kirchmann | C. U. Ludwig |
| 2018 | A. van Vleuten | A. van der Breggen | A. Moolman-Pasio |
| 2017 | A. van Vleuten | E. Deignan | E. Longo Borghini |
| 2016 | C. Hosking | L. Lepistö | M. Vos |
| 2015 | A. van der Breggen | J. D'hoore | A. Pieters |
| 2014 | M. Vos | K. Wild | L. Kirchmann |

## RIDER RESULTS

| WINS | RIDER |
|---|---|
| 2 | A. van Vleuten, M. Vos |

| PODIUMS | RIDER |
|---|---|
| 5 | M. Vos |
| 2 | E. Deignan, L. Kirchmann, C. U. Ludwig, A. van der Breggen, A. van Vleuten, D. Vollering |

## COUNTRY RESULTS

| WINS | COUNTRY |
|---|---|
| 6 | Netherlands |
| 1 | Australia, United Kingdom |

| PODIUMS | COUNTRY |
|---|---|
| 13 | Netherlands |
| 2 | Canada, Denmark, United Kingdom |
| 1 | Australia, Belgium, Finland, Italy, South Africa |

# WOMEN'S HISTORICAL RESULTS

# LADIES TOUR OF NORWAY

## RESULTS BY YEAR

| YEAR | 1ST | 2ND | 3RD |
|---|---|---|---|
| 2021 | A. van Vleuten | A. Moolman-Pasio | K. Faulkner |
| 2020 | Race cancelled | | |
| 2019 | M. Vos | C. Rivera | L. Kirchmann |
| 2018 | M. Vos | E. Fahlin | C. Rivera |
| 2017 | M. Vos | M. Guarnier | E. van Dijk |
| 2016 | L. Brand | T. De Jong | A. Koster |
| 2015 | M. Guarnier | S. Olds | A. Spratt |
| 2014 | A. van der Breggen | M. Vos | K. Niewiadoma |

## RIDER RESULTS

| WINS | RIDER |
|---|---|
| 3 | M. Vos |

| PODIUMS | RIDER |
|---|---|
| 4 | M. Vos |
| 2 | M. Guarnier, C. Rivera |

## COUNTRY RESULTS

| WINS | COUNTRY |
|---|---|
| 6 | Netherlands |
| 1 | United States |

| PODIUMS | COUNTRY |
|---|---|
| 10 | Netherlands |
| 6 | United States |
| 1 | Australia, Canada, Poland, South Africa, Sweden |

WOMEN'S HISTORICAL RESULTS

# WOMEN'S TOUR

## RESULTS BY YEAR

| YEAR | 1ST | 2ND | 3RD |
|---|---|---|---|
| 2021 | D. Vollering | J. Labous | C. Copponi |
| 2020 | Race cancelled | | |
| 2019 | E. Deignan | K. Niewiadoma | A. Pieters |
| 2018 | C. Rivera | M. Vos | D. Rowe |
| 2017 | K. Niewiadoma | C. Majerus | H. Barnes |
| 2016 | E. Deignan | A. Moolman-Pasio | E. Longo Borghini |
| 2015 | L. Brennauer | J. D'hoore | C. Majerus |
| 2014 | M. Vos | E. Johansson | R. Ratto |

## RIDER RESULTS

| WINS | RIDER |
|---|---|
| 2 | E. Deignan |

| PODIUMS | RIDER |
|---|---|
| 2 | E. Deignan, C. Majerus, M. Vos |

## COUNTRY RESULTS

| WINS | COUNTRY |
|---|---|
| 2 | Netherlands, United Kingdom |
| 1 | Germany, Poland, United States |

| PODIUMS | COUNTRY |
|---|---|
| 4 | Netherlands, United Kingdom |
| 2 | France, Italy, Luxembourg, Poland |
| 1 | Belgium, Germany, South Africa, Sweden, United States |

# MADRID CHALLENGE

## RESULTS BY YEAR

| YEAR | 1ST | 2ND | 3RD |
|---|---|---|---|
| 2021 | A. van Vleuten | M. Reusser | E. Chabbey |
| 2020 | L. Brennauer | E. Longo Borghini | L. Wiebes |
| 2019 | L. Brennauer | L. Brand | P. Mathiesen |
| 2018 | E. van Dijk | C. Rivera | A. Cordon |
| 2017 | J. D'hoore | C. Rivera | R. Fournier |
| 2016 | J. D'hoore | C. Hosking | M. Bastianelli |
| 2015 | S. Olds | G. Bronzini | K. Wild |

## RIDER RESULTS

| WINS | RIDER |
|---|---|
| 2 | L. Brennauer, J. D'hoore |

| PODIUMS | RIDER |
|---|---|
| 2 | L. Brennauer, J. D'hoore, C. Rivera |

## COUNTRY RESULTS

| WINS | COUNTRY |
|---|---|
| 2 | Belgium, Germany, Netherlands |
| 1 | United States |

| PODIUMS | COUNTRY |
|---|---|
| 5 | Netherlands |
| 3 | Italy, United States |
| 2 | Belgium, France, Germany, Switzerland |
| 1 | Australia, Denmark |

WOMEN'S HISTORICAL RESULTS

# STRADE BIANCHE

## RESULTS BY YEAR

| YEAR | 1ST | 2ND | 3RD |
|---|---|---|---|
| 2021 | C. van den Broek-Blaak | E. Longo Borghini | A. van der Breggen |
| 2020 | A. van Vleuten | M. García | L. Thomas |
| 2019 | A. van Vleuten | A. Langvad | K. Niewiadoma |
| 2018 | A. van der Breggen | K. Niewiadoma | E. Longo Borghini |
| 2017 | E. Longo Borghini | K. Niewiadoma | E. Deignan |
| 2016 | E. Deignan | K. Niewiadoma | E. Johansson |
| 2015 | M. Guarnier | E. Deignan | E. Longo Borghini |

## RIDER RESULTS

| WINS | RIDER |
|---|---|
| 2 | A. van Vleuten |

| PODIUMS | RIDER |
|---|---|
| 4 | E. Longo Borghini, K. Niewiadoma |
| 3 | E. Deignan |
| 2 | A. van der Breggen, A. van Vleuten |

## COUNTRY RESULTS

| WINS | COUNTRY |
|---|---|
| 4 | Netherlands |
| 1 | Italy, United Kingdom, United States |

| PODIUMS | COUNTRY |
|---|---|
| 5 | Netherlands |
| 4 | Italy, Poland |
| 3 | United Kingdom |
| 2 | United States |
| 1 | Denmark, Spain, Sweden |

HISTORICAL RESULTS

WOMEN'S HISTORICAL RESULTS

# CADEL EVANS GREAT OCEAN ROAD RACE

## RESULTS BY YEAR

| YEAR | 1ST | 2ND | 3RD |
|---|---|---|---|
| 2021 | Race cancelled | | |
| 2020 | L. Lippert | A. Sierra | A. Spratt |
| 2019 | A. Sierra | L. Kennedy | A. Spratt |
| 2018 | C. Hosking | G. Elvin | G. Bronzini |
| 2017 | A. van Vleuten | R. Winder | M. Hagiwara |
| 2016 | A. Spratt | R. Neylan | D. Rowe |

## RIDER RESULTS

| WINS | RIDER |
|---|---|
| | No riders have won this race more than once. |

| PODIUMS | RIDER |
|---|---|
| 3 | A. Spratt |
| 2 | A. Sierra |

## COUNTRY RESULTS

| WINS | COUNTRY |
|---|---|
| 2 | Australia |
| 1 | Cuba, Germany, Netherlands |

| PODIUMS | COUNTRY |
|---|---|
| 7 | Australia |
| 2 | Cuba |
| 1 | Germany, Italy, Japan, Netherlands, United Kingdom, United States |

WOMEN'S HISTORICAL RESULTS

# RIDELONDON

## RESULTS BY YEAR

| YEAR | 1ST | 2ND | 3RD |
|---|---|---|---|
| 2021 | Race cancelled | | |
| 2020 | Race cancelled | | |
| 2019 | L. Wiebes | E. Balsamo | C. Rivera |
| 2018 | K. Wild | M. Vos | E. Balsamo |
| 2017 | C. Rivera | L. Lepistö | L. Brennauer |
| 2016 | K. Wild | N. Kessler | L. Kirchmann |

## RIDER RESULTS

| WINS | RIDER |
|---|---|
| 2 | K. Wild |

| PODIUMS | RIDER |
|---|---|
| 2 | E. Balsamo, K. Wild |

## COUNTRY RESULTS

| WINS | COUNTRY |
|---|---|
| 3 | Netherlands |
| 1 | United States |

| PODIUMS | COUNTRY |
|---|---|
| 5 | Netherlands |
| 2 | Italy, United States |
| 1 | Canada, Finland, Germany |

HISTORICAL RESULTS

WOMEN'S HISTORICAL RESULTS

# LIÈGE-BASTOGNE-LIÈGE

## RESULTS BY YEAR

| YEAR | 1ST | 2ND | 3RD |
|---|---|---|---|
| 2021 | D. Vollering | A. van Vleuten | E. Longo Borghini |
| 2020 | E. Deignan | G. Brown | E. van Dijk |
| 2019 | A. van Vleuten | F. Mackaij | D. Vollering |
| 2018 | A. van der Breggen | A. Spratt | A. van Vleuten |
| 2017 | A. van der Breggen | E. Deignan | K. Niewiadoma |

## RIDER RESULTS

| WINS | RIDER |
|---|---|
| 2 | A. van der Breggen |

| PODIUMS | RIDER |
|---|---|
| 3 | A. van Vleuten |
| 2 | E. Deignan, A. van der Breggen, D. Vollering |

## COUNTRY RESULTS

| WINS | COUNTRY |
|---|---|
| 4 | Netherlands |
| 1 | United Kingdom |

| PODIUMS | COUNTRY |
|---|---|
| 9 | Netherlands |
| 2 | Australia, United Kingdom |
| 1 | Italy, Poland |

WOMEN'S HISTORICAL RESULTS

# TOUR OF GUANGXI

## RESULTS BY YEAR

| YEAR | 1ST | 2ND | 3RD |
|---|---|---|---|
| 2021 | Race cancelled | | |
| 2020 | Race cancelled | | |
| 2019 | C. Hosking | A. Jackson | M. Vos |
| 2018 | A. Sierra | H. Barnes | S. Mustonen |
| 2017 | M. V. Sperotto | A. Cure | L. Van der Haar |

## RIDER RESULTS

| WINS | RIDER |
|---|---|
| | No riders have won this race more than once. |

| PODIUMS | RIDER |
|---|---|
| | No riders have finished on the podium of this race more than once. |

## COUNTRY RESULTS

| WINS | COUNTRY |
|---|---|
| 1 | Australia, Cuba, Italy |

| PODIUMS | COUNTRY |
|---|---|
| 2 | Australia, United Kingdom |

HISTORICAL RESULTS

WOMEN'S HISTORICAL RESULTS

# BRUGGE-DE PANNE

## RESULTS BY YEAR

| YEAR | 1ST | 2ND | 3RD |
|---|---|---|---|
| 2021 | G. Brown | E. Norsgaard | J. D'hoore |
| 2020 | L. Wiebes | L. Brennauer | L. Kopecky |
| 2019 | K. Wild | L. Wiebes | L. Kopecky |
| 2018 | J. D'hoore | C. Hosking | C. Majerus |

## RIDER RESULTS

| WINS | RIDER |
|---|---|
| | No riders have won this race more than once. |

| PODIUMS | RIDER |
|---|---|
| 2 | J. D'hoore, L. Kopecky, L. Wiebes |

## COUNTRY RESULTS

| WINS | COUNTRY |
|---|---|
| 2 | Netherlands |
| 1 | Australia, Belgium |

| PODIUMS | COUNTRY |
|---|---|
| 4 | Belgium |
| 3 | Netherlands |
| 2 | Australia |
| 1 | Denmark, Germany, Luxembourg, Ukraine |

# BRITISH DOMESTIC RACING

The British domestic racing calendar in 2020 was wiped clear. Both the flagship national tours for the men and women – the Tour of Britain and the Women's Tour – had been instantly cancelled, along with the teams-based criterium event, the Tour Series. The Tour de Yorkshire was also struck off (and would be cancelled again in 2021). And both the National Road and Circuit Series fell by the way. It was a wipe-out. For most of the domestic pros – with the exception of those fortunate enough to ride for teams that received occasional invitations to race overseas – there was no racing at all until, tentatively, it returned in 2021 with a heavily curtailed programme.

MEN'S NATIONAL CIRCUIT SERIES

# OTLEY GP
30 June 2021
Round 1

## WEATHER

TEMPERATURE: 13°C
WIND: NE 20km/h

## RESULTS

| POS | NAME | TEAM | TIME |
|---|---|---|---|
| 1. | M. Gibson | RWC | 59:16 |
| 2. | R. Scott | DHB | s.t. |
| 3. | J. Tarling | FLA | s.t. |
| 4. | S. Watson | TIN | s.t. |
| 5. | H. Tanfield | TQA | s.t. |
| 6. | B. Turner | TRI | s.t. |
| 7. | R. Wood | DHB | s.t. |
| 8. | M. Bostock | DHB | s.t. |
| 9. | R. Britton | TIN | s.t. |
| 10. | J. Brown | DHB | s.t. |
| 11. | F. Scheske | RWC | s.t. |
| 12. | T. Shoreman | RT23 | s.t. |
| 13. | J. Walker | CRM | s.t. |
| 14. | J. Price | SRT | s.t. |
| 15. | T. Couzens | SRT | s.t. |
| 16. | T. Mazzone | PIR | s.t. |
| 17. | S. Culverwell | TRI | s.t. |
| 18. | L. Mazzone | CRM | s.t. |
| 19. | O. Peckover | SCB | s.t. |
| 20. | S. McInnes | CCC | s.t. |

# ILKLEY
23 July 2021
Round 2

## WEATHER

TEMPERATURE: 18°C
WIND: E 13km/h

## RESULTS

| POS | NAME | TEAM | TIME |
|---|---|---|---|
| 1. | R. Wood | DHB | 59:52 |
| 2. | J. Scott | DHB | 0:06 |
| 3. | T. Mein | DHB | s.t. |
| 4. | A. Peters | SCB | s.t. |
| 5. | O. Peckover | SCB | 0:08 |
| 6. | R. Scott | DHB | s.t. |
| 7. | J. Walker | CRM | s.t. |
| 8. | M. Bostock | DHB | 0:12 |
| 9. | L. Mazzone | CRM | s.t. |
| 10. | O. Rees | TRI | s.t. |
| 11. | J. Brown | DHB | 0:19 |
| 12. | O. Roberts | WRA | +1 Lap |
| 13. | C. Jeffers | RWC | s.t. |
| 14. | J. Rootkin-Gray | TIN | s.t. |
| 15. | A. Slater | CBA | s.t. |
| 16. | M. Poole | FEN | s.t. |
| 17. | J. Tarling | FLA | s.t. |
| 18. | T. Barnes | CRM | s.t. |
| 19. | T. Couzens | SRT | s.t. |
| 20. | E. Beecher | CRM | s.t. |

MEN'S NATIONAL ROAD SERIES

# LANCASTER GP
15 August 2021
Lancaster–Lancaster
161km

## WEATHER

TEMPERATURE  WIND
17°C         W 19km/h

## RESULTS

| POS | NAME | TEAM | TIME |
|---|---|---|---|
| 1. | J. Whitehead | PBP | 4:02:49 |
| 2. | J. Scott | DHB | s.t. |
| 3. | F. Crockett | WCC | 0:04 |
| 4. | I. Peatfield | CRM | 0:07 |
| 5. | B. Granger | ZRT | 0:15 |
| 6. | R. Christensen | DHB | 0:23 |
| 7. | G. Kimber | SRT | 0:28 |
| 8. | S. Beckett | WRA | s.t. |
| 9. | L. Mazzone | CRM | 0:35 |
| 10. | D. Tulett | DHB | s.t. |
| 11. | O. Roberts | WRA | s.t. |
| 12. | J. Shaw | RWC | s.t. |
| 13. | A. Mitchell | CRM | s.t. |
| 14. | M. Dobbins | RT23 | s.t. |
| 15. | C. Biddle | VRE | s.t. |
| 16. | C. McGoldrick | PTJ | s.t. |
| 17. | S. Lampier | PIR | s.t. |
| 18. | O. Hucks | NOP | s.t. |
| 19. | P. Cocker | RTD | s.t. |
| 20. | M. King | PBP | s.t. |

BRITISH DOMESTIC RACING

MEN'S NATIONAL ROAD SERIES

# RYEDALE GP
22 August 2021
Ampleforth–Ampleforth
150.6km

## WEATHER

TEMPERATURE
19°C

WIND
W 17km/h

## RESULTS

| POS | NAME | TEAM | TIME |
|---|---|---|---|
| 1. | A. Peters | SCB | 3:47:30 |
| 2. | T. Barnes | CRM | s.t. |
| 3. | O. Rees | TRI | s.t. |
| 4. | I. Mundy | RTD | s.t. |
| 5. | M. Stedman | DHB | s.t. |
| 6. | C. Macleod | DHB | 0:14 |
| 7. | O. Peckover | SCB | 0:18 |
| 8. | I. Peatfield | CRM | 0:20 |
| 9. | J. Scott | DHB | 0:26 |
| 10. | F. Crockett | WCC | s.t. |
| 11. | M. Dobbins | RT23 | s.t. |
| 12. | S. Lampier | PIR | s.t. |
| 13. | R. Lamb | SCB | s.t. |
| 14. | O. Roberts | WRA | 0:29 |
| 15. | M. Chadwick | CBA | s.t. |
| 16. | L. Mazzone | CRM | s.t. |
| 17. | G. Kimber | SRT | 0:36 |
| 18. | S. Beckett | WRA | s.t. |
| 19. | R. Christensen | DHB | s.t. |
| 20. | D. Clayton | DHB | s.t. |

MEN'S NATIONAL ROAD SERIES

# BEAUMONT TROPHY

26 September 2021
Stamfordham–Stamfordham
182km

## WEATHER

**TEMPERATURE**
21°C

**WIND**
S 19km/h

## RESULTS

| POS | NAME | TEAM | TIME |
|---|---|---|---|
| 1. | J. Scott | DHB | 4:19:08 |
| 2. | A. Richardson | AFC | 0:02 |
| 3. | M. Gibson | RWC | 1:08 |
| 4. | R. Lamb | SCB | s.t. |
| 5. | M. King | PBP | s.t. |
| 6. | M. Stedman | DHB | s.t. |
| 7. | R. Scott | DHB | s.t. |
| 8. | Z. Kyffin | RWC | 1:16 |
| 9. | T. Mazzone | PIR | 1:51 |
| 10. | A. George | TIN | s.t. |
| 11. | G. Lewis | RWC | s.t. |
| 12. | J. Hill | USN | s.t. |
| 13. | I. Mundy | RTD | s.t. |
| 14. | A. Freeman | RTD | s.t. |
| 15. | J. Price | SRT | s.t. |
| 16. | S. Garry | NOP | s.t. |
| 17. | M. Dobbins | RT23 | s.t. |
| 18. | F. Crockett | WCC | s.t. |
| 19. | W. Bjergfelt | SCB | s.t. |
| 20. | I. Peatfield | CRM | s.t. |

BRITISH DOMESTIC RACING

MEN'S TOUR SERIES

# GUISBOROUGH
8 August 2021
Round 1
1 hour + 3 laps

## WEATHER

TEMPERATURE  
19°C

WIND  
SW 33km/h

## INDIVIDUAL RESULTS

| POS | NAME | TEAM | TIME |
|---|---|---|---|
| 1. | M. Gibson | RWC | 1:04:30 |
| 2. | J. Holt | WRA | 1:27 |
| 3. | L. Mazzone | CRM | 1:28 |
| 4. | I. Mundy | RTD | s.t. |
| 5. | C. Page | RWC | 1:29 |
| 6. | B. Quick | TRI | s.t. |
| 7. | O. Roberts | WRA | s.t. |
| 8. | A. Tennant | DHB | 1:30 |
| 9. | M. King | PBP | s.t. |
| 10. | R. Wood | DHB | s.t. |
| 11. | J. Walker | CRM | s.t. |
| 12. | C. Jeffers | RWC | s.t. |
| 13. | D. Barnes | TSW | s.t. |
| 14. | W. Roberts | WRA | s.t. |
| 15. | F. Crockett | NAT | 1:31 |
| 16. | P. Cocker | RTD | s.t. |
| 17. | L. Watson | TSW | s.t. |
| 18. | T. Mazzone | PIR | 1:32 |
| 19. | C. McGlinchey | TSW | s.t. |
| 20. | M. Dobbins | NAT | s.t. |

## TEAM RESULTS

| POS | NAME | TEAM | POINTS |
|---|---|---|---|
| 1. | Ribble Weldtite Pro Cycling | RWC | 13pts |
| 2. | Crimson Orientation Marketing RT | CRM | 12pts |
| 3. | Scotland | NAT | 11pts |
| 4. | Tekkerz | TEK | 10pts |
| 5. | Wales Racing Academy | WRA | 9pts |
| 6. | Canyon dhb SunGod | DHB | 8pts |
| 7. | Team Spectra Wiggle p/b Vitus | TSW | 7pts |
| 8. | Richardsons Trek DAS | RTD | 6pts |
| 9. | Spirit Bontrager BSS Rotor | SRT | 5pts |
| 10. | Trinity Racing | TRI | 4pts |
| 11. | Saint Piran | PIR | 3pts |
| 12. | Team PB Performance | PBP | 2pts |
| 13. | Bikestrong-KTM | BIK | 1pt |

MEN'S TOUR SERIES

# SUNDERLAND
10 August 2021
Round 2
1 hour + 3 laps

## WEATHER

| TEMPERATURE | WIND |
|---|---|
| 17°C | W 17km/h |

## INDIVIDUAL RESULTS

| POS | NAME | TEAM | TIME |
|---|---|---|---|
| 1. | W. Roberts | WRA | 1:06:16 |
| 2. | O. Rees | TRI | 0:01 |
| 3. | J. Holt | WRA | s.t. |
| 4. | C. Tanfield | DHB | s.t. |
| 5. | T. Barnes | CRM | 0:02 |
| 6. | M. Gibson | RWC | 0:03 |
| 7. | R. Christensen | DHB | 0:05 |
| 8. | C. Page | RWC | 0:13 |
| 9. | J. Brown | DHB | s.t. |
| 10. | A. Tennant | DHB | s.t. |
| 11. | C. McGlinchey | TSW | s.t. |
| 12. | L. Mazzone | CRM | 0:14 |
| 13. | F. Crockett | NAT | s.t. |
| 14. | J. Price | SRT | s.t. |
| 15. | M. King | PBP | 0:15 |
| 16. | S. Lampier | PIR | s.t. |
| 17. | A. Freeman | RTD | s.t. |
| 18. | R. Wood | DHB | s.t. |
| 19. | O. Roberts | WRA | 0:16 |
| 20. | S. Bradbury | PIR | s.t. |

## TEAM RESULTS

| POS | NAME | TEAM | POINTS |
|---|---|---|---|
| 1. | Canyon dhb SunGod | DHB | 13pts |
| 2. | Wales Racing Academy | WRA | 12pts |
| 3. | Ribble Weldtite Pro Cycling | RWC | 11pts |
| 4. | Crimson Orientation Marketing RT | CRM | 10pts |
| 5. | Saint Piran | PIR | 9pts |
| 6. | Spirit Bontrager BSS Rotor | SRT | 8pts |
| 7. | Team Spectra Wiggle p/b Vitus | TSW | 7pts |
| 8. | Tekkerz | TEK | 6pts |
| 9. | Trinity Racing | TRI | 5pts |
| 10. | Scotland | NAT | 4pts |
| 11. | Bikestrong-KTM | BIK | 3pts |
| 12. | Team PB Performance | PBP | 2pts |
| 13. | Richardsons Trek DAS | RTD | 1pt |

## TEAM STANDINGS

| POS | NAME | TEAM | POINTS |
|---|---|---|---|
| 1. | Ribble Weldtite Pro Cycling | RWC | 24pts |
| 2. | Crimson Orientation Marketing RT | CRM | 22pts |
| 3. | Canyon dhb SunGod | DHB | 21pts |
| 4. | Wales Racing Academy | WRA | 21pts |
| 5. | Tekkerz | TEK | 16pts |
| 6. | Scotland | NAT | 15pts |
| 7. | Team Spectra Wiggle p/b Vitus | TSW | 14pts |
| 8. | Spirit Bontrager BSS Rotor | SRT | 13pts |
| 9. | Saint Piran | PIR | 12pts |
| 10. | Trinity Racing | TRI | 9pts |
| 11. | Richardsons Trek DAS | RTD | 7pts |
| 12. | Bikestrong-KTM | BIK | 4pts |
| 13. | Team PB Performance | PBP | 4pts |

BRITISH DOMESTIC RACING

MEN'S TOUR SERIES

# CASTLE DOUGLAS
12 August 2021
Round 3
1 hour + 3 laps

## WEATHER

**TEMPERATURE**
17°C

**WIND**
S 22km/h

## INDIVIDUAL RESULTS

| POS | NAME | TEAM | TIME |
| --- | --- | --- | --- |
| 1. | C. Tanfield | DHB | 1:06:32 |
| 2. | A. Briggs | TEK | s.t. |
| 3. | J. Brown | DHB | 0:01 |
| 4. | L. Mazzone | CRM | s.t. |
| 5. | M. Gibson | RWC | 0:02 |
| 6. | O. Roberts | WRA | s.t. |
| 7. | I. Mundy | RTD | s.t. |
| 8. | B. Quick | TRI | s.t. |
| 9. | J. Holt | WRA | 0:04 |
| 10. | J. Scott | DHB | s.t. |
| 11. | F. Crockett | NAT | s.t. |
| 12. | J. Walker | CRM | 0:05 |
| 13. | R. Wood | DHB | s.t. |
| 14. | T. Barnes | CRM | s.t. |
| 15. | R. Christensen | DHB | 0:06 |
| 16. | J. Price | SRT | 0:13 |
| 17. | B. Symonds | PIR | 0:14 |
| 18. | C. Page | RWC | 0:37 |
| 19. | S. Wylie | TSR | s.t. |
| 20. | G. Kimber | SRT | 0:38 |

## TEAM RESULTS

| POS | NAME | TEAM | POINTS |
| --- | --- | --- | --- |
| 1. | Canyon dhb SunGod | DHB | 13pts |
| 2. | Wales Racing Academy | WRA | 12pts |
| 3. | Ribble Weldtite Pro Cycling | RWC | 11pts |
| 4. | Crimson Orientation Marketing RT | CRM | 10pts |
| 5. | Team Spectra Wiggle p/b Vitus | TSW | 9pts |
| 6. | Scotland | NAT | 8pts |
| 7. | Saint Piran | PIR | 7pts |
| 8. | Spirit Bontrager BSS Rotor | SRT | 6pts |
| 9. | Richardsons Trek DAS | RTD | 5pts |
| 10. | Tekkerz | TEK | 4pts |
| 11. | Bikestrong-KTM | BIK | 3pts |
| 12. | Team PB Performance | PBP | 2pts |
| 13. | Trinity Racing | TRI | 1pt |

## FINAL TEAM STANDINGS

| POS | NAME | TEAM | POINTS |
| --- | --- | --- | --- |
| 1. | Ribble Weldtite Pro Cycling | RWC | 35pts |
| 2. | Canyon dhb SunGod | DHB | 34pts |
| 3. | Wales Racing Academy | WRA | 33pts |
| 4. | Crimson Orientation Marketing RT | CRM | 32pts |
| 5. | Team Spectra Wiggle p/b Vitus | TSW | 23pts |
| 6. | Scotland | NAT | 23pts |
| 7. | Tekkerz | TEK | 20pts |
| 8. | Saint Piran | PIR | 19pts |
| 9. | Spirit Bontrager BSS Rotor | SRT | 19pts |
| 10. | Richardsons Trek DAS | RTD | 12pts |
| 11. | Trinity Racing | TRI | 10pts |
| 12. | Bikestrong-KTM | BIK | 7pts |
| 13. | Team PB Performance | PBP | 6pts |

WOMEN'S NATIONAL CIRCUIT SERIES

## OTLEY GP
30 June 2021
Round 1

## WEATHER

TEMPERATURE  
16°C

WIND  
NE 15km/h

### RESULTS

| POS | NAME | TEAM | TIME |
|---|---|---|---|
| 1. | E. King | TBR | 33:26 |
| 2. | A. Tacey | DRP | s.t. |
| 3. | J. Holl | TEK | s.t. |
| 4. | E. Barnwell | TBR | s.t. |
| 5. | C. Side | PNO | s.t. |
| 6. | A. Towers | DRP | s.t. |
| 7. | A. Mellor | TSR | s.t. |
| 8. | F. Morgans-Slader | UOM | s.t. |
| 9. | H. Bayes | AWO | s.t. |
| 10. | A. Smith | TBR | s.t. |
| 11. | J. Tindley | PNO | s.t. |
| 12. | E. McDermott | BOO | s.t. |
| 13. | L. Lee | LDN | s.t. |
| 14. | M. Barker | CAT | s.t. |
| 15. | F. Perkins | LON | s.t. |
| 16. | I. Pereira-James | ONF | s.t. |
| 17. | I. Darvill | BOO | s.t. |
| 18. | G. Lister | CCD | s.t. |
| 19. | Z. Backstedt | ACR | s.t. |
| 20. | L. Gadd | STR | s.t. |

## ILKLEY
23 July 2021
Round 2

## WEATHER

TEMPERATURE  
14°C

WIND  
W 20km/h

### RESULTS

| POS | NAME | TEAM | TIME |
|---|---|---|---|
| 1. | M. Barker | CAT | 49:19 |
| 2. | B. Morrow | STR | s.t. |
| 3. | I. Gardner | CAT | 0:03 |
| 4. | J. Finney | CAT | 0:32 |
| 5. | L. Ellmore | DSI | s.t. |
| 6. | E. King | TBR | 0:44 |
| 7. | J. Tindley | PNO | s.t. |
| 8. | I. Darvill | BOO | s.t. |
| 9. | A. Mellor | TSR | s.t. |
| 10. | A. Gornall | PNO | s.t. |
| 11. | R. Seal | TOR | s.t. |
| 12. | M. Couzens | PHM | s.t. |
| 13. | M. Leech | PHM | s.t. |
| 14. | C. Hayes | AWO | s.t. |
| 15. | X. Crees | TSR | s.t. |
| 16. | M. Wilkinson | CRM | 1:39 |
| 17. | S. Stuart | CRM | s.t. |
| 18. | N. Coates | TOR | s.t. |
| 19. | H. Dodd | LDN | 1:56 |
| 20. | F. Hall | LOU | 2:08 |

BRITISH DOMESTIC RACING

WOMEN'S NATIONAL ROAD SERIES

# WOMEN'S CICLE CLASSIC
27 June 2021
Melton Mowbray–Melton Mowbray
105km

## WEATHER

TEMPERATURE | WIND
16°C | NE 19km/h

## RESULTS

| POS | NAME | TEAM | TIME |
|---|---|---|---|
| 1. | A. Smith | TBR | 2:45:23 |
| 2. | E. McDermott | BOO | 2:19 |
| 3. | E. King | TBR | s.t. |
| 4. | A. Tacey | DRP | s.t. |
| 5. | N. Grinczer | CAT | s.t. |
| 6. | A. Mellor | TSR | s.t. |
| 7. | J. Tindley | PNO | s.t. |
| 8. | S. Thackray | IND | s.t. |
| 9. | J. Finney | CAT | s.t. |
| 10. | S. Stuart | CRM | s.t. |
| 11. | Z. Backstedt | ACR | s.t. |
| 12. | G. Lister | CCD | s.t. |
| 13. | F. Perkins | LON | s.t. |
| 14. | F. Hall | LOU | s.t. |
| 15. | L. Gadd | STR | s.t. |
| 16. | D. Shrosbree | LDN | s.t. |
| 17. | C. Side | PNO | s.t. |
| 18. | E. Bennett | DRP | s.t. |
| 19. | B. Morrow | STR | s.t. |
| 20. | S. Fawcett | PNO | s.t. |

WOMEN'S NATIONAL ROAD SERIES

# RYEDALE WOMEN'S GP
22 August 2021
Ampleforth–Ampleforth
94.1km

## WEATHER

TEMPERATURE
17°C

WIND
W 11km/h

## RESULTS

| POS | NAME | TEAM | TIME |
|---|---|---|---|
| 1. | I. Gardner | CAT | 2:44:37 |
| 2. | B. Storrie | ONF | 0:04 |
| 3. | C. Side | PNO | 2:12 |
| 4. | F. Morgans-Slader | AWO | s.t. |
| 5. | C. Hayes | AWO | s.t. |
| 6. | A. Kay | RUP | s.t. |
| 7. | L. Ellmore | DSI | 2:15 |
| 8. | D. Shrosbree | LDN | s.t. |
| 9. | N. Grinczer | CAT | s.t. |
| 10. | B. Morrow | STR | s.t. |
| 11. | N. Coates | TOR | 2:21 |
| 12. | M. Yeoman | TEA | 2:27 |
| 13. | J. Tindley | PNO | s.t. |
| 14. | M. Barker | CAT | 4:11 |
| 15. | E. Shaw | TEA | 4:33 |
| 16. | J. Finney | CAT | 4:35 |
| 17. | L. Gadd | STR | 4:36 |
| 18. | F. Hall | LOU | 4:38 |
| 19. | L. Lee | LDN | s.t. |
| 20. | C. Colc | BIA | s.t. |

WOMEN'S NATIONAL ROAD SERIES

# CURLEW CUP
26 September 2021
Stamfordham–Stamfordham
102km

## WEATHER

TEMPERATURE | WIND
17°C | SE 9km/h

## RESULTS

| POS | NAME | TEAM | TIME |
|---|---|---|---|
| 1. | A. Smith | TIB | 2:42:49 |
| 2. | C. Berry | PNO | s.t. |
| 3. | A. Tacey | DRP | s.t. |
| 4. | M. Greenwood | MAC | s.t. |
| 5. | M. Gammons | TJW | s.t. |
| 6. | E. Shaw | TEA | s.t. |
| 7. | C. Side | PNO | s.t. |
| 8. | H. Lancaster | LOU | s.t. |
| 9. | N. Grinczer | CAT | s.t. |
| 10. | F. Morgans-Slader | AWO | s.t. |
| 11. | L. Lee | LDN | s.t. |
| 12. | A. McWilliam | GRC | s.t. |
| 13. | S. Botteley | ONF | s.t. |
| 14. | L. Gadd | STR | s.t. |
| 15. | F. Hall | LOU | s.t. |
| 16. | I. Darvill | PNO | s.t. |
| 17. | G. Hughes | CRM | s.t. |
| 18. | S. Guerrini | WAT | s.t. |
| 19. | R. Galler | PIR | s.t. |
| 20. | S. Enever | LCW | s.t. |

WOMEN'S TOUR SERIES

# GUISBOROUGH
8 August 2021
Round 1
45 minutes + 3 laps

## WEATHER

TEMPERATURE  WIND
21°C          SW 24km/h

### INDIVIDUAL RESULTS

| POS | NAME | TEAM | TIME |
|---|---|---|---|
| 1. | E. King | NAT | 53:11 |
| 2. | J. Tindley | PNO | s.t. |
| 3. | E. McDermott | BOO | s.t. |
| 4. | A. Smith | NAT | 0:01 |
| 5. | H. Dodd | LDN | s.t. |
| 6. | S. Stuart | CRM | 0:04 |
| 7. | M. Barker | CAT | 0:48 |
| 8. | A. Sharpe | NAT | s.t. |
| 9. | S. Thackray | CAT | 0:49 |
| 10. | F. Morgans-Slader | AWO | s.t. |
| 11. | J. Finney | CAT | s.t. |
| 12. | I. Darvill | BOO | s.t. |
| 13. | L. Lee | LDN | s.t. |
| 14. | C. Side | PNO | s.t. |
| 15. | M. Gammons | TJW | s.t. |
| 16. | L. Ellmore | DSI | 0:50 |
| 17. | A. Gornall | PNO | s.t. |
| 18. | B. Morrow | DSI | s.t. |
| 19. | F. Hall | LOU | 0:51 |
| 20. | K. Scott | CAT | 0:52 |

### TEAM RESULTS

| POS | NAME | TEAM | POINTS |
|---|---|---|---|
| 1. | Great Britain Under-23 Track Team | NAT | 15pts |
| 2. | Pro-Noctis-Redchilli Bikes-Heidi Kjeldsen | PNO | 14pts |
| 3. | Team Boompods | BOO | 13pts |
| 4. | CAMS-Basso | CAT | 12pts |
| 5. | Skoda DSI Cycling Academy | DSI | 11pts |
| 6. | Team LDN-Brother UK | LDN | 10pts |
| 7. | Team Spectra Wiggle p/b Vitus | TSW | 9pts |
| 8. | Jadan-Vive le Velo | TJW | 8pts |
| 9. | Crimson Orientation Marketing RT | CRM | 7pts |
| 10. | Loughborough Lightning-TRG | LOU | 6pts |
| 11. | Awol OShea | AWO | 5pts |
| 12. | Torelli Assure Cayman Islands Scimitar | TOR | 4pts |
| 13. | Brother UK Cycle Team OnForm | ONF | 3pts |
| 14. | Saint Piran | PIR | 2pts |
| 15. | Datalynx Parenesis RT | DPC | 1pt |

WOMEN'S TOUR SERIES

# SUNDERLAND
10 August 2021
Round 2
45 minutes + 3 laps

## WEATHER

**TEMPERATURE**
19°C

**WIND**
W 15km/h

## INDIVIDUAL RESULTS

| POS | NAME | TEAM | TIME |
|---|---|---|---|
| 1. | M. Barker | CAT | 50:17 |
| 2. | J. Tindley | PNO | s.t. |
| 3. | S. Stuart | CRM | 0:01 |
| 4. | J. Finney | CAT | s.t. |
| 5. | E. McDermott | BOO | s.t. |
| 6. | I. Perraira | ONF | s.t. |
| 7. | C. Side | PNO | s.t. |
| 8. | I. Darvill | BOO | s.t. |
| 9. | L. Ellmore | DSI | 0:02 |
| 10. | B. Seal | TOR | s.t. |
| 11. | M. Gammons | TJW | s.t. |
| 12. | B. Morrow | DSI | 0:03 |
| 13. | H. Dodd | LDN | s.t. |
| 14. | E. Edwards | CAT | s.t. |
| 15. | B. Harley-Jepson | TJW | 0:04 |
| 16. | B. Storrie | ONF | s.t. |
| 17. | B. Dew | PIR | s.t. |
| 18. | A. Mellor | TSW | s.t. |
| 19. | X. Crees | TSW | 0:05 |
| 20. | A. Gornall | PNO | s.t. |

## TEAM RESULTS

| POS | NAME | TEAM | POINTS |
|---|---|---|---|
| 1. | CAMS-Basso | CAT | 15pts |
| 2. | Pro-Noctis-Redchilli Bikes-Heidi Kjeldsen | PNO | 14pts |
| 3. | Skoda DSI Cycling Academy | DSI | 13pts |
| 4. | Brother UK Cycle Team OnForm | ONF | 12pts |
| 5. | Jadan-Vive le Velo | TJW | 11pts |
| 6. | Team LDN-Brother UK | LDN | 10pts |
| 7. | Team Boompods | BOO | 9pts |
| 8. | Torelli Assure Cayman Islands Scimitar | TOR | 8pts |
| 9. | Crimson Orientation Marketing RT | CRM | 7pts |
| 10. | Team Spectra Wiggle p/b Vitus | TSW | 6pts |
| 11. | Awol OShea | AWO | 5pts |
| 12. | Saint Piran | PIR | 4pts |
| 13. | Loughborough Lightning-TRG | LOU | 3pts |
| 14. | Datalynx Parenesis RT | DPC | 2pts |

## TEAM STANDINGS

| POS | NAME | TEAM | POINTS |
|---|---|---|---|
| 1. | Pro-Noctis-Redchilli Bikes-Heidi Kjeldsen | PNO | 28pts |
| 2. | CAMS-Basso | CAT | 27pts |
| 3. | Skoda DSI Cycling Academy | DSI | 24pts |
| 4. | Team Boompods | BOO | 22pts |
| 5. | Team LDN-Brother UK | LDN | 20pts |
| 6. | Jadan-Vive le Velo | TJW | 19pts |
| 7. | Great Britain Under-23 Track Team | NAT | 15pts |
| 8. | Brother UK Cycle Team OnForm | ONF | 14pts |
| 9. | Crimson Orientation Marketing RT | CRM | 14pts |
| 10. | Team Spectra Wiggle p/b Vitus | TSW | 14pts |
| 11. | Torelli Assure Cayman Islands Scimitar | TOR | 11pts |
| 12. | Awol OShea | AWO | 11pts |
| 13. | Loughborough Lightning-TRG | LOU | 9pts |
| 14. | Saint Piran | PIR | 8pts |
| 15. | Datalynx Parenesis RT | DPC | 3pts |

WOMEN'S TOUR SERIES

# CASTLE DOUGLAS
12 August 2021
Round 3
45 minutes + 3 laps

## WEATHER

| TEMPERATURE | WIND |
|---|---|
| 17°C | S 22km/h |

## INDIVIDUAL RESULTS

| POS | NAME | TEAM | TIME |
|---|---|---|---|
| 1. | M. Barker | CAT | 50:14 |
| 2. | J. Tindley | PNO | s.t. |
| 3. | J. Finney | CAT | 0:01 |
| 4. | F. Morgans-Slader | AWO | 0:02 |
| 5. | S. Stuart | CRM | 0:04 |
| 6. | A. Gornall | PNO | 0:05 |
| 7. | I. Darvill | BOO | 0:06 |
| 8. | C. Side | PNO | s.t. |
| 9. | L. Ellmore | DSI | 0:07 |
| 10. | A. Mellor | TSW | 0:08 |
| 11. | S. Fawcett | PNO | s.t. |
| 12. | S. Thackray | CAT | s.t. |
| 13. | B. Seal | TOR | 0:09 |
| 14. | B. Harley-Jepson | TJW | 0:10 |
| 15. | H. Dodd | LDN | s.t. |
| 16. | C. Berry | PNO | 0:11 |
| 17. | B. Dew | PIR | 0:12 |
| 18. | X. Crees | TSW | s.t. |
| 19. | A. Baker | LOU | 0:14 |
| 20. | B. Storrie | ONF | 0:15 |

## TEAM RESULTS

| POS | NAME | TEAM | POINTS |
|---|---|---|---|
| 1. | CAMS-Basso | CAT | 15pts |
| 2. | Pro-Noctis-Redchilli Bikes-Heidi Kjeldsen | PNO | 14pts |
| 3. | Team Spectra Wiggle p/b Vitus | TSW | 13pts |
| 4. | Team LDN-Brother UK | LDN | 12pts |
| 5. | Jadan-Vive le Velo | TJW | 11pts |
| 6. | Loughborough Lightning-TRG | LOU | 10pts |
| 7. | Brother UK Cycle Team OnForm | ONF | 9pts |
| 8. | Team Boompods | BOO | 8pts |
| 9. | Awol OShea | AWO | 7pts |
| 10. | Crimson Orientation Marketing RT | CRM | 6pts |
| 11. | Torelli Assure Cayman Islands Scimitar | TOR | 5pts |
| 12. | Saint Piran | PIR | 4pts |
| 13. | Skoda DSI Cycling Academy | DSI | 3pts |
| 14. | Datalynx Parenesis RT | DPC | 2pts |

## FINAL TEAM STANDINGS

| POS | NAME | TEAM | POINTS |
|---|---|---|---|
| 1. | CAMS-Basso | CAT | 42pts |
| 2. | Pro-Noctis-Redchilli Bikes-Heidi Kjeldsen | PNO | 42pts |
| 3. | Team LDN-Brother UK | LDN | 32pts |
| 4. | Jadan-Vive le Velo | TJW | 30pts |
| 5. | Team Boompods | BOO | 30pts |
| 6. | Team Spectra Wiggle p/b Vitus | TSW | 27pts |
| 7. | Skoda DSI Cycling Academy | DSI | 27pts |
| 8. | Brother UK Cycle Team OnForm | ONF | 23pts |
| 9. | Crimson Orientation Marketing RT | CRM | 20pts |
| 10. | Loughborough Lightning-TRG | LOU | 19pts |
| 11. | Awol OShea | AWO | 18pts |
| 12. | Torelli Assure Cayman Islands Scimitar | TOR | 16pts |
| 13. | Great Britain Under-23 Track Team | NAT | 15pts |
| 14. | Saint Piran | PIR | 12pts |
| 15. | Datalynx Parenesis RT | DPC | 5pts |

BRITISH DOMESTIC RACING

# CYCLOCROSS WORLD CUP LOCATIONS

We've grown used to being inundated with graphs and data over the past couple of years, and a map featuring a cluster in Belgium usually signifies bad news. This time, however, it is good news, as it shows where the 2021 Cyclocross World Cup rounds took place – or at least where all 11 were supposed to take place. The pandemic ruled out ventures to French Besançon and Swiss Villars, although thankfully an eastwards journey to Tabor in the Czech Republic survived. It makes sense that Belgium hosts the lion's share of events, with their culture and history of the sport, and courses lined with fans drinking beers and eating frites. But with the rivalry between Mathieu van der Poel and Wout van Aert, as well as Tom Pidcock vying to join them at the top table, the winter discipline seems to be getting more international and blossoming with every passing year.

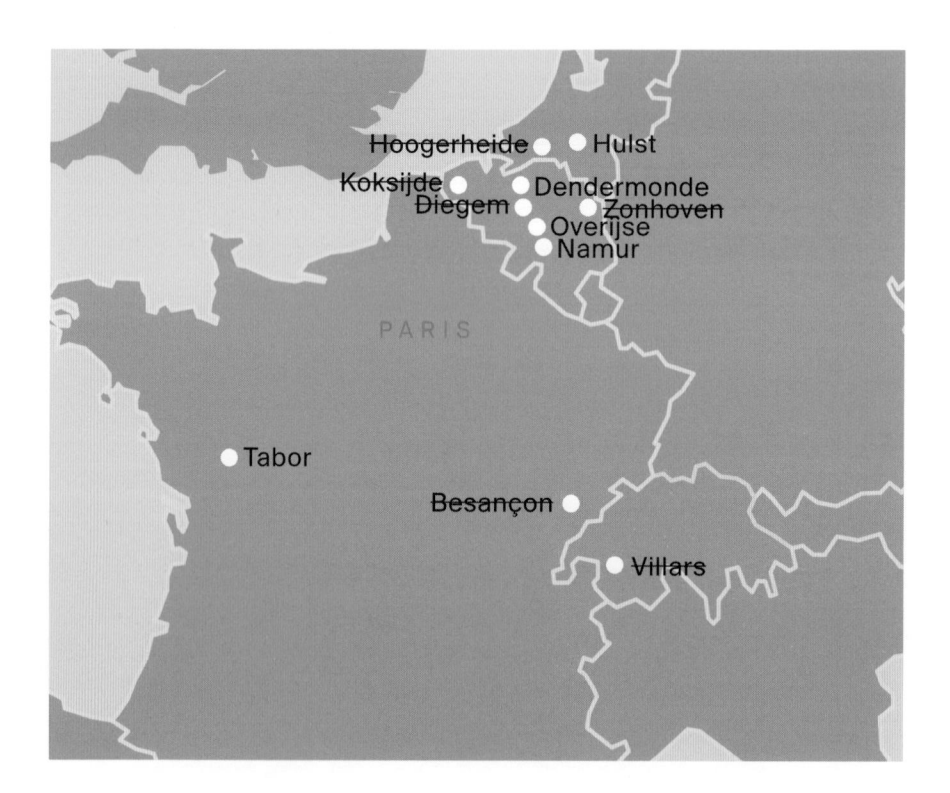

# CYCLOCROSS

Organised cyclocross originated in France in 1902, when the first national championships were held. Very quickly its popularity spread across continental Europe and took seed in North America. Always valued by the earliest of road racers for the training it facilitates in the winter months, to this day cyclocross continues to flourish largely unchanged from its origins. The races are short – normally no more than an hour, and sometimes less – but they are explosive, and every race features a different set of impossible-seeming obstacles, many of which will force the rider to run with their bike. Mud is a prerequisite. The undisputed heartland of cyclocross in modern times is Belgium, which hosts numerous races and whose top stars are handsomely rewarded. Recently, top cyclocross riders like Wout van Aert, Mathieu van der Poel and Tom Pidcock have started to redefine the nature of conventional road racing as they switch between the codes.

CYCLOCROSS WORLD CUP

## 1: TABOR, CZECH REPUBLIC
29 November 2020

### MEN'S RESULTS

| POS | NAME | TEAM | TIME |
|---|---|---|---|
| 1. | M. Vanthourenhout | BEL | 1:02:43 |
| 2. | E. Iserbyt | BEL | 0:05 |
| 3. | W. van Aert | BEL | 0:12 |
| 4. | T. Aerts | BEL | 0:18 |
| 5. | L. van der Haar | NED | 0:21 |
| 6. | C. van Kessel | NED | 0:51 |
| 7. | Q. Hermans | BEL | 1:01 |
| 8. | D. Soete | BEL | 1:05 |
| 9. | K. Kuhn | SUI | 1:27 |
| 10. | D. Sweeck | BEL | 1:42 |

### WOMEN'S RESULTS

| POS | NAME | TEAM | TIME |
|---|---|---|---|
| 1. | L. Brand | NED | 53:43 |
| 2. | C. D. C. Alvarado | NED | 0:24 |
| 3. | D. Betsema | NED | 0:32 |
| 4. | B. K. Vas | HUN | s.t. |
| 5. | A. Worst | NED | 0:50 |
| 6. | P. Pieterse | NED | 1:22 |
| 7. | L. Verdonschot | BEL | 1:31 |
| 8. | A. M. Arzuffi | ITA | s.t. |
| 9. | A. Kay | GBR | 1:45 |
| 10. | Y. Kastelijn | NED | 1:53 |

## 2: NAMUR, BELGIUM
20 December 2020

### MEN'S RESULTS

| POS | NAME | TEAM | TIME |
|---|---|---|---|
| 1. | M. van der Poel | NED | 1:03:59 |
| 2. | W. van Aert | BEL | 0:03 |
| 3. | T. Pidcock | GBR | 0:11 |
| 4. | M. Vanthourenhout | BEL | 1:07 |
| 5. | Q. Hermans | BEL | 2:09 |
| 6. | L. van der Haar | NED | 2:17 |
| 7. | T. Aerts | BEL | 2:53 |
| 8. | D. Soete | BEL | 2:57 |
| 9. | C. van Kessel | NED | 3:25 |
| 10. | R. Kamp | NED | 3:31 |

### WOMEN'S RESULTS

| POS | NAME | TEAM | TIME |
|---|---|---|---|
| 1. | L. Brand | NED | 52:47 |
| 2. | C. Honsinger | USA | 0:29 |
| 3. | D. Betsema | NED | 0:38 |
| 4. | C. D. C. Alvarado | NED | 1:21 |
| 5. | B. K. Vas | HUN | 1:38 |
| 6. | E. Richards | GBR | 1:45 |
| 7. | A. Kay | GBR | 2:14 |
| 8. | A. van Alphen | NED | 2:26 |
| 9. | P. Clauzel | FRA | 2:33 |
| 10. | E. Lechner | ITA | 2:42 |

CYCLOCROSS WORLD CUP

## 3: DENDERMONDE, BELGIUM
27 December 2020

### MEN'S RESULTS

| POS | NAME | TEAM | TIME |
|---|---|---|---|
| 1. | W. van Aert | BEL | 1:06:10 |
| 2. | M. van der Poel | NED | 2:49 |
| 3. | T. Aerts | BEL | 3:06 |
| 4. | M. Vanthourenhout | BEL | 3:42 |
| 5. | L. Sweeck | BEL | 3:58 |
| 6. | C. van Kessel | NED | 4:14 |
| 7. | Q. Hermans | BEL | 4:22 |
| 8. | P. Ronhaar | NED | 4:29 |
| 9. | T. Aerts | BEL | 4:49 |
| 10. | G. Vermeersch | BEL | 5:04 |

### WOMEN'S RESULTS

| POS | NAME | TEAM | TIME |
|---|---|---|---|
| 1. | L. Brand | NED | 45:27 |
| 2. | C. Honsinger | USA | 0:15 |
| 3. | C. D. C. Alvarado | NED | 0:24 |
| 4. | F. van Empel | NED | 0:40 |
| 5. | A. Worst | NED | 0:45 |
| 6. | S. Cant | BEL | 0:48 |
| 7. | B. K. Vas | HUN | 0:54 |
| 8. | D Betsema | NED | 1:22 |
| 9. | M. Bakker | NED | 1:35 |
| 10. | Y. Kastelijn | NED | 2:13 |

## 4: HULST, NETHERLANDS
3 January 2021

### MEN'S RESULTS

| POS | NAME | TEAM | TIME |
|---|---|---|---|
| 1. | M. van der Poel | NED | 1:05:27 |
| 2. | W. van Aert | NED | 1:31 |
| 3. | T. Pidcock | GBR | 1:49 |
| 4. | M. Vanthourenhout | BEL | 2:41 |
| 5. | T. Aerts | BEL | 3:07 |
| 6. | L. van der Haar | NED | 3:19 |
| 7. | Q. Hermans | BEL | 3:32 |
| 8. | L. Sweeck | BEL | 3:37 |
| 9. | R. Kamp | NED | 4:12 |
| 10. | C. van Kessel | NED | 4:46 |

### WOMEN'S RESULTS

| POS | NAME | TEAM | TIME |
|---|---|---|---|
| 1. | D. Betsema | NED | 53:06 |
| 2. | L. Brand | NED | 1:02 |
| 3. | C. D. C. Alvarado | NED | 1:09 |
| 4. | A. Worst | NED | 1:26 |
| 5. | B. K. Vas | HUN | 1:57 |
| 6. | C. Honsinger | USA | 2:10 |
| 7. | P. Pieterse | NED | 2:22 |
| 8. | S. Cant | BEL | 2:23 |
| 9. | M. Bakker | NED | 2:41 |
| 10. | F. van Empel | NED | 2:50 |

CYCLOCROSS WORLD CUP

## 5: OVERIJSE, BELGIUM
24 January 2021

### MEN'S RESULTS

| POS | NAME | TEAM | TIME |
|---|---|---|---|
| 1. | W. van Aert | BEL | 1:05:57 |
| 2. | M. van der Poel | NED | 1:03 |
| 3. | T. Pidcock | GBR | 2:07 |
| 4. | M. Vanthourenhout | BEL | 2:24 |
| 5. | T. Aerts | BEL | 2:49 |
| 6. | L. van der Haar | NED | 3:26 |
| 7. | L. Sweeck | BEL | 3:35 |
| 8. | C. van Kessel | NED | 3:41 |
| 9. | Q. Hermans | BEL | 3:57 |
| 10. | G. Vermeersch | BEL | 4:12 |

### WOMEN'S RESULTS

| POS | NAME | TEAM | TIME |
|---|---|---|---|
| 1. | C. D. C. Alvarado | NED | 49:48 |
| 2. | L. Brand | NED | 0:20 |
| 3. | M. Bakker | NED | 0:21 |
| 4. | C. Honsinger | USA | 0:34 |
| 5. | D. Betsema | NED | 0:40 |
| 6. | S. Cant | BEL | 0:48 |
| 7. | A. Kay | GBR | 0:56 |
| 8. | E. Richards | GBR | 0:58 |
| 9. | B. K. Vas | HUN | 1:15 |
| 10. | M. Vos | NED | 1:21 |

## FINAL CYCLOCROSS WORLD CUP STANDINGS

### MEN'S RESULTS

| POS | NAME | TEAM | POINTS |
|---|---|---|---|
| 1. | W. van Aert | BEL | 165 |
| 2. | M. van der Poel | NED | 140 |
| 3. | M. Vanthourenhout | BEL | 128 |
| 4. | T. Aerts | BEL | 108 |
| 5. | Q. Hermans | BEL | 95 |
| 6. | C. Van Kessel | NED | 91 |
| 7. | T. Pidcock | GBR | 84 |
| 8. | L. Van der Haar | NED | 81 |
| 9. | L. Sweeck | BEL | 77 |
| 10. | K. Kuhn | SUI | 63 |

### WOMEN'S RESULTS

| POS | NAME | TEAM | POINTS |
|---|---|---|---|
| 1. | L. Brand | NED | 180 |
| 2. | C. D. C. Alvarado | NED | 142 |
| 3. | D. Betsema | NED | 129 |
| 4. | C. Honsinger | USA | 102 |
| 5. | B. K. Vas | HUN | 100 |
| 6. | S. Cant | BEL | 86 |
| 7. | A Worst | NED | 79 |
| 8. | M. Bakker | NED | 71 |
| 9. | P. Pieterse | NED | 66 |
| 10. | A. Kay | GBR | 63 |

# CYCLOCROSS WORLD CUP WINNING MARGINS

From the end of 2020 to the early months of 2021, life continued to be disrupted by the coronavirus pandemic. What this meant for those in northern Europe with a penchant for racing bikes through muddy fields was that six of the planned 11 UCI World Cup rounds were cancelled. When things kicked off in Tabor in the Czech Republic, Lucinda Brand showed the form that would see her dominate the season's World Cups, while the men's race featured a rarity in that the top two spaces weren't occupied by Van der Poel and Van Aert. Maybe lacking the impetus provided by his Dutch rival, who was missing from the start line, Van Aert came third. In Namur it was business as usual, though, with Van der Poel edging out Van Aert by just 3 seconds – the smallest winning margin this season – while Brand took the second of three consecutive wins. In East Flanders, Van Aert exacted his revenge with the biggest winning margin of the season: 2 minutes 49 seconds. Brand would eventually get bested in the final two rounds, first by Denise Betsema and then Ceylin del Carmen Alvarado. Van der Poel and Van Aert continued to share the spoils, yet a certain Tom Pidcock was snapping at their heels, recording three third places.

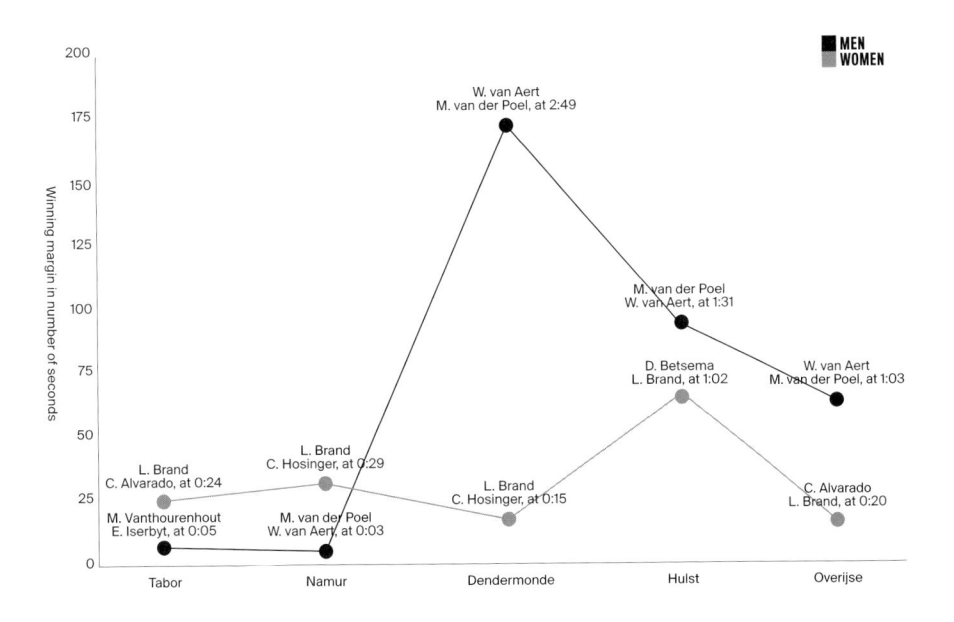

# CYCLOCROSS WORLD CHAMPIONSHIPS

## MEN'S RESULTS

| POS | NAME | TEAM | TIME |
|---|---|---|---|
| 1. | M. van der Poel | NED | 58:57 |
| 2. | W. van Aert | BEL | 0:37 |
| 3. | T. Aerts | BEL | 1:24 |
| 4. | T. Pidcock | GBR | 1:37 |
| 5. | L. Sweeck | BEL | 2:05 |
| 6. | M. Vanthourenhout | BEL | 2:14 |
| 7. | E. Iserbyt | BEL | 2:18 |
| 8. | Q. Hermans | BEL | 2:23 |
| 9. | L. van der Haar | NED | 2:41 |
| 10. | J. Nieuwenhuis | NED | 3:15 |

## WOMEN'S RESULTS

| POS | NAME | TEAM | TIME |
|---|---|---|---|
| 1. | L. Brand | NED | 46:53 |
| 2. | A. Worst | NED | 0:08 |
| 3. | D. Betsema | NED | 0:19 |
| 4. | C. Honsinger | USA | 0:52 |
| 5. | Y. Kastelijn | NED | 1:04 |
| 6. | C. D. C. Alvarado | NED | 1:12 |
| 7. | E. Richards | GBR | 1:13 |
| 8. | S. Cant | BEL | 1:43 |
| 9. | E. Brandau | GER | 2:07 |
| 10. | C. Majerus | LUX | 2:08 |

HISTORICAL CYCLOCROSS WORLD CHAMPIONSHIPS RESULTS

## MEN'S HISTORICAL WORLD CHAMPIONSHIPS RESULTS

| YEAR | GOLD | SILVER | BRONZE |
|---|---|---|---|
| 1950 | Jean Robic (FRA) | Roger Rondeaux (FRA) | Pierre Jodet (FRA) |
| 1951 | Roger Rondeaux (FRA) | André Dufraisse (FRA) | Pierre Jodet (FRA) |
| 1952 | Roger Rondeaux (FRA) | André Dufraisse (FRA) | Albert Meier (SUI) |
| 1953 | Roger Rondeaux (FRA) | Gilbert Bauvin (FRA) | André Dufraisse (FRA) |
| 1954 | André Dufraisse (FRA) | Pierre Jodet (FRA) | Hans Bieri (SUI) |
| 1955 | André Dufraisse (FRA) | Hans Bieri (SUI) | Amerigo Severini (ITA) |
| 1956 | André Dufraisse (FRA) | Georges Meunier (FRA) | Emile Plattner (SUI) |
| 1957 | André Dufraisse (FRA) | Firmin Van Kerrebroek (BEL) | Georges Meunier (FRA) |
| 1958 | André Dufraisse (FRA) | Amerigo Severini (ITA) | Rolf Wolfshohl (GER) |
| 1959 | Renato Longo (ITA) | Rolf Wolfshohl (GER) | Amerigo Severini (ITA) |
| 1960 | Rolf Wolfshohl (GER) | Arnold Hungerbuhler (SUI) | Robert Aubry (FRA) |
| 1961 | Rolf Wolfshohl (GER) | Renato Longo (ITA) | André Dufraisse (FRA) |
| 1962 | Renato Longo (ITA) | Maurice Gandolfo (FRA) | André Dufraisse (FRA) |
| 1963 | Rolf Wolfshohl (GER) | Renato Longo (USA) | André Dufraisse (FRA) |
| 1964 | Renato Longo (ITA) | Roger De Clercq (BEL) | Joseph Mahe (FRA) |
| 1965 | Renato Longo (ITA) | Rolf Wolfshohl (GER) | Amerigo Severini (ITA) |
| 1966 | Eric De Vlaeminck (BEL) | Herman Gretener (SUI) | Rolf Wolfshohl (GER) |
| 1967 | Renato Longo (ITA) | Rolf Wolfshohl (GER) | Herman Gretener (SUI) |
| 1968 | Eric De Vlaeminck (BEL) | Herman Gretener (SUI) | Michel Pelchat (FRA) |
| 1969 | Eric De Vlaeminck (BEL) | Rolf Wolfshohl (GER) | Renato Longo (ITA) |
| 1970 | Eric De Vlaeminck (BEL) | Albert Van Damme (BEL) | Rolf Wolfshohl (GER) |
| 1971 | Eric De Vlaeminck (BEL) | Albert Van Damme (BEL) | René De Clercq (BEL) |
| 1972 | Eric De Vlaeminck (BEL) | Rolf Wolfshohl (GER) | Herman Gretener (SUI) |
| 1973 | Eric De Vlaeminck (BEL) | André Wilhelm (FRA) | Rolf Wolfshohl (GER) |
| 1974 | Albert Van Damme (BEL) | Roger De Vlaeminck (BEL) | Peter Frischknecht (SUI) |
| 1975 | Roger De Vlaeminck (BEL) | Albert Zweifel (SUI) | Peter Frischknecht (SUI) |
| 1976 | Albert Zweifel (SUI) | Peter Frischknecht (SUI) | André Wilhelm (FRA) |
| 1977 | Albert Zweifel (SUI) | Peter Frischknecht (SUI) | Eric De Vlaeminck (BEL) |
| 1978 | Albert Zweifel (SUI) | Peter Frischknecht (SUI) | Klaus-Peter Thaler (GER) |
| 1979 | Albert Zweifel (SUI) | Gilles Blaser (SUI) | Robert Vermeire (BEL) |
| 1980 | Roland Liboton (BEL) | Klaus-Peter Thaler (GER) | Hennie Stamsnijder (NED) |
| 1981 | Hennie Stamsnijder (NED) | Roland Liboton (BEL) | Albert Zweifel (SUI) |
| 1982 | Roland Liboton (BEL) | Albert Zweifel (SUI) | Hennie Stamsnijder (NED) |
| 1983 | Roland Liboton (BEL) | Albert Zweifel (SUI) | Klaus-Peter Thaler (GER) |
| 1984 | Roland Liboton (BEL) | Hennie Stamsnijder (NED) | Albert Zweifel (SUI) |
| 1985 | Klaus-Peter Thaler (GER) | Adri van der Poel (NED) | Claude Michely (LUX) |
| 1986 | Albert Zweifel (SUI) | Pascal Richard (SUI) | Hennie Stamsnijder (NED) |
| 1987 | Klaus-Peter Thaler (GER) | Danny De Bie (BEL) | Christophe Lavainne (FRA) |
| 1988 | Pascal Richard (SUI) | Adri van der Poel (NED) | Beat Breu (SUI) |
| 1989 | Danny De Bie (BEL) | Adri van der Poel (NED) | Christophe Lavainne (FRA) |
| 1990 | Henk Baars (NED) | Adri van der Poel (NED) | Bruno Lebras (FRA) |
| 1991 | Radomír Šimůnek (CZE) | Adri van der Poel (NED) | Bruno Lebras (FRA) |
| 1992 | Mike Kluge (GER) | Karel Camrda (CZE) | Adri van der Poel (NED) |
| 1993 | Dominique Arnould (FRA) | Mike Kluge (GER) | Wim De Vos (NED) |
| 1994 | Paul Herygers (BEL) | Richard Groenendaal (NED) | Erwin Vervecken (BEL) |
| 1995 | Dieter Runkel (SUI) | Richard Groenendaal (NED) | Beat Wabel (SUI) |
| 1996 | Adri van der Poel (NED) | Daniele Pontoni (ITA) | Luca Bramati (ITA) |
| 1997 | Daniele Pontoni (ITA) | Thomas Frischknecht (SUI) | Luca Bramati (ITA) |
| 1998 | Mario De Clercq (BEL) | Erwin Vervecken (BEL) | Henrik Djernis (DEN) |
| 1999 | Mario De Clercq (BEL) | Erwin Vervecken (BEL) | Adri van der Poel (NED) |
| 2000 | Richard Groenendaal (NED) | Mario De Clercq (BEL) | Sven Nys (BEL) |
| 2001 | Erwin Vervecken (BEL) | Petr Dlask (CZE) | Mario De Clercq (BEL) |
| 2002 | Mario De Clercq (BEL) | Tom Vannoppen (BEL) | Sven Nys (BEL) |
| 2003 | Bart Wellens (BEL) | Mario De Clercq (BEL) | Erwin Vervecken (BEL) |
| 2004 | Bart Wellens (BEL) | Mario De Clercq (BEL) | Sven Vanthourenhout (BEL) |
| 2005 | Sven Nys (BEL) | Erwin Vervecken (BEL) | Sven Vanthourenhout (BEL) |
| 2006 | Erwin Vervecken (BEL) | Bart Wellens (BEL) | Francis Mourey (FRA) |
| 2007 | Erwin Vervecken (BEL) | Jonathan Page (USA) | Enrico Franzoi (ITA) |
| 2008 | Lars Boom (NED) | Zdeněk Štybar (CZE) | Sven Nys (BEL) |
| 2009 | Niels Albert (BEL) | Zdeněk Štybar (CZE) | Sven Nys (BEL) |
| 2010 | Zdeněk Štybar (CZE) | Klaas Vantornout (BEL) | Sven Nys (BEL) |
| 2011 | Zdeněk Štybar (CZE) | Sven Nys (BEL) | Kevin Pauwels (BEL) |
| 2012 | Niels Albert (BEL) | Rob Peeters (BEL) | Kevin Pauwels (BEL) |
| 2013 | Sven Nys (BEL) | Klaas Vantornout (BEL) | Lars van der Haar (NED) |
| 2014 | Zdeněk Štybar (CZE) | Sven Nys (BEL) | Kevin Pauwels (BEL) |
| 2015 | Mathieu van der Poel (NED) | Wout van Aert (BEL) | Lars van der Haar (NED) |
| 2016 | Wout van Aert (BEL) | Lars van der Haar (NED) | Kevin Pauwels (BEL) |
| 2017 | Wout van Aert (BEL) | Mathieu van der Poel (NED) | Kevin Pauwels (BEL) |
| 2018 | Wout van Aert (BEL) | Michael Vanthourenhout (BEL) | Mathieu van der Poel (NED) |
| 2019 | Mathieu van der Poel (NED) | Wout van Aert (BEL) | Toon Aerts (BEL) |
| 2020 | Mathieu van der Poel (NED) | Tom Pidcock (GBR) | Toon Aerts (BEL) |
| 2021 | Mathieu van der Poel (NED) | Wout van Aert (BEL) | Toon Aerts (BEL) |

# WOMEN'S HISTORICAL WORLD CHAMPIONSHIPS RESULTS

| YEAR | GOLD | SILVER | BRONZE |
|---|---|---|---|
| 2000 | Hanka Kupfernagel (GER) | Louise Robinson (GBR) | Daphny van den Brand (NED) |
| 2001 | Hanka Kupfernagel (GER) | Corine Dorland (NED) | Daphny van den Brand (NED) |
| 2002 | Laurence Leboucher (FRA) | Hanka Kupfernagel (GER) | Daphny van den Brand (NED) |
| 2003 | Daphny van den Brand (NED) | Hanka Kupfernagel (GER) | Laurence Leboucher (FRA) |
| 2004 | Laurence Leboucher (FRA) | Maryline Salvetat (FRA) | Hanka Kupfernagel (GER) |
| 2005 | Hanka Kupfernagel (GER) | Sabine Spitz (GER) | Mirjam Melchers (NED) |
| 2006 | Marianne Vos (NED) | Hanka Kupfernagel (GER) | Daphny van den Brand (NED) |
| 2007 | Maryline Salvetat (FRA) | Katie Compton (USA) | Laurence Leboucher (FRA) |
| 2008 | Hanka Kupfernagel (GER) | Marianne Vos (NED) | Laurence Leboucher (FRA) |
| 2009 | Marianne Vos (NED) | Hanka Kupfernagel (GER) | Katie Compton (USA) |
| 2010 | Marianne Vos (NED) | Hanka Kupfernagel (GER) | Daphny van den Brand (NED) |
| 2011 | Marianne Vos (NED) | Katie Compton (USA) | Kateřina Nash (CZE) |
| 2012 | Marianne Vos (NED) | Daphny Van Den Brand (NED) | Sanne Cant (BEL) |
| 2013 | Marianne Vos (NED) | Katie Compton (USA) | Lucie Chainel-Lefèvre (FRA) |
| 2014 | Marianne Vos (NED) | Eva Lechner (ITA) | Helen Wyman (GBR) |
| 2015 | Pauline Ferrand-Prévot (FRA) | Sanne Cant (BEL) | Marianne Vos (NED) |
| 2016 | Thalita de Jong (NED) | Caroline Mani (FRA) | Sanne Cant (BEL) |
| 2017 | Sanne Cant (BEL) | Marianne Vos (NED) | Kateřina Nash (CZE) |
| 2018 | Sanne Cant (BEL) | Katie Compton (USA) | Lucinda Brand (NED) |
| 2019 | Sanne Cant (BEL) | Lucinda Brand (NED) | Marianne Vos (NED) |
| 2020 | Ceylin del Carmen Alvarado (NED) | Annemarie Worst (NED) | Lucinda Brand (NED) |
| 2021 | Lucinda Brand (NED) | Annemarie Worst (NED) | Denise Betsema (NED) |

# IN THE CROSS FIRE

BY TOM PIDCOCK

Cyclocross started off for me as a bit of fun, really. I was already on the British Cycling Junior Academy, concentrating on track and road, and I was just doing cross as a little bit of something extra. So there was no pressure. I was only doing it for fun.

The first cross race I did abroad was the European Championships. I went away with the GB team on the boat overnight. It was like going away on a school trip almost. It was a sandy course and I only had mud tyres, so I wasn't very well equipped for it. But I started from the back of the grid and ended up finishing eighth.

Everybody told me, 'Bloody hell! That's amazing!' But all I'd done was finish eighth.

'What do you mean?' I asked them.

'Well, no British rider's ever really done that before.'

So I thought, 'OK. That's cool.' And that was it.

In 2016 I went to my first World Championships in Zolder as a first-year junior. I had a really strong race even though I had started from the back, but I'd thought to myself that I could definitely come back the following year and win it.

Back then I only knew who Sven Nys was. I had no idea who Mathieu van der Poel or Wout van Aert were. Wout actually won the elite race that year. There were around 60,000 people there – 100,000 in total over the two days. I remember climbing to the very top of a caged walkway and I was the only one up there to watch the finish. I took a video on my phone, but it couldn't cope with the noise and couldn't pick it up. It was just too loud at the finish for my phone. It was insane to see how the Belgians responded to a Belgian winning.

Going into the Junior World Championships in 2017, I was the favourite. I had only lost one race that season. It was the biggest goal I'd ever had, even right up until now. I don't think I could ever be that targeted again. I even wore a face mask on the plane on the way over so that I wouldn't get ill. I was that ahead of the times.

I don't think I was nervous. I remember eating breakfast in the morning and thinking that it didn't feel like it could actually be the Worlds that day. And then when we got to the course, it rained in between our practice and the race, and the ground was like sheet ice.

They had gritted the start/finish line but not the first corner, which was gravel. There were frozen puddles there and I knew there'd definitely be a crash there. So we started the race. I stuck to the inside line and just made sure I got around that corner, and behind me there was a massive pile-up.

After that, a French guy got away and took the lead. But after the second lap, I took the lead and got to work consolidating it and growing it and not making any mistakes. Then I heard on the tannoy that it was a British 1-2-3 and Ben Turner and Dan Tulett were fighting each other for second and third. I couldn't believe it. I think they both crashed about five times each on the final lap. I was simply making sure I stayed upright. Then I finished, and then Dan and Ben, and we were all on the podium.

We had all ridden with black armbands. Charlie Craig had died two weeks before. Charlie had been one of the big talents of the youth scene and was for sure going to be a good rider. He'd died in his sleep. He just went to sleep and didn't wake up. Cycling's a small world; everyone knows everyone. To be honest, I couldn't stop crying.

After every goal I achieve, the main feeling is simply relief that it's finished. That's what I always feel. When I stepped up to the elite, it took a while to adjust my mentality, having been used to so much winning. I had to learn to fight for places that I would not normally care about. I think that's an important lesson for the whole of the rest of my career in the World Tour on the road and with the elites in cross – you're not always going to win. You have to try and fight for all the other places as well. But as time's gone on, I've got stronger. So now I can race to win or at least to be on the podium.

The first part of this season, I was right there even though I was 17th in my first World Cup race. But once I got going, it was good.

The day before the Superprestige at Gavere, I had got on the podium for the first time in the season and I went home knowing that I'd be good the next day. I knew it. I could imagine the start and smashing it from the first lap, which is how I used to race as a junior. That's how I won a Tour Series race in Durham and how I won junior Paris–Roubaix. I could sense that I was going to win, which sounds weird, but I'd imagine what I was going to do and then I'd do it. It was the same in Gavere. I needed to start well, go straight to the front and then smash it. It's a risky strategy, but I always go better when I'm in the front riding my own race rather than trying to follow.

As the race went on, Mathieu van der Poel and Toon Aerts came across and I sat behind them a bit. Then I gradually got a gap, and Mathieu kept making mistakes. I actually assumed he'd punctured or something and that he'd get back to me, but then it became clear that he hadn't and that I'd actually just gapped him. I wouldn't say Mathieu was pleased to lose to me exactly, but his rivalry is much more with Wout van Aert, so he congratulated me. That was my first proper win. The first win that really mattered, I guess.

I don't know Mathieu van der Poel and Wout van Aert that well. I've played Fortnite with Mathieu a few times. I quite like chatting to Wout when I see him after the podium. Me and Mathieu talk about cars sometimes. He is not happy unless he wins, whereas Wout measures it. He knows the days when he can go full, and he often wins on those days, apart from at the Worlds this year. They're both strong and explosive. Cross makes you fast. Strong and fast. That shows on the road with them and the way they are. Wout can climb better, as he showed at the Tour, but they can both win sprints and do well in the Classics. That's what they're about. I'm similar. I may not be as strong or as good at sprinting, but I have the same characteristics from cross as they do. I'm getting better at climbing in road races. Climbing and sprinting really.

The worse the weather, the better I am. Take, for example, Namur in 2020. It was the coldest I have ever been, for sure. When I got back to the camper van, I sat under every towel I could find, my whole body shivering uncontrollably until I could actually stand up to get in the shower. And that was after only an hour in the rain. I'd snapped my seat post off on the last lap, so I lost a podium place. But I think that might have been a blessing in disguise because I think I might have died of hypothermia otherwise.

In Namur they basically sent us riding down stairs. They put sandbags down, but they didn't make much difference. Everyone was freezing cold. I was so cold I could barely hold my bars and then we had to go down these stairs, round a corner and then drop onto some cobbles where there was a puddle so deep you didn't even know where the bottom of it was. It was massive and full of sloppy sand. Every lap I'd go around and try to brace myself for where I thought the bottom of this puddle was, but I never once got it right and I always had to put my foot down or just get off.

When you make mistakes, cross has a way of making you look like a numpty. You trip over going up the stairs or catch a handlebar on the fence or you just slide out, slipping around in the mud. You can look quite ridiculous sometimes, even the best riders in the world. Like in the warm-up for Overijse this year, on the first lap. It was a new course that I didn't really know all that well. There was a downhill section into an uphill that you have to run because you can't ride it. I jumped off my bike, slipped straight on my arse and slid straight towards a cameraman. As I got up, I said, 'Did you get that?' He said, 'Of course!' I think the mistakes make it more engaging for the fans. It resonates more; the mistakes make the riders seem more human.

If you're even on just a slightly bad day, you can tell. It makes such a difference to the whole flow of your race, to the whole lot. You lose so much more time and ground from the start than you would in a road race if you felt bad. You start flat out – you sprint into the first corner – so immediately if you're on a bad day there's no time to find your feet like there is in a road race. You're immediately on the back foot.

There is no way on earth anyone could possibly replicate a cross race in training. Even if you tried to simulate it, straight from the start and then going into a sustained effort, you could not come close to what you do in a cross race. But in the race you don't really feel how it hurts. The faster you go, the more your adrenaline flows and the better it feels. That's how I see it. When you are going well, and you can put laps or sections together and nail it perfectly, that's a pretty good feeling. It can be intense. I got more and more involved in it because I was good at it, and it's become my job now.

I could win the World Cup, but who remembers who wins the World Cup? I need to be the world champion. There's nothing else.

# OBITUARIES

The emotion on open display at this year's Tour de France was a particular hallmark of the 2021 edition of the race. It is hard to know why this year should have led so many riders to dedicating wins to recently deceased relatives, and with such feeling. Perhaps the pandemic has heightened vulnerabilities and made us all cherish our families that bit more. But the stunning victory on stage 2 of the Tour by Mathieu van der Poel, which earned him the yellow jersey that had eluded his grandfather Raymond Poulidor, reminded us all of the passage of time and the sudden absence of those we thought might never leave us. This year, as is always the case, many men and women whose contributions to the sport have been worthy of committing to memory have died. These pages are a record that their lives will not easily be forgotten.

# KAMIEL BUYSSE

8 JULY 1934 – 26 OCTOBER 2020

Kamiel Buysse, a professional for seven seasons and grandfather of 2016 Olympic road race champion Greg Van Avermaet, died in Sint-Niklaas at the age of 86.

Born in Zele in East Flanders, just to the east of Ghent, Buysse won the Tour of Yugoslavia in 1956 while racing as an amateur. He stepped up to the pro ranks in the middle of 1958 when he joined the Peugeot-BP team, winning at Putte that season.

The following year was arguably his best. He won a stage at the Tour of Belgium, finishing third overall, took second place at the Ronde van Limburg and lined up for the Belgian national team at the Tour de France. Powerfully built, he was a solid domestique working for team leaders Jan Adriaensens, Jos Hoevenaers and Jean Brankart, who all finished in the top ten in a race won by Federico Bahamontes. Buysse was 61st in Paris.

In 1960, he joined the Wiel's-Flandria managed by Belgian Classics legend Briek Schotte and led by Joseph Planckaert, winning a handful of smaller races in Belgium and taking sixth place in the Tour of Belgium. In 1962 he raced alongside another Belgian king of the Classics, Rik Van Steenbergen, on the Solo-Van Steenbergen team. After two seasons with the Libertas team, he retired from racing at the end of 1964.

His daughter, Bernadette, became one of the country's leading middle-distance runners, winning world military titles in 1980 and 1981. She later married Belgian pro Ronald Van Avermaet, who had represented Belgium at the 1980 Olympics in Moscow.

# MICHEL BRUX

24 DECEMBER 1940 – 31 OCTOBER 2020

French sprinter Michel Brux, who spent three seasons with the Mercier BP team in the mid-1960s and outsprinted world champion Eddy Merckx in 1967 to claim his most renowned victory, died in his home town of Tarbes at the age of 79.

A good sprinter, he won 93 races during his career, mostly in the amateur ranks. Regional champion in 1959, he gained selection for the French team that went to the World Amateur Road Championship in 1962, where he finished 32nd. The following week, once again representing the French amateur team that also featured future Tour de France winner Lucien Aimar, he won a stage of the Tour of Luxembourg.

He took on independent status two years later, racing in Mercier BP colours and claiming 16 victories that season, many against leading professionals. He took out a full professional licence the following season, staying with Mercier BP. However, the team manager Antonin Magne rarely selected him and he only competed in half as many races as the previous year, winning just once, at Saint-Céré, and taking third place in the Bordeaux–Saintes one-day race.

This experience led to him returning to the independent ranks in 1966, although still racing for Mercier BP. It led to a considerable change in his fortunes as he took 15 victories. His most famous success came in 1967, his final season as an independent at the Grand Prix de la Soierie in Charlieu. With 30km remaining, he broke away with young world champion Eddy Merckx and another rider. Merckx tried to ride them off his wheel, but the pair hung on and it was Brux who narrowly won the final sprint.

Following his racing career, he worked for a print company until his retirement. He was survived by his wife and three children.

# JEAN-PIERRE LOTH

12 DECEMBER 1950 – 10 NOVEMBER 2020

Former professional and race organiser Jean-Pierre Loth died of cancer in his home city of Paris at the age of 69.

After racing for the famous ACBB team in Paris, he stepped into the professional ranks in 1976 with Lejeune-BP – a team that featured Ferdinand Bracke, Roger Legeay and Mariano Martinez. He stayed with Lejeune-BP the following season when defending Tour de France champion Lucien Van Impe joined the squad.

Described by *L'Équipe* as 'affable and elegant', Loth went into the hospitality business, establishing a restaurant in Versailles that was popular with actors and other artists appearing at local venues. He also established a professional race, Les Boucles Parisiennes, which he organised between 1987 and 1990, Belgian sprinter Etienne De Wilde winning the first edition and French climber Thierry Claveyrolat the last.

# LOUIS ROSTOLLAN

1 JANUARY 1936 – 13 NOVEMBER 2020

Winner of the Critérium du Dauphiné Libéré, twice the champion at the Tour de Romandie and an eight-time participant in the Tour de France, Louis Rostollan died in the Château-Gombert area of Marseille (where he was born) at the age of 84 as a result of lung cancer.

Rostollan said he never really raced as an amateur. At the end of his teenage years and in his early twenties, he combined work as a bricklayer and builder with his passion for bike racing, competing as an independent in events close to Marseille. In an interview with Vélo101.com in 2016, he revealed that his mother allowed him to focus on his racing as long as he could provide her with 50 francs a week for his keep. Within weeks he was winning races in Provence. In 1957, racing as an independent for the Liberia team, he finished second at the Tour du Sud-Est and sixth at the Dauphiné.

Tall and slim and nicknamed 'Pétrolette' after one of France's first motorbikes, Rostollan was a strong climber, as he showed in winning the Dauphiné in 1958. His victory led to an offer of a professional contract from Liberia that would have earned him 20,000 francs a month. He signed it, but Essor-Leroux team manager Mickey Wiegant insisted he could get him a better deal and offered him twice the money as well as compensation to Liberia. The following season, Wiegant brought the Helyett and Leroux teams together, the result of which was a super squad that featured Jacques Anquetil, André Darrigade, Jo de Roo, Shay Elliott, Jean Stablinski and the upcoming Rostollan.

The Marseillais made his Tour debut in 1959, racing for the Midi-Centre team led by French champion Henri Anglade, who finished second overall behind Federico Bahamontes. Rostollan was 59th. The following season he won Romandie for the first time, was second in the French road championship and was selected for the national team at the Tour, where Roger Rivière was designated as leader.

On the morning of the stage to Avignon that would pass through the Cévennes mountains, the French team's mechanic joined the riders for breakfast. 'There were thirteen of us at the table,' Rostollan told Vélo101.com. 'Our soigneur was really upset about it but because we were young we didn't think anything of the issue. We all laughed at him. Unfortunately, fate intervened and Roger Rivière crashed that day on the descent of the Perjuret. I was the last to see him fall into the void because I was on the bend above him.' Rivière broke his back and never raced again.

After defending his Romandie title in 1961, Rostollan was again selected for the French team for the Tour, where his trade team leader Anquetil was their main hope. The Frenchman cruised to his second yellow-jersey victory and reclaimed the title in the next three seasons, Rostollan at his side throughout. Rostollan also helped in Anquetil's successful quests to win the Giro d'Italia in 1960 and 1964. In the latter, he's best remembered for helping Anquetil fight his way back up to the bunch climbing out of Andorra over the mighty Envalira after his team leader had overindulged at a rest-day barbecue.

He spent the 1965 season with Anquetil at Ford France-Gitane, then rode for two seasons à *la musette* for the Kamomé team, earning no monthly wage and depending on prize money earned by himself and his teammates. He hung up his wheels in 1968, returning to Marseille to work as a builder for the city council. His son Mark was an amateur racer, while his grandson Thomas spent several seasons as a pro, firstly with the La Pomme team in Marseille and latterly with the Armée de Terre team.

# EDDIE BORYSEWICZ

18 MARCH 1939 – 16 NOVEMBER 2020

Edward 'Eddie B' Borysewicz, the Polish cycling coach who oversaw the USA's gold rush at 1984 Los Angeles Olympics and later worked with the likes of Greg LeMond, Andy Hampsten and Lance Armstrong, died in hospital in Drezdenko, Poland, after contracting Covid-19. He was 81.

Born in Kisielewszczyźnie, in what was then eastern Poland but subsequently became part of Belarus, Borysewicz quickly showed talent as an athlete, his father training him to become a national-standard 400-metre runner. His parents moved to the city of Łódź, where he started riding a bike and got invited to join a local cycling club after catching and dropping several of their riders who were training. He progressed through the junior ranks, becoming part of the national track and road team set-up, winning several national titles, notably in the pursuit. However, having been misdiagnosed with tuberculosis and prescribed with medicine that damaged his liver, he began to focus on coaching and became a full-time coach with the Polish national team when he turned 30.

He worked with numerous national and world champions, and travelled to the 1976 Montreal Olympics with the Polish team. Following the Games he travelled to the US to see friends, and a chance meeting in a New Jersey bike shop with a highly placed member of the US Cycling Federation, Mike Fraysse, led to him being appointed their first full-time coach. He set up in an office at the US Olympic training centre at Squaw Valley in California. He dropped a lot of the established riders from the programme and brought in younger riders, establishing a new ethos based on team rather than individual performance. It was here that he gained the nickname 'Eddie B', as the athletes working with him struggled to pronounce his surname.

LeMond was among the junior riders who emerged within the US set-up, and produced one of the most significant early results under Borysewicz when he won the junior world road title in Argentina in 1979. 'He was great, he laid the groundwork for American cycling,' LeMond told Rowery.org in 2020. 'He made these American cyclists believe in themselves, believe that they can go to Europe and race against Europeans. For many years in the US, we believed that the pros, the Russians, the Germans from the East, were good, and we were somewhere at the back. The riders were intimidated … maybe I wasn't, but many were. He gave us a lot of confidence to go to Europe.'

The US boycott of the 1980 Moscow Olympics prevented LeMond and the USA's other cyclists from participating in the Games. Four years later, however, when the Olympics took place in Los Angeles, the fruits of Borysewicz's methods were apparent to the world when the USA claimed four gold, three silver and one bronze medal – their first in the cycling events since 1912. The US team won both the men's and women's road race titles thanks to Alexi Grewal and Connie Carpenter, respectively, while on the track Steve Hegg won the pursuit crown and Mark Gorski took gold in the sprint.

These successes were tainted by the subsequent revelation that seven of the riders on the US team – including medallists Hegg, Rebecca Twigg, Pat McDonough and Leonard Nitz – had undergone 'blood doping', receiving transfusions to boost their red blood cell count. The other athletes on the team had refused to take part in their practice, which wasn't at that point banned by the IOC, although they discouraged its use. Although Borysewicz denied his involvement, he was fined a month's pay the following year.

'As far as I knew, no one on my team had taken anything that was illegal,' Borysewicz said in a 2017 interview with PezCyclingNews.com. 'The year after my greatest triumph was my most difficult. I looked for every advantage for my riders and we were very successful. More than I expected, too! … Three of the four gold medal winners did not use blood boosting, so that was not the reason they won.'

In 1985, Borysewicz wrote *Bicycle Road Racing: Complete Programme for Training and Competition*, a book that became a seminal text. It not only offered insight into training methods, but also focused on bike fit, nutrition, training and tactics.

In 1987, Borysewicz resigned from his role with the US cycling set-up and established a road team. Initially sponsored first by Sunkyong, it became best known as Subaru-Montgomery, backing coming from financial investor Thom Weisel. Lance Armstrong was among the team's early recruits, winning the Canadian Tour of Gastown race in their colours in 1991. The team's line-up later included Britons Rob Holden and Chris Walker (1992), French brothers Marc and Yvon Madiot (1993) and, under the Montgomery-Bell title in 1995, Tyler Hamilton. US Postal came in as the main sponsor the following season, when Andy Hampsten was signed as leader in his last season. In 1997, Borysewicz stepped down and began to coach riders at lower levels from his home in San Diego.

After his house was burned down in wildfires during 2003, his friends helped to raise $120,000 to rebuild it. Greg LeMond was among those who contributed by holding a fundraising cycling camp for his former training mentor. He also presented the Polish coach with the 'Father of Modern American Cycling' award at the Endurance Sports Awards in San Diego, an event that was attended by many members of the 1984 Olympic cycling team.

In his later years, Borysewicz split his time between his homes in California and Poland. He was survived by his wife, Sophie, and his children, Julia and Edward.

# EMMANUEL CRENN

30 JULY 1932 – 18 NOVEMBER 2020

Winner of the Grand Prix de Plouay in 1959 and as many as 150 races during his amateur career, Emmanuel 'Manu' Crenn died at the age of 87 in Plougastel-Daoulas in his home region of Brittany.

Born in Guipavas, he first stood out in the amateur ranks, finishing second in a stage of the 12-day Route de France. He turned pro the following season with the Rochet-Dunlop and stayed with them for the following five years, essentially racing a programme centred on events in Brittany, and also participating in cyclocross events during the winter with considerable success. Winner of two stages of the Circuit of the Ardennes in 1961, he finished third overall in the same event in 1962.

His racing achievements would likely have been much more extensive if his career hadn't been interrupted by two spells in the French army. He was initially called up to do his compulsory military service, then recalled during the French army's campaign in Algeria.

# ROLAND FANGILLE

29 APRIL 1939 – 18 NOVEMBER 2020

Roland Fangille – the founder and organiser for 50 years of the French season-opening Étoile de Bessèges stage race that takes place in the department of Gard in southern France – died in hospital in Alès after contracting Covid-19. He was 81.

Born in the Moselle region in France's north-east, he moved to Gard in the 1960s to establish a wood and carpentry business. A good amateur racer and for two years in the mid-1960s an independent professional, he became president of the local cycling club, the Union Cycliste Bességeoise. In 1971, he organised the first edition of the Étoile de Bessèges, choosing a February date in order to attract the professionals who began the season racing and training in the south of France.

Just two dozen riders signed on for the inaugural edition of what was initially known as the Gran Prix de Bessèges, most of them seasoned performers such as Barry Hoban, who placed third, Cyrille Guimard and Jean-Luc Molinéris, the first winner. The most significant participant, though, was Raymond Poulidor, with whom Fangille established a lifelong friendship. He always insisted that Poulidor was the race's saviour. 'There were only about 20 riders on the start line, but Raymond had promised me he would be there and it was down to his presence that the race made a big impact in the media. I don't know if the race would have survived without him,' Fangille told *L'Équipe* prior to the 50th edition of the race in 2020.

The fortunes of Fangille's race fluctuated considerably over those five decades. Its status and popularity grew steadily as it was expanded to five consecutive one-day races and renamed the Étoile in 1974, when Guimard and Joop Zoetemelk were among the winners. Five years on, it switched from being a one-day series where the 'overall' prize was decided on points to becoming a stage race that was sometimes three days long, but usually four, and almost always attracted a strong field.

The relatively flat stages and shortness of the time trial made it a particular favourite among sprinters. Etienne De Wilde, Jan Svorada, Jean-Paul van Poppel, Robbie McEwen and Joseph Planckaert, all won the overall title, the latter doing so twice. Following victories by his father Willy and uncle Eddy, his successes resulted in it being dubbed the 'Étoile de Planckaert'.

Yet as the sport's move towards *mondialisation* advanced, the race gradually declined in importance and was overlooked by many teams in favour of warm-weather races in Australia and the Middle East. By 2018, Groupama-FDJ and AG2R La Mondiale were the only two WorldTour teams on the start line, with the peloton filled out by smaller Belgian and French teams for the most part.

In 2019, the situation worsened when the municipality of Laudun withdrew its €36,000 backing. For a short period, the race's fate was in the balance, Fangille admitting that it was not only difficult to find replacement sponsors but even to persuade his other backers not to pull their support. At the last minute, though, L'Équipe TV, ASO's sports channel, agreed to provide a live broadcast of the race, which convinced the local government and tourism organisations to stay on board.

Run over four stages in 2019 but restored to five last year for the 50th edition, when no fewer than seven WorldTour teams competed, Bessèges appeared to have stepped away from the brink until the coronavirus pandemic again put its future in doubt. In November 2020, Fangille was hospitalised after contracting Covid-19. As his health deteriorated, he called his daughter, Claudine Allègre-Fangille, and told her that his wish was that the race not go ahead.

'He was afraid that, due to the health situation, the race wouldn't take place in the normal fashion. He would have preferred to cancel the race rather than ask the volunteers to return home right after the stages, to be forced to sacrifice those traditional moments of conviviality each evening in the *permanence*, of not being able to enjoy those moments that he relished so much,' she told *L'Équipe*. 'Together with the organising committee, we still tried to persuade him to organise the race. But then he was taken into hospital. I decided that we had to respect his decision and I had resigned myself to the fact that the Étoile de Bessèges wouldn't take place this year. I didn't want to go on without him.'

Yet her children encouraged her to take over as race organiser and for it to continue in memory of their grandfather. As other early-season races were cancelled or postponed as a result of the coronavirus, the Bessèges organisers received authorisation from the Gard prefecture for it to go ahead. It attracted arguably the best field in its history, with Ineos, Deceuninck-QuickStep and Lotto Soudal among the many WorldTour teams that took part.

'I think my father would be proud of what we've achieved this year. He loved the riders and this race was his life. I think if he could be here he'd be so impressed with the teams and riders we've got, it's turned out to be a great homage to him,' said Allègre-Fangille.

Tour de France race director Thierry Gouvenou, who was lead commissaire at the race, said he'd got to know Fangille well during meetings of the French race organisers' association: 'He was to some extent the patriarch. He had spent decades building up his race, gradually making it better. He often used to say that he had a small team and was a little organiser and couldn't do very much. But we can all see how it's survived and developed. I can only praise the work that he did over 50 years, to have devoted half a century of service to cycling is really impressive. It's fair to say that when you've headed an organisation like this for 50 years, you have to be charismatic, you have to be able to rally people around you. He always managed that and he's left a real legacy.'

# JEAN-PIERRE CARENSO

9 OCTOBER 1934 – 22 NOVEMBER 2020

Former advertising executive and Tour de France director Jean-Pierre Carenso died near Annecy at the age of 86.

Born in Menton, between Nice and Monte Carlo, into a wine-growing family, Carenso was a passionate sports fan as a youngster, riding his bike to watch OGC Nice play football and also hanging around the hotels in Menton where the likes of Louison Bobet, Briek Schotte and other leading stars of the late 1940s stayed while training on the Côte d'Azur prior to the start of each season.

He spent most of his working career in advertising and is best known for the slogan 'Du pain, du vin, du Boursin' that was used to promote the soft cheese so successfully. In the mid-1980s, he was a regular at the Parc des Princes to watch Paris Saint-Germain, and as a consequence became friendly with ASO's directors. He was offered and accepted the post as director-general of *L'Équipe*. Then, in 1989, he became the new co-director of the Tour de France alongside *L'Équipe* journalist Jean-Marie Leblanc, Carenso looking after the race's business side while Leblanc was responsible for the sporting aspect.

Carenso was responsible for slimming down the number of low-paying sponsors and jersey competitions, establishing five principal backers who paid much higher rates. The Tour, for instance, had had a long relationship with Peugeot as its official vehicle supplier, but the French car manufacturer paid no fee for this exposure. After Peugeot turned down Carenso's request for 500,000 French francs for the right to continue, he turned to Fiat, and the Italian manufacturer agreed to pay twelve times that amount.

He stepped down from his role as Tour director in 1994 after falling out with former skiing champion Jean-Claude Killy, who had been brought in as his boss. However, his mark on the race is still evident in those high-paying sponsorship deals with a handful of primary sponsors and other aspects of the Tour's commercial reach and success.

# GASTON DE WACHTER

### 29 JANUARY 1926 – 29 NOVEMBER 2020

Former pro and derny pilot Gaston De Wachter, who led Herman Van Springel to victory in seven editions of Bordeaux–Paris, died at a care and residential centre in Berendrecht, Belgium, at the age of 94.

Born in Schelle, just south of Antwerp, he turned professional with the Bertin team in the middle of 1947 after impressing in the junior ranks during the immediate post-war years. A very competitive sprinter, he lined up in the Tour of Flanders the following year, finishing an impressive 15th. However, he forged his racing reputation in kermesses, winning a handful most years during a competitive career that lasted until 1956.

Fourth in Scheldeprijs in 1952 and winner of the Tour of Limburg the next season, De Wachter went on to establish himself as one of the sport's leading derny riders and became much sought-after on the road and track. His first success at Bordeaux–Paris came in 1961, when he guided Dutchman Wim van Est to victory. Eight years on, he was Walter Godefroot's pilot. In 1970, he began a hugely successful partnership with Herman Van Springel as victory that year was followed by another half-dozen up to 1981.

# ALDO MOSER

7 FEBRUARY 1934 – 3 DECEMBER 2020

Aldo Moser, who took part in 16 editions of the Giro d'Italia and twice wore the leader's *maglia rosa*, died in Trento at the age of 86 due to respiratory issues after being diagnosed with Covid-19.

The eldest of 12 children – including four brothers who all became professional racers, notably 1984 Giro d'Italia winner Francesco – he was born in Palu di Giovo in the Trentino region. As a youngster, he mixed his job delivering bread by bike with his fledgling racing career. He won the amateur edition of the Tour of Lombardy in 1953. That led to a professional contract towards the end of the following season with the team run by the Padova-based manufacturer Torpado. That October he won the Coppa Agostoni and was seventh in the pro edition of Lombardy, finishing in the same group as winner Fausto Coppi.

Winner of the GP di Prato and runner-up at Milan–Turin and Tre Valle Varesine semi-Classic races in 1955, he also made his Giro debut that season, finishing sixth overall as Fiorenzo Magni took the title. His Torpado team won the team time trial at Genova on the sixth stage. His performances that season earned him selection for the Italian road race team at the World Championships on home ground in Frascati, where he was 17th.

A career-best fifth in the Giro d'Italia in 1956, again in Torpado colours, showed he was a strong all-rounder and particularly talented in time trials. He finished third in the 1957 Grand Prix des Nations (then regarded as the unofficial world time trial championship) as well as in the Baracchi Trophy, where he was partnered by Oreste Magni. A year later, he claimed the prestigious Baracchi TT riding with Ercole Baldini, having worn the Giro's *maglia rosa* for a day earlier in the season. In 1959, he added the GP des Nations to his impressive TT palmarès and defended his Baracchi crown with Baldini.

He remained hugely consistent during the 1960s, when he raced for the Emi, Ghigi, San Pellegrino, Lygie, Maino, Vittadello, Pepsi Cola and GBC teams, spending four seasons with his brother Enzo. There were fewer wins but always a substantial list of places of honour, including third place in the 1962 Tour of Switzerland. In 1970, he was joined at GBC by his brother Diego and both were also on the team when Aldo wore the *maglia rosa* for a day in the 1971 *corsa rosa*.

He ended his racing career at Filotex in 1973, when he rode alongside Diego and Francesco, who was in his first professional season, the two of them racing the Giro together, where the young tyro of the family won a stage.

'I grew up admiring him,' Francesco Moser told La Gazzetta dello Sport. 'Without him I'd never have become a good rider. He pushed me to race. He'd had a good Giro in 1969 and convinced me to try racing. He gave me one of his bikes, a GBC from his team. When I moved to Tuscany to race with the Filotex team in 1973, he raced with me so I wasn't alone. He could have retired but raced on to help me. Diego was there too, while Enzo was a *directeur sportif*. He hadn't been well recently. He had heart problems and had been fitted with a pacemaker. Yet we walked together when he had a Covid-19 test on Monday, then he was taken into hospital. Sadly, we were unable to visit him in hospital.'

# ROGER HASSENFORDER

29 JULY 1930 – 3 JANUARY 2021

Winner of eight Tour de France stages, wearer of the yellow jersey for four days during the 1953 race, and later a hotelier and restauranteur in Colmar, Roger Hassenforder was known for high jinks and was nicknamed both 'the joker' and 'Hassen the magnificent'. He died in Colmar residential home at the age of 90.

Born in the Vosges village of Sausheim, the eldest of five siblings, Hassenforder's modest circumstances led to him getting into scrapes from a young age. He would go poaching for rabbits and fish in the local countryside and streams. Hyperactive and often punished for his antics, he struggled at school and left without being able to write. During the war, he got into trouble for stealing guns and mines from the German forces billeted in his region. In one incident, he was caught up in an explosion of his own making and spent six months in a Mulhouse hospital.

Employed, like his father, as a painter in the post-war years, he travelled to work by bike and began to realise it offered him a release. He raced for the first in Mulhouse in 1947 and soon began to win across the Alsace region. In 1950, he started his military service and learned to speak French for the first time, having been brought up speaking an Alsatian dialect. His racing career continued to flourish as well. Winner of the Simplex Trophy for aspiring racers, he received a host of offers from professional teams and opted to join the Mercier squad managed by two-time Tour winner Antonin Magne.

Quick in a sprint, he made a rapid impression, winning the Tour du Sud-Est in his debut 1953 season and a stage at the Dauphiné Libéré. Despite Magne saying he was against the idea, Hassenforder also made his Tour debut riding for the North East-Centre. Second place on the fifth stage into Caen put him into the yellow jersey, which he held for four days until the race went into the Pyrenees, where he finished outside the time limit on stage 10.

He won his first Tour stage in 1955. The following season, after switching to the Saint-Raphaël-Geminiani team, he won four stages – the first three from small groups, and the fourth with a long solo break through the Massif Central to Montluçon. He won two more in 1957, as well as a stage at the Vuelta a España, and celebrated an eighth Tour success in 1959. By that point he'd got a reputation as the peloton's great entertainer, throwing himself into the sea at one Tour stage finish, always ready to clown for the fans.

His career came to an end in 1963. He said he'd made nothing from it and that his parents had to lend him and his wife money so that they could open their hotel and restaurant business at Kaysersberg in 1964. They retired in 1999, selling the business to a Swiss couple who've kept the name Chez Roger Hassenforder to the present day.

# MERCEDES ATECA

23 DECEMBER 1945 – 23 JANUARY 2021

Winner of the first three editions of the Spanish national road race championship and twice a member of the Spanish team at the World Road Race Championships, Mercedes Ateca died in Laredo in her home province of Cantabria at the age of 75.

Born in Udalla, she was one of ten children. There had been no history of bike racing in the family, although her brother Fernando also became a racer and, later, director of the Cafés Baqué team based in the Basque Country. Ateca lived in Paris, where she worked in the hospitality industry and raced in Peugeot colours.

She first represented Spain at the 1978 World Championships in Cologne. The following season, she was the comprehensive winner of the first national road championship, which was held on a 1.25km circuit in Zaragoza. She broke away on the first lap and finished more than 90 seconds clear of the chasers. Ateca retained the title in the two following seasons.

When her racing career ended, she returned to Udalla and, in 1993, opened a restaurant with her sister Isabel that served local dishes but with a French influence. The Cantabrian government paid tribute to her at the Under-23 Tour of Cantabria in 2020: 'This is a sad loss for Cantabrian sport of a woman who was a standard bearer and paved the way for many sportswomen in the country,' said Cantabrian regional government member Pablo Zuloaga. 'Mercedes Ateca will always be remembered as a pioneering woman in women's cycling in Cantabria, as someone who helped to create an important school of cyclists in our autonomous community, putting herself at the forefront of women's achievements.'

# GABRIEL DELOOF

24 SEPTEMBER 1936 – 23 JANUARY 2021

Belgian independent racing champion in 1960 and a professional racer for four seasons, Gabriel Deloof died in his home town of Tielt at the age of 84 after contracting Covid-19.

Winner of the Belgian championship for independent riders in 1960, Deloof turned professional with the Wiel's-Flandria team that was managed by Briek Schotte and led by Joseph Planckaert that summer.

He continued to flit between independent and professional status over the following two seasons. In 1964, when he raced as a full-time professional for the Flandria-Romeo team that featured Dutch Classics star Peter Post, he finished 11th in Het Nieuwsblad and made his Grand Tour debut at the Giro d'Italia, which he abandoned. He retired from racing at the end of that season.

# WINFRIED BÖLKE

25 MAY 1941 – 26 JANUARY 2021

The winner of the German professional road title on three consecutive occasions and twice a starter in the Tour de France, Winfried Bölke died in Dortmund at the age of 79.

Born in Genthin in eastern Germany, he was brought up in Dortmund. A big racing talent from an early age, he won the national amateur road title in 1962 and 1963, finishing fourth and then third in the world amateur championship in those two seasons. He signed a professional contract with Peugeot-BP at the end of 1963 and would remain with the French squad until 1969, racing alongside Tom Simpson, Eddy Merckx and Roger Pingeon during those seasons.

Like many racers in that period, Bölke – known as 'Gustav' to his peers – rode cyclocross and track events in the winter. He was known for his quick finish and his strength in breakaways. In his first pro season he won a stage and the overall title at the Tour de l'Oise and a stage of the Volta a Catalunya, and also finished second to Germany's leading star Rudi Altig in the national road championship.

In 1965, when the championship was held on his home ground in Dortmund, Bölke took the first of three consecutive German titles. Winner of the German Madison in 1967, his versatility was shown by him making his Tour de France debut in German national team colours that season. Narrowly beaten by Belgium's Herman Van Springel on the sixth stage into Metz, he abandoned two days later in the Vosges. He also took part in the 1968 Tour, abandoning on stage 12.

He raced professionally until 1972, when he was diagnosed with heart issues, and worked for Dortmund city council. However, he returned to semi-professional competition in the mid-1980s, terrifying riders two decades younger than him with powerful attacks, reportedly leaving them reflecting how 'Gustav has done us in again'. A recurrence of his heart issues forced him into a second retirement in 1993.

In his later years, he lived in Dortmund in the winter months and on a campsite at Lüdinghausen during the summer months. He still rode with a local group, covering up to 80km through the Soest Börde region of central Germany.

# RYSZARD SZURKOWSKI

12 JANUARY 1946 – 1 FEBRUARY 2021

Four-time winner of the Peace Race, a world amateur road champion, twice an Olympic silver medallist in the team time trial and widely regarded as the best Polish racer of all time, Ryszard Szurkowski died in Radom, Poland, at the age of 75.

Voted Poland's second-most popular athlete of the 20th century, after sprinter Irena Szewińska, Szurkowski was a natural athletic talent. He followed his own path into racing, winning the national cyclocross championship and taking fourth place in the road championship in 1968. These performances drew him to the attention of national team coach Henryk Łasak, and he became part of that set-up. In 1969, he lined up in the Peace Race for the first time and finished second overall to France's Jean-Pierre Danguillaume.

Nicknamed 'Bibi' by his teammates, he quickly built on this initial success. A hugely strong rouleur with acute tactical sense, he took his first Peace Race title in 1970 and went on to win what was the biggest bike race that took place behind the Iron Curtain three more times in the next five years. In total, he raced 89 stages in the event, 52 of them in the leader's jersey.

His performances made him a national sporting hero. 'I remember the stage of the Peace Race to Poznan, we took the first three places in 1970. And you know what? It looked just like in St Peter's Square when people were calling out for John Paul II. Thousands of people stood at the window and chanted our names for us to appear to them in the windows,' he recalled in an interview not long before his death.

He was part of the Polish quartet that took the silver medal in the team time trial at the 1972 Munich Olympics, where they were beaten by the Russians. The following year the Poles got their revenge at the World Amateur Championships, winning the gold medal. Szurkowski then went on to win the road race, attacking from a four-man group 1,300 metres from the finish line. He took silver the following year and won another gold in the TTT in 1975.

Winner of the Polish road title on five occasions and the record-holder for stage wins (15) at his national tour, although he never managed to win the overall title, he also won big races in the West, including the Circuit de la Sarthe (1969), the Tour of Scotland (1972) and the Tour du Limousin (1974). In 1974 he also competed at Paris–Nice, finishing 28th on GC. He was courted by several professional teams, including Eddy Merckx's Molteni, but the Polish Cycling Union refused to allow him to turn pro.

He won a second Olympic silver medal in the TTT at the 1976 Montreal Olympics, where the Poles once again finished behind the Russians, and retired from the national team in 1980. He went on to become a successful coach/*directeur sportif* both at national and international level, overseeing Lech Piasecki's successes in the Peace Race and world amateur road championship in 1985. At the Seoul Olympics in 1988, the Polish team he was directing once again took the silver medal in the team time trial.

That same year, as Poland moved towards political and economic liberalisation, he set up Poland's first professional racing team, Exbud Kielce, and later founded the Szurkowski sports club in Warsaw, where he also ran a cycling shop. During that same period, he was also a non-partisan member of the Polish parliament. He went on to become director of the Polish stages of the Peace Race and, from 2010 to 2011, president of the Polish Cycling Union.

In 2011, his son Norbert died in the terrorist attacks on the World Trade Center, where he was decorating offices of financial services company Cantor Fitzgerald. Tragedy struck again in June 2018, when Szurkowski crashed heavily during an event for ex-racers and was left paralysed from the waist down. A fundraiser to help his rehabilitation was supported by many of Poland's leading sports stars, including tennis player Agnieszka Radwańska, footballer Robert Lewandowski, Tour of Poland race organiser Czesław Lang and ex-racer Zenon Jaskuła.

Affected by digestive issues, pneumonia and cancer, he was asked on his 75th birthday, just days before his death, what his biggest wish was. 'Just one,' he replied. 'I wish could take my first independent step and be able to return to the bicycle, even a three-wheel one.'

Married three times, he is survived by his wife Iwona Arkuszewska-Szurkowska.

# ANDRÉ DUFRAISSE

30 JUNE 1926 – 21 FEBRUARY 2021

Five-time world cyclocross champion and seven times the French national champion, André Dufraisse died in Limoges at the age of 94.

Born in the hamlet of Silord in the Limousin, the only child of a builder and a farm worker, he began racing cyclocross in the immediate post-war years. Initially known for his strength when running rather than his riding technique, Dufraisse progressed quickly. In 1951 he was runner-up in the French championship, then went on to finish in the same position in the world championship in Luxembourg behind compatriot Roger Rondeaux.

By then he was also racing on the road in the colours of the Rochet-Dunlop team. Although he managed to gain selection for the West/South-West team for the 1952 Tour de France, he abandoned on the third stage. He did stand out occasionally on the road after that – winning the 1953 edition Arantzazu hill-climb in Spain, for instance – but he focused increasingly on cyclocross.

Runner-up at the Worlds to Rondeaux in 1952 and third behind him in 1953, Dufraisse took the world crown in 1954 at Crenna in Italy. Nicknamed 'the woodland virtuoso', he won the next four editions, the last of them on home ground in Limoges. 'That was the hardest title to win because I'd had sciatica for several days beforehand, but it was also the most emotional because it was in Limoges,' he recalled.

He retired from racing in 1966 and worked in a service station in Limoges, later taking over as manager. He then worked for a quartz-finishing company and later opened a bar carrying his own name and with a façade painted with a rainbow jersey. He kept riding into his final years, often covering 40km in his late eighties. Dufraisse's achievements led to him receiving the Legion of Honour from fellow Limousin Raymond Poulidor, who was also a good friend.

# BERNARD GUYOT

19 NOVEMBER 1945 – 28 FEBRUARY 2021

Winner of the Peace Race, five times a Tour de France participant and runner-up in Paris–Nice, the Grand Prix des Nations and the French road championship, Bernard Guyot died in Péronne at the age of 75.

Born in Savigny-sur-Orge, near Paris, he was the most talented of three brothers who all raced at a high level – his younger brother Claude was a pro for four seasons and Serge raced for the US Créteil amateur team. Guyot was a member of the French road team at the 1964 Olympics in Tokyo, where he was disqualified for giving a wheel to teammate Lucien Aimar.

Tenth in the Tour de l'Avenir the following season, winning two stages in the process, he became the first French rider to taste victory at the Peace Race in 1966, when he also finished fourth in the Avenir and in the world team time trial championship. He turned pro with the Pelforth-Sauvage team in 1967 – led by Dutchman Jan Janssen and also featuring future Tour director Jean-Marie Leblanc in its ranks – and blazed a trail through that season.

Winner of the Tour de l'Hérault and the Tour du Morbihan, Guyot was runner-up to Tom Simpson at Paris–Nice, where he triumphed in the time trial on the final day using what was then an unusually large gear of 55x13. Second in the Baracchi Trophy, where he partnered Jacques Anquetil, and runner-up to Felice Gimondi in the Grand Prix des Nations, he won that season's Prestige Pernod prize as France's best rider and finished ninth in the SuperPrestige international ranking, which was topped by teammate Janssen.

Riding alongside his brother Claude at Pelforth in 1968, he was fourth in Paris–Nice and was selected for the France A team at the Tour, which was led by defending champion Roger Pingeon and Raymond Poulidor. Guyot finished 27th as the title went to Janssen.

Sonolor came in as the team's principal sponsor in 1969, when Guyot was one of the leaders. But he failed to produce the results that his early start to pro racing had suggested he was capable of. He finished 50th at the Tour, which had reverted to a trade-team format, his performance overshadowed by a newly signed Belgian climber, Lucien Van Impe, who was 12th.

Over the next three seasons with Sonolor, Guyot's form continued to fade. He rode the Tour three more times and finished runner-up in the 1972 French championship behind Roland Berland. He retired at the end of the 1974 season and became a driver for a company based in Péronne in north-east France.

# DICK ENTHOVEN

2 AUGUST 1936 – 21 MARCH 2021

Winner of the Tour of Holland in 1961 and three times a Tour de France rider, Dutchman Dick Enthoven died in Stekene, Belgium, at the age of 84.

The Dutch amateur champion in 1959, when he also finished third overall at the Tour of Poland, Enthoven turned professional towards the end of that season with the Saint-Raphaël-Geminiani team, making his debut at Paris–Tours. He stayed with the French team for the next two seasons, winning his home tour in 1961, when he also made his Tour debut for the Dutch team, abandoning on the 10th stage.

In 1962, he switched to the Pelforth-Sauvage team, finishing seventh in the Dauphiné Libéré. He rode the Tour in their colours as well, but once again failed to finish. The following season, he did make it to Paris, finishing in 34th place. He joined the Wiel's-Groene Leeuw team in 1965, but retired halfway through that season. He then worked on road construction in Belgium, where he had set up home with his family during his racing career.

His son Edwin also became a professional, riding briefly for Collstrop in 1993 and for Zetelhallen in 1994.

# MANFRED AEBI

## 21 AUGUST 1932 – 6 APRIL 2021

Swiss watch company executive Manfred Aebi, who represented the Rodania brand in Belgium and composed the promotional jingle that announced the arrival of the riders in many Belgian races for six decades, died due to a thrombosis at the age of 88.

Aebi was sent to Belgium by Rodania in 1951. He planned to stay briefly, but met his future wife, Simone Verlinden, and never left. He had very little budget with which to promote the Rodania brand but quickly realised that cycling offered him a great opportunity to do so. Initially he travelled in a car ahead of races and shouted slogans through a PA system, but his words were often lost on the wind or in the clatter of race vehicles.

Travelling back from a race one afternoon, he heard the start of Beethoven's fifth symphony. 'It fitted perfectly with the name Rodania. Tadadadaaaa… Ro-da-ni-aaaa was born,' he later explained. The jingle became an indelible part of Belgian bike racing, sounding out just ahead of races, alerting fans to the riders' imminent arrival.

In 1990, Aebi bought up the Rodania company and moved it to Brussels, but the link with cycling continued until 2018. It was reintroduced at some races at the start of this season, just weeks before Aebi's death.

# FRANCIS SIGUENZA

30 NOVEMBER 1930 – 11 APRIL 2021

A Spaniard born in Nîmes who took on French nationality, Francis Siguenza was one of the few riders from the department of Gard to have raced at the Tour de France, making four appearances in the race in the mid-1950s. A former teammate of Hugo Koblet, Ferdi Kübler and Jacques Anquetil, he died in Vienne aged 90.

He was a good amateur racer, and turned pro in August 1952 with La Perle-Hutchinson, remaining with the team for the next three seasons. Winner of the Grand Prix de Monaco and runner-up in the Tour de l'Ouest in 1953, he made his Tour debut for the Sud-Est team in the following season, finishing 61st in Paris. A good time triallist, he was fifth in the Grand Prix des Nations that same year.

Nicknamed 'Zig-Zag', Siguenza flirted with glory on the fifth stage of the 1955 Tour into Colmar. Riding for Ile de France, he was part of the stage-winning break of four, but was the last of them to cross the line as local man Roger Hassenforder claimed victory. He would finish 44th on GC.

He joined Rochet-Dunlop in 1956. Once again he rode in Ile de France colours at the Tour, where Ireland's Shay Elliott was one of his teammates. Like the previous year, he reached Paris in 44th place. Winner of races on home ground in Alès and Nîmes in 1957, he was back in the Sud-Est team at the 1957 Tour, which he completed once again, in 53rd place. He then spent a season with Peugeot and then another with UCPF, before switching to independent status in 1960 and for the following two seasons.

# JESÚS HOYOS

UNKNOWN – 30 APRIL 2021

The team doctor at the Banesto/Caisse d'Épargne/Movistar team for 24 years, Jesús Hoyos died in hospital in Alicante due to pancreatic cancer. He was 62.

He graduated from the School of Sporting Medicine at Madrid's Complutense University. He worked in Iraq, treating workers who were building the defensive bunkers for Saddam Hussein's forces for heat-related illnesses. He came into the sport at the end of the 1980s, when he worked for the Caja Rural team. He later worked with the Artiach team and arrived at Banesto in 1997, remaining with the team until the spring of 2020, when his illness forced him to step away from the sport.

Hoyos died on the day that Movistar's Marc Soler won the third stage at the Tour de Romandie. Soler dedicated his victory to Hoyos, saying his loss had caused 'huge grief for everyone'.

'He was above all an upright man who didn't want to say anything to anyone about his cancer, who didn't want anyone to worry about him,' said Movistar *directeur sportif* José Luis Arrieta.

# WILFRIED PEFFGEN

1 OCTOBER 1942 – 9 MAY 2021

A track racing specialist who won the world motor-pacing title three times and the European title on six occasions, Wilfried Peffgen also won 16 Six-Day races, the German road title and appeared in the Tour de France on four occasions. He died in his home city of Cologne at the age of 78.

Blessed with natural athletic talent, Peffgen was a football and handball player before turning to cycling in his teenage years. He won the German junior road title in 1959 at the age of 16. When he stepped up into the senior ranks, he finished fourth in the 1962 German amateur road championship and was runner-up two years later, when he was selected for the German team for the Tokyo Olympics, where he finished sixth.

German amateur champion in 1965 and seventh in the world amateur championship, he turned pro that season with the German Ruberg-Campagnolo team. That December he made the first of 188 Six-Day appearances on his home track in Cologne.

In 1967, still riding for Ruberg, he made his Tour debut in support of Germany's top racer, Rudi Altig. Peffgen abandoned the race after breaking his collarbone on the 13th stage to Carpentras (on which Tom Simpson died).

He joined Altig at the Salvarani team in 1968 and made his debut in the Vuelta a España, winning the seventh stage into Benidorm and then helping team leader Felice Gimondi to take the overall title. He then rode in support of Gimondi at the Giro d'Italia, where the Italian was third behind another debutant, Eddy Merckx. Peffgen finished 50th.

In 1970, Peffgen moved to GBC for two seasons, then, in 1972, he moved on to Rokado. It was in their colours that he became the German road champion. He wore the national champion's jersey at the Tour, where he was 63rd. He made his final Tour appearance in 1973, abandoning on the fifth stage.

By that point, his racing career was much more focused on the track. He took his first Six-Day win in Münster in 1972 with his regular partner, Albert Fritz, with whom he would go on to take another dozen Sixes among his total of 16 victories. European Madison champion with Sigi Renz, he won the world and European motor-pacing titles in 1976, paced by his long-time derny rider Dieter Durst, adding two more world titles in 1978 and 1980, while also defending the European crown every year through to 1981. He rode his last Six-Day event, in Cologne, in 1983.

A locksmith by trade, since 1967 he had run a petrol station in Cologne with his wife. He set up a bike shop in Cologne after his retirement from competition and became the director of the Dortmund Six, staying in that role until 2009.

# MARCEL QUEHEILLE

16 MARCH 1930 – 17 JULY 2021

Winner of a stage of the 1959 Tour de France, in which he appeared on four occasions, Marcel Queheille died in Oloron-Sainte-Marie at the age of 91.

Born in Sauguis-Saint-Étienne in the foothills of the Pyrenees in the French Basque Country, Queheille grew up idolising Fausto Coppi but worked long hours as a carpenter and didn't have time to indulge his passion. However, in his early twenties, he began to devote a little time to racing and saw good results, taking 18 victories between 1953 and 1955.

Just 1.60 metres tall and weighing a mere 55kg, he was always destined to be a climber, and this is where he began to thrive. Second in the Route de France in 1956, when he was riding as an independent, he turned professional with Mercier-BP-Hutchinson in June of the following year, just before making his Tour debut for the Sud-Ouest team. He finished 30th in Paris, taking second place on the long stage through the Pyrenees to Ax-les-Thermes behind Jean Bourlès.

After winning a stage at the Dauphiné Libéré, he returned to the Tour with the Sud-Ouest team two years later and took the biggest victory of his career, on stage 9 into the Basque city of Bayonne. It helped him to 26th place on GC. Second in the Grand Prix de Midi-Libre in 1960, Queheille rode the Tour in the purple colours of the Centre-Midi team, finishing 50th.

The Basque rider moved to the Kas team in 1961 and made his debut at the Vuelta a España, where he was 26th. A member of the Ouest/Sud-Ouest team at the Tour, he claimed his best GC finish, reaching Paris in 21st place and also taking the prize as the most combative rider.

Signed by the Helyett-Saint-Raphaël team towards the end of that season, he lined up in a very strong team at the 1962 Vuelta alongside Jacques Anquetil, Rudi Altig (who would take the title), Shay Elliott (who was third) and Jean Stablinski (who was sixth). Queheille crashed on the second stage to Tortona. Given a bike that was too big for him by team director Raphaël Geminiani, the Frenchman finished outside the time limit. He wasn't retained at the end of that season but found a place on a small Spanish team, Pinturas Ega. He lined up at the Vuelta again but abandoned once more, his professional career ending soon afterwards.

He moved back into carpentry, working for a company that manufactured high-quality furniture and, later, managing a showroom of their products. He still kept riding, climbing 70 or more climbs per year in the Pyrenees until well into his eighties.

# FABIO TABORRE

5 JUNE 1985 – 12 SEPTEMBER 2021

Italian former professional Fabio Taborre, winner of the GP Camaiore and Memorial Pantani before being banned from racing for a doping violation, died at his home in Pescara as a result of heart disease. He was 36.

Taborre turned pro in 2009 with the Diquigiovanni-Androni team managed by Gianni Savio. He moved to Acqua e Sapone in 2011, making his Giro d'Italia debut with them that season. He claimed his first pro win later that summer, leading in a three-man break at the GP Camaiore. He dedicated the victory to his sister Chiara, who had died in a car accident two years earlier. Always a strong performer in hilly terrain, with a quick turn of speed in a small group, he underlined that with victory in the 2011 Memorial Pantani, beating Davide Rebellin and Dan Martin in the sprint.

Winner of a stage at the Tour of Austria in 2012, Taborre moved to Vini Fantini in 2013. He raced at the Giro again, abandoning halfway through the event. After a season with Neri Sottoli, he returned to Androni in 2015, but was sacked by the team after testing positive for FG-4592, a drug being developed to treat anaemia that boosted EPO production in the body. He received a four-year ban for the doping violation, which also led to him being sued by the Androni team.

In 2017, he was arrested after police in the town of Montesilvano, near Pescara, found him and an accomplice recovering two stolen vehicles. The pair were also linked to a series of burglaries carried out in the area.

'He was like a younger brother,' Androni DS Alessandro Spezialetti, who comes from the same region, told *Il Centro*. 'He asked and listened to my advice, as well as to Danilo Di Luca and Ruggero Marzoli. He trusted me, he was respectful. He was a good cyclist, he did his best and he had some great moments. He was quiet, but a really good guy.'

# CHRIS ANKER SØRENSEN

## 5 SEPTEMBER 1984 – 18 SEPTEMBER 2021

Danish road champion in 2015, one of the stalwarts of the CSC/Saxo Bank team and winner of a stage at the Giro d'Italia in 2010, Chris Anker Sørensen died in Zeebrugge, Belgium, after being hit by a truck while riding the time trial course of the 2021 World Championships in his role as a commentator with Danish TV channel TV2. He was 37.

Born in the town of Hammel, Sørensen turned pro with the Designa Køkken team in 2005 and was taken on as a stagiaire by CSC that August. Eleventh on GC in the Tour of Britain a month later, he joined the team managed by Bjarne Riis in 2007, when he was fifth overall in the Tour of Germany, which was won by his teammate Jens Voigt, and soon after made his Grand Tour debut at the Vuelta a España, where he finished a very promising 19th while helping CSC leader Carlos Sastre to second place on the final podium.

A strong climber, he underlined his ability in the mountains the following season with two prestigious summit victories. His debut pro win came at La Toussuire in the Critérium du Dauphiné. The following month, he added a second success on the hugely challenging ascent of the Kitzbüheler Horn at the Tour of Austria. He made his first appearance at the Tour de France in 2009, once again playing a key role in the mountains for his leader, Andy Schleck, in what had become the Saxo Bank team.

Generally tasked with being the lieutenant to Riis's team leaders in the mountains in the leading events on the race calendar, Sørensen seized the opportunity to ride for himself on the Terminillo stage of the 2010 Giro d'Italia, breaking away in the mist with 6km remaining to take what would prove to be the most prestigious victory of his career.

A distant second behind Thomas Voeckler at Luchon in the 2012 Tour, his battling performance in the mountains during that race resulted in Sørensen finishing on the final podium in Paris after being awarded the prize of the race's most aggressive rider. Winner of the Danish road title in 2015, he moved from Tinkoff-Saxo Bank at the end of that season to the French Fortuneo team, making his fifth and final Tour appearance that year in their colours.

He stepped down to continental ranks for the Riwal team in 2017, combining his racing commitments with a new career as a commentator for TV2. He retired from racing in 2018 and moved into a team management role with Riwal.

'He was living life, riding a lot, and cycling was his religion,' Andy Schleck told *Cyclingnews*. 'You won't find anyone in the sport with a bad word to say about him. He was just a great man and a great friend. This is a huge loss for all of cycling. He started as a fan, he lived his dream as a rider and then stayed in the sport because he wanted to give something back. As I said, he was a role model. My heart goes out to his family, his children and everyone who was lucky enough to be influenced by him. We rode together for six years and all I can say is that he was a role model teammate. He was a rider who put aside his own ambitions when it came to results and always put the team first. He was the perfect teammate. He knew that he had good qualities as a climber, he was a pure climber, but he put all his energies into helping his friends and teammates.'

Sørensen leaves behind his wife, Michelle Moestrup, and daughters Lærke and Laura.

# ROBERT GIBANEL

6 JULY 1932 – 28 SEPTEMBER 2021

A two-time Tour de France participant who ran a bike shop and gained a reputation as a sculptor in his post-racing years, Robert Gibanel died in his hometown of Jurançon at the age of 89.

A highly successful independent rider in his native Béarn, in the shadow of the Pyrenees, he turned professional in 1956 with Elvish and made his Tour debut that year with the South-West regional team, finishing 73rd. He's better remembered, though, for his courageous performance over the cobbles from Roubaix to Charleroi in 1957. He crashed heavily on the pavé, sustaining injuries that meant he couldn't dismount from his bike without assistance at the finish. The Tour doctor was shocked to discover that he'd ridden in with a broken pelvis.

Gibanel stepped down from the pro ranks the following season, but continued to enjoy considerable success as an independent until his competitive retirement in 1963. He subsequently ran a successful bike shop, worked as a chocolate confectioner and gained considerable renown as a sculptor, his works featuring in many exhibitions.

# JACQUES VIVIER

9 OCTOBER 1930 – 28 SEPTEMBER 2021

Winner of two Tour de France stages in the early 1950s and a highly reputed wood merchant in his post-racing years, Jacques Vivier died in his native Limousin at the age of 90.

Winner of the first edition of the Route de France in 1951 and French military champion that same year, Vivier turned professional with the Royal Fabric team in 1952. He made his Tour debut that season for the West/South-West team, winning the stage into Limoges in his home region, as he finished 49th on GC.

Tour winner Fausto Coppi could see the young rider was very talented and tried to take Vivier under his wing, but the Frenchman never gave his full commitment to the sport, regarding it as a means of making money rather than something that brought him huge pleasure or filled him with ambition. Each year, he did the training that was needed to remain competitive, but no more. That was, though, often enough for him to thrive, notably in the 1954 Tour, when he won another stage.

He retired from racing at the end of the 1957 season and later said he put his bike in his barn and never looked at it again. He became a wood merchant in the Limousin.

# HEIKO SALZWEDEL

16 APRIL 1957 – 29 SEPTEMBER 2021

German cycling coach and team manager Heiko Salzwedel, who was driving force behind Olympic and World Championship track and road success in several countries, most notably Australia, Great Britain and Denmark, died in Berlin after spending three weeks in a coma following a pulmonary embolism. He was 64.

Having worked as a coach for junior teams within his native East Germany, Salzwedel took up a position as the elite-level coach in the Australian state of New South Wales in 1990. He soon relocated to Canberra, though, to take up a new role as the road and mountain bike coach at the Australian Institute of Sport. Salzwedel established the foundation of what would quickly become a hugely successful programme, envied across the cycling world. Among its biggest early successes was the 1992 Olympic road title taken by Kathy Watt in Barcelona, where she also claimed silver in the individual pursuit. He worked with a string of athletes who went on to make a major impact in a variety of disciplines including Robbie McEwen, Henk Vogels, Patrick Jonker and Cadel Evans, a precocious MTB talent who Salzwedel believed would reach his prime at the Tour de France, which of course Evans won in 2011.

In 1996, Salzwedel played a pivotal role in the establishment of the Giant-AIS road team. Two years later, he returned to Germany to become performance director at the country's cycling federation. In 2001, he took up a similar role at British Cycling, the first of three spells he had with the organisation. In the second spell between 2008 and the end of the 2012 London Olympics, Salzwedel was at the heart of Britain's all-conquering success on the track. He returned to the organisation in 2014, overseeing Bradley Wiggins' successful attempt to break the world hour record in 2015 and a further string of successes at the 2016 Rio Olympics.

In between these periods with British Cycling, from 2005 to 2008 he worked as national track coach for the Danish federation, where performance levels rose considerably under his aegis, and, in 2012, played a key role in the foundation of the RusVelo road cycling team, now known as Gazprom.

He left his role with British Cycling towards the end of 2017, going into semi-retirement in Berlin, although he continued to work with some of the country's leading track names, including world champions Roger Kluge and Max Levy.

'There is nowhere that Heiko has travelled in the world that – when allowed to take control – he has not achieved success,' said Phill Bates, former head of Australia's road commission and also a close friend of the German coach, in a tribute on Australian's SBS TV channel. 'I have met few people in the sport of cycling that ever amazed me and Heiko was on top of the list. The cyclists that learned the art of racing under his guidance will never forget him. His passion, drive and knowledge made him one of the best coaches the world has seen. He may have been accused of being a tough taskmaster and unrelenting, but he knew his game.'

In a tribute on Facebook, Kathy Watt wrote, 'Heiko became a great friend, intelligent coach and we shared many great times together at the AIS and on training camps and competitions both within Australia and around the world. He was a person with great strength of character and good humour who fully supported the athletes he worked with. My condolences to his family. He will be missed by many people in Australia (not just in the cycling community) and worldwide.'

He is survived by his wife, Cindy, and two sons.

# JOSÉ PÉREZ FRANCÉS

27 DECEMBER 1936 – 30 SEPTEMBER 2021

Third in the 1963 edition of the Tour de France and four times a podium finisher at the Vuelta a España, José Pérez Francés died in his adopted home city of Barcelona at the age of 84.

Born in the northern province of Cantabria, he took the Spanish amateur title in 1955 and continued to make an impact as an amateur and then as an independent semi-professional prior to joining the Ferrys team, where he would spend the next seven years of his career, in 1960.

Runner-up and a stage winner at the Volta a Catalunya that first season, he also made his debut at the Vuelta a España but failed to finish. The following year, he finished third in his national tour behind winner Angelino Soler, winning the stage into Albacete, and impressed too on his debut at the Tour de France, reaching Paris in seventh place on GC.

He was the distant runner-up to Rudi Altig in the 1962 edition of the Vuelta and continued almost immediately on to the Giro d'Italia, where he finished sixth. He returned to the Tour in 1963, taking third place behind Jacques Anquetil and Federico Bahamontes, with whom he had a very frosty relationship that resulted in them not exchanging a word for several years.

Third again at the Vuelta in 1964, he's best remembered for his epic stage-winning break in 1965 between Ax-les-Thermes and his home city of Barcelona. He went clear just 17km into the stage, with 233km remaining, and built up a huge lead that the peloton never succeeded in closing down. As he rode through Catalunya in baking heat, fans flocked to the roadside to watch his progress and cheer him on, many dousing him with water in the roasting conditions. His successful sortie remains one of just seven solo wins of more than 200km in the Tour's history and helped him to sixth place on GC that year.

He joined Kas in 1967 and it was in their colours that he finished second to Felice Gimondi in the 1968 Vuelta, winning a stage on the way. He retired at the end of the 1969 season, which he spent with Bic. He was renowned for riding his bike every day and continued to race into the 1990s, when he was Spanish veteran champion. He refused to be a guest of honour when the Tour returned to Barcelona for a stage finish in 2009, explaining that he probably wouldn't watch the race because it would interfere with his daily ride, though it was later said he did stop at the roadside to see it pass. In 2014 he told *El Periódico*, 'I have to go out with younger riders nowadays because those of my age can't keep up with my rhythm.'

# NORMAN HILL

12 MARCH 1939 – 1 OCTOBER 2021

A regular on the Six-Day scene at the end of the 1960s and in the early 1970s, British track and kermesse rider Norman Hill died of heart failure at the age of 81.

A member of the Kentish Wheelers and an apprentice in machine-shop engineering, he moved to Switzerland to work for the Schindler Elevator company in the early 1960s and often raced amateur events on the track in Zurich. It wasn't until he moved to the Netherlands later in that decade that he began to race at a higher level. He made his first Six-Day appearance at the Skol Six in London in 1967 and went on to participate in another 15 events over the following seasons, specialising in Derny racing. He met his future wife, Harma, at one such event in Groningen, where she was a podium miss.

Hill participated in the World Derny (Stayer) Championship on four occasions, and also raced kermesses in Belgium and the Netherlands as a 'weekend warrior'. Following an appearance in the Los Angeles Six in the early 1970s, Hill stayed on in California to become the coach at the Hollywood Wheelmen Cycling Club. That led to him becoming the manager and coach of the Vancouver track in Canada. After two years there, he set up a bike shop in the city, before switching back into the lift industry, ultimately working for OTIS and then setting up his own lift consultancy.

# BERNARD TAPIE

26 JANUARY 1943 – 3 OCTOBER 2021

Bernard Tapie, the French businessman who set up La Vie Claire team in the mid-1980s that won two Tours de France as well as the Giro d'Italia and became a hugely successful and controversial figure within his home country, died of cancer in Marseille aged 78.

Born and raised in a working-class suburb of Paris, he was the older of two sons to Jean-Baptiste, who was a refrigeration engineer, and Raymonde who was a nurse. After leaving school, Tapie began a long and extremely varied business career in what would turn out to be his typically flamboyant fashion, selling televisions by day and singing in Parisian clubs at night. He dabbled in motor-racing, made a vain attempt to launch a pop career, but found his niche in buying up and turning around failing companies, which made him extremely wealthy.

He first became involved in cycling when, in 1983, he bought the French manufacturer Look, which specialised in ski bindings as well as bike and componentry construction. Through contacts in the sport, he met four-time Tour de France winner Bernard Hinault in the winter of 1983/84. The Breton had fallen out with his team manager at Renault, Cyrille Guimard, and was looking for a new sponsor to support him and a dozen or so other riders. Hinault said that when he met Tapie there was an instant rapport between them. A deal was quickly sorted out, Tapie investing the equivalent of €2.7 million in a team that would carry the name of the health-food chain he owned, La Vie Claire. At the launch, Tapie said he would shake up the 'medieval' world of cycling.

The team was ground-breaking from the start. Its Piet Mondrian-style jerseys would become iconic. On the performance side, Tapie brought in Swiss coach Paul Köchli, who was a mentor of Guimard's and introduced a dynamic approach to racing: what could effectively be called 'total cycling', with the team's riders all focused on attack and making the race at the front – the epitome of the *course en tête* strategy. Hinault and Tapie also began to test and invest in clipless pedals, eventually leading to the development of the Look PP65, which Hinault rode as he claimed a fifth Tour victory in 1985.

Believing riders were underpaid, Tapie boosted salaries, which not only drew in Hinault and some of France's top riders but also resulted in Greg LeMond leaving the Renault fold at the end of the 1984 season. The first contact with the American took place during that year's Tour when the race halted at Alpe d'Huez. LeMond was approached by a motorcyclist in leathers, 'like a James Bond girl who held out a helmet and said, "Come with me, Monsieur Tapie is waiting for you."' The American was whisked to La Vie Claire's hotel, where he met Tapie and Hinault and agreed a million-dollar contract that was spread over three seasons. LeMond was also promised a cut of all Look clipless pedals sold in the United States but said he never received a penny of this money.

Hinault won the Giro in 1985, then added the Tour title that summer, with LeMond a podium finisher on both occasions and playing a key role in those victories. Subsequently, Hinault promised that he would support the American's bid to win the 1986 Tour. That edition became an all-time classic, Hinault playing mind games with his American teammate but LeMond eventually prevailing. Their unpredictable partnership produced the legendary moment when they crossed the line at Alpe d'Huez arm in arm, the Frenchman the stage winner but his younger teammate the anointed champion and in the yellow jersey.

Following Hinault's retirement at the end of that season and LeMond's life-threatening hunting accident the following spring, what had become the Toshiba team focused on Frenchman Jean-François Bernard, who would finish third in the 1987 Tour. Tapie, though, was losing interest in cycling and left the sport in 1989 to focus on his new passion, the football team Olympique de Marseille, which he had bought in 1986. A sleeping giant of the sport in France, he adopted the same strategy as he had with La Vie Claire, paying big money for the best players, which led to the team's victory in the 1993 Champions League.

That victory led to one of many legal controversies that Tapie would become mired in during the last three decades of his life. He was found guilty of corruption after it was revealed that he'd bribed a rival French team to lose a game to Marseille in the run-up to their 1993 success. The team were stripped of the French title and Tapie received an eight-month jail sentence. On his release, he was banned from involvement in football and politics, where he was also active, becoming an MP in 1989 and subsequently serving as a minister in socialist president François Mitterrand's government.

In that period he also became embroiled in a legal case that would drag on for the rest of his life. Forced to sell his majority stake in sports equipment manufacturer Adidas to avoid any conflict of interest, he ended up suing the part state-owned Crédit Lyonnais bank that had advised him on the deal on the basis that the company had been undervalued (it had been sold the following year for twice the sum Tapie had received for it). In 2008, he was paid €403 million in compensation and damages, only for an appeal court to overturn that judgment seven years later and order him to repay the full sum. Tapie claimed he'd spent it all, resulting in a legal process continuing up until his death without any resolution. He spent two further short spells in prison as a result of tax fraud.

'When you've won the Tour de France, the Champions League, you've been a minister, a singer, an actor... what have I not done?' he said in an interview with *Le Monde* in 2017 following an announcement that he had stomach cancer. 'I can't say I haven't been spoiled rotten by life.'

Tapie was twice married, first in 1964 to Michèle Layec, with whom he had two children, Nathalie and Stéphane. After they divorced, he married Dominique Mialet-Damianos in 1987, with whom he also had two children, Laurent and Sophie.

# CONTRIBUTORS

KATHRYN BERTINE was born in New York. As well as having competed as a figure skater and triathlete, she also represented St Kitts and Nevis as international cyclist. This was while attempting to qualify for the 2008 Olympic Games as part of her work as a staff writer for ESPN. Subsequently, she went on to ride in the professional women's peloton and became a driving force for gender equality in the sport, campaigning in particular for the return of the women's Tour de France. In 2022, this will happen.

NED BOULTING has been covering road racing since 2003. He commentates on the Tour de France for ITV in the UK and has published widely in a variety of magazines. He is the author of a number of books on road racing and co-hosts a loosely cycling-based podcast with former professional racer David Millar. When there is no pandemic, he also tours a theatrical one-man show about the Tour de France.

SIMON BROTHERTON is BBC TV's cycling commentator and has covered the Tour de France for BBC Radio 22 times. Tokyo 2020 was the seventh Olympic Games he has commentated on and his second Paralympics for Channel 4. He spends much of the year covering football and is a familiar voice on *BBC Match of the Day* and BT Sport in the UK and Champions League matches around the world. His résumé includes six World Cups and seven European Championships including Euro 2020.

Cycling writer PETER COSSINS is the author of *Full Gas* and *The Yellow Jersey*, winners of the cycling book of the year at the Daily Telegraph Sports Book Awards in 2019 and 2020, respectively. His latest book is *A Cyclist's Guide to the Pyrenees*.

DANIEL FRIEBE is a multi-lingual cycling journalist, TV reporter and podcast host. He is the author of *Eddy Merckx: The Cannibal*, *Mountain High* and *Mountain Higher*, and collaborated with Mark Cavendish on *Boy Racer* and *At Speed*. Since 2016, he has been part of ITV's Tour de France presentation team, broadcasting to the UK. He is one of three co-hosts of The Cycling Podcast.

PETER KAMASA was born in exile in Tanzania, his Tutsi parents having fled Rwanda in 1959. After the 1994 genocide, during which he lost 20 family members, he moved to the country of his parents' birth, where he began a career in sports journalism. He has covered nine editions of the Tour du Rwanda.

LUKAS KNÖFLER started working in cycling communications in 2013 and has seen the inside of the scene from many angles. He has worked as a press officer for teams and races and written for several online and print publications. Since 2018, he has been the Women's WorldTour correspondent for cyclingnews.com.

JONNY LONG is a journalist and weekend editor for *Cycling Weekly*, having also been a freelancer for *Vice*, *TimeOut* and the *Telegraph*. He first worked on the Tour de France in 2011 for ITV as a production assistant and was also employed for a couple of years to fetch the sandwiches on their Vuelta a España coverage.

CECILIE UTTRUP LUDWIG is a professional cyclist from Denmark, riding with FDJ Nouvelle-Aquitaine Futuroscope in 2021. She is a Classics specialist, well known for her attacking style, consistency and outspoken interviews. She is a resident of Girona, where she trains with the 'Danish mafia'. 2021 was her breakthrough year.

DAN MARTIN announced in early September that he would retire at the end of the 2021. The Irishman – nephew of the former World Champion and Tour de France winner Stephen Roche – thus called time on a career that yielded wins at both Liège–Bastogne–Liège and Il Lombardia. In 2021 he took a stage of the Giro, which 'completed the set' of Grand Tour stage victories.

LUCY MARTIN is a former professional cyclist who represented Great Britain at the London 2012 Olympic road race as part of the silver medal winning support team for Lizzie Deignan. She came through the British Cycling ranks, developing from the Talent Team to the British Under-23 academy and later she was a member of the Elite Podium Programme. She competed on both the road and track, picking up the silver medal at the 2008 Manchester World Cup in the points race aged just 18 and went on to represent her country in three elite women's World Road Race championships and England at the 2010 Commonwealth Games in Delhi in both track and road events. For the past six years she has been working for Team BikeExchange (formerly Mitchelton-Scott) men's and women's WorldTour cycling team as Digital & Communications Manager, and as a cycling commentator for ITV, Eurosport and the UCI.

KIT NICHOLSON has been cycling on the road since 2013, building up gradually from the country lanes south of Cambridge to the mountains of Europe. Her lifelong passion for writing was first combined with cycling in 2015 and she has worked closely with Fausto Agency ever since, writing for clients including Bianchi, Brooks, Amgen Tour of California, MET, Conquista, Eurosport and the Rally Cycling team. In 2021, she started working with CyclingTips as the website's weekend news editor. She's currently based in Edinburgh and is more often to be found exploring the mountains on foot than on two wheels, but she continues to write about the sport while also working on fiction projects.

TOM PIDCOCK began his professional road career in 2021, having signed for Ineos Grenadiers. Long touted as one of the most exciting prospects in world cycling, the Briton balanced his traditional cyclocross winter programme with a long Classics campaign, a first Grand Tour and the Tokyo Olympics Games, in which he took a gold medal in mountain biking.

MATT RENDELL is the author of *The Death of Marco Pantani*, *Kings of the Mountains: How Colombia's Cycling Heroes Changed Their Nation's History* and, most recently, *Colombia Es Pasión* about South America's current WorldTour riders. A regular contributor to cycling coverage on TV and in print, his forte is long form: he has written five books about Colombian cycling, exhibiting less interest in who is first across a white line defacing a road, and more in matters of national and individual identity. He has worked inside WorldTour teams, for event organisers, and in a range of roles – from logistics to cameraman to race commentator and director – for TV coverage.

# ACKNOWLEDGEMENTS

Getting The Road Book onto people's shelves for the fourth year and once again in the middle of a pandemic has been a genuine accomplishment in which we all take great pride. We do so with the support of many people. The staff at Directeur consistently take our sometimes vague ideas and turn them into beautiful presentations that help us to communicate with our readership. Steve Leard's design work lends the volume the final touches of quality that raise it up to the standards we demand for our readers. Jonathan Baker's typesetting and the printers at Imago deliver for us a constantly evolving and improving product. And, in the background, Bruce Sandell and Humphrey Cobbold offer their continued and invaluable advice and support. Thank you to all these colleagues for their collaborative work.

The book lives or falls by the presentation and accuracy of the thousands and thousands of lines of data that document the year, for which we have Robert Smith to thank. Matthew Green's wonderful illustrations are once again central to the look and feel of the book and sit perfectly within its pages. Russ Ellis – working this year with Chris Auld, Bram Berkien and Getty Images – has pulled together for us another beautiful gallery of photographs that channel the emotional meaning of the races. Our staff of writers have been with us since the beginning and continue to deliver crisp prose that will stand the test of time and we hope make perfect sense to readers fifty or a hundred years hence. In that spirit, thanks once more to Kit Nicholson, Lucy Martin, Lukas Knöfler, Matt Rendell, Peter Cossins and Simon Brotherton.

This year more than ever we are proud to present a wide variety of different essays. Some have been written by current riders: Dan Martin (to whom we wish a long and happy post-racing life), Cecilie Uttrup Ludwig and Tom Pidcock. Other contributions have come from three different continents and feature many different voices: Tomas Van Den Spiegel, Kathryn Bertine, Kit Nicholson (again), Daniel Friebe and Peter Kamasa.

We greatly value the opinion of our jury, which this year is composed of Christian Prudhomme, Giorgia Bronzini, David Millar, Sean Kelly, Orla Chennaoui, Rolf Sørensen, Ryder Hesjedal, Phil Liggett and Daniel Mangeas. My thanks to them for their last-minute deliberations.

And finally there are four people without whom this book would not exist. Harry Scott's tireless work behind the scenes at The Road Book keeps the whole project ticking over. Jonny Long's excellent writing, imaginative infographics and general support makes him completely indispensable. Charlotte Atyeo's passion for the book, attention to detail and cracking of the whip safeguards our standards year in, year out. And Jay Marks continues to lead the way. Thank you, Jay.

But, as ever, our biggest thanks go to you, the reader.

NED BOULTING

Gallery images reproduced with thanks to Russ Ellis (@cyclingimages), Chris Auld (@cauldphoto), Tornanti_cc, Bram Berkien and Getty Images.

Men's WorldTour rider photographs reproduced with thanks to: AG2R Citroën Team (Vincent Curutchet); Astana Premier Tech (Getty Sport); Bahrain Victorious (Bettiniphoto and Beynon Films); Bora-Hansgrohe (Bora-Hansgrohe/Christof Kreutzer); Cofidis (Chris Auld); Deceuninck-QuickStep (Wout Beel); EF Education-Nippo; Groupama-FDJ; Ineos Grenadiers; Intermarché-Wanty-Gobert Matériaux (Photonews/Intermarché-Wanty-Gobert); Israel Start-Up Nation (Tony Vilches); Jumbo-Visma; Lotto Soudal (Facepeeters); Movistar Team (Photo Gomez Sport/Movistar Team); Team DSM (Team DSM/Vincent Riemersma/Keep Challenging); Team Qhubeka NextHash; Trek-Segafredo (Trek-Segafredo/Jojo Harper); UAE Team Emirates (@PhotoFizza).

Women's WorldTour rider photographs reproduced with thanks to: Alé BTC Ljubljana (Paolo Codeluppi): A.R. Monex; Canyon-SRAM Racing; Ceratizit-WNT (Ceratizit-WNT Racing/Sean Hardy); FDJ Nouvelle-Aquitaine Futuroscope (Thomas Maheux); Jumbo-Visma; Liv Racing; Movistar Team Women (Photo Gomez Sport/Movistar Team); Parkhotel Valkenburg; Rally Cycling; Team BikeExchange (Getty); Team DSM (Team DSM/Vincent Riemersma/Keep Challenging); Team SD Worx; Tibco-SVB; Trek-Segafredo (Trek-Segafredo/Jojo Harper); Valcar Travel & Service (Da Re)